Modern Developments in Investment Management

A Book of Readings

Second Edition

EDITED BY

JAMES LORIE AND

RICHARD BREALEY

Dryden Press
Hinsdale, Illinois

To Vanna and Diana
without whose constant help and encouragement this book was written

The authors wish to thank all sources
for the use of their material.
Credit lines for some of the copyrighted materials
appearing in this work are placed in the
Acknowledgments section on page VIII.
This page is to be considered
an extension of the copyright page.

Library of Congress Catalog Card Number: 77-81246
ISBN: 0-03-040716-8

Printed in the United States of America
89 090 987654321

Preface

The first edition of *Modern Developments* was published in 1972. Our aim then was to gather a selection of articles that would elucidate the important ideas in the modern theory of investment management. We believed that readers would find it convenient to have in one volume the more important, respectable, and instructive articles that were unpublished or dispersed in numerous journals. Several other books of readings were available but none of them adequately reflected our views of what was important and relevant.

The essays that we selected were distinguished for their lucid explanation of three pivotal ideas. These ideas are: (1) capital markets in the USA are highly efficient — meaning that current prices reflect in an unbiased way what is knowable about the companies whose securities are traded; (2) portfolio management is a different subject from security analysis, (security analysis is designed to indicate the likely or possible returns from investing in particular securities, whereas portfolio management has to do with the selection and surveillance of a bundle of securities that match the aspirations, fortitude, and tax status of the beneficiary); and (3) the relative prices of securities are determined by the expected return to the investor and also by the uncertainty about the return. Modern theory has taught us something about the way in which the market determines the premium for enduring uncertainty or risk.

In this second edition we have dropped seven articles and added eleven new ones. Our basic aims are unchanged and we have simply let time do its work. Some of the new articles largely update the old ones. In other cases, the additions reflect some of the concerns that have increasingly occupied investment managers over the past five years. For example, the growth in pension funds and new pension legislation have caused investment managers and academics to think more carefully about the appropriate investment policy for such funds. The article by O'Brien and Tito suggests a practical approach to this problem. Similarly, the development of markets in traded options has generated an interest in option valuation. Therefore, we have included Fischer Black's essay which shows you how to price options. The major swings in bond prices during the 1970s have led many investment managers to re-evaluate their techniques for appraising bonds. Schaefer's article on yields to maturity and Telser's article on the term structure of interest rates offer some basic reading on bond management.

As in the original edition, we have tried to keep a balance between three different kinds of articles. First there are those that are pioneering and that shed light on the evolution of modern financial theory. Among them are Roberts' essay in 1959 on efficient markets (Chapter 8), Markowitz's famous article of 1952 on portfolio selection (Chapter 16), and Williams' work of 1938 on security valuation (Chapter 31).

III

A second group of articles is concerned with developing existing theory or testing its validity. For example, we have included a selection of studies that test the efficient market theory, that consider the practical problems of applying portfolio theory or that try to estimate actual asset values. Finally we have included some review articles that summarize and interpret the important works on the subjects with which they deal. They should prove useful for the indolent or for those who do not have enough time to read more extensively.

In going through the book, some readers may encounter certain terms or ideas that are unfamiliar or obscure to them; invariably they will find them explained in later essays. There was no way of anticipating the individual needs of each reader, but in our introductory chapters we have tried to smooth the reader's way by outlining the implications of each essay and explaining some of the concepts which may prove taxing for those whose technical knowledge of algebra and statistics is slight.

When we made our first selection of readings, we were surprised to find that almost half of them were in some way associated with the Center for Research in Security Prices. Either they were first presented at the Center's semiannual meetings, or they were based on the Center's data files, or they were written by authors directly associated with the Center. The influence of the Center is no less apparent in this second edition. We should therefore like to take this opportunity to express our appreciation to Merrill Lynch, Pierce, Fenner & Smith, Inc., for their sponsorship of the Center and for their contribution to the development of modern investment theory.

Acknowledgments

The editors of a book of readings have a major and obvious debt to the authors and publishers who have given permission for their works to be reprinted. Babu Jones provided invaluable assistance in many ways which made it possible for this edition to come out as well and as quickly as it has.

We would also like to acknowledge the financial support of the Graduate School of Business of the University of Chicago and its Center for Research in Security Prices (sponsored by Merrill Lynch, Pierce, Fenner and Smith Inc.) and of the London Graduate School of Business Studies.

Contents

V

Acknowledgments

The following are credit lines that, for various reasons, do not appear on the first page of the article. Page 78: Reprinted with permission from *The Stock Market: Theories and Evidence* by J. Lorie and M. Hamilton (Homewood, IL: Richard D. Irwin, Inc., 1973 c.), chap. 3. Page 94: Reprinted with permission from the September 29, 1966, issue of the *Commercial and Financial Chronicle*, 110 Wall Street, New York, New York. Page 275: C. Jackson Grayson, Chapter 10, "Utility," from *Decisions Under Uncertainty: Drilling Decisions by Oil and Gas Operators,* Division of Research, Harvard Business School, 1960, pp. 279-313. Copyright © 1960, by the President and Fellows of Harvard College. Reprinted by permission. Page 342: Reprinted from *The Financial Analysts Journal,* XXVIII (January/February 1972), 74-79, by permission of the author and the publisher. Page 348: Reprinted from *The Financial Analysts Journal,* XXIX (March/April 1973), 50-65, by permission of the authors and the publisher. Page 397: Reprinted from *The Financial Analysts Journal,* XXXII (January/February 1976), 23-31, by permission of the author and the publisher. Page 406: Paper presented to the Seminar on the Analysis of Security Prices, November 1972. Reprinted by permission of the authors. Page 424: Reprinted by permission of the publisher, from *Methodology in Finance – Investments* by James L. Bicksler (Lexington, Mass.: Lexington Books, D.C. Heath and Company, 1972). Page 442: Reprinted from *Journal of Portfolio Management,* Winter 1975, 29-34, by permission of the author and the publisher. © 1975 Institutional Investor Systems, Inc. Page 448: Reprinted from *The Journal of Finance,* XXVII, No. 5 (1972), by permission of the author and the publisher. Page 612: Reprinted from *The Financial Analysts Journal,* XXVIII (September/October 1972), 41-43, by permission of the author and the publisher. Page 617: Reprinted from *The Journal of Business,* January 1961, pp. 10-30, by permission of the authors and the University of Chicago Press. © 1961 the University of Chicago. Page 669: Reprinted from the National Bureau of Economic Research, *53rd Annual Report,* September 1973, by permission of the author and NBER. Page 684: Reprinted from *The Financial Analysts Journal,* XXXI (July/August 1975), 36-41 and 61-72, by permission of the author and the publisher. Page 702: Reprinted from *The Financial Analysts Journal,* XXXIII (May/June 1977), by permission of the author and the publisher. Page 711: Reprinted from *The Journal of Political Economy,* August 1967, pp. 546-561, by permission of the author and the University of Chicago Press. © 1967 the University of Chicago.

PART I

THE BEHAVIOR OF THE STOCK MARKET

Measurement of the Behavior of Individual Stocks and of the Market

1

INTRODUCTION: THE RECORD

In recent years, costly and complicated efforts have been made to measure accurately the behavior of the stock market and of individual stocks. Measurements have been made of average rates of return from different investment strategies in individual stocks, of the characteristics of market indexes and the relationships among indexes, of the frequency distributions of returns on individual stocks, and of certain salient characteristics of those distributions. All of these efforts may seem to some to be quite academic and of little importance to the investor who is trying to figure out which stocks are most likely to show unusual appreciation. We believe that persons who feel that way about refined measurements are wrong. Not only are such measurements of interest in themselves, but they test the validity of theories that have considerable relevance to the problems of practical portfolio management.

It is perhaps astonishing that refined measurements were made for the first time so recently. The necessary data are freely available in this country at least, and the supply of practitioners and graduate students has never been deemed seriously inadequate by any influential, vocal segment of society. The reasons for the recency of these studies are at least twofold. First, powerful computers have been necessary to carry them out, and such computers have been available at reasonable cost only within the last fifteen years. To those who have become accustomed to computers, it may be startling to realize that as recently as 1953 International Business Machines did not have a commercial, digital tape-driven computer.

Moreover, recognition of the importance of scientific measurement depended on the development of the theory of efficient markets and portfolio selection. Previously, almost every investor · considered the central problem to be that of competent security analysis, a task for which it was unnecessary to know anything either about the performance of the market or about the rates of return on individual securities. Interest in these subjects, therefore, was stimulated by an increasing awareness of the importance of a correct assessment of the long-term prospects for the market and of the interrelationships between the returns on the market and those on individual securities.

The first article (Chapter 2) is a comprehensive report by Fisher and Lorie on the average rates of return from a policy of investing equal amounts of money in each common stock listed on the New York Stock Exchange. The report covers the period from January, 1926, through December, 1965, and numerous subperiods. It lists rates of return for persons in different tax categories; for those who reinvest dividends as well as for those who consume them.

Fisher and Lorie have recently updated some of their figures through 1976 and added some interesting data on short-term bonds, long-term bonds and a basket of consumption goods. These results are summarized in Tables 1 to 6.[1] They indicate that on the average for all reasonably long periods, average rates of return on common stocks have substantially exceeded average rates on bonds. That finding is of considerable importance in itself and provides some evidence that investors on the whole are risk adverse and require additional compensation for the more exciting investments in common stocks.

There has also been some recent work on rates of return on stocks in the over-the-counter market. Pratt's study [3] contains interesting quantitative information but few surprises. As expected, average rates for stocks traded in the over-the-counter market have been higher than those for stocks in the more mature companies, which are listed on the New York Stock Exchange—a finding consistent with modern theories about the relationship between risk and return in a world of risk averters.

After the study on average rates of return, work was undertaken on the nature of the frequency distribution of rates of return from individual stocks and from portfolios containing different numbers of stocks. The major work on this subject is presented in the second included article (Chapter 3).

Chapters 4 and 5 are on indexes. From even a casual reading of the financial press and unsystematic introspection, it is clear that investors are interested in what is happening to "the market." Their interest has caused the production of several measures of the market. Such measures have very direct relevance for portfolio management, since one crucial datum is the sensitivity of the individual security to market movements. Also, since the increased acceptance of the efficient-market hypothesis, the performance of the market has become a useful bench mark for

---

1. Lawrence Fisher and James H. Lorie, *A Half Century of Returns on Stocks and Bonds: Rates of Return on Investments in Common Stocks and on U.S. Treasury Securities, 1926-1976* (Chicago: Graduate School of Business, University of Chicago, 1977).

2. Shannon P. Pratt, "Differences in the Behavior of the Over-the-Counter Market and the New York Stock Exchange" (an unpublished paper presented to the Seminar on the Analysis of Security Prices, University of Chicago, November 1971).

evaluating the performance of actual portfolios. Beyond that, investors are naturally interested in the interrelationships between the market and other economic events, such as changes in the level of economic output and in corporate profits, the rate of inflation, and international monetary developments.

The various measures of the market are based on different samples of securities, different methods of weighting the component securities, and different methods of averaging. The extract from the Lorie-Hamilton article (Chapter 4) discusses the construction of some frequently quoted indexes and examines the interrelationships among the various measures. In the following chapter, Cootner discusses some popular fallacies concerning the use of stock market indexes.

TABLE 1
TIME-WEIGHTED RATES OF RETURN* ON COMMON STOCKS: DIVIDENDS REINVESTED,
CASH TO PORTFOLIO,
EQUAL INITIAL WEIGHTING,
TAX EXEMPT,
CURRENT DOLLARS

ACQUIRED AT END OF MONTH

HELD UNTIL	12/25	12/26	12/27	12/28	12/29	12/30	12/31	12/32	12/33	12/34	12/35	12/36	12/37	12/38	12/39	12/40	12/41	12/42	12/43	12/44
12/26	0.8
12/27	15.9	29.3
12/28	23.7	37.4	45.7
12/29	8.2	9.8	0.9	-29.4
12/30	-2.2	-3.7	-12.9	-31.7	-30.0
12/31	-11.3	-13.6	-21.6	-36.3	-41.2	-48.2
12/32	-10.4	-12.6	-19.7	-30.0	-32.1	-30.7
12/33	-2.7	-3.3	-7.5	-15.5	-12.0	-1.4	-9.8
12/34	-1.0	-1.5	-4.9	-11.1	-7.0	2.3	37.1	106.0
12/35	4.7	4.7	2.4	-2.6	1.6	9.3	28.3	54.4	15.3
12/36	0.7	-0.6	-2.4	-5.6	-3.8	13.9	35.6	53.5	32.1	50.7
12/37	2.9	2.6	0.6	-6.2	-0.8	3.1	16.1	57.3	37.1	50.6	46.8
12/38	2.8	2.4	0.5	-2.9	0.8	6.7	14.7	23.0	8.1	6.0	-11.7	-46.1
12/39	2.2	1.7	0.1	-2.6	0.8	6.7	15.6	25.0	13.0	12.1	6.0	-12.2	-14.8
12/40	1.5	1.0	-0.7	-3.3	-0.6	5.8	14.8	20.3	10.3	8.8	-1.3	-11.2	-30.7
12/41	3.6	3.5	3.5	-1.9	7.0	7.0	13.7	16.9	8.4	4.4	-0.9	-9.2	6.7
12/42	3.6	3.6	3.5	0.1	4.5	7.0	13.7	16.3	10.2	5.2	0.1	-9.2	4.7
12/43	4.4	6.4	5.5	1.6	4.9	11.1	17.6	16.1	14.3	11.9	4.5	0.7	13.7
12/44	5.6	6.6	5.5	3.8	4.5	11.1	17.6	17.8	15.7	12.1	6.2	4.5	17.1
12/45	5.4	6.4	4.6	3.1	6.7	9.7	15.5	16.8	13.3	12.0	6.1	5.3	17.4
12/46	5.1	5.1	4.2	2.6	5.8	9.2	15.7	15.5	11.4	10.9	6.1	5.8	15.6
12/47	5.8	5.8	4.9	3.4	5.7	9.0	13.4	14.7	11.0	10.4	8.0	6.4	14.7
12/48	6.5	6.6	5.9	4.4	6.4	10.2	15.0	14.7	13.0	12.4	10.5	9.4	14.8
12/49	7.1	7.2	6.5	5.1	7.4	10.5	15.1	14.7	13.2	12.9	10.5	10.9	14.9
12/50	8.0	8.2	7.5	6.4	7.6	11.5	15.6	15.4	13.1	13.0	10.0	9.1	14.9
12/51	8.4	8.6	8.2	6.9	8.1	11.8	15.6	15.6	13.2	12.7	10.0	8.4	13.4
12/52	8.5	8.7	8.1	7.1	8.7	11.9	17.2	15.4	14.5	14.1	12.4	11.2	13.9
12/53	7.8	7.9	7.3	6.3	8.3	10.7	14.4	15.6	14.6	12.6	11.5	9.8	14.0
12/54	9.0	9.0	8.6	8.1	9.7	12.9	16.9	15.7	15.0	13.2	12.7	11.7	15.7
12/55	9.0	9.2	8.6	7.7	9.4	11.7	15.1	16.7	14.5	12.9	12.9	11.2	15.2
12/56	8.8	8.8	8.4	7.7	9.4	11.7	15.1	16.7	14.5	13.0	13.0	11.2	14.9
12/57	9.4	9.6	9.3	8.5	10.0	12.3	15.1	16.7	14.5	14.6	13.0	10.7	14.1
12/58	8.8	8.9	8.4	7.3	9.4	11.3	14.7	15.7	13.3	13.3	11.8	10.7	14.1
12/59	9.4	9.3	9.1	8.6	9.4	11.6	15.0	15.6	13.4	13.6	12.3	11.3	14.5
12/60	9.2	9.2	8.8	8.2	9.2	11.7	14.4	15.1	14.0	13.2	12.1	10.9	13.2
12/61	9.4	9.4	9.2	8.5	9.6	12.0	14.8	15.9	14.0	14.0	11.9	11.0	13.2
12/62	8.9	8.9	9.2	8.5	9.2	11.6	14.2	15.9	14.1	14.0	12.9	12.0	14.8
12/63	9.2	9.3	9.5	9.2	9.6	12.3	15.0	14.8	13.1	14.1	12.9	12.0	13.7
12/64	9.2	9.3	9.4	9.4	9.9	11.3	13.5	14.4	13.5	13.1	11.5	11.7	13.7
12/65	9.4	9.4	9.9	9.2	10.5	11.6	13.6	14.4	12.7	12.1	11.7	10.9	13.4
12/66	8.9	8.6	8.6	8.3	9.2	11.4	13.2	14.4	12.7	12.4	10.7	9.9	12.0
12/67	9.2	9.5	9.7	9.0	9.6	11.7	15.1	14.0	13.3	14.0	11.7	9.9	11.9
12/68	9.4	9.6	9.2	8.9	10.1	11.7	15.9	14.0	14.1	13.2	11.6	9.7	11.1
12/69	9.3	9.4	8.9	8.2	9.7	11.4	14.8	14.1	14.1	13.1	11.4	10.5	11.4
12/70	9.1	9.3	8.7	8.1	9.4	11.1	13.5	14.1	13.1	13.1	11.5	10.2	11.0
12/71	9.3	9.4	8.9	8.4	9.3	11.3	13.6	14.4	12.8	12.7	11.7	10.9	11.7
12/72	9.3	9.4	9.4	8.2	9.6	12.7	13.6	14.4	12.7	12.1	10.7	9.9	11.2
12/73	8.8	8.8	8.4	7.8	9.2	11.6	13.3	14.4	11.8	11.7	10.7	9.9	11.9
12/74	8.1	8.6	8.4	7.1	8.3	10.5	12.7	13.3	11.4	11.6	10.5	9.7	11.0
12/75	8.6	8.6	8.3	7.7	9.2	11.6	12.2	13.0	11.5	11.4	10.4	9.7	11.2
12/76	9.0	9.0	8.1	8.1	9.4	10.7	13.4	12.0	12.0	11.9	10.2	10.2	12.2

1   1836   111131

TABLE 1 CONTINUED

ACQUIRED AT END OF MONTH

HELD UNTIL	12/45	12/46	12/47	12/48	12/49	12/50	12/51	12/52	12/53	12/54	12/55	12/56	12/57	12/58	12/59	12/60	12/61	12/62	12/63	12/64
12/46	-9.5																			
12/47	-4.2	0.0																		
12/48	-3.4	-0.8	-3.1																	
12/49	2.1	5.7	8.3	19.7																
12/50	7.9	12.6	16.7	27.3	35.9															
12/51	9.5	13.5	16.5	23.4	25.3	14.8	6.9													
12/52	9.4	13.0	15.3	19.9	19.9	12.5	3.5	-3.2												
12/53	8.0	10.6	12.1	15.2	13.7	7.6	1.6	2.9	45.2											
12/54	12.7	15.7	17.9	21.5	21.7	18.6	18.6	22.3	37.4	19.1										
12/55	13.6	16.3	18.3	21.5	21.9	18.6	19.2	22.3	37.0	13.5	6.6									
12/56	13.4	15.8	17.3	20.0	20.1	17.1	17.1	18.8	27.0	3.6	-3.7	-13.8								
12/57	10.7	12.5	13.6	15.5	14.9	12.1	11.3	11.3	14.7	14.7	13.1	14.8	58.1							
12/58	13.5	15.5	16.4	19.0	18.4	16.7	16.7	17.8	22.2	14.7	17.2	17.2	34.1	14.5						
12/59	13.5	15.5	16.8	18.8	18.4	16.8	16.8	17.8	21.5	15.3	15.3	12.9	22.0	6.5	-1.9					
12/60	12.5	14.3	15.4	17.1	16.8	15.1	15.0	15.6	18.1	12.8	11.3	10.4	15.2	6.4	3.9	27.6				
12/61	13.4	15.2	16.2	17.8	17.5	16.2	16.1	19.3	19.3	10.7	9.6	10.4	15.9	13.7	7.5	5.9	-13.4			
12/62	11.5	13.0	13.9	15.1	14.7	13.2	13.0	13.7	14.0	11.6	9.5	14.1	14.1	6.9	9.7	12.6	7.2	17.4		
12/63	12.3	13.7	14.4	15.5	15.2	13.9	13.7	14.0	15.6	11.6	11.4	12.3	14.3	10.5	9.7	12.4	13.0	14.6	28.5	
12/64	12.3	13.7	14.4	15.5	15.2	13.9	13.7	14.0	15.4	12.2	10.4	11.4	13.4	10.2	9.7	12.1	12.0	13.4	17.3	10.1
12/65	12.8	14.4	15.1	16.2	15.9	14.7	14.5	15.4	13.4	11.5	10.7	11.4	14.9	10.2	9.7	12.1	12.0	16.2	13.4	22.6
12/66	11.7	13.1	13.1	14.8	14.5	13.1	12.9	13.2	14.4	11.5	10.7	11.4	13.4	14.5	13.4	12.1	12.7	14.2	13.7	10.7
12/67	12.9	14.2	14.9	15.9	15.8	14.5	14.9	14.8	16.7	14.2	13.6	14.6	18.0	14.5	13.4	17.3	12.7	17.3	10.7	23.2
12/68	13.2	14.5	15.2	16.2	16.0	14.9	14.9	15.3	16.1	14.7	10.7	11.6	14.2	10.4	10.2	12.7	10.7	10.7	12.7	7.6
12/69	11.7	12.8	13.4	14.3	14.0	12.9	12.8	13.0	14.1	10.9	10.7	11.6	14.2	9.4	9.4	11.5	12.7	12.6	11.3	11.0
12/70	11.2	12.2	12.9	13.5	13.2	12.2	12.0	12.2	13.2	10.9	10.4	11.3	13.4	10.6	9.2	11.5	11.5	12.6	11.9	11.0
12/71	11.4	12.5	13.0	13.8	13.5	12.5	12.4	12.6	13.5	11.2	10.9	11.3	13.3	10.6	10.3	11.5	11.5	9.3	7.7	4.6
12/72	11.5	12.5	12.9	13.7	13.5	12.5	12.3	12.6	13.6	11.4	10.7	11.3	13.3	10.6	10.3	5.5	5.5	4.5	7.7	3.0
12/73	10.2	11.0	11.4	12.0	11.5	10.8	10.5	10.5	11.4	9.4	8.7	6.9	10.5	8.0	7.7	5.7	5.2	6.7	7.4	6.4
12/74	8.9	10.4	9.4	10.4	10.1	10.0	10.1	10.8	7.4	9.0	8.7	6.9	10.5	7.7	7.3	8.1	6.7	4.2	7.4	6.4
12/75	9.9	10.4	10.9	11.5	11.2	10.3	10.1	10.1	11.2	9.0	8.4	8.6	9.3	5.6	5.2	6.1	1.6	4.1	7.1	6.4
12/76	10.5	11.3	11.6	12.2	12.0	11.0	10.9	10.9	11.5	9.9	9.4	9.6	11.0	8.2	8.7	9.6	9.6	—	—	—

ACQUIRED AT END OF MONTH

HELD UNTIL	12/65	12/66	12/67	12/68	12/69	12/70	12/71	12/72	12/73	12/74	12/75
12/66	-8.2										
12/67	17.9	51.5									
12/68	21.0	40.3	28.5								
12/69	9.3	16.1	1.7	-20.1							
12/70	6.4	10.8	0.4	-11.8	-4.4						
12/71	8.3	12.4	4.6	-2.5	6.8	17.0					
12/72	8.7	12.1	5.9	0.9	8.0	13.4	6.7				
12/73	4.1	6.0	0.5	-4.2	-0.5	-1.1	-9.9	-28.1			
12/74	0.4	1.6	-3.5	-7.9	-5.6	-7.4	-14.6	-26.0	-27.2		
12/75	4.3	5.9	1.7	-1.6	1.7	1.8	-2.0	-4.4	6.4	53.8	
12/76	6.7	8.4	4.8	2.2	6.0	7.1	5.0	3.4	14.9	48.3	40.1

5

TABLE 2

TIME-WEIGHTED RATES OF RETURN* ON COMMON STOCKS: DIVIDENDS REINVESTED.
CASH TO PORTFOLIO.
EQUAL INITIAL WEIGHTING.
TAX EXEMPT.
DEFLATED BY THE CONSUMER PRICE INDEX

ACQUIRED AT END OF MONTH

HELD UNTIL	12/25	12/26	12/27	12/28	12/29	12/30	12/31	12/32	12/33	12/34	12/35	12/36	12/37	12/38	12/39	12/40	12/41	12/42	12/43	12/44
12/26	2.4																			
12/27	18.0	30.0																		
12/28	25.6	34.5	47.1																	
12/29	9.4	10.8	1.3	−29.6																
12/30	−0.1	−1.5	−10.9	−29.6	−34.0															
12/31	−8.2	−10.3	−18.1	−32.8	−34.2	−42.7														
12/32	−6.7	−8.1	−14.0	−25.1	−25.6	−23.1	0.5													
12/33	1.1	0.9	−3.1	−11.0	−5.9	7.5	44.4	105.0												
12/34	2.1	1.9	−1.4	−7.4	−2.3	7.1	32.0	52.5	13.0											
12/35	5.1	4.9	2.2	−2.6	3.1	12.7	34.9	50.7	29.0	46.4										
12/36	2.6	2.1	−0.5	−4.4	−0.8	16.7	36.8	49.4	34.3	47.5	45.0									
12/37																				

TABLE 2 CONTINUED

ACQUIRED AT END OF MONTH

HELD UNTIL	12/45	12/46	12/47	12/48	12/49	12/50	12/51	12/52	12/53	12/54	12/55	12/56	12/57	12/58	12/59	12/60	12/61	12/62	12/63	12/64
12/47	-23.4																			
12/48	-15.6	-8.2																		
12/49	-12.0	-6.3	-5.7																	
12/50	-6.4	2.4	7.8	21.9																
12/51	1.3	4.4	14.2	24.9	28.5															
12/52	2.9	8.8	13.0	19.5	18.4	8.4														
12/53	3.7	9.0	12.3	16.8	15.1	8.8	6.0													
12/54	7.9	7.1	9.6	12.7	10.1	5.0	2.7	-3.8												
12/55	9.3	12.6	15.7	19.4	18.7	16.0	18.2	22.9	55.0											
12/56	9.2	13.5	16.3	19.7	18.5	16.9	18.8	22.1	37.5	14.6										
12/57	6.7	13.0	15.2	18.0	17.5	15.2	16.1	17.8	25.8	11.7	3.6									
12/58	6.5	9.7	11.4	13.4	12.3	10.0	9.9	9.9	13.1	1.4	-6.4	-16.3								
12/59	9.7	12.7	14.7	16.8	16.2	14.7	15.2	15.7	19.7	12.5	10.3	14.1	55.3							
12/60	8.8	12.8	14.7	16.7	16.2	14.7	15.3	16.2	19.7	20.4	11.6	14.8	33.9	12.4						
12/61	8.8	11.6	13.3	15.0	14.3	13.1	13.5	14.0	16.4	13.2	9.0	10.7	20.1	4.9	-7.4					
12/62	9.9	12.6	14.7	15.8	15.4	14.2	14.6	15.3	17.7	10.7	10.1	14.1	22.2	12.4	11.8	26.8				
12/63	8.2	10.6	11.9	13.2	12.5	11.4	11.7	13.3	14.9	13.0	8.7	8.7	13.7	5.1	2.7	5.0	-14.4			
12/64	8.8	11.1	12.3	13.5	12.9	11.8	12.2	13.7	14.4	9.4	9.7	9.7	14.4	4.1	4.4	7.5	6.2	12.9		
12/65	9.1	11.3	12.5	13.1	13.1	12.0	12.5	14.0	14.0	10.5	10.6	10.6	14.4	11.1	11.1	9.2	4.3	14.9	15.2	
12/66	9.7	11.3	12.9	13.1	12.8	11.8	12.2	13.4	14.0	11.6	10.4	11.8	13.0	6.5	7.9	11.5	7.6	28.4	21.9	26.1
12/67	8.4	11.1	13.1	13.3	13.0	12.8	12.5	13.4	12.8	9.6	6.7	9.4	15.3	4.1	4.4	10.1	12.6	12.6	16.4	7.9
12/68	9.7	11.7	11.7	12.3	11.9	11.3	11.5	13.0	12.8	11.5	10.4	11.6	15.0	4.8	7.9	12.0	7.6	16.2	18.7	19.3
12/69	9.7	11.8	12.9	13.4	13.6	12.7	13.7	14.6	14.4	11.9	11.3	12.2	15.0	12.2	12.3	13.0	13.0	16.2	18.7	8.7
12/70	9.9	10.9	11.4	11.4	10.5	10.6	10.8	10.8	11.7	4.2	4.5	7.0	10.4	2.9	2.0	9.3	5.3	9.0	6.8	5.3
12/71	8.0	9.3	10.1	10.5	10.9	10.5	10.6	12.2	12.9	11.6	10.4	11.6	13.0	7.2	6.4	7.2	5.3	9.0	7.0	6.7
12/72	9.3	9.6	10.9	10.9	10.7	9.9	10.0	10.9	12.8	7.6	7.9	8.8	10.3	7.6	6.6	7.3	4.4	9.8	7.9	6.2
12/73	6.6	7.9	8.5	9.1	9.9	9.4	9.8	11.6	10.0	4.6	5.5	5.7	7.2	4.7	4.3	4.9	4.2	7.9	3.4	-2.1
12/74	5.0	6.2	6.6	7.1	7.8	7.4	7.4	5.5	6.7	3.9	3.1	5.7	7.2	1.8	1.3	1.6	-0.1	1.0	-0.4	1.0
12/75	5.8	7.0	7.5	7.6	6.8	6.7	6.7	7.2	7.2	5.3	4.5	4.6	5.9	3.4	1.6	2.7	2.1	3.7	2.3	1.0
12/76	6.4	7.6	8.1	8.7	8.3	7.5	7.4	6.1	6.1	6.1	5.5	6.0	4.9	4.4	4.4	5.1	3.7	5.0	4.1	3.0

ACQUIRED AT END OF MONTH

HELD UNTIL	12/65	12/66	12/67	12/68	12/69	12/70	12/71	12/72	12/73	12/74	12/75
12/66	-11.1										
12/67	14.2	47.0									
12/68	16.7	35.1	22.7								
12/69	4.8	11.0	-3.6	-24.1							
12/70	1.6	5.7	-4.8	-16.6	-9.3						
12/71	3.8	7.5	-0.3	-7.2	2.3	13.2					
12/72	4.3	7.4	1.2	-3.6	3.7	9.7	3.2				
12/73	-0.7	1.0	-4.5	-9.1	-6.5	-6.0	-15.0	-33.9			
12/74	-4.4	-4.0	-9.2	-13.5	-11.4	-13.3	-21.0	-33.0	-35.1		
12/75	-1.3	-0.1	-4.4	-7.7	-4.7	-4.8	-9.1	-14.4	-2.9	43.8	
12/76	1.0	2.4	-1.3	-3.0	-0.4	0.5	-2.1	-4.4	8.3	40.0	31.6

TABLE 3

TIME-WEIGHTED RATES OF RETURN* ON SHORT-TERM U.S. TREASURY SECURITIES: INTEREST REINVESTED,
TAX EXEMPT,
CURRENT DOLLARS

ACQUIRED AT END OF MONTH

HELD UNTIL	12/25	12/26	12/27	12/28	12/29	12/30	12/31	12/32	12/33	12/34	12/35	12/36	12/37	12/38	12/39	12/40	12/41	12/42	12/43	12/44
12/26	3.9																			
12/27	3.5	3.2																		
12/28	3.5	3.2	3.3																	
12/29	3.9	3.9	4.2	5.1																
12/30	3.8	3.8	4.0	4.3	3.5															
12/31	3.4	3.3	3.3	3.3	2.5	1.5														
12/32	3.4	3.3	3.4	3.4	2.8	2.5	3.5													
12/33	3.0	3.0	2.9	2.8	2.4	1.8	1.9	0.4												
12/34	3.0	2.9	2.9	2.7	2.3	2.0	1.8	1.5	2.6											
12/35	2.8	2.8	2.6	2.5	2.0	1.7	1.4	1.1	1.7	0.7										
12/36	2.6	2.6	2.4	2.2	1.8	1.6	1.4	1.1	1.3	0.7	0.7									
12/37	2.6	2.4	2.4	2.2	1.8	1.4	1.3	0.9	1.1	0.6	0.5	0.3								
12/38	2.2	2.2	2.1	2.0	1.6	1.3	1.2	1.0	1.0	0.6	0.6	0.4	0.5							
12/39	2.1	2.1	2.0	1.8	1.5	1.2	1.1	0.9	0.9	0.5	0.4	0.4	0.7	0.9						
12/40	2.0	2.0	1.8	1.7	1.4	1.1	1.0	0.7	0.7	0.5	0.4	0.4	0.6	0.7	0.4					
12/41	1.9	1.9	1.7	1.5	1.3	1.0	1.0	0.7	0.7	0.5	0.4	0.4	0.4	0.3	0.2	-0.4				
12/42	1.8	1.8	1.7	1.4	1.2	1.0	0.9	0.7	0.7	0.5	0.5	0.5	0.6	0.4	0.4	0.0	0.9			
12/43	1.7	1.7	1.6	1.4	1.2	1.0	0.9	0.7	0.6	0.5	0.5	0.6	0.6	0.5	0.4	0.3	0.8	0.9		
12/44	1.7	1.6	1.5	1.3	1.1	0.9	0.8	0.7	0.6	0.6	0.6	0.6	0.6	0.5	0.5	0.5	0.6	0.8	0.9	0.9
12/45	1.6	1.6	1.5	1.3	1.1	0.9	0.8	0.7	0.6	0.5	0.5	0.6	0.6	0.5	0.5	0.6	0.7	0.8	0.9	0.8
12/46	1.6	1.6	1.5	1.3	1.1	0.9	0.9	0.7	0.6	0.6	0.6	0.6	0.6	0.6	0.6	0.7	0.8	0.9	0.8	0.8
12/47	1.6	1.6	1.4	1.3	1.1	0.9	0.9	0.7	0.6	0.6	0.6	0.6	0.7	0.6	0.7	0.7	0.9	0.9	0.9	1.0
12/48	1.5	1.5	1.4	1.3	1.1	0.9	0.9	0.8	0.8	0.7	0.7	0.7	0.7	0.7	0.7	0.8	0.9	0.8	0.8	1.0
12/49	1.5	1.4	1.4	1.3	1.1	0.9	0.9	0.8	0.8	0.7	0.7	0.7	0.8	0.8	0.8	0.9	0.9	1.0	1.0	1.1
12/50	1.5	1.4	1.3	1.3	1.1	0.9	0.9	0.9	0.9	0.8	0.8	0.8	0.8	0.8	0.9	0.9	1.0	1.1	1.1	1.1
12/51	1.5	1.4	1.3	1.3	1.1	1.0	1.0	0.9	0.9	0.8	0.9	0.9	0.9	0.9	0.9	1.0	1.1	1.1	1.1	1.2
12/52	1.5	1.4	1.3	1.3	1.2	1.0	1.0	1.0	1.0	0.9	0.9	0.9	1.0	1.0	1.0	1.1	1.2	1.2	1.2	1.3
12/53	1.5	1.4	1.4	1.3	1.2	1.1	1.1	1.0	1.0	1.0	1.0	1.0	1.0	1.1	1.1	1.2	1.2	1.3	1.3	1.3
12/54	1.6	1.5	1.4	1.4	1.2	1.2	1.2	1.1	1.1	1.1	1.1	1.1	1.2	1.2	1.2	1.3	1.3	1.3	1.4	1.4
12/55	1.6	1.5	1.5	1.4	1.3	1.2	1.2	1.2	1.2	1.2	1.2	1.2	1.3	1.3	1.3	1.4	1.4	1.4	1.5	1.5
12/56	1.6	1.6	1.5	1.5	1.3	1.3	1.3	1.2	1.3	1.3	1.3	1.3	1.3	1.4	1.4	1.5	1.5	1.6	1.6	1.6
12/57	1.7	1.6	1.5	1.5	1.4	1.3	1.3	1.3	1.4	1.4	1.4	1.4	1.4	1.5	1.5	1.6	1.6	1.7	1.7	1.7
12/58	1.7	1.6	1.6	1.5	1.4	1.4	1.4	1.4	1.4	1.4	1.4	1.4	1.5	1.5	1.5	1.6	1.6	1.7	1.7	1.7
12/59	1.7	1.6	1.6	1.5	1.5	1.4	1.5	1.4	1.5	1.5	1.5	1.5	1.6	1.6	1.6	1.7	1.8	1.8	1.9	1.9
12/60	1.8	1.7	1.7	1.7	1.6	1.5	1.5	1.5	1.6	1.6	1.6	1.7	1.7	1.7	1.7	1.8	1.9	1.9	2.0	2.0
12/61	1.8	1.8	1.7	1.7	1.6	1.6	1.6	1.6	1.6	1.6	1.7	1.7	1.8	1.8	1.8	1.9	2.0	2.0	2.1	2.1
12/62	1.9	1.8	1.8	1.7	1.7	1.6	1.6	1.6	1.7	1.7	1.7	1.8	1.8	1.8	1.8	1.9	2.0	2.1	2.1	2.1
12/63	1.9	1.8	1.8	1.8	1.7	1.7	1.7	1.7	1.7	1.7	1.8	1.8	1.9	1.9	1.9	2.0	2.1	2.1	2.2	2.1
12/64	2.0	1.9	1.9	1.8	1.8	1.7	1.8	1.7	1.8	1.8	1.9	1.9	1.9	2.0	2.0	2.1	2.2	2.2	2.3	2.2
12/65	2.0	2.0	1.9	1.9	1.8	1.8	1.8	1.8	1.9	1.9	1.9	2.0	2.0	2.1	2.1	2.1	2.3	2.3	2.4	2.3
12/66	2.1	2.0	2.0	2.0	1.9	1.9	1.9	1.9	2.0	2.0	2.1	2.1	2.1	2.2	2.3	2.3	2.5	2.5	2.6	2.5
12/67	2.1	2.1	2.0	2.0	1.9	1.9	1.9	1.9	2.0	2.0	2.1	2.2	2.3	2.3	2.4	2.4	2.6	2.6	2.8	2.7
12/68	2.2	2.2	2.1	2.1	2.0	2.0	2.0	2.0	2.1	2.2	2.3	2.3	2.4	2.4	2.5	2.5	2.7	2.7	2.8	2.8
12/69	2.3	2.3	2.2	2.2	2.1	2.2	2.2	2.3	2.3	2.4	2.4	2.5	2.5	2.6	2.7	2.7	2.9	2.9	3.0	3.1
12/70	2.5	2.5	2.5	2.4	2.3	2.3	2.3	2.4	2.4	2.5	2.5	2.6	2.7	2.7	2.8	2.8	3.0	3.0	3.1	3.1
12/71	2.6	2.6	2.5	2.5	2.4	2.4	2.4	2.5	2.5	2.6	2.6	2.7	2.7	2.8	2.8	2.9	3.1	3.1	3.2	3.2
12/72	2.6	2.6	2.6	2.6	2.5	2.5	2.5	2.6	2.6	2.6	2.7	2.7	2.8	2.8	2.9	3.0	3.1	3.1	3.3	3.3
12/73	2.7	2.7	2.7	2.7	2.6	2.6	2.6	2.7	2.7	2.7	2.8	2.8	2.9	2.9	3.0	3.1	3.2	3.2	3.1	3.4
12/74	2.8	2.8	2.8	2.7	2.7	2.7	2.7	2.8	2.8	2.8	2.9	2.9	3.0	3.1	3.1	3.2	3.3	3.5	3.5	3.4
12/75	2.9	2.9	2.9	2.9	2.8	2.8	2.9	2.9	2.9	2.9	3.0	3.0	3.1	3.2	3.3	3.3	3.5	3.5	3.6	3.7
12/76	3.0	3.0	3.0	3.0	2.9	2.9	3.0	3.0	3.0	3.0	3.1	3.2	3.2	3.3	3.4	3.4	3.5	3.7	3.8	3.8

1 0 71

TABLE 3   CONTINUED

ACQUIRED AT END OF MONTH

HELD UNTIL	12/45	12/46	12/47	12/48	12/49	12/50	12/51	12/52	12/53	12/54	12/55	12/56	12/57	12/58	12/59	12/60	12/61	12/62	12/63	12/64
12/46	0.8																			
12/47	0.8	0.8																		
12/48	0.9	0.9	1.0																	
12/49	1.0	1.0	1.2	1.3																
12/50	1.0	1.0	1.1	1.2	1.0															
12/51	1.1	1.2	1.2	1.3	1.3	1.6														
12/52	1.2	1.3	1.4	1.5	1.5	1.7	1.9													
12/53	1.4	1.4	1.6	1.7	1.7	2.1	2.1	2.7												
12/54	1.4	1.5	1.5	1.7	1.8	1.9	2.1	2.2	1.3											
12/55	1.5	1.5	1.6	1.8	1.9	2.0	2.2	2.3	1.7	1.0										
12/56	1.7	1.7	1.8	1.9	2.0	2.1	2.3	2.4	2.0	1.8	2.5									
12/57	1.7	1.7	1.8	1.9	2.0	2.1	2.4	2.4	2.0	1.8	2.4	3.7								
12/58	1.8	1.8	1.9	2.0	2.1	2.2	2.6	2.7	2.3	2.3	2.8	2.9	2.1							
12/59	2.0	1.9	2.0	2.3	2.3	2.5	2.7	2.7	2.4	2.3	2.8	3.1	2.5	3.0						
12/60	2.1	2.1	2.2	2.3	2.4	2.5	2.7	2.7	2.4	2.3	2.9	3.3	3.4	4.1	5.2					
12/61	2.1	2.1	2.2	2.3	2.4	2.6	2.7	2.7	2.4	2.4	3.0	3.3	3.3	3.5	4.0	2.8				
12/62	2.2	2.2	2.3	2.4	2.5	2.6	2.8	2.8	2.8	2.9	3.1	3.3	3.3	3.6	3.7	3.0	3.2			
12/63	2.3	2.3	2.4	2.5	2.6	2.7	2.9	2.9	2.9	3.0	3.2	3.4	3.3	3.5	3.6	3.2	3.1	3.0		
12/64	2.5	2.4	2.6	2.6	2.7	2.8	3.0	3.0	3.0	3.1	3.3	3.4	3.4	3.6	3.9	3.3	3.3	3.1	3.0	
12/65	2.6	2.6	2.7	2.8	2.9	3.0	3.1	3.1	3.1	3.3	3.5	3.6	3.6	3.8	3.9	3.6	3.5	3.4	3.4	3.8
12/66	2.8	2.7	2.8	2.9	3.0	3.1	3.4	3.4	3.4	3.4	3.6	3.7	3.8	3.8	4.1	3.8	3.7	3.6	3.6	3.5
12/67	2.9	2.8	3.0	3.1	3.2	3.3	3.7	3.7	3.5	3.9	3.8	3.9	4.0	3.9	4.3	3.9	4.1	4.0	4.2	4.4
12/68	3.0	3.0	3.1	3.2	3.3	3.4	3.9	4.0	4.1	4.2	4.1	4.2	4.2	4.2	4.3	4.0	4.2	4.2	4.5	4.6
12/69	3.2	3.2	3.4	3.5	3.6	3.9	4.0	4.1	4.2	4.4	4.4	4.6	4.6	4.9	4.9	4.5	4.7	4.9	5.1	5.1
12/70	3.3	3.3	3.5	3.6	3.8	3.8	4.0	4.2	4.3	4.4	4.6	4.7	4.8	5.0	5.1	5.0	5.1	5.3	5.2	5.5
12/71	3.4	3.4	3.6	3.7	3.9	3.9	4.1	4.3	4.4	4.5	4.7	4.8	4.8	5.0	5.2	5.1	5.2	5.3	5.4	5.5
12/72	3.5	3.5	3.7	3.8	4.0	4.1	4.2	4.4	4.5	4.6	4.8	4.8	4.9	5.1	5.4	5.2	5.4	5.4	5.4	5.8
12/73	3.7	3.6	3.8	3.9	4.1	4.2	4.3	4.5	4.7	4.8	5.0	5.2	5.1	5.3	5.6	5.4	5.6	5.8	6.1	6.1
12/74	3.8	3.8	3.9	4.0	4.2	4.5	4.6	4.7	4.8	4.9	5.0	5.2	5.2	5.4	5.7	5.8	6.1	6.3	6.1	6.3
12/75	3.9	3.9	4.0	4.1	4.3	4.4	4.5	4.7	4.8	4.9	5.1	5.3	5.4	5.5	5.7	5.7	5.9	6.1	6.7	6.4
12/76	4.0	4.0	4.1	4.2	4.3	4.5	4.6	4.7	4.8	4.9	5.1	5.3	5.4	5.5	5.7	5.7	5.9	6.1	6.4	6.4

ACQUIRED AT END OF MONTH

HELD UNTIL	12/65	12/66	12/67	12/68	12/69	12/70	12/71	12/72	12/73	12/74	12/75
12/66	5.3										
12/67	5.3	5.2									
12/68	5.5	5.7	6.1								
12/69	5.9	6.1	6.6	7.0							
12/70	6.1	7.0	7.4	7.8	8.9						
12/71	6.7	6.9	7.0	7.8	8.7	6.5					
12/72	6.3	6.5	6.1	7.0	8.2	5.5	4.5				
12/73	6.3	6.5	6.7	6.8	6.8	5.8	5.4	6.2			
12/74	6.6	6.8	6.8	6.8	6.8	6.5	7.5	7.5	8.8		
12/75	6.7	6.9	7.1	7.1	7.3	6.8	7.7	7.7	8.4	8.0	
12/76	6.8	7.0	7.2	7.3	7.3	6.9	7.0	7.6	8.1	7.7	7.4

TABLE 4

TIME-WEIGHTED RATES OF RETURN* ON SHORT-TERM U.S. TREASURY SECURITIES: INTEREST REINVESTED.
TAX EXEMPT.
DEFLATED BY THE CONSUMER PRICE INDEX

ACQUIRED AT END OF MONTH

HELD UNTIL	12/25	12/26	12/27	12/28	12/29	12/30	12/31	12/32	12/33	12/34	12/35	12/36	12/37	12/38	12/39	12/40	12/41	12/42	12/43	12/44
12/26	5.4																			
12/27	5.4	5.4																		
12/28	5.0	4.8	4.3																	
12/29	5.0	4.9	4.6	4.9																
12/30	6.0	6.2	6.4	7.5	10.2															
12/31	7.0	7.3	7.4	9.0	11.1	12.1														
12/32	8.2	8.6	9.3	10.6	12.5	13.7	15.4													
12/33	7.1	7.7	7.7	8.3	9.2	8.9	7.3	-0.1												
12/34	6.3	6.6	6.6	7.0	7.4	6.8	5.0	0.2	0.6											
12/35	5.5	5.5	5.8	5.6	5.8	5.0	3.2	-0.6	-0.7	-2.2										
12/36	4.2	4.1	4.0	4.9	4.8	4.0	2.4	-1.0	-1.2	-1.3	-0.5									
12/37	4.2	4.1	3.7	4.0	3.9	3.0	1.6	-0.3	-1.0	-1.4	-1.6	-2.7								
12/38	4.0	3.9	3.4	3.9	3.6	3.0	1.8	-0.1	-0.5	-0.5	0.0	0.3	3.3							
12/39	3.7	3.5	3.4	3.7	3.2	2.9	1.5	-0.1	-0.3	-0.2	0.2	0.6	2.4	1.4						
12/40	2.8	2.6	2.5	3.3	2.1	2.5	0.4	-1.2	-1.3	-1.6	-1.4	-1.6	-1.4	0.5	-0.5					
12/41	2.1	1.7	1.7	2.3	1.3	1.4	-0.4	-1.9	-2.1	-2.4	-2.4	-2.7	-2.7	-2.9	-5.0	-9.2				
12/42	1.9	1.7	1.5	1.5	1.0	0.6	-0.6	-1.9	-2.0	-2.3	-2.3	-2.5	-2.6	-4.2	-5.1	-8.6	-8.1			
12/43	1.7	1.3	1.3	1.3	0.7	0.4	-0.7	-1.8	-2.0	-2.2	-2.2	-2.4	-2.5	-3.4	-4.1	-6.5	-5.2	-2.2		
12/44	1.6	1.2	1.2	1.1	0.7	0.2	-0.6	-1.7	-1.9	-2.1	-2.1	-2.3	-2.3	-3.4	-3.8	-4.5	-3.3	-1.7	-1.3	
12/45	0.7	0.1	-0.1	-0.4	-0.2	-0.7	-1.7	-2.8	-3.0	-3.3	-3.4	-4.0	-4.6	-5.0	-5.5	-6.3	-5.7	-5.0	-4.6	-8.0
12/46	0.3	0.1	0.1	-0.4	-0.7	-1.7	-2.1	-3.1	-3.3	-3.6	-3.7	-4.2	-5.0	-5.7	-6.4	-6.6	-6.0	-5.5	-6.4	-8.4
12/47	0.4	0.0	0.0	-0.5	-0.5	-1.3	-2.0	-2.7	-2.8	-3.0	-3.1	-3.4	-3.9	-4.5	-4.9	-4.9	-4.3	-4.3	-4.7	-6.4
12/48	0.2	-0.2	-0.2	-0.6	-0.7	-1.3	-1.7	-2.8	-3.2	-3.2	-3.4	-4.0	-4.2	-4.6	-5.3	-5.4	-5.0	-4.9	-4.4	-6.4
12/49	0.0	-0.2	-0.1	-0.6	-0.5	-1.2	-1.9	-2.7	-2.8	-3.4	-3.4	-3.9	-3.9	-4.5	-4.9	-4.7	-4.7	-3.9	-4.1	-4.6
12/50	0.1	-0.2	-0.1	-0.4	-0.7	-1.2	-1.7	-2.8	-2.9	-3.1	-3.2	-3.4	-3.4	-4.0	-4.5	-4.9	-4.3	-3.9	-3.9	-4.3
12/51	0.1	-0.1	-0.1	-0.5	-0.5	-1.4	-2.0	-3.0	-3.2	-3.2	-3.2	-3.5	-3.5	-4.0	-4.4	-4.8	-4.3	-4.1	-3.9	-4.3
12/52	0.2	0.0	0.0	-0.5	-0.6	-1.3	-1.7	-2.8	-2.9	-2.7	-2.7	-2.9	-3.1	-3.4	-4.0	-4.3	-3.9	-3.9	-3.6	-4.0
12/53	0.2	-0.1	0.0	-0.6	-0.7	-1.3	-1.9	-2.4	-2.8	-2.5	-2.4	-2.6	-2.6	-3.5	-3.6	-3.9	-3.4	-3.4	-2.9	-3.4
12/54	0.2	-0.1	0.0	-0.4	-0.5	-1.0	-1.7	-2.3	-2.4	-2.2	-2.1	-2.4	-2.4	-2.9	-3.2	-3.4	-3.0	-2.5	-2.3	-3.0
12/55	0.2	-0.1	-0.1	-0.3	-0.5	-0.9	-1.5	-2.1	-2.3	-2.2	-2.3	-2.4	-2.3	-2.7	-3.0	-3.2	-2.6	-2.3	-2.1	-2.6
12/56	0.2	0.0	0.0	-0.5	-0.4	-0.9	-1.4	-2.0	-2.1	-2.0	-2.0	-2.2	-2.3	-2.6	-2.8	-2.8	-2.4	-2.0	-1.9	-2.2
12/57	0.2	0.1	0.2	-0.3	-0.4	-0.8	-1.3	-1.9	-1.9	-1.7	-1.9	-2.0	-2.0	-2.3	-2.6	-2.6	-2.2	-1.8	-1.6	-2.0
12/58	0.2	0.1	0.3	-0.2	-0.4	-0.7	-1.1	-1.8	-1.8	-1.5	-1.6	-1.8	-1.8	-2.0	-2.3	-2.4	-2.1	-1.8	-1.5	-1.8
12/59	0.4	0.3	0.4	-0.1	-0.2	-0.6	-1.0	-1.6	-1.6	-1.3	-1.4	-1.5	-1.6	-1.7	-2.0	-2.1	-1.7	-1.3	-1.1	-1.4
12/60	0.5	0.4	0.5	-0.1	0.1	-0.4	-0.9	-1.5	-1.4	-1.2	-1.3	-1.4	-1.4	-1.6	-1.8	-1.7	-1.4	-1.3	-1.1	-1.3
12/61	0.5	0.5	0.5	0.0	0.1	-0.3	-0.8	-1.3	-1.3	-1.1	-1.1	-1.2	-1.3	-1.5	-1.7	-1.7	-1.3	-1.0	-0.9	-1.1
12/62	0.6	0.5	0.5	0.1	0.1	-0.3	-0.7	-1.2	-1.2	-1.0	-1.0	-1.1	-1.1	-1.4	-1.5	-1.4	-1.2	-0.9	-0.8	-1.0
12/63	0.6	0.5	0.6	0.2	0.2	-0.2	-0.6	-1.0	-1.1	-0.9	-0.9	-1.0	-1.1	-1.3	-1.4	-1.3	-1.0	-0.8	-0.7	-0.9
12/64	0.5	0.4	0.5	0.1	0.1	-0.3	-0.7	-1.1	-1.2	-0.9	-0.9	-1.0	-1.0	-1.2	-1.3	-1.2	-0.9	-0.7	-0.6	-0.8
12/65	0.6	0.5	0.5	0.2	0.2	-0.2	-0.6	-1.0	-1.0	-0.8	-0.8	-0.9	-0.9	-1.1	-1.1	-1.1	-0.7	-0.6	-0.5	-0.6
12/66	0.6	0.5	0.5	0.2	0.1	-0.2	-0.5	-0.9	-0.9	-0.8	-0.8	-0.8	-0.9	-1.0	-1.0	-1.0	-0.7	-0.5	-0.4	-0.5
12/67	0.6	0.5	0.5	0.2	0.2	-0.1	-0.4	-0.8	-0.8	-0.7	-0.7	-0.8	-0.8	-0.9	-1.0	-0.9	-0.7	-0.4	-0.4	-0.4
12/68	0.6	0.5	0.5	0.3	0.3	-0.1	-0.4	-0.7	-0.8	-0.6	-0.6	-0.7	-0.7	-0.8	-0.8	-0.8	-0.5	-0.5	-0.3	-0.3
12/69	0.6	0.5	0.5	0.3	0.3	-0.1	-0.4	-0.7	-0.7	-0.6	-0.6	-0.6	-0.7	-0.8	-0.8	-0.7	-0.5	-0.3	-0.3	-0.3
12/70	0.7	0.6	0.6	0.4	0.4	0.0	-0.3	-0.6	-0.6	-0.5	-0.5	-0.6	-0.6	-0.7	-0.7	-0.7	-0.4	-0.3	-0.2	-0.2
12/71	0.8	0.7	0.7	0.5	0.5	0.1	-0.2	-0.5	-0.5	-0.4	-0.4	-0.5	-0.5	-0.6	-0.6	-0.6	-0.3	-0.2	-0.1	-0.1
12/72	0.7	0.6	0.6	0.4	0.4	0.0	-0.2	-0.5	-0.5	-0.5	-0.5	-0.5	-0.5	-0.6	-0.6	-0.6	-0.4	-0.2	-0.1	-0.1
12/73	0.7	0.5	0.5	0.3	0.3	-0.2	-0.3	-0.6	-0.6	-0.5	-0.5	-0.6	-0.5	-0.6	-0.6	-0.6	-0.3	-0.2	-0.1	-0.1
12/74	0.6	0.5	0.4	0.2	0.2	0.0	-0.2	-0.5	-0.5	-0.5	-0.5	-0.5	-0.4	-0.5	-0.6	-0.6	-0.3	-0.2	-0.0	-0.0
12/75	0.6	0.5	0.4	0.4	0.3	0.0	-0.2	-0.5	-0.5	-0.5	-0.5	-0.5	-0.5	-0.6	-0.6	-0.6	-0.2	-0.1	-0.0	-0.0
12/76	0.7	0.6	0.5	0.4	0.3	0.1	-0.2	-0.5	-0.5	-0.5	-0.5	-0.6	-0.4	-0.6	-0.6	-0.6	-0.3	-0.1	-0.0	-0.0

TABLE 4   CONTINUED

ACQUIRED AT END OF MONTH

HELD UNTIL	12/45	12/46	12/47	12/48	12/49	12/50	12/51	12/52	12/53	12/54	12/55	12/56	12/57	12/58	12/59	12/60	12/61	12/62	12/63	12/64
12/46	-14.7																			
12/47	-11.2	-7.5																		
12/48	-8.1	-4.6	-1.6																	
12/49	-5.4	-2.1	0.7	3.1																
12/50	-5.2	-2.7	-1.0	-0.8	-4.0															
12/51	-5.0	-3.0	-1.8	-1.8	-4.3	1.0														
12/52	-4.2	-2.3	-1.3	-1.2	-2.6	1.5	2.1													
12/53	-3.4	-1.7	-0.7	-0.7	-1.4	1.7	2.1	2.1												
12/54	-2.8	-1.2	-0.3	-0.1	-0.7	1.5	1.1	1.4	0.8											
12/55	-2.5	-1.0	-0.2	0.0	-0.1	1.0	1.0	0.8	0.7	-0.3										
12/56	-2.3	-1.0	-0.2	0.0	0.2	1.3	1.4	1.3	1.3	0.2	0.6									
12/57	-2.0	-0.8	-0.1	0.1	0.3	1.4	1.5	1.4	1.3	1.3	1.5	0.3								
12/58	-1.9	-0.7	0.1	0.2	0.4	1.4	1.6	1.4	1.4	1.4	1.6	0.8	0.9							
12/59	-1.6	-0.6	0.3	0.5	0.6	1.5	1.6	1.6	1.5	1.5	1.8	1.9	1.8	1.5						
12/60	-1.3	-0.3	0.5	0.6	0.7	1.4	1.6	1.6	1.5	1.6	1.8	1.9	1.9	2.4	3.7					
12/61	-1.1	-0.1	0.6	0.7	0.9	1.5	1.7	1.6	1.6	1.6	1.8	1.9	1.9	2.1	2.9	2.1				
12/62	-0.9	0.0	0.6	0.8	1.0	1.4	1.6	1.6	1.6	1.6	1.8	1.8	1.9	2.1	2.3	1.8	2.0			
12/63	-0.8	0.1	0.8	0.9	1.1	1.5	1.7	1.7	1.7	1.7	1.9	1.8	2.0	2.0	2.2	2.0	2.0	2.0		
12/64	-0.6	0.2	0.8	1.0	1.2	1.5	1.7	1.7	1.7	1.7	1.9	1.8	2.0	2.1	2.2	2.0	1.9	2.0	2.1	
12/65	-0.4	0.3	0.9	1.0	1.2	1.5	1.7	1.7	1.7	1.7	1.8	1.9	2.0	2.2	2.2	2.1	2.0	2.1	2.1	2.7
12/66	-0.3	0.4	0.9	1.0	1.3	1.3	1.8	1.7	1.8	1.7	2.0	2.0	2.1	2.2	2.2	2.1	2.1	2.0	2.0	2.3
12/67	-0.2	0.5	0.9	1.0	1.3	1.3	1.5	1.7	1.7	1.7	1.9	1.9	2.1	2.1	2.2	2.1	2.1	2.0	2.1	2.1
12/68	-0.1	0.5	0.9	1.1	1.2	1.3	1.5	1.6	1.6	1.6	1.8	1.8	2.0	2.0	2.2	1.9	1.8	1.6	1.8	1.8
12/69	-0.3	0.7	0.9	1.0	1.2	1.5	1.7	1.7	1.7	1.7	1.9	1.9	1.9	2.1	2.0	2.0	2.0	2.0	2.0	1.8
12/70	-0.5	0.8	1.1	1.2	1.4	1.4	1.7	1.8	1.8	1.7	1.8	2.0	2.1	2.2	2.2	2.1	2.1	2.1	2.1	2.0
12/71	-0.4	0.8	1.1	1.3	1.5	1.4	1.7	1.7	1.7	1.7	1.8	1.9	2.0	2.1	2.2	2.0	2.0	2.0	2.0	2.1
12/72	-0.3	0.7	1.0	1.1	1.4	1.3	1.5	1.5	1.5	1.5	1.5	1.6	1.7	1.8	1.8	1.7	1.7	1.7	1.6	1.8
12/73	-0.2	0.5	0.9	1.2	1.3	1.1	1.3	1.3	1.3	1.3	1.3	1.3	1.4	1.5	1.5	1.3	1.3	1.2	1.2	1.4
12/74	-0.1	0.6	0.9	0.9	1.1	1.3	1.3	1.3	1.3	1.2	1.3	1.4	1.4	1.5	1.5	1.4	1.3	1.3	1.4	1.3
12/75	-0.0	0.6	0.9	0.9	1.0	1.3	1.3	1.3	1.3	1.3	1.3	1.4	1.5	1.5	1.5	1.3	1.3	1.3	1.3	1.2
12/76	0.1	0.6	0.9	1.0	1.1	1.4	1.4	1.4	1.3	1.3	1.4	1.4	1.5	1.5	1.5	1.4	1.3	1.3	1.3	1.2

ACQUIRED AT END OF MONTH

HELD UNTIL	12/65	12/66	12/67	12/68	12/69	12/70	12/71	12/72	12/73	12/74	12/75
12/66	1.9										
12/67	2.0	2.1									
12/68	1.8	1.7	1.3								
12/69	1.5	1.4	1.1	0.8							
12/70	2.1	2.3	2.1	2.5	4.1						
12/71	2.2	2.3	2.3	2.7	7.6	3.0					
12/72	2.1	2.1	2.1	2.3	2.7	2.1	1.1				
12/73	1.5	1.4	1.3	1.4	1.4	1.4	-0.7	-3.0			
12/74	1.0	0.9	0.7	0.6	0.5	0.6	-0.9	-1.5	-1.1		
12/75	0.9	0.9	0.7	0.6	0.6	0.6	-0.1	-0.5	0.1	1.0	
12/76	1.1	1.0	0.9	0.9	0.9	0.9	-0.2	0.3	0.1	1.7	2.5

TABLE 5

TIME-WEIGHTED RATES OF RETURN* ON LONG-TERM U.S. TREASURY BONDS: INTEREST REINVESTED.
TAX EXEMPT.
CURRENT DOLLARS

ACQUIRED AT END OF MONTH

HELD UNTIL	12/25	12/26	12/27	12/28	12/29	12/30	12/31	12/32	12/33	12/34	12/35	12/36	12/37	12/38	12/39	12/40	12/41	12/42	12/43	12/44
12/26	7.2																			
12/27	7.7	8.2																		
12/28	4.7	3.5	-0.9																	
12/29	4.7	3.8	1.7	4.4																
12/30	5.0	4.4	3.2	5.3	6.2															
12/31	2.8	1.9	0.4	0.8	-0.9	-7.6														
12/32	3.4	2.9	2.0	3.4	3.1	1.5	11.5													
12/33	3.4	2.9	2.0	2.6	2.2	0.8	5.3	-0.5												
12/34	4.0	3.6	3.0	3.7	3.5	2.8	6.6	4.2	9.0											
12/35	3.8	3.8	3.1	3.8	3.8	3.3	6.5	4.5	7.1	5.1										
12/36	4.2	4.2	3.7	4.3	4.3	4.0	6.5	5.2	7.2	6.3	7.5									
12/37	4.1	4.0	3.4	3.9	3.8	3.5	5.5	4.5	5.6	4.7	4.1	0.7								
12/38	4.2	4.2	3.6	4.1	4.0	3.8	5.5	4.8	5.7	5.1	4.6	3.2	5.6							
12/39	4.2	4.0	3.5	4.0	4.0	3.6	5.6	4.9	5.7	5.1	5.1	4.6	5.9	6.5						
12/40	4.5	4.2	3.8	4.3	4.2	4.1	5.7	5.1	5.7	5.1	5.1	4.6	5.6	6.0	5.5					
12/41	4.2	4.1	3.6	4.1	4.0	3.9	5.0	4.5	4.8	4.4	4.3	3.8	4.4	4.3	3.7	1.1				
12/42	4.1	4.0	3.6	4.1	4.0	3.7	4.7	4.3	4.4	4.1	3.9	3.5	4.0	3.6	3.2	2.1	2.1			
12/43	4.0	3.9	3.6	4.0	3.9	3.7	4.6	4.1	4.4	4.1	4.5	3.4	3.8	3.5	2.9	2.3	2.3	3.2		
12/44	4.1	4.0	3.7	4.3	4.2	4.1	5.0	4.5	4.9	4.6	4.5	4.2	4.6	4.5	4.2	3.9	4.7	5.1	10.7	
12/45	4.3	4.2	4.0	4.3	4.2	4.1	5.0	4.6	4.9	4.6	4.5	4.2	4.6	4.4	4.2	3.9	4.4	4.5	6.7	5.2
12/46	3.8	3.6	3.5	3.6	3.6	3.5	4.2	3.7	4.0	3.6	3.5	3.2	3.3	3.2	2.8	2.4	2.6	2.4	3.1	2.6
12/47	3.8	3.6	3.4	3.6	3.6	3.5	4.0	3.7	3.8	3.6	3.5	3.2	3.4	3.2	2.8	2.5	2.7	2.6	3.1	2.6
12/48	3.9	3.8	3.5	3.8	3.7	3.6	4.1	3.9	4.1	3.8	3.7	3.4	3.7	3.5	3.2	2.9	3.2	3.2	3.5	3.1
12/49	3.7	3.7	3.4	3.7	3.6	3.4	4.0	3.6	3.9	3.6	3.5	3.4	3.7	3.5	3.2	2.9	3.2	3.0	3.4	2.9
12/50	3.4	3.3	3.1	3.4	3.3	3.1	3.6	3.4	3.6	3.1	3.0	2.8	2.8	2.6	2.3	2.0	2.0	2.0	2.0	1.6
12/51	3.3	3.2	3.0	3.3	3.2	3.1	3.5	3.3	3.4	3.1	2.9	2.7	2.7	2.5	2.3	2.1	2.1	1.9	1.9	1.5
12/52	3.3	3.2	3.1	3.2	3.2	3.0	3.5	3.1	3.4	3.0	3.0	2.6	2.7	2.4	2.2	2.0	2.1	1.8	2.0	1.6
12/53	3.4	3.3	3.1	3.3	3.2	3.0	3.5	3.3	3.4	3.1	3.0	2.7	2.9	2.7	2.5	2.3	2.3	2.1	2.3	1.7
12/54	3.4	3.3	3.2	3.3	3.2	3.1	3.5	3.4	3.4	3.1	3.0	2.8	2.9	2.7	2.5	2.3	2.0	2.0	2.0	1.4
12/55	3.0	2.8	2.6	3.0	3.0	2.8	3.2	3.0	3.2	2.7	2.6	2.4	2.5	2.4	2.1	1.8	1.6	1.6	1.6	1.1
12/56	3.2	3.1	2.9	3.1	3.0	2.8	3.2	2.9	3.1	2.8	2.6	2.4	2.5	2.4	2.2	1.9	1.7	1.7	1.5	1.2
12/57	2.7	2.6	2.4	2.6	2.6	2.4	2.7	2.4	2.6	2.3	2.3	2.3	2.4	2.1	1.8	1.4	1.4	1.3	1.4	1.0
12/58	3.0	2.9	2.8	2.8	2.8	2.6	2.8	2.7	2.7	2.4	2.4	2.3	2.4	2.2	2.2	2.0	2.0	2.0	2.0	2.0
12/59	3.0	2.9	2.6	2.8	2.7	2.6	2.8	2.7	2.7	2.4	2.4	2.3	2.4	2.3	2.1	1.9	1.9	1.7	1.9	1.9
12/60	3.0	3.0	2.8	2.9	2.8	2.7	2.8	2.8	2.8	2.6	2.6	2.5	2.6	2.4	2.2	2.1	2.0	2.0	2.1	1.8
12/61	3.0	3.0	2.8	2.9	2.8	2.7	2.9	2.7	2.9	2.6	2.5	2.3	2.5	2.3	2.1	2.1	2.1	1.9	2.0	2.0
12/62	3.0	2.9	2.8	2.8	2.8	2.7	2.9	2.8	2.8	2.6	2.6	2.4	2.5	2.4	2.2	2.1	1.3	1.1	1.9	1.9
12/63	3.0	2.9	2.7	2.8	2.8	2.7	2.8	2.8	2.9	2.6	2.6	2.4	2.5	2.4	2.2	2.1	2.0	2.0	2.0	2.0
12/64	3.0	2.9	2.8	2.9	2.8	2.7	2.9	2.8	2.9	2.7	2.6	2.4	2.5	2.3	2.2	2.1	2.1	2.1	2.1	2.0
12/65	3.0	2.9	2.7	2.8	2.7	2.6	2.8	2.7	2.8	2.6	2.5	2.4	2.5	2.4	2.2	2.1	2.1	2.1	2.1	2.0
12/66	3.0	2.9	2.7	2.7	2.7	2.5	2.7	2.6	2.7	2.4	2.4	2.2	2.4	2.2	2.0	2.0	1.8	1.8	1.7	1.7
12/67	2.8	2.7	2.5	2.6	2.6	2.4	2.5	2.5	2.5	2.3	2.3	2.2	2.2	2.1	2.0	1.8	1.9	1.8	1.4	1.4
12/68	2.8	2.6	2.5	2.6	2.6	2.4	2.6	2.5	2.6	2.4	2.3	2.2	2.3	2.1	1.6	1.5	1.5	1.4	1.4	1.3
12/69	2.5	2.4	2.2	2.3	2.3	2.2	2.2	2.2	2.3	2.1	2.0	1.8	1.9	1.8	1.6	1.5	1.5	1.3	1.4	1.3
12/70	2.9	2.8	2.6	2.7	2.7	2.6	2.6	2.6	2.6	2.5	2.5	2.3	2.4	2.3	2.2	2.1	2.0	2.1	2.5	2.0
12/71	3.1	3.0	2.9	3.0	2.9	2.9	3.2	2.7	3.0	2.9	2.9	2.7	2.8	2.7	2.6	2.5	2.5	2.4	2.6	2.4
12/72	3.2	3.0	2.9	3.0	2.9	2.9	3.1	3.0	3.1	3.0	2.8	2.8	2.8	2.7	2.6	2.5	2.5	2.5	2.6	2.5
12/73	3.1	3.0	3.0	3.0	2.9	2.9	3.2	3.1	3.1	2.9	2.9	2.7	2.8	2.7	2.6	2.5	2.5	2.6	2.7	2.6
12/74	3.2	3.0	2.9	3.1	2.9	2.9	3.2	3.0	3.1	2.9	2.9	2.8	2.8	2.7	2.6	2.5	2.1	2.6	2.7	2.6
12/75	3.2	3.0	3.0	3.1	3.0	3.0	3.0	3.1	3.1	2.9	2.9	2.8	2.9	2.8	2.7	2.6	2.7	2.7	2.7	2.7
12/76	3.4	3.4	3.3	3.4	3.3	3.3	3.5	3.4	3.5	3.3	3.3	3.2	3.2	3.2	3.1	3.0	3.1	3.1	3.1	3.1
	12/25	12/26	12/27	12/28	12/29	12/30	12/31	12/32	12/33	12/34	12/35	12/36	12/37	12/38	12/39	12/40	12/41	12/42	12/43	12/44

TABLE 5   CONTINUED

ACQUIRED AT END OF MONTH

HELD UNTIL	12/45	12/46	12/47	12/48	12/49	12/50	12/51	12/52	12/53	12/54	12/55	12/56	12/57	12/58	12/59	12/60	12/61	12/62	12/63	12/64
12/46	-0.1																			
12/47	-1.4	-2.6																		
12/48	0.2	0.3	3.4																	
12/49	1.7	2.3	4.9	6.4																
12/50	1.4	1.8	3.3	3.2	0.1															
12/51	0.5	0.6	1.4	0.8	-2.0	-3.9														
12/52	1.0	0.7	1.7	0.9	-0.9	-1.4	1.2													
12/53	1.4	1.1	2.2	1.4	0.2	0.2	2.4	3.6												
12/54	1.6	1.6	1.7	2.0	1.1	1.4	3.2	4.2	4.9											
12/55	1.1	1.2	1.8	1.5	0.5	0.8	2.0	2.3	1.6	-1.5										
12/56	0.5	0.6	0.9	1.6	0.7	0.9	2.0	0.4	-0.6	-3.2	-4.9									
12/57	1.2	1.4	1.3	0.6	-0.2	-0.2	0.6	1.8	1.8	0.8	2.0	9.4								
12/58	0.8	0.9	1.8	1.5	1.0	1.1	1.9	1.2	0.7	-0.4	0.5	2.6	-3.7							
12/59	0.5	0.9	1.4	1.6	1.4	1.6	2.1	0.5	-0.8	-1.0	-0.9	0.5	-3.6	-3.5						
12/60	1.4	1.5	1.9	1.8	1.1	1.7	1.7	2.0	1.6	1.3	1.9	3.7	1.9	3.1	13.8					
12/61	1.3	1.4	1.9	1.9	1.6	1.9	2.2	2.2	1.6	1.1	2.9	3.3	2.2	3.3	6.6	-0.0				
12/62	1.5	1.6	2.0	1.6	1.1	2.1	2.1	1.9	2.0	1.6	3.0	3.1	2.3	3.2	6.2	2.4	5.4			
12/63	1.6	1.7	2.0	1.1	1.2	1.7	2.1	2.1	2.1	1.8	2.4	3.0	2.0	3.1	4.7	2.6	3.3	1.3		
12/64	1.7	1.8	1.6	1.9	1.6	1.8	1.7	1.8	1.9	1.7	3.0	2.4	2.3	2.9	4.0	2.1	2.7	2.5	3.7	0.3
12/65	1.4	1.5	1.2	1.7	1.3	1.3	1.1	1.1	1.6	1.4	2.8	3.0	2.3	3.1	4.0	2.5	3.0	2.4	2.0	2.3
12/66	1.0	1.0	2.0	1.3	0.8	1.1	2.1	1.8	1.6	1.4	2.8	2.2	1.6	2.1	2.8	1.5	1.7	0.8	0.7	-0.3
12/67	1.7	1.8	2.0	1.8	0.9	2.1	2.7	2.8	2.0	1.4	2.9	1.3	0.7	1.1	2.8	1.3	1.7	1.1	-1.0	-0.4
12/68	2.2	2.4	2.5	2.4	2.4	2.4	2.7	2.8	2.7	2.6	3.5	3.4	3.0	3.5	3.2	2.2	2.4	2.1	-0.6	-1.4
12/69	2.3	2.4	2.6	2.5	2.3	2.5	2.7	2.8	2.8	2.6	3.0	3.0	3.0	3.4	3.9	3.2	3.6	3.5	3.7	-1.9
12/70	2.2	2.4	2.7	2.5	2.3	2.4	2.8	2.8	2.8	2.7	2.9	3.4	3.2	3.5	4.0	3.3	3.5	3.6	3.5	3.7
12/71	2.4	2.5	2.7	2.7	2.5	2.6	2.9	3.0	2.9	2.9	3.1	3.5	3.2	3.6	4.1	3.5	3.7	3.6	3.8	3.8
12/72	2.9	3.0	3.2	3.2	3.1	3.2	3.5	3.6	3.6	3.5	3.7	4.2	3.9	4.4	4.9	4.3	4.6	4.6	4.8	4.9

ACQUIRED AT END OF MONTH

HELD UNTIL	12/65	12/66	12/67	12/68	12/69	12/70	12/71	12/72	12/73	12/74	12/75
12/66	4.3										
12/67	-0.6	-5.3									
12/68	0.4	-1.5	2.4								
12/69	-1.9	-3.9	-3.2	-8.4							
12/70	2.2	1.7	4.8	5.1	20.5						
12/71	4.3	4.3	6.5	8.4	17.8	15.2					
12/72	4.5	3.9	6.5	7.6	13.5	10.2	5.4				
12/73	3.0	3.9	5.5	6.1	10.0	6.8	2.3	0.2			
12/74	4.0	4.1	5.3	5.8	8.9	6.2	3.3	2.3	4.4		
12/75	4.2	4.1	5.7	5.8	8.4	6.1	4.0	3.5	5.2	6.0	
12/76	5.3	5.4	6.7	7.3	9.7	8.0	6.6	6.9	9.3	11.8	17.9

TABLE 6

TIME-WEIGHTED RATES OF RETURN* ON LONG-TERM U.S. TREASURY BONDS: INTEREST REINVESTED.
TAX EXEMPT,
DEFLATED BY THE CONSUMER PRICE INDEX

ACQUIRED AT END OF MONTH

HELD UNTIL	12/25	12/26	12/27	12/28	12/29	12/30	12/31	12/32	12/33	12/34	12/35	12/36	12/37	12/38	12/39	12/40	12/41	12/42	12/43	12/44
12/26	8.8																			
12/27	9.7	10.5																		
12/28	6.3	5.1	0.0																	
12/29	5.8	4.8	2.1	4.2																
12/30	7.2	6.8	5.6	8.5	13.0															
12/31	6.4	5.7	4.7	6.4	7.5	2.1														
12/32	8.7	8.7	8.4	10.6	12.8	12.7	24.3													
12/33	7.5	7.3	7.1	8.2	8.7	7.7	10.9	-1.0												
12/34	7.4	7.2	7.0	8.0	8.7	7.7	9.6	2.9	6.9											
12/35	6.9	6.7	6.5	7.1	7.4	6.5	7.4	3.5	5.0	2.1										
12/36	6.8	6.6	6.3	7.0	7.4	6.5	7.1	3.3	4.4	4.1	6.2									
12/37	6.2	6.0	5.7	6.2	6.4	5.8	6.2	3.3	3.2	3.6	4.1	-2.3								
12/38	6.2	6.1	5.9	6.3	6.4	5.6	6.2	3.9	4.7	4.3	4.7	3.0	8.6							
12/39	6.2	6.1	5.7	6.2	6.3	5.8	6.0	3.9	4.7	4.3	4.7	4.4	7.8	7.0						
12/40	6.2	6.0	5.6	6.1	6.3	5.6	6.0	2.5	3.0	2.5	2.5	1.8	2.8	5.7	4.5					
12/41	5.2	5.0	4.6	5.0	5.2	4.3	4.5	1.7	1.6	1.1	1.0	0.3	0.7	-1.0	-1.9	-7.9				
12/42	5.2	4.3	4.2	4.2	4.3	3.5	3.6	1.5	2.1	1.7	1.7	0.3	0.7	-0.8	-2.0	-6.7	-5.6			
12/43	4.2	3.8	3.6	3.8	3.1	2.9	3.0	1.4	1.6	1.1	1.0	-1.2	-1.6	-1.6	-2.6	-4.9	-3.3	-2.3		
12/44	4.2	4.0	3.7	3.9	3.3	3.3	3.4	2.1	2.1	1.7	1.7	-0.2	-0.5	-1.6	-2.3	-3.8	-0.5	-3.0	-1.0	-8.3
12/45	4.3	3.9	3.7	2.7	2.6	2.6	3.4	0.7	0.2	0.5	0.8	-0.6	-1.6	-2.2	-4.1	-2.9	-2.3	-4.0	-2.6	-4.5
12/46	3.2	2.9	2.6	2.0	1.8	1.2	1.1	-0.2	-0.2	-0.7	-0.9	-1.6	-1.3	-3.1	-3.4	-3.1	-2.9	-4.2	-3.7	-4.7
12/47	2.5	2.2	1.8	1.9	1.8	1.5	1.1	-0.1	-0.1	-0.6	-0.8	-0.7	-0.9	-1.7	-2.7	-4.1	-3.2	-4.2	-3.7	-4.8
12/48	2.7	2.2	2.0	1.9	1.9	1.2	1.1	-0.3	-0.2	-0.4	-0.5	-0.7	-0.9	-1.3	-2.3	-2.8	-2.5	-2.1	-2.4	-3.2
12/49	2.4	2.1	1.9	1.9	1.7	1.5	1.1	0.4	0.6	0.0	-0.2	-0.6	-0.5	-1.3	-2.0	-2.8	-2.5	-2.3	-2.0	-2.8
12/50	1.9	1.6	1.7	1.2	1.2	1.2	0.6	-0.2	-0.1	-0.9	-1.1	-1.2	-1.1	-1.9	-2.4	-3.3	-2.9	-3.1	-2.1	-3.2
12/51	1.8	1.6	1.2	1.8	1.2	1.5	0.9	-0.5	-0.5	-0.9	-1.1	-1.8	-1.1	-2.3	-2.4	-3.1	-2.7	-2.6	-2.2	-2.6
12/52	1.9	1.8	1.3	1.3	1.1	1.2	0.8	-0.2	-0.2	-0.5	-0.8	-0.7	-0.8	-1.3	-1.9	-2.3	-2.1	-2.1	-1.5	-1.8
12/53	1.9	2.0	1.1	1.5	1.5	1.5	0.6	0.2	0.4	-0.2	-0.6	-1.2	-1.1	-2.1	-2.4	-2.6	-2.4	-2.0	-1.6	-1.9
12/54	2.0	1.6	1.3	1.0	1.2	1.2	0.9	0.3	0.5	0.4	0.5	-0.3	-0.2	-1.3	-1.9	-2.1	-1.9	-1.5	-1.6	-1.7
12/55	1.5	1.5	1.0	1.7	0.6	0.6	0.4	-0.5	-0.1	-0.7	-0.8	-0.6	-0.7	-1.1	-1.3	-1.7	-1.5	-1.5	-1.9	-1.7
12/56	1.7	1.2	1.2	1.0	0.9	0.9	0.7	-0.2	-0.2	-0.7	-0.8	-0.8	-1.1	-1.4	-1.4	-1.7	-1.1	-1.9	-1.0	-1.8
12/57	1.5	1.0	1.1	1.1	1.0	1.0	0.7	0.1	-0.2	-0.3	-0.5	-0.8	-0.8	-1.3	-1.6	-1.7	-1.7	-1.6	-1.1	-1.7
12/58	1.6	1.1	1.1	1.0	1.0	0.9	0.6	-0.1	-0.1	-0.5	-0.8	-0.6	-0.6	-1.0	-1.4	-1.4	-1.5	-1.5	-1.9	-1.4
12/59	1.6	1.3	1.2	1.0	1.1	1.0	0.7	-0.2	-0.5	-0.2	-0.5	-0.6	-0.4	-1.0	-1.1	-1.4	-1.6	-1.2	-1.2	-1.2
12/60	1.5	1.4	1.1	1.0	1.0	0.6	0.4	-0.2	-0.2	-0.5	-0.8	-0.4	-0.7	-1.0	-1.1	-1.4	-1.2	-1.9	-1.3	-1.3
12/61	1.5	1.3	1.0	1.0	1.0	0.7	0.5	-0.1	-0.1	-0.4	-0.6	-0.6	-0.7	-0.9	-1.0	-1.3	-1.1	-1.7	-1.2	-1.0
12/62	1.4	1.5	1.4	1.1	1.1	0.7	0.4	-0.2	-0.1	-0.4	-0.5	-0.4	-0.5	-0.8	-0.9	-1.1	-1.1	-1.5	-1.1	-0.9
12/63	1.5	1.3	1.3	1.1	1.0	0.8	0.5	0.0	0.0	-0.4	-0.4	-0.3	-0.4	-0.7	-0.9	-1.0	-1.0	-1.2	-1.2	-1.1
12/64	1.5	1.4	1.3	1.1	1.0	0.7	0.4	0.0	0.0	-0.3	-0.4	-0.5	-0.5	-0.8	-0.8	-1.0	-0.9	-1.0	-1.3	-1.4
12/65	1.4	1.3	1.1	1.0	0.7	0.4	0.4	-0.2	-0.3	-0.5	-0.6	-0.5	-0.5	-0.7	-0.8	-0.9	-0.9	-1.1	-1.2	-1.1
12/66	1.2	1.0	1.0	0.7	0.7	0.4	0.0	-0.2	-0.3	-0.4	-0.6	-0.4	-0.7	-1.0	-0.8	-0.9	-0.9	-1.0	-0.8	-1.1
12/67	0.8	1.0	0.8	0.8	0.4	0.4	-0.1	-0.2	-0.4	-0.5	-0.5	-0.6	-0.7	-0.8	-0.9	-1.0	-0.7	-0.7	-0.7	-0.8
12/68	1.0	0.6	0.7	0.7	0.5	-0.0	0.1	-0.3	-0.3	-0.5	-0.6	-0.5	-0.4	-0.7	-0.8	-0.8	-0.8	-0.9	-0.8	-0.7
12/69	0.9	0.9	0.7	0.7	0.3	0.3	0.3	-0.3	-0.3	-0.4	-0.6	-0.4	-0.5	-0.7	-0.7	-0.9	-0.9	-1.1	-1.0	-1.1
12/70	1.0	0.9	0.9	0.6	0.6	0.3	0.3	-0.2	-0.3	-0.5	-0.6	-0.6	-0.6	-0.8	-0.9	-0.9	-1.0	-1.1	-1.1	-1.1
12/71	1.3	0.9	1.1	0.9	0.7	0.4	0.3	-0.0	0.0	-0.2	-0.4	-0.4	-0.4	-0.7	-0.8	-0.9	-0.7	-0.9	-0.4	-1.1
12/72	1.1	1.1	1.1	1.1	0.7	0.4	0.4	-0.0	0.0	-0.4	-0.6	-0.5	-0.7	-0.8	-0.8	-1.0	-1.0	-0.5	-0.6	-1.1
12/73	1.0	0.7	1.1	1.0	0.7	0.2	0.3	-0.3	-0.3	-0.5	-0.6	-0.6	-0.6	-0.7	-0.9	-0.9	-1.0	-1.1	-1.0	-1.1
12/74	0.9	0.7	0.5	0.6	0.2	0.2	-0.3	-0.3	-0.3	-0.5	-0.6	-0.7	-0.7	-0.7	-1.0	-1.0	-1.1	-1.0	-1.1	-1.0
12/75	0.9	0.7	0.5	0.8	0.2	0.2	-0.1	-0.3	-0.3	-0.5	-0.6	-0.4	-0.4	-0.6	-0.8	-0.9	-1.0	-1.1	-1.0	-1.0
12/76	1.1	0.9	0.7	0.8	0.7	0.4	0.4	-0.1	-0.1	-0.2	-0.3	-0.4	-0.4	-0.6	-0.8	-1.0	-1.0	-0.7	-0.8	-0.6

TABLE 6   CONTINUED

ACQUIRED AT END OF MONTH

HELD UNTIL	12/45	12/46	12/47	12/48	12/49	12/50	12/51	12/52	12/53	12/54	12/55	12/56	12/57	12/58	12/59	12/60	12/61	12/62	12/63	12/64
12/46	-15.5																			
12/47	-13.1	-10.7																		
12/48	-8.7	-5.2	0.7																	
12/49	-4.7	-0.8	4.5	8.4																
12/50	-4.9	-2.0	1.1	1.3	-9.3															
12/51	-5.6	-3.5	-1.6	-2.4	-7.4	-4.6	0.3													
12/52	-4.8	-2.9	-1.2	-1.7	-4.9	-2.1	1.6	3.0												
12/53	-3.9	-2.1	-0.6	-0.8	-3.0	-0.3	2.9	4.2	5.4											
12/54	-2.9	-1.2	0.3	0.2	-1.4	-0.6	1.6	2.1	1.7	-1.9										
12/55	-2.8	-1.2	0.2	-0.1	-2.3	-1.8	-0.3	-0.4	-1.5	-4.8	-7.6									
12/56	-3.2	-1.9	-0.9	-1.1	-1.3	-0.7	-0.7	-0.2	-0.8	-1.3	-0.4	6.2								
12/57	-2.5	-1.2	-1.1	-1.3	-1.8	-1.3	-0.1	-0.9	-1.5	-2.3	-2.4	0.2	-5.4							
12/58	-2.7	-1.5	-0.7	-0.8	-2.1	-1.7	-0.7	0.7	0.3	-2.8	-3.1	-1.7	-5.2	-5.0						
12/59	-2.9	-1.8	-0.7	-0.7	-0.9	-0.4	0.4	0.5	0.7	-0.5	-0.2	1.7	0.7	3.2	12.1					
12/60	-1.9	-0.9	-1.0	-1.2	-0.5	-0.5	0.5	0.9	0.6	-0.5	-0.3	1.7	0.8	1.9	5.5	-0.7				
12/61	-1.8	-0.9	-0.1	-0.1	-0.1	-0.1	0.5	0.7	0.5	0.0	0.3	1.5	0.9	2.4	5.0	1.7	4.1			
12/62	-1.5	-0.6	-0.1	-0.1	-0.3	0.1	0.4	0.9	0.7	0.2	0.5	1.2	0.6	2.0	3.4	1.0	1.9	-0.3		
12/63	-1.4	-0.4	0.1	0.1	-0.4	-0.0	0.7	0.7	0.5	0.1	0.3	0.3	0.6	1.5	2.6	1.4	2.1	-1.1	7.5	
12/64	-1.2	-0.4	0.1	0.2	-0.3	-0.5	0.7	0.7	-0.1	-0.5	-0.4	0.1	-0.3	0.6	2.4	0.8	1.2	-0.4	0.5	-1.6
12/65	-1.3	-0.4	0.2	0.2	-0.8	-0.6	0.5	0.1	-0.2	-0.6	-0.5	-1.0	-0.5	0.0	1.0	-0.5	-0.5	-1.5	-1.6	-0.3
12/66	-1.2	-0.4	0.2	-0.3	-1.5	-1.3	-0.0	-0.0	-0.3	-1.6	-1.5	-0.0	-1.6	-0.1	-0.0	-0.7	-0.7	-1.3	-1.8	-3.0
12/67	-1.5	-0.8	-0.3	-1.1	-0.6	-0.0	-0.8	-0.9	-1.1	-0.6	-0.6	0.7	-0.5	-1.3	-0.9	-2.3	-2.4	-3.3	-3.4	-5.1
12/68	-2.0	-0.3	-1.1	-1.1	-0.0	0.1	0.5	-0.1	0.3	0.0	0.2	0.8	0.3	-0.3	-2.3	0.3	0.4	-0.0	-0.1	-0.3
12/69	-1.4	-1.4	-0.4	-0.4	-0.2	-0.3	0.5	0.5	0.4	-0.3	-0.2	0.2	0.9	0.8	-0.4	0.5	0.6	0.2	0.2	0.0
12/70	-1.0	-0.8	0.1	0.1	-0.8	-0.6	0.1	0.1	-0.0	-0.6	-0.6	-0.2	-0.1	0.9	1.3	-0.7	-0.7	-0.5	-0.8	-0.9
12/71	-0.9	-0.3	-0.1	-0.1	-0.6	-0.6	-0.2	-0.2	-0.4	-0.7	-0.6	-0.2	-0.5	-0.2	0.5	-0.7	-0.7	-1.1	-1.2	-1.5
12/72	-1.1	-0.3	-0.1	-0.4	-0.3	-0.1	-0.6	-0.2	-0.2	-0.7	-0.6	-0.2	-0.6	-0.2	0.1	0.1	0.1	-0.2	-1.1	-1.5
12/73	-1.1	-0.6	-0.4	-0.5																
12/74	-1.3	-0.8	-0.5	-0.0																
12/75	-1.3	-0.8	-0.0																	
12/76	-0.9	-0.4																		

ACQUIRED AT END OF MONTH

HELD UNTIL	12/65	12/66	12/67	12/68	12/69	12/70	12/71	12/72	12/73	12/74	12/75
12/66	0.9										
12/67	-3.7	-8.1									
12/68	-3.2	-5.2	-2.3								
12/69	-5.9	-8.1	-8.1	-13.6							
12/70	-2.2	-3.0	-1.2	-0.7	14.2						
12/71	-0.0	-0.2	-0.7	3.2	12.8	11.5					
12/72	0.2	0.1	1.8	2.9	4.6	6.6	1.9				
12/73	-0.1	-1.1	0.1	0.6	1.5	1.5	-3.1	-7.9			
12/74	-0.8	-1.8	-0.7	-0.7	1.6	-0.7	-4.4	-7.4	-7.0		
12/75	-1.5	-1.7	-0.9	-0.7	-0.7	-0.7	-3.6	-5.3	-4.0	-0.9	
12/76	-0.3	-0.4	0.5	0.8	3.1	1.4	-0.5	-1.2	1.2	5.6	12.5

2

RATES OF RETURN ON INVESTMENTS IN COMMON STOCK: THE YEAR-BY-YEAR RECORD, 1926–65 *

Lawrence Fisher † and James H. Lorie ‡

THE FINDINGS

IN JANUARY, 1964, "Rates of Return on Investments in Common Stocks" appeared in this *Journal*.[1] That article contained rates of return on all common stocks listed on the New York Stock Exchange for twenty-two periods

* Funds to support the work reported in this article came primarily from Merrill Lynch, Pierce, Fenner & Smith, Inc. In addition, the work of the Center for Research in Security Prices was supported by the National Science Foundation.

We would like to acknowledge the help of Milton Davis and Irving Levenstein in collecting and checking data; that of Mark C. Case, Marvin Lipson, John Pomeranz, Richard Roll, Daniel Rosenfels, and Jesse Seymour in the writing of computer programs for the general handling of the basic file of data analyzed for this study; that of Owen M. Hewett in revising the computer programs used for the study itself so as to provide a vast increase in the amount of information obtained; and the staff of the Computation Center of the University of Chicago for general assistance in data processing. Nearly all price data for the period after 1960 were provided on magnetic tape by Merrill Lynch, Pierce, Fenner & Smith, Inc.

† Associate professor of finance and associate director of the Center for Research in Security Prices (sponsored by Merrill Lynch, Pierce, Fenner & Smith, Inc.), Graduate School of Business, University of Chicago.

‡ Professor of business administration and director of the Center for Research in Security Prices (sponsored by Merrill Lynch, Pierce, Fenner & Smith, Inc.), Graduate School of Business, University of Chicago.

between January 30, 1926, and December 30, 1960. It was "news" in the sense that it presented the first comprehensive and refined measurement of the performance of stocks listed on the New York Stock Exchange for a significant number of time periods under a variety of assumptions about taxes and reinvestment of dividends. The relatively high rates of return reported in that study apparently surprised many people. The present article may be considered "news" insofar as it provides detailed confirmation of the earlier findings and extends them through December, 1965. It presents results for portfolios of all common stocks listed on the New York Stock Exchange, assuming equal initial investments in the stock of each corporation, from the end of each year to the end of each subsequent year, a total of 820 time periods.[2] In all, data for 1,856 stocks were used in the calculations. On the average, each stock affected the results for about 330 time periods.

The rates shown in Table 1 are aver-

[1] L. Fisher and J. H. Lorie, "Rates of Return on Investments in Common Stock," *Journal of Business*, XXXVII, No. 1 (January, 1964), 1–21.

[2] The single exception is that the first starting date is the end of January, 1926, rather than the end of December, 1925.

age annual rates of return compounded annually, assuming equal initial investments in the common stocks listed on the New York Stock Exchange.[3] Of course, no one actually made such investments, and there may therefore be interest in the relationship between these rates and a feasible policy, such as—say—random selection of stocks. It is impossible to make a definitive statement about the relationship between the rates in Table 1 and the rates resulting from a policy of random selection, but it is possible to say something about the relationship between the ratios of terminal wealth to initial investment which are implied by the rates of Table 1 and the corresponding ratios of terminal wealth to initial investment that would result from simple random selection.[4] These ratios would be the same on the average. That is, an investor who selected stocks at random would, on the average, have ended up with the same wealth as the investor who earned the rates in Table 1.

As in the earlier article, data are presented for different tax brackets with dividends reinvested, dividends not reinvested but taken into account with respect to both time and amount, and dividends ignored. The data are shown in detail as average annual rates of return on investment or annual rates of price change.

The methods of computation used in the first study were effectively the same as the methods of computation for this study. However, statistics from the present study frequently differ from those in the first study for comparable periods by a fraction of 1 per cent per annum.[5] For example, the average annual rate of return compounded annually, assuming tax exemption and reinvestment of dividends for the period January, 1926–December, 1960, was reported as 9.0 per cent in the first study and is 8.8 per cent here. Most of the rates of return either remain unchanged or are changed by 0.1 per cent. Some of the changes are up, but most are down. The changes are due primarily to corrections in the master file of data upon which the studies are based. In addition, there are minor changes in the method of measuring return. These changes in method may have caused occasional differences in the rounded values of the rates of return presented. The changes allowed the organization of the master file to be simplified and permitted the calculation and retention of detailed data on the return for each stock covered by the study.[6]

This article will be followed by another which will present frequency distributions of the rates of return on investments in individual stocks for each of many of the time periods presented here. It will present summaries of these data in a way which, we believe, provides new information on the variability of rates of return among stocks and hence provides new information about the riskiness of investment in common stocks and on the effectiveness of diversification.

[3] For a more detailed statement of the investment policy underlying this and other tables, see below.

[4] By "simple random selection" is meant any scheme which produces equal expectations of the amount of initial investment in each stock—a scheme, for example, such as equal probabilities of selection with equal investment in the stocks selected.

[5] See Appendix.

[6] The data that have been retained for each company are on rates of return with reinvestment of dividends and with dividends ignored for the 820 periods reported in the text. Tables 1 and 3 may be viewed as summaries of these data. Although these data contain less than 1 per cent of such data potentially available from the master file, their storage requires twice as many reels of magnetic tape. Retention of data on the return to each stock without reinvestment of dividends was not feasible.

The highlights of this study are the following:

1. For the period from December, 1960, to December, 1965, rates of return were high. In 1962, the rate of return was negative, −13.3 per cent; but in each of the other four years, the rate of return exceeded 16 per cent and, in 1965, was 28.3 per cent. The average for the five years was 15.9 per cent per annum, compounded annually. These rates are not dramatically different from other rates since the end of 1948 or even the entire period since 1931.

2. In all the 820 overlapping, and therefore not independent, time periods within the forty years, the longest periods of time with negative rates of return on common stocks listed on the New York Stock Exchange were the fourteen-year periods beginning at the end of 1927 and the end of 1928, and the twelve years beginning at the end of 1929. Aside from periods beginning in these years, the next longest period with a negative rate was six years. In all, only seventy-two of the periods showed negative rates of return.

3. The longest period of time for which rates of return were less than 5.0 per cent was the period between December, 1928, and December, 1950—twenty-two years. If one considers only the period after the market crash of 1929–32, the longest period for which rates were less than 5 per cent was the eight years from December, 1936, to December, 1944.

4. During the last twenty years covered by the study, rates were consistently high. In the 210 overlapping time periods considered, positive rates of return were earned in 199 periods—95 per cent of the total. In this period, there was no interval of more than four years in which our hypothetical investor earned a rate of return of less than 7 per cent.

There was no ten-year period in which the investor earned less than 11 per cent.

5. As many have suspected, the cumulative effect of the personal income tax on wealth is great. As explained in the earlier article,[7] after-tax rates of return were calculated assuming the marginal rates applicable to individuals with taxable incomes of $10,000 and $50,000 in 1960 and comparable incomes in other years (e.g., $12,200 and $61,200 in 1965 or $1,780 and $8,950 in 1933). For the period January, 1926–December, 1965, the terminal wealth of a tax-exempt investor who reinvested dividends would have been 1.36 times as great as that of the investor in the lower tax category and 2.26 times that of the investor in the higher tax category, if they had all sold their holdings at the end of 1965. For December, 1945–December, 1965, the ratios were 1.30 and 1.97, respectively.[8]

The above findings are some of the generalizations which are permitted by the greater detail of the present study. The first study pointed out, perhaps adequately, that it is also possible to lose money by investing in common stocks and that losses were dramatic during the market crash of 1929–32.

METHOD

Except for the change described in step 5(*b*) below, the method for finding the rate of return for a time period used here is the same as that used in the

[7] *Op. cit.*, p. 6.

[8] These findings were obtained from the data used to calculate the rates of return shown in Table 1. Ratios for other periods may be obtained from Tables 1 and 3 by applying the formula

$$\text{Ratio} = \left(\frac{1 + r_1}{1 + r_2}\right)^L,$$

where r_1 is the tax-exempt rate of return for a period (as a decimal fraction), r_2 is the taxable rate of return, and L is the length of the period.

earlier study.[9] For those unfamiliar with the earlier study, the complete method will be summarized here.

The methods of finding any single number in Tables 1–3 will be described. There is a total of 14,760 numbers in these tables. For numbers referring to rates of return with reinvestment of dividends or rates of change in prices (rates with dividends ignored), the first step is to find the wealth of an investor at the end of a specified time period, assuming a specified investment policy. (The specified investment policy is indicated by the description of the method and the title of the table.) The final step is to find the constant rate of return, expressed as an annual rate compounded annually, which, when applied to the initial investment, would have produced that terminal wealth. For numbers referring to rates of return without reinvestment of dividends, the first step is to specify the stream of dividends withdrawn from the portfolio and the terminal wealth. The final step is to find the rate of return (discount rate or internal rate of return) which makes the present value of the stream of dividends and terminal wealth equal to the initial investment. The rate of return or discount is conceptually identical with the familiar yield-to-maturity of a bond.

The rates of return reported may be viewed as rather complex averages of rates for the months in each period. For rates with reinvestment of dividends, the months are equally weighted. For rates without reinvestment, the earlier months receive higher weights than later months.

The investment policies are as follows:

1. Initial investment

   In all cases, at the beginning of a period, an equal amount of money is used to purchase

[9] For details, see Fisher and Lorie, *op. cit.*, pp. 15–17.

the common stock of each company whose common stock is listed on the New York Stock Exchange at that time.

2. Dividends

   a) For rates based on reinvestment of dividends, dividends after income taxes are reinvested in the stock paying the dividend.

   b) For rates based on consumption of dividends, it is assumed that ordinary cash dividends, other dividends treated the same for tax purposes, and cash dividends that were taxed as "returns of capital" were spent. Other "dividends," such as stock dividends and partial liquidations, are reinvested on the grounds that they are really capital changes.

   c) For rates computed without regard to dividends, cash and cash-equivalent dividends described in *b* above are ignored and others are reinvested.

3. Subscription rights

   It is assumed that the recipient of subscription rights to more of the same stock sells enough of them so that the proceeds after capital-gains taxes are just sufficient to exercise the remainder. Other rights are treated as cash dividends if taxable and as partial liquidations if non-taxable.

4. Spinoffs

   a) Non-taxable distributions of the common stock of listed companies are retained. Distributions of unlisted stocks are sold, and the proceeds are reinvested in the stock of the distributing company.

   b) Taxable distributions of stock in another company, when dividends are reinvested, are sold to the extent necessary to pay taxes, and the remainder is retained if the stock is a listed common stock. If the stock is not a listed common stock, the dividend is treated as if it were cash. In calculating rates based on the assumption that dividends are either consumed or ignored, such distributions were treated as if they were cash dividends.

5. Delistings

   a) When two companies with listed common stock merge, the proceeds to the investor in the acquired company are invested in the stock of the surviving company.

   b) When delisting occurs for reasons other than merger into a company with listed common stock, the stock of the delisted company is sold, and the proceeds are invested in a dummy stock whose performance is given by Fisher's index.[10]

6. End of the period

For rates based on the assumption that the final portfolio is converted to cash, the value of the holdings is calculated after the payment of commissions and taxes.

The only change in method between the first and present studies is minor and did not affect the results perceptibly. In the first study, when a stock was delisted without being merged into another company whose common stock was listed, the stock was assumed to have been sold over the counter, and the funds were reinvested in equal amounts in the common stock of each company then listed on the New York Stock Exchange. In the

present study, the funds were reinvested in a dummy stock derived from Fisher's indexes. These indexes are based upon an equal weighting of the performance of all common stocks on the New York Stock Exchange, so that immediately afterward the effect of investing in the dummy stock is virtually the same as the effect of investing equal amounts in each stock listed. In the computation of the index, however, the investment in each common stock is nearly equalized monthly. From analysis of fifty-five of the 820 periods, it appears that this change in method caused no difference in the rate of return for any period that was as great as 0.1 per cent.[11, 12]

[10] Lawrence Fisher, "Some New Stock-Market Indexes," *Journal of Business*, XXXIX, No. 1, Part II (January, 1966), 191–225. The indexes used are revised values of the Combination Investment-Performance and Price Indexes. Each month's price was taken as the value of the Combination Price Index. Each month's dividend was found by multiplying the previous month's "price" by the difference between the link relatives for the Investment-Performance and Price Indexes. The percentage rate of brokerage commission was the arithmetic mean of the percentage rates for each common stock listed that month.

[11] The periods analyzed were all those that were a multiple of four years in length and began in January, 1926, or in December of 1929 and each fourth year thereafter through 1961. The cases analyzed all assumed tax exemption and reinvestment of dividends. In the process of analysis, some possible improvements in the method of computing the index were revealed. Making these improvements would change some values of the index significantly, but the changed values of the index would not significantly affect the rates of return in this article.

[12] There were several reasons for the change in method. The major ones were to simplify organization of the file of data and to facilitate the calculation of the rates of return on individual stocks.

FROM

To	1/26	12/26	12/27	12/28	12/29	12/30	12/31	12/32	12/33	12/34	12/35	12/36	12/37	12/38	12/39	12/40	12/41	12/42	12/43	12/44
12/26	-1.6																			
12/27	15.3	30.0																		
12/28	23.9	37.7	45.5																	
12/29	7.8	9.6	0.1	-30.0																
12/30	-2.3	-3.5	-13.0	-31.7	-37.2															
12/31	-11.1	-13.5	-21.7	-36.3	-40.8	-47.8														
12/32	-11.0	-12.7	-19.0	-30.3	-32.1	-31.0	-11.1													
12/33	-2.7	-3.2	-7.7	-15.6	-11.8	-1.3	36.9	108.4												
12/34	-1.2	-1.6	-5.2	-11.3	-7.0	2.4	28.2	55.0	13.8											
12/35	2.2	2.1	-0.8	-5.7	-0.5	9.3	32.9	53.5	31.2	50.4										
12/36	6.6	5.5	3.1	-0.4	5.3	15.3	37.5	54.5	40.9	56.8	63.9									
12/37	0.5	0.1	-2.3	-6.2	-2.8	3.3	16.1	23.1	8.2	6.6	-10.9	-46.0								
12/38	2.8	2.5	0.4	-2.9	0.9	7.0	18.7	25.1	12.9	12.4	1.1	-16.2	30.7							
12/39	2.6	2.3	0.3	-2.6	0.9	6.0	15.7	20.5	10.1	9.0	0.4	-11.2	12.9	-3.3						
12/40	1.9	1.6	-0.2	-3.0	0.2	4.7	13.0	16.9	7.9	6.4	-1.1	-9.8	6.3	-5.0	-9.9					
12/41	1.2	0.9	-0.8	-3.3	-0.5	3.5	10.8	13.8	5.8	4.2	-1.9	-9.2	2.6	-5.5	-9.0	-10.2				
12/42	2.0	1.9	0.4	-1.9	0.9	4.8	11.6	14.3	7.2	6.0	0.9	-4.9	6.1	0.6	1.1	7.6	31.1			
12/43	3.5	3.6	2.2	0.2	3.1	7.2	13.8	16.5	10.2	9.7	5.5	0.9	12.3	9.4	12.1	22.2	47.1	56.7		
12/44	4.6	4.7	3.5	1.7	4.7	8.7	15.2	17.9	12.3	12.0	8.4	4.6	15.7	13.7	17.1	26.8	45.6	49.3	38.1	
12/45	6.3	6.5	5.5	3.9	7.0	11.3	17.6	20.4	15.4	15.5	12.4	9.3	20.3	19.4	23.7	33.6	51.4	55.4	50.1	59.8
12/46	5.5	5.7	4.7	3.2	6.0	9.9	15.6	18.0	13.3	13.1	10.2	7.2	16.3	15.0	17.8	24.2	34.8	34.5	26.0	20.2
12/47	5.3	5.6	4.6	3.1	5.8	9.3	14.6	16.8	12.4	12.1	9.4	6.7	14.7	13.6	15.5	20.3	27.5	26.3	18.9	13.2
12/48	5.1	5.2	4.2	2.8	5.2	8.5	13.5	15.5	11.3	11.0	8.4	5.8	12.7	11.7	13.3	17.0	22.5	20.8	14.2	9.1
12/49	5.7	5.8	4.9	3.6	6.0	9.1	13.8	15.7	11.7	11.5	9.1	6.8	13.3	12.3	13.9	17.3	22.2	20.8	15.2	11.4
12/50	6.5	6.7	5.9	4.6	7.0	10.2	14.9	16.7	12.9	12.8	10.6	8.5	14.8	14.1	15.6	19.0	23.5	22.4	17.9	15.0
12/51	6.9	7.1	6.4	5.1	7.5	10.6	15.1	16.7	13.1	13.1	11.0	9.0	14.8	14.1	15.6	18.6	22.6	21.6	17.7	15.2
12/52	7.0	7.2	6.5	5.3	7.6	10.5	14.8	16.4	13.0	13.0	11.0	9.0	14.5	13.8	15.1	17.9	21.5	20.4	16.8	14.5
12/53	6.6	6.8	6.1	5.0	7.1	9.8	13.9	15.3	12.2	12.1	10.2	8.3	13.3	12.5	13.7	16.1	19.3	18.1	14.8	12.5
12/54	8.0	8.2	7.6	6.4	8.7	11.4	15.5	17.0	14.0	14.1	12.2	10.5	15.5	14.8	16.2	18.7	21.9	21.0	18.2	16.4
12/55	8.4	8.6	8.0	6.9	9.2	11.9	15.9	17.4	14.5	14.6	12.7	11.1	15.9	15.2	16.6	18.8	21.8	21.1	18.6	16.9
12/56	8.5	8.7	8.1	7.0	9.2	11.8	15.7	17.1	14.4	14.4	12.6	11.1	15.6	15.1	16.2	18.2	20.8	20.2	17.9	16.4
12/57	7.8	7.9	7.3	6.3	8.3	10.7	14.3	15.5	12.9	12.9	11.2	9.7	13.9	13.2	14.2	15.9	18.3	17.5	15.1	13.6
12/58	8.8	9.0	8.4	7.5	9.5	11.9	15.5	16.7	14.3	14.4	12.7	11.3	15.5	15.0	16.0	17.8	20.2	19.4	17.3	16.0
12/59	8.9	9.1	8.5	7.6	9.7	12.1	15.6	16.8	14.4	14.5	12.8	11.5	15.6	15.0	16.0	17.6	19.9	19.1	17.1	15.8
12/60	8.8	9.0	8.3	7.5	9.4	11.6	14.9	16.1	13.9	13.9	12.3	11.1	14.8	14.2	15.1	16.6	18.7	17.9	15.9	14.6
12/61	9.3	9.5	8.9	8.1	9.9	12.2	15.4	16.6	14.4	14.5	13.0	11.8	15.4	15.0	15.8	17.3	19.3	18.5	16.5	15.4
12/62	8.6	8.8	8.2	7.3	9.1	11.2	14.3	15.3	13.2	13.3	11.8	10.7	14.0	13.5	14.3	15.6	17.3	16.5	14.6	13.5
12/63	8.9	9.1	8.5	7.7	9.5	11.6	14.6	15.6	13.5	13.6	12.2	11.0	14.3	13.8	14.6	15.8	17.4	16.7	14.9	13.9
12/64	9.1	9.3	8.8	7.9	9.6	11.6	14.5	15.6	13.6	13.7	12.4	11.3	14.4	14.0	14.7	15.8	17.4	16.7	15.0	14.0
12/65	9.3	9.5	9.0	8.2	10.0	12.0	14.9	15.9	13.9	14.0	12.6	11.6	14.6	14.2	14.9	16.0	17.5	16.9	15.4	14.4

FROM

To	1/26	12/26	12/27	12/28	12/29	12/30	12/31	12/32	12/33	12/34	12/35	12/36	12/37	12/38	12/39	12/40	12/41	12/42	12/43	12/44
12/26	-2.2																			
12/27	15.1	29.3																		
12/28	23.7	37.4	44.9																	
12/29	7.7	9.4	-0.2	-30.4																
12/30	-2.4	-3.6	-13.2	-31.9	-37.7															
12/31	-11.3	-13.7	-21.9	-36.5	-41.2	-48.7														
12/32	-11.1	-12.9	-19.2	-30.5	-32.4	-31.7	-12.9													
12/33	-2.8	-3.3	-7.8	-15.8	-12.0	-1.7	36.0	105.7												
12/34	-1.3	-1.7	-5.3	-11.4	-7.1	2.2	27.7	54.2	12.5											
12/35	2.1	2.0	-0.9	-5.8	-0.6	9.2	32.6	53.1	30.7	49.0										
12/36	6.5	5.4	3.1	-0.5	5.2	15.2	37.3	54.3	40.6	56.3	62.8									
12/37	0.5	0.1	-2.4	-6.3	-2.9	3.2	16.0	22.8	7.9	6.2	-11.4	-46.6								
12/38	2.7	2.5	0.4	-2.9	0.8	6.9	18.6	25.0	12.7	12.2	0.8	-16.5	29.3							
12/39	2.5	2.3	0.3	-2.7	0.8	5.9	15.6	20.3	10.0	8.8	0.1	-11.5	12.4	-4.4						
12/40	1.9	1.6	-0.3	-3.0	0.1	4.6	12.9	16.8	7.7	6.2	-1.2	-10.0	5.9	-5.5	-10.9					
12/41	1.2	0.8	-0.9	-3.3	-0.6	3.4	10.7	13.7	5.7	4.1	-2.1	-9.4	2.3	-5.9	-9.5	-11.4				
12/42	2.0	1.8	0.3	-2.0	0.8	4.7	11.4	14.1	7.0	5.9	0.7	-5.0	5.9	0.3	0.6	6.8	29.0			
12/43	3.5	3.5	2.2	0.1	3.1	7.1	13.7	16.4	10.1	9.6	5.3	0.8	12.2	9.2	11.8	21.8	46.1	54.7		
12/44	4.5	4.7	3.5	1.6	4.6	8.7	15.1	17.8	12.2	11.9	8.3	4.5	15.5	13.5	16.9	26.5	45.1	48.5	36.8	
12/45	6.2	6.5	5.5	3.8	7.0	11.2	17.5	20.4	15.3	15.4	12.4	9.2	20.2	19.2	23.5	33.4	51.1	55.0	49.5	58.7
12/46	5.5	5.7	4.7	3.2	6.0	9.8	15.5	17.9	13.2	13.0	10.2	7.2	16.2	14.9	17.7	24.0	34.5	34.2	25.6	19.7
12/47	5.3	5.5	4.5	3.1	5.7	9.3	14.6	16.7	12.3	12.0	9.4	6.6	14.5	13.5	15.4	20.1	27.3	26.0	18.6	12.8
12/48	5.0	5.1	4.2	2.7	5.2	8.5	13.4	15.4	11.2	10.9	8.3	5.7	12.6	11.6	13.1	16.9	22.3	20.5	14.0	8.9
12/49	5.7	5.8	4.9	3.5	5.9	9.0	13.8	15.6	11.7	11.4	9.0	6.7	13.2	12.2	13.8	17.1	22.1	20.6	15.0	11.1
12/50	6.5	6.6	5.8	4.5	7.0	10.2	14.9	16.6	12.8	12.8	10.6	8.4	14.7	14.0	15.5	18.9	23.3	22.3	17.8	14.8
12/51	6.9	7.1	6.3	5.1	7.4	10.5	15.1	16.7	13.1	13.1	10.9	8.9	14.7	14.0	15.5	18.5	22.5	21.5	17.6	15.1
12/52	7.0	7.2	6.5	5.3	7.6	10.5	14.8	16.3	13.0	12.9	10.9	9.0	14.4	13.7	15.1	17.8	21.4	20.3	16.7	14.4
12/53	6.6	6.8	6.1	4.9	7.1	9.7	13.8	15.3	12.1	12.1	10.1	8.3	13.2	12.4	13.6	16.0	19.2	18.0	14.6	12.4
12/54	8.0	8.2	7.5	6.4	8.6	11.3	15.5	17.0	14.0	14.0	12.2	10.5	15.4	14.7	16.1	18.6	21.8	20.9	18.1	16.3
12/55	8.4	8.6	8.0	6.9	9.1	11.9	15.9	17.3	14.4	14.5	12.7	11.0	15.8	15.2	16.5	18.8	21.7	21.0	18.5	16.8
12/56	8.5	8.6	8.0	7.0	9.2	11.8	15.7	17.0	14.3	14.4	12.6	11.0	15.6	15.0	16.1	18.1	20.7	20.1	17.9	16.3
12/57	7.7	7.9	7.2	6.3	8.3	10.6	14.3	15.4	12.9	12.9	11.1	9.7	13.8	13.2	14.1	15.9	18.2	17.4	15.0	13.5
12/58	8.8	9.0	8.4	7.5	9.5	11.9	15.5	16.7	14.2	14.3	12.6	11.3	15.5	14.9	15.9	17.7	20.1	19.4	17.2	15.9
12/59	8.9	9.1	8.5	7.6	9.6	12.1	15.5	16.7	14.3	14.4	12.8	11.5	15.5	15.0	15.9	17.6	19.8	19.1	17.0	15.7
12/60	8.7	8.9	8.3	7.4	9.3	11.6	14.9	16.0	13.8	13.9	12.3	11.0	14.7	14.1	15.0	16.5	18.6	17.8	15.8	14.6
12/61	9.3	9.5	8.9	8.0	9.9	12.1	15.4	16.5	14.4	14.5	12.9	11.8	15.4	14.9	15.7	17.3	19.2	18.4	16.5	15.4
12/62	8.6	8.8	8.2	7.3	9.1	11.2	14.2	15.3	13.2	13.3	11.8	10.6	14.0	13.5	14.2	15.5	17.3	16.5	14.6	13.5
12/63	8.9	9.1	8.5	7.6	9.4	11.5	14.5	15.6	13.5	13.6	12.1	11.0	14.2	13.8	14.5	15.7	17.4	16.6	14.8	13.8
12/64	9.1	9.3	8.7	7.9	9.6	11.6	14.5	15.5	13.6	13.6	12.3	11.2	14.4	14.0	14.6	15.8	17.3	16.7	15.0	14.0
12/65	9.3	9.5	9.0	8.2	9.9	12.0	14.9	15.8	13.9	14.0	12.6	11.5	14.6	14.2	14.9	16.0	17.5	16.9	15.3	14.4

TABLE 1
RATES OF RETURN ON INVESTMENT IN COMMON STOCKS LISTED ON THE NEW YORK STOCK EXCHANGE
WITH REINVESTMENT OF DIVIDENDS (Per Cent Per Annum Compounded Annually)
PART A—CASH-TO-PORTFOLIO, TAX EXEMPT

FROM

12/45	12/46	12/47	12/48	12/49
-9.9				
-4.4	-0.5			
-3.5	-1.0	-2.9		
1.9	5.4	8.2	19.3	
7.8	12.4	16.6	27.0	35.8

FROM

12/45	12/46	12/47	12/48	12/49	12/50	12/51	12/52	12/53	12/54
9.4	13.3	16.4	23.1	25.2	14.9				
9.4	12.9	15.2	19.7	19.8	12.4	8.9			
7.9	10.5	12.1	15.0	13.7	7.5	3.5	-3.1		
12.5	15.5	17.7	21.3	21.6	17.9	18.5	22.8	54.8	
13.4	16.2	18.2	21.4	21.7	18.5	19.1	22.2	37.2	19.0

FROM

12/45	12/46	12/47	12/48	12/49	12/50	12/51	12/52	12/53	12/54	12/55	12/56	12/57	12/58	12/59
13.3	15.6	17.2	19.8	20.0	17.0	16.9	18.6	26.7	13.3	6.5				
10.5	12.3	13.5	15.3	14.8	12.0	11.1	11.1	14.5	3.4	-3.7	-12.9			
13.2	15.2	16.7	18.7	18.6	16.5	16.5	17.5	21.9	14.5	13.0	17.4	57.9		
13.3	15.3	16.6	18.6	18.6	16.6	16.6	17.6	21.2	15.0	14.0	17.6	36.0	14.4	
12.2	14.0	15.2	16.8	16.5	14.9	14.8	15.3	17.8	12.4	11.2	13.1	21.9	6.4	-1.9

FROM

12/45	12/46	12/47	12/48	12/49	12/50	12/51	12/52	12/53	12/54	12/55	12/56	12/57	12/58	12/59	12/60	12/61	12/62	12/63	12/64
13.2	14.9	16.0	17.5	17.3	16.0	16.0	16.6	19.0	14.6	13.9	16.1	23.7	13.6	12.9	27.6				
11.3	12.8	13.7	14.9	14.5	13.1	12.8	13.0	14.7	10.5	9.4	10.4	15.1	6.3	3.8	5.9	-13.3			
11.8	13.2	14.0	15.2	14.9	13.5	13.3	13.5	15.0	11.3	10.4	11.5	15.7	8.7	7.4	10.4	2.0	17.7		
12.1	13.4	14.2	15.3	15.0	13.7	13.5	13.8	15.3	11.9	11.2	12.3	16.2	10.4	9.7	12.8	7.6	18.5	16.3	
12.6	14.1	14.9	15.9	15.8	14.5	14.3	14.7	16.2	13.1	12.5	13.6	17.7	12.7	12.4	15.9	12.9	22.6	23.4	28.3

TABLE 1.
RATES OF RETURN ON INVESTMENT IN COMMON STOCKS LISTED ON THE NEW YORK STOCK EXCHANGE
WITH REINVESTMENT OF DIVIDENDS (Per Cent Per Annum Compounded Annually)
PART B—CASH-TO-CASH, TAX EXEMPT

FROM

12/45	12/46	12/47	12/48	12/49
-10.6				
-4.9	-1.5			
-3.8	-1.5	-4.0		
1.6	5.1	7.6	18.0	
7.6	12.1	16.2	26.4	34.5

FROM

12/45	12/46	12/47	12/48	12/49	12/50	12/51	12/52	12/53	12/54
9.2	13.1	16.1	22.8	24.6	13.8				
9.3	12.7	15.0	19.5	19.4	11.9	7.8			
7.7	10.3	11.9	14.8	13.4	7.1	2.9	-4.3		
12.4	15.4	17.6	21.1	21.4	18.1	22.2	53.2		
13.3	16.1	18.1	21.2	21.6	18.3	18.8	21.8	36.5	17.8

FROM

12/45	12/46	12/47	12/48	12/49	12/50	12/51	12/52	12/53	12/54	12/55	12/56	12/57	12/58	12/59
13.2	15.5	17.1	19.7	19.8	16.8	16.7	18.3	26.3	12.8	5.4				
10.5	12.2	13.4	15.2	14.6	11.8	10.9	10.9	14.5	3.0	-4.2	-13.9			
13.2	15.1	16.6	18.6	18.5	16.4	16.3	17.3	21.6	14.2	12.6	16.8	56.1		
13.2	15.2	16.6	18.5	18.5	16.4	16.5	17.4	20.9	14.8	13.7	17.2	35.2	13.2	
12.2	13.9	15.1	16.7	16.4	14.7	14.7	15.2	17.6	12.2	11.0	12.8	21.4	5.8	-3.1

FROM

12/45	12/46	12/47	12/48	12/49	12/50	12/51	12/52	12/53	12/54	12/55	12/56	12/57	12/58	12/59	12/60	12/61	12/62	12/63	12/64
13.1	14.8	16.0	17.4	17.2	15.9	15.9	16.5	18.8	14.4	13.7	15.9	23.3	13.2	12.3	26.2				
11.3	12.7	13.6	14.8	14.4	13.0	12.7	12.9	14.5	10.3	9.2	10.2	14.8	6.0	3.4	5.2	-14.4			
11.7	13.2	14.0	15.1	14.8	13.4	13.2	13.4	14.9	11.2	10.3	11.3	15.5	8.5	7.1	10.0	1.4	16.3		
12.0	13.4	14.1	15.2	15.0	13.6	13.4	13.7	15.2	11.8	11.1	12.2	16.0	10.2	9.4	12.5	7.2	17.8	15.0	
12.6	14.1	14.8	15.9	15.7	14.4	14.3	14.6	16.2	13.0	12.4	13.5	17.5	12.5	12.3	15.7	12.6	22.2	22.7	26.9

Measurement of the Behavior of Individual Stocks and of the Market

To	1/26	12/26	12/27	12/28	12/29	12/30	12/31	12/32	12/33	12/34	12/35	12/36	12/37	12/38	12/39	12/40	12/41	12/42	12/43	12/44
12/26	-1.6																			
12/27	15.3	30.0																		
12/28	23.9	37.7	45.5																	
12/29	7.8	9.6	0.1	-30.0																
12/30	-2.3	-3.5	-13.0	-31.7	-37.2															
12/31	-11.1	-13.5	-21.7	-36.3	-40.8	-47.8														
12/32	-11.0	-12.7	-19.0	-30.3	-32.1	-31.0	-11.1													
12/33	-2.7	-3.2	-7.7	-15.6	-11.8	-1.3	36.9	108.4												
12/34	-1.2	-1.6	-5.2	-11.3	-7.0	2.4	28.2	55.0	13.8											
12/35	2.2	2.1	-0.8	-5.7	-0.5	9.3	32.9	53.5	31.2	50.4										
12/36	6.6	5.5	3.1	-0.4	5.3	15.3	37.5	54.5	40.9	56.8	63.9									
12/37	0.5	0.1	-2.3	-6.2	-2.8	3.3	16.1	23.1	8.2	6.6	-10.9	-46.0								
12/38	2.8	2.5	0.4	-2.9	0.9	7.0	18.7	25.1	12.9	12.4	1.1	-16.2	30.7							
12/39	2.6	2.3	0.3	-2.6	0.9	6.0	15.7	20.5	10.1	9.0	0.4	-11.2	12.9	-3.3						
12/40	1.9	1.6	-0.3	-3.0	0.2	4.6	13.0	16.9	7.8	6.3	-1.1	-9.8	6.2	-5.1	-10.0					
12/41	1.2	0.8	-0.9	-3.3	-0.6	3.4	10.7	13.7	5.7	4.1	-2.1	-9.4	2.3	-5.8	-9.4	-10.8				
12/42	1.9	1.8	0.2	-2.1	0.7	4.6	11.3	14.0	6.9	5.8	0.6	-5.2	5.7	0.2	0.5	6.8	30.0			
12/43	3.3	3.4	2.0	-0.0	2.9	6.9	13.5	16.1	9.9	9.3	5.1	0.5	11.8	8.8	11.3	21.2	45.8	55.1		
12/44	4.3	4.4	3.3	1.4	4.4	8.4	14.8	17.4	11.8	11.6	7.9	4.0	15.0	13.0	16.2	25.7	44.2	47.7	36.6	
12/45	6.0	6.3	5.2	3.6	6.7	10.9	17.1	19.9	14.9	15.0	11.9	8.7	19.6	18.5	22.7	32.5	50.1	53.9	48.7	58.4
12/46	5.2	5.4	4.4	2.9	5.7	9.4	15.1	17.4	12.7	12.5	9.6	6.6	15.5	14.2	16.8	23.1	33.6	33.2	24.7	19.0
12/47	5.0	5.2	4.2	2.7	5.3	8.8	14.1	16.2	11.7	11.4	8.7	5.9	13.8	12.7	14.4	19.0	26.2	24.9	17.6	11.9
12/48	4.7	4.8	3.8	2.3	4.7	8.0	12.9	14.8	10.6	10.2	7.6	5.0	11.8	10.7	12.2	15.8	21.2	19.4	12.9	7.9
12/49	5.3	5.4	4.4	3.1	5.4	8.5	13.1	14.9	11.0	10.7	8.3	6.0	12.3	11.3	12.7	16.0	20.9	19.4	13.8	10.1
12/50	6.0	6.2	5.4	4.1	6.4	9.6	14.2	15.9	12.1	12.0	9.8	7.6	13.8	13.0	14.4	17.7	22.2	21.0	16.5	13.6
12/51	6.4	6.6	5.8	4.5	6.9	9.9	14.3	15.9	12.3	12.3	10.1	8.0	13.8	13.0	14.4	17.4	21.3	20.2	16.3	13.9
12/52	6.5	6.7	5.9	4.7	7.0	9.8	14.0	15.5	12.2	12.1	10.1	8.1	13.4	12.6	13.9	16.6	20.2	19.0	15.4	13.2
12/53	6.1	6.3	5.5	4.3	6.4	9.0	13.0	14.4	11.3	11.2	9.2	7.4	12.2	11.3	12.5	14.8	18.0	16.7	13.4	11.2
12/54	7.4	7.6	6.9	5.8	8.0	10.6	14.7	16.1	13.1	13.1	11.3	9.5	14.4	13.7	15.0	17.4	20.6	19.6	16.8	15.0
12/55	7.8	8.0	7.3	6.3	8.5	11.1	15.1	16.5	13.6	13.6	11.8	10.1	14.8	14.1	15.3	17.6	20.5	19.7	17.3	15.6
12/56	7.9	8.0	7.4	6.4	8.5	11.0	14.9	16.2	13.4	13.5	11.7	10.1	14.5	14.0	15.0	16.9	19.5	18.8	16.6	15.1
12/57	7.1	7.3	6.6	5.6	7.6	9.9	13.5	14.6	12.0	12.0	10.2	8.7	12.8	12.1	13.0	14.7	17.0	16.2	13.9	12.3
12/58	8.2	8.4	7.8	6.8	8.8	11.2	14.7	15.8	13.4	13.5	11.8	10.4	14.4	13.9	14.8	16.6	19.0	18.2	16.0	14.7
12/59	8.3	8.5	7.9	6.9	9.0	11.3	14.8	15.9	13.5	13.6	11.9	10.6	14.5	14.0	14.8	16.5	18.7	17.9	15.9	14.6
12/60	8.2	8.4	7.7	6.8	8.7	10.8	14.1	15.2	13.0	13.0	11.4	10.1	13.7	13.1	13.9	15.4	17.5	16.7	14.7	13.5
12/61	8.7	8.9	8.3	7.4	9.2	11.4	14.6	15.7	13.5	13.6	12.1	10.9	14.4	13.9	14.7	16.1	18.1	17.3	15.4	14.3
12/62	8.0	8.2	7.6	6.7	8.4	10.4	13.4	14.4	12.3	12.4	10.9	9.7	13.0	12.5	13.2	14.5	16.2	15.4	13.5	12.4
12/63	8.3	8.4	7.9	7.0	8.7	10.8	13.7	14.7	12.6	12.7	11.2	10.1	13.3	12.8	13.4	14.6	16.3	15.5	13.7	12.7
12/64	8.4	8.6	8.1	7.	8.9	10.9	13.7	14.7	12.7	12.8	11.4	10.3	13.4	12.9	13.6	14.7	16.2	15.5	13.9	12.9
12/65	8.7	8.8	8.3	7.5	9.2	11.2	14.1	15.0	13.0	13.1	11.7	10.6	13.6	13.1	13.8	14.9	16.4	15.8	14.2	13.3

To	1/26	12/26	12/27	12/28	12/29	12/30	12/31	12/32	12/33	12/34	12/35	12/36	12/37	12/38	12/39	12/40	12/41	12/42	12/43	12/44
12/26	-2.2																			
12/27	15.1	29.3																		
12/28	23.7	37.4	44.9																	
12/29	7.7	9.4	-0.2	-30.4																
12/30	-2.4	-3.6	-13.2	-31.9	-37.7															
12/31	-11.3	-13.7	-21.9	-36.5	-41.2	-48.7														
12/32	-11.1	-12.9	-19.2	-30.5	-32.4	-31.7	-12.9													
12/33	-2.8	-3.3	-7.8	-15.8	-12.0	-1.7	36.0	105.7												
12/34	-1.3	-1.7	-5.3	-11.4	-7.1	2.2	27.7	54.2	12.5											
12/35	2.1	2.0	-0.9	-5.8	-0.6	9.2	32.6	53.1	30.7	49.0										
12/36	6.5	5.4	3.1	-0.5	5.2	15.2	37.3	54.3	40.6	56.3	62.8									
12/37	0.5	0.1	-2.4	-6.3	-2.9	3.2	16.0	22.8	7.9	6.2	-11.4	-46.6								
12/38	2.7	2.5	0.4	-2.9	0.8	6.9	18.6	25.0	12.7	12.2	0.8	-16.5	29.3							
12/39	2.5	2.3	0.3	-2.7	0.8	5.9	15.6	20.3	10.0	8.8	0.1	-11.5	12.4	-4.4						
12/40	1.9	1.6	-0.2	-2.8	0.2	4.5	12.7	16.5	7.6	6.1	-1.1	-9.5	5.8	-5.2	-10.5					
12/41	1.4	1.1	-0.5	-2.7	-0.3	3.4	10.3	13.2	5.6	4.1	-1.6	-8.1	2.3	-5.1	-8.4	-10.2				
12/42	2.1	1.9	0.6	-1.5	0.9	4.5	10.9	13.4	6.7	5.6	0.9	-4.1	5.4	0.5	0.7	5.7	25.1			
12/43	3.3	3.3	2.1	0.1	2.8	6.6	12.9	15.5	9.4	8.9	4.9	0.6	11.0	8.1	10.4	19.3	41.1	47.9		
12/44	4.2	4.3	3.2	1.4	4.2	8.0	14.1	16.6	11.1	10.9	7.4	3.8	13.9	11.9	14.8	23.4	40.2	42.5	31.4	
12/45	5.7	5.9	4.9	3.4	6.3	10.3	16.4	19.0	14.0	14.1	11.1	8.0	18.3	17.2	21.0	30.1	46.3	49.2	43.4	50.6
12/46	5.0	5.2	4.2	2.7	5.4	9.0	14.4	16.7	12.0	11.8	9.0	6.1	14.5	13.2	15.6	21.4	31.1	30.5	22.3	16.9
12/47	4.8	5.0	4.0	2.6	5.1	8.4	13.5	15.5	11.2	10.9	8.3	5.6	13.0	11.9	13.5	17.8	24.5	23.1	16.0	10.7
12/48	4.6	4.7	3.7	2.3	4.6	7.7	12.5	14.4	10.3	9.9	7.3	4.8	11.4	10.3	11.6	15.1	20.2	18.5	12.1	7.4
12/49	5.1	5.2	4.3	3.0	5.3	8.2	12.8	14.6	10.7	10.4	8.0	5.7	11.9	10.9	12.2	15.4	20.1	18.5	13.1	9.5
12/50	5.9	6.0	5.2	3.9	6.2	9.3	13.9	15.5	11.7	11.6	9.4	7.3	13.3	12.5	13.9	17.1	21.3	20.1	15.7	12.9
12/51	6.2	6.4	5.6	4.4	6.6	9.6	14.0	15.5	11.9	11.9	9.7	7.7	13.3	12.5	13.8	16.7	20.4	19.3	15.5	13.1
12/52	6.3	6.5	5.7	4.5	6.7	9.5	13.6	15.1	11.8	11.7	9.7	7.7	12.9	12.1	13.4	15.9	19.4	18.2	14.7	12.4
12/53	5.9	6.1	5.4	4.2	6.2	8.8	12.7	14.1	11.0	10.8	8.9	7.1	11.8	10.9	12.0	14.3	17.3	16.1	12.8	10.6
12/54	7.2	7.4	6.7	5.6	7.7	10.3	14.3	15.7	12.7	12.7	10.9	9.2	13.9	13.2	14.5	16.8	19.9	18.9	16.1	14.3
12/55	7.6	7.7	7.1	6.0	8.2	10.8	14.7	16.1	13.2	13.2	11.4	9.7	14.3	13.6	14.8	17.0	19.8	19.0	16.6	14.9
12/56	7.7	7.8	7.2	6.1	8.2	10.7	14.5	15.8	13.1	13.1	11.3	9.7	14.1	13.5	14.5	16.4	18.9	18.2	16.0	14.4
12/57	7.0	7.1	6.5	5.5	7.4	9.6	13.2	14.3	11.7	11.7	10.0	8.5	12.5	11.8	12.6	14.3	16.5	15.7	13.4	11.9
12/58	8.0	8.2	7.5	6.6	8.5	10.9	14.4	15.5	13.0	13.1	11.4	10.0	14.0	13.5	14.4	16.1	18.4	17.6	15.5	14.2
12/59	8.1	8.3	7.6	6.7	8.7	11.0	14.4	15.6	13.2	13.2	11.5	10.2	14.1	13.5	14.4	16.0	18.2	17.4	15.3	14.1
12/60	7.9	8.1	7.4	6.6	8.4	10.5	13.8	14.9	12.6	12.7	11.1	9.8	13.3	12.7	13.5	15.0	17.0	16.2	14.2	13.0
12/61	8.4	8.6	8.0	7.1	8.9	11.0	14.2	15.3	13.1	13.2	11.6	10.4	13.9	13.4	14.1	15.6	17.5	16.7	14.7	13.7
12/62	7.7	7.9	7.3	6.4	8.1	10.1	13.1	14.1	12.0	12.0	10.5	9.4	12.6	12.1	12.7	14.0	15.7	14.9	13.0	11.9
12/63	8.0	8.2	7.6	6.7	8.4	10.5	13.4	14.3	12.3	12.3	10.9	9.7	12.8	12.3	13.0	14.2	15.8	15.0	13.2	12.2
12/64	8.2	8.4	7.9	7.0	8.7	10.6	13.4	14.4	12.4	12.5	11.1	10.0	13.1	12.6	13.2	14.3	15.8	15.1	13.5	12.5
12/65	8.5	8.6	8.1	7.3	9.0	10.9	13.8	14.7	12.7	12.8	11.3	10.3	13.3	12.8	13.4	14.5	16.0	15.3	13.8	12.9

TABLE 1
RATES OF RETURN ON INVESTMENT IN COMMON STOCKS LISTED ON THE NEW YORK STOCK EXCHANGE WITH REINVESTMENT OF DIVIDENDS (Per Cent Per Annum Compounded Annually) PART C—CASH-TO-PORTFOLIO, LOWER TAX RATE

FROM

12/45	12/46	12/47	12/48	12/49	12/50	12/51	12/52	12/53	12/54	12/55	12/56	12/57	12/58	12/59	12/60	12/61	12/62	12/63	12/64
-10.8																			
-5.6	-1.9																		
-4.7	-2.3	-4.1																	
0.6	4.1	6.9	17.9																
6.5	11.0	15.2	25.5	34.2															
8.0	11.9	15.0	21.7	23.7	13.4														
8.1	11.5	13.8	18.3	18.3	11.0	7.5													
6.5	9.1	10.7	13.6	12.3	6.2	2.2	-4.4												
11.1	14.1	16.4	19.9	20.2	16.5	17.2	21.5	53.5											
12.1	14.8	16.9	20.0	20.4	17.2	17.9	21.1	36.2	18.2										
12.0	14.3	15.9	18.5	18.7	15.8	15.8	17.5	25.7	12.6	5.8									
9.3	11.1	12.3	14.1	13.6	10.9	10.1	10.2	13.6	2.7	-4.4	-13.6								
12.1	14.0	15.5	17.5	17.5	15.4	15.4	16.5	21.0	13.7	12.2	16.6	56.9							
12.2	14.1	15.5	17.4	17.5	15.5	15.6	16.6	20.3	14.3	13.2	16.8	35.2	13.8						
11.1	12.9	14.1	15.7	15.5	13.9	13.8	14.4	17.0	11.7	10.5	12.4	21.1	5.8	-2.6					
12.1	13.8	14.9	16.4	16.3	15.0	15.1	15.7	18.2	13.8	13.2	15.4	22.9	12.9	12.1	26.7				
10.3	11.7	12.6	13.8	13.5	12.1	11.9	12.1	13.8	9.7	8.6	9.7	14.3	5.6	3.0	5.1	-14.0			
10.7	12.1	13.0	14.1	13.8	12.5	12.3	12.6	14.2	10.5	9.6	10.7	14.9	8.0	6.6	9.6	1.3	16.9		
11.0	12.4	13.1	14.2	14.0	12.7	12.6	12.9	14.5	11.1	10.4	11.5	15.4	9.7	8,9	11.9	6.9	17.7	15.6	
11.6	13.1	13.8	14.9	14.8	13.5	13.4	13.8	15.4	12.3	11.7	12.8	16.8	11.9	11.7	15.1	12.1	21.7	22.6	27.5

TABLE 1.
RATES OF RETURN ON INVESTMENT IN COMMON STOCKS LISTED ON THE NEW YORK STOCK EXCHANGE WITH REINVESTMENT OF DIVIDENDS (Per Cent Per Annum Compounded Annually) PART D—CASH-TO-CASH, LOWER TAX RATE

FROM

12/45	12/46	12/47	12/48	12/49	12/50	12/51	12/52	12/53	12/54	12/55	12/56	12/57	12/58	12/59	12/60	12/61	12/62	12/63	12/64
-9.7																			
-4.8	-2.0																		
-4.2	-2.1	-4.2																	
0.7	3.9	6.3	15.7																
6.1	10.3	14.1	23.4	30.5															
7.6	11.1	14.0	20.0	21.6	11.7														
7.6	10.8	12.9	16.9	16.8	10.0	6.3													
6.2	8.6	10.1	12.7	11.4	5.7	1.9	-4.4												
10.6	13.4	15.4	18.7	18.9	15.3	15.7	19.4	47.3											
11.5	14.1	16.0	18.9	19.2	16.1	16.5	19.3	32.9	15.7										
11.4	13.6	15.1	17.6	17.7	14.8	14.7	16.2	23.7	11.3	4.6									
9.0	10.6	11.8	13.5	12.9	10.3	9.5	9.5	12.7	2.5	-4.0	-12.7								
11.5	13.4	14.8	16.7	16.6	14.6	14.5	15.5	19.6	12.6	11.1	14.8	50.1							
11.6	13.5	14.8	16.7	16.7	14.7	14.7	15.7	19.1	13.2	12.1	15.3	31.8	11.7						
10.6	12.3	13.4	15.0	14.7	13.1	13.0	13.5	15.9	10.8	9.6	11.3	19.1	5.0	-3.0					
11.5	13.1	14.2	15.6	15.4	14.1	14.1	14.6	16.9	12.7	12.0	13.9	20.7	11.4	10.4	22.4				
9.8	11.2	12.0	13.1	12.8	11.4	11.2	11.3	12.9	9.0	7.9	8.8	13.0	5.0	2.7	4.3	-12.8			
10.2	11.6	12.4	13.4	13.2	11.8	11.6	11.8	13.3	9.8	8.9	9.9	13.7	7.2	5.9	8.5	0.9	13.9		
10.6	11.9	12.7	13.7	13.5	12.2	12.0	12.3	13.8	10.5	9.8	10.8	14.4	8.9	8.1	10.9	6.1	15.7	13.0	
11.1	12.6	13.3	14.3	14.2	12.9	12.8	13.1	14.6	11.6	11.0	12.0	15.8	11.0	10.7	13.8	10.9	19.6	20.0	23.5

FROM

To	1/26	12/26	12/27	12/28	12/29	12/30	12/31	12/32	12/33	12/34	12/35	12/36	12/37	12/38	12/39	12/40	12/41	12/42	12/43	12/44
12/26	-1.7																			
12/27	15.3	29.9																		
12/28	23.8	37.6	45.4																	
12/29	7.7	9.5	0.0	-30.0																
12/30	-2.3	-3.6	-13.1	-31.7	-37.2															
12/31	-11.1	-13.5	-21.7	-36.2	-40.8	-47.8														
12/32	-10.9	-12.7	-18.9	-30.1	-31.9	-30.9	-11.1													
12/33	-2.6	-3.1	-7.5	-15.3	-11.5	-1.1	37.0	108.5												
12/34	-1.1	-1.5	-5.1	-11.0	-6.7	2.6	28.2	55.0	13.7											
12/35	2.3	2.2	-0.7	-5.4	-0.3	9.5	32.9	53.4	31.2	50.3										
12/36	6.6	5.5	3.2	-0.2	5.4	15.4	37.3	54.3	40.7	56.4	63.2									
12/37	0.5	0.1	-2.4	-6.1	-2.8	3.2	15.9	22.8	7.8	6.1	-11.4	-46.3								
12/38	2.7	2.5	0.4	-2.8	0.9	6.8	18.4	24.8	12.6	12.0	0.7	-16.4	30.4							
12/39	2.5	2.2	0.3	-2.6	0.8	5.8	15.4	20.1	9.8	8.6	-0.0	-11.5	12.6	-3.7						
12/40	1.8	1.5	-0.4	-3.0	0.1	4.4	12.6	16.5	7.4	5.9	-1.5	-10.2	5.8	-5.5	-10.5					
12/41	0.9	0.6	-1.1	-3.5	-0.9	3.0	10.1	13.0	5.0	3.4	-2.8	-10.0	1.5	-6.7	-10.4	-12.3				
12/42	1.6	1.4	-0.1	-2.3	0.3	4.1	10.6	13.2	6.1	4.9	-0.3	-6.0	4.6	-1.0	-0.9	4.9	27.5			
12/43	2.9	2.9	1.6	-0.4	2.4	6.3	12.7	15.2	8.9	8.4	4.1	-0.5	10.5	7.4	9.7	19.2	43.4	52.5		
12/44	3.9	4.0	2.8	1.0	3.8	7.7	13.9	16.4	10.8	10.5	6.8	3.0	13.6	11.5	14.5	23.7	42.0	45.3	34.4	
12/45	5.5	5.7	4.7	3.2	6.1	10.1	16.2	18.8	13.8	13.8	10.7	7.6	18.2	17.1	21.0	30.6	48.1	51.8	46.6	56.4
12/46	4.6	4.8	3.8	2.4	5.0	8.6	14.1	16.3	11.6	11.3	8.4	5.4	14.1	12.7	15.1	21.1	31.7	31.3	22.9	17.4
12/47	4.4	4.5	3.6	2.1	4.6	7.9	13.0	15.0	10.5	10.2	7.5	4.7	12.3	11.2	12.7	17.1	24.3	23.0	15.7	10.1
12/48	4.0	4.1	3.1	1.7	3.9	7.0	11.7	13.5	9.3	9.0	6.3	3.7	10.3	9.2	10.4	14.0	19.3	17.5	11.1	6.2
12/49	4.6	4.6	3.7	2.4	4.6	7.5	12.0	13.6	9.7	9.4	6.9	4.6	10.8	9.7	11.0	14.2	19.1	17.6	12.0	8.3
12/50	5.3	5.4	4.6	3.3	5.5	8.5	13.0	14.6	10.8	10.6	8.4	6.2	12.2	11.4	12.7	15.9	20.3	19.1	14.7	11.8
12/51	5.6	5.8	5.0	3.8	5.9	8.8	13.1	14.5	10.9	10.8	8.7	6.6	12.1	11.3	12.6	15.4	19.4	18.2	14.4	12.0
12/52	5.7	5.8	5.1	3.9	6.0	8.6	12.7	14.1	10.7	10.7	8.6	6.6	11.8	10.9	12.1	14.7	18.4	17.1	13.5	11.3
12/53	5.2	5.3	4.6	3.5	5.4	7.8	11.7	12.9	9.8	9.7	7.7	5.8	10.5	9.6	10.7	12.9	16.1	14.8	11.4	9.2
12/54	6.5	6.6	6.0	4.9	6.9	9.4	13.3	14.6	11.6	11.6	9.7	8.0	12.6	11.9	13.1	15.4	18.6	17.6	14.8	13.0
12/55	6.9	7.0	6.3	5.3	7.3	9.8	13.7	14.9	12.0	12.1	10.2	8.5	13.0	12.3	13.5	15.6	18.6	17.8	15.3	13.6
12/56	6.9	7.0	6.4	5.4	7.3	9.7	13.4	14.6	11.9	11.9	10.1	8.5	12.7	12.2	13.1	15.0	17.6	16.8	14.6	13.1
12/57	6.2	6.3	5.6	4.6	6.4	8.6	12.0	13.0	10.5	10.5	8.7	7.1	11.1	10.4	11.2	12.8	15.1	14.2	11.9	10.4
12/58	7.2	7.4	6.7	5.8	7.6	9.9	13.2	14.3	11.8	11.9	10.2	8.8	12.7	12.1	13.0	14.1	17.0	16.2	14.1	12.8
12/59	7.3	7.5	6.8	5.9	7.8	10.0	13.3	14.3	11.9	12.0	10.3	9.0	12.7	12.2	13.0	14.5	16.8	16.0	13.9	12.7
12/60	7.2	7.3	6.6	5.7	7.5	9.5	12.6	13.6	11.4	11.5	9.8	8.5	12.0	11.4	12.1	13.5	15.6	14.8	12.8	11.7
12/61	7.7	7.9	7.2	6.3	8.0	10.1	13.2	14.1	12.0	12.1	10.5	9.3	12.6	12.1	12.8	14.2	16.2	15.4	13.5	12.5
12/62	7.0	7.1	6.5	5.6	7.2	9.1	12.0	12.9	10.8	10.8	9.3	8.1	11.3	10.7	11.4	12.6	14.3	13.5	11.6	10.6
12/63	7.2	7.4	6.8	5.9	7.5	9.4	12.3	13.1	11.1	11.1	9.6	8.5	11.5	11.0	11.6	12.8	14.4	13.6	11.9	11.0
12/64	7.4	7.6	7.0	6.2	7.7	9.5	12.2	13.1	11.1	11.2	9.8	8.7	11.6	11.2	11.8	12.8	14.4	13.7	12.0	11.2
12/65	7.7	7.8	7.2	6.4	8.0	9.9	12.6	13.4	11.5	11.5	10.1	9.0	11.9	11.4	12.0	13.1	14.6	13.9	12.4	11.6

FROM

To	1/26	12/26	12/27	12/28	12/29	12/30	12/31	12/32	12/33	12/34	12/35	12/36	12/37	12/38	12/39	12/40	12/41	12/42	12/43	12/44
12/26	-1.8																			
12/27	14.4	27.8																		
12/28	22.7	35.5	42.3																	
12/29	7.5	9.1	0.1	-28.4																
12/30	-2.0	-3.1	-12.0	-29.4	-35.3															
12/31	-10.1	-12.3	-19.9	-33.3	-38.3	-46.1														
12/32	-9.0	-10.6	-16.0	-25.4	-27.7	-27.9	-11.4													
12/33	-2.1	-2.5	-6.5	-13.4	-10.4	-1.2	33.4	96.4												
12/34	-0.8	-1.1	-4.3	-9.7	-6.1	2.2	25.9	50.3	11.5											
12/35	2.3	2.2	-0.5	-4.9	-0.3	8.8	30.9	50.2	28.6	45.1										
12/36	5.3	5.3	3.1	-0.1	5.0	14.4	35.4	51.4	37.9	52.1	57.1									
12/37	0.7	0.3	-1.9	-5.3	-2.4	3.1	15.1	21.5	7.4	5.7	-10.3	-42.5								
12/38	2.7	2.5	0.6	-2.4	0.9	6.4	17.4	23.4	11.7	11.2	0.7	-14.8	26.4							
12/39	2.5	2.3	0.5	-2.2	0.9	5.5	14.5	19.0	9.1	8.0	0.1	-10.1	11.1	-3.9						
12/40	2.0	1.7	0.1	-2.2	0.3	4.2	11.8	15.4	6.9	5.5	-0.9	-8.2	5.1	-4.6	-9.3					
12/41	1.8	1.6	0.3	-1.4	0.3	3.2	9.0	11.4	4.9	3.8	-0.5	-5.1	2.1	-3.1	-5.6	-7.2				
12/42	2.2	2.1	1.0	-0.6	1.2	3.9	9.1	11.3	5.5	4.7	1.2	-2.4	4.1	0.6	0.6	4.0	16.6			
12/43	2.9	2.9	1.8	0.1	2.3	5.6	11.4	13.7	7.9	7.4	3.7	0.0	8.9	6.2	8.0	15.3	33.9	38.7		
12/44	3.6	3.7	2.7	1.1	3.4	6.8	12.4	14.8	9.5	9.1	5.9	2.6	11.5	9.5	11.9	19.3	34.1	35.5	25.3	
12/45	5.0	5.1	4.2	2.7	5.3	8.9	14.5	17.0	12.1	12.0	9.1	6.3	15.5	14.3	17.6	25.6	40.4	42.3	36.4	41.9
12/46	4.2	4.4	3.5	2.1	4.4	7.6	12.7	14.8	10.2	9.9	7.3	4.6	12.1	10.7	12.7	17.8	26.7	25.8	18.2	13.5
12/47	4.0	4.1	3.3	2.0	4.1	7.1	11.8	13.6	9.4	9.0	6.5	4.0	10.6	9.5	10.8	14.6	20.6	19.2	12.7	8.1
12/48	3.8	3.8	2.9	1.7	3.7	6.5	10.9	12.6	8.6	8.2	5.7	3.3	9.2	8.2	9.3	12.4	17.1	15.4	9.5	5.3
12/49	4.3	4.3	3.5	2.3	4.2	6.9	11.2	12.7	8.9	8.6	6.3	4.2	9.7	8.7	9.8	12.6	17.1	15.5	10.5	7.2
12/50	4.9	5.0	4.2	3.0	5.0	7.8	12.1	13.6	9.9	9.7	7.6	5.5	11.0	10.2	11.3	14.2	18.2	17.0	12.8	10.2
12/51	5.1	5.2	4.5	3.4	5.3	8.0	12.0	13.4	9.9	9.8	7.7	5.8	10.8	10.0	11.1	13.7	17.2	16.0	12.4	10.2
12/52	5.2	5.3	4.6	3.5	5.3	7.8	11.7	13.0	9.7	9.6	7.6	5.8	10.5	9.7	10.7	13.0	16.3	15.0	11.7	9.6
12/53	4.8	4.9	4.2	3.1	4.9	7.2	10.8	12.0	9.0	8.8	6.9	5.2	9.5	8.6	9.5	11.5	14.3	13.1	9.9	8.0
12/54	5.9	6.0	5.4	4.3	6.2	8.5	12.3	13.5	10.6	10.5	8.7	7.0	11.4	10.6	11.7	13.8	16.8	15.7	13.0	11.3
12/55	6.3	6.4	5.7	4.7	6.6	9.0	12.7	13.9	11.0	11.0	9.2	7.6	11.8	11.0	12.1	14.1	16.8	15.9	13.5	11.9
12/56	6.3	6.4	5.8	4.8	6.6	8.9	12.5	13.6	10.9	10.9	9.1	7.6	11.6	11.0	11.8	13.6	16.0	15.2	13.0	11.5
12/57	5.7	5.8	5.1	4.2	5.9	7.9	11.2	12.2	9.7	9.6	7.9	6.4	10.1	9.4	10.1	11.6	13.8	12.9	10.7	9.3
12/58	6.6	6.7	6.1	5.2	6.9	9.1	12.3	13.3	10.9	10.9	9.2	7.9	11.6	11.0	11.8	13.3	15.6	14.7	12.6	11.4
12/59	6.7	6.8	6.2	5.3	7.1	9.2	12.4	13.4	11.0	11.0	9.4	8.1	11.7	11.1	11.8	13.3	15.4	14.5	12.5	11.3
12/60	6.6	6.7	6.0	5.2	6.8	8.8	11.8	12.8	10.6	10.6	9.0	7.7	11.0	10.4	11.0	12.4	14.3	13.5	11.5	10.4
12/61	7.1	7.2	6.6	5.7	7.3	9.3	12.3	13.3	11.1	11.1	9.6	8.4	11.6	11.1	11.7	13.1	14.9	14.1	12.2	11.2
12/62	6.4	6.5	5.9	5.1	6.6	8.5	11.3	12.1	10.0	10.0	8.5	7.4	10.4	9.9	10.4	11.6	13.3	12.4	10.6	9.5
12/63	6.7	6.8	6.2	5.4	6.9	8.8	11.6	12.4	10.3	10.3	8.9	7.7	10.6	10.1	10.7	11.8	13.4	12.6	10.8	9.9
12/64	6.9	7.0	6.4	5.6	7.1	8.9	11.5	12.4	10.4	10.4	9.1	7.9	10.8	10.3	10.8	11.9	13.4	12.7	11.0	10.1
12/65	7.1	7.2	6.6	5.9	7.4	9.2	11.9	12.7	10.7	10.7	9.3	8.3	11.0	10.5	11.1	12.1	13.6	12.9	11.4	10.5

TABLE 1.
RATES OF RETURN ON INVESTMENT IN COMMON STOCKS LISTED ON THE NEW YORK STOCK EXCHANGE
WITH REINVESTMENT OF DIVIDENDS (Per Cent Per Annum Compounded Annually)
PART E—CASH-TO-PORTFOLIO, HIGHER TAX RATE

FROM					FROM					FROM					FROM				
12/45	12/46	12/47	12/48	12/49	12/50	12/51	12/52	12/53	12/54	12/55	12/56	12/57	12/58	12/59	12/60	12/61	12/62	12/63	12/64
-12.1																			
-7.2	-3.8																		
-6.3	-4.0	-5.6																	
-1.1	2.3	5.2	16.0																
4.7	9.1	13.4	23.5	32.1															
6.2	10.0	13.1	19.6	21.6	11.3														
6.2	9.5	11.9	16.2	16.2	8.9	5.5													
4.6	7.1	8.7	11.6	10.1	4.1	0.1	-6.4												
9.2	12.1	14.3	17.8	18.0	14.3	15.0	19.3	51.1											
10.2	12.8	14.9	17.9	18.3	15.1	15.8	19.0	34.2	16.5										
10.0	12.3	13.9	16.4	16.7	13.7	13.8	15.6	23.8	10.9	4.1									
7.5	9.2	10.4	12.1	11.6	8.9	8.1	8.3	11.8	1.0	-6.0	-15.1								
10.2	12.1	13.5	15.5	15.5	13.4	13.5	14.6	19.1	11.9	10.5	14.8	54.7							
10.3	12.2	13.6	15.5	15.5	13.6	13.8	14.8	18.5	12.6	11.6	15.1	33.4	12.4						
9.3	11.0	12.2	13.8	13.6	12.0	12.0	12.7	15.3	10.1	8.9	10.8	19.5	4.4	-3.9					
10.3	12.0	13.1	14.6	14.4	13.2	13.3	14.0	16.5	12.2	11.6	13.8	21.3	11.6	10.8	25.4				
8.5	9.9	10.8	12.0	11.7	10.3	10.2	10.5	12.2	8.2	7.1	8.2	12.9	4.3	1.8	4.0	-14.9			
9.0	10.4	11.2	12.3	12.1	10.8	10.6	10.9	12.6	9.0	8.2	9.3	13.5	6.7	5.3	8.4	0.2	15.5		
9.3	10.6	11.4	12.5	12.3	11.0	10.9	11.3	12.9	9.6	9.0	10.1	13.9	8.4	7.6	10.7	5.7	16.4	14.5	
9.9	11.3	12.1	13.2	13.1	11.8	11.8	12.2	13.9	10.8	10.3	11.4	15.4	10.6	10.4	13.9	11.0	20.5	21.5	26.3

TABLE 1.
RATES OF RETURN ON INVESTMENT IN COMMON STOCKS LISTED ON THE NEW YORK STOCK EXCHANGE
WITH REINVESTMENT OF DIVIDENDS (Per Cent Per Annum Compounded Annually)
PART F—CASH-TO-CASH, HIGHER TAX RATE

FROM					FROM					FROM					FROM				
12/45	12/46	12/47	12/48	12/49	12/50	12/51	12/52	12/53	12/54	12/55	12/56	12/57	12/58	12/59	12/60	12/61	12/62	12/63	12/64
-9.1																			
-5.2	-3.0																		
-4.6	-2.9	-4.4																	
-0.4	2.3	4.5	12.6																
4.2	7.8	11.2	19.2	25.1															
5.3	8.4	10.9	15.9	17.1	8.6														
5.4	8.0	9.9	13.3	13.0	7.1	3.9													
4.1	6.1	7.4	9.7	8.4	3.5	0.3	-4.9												
7.8	10.3	12.1	14.9	14.9	11.6	11.9	14.9	38.0											
-8.7	11.0	12.7	15.3	15.4	12.4	12.8	15.1	26.7	12.1										
8.7	10.6	12.0	14.1	14.1	11.4	11.3	12.6	19.1	8.4	2.9									
6.5	8.0	9.0	10.5	10.0	7.6	6.9	7.0	9.7	1.2	-4.2	-11.5								
8.8	10.5	11.8	13.5	13.3	11.4	11.3	12.2	15.8	9.6	8.2	11.3	40.4							
9.0	10.7	11.9	13.6	13.5	11.6	11.6	12.4	15.5	10.2	9.2	11.9	25.8	8.8						
8.2	9.7	10.8	12.2	11.9	10.3	10.2	10.7	12.9	8.3	7.2	8.6	15.4	3.3	-3.3					
9.1	10.6	11.6	12.9	12.6	11.4	11.4	11.9	14.0	10.1	9.5	11.2	17.2	9.0	8.2	18.5				
7.5	8.8	9.6	10.6	10.3	9.0	8.7	8.9	10.4	6.9	5.9	6.7	10.5	3.5	1.5	2.9	-11.7			
8.0	9.2	10.0	11.0	10.7	9.4	9.2	9.4	10.8	7.6	6.8	7.7	11.1	5.4	4.3	6.5	0.0	11.1		
8.3	9.5	10.2	11.2	10.9	9.7	9.5	9.8	11.2	8.2	7.5	8.4	11.6	6.8	6.1	8.5	4.4	12.4	10.2	
8.8	10.2	10.9	11.8	11.7	10.4	10.3	10.7	12.1	9.3	8.7	9.6	13.1	8.7	8.5	11.2	8.6	16.1	16.4	19.2

FROM / **To**

To	1/26	12/26	12/27	12/28	12/29	12/30	12/31	12/32	12/33	12/34	12/35	12/36	12/37	12/38	12/39	12/40	12/41	12/42	12/43	12/44
12/26	-1.8																			
12/27	14.9	29.9																		
12/28	23.3	37.5	45.6																	
12/29	8.0	10.1	0.6	-30.0																
12/30	-1.2	-2.3	-12.1	-31.5	-36.9															
12/31	-8.9	-11.3	-20.1	-35.8	-40.5	-47.6														
12/32	-9.1	-11.0	-18.1	-30.5	-32.4	-31.4	-11.5													
12/33	-2.5	-3.0	-8.0	-16.9	-13.1	-2.4	36.3	108.8												
12/34	-1.4	-1.8	-5.9	-12.9	-8.4	1.3	27.9	55.5	13.7											
12/35	1.5	1.5	-1.8	-7.5	-2.1	8.3	32.7	54.0	31.1	50.4										
12/36	6.3	4.9	2.2	-1.9	4.0	14.5	37.5	55.3	41.1	57.2	64.2									
12/37	0.4	0.0	-2.9	-7.5	-3.7	3.2	17.4	25.5	9.5	8.0	-9.9	-45.9								
12/38	2.1	1.9	-0.6	-4.7	-0.5	6.4	19.5	27.0	13.6	13.2	1.2	-16.9	30.5							
12/39	1.9	1.7	-0.7	-4.4	-0.5	5.5	16.6	22.5	10.8	9.7	0.3	-12.2	12.8	-3.6						
12/40	1.5	1.2	-1.1	-4.6	-1.0	4.2	14.2	19.3	8.6	7.0	-1.2	-10.7	6.3	-5.3	-10.1					
12/41	1.0	0.7	-1.4	-4.7	-1.5	3.4	12.4	16.6	6.8	5.1	-2.0	-10.1	2.8	-5.7	-9.1	-10.1				
12/42	1.5	1.4	-0.6	-3.7	-0.5	4.3	12.8	16.7	7.8	6.4	0.4	-6.2	5.9	-0.0	0.4	7.1	31.1			
12/43	2.6	2.6	0.9	-1.9	1.4	6.2	14.5	18.3	10.3	9.6	4.6	-0.8	11.7	8.4	11.2	21.8	47.7	57.8		
12/44	3.4	3.5	1.9	-0.6	2.8	7.6	15.5	19.3	12.0	11.6	7.2	2.7	14.8	12.5	16.0	26.3	46.3	50.2	38.2	
12/45	4.7	5.0	3.6	1.3	4.8	9.7	17.4	21.2	14.6	14.6	10.9	7.1	19.1	17.8	22.3	32.9	52.0	56.1	50.1	59.8
12/46	4.2	4.4	3.0	0.9	4.1	8.6	15.8	19.4	12.9	12.7	9.1	5.4	15.7	14.1	17.1	24.2	36.1	35.9	26.7	20.9
12/47	4.2	4.4	3.0	0.9	4.0	8.2	15.2	18.5	12.2	11.9	8.5	5.1	14.4	13.0	15.2	20.7	29.2	28.1	19.8	13.8
12/48	4.1	4.2	2.8	0.8	3.7	7.8	14.5	17.6	11.5	11.1	7.7	4.4	12.9	11.5	13.4	18.0	24.8	23.1	15.5	10.0
12/49	4.5	4.6	3.3	1.4	4.2	8.1	14.6	17.6	11.8	11.4	8.2	5.2	13.3	12.0	13.8	18.1	24.4	22.8	16.1	11.8
12/50	5.1	5.2	4.0	2.2	5.0	8.9	15.3	18.2	12.5	12.3	9.4	6.6	14.3	13.3	15.1	19.4	25.2	23.9	18.3	14.8
12/51	5.4	5.5	4.4	2.7	5.4	9.2	15.4	18.1	12.7	12.6	9.8	7.0	14.4	13.3	15.1	19.0	24.4	23.1	18.1	15.1
12/52	5.5	5.6	4.6	2.9	5.5	9.2	15.2	17.9	12.7	12.5	9.8	7.2	14.2	13.1	14.9	18.5	23.5	22.2	17.4	14.5
12/53	5.3	5.4	4.4	2.7	5.3	8.8	14.7	17.4	12.2	12.0	9.3	6.8	13.4	12.3	13.9	17.3	21.9	20.4	15.8	13.0
12/54	6.1	6.3	5.3	3.8	6.3	9.8	15.5	18.1	13.2	13.2	10.6	8.3	14.8	13.8	15.5	18.9	23.4	22.3	18.2	15.9
12/55	6.4	6.6	5.7	4.2	6.7	10.1	15.8	18.3	13.5	13.5	11.0	8.8	15.1	14.1	15.8	19.0	23.3	22.2	18.5	16.3
12/56	6.5	6.7	5.8	4.3	6.8	10.1	15.6	18.1	13.5	13.4	11.0	8.8	14.9	14.1	15.5	18.5	22.5	21.5	18.0	15.9
12/57	6.1	6.3	5.4	3.9	6.3	9.5	15.0	17.4	12.7	12.6	10.2	8.0	13.9	12.9	14.3	17.1	20.9	19.8	16.1	13.9
12/58	6.8	7.0	6.1	4.7	7.1	10.3	15.6	17.9	13.5	13.5	11.1	9.2	14.9	14.1	15.4	18.2	22.0	20.9	17.5	15.6
12/59	6.9	7.1	6.2	4.9	7.2	10.4	15.6	17.9	13.5	13.5	11.2	9.3	14.9	14.1	15.4	18.1	21.7	20.7	17.3	15.5
12/60	6.8	7.0	6.1	4.8	7.1	10.1	15.3	17.6	13.3	13.2	11.0	9.1	14.4	13.6	14.9	17.4	21.0	19.9	16.5	14.7
12/61	7.2	7.4	6.5	5.2	7.5	10.5	15.5	17.8	13.5	13.6	11.4	9.6	14.8	14.0	15.3	17.8	21.2	20.1	16.9	15.2
12/62	6.8	7.0	6.1	4.8	7.0	10.0	15.0	17.3	12.9	12.9	10.7	8.9	14.0	13.2	14.4	16.8	20.2	19.0	15.7	13.9
12/63	7.0	7.2	6.3	5.1	7.3	10.2	15.1	17.4	13.1	13.1	10.9	9.1	14.2	13.4	14.6	16.9	20.1	19.0	15.8	14.1
12/64	7.1	7.3	6.5	5.3	7.4	10.2	15.1	17.3	13.1	13.1	11.0	9.3	14.2	13.4	14.6	16.9	20.1	19.0	15.9	14.3
12/65	7.3	7.5	6.7	5.5	7.7	10.5	15.3	17.4	13.3	13.3	11.2	9.6	14.4	13.6	14.8	17.0	20.1	19.0	16.1	14.5

FROM / **To**

To	1/26	12/26	12/27	12/28	12/29	12/30	12/31	12/32	12/33	12/34	12/35	12/36	12/37	12/38	12/39	12/40	12/41	12/42	12/43	12/44
12/26	-2.3																			
12/27	14.7	29.2																		
12/28	23.2	37.2	45.0																	
12/29	7.9	9.9	0.3	-30.3																
12/30	-1.4	-2.4	-12.3	-31.7	-37.4															
12/31	-9.0	-11.4	-20.3	-36.0	-40.8	-48.4														
12/32	-9.2	-11.1	-18.3	-30.7	-32.7	-32.0	-13.3													
12/33	-2.6	-3.1	-8.1	-17.1	-13.3	-2.8	35.4	106.1												
12/34	-1.5	-1.8	-6.0	-13.0	-8.6	1.0	27.4	54.6	12.4											
12/35	1.5	1.4	-1.9	-7.6	-2.2	8.1	32.4	53.6	30.6	49.0										
12/36	6.2	4.9	2.1	-2.0	3.9	14.4	37.4	55.1	40.9	56.7	63.1									
12/37	0.3	-0.0	-2.9	-7.6	-3.8	3.0	17.2	25.3	9.3	7.7	-10.4	-46.5								
12/38	2.1	1.9	-0.7	-4.7	-0.6	6.3	19.3	26.8	13.4	9.5	0.9	-17.3	29.2							
12/39	1.9	1.7	-0.7	-4.4	-0.6	5.4	16.5	22.4	10.6	9.5	0.1	-12.4	12.3	-4.6						
12/40	1.4	1.2	-1.1	-4.6	-1.1	4.2	14.1	19.1	8.5	6.8	-1.3	-10.9	5.9	-5.8	-11.1					
12/41	1.0	0.7	-1.5	-4.7	-1.6	3.3	12.3	16.5	6.7	4.9	-2.1	-10.2	2.6	-6.0	-9.6	-11.3				
12/42	1.5	1.3	-0.7	-3.7	-0.5	4.2	12.7	16.6	7.7	6.3	0.3	-6.3	5.7	-0.3	-0.1	6.3	29.0			
12/43	2.6	2.6	0.8	-2.0	1.3	6.2	14.4	18.2	10.2	9.5	4.5	-0.9	11.6	8.2	10.9	21.3	46.7	55.8		
12/44	3.4	3.5	1.9	-0.6	2.7	7.5	15.5	19.2	11.9	11.5	7.2	2.6	14.7	12.4	15.8	26.0	45.7	49.4	36.9	
12/45	4.7	4.9	3.5	1.3	4.8	9.6	17.4	21.1	14.5	14.6	10.8	7.0	19.0	17.7	22.2	32.7	51.7	55.7	49.5	58.7
12/46	4.2	4.4	3.0	0.8	4.1	8.6	15.8	19.3	12.9	12.6	9.0	5.4	15.6	14.0	17.0	24.1	35.9	35.6	26.4	20.4
12/47	4.2	4.3	3.0	0.9	4.0	8.2	15.1	18.4	12.2	11.9	8.5	5.0	14.3	12.9	15.1	20.5	29.0	27.8	19.6	13.4
12/48	4.1	4.1	2.8	0.8	3.7	7.7	14.4	17.5	11.4	11.0	7.7	4.4	12.8	11.5	13.3	17.9	24.7	22.9	15.3	9.7
12/49	4.4	4.6	3.3	1.3	4.2	8.1	14.6	17.6	11.7	11.4	8.2	5.2	13.2	11.9	13.7	18.0	24.3	22.6	16.0	11.6
12/50	5.0	5.2	4.0	2.2	5.0	8.9	15.3	18.1	12.5	12.3	9.4	6.5	14.3	13.2	15.1	19.3	25.1	23.8	18.1	14.6
12/51	5.3	5.5	4.4	2.6	5.4	9.2	15.4	18.1	12.7	12.5	9.7	7.0	14.3	13.3	15.1	19.0	24.3	23.0	18.0	14.9
12/52	5.4	5.6	4.6	2.8	5.5	9.2	15.2	17.9	12.6	12.5	9.7	7.1	14.2	13.1	14.8	18.5	23.5	22.1	17.3	14.4
12/53	5.2	5.4	4.4	2.7	5.3	8.8	14.7	17.4	12.2	12.0	9.2	6.7	13.4	12.2	13.9	17.2	21.8	20.4	15.7	12.9
12/54	6.1	6.3	5.3	3.8	6.3	9.8	15.5	18.1	13.2	13.1	10.6	8.3	14.8	13.8	15.5	18.8	23.4	22.2	18.2	15.8
12/55	6.4	6.6	5.7	4.2	6.7	10.1	15.7	18.3	13.5	13.5	11.0	8.8	15.0	14.1	15.7	19.0	23.2	22.2	18.4	16.2
12/56	6.5	6.7	5.8	4.3	6.8	10.1	15.6	18.1	13.4	13.4	11.0	8.8	14.9	14.0	15.5	18.5	22.5	21.5	17.9	15.8
12/57	6.1	6.3	5.3	3.9	6.3	9.5	14.9	17.4	12.7	12.6	10.1	8.0	13.9	12.9	14.3	17.1	20.9	19.7	16.0	13.9
12/58	6.8	7.0	6.1	4.7	7.1	10.2	15.5	17.9	13.4	13.4	11.1	9.1	14.8	14.0	15.4	18.2	21.9	20.9	17.4	15.5
12/59	6.9	7.1	6.2	4.8	7.2	10.4	15.6	17.9	13.5	13.5	11.2	9.3	14.9	14.1	15.4	18.0	21.7	20.6	17.3	15.4
12/60	6.8	7.0	6.1	4.8	7.1	10.1	15.2	17.6	13.2	13.2	10.9	9.0	14.4	13.5	14.8	17.4	20.9	19.8	16.5	14.7
12/61	7.2	7.4	6.5	5.2	7.5	10.5	15.5	17.8	13.5	13.5	11.3	9.6	14.8	14.0	15.2	17.7	21.2	20.1	16.9	15.2
12/62	6.8	7.0	6.1	4.8	7.0	10.0	15.0	17.3	12.9	12.9	10.7	8.9	14.0	13.2	14.4	16.8	20.1	19.0	15.7	13.9
12/63	7.0	7.2	6.3	5.1	7.2	10.2	15.1	17.4	13.1	13.1	10.9	9.1	14.1	13.3	14.5	16.9	20.1	19.0	15.8	14.1
12/64	7.1	7.3	6.5	5.3	7.4	10.2	15.1	17.3	13.1	13.1	11.0	9.3	14.2	13.4	14.6	16.9	20.0	19.0	15.9	14.2
12/65	7.3	7.5	6.7	5.5	7.6	10.5	15.2	17.4	13.3	13.3	11.2	9.5	14.3	13.6	14.7	17.0	20.1	19.0	16.0	14.5

TABLE 2.

RATES OF RETURN ON INVESTMENT IN COMMON STOCKS LISTED ON THE NEW YORK STOCK EXCHANGE
WITHOUT REINVESTMENT OF DIVIDENDS (Per Cent Per Annum Compounded Annually)
PART A—CASH-TO-PORTFOLIO, TAX EXEMPT

FROM

12/45	12/46	12/47	12/48	12/49	12/50	12/51	12/52	12/53	12/54	12/55	12/56	12/57	12/58	12/59	12/60	12/61	12/62	12/63	12/64
-9.8																			
-4.6	-0.7																		
-3.6	-1.0	-2.8																	
1.2	4.9	7.7	18.9																
6.6	11.4	15.7	26.5	35.7															
8.1	12.4	15.8	23.1	25.6	15.0														
8.3	12.1	14.8	20.0	20.3	12.5	8.8													
7.2	10.2	12.2	15.8	14.6	7.9	3.6	-3.2												
10.9	14.4	16.9	21.1	21.5	17.3	17.8	22.1	54.8											
11.8	15.0	17.4	21.2	21.6	18.0	18.5	21.8	37.7	19.0										
11.7	14.6	16.5	19.8	20.1	16.6	16.6	18.5	27.4	13.5	6.6									
9.8	12.2	13.7	16.3	15.7	12.4	11.6	11.8	15.9	4.0	-3.3	-12.7								
11.9	14.4	16.2	18.9	18.8	16.2	16.2	17.4	22.5	14.3	12.6	16.9	58.1							
12.0	14.4	16.2	18.8	18.8	16.3	16.4	17.5	21.8	14.9	13.7	17.3	36.5	14.6						
11.3	13.6	15.2	17.4	17.2	15.0	14.9	15.6	18.7	12.5	11.1	13.1	22.6	6.6	-2.1					
12.0	14.2	15.8	17.9	17.7	15.8	15.8	16.6	19.7	14.4	13.6	15.9	24.2	13.5	12.7	27.9				
10.7	12.7	14.0	15.8	15.5	13.4	13.1	13.5	15.8	10.7	9.4	10.6	15.9	6.5	3.8	6.1	-13.5			
11.0	13.0	14.3	16.0	15.7	13.7	13.5	13.8	16.0	11.4	10.4	11.6	16.5	8.8	7.2	10.6	1.8	18.0		
11.3	13.2	14.4	16.1	15.8	13.9	13.7	14.1	16.2	11.9	11.0	12.3	16.7	10.3	9.4	12.8	7.3	18.6	16.4	
11.7	13.7	14.9	16.5	16.3	14.5	14.3	14.8	16.9	13.0	12.2	13.5	18.1	12.4	12.1	15.8	12.5	22.7	23.4	28.3

TABLE 2.

RATES OF RETURN ON INVESTMENT IN COMMON STOCKS LISTED ON THE NEW YORK STOCK EXCHANGE
WITHOUT REINVESTMENT OR DIVIDENDS (Per Cent Per Annum Compounded Annually)
PART B—CASH-TO-CASH, TAX EXEMPT

FROM

12/45	12/46	12/47	12/48	12/49	12/50	12/51	12/52	12/53	12/54	12/55	12/56	12/57	12/58	12/59	12/60	126/1	12/62	12/63	12/64
-10.5																			
-5.0	-1.7																		
-3.9	-1.5	-3.8																	
1.0	4.6	7.2	17.7																
6.4	11.1	15.4	25.9	34.4															
8.0	12.2	15.6	22.7	25.0	13.9														
8.2	12.0	14.6	19.7	20.0	12.0	7.7													
7.1	10.1	12.0	15.6	14.3	7.5	3.0	-4.3												
10.9	14.3	16.8	20.9	21.3	17.1	17.4	21.5	53.3											
11.7	14.9	17.3	21.0	21.5	17.8	18.3	21.4	37.0	17.9										
11.6	14.5	16.4	19.7	19.9	16.5	16.4	18.2	27.0	13.0	5.5									
9.7	12.1	13.7	16.2	15.6	12.3	11.4	11.6	15.6	3.7	-3.8	-13.7								
11.8	14.3	16.1	18.8	18.7	16.1	16.0	17.2	22.2	14.0	12.2	16.3	56.3							
11.9	14.4	16.1	18.7	18.7	16.2	16.3	17.4	21.6	14.7	13.4	16.9	35.8	13.3						
11.2	13.5	15.1	17.3	17.1	14.9	14.8	15.5	18.6	12.4	10.9	12.8	22.2	6.0	-3.2					
11.9	14.2	15.7	17.8	17.6	15.7	15.7	16.5	19.5	14.3	13.5	15.7	23.9	13.1	12.1	26.5				
10.6	12.7	14.0	15.8	15.4	13.4	13.1	13.4	15.7	10.6	9.3	10.4	15.7	6.2	3.4	5.5	-14.6			
11.0	13.0	14.2	16.0	15.6	13.7	13.4	13.7	15.9	11.3	10.2	11.4	16.3	8.5	7.0	10.2	1.2	16.6		
11.2	13.1	14.3	16.0	15.7	13.8	13.6	14.0	16.1	11.8	10.9	12.1	16.6	10.1	9.2	12.5	6.9	18.0	15.1	
11.6	13.6	14.8	16.5	16.3	14.4	14.3	14.7	16.8	12.9	12.1	13.4	17.9	12.3	11.9	15.6	12.2	22.3	22.8	27.0

FROM

To	1/26	12/26	12/27	12/28	12/29	12/30	12/31	12/32	12/33	12/34	12/35	12/36	12/37	12/38	12/39	12/40	12/41	12/42	12/43	12/44
12/26	-1.8																			
12/27	14.9	29.9																		
12/28	23.3	37.5	45.6																	
12/29	8.0	10.1	0.6	-30.0																
12/30	-1.2	-2.3	-12.1	-31.5	-36.9															
12/31	-8.9	-11.3	-20.1	-35.8	-40.5	-47.6														
12/32	-9.1	-11.0	-18.1	-30.5	-32.4	-31.4	-11.5													
12/33	-2.5	-3.0	-8.0	-16.9	-13.1	-2.4	36.3	108.8												
12/34	-1.4	-1.8	-5.9	-12.9	-8.4	1.3	27.9	55.5	13.7											
12/35	1.5	1.5	-1.8	-7.5	-2.1	8.3	32.7	54.0	31.1	50.4										
12/36	6.3	4.9	2.2	-1.9	4.0	14.5	37.5	55.3	41.1	57.2	64.2									
12/37	0.4	0.0	-2.9	-7.5	-3.7	3.2	17.4	25.5	9.5	8.0	-9.9	-45.9								
12/38	2.1	1.9	-0.6	-4.7	-0.5	6.4	19.5	27.0	13.6	13.2	1.2	-16.9	30.5							
12/39	1.9	1.7	-0.7	-4.4	-0.5	5.5	16.6	22.5	10.8	9.7	0.3	-12.2	12.8	-3.6						
12/40	1.5	1.2	-1.1	-4.6	-1.0	4.2	14.2	19.2	8.5	7.0	-1.2	-10.7	6.2	-5.4	-10.3					
12/41	1.0	0.7	-1.5	-4.7	-1.6	3.3	12.3	16.5	6.7	4.9	-2.1	-10.2	2.6	-6.0	-9.5	-10.7				
12/42	1.5	1.3	-0.7	-3.7	-0.6	4.2	12.6	16.5	7.6	6.2	0.2	-6.4	5.6	-0.4	-0.1	6.4	29.9			
12/43	2.5	2.5	0.8	-2.0	1.3	6.1	14.3	18.0	10.0	9.4	4.3	-1.0	11.3	8.0	10.5	20.9	46.3	56.0		
12/44	3.3	3.4	1.8	-0.7	2.6	7.4	15.3	19.0	11.7	11.3	6.9	2.4	14.3	12.0	15.3	25.3	44.8	48.4	36.7	
12/45	4.6	4.8	3.5	1.2	4.7	9.5	17.2	20.9	14.3	14.3	10.6	6.8	18.6	17.3	21.6	32.0	50.6	54.5	48.7	58.5
12/46	4.1	4.3	2.9	0.7	3.9	8.3	15.5	19.0	12.5	12.2	8.7	5.0	15.1	13.5	16.3	23.1	34.6	34.3	25.3	19.5
12/47	4.0	4.2	2.8	0.7	3.7	7.9	14.7	18.0	11.8	11.4	8.0	4.6	13.6	12.3	14.2	19.4	27.6	26.3	18.3	12.4
12/48	3.8	3.9	2.6	0.5	3.4	7.4	14.0	17.0	10.9	10.5	7.1	3.8	12.0	10.7	12.3	16.6	23.0	21.2	13.9	8.5
12/49	4.2	4.3	3.0	1.1	3.9	7.7	14.1	17.0	11.2	10.8	7.7	4.7	12.4	11.1	12.7	16.7	22.7	21.0	14.6	10.4
12/50	4.8	5.0	3.8	2.0	4.7	8.5	14.8	17.6	12.0	11.8	8.8	6.0	13.5	12.4	14.1	18.1	23.5	22.1	16.8	13.5
12/51	5.1	5.3	4.2	2.4	5.1	8.8	14.9	17.5	12.1	12.0	9.2	6.5	13.5	12.5	14.1	17.7	22.7	21.4	16.6	13.7
12/52	5.2	5.4	4.3	2.6	5.2	8.8	14.7	17.2	12.0	11.9	9.2	6.6	13.3	12.2	13.8	17.2	21.8	20.4	15.9	13.2
12/53	5.0	5.1	4.1	2.4	4.9	8.3	14.1	16.6	11.5	11.3	8.6	6.1	12.5	11.3	12.7	15.8	20.0	18.6	14.2	11.5
12/54	5.8	6.1	5.1	3.5	6.0	9.4	15.0	17.5	12.6	12.6	10.1	7.8	13.9	12.9	14.5	17.6	21.8	20.6	16.8	14.6
12/55	6.2	6.3	5.4	3.9	6.4	9.7	15.2	17.6	12.9	12.9	10.5	8.3	14.2	13.3	14.8	17.7	21.6	20.6	17.2	15.1
12/56	6.3	6.4	5.5	4.1	6.5	9.7	15.1	17.4	12.9	12.8	10.4	8.3	14.0	13.2	14.5	17.2	20.8	19.8	16.6	14.7
12/57	5.8	6.0	5.0	3.6	5.9	9.0	14.3	16.6	12.0	11.9	9.5	7.4	12.9	12.0	13.2	15.7	19.1	18.0	14.6	12.7
12/58	6.5	6.7	5.8	4.5	6.8	9.8	15.0	17.2	12.9	12.8	10.6	8.6	14.0	13.2	14.4	16.9	20.3	19.3	16.2	14.4
12/59	6.6	6.8	5.9	4.6	6.9	10.0	15.0	17.2	12.9	12.9	10.7	8.8	14.0	13.3	14.4	16.8	20.1	19.0	16.0	14.4
12/60	6.6	6.8	5.8	4.5	6.8	9.7	14.6	16.9	12.6	12.6	10.4	8.5	13.5	12.7	13.8	16.1	19.2	18.2	15.2	13.6
12/61	7.0	7.2	6.2	5.0	7.2	10.1	14.9	17.1	12.9	12.9	10.8	9.1	13.9	13.2	14.3	16.5	19.5	18.5	15.6	14.1
12/62	6.5	6.7	5.8	4.5	6.6	9.5	14.3	16.5	12.3	12.2	10.1	8.3	13.1	12.3	13.3	15.4	18.4	17.2	14.3	12.7
12/63	6.7	6.9	6.1	4.8	6.9	9.7	14.4	16.6	12.4	12.4	10.3	8.6	13.2	12.4	13.5	15.5	18.4	17.3	14.4	13.0
12/64	6.8	7.0	6.2	5.0	7.0	9.8	14.4	16.5	12.5	12.4	10.4	8.8	13.3	12.5	13.5	15.5	18.3	17.2	14.5	13.1
12/65	7.0	7.2	6.4	5.3	7.3	10.0	14.6	16.6	12.6	12.6	10.6	9.0	13.4	12.7	13.7	15.6	18.3	17.3	14.7	13.4

FROM

To	1/26	12/26	12/27	12/28	12/29	12/30	12/31	12/32	12/33	12/34	12/35	12/36	12/37	12/38	12/39	12/40	12/41	12/42	12/43	12/44
12/26	-2.3																			
12/27	14.7	29.2																		
12/28	23.2	37.2	45.6																	
12/29	7.9	9.9	0.3	-30.3																
12/30	-1.4	-2.4	-12.3	-31.7	-37.4															
12/31	-9.0	-11.4	-20.3	-36.0	-40.8	-48.4														
12/32	-9.2	-11.1	-18.3	-30.7	-32.7	-32.0	-13.3													
12/33	-2.6	-3.1	-8.1	-17.1	-13.3	-2.8	35.4	106.1												
12/34	-1.5	-1.8	-6.0	-13.0	-8.6	1.0	27.4	54.6	12.4											
12/35	-1.5	1.4	-1.9	-7.6	-2.2	8.1	32.4	53.6	30.6	49.0										
12/36	6.2	4.9	2.1	-2.0	3.9	14.4	37.4	55.1	40.9	56.7	63.1									
12/37	0.3	-0.0	-2.9	-7.6	-3.8	3.0	17.2	25.3	9.3	7.7	-10.4	-46.5								
12/38	2.1	1.9	-0.7	-4.7	-0.6	6.3	19.3	26.8	13.4	12.9	0.9	-17.3	29.2							
12/39	1.9	1.7	-0.7	-4.4	-0.6	5.4	16.5	22.4	10.6	9.5	0.1	-12.4	12.3	-4.6						
12/40	1.5	1.2	-1.0	-4.3	-1.0	4.1	13.9	18.8	8.3	6.7	-1.2	-10.3	5.8	-5.5	-10.7					
12/41	1.2	0.9	-1.1	-4.0	-1.3	3.2	11.9	15.9	6.5	4.9	-1.6	-8.8	2.5	-5.2	-8.5	-10.1				
12/42	1.7	1.5	-0.3	-3.0	-0.3	4.0	12.1	15.8	7.3	6.0	0.6	-5.2	5.3	-0.1	0.1	5.6	25.1			
12/43	2.5	2.5	0.9	-1.7	1.3	5.8	13.8	17.4	9.6	8.9	4.1	-0.8	10.5	7.4	9.7	19.0	41.6	48.7		
12/44	3.2	3.3	1.8	-0.5	2.5	7.0	14.6	18.3	11.1	10.6	6.5	2.3	13.3	11.0	14.0	23.1	40.7	43.1	31.5	
12/45	4.4	4.6	3.3	1.2	4.4	8.9	16.4	20.1	13.5	13.5	9.9	6.3	17.4	16.1	20.0	29.6	46.8	49.7	43.4	50.6
12/46	3.9	4.1	2.8	0.7	3.7	7.9	14.9	18.3	11.9	11.6	8.2	4.7	14.1	12.5	15.1	21.5	32.2	31.5	22.9	17.3
12/47	3.9	4.0	2.7	0.8	3.6	7.5	14.2	17.4	11.2	10.9	7.6	4.3	12.9	11.5	13.3	18.2	25.8	24.4	16.7	11.2
12/48	3.8	3.8	2.5	0.6	3.3	7.1	13.6	16.6	10.6	10.2	6.9	3.7	11.6	10.2	11.8	15.9	22.1	20.2	13.1	8.0
12/49	4.1	4.2	3.0	1.1	3.7	7.5	13.8	16.7	10.9	10.5	7.4	4.5	12.0	10.6	12.2	16.1	21.8	20.1	13.9	9.8
12/50	4.7	4.8	3.7	1.9	4.5	8.3	14.5	17.2	11.6	11.4	8.5	5.8	13.0	12.0	13.6	17.4	22.7	21.3	16.0	12.8
12/51	5.0	5.1	4.0	2.3	4.9	8.5	14.5	17.2	11.8	11.6	8.8	6.2	13.0	12.0	13.5	17.1	21.9	20.5	15.8	13.0
12/52	5.0	5.2	4.2	2.5	5.0	8.5	14.3	16.9	11.7	11.5	8.8	6.3	12.8	11.7	13.2	16.5	21.0	19.6	15.1	12.5
12/53	4.8	5.0	4.0	2.3	4.7	8.1	13.8	16.3	11.2	11.0	8.3	5.9	12.1	10.9	12.3	15.3	19.4	17.9	13.6	11.0
12/54	5.6	5.9	4.9	3.4	5.8	9.1	14.7	17.2	12.3	12.2	9.7	7.5	13.5	12.5	14.0	17.0	21.2	19.9	16.2	14.0
12/55	6.0	6.2	5.2	3.8	6.2	9.5	14.9	17.4	12.6	12.6	10.2	7.9	13.8	12.9	14.3	17.2	21.1	20.0	16.5	14.5
12/56	6.1	6.3	5.4	3.9	6.3	9.4	14.8	17.2	12.6	12.5	10.1	8.0	13.7	12.8	14.1	16.8	20.3	19.3	16.0	14.1
12/57	5.7	5.8	4.9	3.5	5.7	8.8	14.1	16.4	11.8	11.7	9.3	7.2	12.6	11.7	12.9	15.3	18.7	17.6	14.2	12.2
12/58	6.4	6.5	5.6	4.3	6.5	9.6	14.7	17.0	12.6	12.6	10.3	8.3	13.7	12.9	14.1	16.5	19.9	18.8	15.7	13.9
12/59	6.4	6.6	5.7	4.4	6.7	9.8	14.8	17.0	12.7	12.6	10.4	8.5	13.7	12.9	14.1	16.4	19.7	18.6	15.6	13.9
12/60	6.4	6.6	5.6	4.4	6.5	9.5	14.4	16.7	12.4	12.3	10.1	8.3	13.2	12.4	13.5	15.7	18.9	17.8	14.7	13.1
12/61	6.7	6.9	6.0	4.8	6.9	9.8	14.6	16.8	12.6	12.6	10.5	8.7	13.6	12.8	13.8	16.1	19.1	18.0	15.1	13.5
12/62	6.3	6.5	5.6	4.3	6.4	9.3	14.1	16.3	12.0	11.9	9.8	8.0	12.8	11.9	13.0	15.1	18.0	16.8	13.9	12.3
12/63	6.5	6.7	5.9	4.6	6.7	9.5	14.2	16.4	12.2	12.1	10.0	8.3	12.9	12.1	13.1	15.2	18.0	16.9	14.0	12.5
12/64	6.7	6.9	6.1	4.8	6.9	9.6	14.2	16.4	12.3	12.2	10.2	8.5	13.1	12.3	13.3	15.3	18.0	17.0	14.2	12.7
12/65	6.9	7.0	6.2	5.1	7.1	9.8	14.4	16.5	12.4	12.4	10.4	8.8	13.2	12.4	13.4	15.4	18.0	17.0	14.4	13.0

TABLE 2.
RATES OF RETURN ON INVESTMENT IN COMMON STOCKS LISTED ON THE NEW YORK STOCK EXCHANGE
WITHOUT REINVESTMENT OF DIVIDENDS (Per Cent Per Annum Compounded Annually)
PART C—CASH-TO-PORTFOLIO, LOWER TAX RATE

FROM					FROM					FROM					FROM				
12/45	12/46	12/47	12/48	12/49	12/50	12/51	12/52	12/53	12/54	12/55	12/56	12/57	12/58	12/59	12/60	12/61	12/62	12/63	12/64
-10.7																			
-5.7	-2.0																		
-4.8	-2.2	-3.9																	
0.1	3.7	6.6	17.6																
5.5	10.2	14.6	25.2	34.1															
7.1	11.2	14.5	21.6	24.0	13.5														
7.2	10.9	13.5	18.5	18.8	11.1	7.4													
6.0	8.9	10.8	14.2	13.0	6.5	2.3	-4.4												
9.9	13.2	15.7	19.7	20.1	16.1	16.6	20.9	53.5											
10.8	13.9	16.3	19.9	20.3	16.8	17.4	20.8	36.6	18.2										
10.8	13.5	15.4	18.5	18.8	15.5	15.5	17.5	26.4	12.7	5.8									
8.8	11.0	12.5	14.9	14.4	11.2	10.4	10.7	14.8	3.2	-4.1	-13.4								
11.0	13.3	15.1	17.6	17.6	15.2	15.2	16.5	21.5	13.5	11.9	16.2	57.0							
11.1	13.4	15.2	17.6	17.6	15.3	15.4	16.6	20.8	14.2	13.0	16.6	35.6	13.9						
10.4	12.5	14.1	16.2	16.0	13.9	13.9	14.7	17.8	11.8	10.4	12.4	21.7	5.9	-2.7					
11.1	13.2	14.7	16.7	16.6	14.8	14.9	15.7	18.7	13.7	12.9	15.2	23.3	12.8	11.9	26.9				
9.8	11.6	12.9	14.6	14.2	12.4	12.2	12.5	14.8	9.9	8.7	9.8	15.0	5.7	3.0	5.3	-14.1			
10.1	12.0	13.2	14.8	14.5	12.7	12.5	12.9	15.0	10.6	9.6	10.8	15.5	8.0	6.5	9.7	1.1	17.1		
10.4	12.1	13.3	14.9	14.6	12.9	12.7	13.2	15.2	11.1	10.3	11.5	15.8	9.6	8.7	11.9	6.6	17.8	15.6	
10.8	12.7	13.8	15.3	15.2	13.5	13.4	13.9	15.9	12.2	11.5	12.7	17.2	11.7	11.4	15.0	11.8	21.8	22.6	27.5

TABLE 2.
RATES OF RETURN ON INVESTMENT IN COMMON STOCKS LISTED ON THE NEW YORK STOCK EXCHANGE
WITHOUT REINVESTMENT OF DIVIDENDS (Per Cent Per Annum Compounded Annually)
PART D—CASH-TO-CASH, LOWER TAX RATE

FROM					FROM					FROM					FROM				
12/45	12/46	12/47	12/48	12/49	12/50	12/51	12/52	12/53	12/54	12/55	12/56	12/57	12/58	12/59	12/60	12/61	12/62	12/63	12/64
-9.6																			
-4.9	-2.1																		
-4.2	-2.0	-4.0																	
0.3	3.5	6.0	15.5																
5.3	9.6	13.5	23.0	30.5															
6.7	10.5	13.6	20.0	21.9	11.8														
6.9	10.2	12.6	17.2	17.2	10.1	6.2													
5.8	8.5	10.2	13.3	12.1	6.0	2.0	-4.4												
9.4	12.5	14.9	18.6	18.8	14.9	15.2	18.9	47.3											
10.3	13.2	15.4	18.8	19.2	15.7	16.1	19.0	33.2	15.8										
10.3	12.9	14.7	17.6	17.8	14.6	14.5	16.2	24.3	11.4	4.7									
8.4	10.6	12.0	14.2	13.7	10.7	9.9	10.1	13.8	3.0	-3.7	-12.6								
10.5	12.8	14.5	16.9	16.8	14.4	14.3	15.5	20.1	12.5	10.8	14.5	50.3							
10.6	12.9	14.6	16.9	16.9	14.6	14.6	15.7	19.6	13.1	11.9	15.1	32.2	11.8						
9.9	12.0	13.5	15.5	15.3	13.2	13.1	13.8	16.7	10.9	10.9	11.3	19.7	5.1	-3.1					
10.6	12.6	14.0	15.9	15.7	14.0	14.0	14.7	17.5	12.6	11.8	13.8	21.1	11.3	10.3	22.6				
9.3	11.1	12.3	14.0	13.6	11.7	11.5	11.8	13.8	9.2	8.0	9.0	13.7	5.1	2.7	4.5	-12.9			
9.7	11.5	12.6	14.2	13.9	12.1	11.8	12.1	14.1	9.9	8.9	9.9	14.3	7.3	5.8	8.6	0.8	14.1		
10.0	11.8	12.8	14.4	14.1	12.4	12.2	12.6	14.5	10.5	9.7	10.8	14.8	8.8	8.0	10.9	5.9	15.8	13.1	
10.4	12.3	13.4	14.9	14.7	13.0	12.8	13.3	15.2	11.5	10.8	11.9	16.1	10.8	10.5	13.8	10.7	19.7	20.1	23.6

Measurement of the Behavior of Individual Stocks and of the Market

To	1/26	12/26	12/27	12/28	12/29	12/30	12/31	12/32	12/33	12/34	12/35	12/36	12/37	12/38	12/39	12/40	12/41	12/42	12/43	12/44
12/26	-1.8																			
12/27	14.9	29.8																		
12/28	23.3	37.4	45.5																	
12/29	7.9	10.0	0.5	-30.0																
12/30	-1.3	-2.3	-12.2	-31.5	-36.9															
12/31	-9.0	-11.3	-20.1	-35.7	-40.4	-47.5														
12/32	-9.1	-10.9	-18.0	-30.3	-32.2	-31.3	-11.5													
12/33	-2.4	-2.9	-7.8	-16.6	-12.8	-2.1	36.4	108.9												
12/34	-1.3	-1.7	-5.7	-12.6	-8.2	1.5	27.9	55.5	13.7											
12/35	1.7	1.6	-1.6	-7.1	-1.8	8.5	32.7	54.0	31.1	50.3										
12/36	6.4	5.0	2.4	-1.6	4.2	14.6	37.4	55.1	40.9	56.8	63.5									
12/37	0.4	0.0	-2.8	-7.3	-3.6	3.1	17.0	25.0	9.1	7.5	-10.5	-46.2								
12/38	2.1	1.9	-0.5	-4.4	-0.4	6.3	19.1	26.5	13.2	12.7	0.8	-17.1	30.3							
12/39	1.9	1.7	-0.6	-4.2	-0.5	5.3	16.2	22.0	10.4	9.2	-0.1	-12.3	12.5	-3.9						
12/40	1.4	1.1	-1.1	-4.4	-1.0	4.0	13.7	18.6	8.1	6.5	-1.6	-10.9	5.8	-5.7	-10.7					
12/41	0.8	0.5	-1.6	-4.7	-1.8	2.9	11.7	15.7	6.0	4.2	-2.7	-10.6	1.8	-6.8	-10.5	-12.2				
12/42	1.3	1.1	-0.8	-3.7	-0.7	3.8	11.9	15.5	6.8	5.4	-0.5	-6.9	4.6	-1.4	-1.3	4.6	27.5			
12/43	2.4	2.3	0.6	-2.0	1.1	5.7	13.6	17.1	9.3	8.5	3.6	-1.6	10.3	6.9	9.2	19.0	43.7	53.0		
12/44	3.2	3.2	1.7	-0.7	2.4	6.9	14.5	18.0	10.9	10.5	6.2	1.8	13.3	10.9	14.0	23.5	42.3	45.7	34.4	
12/45	4.5	4.7	3.4	1.3	4.5	9.1	16.5	20.0	13.6	13.6	10.0	6.3	17.7	16.4	20.4	30.3	48.4	52.1	46.6	56.5
12/46	3.9	4.0	2.7	0.7	3.6	7.8	14.7	17.9	11.7	11.3	7.9	4.4	13.9	12.3	14.8	21.2	32.3	31.8	23.2	17.7
12/47	3.7	3.8	2.6	0.6	3.4	7.3	13.8	16.7	10.8	10.4	7.1	3.8	12.3	10.9	12.6	17.4	25.0	23.7	16.1	10.4
12/48	3.5	3.5	2.2	0.3	2.9	6.6	12.8	15.6	9.8	9.3	6.1	2.9	10.5	9.2	10.6	14.5	20.4	18.5	11.6	6.5
12/49	3.9	3.9	2.7	0.9	3.4	7.0	12.9	15.6	10.0	9.6	6.6	3.8	10.9	9.6	11.0	14.6	20.1	18.4	12.4	8.5
12/50	4.5	4.6	3.5	1.8	4.3	7.9	13.7	16.2	10.9	10.6	7.8	5.2	12.1	11.1	12.5	16.1	21.1	19.7	14.8	11.6
12/51	4.8	4.9	3.9	2.2	4.7	8.1	13.7	16.1	11.0	10.8	8.1	5.6	12.0	11.0	12.4	15.7	20.2	18.9	14.5	11.9
12/52	4.8	5.0	3.9	2.4	4.7	8.0	13.5	15.8	10.9	10.7	8.1	5.6	11.8	10.7	12.1	15.1	19.3	17.9	13.8	11.2
12/53	4.5	4.6	3.6	2.1	4.3	7.4	12.7	15.0	10.2	10.0	7.4	5.1	10.8	9.6	10.9	13.5	17.3	15.9	11.9	9.5
12/54	5.5	5.6	4.7	3.3	5.5	8.6	13.8	16.0	11.5	11.4	9.0	6.9	12.4	11.5	12.9	15.6	19.3	18.2	14.8	12.8
12/55	5.8	6.0	5.1	3.7	6.0	9.0	14.1	16.2	11.8	11.8	9.5	7.4	12.8	11.9	13.2	15.7	19.2	18.2	15.2	13.3
12/56	5.9	6.0	5.1	3.8	6.0	8.9	13.9	15.9	11.7	11.7	9.4	7.4	12.5	11.8	12.9	15.2	18.3	17.4	14.6	12.9
12/57	5.3	5.5	4.6	3.2	5.3	8.1	12.9	14.9	10.7	10.6	8.3	6.3	11.2	10.4	11.3	13.4	16.3	15.3	12.4	10.6
12/58	6.1	6.3	5.4	4.2	6.3	9.1	13.7	15.7	11.7	11.6	9.5	7.7	12.5	11.8	12.7	14.8	17.8	16.8	14.1	12.7
12/59	6.2	6.4	5.5	4.3	6.4	9.2	13.8	15.7	11.7	11.7	9.6	7.9	12.5	11.8	12.8	14.7	17.5	16.6	14.0	12.6
12/60	6.1	6.3	5.4	4.2	6.2	8.9	13.3	15.2	11.4	11.3	9.2	7.6	11.9	11.2	12.0	13.9	16.6	15.6	13.1	11.7
12/61	6.6	6.7	5.8	4.7	6.7	9.3	13.7	15.5	11.7	11.8	9.7	8.2	12.4	11.7	12.6	14.4	17.0	16.0	13.6	12.3
12/62	6.0	6.2	5.3	4.1	6.1	8.6	12.9	14.7	10.9	10.9	8.9	7.3	11.4	10.7	11.5	13.2	15.6	14.6	12.1	10.8
12/63	6.3	6.4	5.6	4.4	6.3	8.9	13.1	14.8	11.1	11.1	9.1	7.6	11.6	10.9	11.7	13.3	15.6	14.6	12.3	11.1
12/64	6.4	6.5	5.8	4.7	6.5	8.9	13.0	14.7	11.2	11.1	9.3	7.8	11.7	11.0	11.8	13.3	15.5	14.6	12.4	11.3
12/65	6.6	6.7	6.0	4.9	6.8	9.2	13.3	14.9	11.4	11.4	9.5	8.1	11.9	11.2	12.0	13.5	15.6	14.8	12.7	11.6

To	1/26	12/26	12/27	12/28	12/29	12/30	12/31	12/32	12/33	12/34	12/35	12/36	12/37	12/38	12/39	12/40	12/41	12/42	12/43	12/44
12/26	-2.0																			
12/27	14.0	27.7																		
12/28	22.2	35.4	42.4																	
12/29	7.6	9.5	0.5	-28.4																
12/30	-1.0	-2.0	-11.1	-29.2	-35.0															
12/31	-8.1	-10.3	-18.5	-32.8	-37.9	-45.8														
12/32	-7.5	-9.1	-15.2	-25.5	-27.9	-28.2	-11.8													
12/33	-1.9	-2.3	-6.8	-14.4	-11.4	-2.2	32.8	96.8												
12/34	-0.9	-1.2	-4.9	-11.0	-7.3	1.2	25.6	50.7	11.5											
12/35	1.7	1.7	-1.4	-6.4	-1.7	7.8	30.7	50.7	28.5	45.1										
12/36	6.1	4.8	2.3	-1.4	3.9	13.6	35.5	52.2	38.2	52.5	57.4									
12/37	0.6	0.3	-2.4	-6.4	-3.2	2.9	16.2	23.7	8.5	7.0	-9.4	-42.4								
12/38	2.1	2.0	-0.3	-3.8	-0.3	5.9	18.1	25.1	12.3	11.8	0.8	-15.4	26.3							
12/39	2.0	1.8	-0.4	-3.6	-0.3	5.0	15.4	20.8	9.7	8.6	0.1	-10.8	11.0	-4.1						
12/40	1.6	1.4	-0.6	-3.4	-0.6	3.8	12.8	17.4	7.5	6.0	-1.0	-8.8	5.1	-4.8	-9.4					
12/41	1.6	1.4	-0.1	-2.3	-0.4	3.0	10.2	13.7	5.5	4.3	-0.5	-5.6	2.3	-3.2	-5.6	-7.2				
12/42	1.9	1.8	0.5	-1.5	0.3	3.5	10.2	13.3	6.0	5.0	1.0	-2.9	4.1	0.4	0.4	3.8	16.6			
12/43	2.4	2.4	0.9	-1.2	1.2	5.1	12.3	15.6	8.2	7.5	3.3	-0.8	8.7	5.8	7.6	15.2	34.2	39.0		
12/44	3.0	3.0	1.7	-0.3	2.2	6.1	13.2	16.4	9.6	9.1	5.4	1.7	11.2	9.1	11.5	19.2	34.4	35.8	25.4	
12/45	4.1	4.2	3.0	1.2	3.9	8.0	14.9	18.3	12.0	11.9	8.5	5.2	15.1	13.7	17.1	25.5	40.7	42.6	36.5	42.0
12/46	3.6	3.7	2.5	0.7	3.2	6.9	13.4	16.4	10.3	10.0	6.8	3.7	11.9	10.4	12.5	17.9	27.3	26.3	18.5	13.7
12/47	3.4	3.5	2.4	0.7	3.0	6.5	12.6	15.5	9.6	9.2	6.2	3.3	10.6	9.3	10.7	14.8	21.4	19.8	13.0	8.3
12/48	3.3	3.3	2.2	0.5	2.7	6.1	12.0	14.7	9.0	8.5	5.5	2.7	9.5	8.2	9.4	12.8	18.1	16.2	10.0	5.7
12/49	3.6	3.7	2.6	0.9	3.1	6.4	12.2	14.7	9.3	8.8	6.0	3.4	9.9	8.6	9.9	13.1	18.0	16.3	10.8	7.4
12/50	4.2	4.3	3.2	1.7	3.9	7.2	12.9	15.3	10.0	9.8	7.1	4.6	10.9	9.9	11.2	14.4	19.0	17.6	12.9	10.1
12/51	4.4	4.5	3.5	2.0	4.2	7.4	12.8	15.1	10.1	9.8	7.3	4.9	10.8	9.8	11.0	13.9	18.0	16.7	12.5	10.2
12/52	4.4	4.5	3.6	2.1	4.2	7.3	12.6	14.8	9.9	9.7	7.2	5.0	10.6	9.5	10.7	13.4	17.3	15.8	11.9	9.6
12/53	4.2	4.3	3.3	1.9	3.9	6.8	12.0	14.2	9.4	9.1	6.7	4.5	9.7	8.6	9.7	12.1	15.6	14.2	10.4	8.2
12/54	5.0	5.1	4.2	2.9	5.0	7.9	13.0	15.1	10.6	10.4	8.1	6.1	11.3	10.3	11.6	14.1	17.6	16.4	13.1	11.1
12/55	5.3	5.4	4.6	3.3	5.3	8.3	13.2	15.3	10.9	10.8	8.5	6.5	11.6	10.7	11.9	14.3	17.5	16.5	13.5	11.7
12/56	5.4	5.5	4.6	3.4	5.4	8.2	13.1	15.1	10.9	10.7	8.5	6.6	11.5	10.7	11.7	13.8	16.8	15.9	13.0	11.3
12/57	4.9	5.0	4.2	2.9	4.8	7.5	12.3	14.3	10.0	9.8	7.6	5.7	10.4	9.5	10.4	12.3	15.1	14.0	11.2	9.5
12/58	5.6	5.8	4.9	3.7	5.7	8.4	13.0	14.9	10.9	10.8	8.7	6.9	11.5	10.7	11.7	13.7	16.5	15.5	12.8	11.3
12/59	5.7	5.9	5.0	3.8	5.8	8.5	13.1	15.0	11.0	10.9	8.8	7.1	11.6	10.8	11.7	13.6	16.3	15.3	12.7	11.3
12/60	5.7	5.8	4.9	3.8	5.6	8.2	12.7	14.6	10.7	10.6	8.5	6.8	11.1	10.3	11.1	12.9	15.5	14.5	11.9	10.5
12/61	6.1	6.2	5.3	4.2	6.1	8.7	13.0	14.8	11.0	11.0	9.0	7.4	11.5	10.8	11.6	13.4	15.9	14.9	12.4	11.1
12/62	5.6	5.7	4.9	3.7	5.5	8.1	12.4	14.2	10.3	10.2	8.2	6.6	10.7	9.9	10.7	12.3	14.7	13.6	11.1	9.8
12/63	5.8	5.9	5.1	4.0	5.8	8.3	12.5	14.3	10.5	10.4	8.4	6.9	10.8	10.1	10.9	12.5	14.7	13.7	11.3	10.1
12/64	5.9	6.1	5.3	4.2	6.0	8.4	12.5	14.2	10.6	10.5	8.6	7.1	10.9	10.2	11.0	12.5	14.7	13.7	11.5	10.3
12/65	6.1	6.3	5.5	4.5	6.3	8.7	12.8	14.4	10.8	10.7	8.9	7.4	11.1	10.4	11.2	12.7	14.8	13.9	11.8	10.6

TABLE 2.
RATES OF RETURN ON INVESTMENT IN COMMON STOCKS LISTED ON THE NEW YORK STOCK EXCHANGE
WITHOUT REINVESTMENT OF DIVIDENDS (Per Cent Per Annum Compounded Annually)
PART E—CASH-TO-PORTFOLIO, HIGHER TAX RATE

FROM																				
12/45	12/46	12/47	12/48	12/49																
-12.0																				
-7.3	-3.9																			
-6.3	-3.9	-5.5			FROM															
-1.4	2.1	5.0	15.8																	
4.1	8.6	12.9	23.3	32.0	12/50	12/51	12/52	12/53	12/54											
5.6	9.5	12.8	19.6	21.8	11.4															
5.7	9.2	11.7	16.4	16.5	9.0	5.4														
4.3	7.0	8.8	12.0	10.6	4.3	0.2	-6.4			FROM										
8.5	11.6	14.0	17.7	18.0	14.1	14.7	19.0	51.2												
9.4	12.3	14.5	17.9	18.3	14.9	15.6	18.9	34.4	16.6	12/55	12/56	12/57	12/58	12/59						
9.3	11.8	13.6	16.5	16.7	13.6	13.6	15.5	24.2	11.0	4.1										
7.1	9.1	10.5	12.6	12.1	9.1	8.4	8.7	12.5	1.4	-5.8	-15.0									
9.5	11.7	13.3	15.6	15.6	13.3	13.4	14.6	19.4	11.9	10.3	14.6	54.8			FROM					
9.7	11.8	13.4	15.6	15.6	13.5	13.7	14.8	18.8	12.5	11.4	15.0	33.7	12.4							
8.9	10.8	12.3	14.2	13.9	12.1	12.1	12.8	15.7	10.2	8.9	10.8	19.8	4.5	-3.9	12/60	12/61	12/62	12/63	12/64	
9.7	11.6	13.0	14.8	14.6	13.1	13.2	14.0	16.8	12.2	11.5	13.7	21.6	11.5	10.7	25.6					
8.2	9.9	11.0	12.5	12.1	10.5	10.3	10.7	12.7	8.3	7.2	8.3	13.3	4.4	1.9	4.1	-15.0				
8.6	10.3	11.3	12.7	12.4	10.9	10.7	11.1	13.1	9.1	8.2	9.3	13.8	6.7	5.3	8.5	0.1	15.7			
8.9	10.5	11.5	12.8	12.6	11.1	11.0	11.4	13.3	9.6	8.9	10.1	14.2	8.3	7.5	10.7	5.6	16.5	14.5		
9.4	11.1	12.1	13.4	13.3	11.8	11.8	12.3	14.2	10.8	10.2	11.4	15.6	10.6	10.3	13.9	10.8	20.6	21.5	26.3	

TABLE 2.
RATES OF RETURN ON INVESTMENT IN COMMON STOCKS LISTED ON THE NEW YORK STOCK EXCHANGE
WITHOUT REINVESTMENT OF DIVIDENDS (Per Cent Per Annum Compounded Annually)
PART F—CASH-TO-CASH, HIGHER TAX RATE

FROM																				
12/45	12/46	12/47	12/48	12/49																
-9.1																				
-5.2	-3.0																			
-4.6	-2.8	-4.3			FROM															
-0.7	2.1	4.3	12.4																	
3.7	7.4	10.9	19.0	25.1	12/50	12/51	12/52	12/53	12/54											
4.8	8.0	10.6	16.0	17.2	8.6															
4.9	7.7	9.8	13.4	13.3	7.1	3.9														
3.9	6.1	7.5	10.0	8.8	3.7	0.4	-4.9			FROM										
7.2	9.9	11.8	14.9	14.9	11.4	11.6	14.7	38.0												
8.1	10.5	12.4	15.2	15.4	12.3	12.6	15.0	26.9	12.2	12/55	12/56	12/57	12/58	12/59						
8.0	10.2	11.8	14.2	14.2	11.3	11.2	12.6	19.4	8.5	2.9										
6.3	8.0	9.2	11.0	10.4	7.8	7.1	7.2	10.3	1.4	-4.1	-11.4									
8.3	10.2	11.7	13.7	13.5	11.3	11.2	12.2	16.1	9.5	8.1	11.1	40.4			FROM					
8.5	10.4	11.8	13.7	13.6	11.6	11.6	12.4	15.8	10.2	9.1	11.8	26.1	8.8							
7.8	9.6	10.8	12.5	12.2	10.4	10.3	10.9	13.3	8.4	7.2	8.6	15.7	3.4	-3.4	12/60	12/61	12/62	12/63	12/64	
8.6	10.3	11.5	13.1	12.9	11.3	11.3	12.0	14.4	10.1	9.4	11.1	17.5	9.0	8.1	18.7					
7.3	8.8	9.8	11.1	10.7	9.2	8.9	9.2	10.9	7.0	6.0	6.8	10.8	3.6	1.5	3.1	-11.7				
7.7	9.2	10.2	11.4	11.1	9.5	9.3	9.6	11.3	7.7	6.8	7.7	11.5	5.4	4.2	6.6	-0.0	11.2			
8.0	9.4	10.3	11.6	11.3	9.8	9.6	9.9	11.6	8.2	7.5	8.4	11.9	6.8	6.0	8.5	4.3	12.5	10.3		
8.5	10.1	11.0	12.2	12.0	10.5	10.4	10.8	12.4	9.2	8.6	9.6	13.3	8.7	8.4	11.2	8.5	16.2	16.4	19.0	

FROM

To	1/26	12/26	12/27	12/28	12/29	12/30	12/31	12/32	12/33	12/34	12/35	12/36	12/37	12/38	12/39	12/40	12/41	12/42	12/43	12/44
12/26	-5.7																			
12/27	10.8	25.2																		
12/28	19.5	33.3	41.7																	
12/29	3.7	5.8	-3.1	-32.6																
12/30	-6.2	-7.2	-16.3	-34.7	-40.1															
12/31	-15.0	-17.1	-24.9	-39.4	-43.8	-50.2														
12/32	-15.0	-16.6	-22.6	-33.9	-35.6	-34.1	-14.5													
12/33	-7.0	-7.3	-11.5	-19.6	-15.6	-4.8	33.4	105.1												
12/34	-5.6	-5.8	-9.2	-15.5	-11.0	-1.1	25.0	52.1	11.2											
12/35	-2.2	-2.1	-4.8	-9.9	-4.5	5.9	29.9	50.7	28.4	47.3										
12/36	3.1	1.6	-0.6	-4.1	1.7	12.1	34.6	51.6	38.0	53.5	59.7									
12/37	-3.9	-4.2	-6.6	-10.6	-7.0	-0.6	12.5	19.5	4.7	3.0	-14.4	-48.8								
12/38	-1.8	-1.9	-3.9	-7.4	-3.5	3.1	15.1	21.5	9.3	8.9	-2.6	-19.8	26.7							
12/39	-2.0	-2.2	-4.1	-7.2	-3.6	2.0	11.9	16.7	6.3	5.3	-3.5	-15.1	9.0	-6.9						
12/40	-2.7	-3.0	-4.7	-7.6	-4.4	0.3	8.9	12.8	3.7	2.2	-5.2	-14.0	1.9	-9.2	-14.2					
12/41	-3.5	-3.8	-5.4	-8.0	-5.3	-1.1	6.4	9.2	1.2	-0.3	-6.6	-14.0	-2.5	-10.5	-14.2	-16.0				
12/42	-2.9	-3.1	-4.5	-6.9	-4.2	-0.1	6.7	9.2	2.2	1.0	-4.2	-10.1	0.5	-5.0	-5.0	0.9	23.3			
12/43	-1.4	-1.4	-2.6	-4.9	-1.9	2.3	9.0	11.5	5.3	4.7	0.4	-4.4	6.8	3.9	6.1	15.8	40.3	49.7		
12/44	-0.4	-0.2	-1.3	-3.3	-0.3	3.9	10.4	13.0	7.3	7.1	3.4	-0.7	10.2	8.3	11.2	20.7	39.4	43.0	32.0	
12/45	1.4	1.7	0.8	-1.0	2.2	6.5	12.9	15.6	10.5	10.7	7.5	4.2	15.1	14.1	18.1	28.0	46.0	49.9	44.5	54.4
12/46	0.7	1.0	-0.0	-1.7	1.2	5.1	10.8	13.2	8.4	8.3	5.4	2.2	11.1	9.9	12.3	18.7	29.7	29.4	21.1	15.7
12/47	0.6	0.8	-0.1	-1.8	0.9	4.5	9.8	11.9	7.4	7.2	4.5	1.5	9.4	8.4	10.0	14.7	22.2	21.0	13.6	8.1
12/48	0.2	0.3	-0.6	-2.2	0.3	3.6	8.5	10.3	6.1	5.9	3.2	0.4	7.2	6.3	7.6	11.3	17.0	15.3	8.6	3.6
12/49	0.7	0.8	-0.0	-1.5	0.8	3.9	8.6	10.3	6.4	6.2	3.7	1.3	7.6	6.7	8.0	11.3	16.6	15.0	9.3	5.4
12/50	1.5	1.7	0.9	-0.5	1.8	5.0	9.7	11.3	7.5	7.4	5.1	2.8	8.9	8.2	9.5	12.9	17.6	16.3	11.6	8.6
12/51	1.9	2.1	1.4	-0.0	2.2	5.3	9.8	11.2	7.6	7.6	5.4	3.2	8.9	8.2	9.5	12.5	16.7	15.4	11.3	8.8
12/52	1.9	2.1	1.5	0.1	2.3	5.2	9.4	10.8	7.5	7.5	5.4	3.2	8.6	7.9	9.0	11.8	15.7	14.4	10.5	8.2
12/53	1.5	1.8	1.1	-0.2	1.8	4.4	8.4	9.7	6.6	6.6	4.6	2.6	7.4	6.6	7.7	10.1	13.5	12.1	8.5	6.3
12/54	2.9	3.1	2.5	1.3	3.4	6.0	10.1	11.4	8.4	8.5	6.5	4.7	9.5	8.9	10.1	12.5	16.0	14.9	11.9	10.1
12/55	3.3	3.5	2.9	1.8	3.9	6.5	10.5	11.8	8.8	9.0	7.1	5.3	9.9	9.3	10.5	12.8	15.9	15.0	12.3	10.7
12/56	3.4	3.6	3.1	2.0	3.9	6.5	10.3	11.5	8.7	8.9	7.0	5.3	9.7	9.3	10.2	12.2	14.9	14.1	11.7	10.2
12/57	2.7	2.9	2.3	1.2	3.1	5.4	8.9	9.9	7.4	7.5	5.7	4.1	8.1	7.5	8.3	10.0	12.5	11.6	9.1	7.7
12/58	3.8	4.0	3.4	2.4	4.3	6.7	10.2	11.3	8.8	8.9	7.2	5.7	9.7	9.3	10.1	11.9	14.5	13.7	11.3	10.1
12/59	4.0	4.2	3.5	2.6	4.5	6.9	10.3	11.4	8.9	9.1	7.4	6.0	9.8	9.4	10.2	11.8	14.2	13.4	11.3	10.1
12/60	3.9	4.1	3.4	2.4	4.2	6.5	9.7	10.7	8.5	8.6	7.0	5.6	9.1	8.6	9.4	10.9	13.1	12.3	10.2	9.1
12/61	4.5	4.7	4.0	3.0	4.9	7.1	10.3	11.3	9.0	9.2	7.6	6.3	9.8	9.4	10.1	11.6	13.7	12.9	10.9	9.9
12/62	3.8	3.9	3.4	2.4	4.1	6.2	9.2	10.1	7.9	8.1	6.6	5.3	8.5	8.1	8.7	10.1	12.0	11.2	9.2	8.1
12/63	4.1	4.3	3.7	2.7	4.5	6.6	9.5	10.4	8.3	8.4	6.9	5.7	8.8	8.4	9.1	10.3	12.1	11.3	9.5	8.5
12/64	4.3	4.5	4.0	3.0	4.7	6.7	9.5	10.4	8.4	8.5	7.2	6.0	9.0	8.6	9.2	10.4	12.1	11.4	9.7	8.8
12/65	4.6	4.8	4.2	3.4	5.1	7.1	10.0	10.8	8.8	8.9	7.5	6.3	9.3	8.9	9.6	10.7	12.4	11.7	10.1	9.3

FROM

To	1/26	12/26	12/27	12/28	12/29	12/30	12/31	12/32	12/33	12/34	12/35	12/36	12/37	12/38	12/39	12/40	12/41	12/42	12/43	12/44
12/26	-6.2																			
12/27	10.6	24.5																		
12/28	19.4	33.1	41.1																	
12/29	3.6	5.6	-3.4	-33.0																
12/30	-6.3	-7.3	-16.5	-34.9	-40.6															
12/31	-15.1	-17.3	-25.1	-39.6	-44.1	-51.0														
12/32	-15.2	-16.7	-22.8	-34.1	-35.9	-34.7	-16.2													
12/33	-7.1	-7.4	-11.6	-19.7	-15.9	-5.2	32.5	102.3												
12/34	-5.7	-5.9	-9.3	-15.6	-11.1	-1.4	24.5	51.2	9.9											
12/35	-2.3	-2.2	-4.9	-9.9	-4.6	5.8	29.6	50.3	27.8	45.9										
12/36	3.1	1.6	-0.6	-4.2	1.6	12.0	34.4	51.4	37.7	53.0	58.6									
12/37	-4.0	-4.3	-6.6	-10.7	-7.1	-0.7	12.3	19.3	4.4	2.7	-14.9	-49.4								
12/38	-1.8	-2.0	-4.0	-7.5	-3.6	2.9	14.9	21.4	9.1	8.6	-2.9	-20.1	25.4							
12/39	-2.1	-2.3	-4.1	-7.3	-3.7	1.9	11.7	16.5	6.2	5.1	-3.7	-15.4	8.4	-7.9						
12/40	-2.8	-3.0	-4.8	-7.7	-4.5	0.3	8.8	12.7	3.6	2.1	-5.4	-14.2	1.5	-9.7	-15.2					
12/41	-3.6	-3.9	-5.5	-8.1	-5.4	-1.2	6.3	9.1	1.1	-0.5	-6.8	-14.2	-2.7	-10.8	-14.8	-17.1				
12/42	-3.0	-3.1	-4.6	-7.0	-4.3	-0.2	6.6	9.1	2.1	0.9	-4.4	-10.3	0.3	-5.3	-5.4	0.1	21.3			
12/43	-1.5	-1.4	-2.7	-4.9	-2.0	2.3	8.9	11.4	5.1	4.6	0.3	-4.5	6.6	3.7	5.8	15.3	39.2	47.7		
12/44	-0.4	-0.2	-1.3	-3.3	-0.4	3.8	10.3	12.9	7.2	7.0	3.3	-0.8	10.1	8.1	11.0	20.4	38.9	42.3	30.8	
12/45	1.4	1.7	0.7	-1.1	2.1	6.5	12.9	15.5	10.5	10.6	7.5	4.1	15.0	14.0	17.9	27.8	45.7	49.5	44.0	53.3
12/46	0.7	0.9	-0.0	-1.7	1.1	5.1	10.8	13.1	8.4	8.2	5.3	2.1	11.0	9.8	12.2	18.5	29.4	29.1	20.7	15.2
12/47	0.5	0.7	-0.2	-1.8	0.8	4.4	9.7	11.8	7.4	7.1	4.4	1.4	9.3	8.3	9.8	14.5	21.9	20.7	13.3	7.7
12/48	0.2	0.3	-0.6	-2.2	0.2	3.5	8.5	10.3	6.1	5.8	3.1	0.3	7.1	6.2	7.5	11.2	16.8	15.0	8.4	3.4
12/49	0.7	0.8	-0.1	-1.6	0.7	3.9	8.6	10.3	6.4	6.1	3.6	1.2	7.5	6.6	7.9	11.2	16.4	14.8	9.1	5.2
12/50	1.5	1.6	0.9	-0.6	1.8	5.0	9.6	11.2	7.4	7.3	5.0	2.7	8.8	8.2	9.4	12.8	17.5	16.2	11.5	8.5
12/51	1.8	2.0	1.3	-0.1	2.2	5.2	9.7	11.1	7.6	7.6	5.4	3.1	8.8	8.1	9.4	12.4	16.6	15.3	11.2	8.7
12/52	1.9	2.1	1.4	0.1	2.3	5.1	9.4	10.8	7.4	7.4	5.3	3.2	8.5	7.8	9.0	11.7	15.6	14.3	10.4	8.1
12/53	1.5	1.7	1.0	-0.2	1.8	4.4	8.4	9.7	6.6	6.5	4.5	2.5	7.3	6.5	7.6	10.0	13.3	12.0	8.4	6.2
12/54	2.9	3.1	2.4	1.3	3.3	6.0	10.0	11.3	8.3	8.4	6.5	4.7	9.5	8.8	10.0	12.5	15.9	14.8	11.8	10.0
12/55	3.3	3.5	2.9	1.8	3.9	6.5	10.5	11.7	8.8	8.9	7.1	5.3	9.9	9.3	10.4	12.7	15.8	14.9	12.3	10.6
12/56	3.4	3.6	3.0	1.9	3.9	6.4	10.2	11.4	8.7	8.8	7.0	5.3	9.6	9.2	10.1	12.1	14.8	14.1	11.6	10.1
12/57	2.7	2.9	2.3	1.2	3.0	5.3	8.9	9.9	7.4	7.4	5.6	4.0	8.0	7.4	8.2	9.9	12.4	11.5	9.1	7.6
12/58	3.8	4.0	3.4	2.4	4.3	6.7	10.2	11.2	8.7	8.9	7.2	5.7	9.7	9.3	10.1	11.9	14.4	13.6	11.3	10.0
12/59	4.0	4.2	3.5	2.5	4.5	6.9	10.3	11.3	8.9	9.0	7.3	5.9	9.8	9.4	10.1	11.8	14.2	13.4	11.2	10.0
12/60	3.9	4.1	3.3	2.4	4.2	6.4	9.7	10.7	8.4	8.6	6.9	5.5	9.1	8.6	9.3	10.8	13.1	12.3	10.1	9.0
12/61	4.5	4.6	4.0	3.0	4.8	7.1	10.3	11.2	9.0	9.2	7.6	6.3	9.8	9.4	10.1	11.6	13.7	12.9	10.9	9.8
12/62	3.8	3.9	3.3	2.3	4.1	6.1	9.2	10.0	7.9	8.1	6.5	5.2	8.5	8.1	8.7	10.0	11.9	11.1	9.1	8.1
12/63	4.1	4.3	3.7	2.7	4.4	6.5	9.5	10.3	8.2	8.4	6.9	5.6	8.8	8.4	9.0	10.3	12.1	11.3	9.4	8.5
12/64	4.3	4.5	3.9	3.0	4.6	6.6	9.5	10.3	8.4	8.5	7.1	5.9	9.0	8.6	9.2	10.3	12.1	11.4	9.6	8.8
12/65	4.6	4.8	4.2	3.4	5.1	7.1	10.0	10.7	8.7	8.9	7.4	6.3	9.3	8.9	9.5	10.7	12.3	11.7	10.1	9.2

TABLE 3.
RATES OF CHANGE IN VALUE OF INVESTMENTS IN COMMON STOCKS LISTED ON THE NEW YORK STOCK EXCHANGE, IGNORING DIVIDENDS (Per Cent Per Annum Compounded Annually)
PART A—CASH-TO-PORTFOLIO, TAX EXEMPT

FROM

12/45	12/46	12/47	12/48	12/49	12/50	12/51	12/52	12/53	12/54	12/55	12/56	12/57	12/58	12/59	12/60	12/61	12/62	12/63	12/64
-13.6																			
-9.2	-6.2																		
-8.9	-7.0	-9.2																	
-4.1	-1.2	1.2	11.6																
1.3	5.3	9.1	18.9	27.2															
2.9	6.3	9.1	15.5	17.6	8.1														
3.0	6.0	8.1	12.5	12.8	6.0	2.8													
1.6	3.8	5.3	8.2	7.1	1.4	-2.3	-8.6												
6.1	8.8	10.9	14.4	14.8	11.5	12.2	16.5	47.7											
7.1	9.6	11.5	14.7	15.3	12.3	13.1	16.4	31.3	14.0										
7.0	9.2	10.7	13.3	13.7	11.0	11.2	13.1	21.3	8.6	2.0									
4.6	6.2	7.3	9.2	8.8	6.3	5.7	6.0	9.5	-1.1	-8.0	-17.1								
7.3	9.1	10.5	12.7	12.8	10.9	11.1	12.3	16.8	9.7	8.2	12.5	52.0							
7.5	9.4	10.7	12.8	13.0	11.2	11.4	12.6	16.3	10.5	9.5	13.0	31.4	10.7						
6.7	8.3	9.5	11.3	11.2	9.7	9.9	10.6	13.2	8.1	7.0	8.9	17.7	2.9	-5.4					
7.7	9.3	10.5	12.1	12.0	10.9	11.1	11.9	14.5	10.3	9.7	12.0	19.6	10.0	9.3	23.8				
6.0	7.4	8.3	9.6	9.4	8.2	8.1	8.5	10.3	6.3	5.3	6.4	11.3	2.8	0.4	2.5	-16.2			
6.5	7.9	8.7	9.9	9.8	8.7	8.6	9.0	10.7	7.2	6.4	7.6	12.0	5.2	3.9	7.0	-1.2	14.2		
6.9	8.2	9.0	10.2	10.1	9.0	8.9	9.4	11.0	7.8	7.2	8.4	12.4	6.8	6.1	9.2	4.2	14.9	12.9	
7.5	9.0	9.8	10.9	11.0	9.8	9.9	10.4	12.1	9.1	8.6	9.8	14.0	9.1	8.9	12.4	9.5	19.1	19.9	24.7

TABLE 3.
RATES OF CHANGE IN VALUE OF INVESTMENTS IN COMMON STOCKS LISTED ON THE NEW YORK STOCK EXCHANGE, IGNORING DIVIDENDS (Per Cent Per Annum Compounded Annually)
PART B—CASH-TO-CASH, TAX EXEMPT

FROM

12/45	12/46	12/47	12/48	12/49	12/50	12/51	12/52	12/53	12/54	12/55	12/56	12/57	12/58	12/59	12/60	12/61	12/62	12/63	12/64
-14.3																			
-9.6	-7.1																		
-9.2	-7.5	-10.2																	
-4.3	-1.5	0.6	10.4																
1.2	5.1	8.7	18.3	26.0															
2.7	6.1	8.8	15.2	17.1	7.0														
2.9	5.9	7.9	12.3	12.4	5.5	1.8													
1.4	3.7	5.1	8.0	6.7	1.0	-2.9	-9.6												
6.0	8.7	10.7	14.2	14.6	11.2	11.9	15.9	46.2											
7.0	9.5	11.4	14.5	15.1	12.1	12.9	16.0	30.6	12.9										
6.9	9.1	10.5	13.2	13.6	10.8	11.0	12.8	20.9	8.0	0.9									
4.5	6.1	7.2	9.1	8.7	6.2	5.5	5.7	9.1	-1.5	-8.6	-18.1								
7.2	9.1	10.4	12.5	12.6	10.7	10.9	12.1	16.5	9.4	7.9	11.9	50.3							
7.4	9.3	10.6	12.7	12.8	11.1	11.3	12.4	16.1	10.2	9.2	12.6	30.6	9.5						
6.6	8.2	9.4	11.2	11.1	9.6	9.7	10.5	13.1	7.9	6.7	8.6	17.3	2.3	-6.5					
7.6	9.2	10.4	12.0	12.0	10.8	11.0	11.8	14.4	10.1	9.5	11.7	19.3	9.6	8.7	22.5				
5.9	7.3	8.2	9.5	9.3	8.1	8.0	8.3	10.1	6.1	5.1	6.2	11.0	2.5	-0.0	1.9	-17.2			
6.5	7.8	8.7	9.9	9.8	8.6	8.5	8.9	10.6	7.0	6.2	7.4	11.7	5.0	3.6	6.5	-1.8	12.8		
6.8	8.1	8.9	10.1	10.0	8.9	8.9	9.3	10.9	7.7	7.1	8.2	12.2	6.6	5.9	8.9	3.8	14.3	11.5	
7.4	8.9	9.7	10.9	10.9	9.7	9.8	10.3	12.0	9.0	8.5	9.7	13.8	9.0	8.7	12.2	9.2	18.7	19.3	23.4

FROM

To	1/26	12/26	12/27	12/28	12/29	12/30	12/31	12/32	12/33	12/34	12/35	12/36	12/37	12/38	12/39	12/40	12/41	12/42	12/43	12/44
12/26	-5.7																			
12/27	10.8	25.2																		
12/28	19.5	33.3	41.7																	
12/29	3.7	5.8	-3.1	-32.6																
12/30	-6.2	-7.2	-16.3	-34.7	-40.1															
12/31	-15.0	-17.1	-24.9	-39.4	-43.8	-50.2														
12/32	-15.0	-16.6	-22.6	-33.9	-35.6	-34.1	-14.5													
12/33	-7.0	-7.3	-11.5	-19.6	-15.6	-4.8	33.4	105.1												
12/34	-5.6	-5.8	-9.2	-15.5	-11.0	-1.1	25.0	52.1	11.2											
12/35	-2.2	-2.1	-4.8	-9.9	-4.5	5.9	29.9	50.7	28.4	47.3										
12/36	3.1	1.6	-0.6	-4.1	1.7	12.1	34.6	51.6	38.0	53.5	59.7									
12/37	-3.9	-4.2	-6.6	-10.6	-7.0	-0.6	12.5	19.5	4.7	3.0	-14.4	-48.8								
12/38	-1.8	-1.9	-3.9	-7.4	-3.5	3.1	15.1	21.5	9.3	8.9	-2.6	-19.8	26.7							
12/39	-2.0	-2.2	-4.1	-7.2	-3.6	2.0	11.9	16.7	6.3	5.3	-3.5	-15.1	9.0	-6.9						
12/40	-2.7	-3.0	-4.7	-7.6	-4.4	0.4	8.9	12.8	3.7	2.2	-5.2	-14.0	1.9	-9.2	-14.2					
12/41	-3.5	-3.8	-5.4	-8.0	-5.3	-1.1	6.4	9.2	1.2	-0.3	-6.6	-14.0	-2.5	-10.5	-14.2	-16.0				
12/42	-2.9	-3.0	-4.5	-6.9	-4.2	-0.1	6.7	9.2	2.2	1.1	-4.2	-10.1	0.5	-5.0	-5.0	0.9	23.3			
12/43	-1.4	-1.4	-2.6	-4.8	-1.9	2.3	9.0	11.5	5.3	4.8	0.4	-4.3	6.8	3.9	6.1	15.8	40.2	49.7		
12/44	-0.3	-0.2	-1.3	-3.3	-0.3	3.9	10.4	13.0	7.3	7.1	3.4	-0.6	10.2	8.3	11.2	20.7	39.3	43.0	32.0	
12/45	1.5	1.7	0.8	-1.0	2.2	6.5	12.9	15.6	10.5	10.7	7.6	4.2	15.1	14.1	18.1	27.9	45.9	49.8	44.5	54.4
12/46	0.7	1.0	0.0	-1.6	1.2	5.1	10.8	13.2	8.4	8.3	5.4	2.2	11.1	9.9	12.3	18.7	29.6	29.4	21.0	15.6
12/47	0.6	0.8	-0.1	-1.7	0.9	4.5	9.8	11.9	7.4	7.2	4.5	1.6	9.4	8.4	10.0	14.6	22.1	20.9	13.6	8.1
12/48	0.2	0.3	-0.6	-2.1	0.3	3.6	8.5	10.3	6.1	5.9	3.2	0.4	7.2	6.3	7.6	11.3	17.0	15.2	8.6	3.6
12/49	0.7	0.9	-0.0	-1.5	0.8	3.9	8.6	10.3	6.4	6.2	3.7	1.3	7.6	6.7	8.0	11.3	16.5	15.0	9.2	5.4
12/50	1.5	1.7	0.9	-0.5	1.8	5.0	9.7	11.3	7.5	7.4	5.1	2.8	8.9	8.2	9.5	12.9	17.6	16.3	11.6	8.6
12/51	1.9	2.1	1.4	0.0	2.3	5.3	9.8	11.2	7.6	7.6	5.4	3.2	8.9	8.2	9.4	12.4	16.6	15.4	11.3	8.8
12/52	2.0	2.2	1.5	0.2	2.3	5.2	9.4	10.8	7.5	7.5	5.4	3.3	8.6	7.9	9.0	11.8	15.6	14.3	10.5	8.2
12/53	1.6	1.8	1.1	-0.2	1.8	4.4	8.4	9.7	6.6	6.6	4.6	2.6	7.4	6.6	7.6	10.0	13.4	12.1	8.5	6.3
12/54	2.9	3.1	2.5	1.3	3.4	6.0	10.1	11.3	8.4	8.5	6.5	4.7	9.5	8.8	10.1	12.5	15.9	14.9	11.9	10.0
12/55	3.3	3.5	3.0	1.8	3.9	6.5	10.5	11.7	8.8	9.0	7.1	5.3	9.9	9.3	10.5	12.7	15.8	15.0	12.3	10.6
12/56	3.4	3.6	3.1	2.0	3.9	6.5	10.3	11.5	8.7	8.9	7.0	5.3	9.7	9.2	10.1	12.1	14.8	14.1	11.7	10.2
12/57	2.7	2.9	2.3	1.2	3.1	5.4	8.9	9.9	7.4	7.5	5.7	4.1	8.0	7.5	8.2	10.0	12.4	11.6	9.1	7.6
12/58	3.8	4.0	3.4	2.4	4.3	6.7	10.2	11.2	8.8	8.9	7.2	5.7	9.7	9.3	10.1	11.9	14.4	13.6	11.3	10.0
12/59	4.0	4.2	3.5	2.6	4.5	6.9	10.3	11.3	8.9	9.0	7.4	6.0	9.8	9.4	10.1	11.8	14.2	13.4	11.2	10.0
12/60	3.9	4.1	3.4	2.5	4.3	6.5	9.7	10.7	8.4	8.6	6.9	5.6	9.1	8.6	9.3	10.8	13.1	12.3	10.2	9.1
12/61	4.5	4.7	4.0	3.1	4.9	7.1	10.3	11.2	9.0	9.2	7.6	6.3	9.8	9.4	10.1	11.6	13.7	12.9	10.9	9.9
12/62	3.8	4.0	3.4	2.4	4.1	6.2	9.2	10.0	7.9	8.1	6.5	5.3	8.5	8.1	8.7	10.0	11.9	11.1	9.1	8.1
12/63	4.1	4.3	3.7	2.8	4.5	6.5	9.5	10.3	8.2	8.4	6.9	5.7	8.8	8.4	9.0	10.2	12.0	11.3	9.4	8.5
12/64	4.3	4.5	4.0	3.0	4.7	6.6	9.5	10.3	8.4	8.5	7.1	5.9	9.0	8.6	9.2	10.3	12.0	11.4	9.6	8.8
12/65	4.6	4.8	4.2	3.4	5.1	7.1	10.0	10.7	8.7	8.9	7.4	6.3	9.3	8.9	9.5	10.6	12.3	11.6	10.0	9.2

FROM

To	1/26	12/26	12/27	12/28	12/29	12/30	12/31	12/32	12/33	12/34	12/35	12/36	12/37	12/38	12/39	12/40	12/41	12/42	12/43	12/44
12/26	-6.2																			
12/27	10.6	24.5																		
12/28	19.4	33.1	41.1																	
12/29	3.6	5.6	-3.4	-33.0																
12/30	-6.3	-7.3	-16.5	-34.9	-40.6															
12/31	-15.1	-17.3	-25.1	-39.6	-44.1	-51.0														
12/32	-15.2	-16.7	-22.8	-34.1	-35.9	-34.7	-16.2													
12/33	-7.1	-7.4	-11.6	-19.7	-15.9	-5.2	32.5	102.3												
12/34	-5.7	-5.9	-9.3	-15.6	-11.1	-1.4	24.5	51.2	9.9											
12/35	-2.3	-2.2	-4.9	-9.9	-4.6	5.8	29.6	50.3	27.8	45.9										
12/36	3.1	1.6	-0.6	-4.2	1.6	12.0	34.4	51.4	37.7	53.0	58.6									
12/37	-4.0	-4.3	-6.6	-10.7	-7.1	-0.7	12.3	19.3	4.4	2.7	-14.9	-49.4								
12/38	-1.8	-2.0	-4.0	-7.5	-3.6	2.9	14.9	21.4	9.1	8.6	-2.9	-20.1	25.4							
12/39	-2.1	-2.3	-4.1	-7.3	-3.7	1.9	11.7	16.5	6.2	5.1	-3.7	-15.4	8.4	-7.9						
12/40	-2.7	-2.9	-4.6	-7.3	-4.3	0.2	8.5	12.3	3.4	2.0	-5.2	-13.6	1.5	-9.3	-14.6					
12/41	-3.3	-3.5	-4.9	-7.1	-4.9	-1.1	5.8	8.5	1.0	-0.4	-6.0	-12.4	-2.5	-9.7	-13.2	-15.4				
12/42	-2.6	-2.8	-3.9	-6.0	-3.8	-0.2	6.0	8.3	1.8	0.8	-3.8	-8.7	0.2	-4.6	-4.7	0.1	18.5			
12/43	-1.4	-1.4	-2.4	-4.4	-1.9	2.0	8.3	10.6	4.7	4.2	0.2	-4.0	5.9	3.3	5.2	13.8	35.5	42.5		
12/44	-0.4	-0.3	-1.2	-3.0	-0.4	3.4	9.5	11.9	6.6	6.3	2.9	-0.7	9.1	7.2	9.8	18.4	35.2	37.7	26.9	
12/45	1.2	1.5	0.6	-1.0	1.8	5.9	12.0	14.6	9.6	9.8	6.8	3.7	13.7	12.7	16.3	25.4	42.0	45.0	39.2	46.6
12/46	0.5	0.8	-0.1	-1.6	1.0	4.6	10.0	12.3	7.7	7.5	4.8	1.8	10.0	8.9	11.1	16.9	27.0	26.5	18.5	13.4
12/47	0.4	0.6	-0.2	-1.7	0.7	4.0	9.0	11.0	6.7	6.5	4.0	1.2	8.4	7.5	8.9	13.2	20.1	18.9	11.9	6.8
12/48	0.1	0.2	-0.6	-2.1	0.1	3.3	8.0	9.8	5.7	5.4	2.9	0.3	6.7	5.8	6.9	10.4	15.8	14.1	7.7	3.1
12/49	0.6	0.7	-0.1	-1.5	0.6	3.6	8.2	9.8	6.0	5.8	3.4	1.1	7.0	6.1	7.4	10.5	15.5	13.9	8.4	4.8
12/50	1.3	1.5	0.8	-0.6	1.6	4.7	9.2	10.7	7.0	6.9	4.7	2.5	8.3	7.6	8.9	12.1	16.5	15.2	10.7	7.8
12/51	1.7	1.9	1.2	-0.1	2.0	4.9	9.2	10.6	7.1	7.1	5.0	2.8	8.2	7.6	8.7	11.6	15.6	14.3	10.4	8.0
12/52	1.7	1.9	1.3	0.0	2.1	4.7	8.9	10.2	6.9	7.0	4.9	2.9	7.9	7.2	8.3	10.9	14.6	13.3	9.6	7.4
12/53	1.3	1.5	0.9	-0.3	1.6	4.0	7.9	9.2	6.1	6.1	4.1	2.3	6.8	6.0	7.0	9.3	12.5	11.2	7.7	5.6
12/54	2.6	2.9	2.3	1.1	3.1	5.6	9.6	10.8	7.9	8.0	6.1	4.3	8.9	8.3	9.4	11.8	15.1	14.0	11.1	9.3
12/55	3.1	3.3	2.7	1.6	3.6	6.2	10.0	11.3	8.4	8.5	6.7	4.9	9.3	8.7	9.8	12.0	15.0	14.2	11.5	9.9
12/56	3.2	3.4	2.8	1.8	3.6	6.1	9.8	11.0	8.3	8.4	6.6	4.9	9.1	8.7	9.6	11.5	14.1	13.3	11.0	9.5
12/57	2.5	2.7	2.1	1.1	2.8	5.0	8.5	9.5	7.0	7.1	5.3	3.7	7.6	7.0	7.7	9.4	11.8	10.9	8.5	7.1
12/58	3.6	3.7	3.1	2.2	4.0	6.3	9.8	10.8	8.3	8.5	6.8	5.3	9.2	8.8	9.6	11.3	13.8	12.9	10.6	9.4
12/59	3.7	3.9	3.3	2.3	4.2	6.5	9.9	10.9	8.5	8.6	7.0	5.6	9.3	8.9	9.6	11.2	13.6	12.7	10.6	9.4
12/60	3.6	3.8	3.1	2.2	3.9	6.1	9.3	10.2	8.0	8.1	6.5	5.2	8.6	8.1	8.8	10.3	12.4	11.6	9.5	8.4
12/61	4.2	4.3	3.6	2.7	4.5	6.6	9.8	10.7	8.5	8.7	7.1	5.9	9.2	8.8	9.4	10.9	12.9	12.1	10.1	9.1
12/62	3.5	3.6	3.1	2.1	3.7	5.8	8.7	9.6	7.4	7.6	6.1	4.8	8.0	7.5	8.1	9.4	11.2	10.4	8.5	7.5
12/63	3.8	4.0	3.4	2.5	4.1	6.1	9.1	9.9	7.8	7.9	6.4	5.2	8.3	7.9	8.5	9.7	11.4	10.6	8.8	7.9
12/64	4.1	4.2	3.7	2.8	4.4	6.3	9.1	10.0	8.0	8.1	6.8	5.6	8.6	8.2	8.7	9.9	11.6	10.9	9.1	8.3
12/65	4.3	4.5	4.0	3.1	4.8	6.8	9.6	10.3	8.3	8.5	7.1	6.0	8.8	8.4	9.0	10.2	11.8	11.1	9.5	8.7

TABLE 3.
RATES OF CHANGE IN VALUE OF INVESTMENTS IN COMMON STOCKS LISTED ON THE NEW YORK STOCK EXCHANGE, IGNORING DIVIDENDS (Per Cent Per Annum Compounded Annually)
PART C—CASH-TO-PORTFOLIO, LOWER TAX RATE

FROM 12/45	12/46	12/47	12/48	12/49	12/50	12/51	12/52	12/53	12/54	12/55	12/56	12/57	12/58	12/59	12/60	12/61	12/62	12/63	12/64
-13.6																			
-9.2	-6.2																		
-8.9	-7.0	-9.2																	
-4.1	-1.2	1.2	11.6																
1.3	5.3	9.1	18.9	27.2															
2.9	6.3	9.1	15.5	17.6	8.0														
3.0	6.0	8.1	12.5	12.8	6.0	2.8													
1.6	3.8	5.3	8.2	7.0	1.4	-2.3	-8.6												
6.1	8.8	10.8	14.4	14.8	11.5	12.2	16.5	47.7											
7.1	9.6	11.5	14.7	15.2	12.3	13.1	16.4	31.3	14.0										
7.0	9.1	10.6	13.3	13.7	11.0	11.2	13.0	21.2	8.5	1.9									
4.6	6.2	7.3	9.2	8.8	6.3	5.7	6.0	9.4	-1.1	-8.1	-17.1								
7.3	9.1	10.5	12.6	12.7	10.9	11.0	12.3	16.7	9.6	8.2	12.5	52.0							
7.5	9.3	10.7	12.7	12.9	11.2	11.4	12.6	16.3	10.4	9.5	13.0	31.3	10.7						
6.6	8.3	9.5	11.2	11.2	9.7	9.8	10.6	13.2	8.1	6.9	8.9	17.7	2.8	-5.4					
7.7	9.3	10.4	12.0	12.0	10.9	11.1	11.9	14.4	10.3	9.7	11.9	19.6	9.9	9.2	23.8				
6.0	7.3	8.2	9.5	9.3	8.1	8.0	8.4	10.2	6.3	5.3	6.4	11.2	2.8	0.3	2.5	-16.2			
6.5	7.8	8.7	9.9	9.8	8.6	8.6	9.0	10.7	7.1	6.3	7.5	11.9	5.2	3.8	6.9	-1.2	14.2		
6.9	8.1	8.9	10.1	10.0	8.9	8.9	9.4	11.0	7.8	7.2	8.3	12.3	6.8	6.1	9.2	4.2	14.9	12.9	
7.5	8.9	9.7	10.9	10.9	9.8	9.8	10.3	12.0	9.0	8.5	9.7	13.9	9.1	8.9	12.4	9.5	19.0	19.9	24.7

TABLE 3
RATES OF CHANGE IN VALUE OF INVESTMENTS IN COMMON STOCKS LISTED ON THE NEW YORK STOCK EXCHANGE, IGNORING DIVIDENDS (Per Cent Per Annum Compounded Annually)
PART D—CASH-TO-CASH, LOWER TAX RATE

FROM 12/45	12/46	12/47	12/48	12/49	12/50	12/51	12/52	12/53	12/54	12/55	12/56	12/57	12/58	12/59	12/60	12/61	12/62	12/63	12/64
-12.5																			
-8.4	-6.2																		
-8.3	-6.8	-9.3																	
-3.9	-1.4	0.6	9.5																
1.1	4.6	8.0	16.8	23.6															
2.5	5.5	8.0	13.8	15.4	6.3														
2.6	5.3	7.2	11.1	11.2	4.9	1.6													
1.3	3.3	4.6	7.2	6.1	0.9	-2.5	-8.6												
5.5	8.0	9.9	13.1	13.4	10.2	10.8	14.5	41.6											
6.5	8.8	10.6	13.5	14.0	11.1	11.8	14.6	27.9	11.6										
6.4	8.4	9.8	12.3	12.6	10.0	10.1	11.7	19.1	7.3	0.8									
4.1	5.6	6.6	8.4	8.0	5.7	5.0	5.2	8.3	-1.3	-7.7	-16.3								
6.7	8.4	9.7	11.7	11.8	10.0	10.1	11.2	15.3	8.5	7.1	10.7	45.3							
6.9	8.7	10.0	11.9	12.0	10.3	10.5	11.5	15.0	9.4	8.4	11.5	27.9	8.6						
6.1	7.6	8.8	10.4	10.3	8.9	9.0	9.6	12.0	7.2	6.1	7.7	15.6	2.0	-5.8					
7.0	8.5	9.6	11.1	11.0	9.9	10.0	10.7	13.1	9.1	8.5	10.5	17.3	8.4	7.6	19.5				
5.4	6.7	7.5	8.7	8.5	7.3	7.2	7.5	9.2	5.5	4.5	5.5	9.8	2.2	0.0	1.6	-15.0			
5.9	7.2	8.0	9.1	9.0	7.8	7.7	8.1	9.7	6.3	5.5	6.6	10.5	4.4	3.1	5.7	-1.6	11.2		
6.4	7.6	8.4	9.5	9.4	8.3	8.3	8.7	10.2	7.1	6.5	7.5	11.3	6.0	5.3	8.1	3.5	12.9	10.4	
7.0	8.4	9.2	10.2	10.2	9.1	9.1	9.6	11.2	8.3	7.8	8.9	12.8	8.2	7.9	11.1	8.3	16.9	17.3	20.8

To	1/26	12/26	12/27	12/28	12/29	12/30	12/31	12/32	12/33	12/34	12/35	12/36	12/37	12/38	12/39	12/40	12/41	12/42	12/43	12/44
12/26	-5.7																			
12/27	10.8	25.2																		
12/28	19.5	33.3	41.6																	
12/29	3.7	5.7	-3.2	-32.6																
12/30	-6.2	-7.2	-16.3	-34.6	-40.1															
12/31	-15.0	-17.1	-24.9	-39.3	-43.7	-50.1														
12/32	-14.9	-16.5	-22.5	-33.6	-35.3	-33.9	-14.4													
12/33	-6.8	-7.1	-11.2	-19.2	-15.3	-4.5	33.5	105.2												
12/34	-5.5	-5.6	-9.0	-15.1	-10.7	-0.9	25.1	52.1	11.2											
12/35	-2.0	-1.9	-4.5	-9.4	-4.1	6.1	30.0	50.7	28.4	47.4										
12/36	3.3	1.8	-0.3	-3.7	2.0	12.3	34.6	51.6	38.0	53.5	59.5									
12/37	-3.8	-4.1	-6.3	-10.2	-6.8	-0.5	12.5	19.5	4.7	3.0	-14.5	-48.8								
12/38	-1.6	-1.8	-3.7	-7.0	-3.2	3.2	15.1	21.5	9.3	8.8	-2.6	-19.6	26.8							
12/39	-1.9	-2.0	-3.8	-6.8	-3.3	2.1	11.9	16.6	6.3	5.3	-3.4	-14.9	9.1	-6.8						
12/40	-2.6	-2.8	-4.5	-7.2	-4.1	0.5	8.9	12.8	3.7	2.3	-5.2	-13.8	2.0	-9.1	-14.1					
12/41	-3.4	-3.6	-5.2	-7.7	-5.1	-1.0	6.4	9.2	1.2	-0.3	-6.5	-13.8	-2.4	-10.4	-14.2	-15.9				
12/42	-2.7	-2.9	-4.2	-6.6	-3.9	0.0	6.7	9.2	2.3	1.1	-4.1	-9.9	0.6	-4.9	-4.9	0.9	23.1			
12/43	-1.2	-1.2	-2.3	-4.4	-1.7	2.5	9.0	11.5	5.3	4.8	0.5	-4.2	6.8	3.9	6.1	15.7	40.0	49.6		
12/44	-0.1	0.0	-1.0	-2.8	0.0	4.0	10.4	12.9	7.4	7.1	3.5	-0.4	10.2	8.3	11.2	20.6	39.2	42.9	32.1	
12/45	1.7	2.0	1.1	-0.5	2.5	6.7	12.9	15.6	10.6	10.7	7.6	4.4	15.1	14.1	18.1	27.9	45.7	49.7	44.5	54.4
12/46	0.9	1.2	0.3	-1.2	1.5	5.2	10.8	13.2	8.5	8.3	5.4	2.4	11.1	9.9	12.3	18.6	29.4	29.3	21.0	15.6
12/47	0.8	1.0	0.1	-1.4	1.1	4.6	9.8	11.9	7.5	7.3	4.5	1.7	9.4	8.4	10.0	14.6	22.0	20.8	13.6	8.0
12/48	0.4	0.5	-0.3	-1.8	0.5	3.7	8.5	10.3	6.2	5.9	3.3	0.6	7.3	6.3	7.6	11.2	16.9	15.1	8.6	3.6
12/49	0.9	1.0	0.2	-1.2	1.0	4.0	8.6	10.3	6.4	6.2	3.8	1.4	7.6	6.7	8.0	11.3	16.5	14.9	9.2	5.4
12/50	1.7	1.9	1.1	-0.2	2.0	5.1	9.7	11.2	7.5	7.4	5.2	2.9	8.9	8.2	9.5	12.8	17.5	16.2	11.6	8.6
12/51	2.0	2.3	1.6	0.3	2.4	5.4	9.8	11.2	7.6	7.6	5.5	3.3	8.9	8.2	9.4	12.4	16.5	15.3	11.3	8.8
12/52	2.1	2.3	1.7	0.5	2.5	5.2	9.4	10.8	7.5	7.5	5.4	3.3	8.6	7.9	9.0	11.7	15.6	14.3	10.5	8.2
12/53	1.7	1.9	1.3	0.1	2.0	4.5	8.4	9.7	6.6	6.6	4.6	2.7	7.4	6.6	7.6	10.0	13.3	12.0	8.5	6.3
12/54	3.0	3.3	2.7	1.6	3.5	6.1	10.0	11.3	8.4	8.4	6.6	4.8	9.5	8.8	10.0	12.5	15.9	14.8	11.9	10.0
12/55	3.5	3.7	3.1	2.1	4.0	6.6	10.5	11.7	8.8	9.0	7.1	5.4	9.9	9.3	10.4	12.7	15.8	14.9	12.3	10.6
12/56	3.5	3.7	3.2	2.2	4.1	6.5	10.2	11.4	8.7	8.8	7.0	5.4	9.6	9.2	10.1	12.1	14.8	14.0	11.6	10.1
12/57	2.8	3.0	2.4	1.4	3.2	5.4	8.9	9.9	7.4	7.4	5.7	4.1	8.0	7.4	8.2	9.9	12.4	11.5	9.1	7.6
12/58	3.9	4.1	3.5	2.6	4.4	6.7	10.2	11.2	8.7	8.9	7.2	5.8	9.7	9.2	10.1	11.8	14.3	13.5	11.3	10.0
12/59	4.1	4.3	3.7	2.8	4.6	6.9	10.3	11.3	8.9	9.0	7.4	6.0	9.8	9.3	10.1	11.7	14.1	13.3	11.2	10.0
12/60	4.0	4.2	3.5	2.7	4.4	6.5	9.7	10.6	8.4	8.5	6.9	5.6	9.1	8.6	9.3	10.8	13.0	12.2	10.1	9.0
12/61	4.6	4.8	4.1	3.3	5.0	7.1	10.3	11.2	9.0	9.2	7.6	6.4	9.7	9.3	10.0	11.5	13.6	12.8	10.8	9.8
12/62	3.9	4.0	3.5	2.6	4.2	6.2	9.1	10.0	7.9	8.0	6.5	5.3	8.5	8.0	8.6	9.9	11.8	11.0	9.1	8.1
12/63	4.2	4.4	3.8	2.9	4.5	6.5	9.5	10.3	8.2	8.3	6.8	5.7	8.7	8.3	8.9	10.1	11.9	11.2	9.3	8.5
12/64	4.4	4.6	4.1	3.2	4.7	6.6	9.4	10.3	8.3	8.4	7.1	5.9	8.9	8.5	9.1	10.2	11.9	11.3	9.6	8.7
12/65	4.7	4.8	4.3	3.6	5.1	7.1	9.9	10.7	8.7	8.8	7.4	6.3	9.2	8.8	9.4	10.5	12.2	11.5	10.0	9.2

To	1/26	12/26	12/27	12/28	12/29	12/30	12/31	12/32	12/33	12/34	12/35	12/36	12/37	12/38	12/39	12/40	12/41	12/42	12/43	12/44
12/26	-5.8																			
12/27	10.0	23.1																		
12/28	18.4	31.3	38.6																	
12/29	3.4	5.3	-3.2	-31.0																
12/30	-5.9	-6.8	-15.3	-32.3	-38.2															
12/31	-14.0	-16.0	-23.1	-36.3	-41.2	-48.5														
12/32	-13.0	-14.4	-19.4	-28.6	-31.0	-30.9	-14.8													
12/33	-6.2	-6.5	-10.1	-17.0	-14.0	-4.6	29.9	93.2												
12/34	-5.0	-5.2	-8.1	-13.4	-9.8	-1.2	22.7	47.4	9.0											
12/35	-2.0	-1.9	-4.3	-8.7	-4.0	5.5	27.9	47.4	25.9	42.2										
12/36	3.0	1.6	-0.4	-3.5	1.6	11.3	32.6	48.6	35.2	49.1	53.4									
12/37	-3.5	-3.8	-5.8	-9.2	-6.3	-0.6	11.5	18.0	4.1	2.5	-13.5	-45.0								
12/38	-1.6	-1.7	-3.4	-6.3	-3.1	2.7	13.9	19.9	8.3	7.9	-2.6	-17.9	22.9							
12/39	-1.8	-1.9	-3.5	-6.1	-3.1	1.7	10.8	15.3	5.6	4.6	-3.3	-13.4	7.5	-7.0						
12/40	-2.3	-2.5	-3.9	-6.1	-3.7	0.2	7.8	11.3	3.1	1.8	-4.5	-11.6	1.3	-8.2	-12.9					
12/41	-2.4	-2.5	-3.3	-4.8	-3.5	-0.9	4.5	6.6	0.7	-0.3	-4.1	-8.4	-1.9	-6.8	-9.3	-10.9				
12/42	-1.9	-1.9	-2.6	-3.9	-2.6	-0.3	4.4	6.2	1.3	0.6	-2.5	-5.6	0.0	-3.1	-3.1	0.1	12.3			
12/43	-1.1	-1.1	-1.9	-3.5	-1.5	1.7	7.4	9.5	4.1	3.7	0.2	-3.3	5.1	2.8	4.4	11.9	30.5	35.8		
12/44	-0.3	-0.2	-0.9	-2.4	-0.3	3.1	8.7	10.9	5.9	5.6	2.6	-0.6	8.0	6.4	8.7	16.2	31.2	33.0	23.1	
12/45	1.2	1.4	0.7	-0.7	1.7	5.4	11.1	13.5	8.7	8.8	6.1	3.3	12.4	11.4	14.6	22.9	37.9	40.1	34.3	40.0
12/46	0.6	0.8	0.1	-1.2	0.9	4.1	9.2	11.3	6.9	6.8	4.2	1.6	9.0	7.9	9.9	15.2	24.3	23.6	16.2	11.6
12/47	0.4	0.6	-0.1	-1.3	0.7	3.6	8.3	10.2	6.1	5.9	3.5	1.1	7.5	6.7	7.9	11.8	18.1	16.8	10.4	5.9
12/48	0.2	0.3	-0.4	-1.6	0.2	3.0	7.4	9.1	5.2	4.9	2.6	0.3	6.0	5.2	6.2	9.4	14.4	12.7	6.9	2.7
12/49	0.6	0.7	0.0	-1.1	0.7	3.3	7.6	9.1	5.5	5.2	3.1	1.0	6.4	5.5	6.6	9.5	14.1	12.6	7.5	4.2
12/50	1.3	1.4	0.8	-0.3	1.5	4.3	8.5	10.0	6.4	6.3	4.3	2.3	7.6	6.9	8.0	11.0	15.1	13.9	9.6	6.9
12/51	1.5	1.7	1.1	0.0	1.8	4.4	8.4	9.7	6.4	6.4	4.4	2.5	7.3	6.7	7.7	10.3	14.0	12.8	9.1	6.9
12/52	1.6	1.7	1.2	0.2	1.8	4.3	8.1	9.4	6.2	6.2	4.3	2.5	7.1	6.4	7.4	9.8	13.2	11.9	8.4	6.4
12/53	1.2	1.4	0.9	-0.1	1.4	3.6	7.2	8.4	5.5	5.4	3.6	2.0	6.0	5.3	6.2	8.3	11.2	9.9	6.7	4.8
12/54	2.4	2.6	2.1	1.1	2.8	5.1	8.8	10.0	7.2	7.2	5.4	3.8	8.1	7.4	8.5	10.6	13.7	12.6	9.8	8.1
12/55	2.8	3.0	2.5	1.5	3.3	5.6	9.3	10.4	7.6	7.7	6.0	4.4	8.5	7.9	8.9	10.9	13.7	12.9	10.3	8.7
12/56	2.9	3.1	2.6	1.6	3.3	5.6	9.1	10.2	7.6	7.7	5.9	4.4	8.3	7.9	8.6	10.4	12.9	12.1	9.8	8.4
12/57	2.3	2.4	1.9	1.0	2.5	4.6	7.8	8.8	6.3	6.4	4.7	3.3	6.8	6.3	7.0	8.5	10.7	9.8	7.6	6.2
12/58	3.3	3.4	2.9	2.0	3.6	5.8	9.1	10.1	7.7	7.8	6.1	4.8	8.4	8.0	8.7	10.3	12.6	11.8	9.6	8.4
12/59	3.4	3.6	3.0	2.2	3.8	6.0	9.2	10.2	7.8	7.9	6.3	5.0	8.6	8.1	8.8	10.3	12.5	11.7	9.6	8.4
12/60	3.3	3.5	2.9	2.1	3.6	5.6	8.7	9.6	7.4	7.5	6.0	4.7	7.9	7.4	8.1	9.5	11.5	10.7	8.7	7.6
12/61	3.9	4.1	3.4	2.6	4.2	6.2	9.3	10.2	8.0	8.1	6.6	5.4	8.6	8.2	8.8	10.2	12.1	11.3	9.4	8.4
12/62	3.3	3.4	2.9	2.0	3.5	5.4	8.2	9.0	7.0	7.1	5.6	4.5	7.4	7.0	7.5	8.8	10.5	9.7	7.8	6.8
12/63	3.6	3.7	3.2	2.4	3.8	5.8	8.6	9.3	7.3	7.4	6.0	4.8	7.7	7.3	7.9	9.0	10.7	9.9	8.1	7.2
12/64	3.8	3.9	3.4	2.6	4.1	5.9	8.6	9.4	7.4	7.5	6.2	5.1	7.9	7.5	8.0	9.1	10.7	10.0	8.4	7.5
12/65	4.1	4.2	3.7	3.0	4.4	6.3	9.1	9.8	7.8	7.9	6.5	5.5	8.2	7.8	8.4	9.5	11.0	10.3	8.8	8.0

TABLE 3.
RATES OF CHANGE IN VALUE OF INVESTMENTS IN COMMON STOCKS LISTED ON THE NEW YORK STOCK EXCHANGE, IGNORING DIVIDENDS (Per Cent Per Annum Compounded Annually)
PART E—CASH-TO-PORTFOLIO, HIGHER TAX RATE

FROM

12/45	12/46	12/47	12/48	12/49	12/50	12/51	12/52	12/53	12/54	12/55	12/56	12/57	12/58	12/59	12/60	12/61	12/62	12/63	12/64
-13.6																			
-9.2	-6.2																		
-8.9	-7.0	-9.2																	
-4.1	-1.2	1.2	11.6																
1.3	5.3	9.1	18.9	27.2															
2.8	6.3	9.1	15.5	17.6	8.0														
3.0	6.0	8.1	12.5	12.7	6.0	2.8													
1.6	3.8	5.3	8.2	7.0	1.4	-2.3	-8.6												
6.1	8.8	10.8	14.3	14.7	11.4	12.2	16.5	47.7											
7.1	9.6	11.5	14.6	15.2	12.3	13.1	16.4	31.3	14.0										
7.0	9.1	10.6	13.2	13.6	10.9	11.2	13.0	21.2	8.5	1.9									
4.6	6.2	7.2	9.1	8.8	6.3	5.7	5.9	9.4	-1.2	-8.1	-17.1								
7.3	9.1	10.5	12.6	12.7	10.8	11.0	12.2	16.6	9.6	8.2	12.4	51.9							
7.5	9.3	10.7	12.7	12.9	11.1	11.4	12.5	16.2	10.4	9.5	13.0	31.3	10.7						
6.6	8.3	9.5	11.2	11.1	9.7	9.8	10.5	13.1	8.1	6.9	8.8	17.6	2.8	-5.4					
7.6	9.3	10.4	12.0	11.9	10.8	11.1	11.8	14.4	10.2	9.7	11.9	19.5	9.9	9.2	23.7				
5.9	7.3	8.2	9.4	9.3	8.1	8.0	8.4	10.2	6.2	5.3	6.4	11.1	2.8	0.3	2.4	-16.2			
6.5	7.8	8.6	9.8	9.7	8.6	8.5	8.9	10.6	7.1	6.3	7.5	11.8	5.2	3.8	6.9	-1.2	14.1		
6.8	8.1	8.9	10.0	10.0	8.9	8.9	9.3	10.9	7.8	7.1	8.3	12.2	6.8	6.0	9.1	4.2	14.8	12.9	
7.4	8.9	9.7	10.8	10.8	9.7	9.8	10.3	11.9	9.0	8.5	9.7	13.8	9.1	8.9	12.3	9.5	19.0	19.8	24.6

TABLE 3
RATES OF CHANGE IN VALUE OF INVESTMENTS IN COMMON STOCKS LISTED ON THE NEW YORK STOCK EXCHANGE, IGNORING DIVIDENDS (Per Cent Per Annum Compounded Annually)
PART F—CASH-TO-CASH, HIGHER TAX RATE

FROM

12/45	12/46	12/47	12/48	12/49	12/50	12/51	12/52	12/53	12/54	12/55	12/56	12/57	12/58	12/59	12/60	12/61	12/62	12/63	12/64
-10.7																			
-7.1	-5.3																		
-7.1	-5.9	-8.1																	
-3.4	-1.2	0.5	8.2																
0.9	4.1	7.0	14.6	20.4															
2.1	4.7	6.8	11.7	13.0	5.3														
2.2	4.5	6.1	9.5	9.4	4.1	1.3													
1.1	2.8	3.9	6.1	5.1	0.8	-2.1	-7.1												
4.7	6.9	8.6	11.4	11.6	8.7	9.1	12.2	34.6											
5.6	7.7	9.2	11.8	12.2	9.5	10.1	12.4	23.7	9.7										
5.6	7.4	8.6	10.8	11.0	8.6	8.6	10.0	16.3	6.1	0.7									
3.6	4.9	5.8	7.3	6.9	4.8	4.3	4.4	7.1	-1.1	-6.3	-13.5								
5.9	7.5	8.6	10.4	10.4	8.7	8.7	9.6	13.2	7.2	6.0	9.0	37.7							
6.1	7.7	8.9	10.6	10.7	9.0	9.2	10.0	13.1	8.0	7.1	9.7	23.7	7.1						
5.4	6.8	7.8	9.3	9.2	7.8	7.9	8.4	10.6	6.2	5.2	6.6	13.4	1.7	-4.9					
6.3	7.8	8.7	10.1	10.0	8.9	9.1	9.7	11.8	8.1	7.5	9.2	15.3	7.3	6.6	16.8				
4.9	6.1	6.8	7.9	7.7	6.6	6.5	6.7	8.2	4.8	4.0	4.8	8.6	1.9	-0.0	1.4	-12.9			
5.4	6.6	7.3	8.3	8.2	7.1	7.0	7.3	8.7	5.6	4.9	5.8	9.4	3.8	2.7	5.0	-1.3	9.6		
5.7	6.8	7.5	8.6	8.5	7.4	7.3	7.7	9.0	6.2	5.6	6.5	9.8	5.2	4.5	6.9	2.9	10.9	8.7	
6.3	7.6	8.3	9.3	9.3	8.2	8.2	8.6	10.0	7.3	6.8	7.8	11.3	7.1	6.9	9.6	7.1	14.5	14.8	17.5

APPENDIX

REVISION OF DATA PUBLISHED PREVIOUSLY

Tables A1, A2, and A3 are revisions of Tables 1, 2, and 3 of the first study.[13] The notes to the figures show the extent of change. Where the changes are substantial, that is, more than 0.1 per cent per annum, they are due to revision in the data used for the computations. The small changes, however, may be due to either changes in the data or changes in the investment policy discussed in the text.

[13] Fisher and Lorie, *op. cit.*, pp. 4, 5, 7.

TABLE A1

REVISION OF
"TABLE 1—RATES OF RETURN ON INVESTMENT IN COMMON STOCKS LISTED ON THE
NEW YORK STOCK EXCHANGE WITH REINVESTMENT OF DIVIDENDS
(Per Cent per Annum Compounded Annually)"*

	INCOME CLASS					
PERIOD	Tax Exempt		$10,000 in 1960		$50,000 in 1960	
	Cash-to-Portfolio†	Cash-to-Cash‡	Cash-to-Portfolio	Cash-to-Cash	Cash-to-Portfolio	Cash-to-Cash
1/26–12/60	8.8b	8.7c	8.2b	7.9c	7.2b	6.6b
1/26– 9/29	20.3a	20.2a	20.3a	20.2a	20.3	19.4
1/26– 6/32	−17.2g	−17.3e	−17.2g	−17.3e	−17.1f	−13.8d
1/26–12/40	1.9e	1.9d	1.9e	1.9e	1.8d	2.0d
1/26–12/50	6.5c	6.5c	6.0c	5.9b	5.3b	4.9b
9/29– 6/32	−48.8d	−49.1c	−48.8d	−49.1c	−48.7c	−40.9c
9/29–12/40	− 3.1a	− 3.2a	− 3.1a	− 3.0a	− 3.2b	− 2.4a
9/29–12/50	4.8a	4.8	4.3	4.1	3.5	3.2
9/29–12/60	7.6a	7.6a	7.0	6.7a	5.9	5.3a
6/32–12/40	20.9d	20.8c	20.9c	20.4d	20.4d	19.2c
6/32–12/50	18.5a	18.4b	17.7a	17.3b	16.4a	15.4a
6/32–12/60	17.3a	17.3	16.5	16.1a	14.9a	14.1
12/50–12/52	12.4a	11.9a	11.0a	10.0	8.9a	7.1
12/50–12/54	17.9	17.6	16.5a	15.3	14.3a	11.6
12/50–12/56	17.0	16.8	15.8	14.8	13.7	11.4
12/50–12/58	16.5	16.4	15.4	14.6	13.4	11.4
12/50–12/60	14.9z	14.7	13.9z	13.1	12.0	10.3
12/55–12/56	6.5z	5.4	5.8z	4.6	4.1z	2.9z
12/55–12/57	− 3.7	− 4.2	− 4.4	− 4.0	− 6.0	− 4.2
12/55–12/58	13.0	12.6	12.2	11.1	10.5	8.2
12/55–12/59	14.0	13.7	13.2a	12.1a	11.6	9.2
12/55–12/60	11.2	11.0z	10.5	9.6	8.9	7.2

* Fisher and Lorie, *op. cit.*, p. 4. Revisions are indicated by the following codes:

Downward Revisions		Upward Revisions	
a	0.1% per annum	z	0.1% per annum
b	0.2% per annum		
c	0.3% per annum		
d	0.4% per annum		
e	0.5% per annum		
f	0.6% per annum		
g	0.7% per annum		

† "Cash-to-Portfolio" means the net rate of return which would have been realized after paying commissions and taxes (if any) on each transaction but continuing to hold the portfolio at the end of each period.

‡ "Cash-to-Cash" means the net return which would have been realized after paying commissions and taxes (if any) on each transaction including the sale of the portfolio at the end of each period.

TABLE A2

REVISION OF
"TABLE 2—RATES OF RETURN ON INVESTMENT IN COMMON STOCKS LISTED ON THE NEW YORK STOCK EXCHANGE WITHOUT REINVESTMENT OF DIVIDENDS

(Per Cent per Annum Compounded Annually)"*

| | INCOME CLASS | | | | | |
| | Tax Exempt | | $10,000 in 1960 | | $50,000 in 1960 | |
PERIOD	Cash-to-Portfolio†	Cash-to-Cash‡	Cash-to-Portfolio	Cash-to-Cash	Cash-to-Portfolio	Cash-to-Cash
1/26–12/60	6.8a	6.8a	6.6a	6.4b	6.1a	5.7a
1/26– 9/29	19.9z	19.8z	19.9z	19.8z	19.8	18.9
1/26– 6/32	−13.8f	−13.9e	−13.8f	−13.9e	−13.8f	−11.2d
1/26–12/40	1.5a	1.4b	1.5a	1.5b	1.4b	1.6b
1/26–12/50	5.1	5.0a	4.8a	4.7	4.5	4.2
9/29– 6/32	−48.7e	−49.0d	−48.7e	−49.0d	−48.5d	−40.7c
9/29–12/40	− 4.9	− 5.0	− 4.9	− 4.7	− 4.8	− 3.8
9/29–12/50	2.4z	2.3z	2.1z	2.0	1.9z	1.7
9/29–12/60	4.9	4.9	4.7z	4.5z	4.3	3.8
6/32–12/40	24.0e	23.9e	24.0e	23.6e	23.4d	22.0e
6/32–12/50	21.1c	21.1c	20.5c	20.2c	19.0c	18.1d
6/32–12/60	20.2c	20.2c	19.4c	19.2c	17.5c	17.0c
12/50–12/52	12.5a	12.0a	11.1a	10.1	9.0a	7.1a
12/50–12/54	17.3	17.1	16.1	14.9	14.1	11.4a
12/50–12/56	16.6	16.5	15.5	14.6	13.6	11.3
12/50–12/58	16.2	16.1	15.2	14.4	13.3	11.3
12/50–12/60	15.0	14.9	13.9a	13.2§	12.1	10.4
12/55–12/56	6.6z	5.5z	5.8z	4.7z	4.1z	2.9z
12/55–12/57	− 3.3	− 3.8	− 4.1	− 3.7	− 5.8	− 4.1
12/55–12/58	12.6	12.2	11.9	10.8	10.3	8.1
12/55–12/59	13.7	13.4	13.0	11.9a	11.4	9.1
12/55–12/60	11.1	10.9	10.4	9.6	8.9	7.2

* Fisher and Lorie, *op. cit.*, p. 5. Revisions are indicated by the following codes:

Downward Revisions	Upward Revisions
a .... 0.1% per annum	z .... 0.1% per annum
b .... 0.2% per annum	
c .... 0.3% per annum	
d .... 0.4% per annum	
e .... 0.5% per annum	
f .... 0.6% per annum	

† "Cash-to-Portfolio" means the net rate of return which would have been realized after paying commissions and taxes (if any) on each transaction but continuing to hold the portfolio at the end of each period.

‡ "Cash-to-Cash" means the net return which would have been realized after paying commissions and taxes (if any) on each transaction including the sale of the portfolio at the end of each period.

§ The calculated figure was 13.2 per cent. The figure "18.2" appeared because of a printing error.

TABLE A3

REVISION OF

"TABLE 3—RATES OF CHANGE IN VALUE OF INVESTMENT IN COMMON STOCKS LISTED
ON THE NEW YORK STOCK EXCHANGE, IGNORING DIVIDENDS
(Per Cent per Annum Compounded Annually)"*

PERIOD	INCOME CLASS					
	Tax Exempt		$10,000 in 1960		$50,000 in 1960	
	Cash-to-Portfolio†	Cash-to-Cash‡	Cash-to-Portfolio	Cash-to-Cash	Cash-to-Portfolio	Cash-to-Cash
1/26–12/60	3.9	3.9z	3.9	3.6	4.0	3.3
1/26– 9/29	16.1w	16.0w	16.1w	16.0w	16.1w	15.2w
1/26– 6/32	−21.0	−21.1z	−21.0	−21.1z	−20.9	−17.6y
1/26–12/40	− 2.7z	− 2.8z	− 2.7z	− 2.7z	− 2.6z	− 2.3z
1/26–12/50	1.5y	1.5y	1.5z	1.3z	1.7y	1.3y
9/29– 6/32	−51.7b	−52.0a	−51.7b	−52.0a	−51.5b	−43.5a
9/29–12/40	− 7.8y	− 7.9z	− 7.8y	− 7.5y	− 7.4y	− 6.3z
9/29–12/50	− 0.4z	− 0.4y	− 0.3y	− 0.4y	0.0y	− 0.2z
9/29–12/60	2.5	2.5z	2.6z	2.3z	2.8z	2.2z
6/32–12/40	16.8a	16.6b	16.8a	16.2b	16.7a	15.1
6/32–12/50	13.1	13.0	13.1z	12.5	13.0·	11.7
6/32–12/60	12.0z	12.0z	12.0z	11.5z	11.9z	10.9z
12/50–12/52	6.0z	5.5z	6.0z	4.9z	6.0z	4.1z
12/50–12/54	11.5z	11.2z	11.5y	10.2z	11.4z	8.7z
12/50–12/56	11.0y	10.8z	11.0y	10.0y	10.9z	8.6y
12/50–12/58	10.9y	10.7z	10.9y	10.0y	10.8z	8.7y
12/50–12/60	9.7z	9.6y	9.7y	8.9y	9.7y	7.8y
12/55–12/56	2.0v	0.9v	1.9v	0.8w	1.9v	0.7v
12/55–12/57	− 8.0x	− 8.6y	− 8.1y	− 7.7y	− 8.1y	− 6.3x
12/55–12/58	8.2y	7.9x	8.2y	7.1y	8.2y	6.0y
12/55–12/59	9.5y	9.2y	9.5y	8.4y	9.5y	7.1y
12/55–12/60	7.0x	6.7y	6.9y	6.1x	6.9y	5.2y

* Fisher and Lorie, *op. cit.*, p. 7. Revisions are indicated by the following codes:

Downward Revisions		Upward Revisions	
a	0.1% per annum	z	0.1% per annum
b	0.2% per annum	y	0.2% per annum
		x	0.3% per annum
		w	0.4% per annum
		v	0.5% per annum

† "Cash-to-Portfolio" means the net rate of change which would have been realized after paying commissions and taxes (if any) on each transaction but continuing to hold the portfolio at the end of each period.

‡ "Cash-to-Cash" means the net rate of change which would have been realized after paying commissions and taxes (if any) on each transaction including the sale of the portfolio at the end of each period.

The logical organization of the file of data on magnetic tape is similar to that described in Fisher and Lorie's earlier article (*op. cit.*). A detailed statement is available from the Center for Research in Security Prices (sponsored by Merrill Lynch, Pierce, Fenner & Smith, Inc.), Graduate School of Business, University of Chicago, Chicago, Illinois 60637.

3

SOME STUDIES OF VARIABILITY OF RETURNS ON INVESTMENTS IN COMMON STOCKS *

Lawrence Fisher † and James H. Lorie ‡

INTRODUCTION

We report here the findings of three studies we have conducted on the variability of returns on investments in common stocks listed on the New York Stock Exchange. One study examines the frequency distributions of returns on individual stocks for fifty-five specific periods ranging from one to forty years in length during the period 1926–65. A second examines the aggregated distributions of returns from investments in individual common stocks for nonoverlapping periods of equal length from one to twenty years. Aggregating frequency distributions of all such one-, five-, ten-, or twenty-year periods permits broader generalization about the behavior of the market, since these aggregated distribu-

tions are not dominated by the behavior of the market in any single period.

The third study deals with returns from investment in portfolios containing different numbers of common stocks on the New York Stock Exchange. Distributions were found for portfolios of six size ranges from one through 128 and for portfolios containing all such common stocks. The tables dealing with aggregated frequency distributions, paralleling the second study, are of greater general interest, we think, and are discussed in the text. The tables from which they were derived and which deal with specific periods, paralleling the first study, are of less direct interest and are presented in Appendix A.

Before discussing our results, we would like to indicate why we undertook these studies and the ways in which they are related to our earlier studies on average rates of return[1] and on outcomes for random investments.[2]

* We are indebted to Harry Roberts for aid in understanding Gini's mean difference. Our exposition has benefitted from reactions to presentations at seminars at the University of Chicago and several other universities. Most of the many computer programs required for this study were prepared by Marvin Lipson. Some additional programming was done by Mark Case and Owen M. Hewett.

† Professor of finance, Graduate School of Business, University of Chicago, and associate director of the Center for Research in Security Prices (sponsored by Merrill Lynch, Pierce, Fenner & Smith, Inc.).

‡ Professor of business administration, Graduate School of Business, University of Chicago, and director of the Center for Research in Security Prices (sponsored by Merrill Lynch, Pierce, Fenner & Smith, Inc.).

[1] Lawrence Fisher and James H. Lorie, "Rates of Return on Investments in Common Stocks," *Journal of Business* 37 (January 1964):1–21; Lawrence Fisher and James H. Lorie, "Rates of Return on Investments in Common Stocks: The Year-by-Year Record, 1926–65," *Journal of Business* 41 (July 1968):291–316.

[2] Lawrence Fisher, "Outcomes for 'Random' Investments in Common Stocks Listed on the New York Stock Exchange," *Journal of Business* 38 (April 1965):149–61.

For several reasons, studies of variability may be interesting. One of the most controversial and important subjects in the field of finance is risk. There is controversy about both methods of estimation and the nature of the relationship between risk and rates of return. The studies reported here do not deal directly with either of those controversial aspects of risk, but they do bear upon the general subject by providing the first comprehensive and well-based estimates of the effect of increasing the size of portfolios on the variability of returns—one of the most widely used estimates of risk. The earlier studies of average rates of return provided bench marks which have been widely used in evaluating the performance of average rates of return from portfolios; the studies reported here can be thought of as providing bench marks for evaluating the effectiveness of diversification in reducing variability of returns.

Another way of looking at the present studies would be to say that the earlier studies on average rates of return indicate only the average experience from investing in common stocks listed on the New York Stock Exchange without any indication of the inherent riskiness. The studies reported here indicate something about riskiness by providing detailed information on frequency distributions of returns.

These studies should prove more useful than the first author's earlier study of outcomes for random investments in common stocks, which also deals with variability of returns, because in these studies we are able to look at the variability of returns on portfolios as well as return on individual stocks. We can now look at portfolios because the current studies hold constant the holding period of the investments whose frequency distributions are reported. Looking at portfolios is obviously desirable, since almost all investors with significant investments hold portfolios of more than one common stock. Moreover, there is much interest in the effect of changing the size of portfolios on variability in return.

The current studies are also superior in that they, unlike the earlier study on outcomes for random investments, take into account the value of investments even after they consist of assets other than the common stock in which the investment was originally made. This change in assets can occur where there are mergers, spin-offs, or delistings.

A section on general methodology follows these introductory remarks. It includes some comments on statistics that we have computed in the course of all three studies. Next are sections on the three studies, and finally appendixes containing the basic data for the last study. The results are presented primarily in tables which, we hope, will provide reference material for specialists in the field. Since we have spent considerable time examining the material in the tables, we will make a few comments. However, most analysis will be left to the reader.

GENERAL METHODS OF ANALYSIS

The distributions which will be described are in all cases the distributions of "wealth ratios." The wealth ratio is the ratio of the value of the investment at the end of the period to the amount invested. Much of the work in this field has been in terms of rates of return, since such rates are necessary in comparing investment results for periods of different lengths. We are free to use wealth ratios because we compare only periods of equal length.

We have used wealth ratios for two reasons. First, introspection and observation have persuaded us that it is extremely difficult to understand the significance of differences among annual rates of return for long periods of time. For example, few persons easily see that a difference between 5 percent per annum, compounded annually, and 10 percent per annum over a forty-year period produces wealth ratios which are strikingly different—approximately 7 and 45, respectively. The wealth ratio produced by the 10 percent annual return is 543 percent greater than the ratio produced by

period in question exceeds the compounding interval, and to an overestimate if the period is less than the compounding interval. This is exemplified in table 1.

Harry Markowitz[4] uses returns, but they are not necessarily annual rates. They are simply one less than the corresponding wealth ratios, and they are typically expressed as percentages. In table 1, the Markowitz returns for stocks A, B, and C would be 0, 300 percent, and

TABLE 1

ILLUSTRATION OF RELATIONSHIP BETWEEN
WEALTH RATIOS AND RATES OF RETURN

Stock	Wealth Ratio After 10 Years	Annual Rate of Return Compounded Annually (Percent)
A	1	0
B	4	14.9
C	7	21.5
Mean	4	12.1

The wealth ratio implied by an investment returning 12.1 percent annually and held for ten years is 3.14, not 4.0. Thus, using the mean rate of return to deduce the mean wealth ratio would lead to a significant underestimate.

the 5 percent return. The corresponding wealth ratios for annual rates of return of 9 percent and 10 percent are 31 and 45, respectively. The wealth ratio for the 10 percent rate of return exceeds that for the 9 percent rate of return by 44 percent.

The second reason for presenting data on wealth ratios rather than on rates of return is that data on rates of return are frequently misinterpreted. The most common mistake is to assume that one can deduce the mean wealth ratio from knowledge of the mean rate of return.[3] Such an attempt leads to an underestimate of the mean wealth ratio if the

600 percent, respectively. We have used wealth ratios rather than Markowitz's returns, since the latter are easily confused with *annual* rates of return.

We recognize, however, that some readers do think about returns from investments as annual rates. In order to

[3] See, for example, Marc Nerlove, "Factors Affecting Differences among Rates of Return on Investments in Individual Common Stocks," *Review of Economics and Statistics* 50 (August 1968): 312–31; and Eugene F. Brigham and James L. Pappas, "Rates of Return on Common Stock," *Journal of Business* 42 (July 1969):302–20.

[4] Harry Markowitz, *Portfolio Selection: Efficient Diversification of Investments* (New York: John Wiley & Sons, 1959).

facilitate translation from wealth ratios to annual rates of return, we present table 2, which simply indicates for periods of various lengths the rates of return corresponding to various wealth ratios.

In computing wealth ratios, commissions were charged when investments were originally made and when each dividend was reinvested, but the value of the investment at the end of each period was calculated on the basis of the market price on that date without taking into account any contingent transaction costs or taxes.[5]

For each frequency distribution of wealth ratios the following statistics are reported:

1. *a*) 5th centile
   b) 10th centile
   c) 20th centile
   d) 30th centile
   e) 40th centile
   f) 50th centile (median)
   g) 60th centile
   h) 70th centile
   i) 80th centile
   j) 90th centile
   k) 95th centile
2. The maximum
3. The minimum
4. The arithmetic mean
5. Measures of absolute dispersion
   a) The standard deviation
   b) The mean deviation
   c) Gini's mean difference
6. Measures of relative dispersion
   a) Coefficient of variation
   b) Relative mean deviation
   c) Gini's coefficient of concentration
7. Momental skewness
8. Kurtosis

[5] The wealth ratios used were, in fact, the wealth ratios used to construct the table of annual rates of return with reinvestment of dividends for the tax-exempt investor in the cash-to-portfolio computations (part A of table 1 of the Fisher and Lorie 1968 article). For the methods of treating investments in stocks which were merged into or spun off other issues or which were delisted, see the 1968 article, p. 295, and the 1964 article, pp. 15–17.

All of the foregoing statistics should be familiar, with the possible exception of Gini's mean difference and Gini's coefficient of concentration. These statistics are discussed, among other places, in Gini's own work[6] and in a text of Kendall and Stuart.[7] Even so, it may be helpful for us to say something here about Gini's statistics.

In principle, to compute Gini's mean difference, one merely finds the absolute value of the difference between the elements of each possible pair of observations and divides by the number of such pairs. For example, consider the following three observations: 2, 4, 7. The following pairs are considered: 2 and 4, 2 and 7, and 4 and 7. The absolute values of the differences between the elements of these pairs are 2, 5, and 3, respectively. Thus Gini's mean difference is 10 divided by 3, or $3\frac{1}{3}$. If there are N observations, the number of possible pairs is equal to $N(N-1)/2$. When N is very large—as in our third study, for example—the volume of computations necessary for exact calculation is unbearable and estimation must be used.

The relationship between Gini's mean difference and Gini's coefficient of concentration is nearly analogous to that between the standard deviation and the coefficient of variation. To compute the coefficient of variation, one divides the standard deviation by the mean. To compute Gini's coefficient of concentration, one divides Gini's mean difference by *twice* the mean.

The discourteous reader might ask at this point why, instead of using statistics

[6] Corrado Gini, *Memorie di metodologia statistica*, 2d ed. rev. Ernesto Pizzetti and T. Salvemini (Rome: Libreria Eredi Virgilio Veschi, 1955).

[7] Maurice G. Kendall and Alan Stuart, *Advanced Theory of Statistics in Three Volumes*, 2d ed. (New York: Hafner Publishing Co., 1963), vol. 1.

TABLE 2

WEALTH RATIOS AND CORRESPONDING ANNUAL RATES OF RETURN
(COMPOUNDED ANNUALLY) FOR SPECIFIED PERIODS

Holding Period

5 Years		10 Years		20 Years		39 11/12 Years	
Wealth Ratio	Rate of Return	Wealth Ratio	Rate of Return	Wealth Ratio	Rate of Return	Wealth Ratio	Rate of Return
.01	-60.2	.01	-36.9	.01	-20.6	.01	-10.9
.02	-54.3	.02	-32.4	.02	-17.8	.02	-9.3
.03	-50.4	.03	-29.6	.03	-16.1	.05	-7.2
.04	-47.5	.04	-27.5	.05	-13.9	.1	-5.6
.05	-45.1	.05	-25.9	.1	-10.9	.2	-4.0
.07	-41.2	.1	-20.6	.2	-7.7	.3	-3.0
.1	-36.9	.2	-14.9	.3	-5.8	.4	-2.3
.2	-27.5	.3	-11.3	.4	-4.5	.6	-1.3
.3	-21.4	.4	-8.8	.5	-3.4	1.0	0.0
.4	-16.7	.5	-6.7	.7	-1.8	1.5	1.0
.5	-12.9	.6	-5.0	.9	-0.5	2.2	2.0
.6	-9.7	.7	-3.5	1.1	0.5	3.2	3.0
.7	-6.9	.8	-2.2	1.4	1.7	4.6	3.9
.8	-4.4	.9	-1.0	1.8	3.0	6.4	4.8
.9	-2.1	1.1	1.0	2.3	4.3	8.6	5.5
1.0	0.	1.3	2.7	2.8	5.3	12.	6.4
1.1	1.9	1.5	4.1	3.4	6.3	15.	7.0
1.3	5.4	1.8	6.1	4.0	7.2	18.	7.5
1.4	7.0	2.0	7.2	4.7	8.0	22.	8.1
1.6	9.9	2.2	8.2	5.4	8.8	25.	8.4
1.7	11.2	2.4	9.1	5.9	9.3	28.	8.7
1.8	12.5	2.6	10.0	6.4	9.7	31.	9.0
1.9	13.7	2.7	10.4	6.8	10.1	34.	9.2
2.0	14.9	2.8	10.8	7.0	10.2	35.	9.3
2.1	16.0	2.9	11.2	7.1	10.3	36.	9.4
2.2	17.1	3.0	11.6	7.2	10.4	37.	9.5
2.3	18.1	3.1	12.0	7.3	10.5	38.	9.5
2.4	19.1	3.2	12.3	7.4	10.5	39.	9.6
2.5	20.1	3.3	12.7	7.6	10.7	40.	9.7
2.6	21.1	3.4	13.0	7.9	10.9	42.	9.8
2.7	22.0	3.5	13.3	8.3	11.2	44.	9.9
2.8	22.9	3.7	14.0	8.8	11.5	48.	10.2
2.9	23.7	4.0	14.9	9.4	11.9	53.	10.5
3.0	24.6	4.3	15.7	11.	12.7	60.	10.8
3.2	26.2	4.8	17.0	12.	13.2	70.	11.2
3.6	29.2	5.3	18.1	13.	13.7	80.	11.6
4.1	32.6	6.0	19.6	14.	14.1	90.	11.9
4.6	35.7	6.9	21.3	15.	14.5	100.	12.2
5.3	39.6	7.9	23.0	17.	15.2	120.	12.7
6.2	44.0	9.2	24.8	20.	16.2	150.	13.4
7.2	48.4	11.	27.1	22.	16.7	200.	14.2
8.6	53.8	13.	29.2	26.	17.7	250.	14.8
11.	61.5	16.	32.0	30.	18.5	300.	15.4
13.	67.0	19.	34.2	35.	19.5	350.	15.8
16.	74.1	23.	36.8	42.	20.5	400.	16.2
19.	80.2	29.	40.0	50.	21.6	500.	16.8
24.	88.8	36.	43.1	60.	22.7	700.	17.8
30.	97.4	46.	46.6	73.	23.9	1,000.	18.9
38.	107.0	58.	50.1	90.	25.2	1,300.	19.7
49.	117.8	75.	54.0	111.	26.6	1,715.	20.5

that are familiar to readers of English, we must refer to Gini's statistics. In the first place, Gini's mean difference gives us some information that is interesting in itself. It tells us the expected value of the difference in returns between two portfolios of any given size, including portfolios of one stock. In the second place, Gini's coefficient of concentration is useful in summarizing differences in returns

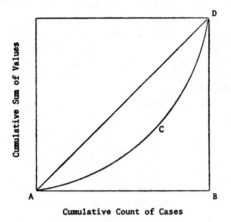

Cumulative Count of Cases

Fig. 1.—A Lorenz curve

to portfolios. The coefficient was originally developed to summarize differences in wealth or income and thus applies to our studies of differences among wealth ratios.

Many readers will be familiar with the Lorenz curve as exemplified in figure 1. Gini's coefficient of concentration measures the ratio of the area between the Lorenz curve *ACD* and the line *AD* to the total area of the triangle *ABD*. When applied to returns on portfolios, the interpretation is straightforward. If portfolios are ranked by the size of returns from the smallest to the largest, the locus of a Lorenz curve is readily drawn. The number of portfolios, *M*, is shown on the

horizontal axis; and the sum of the wealth ratios of these *M* (smallest) portfolios is shown on the vertical axis. If all portfolios had equal returns, the Lorenz curve would be identical with line *AD*. If all portfolios except one had zero wealth ratios and that one had a positive wealth ratio, the Lorenz curve would be virtually identical with curve *ABD*. In the former case, Gini's coefficient of concentration would be zero; in the latter case, one.

In the third place, we use Gini's statistics because many of the distributions we report here depart greatly from normality. For such distributions, the standard deviation of even a large sample may not give a very meaningful indication of the dispersion of the population. Gini's mean difference and coefficient of concentration are nonparametric measures and are invulnerable to this consequence of departure from normality. The mean deviation from the mean is also invulnerable to this adverse consequence of departure from normality. Gini's mean difference differs from the mean deviation by giving greater weight to extreme observations, thus taking care of a frequently made criticism of the mean deviation.

We use measures both of absolute and of relative dispersion. The absolute measures are interesting in themselves, but reliance on them exclusively would conceal some relationships which, as we will see, have been remarkably invariant for long periods of time.

THE STUDIES

STUDY 1: DISTRIBUTIONS OF WEALTH RATIOS FOR INVESTMENTS IN SINGLE STOCKS

The frequency distributions of wealth ratios for investments in single stocks for fifty-five time periods are summarized in table 3. Many of their general features should not surprise anyone. In general, the mean wealth ratios shown in column 16 increase with the length of the holding period, although there is substantial overlap. (For example, the greatest mean for a one-year period is greater than five of the eight means for five-year periods, and the worst mean for a five-year period exceeds only four of the 40 one-year means.)

The distributions for longer holding periods tend to have greater dispersion than the distributions for shorter periods, both absolutely and relatively. This tendency may be seen by looking at corresponding entries in columns (17–22) or by comparing ranges defined by columns (6) and (8), (5) and (9), (4) and (10), (3) and (11), (2) and (12), or (13) and (14).

For all periods studied, skewness of the distribution of wealth ratios was positive. This implies, as almost every investor knows, that the probability of deviating from the mean by very large amounts on the high side is greater than the probability of extremely large deviations on the low side. This skewness almost inevitably results from the simple arithmetic fact that it is impossible to lose more than 100 percent of one's investment, assuming that one does not buy on margin, while it is possible to make much more than 100 percent on one's money when one is lucky or wise. For all periods of five years or more, the maximum wealth ratio was at least 4.5 times as large as the mean wealth ratio. In fact, the maximum ratio was more than twice the mean in nine of the 40 one-year periods.

As would be expected with positive skewness, the mean is almost invariably greater than the median. There are a few exceptions for one-year periods when the

positive skewness is slight. For almost all one-year periods and for all periods longer than one year the mean exceeds the median. The longer the period, the greater the difference.

For all periods except 1929, the kurtosis of the frequency distributions is greater than 3.0. That is, a greater proportion of the observations fall near the mean than is true for normal distributions.[8] Nearness to the mean is measured in terms of standard deviations. In these particular distributions, the kurtosis is relatively small when skewness is slight. Thus the "peakedness" is caused largely by the presence of a few very large wealth ratios.

In table 3, it is interesting to note the lower levels of relative dispersion after 1943. For example, Gini's coefficient of concentration was always at least 0.16 from 1926 through 1943; thereafter, the coefficient was always less than 0.16.

While discussing dispersion, it is interesting to compare the six measures of dispersion: the standard deviation, the mean deviation, the mean difference, the coefficient of variation, the relative mean deviation, and Gini's coefficient of concentration. The important fact is that the standard deviation and measure of relative dispersion derived from it, the coefficient of variation, are more variable from period to period than are the other measures. We believe that the greater instability in the standard deviation and the coefficient of variation lends support to Mandelbrot's hypothesis that the dis-

[8] As Kaplansky has stated (I. Kaplansky, "A Common Error concerning Kurtosis," *Journal of the American Statistical Association* 40 [June 1945]: 259), it is a vulgar error blandly or blindly to assume that high kurtosis necessarily implies great concentration around the rear. Since we have examined them in great detail, we know that the common interpretation is correct for these distributions.

tributions of returns on individual stocks over time have infinite variance.[9]

It is also mildly interesting to note that for our data the relationship between Gini's mean difference and the mean deviation was remarkably stable—always being near the ratio that would be

[9] Benoit Mandelbrot, "Variation of Certain Speculative Prices," *Journal of Business* 36 (October 1963):394–419.

expected if the distributions were normal. For normal distributions, the ratio of Gini's mean difference to the mean deviation is $\sqrt{2}$.[10] Thus, it appears that

[10] Derived from Kendall and Stuart, pp. 139, 241. For normal distributions the mean deviation is $\sqrt{(2/\pi)}$ $(=0.80)$ times the standard deviation, and Gini's mean difference is $2/\sqrt{\pi}$ $(=1.13)$ times standard deviation. Note also that in table 3 the standard deviation is usually greater than Gini's mean difference.

TABLE 3

FREQUENCY DISTRIBUTIONS OF WEALTH RATIOS FROM INVESTMENTS
IN INDIVIDUAL STOCKS LISTED ON THE NYSE, 1926-65

					Centiles of the Frequency Distributions						
Period of Investment	5th	10th	20th	30th	40th	(Median) 50th	60th	70th	80th	90th	95th
(1)	(2)	(3)	(4)	(5)	(6)	(7)	(8)	(9)	(10)	(11)	(12)
ONE-YEAR PERIODS											
1/30/26-12/31/26	.429	.560	.722	.845	.917	.991	1.060	1.115	1.183	1.316	1.485
12/31/26-12/31/27	.640	.752	.888	1.053	1.132	1.225	1.330	1.457	1.601	1.834	2.274
12/31/27-12/31/28	.725	.834	.976	1.064	1.153	1.251	1.376	1.512	1.711	2.136	2.795
12/31/28-12/31/29	.197	.279	.405	.518	.604	.700	.774	.873	.977	1.123	1.218
12/31/29-12/31/30	.205	.265	.367	.442	.521	.593	.674	.757	.868	.986	1.106
12/31/30-12/31/31	.158	.215	.292	.347	.401	.467	.536	.615	.738	.909	1.044
12/31/31-12/31/32	.353	.449	.561	.654	.729	.828	.931	1.035	1.173	1.377	1.662
12/31/32-12/30/33	.657	.856	1.189	1.402	1.628	1.849	2.075	2.394	2.742	3.331	4.338
12/30/33-12/31/34	.566	.645	.759	.849	.938	1.029	1.134	1.262	1.428	1.728	2.017
12/31/34-12/31/35	.761	.864	1.029	1.134	1.232	1.353	1.492	1.656	1.927	2.342	2.747
12/31/35-12/31/36	.854	.943	1.052	1.154	1.235	1.334	1.446	1.583	1.773	2.130	2.461
12/31/36-12/31/37	.276	.315	.373	.420	.472	.517	.562	.624	.687	.798	.888
12/31/37-12/31/38	.693	.838	.986	1.090	1.186	1.260	1.350	1.458	1.594	1.798	2.020
12/31/38-12/30/39	.554	.626	.704	.790	.869	.947	1.021	1.089	1.183	1.319	1.478
12/30/39-12/31/40	.477	.584	.713	.795	.852	.904	.952	1.005	1.069	1.194	1.331
12/31/40-12/31/41	.445	.545	.666	.751	.820	.879	.947	1.016	1.096	1.234	1.412
12/31/41-12/31/42	.844	.907	.986	1.054	1.120	1.190	1.273	1.380	1.527	1.766	2.106
12/31/42-12/31/43	1.032	1.088	1.195	1.249	1.331	1.403	1.499	1.624	1.812	2.130	2.560
12/31/43-12/30/44	1.029	1.088	1.151	1.202	1.245	1.304	1.372	1.447	1.556	1.750	2.025
12/30/44-12/31/45	1.179	1.238	1.316	1.372	1.427	1.500	1.578	1.672	1.805	2.074	2.329
12/31/45-12/31/46	.529	.592	.698	.785	.847	.898	.944	1.002	1.083	1.187	1.308
12/31/46-12/31/47	.617	.701	.795	.857	.910	.962	1.025	1.091	1.175	1.312	1.456
12/31/47-12/31/48	.600	.703	.798	.858	.916	.967	1.007	1.050	1.107	1.212	1.321
12/31/48-12/31/49	.840	.906	.997	1.061	1.122	1.178	1.233	1.302	1.374	1.481	1.617
12/31/49-12/30/50	.904	.965	1.047	1.123	1.207	1.298	1.384	1.487	1.614	1.817	2.015
12/30/50-12/31/51	.832	.905	.981	1.039	1.081	1.122	1.172	1.228	1.294	1.417	1.554
12/31/51-12/31/52	.771	.841	.920	.980	1.037	1.088	1.137	1.184	1.245	1.333	1.424
12/31/52-12/31/53	.602	.704	.805	.864	.918	.969	1.021	1.064	1.112	1.221	1.320
12/31/53-12/31/54	1.095	1.164	1.251	1.327	1.407	1.480	1.565	1.660	1.786	1.995	2.256
12/31/54-12/30/55	.829	.924	1.003	1.049	1.093	1.144	1.193	1.261	1.354	1.516	1.687
12/30/55-12/31/56	.711	.789	.880	.941	.989	1.026	1.082	1.141	1.236	1.378	1.518
12/30/56-12/31/57	.496	.567	.658	.721	.791	.856	.923	.996	1.060	1.149	1.228
12/31/57-12/31/58	1.112	1.199	1.294	1.363	1.434	1.491	1.552	1.647	1.780	2.001	2.326
12/31/58-12/31/59	.759	.845	.934	.988	1.028	1.080	1.149	1.214	1.323	1.527	1.715
12/31/59-12/30/60	.591	.652	.749	.825	.887	.948	1.022	1.100	1.196	1.325	1.447
12/30/60-12/29/61	.852	.935	1.037	1.114	1.176	1.235	1.301	1.373	1.460	1.621	1.818
12/29/61-12/31/62	.544	.616	.696	.761	.813	.856	.909	.965	1.019	1.114	1.207
12/31/62-12/31/63	.808	.894	.985	1.041	1.089	1.137	1.186	1.247	1.344	1.488	1.657
12/31/63-12/31/64	.765	.875	.978	1.049	1.099	1.142	1.194	1.248	1.323	1.466	1.622
12/31/64-12/31/65	.856	.923	.995	1.056	1.116	1.196	1.275	1.387	1.510	1.732	1.963
FIVE-YEAR PERIODS											
1/30/26-12/31/30	.041	.095	.192	.340	.518	.682	.876	1.116	1.443	1.884	2.476
12/31/30-12/31/35	.098	.227	.417	.660	.897	1.147	1.412	1.766	2.293	3.296	4.601
12/31/35-12/31/40	.119	.218	.364	.539	.673	.832	.959	1.134	1.336	1.736	2.061
12/31/40-12/31/45	1.459	1.721	2.084	2.408	2.708	3.155	3.688	4.335	5.556	7.601	10.036
12/31/45-12/30/50	.477	.627	.865	1.007	1.148	1.302	1.481	1.702	1.960	2.409	2.838
12/30/50-12/30/55	.853	1.142	1.440	1.691	1.907	2.107	2.337	2.621	3.002	3.775	4.568
12/30/55-12/30/60	.532	.707	.939	1.130	1.292	1.477	1.656	1.883	2.181	2.708	3.396
12/30/60-12/31/65	.761	.977	1.256	1.440	1.605	1.778	1.979	2.241	2.595	3.402	4.445
TEN-YEAR PERIODS											
1/30/26-12/31/35	.016	.048	.152	.256	.461	.688	1.007	1.368	1.850	2.730	4.297
12/31/35-12/31/45	.614	1.056	1.592	1.912	2.210	2.557	2.999	3.493	4.216	5.500	7.664
12/31/45-12/30/55	.621	.982	1.505	1.895	2.302	2.750	3.270	4.059	5.100	7.169	9.001
12/30/55-12/31/65	.836	1.157	1.654	2.035	2.427	2.814	3.208	3.681	4.289	5.473	7.075
20-YEAR PERIODS											
1/30/26-12/31/45	.000	.052	.324	.772	1.273	1.864	2.772	3.914	5.133	7.395	11.389
12/31/45-12/31/65	.912	1.886	3.357	4.549	6.269	8.242	10.111	12.529	16.068	21.992	30.115
40-YEAR PERIOD											
1/30/26-12/31/65	.000	.258	1.283	3.724	8.257	14.323	21.581	33.613	50.787	82.532	127.554

for the particular distribution we describe here, either measure provides a good estimate of the other. The mean deviation is usually easier to calculate.

STUDY 2: DISTRIBUTIONS OF WEALTH RATIOS
AGGREGATED FOR NONOVER-
LAPPING PERIODS

In table 4 we present data on aggregated frequency distributions of wealth ratios from investments in individual stocks on the New York Stock Exchange. When one considers individual periods separately, as in table 3, it is hard to make generalizations about the variability of experience in investing in stocks on the New York Stock Exchange because of the substantial changes from period to period.

We cannot, for example, tell the probability of gaining or losing a given

Period of Investment	Minimum	Maximum	Arithmetic Mean	Standard Deviation	Mean Deviation	Gini's Mean Difference	Coefficient of Variation	Relative Mean Deviation	Coefficient of Concentration	Skewness	Kurtosis	Number of Companies
(13)	(14)	(15)	(16)	(17)	(18)	(19)	(20)	(21)	(22)	(23)	(24)	(25)
ONE-YEAR PERIODS												
1/30/26-12/31/26	.073	2.970	.985	.343	.242	.355	.348	.245	.180	1.304	8.891	510
12/31/26-12/31/27	.000	7.889	1.300	.577	.374	.546	.444	.288	.210	3.660	36.275	543
12/31/27-12/31/28	.398	13.226	1.453	.904	.498	.712	.622	.343	.245	5.844	60.390	589
12/31/28-12/31/29	.000	1.851	.700	.318	.259	.361	.454	.370	.258	.261	2.718	627
12/31/29-12/31/30	.046	2.105	.620	.286	.229	.318	.461	.369	.257	.685	4.047	717
12/31/30-12/31/31	.000	2.204	.522	.291	.221	.311	.558	.425	.298	1.323	6.365	737
12/31/31-12/31/32	.000	3.308	.891	.435	.319	.455	.488	.358	.255	1.481	7.462	732
12/31/32-12/30/33	.000	20.841	2.083	1.366	.873	1.253	.656	.419	.301	4.686	54.283	709
12/30/33-12/31/34	.090	9.481	1.139	.574	.364	.517	.504	.319	.227	5.358	67.343	707
12/31/34-12/31/35	.000	6.077	1.507	.675	.485	.687	.448	.322	.228	1.830	9.327	706
12/31/35-12/31/36	.178	17.234	1.483	.814	.424	.605	.549	.286	.204	10.719	197.482	719
12/31/36-12/31/37	.109	1.372	.541	.195	.153	.215	.360	.283	.199	.815	4.073	744
12/31/37-12/31/38	.000	7.187	1.307	.497	.320	.469	.380	.245	.179	3.998	44.628	780
12/31/38-12/30/39	.000	2.830	.967	.313	.234	.334	.324	.242	.173	1.140	6.735	775
12/30/39-12/31/40	.000	2.748	.901	.276	.195	.288	.306	.216	.160	.823	8.584	778
12/31/40-12/31/41	.000	2.941	.898	.312	.227	.330	.348	.253	.184	1.101	7.515	788
12/31/41-12/31/42	.560	5.907	1.311	.501	.320	.452	.382	.244	.172	3.358	21.015	797
12/31/42-12/31/43	.293	7.469	1.564	.644	.389	.550	.412	.249	.176	4.134	30.193	800
12/31/43-12/31/44	.417	4.389	1.383	.353	.237	.339	.256	.171	.123	2.451	14.494	810
12/30/44-12/31/45	.649	4.700	1.598	.422	.283	.400	.264	.177	.125	2.807	16.262	826
12/31/45-12/31/46	.254	2.230	.901	.242	.184	.266	.268	.204	.147	.609	4.739	853
12/31/46-12/31/47	.348	2.577	.994	.260	.195	.280	.262	.196	.141	1.031	5.812	904
12/31/47-12/31/48	.337	4.544	.969	.259	.169	.250	.268	.175	.129	3.571	44.575	939
12/31/48-12/31/49	.095	2.885	1.194	.254	.189	.271	.213	.158	.114	.967	7.704	963
12/31/49-12/30/50	.645	3.917	1.358	.378	.283	.397	.279	.208	.146	1.622	8.628	990
12/30/50-12/31/51	.135	4.047	1.149	.242	.168	.245	.211	.146	.107	2.249	24.699	1,010
12/31/51-12/31/52	.113	1.866	1.089	.201	.157	.223	.185	.144	.103	.207	3.915	1,029
12/31/52-12/31/53	.000	2.135	.968	.215	.162	.234	.222	.168	.121	.389	4.939	1,044
12/31/53-12/31/54	.608	5.441	1.548	.392	.279	.397	.253	.180	.128	2.205	15.744	1,045
12/31/54-12/30/55	.163	2.886	1.190	.270	.194	.280	.227	.163	.118	1.391	7.370	1,052
12/30/55-12/31/56	.142	4.282	1.065	.268	.188	.273	.251	.176	.128	2.342	24.249	1,055
12/31/56-12/31/57	.268	2.266	.864	.242	.191	.268	.280	.221	.155	.638	5.395	1,056
12/31/57-12/31/58	.803	5.077	1.579	.440	.285	.412	.279	.181	.131	2.873	16.763	1,077
12/31/58-12/31/59	.428	3.372	1.144	.310	.219	.314	.271	.191	.137	1.824	9.521	1,067
12/31/59-12/30/60	.253	2.380	.981	.276	.215	.303	.282	.219	.154	.886	5.001	1,088
12/30/60-12/29/61	.000	3.810	1.276	.330	.229	.335	.259	.180	.131	1.885	12.084	1,119
12/29/61-12/31/62	.146	1.741	.865	.206	.159	.228	.239	.184	.132	.364	4.102	1,142
12/31/62-12/31/63	.000	3.214	1.176	.287	.198	.291	.244	.168	.124	1.680	10.576	1,162
12/31/63-12/31/64	.326	3.130	1.163	.265	.188	.278	.228	.162	.120	1.043	7.656	1,191
12/31/64-12/31/65	.289	5.426	1.282	.410	.283	.401	.320	.221	.156	2.554	16.991	1,227
FIVE-YEAR PERIODS												
1/30/26-12/31/30	.000	4.487	.877	.778	.600	.822	.887	.684	.468	1.412	5.405	510
12/31/30-12/31/35	.000	11.841	1.568	1.585	1.079	1.506	1.011	.688	.480	2.463	11.345	737
12/31/35-12/31/40	.000	10.457	.949	.822	.519	.741	.867	.547	.391	4.460	41.754	719
12/31/40-12/31/45	.000	48.855	4.264	3.990	2.289	3.150	.936	.537	.369	5.010	41.665	788
12/31/45-12/30/50	.063	6.514	1.455	.771	.576	.811	.530	.396	.279	1.525	7.489	853
12/30/50-12/30/55	.113	10.794	2.335	1.217	.861	1.240	.521	.369	.266	1.836	9.107	1,010
12/30/55-12/30/60	.102	35.876	1.701	1.508	.737	1.067	.886	.433	.314	12.294	257.373	1,055
12/30/60-12/31/65	.159	18.598	2.086	1.382	.851	1.221	.663	.408	.293	4.087	34.270	1,119
TEN-YEAR PERIODS												
1/30/26-12/31/35	.000	24.679	1.238	1.852	1.086	1.480	1.496	.877	.598	5.481	56.199	510
12/31/35-12/31/45	.000	74.724	3.226	3.675	1.708	2.459	1.139	.529	.381	11.440	205.680	719
12/31/45-12/30/55	.047	21.753	3.526	2.766	2.012	2.779	.785	.571	.394	1.958	8.668	853
12/30/55-12/31/65	.084	22.340	3.241	2.350	1.506	2.166	.725	.465	.334	3.278	20.969	1,055
20-YEAR PERIODS												
1/30/26-12/31/45	.000	40.763	3.361	4.759	2.943	4.018	1.416	.876	.598	3.718	22.395	510
12/31/45-12/31/65	.116	110.916	10.766	10.593	7.083	9.866	.984	.658	.458	3.111	19.804	853
40-YEAR PERIOD												
1/30/26-12/31/65	.000	1715.239	35.124	89.807	36.247	48.377	2.557	1.032	.689	13.439	242.255	510

amount by selecting a stock at random during a year selected at random. We know only the distribution of experience for the individual periods. To answer a variety of interesting questions (at least for the forty years 1926–65), we must combine the frequency distributions for each period, giving equal weight to each period's distribution.

Suppose one were interested in knowing the relative frequency with which one would have lost more than 20 percent of his money if he had bought a stock at random and held it for a year during the

forty-year period 1926–65. By reference to table 4, one can see that there was about a 20 percent chance of losing about 20 percent or more of one's money by investing in a stock for one year. Similarly, there was about a 37 percent chance of making 20 percent or more by investing in a stock for one year.

When one turns to the five-year periods, one can answer the same kinds of questions. For example, one lost about 20 percent or more of his money approximately 23 percent of the time. Conversely, one made at least 20 percent

TABLE 4

AGGREGATED FREQUENCY DISTRIBUTIONS OF WEALTH RATIOS
FROM INVESTMENTS IN INDIVIDUAL STOCKS
LISTED ON THE NYSE, 1926–65

Statistic	Periods					
	40 One-Year	20 One-Year (1926-45)	20 One-Year (1946-65)	8 Five-Year	4 Ten-Year	2 Twenty-Year
5th centil	.466	.356	.663	.201	.130	.052
10th centile	.613	.480	.763	.391	.340	.288
20th centile	.796	.675	.879	.726	.894	1.006
30th centile	.911	.828	.961	.990	1.416	1.871
40th centile	1.003	.958	1.026	1.240	1.833	3.028
50th centile (median)	1.085	1.075	1.091	1.491	2.245	4.222
60th centile	1.173	1.192	1.161	1.762	2.709	5.626
70th centile	1.277	1.326	1.245	2.096	3.282	7.940
80th centile	1.423	1.500	1.359	2.564	4.099	11.194
90th centile	1.675	1.830	1.551	3.581	5.479	17.263
95th centile	1.975	2.230	1.743	4.875	7.451	22.878
Minimum	0.000	0.000	0.000	0.000	0.000	0.000
Maximum	20.841	20.841	5.441	48.855	74.724	110.916
Mean	1.148	1.158	1.138	1.904	2.808	7.064
Standard deviation	.554	.699	.355	2.064	2.892	9.008
Mean deviation	.351	.447	.255	1.145	1.761	5.956
Gini's mean difference	.518	.653	.367	1.640	2.505	8.052
Coefficient of variation	.483	.604	.312	1.084	1.030	1.275
Relative mean deviation	.306	.386	.224	.601	.627	.843
Gini's coefficient of concentration	.226	.282	.161	.431	.446	.570
Skewness	5.339	5.062	1.791	7.197	7.315	3.485
Kurtosis	111.090	86.788	12.734	107.852	144.189	24.393
Number of cases	35,407	14,394	21,013	6,791	3,137	1,363

about half of the time. Naturally, the absolute variation in the wealth ratios increases as one moves from a one-year to a five-year holding period. Most of the increase is above the mean rather than below, as one would expect during periods when investors in common stocks generally received positive returns. It is important to note, however, that dispersion in the annual rates of return declines as the length of period increases. One can see this by interpreting the data in table 4 in connection with the conversion table presented earlier (table 2).

For ten-year periods, one lost 20 percent or more of his money less than 20 percent of the time and made a profit of at least 20 percent about three-quarters of the time (table 4). It is possible to make other similar observations from table 4.

STUDY 3: THE EFFECT OF INCREASING THE
NUMBER OF STOCKS IN A PORTFOLIO ON
THE DISTRIBUTION OF RETURNS

Some preliminary comments.—Now we shall discuss the most interesting study in this article. The study concerns the wealth ratios resulting from investment in portfolios of specified numbers of stocks, ranging from one through 128 and in all stocks listed on the New York Stock Exchange. The ratios refer to all of the 40 one-year periods, the eight possible nonoverlapping five-year periods, the four possible ten-year periods, and the two 20-year periods. We also present data for the first twenty years and the last twenty years of the forty-year period so as to permit a comparison of the twenty years ending with the last year of World War II and the first twenty years of the postwar period.

Much of the previous work on the effect of portfolio size on the dispersion of wealth ratios is discussed and summarized in Brealey.[11] Other empirical work has been done by Evans and Archer.[12] This work has generally been concerned only with the effect of diversification on the standard deviation of returns or on the standard deviation of annual rates of return over time. These studies are subject to a serious bias in that they are based on investment only in stocks which were listed throughout the period of study. The elimination of stocks which merged into other stocks or were delisted is the source of the bias.

Additional empirical work is not required to find the effect of diversification on the variance or standard deviation of returns when the mean and variance for each period are known. This is true for the following reasons: (1) the variance for any period for portfolios (randomly selected) of more than one stock can be calculated from knowledge of the variance of returns from investment in portfolios of one stock, and (2) the variance for several periods considered together (that is, aggregated) can be calculated from knowledge of the means and variances for the individual periods. The variance among wealth ratios of stocks or portfolios is equal to the sum of their average variances for the periods under consideration and the variance of the means. Diversification by random selection reduces the average variance within each period but does not affect the variance of the means.

If we had been content to rely on the variance and its derivative statistics, we could have avoided much expense in

---

[11] Richard A. Brealey, *An Introduction to Risk and Return from Common Stocks* (Cambridge, Mass.: M.I.T. Press, 1969).

[12] John L. Evans and Stephen H. Archer, "Diversification and the Reduction of Dispersion: An Empirical Analysis," *Journal of Finance* 23 (December 1968): 761–67.

using the computer merely by algebraically calculating the statistics. We incurred the computer expense because the variance and its derivatives have been under suspicion since Mandelbrot's work seven years ago.[13]

Table 5 shows the frequency distribution of returns for portfolios of different sizes. The frequency distributions for portfolios containing one stock were derived from complete enumeration of all possible such portfolios for the nonoverlapping periods selected. These distributions are also shown in table 4. We also

[13] Mandelbrot (n. 9 above).

used complete enumeration to find the frequency distributions for portfolios containing two different stocks. We assumed equal initial investment in each stock and also assumed that dividends were reinvested in the stock which paid them.

For portfolios containing 8, 16, 32, and 128 stocks, we used simple random selection of individual stocks without replacement. It is possible, however, that this process produced two or more identical portfolios. We were unable to construct frequency distributions of portfolios of these sizes on the basis of complete

TABLE 5

AGGREGATED FREQUENCY DISTRIBUTIONS OF WEALTH RATIOS FROM INVESTMENTS
IN RANDOMLY SELECTED PORTFOLIOS CONTAINING SPECIFIED NUMBERS
OF STOCKS LISTED ON THE NYSE, 1926-65

Number and Length of Periods	Size of Portfolio/ Sampling Method	Centiles of the Aggregated Frequency Distributions										
		5th	10th	20th	30th	40th	(Median) 50th	60th	70th	80th	90th	95th
(1)	(2)	(3)	(4)	(5)	(6)	(7)	(8)	(9)	(10)	(11)	(12)	(13)
PERIODS						40 YEARS 1926-1965						
40 ONE-YEAR	1E	.466	.613	.796	.911	1.003	1.085	1.173	1.277	1.423	1.675	1.975
	2E	.539	.681	.838	.939	1.021	1.099	1.182	1.280	1.409	1.622	1.855
	8S	.582	.745	.883	.964	1.044	1.121	1.196	1.286	1.406	1.569	1.719
	8R	.584	.747	.883	.964	1.045	1.122	1.198	1.288	1.407	1.570	1.718
	16S	.583	.763	.893	.965	1.046	1.129	1.202	1.290	1.408	1.561	1.680
	16R	.587	.763	.894	.965	1.046	1.130	1.205	1.293	1.409	1.566	1.684
	32S	.581	.775	.899	.964	1.043	1.136	1.205	1.295	1.408	1.555	1.648
	32R	.588	.768	.902	.968	1.041	1.140	1.214	1.299	1.406	1.565	1.657
	128S	.576	.781	.900	.966	1.035	1.147	1.200	1.301	1.403	1.555	1.606
	All	.580	.782	.900	.968	1.030	1.147	1.192	1.303	1.418	1.556	1.588
8 FIVE-YEAR	1E	.201	.391	.726	.990	1.240	1.491	1.762	2.096	2.564	3.581	4.875
	2E	.418	.605	.879	1.109	1.328	1.553	1.803	2.110	2.555	3.444	4.533
	8S	.678	.804	1.021	1.239	1.435	1.627	1.842	2.101	2.473	3.355	4.278
	8R	.680	.805	1.023	1.242	1.437	1.631	1.848	2.107	2.480	3.423	4.366
	16S	.748	.847	1.036	1.287	1.470	1.641	1.847	2.093	2.405	3.508	4.308
	16R	.746	.845	1.036	1.292	1.473	1.650	1.866	2.113	2.415	3.695	4.490
	32S	.794	.868	1.023	1.336	1.491	1.639	1.845	2.097	2.360	3.674	4.327
	32R	.769	.849	1.018	1.347	1.503	1.665	1.916	2.171	2.404	4.051	4.672
	128S	.851	.891	.976	1.416	1.517	1.633	1.818	2.109	2.316	3.987	4.335
	All						1.635					
4 TEN-YEAR	1E	.130	.340	.894	1.416	1.833	2.245	2.709	3.282	4.099	5.479	7.451
	2E	.360	.683	1.250	1.727	2.129	2.496	2.885	3.340	3.959	5.086	6.235
	8S	.736	.979	1.607	2.233	2.571	2.838	3.097	3.383	3.746	4.324	4.881
	8R	.754	.992	1.618	2.255	2.596	2.861	3.118	3.404	3.763	4.335	4.879
	16S	.870	1.065	1.545	2.452	2.749	2.968	3.173	3.387	3.661	4.062	4.436
	16R	.888	1.080	1.551	2.504	2.804	3.016	3.221	3.433	3.690	4.090	4.447
	32S	.972	1.123	1.471	2.636	2.889	3.061	3.226	3.389	3.603	3.904	4.172
	32R	.898	1.026	1.334	2.797	3.036	3.207	3.357	3.524	3.696	3.992	4.314
	128S	1.109	1.185	1.351	2.895	3.070	3.185	3.284	3.384	3.525	3.671	3.829
	All						3.233					
2 TWENTY-YR	1E	.052	.288	1.006	1.871	3.028	4.222	5.626	7.940	11.194	17.263	22.878
	2E	.517	.959	1.893	2.763	3.722	4.981	6.601	8.647	11.282	15.653	20.082
	8S	1.608	2.010	2.661	3.390	4.465	6.201	7.895	9.424	11.129	13.516	15.839
	8R	1.660	2.060	2.717	3.464	4.531	6.242	7.888	9.408	11.100	13.468	15.770
	16S	2.012	2.360	2.911	3.502	4.335	6.359	8.501	9.845	11.135	12.984	14.497
	16R	2.100	2.437	2.992	3.587	4.418	6.423	8.523	9.856	11.105	12.924	14.378
	32S	2.350	2.665	3.070	3.514	4.078	6.467	9.058	10.174	11.110	12.523	13.417
	32R	2.293	2.569	2.980	3.393	3.848	6.376	9.147	10.206	11.092	12.449	13.352
	128S	2.791	2.962	3.272	3.506	3.739	6.377	9.924	10.447	10.971	11.494	12.574
	All						7.064					

53

enumeration because of the enormous volume of necessary computation. For example, the number of possible portfolios containing eight different stocks that could be selected from a list of 1,000 stocks is more than 24 quintillion.[14] At current costs for computer time, complete enumeration of all such portfolios of eight stocks would have cost approximately $150 trillion. Instead of complete enumeration, we used a sample of all possible portfolios. The sample numbers are indicated in the table. The smallest sample size was approximately 32,000

[14] 2.4115×10^{19}.

portfolios in a given period.[15] We believe that with random samples of this size there are no significant biases or errors in the portrayals in the frequency distributions for the specified periods.

As indicated earlier, there were two methods of random sampling. The first has already been described as simple random sampling without replacement. Samples of this type are designated in the

[15] These sample sizes were selected so as to make the total number of stocks selected approximately the same regardless of the size of the portfolio. The actual numbers (32,768, etc.) are powers of two, which were convenient to use in the computer programming.

Number and Length of Periods	Size of Portfolio and Sampling Method	Sample Minimum	Sample Maximum	Arithmetic Mean	Standard Deviation	Mean Deviation	Gini's Mean Difference	Coefficient of Variation	Relative Mean Deviation	Coefficient of Concentration	Skewness	Kurtosis	Number of Portfolios Examined
(14)	(15)	(16)	(17)	(18)	(19)	(20)	(21)	(22)	(23)	(24)	(25)	(26)	(27)
PERIODS				40 YEARS 1926-1965									
40 ONE-YEAR	1E	.000	20.841	1.148	.554	.351	.518	.483	.306	.226	5.339	111.090	35,407
	2E	.000	14.428	1.148	.451	.307	.449	.393	.268	.196	3.097	41.128	16,357,749
	8S	.164	6.272	1.148	.354	.265	.381	.308	.231	.166	1.028	7.606	5,242,880
	8R	.185	6.171	1.148	.353	.264	.381	.307	.230	.166	1.037	7.837	2,621,440
	16S	.273	4.434	1.148	.335	.257	.367	.292	.224	.160	.680	5.069	2,621,440
	16R	.284	4.406	1.149	.334	.257	.367	.290	.223	.160	.661	5.075	1,310,720
	32S	.344	3.533	1.148	.325	.253	.359	.283	.220	.157	.502	4.136	1,310,720
	32R	.373	3.261	1.150	.324	.253	.359	.281	.220	.156	.474	4.074	655,360
	128S	.434	2.525	1.148	.318	.249	.353	.277	.217	.154	.380	3.618	655,360
	All	.522	2.083	1.148	.315	.247	.350	.275	.216	.152	.345	3.493	40
8 FIVE-YEAR	1E	.000	48.855	1.904	2.064	1.145	1.640	1.084	.601	.431	7.197	107.852	6,791
	2E	.000	45.698	1.904	1.623	.995	1.417	.852	.523	.372	4.713	47.629	3,023,639
	8S	.103	16.196	1.904	1.190	.827	1.171	.625	.434	.307	2.239	11.032	1,048,576
	8R	.122	15.239	1.918	1.209	.837	1.189	.631	.436	.310	2.212	10.601	524,288
	16S	.268	11.391	1.905	1.103	.787	1.113	.579	.413	.292	1.794	7.059	524,288
	16R	.278	10.258	1.934	1.145	.809	1.154	.592	.418	.298	1.754	6.528	262,144
	32S	.427	8.355	1.903	1.051	.762	1.075	.552	.401	.282	1.557	5.316	262,144
	32R	.428	7.618	1.966	1.145	.814	1.165	.582	.414	.296	1.537	4.981	131,072
	128S	.668	5.713	1.906	1.019	.745	1.043	.535	.391	.274	1.409	4.293	131,072
	All	.877	4.264	1.904	1.007	.743	1.021	.529	.390	.268	1.362	4.017	8
4 TEN-YEAR	1E	.000	74.724	2.808	2.892	1.761	2.505	1.030	.627	.446	7.315	144.189	3,137
	2E	.000	51.189	2.808	2.144	1.418	2.039	.763	.505	.363	4.564	62.255	1,307,279
	8S	.049	16.967	2.804	1.325	.991	1.431	.472	.354	.255	1.037	8.955	524,288
	8R	.079	16.527	2.824	1.342	.994	1.436	.475	.352	.254	1.205	10.180	262,144
	16S	.192	10.241	2.806	1.137	.881	1.254	.405	.314	.223	.104	3.940	262,144
	16R	.228	9.974	2.849	1.164	.898	1.270	.409	.315	.223	.236	4.525	131,072
	32S	.475	6.930	2.806	1.030	.822	1.131	.367	.293	.201	-0.459	2.580	131,072
	32R	.476	7.813	2.896	1.150	.940	1.239	.397	.325	.214	-0.371	2.801	65,536
	128S	.797	4.637	2.808	.942	.786	.974	.336	.280	.174	-0.945	2.255	65,536
	All	1.238	3.526	2.808	.914	.785	.860	.326	.280	.153	-1.094	2.293	4
2 TWENTY-YR	1E	.000	110.916	7.064	9.008	5.956	8.052	1.275	.843	.570	3.485	24.393	1,363
	2E	.000	94.155	7.064	6.883	4.983	6.778	.974	.705	.480	2.327	12.326	493,173
	8S	.172	36.448	7.070	4.702	3.903	5.189	.665	.552	.367	.893	3.586	262,144
	8R	.154	36.448	7.086	4.656	3.857	5.139	.657	.544	.363	.893	3.591	131,072
	16S	.545	28.019	7.063	4.221	3.735	4.748	.598	.529	.336	.510	2.265	131,072
	16R	.646	24.726	7.095	4.156	3.678	4.679	.586	.518	.330	.498	2.237	65,536
	32S	1.208	21.171	7.058	3.961	3.701	4.438	.561	.524	.314	.272	1.603	65,536
	32R	1.190	19.714	7.002	3.999	3.769	4.465	.571	.538	.319	.243	1.522	32,768
	128S	2.213	14.266	7.061	3.758	3.699	4.053	.532	.524	.287	.065	1.127	32,768
	All	3.361	10.766	7.064	3.702	3.702	3.702	.524	.524	.262	.000	1.000	2

TABLE 5, CONTINUED

AGGREGATED FREQUENCY DISTRIBUTIONS OF WEALTH RATIOS FROM INVESTMENTS
IN RANDOMLY SELECTED PORTFOLIOS CONTAINING SPECIFIED NUMBERS
OF STOCKS LISTED ON THE NYSE, 1926-65

Number and Length of Periods	Size of Portfolio/ Sampling Method	Centiles of the Aggregated Frequency Distributions										
		5th	10th	20th	30th	40th	(Median) 50th	60th	70th	80th	90th	95th
(1)	(2)	(3)	(4)	(5)	(6)	(7)	(8)	(9)	(10)	(11)	(12)	(13)
PERIODS		20 YEARS 1926-1945										
20 ONE-YEAR	1E	.356	.480	.675	.828	.958	1.075	1.192	1.326	1.500	1.830	2.230
	2E	.438	.545	.718	.859	.979	1.098	1.218	1.344	1.497	1.761	2.070
	8S	.510	.582	.760	.892	1.001	1.145	1.272	1.378	1.497	1.675	1.891
	8R	.512	.584	.760	.893	1.002	1.149	1.275	1.380	1.499	1.677	1.987
	16S	.524	.583	.771	.902	.995	1.167	1.295	1.389	1.498	1.649	1.837
	16R	.527	.587	.769	.903	.998	1.173	1.298	1.392	1.504	1.656	1.828
	32S	.530	.581	.779	.908	.986	1.189	1.311	1.396	1.496	1.622	1.816
	32R	.532	.588	.769	.913	.994	1.196	1.318	1.400	1.505	1.640	1.796
	128S	.533	.576	.781	.909	.976	1.221	1.322	1.400	1.501	1.593	1.766
	All	.531	.580	.795	.900	.976	1.219	1.309	1.418	1.495	1.581	1.841
4 FIVE-YEAR	1E	.100	.207	.435	.673	.920	1.200	1.561	2.022	2.722	4.123	6.168
	2E	.286	.421	.622	.798	.983	1.206	1.535	2.091	2.878	4.217	5.517
	8S	.586	.678	.804	.914	1.036	1.195	1.454	2.028	3.222	4.243	5.082
	8R	.591	.680	.806	.917	1.039	1.199	1.460	2.035	3.303	4.327	5.177
	16S	.677	.748	.847	.935	1.038	1.194	1.461	1.895	3.472	4.307	4.950
	16R	.677	.746	.845	.934	1.039	1.201	1.480	1.909	3.658	4.489	5.113
	32S	.740	.794	.868	.937	1.023	1.194	1.482	1.795	3.674	4.327	4.783
	32R	.712	.769	.849	.924	1.018	1.222	1.527	1.844	4.051	4.672	5.080
	128S	.821	.851	.891	.929	.976	1.191	1.536	1.680	3.987	4.335	4.549
	All						1.258					
2 TEN-YEAR	1E	.036	.133	.386	.772	1.255	1.702	2.084	2.596	3.367	4.578	6.213
	2E	.195	.362	.700	1.043	1.427	1.859	2.277	2.725	3.302	4.273	5.435
	8S	.590	.736	.979	1.246	1.621	2.108	2.498	2.842	3.236	3.812	4.350
	8R	.607	.754	.992	1.258	1.631	2.141	2.537	2.891	3.293	3.870	4.400
	16S	.749	.870	1.065	1.268	1.545	2.217	2.640	2.925	3.221	3.639	4.055
	16R	.763	.888	1.080	1.276	1.551	2.307	2.740	3.037	3.344	3.788	4.268
	32S	.871	.972	1.123	1.271	1.471	2.242	2.756	2.994	3.233	3.568	3.911
	32R	.813	.898	1.026	1.157	1.334	2.305	3.073	3.326	3.590	3.991	4.961
	128S	1.043	1.109	1.185	1.264	1.351	1.967	2.952	3.109	3.270	3.481	3.672
	All						2.232					

TABLE 5, CONTINUED

AGGREGATED FREQUENCY DISTRIBUTIONS OF WEALTH RATIOS FROM INVESTMENTS
IN RANDOMLY SELECTED PORTFOLIOS CONTAINING SPECIFIED NUMBERS
OF STOCKS LISTED ON THE NYSE, 1926-65

Number and Length of Periods	Size of Portfolio/ Sampling Method	Centiles of the Aggregated Frequency Distributions										
		5th	10th	20th	30th	40th	(Median) 50th	60th	70th	80th	90th	95th
(1)	(2)	(3)	(4)	(5)	(6)	(7)	(8)	(9)	(10)	(11)	(12)	(13)
PERIODS		20 YEARS 1945-1965										
20 ONE-YEAR	1E	.663	.763	.879	.961	1.026	1.091	1.161	1.245	1.359	1.551	1.743
	2E	.746	.820	.913	.982	1.042	1.100	1.162	1.236	1.335	1.497	1.650
	8S	.829	.876	.944	1.005	1.063	1.114	1.163	1.218	1.299	1.454	1.567
	8R	.831	.876	.944	1.005	1.062	1.113	1.163	1.219	1.300	1.454	1.566
	16S	.847	.887	.948	1.007	1.069	1.120	1.165	1.214	1.285	1.450	1.557
	16R	.849	.888	.948	1.005	1.067	1.120	1.166	1.216	1.287	1.448	1.559
	32S	.857	.891	.951	1.004	1.074	1.127	1.167	1.210	1.277	1.453	1.558
	32R	.860	.894	.954	1.003	1.065	1.128	1.174	1.219	1.282	1.443	1.560
	128S	.864	.887	.962	.994	1.078	1.140	1.169	1.199	1.277	1.456	1.561
	All	.865	.883	.968	.987	1.077	1.147	1.169	1.192	1.279	1.453	1.563
4 FIVE-YEAR	1E	.579	.797	1.057	1.264	1.460	1.656	1.875	2.131	2.474	3.149	3.916
	2E	.861	1.015	1.227	1.399	1.560	1.724	1.903	2.116	2.407	2.924	3.481
	8S	1.175	1.280	1.427	1.554	1.678	1.810	1.953	2.115	2.312	2.600	2.865
	8R	1.177	1.281	1.428	1.556	1.682	1.816	1.960	2.121	2.316	2.602	2.868
	16S	1.267	1.351	1.473	1.583	1.702	1.837	1.982	2.130	2.291	2.506	2.688
	16R	1.267	1.350	1.471	1.586	1.712	1.855	2.004	2.148	2.305	2.516	2.702
	32S	1.331	1.397	1.495	1.590	1.710	1.863	2.016	2.151	2.284	2.448	2.573
	32R	1.329	1.393	1.494	1.600	1.743	1.942	2.099	2.219	2.336	2.483	2.610
	128S	1.400	1.435	1.507	1.603	1.712	1.923	2.054	2.165	2.267	2.364	2.431
	All						1.894					
2 TEN-YEAR	1E	.749	1.073	1.576	1.960	2.358	2.787	3.233	3.843	4.661	6.361	8.260
	2E	1.290	1.590	2.003	2.340	2.661	2.992	3.361	3.824	4.483	5.610	6.839
	8S	2.144	2.350	2.620	2.836	3.034	3.241	3.463	3.719	4.068	4.643	5.146
	8R	2.160	2.364	2.630	2.845	3.040	3.244	3.465	3.718	4.059	4.628	5.118
	16S	2.439	2.614	2.831	2.993	3.151	3.308	3.479	3.669	3.922	4.290	4.620
	16R	2.451	2.626	2.845	3.005	3.161	3.313	3.479	3.663	3.906	4.256	4.559
	32S	2.661	2.800	2.962	3.105	3.224	3.342	3.472	3.613	3.785	4.020	4.268
	32R	2.721	2.867	3.020	3.153	3.262	3.371	3.493	3.619	3.773	3.992	4.201
	128S	2.924	3.021	3.147	3.219	3.291	3.363	3.445	3.535	3.625	3.738	3.904
	All						3.383					

Number and Length of Periods	Size of Portfolio and Sampling Method	Sample Minimum	Sample Maximum	Arithmetic Mean	Standard Deviation	Mean Deviation	Gini's Mean Difference	Coefficient of Variation	Relative Mean Deviation	Coefficient of Concentration	Skewness	Kurtosis	Number of Portfolios Examined
(14)	(15)	(16)	(17)	(18)	(19)	(20)	(21)	(22)	(23)	(24)	(25)	(26)	(27)

PERIODS   20 YEARS 1926-1945

20 ONE-YEAR	1E	.000	20.841	1.158	.699	.447	.653	.604	.386	.282	5.062	86.788	14,394
	2E	.000	14.428	1.158	.569	.399	.574	.492	.344	.248	2.880	31.712	5,246,994
	8S	.164	6.272	1.158	.448	.355	.493	.387	.306	.213	.869	5.628	2,621,440
	8R	.185	6.171	1.159	.447	.354	.492	.386	.306	.212	.874	5.805	1,310,720
	16S	.273	4.434	1.158	.425	.348	.476	.367	.301	.205	.529	3.691	1,310,720
	16R	.284	4.406	1.159	.422	.347	.474	.364	.300	.204	.507	3.709	655,360
	32S	.344	3.533	1.157	.412	.345	.465	.356	.298	.201	.358	2.993	655,360
	32R	.373	3.261	1.162	.410	.345	.464	.353	.297	.200	.322	2.946	327,680
	128S	.434	2.525	1.158	.403	.343	.455	.348	.296	.196	.237	2.606	327,680
	All	.522	2.083	1.158	.400	.341	.450	.346	.295	.194	.204	2.514	20
4 FIVE-YEAR	1E	.000	48.855	1.914	2.615	1.485	2.050	1.366	.776	.535	6.257	75.783	2,754
	2E	.000	45.698	1.914	2.091	1.355	1.825	1.092	.708	.477	3.996	32.107	969,210
	8S	.103	16.196	1.914	1.588	1.226	1.561	.830	.640	.408	1.805	6.781	524,288
	8R	.122	15.239	1.937	1.615	1.244	1.591	.834	.642	.411	1.762	6.447	262,144
	16S	.268	11.391	1.917	1.490	1.196	1.494	.778	.624	.390	1.413	4.158	262,144
	16R	.278	10.258	1.962	1.549	1.235	1.557	.789	.629	.397	1.346	3.765	131,072
	32S	.427	8.355	1.912	1.431	1.177	1.442	.748	.615	.377	1.212	3.056	131,072
	32R	.428	7.618	1.999	1.562	1.258	1.577	.781	.629	.395	1.147	2.761	65,536
	128S	.668	5.713	1.917	1.397	1.170	1.394	.729	.611	.363	1.070	2.391	65,536
	All	.877	4.264	1.914	1.383	1.175	1.347	.722	.614	.352	1.032	2.223	4
2 TEN-YEAR	1E	.000	74.724	2.232	3.075	1.845	2.302	1.378	.826	.516	10.879	225.901	1,229
	2E	.000	51.189	2.232	2.284	1.550	1.935	1.023	.695	.433	6.927	98.839	387,916
	8S	.049	16.967	2.227	1.415	1.189	1.459	.636	.534	.328	2.162	14.642	262,144
	8R	.079	16.527	2.269	1.473	1.202	1.497	.649	.530	.330	2.326	15.430	131,072
	16S	.192	10.241	2.229	1.222	1.091	1.327	.548	.489	.298	1.079	5.646	131,072
	16R	.228	9.974	2.316	1.322	1.134	1.420	.571	.490	.307	1.191	5.836	65,536
	32S	.475	6.930	2.230	1.113	1.039	1.239	.499	.466	.278	.511	2.630	65,536
	32R	.476	7.813	2.390	1.398	1.268	1.540	.585	.530	.322	.562	2.448	32,768
	128S	.797	4.637	2.228	1.023	1.000	1.118	.459	.449	.251	.103	1.233	32,768
	All	1.238	3.226	2.232	.994	.994	.994	.445	.445	.223	.000	1.000	2

Number and Length of Periods	Size of Portfolio and Sampling Method	Sample Minimum	Sample Maximum	Arithmetic Mean	Standard Deviation	Mean Deviation	Gini's Mean Difference	Coefficient of Variation	Relative Mean Deviation	Coefficient of Concentration	Skewness	Kurtosis	Number of Portfolios Examined
(14)	(15)	(16)	(17)	(18)	(19)	(20)	(21)	(22)	(23)	(24)	(25)	(26)	(27)

PERIODS   20 YEARS 1945-1965

20 ONE-YEAR	1E	.000	5.441	1.138	.355	.255	.367	.312	.224	.161	1.791	12.734	21,013
	2E	.174	4.951	1.138	.287	.216	.307	.252	.189	.135	1.233	7.080	11,110,755
	8S	.534	2.644	1.138	.223	.174	.246	.196	.153	.108	.769	3.673	2,621,440
	8R	.535	2.580	1.138	.222	.174	.246	.195	.153	.108	.772	3.654	1,310,720
	16S	.637	2.214	1.138	.210	.165	.233	.185	.145	.103	.708	3.259	1,310,720
	16R	.658	2.141	1.138	.210	.166	.233	.184	.146	.103	.710	3.228	655,360
	32S	.697	1.989	1.138	.203	.160	.227	.179	.141	.100	.681	3.059	655,360
	32R	.711	1.930	1.139	.202	.161	.226	.178	.142	.099	.670	3.007	327,680
	128S	.777	1.765	1.138	.198	.156	.221	.174	.137	.097	.664	2.917	327,680
	All	.864	1.579	1.138	.197	.154	.218	.173	.136	.096	.659	2.875	20
4 FIVE-YEAR	1E	.063	35.876	1.894	1.296	.806	1.152	.684	.425	.304	6.646	129.423	4,037
	2E	.107	24.524	1.894	.947	.635	.903	.500	.335	.238	4.318	57.353	2,054,429
	8S	.553	7.417	1.894	.557	.428	.597	.294	.226	.158	1.458	8.981	524,288
	8R	.639	7.554	1.899	.562	.430	.600	.296	.226	.158	1.528	9.5C0	262,144
	16S	.846	5.052	1.894	.460	.377	.514	.243	.199	.136	.699	3.666	262,144
	16R	.886	4.934	1.906	.470	.383	.524	.247	.201	.138	.732	3.866	131,072
	32S	.910	3.507	1.895	.404	.348	.462	.213	.184	.122	.309	2.168	131,072
	32R	1.022	3.471	1.932	.422	.370	.484	.218	.191	.125	.167	1.972	65,536
	128S	1.197	2.746	1.894	.355	.320	.408	.187	.169	.108	.052	1.596	65,536
	All	1.455	2.335	1.894	.340	.316	.378	.179	.167	.100	.004	1.461	4
2 TEN-YEAR	1E	.047	22.340	3.383	2.571	1.677	2.485	.760	.496	.367	2.499	13.148	1,908
	2E	.064	21.851	3.383	1.820	1.286	1.865	.538	.380	.276	1.775	8.049	919,363
	8S	.837	9.564	3.381	.917	.793	1.004	.271	.235	.148	.915	4.242	262,144
	8R	1.035	9.523	3.380	.902	.787	.990	.267	.233	.146	.886	4.139	131,072
	16S	1.451	7.562	3.385	.653	.671	.726	.193	.198	.107	.668	3.613	131,072
	16R	1.523	6.935	3.381	.630	.662	.703	.186	.196	.104	.611	3.488	65,536
	32S	1.999	5.787	3.382	.469	.605	.527	.139	.179	.078	.494	3.230	65,536
	32R	1.912	5.420	3.401	.425	.613	.479	.125	.180	.070	.358	3.029	32,768
	128S	2.6C0	4.409	3.379	.256	.572	.290	.076	.169	.043	.289	2.821	32,768
	All	3.241	3.526	3.383	.143	.143	.143	.042	.042	.021	.000	1.000	2

table with the letter *S*. A second method of random sampling was also used, and the results of this method are indicated in the table with the letter *R*. In the second method, we took steps to insure that the portfolios were well diversified by industry. All the common stocks on the New York Stock Exchange were assigned to thirty-four industry groups.[16] Our

[16] See Appendix, table A1.

method of random selection insured that no more than one stock fell in any single industry group. The greater the number of stocks in an industry, the greater the probability of including that industry in the portfolio. But the greater the number in the industry, the smaller the probability of including any particular stock.

We will not distinguish between these two different random methods of sampling in discussing the results, since the

TABLE 6

DISPERSION OF RETURNS ON N-STOCK PORTFOLIOS AS PERCENTAGE
OF DISPERSION OF ONE-STOCK PORTFOLIOS
(Based on portfolios of stocks from NYSE for 1926-65 or as specified)

MEASURE OF RELATIVE DISPERSION For holding period(s)	Number of Stocks in Portfolio						
	1	2	8	16	32	128	All (Market)
Coefficient of Variation							
40 one-year	100	81	64	60	59	57	57
20 one-year (1926-45)	100	81	64	61	59	58	57
20 one-year (1946-65)	100	81	63	59	57	56	55
8 five-year	100	79	58	53	51	49	49
4 ten-year	100	74	46	39	36	33	32
2 twenty-year	100	76	52	47	44	42	41
Relative Mean Deviation							
40 one-year	100	88	75	73	72	71	71
20 one-year (1926-45)	100	89	79	78	77	77	76
20 one-year (1946-65)	100	85	68	65	63	61	61
8 five-year	100	87	72	69	67	65	65
4 ten-year	100	81	56	50	47	45	45
2 twenty-year	100	84	65	63	62	62	62
Gini's Coefficient of Concentration							
40 one-year	100	87	74	71	69	68	68
20 one-year (1926-45)	100	88	76	73	71	70	69
20 one-year (1946-65)	100	84	67	64	62	60	59
8 five-year	100	84	67	64	62	60	59
4 ten-year	100	81	57	50	45	39	34
2 twenty-year	100	84	64	59	55	50	46

two methods of selecting the sample did not produce significantly different results. Although there was a slight reduction in dispersion within individual periods as a result of the constrained random sampling, this reduction was almost exactly offset by the increased dispersion of the means among periods. Thus, when periods were aggregated, the distributions from the two methods of sampling became almost the same.

The findings.—In considering the findings discussed here, it is important to remember that initial equal investments were made in each stock included in any portfolio and that there was no subsequent reallocation of resources to preserve the equality of investment. This is not an investment strategy we advocate; again, it was chosen to make certain that the distributions were affected only by the number of stocks in the portfolio.

TABLE 7

DISPERSION OF RETURNS ON N-STOCK PORTFOLIOS AS PERCENTAGE
OF DISPERSION OF MARKET PORTFOLIOS
(Based on portfolios of stocks from NYSE for 1926-65 or as specified)

MEASURE OF RELATIVE DISPERSION For holding period(s)	Number of Stocks in Portfolio						
	1	2	8	16	32	128	All (Market)
Coefficient of Variation							
40 one-year	176	143	112	106	103	101	100
20 one-year (1926-45)	175	142	112	106	103	101	100
20 one-year (1946-65)	180	146	113	107	103	101	100
8 five-year	205	161	118	109	104	101	100
4 ten-year	316	234	145	124	113	103	100
2 twenty-year	243	186	127	114	107	102	100
Relative Mean Deviation							
40 one-year	142	124	107	104	102	101	100
20 one-year (1926-45)	131	117	104	102	101	100	100
20 one-year (1946-65)	165	140	113	107	104	101	100
8 five-year	154	134	111	106	103	100	100
4 ten-year	224	181	126	112	105	100	100
2 twenty-year	161	135	105	101	100	100	100
Gini's Coefficient of Concentration							
40 one-year	148	128	109	105	103	101	100
20 one-year (1926-45)	145	127	110	106	103	101	100
20 one-year (1946-65)	169	141	113	107	104	101	100
8 five-year	161	139	115	109	105	102	100
4 ten-year	291	237	167	146	132	113	100
2 twenty-year	217	183	140	128	120	110	100

There is only one important generalization about table 5. It is that portfolios containing eight stocks have frequency distributions strikingly similar to those of portfolios containing larger numbers of stocks—including all listed stocks—except for the tails beyond the fifth and ninetieth centiles. The tails beyond those centiles get progressively shorter as the number of stocks in the portfolio increases. This fact causes the measures of dispersion to get smaller, despite the nearly identical distributions between the fifth and ninetieth centiles.

Tables 6, 7, and 8 summarize the information in table 5 with respect to the effect on relative dispersion of changing the number of stocks in a portfolio. The tables are easily read. The market as a whole generally had 50–75 percent as

TABLE 8

PERCENT OF POSSIBLE REDUCTION IN RELATIVE DISPERSION ACHIEVED
THROUGH INCREASING THE NUMBER OF STOCKS IN THE PORTFOLIO
(Based on portfolios of stocks from NYSE for 1926-65 or as specified)

MEASURE OF RELATIVE DISPERSION For holding period(s)	Number of Stocks in Portfolio						
	1	2	8	16	32	128	All (Market)
Coefficient of Variation							
40 one-year	0	43	84	92	96	99	100
20 one-year (1926-45)	0	43	84	92	96	99	100
20 one-year (1946-65)	0	43	84	92	96	99	100
8 five-year	0	42	83	91	96	99	100
4 ten-year	0	38	79	89	94	99	100
2 twenty-year	0	40	81	90	95	99	100
Relative Mean Deviation							
40 one-year	0	42	84	91	95	98	100
20 one-year (1926-45)	0	45	87	94	96	99	100
20 one-year (1946-65)	0	39	80	89	94	99	100
8 five-year	0	37	79	89	95	99	100
4 ten-year	0	35	79	90	96	100	100
2 twenty-year	0	43	91	99	100	100	100
Gini's Coefficient of Concentration							
40 one-year	0	41	81	90	94	98	100
20 one-year (1926-45)	0	39	79	87	93	98	100
20 one-year (1946-65)	0	40	81	89	94	98	100
8 five-year	0	36	76	85	91	97	100
4 ten-year	0	28	65	76	84	93	100
2 twenty-year	0	29	66	76	83	92	100

much dispersion as did one-stock portfolios, depending on the periods and measure of dispersion (table 6). Conversely, one-stock portfolios have roughly one and one-third to twice as much dispersion as the market (table 7). The opportunity to reduce dispersion by increasing the number of stocks in the portfolio is rapidly exhausted (table 8). Roughly, 40 percent of achievable reduction is obtained by holding two stocks; 80 percent, by holding eight stocks; 90 percent, by holding sixteen stocks; 95 percent, by holding thirty-two stocks; and 99 percent, by holding 128 stocks (table 8).

APPENDIX A

AGGREGATED FREQUENCY DISTRIBUTIONS FOR PORTFOLIOS OF SPECIFIED SIZES

Table A1 shows the frequency distributions of wealth ratios for portfolios of specified sizes for the fifty-five periods. These distributions were aggregated to produce tables 4 and 5.

Since the statistics for portfolios having eight or more stocks were based on samples, it is unlikely that the minimum and maximum wealth ratios for any samples were the true minima and maxima. Table A2 shows the true minima and maxima for portfolios of eight or more stocks for each of the fifty-five periods.

TABLE A1

FREQUENCY DISTRIBUTIONS OF WEALTH RATIOS FROM INVESTMENTS IN RANDOMLY SELECTED PORTFOLIOS
CONTAINING SPECIFIED NUMBERS OF STOCKS LISTED ON THE NYSE, 1926-65

Number and Length of Periods	Size of Portfolio/ Sampling Method	Centiles of the Frequency Distributions										
		5th	10th	20th	30th	40th	(Median) 50th	60th	70th	80th	90th	95th
(1)	(2)	(3)	(4)	(5)	(6)	(7)	(8)	(9)	(10)	(11)	(12)	(13)
ONE-YEAR PERIODS												
1/26-12/26	1E	.429	.560	.722	.845	.917	.991	1.060	1.115	1.183	1.316	1.485
	2E	.626	.703	.796	.865	.923	.976	1.026	1.079	1.143	1.249	1.382
	8S	.802	.839	.886	.919	.949	.977	1.005	1.038	1.077	1.139	1.196
	8R	.801	.838	.884	.918	.947	.960	1.004	1.037	1.078	1.141	1.201
	16S	.853	.881	.914	.938	.960	.980	1.002	1.025	1.053	1.095	1.132
	16R	.851	.879	.912	.935	.957	.978	.999	1.023	1.052	1.095	1.132
	32S	.892	.912	.936	.953	.969	.983	.998	1.015	1.034	1.061	1.084
	32R	.886	.904	.928	.945	.961	.974	.989	1.005	1.024	1.052	1.075
	128S	.942	.952	.963	.971	.978	.985	.992	.999	1.008	1.019	1.029
12/26-12/27	1E	.640	.752	.888	1.053	1.132	1.225	1.330	1.457	1.601	1.834	2.274
	2E	.797	.895	1.011	1.099	1.175	1.248	1.326	1.414	1.532	1.739	1.957
	8S	1.024	1.077	1.142	1.192	1.235	1.273	1.321	1.372	1.435	1.536	1.637
	8R	1.026	1.077	1.140	1.189	1.231	1.273	1.317	1.367	1.430	1.529	1.631
	16S	1.097	1.137	1.185	1.221	1.253	1.285	1.318	1.354	1.400	1.474	1.557
	16R	1.095	1.134	1.182	1.216	1.247	1.278	1.309	1.345	1.389	1.459	1.530
	32S	1.153	1.181	1.216	1.243	1.267	1.291	1.313	1.340	1.374	1.427	1.477
	32R	1.148	1.175	1.210	1.235	1.256	1.278	1.301	1.325	1.355	1.397	1.439
	128S	1.230	1.244	1.262	1.275	1.287	1.299	1.310	1.323	1.338	1.359	1.377
12/27-12/28	1E	.725	.834	.976	1.064	1.153	1.251	1.376	1.512	1.711	2.136	2.795
	2E	.879	.960	1.064	1.148	1.227	1.310	1.402	1.517	1.689	2.049	2.459
	8S	1.095	1.149	1.219	1.276	1.330	1.386	1.449	1.524	1.626	1.811	2.026
	8R	1.096	1.148	1.217	1.274	1.326	1.381	1.442	1.517	1.618	1.802	2.031
	16S	1.176	1.220	1.279	1.326	1.369	1.413	1.460	1.518	1.597	1.731	1.878
	16R	1.167	1.208	1.265	1.309	1.350	1.391	1.438	1.492	1.568	1.699	1.839
	32S	1.244	1.281	1.325	1.362	1.395	1.430	1.468	1.510	1.566	1.662	1.754
	32R	1.207	1.237	1.275	1.306	1.335	1.363	1.393	1.431	1.479	1.558	1.630
	128S	1.344	1.365	1.392	1.412	1.430	1.448	1.466	1.486	1.512	1.547	1.579
12/28-12/29	1E	.197	.279	.405	.518	.604	.700	.774	.873	.977	1.123	1.218
	2E	.339	.412	.505	.574	.636	.694	.752	.816	.890	.994	1.079
	8S	.518	.556	.604	.639	.669	.698	.726	.757	.794	.844	.886
	8R	.520	.558	.604	.637	.667	.696	.723	.753	.789	.838	.879
	16S	.572	.599	.633	.657	.679	.699	.719	.740	.765	.801	.830
	16R	.573	.600	.632	.655	.675	.693	.712	.733	.758	.791	.819
	32S	.609	.629	.653	.670	.685	.699	.713	.728	.746	.770	.790
	32R	.612	.629	.651	.666	.679	.691	.703	.717	.734	.756	.775
	128S	.659	.667	.679	.686	.693	.700	.707	.713	.721	.732	.742
12/29-12/30	1E	.205	.265	.367	.442	.521	.593	.674	.757	.868	.986	1.106
	2E	.313	.370	.446	.504	.557	.607	.658	.715	.783	.882	.967
	8S	.462	.494	.535	.565	.591	.616	.641	.669	.702	.750	.791
	8R	.463	.496	.537	.568	.594	.620	.645	.673	.705	.753	.793
	16S	.506	.531	.560	.581	.600	.618	.636	.655	.679	.711	.739
	16R	.514	.537	.566	.588	.606	.624	.642	.662	.684	.716	.743
	32S	.539	.556	.578	.593	.606	.619	.631	.645	.661	.683	.702
	32R	.550	.566	.588	.603	.615	.628	.640	.653	.669	.692	.711
	128S	.582	.590	.601	.607	.614	.620	.625	.632	.639	.649	.658
12/30-12/31	1E	.158	.215	.292	.347	.401	.467	.536	.615	.738	.909	1.044
	2E	.241	.288	.350	.399	.446	.493	.545	.603	.677	.788	.891
	8S	.367	.397	.434	.463	.489	.514	.540	.568	.603	.656	.702
	8R	.371	.401	.439	.469	.494	.519	.545	.574	.610	.662	.708
	16S	.410	.432	.460	.481	.500	.518	.536	.556	.580	.616	.646
	16R	.420	.443	.472	.493	.511	.529	.548	.568	.593	.628	.658
	32S	.442	.458	.478	.494	.507	.520	.533	.547	.564	.587	.607
	32R	.463	.480	.500	.515	.529	.542	.555	.568	.585	.609	.627
	128S	.483	.491	.502	.509	.515	.521	.527	.534	.541	.552	.560
12/31-12/32	1E	.353	.449	.561	.654	.729	.828	.931	1.035	1.173	1.377	1.662
	2E	.475	.551	.646	.719	.786	.851	.920	1.000	1.103	1.272	1.451
	8S	.663	.707	.763	.805	.842	.877	.915	.957	1.009	1.088	1.160
	8R	.665	.709	.763	.799	.830	.857	.883	.911	.941	.978	1.032
	16S	.726	.759	.799	.830	.857	.883	.906	.935	.970	1.022	1.066
	16R	.723	.756	.797	.827	.854	.879	.906	.927	.953	.989	1.020
	32S	.772	.796	.827	.849	.869	.887	.906	.927	.953	.989	1.020
	32R	.763	.785	.813	.834	.852	.871	.888	.908	.931	.963	.991
	128S	.834	.846	.862	.873	.882	.891	.900	.909	.921	.937	.950
12/32-12/33	1E	.657	.856	1.189	1.402	1.628	1.849	2.075	2.394	2.742	3.331	4.338
	2E	.986	1.165	1.401	1.587	1.755	1.925	2.106	2.319	2.608	3.128	3.691
	8S	1.459	1.568	1.712	1.822	1.919	2.018	2.124	2.245	2.397	2.634	2.865
	8R	1.451	1.557	1.697	1.802	1.900	1.998	2.101	2.221	2.373	2.613	2.839
	16S	1.619	1.704	1.814	1.897	1.971	2.045	2.121	2.208	2.312	2.480	2.662
	16R	1.586	1.669	1.777	1.856	1.929	2.000	2.075	2.160	2.273	2.448	2.658
	32S	1.744	1.806	1.889	1.950	2.005	2.057	2.113	2.176	2.256	2.383	2.517
	32R	1.704	1.768	1.843	1.902	1.956	2.007	2.064	2.128	2.219	2.399	2.576
	128S	1.915	1.950	1.992	2.023	2.052	2.080	2.107	2.138	2.174	2.227	2.274

Number and Length of Periods	Size of Portfolio and Sampling Method	Sample Minimum	Sample Maximum	Arithmetic Mean	Standard Deviation	Mean Deviation	Gini's Mean Difference	Coefficient of Variation	Relative Mean Deviation	Coefficient of Concentration	Skewness	Kurtosis	Number of Portfolios Examined
(14)	(15)	(16)	(17)	(18)	(19)	(20)	(21)	(22)	(23)	(24)	(25)	(26)	(27)

ONE-YEAR PERIODS

Number and Length of Periods	Size of Portfolio and Sampling Method	Sample Minimum	Sample Maximum	Arithmetic Mean	Standard Deviation	Mean Deviation	Gini's Mean Difference	Coefficient of Variation	Relative Mean Deviation	Coefficient of Concentration	Skewness	Kurtosis	Number of Portfolios Examined
1/26-12/26	1E	.073	2.970	.985	.343	.242	.355	.348	.245	.180	1.304	8.891	510
	2E	.174	2.950	.985	.242	.179	.259	.246	.181	.132	.920	5.910	129,795
	8S	.529	1.700	.984	.122	.094	.134	.122	.095	.068	.436	3.637	131,072
	8R	.554	1.843	.984	.122	.095	.135	.124	.096	.069	.499	3.744	65,536
	16S	.674	1.365	.985	.084	.067	.095	.086	.068	.048	.306	3.246	65,536
	16R	.692	1.410	.983	.085	.068	.096	.087	.069	.049	.346	3.283	32,768
	32S	.740	1.257	.985	.058	.046	.066	.059	.047	.033	.197	3.088	32,768
	32R	.789	1.198	.977	.057	.046	.064	.059	.047	.033	.228	3.007	16,384
	128S	.886	1.086	.985	.026	.021	.030	.027	.021	.015	.059	2.939	16,384
12/26-12/27	1E	.000	7.889	1.300	.577	.374	.546	.444	.288	.210	3.660	36.275	543
	2E	.000	6.338	1.300	.408	.278	.404	.314	.214	.155	2.581	19.478	147,153
	8S	.627	2.805	1.300	.203	.150	.215	.156	.115	.083	1.254	6.823	131,072
	8R	.632	2.881	1.296	.199	.148	.212	.154	.114	.082	1.261	6.922	65,536
	16S	.835	2.238	1.300	.143	.108	.155	.110	.083	.060	.895	4.825	65,536
	16R	.834	2.227	1.291	.136	.105	.148	.105	.081	.057	.812	4.718	32,768
	32S	.992	1.805	1.298	.098	.077	.109	.076	.059	.042	.568	3.653	32,768
	32R	.977	1.745	1.284	.089	.072	.099	.069	.056	.039	.449	3.595	16,384
	128S	1.134	1.476	1.300	.045	.036	.050	.034	.027	.019	.210	2.994	16,384
12/27-12/28	1E	.398	13.226	1.453	.904	.498	.712	.622	.343	.245	5.844	60.390	589
	2E	.407	10.450	1.453	.639	.388	.554	.440	.267	.191	4.122	31.444	173,166
	8S	.778	4.001	1.451	.316	.223	.317	.218	.154	.109	2.021	9.670	131,072
	8R	.908	3.069	1.447	.313	.222	.314	.216	.153	.108	2.033	9.757	65,536
	16S	.908	3.069	1.454	.223	.165	.235	.154	.114	.081	1.404	6.161	65,536
	16R	.961	2.802	1.431	.213	.163	.225	.149	.114	.081	1.398	6.136	32,768
	32S	1.053	2.288	1.454	.155	.120	.170	.107	.082	.058	.931	4.254	32,768
	32R	1.061	2.208	1.383	.132	.125	.144	.096	.090	.052	1.015	4.764	16,384
	128S	1.248	1.752	1.453	.071	.057	.080	.049	.039	.028	.360	3.008	16,384
12/28-12/29	1E	.000	1.851	.700	.318	.259	.361	.454	.370	.258	.261	2.718	627
	2E	.026	1.754	.700	.225	.181	.254	.321	.258	.182	.184	2.856	196,251
	8S	.216	1.214	.699	.112	.090	.126	.160	.128	.090	.096	2.981	131,072
	8R	.283	1.169	.697	.109	.087	.123	.156	.125	.088	.083	2.928	65,536
	16S	.360	1.024	.699	.079	.063	.089	.112	.090	.063	.059	2.952	65,536
	16R	.355	1.003	.695	.075	.060	.084	.108	.086	.061	.079	3.045	32,768
	32S	.476	.924	.699	.055	.044	.062	.079	.063	.044	.029	2.956	32,768
	32R	.509	.883	.692	.049	.040	.055	.071	.057	.040	.078	2.977	16,384
	128S	.605	.797	.700	.025	.020	.028	.036	.029	.020	.030	2.948	16,384
12/29-12/30	1E	.046	2.105	.620	.286	.229	.318	.461	.369	.257	.685	4.047	717
	2E	.051	1.961	.620	.202	.160	.226	.326	.258	.182	.483	3.516	256,686
	8S	.241	1.121	.620	.100	.080	.113	.162	.128	.091	.237	3.127	131,072
	8R	.260	1.123	.623	.100	.080	.113	.161	.128	.091	.223	3.095	65,536
	16S	.347	.950	.620	.070	.056	.079	.114	.091	.064	.153	3.021	65,536
	16R	.383	.927	.626	.070	.056	.079	.111	.089	.063	.133	3.009	32,768
	32S	.432	.822	.619	.049	.039	.056	.079	.063	.045	.102	2.970	32,768
	32R	.452	.825	.629	.049	.039	.055	.077	.063	.044	.105	2.978	16,384
	128S	.541	.716	.620	.023	.018	.026	.037	.029	.021	.046	2.995	16,384
12/30-12/31	1E	.000	2.204	.522	.291	.221	.311	.558	.425	.298	1.323	6.365	737
	2E	.000	2.114	.522	.206	.160	.225	.394	.306	.216	.933	4.667	271,216
	8S	.164	1.079	.521	.102	.081	.114	.196	.155	.110	.452	3.358	131,072
	8R	.185	1.132	.527	.103	.081	.115	.196	.154	.109	.458	3.419	65,536
	16S	.273	.910	.521	.072	.057	.081	.138	.110	.078	.328	3.223	65,536
	16R	.284	.899	.533	.072	.058	.081	.135	.108	.076	.286	3.116	32,768
	32S	.344	.770	.522	.050	.040	.057	.096	.077	.054	.190	3.024	32,768
	32R	.373	.730	.543	.050	.043	.056	.092	.079	.052	.143	2.940	16,384
	128S	.434	.614	.521	.023	.019	.026	.045	.036	.025	.084	3.000	16,384
12/31-12/32	1E	.000	3.308	.891	.435	.319	.455	.488	.358	.255	1.481	7.462	732
	2E	.000	3.188	.891	.307	.232	.331	.345	.260	.186	1.045	5.211	267,546
	8S	.375	1.787	.891	.153	.120	.170	.171	.135	.096	.506	3.514	131,072
	8R	.356	1.758	.890	.151	.119	.169	.170	.134	.095	.505	3.516	65,536
	16S	.520	1.521	.890	.108	.085	.121	.121	.096	.068	.379	3.288	65,536
	16R	.513	1.367	.885	.104	.083	.117	.118	.094	.066	.320	3.191	32,768
	32S	.622	1.217	.890	.075	.060	.085	.084	.067	.048	.249	3.083	32,768
	32R	.569	1.151	.873	.069	.058	.078	.080	.066	.045	.189	3.010	16,384
	128S	.770	1.039	.891	.035	.028	.039	.039	.031	.022	.095	3.009	16,384
12/32-12/33	1E	.000	20.841	2.083	1.366	.873	1.253	.656	.419	.301	4.686	54.283	709
	2E	.000	14.428	2.083	.965	.650	.933	.463	.312	.224	3.306	28.455	250,986
	8S	.832	6.272	2.082	.479	.350	.500	.230	.168	.120	1.628	9.059	131,072
	8R	.843	6.171	2.066	.486	.352	.500	.235	.170	.121	1.805	9.873	65,536
	16S	1.142	4.434	2.083	.339	.253	.363	.163	.122	.087	1.147	5.934	65,536
	16R	1.143	4.406	2.049	.353	.264	.371	.172	.129	.091	1.375	6.520	32,768
	32S	1.316	3.533	2.082	.236	.182	.260	.114	.087	.062	.762	4.204	32,768
	32R	1.381	3.261	2.048	.258	.203	.279	.126	.099	.068	.963	4.196	16,384
	128S	1.720	2.525	2.085	.108	.086	.122	.052	.041	.029	.272	3.031	16,384

TABLE A1, CONTINUED

FREQUENCY DISTRIBUTIONS OF WEALTH RATIOS FROM INVESTMENTS IN RANDOMLY SELECTED PORTFOLIOS
CONTAINING SPECIFIED NUMBERS OF STOCKS LISTED ON THE NYSE, 1926-65

Number and Length of Periods	Size of Portfolio/ Sampling Method	Centiles of the Frequency Distributions										
		5th	10th	20th	30th	40th	(Median) 50th	60th	70th	80th	90th	95th
(1)	(2)	(3)	(4)	(5)	(6)	(7)	(8)	(9)	(10)	(11)	(12)	(13)
					ONE-YEAR PERIODS (CONTINUED)							
12/33-12/34	1E	.566	.645	.759	.849	.938	1.029	1.134	1.262	1.428	1.728	2.017
	2E	.690	.760	.855	.930	1.001	1.072	1.150	1.242	1.362	1.558	1.761
	8S	.883	.927	.986	1.031	1.072	1.111	1.155	1.204	1.266	1.364	1.462
	8R	.893	.937	.994	1.039	1.078	1.119	1.161	1.210	1.272	1.372	1.469
	16S	.947	.983	1.027	1.061	1.092	1.122	1.154	1.189	1.234	1.302	1.376
	16R	.967	1.002	1.045	1.078	1.107	1.137	1.167	1.202	1.246	1.314	1.388
	32S	.998	1.024	1.059	1.084	1.105	1.127	1.149	1.176	1.209	1.262	1.324
	32R	1.024	1.050	1.080	1.104	1.125	1.145	1.166	1.189	1.219	1.263	1.312
	128S	1.068	1.082	1.100	1.113	1.125	1.136	1.148	1.161	1.178	1.201	1.220
12/34-12/35	1E	.761	.864	1.029	1.134	1.232	1.353	1.492	1.656	1.927	2.342	2.747
	2E	.907	1.007	1.132	1.230	1.323	1.421	1.532	1.663	1.829	2.117	2.394
	8S	1.163	1.226	1.308	1.370	1.426	1.483	1.542	1.610	1.694	1.824	1.939
	8R	1.169	1.232	1.313	1.375	1.432	1.488	1.546	1.614	1.697	1.825	1.943
	16S	1.254	1.303	1.365	1.411	1.453	1.494	1.537	1.584	1.641	1.726	1.801
	16R	1.269	1.316	1.377	1.423	1.465	1.505	1.546	1.593	1.650	1.735	1.808
	32S	1.327	1.361	1.407	1.441	1.471	1.500	1.529	1.561	1.600	1.658	1.705
	32R	1.350	1.384	1.429	1.462	1.490	1.517	1.546	1.577	1.615	1.670	1.717
	128S	1.420	1.437	1.460	1.477	1.492	1.506	1.519	1.534	1.552	1.577	1.598
12/35-12/36	1E	.854	.943	1.052	1.154	1.235	1.334	1.446	1.583	1.773	2.130	2.461
	2E	.979	1.054	1.152	1.231	1.307	1.385	1.473	1.580	1.722	1.975	2.252
	8S	1.181	1.231	1.296	1.348	1.395	1.442	1.491	1.550	1.624	1.740	1.854
	8R	1.182	1.231	1.295	1.346	1.392	1.439	1.489	1.545	1.619	1.735	1.849
	16S	1.257	1.296	1.346	1.385	1.420	1.455	1.491	1.533	1.586	1.670	1.759
	16R	1.254	1.293	1.344	1.382	1.417	1.450	1.486	1.528	1.580	1.662	1.748
	32S	1.312	1.341	1.380	1.409	1.435	1.460	1.487	1.517	1.555	1.619	1.723
	32R	1.321	1.351	1.386	1.414	1.440	1.464	1.488	1.517	1.552	1.605	1.665
	128S	1.391	1.408	1.429	1.444	1.458	1.473	1.489	1.508	1.536	1.582	1.613
12/36-12/37	1E	.276	.315	.373	.420	.472	.517	.562	.624	.687	.798	.888
	2E	.338	.374	.423	.461	.495	.528	.563	.602	.650	.721	.786
	8S	.434	.455	.482	.502	.520	.537	.555	.574	.597	.631	.659
	8R	.434	.455	.482	.502	.519	.536	.554	.572	.595	.628	.656
	16S	.463	.480	.500	.514	.527	.539	.551	.565	.581	.604	.623
	16R	.464	.480	.498	.513	.525	.536	.549	.562	.577	.599	.618
	32S	.486	.498	.512	.522	.532	.540	.549	.558	.569	.585	.597
	32R	.478	.489	.502	.512	.521	.528	.537	.545	.556	.570	.582
	128S	.514	.521	.527	.532	.537	.541	.545	.549	.554	.561	.568
12/37-12/38	1E	.693	.838	.986	1.090	1.186	1.260	1.350	1.458	1.594	1.798	2.020
	2E	.849	.950	1.065	1.144	1.212	1.277	1.345	1.422	1.517	1.661	1.802
	8S	1.067	1.115	1.174	1.218	1.255	1.291	1.328	1.368	1.419	1.496	1.576
	8R	1.068	1.115	1.172	1.215	1.252	1.287	1.323	1.364	1.413	1.490	1.575
	16S	1.134	1.168	1.210	1.242	1.269	1.295	1.322	1.352	1.389	1.449	1.523
	16R	1.128	1.162	1.205	1.234	1.261	1.286	1.314	1.344	1.383	1.452	1.557
	32S	1.181	1.206	1.236	1.259	1.279	1.299	1.319	1.341	1.370	1.416	1.466
	32R	1.184	1.209	1.240	1.262	1.283	1.302	1.325	1.352	1.391	1.459	1.507
	128S	1.243	1.256	1.272	1.284	1.294	1.304	1.314	1.326	1.339	1.359	1.376
12/38-12/39	1E	.554	.626	.704	.790	.869	.947	1.021	1.089	1.183	1.319	1.478
	2E	.648	.709	.789	.848	.899	.948	.999	1.056	1.125	1.234	1.351
	8S	.798	.832	.874	.906	.934	.960	.988	1.018	1.055	1.111	1.160
	8R	.801	.835	.877	.909	.936	.963	.990	1.022	1.059	1.114	1.164
	16S	.846	.871	.902	.924	.944	.964	.983	1.005	1.030	1.068	1.101
	16R	.852	.877	.907	.931	.951	.970	.990	1.013	1.039	1.078	1.111
	32S	.881	.898	.921	.937	.951	.965	.979	.994	1.011	1.037	1.059
	32R	.905	.924	.947	.964	.979	.993	1.008	1.023	1.042	1.067	1.089
	128S	.925	.934	.946	.954	.961	.967	.974	.980	.989	1.000	1.010
12/39-12/40	1E	.477	.584	.713	.795	.852	.904	.952	1.005	1.069	1.194	1.331
	2E	.597	.672	.755	.811	.858	.899	.939	.982	1.036	1.122	1.204
	8S	.748	.782	.822	.851	.876	.899	.922	.947	.977	1.023	1.064
	8R	.751	.783	.822	.850	.875	.897	.920	.945	.977	1.024	1.069
	16S	.792	.816	.844	.865	.883	.899	.916	.934	.956	.988	1.017
	16R	.796	.819	.846	.866	.884	.901	.918	.937	.960	.993	1.022
	32S	.825	.841	.861	.876	.888	.900	.912	.925	.940	.963	.982
	32R	.837	.854	.874	.889	.902	.914	.927	.940	.957	.979	.999
	128S	.864	.872	.882	.889	.896	.902	.907	.914	.921	.930	.939
12/40-12/41	1E	.445	.545	.666	.751	.820	.879	.947	1.016	1.096	1.234	1.412
	2E	.572	.642	.726	.785	.836	.883	.931	.985	1.051	1.159	1.277
	8S	.729	.764	.807	.838	.866	.891	.918	.948	.984	1.039	1.089
	8R	.730	.766	.808	.839	.866	.893	.919	.948	.985	1.041	1.088
	16S	.777	.802	.833	.856	.875	.894	.914	.935	.960	.998	1.029
	16R	.778	.803	.833	.855	.875	.894	.913	.935	.959	.996	1.027
	32S	.811	.829	.852	.868	.882	.896	.910	.925	.943	.968	.989
	32R	.819	.836	.858	.873	.887	.900	.914	.928	.945	.969	.989
	128S	.856	.865	.876	.884	.891	.898	.904	.911	.920	.932	.941

Number and Length of Periods	Size of Portfolio and Sampling Method	Sample Minimum	Sample Maximum	Arithmetic Mean	Standard Deviation	Mean Deviation	Gini's Mean Difference	Coefficient of Variation	Relative Mean Deviation	Coefficient of Concentration	Skewness	Kurtosis	Number of Portfolios Examined
(14)	(15)	(16)	(17)	(18)	(19)	(20)	(21)	(22)	(23)	(24)	(25)	(26)	(27)

ONE-YEAR PERIODS (CONTINUED)

12/33–12/34	1E	.090	9.481	1.139	.574	.364	.517	.504	.319	.227	5.358	67.343	707
	2E	.154	6.789	1.139	.406	.269	.384	.356	.236	.169	3.780	34.938	249,571
	8S	.626	2.975	1.139	.202	.144	.207	.178	.127	.091	1.874	10.659	131,072
	8R	.627	2.609	1.147	.201	.143	.206	.176	.125	.090	1.866	10.388	65,536
	16S	.744	2.046	1.139	.142	.105	.150	.124	.092	.066	1.258	6.423	65,536
	16R	.721	2.093	1.154	.139	.102	.148	.121	.088	.064	1.293	6.465	32,768
	32S	.856	1.689	1.138	.100	.076	.109	.087	.067	.048	.871	4.473	32,768
	32R	.899	1.642	1.153	.089	.068	.098	.078	.059	.042	.783	4.378	16,384
	128S	.974	1.326	1.139	.046	.037	.052	.040	.032	.023	.302	3.020	16,384
12/34–12/35	1E	.000	6.077	1.507	.675	.485	.687	.448	.322	.228	1.830	9.327	706
	2E	.000	5.683	1.507	.477	.359	.508	.317	.238	.168	1.291	6.137	248,865
	8S	.768	3.035	1.508	.238	.187	.265	.158	.124	.088	.630	3.710	131,072
	8R	.716	3.008	1.512	.237	.186	.263	.157	.123	.087	.640	3.738	65,536
	16S	.946	2.433	1.507	.167	.132	.187	.111	.088	.062	.452	3.390	65,536
	16R	.970	2.499	1.517	.165	.130	.185	.109	.086	.061	.446	3.362	32,768
	32S	1.109	2.103	1.505	.116	.092	.130	.077	.061	.043	.310	3.173	32,768
	32R	1.180	2.020	1.523	.112	.089	.126	.074	.059	.041	.320	3.189	16,384
	128S	1.332	1.731	1.507	.054	.043	.061	.036	.029	.020	.162	2.994	16,384
12/35–12/36	1E	.178	17.234	1.483	.814	.424	.605	.549	.286	.204	10.719	197.482	719
	2E	.186	11.272	1.483	.575	.321	.460	.388	.217	.155	7.563	99.551	258,121
	8S	.853	4.318	1.483	.285	.178	.257	.192	.120	.087	3.723	26.133	131,072
	8R	.869	4.095	1.481	.285	.177	.256	.192	.120	.086	3.777	26.489	65,536
	16S	1.004	3.005	1.485	.204	.133	.194	.137	.089	.065	2.629	13.936	65,536
	16R	1.010	2.834	1.479	.195	.130	.187	.132	.088	.063	2.585	14.164	32,768
	32S	1.138	2.299	1.481	.140	.098	.141	.095	.066	.048	1.787	7.928	32,768
	32R	1.140	2.265	1.478	.122	.087	.125	.082	.059	.042	1.665	8.485	16,384
	128S	1.298	1.748	1.484	.066	.052	.074	.045	.035	.025	.672	3.202	16,384
12/36–12/37	1E	.109	1.372	.541	.195	.153	.215	.360	.283	.199	.815	4.073	744
	2E	.123	1.345	.541	.138	.109	.154	.254	.201	.142	.575	3.529	276,396
	8S	.276	.867	.541	.069	.055	.077	.127	.101	.071	.294	3.134	131,072
	8R	.314	.893	.540	.068	.054	.076	.125	.100	.070	.284	3.126	65,536
	16S	.350	.762	.541	.048	.039	.055	.090	.071	.050	.193	3.044	65,536
	16R	.368	.786	.538	.047	.037	.053	.087	.069	.049	.204	3.069	32,768
	32S	.414	.690	.541	.034	.027	.038	.062	.050	.035	.131	3.009	32,768
	32R	.419	.666	.529	.031	.027	.035	.059	.051	.033	.124	3.038	16,384
	128S	.482	.608	.541	.016	.012	.018	.029	.023	.016	.075	3.006	16,384
12/37–12/38	1E	.000	7.187	1.307	.497	.320	.469	.380	.245	.179	3.998	44.628	780
	2E	.073	6.919	1.307	.351	.236	.344	.269	.181	.132	2.822	23.675	303,810
	8S	.716	3.008	1.307	.175	.126	.183	.134	.097	.070	1.397	7.977	131,072
	8R	.731	2.776	1.305	.176	.126	.183	.135	.097	.070	1.517	8.203	65,536
	16S	.910	2.219	1.307	.123	.092	.132	.094	.070	.051	.979	5.385	65,536
	16R	.863	2.145	1.303	.129	.096	.137	.099	.073	.053	1.179	5.657	32,768
	32S	1.009	1.801	1.307	.086	.066	.095	.066	.051	.036	.636	3.950	32,768
	32R	1.020	1.832	1.318	.098	.074	.107	.074	.056	.041	.822	3.857	16,384
	128S	1.152	1.465	1.306	.040	.032	.045	.031	.024	.017	.279	3.136	16,384
12/38–12/39	1E	.000	2.830	.967	.313	.234	.334	.324	.242	.173	1.140	6.735	775
	2E	.098	2.623	.967	.221	.168	.241	.229	.174	.125	.805	4.852	299,925
	8S	.564	1.553	.967	.110	.087	.123	.114	.090	.064	.390	3.412	131,072
	8R	.561	1.654	.970	.111	.087	.124	.114	.090	.064	.401	3.420	65,536
	16S	.681	1.329	.967	.077	.061	.087	.080	.064	.045	.259	3.172	65,536
	16R	.672	1.391	.974	.079	.063	.089	.081	.064	.045	.285	3.194	32,768
	32S	.742	1.229	.967	.054	.043	.061	.056	.045	.032	.201	3.105	32,768
	32R	.773	1.239	.995	.056	.049	.063	.056	.050	.032	.128	2.969	16,384
	128S	.870	1.089	.967	.025	.020	.029	.026	.021	.015	.069	2.986	16,384
12/39–12/40	1E	.000	2.748	.901	.276	.195	.288	.306	.216	.160	.823	8.584	778
	2E	.000	2.559	.901	.195	.144	.210	.216	.160	.117	.581	5.770	302,253
	8S	.509	1.484	.901	.097	.076	.108	.108	.084	.060	.288	3.650	131,072
	8R	.524	1.446	.901	.097	.076	.108	.108	.084	.060	.361	3.681	65,536
	16S	.572	1.246	.901	.068	.054	.076	.076	.060	.042	.184	3.312	65,536
	16R	.615	1.235	.904	.069	.054	.077	.076	.060	.043	.256	3.286	32,768
	32S	.710	1.116	.901	.048	.038	.054	.053	.042	.030	.147	3.178	32,768
	32R	.749	1.121	.916	.049	.040	.055	.054	.044	.030	.171	3.088	16,384
	128S	.814	.992	.902	.022	.018	.025	.025	.020	.014	.041	2.994	16,384
12/40–12/41	1E	.000	2.941	.898	.312	.227	.330	.348	.253	.184	1.101	7.515	788
	2E	.000	2.689	.898	.221	.166	.239	.246	.184	.133	.777	5.239	310,078
	8S	.450	1.493	.898	.110	.086	.122	.122	.096	.068	.386	3.537	131,072
	8R	.452	1.560	.898	.109	.085	.122	.121	.095	.068	.365	3.505	65,536
	16S	.616	1.306	.898	.077	.061	.087	.086	.068	.048	.263	3.253	65,536
	16R	.635	1.259	.897	.076	.060	.085	.085	.067	.048	.253	3.176	32,768
	32S	.669	1.160	.898	.054	.043	.061	.060	.048	.034	.182	3.049	32,768
	32R	.707	1.132	.902	.052	.041	.058	.057	.046	.032	.150	3.054	16,384
	128S	.801	.992	.898	.026	.020	.029	.028	.023	.016	.085	2.959	16,384

TABLE A1, CONTINUED

FREQUENCY DISTRIBUTIONS OF WEALTH RATIOS FROM INVESTMENTS IN RANDOMLY SELECTED PORTFOLIOS
CONTAINING SPECIFIED NUMBERS OF STOCKS LISTED ON THE NYSE, 1926-65

Number and Length of Periods	Size of Portfolio/ Sampling Method	Centiles of the Frequency Distributions										
		5th	10th	20th	30th	40th	(Median) 50th	60th	70th	80th	90th	95th
(1)	(2)	(3)	(4)	(5)	(6)	(7)	(8)	(9)	(10)	(11)	(12)	(13)

ONE-YEAR PERIODS (CONTINUED)

Number and Length of Periods	Size of Portfolio/ Sampling Method	5th	10th	20th	30th	40th	50th	60th	70th	80th	90th	95th
12/41-12/42	1E	.844	.907	.986	1.054	1.120	1.190	1.273	1.380	1.527	1.766	2.106
	2E	.940	.990	1.060	1.119	1.175	1.234	1.299	1.376	1.484	1.686	1.965
	8S	1.085	1.122	1.169	1.207	1.243	1.279	1.320	1.368	1.436	1.549	1.653
	8R	1.098	1.135	1.184	1.223	1.259	1.295	1.335	1.385	1.453	1.563	1.664
	16S	1.141	1.170	1.208	1.238	1.266	1.294	1.325	1.360	1.407	1.479	1.543
	16R	1.170	1.200	1.240	1.271	1.299	1.327	1.359	1.395	1.441	1.511	1.575
	32S	1.184	1.207	1.238	1.260	1.282	1.303	1.325	1.351	1.382	1.428	1.468
	32R	1.239	1.264	1.295	1.319	1.338	1.359	1.380	1.405	1.434	1.477	1.516
	128S	1.247	1.260	1.276	1.289	1.300	1.310	1.320	1.332	1.346	1.364	1.380
12/42-12/43	1E	1.032	1.088	1.195	1.249	1.331	1.403	1.499	1.624	1.812	2.130	2.560
	2E	1.123	1.182	1.260	1.325	1.389	1.457	1.536	1.634	1.770	2.025	2.327
	8S	1.287	1.330	1.387	1.433	1.476	1.520	1.569	1.627	1.707	1.852	2.022
	8R	1.301	1.342	1.398	1.444	1.486	1.531	1.581	1.639	1.719	1.868	2.037
	16S	1.352	1.386	1.432	1.468	1.503	1.537	1.574	1.619	1.680	1.779	1.872
	16R	1.378	1.413	1.459	1.496	1.532	1.566	1.604	1.651	1.715	1.817	1.906
	32S	1.404	1.433	1.469	1.498	1.524	1.551	1.578	1.611	1.652	1.715	1.769
	32R	1.454	1.482	1.519	1.547	1.575	1.602	1.632	1.666	1.708	1.769	1.826
	128S	1.483	1.499	1.519	1.534	1.548	1.561	1.575	1.589	1.607	1.632	1.653
12/43-12/44	1E	1.029	1.088	1.151	1.202	1.245	1.304	1.372	1.447	1.556	1.750	2.025
	2E	1.097	1.143	1.200	1.246	1.289	1.334	1.383	1.442	1.526	1.684	1.853
	8S	1.212	1.242	1.282	1.312	1.339	1.367	1.397	1.432	1.477	1.548	1.613
	8R	1.215	1.245	1.284	1.313	1.340	1.367	1.396	1.429	1.472	1.538	1.599
	16S	1.255	1.279	1.309	1.333	1.353	1.374	1.396	1.421	1.453	1.500	1.542
	16R	1.262	1.284	1.313	1.335	1.355	1.374	1.394	1.417	1.446	1.488	1.527
	32S	1.290	1.308	1.331	1.348	1.364	1.378	1.394	1.411	1.432	1.462	1.488
	32R	1.303	1.321	1.341	1.356	1.370	1.385	1.399	1.414	1.433	1.460	1.484
	128S	1.336	1.346	1.359	1.368	1.375	1.382	1.390	1.398	1.407	1.421	1.432
12/44-12/45	1E	1.179	1.238	1.316	1.372	1.427	1.500	1.578	1.672	1.805	2.074	2.329
	2E	1.264	1.312	1.377	1.430	1.482	1.535	1.596	1.670	1.772	1.941	2.122
	8S	1.397	1.432	1.476	1.511	1.543	1.575	1.609	1.650	1.704	1.795	1.882
	8R	1.401	1.435	1.480	1.516	1.549	1.582	1.617	1.657	1.712	1.804	1.894
	16S	1.447	1.475	1.510	1.537	1.562	1.586	1.613	1.642	1.680	1.738	1.789
	16R	1.457	1.486	1.521	1.549	1.573	1.600	1.627	1.657	1.694	1.752	1.803
	32S	1.490	1.510	1.536	1.557	1.575	1.593	1.611	1.632	1.659	1.697	1.729
	32R	1.513	1.533	1.560	1.581	1.598	1.617	1.635	1.656	1.679	1.714	1.746
	128S	1.544	1.555	1.569	1.580	1.589	1.597	1.606	1.616	1.627	1.643	1.657
12/45-12/46	1E	.529	.592	.698	.785	.847	.898	.944	1.002	1.083	1.187	1.308
	2E	.636	.692	.760	.810	.854	.895	.935	.980	1.034	1.115	1.190
	8S	.766	.794	.830	.855	.877	.898	.920	.943	.971	1.010	1.045
	8R	.772	.799	.832	.856	.878	.898	.919	.941	.968	1.007	1.041
	16S	.806	.826	.851	.869	.885	.900	.915	.931	.951	.978	1.002
	16R	.813	.832	.855	.871	.886	.900	.914	.930	.949	.975	.996
	32S	.833	.848	.866	.879	.891	.901	.912	.924	.937	.956	.973
	32R	.842	.854	.870	.882	.892	.901	.910	.920	.932	.949	.964
	128S	.870	.876	.885	.891	.896	.902	.907	.912	.918	.928	.935
12/46-12/47	1E	.617	.701	.795	.857	.910	.962	1.025	1.091	1.175	1.312	1.456
	2E	.727	.780	.845	.893	.935	.977	1.020	1.069	1.131	1.229	1.322
	8S	.853	.882	.917	.944	.967	.989	1.012	1.037	1.068	1.113	1.154
	8R	.852	.880	.915	.941	.964	.987	1.009	1.035	1.066	1.110	1.149
	16S	.894	.914	.940	.955	.976	.992	1.009	1.027	1.048	1.079	1.106
	16R	.890	.911	.936	.955	.972	.987	1.003	1.020	1.041	1.071	1.097
	32S	.922	.937	.955	.969	.981	.992	1.004	1.016	1.031	1.052	1.070
	32R	.920	.933	.950	.963	.974	.984	.995	1.006	1.019	1.038	1.054
	128S	.959	.966	.976	.983	.989	.994	1.000	1.006	1.013	1.023	1.030
12/47-12/48	1E	.600	.703	.798	.858	.916	.967	1.007	1.050	1.107	1.212	1.321
	2E	.715	.772	.840	.886	.924	.959	.994	1.032	1.079	1.156	1.238
	8S	.839	.865	.898	.922	.942	.962	.981	1.003	1.030	1.072	1.113
	8R	.842	.868	.900	.923	.943	.962	.981	1.003	1.029	1.072	1.113
	16S	.875	.894	.918	.935	.950	.964	.978	.994	1.014	1.045	1.076
	16R	.879	.898	.920	.937	.951	.965	.979	.995	1.014	1.044	1.074
	32S	.901	.915	.932	.944	.955	.966	.976	.988	1.002	1.026	1.049
	32R	.904	.917	.933	.944	.954	.964	.974	.985	.999	1.019	1.038
	128S	.934	.942	.951	.957	.963	.968	.974	.980	.987	.998	1.007
12/48-12/49	1E	.840	.906	.997	1.061	1.122	1.178	1.233	1.302	1.374	1.481	1.617
	2E	.930	.986	1.052	1.100	1.143	1.183	1.224	1.269	1.325	1.411	1.495
	8S	1.055	1.085	1.121	1.146	1.169	1.190	1.211	1.235	1.265	1.308	1.347
	8R	1.059	1.088	1.123	1.149	1.171	1.192	1.214	1.238	1.266	1.309	1.347
	16S	1.094	1.115	1.141	1.161	1.177	1.192	1.208	1.225	1.246	1.276	1.302
	16R	1.103	1.122	1.148	1.166	1.181	1.196	1.212	1.229	1.249	1.279	1.304
	32S	1.123	1.138	1.157	1.171	1.182	1.193	1.206	1.217	1.231	1.252	1.269
	32R	1.141	1.155	1.173	1.185	1.197	1.207	1.218	1.230	1.243	1.263	1.281
	128S	1.160	1.167	1.176	1.183	1.189	1.194	1.199	1.205	1.212	1.221	1.229

Number and Length of Periods	Size of Portfolio and Sampling Method	Sample Minimum	Sample Maximum	Arithmetic Mean	Standard Deviation	Mean Deviation	Gini's Mean Difference	Coefficient of Variation	Relative Mean Deviation	Coefficient of Concentration	Skewness	Kurtosis	Number of Portfolios Examined
(14)	(15)	(16)	(17)	(18)	(19)	(20)	(21)	(22)	(23)	(24)	(25)	(26)	(27)

ONE-YEAR PERIODS (CONTINUED)

Number and Length of Periods	Size	Min	Max	Arith Mean	Std Dev	Mean Dev	Gini	Coef Var	Rel Mean Dev	Coef Conc	Skewness	Kurtosis	No. Port.
12/41-12/42	1E	.560	5.907	1.311	.501	.320	.452	.382	.244	.172	3.358	21.015	797
	2E	.584	5.268	1.311	.354	.242	.344	.270	.184	.131	2.370	11.947	317,206
	8S	.883	2.496	1.312	.177	.135	.190	.135	.103	.073	1.148	4.989	131,072
	8R	.913	2.638	1.327	.176	.133	.191	.133	.100	.072	1.120	5.007	65,536
	16S	.985	2.155	1.312	.124	.097	.137	.095	.074	.052	.820	4.007	65,536
	16R	.979	2.148	1.344	.125	.098	.138	.093	.073	.051	.765	3.954	32,768
	32S	1.055	1.840	1.312	.087	.069	.097	.066	.053	.037	.570	3.458	32,768
	32R	1.112	1.778	1.366	.084	.078	.094	.062	.057	.034	.491	3.452	16,384
	128S	1.177	1.517	1.311	.040	.032	.046	.031	.025	.017	.211	2.995	16,384
12/42-12/43	1E	.293	7.469	1.564	.644	.389	.550	.412	.249	.176	4.134	30.193	800
	2E	.459	7.459	1.564	.455	.299	.424	.291	.191	.136	2.918	16.507	319,600
	8S	1.063	3.513	1.565	.228	.169	.240	.146	.108	.077	1.454	6.316	131,072
	8R	1.035	3.128	1.577	.228	.168	.240	.145	.106	.076	1.425	6.084	65,536
	16S	1.169	2.609	1.564	.161	.124	.175	.103	.079	.056	1.039	4.672	65,536
	16R	1.182	2.570	1.594	.163	.124	.178	.102	.078	.056	.946	4.202	32,768
	32S	1.258	2.158	1.564	.112	.088	.125	.072	.056	.040	.673	3.631	32,768
	32R	1.311	2.343	1.616	.114	.095	.127	.070	.059	.039	.630	3.482	16,384
	128S	1.378	1.792	1.564	.052	.041	.058	.033	.027	.019	.286	3.081	16,384
12/43-12/44	1E	.417	4.389	1.383	.353	.237	.339	.256	.171	.123	2.451	14.494	810
	2E	.417	3.850	1.383	.250	.178	.255	.181	.129	.092	1.730	8.708	327,645
	8S	.992	2.151	1.384	.125	.096	.137	.090	.070	.049	.854	4.337	131,072
	8R	.979	2.151	1.382	.119	.093	.131	.086	.067	.047	.783	4.185	65,536
	16S	1.091	1.955	1.383	.088	.069	.098	.064	.050	.035	.618	3.708	65,536
	16R	1.105	1.828	1.382	.081	.064	.090	.059	.046	.033	.524	3.497	32,768
	32S	1.186	1.681	1.383	.061	.048	.068	.044	.035	.025	.401	3.268	32,768
	32R	1.199	1.635	1.388	.055	.044	.062	.039	.032	.022	.335	3.078	16,384
	128S	1.284	1.497	1.383	.029	.023	.032	.021	.017	.012	.153	3.001	16,384
12/44-12/45	1E	.649	4.700	1.598	.422	.283	.400	.264	.177	.125	2.807	16.262	826
	2E	.691	4.606	1.598	.299	.212	.301	.187	.133	.094	1.982	9.587	340,725
	8S	1.170	2.581	1.597	.149	.114	.162	.093	.072	.051	.974	4.518	131,072
	8R	1.155	2.601	1.604	.150	.115	.164	.094	.072	.051	.934	4.343	65,536
	16S	1.275	2.205	1.598	.105	.082	.116	.065	.052	.036	.657	3.678	65,536
	16R	1.248	2.236	1.611	.106	.083	.118	.066	.052	.037	.622	3.587	32,768
	32S	1.369	2.005	1.599	.074	.058	.082	.046	.036	.026	.484	3.351	32,768
	32R	1.399	1.952	1.621	.071	.058	.080	.044	.036	.025	.395	3.176	16,384
	128S	1.478	1.770	1.598	.034	.027	.039	.021	.017	.012	.183	3.028	16,384
12/45-12/46	1E	.254	2.230	.901	.242	.184	.266	.268	.204	.147	.609	4.739	853
	2E	.271	2.113	.901	.171	.133	.190	.189	.148	.105	.430	3.861	363,378
	8S	.537	1.345	.901	.085	.067	.096	.094	.075	.053	.225	3.213	131,072
	8R	.604	1.329	.901	.082	.065	.092	.090	.072	.051	.227	3.164	65,536
	16S	.674	1.189	.901	.059	.047	.067	.066	.052	.051	.227	3.106	65,536
	16R	.679	1.160	.902	.056	.044	.063	.062	.049	.035	.159	3.060	32,768
	32S	.740	1.078	.902	.042	.033	.047	.047	.037	.026	.159	3.028	32,768
	32R	.762	1.087	.902	.037	.029	.042	.041	.033	.023	.093	3.052	16,384
	128S	.830	.981	.902	.020	.016	.022	.022	.017	.012	.049	2.965	16,384
12/46-12/47	1E	.348	2.577	.994	.260	.195	.280	.262	.196	.141	1.031	5.812	904
	2E	.369	2.342	.994	.184	.142	.202	.185	.142	.102	.728	4.395	408,156
	8S	.663	1.592	.994	.092	.072	.103	.092	.073	.052	.374	3.364	131,072
	8R	.663	1.455	.992	.091	.072	.072	.102	.092	.073	.051	.342	3.287	65,536
	16S	.771	1.298	.995	.064	.051	.073	.065	.052	.036	.252	3.141	65,536
	16R	.767	1.297	.989	.063	.050	.070	.063	.051	.036	.213	3.102	32,768
	32S	.824	1.235	.994	.045	.036	.051	.045	.036	.026	.195	3.082	32,768
	32R	.831	1.174	.985	.041	.034	.046	.041	.034	.023	.155	3.006	16,384
	128S	.914	1.078	.994	.021	.017	.024	.022	.017	.012	.066	2.988	16,384
12/47-12/48	1E	.337	4.544	.969	.259	.169	.250	.268	.175	.129	3.571	44.575	939
	2E	.342	3.691	.969	.183	.126	.184	.189	.130	.095	2.521	23.673	440,391
	8S	.634	1.776	.969	.092	.067	.097	.094	.069	.050	1.258	8.080	131,072
	8R	.594	1.675	.969	.090	.066	.095	.093	.068	.049	1.280	8.075	65,536
	16S	.738	1.411	.969	.064	.048	.070	.067	.050	.036	.913	5.552	65,536
	16R	.749	1.400	.970	.062	.047	.067	.064	.048	.035	.817	5.088	32,768
	32S	.801	1.202	.969	.045	.035	.050	.047	.036	.026	.607	4.046	32,768
	32R	.815	1.194	.967	.041	.032	.046	.043	.033	.024	.484	3.737	16,384
	128S	.898	1.061	.969	.022	.017	.024	.022	.018	.013	.252	3.073	16,384
12/48-12/49	1E	.095	2.885	1.194	.254	.189	.271	.213	.158	.114	.967	7.704	963
	2E	.236	2.845	1.194	.180	.136	.196	.150	.114	.082	.683	5.337	463,203
	8S	.807	1.737	1.194	.089	.070	.099	.075	.059	.042	.345	3.572	131,072
	8R	.851	1.666	1.196	.088	.069	.099	.074	.058	.041	.329	3.535	65,536
	16S	.947	1.539	1.194	.063	.050	.071	.053	.042	.030	.231	3.281	65,536
	16R	.966	1.524	1.199	.062	.049	.069	.051	.041	.029	.285	3.395	32,768
	32S	1.033	1.391	1.194	.044	.035	.050	.037	.029	.021	.170	3.082	32,768
	32R	1.054	1.413	1.208	.042	.035	.047	.035	.029	.020	.209	3.137	16,384
	128S	1.115	1.270	1.194	.021	.017	.023	.017	.014	.010	.046	3.016	16,384

TABLE A1, CONTINUED

FREQUENCY DISTRIBUTIONS OF WEALTH RATIOS FROM INVESTMENTS IN RANDOMLY SELECTED PORTFOLIOS
CONTAINING SPECIFIED NUMBERS OF STOCKS LISTED ON THE NYSE, 1926-65

Number and Length of Periods	Size of Portfolio/ Sampling Method	Centiles of the Frequency Distributions										
		5th	10th	20th	30th	40th	(Median) 50th	60th	70th	80th	90th	95th
(1)	(2)	(3)	(4)	(5)	(6)	(7)	(8)	(9)	(10)	(11)	(12)	(13)

ONE-YEAR PERIODS (CONTINUED)

12/49-12/50	1E	.904	.965	1.047	1.123	1.207	1.298	1.384	1.487	1.614	1.817	2.015
	2E	1.000	1.057	1.138	1.203	1.263	1.322	1.385	1.457	1.548	1.694	1.836
	8S	1.161	1.198	1.246	1.283	1.315	1.347	1.380	1.417	1.463	1.532	1.595
	8R	1.163	1.200	1.246	1.281	1.312	1.342	1.373	1.408	1.452	1.516	1.576
	16S	1.215	1.243	1.278	1.305	1.329	1.352	1.376	1.403	1.435	1.481	1.523
	16R	1.212	1.238	1.272	1.296	1.317	1.338	1.359	1.382	1.410	1.452	1.489
	32S	1.256	1.276	1.302	1.322	1.338	1.355	1.371	1.390	1.413	1.444	1.471
	32R	1.238	1.255	1.278	1.294	1.309	1.322	1.336	1.351	1.368	1.394	1.416
	128S	1.308	1.319	1.332	1.342	1.350	1.358	1.366	1.375	1.385	1.399	1.412
12/50-12/51	1E	.832	.905	.981	1.039	1.081	1.122	1.172	1.228	1.294	1.419	1.554
	2E	.909	.963	1.022	1.064	1.100	1.134	1.170	1.211	1.264	1.348	1.426
	8S	1.022	1.049	1.081	1.104	1.124	1.143	1.163	1.185	1.211	1.252	1.289
	8R	1.023	1.049	1.080	1.103	1.123	1.142	1.161	1.183	1.209	1.248	1.283
	16S	1.057	1.076	1.099	1.116	1.131	1.145	1.159	1.175	1.194	1.223	1.250
	16R	1.058	1.076	1.097	1.114	1.128	1.142	1.156	1.171	1.189	1.216	1.239
	32S	1.083	1.097	1.113	1.125	1.136	1.147	1.157	1.168	1.182	1.203	1.221
	32R	1.080	1.093	1.109	1.119	1.129	1.138	1.147	1.157	1.169	1.186	1.199
	128S	1.116	1.123	1.132	1.138	1.143	1.148	1.153	1.159	1.166	1.175	1.184
12/51-12/52	1E	.771	.841	.920	.980	1.037	1.088	1.137	1.184	1.245	1.333	1.424
	2E	.864	.912	.971	1.014	1.050	1.085	1.120	1.158	1.203	1.269	1.329
	8S	.973	.999	1.029	1.051	1.070	1.088	1.106	1.125	1.148	1.180	1.208
	8R	.976	1.001	1.030	1.051	1.070	1.086	1.104	1.122	1.145	1.175	1.201
	16S	1.006	1.024	1.046	1.062	1.075	1.088	1.101	1.115	1.130	1.153	1.171
	16R	1.007	1.024	1.044	1.060	1.072	1.084	1.096	1.108	1.124	1.145	1.162
	32S	1.031	1.043	1.059	1.070	1.079	1.088	1.097	1.107	1.118	1.134	1.147
	32R	1.024	1.035	1.049	1.059	1.068	1.076	1.084	1.093	1.103	1.118	1.129
	128S	1.060	1.066	1.073	1.079	1.084	1.088	1.093	1.097	1.103	1.110	1.117
12/52-12/53	1E	.602	.704	.805	.864	.918	.969	1.021	1.064	1.112	1.221	1.320
	2E	.727	.781	.845	.891	.930	.965	1.000	1.038	1.083	1.154	1.220
	8S	.845	.872	.904	.928	.947	.965	.985	1.005	1.030	1.065	1.095
	8R	.848	.873	.905	.928	.947	.966	.984	1.005	1.029	1.065	1.095
	16S	.881	.900	.922	.939	.953	.967	.980	.995	1.012	1.037	1.057
	16R	.883	.902	.924	.940	.954	.967	.981	.996	1.013	1.037	1.057
	32S	.906	.920	.936	.948	.958	.967	.977	.987	.999	1.016	1.030
	32R	.918	.931	.946	.957	.967	.975	.984	.994	1.006	1.023	1.036
	128S	.939	.945	.953	.959	.964	.968	.973	.978	.984	.992	.999
12/53-12/54	1E	1.095	1.164	1.251	1.327	1.407	1.480	1.565	1.660	1.786	1.995	2.256
	2E	1.193	1.254	1.333	1.394	1.451	1.507	1.568	1.639	1.733	1.890	2.035
	8S	1.349	1.386	1.434	1.470	1.503	1.535	1.568	1.605	1.651	1.722	1.791
	8R	1.355	1.392	1.439	1.474	1.506	1.536	1.569	1.605	1.651	1.720	1.787
	16S	1.404	1.431	1.466	1.493	1.518	1.541	1.565	1.591	1.624	1.674	1.720
	16R	1.412	1.438	1.473	1.499	1.522	1.544	1.567	1.593	1.625	1.672	1.718
	32S	1.444	1.465	1.491	1.511	1.528	1.545	1.562	1.580	1.604	1.637	1.667
	32R	1.457	1.476	1.500	1.519	1.535	1.551	1.566	1.585	1.607	1.639	1.666
	128S	1.496	1.507	1.520	1.530	1.539	1.547	1.556	1.565	1.575	1.590	1.604
12/54-12/55	1E	.829	.924	1.003	1.049	1.093	1.144	1.193	1.261	1.354	1.516	1.687
	2E	.932	.983	1.042	1.084	1.123	1.161	1.204	1.256	1.323	1.432	1.544
	8S	1.047	1.075	1.110	1.136	1.159	1.182	1.205	1.232	1.266	1.315	1.358
	8R	1.047	1.075	1.108	1.134	1.156	1.179	1.203	1.229	1.262	1.311	1.354
	16S	1.086	1.107	1.133	1.153	1.170	1.186	1.203	1.222	1.244	1.278	1.305
	16R	1.082	1.103	1.128	1.148	1.165	1.181	1.198	1.217	1.239	1.272	1.301
	32S	1.115	1.130	1.149	1.163	1.176	1.187	1.199	1.212	1.228	1.250	1.269
	32R	1.112	1.128	1.147	1.161	1.173	1.185	1.19	1.210	1.225	1.249	1.267
	128S	1.153	1.161	1.170	1.177	1.183	1.189	1.195	1.201	1.209	1.219	1.228
12/55-12/56	1E	.711	.789	.880	.941	.989	1.026	1.082	1.141	1.236	1.378	1.518
	2E	.805	.859	.923	.968	1.007	1.045	1.087	1.136	1.197	1.290	1.376
	8S	.926	.954	.989	1.015	1.037	1.059	1.081	1.106	1.136	1.180	1.221
	8R	.924	.952	.987	1.012	1.034	1.054	1.076	1.100	1.128	1.171	1.211
	16S	.965	.986	1.011	1.030	1.046	1.061	1.077	1.094	1.116	1.147	1.177
	16R	.960	.980	1.004	1.022	1.037	1.051	1.066	1.083	1.101	1.130	1.155
	32S	.993	1.008	1.027	1.040	1.051	1.062	1.074	1.086	1.101	1.124	1.145
	32R	.985	.999	1.015	1.027	1.037	1.047	1.057	1.068	1.080	1.099	1.115
	128S	1.031	1.037	1.047	1.054	1.060	1.065	1.071	1.077	1.084	1.095	1.104
12/56-12/57	1E	.496	.567	.658	.721	.791	.856	.923	.996	1.060	1.149	1.228
	2E	.597	.652	.721	.773	.817	.859	.901	.947	1.001	1.075	1.139
	8S	.729	.757	.793	.819	.841	.862	.883	.906	.933	.973	1.008
	8R	.739	.765	.798	.822	.843	.863	.883	.906	.932	.971	1.005
	16S	.767	.788	.814	.832	.848	.863	.878	.894	.914	.941	.965
	16R	.780	.799	.822	.838	.853	.867	.881	.896	.915	.941	.965
	32S	.797	.811	.829	.842	.853	.864	.875	.886	.899	.919	.935
	32R	.816	.829	.845	.856	.866	.875	.885	.896	.908	.926	.940
	128S	.831	.839	.847	.853	.859	.864	.869	.875	.882	.891	.898

Number and Length of Periods	Size of Portfolio and Sampling Method	Sample Minimum	Sample Maximum	Arithmetic Mean	Standard Deviation	Mean Deviation	Gini's Mean Difference	Coefficient of Variation	Relative Mean Deviation	Coefficient of Concentration	Skewness	Kurtosis	Number of Portfolios Examined
(14)	(15)	(16)	(17)	(18)	(19)	(20)	(21)	(22)	(23)	(24)	(25)	(26)	(27)

ONE-YEAR PERIODS (CONTINUED)

Number and Length of Periods	Size	Sample Minimum	Sample Maximum	Arithmetic Mean	Standard Deviation	Mean Deviation	Gini's Mean Difference	Coeff. of Variation	Relative Mean Deviation	Coeff. of Concentration	Skewness	Kurtosis	Number Examined
12/49-12/50	1E	.645	3.917	1.358	.378	.283	.397	.279	.208	.146	1.622	8.628	990
	2E	.650	3.915	1.358	.267	.204	.289	.197	.150	.106	1.145	5.797	489,555
	8S	.936	2.186	1.358	.133	.105	.148	.098	.077	.055	.555	3.641	131,072
	8R	.909	2.041	1.352	.126	.100	.141	.093	.074	.052	.506	3.550	65,536
	16S	1.053	2.044	1.358	.094	.075	.106	.069	.055	.039	.401	3.376	65,536
	16R	1.028	1.765	1.343	.084	.068	.094	.062	.051	.035	.317	3.221	32,768
	32S	1.124	1.660	1.358	.066	.052	.074	.048	.039	.027	.283	3.153	32,768
	32R	1.128	1.555	1.324	.054	.052	.061	.041	.039	.023	.187	3.053	16,384
	128S	1.249	1.514	1.359	.031	.025	.035	.023	.018	.013	.130	3.030	16,384
12/50-12/51	1E	.135	4.047	1.149	.242	.168	.245	.211	.146	.107	2.249	24.699	1,010
	2E	.311	3.253	1.149	.171	.124	.179	.149	.108	.078	1.588	13.792	509,545
	8S	.780	1.765	1.148	.085	.065	.093	.074	.056	.040	.766	5.465	131,072
	8R	.826	1.815	1.147	.083	.064	.091	.072	.055	.040	.734	5.462	65,536
	16S	.892	1.574	1.149	.060	.046	.066	.052	.040	.029	.551	4.258	65,536
	16R	.962	1.496	1.145	.057	.044	.063	.049	.039	.027	.462	4.059	32,768
	32S	.984	1.415	1.149	.042	.033	.047	.037	.029	.020	.412	3.632	32,768
	32R	.996	1.335	1.139	.037	.030	.041	.032	.026	.018	.261	3.525	16,384
	128S	1.082	1.246	1.149	.020	.016	.023	.017	.014	.010	.182	3.075	16,384
12/51-12/52	1E	.113	1.866	1.089	.201	.157	.223	.185	.144	.103	.207	3.915	1,029
	2E	.291	1.832	1.089	.142	.112	.159	.131	.103	.073	.146	3.452	528,906
	8S	.737	1.401	1.089	.071	.057	.080	.065	.052	.037	.070	3.082	131,072
	8R	.769	1.416	1.087	.069	.054	.077	.063	.050	.036	.053	3.131	65,536
	16S	.884	1.334	1.088	.050	.040	.056	.046	.037	.026	.031	3.038	65,536
	16R	.912	1.285	1.084	.047	.038	.053	.043	.035	.024	.052	3.037	32,768
	32S	.952	1.261	1.088	.035	.028	.040	.032	.026	.018	.032	2.999	32,768
	32R	.938	1.211	1.076	.032	.027	.036	.029	.025	.017	.017	2.960	16,384
	128S	1.023	1.152	1.088	.017	.013	.019	.015	.012	.009	.039	2.994	16,384
12/52-12/53	1E	.000	2.135	.968	.215	.162	.234	.222	.168	.121	.389	4.939	1,044
	2E	.174	1.990	.968	.152	.117	.168	.157	.121	.087	.274	3.962	544,446
	8S	.662	1.384	.968	.076	.060	.085	.079	.062	.044	.150	3.237	131,072
	8R	.650	1.382	.968	.075	.059	.084	.078	.061	.044	.170	3.225	65,536
	16S	.755	1.195	.967	.054	.043	.060	.055	.044	.031	.094	3.061	65,536
	16R	.776	1.234	.969	.053	.042	.060	.055	.044	.031	.117	3.078	32,768
	32S	.816	1.124	.968	.037	.030	.042	.039	.031	.022	.071	3.069	32,768
	32R	.848	1.122	.976	.036	.029	.040	.037	.030	.021	.123	3.086	16,384
	128S	.903	1.049	.968	.018	.014	.020	.018	.015	.010	.031	3.022	16,384
12/53-12/54	1E	.608	5.441	1.548	.392	.279	.397	.253	.180	.128	2.205	15.744	1,045
	2E	.659	4.841	1.548	.277	.204	.291	.179	.132	.094	1.557	9.338	545,490
	8S	1.078	2.485	1.548	.138	.106	.151	.089	.069	.049	.770	4.508	131,072
	8R	1.098	2.462	1.550	.136	.104	.149	.088	.067	.048	.842	4.884	65,536
	16S	1.238	2.120	1.548	.097	.076	.108	.063	.049	.035	.557	3.786	65,536
	16R	1.267	2.061	1.552	.094	.073	.105	.061	.047	.034	.595	3.913	32,768
	32S	1.341	1.989	1.548	.068	.054	.076	.044	.035	.025	.368	3.333	32,768
	32R	1.326	1.930	1.555	.065	.051	.072	.042	.033	.023	.424	3.488	16,384
	128S	1.427	1.699	1.548	.032	.026	.037	.021	.017	.012	.172	3.096	16,384
12/54-12/55	1E	.163	2.886	1.190	.270	.194	.280	.227	.163	.118	1.391	7.370	1,052
	2E	.357	2.747	1.190	.191	.144	.206	.160	.121	.086	.982	5.172	552,826
	8S	.830	1.731	1.190	.095	.075	.106	.080	.063	.045	.481	3.485	131,072
	8R	.842	1.757	1.187	.094	.074	.105	.079	.063	.044	.490	3.536	65,536
	16S	.946	1.577	1.190	.067	.053	.075	.056	.045	.032	.332	3.263	65,536
	16R	.962	1.520	1.185	.067	.053	.075	.056	.045	.032	.328	3.221	32,768
	32S	1.026	1.415	1.189	.047	.037	.053	.039	.031	.022	.239	3.139	32,768
	32R	1.032	1.404	1.187	.047	.038	.053	.040	.032	.022	.208	3.098	16,384
	128S	1.105	1.290	1.190	.022	.018	.025	.019	.015	.011	.094	2.973	16,384
12/55-12/56	1E	.142	4.282	1.065	.268	.188	.273	.251	.176	.128	2.342	24.249	1,055
	2E	.221	3.510	1.065	.189	.138	.199	.178	.130	.093	1.654	13.570	555,985
	8S	.709	1.852	1.065	.094	.072	.103	.089	.068	.048	.796	5.413	131,072
	8R	.741	1.730	1.060	.091	.070	.099	.086	.066	.047	.738	5.372	65,536
	16S	.769	1.452	1.065	.066	.051	.073	.062	.048	.034	.581	4.296	65,536
	16R	.807	1.398	1.054	.060	.049	.067	.057	.046	.032	.409	3.966	32,768
	32S	.902	1.303	1.065	.046	.036	.051	.043	.034	.024	.371	3.535	32,768
	32R	.902	1.271	1.048	.040	.035	.044	.038	.033	.021	.253	3.420	16,384
	128S	.975	1.171	1.066	.022	.018	.025	.021	.016	.012	.152	3.096	16,384
12/56-12/57	1E	.268	2.266	.864	.242	.191	.268	.280	.221	.155	.638	5.395	1,056
	2E	.274	2.242	.864	.171	.134	.190	.198	.155	.110	.451	4.189	557,040
	8S	.534	1.313	.864	.085	.067	.095	.098	.078	.055	.226	3.297	131,072
	8R	.563	1.379	.866	.081	.064	.091	.094	.074	.053	.277	3.391	65,536
	16S	.637	1.179	.864	.060	.048	.068	.069	.055	.039	.158	3.161	65,536
	16R	.658	1.137	.869	.056	.044	.063	.065	.051	.036	.227	3.197	32,768
	32S	.697	1.050	.865	.042	.033	.047	.049	.039	.027	.114	3.073	32,768
	32R	.761	1.027	.877	.038	.031	.042	.043	.036	.024	.167	2.990	16,384
	128S	.777	.957	.864	.020	.016	.023	.023	.019	.013	.037	3.013	16,384

TABLE A1, CONTINUED

FREQUENCY DISTRIBUTIONS OF WEALTH RATIOS FROM INVESTMENTS IN RANDOMLY SELECTED PORTFOLIOS
CONTAINING SPECIFIED NUMBERS OF STOCKS LISTED ON THE NYSE, 1926-65

Number and Length of Periods	Size of Portfolio/ Sampling Method	Centiles of the Frequency Distributions										
		5th	10th	20th	30th	40th	(Median) 50th	60th	70th	80th	90th	95th
(1)	(2)	(3)	(4)	(5)	(6)	(7)	(8)	(9)	(10)	(11)	(12)	(13)
		ONE-YEAR PERIODS (CONTINUED)										
12/57-12/58	1E	1.112	1.199	1.294	1.363	1.434	1.491	1.552	1.647	1.780	2.001	2.326
	2E	1.223	1.282	1.357	1.413	1.464	1.517	1.575	1.646	1.744	1.922	2.145
	8S	1.373	1.407	1.453	1.488	1.521	1.554	1.590	1.633	1.690	1.786	1.875
	8R	1.373	1.409	1.456	1.491	1.523	1.556	1.591	1.634	1.691	1.785	1.873
	16S	1.423	1.450	1.486	1.514	1.539	1.565	1.592	1.623	1.664	1.724	1.778
	16R	1.428	1.455	1.491	1.518	1.544	1.569	1.595	1.627	1.665	1.723	1.776
	32S	1.464	1.485	1.513	1.534	1.553	1.572	1.592	1.614	1.641	1.680	1.716
	32R	1.470	1.490	1.516	1.536	1.553	1.570	1.589	1.609	1.634	1.669	1.699
	128S	1.520	1.532	1.547	1.558	1.568	1.577	1.586	1.597	1.609	1.626	1.641
12/58-12/59	1E	.759	.845	.934	.988	1.028	1.080	1.149	1.214	1.323	1.527	1.715
	2E	.862	.914	.977	1.022	1.064	1.107	1.155	1.213	1.290	1.418	1.552
	8S	.986	1.016	1.053	1.082	1.107	1.133	1.160	1.191	1.230	1.289	1.342
	8R	.989	1.018	1.054	1.083	1.109	1.134	1.161	1.191	1.230	1.290	1.342
	16S	1.030	1.051	1.079	1.101	1.120	1.139	1.158	1.180	1.207	1.246	1.279
	16R	1.031	1.053	1.082	1.103	1.122	1.140	1.159	1.181	1.207	1.245	1.279
	32S	1.060	1.077	1.099	1.115	1.128	1.142	1.156	1.171	1.189	1.215	1.239
	32R	1.068	1.084	1.104	1.120	1.133	1.145	1.158	1.171	1.189	1.213	1.235
	128S	1.102	1.111	1.122	1.130	1.136	1.143	1.150	1.157	1.166	1.178	1.187
12/59-12/60	1E	.591	.652	.749	.825	.887	.948	1.022	1.100	1.196	1.325	1.447
	2E	.692	.746	.816	.870	.919	.965	1.013	1.067	1.132	1.229	1.319
	8S	.828	.859	.897	.926	.951	.976	1.000	1.027	1.059	1.107	1.148
	8R	.835	.864	.901	.929	.953	.976	1.000	1.025	1.057	1.103	1.143
	16S	.871	.894	.923	.943	.961	.978	.996	1.015	1.038	1.071	1.099
	16R	.878	.900	.927	.946	.963	.979	.996	1.014	1.036	1.069	1.095
	32S	.902	.919	.940	.955	.968	.980	.992	1.005	1.021	1.043	1.062
	32R	.918	.934	.953	.967	.980	.992	1.003	1.016	1.031	1.052	1.070
	128S	.943	.951	.961	.968	.975	.981	.987	.993	1.000	1.010	1.019
12/60-12/61	1E	.852	.935	1.037	1.114	1.176	1.235	1.301	1.373	1.460	1.621	1.818
	2E	.964	1.025	1.099	1.154	1.201	1.247	1.296	1.352	1.424	1.547	1.685
	8S	1.106	1.140	1.181	1.211	1.238	1.265	1.292	1.324	1.364	1.426	1.485
	8R	1.110	1.143	1.185	1.215	1.243	1.270	1.298	1.330	1.370	1.435	1.495
	16S	1.152	1.176	1.207	1.230	1.250	1.269	1.290	1.313	1.341	1.384	1.422
	16R	1.162	1.187	1.219	1.242	1.263	1.283	1.304	1.327	1.357	1.400	1.440
	32S	1.186	1.204	1.227	1.244	1.259	1.273	1.288	1.304	1.323	1.351	1.376
	32R	1.214	1.232	1.255	1.273	1.288	1.303	1.318	1.334	1.355	1.384	1.411
	128S	1.231	1.241	1.252	1.261	1.268	1.275	1.282	1.289	1.298	1.311	1.322
12/61-12/62	1E	.544	.616	.696	.761	.813	.856	.909	.965	1.019	1.114	1.207
	2E	.634	.684	.745	.788	.825	.860	.896	.934	.980	1.048	1.110
	8S	.747	.773	.803	.826	.845	.863	.881	.901	.925	.958	.986
	8R	.748	.773	.803	.825	.844	.862	.880	.899	.923	.957	.985
	16S	.781	.800	.821	.837	.851	.864	.877	.891	.908	.931	.951
	16R	.779	.797	.819	.834	.848	.861	.874	.888	.905	.928	.947
	32S	.805	.818	.834	.845	.855	.864	.874	.883	.895	.912	.926
	32R	.802	.814	.829	.840	.850	.859	.868	.878	.889	.904	.917
	128S	.835	.842	.850	.855	.860	.864	.869	.874	.879	.887	.894
12/62-12/63	1E	.808	.894	.985	1.041	1.089	1.137	1.186	1.247	1.344	1.488	1.657
	2E	.902	.960	1.026	1.072	1.111	1.150	1.192	1.241	1.306	1.417	1.539
	8S	1.026	1.056	1.093	1.120	1.144	1.167	1.191	1.218	1.253	1.307	1.358
	8R	1.027	1.058	1.094	1.121	1.146	1.169	1.194	1.222	1.257	1.312	1.363
	16S	1.067	1.089	1.116	1.136	1.154	1.171	1.189	1.209	1.233	1.269	1.302
	16R	1.072	1.093	1.121	1.142	1.159	1.177	1.195	1.216	1.240	1.277	1.308
	32S	1.099	1.114	1.134	1.149	1.161	1.174	1.186	1.200	1.217	1.241	1.262
	32R	1.114	1.130	1.150	1.165	1.178	1.189	1.203	1.216	1.233	1.256	1.276
	128S	1.137	1.145	1.155	1.163	1.169	1.175	1.182	1.188	1.197	1.208	1.217
12/63-12/64	1E	.765	.875	.978	1.049	1.099	1.142	1.194	1.248	1.323	1.466	1.622
	2E	.883	.947	1.021	1.070	1.111	1.149	1.188	1.233	1.292	1.390	1.491
	8S	1.018	1.048	1.085	1.112	1.136	1.158	1.180	1.205	1.236	1.283	1.324
	8R	1.021	1.051	1.088	1.115	1.138	1.161	1.184	1.210	1.240	1.287	1.328
	16S	1.059	1.081	1.107	1.127	1.144	1.160	1.177	1.195	1.217	1.249	1.276
	16R	1.065	1.088	1.115	1.135	1.152	1.169	1.185	1.204	1.226	1.257	1.285
	32S	1.090	1.105	1.124	1.138	1.150	1.162	1.174	1.186	1.202	1.223	1.241
	32R	1.112	1.128	1.147	1.161	1.173	1.184	1.196	1.209	1.223	1.244	1.261
	128S	1.126	1.134	1.144	1.151	1.157	1.163	1.169	1.175	1.182	1.192	1.200
12/64-12/65	1E	.856	.923	.995	1.056	1.116	1.196	1.275	1.387	1.510	1.732	1.963
	2E	.937	.991	1.062	1.120	1.175	1.231	1.292	1.364	1.459	1.626	1.817
	8S	1.081	1.117	1.163	1.200	1.232	1.264	1.299	1.338	1.389	1.467	1.543
	8R	1.088	1.123	1.168	1.203	1.235	1.266	1.300	1.339	1.388	1.464	1.535
	16S	1.134	1.161	1.197	1.224	1.248	1.273	1.297	1.326	1.360	1.413	1.464
	16R	1.141	1.168	1.202	1.228	1.251	1.274	1.298	1.325	1.359	1.409	1.455
	32S	1.174	1.195	1.222	1.243	1.261	1.278	1.296	1.316	1.340	1.376	1.409
	32R	1.180	1.199	1.223	1.241	1.257	1.272	1.288	1.305	1.326	1.357	1.385
	128S	1.227	1.239	1.253	1.263	1.272	1.281	1.290	1.300	1.311	1.328	1.341

Number and Length of Periods	Size of Portfolio and Sampling Method	Sample Minimum	Sample Maximum	Arithmetic Mean	Standard Deviation	Mean Deviation	Gini's Mean Difference	Coefficient of Variation	Relative Mean Deviation	Coefficient of Concentration	Skewness	Kurtosis	Number of Portfolios Examined
(14)	(15)	(16)	(17)	(18)	(19)	(20)	(21)	(22)	(23)	(24)	(25)	(26)	(27)
						ONE-YEAR PERIODS (CONTINUED)							
12/57-12/58	1E	.803	5.077	1.579	.440	.285	.412	.279	.181	.131	2.873	16.763	1,077
	2E	.817	4.951	1.579	.311	.217	.311	.197	.137	.098	2.029	9.846	579,426
	8S	1.136	2.644	1.579	.155	.119	.168	.098	.075	.053	.983	4.532	131,072
	8R	1.157	2.580	1.580	.153	.118	.167	.097	.075	.053	.952	4.407	65,536
	16S	1.261	2.214	1.578	.109	.086	.121	.069	.054	.038	.713	3.851	65,536
	16R	1.247	2.141	1.581	.106	.084	.118	.067	.053	.037	.624	3.559	32,768
	32S	1.319	1.957	1.579	.077	.061	.086	.049	.039	.027	.493	3.347	32,768
	32R	1.356	1.870	1.576	.070	.056	.079	.045	.036	.025	.400	3.212	16,384
	128S	1.456	1.765	1.578	.037	.029	.041	.023	.018	.013	.211	3.100	16,384
12/58-12/59	1E	.428	3.372	1.144	.310	.219	.314	.271	.191	.137	1.824	9.521	1,067
	2E	.464	3.147	1.144	.219	.163	.232	.191	.142	.102	1.288	6.242	568,711
	8S	.794	1.875	1.144	.109	.086	.121	.096	.075	.053	.639	3.793	131,072
	8R	.802	1.739	1.146	.108	.085	.120	.095	.074	.053	.630	3.714	65,536
	16S	.888	1.541	1.145	.076	.061	.086	.067	.053	.037	.442	3.322	65,536
	16R	.887	1.531	1.146	.076	.060	.085	.066	.052	.037	.448	3.395	32,768
	32S	.947	1.428	1.145	.054	.043	.061	.047	.038	.027	.309	3.197	32,768
	32R	.990	1.362	1.147	.051	.040	.057	.044	.035	.025	.289	3.142	16,384
	128S	1.055	1.244	1.144	.026	.021	.029	.022	.018	.013	.127	2.958	16,384
12/59-12/60	1E	.253	2.380	.981	.276	.215	.303	.282	.219	.154	.886	5.001	1,088
	2E	.322	2.360	.981	.195	.153	.217	.199	.156	.110	.626	3.993	591,328
	8S	.631	1.457	.980	.097	.077	.109	.099	.079	.056	.298	3.203	131,072
	8R	.676	1.481	.981	.094	.075	.106	.096	.076	.054	.328	3.262	65,536
	16S	.702	1.299	.981	.069	.055	.078	.070	.056	.040	.213	3.110	65,536
	16R	.736	1.323	.982	.066	.052	.074	.067	.053	.038	.252	3.141	32,768
	32S	.803	1.179	.981	.048	.038	.054	.049	.039	.028	.138	2.971	32,768
	32R	.813	1.173	.992	.046	.038	.052	.046	.038	.026	.135	3.000	16,384
	128S	.887	1.070	.981	.023	.018	.026	.023	.019	.013	.030	2.907	16,384
12/60-12/61	1E	.000	3.810	1.276	.330	.229	.335	.259	.180	.131	1.885	12.084	1,119
	2E	.247	3.785	1.276	.233	.170	.246	.183	.133	.096	1.331	7.519	625,521
	8S	.845	2.154	1.276	.116	.090	.128	.091	.071	.050	.660	4.099	131,072
	8R	.883	2.036	1.281	.118	.091	.131	.092	.071	.051	.671	4.059	65,536
	16S	.997	1.838	1.276	.083	.065	.092	.065	.051	.036	.477	3.567	65,536
	16R	.998	1.844	1.290	.085	.067	.095	.066	.052	.037	.494	3.633	32,768
	32S	1.083	1.616	1.276	.058	.046	.065	.045	.036	.025	.322	3.228	32,768
	32R	1.114	1.605	1.306	.060	.052	.067	.046	.040	.026	.355	3.278	16,384
	128S	1.179	1.388	1.275	.027	.022	.031	.021	.017	.012	.142	3.035	16,384
12/61-12/62	1E	.146	1.741	.865	.206	.159	.228	.239	.184	.132	.364	4.102	1,142
	2E	.203	1.737	.865	.146	.114	.163	.169	.132	.094	.257	3.546	651,511
	8S	.552	1.232	.864	.073	.058	.082	.084	.067	.047	.121	3.133	131,072
	8R	.535	1.228	.864	.072	.057	.081	.083	.066	.047	.142	3.155	65,536
	16S	.653	1.090	.865	.051	.041	.058	.059	.047	.033	.094	3.073	65,536
	16R	.670	1.096	.862	.051	.041	.057	.059	.047	.033	.116	3.070	32,768
	32S	.709	1.022	.865	.036	.029	.041	.042	.033	.024	.076	2.989	32,768
	32R	.711	1.004	.859	.035	.028	.040	.041	.033	.023	.066	3.079	16,384
	128S	.800	.939	.865	.017	.014	.019	.020	.016	.011	.045	3.038	16,384
12/62-12/63	1E	.000	3.214	1.176	.287	.198	.291	.244	.168	.124	1.680	10.576	1,162
	2E	.175	3.177	1.176	.203	.148	.215	.173	.126	.091	1.187	6.769	674,541
	8S	.775	1.807	1.176	.102	.079	.112	.086	.067	.048	.602	3.966	131,072
	8R	.734	1.872	1.178	.102	.080	.114	.087	.068	.048	.571	3.815	65,536
	16S	.922	1.569	1.176	.072	.056	.080	.061	.048	.034	.406	3.433	65,536
	16R	.936	1.537	1.182	.072	.057	.081	.061	.048	.034	.387	3.358	32,768
	32S	1.002	1.426	1.176	.050	.040	.056	.042	.034	.024	.286	3.191	32,768
	32R	1.000	1.449	1.192	.049	.041	.055	.041	.034	.023	.242	3.164	16,384
	128S	1.094	1.275	1.176	.024	.019	.027	.020	.016	.012	.148	3.005	16,384
12/63-12/64	1E	.326	3.130	1.163	.265	.188	.278	.228	.162	.120	1.043	7.656	1,191
	2E	.347	2.763	1.163	.188	.140	.203	.161	.120	.087	.736	5.315	708,645
	8S	.772	1.740	1.163	.094	.073	.104	.081	.063	.045	.369	3.598	131,072
	8R	.786	1.671	1.166	.094	.074	.105	.081	.063	.045	.362	3.470	65,536
	16S	.890	1.522	1.163	.066	.052	.074	.057	.045	.032	.250	3.246	65,536
	16R	.894	1.480	1.171	.066	.053	.075	.057	.045	.032	.201	3.177	32,768
	32S	.981	1.383	1.163	.046	.037	.052	.040	.032	.022	.170	3.156	32,768
	32R	1.026	1.400	1.186	.045	.040	.051	.038	.034	.021	.143	3.087	16,384
	128S	1.083	1.252	1.163	.022	.018	.025	.019	.015	.011	.056	2.957	16,384
12/64-12/65	1E	.289	5.426	1.282	.410	.283	.401	.320	.221	.156	2.554	16.991	1,227
	2E	.371	4.762	1.282	.290	.209	.298	.226	.163	.116	1.804	9.964	752,151
	8S	.876	2.367	1.282	.144	.111	.158	.112	.087	.061	.887	4.654	131,072
	8R	.859	2.340	1.283	.140	.108	.153	.109	.084	.060	.866	4.627	65,536
	16S	.963	1.937	1.282	.102	.080	.113	.079	.062	.044	.656	3.996	65,536
	16R	.977	1.824	1.283	.096	.076	.107	.075	.059	.042	.569	3.454	32,768
	32S	1.065	1.737	1.283	.071	.056	.080	.056	.044	.031	.445	3.444	32,768
	32R	1.087	1.559	1.276	.062	.050	.070	.049	.039	.027	.362	3.307	16,384
	128S	1.164	1.431	1.282	.034	.027	.039	.027	.021	.015	.177	2.958	16,384

TABLE A1, CONTINUED

FREQUENCY DISTRIBUTIONS OF WEALTH RATIOS FROM INVESTMENTS IN RANDOMLY SELECTED PORTFOLIOS
CONTAINING SPECIFIED NUMBERS OF STOCKS LISTED ON THE NYSE, 1926-65

Number and Length of Periods	Size of Portfolio/ Sampling Method	Centiles of the Frequency Distributions										
		5th	10th	20th	30th	40th	(Median) 50th	60th	70th	80th	90th	95th
(1)	(2)	(3)	(4)	(5)	(6)	(7)	(8)	(9)	(10)	(11)	(12)	(13)
						FIVE-YEAR PERIODS						
1/26-12/30	1E	.041	.095	.192	.340	.518	.682	.876	1.116	1.443	1.884	2.476
	2E	.159	.254	.402	.530	.653	.782	.921	1.083	1.299	1.630	1.921
	8S	.469	.542	.642	.718	.786	.853	.923	1.001	1.098	1.241	1.361
	8R	.471	.545	.643	.718	.786	.854	.925	1.003	1.099	1.239	1.364
	16S	.582	.639	.714	.769	.819	.867	.916	.971	1.037	1.131	1.210
	16R	.584	.639	.709	.763	.812	.859	.908	.961	1.026	1.119	1.200
	32S	.667	.708	.762	.802	.838	.872	.906	.944	.990	1.056	1.109
	32R	.632	.670	.717	.752	.784	.814	.845	.879	.918	.973	1.019
	128S	.779	.798	.825	.844	.862	.877	.892	.908	.931	.955	.983
12/30-12/35	1E	.098	.227	.417	.660	.897	1.147	1.412	1.766	2.293	3.296	4.601
	2E	.340	.494	.715	.902	1.086	1.283	1.518	1.811	2.225	3.005	3.854
	8S	.813	.931	1.095	1.229	1.355	1.484	1.626	1.792	2.004	2.323	2.605
	8R	.826	.943	1.105	1.238	1.363	1.489	1.631	1.795	2.008	2.335	2.622
	16S	1.000	1.100	1.233	1.338	1.434	1.530	1.633	1.749	1.894	2.101	2.288
	16R	1.016	1.115	1.251	1.359	1.455	1.552	1.651	1.763	1.907	2.121	2.312
	32S	1.150	1.229	1.332	1.409	1.480	1.549	1.620	1.700	1.795	1.927	2.054
	32R	1.181	1.265	1.371	1.453	1.526	1.593	1.668	1.749	1.844	1.987	2.109
	128S	1.363	1.410	1.462	1.500	1.536	1.569	1.601	1.640	1.680	1.745	1.798
12/35-12/40	1E	.119	.218	.364	.539	.673	.832	.959	1.134	1.336	1.736	2.061
	2E	.299	.401	.541	.651	.754	.857	.967	1.092	1.253	1.516	1.820
	8S	.578	.643	.725	.789	.847	.903	.964	1.035	1.128	1.279	1.452
	8R	.587	.648	.729	.790	.847	.903	.963	1.034	1.129	1.286	1.465
	16S	.673	.723	.785	.834	.877	.920	.966	1.018	1.088	1.206	1.335
	16R	.679	.726	.788	.836	.879	.922	.969	1.024	1.095	1.219	1.352
	32S	.744	.781	.829	.866	.898	.932	.967	1.006	1.057	1.140	1.213
	32R	.772	.806	.856	.894	.929	.964	.999	1.042	1.097	1.187	1.261
	128S	.842	.865	.889	.911	.928	.945	.963	.983	1.005	1.040	1.069
12/40-12/45	1E	1.459	1.721	2.084	2.408	2.708	3.155	3.688	4.335	5.556	7.601	10.036
	2E	1.883	2.116	2.470	2.794	3.124	3.501	3.982	4.584	5.382	6.974	9.008
	8S	2.671	2.889	3.197	3.452	3.699	3.954	4.241	4.594	5.082	5.985	6.993
	8R	2.745	2.967	3.281	3.539	3.781	4.035	4.326	4.681	5.177	6.063	7.052
	16S	3.020	3.209	3.472	3.681	3.874	4.081	4.307	4.579	4.950	5.586	6.214
	16R	3.194	3.387	3.658	3.869	4.066	4.268	4.489	4.757	5.113	5.708	6.283
	32S	3.308	3.466	3.674	3.845	4.002	4.159	4.327	4.524	4.783	5.193	5.547
	32R	3.680	3.845	4.051	4.212	4.361	4.510	4.672	4.850	5.080	5.428	5.727
	128S	3.761	3.866	3.987	4.080	4.167	4.250	4.335	4.432	4.549	4.714	4.843
12/45-12/50	1E	.477	.627	.865	1.007	1.148	1.302	1.481	1.702	1.960	2.409	2.838
	2E	.726	.846	1.008	1.135	1.254	1.375	1.505	1.657	1.851	2.159	2.450
	8S	1.052	1.126	1.225	1.299	1.366	1.432	1.501	1.578	1.671	1.812	1.935
	8R	1.052	1.126	1.224	1.297	1.365	1.430	1.498	1.576	1.670	1.813	1.937
	16S	1.161	1.220	1.291	1.348	1.397	1.445	1.494	1.546	1.612	1.708	1.791
	16R	1.159	1.215	1.286	1.340	1.389	1.436	1.484	1.537	1.602	1.696	1.779
	32S	1.238	1.285	1.341	1.380	1.416	1.450	1.485	1.522	1.569	1.633	1.682
	32R	1.241	1.284	1.333	1.369	1.402	1.434	1.465	1.502	1.541	1.603	1.658
	128S	1.346	1.364	1.400	1.419	1.435	1.452	1.469	1.492	1.514	1.537	1.575
12/50-12/55	1E	.853	1.142	1.440	1.691	1.907	2.107	2.337	2.621	3.002	3.775	4.568
	2E	1.230	1.420	1.662	1.848	2.017	2.187	2.374	2.600	2.908	3.425	3.954
	8S	1.711	1.826	1.973	2.086	2.189	2.288	2.396	2.521	2.674	2.907	3.118
	8R	1.710	1.825	1.968	2.081	2.183	2.280	2.387	2.509	2.661	2.893	3.099
	16S	1.877	1.965	2.078	2.163	2.239	2.314	2.392	2.477	2.583	2.740	2.879
	16R	1.868	1.955	2.066	2.150	2.224	2.295	2.369	2.453	2.556	2.701	2.834
	32S	2.004	2.064	2.149	2.215	2.270	2.324	2.377	2.440	2.512	2.616	2.703
	32R	2.000	2.060	2.141	2.204	2.254	2.305	2.355	2.410	2.475	2.574	2.662
	128S	2.159	2.202	2.239	2.276	2.306	2.332	2.359	2.385	2.429	2.474	2.517
12/55-12/60	1E	.532	.707	.939	1.130	1.292	1.477	1.656	1.883	2.181	2.708	3.396
	2E	.798	.937	1.121	1.266	1.399	1.533	1.678	1.849	2.081	2.497	3.043
	8S	1.168	1.253	1.366	1.454	1.534	1.614	1.701	1.805	1.938	2.162	2.416
	8R	1.176	1.258	1.369	1.455	1.534	1.615	1.702	1.805	1.944	2.169	2.423
	16S	1.292	1.360	1.449	1.517	1.579	1.641	1.707	1.783	1.884	2.050	2.241
	16R	1.305	1.371	1.458	1.524	1.586	1.648	1.714	1.791	1.894	2.071	2.286
	32S	1.390	1.442	1.511	1.564	1.611	1.659	1.710	1.765	1.840	1.967	2.120
	32R	1.426	1.480	1.546	1.598	1.645	1.693	1.745	1.808	1.894	2.091	2.674
	128S	1.527	1.555	1.596	1.627	1.654	1.680	1.712	1.746	1.796	1.885	1.961
12/60-12/65	1E	.761	.977	1.256	1.440	1.605	1.778	1.979	2.241	2.595	3.402	4.445
	2E	1.067	1.222	1.421	1.576	1.720	1.870	2.040	2.255	2.568	3.160	3.826
	8S	1.474	1.571	1.702	1.806	1.902	2.001	2.110	2.240	2.407	2.682	2.975
	8R	1.483	1.584	1.717	1.823	1.920	2.020	2.130	2.261	2.432	2.710	3.022
	16S	1.619	1.698	1.801	1.884	1.960	2.037	2.117	2.210	2.331	2.524	2.724
	16R	1.653	1.737	1.846	1.930	2.007	2.082	2.167	2.265	2.392	2.610	2.831
	32S	1.737	1.799	1.882	1.947	2.005	2.062	2.122	2.188	2.275	2.410	2.533
	32R	1.839	1.905	1.993	2.060	2.122	2.183	2.249	2.322	2.411	2.543	2.649
	128S	1.896	1.938	1.982	2.022	2.051	2.080	2.112	2.148	2.184	2.249	2.286

Number and Length of Periods (14)	Size of Portfolio and Sampling Method (15)	Sample Minimum (16)	Sample Maximum (17)	Arithmetic Mean (18)	Standard Deviation (19)	Mean Deviation (20)	Gini's Mean Difference (21)	Coefficient of Variation (22)	Relative Mean Deviation (23)	Coefficient of Concentration (24)	Skewness (25)	Kurtosis (26)	Number of Portfolios Examined (27)
					FIVE-YEAR PERIODS								
1/26-12/30	1E	.000	4.487	.877	.778	.600	.822	.887	.684	.468	1.412	5.405	510
	2E	.000	4.445	.877	.550	.432	.602	.627	.492	.343	.996	4.184	129,795
	8S	.103	2.467	.876	.272	.216	.305	.310	.247	.174	.484	3.267	131,072
	8R	.122	2.259	.877	.272	.217	.305	.310	.247	.174	.496	3.293	65,536
	16S	.268	1.857	.878	.191	.152	.215	.218	.174	.123	.334	3.124	65,536
	16R	.278	1.801	.871	.187	.150	.210	.215	.172	.121	.369	3.130	32,768
	32S	.427	1.483	.878	.134	.107	.151	.153	.122	.086	.252	3.018	32,768
	32R	.428	1.354	.818	.116	.106	.131	.142	.130	.080	.194	2.985	16,384
	128S	.668	1.099	.877	.059	.047	.066	.067	.054	.038	.074	2.926	16,384
12/30-12/35	1E	.000	11.841	1.568	1.585	1.079	1.506	1.011	.688	.480	2.463	11.345	737
	2E	.000	11.085	1.568	1.120	.820	1.145	.714	.523	.365	1.738	7.140	271,216
	8S	.203	5.424	1.569	.557	.438	.614	.355	.279	.196	.856	4.029	131,072
	8R	.266	4.853	1.577	.556	.436	.612	.353	.276	.194	.868	4.036	65,536
	16S	.486	3.941	1.573	.396	.314	.442	.252	.200	.141	.612	3.505	65,536
	16R	.445	3.650	1.591	.395	.311	.441	.248	.196	.139	.588	3.435	32,768
	32S	.745	2.750	1.567	.274	.219	.308	.175	.139	.098	.388	3.126	32,768
	32R	.808	3.050	1.614	.282	.225	.317	.175	.139	.098	.415	3.265	16,384
	128S	1.089	2.149	1.572	.128	.102	.144	.081	.065	.046	.186	3.082	16,384
12/35-12/40	1E	.000	10.457	.949	.822	.519	.741	.867	.547	.391	4.460	41.754	719
	2E	.000	9.666	.949	.581	.384	.552	.613	.405	.291	3.147	22.236	258,121
	8S	.226	3.512	.947	.289	.210	.301	.306	.222	.159	1.557	7.697	131,072
	8R	.263	3.312	.950	.292	.211	.305	.307	.222	.159	1.603	7.606	65,536
	16S	.400	2.406	.948	.203	.153	.219	.214	.162	.115	1.068	5.072	65,536
	16R	.411	2.352	.954	.207	.156	.223	.217	.163	.117	1.112	5.186	32,768
	32S	.552	1.656	.948	.142	.111	.157	.150	.117	.083	.718	3.817	32,768
	32R	.572	1.752	.982	.149	.116	.165	.151	.118	.084	.685	3.657	16,384
	128S	.732	1.249	.949	.066	.053	.074	.069	.056	.039	.290	3.019	16,384
12/40-12/45	1E	.000	48.855	4.264	3.990	2.289	3.150	.936	.537	.369	5.010	41.665	788
	2E	.000	45.698	4.264	2.819	1.780	2.486	.661	.418	.292	3.536	22.205	310,078
	8S	1.553	16.196	4.263	1.400	1.017	1.436	.328	.238	.168	1.734	7.502	131,072
	8R	1.539	15.239	4.344	1.393	1.001	1.434	.321	.230	.165	1.681	7.202	65,536
	16S	2.095	11.391	4.269	.991	.752	1.062	.232	.176	.124	1.225	5.219	65,536
	16R	2.278	10.258	4.434	.952	.717	1.031	.215	.162	.116	1.078	4.642	32,768
	32S	2.617	8.355	4.255	.686	.538	.756	.161	.126	.089	.814	3.931	32,768
	32R	2.967	7.618	4.583	.624	.530	.695	.136	.116	.076	.660	3.591	16,384
	128S	3.218	5.713	4.270	.324	.259	.365	.076	.061	.043	.335	3.017	16,384
12/45-12/50	1E	.063	6.514	1.455	.771	.576	.811	.530	.396	.279	1.525	7.489	853
	2E	.107	6.024	1.455	.545	.418	.591	.374	.287	.203	1.076	5.228	363,378
	8S	.553	3.177	1.454	.271	.214	.302	.186	.147	.104	.530	3.559	131,072
	8R	.639	2.884	1.453	.270	.213	.301	.186	.147	.104	.520	3.432	65,536
	16S	.846	2.697	1.455	.191	.152	.214	.131	.104	.074	.362	3.268	65,536
	16R	.886	2.333	1.447	.188	.150	.211	.130	.104	.073	.371	3.219	32,768
	32S	.910	2.128	1.455	.133	.106	.150	.092	.073	.052	.217	3.113	32,768
	32R	1.022	1.910	1.439	.123	.099	.138	.085	.069	.048	.235	3.012	16,384
	128S	1.197	1.706	1.455	.063	.050	.071	.043	.034	.024	.097	3.004	16,384
12/50-12/55	1E	.113	10.794	2.335	1.217	.861	1.240	.521	.369	.266	1.836	9.107	1,010
	2E	.145	9.896	2.335	.860	.643	.915	.368	.275	.196	1.296	6.035	509,545
	8S	1.059	5.107	2.335	.430	.338	.477	.184	.145	.102	.644	3.739	131,072
	8R	1.067	4.842	2.326	.423	.334	.470	.182	.143	.101	.628	3.643	65,536
	16S	1.299	4.119	2.337	.302	.240	.339	.129	.103	.072	.466	3.362	65,536
	16R	1.406	3.880	2.316	.292	.233	.327	.126	.100	.071	.431	3.314	32,768
	32S	1.595	3.364	2.334	.212	.169	.238	.091	.072	.051	.323	3.162	32,768
	32R	1.698	3.140	2.312	.196	.157	.220	.085	.068	.048	.273	3.084	16,384
	128S	1.943	2.746	2.334	.100	.080	.113	.043	.034	.024	.131	3.008	16,384
12/55-12/60	1E	.102	35.876	1.701	1.508	.737	1.067	.886	.433	.314	12.294	257.373	1,055
	2E	.107	24.524	1.701	1.066	.562	.813	.626	.330	.239	8.681	129.571	555,985
	8S	.629	7.417	1.701	.536	.322	.467	.315	.189	.137	4.319	33.403	131,072
	8R	.666	7.554	1.709	.555	.326	.474	.325	.191	.139	4.426	33.331	65,536
	16S	.889	5.052	1.701	.373	.240	.348	.219	.141	.102	3.001	17.842	65,536
	16R	.896	4.934	1.722	.413	.251	.371	.240	.146	.108	3.133	16.777	65,536
	32S	1.066	3.480	1.702	.265	.181	.262	.156	.106	.077	2.104	9.975	32,768
	32R	1.115	3.471	1.773	.335	.213	.323	.189	.120	.091	1.971	6.963	32,768
	128S	1.389	2.314	1.701	.125	.097	.137	.074	.057	.040	.883	3.833	16,384
12/60-12/65	1E	.159	18.598	2.086	1.382	.851	1.221	.663	.408	.293	4.087	34.270	1,119
	2E	.187	16.508	2.086	.977	.654	.931	.468	.314	.223	2.886	18.560	625,521
	8S	.869	6.516	2.085	.486	.361	.513	.233	.173	.123	1.444	6.908	131,072
	8R	.878	5.599	2.106	.495	.365	.523	.235	.173	.124	1.410	6.435	65,536
	16S	1.209	4.381	2.083	.342	.262	.372	.164	.126	.089	.996	4.792	65,536
	16R	1.205	4.128	2.137	.355	.270	.388	.166	.126	.091	.914	4.182	32,768
	32S	1.383	3.507	2.088	.241	.189	.267	.115	.090	.064	.703	3.883	32,768
	32R	1.495	3.293	2.205	.244	.210	.275	.111	.095	.062	.419	3.071	16,384
	128S	1.731	2.650	2.086	.115	.092	.129	.055	.044	.031	.312	3.120	16,384

TABLE A1, CONTINUED

FREQUENCY DISTRIBUTIONS OF WEALTH RATIOS FROM INVESTMENTS IN RANDOMLY SELECTED PORTFOLIOS
CONTAINING SPECIFIED NUMBERS OF STOCKS LISTED ON THE NYSE, 1926-65

Number and Length of Periods	Size of Portfolio/ Sampling Method	Centiles of the Frequency Distributions										
		5th	10th	20th	30th	40th	(Median) 50th	60th	70th	80th	90th	95th
(1)	(2)	(3)	(4)	(5)	(6)	(7)	(8)	(9)	(10)	(11)	(12)	(13)
TEN-YEAR PERIODS												
1/26-12/35	1E	.016	.048	.152	.256	.461	.688	1.007	1.368	1.850	2.730	4.297
	2E	.115	.196	.365	.540	.716	.908	1.106	1.373	1.790	2.593	3.633
	8S	.488	.590	.736	.859	.979	1.104	1.246	1.420	1.641	2.002	2.353
	8R	.502	.607	.754	.875	.992	1.116	1.259	1.428	1.647	2.009	2.370
	16S	.657	.749	.870	.971	1.065	1.162	1.268	1.390	1.545	1.790	2.102
	16R	.672	.763	.888	.985	1.080	1.174	1.276	1.395	1.551	1.816	2.169
	32S	.796	.871	.972	1.050	1.123	1.194	1.271	1.357	1.471	1.667	1.859
	32R	.743	.813	.898	.964	1.026	1.087	1.157	1.234	1.334	1.520	1.705
	128S	1.008	1.043	1.109	1.147	1.185	1.223	1.264	1.306	1.351	1.434	1.476
12/35-12/45	1E	.614	1.056	1.592	1.912	2.210	2.557	2.999	3.493	4.216	5.500	7.664
	2E	1.221	1.515	1.890	2.186	2.464	2.751	3.068	3.462	4.030	5.194	6.442
	8S	1.987	2.174	2.419	2.616	2.797	2.987	3.193	3.434	3.760	4.317	4.996
	8R	2.024	2.211	2.457	2.657	2.843	3.035	3.248	3.495	3.819	4.370	5.105
	16S	2.257	2.414	2.614	2.767	2.914	3.057	3.217	3.387	3.638	4.054	4.599
	16R	2.365	2.502	2.714	2.884	3.029	3.181	3.342	3.538	3.787	4.268	4.886
	32S	2.467	2.608	2.755	2.886	2.994	3.103	3.233	3.363	3.568	3.911	4.454
	32R	2.755	2.895	3.073	3.205	3.326	3.454	3.590	3.742	3.991	4.361	5.642
	128S	2.805	2.873	2.952	3.030	3.109	3.190	3.270	3.351	3.481	3.672	3.852
12/45-12/55	1E	.621	.982	1.505	1.895	2.302	2.750	3.270	4.059	5.100	7.169	9.001
	2E	1.211	1.512	1.943	2.315	2.690	3.089	3.550	4.121	4.908	6.125	7.333
	8S	2.128	2.367	2.682	2.939	3.175	3.410	3.652	3.914	4.303	4.827	5.329
	8R	2.142	2.377	2.686	2.935	3.161	3.389	3.634	3.914	4.271	4.780	5.250
	16S	2.482	2.678	2.935	3.135	3.306	3.479	3.654	3.858	4.093	4.450	4.768
	16R	2.479	2.668	2.912	3.104	3.267	3.431	3.603	3.795	4.021	4.362	4.676
	32S	2.747	2.903	3.111	3.244	3.376	3.502	3.627	3.769	3.941	4.194	4.382
	32R	2.786	2.915	3.106	3.221	3.337	3.453	3.571	3.689	3.861	4.042	4.272
	128S	3.129	3.185	3.295	3.400	3.463	3.525	3.588	3.650	3.723	3.897	3.984
12/55-12/65	1E	.836	1.157	1.654	2.035	2.427	2.814	3.208	3.681	4.289	5.473	7.075
	2E	1.382	1.669	2.054	2.361	2.640	2.923	3.232	3.602	4.112	5.036	6.036
	8S	2.158	2.336	2.576	2.759	2.933	3.103	3.295	3.518	3.814	4.336	4.885
	8R	2.170	2.350	2.591	2.774	2.949	3.122	3.315	3.544	3.849	4.372	4.901
	16S	2.414	2.565	2.747	2.899	3.029	3.165	3.309	3.479	3.687	4.025	4.346
	16R	2.432	2.598	2.782	2.934	3.071	3.211	3.353	3.534	3.747	4.075	4.377
	32S	2.624	2.723	2.885	2.993	3.101	3.208	3.314	3.434	3.595	3.819	4.003
	32R	2.684	2.831	2.962	3.089	3.195	3.298	3.403	3.538	3.674	3.916	4.072
	128S	2.879	2.934	3.043	3.128	3.182	3.235	3.289	3.342	3.398	3.560	3.642
20-YEAR PERIODS												
1/26-12/45	1E	.000	.052	.324	.772	1.273	1.864	2.772	3.914	5.133	7.395	11.389
	2E	.249	.523	.982	1.496	2.010	2.527	3.072	3.770	4.797	7.002	9.909
	8S	1.319	1.608	2.010	2.345	2.662	3.006	3.396	3.848	4.532	5.659	6.734
	8R	1.366	1.660	2.061	2.393	2.717	3.063	3.470	3.941	4.593	5.751	6.813
	16S	1.783	2.012	2.360	2.645	2.911	3.177	3.502	3.835	4.337	5.062	5.592
	16R	1.854	2.100	2.437	2.728	2.992	3.267	3.587	3.928	4.419	5.149	5.676
	32S	2.185	2.350	2.665	2.867	3.070	3.281	3.514	3.746	4.078	4.520	4.956
	32R	2.095	2.293	2.569	2.787	2.980	3.172	3.393	3.620	3.848	4.338	4.597
	128S	2.706	2.791	2.962	3.132	3.272	3.389	3.506	3.623	3.739	3.856	4.215
12/45-12/65	1E	.912	1.886	3.357	4.549	6.269	8.242	10.111	12.529	16.068	21.992	30.115
	2E	2.648	3.608	5.140	6.452	7.741	9.138	10.688	12.552	15.132	19.496	24.671
	8S	5.790	6.623	7.674	8.562	9.372	10.231	11.115	12.220	13.514	15.838	18.168
	8R	5.805	6.646	7.673	8.552	9.358	10.210	11.088	12.175	13.466	15.769	18.061
	16S	6.947	7.590	8.493	9.174	9.844	10.489	11.135	11.939	12.984	14.497	15.874
	16R	6.994	7.634	8.515	9.195	9.856	10.480	11.105	11.871	12.924	14.378	15.811
	32S	7.992	8.383	9.058	9.706	10.174	10.642	11.110	11.629	12.523	13.417	14.352
	32R	8.128	8.468	9.147	9.764	10.206	10.649	11.092	11.547	12.449	13.352	14.072
	128S	8.903	9.662	9.924	10.185	10.447	10.709	10.971	11.232	11.494	12.574	13.164
40-YEAR PERIOD												
1/26-12/65	1E	.000	.258	1.283	3.724	8.257	14.323	21.581	33.613	50.787	82.532	127.554
	2E	1.041	2.663	6.631	10.964	15.669	21.557	28.267	37.228	50.393	76.499	107.820
	8S	10.323	12.954	17.309	21.097	24.948	28.812	33.363	39.326	45.335	60.472	76.912
	8R	10.505	13.251	17.570	21.354	25.136	28.917	33.404	39.255	45.106	60.046	75.798
	16S	15.068	17.211	21.496	24.556	27.547	30.538	34.621	39.153	43.685	56.084	64.379
	16R	15.190	17.236	21.328	24.320	27.194	30.068	33.820	38.339	42.857	54.034	63.398
	32S	18.151	21.735	24.177	26.618	29.060	31.551	35.280	39.010	42.740	54.865	72.821
	32R	16.895	19.399	22.798	24.802	26.806	28.810	30.814	34.606	39.154	43.701	57.493
	128S	23.045	24.410	27.140	29.870	32.555	35.182	37.809	40.436	43.063	48.040	56.520

TABLE A2, CONTINUED

MINIMUM AND MAXIMUM WEALTH RATIOS FROM INVESTMENTS IN INFINITE NUMBERS
OF RANDOMLY SELECTED PORTFOLIOS CONTAINING SPECIFIED NUMBERS
OF STOCKS LISTED ON THE NYSE, 1926-65[a]

Size of Portfolio/ Sampling Method	1926-30 MIN	MAX	1931-35 MIN	MAX	1936-40 MIN	MAX	1941-45 MIN	MAX
8S	0.006	3.719	0.	9.572	0.004	5.817	0.756	31.511
8K	0.013	3.591	0.	9.407	0.021	5.789	0.958	26.887
16S	0.016	3.345	0.	8.352	0.021	4.484	1.003	24.365
16R	0.031	3.135	0.013	7.958	0.057	4.220	1.224	20.627
32S	0.028	2.922	0.020	7.027	0.052	3.421	1.575	18.623
32R	0.126	2.175	0.119	5.657	0.148	3.020	1.663	14.447
128S	0.120	1.965	0.181	4.280	0.184	2.136	1.582	10.566

Size of Portfolio/ Sampling Method	1946-50 MIN	MAX	1951-55 MIN	MAX	1956-60 MIN	MAX	1961-65 MIN	MAX
8S	0.232	4.928	0.281	8.402	0.180	12.182	0.308	11.463
8K	0.232	4.752	0.312	8.057	0.224	11.794	0.351	9.420
16S	0.292	4.328	0.375	7.533	0.242	8.973	0.387	9.273
16R	0.115	4.105	0.431	6.905	0.304	8.221	0.431	7.693
32S	0.338	3.801	0.497	6.550	0.312	6.790	0.467	7.610
32R	0.482	3.221	0.751	5.376	0.499	5.677	0.678	5.795
128S	0.540	2.836	0.886	4.742	0.543	3.987	0.753	4.895

Size of Portfolio/ Sampling Method	1926-35 MIN	MAX	1936-45 MIN	MAX	1946-55 MIN	MAX	1956-65 MIN	MAX
8S	0.	10.651	0.067	25.166	0.155	16.431	0.200	19.032
8K	0.	9.855	0.073	24.508	0.158	16.215	0.214	16.832
16S	0.004	8.559	0.073	18.215	0.221	14.600	0.301	15.819
16R	0.005	7.041	0.291	17.543	0.254	13.488	0.370	13.017
32S	0.070	6.550	0.241	12.258	0.310	12.608	0.456	12.382
32R	0.070	4.320	0.731	12.258	0.603	9.511	0.732	9.761
128S	0.081	3.347	0.888	7.561	0.769	8.755	0.865	7.800

Size of Portfolio/ Sampling Method	1926-45 MIN	MAX	1946-65 MIN	MAX
8S	0.	29.113	0.	483.576
8K	0.	28.131	0.	490.
16S	0.002	23.406	0.006	332.143
16R	0.001	20.750	0.005	307.518
32S	0.142	17.654	0.316	234.007
32R	0.142	12.785	0.919	178.207
128S	0.157	8.998	0.637	106.832

*The corresponding minima and maxima for portfolios of one and two stocks are shown in Table 5.

TABLE A2, CONTINUED

MINIMUM AND MAXIMUM WEALTH RATIOS FROM INVESTMENTS IN INFINITE NUMBERS
OF RANDOMLY SELECTED PORTFOLIOS CONTAINING SPECIFIED NUMBERS
OF STOCKS LISTED ON THE NYSE, 1926-65[a]

Size of Portfolio/ Sampling Method	1946 MIN	MAX	1947 MIN	MAX	1948 MIN	MAX	1949 MIN	MAX
8S	0.353	1.821	0.437	2.077	0.381	2.400	0.481	2.313
8K	0.379	1.742	0.437	1.994	0.416	2.307	0.493	2.272
16S	0.394	1.671	0.478	1.904	0.425	2.012	0.591	2.118
16R	0.468	1.575	0.485	1.787	0.479	1.897	0.632	2.103
32S	0.437	1.533	0.521	1.757	0.469	1.747	0.683	1.928
32R	0.555	1.378	0.598	1.498	0.583	1.568	0.766	1.795
128S	0.547	1.292	0.640	1.453	0.620	1.375	0.833	1.629

Size of Portfolio/ Sampling Method	1950 MIN	MAX	1951 MIN	MAX	1952 MIN	MAX	1953 MIN	MAX
8S	0.703	3.196	0.507	2.328	0.505	1.733	0.378	1.798
8K	0.725	2.866	0.510	2.241	0.506	1.690	0.403	1.775
16S	0.752	2.867	0.581	2.057	0.587	1.684	0.444	1.684
16R	0.787	2.450	0.599	1.983	0.600	1.596	0.473	1.632
32S	0.790	2.578	0.650	1.873	0.653	1.612	0.496	1.561
32R	0.790	2.536	0.741	1.641	0.697	1.465	0.608	1.453
128S	0.905	2.068	0.816	1.575	0.772	1.433	0.619	1.339

Size of Portfolio/ Sampling Method	1954 MIN	MAX	1955 MIN	MAX	1956 MIN	MAX	1957 MIN	MAX
8S	0.732	3.609	0.548	2.437	0.421	2.376	0.320	1.855
8K	0.772	3.442	0.556	2.437	0.427	2.093	0.339	1.855
16S	0.823	3.145	0.556	2.274	0.427	2.093	0.395	1.655
16R	0.874	3.015	0.651	2.232	0.525	1.929	0.395	1.629
32S	0.920	2.853	0.701	2.084	0.559	1.870	0.384	1.501
32R	1.016	2.530	0.766	1.889	0.653	1.638	0.493	1.410
128S	1.081	2.304	0.835	1.722	0.701	1.555	0.493	1.268

Size of Portfolio/ Sampling Method	1958 MIN	MAX	1959 MIN	MAX	1960 MIN	MAX	1961 MIN	MAX
8S	0.879	4.306	0.527	2.709	0.408	2.168	0.522	3.093
8K	0.884	3.942	0.558	2.694	0.408	2.093	0.526	3.029
16S	0.921	3.864	0.572	2.482	0.450	1.774	0.611	2.765
16R	0.942	3.305	0.630	2.308	0.460	1.872	0.636	2.687
32S	0.973	3.339	0.630	2.232	0.488	1.792	0.687	2.452
32R	1.054	2.734	0.729	1.618	0.571	1.618	0.776	2.261
128S	1.138	2.458	0.761	1.770	0.587	1.493	0.837	1.916

Size of Portfolio/ Sampling Method	1962 MIN	MAX	1963 MIN	MAX	1964 MIN	MAX	1965 MIN	MAX
8S	0.283	1.629	0.439	2.731	0.424	2.364	0.509	3.665
8K	0.296	1.553	0.440	2.653	0.467	2.300	0.517	3.414
16S	0.350	1.516	0.532	2.222	0.501	2.222	0.553	3.232
16R	0.164	1.461	0.551	2.335	0.566	2.084	0.593	2.701
32S	0.439	1.420	0.607	2.208	0.575	2.037	0.653	2.866
32R	0.474	1.305	0.710	1.957	0.720	1.828	0.723	2.300
128S	0.531	1.237	0.779	1.752	0.745	1.682	0.818	2.154

*The corresponding minima and maxima for portfolios of one and two stocks are shown in Table 5.

APPENDIX B

INDUSTRY GROUPS USED IN THE RESTRICTED
SAMPLING PROCESS

Samples shown with an *R* in tables 5, A1, and A2 were random samples subject to the restriction that no more than one stock in a given industry be included in any given portfolio. This procedure, as well as simple random sampling, was employed for portfolios of eight, sixteen, and thirty-two stocks.

We classified the companies listed on the New York Stock Exchange into thirty-six industry groups. In defining an index group for this purpose, we used the Securities and Exchange Commission (SEC) two-digit groupings[17] subject to the restriction that there be at least one stock in each group at the beginning of each period. This restriction made it necessary to aggregate several two-digit groups in a number of instances. Table B1 contains the list of industry groups we used.

[17] The SEC two-digit groups correspond closely to the Standard Industrial Classification (SIC) groups.

TABLE B1

LIST OF INDUSTRY GROUPS USED IN RESTRICTED RANDOM SAMPLES

Industry Group	Description	Industry Group	Description
10	Metal mining	38	Instruments and related products
11–12	Coal mining	39	Miscellaneous manufacturing industries
13	Crude petroleum	40, 47	Railroads; miscellaneous transportation services
20	Food and kindred products		
21	Tobacco manufacturing	41–42	Local and highway transportation and public warehousing
22	Textile-mill products		
23.	Apparel and other finished textiles	44	Water transportation
24–25	Lumber and wood products; furniture and fixtures	48	Wire and radio communication
		49	Electric, gas, and water utilities
26	Paper and allied products	53	Department stores, mail order houses and vending-machine operators
27	Printing, publishing, and allied industries		
28	Chemical and allied products	54	Food stores
29	Products of petroleum and coal	56	Retail clothing and shoe stores
30	Rubber products	58	Restaurants
31*	Leather and leather products	50–52, 55, 57, 59	Other wholesale and retail trade
32*	Stone, clay, and glass products		
33*	Primary metal industries	60–63	Banks, savings and loan associations, finance companies, and insurance
34	Fabricated metal products		
35	Machinery except electrical	67	Investment companies
36	Electrical machinery	70–79	Services
37	Transportation equipment	All other	

* Because of a programming error, these industry groups were combined.

TABLE A2, CONTINUED

MINIMUM AND MAXIMUM WEALTH RATIOS FROM INVESTMENTS IN INFINITE NUMBERS
OF RANDOMLY SELECTED PORTFOLIOS CONTAINING SPECIFIED NUMBERS
OF STOCKS LISTED ON THE NYSE, 1926-65*

Size of Portfolio/ Sampling Method	1926-30 MIN	MAX	1931-35 MIN	MAX	1936-40 MIN	MAX	1941-45 MIN	MAX
8S	0.006	3.719	0.	9.572	0.004	5.817	0.756	31.511
8R	0.013	3.591	0.	8.352	0.021	5.789	0.958	26.887
16S	0.016	3.345	0.013	7.958	0.021	4.494	1.003	26.365
16R	0.031	3.135	0.020	7.027	0.057	4.220	1.224	20.627
32S	-0.028	2.922	0.119	5.657	0.052	3.421	1.175	18.623
32R	0.126	2.175	0.181	4.280	0.148	3.020	1.663	14.447
128S	0.120	1.965			0.184	2.136	1.582	10.566

Size of Portfolio/ Sampling Method	1946-50 MIN	MAX	1951-55 MIN	MAX	1956-60 MIN	MAX	1961-65 MIN	MAX
8S	0.232	4.928	0.281	8.402	0.180	12.182	0.308	11.463
8R	0.232	4.752	0.312	8.057	0.224	11.794	0.351	9.420
16S	0.292	4.328	0.375	7.533	0.242	8.973	0.387	9.273
16R	0.315	4.105	0.431	6.905	0.304	6.790	0.431	7.693
32S	0.338	3.601	0.338	6.550	0.312	8.221	0.467	7.610
32R	0.482	3.021	0.751	5.376	0.499	5.677	0.678	5.795
128S	0.540	2.836	0.886	4.742	0.543	3.987	0.753	4.895

Size of Portfolio/ Sampling Method	1926-35 MIN	MAX	1936-45 MIN	MAX	1946-55 MIN	MAX	1956-65 MIN	MAX
8S	0.	10.651	0.067	25.166	0.155	16.431	0.200	19.032
8R	0.	9.655	0.079	24.508	0.158	16.215	0.214	16.832
16S	0.004	8.559	0.079	21.215	0.224	14.608	0.301	15.819
16R	0.005	7.041	0.291	17.543	0.316	12.608	0.456	13.817
32S	0.070	6.500	0.241	13.577	0.603	9.511	0.456	13.381
32R	0.081	4.320	0.731	12.258	0.769	8.765	0.732	9.761
128S		3.347	0.888	7.541			0.865	7.800

Size of Portfolio/ Sampling Method	1926-45 MIN	MAX	1936-65 MIN	MAX	1946-65 MIN	MAX	1926-65 MIN	MAX
8S	0.	29.113	0.	29.113	0.197	73.778	0.	483.576
8R	0.	28.161	0.	28.161	0.202	73.778	0.	459.290
16S	0.002	23.406	0.002	23.406	0.275	59.439	0.002	332.143
16R	0.002	20.750	0.002	20.750	0.340	55.418	0.006	307.518
32S	0.001	12.756	0.001	12.756	0.417	48.120	0.005	234.007
32R	0.157	8.998	0.157	8.998	1.211	39.077	0.919	178.207
128S					1.418	29.602	0.637	106.832

*The corresponding minima and maxima for portfolios of one and two stocks are shown in Table 5.

TABLE A2, CONTINUED

MINIMUM AND MAXIMUM WEALTH RATIOS FROM INVESTMENTS IN INFINITE NUMBERS
OF RANDOMLY SELECTED PORTFOLIOS CONTAINING SPECIFIED NUMBERS
OF STOCKS LISTED ON THE NYSE, 1926-65*

Size of Portfolio/ Sampling Method	1946 MIN	MAX	1947 MIN	MAX	1948 MIN	MAX	1949 MIN	MAX
8S	0.353	1.821	0.437	2.077	0.381	2.400	0.481	2.313
8R	0.409	1.742	0.478	1.994	0.416	2.307	0.493	2.272
16S	0.394	1.671	0.485	1.904	0.425	2.012	0.591	2.118
16R	0.468	1.575	0.521	1.787	0.479	1.897	0.632	2.033
32S	0.437	1.533	0.521	1.757	0.469	1.757	0.683	1.928
32R	0.555	1.378	0.598	1.498	0.583	1.568	0.766	1.795
128S	0.547	1.292	0.640	1.453	0.620	1.375	0.833	1.629

Size of Portfolio/ Sampling Method	1950 MIN	MAX	1951 MIN	MAX	1952 MIN	MAX	1953 MIN	MAX
8S	0.703	3.196	0.507	2.328	0.505	1.733	0.378	1.798
8R	0.725	2.866	0.510	2.241	0.506	1.690	0.403	1.775
16S	0.752	2.867	0.581	2.057	0.587	1.684	0.444	1.684
16R	0.787	2.450	0.599	1.983	0.600	1.596	0.473	1.632
32S	0.789	2.578	0.650	1.873	0.653	1.612	0.496	1.561
32R	0.910	2.086	0.741	1.691	0.697	1.465	0.608	1.453
128S	0.905	2.068	0.816	1.575	0.772	1.433	0.619	1.339

Size of Portfolio/ Sampling Method	1954 MIN	MAX	1955 MIN	MAX	1956 MIN	MAX	1957 MIN	MAX
8S	0.712	3.609	0.548	2.437	0.421	2.376	0.320	1.855
8R	0.723	3.465	0.556	2.437	0.427	2.274	0.339	1.655
16S	0.833	3.942	0.628	2.274	0.492	2.092	0.350	1.655
16R	0.874	3.015	0.650	2.232	0.525	1.929	0.395	1.629
32S	0.920	2.853	0.701	2.084	0.559	1.870	0.384	1.501
32R	1.016	2.530	0.766	1.889	0.653	1.638	0.493	1.410
128S	1.081	2.304	0.835	1.722	0.701	1.555	0.493	1.268

Size of Portfolio/ Sampling Method	1958 MIN	MAX	1959 MIN	MAX	1960 MIN	MAX	1961 MIN	MAX
8S	0.879	4.306	0.527	2.709	0.408	2.188	0.522	3.093
8R	0.884	3.942	0.558	2.694	0.408	2.093	0.526	3.029
16S	0.921	3.864	0.572	2.482	0.450	1.974		
16R	0.942	3.305	0.630	2.308	0.460	1.872	0.636	2.687
32S	0.973	3.339	0.630	2.232	0.488	1.792	0.687	2.452
32R	1.054	2.734	0.729	1.924	0.571	1.618	0.776	2.261
128S	1.108	2.458	0.761	1.770	0.587	1.493	0.837	1.916

Size of Portfolio/ Sampling Method	1962 MIN	MAX	1963 MIN	MAX	1964 MIN	MAX	1965 MIN	MAX
8S	0.283	1.629	0.439	2.731	0.424	2.364	0.509	3.665
8R	0.306	1.573	0.440	2.653	0.467	2.300	0.517	3.414
16S	0.390	1.516	0.501	2.443	0.501	2.222	0.582	3.232
16R	0.364	1.461	0.551	2.335	0.566	2.084	0.593	2.901
32S	0.439	1.420	0.607	2.208	0.575	1.911	0.633	2.866
32R	0.474	1.305	0.710	1.957	0.720	1.828	0.723	2.300
128S	0.511	1.237	0.779	1.752	0.745	1.682	0.818	2.154

*The corresponding minima and maxima for portfolios of one and two stocks are shown in Table 5.

APPENDIX B

INDUSTRY GROUPS USED IN THE RESTRICTED SAMPLING PROCESS

Samples shown with an *R* in tables 5, A1, and A2 were random samples subject to the restriction that no more than one stock in a given industry be included in any given portfolio. This procedure, as well as simple random sampling, was employed for portfolios of eight, sixteen, and thirty-two stocks.

We classified the companies listed on the New York Stock Exchange into thirty-six industry groups. In defining an index group for this purpose, we used the Securities and Exchange Commission (SEC) two-digit groupings[17] subject to the restriction that there be at least one stock in each group at the beginning of each period. This restriction made it necessary to aggregate several two-digit groups in a number of instances. Table B1 contains the list of industry groups we used.

[17] The SEC two-digit groups correspond closely to the Standard Industrial Classification (SIC) groups.

TABLE B1

LIST OF INDUSTRY GROUPS USED IN RESTRICTED RANDOM SAMPLES

Industry Group	Description	Industry Group	Description
10	Metal mining	38	Instruments and related products
11–12	Coal mining	39	Miscellaneous manufacturing industries
13	Crude petroleum	40, 47	Railroads; miscellaneous transportation services
20	Food and kindred products		
21	Tobacco manufacturing	41–42	Local and highway transportation and public warehousing
22	Textile-mill products		
23	Apparel and other finished textiles	44	Water transportation
24–25	Lumber and wood products; furniture and fixtures	48	Wire and radio communication
		49	Electric, gas, and water utilities
26	Paper and allied products	53	Department stores, mail order houses and vending-machine operators
27	Printing, publishing, and allied industries		
28	Chemical and allied products	54	Food stores
29	Products of petroleum and coal	56	Retail clothing and shoe stores
30	Rubber products	58	Restaurants
31*	Leather and leather products	50–52, 55, 57, 59	Other wholesale and retail trade
32*	Stone, clay, and glass products		
33*	Primary metal industries	60–63	Banks, savings and loan associations, finance companies, and insurance
34	Fabricated metal products		
35	Machinery except electrical	67	Investment companies
36	Electrical machinery	70–79	Services
37	Transportation equipment	All other	

* Because of a programming error, these industry groups were combined.

4

STOCK MARKET INDEXES

James H. Lorie and Mary T. Hamilton

INTRODUCTION

We have reluctantly concluded that it is necessary to include the rather dull subject of stock market indexes. There are several reasons. In talking about investments, it is necessary to talk about movements in "the market" and it is interesting to compare such movements with other things such as industrial production, changes in the money supply, corporate profits, etc. Rates of return on "the market" itself can be a valuable bench mark for judging the performance of actual portfolios. Further, modern portfolio theory requires knowledge of the relationship of prices of individual stocks to movements in the market in order to allocate funds rationally among stocks. For these and other purposes, it is essential that there be a summary measure of the behavior of "the market." Indexes serve the purpose. Since there are several in general use, it seems sensible to discuss the principles underlying them, the uses for which each is best suited, and the relationships among changes in them.

SOME PROBLEMS

We do not present a detailed, technical discussion on indexes in general since such discussions are available in numerous books on statistics.[1] Nevertheless, we shall discuss three important issues which arise in constructing indexes. The issues are the following:

1. Selecting stocks for inclusion.
2. Determining the relative importance or weight of each included stock.
3. Combining or averaging included stocks.

In briefer terms, these are the problems of sampling, weighting, and averaging.

[1] "Index Numbers," *Encyclopedia of Social Sciences,* Vol. 7, pp. 154–69.
Alfred Cowles, 3rd, and Associates, *op. cit.*
Irving Fisher, *The Making of Index Numbers: A Study of Their Varieties, Tests, and Reliability* (Boston and New York: Houghton Mifflin Company, 1922).

Sampling

An index can be based on a sample of stocks or upon all of them. Movements in the New York Stock Exchange could be represented by movements of, say, 100 stocks or by movements in the entire list. When indexes were first constructed, technology of data processing made it impractical to include more than a few stocks. For example, when the Dow-Jones Industrial Average was first published in 1884 only 11 stocks were included. Modern computers make it relatively easy to include large numbers of stocks. As a result, the two newest important indexes—those of the New York Stock Exchange and the American Stock Exchange—are based on all stocks listed on the respective exchanges.

Since there are indexes of the two major exchanges which include all stocks, it may seem unnecessary to discuss the sampling problem. But, such discussion is helpful since two important measures of the market—the Standard & Poor's Indexes and the Dow-Jones Averages—are based on samples and because there is no comprehensive index of stocks which are not listed on any exchange. The usefulness of indexes based on samples is importantly influenced by the degree to which one can confidently infer movements in excluded stocks on the basis of movements in included stocks. For stocks on the New York and American stock exchanges, at least, such inferences can be made with great confidence from both the Standard & Poor's Index and the Dow-Jones Average.

The adequacy of indexes based on samples is caused by two factors: the fact that stocks of relatively few companies constitute a large proportion of the value of the stocks of all companies; and the tendency of all stocks to move together.

For some purposes, the very substantial concentration of value in relatively few companies contributes to the power of small samples. If each company is considered to be equally important, this concentration is of no help. If, however, large companies are considered more important than small, as is true when one is interested in changes in the market value of all stocks, the concentration of value is very helpful.

An investigation indicates that about half of the variation in the prices of individual stocks was accounted for by movements in the market.[1] Although the proportion has been declining, it is still substantial. Obviously, if all stocks moved together in perfect lock step, a single stock would represent the market with perfect fidelity. Although the degree of co-movement is not that high, it is still sufficient to help make relatively small samples valuable as indicators of general market movements.

The extent to which these factors cause small samples to represent accurately movements in the general market is indicated by a recent study of the variability in prices of stocks listed on the New York Stock Exchange.[2] For random samples of as few as eight stocks, the degree of

---

[1] Benjamin F. King, "Market and Industry Factors in Stock Price Behavior," *Journal of Business Security Prices: A Supplement,* Vol. 39, No. 1, Part 2 (January, 1966), pp. 179–90.
[2] Fisher and Lorie (1970), *op. cit.*

conformity is striking. For example, for the 40 individual years ending in 1965, the frequency distributions of wealth ratios of all stocks in each year and the frequency distributions of ratios for portfolios of eight stocks selected at random were virtually identical except for the extreme tails, as is indicated in Figure 4.1. Although almost indistinguishable, there are two curves.

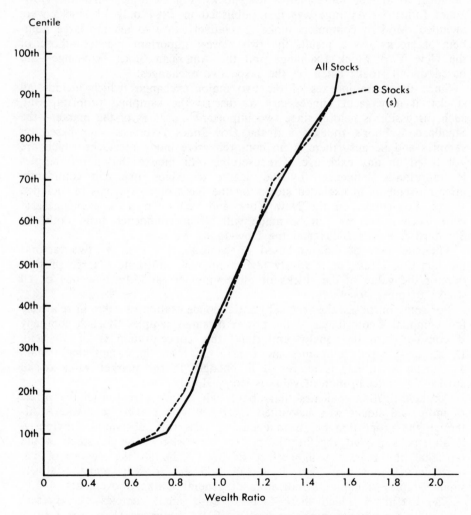

Figure 4.1 Aggregated Frequency Distribution of Wealth Ratios from Investments in Randomly Selected Portfolios of All Stocks and Eight Stocks

The degree of conformity of portfolios of size 16 and 32 stocks is even greater. This means that rates of return based on samples of 16 or 32 can be expected to provide good estimates of rates on all stocks. In

1965, for example, the mean wealth ratio for all stocks was 1.28, and randomly selected portfolios of size 16 could be expected to be between 1.38 and 1.18 about two-thirds of the time.

If one deliberately tries to pick portfolios which aren't representative, the degree of conformity will obviously be much less. This is true of some mutual funds which are specialized by industry. Thus the Chemical Fund or the Oceanographic Fund should not be expected to be representative of stocks in general. Unless there is a deliberate attempt at specialization, almost any sample of stocks of reasonable size will tend to represent well movements in all stocks. The best example is the Dow-Jones Industrial Average whose properties and degree of conformity with general market movements are discussed below.

When the purpose of the index is to represent changes in the value of all stocks, small samples can be used with very great confidence. For example, the stocks included in the Standard & Poor's 500 stock index constituted in 1970 about 80 per cent of the value of all stocks listed on the New York Stock Exchange. Even the Dow-Jones Composite Average, based on only 65 stocks, included stocks having a value equal to 27.5 per cent of all stocks listed in December, 1970.

Weighting

The prices of each stock included in an index must be combined in order to determine the value of the index. For that purpose, it is necessary each time the index is computed to determine the relative importance of each included stock.

Even if the persons computing the index don't recognize the weighting problem, they deal with it. For example, the Dow-Jones Industrial Averages are constructed so as to give each included stock a weight proportional to its price. No one has ever been able to devise a rational justification for this except simplicity. Yet, the Dow-Jones Averages are widely used and are valuable indicators of general market movements.

The reason for weighting is to insure that the index reflects the relative importance of each stock in a way suited to the index. The most common ways of weighting stocks are in accordance with market value or by assigning equal weights to relative price changes.[1] The former method is appropriate for indicating changes in the aggregate market value of stocks represented by the index while the latter is more appropriate for indicating movements in the prices of typical or average stocks. Changes in general market value are more important for studies of relationships between stock prices and other things in the national economy. Value-weighted indexes also have the desirable property of "macro-consistency." That is, it is possible for all investors to hold portfolios in which the individual stocks have a relative importance equal to the relative magnitude of the values of all outstanding shares.

On the other hand, indexes based upon equal weighting are better

---

[1] By equal weighting, we mean an index based on the assumption that equal dollar amounts are invested in each stock. We do not mean the process used in constructing the Dow-Jones Averages by which the prices of included stocks are added up and divided by the number of stocks (adjusted for stock splits).

indicators of the expected change in prices of stocks selected at random. For some purposes, such an index is a more appropriate bench mark than a value-weighted index.

An intuitive feeling for the major implications of the two most common ways of weighting can be achieved by realizing the simple fact that value-weighted indexes attach relatively great importance to large companies and that the stocks of those companies may behave differently from the stocks of small companies. The main expected difference is the greater volatility in the fortunes and stock prices of small companies and the greater tendency for the prices of stocks of large companies to be moved by the general economic tides in the economy as a whole.

Although the stocks in the Dow-Jones Averages are not value-weighted, the selection produces almost the same results. That is, the stocks included are the stocks of very large companies. As a consequence, movements in the Dow-Jones Averages are much the same with respect to volatility and trend as indexes based on value-weighting.

Another property of value-weighting is the automatic adjustment for stock splits. If there is no change in aggregate market value, the relative importance of the split stock remains the same and the index is not affected.

Indexes which are not weighted by market value have no such automatic adjustment. If the method of adjustment changes the relative importance of the split stock, it may impart a bias to the index. When one of the stocks in the Dow-Jones Average is split, adjustment is made by changing the divisor used in the calculation of the value of the average. The adjustment process is illustrated by the following simple hypothetical example:

TABLE 4.1

HYPOTHETICAL INDEX ADJUSTED FOR STOCK SPLIT

Stock	Before split		After split	
	No. shares	*Price per share*	*No. shares*	*Price per share*
A	10	$20	20	$10
B	10	$10	10	$10
C	10	$ 6	10	$ 6
Average		$12		$12
Divisor		3		2.167

The divisor for the average after stock A splits is reduced from 3 to 2.0 in order to preserve the value of the index.

Although an adjustment is necessary to avoid the absurdity of having the value of the average change in response to stock splits, the adjustment process and the method of weighting can produce a bias. Since stocks in the Dow-Jones Averages are weighted according to their market price, the adjustment for a stock split reduces the relative importance of that stock. If stocks that split behave differently from others, the Dow-Jones Averages will be biased. There is some evidence that stocks which split are those in companies which have been doing particularly well.[1] As a consequence, the weighting and adjustment process for the Dow-Jones Averages produces a downward bias.

Methods of Averaging

Given a group of prices of common stocks, either weighted or un-weighted, one has to combine them into a single number in order to create a descriptive measure. Although statistics books list and discuss several kinds of averages or measures of central tendency, and although in the history of stock market indexes many different kinds of averages have been used, at the present time in the United States only two averages are used in constructing the major stock market indexes. These are the arithmetic mean and the geometric mean.[2] All of the most widely used indexes such as the New York Stock Exchange Indexes, the Standard & Poor's Indexes, the Dow-Jones Averages, and the American Stock Exchange Index are based on arithmetic means of prices or price changes. The only index based on a geometric mean is the Value Line Index.

Before going into the question of methods of averaging, it's worth noting that indexes, though typically based on averages, are not quite the same as averages. The difference consists of the fact that the index is constructed by setting the value of the average equal to some arbitrary but generally rounded number at some point in time in order to facilitate comparisons of the value of the index at subsequent (or previous) points in time. For example, most federal economic statistics are indexes which are arbitrarily assigned a value of one hundred for the base period 1957–59. The Consumer Price Index in January, 1969, had a value of 124.1, meaning that

TABLE 4.2

Stock	Base period price	Current period price
X	$100	$125
Y	$ 50	$ 75
Z	$ 30	$ 15
Average	$ 60	$ 71.67
Index	100	119.45

The average of the stock prices was $60 in the base period. In the current period, the average is $71.67 or about 19 per cent above the base average. The index is therefore 119.45. One additional point is worth noting. The index in the example refers to an unweighted arithmetic average of prices, so the $25 or 25 per cent increase in the price of stock X has the same effect on the index as the $25 or 50 per cent increase in the price of Y.

---

[1] Eugene F. Fama, Lawrence Fisher, Michael C. Jensen, and Richard Roll, "The Adjustment of Stock Prices to New Information," *International Economic Review*, Vol. 10, No. 1 (February, 1969), pp. 1–21.

[2] Strictly speaking, an approximation of the geometric mean must be used since it is computed by multiplication rather than addition. If the price of a stock falls to zero, the index would be zero.

the index was 24.1 per cent greater than the base period 1957–59. The value of the Standard & Poor's Index of prices of 425 industrial stocks in January, 1969, was 110.97, and in the base period of 1941–43 the value of the index was set at 10.0. An average, on the other hand, does not involve the selection of an arbitrary value for some base period; it is simply an average. The Dow-Jones Averages are not indexes, technically. They are simply the arithmetic mean of the prices of the stocks included at each point in time, adjusted for stock splits. The simple example in Table 4.2 illustrates the difference.

For some purposes, it is important to understand the differences which result from the different methods of averaging. If there is any variation through time in the prices making up the index, there will be a difference between the value of an arithmetic mean of the prices and the geometric mean. The index based on the geometric mean will increase more slowly and decrease more rapidly than an arithmetic mean. The degree of divergence increases with the degree of variability in the component prices. This is illustrated by the following simple example based on three stocks which go up for two successive periods and then decline for two successive periods:

TABLE 4.3

INDEXES BASED ON ARITHMETIC AND GEOMETRIC
AVERAGES OF STOCK PRICES

		Period			
Stock	*Base*	*1*	*2*	*3*	*4*
X	$10	$12	$15	$10	$ 6
Y	$10	$15	$20	$15	$ 2
Z	$10	$21	$31	$ 8	$ 4
Average:					
Arithmetic	$10	$16	$22	$11	$ 4
Geometric	$10	$15.6	$21	$10.6	$ 3.6
Index:					
Arithmetic	100	160	220	110	40
Geometric	100	156	210	106	36

The examples not only illustrate the differences between movements in indexes when stock prices rise and fall but also illustrate the methods of computing an arithmetic mean and a geometric mean. The arithmetic mean is the sum of the individual prices divided by the number of prices while the geometric mean is the nth root of the product of the prices.

Some people claim that the arithmetic mean has an upward bias and some that the geometric mean has a downward bias. In one sense, the arithmetic mean is certainly biased upwards. For example, if a $10 stock moves to $20, and a $20 stock falls to $10, the arithmetic average of the relative changes is plus 25 per cent. If each stock returns to its original price, the arithmetic average of the relative changes is still 25 per cent.

However, the total value of the stocks is unchanged. The geometric mean adjusts for this. A corollary of this property of arithmetic averages is that over long periods of time, an arithmetic index will outperform most of the components. This is due in part, however, to the economic characteristics of stock prices. Since there is a lower, but no upper, limit to price changes, their distribution will not be symmetric.

It is interesting to consider the magnitude of the differences in indexes that can be caused by the choice of the method of averaging. It has been estimated that a geometric average of the Dow-Jones stocks would have 2.4 percentage points less gain per year than the arithmetic average, whereas an arithmetic index of the Value Line stocks would have three percentage points more per year than the geometric index. Similarly, Standard & Poor's Industrial Index was about 17 in June, 1950. In July, 1966, it reached 90. If a geometric mean had been used, it would only have been about 60.[1]

An interesting solution to the problem is that used by Fisher.[2] For the period 1926–60, he computed both an arithmetic and a geometric index of equally weighted relative price changes. When compared to the Fisher-Lorie rates of return presented in Chapter 3, he found the arithmetic index had an upward bias and the geometric a downward bias, greater in magnitude. He therefore computed a combined index with weights of 0.56 and 0.44 for the arithmetic and geometric indexes, respectively. Movements of this index relative to some of those currently available are considered in a subsequent section.

THE MAJOR INDEXES

There are a variety of indexes of stock prices currently available. They differ in construction and in purposes for which they are best suited. We will limit our discussion to five of the most widely known. We will also comment briefly on investment performance indexes.

The Dow-Jones Industrial Average

The Dow-Jones Industrial Average is probably the most familar of stock price measures, and widely quoted by professional investors and friendly taxi cab drivers. At the same time, it is often the most misunderstood. Essentially, the measure is an "unweighted" arithmetic average of the prices of 30 industrial stocks. The term "unweighted" is somewhat of a misnomer in that the influence of a particular stock on the change in the average is proportional to its price. For example, an increase of 10 per cent in the price of a $10 stock has twice the effect of a 10 per cent increase in a $5 stock.

The average has undergone changes both in composition and in computation since its appearance in 1884 in a daily letter issued by Dow-Jones & Co. At that time, it included 11 stocks. A twelfth was soon added. In

[1] Paul Cootner, "Stock Market Indexes—Fallacies and Illusions," *Commercial and Financial Chronicle*, September 29, 1966, p. 18.
[2] Lawrence Fisher, "Some New Stock Market Indexes," *Journal of Business, Security Prices: A Supplement*, Vol. 39, No. 1, Part II (January, 1966), pp. 191–225.

1916, the sample was enlarged to 20, and in 1928, to 30. Upon occasion there have been substitutions in the stock list designed to improve the representativeness of the average. There have been approximately 30 of these since 1928.

Originally, the average was computed by summing the prices of the component stocks and dividing by 11. Adjustments for stock splits or dividends of 10 per cent or more [1] were made by multiplying the new price of the stock by an appropriate factor. For example, if a stock split two for one, the new price was multiplied by two in order to compute the average. In 1928, this procedure was changed. Since then, instead of summing the prices (some with multipliers) and dividing by the number of stock issues, the price totals (with no multipliers) are divided by a number adjusted so that the average is unaffected on the transition date. Each new stock split or dividend reduces the divisor, so that by December, 1970, the divisor was approximately 1.0. One result is that there is no equivalence between points in the average and dollars and cents.

A more important feature of the adjustment, however, is that the change in the divisor reduces the importance of the split stock relative to that of the other stocks. The possibility of bias resulting from this computation was mentioned in the preceding section. The actual DJI stood at 192.91 at the end of 1945 and 969.26 at the end of 1965. If a constant divisor had been used throughout this period, with adjustments made in the original way, the average would have been 1086.59 at the end of 1965. [2]

Despite the popularity of the Dow-Jones Industrial Average, criticisms are abundant. A frequent, but superficial, objection is that it is widely misconstrued as being the actual stock price average. More fundamental criticisms are aimed at the representativeness of the sample and the method of computation. The 30 stocks are large, well-established companies; in 1970, they constituted 23.8 per cent of the market value of all stocks on the New York Stock Exchange. It has been argued that these "blue chips" are not representative of an average portfolio and are therefore poor measures of market performance.

The major criticisms of the methodology focus on the whimsical system of implicit price weights, the possibility of bias resulting from the adjustments, and the failure to adjust for small stock dividends. These are usually added to the reported cash dividend total. For example, in 1964, the value of small stock dividends for which no division adjustment was made constituted 19 per cent of total dividends reported. [3]

Some proponents of the Average who accept the sample have suggested changing the computational procedure by introducing explicitly market value or equal weights. Some also argue for replacing the arithmetic mean with a geometric mean. One proponent has actually recomputed the Average, using market value weights and arithmetic and geometric means with equal weights. If the value of each of these variants was 192.91 at the end of 1945 (the actual value of the DJI), by the end of 1965 they

---

[1] Stock dividends of less than 100 per cent were ignored.

[2] Robert D. Milne, "The Dow-Jones Industrial Average Re-examined," *Financial Analysts Journal*, Vol. 22, No. 6 (November–December, 1966), p. 86.

[3] *Ibid.*, p. 86.

would have the following values in comparison to the actual DJI of 969.26: [1]

Market value weights	1026.84
Equal weights–arithmetic average	1096.92
Equal weights–geometric average	813.40

The relationship between the 1965 value of the various averages is what one would expect, given the properties of different methods of computation. Over the 20-year period, the performance is quite similar, but for short periods there can be considerable diversity in the changes of the averages.

The Standard and Poor's "500"

The Standard and Poor's composite index of 500 stocks includes 425 industrials, 25 railroads, and 25 utilities. In contrast to the Dow-Jones Averages, the relative importance of the prices of the component stocks is determined by the number of shares outstanding. The index is officially described as a "base-weighted" aggregative, but, in fact, the weights are adjusted for stock dividends, new issues, etc. The aggregate market value of the stocks in the index is expressed as a percentage of the average market value in 1941–43. This percentage is divided by 10, which was selected as the value of the index in the base period. This was done in order to make the index in line with the actual average of stock prices.[2]

The present index of daily prices was first published in 1957, although other, less comprehensive indexes were published before that. It has been extended back to 1928 on a daily basis. In coverage, it is considerably broader than the DJI. In 1965, the aggregate market value of the 500 stocks was 79.3 per cent of all stocks on the New York Stock Exchange. Interestingly, the market value of Dow-Jones Industrial stocks on that date —all of which are included in the 500—was 29.8 per cent of the "500" market value. However, the importance of individual stocks in the indexes can be very different. For example, the implicit weight of AT&T in the Dow-Jones Industrial was 2.8 per cent in 1965. In the Standard & Poor's "500," its market value weight was 7.5 per cent. If the Dow-Jones Industrial used market value weights, that of AT&T would have been 18.6 per cent.

The composite index has several advantages. The coverage is broad, and the weighting is explicit. Moreover, no adjustments for splits is necessary. Critics have argued that the index is dominated by large companies, and that value weights can create an upward bias. These criticisms are much less universal than those aimed at the Dow-Jones Industrials.

The New York Stock Exchange Composite

In 1965, the New York Stock Exchange inaugurated its own composite index covering all common stocks listed on the exchange. It is similar in

---

[1] *Ibid.*

[2] When the present index was first published in 1957, its value was 47; the average price for all shares on the New York Stock Exchange was $45.23.

concept to the Standard & Poor's indexes in that it is an index of market value or, alternatively, a value-weighted price index. It is intended to measure changes in the average stock price which result from market action alone. The aggregate market value is related to the value in the base period, December 31, 1965. The index on that date was set as 50; the actual stock price average was $53.33.

No adjustment for splits is needed, but the base is adjusted to account for any changes in capitalization, new listings, delistings, etc. The adjustment is such that the relationship between the adjusted base value and the current market value after the change is the same as that between the current market value before the change and the prior base value. In this way, the index is unaffected by factors other than price changes in the market. The daily close index has been extended back to May 28, 1964.

The American Stock Exchange Price Level Index

The American Stock Exchange also developed its own index in 1966. It is un unweighted index of price movements of all its traded stocks and warrants derived by adding, or subtracting, the average net price change each day to or from, the previous index value. It is therefore quite different from the usual stock market measures. Since only net changes are considered, no account is taken of the relationship of the next change to the price of a stock. In this sense, it is comparable to the Dow-Jones Averages.

The use of net price changes has several interesting features. It avoids the problem of splits in that the only time the index is affected is on the day after the split. In practice, the previous day's closing index is adjusted when stock splits, dividends, or cash dividends occur. When new listings appear, the divisor used to obtain the average net change is increased correspondingly.

The base price is $16.88, the average price on April 29, 1966. Since values for the other periods are calculated by adding or subtracting net price changes, the index would more appropriately be called an average. It is available back to October 1, 1962.

The Value Line 1,400 Composite Average

The Value Line Composite Average first appeared in 1963. It consists of 1,217 industrials, 154 utilities, and 29 rails. It is the only widely used index which is based on a geometric average of relative price changes of the component stocks. Although labeled an average, it is, in fact, an index with a value of 100 on June 30, 1961. The adjustment for stock splits or dividends is made by adjusting the closing price of the stock on the previous day to compute the relative change.

Investment Performance Indexes

An investment performance index is essentially an index of rates of return. It differs from a price index in that it takes into account cash dividends. Alfred Cowles [1] was the first to publish a time series of this type.

[1] Alfred Cowles 3rd and Associates, *Common Stock Indexes, 1871–1937,* Cowles Commission Monograph, Principia Press, Inc. (Bloomington, Indiana, 1938).

Although no performance indexes are available on a current basis, Fisher [1] has developed an index based on all of the 1,715 common stocks listed on the New York Stock Exchange for all or part of the period from the end of January, 1926, through the end of December, 1960. We will not go into the details of the construction, but it is interesting to look at some of the effects of taking dividends into account. The table below presents changes for selected periods in the investment performance index and a comparable price index by industry.

TABLE 4.4

RATES OF CHANGE IN TWO INDEXES OF
COMMON STOCK PERFORMANCE
(Annual Rates Compounded Annually)

	Period					
	1/26–12/60		12/40–12/60		12/50–12/60	
Security Group	IPI[a]	PI[b]	IPI[a]	PI[b]	IPI[a]	PI[b]
Railroads	4.0	0.5	17.1	12.0	6.8	2.0
Local and highway transportation	5.6	−0.4	16.7	8.6	11.6	5.5
Water transportation	4.4	−1.7	14.2	5.3	9.4	1.4
Airlines	3.6	2.4	6.1	4.0	5.0	2.1
All common stocks	8.9	4.0	16.0	9.9	13.3	7.9

[a] Investment Performance Index.
[b] Price Index.

The different indexes can lead the uncautious to different conclusions. For example, for the period 1926–60, the price indexes indicate that rails outperformed stocks in local and highway transportation companies, while the more comprehensive investment performance indexes indicated the reverse (Table 4.4).

RELATIONSHIPS BETWEEN THE INDEXES

The preceding discussion raises an obvious question: of what practical importance is the choice of an index? Some insight can be derived from looking at comparative movements over time of the various indexes. In the figure below, the Dow-Jones Industrial Average and the Standard & Poor's 500 are plotted at quarterly intervals from 1926 to 1970. (These have been shifted to a base of 1960 = 100.) Fisher's Combination Index also appears for the years for which it is available.[2]

At first glance one might conclude that differences in coverage and con-

[1] Lawrence Fisher, "Some New Stock Market Indexes," *Journal of Business, Security Prices: A Supplement,* Vol. 39, No. 1, Part II (January, 1966), pp. 191–225.
[2] The Combination Index is the weighted average of arithmetic and geometric averages referred to on p. 77 of this chapter.

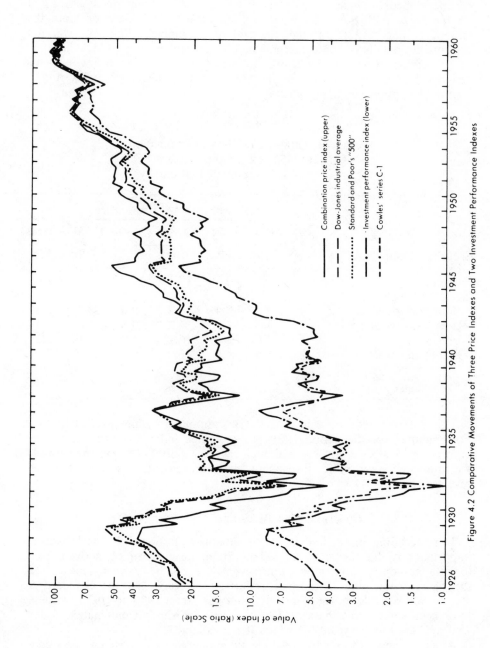

Value of Index (Ratio Scale)

—— Combination price index (upper)
— — Dow-Jones industrial average
·········· Standard and Poor's "500"
—··— Investment performance index (lower)
—·—· Cowles' series C-1

Figure 4.2 Comparative Movements of Three Price Indexes and Two Investment Performance Indexes

struction are of little importance, since the major indexes do move together over long periods of time. The Dow-Jones Industrial Average and Standard & Poor's 500 exhibit great similarity over the 45-year period, and no doubt the New York Stock Exchange Composite, if available, would have behaved in much the same way. This similarity is inevitable, given the coverage of the indexes. On December 31, 1970, the market value of the Dow-Jones Industrials was 151.6 billion. This represents 23.8 per cent of the market value of all common stocks listed on the New York Stock Exchange and about 30 per cent of the market value of the Standard & Poor's 500. The overlap guarantees no marked divergence in the long run. Between 1926 and 1970, the Dow-Jones Industrial Average increased 429 per cent, while the Standard & Poor's 500 increased 622 per cent. Within

TABLE 4.5

CORRELATIONS BETWEEN INDEXES OF PRICES
OF STOCKS ON THE NEW YORK STOCK EXCHANGE [a]

Index	Period	Correlation coefficient
Dow-Jones Composite and:		
Dow-Jones Industrial	Jan., 1926–Dec., 1966	0.969
Standard & Poor's "500"	Jan., 1926–Dec., 1966	0.977
Standard & Poor's "425"	Jan., 1926–Dec., 1966	0.959
New York Stock Exchange Composite [b]	Jan., 1939–Dec., 1966	0.906
Dow-Jones Industrial and:		
Standard & Poor's "500"	Jan., 1926–Dec., 1966	0.976
Standard & Poor's "425"	Jan., 1926–Dec., 1966	0.969
New York Stock Exchange Composite [b]	Jan., 1939–Dec., 1966	0.908
Fisher's Combination Price Index	Jan., 1926–Dec., 1960	0.985
Standard & Poor's "500" and:		
Standard & Poor's "425"	Jan., 1926–Dec., 1966	0.981
New York Stock Exchange Composite [b]	Jan., 1939–Dec., 1966	0.913
Fisher's Combination Price Index	Jan., 1926–Dec., 1960	0.919
Standard & Poor's "425" and:		
New York Composite	Jan., 1926–Dec., 1966	0.909

[a] Correlations are between closing values on the last Friday of the month.
[b] Although the New York Stock Exchange Index was started in 1966, it was extended back to 1939 on the basis of linkage with Securities Exchange Commission Stock Price Index.

the period, the two indexes crossed 17 times. The Combination Index crossed each of the other two 15 times.

The close relationships between various indexes is illustrated further in the table above. The simple correlation between each pair of indexes measures the degree to which they tend to move up and down together.[1] All of the correlations are above 0.9, indicating a high degree of relationship. A coefficient of 0.9 means that over 80 per cent of the variance in one index is "explained" by the variation in the other.

Although long-run movements are similar, indexes may differ markedly over short periods of time. This is reflected both in turning points and volatility. On one occasion, there was a significant difference in the turning points of the market as a whole as measured by a comprehensive equal-weighted index and the Dow-Jones Averages or Standard & Poor's Indexes. In 1929, the equal-weighted index reached its peak six months before the month-end peak in the other two. This suggests that the prices of stocks in relatively small companies turned down before the prices of stocks in large companies. In this instance, at least, the use of the index giving greater weight to small companies could have had enormous value. The equal-weighted index also reached its trough in 1932, one month before either of the other two indexes. All other turning points coincide.

Some indication of the relative volatility of various indexes is illustrated in the table below. The mean relative monthly price changes and two measures of dispersion are presented for nine indexes. The period covered is July, 1964, to June, 1969, except for the New York Stock Exchange Indexes, which are for the period since January, 1966.

TABLE 4.6

ABSOLUTE MONTHLY CHANGES IN STOCK MARKET INDEXES
JULY, 1964–JUNE, 1969

Index	Mean	Standard deviation	Mean deviation
Dow-Jones Composite	0.06%	3.36	2.66
Dow-Jones Industrial	0.14%	3.38	2.67
Standard & Poor's "500"	0.35%	3.08	2.48
Standard & Poor's "425"	0.40%	3.19	2.59
New York Stock Exchange Composite [a]	0.41%	3.33	2.59
New York Stock Exchange Industrial	0.39%	3.95	3.11
Value Line Composite	0.61%	4.02	3.08
Value Line Industrial	0.76%	4.29	3.28
American Stock Exchange	1.95%	5.60	4.33

[a] Period covered is January, 1966–June, 1969.

The mean relative price change in the Dow-Jones Composite was 0.06 per cent. For the Standard & Poor's Composite, the mean change was 0.35

[1] The range of the correlation coefficient is −1 to +1. A value of ±1.0 would indicate perfect correlation, while a value of 0.0 would indicate no correlation.

per cent, or almost six times larger. In other words, the volatility of two measures designed to represent the New York Stock Exchange was dramatically different.

CONCLUDING REMARKS

Irwin Friend *et al.* found that the average annual rate of return (compounded annually) on investment in 136 mutual funds was 10.7 per cent for the period January, 1960 through June, 1968, that the rate from equal investment in all listed stocks would have been 12.4 per cent, and that the rate from investment in all stocks in amounts proportional to their initial market value would have provided a return of 9.9 per cent.[1] Their findings illustrate two points: (1) For some purposes, understanding the construction of indexes can make a crucial difference in interpreting the results of research; and (2) differences among available indexes are not likely to be great.

---

[1] Irwin Friend, Marshall Blume, and Jean Crockett, *Mutual Funds and Other Institutional Investors*, McGraw-Hill Book Company (New York, 1970), p. 19.

5

STOCK MARKET INDEXES:
FALLACIES AND ILLUSIONS

Paul H. Cootner

Stock market indexes come in different sizes and shapes and serve different purposes. But like being unable to know a player without a program, it behooves the stock analyst to make certain the right index is being used and its flaws are properly discounted for the purpose intended. Dr. Cootner's paper contrasts the differences and applicability of the popular geometric and arithmetic weighted and unweighted indexes, notes major fallacies held, and explains differences involved in comparing median, average and typical stock market and portfolio performances. Discussion includes the Dow-Jones, Standard & Poor's, and Value Line indexes.

The U. S. stock market is one of the most closely observed economic phenomena in the world. To measure its fluctuations, analysts have concocted a wide variety of indexes. Despite this intense observation and measurement, and the wide choice of available measures, there has been intense dissatisfaction about these indexes of performance. In the last few months, at least three new stock price indexes have appeared in an attempt to assuage one or more of the complaints.

Regardless of these new indexes, I predict that dissatisfaction will continue—not because the indexes are in fact unsatisfactory but because many analysts are clearly unaware of what they really measure or what they are supposed to measure.

Now, confusion about index numbers is not something peculiar to investment analysts. Economists, statisticians and social scientists have engaged in confused controversy for years about similar indexes. Nevertheless, there are some agreed principles about index numbers which may cast some light on the problems faced by security analysts in evaluating investment performance. In this article, I intend to state some of these principles and, by doing so, I hope to clear up three widespread fallacies about existing stock market indexes.

Reprinted with permission from the September 29, 1966 issue of the *Commercial and Financial Chronicle,* 25 Park Place, New York, New York 10007.

FALLACIES

My discussion will not *exhaust* the list of fallacies: some are too silly for extensive discussion. Take, for example, the complaint that the Dow-Jones is a "bad" index because a drop of 18 points "scares the public" by its magnitude, even though it is only a 2% decline. I simply defer discussion of this complaint until I hear a similar complaint about 2% (18 point) *rises*.

(1) Despite the protestations of its proponents, it simply is not true that a "geometric" index, like, for example, the currrent Value Line index, is more representative of stock market performance than arithmetic indexes like the Dow-Jones or Standard and Poors. Indeed for almost all relevant uses, the Value Line index is a very poor choice.

(2) Similarly, it is not true that arithmetic indexes are unrepresentative of the market simply because we find that, over long periods, most of the component stocks have done much worse than the average and the rise is mostly due to outstanding performance of a very few issues. In fact, this is exactly what we would expect to find and it is simply evidence that the index is behaving as it should.

(3) Weighted averages like the Standard and Poors or the New York Stock Exchange indexes are more representative of the performance of the average portfolio than unweighted averages like the Quotron index, despite the fact that many actual portfolios do not customarily hold securities in amounts proportional to the number of shares outstanding. The loose reasoning that it is better to compare unweighted portfolios with unweighted indexes misses an important point.

Let us open the discussion with the first of these propositions. When I say that a geometric index is inferior to an arithmetic index, I do not mean that every investment advisor should not yearn to be compared with such an index. Indeed, quite the reverse. If there were a *Society for the Protection of Security Analysts,* it should lobby for legislation to make such an index mandatory. The reason for this is simple and can be expressed in the following mathematical theorem:

As long as there is any variability among its components, any geometric index will grow more slowly, or decline more swiftly than the corresponding arithmetic index.

DOWNWARD BIAS

I would like to stress that this is a *mathematical* theorem. It does not depend upon any particular facts about the stock market. It will always be true. I stress this because some analysts I know have tried to "disprove" it by pointing out that over some recent periods the Value Line 1100 stock index has outperformed the 30 stock Dow-Jones. The moral behind this is quite clear. In those particular periods, the 1070 stocks which are not in the Dow have performed so well that they have overcome the natural downward bias of a geometric index. The point is that an 1100 stock *arithmetic* index would have done even better. In defending the Dow against geometric indexes, I do *not* say that the Dow is necessarily a good index.

It is not. I only point out that the Dow's infirmities should be *properly* diagnosed, and it should not be criticized for its virtues.

Now one might ask: Is the *magnitude* of this downward bias of a geometric index truly important? Here we turn to statistical analysis rather than theory. My tests indicate that the effect is very important and more important for comprehensive indexes like the Value Line than for select indexes like the Dow. The reason for this is that the amount of the bias is related to the variability of the prices of the component stocks. Thus, for high-grade stocks with relatively little variance the bias is less than for highly speculative stocks. Thus, I estimate that a geometric index of the Dow stocks would show a 2.4% smaller gain per annum than the Dow itself. Similarly, I would guess that the Value Line index grows 3% per year more slowly than a comparable arithmetic index. To put this bias in more understandable terms, let us compare the behavior of a comprehensive arithmetic index like the S&P 425 Industrials with the probable value of a comparable geometric index. If two such indexes had started out together at 17 on June 30, 1950, the geometric index would probably be only 60 today against 90 for the actual value of the index on July 27. It is appropriate to note that if the Value Line Industrials had been started at the same value as the S&P industrials on June 30, 1950, it would be selling at exactly the predicted level. Nor do I choose to make the most dramatic case—a geometric S&P index based on the 1929 peak would have surpassed that level by only 30%, a rate of increase of less than 1% per year while the arithmetic index is more than three and one-half times as high as in 1929. The Value Line index has doubled in the same period.

Though many users of geometric indexes are not aware of this bias, several proponents of geometric indexes claim the bias is the other way around. They claim that it is the arithmetic indexes which are *upward* biased. While early descriptions of the geometric index were very confused about why it differed from arithmetic indexes, recent expositions are more accurate. Thus Value Line, which claims arithmetic indexes are upward biased, describes its index as measuring median performance and "more closely approximating the performance of a random selection of stocks than any other average."

Median Versus Average Performance

Now, the *median* of a group of stocks does not measure their average performance. It marks the dividing line between the 50% of the stocks that will do better and the 50% of the stocks that will do worse. Thus, on the average we would expect 550 of the 1100 stocks to do better than the geometric index and 550 to do worse. The median is a perfectly respectable statistical measure and is frequently quite useful. For example, if an Arabian oil sheikdom has 50,000 inhabitants who earn $100 a year and a sheik who earns $100,000,000 it is more descriptive to say that the country has a median income of $100 than to say it has an average income of $2,100. The question before us is, How significant is the *median* performance of stock prices?

It is not very significant at all, because it removes from consideration one of the most attractive reasons for buying stock: the fact that you can only take limited losses from stock investment but your gains are unlimited. As a practical matter it can easily be shown that stocks are about equally likely to double as they are to fall 50%, and equally likely to triple as to fall to ⅓ of their value. So let us assume an investor holds three stocks priced at $100. One year later he finds that one of them is at $200, one at $50 and the third is unchanged. The median value of his portfolio in both years is $100 and so is a geometric index of his portfolio. This does not, however, mean that he is no better off at the end of the year than at the beginning. During the year his $300 worth of stock has grown to $350, a gain of almost 17%. One would surely want an index to reflect this gain.

Now you may feel that my example is unfair because some other choice of numbers might produce a different result. That however is not the case. Here a corollary of our theorem comes into play.

For *any* sample of stocks in which the geometric index is equal to the median, the arithmetic index will be larger than the geometric, except, of course, if all the stocks have the same price.

Now, Value Line is undoubtedly correct in asserting that the geometric average is usually representative of the median for stocks and so its average will always lie below the average arithmetic return to the stockholder.

PORTFOLIO PERFORMANCE

No matter how one responds to the difference between median and average returns when discussing *individual* stocks, the geometric index loses all of its rationale when discussing portfolios. Contrary to the belief in the Value Line quote cited above, the geometric average is poorer at measuring the performance of a portfolio than any comparable arithmetic index.

The reason for all this stems from the well-known fact that underlies the insurance industry. The average life expectancy of a new-born baby is about 66 years. Now, any individual baby might die as soon as the next day or might live past 100. But a group of babies chosen at random is likely to have an average life-span of 66 years, and the larger the group of babies chosen, the less likely is their average age at death to differ from 66 years.

The same rule applies to stock portfolios. As a result groups of two or more stocks will behave more like the average of all stocks than their median. As the number of stocks in the portfolio increases, the range of likely outcomes squeezes closer to the arithmetic average of all stocks, so that we will soon find that *substantially more than half* of all random portfolios will outperform a geometric index. In other words, when we shift our discussion from individual stocks to random portfolios, the geometric index not only fails to measure the average performance but it also fails to measure even median performance. Any widely diversified portfolio is likely to surpass such an index. (In the limiting case of a *portfolio* containing every stock in the index, the portfolio will, of course, *always* outperform the index.)

I hope these examples will establish my point but past experience does not make me sanguine.

ASYMMETRICAL DISTRIBUTION

The second proposition arises out of the same asymmetry of stock prices that played a role in the first fallacy—the limitation on price decline and the lack of such limitation on price rises—but this time we must call on a specific property of stock prices. To a close approximation, stocks are equally likely to rise to N times their initial value as they are to fall to $1/N$ of that initial value. (For the technically inclined, this means that the change in the logarithm of price is symmetrically distributed.) The result of this empirical property can be seen if we plot the percentage price changes in all the stocks on (say) the New York Stock Exchange over an average year. There will be a scattering of stocks with declines over 50%; then a gradual rise in the frequency of smaller declines until we reach a peak for some small positive price change. Then the frequency of larger increases will decline, but there will be many increases larger than 50% and a scattering beyond 100% or even 200%. The result is that the distribution is asymmetrical; it will have a longer "tail" of large price increases than of large price decreases.

Now this asymmetry means as I have already mentioned, that the *average* of these price changes will not coincide with the *most frequent* outcome. There will be roughly the same number of price changes *below* the most frequent outcome as there are *above* that outcome, but the larger increases will be more important in making up the average because they are not limited to less than 100%.

As a practical matter this means that a much larger number of stocks will rise by less than the average for the market than will rise by more than the average. As an example, we are likely to find that in a year when the market has risen by 7%, that almost half of the stocks have declined and 58% of the stocks have risen by less than 7%. If stocks were to continue to rise at that 7% per year rate, we would find after four years in which the market rose 32%, almost half of the stocks would still be lower than they were at the start of the period. Furthermore, 64% would have risen less than the average.

Even after 10 years, 47% of the stocks would show a decline even though the averages showed a rise of 101%. Seventy one per cent of the stocks would have risen by less than average.

Look what this means for the Dow-Jones averages in a ten year period in which it had doubled. Of the thirty stocks in the average, we would expect 14 to have declines, and 7 others to have risen by less than the averages. In all 21 would show less than a 7% annual rate of growth. On the other hand three would have grown by more than 15% per annum and one would have been 8 times its initial level. Note further that this kind of performance would be average behavior. It would not be out of the question for some alert analyst, looking for an excuse for bad performance, to find still more striking behavior.

The point is that this is not bizarre behavior—it is to be expected and is no indictment of the Dow or any other arithmetic index. If one insists on an index that measures median performance—i.e., an index in which only half of the components do worse than average—he should choose a geometric index, but such an index will not measure the performance of any portfolio on earth. In fact, all this should be no surprise to real portfolio managers. Breathes there such a manager who would care to see both the three *best* and three worst performers removed before his performance was evaluated?

Unweighted Indexes

The last of the current fallacies that I will discuss is the current penchant for unweighted indexes. In this case, the fallacy is more narrow than in previous cases. There *are* cases in which unweighted indexes are a better standard than weighted ones, but this does not apply to most of the examples used in the financial press.

Optimal Index

The usual argument against weighted indexes is that individual portfolios are not so weighted. Now I am not sure of the empirical validity of that argument but I am willing to concede the point. Assume that all portfolios hold either equal dollar amounts or an equal number of shares of every stock in the portfolio. Now, under those conditions, what is the optimal index, weighted or unweighted?

Before answering, note that all outstanding shares must be held by someone. So if each portfolio contains only 100 shares of AT&T, there must be many more portfolios with AT&T than with Lukens Steel. In evaluating a portfolio chosen at random, we want to know how 100 shares of every stock performed, but we also want to know the likelihood that that portfolio contains the stock in question. That probability, under our assumptions, is measured by the number of outstanding shares. That is, even though each portfolio holds an equal number of shares of each component company, the number of portfolios holding the stock of any company must be proportioned to the number of shares of that company outstanding. Therefore, for a portfolio chosen at random, the performance it is likely to have is equal to an index of prices weighted by the number of shares outstanding. Thus, it is not true, as some analysts loosely argue, that because "a typical portfolio is unweighted," the expected outcome of such a portfolio is best measured by an unweighted index. What *is* true is that if (say) large companies do much worse than small ones, one would expect a larger *number* of portfolios to do worse than an unweighted average and a small number to do much better and *vice versa*. But a weighted average will still represent the average portfolio.

In what situation, then, *is* an unweighted index preferable? It is, for example, the right basis of comparison for an investment advisor with a relatively small clientele who intends to select 10 individual stocks to "outperform the market" without giving any *portfolio* advice. In this case he is trying to demonstrate his ability to choose the stocks which will perform best and his customer can, and would be expected to, invest equally in all. In such a case, the selective ability of the advisor is measured by a simple unweighted arithmetic index. Any portfolio decisions are made by the customer and are a different matter from the choice of stocks.

An Illusion

There is, however, one exception to this rule. If the advisor's clientele is a very large or a very wealthy one, the unweighted average can become inappropriate. The point is that it may be impossible for the clientele to invest equally in the securities without distorting the prices. Recommendation of two companies—one with 100,000 shares outstanding and the other with 100,000,000 shares should not be equally weighted if customers are expected to want 100,000 shares of each. In such a case, the potential appreciation in the first company is likely to be quite illusory for most clients.

In short, we can see a good reason for a broadly based unweighted arithmetic average and one weighted by outstanding shares. The new Quotron index is an example of the former and the old Standard and Poor's indexes or the newer New York Stock Exchange index are examples of the latter. It is quite unlikely that we would find any substantial difference in the behavior of the latter two indexes, despite the larger number of companies covered by the Stock Exchange index because the preponderance of market value is covered by both. Weighted indexes of the American Stock Exchange or the over-the-counter stocks, on the other hand, may behave quite differently because of the different type of stocks.

Unweighted averages will, of course, be more sensitive to composition, but past experience does not indicate much difference from weighted indexes *most of the time*. The Dow-Jones index, for example, is quite bizarre in its construction and falls under neither of my two classifications. Nevertheless, over quite long periods it has had much the same behavior as more sophisticated indexes.

Regardless of the particular indexes used, the most vital need in the security field is analysts who know enough about index numbers and the behavior of stock prices so that they can use measures appropriate to the purpose. The prestige of the field of security analysis can only suffer if analysts continue to use misleading indexes to measure their performance and to condemn good measures for behavior which merely reflects the performance of the marketplace.

Market Efficiency

6

INTRODUCTION: A STARTLING IDEA—CURRENT PRICES REFLECT WHAT IS KNOWABLE

The most important idea in this book, and one of the most important ideas in the field of investments, is that capital markets are "efficient." This does not mean that papers get shuffled cheaply and quickly; rather, it means that new information is widely, quickly, and cheaply available to investors, that this information includes what is knowable and relevant for judging securities, and that it is very rapidly reflected in security prices. This idea was considered bizarre in 1960 but by 1970 was very generally accepted by academicians and by many important financial institutions. This second section of the book includes essays in which the idea is explained and its validity is tested. Before commenting briefly on the individual articles, we will try to explain why the subject is so important.

If current prices reflect what is knowable and relevant for judging securities, it is extremely difficult consistently to discover bargains that will provide extraordinarily high returns or to invest in overpriced securities that will provide extraordinarily low returns. In order to do unusually well in choosing investments, one must foresee the future better than others. Expending effort to see the future only as well may be intrinsically satisfying, but it is not the source of superior or inferior performance.

The implications of this theory of investment management are twofold. First, if security analysis is to make any contribution to performance, the analyst must devise original ways of examining companies that have the promise of yielding superior insights. Secondly, emphasis should shift from conventional security analysis not only to unconventional analysis but also to the tasks of investment counseling and portfolio management. The first seeks to prescribe an unambiguous—*i.e.*, operationally meaningful—investment policy, while the other aims at selecting a portfolio of securities that is consistent with this policy.

The efficient-market hypothesis has three forms, which are discussed and explained in the next chapter. The first, or "weak," form, states that current prices reflect what is knowable from the study of historical prices and trading volume. This form has been termed the "random-walk" hypothesis, since the major tests of its validity were statistical tests for random-ness in successive price changes. The random-walk hypothesis was almost universally derided in the financial community as implying that the market was senseless or irrational; but, properly understood, the random behavior of stock prices is a consequence of intense competition between a large number of competent and avaricious investors. An important implication of the weak form is that technical analysis of stock prices is unlikely to be worthwhile.

The second, or "semistrong," form of the efficient-market hypothesis states that current prices reflect all public information about the companies whose securities are traded. If this is true, the purchase or sale of securities on the strength of such information is more likely to enrich the broker than the investor.

Finally, the third, or "strong," form of the efficient-market hypothesis suggests that current prices reflect not only the kind of public knowledge that stems from entries on the "broad tape" or from press releases but also the results of the probing inquiries of an ardent host of security analysts. Consequently, prices are liable to reflect not only everything that is known but also everything that is knowable. It would be impossible in these circumstances for any investor to achieve consistently superior performance.

It is extremely unlikely, in principle, that the efficient-market hypothesis is strictly true, particularly in its strongest form. For example, as long as information is not wholly free, one might expect investors to require some offsetting gain before they are willing to purchase it. Nor does the empirical evidence justify unqualified acceptance of the efficient-market hypothesis even in its weakest form. The important question, therefore, is not whether the theory is universally true, but whether it is sufficiently correct to provide useful insights into market behavior. There is now overwhelming evidence to suggest that the random-walk hypothesis is such a close approximation to reality that technical analysis cannot provide any guidance to the investment manager. When one turns to the stronger forms of the hypothesis, the evidence becomes less voluminous and the correspondence between theory and reality less exact. Nevertheless, the overriding impression is that of a highly competitive and efficient marketplace in which the opportunities for superior performance are rare.

The first included article in this section (Chapter 7) is a brilliant review by Fama that summarizes the theoretical arguments and the associated empirical work. It deserves careful study.

Fama refers to two important concepts that will recur frequently in succeeding chapters. Since they are not considered in any detail until Part II, it may be useful to summarize them here. The notion of market efficiency does not imply that some stocks cannot offer prospects of greater gain than others, for such attractions may be offset by corresponding disadvantages. Therefore, instead of simply examining the changes in price that follow the announcement of information, it may be more instructive to ascertain the extent to which such changes were unexpected or abnormal. For this purpose, expectations may be defined in terms of the historic relationship between the price movements of the individual security and those of a market index. Some stocks have traditionally responded to market movements with more than proportionate changes; others, with less than proportionate changes. The interesting price movements are those that are significantly different from what would have been expected on the basis of these historical relationships. This idea of a consistent relationship between the movements of the stock and those of a market index is often referred to as the "market model."

Tests of the strong form of the efficient-market hypothesis have been principally concerned with assessing whether one group of securities has given an unusually high rate of return relative to another group. For this purpose, it has proved useful to rely on a theory of market equilibrium that extends the concept outlined in the last paragraph. This theory (commonly known as the "capital asset pricing theory") states that the expected return on a security consists of the rate of interest plus a risk premium that is proportional to the stock's sensitivity to market movement. Therefore, if the risk premium on any portfolio is merely in line with its sensitivity, we should have some evidence that fund managers are unable to distinguish securities with unexpectedly high returns.

After Fama's review article, we include two discussions of the random-walk hypothesis. The first, by Harry Roberts, is simple and dramatic. For several decades, many technicians have been interpreting apparent patterns in the prices of common stocks and in indexes of the market. Roberts presents some evidence that the apparent patterns are indistinguishable from those generated by the sums of random numbers. Further, when price differences rather than prices are plotted, the regularities disappear, and the resulting data are indistinguishable from a sequence of random numbers. The article is important, because it challenged in a plausible and persuasive way beliefs that were prevalent in the financial community. It therefore inspired other investigators to undertake some very careful statistical tests of the random-walk phenomenon and to examine the possible economic rationale for their findings.

These early statistical studies were artificial in that they did not test procedures actually used by technicians. Jensen and Bennington are among those who have sought to remedy this deficiency. Their article (Chapter 9) reports a comprehensive analysis of the profitability of a popular technical criterion—the relative-strength rule.

The next article, by Fama, Fisher, Jensen, and Roll (Chapter 10), tests the semistrong form of the efficient-market hypothesis. The method used in this study has become a model for subsequent empirical work in the field. From an analysis of the abnormal price changes in the months leading up to and following a stock split, the authors conclude that, although splits do not of themselves affect the aggregate value of the shares, they do convey information about the company's prospects. The market is able to assess the value of this information rapidly and accurately. The study, however, is important less because stock splits themselves are important than because it suggests that current prices reflect not only direct information about the company's earning power but also information that requires rather more interpretation.

The article by Scholes (Chapter 11) extends still further the definition of "public information." Secondary distributions, he argues, warn investors that the seller may be in possession of private information. This is reflected in the stock price, which immediately falls by an amount roughly matching the expected value of the information. Scholes's finding is disturbing, for it suggests that even superior knowledge is of little value if its existence is revealed in the investor's actions. Note, however, that we should be careful not to interpret such findings too rigidly. There is evidence in Scholes's work of abnormal price drift after the secondary distribution, although it is small and may even be fortuitous. Scholes's paper is a storehouse of information on many topics. In particular, his discovery that the stock price is largely unaffected by the size of the offering constitutes important evidence of the liquidity of the stock market and the elasticity of demand for a particular security.

Chapters 12 and 13 contain evidence on the strong form of the efficient-market hypothesis. The former reports the results of a study by Jensen of the performance of mutual funds. Jensen's analysis makes extensive use of the capital asset pricing theory. Many readers may find it easier, therefore, to skip portions of the second section and return to it at a later stage. He concludes that, on average, any differences between their return and that of the market as a whole simply reflect differences in risk. Other studies of institutional investment have reached similar conclusions. We reproduce in the following pages four tables extracted from the Securities and Exchange Commission's study of institutional investing.[1] The performance measure (*a*) is very similar to that employed by Jensen and denotes the extra return that could have been achieved by investing a certain sum in the portfolio and the remainder in treasury bills in such a way as to ensure the same over-all degree of volatility as the market would have provided. The SEC's findings differ slightly according to type of fund and time period. Nevertheless, it is abundantly clear that none of these groups was in possession of very valuable monopolistic information. There is some evidence that one or two privileged classes of investors may have some advantage. Although they are not quantitatively important, they are interesting. We have therefore included an article by Pratt and DeVere on the implication of insider trading.

---

[1] U.S. Congress, *Institutional Investor Study Report of the Securities and Exchange Commission*, 92d Cong., 1st sess., 1971, H. Doc. No. 92–64, Vol. 2, pp. 333, 334, 466, and 744.

MUTUAL FUND PERFORMANCE 1960–69—125 FUNDS

PERFORMANCE SUMMARY (All Funds with Complete Data for 1960–69 Period)*

Evaluation Period	Volatility Range (Beta range)	No. Funds	No. Obs. (months)	Average Values (unweighted)					
				Monthly Fund Return %/month	Monthly Market Return %/month	Performance Measure (ALPHA) %/month	Volatility Measure (BETA)	Degree of Diversification	Total Assets ($ mil) at beg. of Obs.Period
Jan. '60–	0–0.4	3	120	0.43	0.77	0.007	0.23	0.27	27.3
	0.4–0.8	35	120	0.63	0.77	0.004	.68	0.59	94.3
Dec. '69	0.8–1.0	44	120	0.79	0.77	0.066	0.91	0.62	137.4
	1.0–1.2	30	120	0.86	0.77	0.056	1.07	0.66	73.7
	1.2+	13	120	1.05	0.77	0.130	1.33	0.56	90.8
	Total	125	120	0.78	0.77	0.051	0.91	0.61	102.6
Jan. '60–	0–0.4	4	60	0.60	1.05	0.245	0.16	0.20	22.6
	0.4–0.8	47	60	0.83	1.05	0.064	0.65	0.64	96.7
Dec. '64	0.8–1.0	43	60	0.82	1.05	−0.157	0.91	0.71	133.1
	1.0–1.2	22	60	0.73	1.05	−0.415	1.11	0.73	76.9
	1.2+	9	60	1.14	1.05	−0.162	1.30	0.62	84.8
	Total	125	60	0.82	1.05	−0.107	0.85	0.66	102.6
Jan. '65–	0–0.4	3	60	0.17	0.49	−0.250	0.26	0.29	39.6
	0.4–0.8	22	60	0.46	0.49	0.001	0.69	0.55	178.2
Dec. '69	0.8–1.0	46	60	0.68	0.49	0.194	0.91	0.62	223.9
	1.0–1.2	30	60	0.73	0.49	0.236	1.08	0.67	297.6
	1.2+	24	60	1.20	0.49	0.673	1.41	0.57	104.8
	Total	125	60	0.74	0.49	0.252	0.99	0.60	206.2

*TABLE IV–103. INSTITUTIONAL INVESTORS STUDY REPORT OF THE SECURITIES AND EXCHANGE COMMISSION.

MUTAL FUND PERFORMANCE 1960–69—236 FUNDS

PERFORMANCE SUMMARY (All Funds with at Least 9 Observations)*

Evaluation Period	Volatility Range (Beta range)	No. Funds	No. Obs. (months)	Average Values (unweighted)					
				Monthly Fund Return %/month	Monthly Market Return %/month	Performance Measure (ALPHA) %/month	Volatility Measure (BETA)	Degree of Diversification	Total Assets ($ mil) at beg. of Obs.Period
Jan. '60– Dec. '69	0–0.4	4	115	0.40	0.76	−0.010	0.20	0.23	27.6
	0.4–0.8	43	111	0.57	0.73	−0.030	0.69	0.56	119.3
	0.8–1.0	63	101	0.69	0.69	0.033	0.91	0.59	125.4
	1.0–1.2	56	97	0.69	0.66	−0.001	1.08	0.63	64.4
	1.2 +	70	62	0.81	0.49	0.327	1.51	0.58	40.1
	Total	236	90	0.70	0.63	0.100	1.08	0.58	82.9
Jan. '60– Dec. '64	0–0.4	7	49	0.50	1.11	0.11	0.18	0.16	17.7
	0.4–0.8	53	57	0.82	1.07	0.04	0.65	0.61	132.0
	0.8–1.0	44	59	0.83	1.07	−0.17	0.91	0.71	130.0
	1.0–1.2	34	52	0.64	1.11	−0.57	1.10	0.70	59.4
	1.2 +	20	52	0.90	1.08	−0.42	1.28	0.64	61.2
	Total	158	56	0.78	1.08	−0.20	0.88	0.64	101.8
Jan. '65– Dec. '69	0–0.4	4	60	0.17	0.49	−0.24	0.22	0.24	37.4
	0.4–0.8	28	58	0.37	0.47	−0.08	0.69	0.52	256.7
	0.8–1.0	69	56	0.63	0.47	0.160	0.92	0.60	193.8
	1.0–1.2	50	53	0.60	0.44	0.15	1.09	0.63	204.5
	1.2 +	85	46	0.93	0.41	0.56	1.53	0.58	59.5
	Total	236	52	0.69	0.44	0.27	1.13	0.58	153.9

* TABLE IV–104. INSTITUTIONAL INVESTOR STUDY REPORT OF THE SECURITIES AND EXCHANGE COMMISSION.

BANK COLLECTIVE INVESTMENT FUND PERFORMANCE 1967–69

(Summary of Performance Data and Other Characteristics
for 48 Bank Collective Investment Funds
by Volatility Range 1967–69)*

Volatility Range	Number of Funds	Average Number of Observations Per Fund	Unadjusted Monthly Fund Return % /Month	Monthly Market Return % /Month	Performance Measure (Alpha) % /Month	Volatility Measure (Average Beta)	Portfolio Turnover (1969) %	Fund Size (Average Common Stock) $ millions	Bank Size (Average Trust Department Assets) $ Billions
0.4–0.8	7	13.4	.33	.50	−.22	.65	8.2	31.6	5.0
0.8–1.0	19	22.8	.49	.57	−.09	.92	27.7	23.1	4.3
1.0–1.2	20	26.6	.48	.44	.06	1.09	50.9	39.3	3.2
Over 1.2	2	26	1.42	.62	.79	1.39	38.0	19.5	1.8
Total	48	23.1	.50	.51	−.01	.97	35.0	30.9	3.8

*TABLE V–22. INSTITUTIONAL INVESTOR STUDY REPORT OF THE SECURITIES AND EXCHANGE COMMISSION.

PERFORMANCE OF INSURANCE COMPANY SEPARATE ACCOUNTS

(Summary of Investment Return Data for the Separate
Accounts Classified by Volatility)*

Volatility Range	Number of Account	Average Number of Observations Per Account	Monthly Account Return Percent Per Month	Monthly Market Return Percent Per Month	Performance Measure (Alpha) Percent Per Month	Volatility Measure (average Beta)	Portfolio Turnover (1969)	Account Size (Average Common Stock Holdings) $ Millions	Advisor Size (Average Assets) $ Billions
0–0.4	3	40.7	.53	.46	−.09	.20	75.4	1.3	2.0
0.4–0.8	13	41.3	.32	.22	−.06	.64	43.7	23.2	14.8
0.8–1.0	30	48.1	.42	.31	.08	.93	34.9	11.1	5.5
1.0–1.2	24	52.0	.54	.40	.16	1.08	60.4	48.7	4.2
Over 1.2	10	27.1	.36	.25	.30	1.36	64.8	2.9	2.8
Total	80	45.3	.44	.32	.10	.95	49.2	23.0	6.2

NOTE: All averages are unweighted.
* TABLE VI–116. INSTITUTIONAL INVESTOR STUDY REPORT OF THE SECURITIES AND EXCHANGE COMMISSION.

7

EFFICIENT CAPITAL MARKETS: A REVIEW OF THEORY AND EMPIRICAL WORK *

Eugene F. Fama

0. Introduction

The primary role of the capital market is allocation of ownership of the economy's capital stock. In general terms, the ideal is a market in which prices provide accurate signals for resource allocation: that is, a market in which firms can make production-investment decisions, and investors can choose among the securities that represent ownership of firms' activities under the assumption that security prices at any time "fully reflect" all available information. A market in which prices always "fully reflect" available information is called "efficient".

This paper reviews the theoretical and empirical literature on the efficient markets model. After a discussion of the theory, empirical work concerned with the adjustment of security prices to three relevant information subsets is considered. First, *weak form* tests, in which the information set is just historical prices, are discussed. Then *semi-strong form* tests, in which the concern is whether prices efficiently adjust to other information that is obviously publicly available (e.g., announcements of annual earnings, stock splits, etc.) are considered. Finally, *strong form* tests concerned with whether

* Research on this project was supported by a grant from the National Science Foundation. I am indebted to Arthur Laffer, Robert Aliber, Ray Ball, Michael Jensen, James Lorie, Merton Miller, Charles Nelson, Richard Roll, William Taylor, and Ross Watts for their helpful comments.

Reprinted from *The Journal of Finance*, XXV, No. 2 (May, 1970), 383–417, by permission of the author and the publisher.

given investors or groups have monopolistic access to any information relevant for price formation are reviewed.[1] We shall conclude that, with but a few exceptions, the efficient markets model stands up well.

Though we proceed from theory to empirical work, to keep the proper historical perspective we should note that to a large extent the empirical work in this area preceded the development of the theory. The theory is presented first here in order to more easily judge which of the empirical results are most relevant from the viewpoint of the theory. The empirical work itself, however, will then be reviewed in more or less historical sequence.

Finally, the perceptive reader will surely recognize instances in this paper where relevant studies are not specifically discussed. In such cases my apologies should be taken for granted. The area is so bountiful that some such injustices are unavoidable. But the primary goal here will have been accomplished if a coherent picture of the main lines of the work on efficient markets is presented, along with an accurate picture of the current state of the arts.

1. The theory of efficient markets

1.0. *Expected return or "fair game" models*

The definitional statement that in an efficient market prices "fully reflect" available information is so general that it has no empirically testable implications. To make the model testable, the process of price formation must be specified in more detail. In essence we must define somewhat more exactly what is meant by the term "fully reflect".

One possibility would be to posit that equilibrium prices (or expected returns) on securities are generated as in the "two parameter" Sharpe (1964) — Lintner (1965a, b) world. In general, however, the theoretical models and especially the empirical tests of capital market efficiency have not been this specific. Most of the available work is based only on the assumption that the conditions of market equilibrium can (somehow) be stated in terms of expected returns. In general terms, like the two parameter model such theories would posit that, conditional on some relevant information set,

---

[1] The distinction between weak and strong form tests was first suggested by Harry Roberts.

the equilibrium expected return on a security is a function of its "risk". And different theories would differ primarily in how "risk" is defined.

All members of the class of such "*expected return theories*" can, however, be described notationally as follows:

$$E(\tilde{p}_{j,t+1} \mid \Phi_t) = [1 + E(\tilde{r}_{j,t+1} \mid \Phi_t)] p_{jt}, \tag{1}$$

where E is the expected value operator; p_{jt} is the price of security j at time t; $p_{j,t+1}$ is its price at $t+1$ (with reinvestment of any intermediate cash income from the security); $r_{j,t+1}$ is the one-period percentage return $(p_{j,t+1} - p_{jt})/p_{jt}$; Φ_t is a general symbol for whatever set of information is assumed to be "fully reflected" in the price at t; and the tildes indicate that $p_{j,t+1}$ and $r_{j,t+1}$ are random variables at t.

The value of the equilibrium expected return $E(\tilde{r}_{j,t+1} \mid \Phi_t)$ projected on the basis of the information Φ_t would be determined from the particular expected return theory at hand. The conditional expectation notation of (1) is meant to imply, however, that whatever expected return model is assumed to apply, the information in Φ_t is fully utilized in determining equilibrium expected returns. And this is the sense in which Φ_t is "fully reflected" in the formation of the price p_{jt}.

But we should note immediately that, simple as it is, the assumption that the conditions of market equilibrium can be stated in terms of expected returns elevates the purely mathematical concept of expected value to a status not necessarily implied by the general notion of market efficiency. The expected value is just one of many possible summary measures of a distribution of returns, and market efficiency *per se* (i.e., the general notion that prices "fully reflect" available information) does not imbue it with any special importance. Thus, the results of tests based on this assumption depend to some extent on its validity as well as on the efficiency of the market. But some such assumption is the unavoidable price one must pay to give the theory of efficient markets empirical content.

The assumptions that the conditions of market equilibrium can be stated in terms of expected returns and that equilibrium expected returns are formed on the basis of (and thus "fully reflect") the information set Φ_t have a major empirical implication — they rule out the possibility of trading systems based only on information in Φ_t that have expected profits or returns in excess of equilibrium expected profits on returns. Thus let

$$x_{j,t+1} = p_{j,t+1} - E(\tilde{p}_{j,t+1} \mid \Phi_t). \tag{2}$$

Then:

$$E(\tilde{x}_{j,t+1} | \Phi_t) = 0, \tag{3}$$

which, *by definition*, says that the sequence $\{x_{jt}\}$ is a "*fair game*" with respect to the information sequence $\{\Phi_t\}$. Or, equivalently, let:

$$z_{j,t+1} = r_{j,t+1} - E(\tilde{r}_{j,t+1} | \Phi_t). \tag{4}$$

Then:

$$E(\tilde{z}_{j,t+1} | \Phi_t) = 0, \tag{5}$$

so that the sequence $\{z_{jt}\}$ is also a "fair game" with respect to the information sequence $\{\Phi_t\}$.

In economic terms, $x_{j,t+1}$ is the excess market value of security j at time $t+1$: it is the difference between the observed price and the expected value of the price that was projected at t on the basis of the information Φ_t. And similarly, $z_{j,t+1}$ is the return at $t+1$ in excess of the equilibrium expected return projected at t. Let:

$$\alpha(\Phi_t) = [\alpha_1(\Phi_t), \alpha_2(\Phi_t), ..., \alpha_n(\Phi_t)]$$

be any trading system based on Φ_t which tells the investor the amounts $\alpha_j(\Phi_t)$ of funds available at t that are to be invested in each of the n available securities. The total excess market value at $t+1$ that will be generated by such a system is:

$$V_{t+1} = \sum_{j=1}^{n} \alpha_j(\Phi_t) \left[r_{j,t+1} - E(\tilde{r}_{j,t+1} | \Phi_t) \right],$$

which, from the "fair game" property of (5) has expectation:

$$E(\tilde{V}_{t+1} | \Phi_t) = \sum_{j=1}^{n} \alpha_j(\Phi_t) E(\tilde{z}_{j,t+1} | \Phi_t) = 0.$$

The expected return or "fair game" efficient markets model has other important testable implications, but these are better saved for the later discussion of the empirical work.[2] Now we turn to two special cases of the

---

[2] Though we shall sometimes refer to the model summarized by (1) as the "fair game" model, keep in mind that the "fair game" properties of the model are *implications* of the assumptions that (i) the conditions of market equilibrium can be stated in terms of expected returns, and (ii) the information Φ_t is fully utilized by the market in forming equilibrium expected returns and thus current prices. — The role of "fair game" models in the theory of efficient markets was first recognized and studied rigorously by Samuelson (1965) and Mandelbrot (1966). Their work will be discussed in more detail later.

model, the submartingale and the random walk, that (as we shall see later) play an important role in the empirical literature.

1.1. *The submartingale model*

Suppose we assume in (1) that for all t and Φ_t:

$$E(\tilde{p}_{j,t+1} | \Phi_t) \geq p_{jt}, \text{ or equivalently, } E(\tilde{r}_{j,t+1} | \Phi_t) \geq 0. \tag{6}$$

This is a statement that the price sequence $\{p_{jt}\}$ for security j follows a *submartingale* with respect to the information sequence $\{\Phi_t\}$, which is to say nothing more than that the expected value of next period's price, as projected on the basis of the information Φ_t, is equal to or greater than the current price. If (6) holds as an equality (so that expected returns and price changes are zero), then the price sequence follows a *martingale*.

A submartingale in prices has one important empirical implication. Consider the set of "one security and cash" mechanical trading rules by which we mean systems that concentrate on individual securities and that define the conditions under which the investor would hold a given security, sell it short, or simply hold cash at any time t. Then the assumption of (6) that expected returns conditional on Φ_t are non-negative directly implies that such trading rules based only on the information in Φ_t cannot have greater expected profits than a policy of always buying-and-holding the security during the future period in question. Tests of such rules will be an important part of the empirical evidence on the efficient markets model.[3]

1.2. *The random walk model*

In the early treatments of the efficient markets model, the statement that the current price of a security "fully reflects" available information was assumed

---

[3] Note that the expected profitability of "one security and cash" trading systems vis-à-vis buy-and-hold is not ruled out by the general expected return or "fair game" efficient markets model. The latter rules out systems with expected profits in excess of equilibrium expected returns, but since in principle it allows equilibrium expected returns to be negative, holding cash (which always has zero actual and thus expected return) may have higher expected return than holding some security. — And negative equilibrium expected returns for some securities are quite possible. For example, in the Sharpe (1964) — Lintner (1965a, b) model the equilibrium expected return on a security depends on the extent to which the dispersion in the security's return distribution is related to dispersion in the returns on all other securities. A security whose returns on average move opposite to the general market is particularly valuable in reducing dispersion of portfolio returns, and so its equilibrium expected return may well be negative.

to imply that successive price changes (or more usually, successive one-period returns) are independent. In addition, it was usually assumed that successive changes (or returns) are identically distributed. Together the two hypotheses constitute the *random walk model*. Formally, the model says:

$$f(r_{j,t+1} \mid \Phi_t) = f(r_{j,t+1}), \tag{7}$$

which is the usual statement that the conditional and marginal probability distributions of an independent random variable are identical. In addition, the density function f must be the same for all t.[4]

Expression (7) of course says much more than the general expected return model summarized by (1). For example, if we restrict (1) by assuming that the expected return on security j is constant over time, then we have:

$$E(\tilde{r}_{j,t+1} \mid \Phi_t) = E(\tilde{r}_{j,t+1}). \tag{8}$$

This says that the mean of the distribution of $r_{j,t+1}$ is independent of Φ_t, the information available at t, whereas the random walk model of (7) in addition says that the entire distribution is independent of Φ_t.[5]

We argue later that it is best to regard the random walk model as an extension of the general expected return or "fair game" efficient markets model in the sense of making a more detailed statement about the economic environment. The "fair game" model just says that the conditions of market equilibrium can be stated in terms of expected returns, and thus it says little about the details of the stochastic process generating returns. A random walk arises within the context of such a model when the environment is (fortuitously) such that the evolution of investor tastes and the process generating new information combine to produce equilibria in which return distributions repeat themselves through time.

---

[4] The terminology is loose. Prices will only follow a random walk if price changes are independent, identically distributed; and even then we should say "random walk with drift" since expected price changes can be non-zero. If one-period returns are independent, identically distributed, prices will not follow a random walk since the distribution of price changes will depend on the price level. But though rigorous terminology is usually desirable, our loose use of terms should not cause confusion; and our usage follows that of the efficient markets literature. — Note also that in the random walk literature, the information set Φ_t in (7) us usually assumed to include only the past return history, $r_{j,t}, r_{j,t+1}, \ldots$

[5] The random walk model does not say, however, that past information is of no value in *assessing* distributions of future returns. Indeed since return distributions are assumed to be stationary through time, past returns are the best source of such information. The random walk model does say, however, that the *sequence* (or the order) of the past returns is of no consequence in assessing distributions of future returns.

Thus it is not surprising that empirical tests of the "random walk" model that are in fact tests of "fair game" properties are more strongly in support of the model than tests of the additional (and, from the viewpoint of expected return market efficiency, superfluous) pure independence assumption. (But it is perhaps equally surprising that, as we shall soon see, the evidence against the independence of returns over time is as weak as it is.)

1.3. *Market conditions consistent with efficiency*

Before turning to the empirical work, however, a few words about the market conditions that might help or hinder efficient adjustment of prices to information are in order. First, it is easy to determine *sufficient* conditions for capital market efficiency. For example, consider a market in which (i) there are no transactions costs in trading securities, (ii) all available information is costlessly available to all market participants, and (iii) all agree on the implications of current information for the current price and distributions of future prices of each security. In such a market, the current price of a security obviously "fully reflects" all available information.

But a frictionless market in which all information is freely available and investors agree on its implications is, of course, not descriptive of markets met in practice. Fortunately, these conditions, while sufficient for market efficiency, are not necessary. For example, as long as transactors take account of all available information, even large transactions costs that inhibit the flow of transactions do not in themselves imply that when transactions do take place, prices will not "fully reflect" available information. Similarly (and speaking, as above, somewhat loosely), the market may be efficient if "sufficient numbers" of investors have ready access to available information. And disagreement among investors about the implications of given information does not in itself imply market inefficiency unless there are investors who can consistently make better evaluations of available information than are implicit in market prices.

But though (i) transactions costs, (ii) information that is not freely available to all investors, and (iii) disagreement among investors about the implications of given information are not necessarily sources of market inefficiency, they are *potential* sources. And all three exist to some extent in real world markets. Measuring their effects on the process of price formation is, of course, the major goal of empirical work in this area.

2. The evidence

All the empirical research on the theory of efficient markets has been concerned with whether prices "fully reflect" particular subsets of available information. Historically, the empirical work evolved more or less as follows. The initial studies were concerned with what we call *weak form* tests in which the information subset of interest is just past price (or return) histories. Most of the results here come from the random walk literature. When extensive tests seemed to support the efficiency hypothesis at this level, attention was turned to *semi-strong form* tests in which the concern is the speed of price adjustment to other obviously publicly available information (e.g., announcements of stock splits, annual reports, new security issues, etc.). Finally, *strong form* tests in which the concern is whether any investor or groups (e.g., managements of mutual funds) have monopolistic access to any information relevant for the formation of prices have recently appeared. We review the empirical research in more or less this historical sequence.

First, however, we should note that what we have called *the* efficient markets model in the discussions of earlier sections is the hypothesis that security prices at any point in time "fully reflect" *all* available information. Though we shall argue that the model stands up rather well to the data, it is obviously an extreme null hypothesis. And, like any other extreme null hypothesis, we do not expect it to be literally true. The categorization of the tests into weak, semi-strong, and strong form will serve the useful purpose of allowing us to pinpoint the level of information at which the hypothesis breaks down. And we shall contend that there is no important evidence against the hypothesis in the weak and semi-strong form tests (i.e., prices seem to efficiently adjust to obviously publicly available information), and only limited evidence against the hypothesis in the strong form tests (i.e., monopolistic access to information about prices does not seem to be a prevalent phenomenon in the investment community).

2.0. *Weak form tests of the efficient markets model*

2.0.0. *Random walks and fair games: a little historical background*

As noted earlier, all of the empirical work on efficient markets can be considered within the context of the general expected return or "fair game" model, and much of the evidence bears directly on the special submartingale expected return model of (6). Indeed, in the early literature, discussions of the efficient markets model were phrased in terms of the even more special random walk model, though we shall argue that most of the early authors were in fact concerned with more general versions of the "fair game" model.

Some of the confusion in the early random walk writings is understandable. Research on secuirty prices did not begin with the development of a theory of price formation which was then subjected to empirical tests. Rather, the impetus for the development of a theory came from the accumulation of evidence in the middle 1950's and early 1960's that the behavior of common stock and other speculative prices could be well approximated by a random walk. Faced with the evidence, economists felt compelled to offer some rationalization. What resulted was a theory of efficient markets stated in terms of random walks, but usually implying some more general "fair game" model.

It was not until the work of Samuelson (1965) and Mandelbrot (1966) that the role of "fair game" expected return models in the theory of efficient markets and the relationships between these models and the theory of random walks were rigorously studied.[6] These papers came somewhat after the major empirical work on random walks. In the earlier work, "theoretical" discussions, though usually intuitively appealing, were always lacking in rigor and often either vague or *ad hoc*. In short, until the Mandelbrot-Samuelson models appeared, there existed a large body of empirical results in search of a rigorous theory.

Thus, though his contributions were ignored for 60 years, the first statement and test of the random walk model was that of Bachelier (1900). But his "fundamental principle" for the behavior of prices was that speculation should be a "fair game"; in particular, the expected profits to the speculator should be zero. With the benefit of the modern theory of

---

[6] Basing their analyses on futures contracts in commodity markets, Mandelbrot and Samuelson show that if the price of such a contract at time t is the expected value at t (given information Φ_t) of the spot price at the termination of the contract, then the fututes price will follow a martingale with respect to the information sequence $\{\Phi_t\}$; that is, the expected price change from period to period will be zero, and the price changes will be a "fair game". If the equilibrium expected return is not assumed to be zero, our more general "fair game" model, summarized by (1), is obtained. — But though the Mandelbrot-Samuelson approach certainly illuminates the process of price formation in commodity markets, we have seen that "fair game" expected return models can be derived in much simpler fashion. In particular, (1) is just a formalization of the assumptions that the conditions of market equilibrium can be stated in terms of expected returns and that the information Φ_t is used in forming market prices at t.

stochastic processes, we know now that the process implied by this fundamental principle is a martingale.

After Bachelier, research on the behavior of security prices lagged until the coming of the computer. In 1953 Kendall examined the behavior of weekly changes in nineteen indices of British industrial share prices and in spot prices for cotton (New York) and wheat (Chicago). After extensive analysis of serial correlations, he suggests, in quite graphic terms:

> The series looks like a wandering one, almost as if once a week the Demon of Chance drew a random number from a symmetrical population of fixed dispersion and added it to the current price to determine the next week's price. (Kendall 1953, p. 13).

Kendall's conclusion had in fact been suggested earlier by Working (1934), though his suggestion lacked the force provided by Kendall's empirical results. And the implications of the conclusion for stock market research and financial analysis were later underlined by Roberts (1959).

But the suggestion by Kendall, Working, and Roberts that series of speculative prices may be well described by random walks was based on observation. None of these authors attempted to provide much economic rationale for the hypothesis, and, indeed, Kendall felt that economists would generally reject it. Osborne (1959) suggested market conditions, similar to those assumed by Bachelier, that would lead to a random walk. But in his model, independence of successive price changes derives from the assumption that the decisions of investors in an individual security are independent from transaction to transaction — which is little in the way of an economic model.

Whenever economists (prior to Mandelbrot and Samuelson) tried to provide economic justification for the random walk, their arguments usually implied a "fair game". For example, Alexander (Cootner 1964, p. 200) states:

> If one were to start out with the assumption that a stock or commodity speculation is a "fair game" with equal expectation of gain or loss or, more accurately, with an expectation of zero gain, one would be well on the way to picturing the behavior of speculative prices as a random walk.

There is an awareness here that the "fair game" assumption is not sufficient to lead to a random walk, but Alexander never expands on the comment. Similarly, Cootner (1964, p. 232) states:

> If any substantial group of buyers thought prices were too low, their buying would force up the prices. The reverse would be true for sellers. Except for appreciation due to earnings retention, the conditional expectation of tomorrow's price, given today's price, is today's price.

> In such a world, the only price changes that would occur are those that result from new information. Since there is no reason to expect that information to be non-random in appearance, the period-to-period price changes of a stock should be random movements, statistically independent of one another.

Though somewhat imprecise, the last sentence of the first paragraph seems to point to a "fair game" model rather than a random walk.[7] In this light, the second paragraph can be viewed as an attempt to describe environmental conditions that would reduce a "fair game" to a random walk. But the specification imposed on the information generating process is insufficient for this purpose; one would, e.g., also have to say something about investor tastes. Finally, lest I be accused of criticizing others too severely for ambiguity, lack of rigor and incorrect conclusions:

> By contrast, the stock market trader has a much more practical criterion for judging what constitutes important dependence in successive price changes. For his purposes the random walk model is valid as long as knowledge of the past behavior of the series of price changes cannot be used to increase expected gains. More specifically, the independence assumption is an adequate description of reality as long as the actual degree of dependence in the series of price changes is not sufficient to allow the past history of the series to be used to predict the future in a way which makes expected profits greater than they would be under a naive buy-and-hold model. (Fama 1965, p. 35).

We know now, of course, that this last condition hardly requires a random walk. It will in fact be met by the submartingale model of (6).

But one should not be too hard on the theoretical efforts of the early empirical random walk literature. The arguments were usually appealing; where they fell short was in awareness of developments in the theory of stochastic processes. Moreover, we shall now see that most of the empirical evidence in the random walk literature can easily be interpreted as tests of more general expected return or "fair game" models.[8]

2.0.1. *Tests of market efficiency in the random walk literature*

As discussed earlier, "fair game" models imply the "impossibility" of various sorts of trading systems. Some of the random walk literature has

---

[7] The appropriate conditioning statement would be "Given the sequence of historical prices".

[8] Our brief historical review is meant only to provide perspective, and it is, of course, somewhat incomplete. For example, we have ignored the important contributions to the early random walk literature in studies of warrants and other options by Sprenkle, Kruizenga, Boness, and others. Much of this early work on options is summarized in Cootner (1964).

been concerned with testing the profitability of such systems. More of the literature has, however, been concerned with tests of serial covariances of returns. We shall now show that, like a random walk, the serial covariances of a "fair game" are zero, so that these tests are also relevant for the expected return models.

If $\{x_t\}$ is a "fair game", its unconditional expectation is zero and its serial covariance can be written in general form as:

$$E(\tilde{x}_{t+\tau}\,\tilde{x}_t) = \int_{x_t} x_t\,E(\tilde{x}_{t+\tau}\,|\,x_t)\,f(x_t)\,\mathrm{d}x_t\,,$$

where f indicates a density function. But if $\{x_t\}$ is a "fair game"[9]:

$$E(\tilde{x}_{t+\tau}\,|\,x_t) = 0\,.$$

From this it follows that for all lags, the serial covariances between lagged values of a "fair game" variable are zero. Thus, observations of a "fair game" variable are linearly independent.[10]

---

[9] More generally, if the sequence $\{x_t\}$ is a fair game with respect to the information sequence $\{\Phi_t\}$ (i.e., $E(\tilde{x}_{t+1}\,|\,\Phi_t) = 0$ for all Φ_t), then $\{x_t\}$ is a fair game with respect to any Φ'_t that is a subset of Φ_t (i.e., $E(\tilde{x}_{t+1}\,|\,\Phi'_t) = 0$ for all Φ'_t). To show this, let $\Phi_t = (\Phi'_t, \Phi''_t)$. Then, using Stieltjes integrals and the symbol F to denote cumulative distribution functions, the conditional expectation

$$E(\tilde{x}_{t+1}\,|\,\Phi'_t) = \int_{\Phi''_t}\int_{x_{t+1}} x_{t+1}\,\mathrm{d}F(x_{t+1}, \Phi''_t\,|\,\Phi'_t)$$

$$= \int_{\Phi''_t}\left[\int_{x_{t+1}} x_{t+1}\,\mathrm{d}F(x_{t+1}\,|\,\Phi'_t, \Phi''_t)\right]\mathrm{d}F(\Phi''_t\,|\,\Phi'_t).$$

But the integral in brackets is just $E(\tilde{x}_{t+1}\,|\,\Phi_t)$ which by the "fair game" assumption is zero, so that:

$$E(x_{t+1}\,|\,\Phi'_t) = 0 \text{ for all } \Phi'_t \subset \Phi_t\,.$$

[10] But though zero serial covariances are consistent with a "fair game", they do not imply such a process. A "fair game" also rules out many types of nonlinear dependence. Thus using arguments similar to those above, it can be shown that if x is a "fair game", $E(\tilde{x}_t\tilde{x}_{t+1}\cdots\tilde{x}_{t+\tau}) = 0$ for all τ, which is not implied by $E(\tilde{x}_t\tilde{x}_{t+\tau}) = 0$ for all τ. For example, consider a three-period case where x must be either ± 1. Suppose the process is $x_{t+2} = \text{sign}\,(x_t x_{t+1})$, i.e.,

x_{2t}	x_{t+}	$\to x_{t+1}$
+	+	$\to$ +
+	−	$\to$ −
−	+	$\to$ −
−	−	$\to$ +

But the "fair game" model does not necessarily imply that the serial covariances of *one-period returns* are zero. In the weak form tests of this model the "fair game" variable is (cf. footnote 9):

$$z_{j,t} = r_{j,t} - E(\tilde{r}_{j,t} r_{j,t-1}, r_{j,t-2}, \ldots).$$

(9)

But the covariance between, e.g., r_{jt} and $r_{j,t+1}$ is:

$$E([\tilde{r}_{j,t+1} - E(\tilde{r}_{j,t+1})][\tilde{r}_{jt} - E(\tilde{r}_{jt})])$$

$$= \int_{r_{jt}} [r_{jt} - E(\tilde{r}_{jt})] [E(\tilde{r}_{j,t+1} \mid r_{jt}) - E(\tilde{r}_{j,t+1})] f(r_{jt}) \, dr_{jt},$$

and (9) does not imply that $E(\tilde{r}_{j,t+1} \mid r_{jt}) = E(\tilde{r}_{j,t+1})$: In the "fair game" efficient markets model, the deviation of the return for $t+1$ from its conditional expectation is a "fair game" variable, but the conditional expectation itself can depend on the return observed for t.[11]

In the random walk literature, this problem is not recognized, since it is assumed that the expected return (and indeed the entire distribution of returns) is stationary through time. In practice, this implies estimating serial covariances by taking cross products of deviations of observed returns from the overall sample mean return. It is somewhat fortuitous, then, that this procedure, which represents a rather gross approximation from the viewpoint of the general expected return efficient markets model, does not seem to greatly affect the results of the covariance tests, at least for common stocks.[12]

For example, table 1 (taken from Fama 1965) shows the serial correlations between successive changes in the natural log of price for each of the thirty

---

If probabilities are uniformly distributed across events,

$$E(\tilde{x}_{t+2} \mid x_{t+1}) = E(\tilde{x}_{t+2} \mid x_t) = E(\tilde{x}_{t+1} \mid x_t) = E(\tilde{x}_{t+2}) = E(\tilde{x}_{t+1}) = E(\tilde{x}_t) = 0,$$

so that all pairwise serial convariances are zero. But the process is not a "fair game", since $E(\tilde{x}_{t+2} \mid x_{t+1}, x_t) \neq 0$, and knowledge of (x_{t+1}, x_t) can be used as the basis of a simple "system" with positive expected profit.

[11] For example, suppose the level of one-period returns follows a martingale so that:

$$E(r_{j,t+1} \mid r_{jt}, r_{j,t+1} \ldots) = r_{jt}.$$

Then covariances between successive returns will be nonzero (though in this special case first differences of returns will be uncorrelated).

[12] The reason is probably that for stocks, changes in equilibrium expected returns for the common differencing intervals of a day, a week, or a month, are trivial relative to other sources of variation in returns. Later, when we consider Roll's (1968) work, we shall see that this is not true for one week returns on U.S. Government Treasury Bills.

stocks of the Dow Jones Industrial Average, for time periods that vary slightly from stock to stock, but usually run from about the end of 1957 to September 26, 1962. The serial correlations of successive changes in $\log_e$ price are shown for differencing intervals or 1, 4, 9, and 16 days.[13]

Table 1 (from Fama 1965)

First-order serial correlation coefficients for 1, 4, 9, and 16 day changes in $\log_e$ price

Stock	Differencing Interval (Days)			
	One	Four	Nine	Sixteen
Allied Chemical	0.017	0.029	−0.091	−0.118
Alcoa	0.118*	0.095	−0.112	−0.044
American Can	−0.087*	−0.124*	−0.060	0.031
A.T. & T.	−0.039	−0.010	−0.009	−0.003
American Tobacco	0.111*	−0.175*	0.033	0.007
Anaconda	0.067*	−0.068	−0.125	0.202
Bethlehem Steel	0.013	−0.122	−0.148	0.112
Chrysler	0.012	0.060	−0.026	0.040
DuPont	0.013	0.069	−0.043	−0.055
Eastman Kodak	0.025	−0.006	−0.053	−0.023
General Electric	0.011	0.020	−0.004	0.000
General Foods	0.061*	−0.005	−0.140	−0.098
General Motors	−0.004	−0.128*	0.009	−0.028
Goodyear	−0.123*	0.001	−0.037	0.033
International Harvester	−0.017	−0.068	−0.244*	0.116
International Nickel	0.096*	0.038	0.124	0.041
International Paper	0.046	0.060	−0.004	−0.010
Johns Manville	0.006	−0.068	−0.002	0.002
Owens Illinois	−0.021	−0.006	0.003	−0.022
Procter & Gamble	0.099*	−0.006	0.098	0.076
Sears	0.097*	−0.070	−0.113	0.041
Standard Oil (Calif.)	0.025	−0.143*	−0.046	0.040
Standard Oil (N.J.)	0.008	−0.109	−0.082	−0.121
Swift & Co.	−0.004	−0.072	0.118	−0.197
Texaco	0.094*	−0.053	−0.047	−0.178
Union Carbide	0.107*	0.049	−0.101	0.124
United Aircraft	0.014	−0.190*	−0.192*	−0.040
U.S. Steel	0.040	−0.006	−0.056	0.236*
Westinghouse	−0.027	−0.097	−0.137	0.067
Woolworth	0.028	−0.033	−0.112	0.040

* Coefficient is twice its computed standard error.

---

[13] The use of changes in $\log_e$ price as the measure of return is common in the random walk literature. It can be justified in several ways. But for current purposes, it is sufficient to note that for price changes less than 15%, the change in $\log_e$ price is approximately the percentage price change or one-period return. And for differencing intervals shorter

The results in table 1 are typical of those reported by others for tests based on serial covariances. (Cf. Kendall (1953); Moore (1962); Alexander (1961), and the results of Granger and Morgenstern (1963) and Godfrey et al. (1964) obtained by means of spectral analysis). Specifically, there is no evidence of substantial linear dependence between lagged price changes or returns. In absolute terms the measured serial correlations are always close to zero.

Looking hard, though, one can probably find evidence of statistically "significant" linear dependence in table 1 (and again this is true of results reported by others). For the daily returns eleven of the serial correlations are more than twice their computed standard errors, and twenty-two out of thirty are positive. On the other hand, twenty-one and twenty-four of the coefficients for the 4 and 9 day differences are negative. But with samples of the size underlying table 1 ($N = 1200$-1700 observations per stock on a daily basis) statistically "significant" deviations from zero covariance are not necessarily a basis for rejecting the efficient markets model. For the results in table 1, the standard errors of the serial correlations were approximated as $(1/(N-1))^{1/2}$, which for the daily data implies that a correlation as small as 0.06 is more than twice its standard error. But a coefficient this size implies that a linear relationship with the lagged price change can be used to explain about 0.36% of the variation in the current price change, which is probably insignificant from an economic viewpoint. In particular, it is unlikely that the small absolute levels of serial correlation that are always observed can be used as the basis of substantially profitable trading systems.[14]

It is, of course, difficult to judge what degree of serial correlation would

---

than one month, returns in excess of 15% are unusual. Thus Fama (1965) reports that for the data of table 1, tests carried out on percentage or one-period returns yielded results essentially identical to the tests based on changes in $\log_e$ price.

[14] Given the evidence of Kendall (1953), Mandelbrot (1963), Fama (1965) and others that large price changes occur much more frequently than would be expected if the generating process were Gaussian, the expression $(1/(N-1))^{1/2}$ understates the sampling dispersion of the serial correlation coefficient, and thus leads to an overstatement of significance levels. In addition, the fact that sample serial correlations are predominantly of one sign or the other is not in itself evidence of linear dependence. If, as the work of King (1966) and Blume (1968) indicates, there is a market factor whose behavior affects the returns on all securities, the sample behavior of this market factor may lead to a predominance of signs of one type in the serial correlations for individual securities, even though the population serial correlations for both the market factor and the returns on individual securities are zero. For a more extensive analysis of these issues see Fama (1965).

imply the existence of trading rules with substantial expected profits. (And indeed we shall soon have to be a little more precise about what is implied by "substantial" profits.) Moreover, zero serial covariances are consistent with a "fair game" model, but as noted earlier (footnote 10), there are types of nonlinear dependence that imply the existence of profitable trading systems, and yet do not imply nonzero serial covariances. Thus, for many reasons it is desirable to directly test the profitability of various trading rules.

The first major evidence on trading rules was Alexander's (1961, 1964). He tests a variety of systems, but the most thoroughly examined can be described as follows: If the price of a security moves up at least $y\%$, buy and hold the security until its price moves down at least $y\%$ from a subsequent high, at which time simultaneously sell and go short. The short position is maintained until the price rises at least $y\%$ above a subsequent low, at which time one covers the short position and buys. Moves less than $y\%$ in either direction are ignored. Such a system is called a $y\%$ filter. It is obviously a "one security and cash" trading rule, so that the results it produces are relevant for the submartingale expected return model of (6).

After extensive tests using daily data on price indices from 1897 to 1959 and filters from 1 to 50%, and after correcting some incorrect presumptions in the initial results of Alexander (1961) (see footnote 25), in his final paper on the subject, Alexander concludes:

> In fact, at this point I should advise any reader who is interested only in practical results, and who is not a floor trader and so must pay commissions, to turn to other sources on how to beat buy and hold. The rest of this article is devoted principally to a theoretical consideration of whether the observed results are consistent with a random walk hypothesis. (Cootner 1964, p. 351).

Later in the paper Alexander concludes that there is some evidence in his results against the independence assumption of the random walk model. But market efficiency does not require a random walk, and from the viewpoint of the submartingale model of (6), the conclusion that the filters cannot beat buy-and-hold is support for the efficient markets hypothesis. Further support is provided by Fama and Blume (1966) who compare the profitability of various filters to buy-and-hold for the individual stocks of the Dow-Jones Industrial Average. (The data are those underlying table 1.)

But again, looking hard one can find evidence in the filter tests of both Alexander and Fama-Blume that is inconsistent with the submartingale efficient markets model, if that model is interpreted in a strict sense. In particular, the results for very small filters (1% in Alexander's tests and 0.5, 1.0, and 1.5% in the tests of Fama-Blume) indicate that it is possible to devise trading schemes based on very short-term (preferably intra-day but at most daily) price swings that will on average outperform buy-and-hold. The average profits on individual transactions from such schemes are miniscule, but they generate transactions so frequently that over longer periods and ignoring commissions they outperform buy-and-hold by a substantial margin. These results are evidence of persistence or positive dependence in very short-term price movements. And, interestingly, this is consistent with the evidence for slight positive linear dependence in successive daily price changes produced by the serial correlations.[15]

But when one takes account of even the minimum trading costs that would be generated by small filters, their advantage over buy-and-hold disappears. For example, even a floor trader (i.e., a person who owns a seat) on the New York Stock Exchange must pay clearinghouse fees on his trades that amount to about 0.1% per turnaround transaction (i.e., sales plus purchase). Fama-Blume show that because small filters produce such frequent trades, these minimum trading costs are sufficient to wipe out their advantage over buy-and-hold.

Thus the filter tests, like the serial correlations, produce empirically noticeable departures from the strict implications of the efficient markets model. But, in spite of any statistical significance they might have, from an

---

[15] Though strictly speaking, such tests of pure independence are not directly relevant for expected return models, it is interesting that the conclusion that very short-term swings in prices persist slightly longer than would be expected under the martingale hypothesis is also supported by the results of non-parametric runs tests applied to the daily data of table 1. (See Fama 1965, Tables 12-15.) For the daily prices changes, the actual number of runs of price changes of the same sign is less than the expected number for 26 out of 30 stocks. Moreover, of the eight stocks for which the actual number of runs is more than two standard errors less than the expected number, five of the same stocks have positive daily, first order serial correlations in table 1 that are more than twice their standard errors. But in both cases the statistical "significance" of the results is largely a reflection of the large sample sizes. Just as the serial correlations are small in absolute terms (the average is 0.026), the differences between the expected and actual number of runs on average are only 3% of the total expected number. — On the other hand, it is also interesting that the runs tests do not support the suggestion of slight negative dependence in 4 and 9 day changes that appeared in the serial correlations. In the runs tests such negative dependence would appear as a tendency for the actual number of runs to exceed the expected number. In fact, for the 4 and 9 day price changes, for 17 and 18 of the 30 stocks in table 1 the actual number of runs is less than the expected number. Indeed, runs tests in general show no consistent evidence of dependence for any differencing interval longer than a day, which seems especially pertinent in light of the comments in footnote 14.

economic viewpoint the departures are so small that it seems hardly justified to use them to declare the market inefficient.

2.0.2. *Other tests of independence in the random walk literature*

It is probably best to regard the random walk model as a special case of the more general expected return model in the sense of making a more detailed specification of the economic environment. That is, the basic model of market equilibrium is the "fair game" expected return model, with a random walk arising when additional environmental conditions are such that distributions of one-period returns repeat themselves through time. From this viewpoint violations of the pure independence assumption of the random walk model are to be expected. But when judged relative to the benchmark provided by the random walk model, these violations can provide insights into the nature of the market environment.

For example, one departure from the pure independence assumption of the random walk model has been noted by Osborne (1962), Fama (1965, Table 17 and Figure 8), and others. In particular, large daily price changes tend to be followed by large daily changes. The signs of the successor changes are apparently random, however, which indicates that the phenomenon represents a denial of the random walk model but not of the market efficiency hypothesis. Nevertheless, it is interesting to speculate why the phenomenon might arise. It may be that when important new information comes into the market, it cannot always be immediately evaluated precisely. Thus, sometimes the initial price will overadjust to the information, and other times it will underadjust. But since the evidence indicates that the price changes on days following the initial large change are random in sign, the initial large change at least represents an unbiased adjustment to the ultimate price effects of the information, and this is sufficient for the expected return efficient markets model.

Niederhoffer and Osborne (1966) document two departures from complete randomness in common stock price changes from transaction to transaction. First, their data indicate that reversals (pairs of consecutive price changes of opposite sign) are from two to three times as likely as continuations (pairs of consecutive price changes of the same sign). Second, a continuation is slightly more frequent after a preceding continuation than after a reversal. That is, let $(+|++)$ indicate the occurrence of a positive price change, given two preceding positive changes. Then the events

$(+|++)$ and $(-|--)$ are slightly more frequent than $(+|+-)$ or $(-|-+)$.[16]

Niederhoffer and Osborne offer explanations for these phenomena based on the market structure of the New York Stock Exchange (N.Y.S.E.). In particular, there are three major types of orders that an investor might place in a given stock: (a) buy limit (buy at a specified price or lower), (b) sell limit (sell at a specified price or higher), and (c) buy or sell at market (at the lowest selling or highest buying price of another investor). A book of unexecuted limit orders in a given stock is kept by the specialist in that stock on the floor of the exchange. Unexecuted sell limit orders are, of course, at higher prices than unexecuted buy limit orders. On both exchanges, the smallest non zero price change allowed is $\frac{1}{8}$ point.

Suppose now that there is more than one unexecuted sell limit order at the lowest price of any such order. A transaction at this price (initiated by an order to buy at market[17]) can only be followed either by a transaction at the same price (if the next market order is to buy) or by a transaction at a lower price (if the next market order is to sell). Consecutive price increases can usually only occur when consecutive market orders to buy exhaust the sell limit orders at a given price.[18] In short, the excessive tendency toward reversal for consecutive non zero price changes could result from bunching of unexecuted buy and sell limit orders.

The tendency for the events $(+|++)$ and $(-|--)$ to occur slightly more frequently than $(+|+-)$ and $(-|-+)$ requires a more involved explanation which we shall not attempt to reproduce in full here. In brief, Niederhoffer and Osborne contend that the higher frequency of $(+|++)$ relative to $(+|+-)$ arises from a tendency for limit orders "to be concentrated at integers (26, 43), halves ($26\frac{1}{2}$, $43\frac{1}{2}$), even eighths and odd eighths in descending order of preference".[19] The frequency of the event $(+|++)$,

---

[16] On a transaction to transaction basis, positive and negative price changes are about equally likely. Thus, under the assumption that price changes are random, any pair of non zero changes should be as likely as any other, and likewise for triplets of consecutive non zero changes.

[17] A buy limit order for a price equal to or greater than the lowest available sell limit price is effectively an order to buy at market, and is treated as such by the broker.

[18] The exception is when there is a gap of more than $\frac{1}{8}$ between the highest unexecuted buy limit and the lowest unexecuted sell limit order, so that market orders (and new limit orders) can be crossed at intermediate prices.

[19] Their empirical documentation for this claim is a few samples of specialists' books for selected days, plus the observation (Osborne 1962) that actual trading prices, at least for volatile high priced stocks, seem to be concentrated at integers, halves, quarters and odd eighths in descending order.

which usually requires that sell limit orders be exhausted at at least two consecutively higher prices (the last of which is relatively more frequently at an odd eighth), more heavily reflects the absence of sell limit orders at odd eighths than the event $(+|+-)$, which usually implies that sell limit orders at only one price have been exhausted and so more or less reflects the average bunching of limit orders at all eighths.

But though Niederhoffer and Osborne present convincing evidence of statistically significant departures from independence in price changes from transaction to transaction, and though their analysis of their findings presents interesting insights into the process of market making on the major exchanges, the types of dependence uncovered do not imply market inefficiency. The best documented source of dependence, the tendency toward excessive reversals in pairs of non zero price changes, seems to be a direct result of the ability of investors to place limit orders as well as orders at market, and this negative dependence in itself does not imply the existence of profitable trading rules. Similarly, the apparent tendency for observed transactions (and, by implication, limit orders) to be concentrated at integers, halves, even eighths and odd eighths in descending order is an interesting fact about investor behavior, but in itself is not a basis on which to conclude that the market is inefficient.[20]

The Niederhoffer-Osborne analysis of market making does, however, point to the existence of market inefficiency, with respect to *strong form* tests of the efficient markets model. In particular, the list of unexecuted buy and sell limit orders in the specialist's book is important information about the likely future behavior of prices, and this information is only available to the specialist. When the specialist is asked for a quote, he gives the prices and can give the quantities of the highest buy limit and lowest sell limit orders on his book, but he is prevented by law from divulging the

---

[20] Niederhoffer and Osborne offer little to refute this conclusion. For example (1966, p. 914): "Although the specific properties reported in this study gave a significance from a statistical point of view, the reader may well ask whether or not they are helpful in a practical sense. Certain trading rules emerge as a result of our analysis. One is that limit and stop orders should be placed at odd eighths, preferably at 7/8 for sell orders and at 1/8 for buy orders. Another is to buy when a stock advances through a barrier and to sell when it sinks through a barrier." The first "trading rule" tells the investor to resist his innate inclination to place orders at integers, but rather to place sell orders $\frac{1}{8}$ below an integer and buy order $\frac{1}{8}$ above. Successful execution of the orders is then more likely, since the congestion of orders that occur at integers is avoided. But the cost of this success is apparent. The second "trading rule" seems no more promising, if indeed it can even be translated into a concrete prescription for action.

book's full contents. The interested reader can easily imagine situations where the structure of limit orders in the book could be used as the basis of a profitable trading rule.[21] But the record seems to speak for itself:

> It should not be assumed that these transactions undertaken by the specialist, and in which he is involved as buyer or seller in 24 per cent of all market volume, are necessarily a burden to him. Typically, the specialist sells above his last purchase on 83 per cent of all his sales, and buys below his last sale on 81 per cent of all his purchases. (Niederhoffer and Osborne 1966, p. 908.)

Thus it seems that the specialist has monopoly power over an important block of information, and, not unexpectedly, uses his monopoly to turn a profit. And this, of course, is evidence of market inefficiency in the strong form sense. The important economic question, of course, is whether the market making function of the specialist could be fulfilled more economically by some non-monopolistic mechanism.[22]

2.0.3. *Distributional evidence*

At this date the weight of the empirical evidence is such that economists would generally agree that whatever dependence exists in series of historical returns cannot be used to make profitable predictions of the future. Indeed, for returns that cover periods of a day or longer, there is little in the evidence that would cause rejection of the stronger random walk model, at least as a good first approximation.

Rather, the last burning issue of the random walk literature has centered on the nature of the distribution of price changes (which, we should note immediately, is an important issue for the efficient markets hypothesis since the nature of the distribution affects both the types of statistical tools relevant for testing the hypothesis and the interpretation of any results obtained). A model implying normally distributed price changes was first

---

[21] See, Niederhoffer and Osborne (1966, p. 908). But it is unlikely that anyone but the specialist could earn substantial profits from knowledge of the structure of unexecuted limit orders on the book. The specialist makes trading profits by engaging in many transactions, each of which has a small average profit; but for any other trader, including those with seats on the exchange, these profits would be eaten up by commissions to the specialist.

[22] With modern computers, it is hard to believe that a more competetive and economical system would not be feasible. It does not seem technologically impossible to replace the entire floor of the N.Y.S.E. with a computer, fed by many remote consoles, that kept all the books now kept by the specialists, that could easily make the entire book on any stock available to anybody (so that interested individuals could then compete to "make a market" in a stock) and that carried out transactions automatically.

proposed by Bachelier (1900), who assumed that price changes from transaction to transaction are independent, identically distributed random variables with finite variances. If transactions are fairly uniformly spread across time, and if the number of transactions per day, week, or month is very large, then the Central Limit Theorem leads us to expect that these price changes will have normal or Gaussian distributions.

Osborne (1959), Moore (1962), and Kendall (1953) all thought their empirical evidence supported the normality hypothesis, but all observed high tails (i.e., higher proportions of large observations) in their data distributions vis-à-vis what would be expected if the distributions were normal. Drawing on these findings and some empirical work of his own, Mandelbrot (1963) then suggested that these departures from normality could be explained by a more general form of the Bachelier model. In particular, if one does not assume that distributions of price changes from transaction to transaction necessarily have finite variances, then the limiting distributions for price changes over longer differencing intervals could be any member of the stable class, which includes the normal as a special case. Non-normal stable distributions have higher tails than the normal, and so can account for this empirically observed feature of distributions of price changes. After extensive testing (involving the data from the stocks in table 1), Fama (1965) concludes that non-normal stable distributions are a better description of distributions of daily returns on common stocks than the normal. This conclusion is also supported by the empirical work of Blume (1968) on common stocks, and it has been extended to U.S. Government Treasury Bills by Roll (1968).

Economists have, however, been reluctant to accept these results, primarily because of the wealth of statistical techniques available for dealing with normal variables and the relative paucity of such techniques for non-normal stable variables.[23] But perhaps the biggest contribution of

---

[23] Some have suggested that the long-tailed empirical distributions might result from processes that are mixtures of normal distributions with different variances. Press (1968), e. g., suggests a Poisson mixture of normals in which the resulting distributions of price changes have long tails but finite variances. On the other hand, Mandelbrot and Taylor (1967) show that other mixtures of normals can still lead to non-normal stable distributions of price changes for finite differencing intervals. — If, as Press' model would imply, distributions of price changes are long-tailed but have finite variances, then distributions of price changes over longer and longer differencing intervals should be progressively closer to the normal. No such convergence to normality was observed in Fama (1953) (though admittedly the techniques used were somewhat rough). Rather,

Mandelbrot's work has been to stimulate research on stable distributions and estimation procedures to be applied to stable variables. (See, e.g., Wise (1963), Fama and Roll (1968), and Blattberg and Sargent (1970), among others.) The advance of statistical sophistication (and the importance of examining distributional assumptions in testing the efficient markets model) is well illustrated in Roll (1968), as compared, e.g., with the early empirical work of Mandelbrot (1963) and Fama (1965).

2.0.4. *"Fair game" models in the treasury till market*

Roll's work is novel in other respects as well. Coming after the efficient markets models of Mandelbrot (1966) and Samuelson (1965), it is the first weak form empirical work that is consciously in the "fair game" rather than the random walk tradition.

More important, as we saw earlier, the "fair game" properties of the general expected return models apply to:

$$z_{jt} = r_{jt} - E(\tilde{r}_{jt} | \Phi_{t-1}). \tag{10}$$

For data on common stocks, tests of "fair game" (and random walk) properties seem to go well when the conditional expected return is estimated as the average return for the sample of data at hand. Apparently the variation in common stock returns about their expected values is so large relative to any changes in the expected values that the latter can safely be ignored. But, as Roll demonstrates, this result does not hold for Treasury Bills. Thus, to test the "fair game" model on Treasury Bills requires explicit economic theory for the evolution of expected returns through time.

Roll uses three existing theories of the term structure (the pure expectations hypothesis of Lutz (1940) and two market segmentation hypotheses, one of which is the familiar "liquidity preference" hypothesis of Hicks (1946) and Kessel 1965) for this purpose.[24] In his models r_{jt} is the rate observed from the term structure at period t for one week loans to commence at

---

except for origin and scale, the distributions for longer differencing intervals seem to have the "high-tailed" characteristics as distributions for shorter differencing intervals, which is as would be expected if the distributions are non-normal stable.

[24] As noted early in our discussions, all available tests of market efficiency are implicitly also tests of expected return models of market equilibrium. But Roll formulates explicitly the economic models underlying his estimates of expected returns, and emphasizes that he is simultaneously testing economic models of the term structure as well as market efficiency.

$t+j-1$, and can be thought of as a "futures" rate. Thus $r_{j+1,t-1}$ is likewise the rate on one week loans to commence at $t+j-1$, but observed in this case at $t-1$. Similarly, L_{jt} is the so-called "liquidity premium" in r_{jt}; that is:

$$r_{jt} = E(\tilde{r}_{0,t+j-1} \,|\, \Phi_t) + L_{jt}.$$

In words, the one-week "futures" rate for period $t+j-1$ observed from the term structure at t is the expectation at t of the "spot" rate for $t+j-1$ plus a "liquidity premium" (which could, however, be positive or negative).

In all three theories of the term structure considered by Roll, the conditional expectation required in (10) is of the form:

$$E(\tilde{r}_{j,t} \,|\, \Phi_{t-1}) = r_{j+1,t-1} + E(L_{jt} \,|\, \Phi_{t-1}) - L_{j+1,t-1}.$$

The three theories differ only in the values assigned to the "liquidity premiums". For example, in the "liquidity preference" hypothesis, investors must always be paid a positive premium for bearing interest rate uncertainty, so that the L_{jt} are always positive. By contrast, in the "pure expectations" hypothesis, all liquidity premiums are assumed to be zero, so that:

$$E(\tilde{r}_{jt} \,|\, \Phi_{t-1}) = r_{j+1,t-1}.$$

After extensive testing, Roll concludes (i) that the two market segmentation hypotheses fit the data better than the pure expectations hypothesis, with perhaps a slight advantage for the "liquidity preference" hypothesis, and (ii) that as far as his tests are concerned, the market for Treasury Bills is efficient. Indeed, it is interesting that when the best fitting term structure model is used to estimate the conditional expected "futures" rate in (10), the resulting variable z_{jt} seems to be serially independent! It is also interesting that if he simply assumed that his data distributions were normal, Roll's results would not be so strongly in support of the efficient markets model. In this case taking account of the observed high tails of the data distributions substantially affected the interpretation of the results.[25]

---

[25] The importance of distributional assumptions is also illustrated in Alexander's work on trading rules. In his initial tests of filter systems, Alexander (1961) assumed that purchases could always be executed exactly (rather than at least) $y\%$ above lows and sales exactly $y\%$ below highs. Mandelbrot (1963) pointed out, however, that though this assumption would do little harm with normally distributed price changes (since price series are then essentially continuous), with non-normal stable distributions it would introduce substantial positive bias into the filter profits (since with such distributions price series will show many discontinuities). In his later tests, Alexander (1964) does indeed find that taking account of the discontinuities (i.e., the presence of large price changes) in his data substantially lowers the profitability of the filters.

2.0.5. *Tests of a multiple security expected return model*

Though the weak form tests support the "fair game" efficient markets model, all of the evidence examined so far consists of what we might call "single security tests". That is, the price or return histories of individual securities are examined for evidence of dependence that might be used as the basis of a trading system for *that* security. We have not discussed tests of whether securities are "appropriately priced" vis-à-vis one another.

But to judge whether differences between average returns are "appropriate" an economic theory of equilibrium expected returns is required. At the moment, the only fully developed theory is that of Sharpe (1964) and Lintner (1965a, b) referred to earlier. In this model (which is a direct outgrowth of the mean-standard deviation portfolio models of investor equilibrium of Markowitz (1959) and Tobin (1958)), the expected return on security j from time t to $t+1$ is:

$$E(\tilde{r}_{j,t+1} \mid \Phi_t) = r_{f,t+1} + \left[\frac{E(\tilde{r}_{m,t+1} \mid \Phi_t) - r_{f,t+1}}{\sigma(\tilde{r}_{m,t+1} \mid \Phi_t)} \right] \frac{\text{cov}(\tilde{r}_{j,t+1}, \tilde{r}_{m,t+1} \mid \Phi_t)}{\sigma(\tilde{r}_{m,t+1} \mid \Phi_t)}, \quad (11)$$

where $r_{f,t+1}$ is the return from t to $t+1$ on an asset that is riskless in money terms; $r_{m,t+1}$ is the return on the "market portfolio" m (a portfolio of all investment assets with each weighted in proportion to the total market value of all its outstanding units); $\sigma^2(\tilde{r}_{m,t+1} \mid \Phi_t)$ is the variance of the return on m; $\text{cov}(\tilde{r}_{j,t+1}, \tilde{r}_{m,t+1} \mid \Phi_t)$ is the covariance between the returns on j and m; and the appearance of Φ_t indicates that the various expected returns, variance and covariance, could in principle depend on Φ_t. Though Sharpe and Lintner derive (11) as a one-period model, the result is given a multi-period interpretation in Fama (1970). The model has also been extended to the case where the one-period returns could have stable distributions with infinite variances by Fama (1971).

In words, (11) says that the expected one-period return on a security is the one-period riskless rate of interest $r_{f,t+1}$ plus a "risk premium" that is proportional to $\text{cov}(\tilde{r}_{j,t+1}, \tilde{r}_{m,t+1} \mid \Phi_t)/\sigma(\tilde{r}_{m,t+1} \mid \Phi_t)$. In the Sharpe-Lintner model each investor holds some combination of the riskless asset and the market portfolio, so that, given a mean-standard deviation framework, the risk of an individual asset can be measured by its contribution to the standard deviation of the return on the market portfolio. This contribution is in fact cov $(\tilde{r}_{j,t+1}, \tilde{r}_{m,t+1}|\Phi_t)/\sigma(\tilde{r}_{m,t+1}|\Phi_t)$.[26] The factor:

$$[E(\tilde{r}_{m,t+1}|\Phi_t)-r_{f,t+1}]/\sigma(\tilde{r}_{m,t+1}|\Phi_t),$$

which is the same for all securities, is then regarded as the market price of risk.

Published empirical tests of the Sharpe-Lintner model are not yet available, though much work is in progress. There is some published work, however, which, though not directed at the Sharpe-Lintner model, is at least consistent with some of its implications. The stated goal of this work has been to determine the extent to which the returns on a given security are related to the returns on other securities. It started (again) with Kendall's (1953) finding that though common stock price changes do not seem to be serially correlated, there is a high degree of cross-correlation between the *simultaneous* returns of different securities. This line of attack was continued by King (1966), who (using factor analysis of a sample of monthly returns on sixty N.Y.S.E. stocks for the period 1926-60) found that on average about 50% of the variance of an individual stock's returns could be accounted for by a "market factor" which affects the returns on all stocks, with "industry factors" accounting for at most an additional 10% of the variance.

For our purposes, however, the work of Fama et al. (1969) (henceforth FFJR) and the more extensive work of Blume (1968) on monthly return data is more relevant. They test the following "market model", originally suggested by Markowitz (1959):

$$\tilde{r}_{j,t+1} = \alpha_j + \beta_j \tilde{r}_{M,t+1} + \tilde{u}_{j,t+1}, \tag{12}$$

where $r_{j,t+1}$ is the rate of return on security j for month t, $r_{M,t+1}$ is the corresponding return on a market index M, α_j and β_j are parameters that can vary from security to security, and $u_{j,t+1}$ is a random disturbance. The tests of FFJR and subsequently those of Blume indicate that (12) is well specified as a linear regression model in that (i) the estimated parameters $\hat{\alpha}_j$ and $\hat{\beta}_j$ remain fairly constant over long periods of time (e.g., the entire post-World War II period in the case of Blume), (ii) $r_{M,t+1}$ and the

---

[26] That is,

$$\sum_i \text{cov}(\tilde{r}_{j,t+1}, \tilde{r}_{m,t+1}|\Phi_t)/\sigma(\tilde{r}_{m,t+1}|\Phi_t) = \sigma(\tilde{r}_{m,t+1}|\Phi_t)$$

estimated $\hat{u}_{j,t+1}$, are close to serially independent, and (iii) the $\hat{u}_{j,t+1}$ seem to be independent of $r_{M,t+1}$.

Thus the observed properties of the "market model" are consistent with the expected return efficient markets model, and, in addition, the "market model" tells us something about the process generating expected returns from security to security. In particular,

$$E(\tilde{r}_{j,t+1}) = \alpha_j + \beta_j E(\tilde{r}_{M,t+1}). \tag{13}$$

The question now is to what extent (13) is consistent with the Sharpe-Lintner expected return model summarized by (11). Rearranging (11) we obtain:

$$E(\tilde{r}_{j,t+1}|\Phi_t) = \alpha_j(\Phi_t) + \beta_j(\Phi_t) E(\tilde{r}_{m,t+1}|\Phi_t), \tag{14}$$

where, noting that the riskless rate $r_{f,t+1}$ is itself part of the information set Φ_t, we have:

$$\alpha_j(\Phi_t) = r_{f,t+1}[1 - \beta_j(\Phi_t)], \tag{15}$$

and:

$$\beta_j(\Phi_t) = \frac{\text{cov}\,(\tilde{r}_{j,t+1}, \tilde{r}_{m,t+1}|\Phi_t)}{\sigma^2(\tilde{r}_{m,t+1}|\Phi_t)}. \tag{16}$$

With some simplifying assumptions, (14) can be reduced to (13). In particular, if the covariance and variance that determine $\beta_j(\Phi_t)$ in (16) are the same for all t and Φ_t, then $\beta_j(\Phi_t)$ in (16) corresponds to β_j in (12) and (13), and the least squares *estimate* of β_j in (12) is in fact just the ratio of the sample values of the covariance and variance in (16). If we also assume that $r_{f,t+1}$ is the same for all t, and that the behavior of the returns on the market portfolio m are closely approximated by the returns on some representative index M, we will have come a long way toward equating (13) and (11). Indeed, the only missing link is whether in the estimated parameters of (12):

$$\hat{\alpha} \cong r_f(1 - \hat{\beta}_j). \tag{17}$$

Neither FFJR nor Blume attack this question directly, though some of Blume's evidence is at least promising. In particular, the magnitudes of the estimated $\hat{\alpha}_j$ are roughly consistent with (17) in the sense that the estimates are always close to zero (as they should be with monthly return data).[27]

In a sense, though, in establishing the apparent empirical validity of the "market model" of (12), both too much and too little have been shown *vis-à-vis* the Sharpe-Lintner expected return model of (11). We know that during the post-World War II period one-month interest rates on riskless assets (e.g., government bills with one month to maturity) have not been constant. Thus, if expected security returns were generated by a version of the "market model" that is fully consistent with the Sharpe-Lintner model, we would, according to (15), expect to observe some non-stationarity in the estimates of α_j. On a monthly basis, however, variation through time in one-period riskless interest rates is probably trivial relative to variation in other factors affecting monthly common stock returns, so that more powerful statistical methods would be necessary to study the effects of changes in the riskless rate.

In any case, since the work of FFJR and Blume on the "market model" was not concerned with relating this model to the Sharpe-Lintner model, we can only say that the results for the former are somewhat consistent with the implications of the latter. But the results for the "market model" are, after all, just a statistical description of the return generating process, and they are probably somewhat consistent with other models of equilibrium expected returns. Thus the only way to generate strong empirical conclusions about the Sharpe-Lintner model is to test it directly. On the other hand, any alternative model of equilibrium expected returns must be somewhat consistent with the "market model", given the evidence in its support.

2.1. *Tests of martingale models of the semi-strong form*

In general, semi-strong form tests of efficient markets models are concerned with whether current prices "fully reflect" all obviously publicly available

---

[27] With least squares applied to monthly return data, the estmate of α_j in (12) is

$$\hat{\alpha}_j = \bar{r}_{J,t} - \hat{\beta}_J \bar{r}_{m,t},$$

where the bars indicate sample mean returns. But, in fact, Blume applies the market model to the wealth relatives $R_{jt} = 1 + r_{jt}$ and $R_{mt} = 1 + r_{mt}$. This yields precisely the same estimate of β_j as least squares applied to (12), but the intercept is now

$$\hat{\alpha}_j = \bar{R}_J \bar{R}_{Mt} = 1 + \bar{r}_{Jt} - \hat{\beta}_J (1 + \bar{r}_{Mt}) = 1 - \hat{\beta}_J + \hat{\alpha}_j.$$

Thus, what Blume in fact finds is that for almost all securities, $\hat{\alpha}_j + \hat{\beta}_j \cong 1$, which implies that $\hat{\alpha}_j$ is close to 0.

information. Each individual test, however, is concerned with the adjustment of security prices to one kind of information generating event (e.g., stock splits, announcements of financial reports by firms, new security issues, etc.). Thus each test only brings supporting evidence for the model, with the idea that by accumulating such evidence the validity of the model will be "established".

In fact, however, though the available evidence is in support of the efficient markets model, it is limited to a few major types of information generating events. The initial major work is apparently the study of stock splits by FFJR, and all the subsequent studies summarized here are adaptations and extensions of the techniques developed in FFJR. Thus, this paper will first be reviewed in some detail, and then the other studies will be considered.

2.1.0. *Splits and the adjustment of stock prices to new information*

Since the only apparent result of a stock split is to multiply the number of shares per shareholder without increasing claims to real assets, splits in themselves are not necessarily sources of new information. The presumption of FFJR is that splits may often be associated with the appearance of more fundamentally important information. The idea is to examine security returns around split dates to see first if there is any "unusual" behavior, and, if so, to what extent it can be accounted for by relationships between splits and other more fundamental variables.

The approach of FFJR to the problem relies heavily on the "market model" of (12). In this model if a stock split is associated with abnormal behavior, this would be reflected in the estimated regression residuals for the months surrounding the split. For a given split, define month 0 as the month in which the effective date of a split occurs, month 1 as the month immediately following the split month, month -1 as the month preceding, etc. Now define the average residual over all split securities for month m (where for each security m is measured relative to the split month) as:

$$u_m = \sum_{j=1}^{N} \frac{\hat{u}_{jm}}{N},$$

where $\hat{u}_{jm}$ is the sample regression residual for security j in month m, and N is the number of splits. Next, define the cumulative average residual

U_m as:

$$U_m = \sum_{k=-29}^{m} u_k.$$

The average residual u_m can be interpreted as the average deviation (in month m relative to split months) of the returns of split stocks from their normal relationships with the market. Similarly, U_m can be interpreted as the cumulative deviation (from month -29 to month m). Finally, define u_m^+, u_m^-, U_m^+, and U_m^- as the average and cumulative average residuals for splits followed by "increased" $(+)$ and "decreased" $(-)$ dividends. An "increase" is a case where the percentage change in dividends on the split share in the year after the split is greater than the percentage change for the N.Y.S.E. as a whole, while a "decrease" is a case of relative dividend decline.

The essence of the results of FFJR are then summarized in fig. 1, which shows the cumulative average residuals U_m, U_m^+, and U_m^- for $-29 \le m \le 30$. The sample includes all 940 stock splits on the N.Y.S.E. from 1927-59, where the exchange was at least five new shares for four old, and where the security was listed for at least 12 months before and after the split.

For all three dividend categories the cumulative average residuals rise in the 29 months prior to the split, and in fact the average residuals (not shown here) are uniformly positive. This cannot be attributed to the splitting process, since in only about 10% of the cases is the time between the announcement and effective dates of a split greater than 4 months. Rather, it seems that firms tend to split their shares during "abnormally" good times — that is, during periods when the prices of their shares have increased more than would be implied by their normal relationships with general market prices, which itself probably reflects a sharp improvement, relative to the market, in the earnings prospects of these firms sometime during the years immediately preceding a split.[28]

---

[28] It is important to note, however, that as FFJR indicate, the persistent upward drift of the cumulative average residuals in the months preceding the split is not a phenomenon that could be used to increase expected trading profits. The reason is that the behavior of the average residuals is not representative of the behavior of the residuals for individual securities. In months prior to the split, successive sample residuals for individual securities seem to be independent. But in most cases, there are a few months in which the residuals are abnormally large and positive. The months of large residuals differ from security to security, however, and these differences in timing explain why the signs of the residuals are uniformly positive for many months preceding the split.

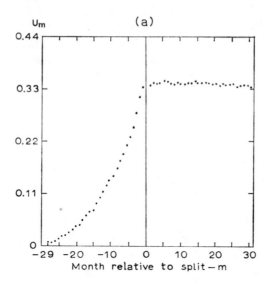

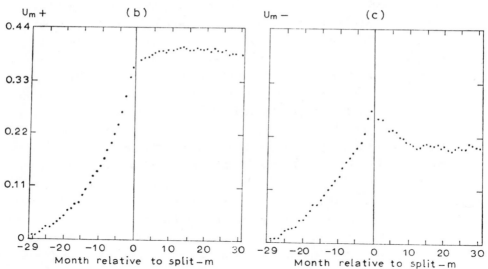

Fig. 1. Cumulative average residuals: (a) all splits. — (b) for dividend "increases". — (c) for dividend "decreases".

After the split month there is almost no further movement in U_m, the cumulative average residual for all splits. This is striking, since 71.5% (672 out of 940) of all splits experienced greater percentage dividend increases in the year after the split than the average for all securities on the

N.Y.S.E. In light of this, FFJR suggest that when a split is announced the market interprets this (and correctly so) as a signal that the company's directors are probably confident that future earnings will be sufficient to maintain dividend payments at a higher level. Thus the large price increases in the months immediately preceding a split may be due to an alteration in expectations concerning the future earning potential of the firm, rather than to any intrinsic effects of the split itself.

If this hypothesis is correct, return behavior subsequent to splits should be substantially different for the cases where the dividend increase materializes than for the cases where it does not. FFJR argue that in fact the differences are in the directions that would be predicted. The fact that the cumulative average residuals for the "increased" dividends (fig. 1b) drift upward but only slightly in the year *after* the split is consistent with the hypothesis that when the split is *declared*, there is a price adjustment in anticipation of future dividend increases. But the behavior of the residuals for stock splits associated with "decreased" dividends offers even stronger evidence for the split hypothesis. The cumulative average residuals for these stocks (fig. 1c) rise in the few months before the split, but then fall dramatically in the few months after the split when the anticipated dividend increase is not forthcoming. When a year has passed after the split, the cumulative average residual has fallen to about where it was 5 months prior to the split, which is about the earliest time reliable information about a split is likely to reach the market. Thus by the time it becomes clear that the anticipated dividend increase is not forthcoming, the apparent effects of the split seem to have been wiped away, and the stock's returns have reverted to their normal relationship with market returns.

Finally, and most important, although the behavior of post-split returns will be very different depending on whether or not dividend "increases" occur, and in spite of the fact that a large majority of split securities do experience dividend "increases", when all splits are examined together (fig. 1a), subsequent to the split there is no net movement up or down in the cumulative average residuals. Thus, apparently the market makes unbiased forecasts of the implications of a split for future dividends, and these forecasts are fully reflected in the price of the security by the end of the split month. After considerably more data analysis than can be summarized here, FFJR conclude that their results lend considerable support to the conclusion that the stock market is efficient, at least with respect to its ability to adjust to the information implicit in a split.

2.1.1. *Other studies of public announcements*

Variants of the method of residual analysis developed in FFJR have been used by others to study the effects of different kinds of public announcements, and all of these also support the efficient markets hypothesis.

Thus using data on 261 major firms for the period 1946-66, Ball and Brown (1968) apply the method to study the effects of annual earnings announcements. They use the residuals from a time series regression of the annual earnings of a firm on the average earnings of all their firms to classify the firm's earnings for a given year as having "increased" or "decreased" relative to the market. Residuals from regressions of monthly common stock returns on an index of returns (i.e., the market model of (12)) are then used to compute cumulative average return residuals separately for the earnings that "increased", and those that "decreased". The cumulative average return residuals rise throughout the year in advance of the announcement for the earnings "increased" category, and fall for the earnings "decreased" category.[29] Ball and Brown (1968, p. 175) conclude that in fact no more than about 10-15% of the information in the annual earnings announcement has not been anticipated by the month of the announcement.

On the macro level, Waud (1970) has used the method of residual analysis to examine the effects of announcements of discount rate changes by Federal Reserve Banks. In this case the residuals are essentially just the deviations of the daily returns on the Standard and Poor's 500 Index from the average daily return. He finds evidence of a statistically significant "announcement effect" on stock returns for the first trading day following an announcement, but the magnitude of the adjustment is small, never exceeding 0.5%. More interesting from the viewpoint of the efficient hypothesis is his conclusion that, if anything, the market anticipates the announcements (or information is somehow leaked in advance). This conclusion is based on the non-random patterns of the signs of average return residuals on the days immediately preceding the announcement.

Further evidence in support of the efficient markets hypothesis is provided in the work of Scholes (1969) on large secondary offerings of common stock (i.e., large underwritten sales of existing common stocks by individuals and institutions) and on new issues of stock. He finds that, on average,

---

[29] But the comment of footnote 28 is again relevant here.

large secondary issues are associated with a decline of between 1 and 2% in the cumulative average residual returns for the corresponding common stocks. Since the magnitude of the price adjustment is unrelated to the size of the issue, Scholes concludes that the adjustment is not due to "selling pressure" (as is commonly believed), but rather results from negative information implicit in the fact that somebody is trying to sell a large block of a firm's stock. Moreover, he presents evidence that the value of the information in a secondary depends to some extent on the vendor. As might be expected, by far the largest negative cumulative average residuals occur where the vendor is the corporation itself or one of its officers, with investment companies a distant second. But the identity of the vendor is not generally known at the time of the secondary, and corporate insiders need only report their transactions in their own company's stock to the S.E.C. within 6 days after a sale. By this time the market on average has fully adjusted to the information in the secondary, as indicated by the fact that the average residuals behave randomly thereafter.

Note, however, that though this is evidence that prices adjust efficiently to public information, it is also evidence that corporate insiders at least sometimes have important information about their firm that is not yet publicly known. Thus Scholes' evidence for secondary distributions provides support for the efficient markets model in the semi-strong form sense, but also some strong-form evidence *against* the model.

Though his results here are only preliminary, Scholes also reports on an application of the method of residual analysis to a sample of 696 new issues of common stock during the period 1926-66. As in the FFJR study of splits, the cumulative average residuals rise in the months preceding the new security offering (suggesting that new issues tend to come after favorable recent events)[30] but behave randomly in the months following the offering (indicating that whatever information is contained in the new issue is on average fully reflected in the price of the month of the offering).

In short, the available semi-strong form evidence on the effects of various sorts of public announcements on common stock returns is all consistent with the efficient markets model. The strong point of the evidence, however, is its consistency rather than its quantity; in fact, few different types of public information have been examined, though those treated are among the obviously most important. Moreover, as we shall now see, the amount

---

[30] Footnote 28 is again relevant here.

of semi-strong form evidence is voluminous compared to the strong form tests that are available.

2.2. *Strong form tests of the efficient markets models*

The strong form tests of the efficient markets model are concerned with whether all available information is fully reflected in prices in the sense that no individual has higher expected trading profits than others because he has monopolistic access to some information. We would not, of course, expect this model to be an exact description of reality, and indeed, the preceding discussions have already indicated the existence of contradictory evidence. In particular, Niederhoffer and Osborne (1966) have pointed out that specialists on the N.Y.S.E. apparently use their monopolistic access to information concerning unfilled limit orders to generate monopoly profits, and Scholes' (1969) evidence indicates that officers of corporations sometimes have monopolistic access to information about their firms.

Since we already have enough evidence to determine that the model is not strictly valid, we can now turn to other interesting questions. Specifically, how far down through the investment community do deviations from the model permeate? Does it pay for the average investor (or the average economist) to expend resources searching out little known information? Are such activities even generally profitable for various groups of market "professionals"? More generally, who are the people in the investment community that have access to "special information"?

Though this is a fascinating problem, only one group has been studied in any depth — the managements of open end mutual funds. Several studies are available (e.g., Sharpe (1965, 1966) and Treynor (1965)), but the most thorough are Jensen's (1968, 1969), and our comments will be limited to his work. We shall first present the theoretical model underlying his tests, and then go on to his empirical results.

2.2.0. *Theoretical framework*

In studying the performance of mutual funds the major goals are to determine (a) whether in general fund managers seem to have access to special information which allows them to generate "abnormal" expected returns, and (b) whether some funds are better at uncovering such special information than others. Since the criterion will simply be the ability of funds to produce higher returns than some norm with no attempt to determine what is responsible for the high returns, the "special information" that leads to high performance could be either keener insight into the implications of publicly available information than is implicit in market prices or monopolistic access to specific information. Thus the tests of the performance of the mutual fund industry are not strictly strong form tests of the efficient markets model.

The major theoretical (and practical) problem in using the mutual fund industry to test the efficient markets model is developing a "norm" against which performance can be judged. The norm must represent the results of an investment policy based on the assumption that prices fully reflect all available information. And if one believes that investors are generally risk averse and so on average must be compensated for any risks undertaken, then one has the problem of finding appropriate definitions of risk and evaluating each fund relative to a norm with its chosen level of risk.

Jensen uses the Sharpe (1964) - Lintner (1965a,b) model of equilibrium expected returns discussed above to derive a norm consistent with these goals. From (14)-(16), in this model the expected return on an asset or portfolio j from t to $t+1$ is:

$$E(\tilde{r}_{j,t+1} \mid \Phi_t) = r_{f,t+1}[1 - \beta_j(\Phi_t)] + E(\tilde{r}_{m,t+1} \mid \Phi_t)\, \beta_j(\Phi_t), \tag{18}$$

where the various symbols are defined as in section 2.0.5. But (18) is an *ex ante* relationship, and to evaluate performance an *ex post* norm is needed. One way the latter can be obtained is to substitute the realized return on the market portfolio for the expected return in (18) with the result[31]:

$$E(\tilde{r}_{j,t+1} \mid \Phi_t, r_{m,t+1}) = r_{f,t+1}[1 - \beta_j(\Phi_t)] + r_{m,t+1}\beta_j(\Phi_t). \tag{19}$$

Geometrically, (19) says that within the context of the Sharpe-Lintner model, the expected return on j (given information Φ_t and the return $r_{m,t+1}$ on the market portfolio) is a linear function of its risk:

$$\beta_j(\Phi_t) = \text{cov}\,(\tilde{r}_{j,t+1}, \tilde{r}_{m,t+1} \mid \Phi_t) / \sigma^2(\tilde{r}_{m,t+1} \mid \Phi_t),$$

as indicated in fig. 2. Assuming that the value of $\beta_j(\Phi_t)$ is somehow known, or can be reliably estimated, if j is a mutual fund, its *ex post* performance

---

[31] The assumption here is that the return $\tilde{r}_{J,t+1}$ is generated according to:

$$\tilde{r}_{J,t+1} = r_{f,t+1}[1 - \beta_J(\Phi_t)] + r_{m,t+1}\beta_J(\Phi_t) + \tilde{u}_{J,t+1},$$

where

$$E(\tilde{u}_{J,t+1} \mid r_{m,t+1}) = 0 \text{ for all } r_{m,t+1}.$$

from t to $t+1$ might now be evaluated by plotting its combination of realized return $r_{j,t+1}$ and risk in fig. 2. If (as for the point a) the combination falls above the expected return line (or, as it is more commonly called, the "market line"), it has done better than would be expected given its level of risk, while if (as for the point b) it falls below the line it has done worse.

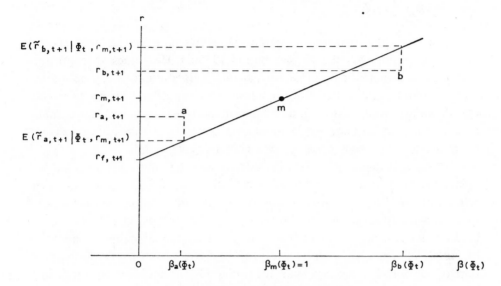

Fig. 2. Performance evaluation graph.

Alternatively, the market line shows the combinations of return and risk provided by portfolios that are simple mixtures of the riskless asset and the market portfolio m. The returns and risks for such portfolios (call them c) are:

$$r_{c,t+1} = \alpha r_{f,t+1} + (1-\alpha) r_{m,t+1}$$

$$\beta_c(\Phi_t) = \frac{\text{cov}\,(\tilde{r}_{c,t+1}, \tilde{r}_{m,t+1}\,|\,\Phi_t)}{\sigma^2(\tilde{r}_{m,t+1}\,|\,\Phi_t)} = \frac{\text{cov}\,((1-\alpha)\tilde{r}_{m,t+1}, \tilde{r}_{m,t+1}\,|\,\Phi_t)}{\sigma^2(\tilde{r}_{m,t+1}\,|\,\Phi_t)} = 1-\alpha,$$

where α is the proportion of portfolio funds invested in the riskless asset. Thus, when $1 \geq \alpha \geq 0$ we obtain the combinations of return and risk along the market line from $r_{f,t+1}$ to m in fig. 2, while when $\alpha < 0$ (and under the assumption that investors can borrow at the same rate that they lend) we obtain the combinations of return and risk along the extension of the line through *m*. In this interpretation, the market line represents the results of a naive investment strategy, which the investor who thinks prices reflect all available information might follow. The performance of a mutual fund is then measured relative to this naive strategy.

2.2.1. *Empirical results*

Jensen uses this risk-return framework to evaluate the performance of 115 mutual funds over the 10-year period 1955-64. He argues at length for measuring return as the nominal 10-year rate with continuous compounding (i.e., the natural log of the ratio of terminal wealth after 10 years to initial wealth) and for using historical data on nominal 1-year rates with continuous compounding to estimate risk. The Standard and Poor Index of 500 major common stocks is used as the proxy for the market portfolio.

The general question to be answered is whether mutual fund managements have any special insights or information which allows them to earn returns above the norm. But Jensen attacks the question on several levels. First, can the funds in general do well enough to compensate investors for loading charges, management fees, and other costs that might be avoided by simply choosing the combination of the riskless asset *f* and the market portfolio *m* with risk level comparable to that of the fund's actual portfolio? The answer seems to be an emphatic no. As far as net returns to investors are concerned, in 89 out of 115 cases, the fund's risk-return combination for the 10-year period is below the market line for the period, and the average over all funds of the deviations of 10 year returns from the market time is -14.6%. That is, on average the consumer's wealth after 10 years of holding mutual funds is about 15% less than if he held the corresponding portfolios along the market line.

But the loading charge that an investor pays in buying into a fund is usually a pure salesman's commission that the fund itself never gets to invest. Thus one might ask whether, ignoring loading charges (i.e., assuming no such charges were paid by the investor), in general fund managements can earn returns sufficiently above the norm to cover all other expenses that are presumably more directly related to the management of the fund portfolios. Again, the answer seems to be no. Even when loading charges are ignored in computing returns, the risk-return combinations for 72 out of 115 funds are below the market line, and the average deviation of 10 year returns from the market line is -8.9%.

Finally, as a somewhat stronger test of the efficient markets model, one would like to know if, ignoring all expenses, fund managements in general showed any ability to pick securities that outperformed the norm. Unfortunately, this question cannot be answered with precision for individual funds since, curiously, data on brokerage commissions are not published regularly. But Jensen suggests the available evidence indicates that the answer to the question is again probably negative. Specifically, adding back all other published expenses of funds to their returns, the risk-return combinations for 58 out of 115 funds were below the market line, and the average deviation of 10 year returns from the line was −2.5%. But part of this result is due to the absence of a correction for brokerage commissions. Estimating these commissions from average portfolio turnover rates for all funds for the period 1953-58 and adding them back to returns for all funds increases the average deviation from the market line from −2.5% to 0.09%, which still is not indicative of the existence of special information among mutual fund managers.

But though mutual fund managers in general do not seem to have access to information not already fully reflected in prices, perhaps there are individual funds that consistently do better than the norm, and so provide at least some strong form evidence against the efficient markets model. If there are such funds, however, they escape Jensen's search. For example, for individual funds, returns above the norm in one subperiod do not seem to be associated with performance above the norm in other subperiods. And regardless of how returns are measured (i.e., net or gross of loading charges and other expenses), the number of funds with large positive deviations of returns from the market line of fig. 2 is less than the number that would be expected by chance with 115 funds under the assumption that fund managements have no special talents in predicting returns.[32]

Jensen argues that though his results apply to only one segment of the

---

[32] On the other hand, there is some suggestion in Scholes' (1969) work on secondary issues that mutual funds may occasionally have access to "special information". After corporate insiders, the next largest negative price changes occur when the secondary seller is an investment company (including mutual funds), though on average the price changes are much smaller (i.e., closer to 0) than when the seller is a corporate insider. — Moreover, Jensen's evidence itself, though not indicative of the existence of special information among mutual fund managers, is not sufficiently precise to conclude that such information never exists. This stronger conclusion would require exact data on unavoidable expenses (including brokerage commissions) of portfolio management incurred by funds.

investment community, they are nevertheless striking evidence in favor of the efficient markets model:

> Although these results certainly do not imply that the strong form of the martingale hypothesis holds for all investors and for all time, they provide strong evidence in support of that hypothesis. One must realize that these analysts are extremely well endowed. Moreover, they operate in the securities markets every day and have wide-ranging contacts and associations in both the business and financial communities. Thus, the fact that they are apparently unable to forecast returns accurately enough to recover their research and transactions costs is a striking piece of evidence in favor of the strong form of the martingale hypothesis at least as far as the extensive subset of information available to these analysts is concerned (Jensen 1969, p. 170).

3. Summary and conclusions

The preceding analysis can be summarized as follows: in general terms, the theory of efficient markets in concerned with whether prices at any point in time "fully reflect" available information. The theory has empirical content, however, only within the context of a more specific model of market equilibrium, that is, a model that specifies the nature of market equilibrium when prices "fully reflect" available information. We have seen that all of the available empirical literature is implicitly or explicitly based on the assumption that the conditions of market equilibrium can be stated in terms of expected returns. This assumption is the basis of the expected return or "fair game" efficient markets models.

The empirical work itself can be divided into three categories depending on the nature of the information subset of interest. *Strong-form* tests are concerned with whether individual investors or groups have monopolistic access to any information relevant for price formation. One would not expect such an extreme model to be an exact description of the world, and it is probably best viewed as a benchmark against which the importance of deviations from market efficiency can be judged. In the less restrictive *semi-strong-form* tests the information subset of interest includes all obviously publicly available information, while in the *weak form* tests the information subset is just historical price or return sequences.

Weak form tests of the efficient markets model are the most voluminous, and it seems fair to say that the results are strongly in support. Though statistically significant evidence for dependence in successive price changes or returns has been found, some of this is consistent with the "fair game" model and the rest does not appear to be sufficient to declare the market inefficient. Indeed, at least for price changes or returns covering a day or longer, there is not much evidence against the more ambitious offspring of the "fair game" model, the random walk.

Thus, there is consistent evidence of positive dependence in day-to-day price changes and returns on common stocks, and the dependence is of a form that can be used as the basis of marginally profitable trading rules. In Fama's (1965) data the dependence shows up as serial correlations that are consistently positive but also consistently close to zero, and as a slight tendency for observed numbers of runs of positive and negative price changes to be less than the numbers that would be expected from a purely random process. More important, the dependence also shows up in the filter tests of Alexander (1961, 1964) and those of Fama and Blume (1966) as a tendency for very small filters to produce profits in excess of buy-and-hold. But any systems (like the filters) that attempt to turn such short-term dependence into trading profits of necessity generate so many transactions that their expected profits would be absorbed by even the minimum commissions (security handling fees) that floor traders on major exchanges must pay. Thus, using a less than completely strict interpretation of market efficiency, this positive dependence does not seem of sufficient importance to warrant rejection of the efficient markets model.

Evidence in contradiction of the "fair game" efficient markets model for price changes or returns covering periods longer than a single day is more difficult to find. Cootner (1962), and Moore (1962) report preponderantly negative (but again small) serial correlations in weekly common stock returns, and this result appears also in the 4-day returns analyzed by Fama (1965). But it does not appear in runs tests of Fama (1965), where, if anything, there is some slight indication of positive dependence, but actually not much evidence of any dependence at all. In any case, there is no indication that whatever dependence exists in weekly returns can be used as the basis of profitable trading rules.

Other existing evidence of dependence in returns provides interesting insights into the process of price formation in the stock market, but it is not relevant for testing the efficient markets model. For example, Fama (1965) shows that large daily price changes tend to be followed by large changes, but of unpredictable sign. This suggests that important information cannot be completely evaluated immediately, but that the initial (first day's) adjustment of prices to the information is unbiased, which is sufficient for the martingale model. More interesting and important, however, is the Niederhoffer-Osborne (1966) finding of a tendency toward excessive reversals in common stock price changes from transaction to transaction. They explain this as a logical result of the mechanism whereby orders to buy and sell at market are matched against existing limit orders on the books of the specialist. Given the way this tendency toward excessive reversals arises, however, there seems to be no way it can be used as the basis of a profitable trading rule. As they rightly claim, their results are a strong refutation of the theory of random walks, at least as applied to price changes from transaction to transaction, but they do not constitute refutation of the economically more relevant "fair game" efficient markets model.

Semi-strong form tests, in which prices are assumed to fully reflect all obviously publicly available information, have also supported the efficient markets hypothesis. Thus Fama *et al.* (1969) find that the information in stock splits concerning the firm's future dividend payments is on average fully reflected in the price of a split share at the time of the split. Ball and Brown (1968) and Scholes (1969) come to similar conclusions with respect to the information contained in (i) annual earning announcements by firms and (ii) new issues and large block secondary issues of common stock. Though only a few different types of information generating events are represented here, they are among the more important, and the results are probably indicative of what can be expected in future studies.

As noted earlier, the strong-form efficient markets model, in which prices are assumed to fully reflect all available information, is probably best viewed as a benchmark against which deviations from market efficiency (interpreted in its strictest sense) can be judged. Two such deviations have in fact been observed. First, Niederhoffer and Osborne (1966) point out that specialists on major security exchanges have monopolistic access to information on unexecuted limit orders, information they use to generate trading profits. This raises the question of whether the "market making" function of the specialist (if indeed this is a meaningful economic function) could not as effectively be carried out by some other mechanism that did not imply monopolistic access to information. Second, Scholes (1969) finds that, not unexpectedly, corporate insiders often have monopolistic access to information about their firms.

At the moment, however, corporate insiders and specialists are the only two groups whose monopolistic access to information has been documented. There is no evidence that deviations from the strong form of the efficient markets model permeate down any further through the investment community. For the purposes of most investors the efficient markets model seems a good approximation to reality.

In short, the evidence in support of the efficient markets model is extensive, and (somewhat uniquely in economics) contradictory evidence is sparse. Nevertheless, we certainly do not want to leave the impression that all issues are closed. The old saw, "much remains to be done", is certainly relevant here. Indeed, as is often the case in successful scientific research, now that we know where we have been in the past, we are able to pose and, hopefully, to answer an even more interesting set of questions for the future. In this case the most pressing field of future endeavor is the development and testing of models of market equilibrium under uncertainty. When the processes generating equilibrium expected returns are better understood, we will have a better framework for more sophisticated tests of market efficiency.

References

Alexander, Sidney S., 1961, Price movements in speculative markets: trends or random walks. *Industrial Management Review* 2, May, 7-26. Reprinted in Cootner (1964), 199-218.

Alexander, Sidney S., 1964, Price movements in speculative markets: trends or random walks, No. 2. In: Cootner (1964), 338-72.

Bachelier, Louis, 1900, *Théorie de la spéculation*. Paris, Gauthier-Villars. Reprinted in English in Cootner (1964), 17-78.

Ball, Ray and Philip Brown, 1968, An empirical evaluation of accounting income numbers. *Journal of Accounting Research* 6, Autumn, 159-78.

Beaver, William, 1968, The information content of annual earnings announcements. In.: *Empirical research in accounting: selected studies*, supplement to Vol. 7 of the *Journal of Accounting Research*, 67-92.

Blattberg, Robert and Thomas Sargent, 1970, Regression with non-Gaussian disturbances: some sampling results. *Econometrica* (forthcoming).

Blume, Marshall, 1968, The assessment of portfolio performance. Unpublished Ph. D. thesis, University of Chicago. A paper summarizing much of this work has appeared in *Journal of Business*, April 1970.

Cootner, Paul, 1962, Stock prices: random vs. systematic changes. *Industrial Management Review* 3, Spring, 24-45. Reprinted in Cootner (1964), 231-52.

Cootner, Paul (ed.), 1964, *The random character of stock market prices*. Cambridge, Mass., The M.I.T. Press.

Fama, Eugene F., 1965, The behavior of stock market prices. *Journal of Business* 38, January, 34-105, 1971.

Fama, Eugene F., 1970, Multiperiod consumption-investment decisions. *American Economic Review*, March, 163-74.

Fama, Eugene F., 1971, Risk, return and equilibrium. *Journal of Political Economy*, January-February.

Fama, Eugene F. and Marshall Blume, 1966, Filter rules and stock market trading profits: *Journal of Business* 39 (Special Supplement, January), 226-41.

Fama, Eugene F., Lawrence Fisher, Michael Jensen, and Richard Roll, 1969, The Adjustment of Stock Prices to New Information. *International Economic Review* 10, February, 1-21.

Fama, Eugene F. and Richard Roll, 1968, Some properties of symmetric stable distributions. *Journal of the American Statistical Association* 63, September, 817-36.

Godfrey, Michael D., C.W.J. Granger, and O. Morgenstern, 1964, The Random Walk Hypothesis of Stock Market Behavior. *Kyklos* 17, 1-30.

Granger, C.W.J. and O. Morgenstern, 1963, Spectral analysis of New York stock market prices. *Kyklos* 16, 1-27. Reprinted in Cootner (1964), 162-187.

Hicks, John R., 1946, *Value and capital*. Oxford, The Clarendon Press.

Jensen, Michael, 1968, The performance of mutual funds in the period 1945-64. *Journal of Finance* 23, May, 389-416.

Jensen, Michael, 1969, Risk, the pricing of capital assets, and the evaluation of investment portfolios. *Journal of Business* 42, April, 167-247.

Kendall, Maurice G., 1953, The analysis of economic time-series. Part I : prices. *Journal of the Royal Statistical Society* 96, Part I, 11-25,

Kessel, Reuben A., 1965, The cyclical behavior of the term structure of interest rates. National Bureau of Economic Research Occasional Paper No. 91. New York, Columbia University Press.

King, Benjamin F., 1966, Market and industry factors in stock price behavior. *Journal of Business* 39 (Special Supplement, January), 139-90.

Lintner, John, 1965a, Security prices, risk, and maximal gains from diversification. *Journal of Finance* 20, December, 587-615.

Lintner, John, 1965b, The valuation of risk assets and the selection of risky investments in stock portfolios and capital budgets. *Review of Economics and Statistics* 47, Februay 13-37.

Lutz, Friedrich A., 1940-41, The structure of interest rates. *Quarterly Journal of Economics* 40.

Mandelbrot, Benoit, 1963, The variation of certain speculative prices. *Journal of Business* 36, October, 394-419.

Mandelbrot, Benoit, 1966, Forecasts of future prices, unbiased markets, and martingale models. *Journal of Business* 39 (Special Supplement, January), 242-55.

Mandelbrot, Benoit and Howard M. Taylor, 1967, On the distribution of stock price differences. *Operations Research* 15, November-December, 1057-62.

Markowitz, Harry, 1959, *Portfolio selection: efficient diversification of investment.* New York, John Wiley & Sons.

Moore, Arnold, 1962, A statistical analysis of common stock prices. Unpublished Ph. D. thesis, Graduate School of Business, University of Chicago.

Niederhoffer, Victor and M.F.M. Osboirne, 1966, Market making and reversal on the stock exchange, *Journal of the American Statistical Association* 61, December, 897-916.

Osborne, M.F.M., 1959, Brownian motion in the stock market. *Operations Research* 7, March-April, 145-73. Reprinted in Cootner (1964), 100-28.

Osborne, M.F.M., 1962, Periodic structure in the brownian motion of stock prices. *Operations Research* 10, May-June, 345-79. Reprinted in Cootner (1964), 262-96.

Press, S. James, 1968, A compound events model for security prices, *Journal of Business* 40, July, 317-35.

Roberts, Harry V., 1959, Stock market 'patterns' and financial analysis: methodological suggestions. *Journal of Finance* 14, March, 1-10.

Roll, Richard, 1968, The efficient market model applied to U.S. treasury till rates. Unpublished Ph. D. thesis, Graduate School of Business, University of Chicago.

Samuelson, Paul A., 1965, Proof that properly anticipated prices fluctuate randomly. *Industrial Management Review* 6, Spring, 41-9.

Scholes, Myron, 1969, A test of the competitive market hypothesis: the market for new issues and secondary offerings. Unpublished Ph. D. thesis, Graduate School of Business, University of Chicago.

Sharpe, William F., 1964, Capital asset prices: a theory of market equilibrium under conditions of risk. *Journal* of *Finance* 19, September, 425-42.

Sharpe, William F., 1965, Risk aversion in the stock market, *Journal of Finance* 20, September, 416-22.

Sharpe, William F., 1966, Mutual fund performance. *Journal of Business* 39 (Special Supplement, January), 119-38.

Tobin, James, 1958, Liquidity preference as behavior towards risk. *Review of Economic Studies* 25, February, 65-85.

Treynor, Jack L., 1965, How to rate management of investment funds. *Harvard Business Review* 43, January-February, 63-75.

Waud, Roger N., 1970, Public interpretation of discount rate changes: evidence on the "Announcement effect". *Econometrica* 38, March, 231-50.

Wise, John, 1963, Linear estimators for linear regression systems having infinite variances. Unpublished paper presented at the Berkeley-Stanford Mathematical Economics Seminar, October.

Working, Holbrook, 1934, A random difference series for use in the analysis of time series. *Journal of the American Statistical Association* 29, March, 11-24.

8

STOCK MARKET "PATTERNS" AND FINANCIAL ANALYSIS: METHODOLOGICAL SUGGESTIONS

Harry V. Roberts *

INTRODUCTION

OF ALL ECONOMIC time series, the history of security prices, both individual and aggregate, has probably been most widely and intensively studied. While financial analysts agree that underlying economic facts and relationships are important, many also believe that the history of the market itself contains "patterns" that give clues to the future, if only these patterns can be properly understood. The Dow theory and its many offspring are evidence of this conviction. In extreme form such theories maintain that *only* the patterns of the past need be studied, since the effect of everything else is reflected "on the tape."

A common and convenient name for analysis of stock-market patterns is "technical analysis." Perhaps no one in the financial world completely ignores technical analysis—indeed, its terminology is ingrained in market reporting—and some rely intensively on it. Technical analysis includes many different approaches, most requiring a good deal of subjective judgment in application. In part these approaches are purely empirical; in part they are based on analogy with physical processes, such as tides and waves.

In light of this intense interest in patterns and of the publicity given to statistics in recent years, it seems curious that there has not been widespread recognition among financial analysts that the patterns of technical analysis may be little, if anything, more than a statistical artifact. At least, it is safe to say that the close resemblance between market behavior over relatively long time periods and that of simple chance devices has escaped general attention,

* I am indebted to Lawrence West and Arnold Moore for help in the preparation of this paper.

Reprinted from *The Journal of Finance*, XIV, No. 1 (March, 1959), 1–10, by permission of the author and the publisher.

though the role of chance variation in very short time periods has often been recognized. One possible explanation is that the usual method of graphing stock prices gives a picture of successive *levels* rather than of *changes,* and levels can give an artificial appearance of "pattern" or "trend." A second is that chance behavior itself produces "patterns" that invite spurious interpretations.

More evidence for this assertion about stock-market behavior is still needed, but almost all the fragmentary evidence known to me is consistent with it. The major published evidence from recent years is a paper about British stock indexes (and American commodity prices) by the British statistician, M. G. Kendall, which appeared in 1953.[1] I have done similar, though less comprehensive, work with recent American data, for both indexes and individual companies, which has been entirely consistent with Kendall's findings. If, for example, weekly *changes* of the Dow Jones Index are examined statistically, it is apparent that these changes behave very much as if they had been generated by an extremely simple chance model. The history of market *levels* behaves very much as if levels had been generated by a *cumulation* of results given by the chance model.

These general conclusions have been reached, probably repeatedly, long before Kendall's study. Thus Holbrook Working, writing in 1934, said:

> It has several times been noted that time series commonly possess in many respects the characteristics of series of cumulated random numbers. The separate items in such time series are by no means random in character, but the changes between successive items tend to be largely random. This characteristic has been noted conspicuously in sensitive commodity prices. . . . King has concluded that stock prices resemble cumulations of purely random changes even more strongly than do commodity prices.[2]

Indeed, the main reason for this paper is to call to the attention of financial analysts empirical results that seem to have been ignored in the past, for whatever reason, and to point out some methodological implications of these results for the study of securities.

From the point of view of the scholar, much more research is needed to establish more precisely the limits to which these generalizations can be carried. For example, do they apply to changes for periods other than weekly? (In my own explorations they have

1. Maurice G. Kendall, "The Analysis of Economic Time Series. I," *Journal of the Royal Statistical Society* (Ser. A), CXVI (1953), 11–25.

2. Holbrook Working, "A Random-Difference Series for Use in the Analysis of Time Series," *Journal of the American Statistical Association,* XXIX (1934), 11.

worked fairly well for both longer and shorter periods.) How well do they apply to individual securities? (Most work has been done on indexes.) What slight departures from the chance model are detectable? Perhaps the traditional academic suspicion about the stock market as an object of scholarly research will be overcome, and this work will be done.[3] This paper, however, is concerned with the methodological problems of the financial analyst who cannot afford to ignore evidence that is easily obtainable from the most casual empirical analysis. From his point of view there should be great interest in the possibility that, to a first approximation, stock-market behavior may be statistically the simplest, by far, of all economic time series.

This paper will describe the chance model more precisely, discuss briefly the common-sense interpretation of the model, and outline a number of methodological suggestions for financial analysts.

THE CHANCE MODEL

Kendall found that changes in security prices behaved nearly as if they had been generated by a suitably designed roulette wheel for which each outcome was statistically independent of past history and for which relative frequencies were reasonably stable through time. This means that, once a person accumulates enough evidence to make good estimates of the relative frequencies (probabilities) of different outcomes of the wheel, he would base his predictions only on these relative frequencies and pay no attention to the pattern of recent spins. Recent spins are relevant to prediction only insofar as they contribute to more precise estimates of relative frequencies. In a gambling expression, this roulette wheel "has no memory."

The chance model just described insists on independence but makes no commitment about the relative frequencies, or probabilities, of different outcomes except that these must be stable over time. A frequency distribution of past changes is a good basis for estimating these probabilities, so long as the independence assumption holds. For concreteness in demonstration, we shall assume that weekly changes of a particular index behave as if they were independent observations on a normal distribution, with mean $+0.5$ and standard deviation 5.0. The details of constructing such a roulette wheel need not concern us here. We shall, in fact, employ for our purpose a published table of random numbers that can be modified easily to

3. Holbrook Working has worked for many years on the behavior of commodities markets, and full publication of his findings is still forthcoming.

conform to the specifications stated above.[4] Assuming that the series starts at 450, we obtain a hypothetical year's experience graphed in Figures 1 and 2.

To even a casual observer of the stock market, Figure 2 is hauntingly realistic, even to the "head-and-shoulders" top. Probably all the classical patterns of technical analysis can be generated artificially by a suitable roulette wheel or random-number table. Figure 1 gives much less evidence of patterns, although intensive and imaginative scrutiny would undoubtedly suggest some. The only *persistent*

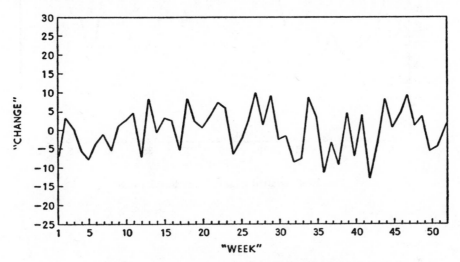

FIG. 1.—Simulated market changes for 52 weeks

patterns of Figure 1 (and its continuation beyond 52 weeks) are (1) the relative frequency of different outcomes and (2) the clustering tendency for similar outcomes. The clustering phenomenon runs contrary to intuitive feelings about chance and raises temporary hopes about predictability. These hopes, however, can be crushed by theoretical analysis that shows clustering to give no information beyond that contained in the relative frequencies.

Figures 3 and 4 give the corresponding diagrams for the Dow Jones Industrial Index for 1956. The general resemblance between Figures 3–4 and Figures 1–2 is unmistakable, although no pains were taken to devise a "roulette" wheel that would simulate closely the actual history of 1956. The major difference in detail between Figures 1 and 3 is that Figure 3 shows greater dispersion. We prob-

4. The RAND Corporation, *A Million Random Digits with 100,000 Normal Deviates* (Glencoe, Ill.: Free Press, 1955).

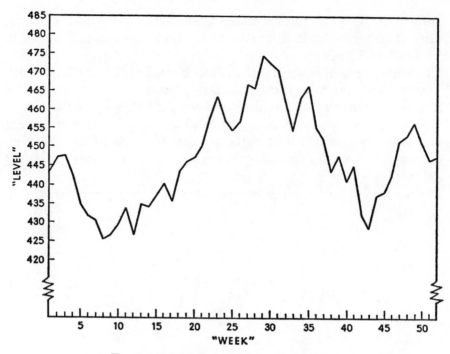

Fɪɢ. 2.—Simulated market levels for 52 weeks

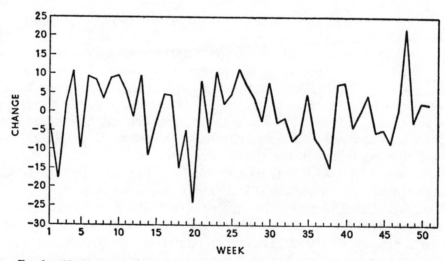

Fɪɢ. 3.—Changes from Friday to Friday (closing) January 6, 1956—December 28, 1956. Dow Jones Industrial Index.

ably could have imitated Figure 3 more closely by using a somewhat larger standard deviation than 5 in constructing the artificial series. It is well, however, to avoid giving the wrong impression by showing *too* striking a parallel in all details. Two artificial series constructed by precisely the same method typically differ from each other just as would two brothers or two years of market history. To put it differently, the chance model cannot duplicate history in any sense other than that in which one evening in a gambling casino duplicates an-

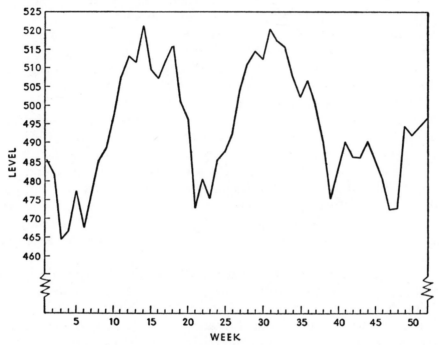

FIG. 4.—Friday closing levels, December 30, 1955—December 28, 1956. Dow Jones Industrial Index.

other. For relatively short periods of history like 52 weeks, there can be substantial differences. In fact, however, the dispersion of Figure 3 is almost surely greater than that of Figure 1 by more than we would expect from the same chance mechanism. We subsequently obtained a better simulation by using a standard deviation of 7 rather than 5.

MEANING OF THE CHANCE MODEL

There are two common reactions to this chance model: (1) while "chance" may be important in extremely short-run stock-market movements, it is inconceivable that the longer-term movement should be a cumulation of short-term "chance" development; (2) once one reflects on the situation, it is obvious that a simple chance model must hold. We shall discuss each reaction briefly.

The first reaction stems partly from a misunderstanding of the term "chance." The chance model of the previous section was meant to illustrate the possibility of constructing a simple mechanical device that would duplicate many of the characteristic features of stock-market movements. Even if the statistical behavior of the market and the mechanical device were completely indistinguishable, it might still be possible to attain a degree of predictability better than that given by knowledge of past relative frequencies alone. To attain such predictability, however, more would be needed than the past history of market prices: e.g., economic theory and knowledge of economic facts might suggest relationships of market prices with other economic variables that might be of predictive value. It seems more likely that economic analysis could give predictive insight into stock-market behavior than that physical analysis could help with a real roulette wheel. Even completely deterministic phenomena, such as the decimal expansions of irrational numbers (e.g., e and π), appear to be "chance" phenomena to an observer who does not understand the underlying mechanism. Phenomena that can be described only as "chance" today, such as the emission of alpha particles in radioactive decay, may ultimately be understood in a deeper sense.

In another sense the reaction against "chance" is sound. Much more empirical work is needed, and it seems likely that departures from simple chance models will be found—if not for stock-market averages, then for individual stocks; if not for weekly periods, then for some other period; if not from the independence assumption, then from the assumption of a stable underlying distribution; etc. Indeed, the analytical proposals of this paper are based on the assumption that such departures will occasionally be found. Holbrook Working has discovered such departures in his commodity market research.[5]

As to the second reaction, that the chance model is obvious, there is a plausible rationale. "If the stock market behaved like a mechanically imperfect roulette wheel, people would notice the imperfections and by acting on them, remove them." This rationale is appealing, if for no other reason than its value as counterweight to the popular view of stock market "irrationality," but it is obviously incomplete.

5. Holbrook Working, "New Ideas and Methods for Price Research," *Journal of Farm Economics,* XXXVIII (1956), 1427–36.

For example, why should not observation of market imperfection lead to greater imperfection rather than less? All we can do is to suggest the importance of the study of such questions.

SUGGESTIONS FOR FINANCIAL ANALYSIS

This section is devoted to statistical suggestions to financial analysts and others who make their living by the study of the market. The fundamental suggestion, of course, is to analyze price *changes* as well as price *levels*. Initially, the weekly change seems worth using, but other time periods may also be useful. This suggestion seems trivial, but it is not. If the simple chance hypothesis is correct, then the statistical behavior of changes, which are independent, is much simpler than that of levels, which are not. There already exists, for example, a body of statistical techniques for analysis of independent data: in fact, modern statistical theory has been largely built up on the assumption of independence. Much of it also assumes, as we did for convenience in the artificial example, that the underlying distribution is a normal distribution in the technical sense of that term. The assumption of normality usually seems far less crucial to the applicability of statistical methods than does that of independence, and some statistical techniques, called "non-parametric," do not make the normality assumption.

If one graphs weekly changes without any formal statistical analysis, he will have taken the most important single step. So long as the stock or stock index behaves like a reasonably good roulette wheel, the visual impression will be similar to that of Figures 1 and 3. If there is a really fundamental shift in the underlying situation, it can be detected visually more readily by an analysis of changes than of levels. Conversely, if there has been no fundamental shift, a graph of changes will be much less likely to give the impression that there has been a shift.

There are formal statistical techniques to supplement visual analysis (though never to replace it entirely, since graphical study is always partial insurance against misapplication of statistical analysis). The most popular field of applied statistics—industrial quality control—draws on these techniques extensively. Though there would undoubtedly be many differences in detail, a financial analyst should find much of interest and relevance in methods of quality control.[6]

6. W. Allen Wallis and Harry V. Roberts, *Statistics: A New Approach* (Glencoe, Ill.: Free Press, 1956), chaps. 16, 18; A. Hald, *Statistical Theory with Engineering Applications* (New York: John Wiley & Sons, Inc., 1952), chap. 13; Eugene L. Grant, *Statistical Quality Control* (rev. ed.; New York: McGraw-Hill Book Co., Inc., 1952).

We shall illustrate briefly how these ideas might be applied in financial analysis. For concreteness, we begin with the data given graphically in Figure 3.

1. The first question is that of independence: Can we regard these weekly changes as independent? Purely to illustrate one test of independence, we shall apply a test based on runs above and below zero. If we denote a positive change by "+" and a negative change by "−", Figure 3 yields the following sequence of +'s and −'s.

$$-\; -\; +\; +\; -\; -\; +\; +\; +\; +\; +\; +\; -\; +\; -\; -\; +\; +\; -\; -\; -\; -\; +\; -\; +\; +\; +\; +\; +\; +$$
$$-\; +\; -\; -\; -\; -\; +\; -\; -\; -\; +\; +\; -\; -\; +\; -\; -\; -\; -\; +\; +\; -\; +\; +$$

A "run" is a consecutive sequence of the same symbol: e.g., − −, + +, −, and + + + + + + are the first four runs. We count 24 runs, which does not differ significantly from the expected number of 26.41.[7]

There are many tests for independence, and experience will show the most useful ones for this kind of application. I would guess that the mean-square successive difference[8] would prove useful. This has the virtue of providing a descriptive measure of the degree of independence or dependence, as well as a test that gives simply an all-or-none verdict or a significance level. A slight degree of dependence may not invalidate subsequent analysis of the kind proposed here, while substantial dependence may open the way for forecasts that exploit the observed pattern, just as one might do by careful study of a defective roulette wheel.

The idea of "rational subgroups" commonly used in industrial practice may be useful,[9] particularly in relating changes for different intervals of time, such as days and weeks.

2. If substantial dependence is found, it may be directly useful for forecasting, using the well-known methods of autoregression. Dependence may also suggest useful avenues for investigation. A sharp jump in the level of price changes for a particular stock, for example, might be found to coincide with a change in management. The company's history since that change would then be the object of an analysis like that described in the preceding paragraph.

3. If a close approximation to independence is found for any moderately large number of weeks (say at least 52, as a rule of thumb), set up "control limits" to aid visual analysis in the future.

7. For mechanical details see Wallis and Roberts, *op. cit.*

8. *Ibid.*

9. Grant, *op. cit.*

These limits can be calculated in many ways.[10] If a point falls outside the control limits, this gives a signal for the analyst to search for an explanation beyond the series itself: e.g., company developments, economic changes, governmental actions. So long as points stay within the limits, there is no need for special attention, although there may also be supplemental warning signals based on gradual shifts that cause trends but do not immediately throw points outside control limits. There will be risks of failing to search when a search is warranted and of searching when nothing is to be found. These risks can be evaluated and the control limits determined accordingly. The aim of the procedure is to economize the time of the financial analyst, who cannot possibly be simultaneously in close contact with the many individual companies that he must be familiar with. It should tend to avoid the numerous false signals that are so strongly suggested by examination of levels rather than changes.

This outline of statistical procedure is meant only to be suggestive. The general nature of the statistical attack is obvious, but the details will be supplied with practical experience guided by sound statistical theory. It may be found, for example, that it is wiser to analyze changes of logarithms or square roots of levels than absolute changes, especially when long periods of time are examined. But much is to be gained simply by viewing a familiar problem from a new vantage point, and minor statistical refinements or blemishes may not be crucial.

These statistical suggestions are only a preliminary to the real work of the financial analyst, which extends far beyond the tape itself and draws on knowledge and skills, including statistical knowledge and skills, that are not discussed here. There is every reason to believe, however, that this method of looking at the tape will facilitate all that takes place afterward. Further statistical analysis, such as multiple regression, will be sounder if based on independent changes rather than dependent levels. Judgment and intuition will proceed more soundly if not hindered by an unnecessary grappling with market "patterns."

10. Wallis and Roberts, *op. cit.*; Hald, *op. cit.*; and Grant, *op. cit.*

9

RANDOM WALKS AND TECHNICAL THEORIES: SOME ADDITIONAL EVIDENCE

Michael C. Jensen and George A. Bennington *

I. INTRODUCTION

THE RANDOM WALK and martingale efficient market theories of security price behavior imply that stock market trading rules based solely on the past price series cannot earn profits greater than those generated by a simple buy-and-hold policy[1]. A vast amount of statistical testing of the behavior of security prices indicates very little evidence of any important dependencies in security price changes through time.[2] Technical analysts or chartists, however, have insisted that this evidence does not imply their methods are invalid and have argued that the dependencies upon which their rules are based are much too subtle to be captured by simple statistical tests. In an effort to meet these criticisms Alexander (1961, 1964) and later Fama and Blume (1966) have examined the profitability of various "filter" trading rules based only on the past price series which purportedly capture the essential characteristics of many technical theories. These studies indicate the "filter" rules do not yield profits net of transactions costs which are higher than those earned by a simple buy-and-hold strategy. Similarly, James (1968) and Van Horne and Parker (1967) have found that various trading rules based upon moving averages of past prices do not yield profits greater than those of a buy-and-hold policy.

Robert A. Levy (1967a, b) has reported empirical results of tests of variations of a technical portfolio trading rule variously called the "relative strength" or "portfolio upgrading" rule. The rule is based solely on the past price series of common stocks, and yet his results seem to indicate that some of the variations of the trading rule perform "significantly" better than a simple buy-and-hold strategy. On the basis of this evidence Levy (1967a) concludes that ". . . the theory of random walks has been refuted." In an invited comment Jensen (1967) pointed out that Levy's results do not support a conclusion as strong as this. In that "Comment" it was pointed out that due to several errors the results reported by Levy overstated the excess returns earned by the profitable trading rules over the returns earned by the buy-and-hold comparison. (These arguments will not be repeated here; the interested reader may consult the original articles for the specific criticisms.) Nevertheless, even after correction for these errors Levy's results still indicated some of the trading rules earned substantially more than the buy-and-hold returns, and

* Assistant Professor and Director of Computing Services respectively at the College of Business Administration, University of Rochester. This Research was supported by the Security Trust Company, Rochester, New York. We wish to express our appreciation to David Besenfelder for his help in the computer programming effort.

1. Cf. Cootner (1964), Fama (1965), Mandelbrot (1966) and Samuelson (1965).

2. For example, cf. Fama (1965), Roll (1968), and the papers in Cootner (1964).

Reprinted from *The Journal of Finance*, XXV, No. 2 (May, 1970), 469–82, by permission of the authors and the publisher.

Jensen (1967) indicated that even these results were inconclusive because of the existence of a subtle form of selection bias.

In his Ph.D. thesis, Levy (1966) reports the results of tests of the profitability of some 68 variations of various trading rules of which very few that were based only on past information yielded returns higher than that given by a buy-and-hold policy.[3] All these rules were tested on the same body of data[4] used in showing the profitability of the additional rules reported by Levy (1967a). Likewise, given enough computer time, we are sure that we can find a mechanical trading rule which "works" on a table of *random numbers*— provided of course that we are allowed to test the rule on the *same* table of numbers which we used to discover the rule. We realize of course that the rule would prove useless on any other table of random numbers, and this is exactly the issue with Levy's results.

As pointed out in the "Comment," the only way to discover whether or not Levy's results are indicative of substantial dependencies in stock prices or are merely the result of this selection bias is to replicate the rules on a different body of data. In a "Reply" Levy (1968) states that additional testing of one of the rules on another body of data[5] yielded returns of 31% per annum. He did not report the buy-and-hold returns for this sample; he did report the returns on the S & P 500-stock index over the same period as slightly less than 10% per annum, and claims the trading rule returns when adjusted[6] to a risk level equal to that of the S & P ". . . would have produced nearly 16% . . .".

The purpose of this paper is to report the results of an extensive set of tests of two of Levy's rules which seemed to earn substantially more than a buy-and-hold policy for his sample of 200 securities in the period 1960-1965.

II. THE TRADING RULE

The "relative strength" trading rule as defined by Levy is as follows:

Define $\bar{P}_{jt}$ to be the average price of the j'th security over the 27 weeks prior to and including time t. Let $PR_{jt} = P_{jt}/\bar{P}_{jt}$ be the ratio of the price at time t to the 27 week average price at time t. (1) Define a percentage X $(0 < X < 100)$ and a "cast out rank" K, and invest an equal dollar amount in the X% of the securities under consideration having the largest ratio PR_{jt} at time t. (2) in weeks $t + \tau$ ($\tau = 1, 2, \ldots$) calculate $PR_{j,t+\tau}$ for all securities, rank them from low to high, and sell all securities currently held with ranks greater than K. (3) Immediately reinvest all proceeds from these sales in the X% of the securities at time $t + \tau$ for which $PR_{j,t+\tau}$ is greatest.

Levy found that the two policies with (X = 10%, K = 160) and (X =

---

3. The results for 20 of these rules, none of which show higher returns after transactions costs than the (correct) buy-and-hold returns of 13.4% [cf. Jensen (1967)], are reported in another article by Levy (1967c).

4. Weekly closing prices on 200 securities listed on the New York Stock Exchange in the 5-year period from October, 1960 to October, 1965.

5. The daily closing prices of 625 New York Stock Exchange securities over the period July 1, 1962 to November 25, 1966.

6. No description of his adjustment method was provided.

5%, K = 140) yielded the maximum returns for his sample (20% and 26.1% unadjusted for risk, while the buy-and-hold returns were 13.4%). We have replicated his tests for these two rules for seven non-overlapping 5-year time periods and for 3 to 5 non-overlapping randomly chosen samples of securities within each time period. The results are presented below.

III. The Data

The data for this study were drawn from the University of Chicago Center for Research in Security Prices Monthly Price Relative File.[7] The file contains monthly closing prices, dividends and commission rates on every security on the New York Stock Exchange over the period January, 1926 to March, 1966. In total the file contains data on 1,952 securities and allows one to construct a complete series of (1) dividends and prices adjusted for all capital changes and (2) the actual round lot commission rate on each security for each month.

IV. The Analysis

In order to keep the broad parameters of our replication as close as possible to the original framework used by Levy, we divided the 40-year period covered by our file into the seven non-overlapping time periods (equal in length to Levy's) given in Table 1. (Note that the last period, October 1960-September 1965, is almost identical to Levy's.) After enumerating all securities listed on the N.Y.S.E. at the beginning of *each* of these periods (see Table 1) we randomly ordered them into subsamples of 200 securities each (the same size sample as that used by Levy).

TABLE 1

SAMPLE INTERVALS AND NUMBER OF SECURITIES LISTED ON THE
N.Y.S.E. AT THE BEGINNING OF EACH TIME PERIOD

Time Period*	Number of Securities Listed on N.Y.S.E. at Beginning of Period
(1) Oct. 1930-Sept. 1935	733
(2) Oct. 1935-Sept. 1940	722
(3) Oct. 1940-Sept. 1945	788
(4) Oct. 1945-Sept. 1950	866
(5) Oct. 1950-Sept. 1955	1010
(6) Oct. 1955-Sept. 1960	1044
(7) Oct. 1960-Sept. 1965	1110

* The first 7 months of these periods are used in establishing the initial rankings for the trading rules. Thus the first returns are calculated for May of the following year. All return data are reported for the interval May 1931 through September 1935, etc.

Thus we obtained 29 separate samples of 200 securities each[8] for use in replicating the trading rule—where Levy had one observation on 200 securities we have 29 observations. These 29 independent samples allow us to obtain a very good estimate of the ability of the trading rules to earn profits superior to that of the buy-and-hold policy in any given time period and over

7. Now distributed by Standard Statistics Inc.

8. Except for the third time period in which there were only 788 securities listed giving us 4 samples for that time period of 197 securities each.

many different time periods. Note also that we have eliminated one additional source of bias in Levy's procedure by not requiring (as he did) that the securities be listed over the entire 5-year sample period. No investor can possibly accomplish this when actually operating a trading rule since he cannot know ahead of time which firms will stay in business and which will not.

The Trading Profits vs. the B & H Returns.—The average returns earned over all seven time periods for all 29 samples by each of the trading rules and the buy-and-hold (B & H) policy are given in Table 2. The returns on the

TABLE 2

AVERAGE RETURNS AND PERFORMANCE MEASURES OVER ALL
PERIODS FOR VARIOUS POLICIES*

Policy	Average Annual Return**		Average Performance Measure $\bar{\delta}$
	Net of Trans. Costs	Gross of Trans. Costs	
(1)	(2)	(3)	(4)
Buy-and-Hold***	.107	.111	—.0018
(X = 10%, K = 160)	.107	.125	—.0049
(X = 5%, K = 140)	.093	.124	—.0254

 * Calculated over all portfolios in Tables 4 and 5.
 ** Continuously compounded.
 *** Weighted Average. Weights are proportional to number of trading rule portfolios in each period.

B & H policy given in Table 2 are the weighted average returns which would have been earned by investing an equal dollar amount in *every* security listed on the N.Y.S.E. at the beginning of each of the 7 periods under consideration (assuming that all dividends were reinvested in their respective securities when received[9]). The returns net of commissions account for the actual transactions costs involved in the initial purchase and final sale (but ignore the transactions costs on the reinvestment of dividends as do the return calculations on the trading rule portfolios).

We can see from Col. 3 of Table 2 that before allowance for commissions costs the trading rules earned approximately 1.4% more than the B & H policy. However, from Col. 2 of Table 2 we see that after allowance for commissions[10] the trading rules earned returns roughly equivalent to or less than the B & H policy. We shall see below however that the trading rules generate portfolios with greater risk than the B & H policy so that after allowance for the differential risk the rules performed somewhat worse than the B & H

9. If a security was delisted during a particular time period the proceeds were assumed to have been reinvested in the Fisher Investment Performance Index (cf. Fisher [1966]) which was constructed to approximate the returns from a buy-and-hold policy including all securities on the N.Y.S.E.. This procedure is unlikely to cause serious bias and saves a considerable amount of computer time. The weights used in calculating the average B & H returns are proportional to the number of trading rule portfolios in each period. This procedure was followed in order to make the B & H average comparable to the trading rule average in which (due to the differing sample sizes) the time periods receive different weights. The simple averages for each time period are given in Tables 3 and 4.

10. Calculated at the actual round lot rate applying to each security at the time of each trade.

policy. Thus at first glance the results of Levy's trading rule simulation on 200 securities are not substantiated in our replication on 29 independent samples of 200 securities selected over a 35 year time interval.

Fama and Blume (1966) and more recently Smidt (1968) have argued persuasively that these results (the higher returns before allowance for transactions costs and returns comparable or lower than the B & H policy after allowance for transactions costs) are just what we would expect in an efficient market in which traders acting upon information are subject to transactions costs. We can expect outside traders to remove dependencies in security prices only up to the limits imposed by the transactions costs. Any dependencies which are not large enough to yield extraordinary profits after allowance for the costs of acting upon them are thus consistent with the economic meaning of the theory of random walks.

Tables 3 and 4 present the summary statistics of the replication of Levy's trading rules for each time period. Columns 3 and 4 contain the annual returns net and gross of actual transactions costs generated by the trading rule when applied to each sample of 200 securities[11] and for the buy-and-hold comparison. The last line of each panel gives the average values of the trading rule statistics for each sample for the period summarized in the panel.

After transactions costs the $(X = 10\%, K = 160)$ trading rule earned more than the B & H policy in only 13 of the 29 cases and the B & H policy showed higher returns in 16 of the 29 cases (see Col. 3 of Table 3). Thus, even ignoring the risk issues, the rule was not able to generate systematically higher returns than the B & H policy. Table 4 shows that the $(X = 5\%, K = 140)$ policy performed even less well, yielding a score of 12 to 17 in favor of the B & H policy.

Note also panel 7 of Tables 3 and 4 which gives the results for a time period almost identical to Levy's. The trading rule returns on all 5 portfolios are far smaller than the 20% and 26% respectively he reported. In fact 12.9% is the highest return we obtained in this period and 5 of the 10 rules earned less than the B & H policy. This is additional evidence that Levy's original high returns were spurious and probably attributable to the selection bias discussed earlier.

As before, gross of transactions costs, both trading rules performed much better relative to the B & H policy; with the $(X = 10\%, K = 160)$ policy earning higher returns than the B & H policy in 19 of the 29 cases and the $(X = 5\%, K = 140)$ policy yielding higher returns in 18 of the 29 cases.

In addition comparison of the mean portfolio return (net of transactions costs) with the B & H return in each subperiod indicates that the B & H returns were higher in 4 out of the 7 periods for the $(X = 10\%, K = 160)$ rule and 5 out of the 7 periods for the $(X = 5\%, K = 140)$ rule. Gross of transactions costs the B & H policy yielded higher returns in 4 of 7 periods for the $(X = 10\%, K = 160)$ policy and 3 of 7 periods for the $(X = 5\%, K = 140)$ policy.

---

11. The data is monthly. Thus the PR_{jt} is defined as the ratio of the price at the end of month t to the average of the closing prices for months t — 6 through month t. The trading rule is then applied at one month intervals for the remainder of the period.

TABLE 3
SUMMARY STATISTICS FOR B & H AND TRADING RULE PORTFOLIOS
FOR VARIOUS TIME PERIODS
(Trading Rule is Levy's (X = 10%, K = 160) Policy)

Time Period	Portfolio	Continuously Compounded Annual Rate of Return		Std. Dev.*	Beta	Delta
		Net of Trans. Costs	Gross of Trans. Costs			
(1)	(2)	(3)	(4)	(5)	(6)	(7)
May 31 to Sep 35 [1]	B & H	0.047	0.051	0.157	0.942	−0.017
	1.	0.088	0.100	0.137	0.774	0.027
	2.	−0.013	0.009	0.112	0.617	−0.066
	3.	−0.032	−0.013	0.151	0.860	−0.093
Portfolio Average		0.014	0.032	0.133	0.750	−0.044
May 36 to Sep 40 [2]	B & H	−.031	−0.027	0.109	0.929	0.004
	1.	−0.081	−0.067	0.095	0.769	−0.057
	2.	−0.048	−0.032	0.106	0.802	−0.020
	3.	−0.103	−0.085	0.104	0.829	−0.078
Portfolio Average		−0.078	−0.062	0.101	0.800	−0.052
May 41 to Sep 45 [3]	B & H	0.300	0.306	0.058	1.032	−0.043
	1.	0.290	0.316	0.059	0.969	−0.032
	2.	0.320	0.347	0.067	1.048	−0.032
	3.	0.237	0.260	0.056	0.881	−0.049
	4.	0.259	0.290	0.071	1.178	−0.116
Portfolio Average		0.277	0.303	0.063	1.019	−0.057
May 46 to Sep 50 [4])	B & H	0.032	0.036	0.049	0.950	0.012
	1.	0.021	0.037	0.055	0.996	−0.000
	2.	0.002	0.019	0.053	0.933	−0.017
	3.	0.031	0.047	0.054	0.983	0.010
	4.	0.006	0.021	0.053	0.952	−0.014
Portfolio Average		0.015	0.031	0.054	0.966	−0.005
May 51 to Sep 55 [5]	B & H	0.157	0.161	0.031	0.989	−0.004
	1.	0.164	0.179	0.039	1.139	−0.016
	2.	0.204	0.219	0.041	1.179	0.013
	3.	0.150	0.170	0.041	1.162	−0.030
	4.	0.162	0.178	0.037	1.026	−0.002
	5.	0.179	0.196	0.033	0.919	0.026
Portfolio Average		0.172	0.188	0.038	1.085	−0.002

* Standard deviation of the monthly returns.

TABLE 3 (Cont'd)

Time Period	Portfolio	Continuously Compounded Annual Rate of Return		Std. Dev.	Beta	Delta
		Net of Trans. Costs	Gross of Trans. Costs			
(1)	(2)	(3)	(4)	(5)	(6)	(7)
May 56 to	B & H	0.090	0.095	0.033	0.968	0.012
Sep 60	1.	0.272	0.281	0.048	0.829	0.174
	2.	0.125	0.141	0.046	1.067	0.040
[6]	3.	0.110	0.128	0.044	1.122	0.024
	4.	0.201	0.216	0.048	1.096	0.104
	5.	0.083	0.099	0.041	1.076	0.002
Portfolio Average		0.158	0.173	0.045	1.038	0.069
May 61 to	B & H	0.096	0.101	0.039	0.956	0.014
Sep 65	1.	0.129	0.146	0.048	1.044	0.040
	2.	0.087	0.105	0.042	0.922	0.008
[7]	3.	0.101	0.120	0.051	1.161	0.010
	4.	0.063	0.081	0.046	1.032	−0.019
	5.	0.103	0.123	0.044	0.953	0.021
Portfolio Average		0.097	0.115	0.046	1.022	0.012

An Alternative Comparison and a Test of Significance.—Tables 3 and 4 contain the B & H returns calculated for an initial equal dollar investment in *every* security on the exchange at the beginning of each period. We have also calculated the B & H returns which would have been realized on *each sample* of 200 securities. The differences between these B & H returns and the trading rule returns for each sample in each time period are given in Table 5. The results are substantially the same as those reported in Tables 3 and 4 in terms of the number of instances in which the trading rules earned higher returns than the B & H policy (see last two lines of Table 5 for a summary).

The mean difference between the B & H and trading rule returns is given for each policy (both net and gross of transactions costs) in Table 5 along with the standard deviation of the differences. The "t" values given at the bottom of Table 5 (none of which is greater than 1.5) indicate that none of the differences is significantly different from zero. Thus even ignoring the issue of differential risk between the B & H and trading rule policies the trading rules do not earn significantly more than the B & H policy.

V. Risk and the Performance of the Trading Rules

In order to compare the riskiness of the portfolios generated by the trading rules with the risk of the B & H policy we have calculated the standard deviation of the monthly returns (after transactions costs), and these are given in column 5 of Tables 3 and 4. Except for the first two subperiods the standard deviations of the trading rule portfolios are uniformly higher than that for the B & H policy. Thus, for equal expected returns a risk averse

TABLE 4
SUMMARY STATISTICS FOR B & H AND TRADING RULE PORTFOLIOS
FOR VARIOUS TIME PERIODS
(Trading Rule is Levy's (X = 5%, K = 160) Policy)

| Time Period | Portfolio | Continuously Compounded Annual Rate of Return | | Std. Dev. | Beta | Delta |
		Net of Trans. Costs	Gross of Trans. Costs			
(1)	(2)	(3)	(4)	(5)	(6)	(7)
May 31	B & H	0.047	0.051	0.157	0.942	−0.017
to						
Sep 35	1.	−0.154	−0.125	0.138	0.728	−0.223
[1]	2.	−0.054	−0.017	0.128	0.672	−0.110
	3.	−0.047	−0.017	0.151	0.822	−01.08
Portfolio Average		−0.085	−0.053	0.139	0.741	−0.147
May 36	B & H	−0.031	−0.027	0.109	0.929	0.004
to						
Sep 40	1.	−0.142	−0.121	0.102	0.806	−0.124
[2]	2.	−0.021	0.004	0.141	0.962	0.016
	3.	−0.157	−0.127	0.103	0.761	−0.143
Portfolio Average		−0.107	−0.081	0.116	0.843	−0.083
May 41	B & H	0.300	0.306	0.058	1.032	−0.043
to						
Sep 45	1.	0.309	0.352	0.072	1.094	−0.053
	2.	0.326	0.368	0.084	1.160	−0.059
[3]	3.	0.203	0.237	0.066	0.995	−0.110
	4.	0.246	0.292	0.081	1.329	−0.170
Portfolio Average		0.271	0.312	0.076	1.145	−0.098
May 46	B & H	0.032	0.036	0.049	0.950	0.012
to						
Sep 50	1.	−0.021	0.005	0.056	1.004	−0.042
	2.	−0.004	0.016	0.056	0.958	−0.024
[4]	3.	0.038	0.060	0.059	1.021	0.017
	4.	−0.003	0.019	0.056	0.965	−0.023
Portfolio Average		0.002	0.025	0.057	0.987	−0.018
May 51	B & H	0.157	0.161	0.031	0.989	−0.004
to						
Sep 55	1.	0.155	0.178	0.038	1.074	−0.015
	2.	0.155	0.178	0.042	1.136	−0.023
[5]	3.	0.188	0.213	0.046	1.228	−0.007
	4.	0.132	0.160	0.036	0.949	−0.019
	5.	0.221	0.241	0.039	0.868	0.067
Portfolio Average		0.170	0.194	0.040	1.051	0.001

TABLE 4 (Cont'd)

| Time Period | Portfolio | Continuously Compounded Annual Rate of Return | | Std. Dev. | Beta | Delta |
		Net of Trans. Costs	Gross of Trans. Costs			
(1)	(2)	(3)	(4)	(5)	(6)	(7)
May 56 to	B & H	0.090	0.095	0.033	0.968	0.012
Sep 60	1.	0.245	0.258	0.046	0.822	0.152
	2.	0.158	0.181	0.058	1.174	0.064
[6]	3.	0.135	0.159	0.051	1.205	0.043
	4.	0.242	0.263	0.056	1.170	0.135
	5.	0.080	0.106	0.046	1.139	−0.004
Portfolio Average		0.172	0.193	0.052	1.102	0.078
May 61 to	B & H	0.096	0.101	0.039	0.956	0.014
Sep 65	1.	0.101	0.130	0.053	1.087	0.013
	2.	0.091	0.119	0.047	0.956	0.010
[7]	3.	0.123	0.149	0.060	1.296	0.023
	4.	0.078	0.107	0.053	1.092	−0.009
	5.	0.073	0.104	0.052	1.019	−0.010
Portfolio Average		0.093	0.122	0.053	1.090	0.005

investor choosing among portfolios on the basis of mean and standard deviation would not be indifferent between them. This brings us to a serious issue.

If securities markets are dominated by risk-averse investors and risky assets are priced so as to earn more on average than less risky assets then any portfolio manager or security analyst will be able to earn above average returns if he systematically selects a portfolio with higher than average risk; so too will a mechanical trading rule. Jensen (1967) has pointed out that there is good reason to believe that Levy's trading rules will tend to select such an above average risk portfolio during time periods in which the market is experiencing generally positive returns. Thus it is important in comparing the returns of the trading rule to those of the B & H policy to make explicit allowance for any differential returns due solely to different degrees of risk.

A Portfolio Evaluation Model.—Jensen (1969) has proposed a model for evaluating the performance of portfolios which takes explicit account of the effects of differential riskiness in comparing portfolios. The model is based upon recent mean-variance general equilibrium models of the pricing of capital assets proposed by Sharpe (1964), Lintner (1965), Mossin (1966), and Fama (1968). The measure of performance, δ_j for any portfolio j in any given holding period suggested by Jensen is

$$\delta_j = R_j - [R_F + (R_M - R_F)\beta_j] \tag{1}$$

where

R_j = the rate of return on portfolio j.
R_F = the riskless rate of interest.

R_M = the rate of return on a market portfolio consisting of an investment in each outstanding asset in proportion to its value.

$\beta_J = \dfrac{\text{cov}(R_J, R_M)}{\sigma^2(R_M)}$ = the systematic risk of the j'th portfolio.

We shall not review the details of the derivation of (1) here; the interested reader is referred to Jensen (1969). However, Figure 1 gives a graphical in-

TABLE 5

DIFFERENCES BETWEEN B & H AND TRADING RULE RETURNS.

(B & H RETURNS CALCULATED FOR EACH SUBSAMPLE OF 200 SECURITIES.)

	B & H Returns—Trading Rule Returns			
	[X = 10%, K = 160]		[X = 5%, K = 140]	
Period	Net of Trans. Costs	Gross of Trans. Costs	Net of Trans. Costs	Gross of Trans. Costs
(1)	(2)	(3)	(4)	(5)
	−0.024	−0.032	0.218	0.193
1	0.057	0.040	0.098	0.066
	0.079	0.065	0.094	0.069
	0.035	0.024	0.096	0.078
2	0.033	0.021	0.006	−0.015
	0.074	0.061	0.128	0.103
	0.012	−0.008	−0.007	−0.044
3	−0.013	−0.033	−0.019	−0.054
	0.039	0.021	0.073	0.044
	0.058	0.034	0.071	0.032
	0.012	0.0	0.054	0.032
4	0.030	0.016	0.036	0.019
	0.008	−0.004	0.001	−0.017
	0.020	0.008	0.029	0.010
	−0.016	−0.027	−0.007	−0.026
	−0.032	−0.043	0.017	−0.002
5	0.003	−0.012	−0.035	−0.055
	−0.012	−0.024	0.018	−0.006
	−0.017	−0.029	−0.059	−0.074
	−0.177	−0.181	−0.150	−0.158
	−0.034	−0.045	−0.067	−0.085
6	−0.022	−0.035	−0.047	−0.066
	−0.100	−0.110	−0.141	−0.157
	−0.004	−0.016	−0.001	−0.023
	−0.033	−0.045	−0.005	−0.029
	0.002	−0.011	−0.002	−0.025
7	0.003	−0.011	−0.019	−0.040
	0.035	0.022	0.020	−0.004
	0.005	−0.010	0.035	0.009
Mean Difference = $\bar{d}$	.001	−.013	.015	−.008
Std. Dev. = $\sigma(\bar{d})$	.050	.048	.075	.072
$t(\bar{d}) = \bar{d}/(\sigma(\bar{d})/\sqrt{29})$	1.07	−1.46	1.08	−.60
Number (−)	12	18	13	18
Number (+)	17	11	16	11

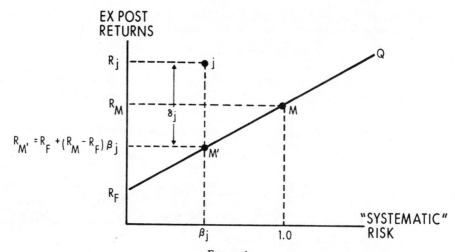

EX POST RETURNS

FIGURE 1
The Measure of Performance δ_j, for a Hypothetical Portfolio

terpretation of the measure of performance δ_j. The point M represents the realized returns on the market portfolio and its "systematic" risk (which from the definition of β, can be seen to be unity). The point R_F is the riskless rate and the equation of the line R_FMQ is

$$E(R|R_M, \beta) = R_F + (R_M - R_F)\beta. \tag{2}$$

If the asset pricing model is valid, the line R_FMQ given by eq. (2) gives us the locus of expected returns on any portfolio conditional on the ex post market returns and the systematic risk of the portfolio, β, in the absence of any forecasting ability by the portfolio manager. Thus the line R_FMQ represents the trade off between risk and return which existed in the market over this particular holding period. The point j represents the ex post returns R_J on a hypothetical portfolio j over this holding period, and β_J is its systematic risk. The vertical distance between the risk-return combination of any portfolio j and the line R_FMQ in Figure 1 is the measure of performance of portfolio j.

In the absence of any forecasting ability by the portfolio manager the expected value of δ_j is zero. That is we expect the realized returns of the portfolio to fluctuate randomly about the line R_FMQ through successive holding intervals. If $\delta_j > 0$ systematically, the portfolio has earned returns higher than that implied solely by its level of risk, and therefore the manager can be judged to have superior forecasting ability. If $\delta_j < 0$ systematically, the portfolio has earned returns less than that implied by its level of risk, and if the model is valid this can only be explained by the absence of forecasting ability and the generation of large expenses by the manager (see Jensen [1969, pp. 227f]).

The measure δ_j may also be interpreted in the following manner: Let M' be a portfolio consisting of a combined investment in the riskless asset and the market portfolio M such that its risk is equal to β_j. Now δ_j may be interpreted as the difference between the return realized on the j'th portfolio and the return $R_{M'}$ which could have been earned on the equivalent risk market portfolio M'. If $\delta_j > 0$, the portfolio j has yielded the investor a return greater than the return on a combined investment in M and F with an identical level of systematic risk.

The measures of systematic risk for each of the portfolios generated by the trading rules and for the B & H policy are given in column 6 of Tables 3 and 4, and the measures of performance δ_j are given in column 7. The market returns and risk free rates used in these estimates are given in Table 6. The

TABLE 6

MARKET AND RISKLESS RETURNS USED IN ESTIMATING
THE PERFORMANCE MEASURES δ_j

Period	Market Return*	Riskless Rate**
1) May 1931-Sept. 1935	.064	.0334
2) May 1936-Sept. 1940	−.039	.0108
3) May 1941-Sept. 1945	.296	.0080
4) May 1946-Sept. 1950	.020	.0104
5) May 1951-Sept. 1955	.149	.0206
6) May 1956-Sept. 1960	.075	.0296
7) May 1961-Sept. 1965	.079	.0344

* Continuously compounded returns on Fisher Investment Performance Index (Fisher [1966]), obtained from most recent Monthly Price Relative Tape distributed by Standard Statistics, Inc.
** Continuously compounded yield to maturity (at the beginning of the period) of a government bond maturing at the end of the period estimated from yield curves presented in the U. S. Treasury Bulletin, except for the first two periods. The rate for the first period is the average yield on long-term government bonds at the beginning of the period taken from the *Eighteenth Annual* Report of the Federal Reserve Board—1931 (Washington, D.C., 1932), p. 79. The rate for the second period is the average yield on U.S. Treasury 3-5 year notes taken from the *Twenty-Third Annual Report of the Board of Governors of the Federal Reserve System—1936* (Washington, D.C., 1937), p. 118.

average δ's for the B & H policy and the trading rule portfolios over all periods are given in column 4 of Table 2. The $\bar{\delta}$ for the B & H policy (after transactions costs) over all 7 periods was −.0018; that is the B & H policy earned on average .18% per year (compounded continuously) less than that implied by its level of risk and the asset pricing model.

On the other hand the average δ for the trading rules (net of transactions cost) was −.49% and −2.54% respectively for the (X = 10%, K = 160) and (X = 5%, K = 140) policies. That is, after explicit adjustment for the systematic riskiness of the two policies, they earned −.49% and −2.54% less than that implied by their level of risk and the asset pricing model. In addition the average δ for the portfolios was greater than the δ for the B & H policy in only 2 periods for both of the trading rules (see Tables 3 and 4). Since the point at issue is whether or not the trading rules perform *significantly better* than the B & H policy the fact that they don't on the average even perform as well means we need not bother with any formal tests of significance.

VI. SUMMARY AND CONCLUSIONS

Our replication of two of Levy's trading rules on 29 independent samples of 200 securities each over successive 5 year time intervals in the period 1931 to 1965 does not support his results. After allowance for transactions costs the trading rules did not on the average earn significantly more than the B & H policy. Furthermore, since the trading rule portfolios were on the average more risky than the B & H portfolios this simple comparison of returns is biased in favor of the trading rules. After explicit adjustment for the level of risk it was shown that net of transactions costs the two trading rules we tested earned on average $-.31\%$ and -2.36% less than an equivalent risk B & H policy. Given these results we conclude that with respect to the performance of Levy's "relative strength" trading rules the behavior of security prices on the N.Y.S.E. is remarkably close to that predicted by the efficient market theories of security price behavior, and Levy's (1967a) conclusion that ". . . the theory of random walks has been refuted," is not substantiated.

REFERENCES

1. Sidney S. Alexander. "Price Movements in Speculative Markets: Trends or Random Walks," *Industrial Management Review*, II (May, 1961), 7-26.
2. Sidney S. Alexander. "Price Movements in Speculative Markets: Trends or Random Walks, Number 2," *Industrial Management Review*, V (Spring, 1964), 25-46.
3. Paul H. Cootner, (ed.). *The Random Character of Stock Market Prices*. (Cambridge, Mass.: M.I.T. Press, 1964).
4. Eugene Fama. "The Behavior of Stock-Market Prices," *Journal of Business*, XXXVII (January, 1965), 34-105.
5. Eugene Fama, and Marshall Blume. "Filter Rules and Stock Market Trading," *Journal of Business*, XXXIX (January, 1966), 226-41.
6. Eugene Fama. "Risk, Return, and Equilibrium: Some Clarifying Comments," *Journal of Finance* (March, 1968), 29-40.
7. Lawrence Fisher. "Some New Stock Market Indexes," *Journal of Business*, XXXIX, Part 2 (January, 1966), 191-225.
8. F. E. James, Jr. "Monthly Moving Averages—An Effective Investment Tool?," *Journal of Financial and Quantitative Analysis* (September, 1968), 315-326.
9. Michael C. Jensen. "Random Walks: Reality or Myth—Comment," *Financial Analysts Journal* (November-December, 1967), 77-85.
10. Michael C. Jensen. "Risk, the Pricing of Capital Assets, and the Evaluation of Investment Portfolios," *Journal of Business*, 42 (April, 1969), 167-247.
11. Robert A. Levy. "An Evaluation of Selected Applications of Stock Market Timing Techniques, Trading Tactics and Trend Analysis," (Unpublished Ph.D. dissertation, The American University, 1966).
12. Robert A. Levy. "Random Walks: Reality or Myth," *Financial Analysts Journal*, (November-December, 1967a).
13. Robert A. Levy. "Relative Strength as a Criterion for Investment Selection," *Journal of Finance*, XXII (December, 1967b), 595-610.
14. Robert A. Levy. "The Principle of Portfolio Upgrading," *The Industrial Management Review* (Fall, 1967c), 82-96.
15. Robert A. Levy. "Random Walks: Reality or Myth—Reply," *Financial Analysts Journal*, (January-February, 1968), 129-132.
16. John Lintner. "Security Prices, Risk, and Maximal Gains from Diversification," *Journal of Finance*, XX (December, 1965), 587-616.
17. Benoit Mandelbrot. "Forecasts of Future Prices, Unbiased Markets and 'Martingale' Models," *Journal of Business*, XXXIX, Part 2 (January, 1966), 242-55.
18. Jan Mossin. "Equilibrium in a Capital Asset Market," *Econometrica*, XXXIV (October, 1966), 768-83.
19. Richard Roll. "The Efficient Market Model Applied to U.S. Treasury Bill Rates," (Unpublished Ph.D. dissertation, University of Chicago, 1968).

10

THE ADJUSTMENT OF STOCK PRICES
TO NEW INFORMATION *

Eugene F. Fama, Lawrence Fisher, Michael C. Jensen,
and Richard Roll [1]

1. INTRODUCTION

THERE IS an impressive body of empirical evidence which indicates that
successive price changes in individual common stocks are very nearly independent.[2] Recent papers by Mandelbrot [11] and Samuelson [16] show rigorously that independence of successive price changes is *consistent* with an
"efficient" market, i.e., a market that adjusts rapidly to new information.

It is important to note, however, that in the empirical work to date the
usual procedure has been to *infer* market efficiency from the observed independence of successive price changes. There has been very little actual
testing of the speed of adjustment of prices to *specific kinds* of new information. The prime concern of this paper is to examine the process by which
common stock prices adjust to the information (if any) that is implicit in a
stock split.

2. SPLITS, DIVIDENDS, AND NEW INFORMATION: A HYPOTHESIS

More specifically, this study will attempt to examine evidence on two related
questions: (1) Is there normally some "unusual" behavior in the rates of
return on a split security in the months surrounding the split?[3] and (2) if
splits are associated with "unusual" behavior of security returns, to what
extent can this be accounted for by relationships between splits and changes

* Manuscript received May 31, 1966, revised October 3, 1966.

[1] This study way suggested to us by Professor James H. Lorie. We are grateful
to Professors Lorie, Merton H. Miller, and Harry V. Roberts for many helpful comments and criticisms.

The research reported here was supported by the Center for Research in Security
Prices, Graduate School of Business, University of Chicago, and by funds made
available to the Center by the National Science Foundation.

[2] Cf.Cootner [2] and the studies reprinted therein, Fama [3], Godfrey, Granger, and
Morgenstern [8] and other empirical studies of the theory of random walks in speculative prices.

[3] A precise definition of "unusual" behavior of security returns will be provided
below.

Reprinted from the *International Economic Review*, X, No. 1 (February, 1969), 1–21,
by permission of the authors and the publisher.

in other more fundamental variables?[4]

In answer to the first question we shall show that stock splits are usually preceded by a period during which the rates of return (including dividends and capital appreciation) on the securities to be split are unusually high. The period of high returns begins, however, long before any information (or even rumor) concerning a possible split is likely to reach the market. Thus we suggest that the high returns far in advance of the split arise from the fact that during the pre-split period these companies have experienced dramatic increases in expected earnings and dividends.

In the empirical work reported below, however, we shall see that the highest average monthly rates of return on split shares occur in the few months immediately preceding the split. This might appear to suggest that the split itself provides some impetus for increased returns. We shall present evidence, however, which suggests that such is not the case. The evidence supports the following reasoning: Although there has probably been a dramatic increase in earnings in the recent past, in the months immediately prior to the split (or its announcement) there may still be considerable uncertainty in the market concerning whether the earnings can be maintained at their new higher level. Investors will attempt to use any information available to reduce this uncertainty, and a proposed split may be one source of such information.

In the past a large fraction of stock splits have been followed closely by dividend increases—and increases greater than those experienced at the same time by other securities in the market. In fact it is not unusual for the dividend change to be announced at the same time as the split. Other studies (cf. Lintner [10] and Michaelsen [14]) have demonstrated that, once dividends have been increased, large firms show great reluctance to reduce them, except under the most extreme conditions. Directors have appeared to hedge against such dividend cuts by increasing dividends only when they are quite sure of their ability to maintain them in the future, i.e., only when they feel strongly that future earnings will be sufficient to maintain the dividends at their new higher rate. Thus dividend changes may be assumed to convey important information to the market concerning management's

[4] There is another question concerning stock splits which this study does not consider. That is, given that splitting is not costless, and since the only apparent result is to multiply the number of shares per shareholder without increasing the shareholder's claims to assets, why do firms split their shares? This question has been the subject of considerable discussion in the professional financial literature. (Cf. Bellemore and Blucher [1].) Suffice it to say that the arguments offered in favor of splitting usually turn out to be two-sided under closer examination — e.g., a split, by reducing the price of a round lot, will reduce transactions costs for some relatively small traders but increase costs for both large and very small traders (i.e., for traders who will trade, exclusively, either round lots or odd lots both before and after the split). Thus the conclusions are never clear-cut. In this study we shall be concerned with identifying the factors which the *market* regards as important in a stock split and with determining how market prices adjust to these factors rather than with explaining why firms split their shares.

assessment of the firm's long-run earning and dividend paying potential.

We suggest, then, that unusually high returns on splitting shares in the months immediately preceding a split reflect the market's anticipation of substantial increases in dividends which, in fact, usually occur. Indeed evidence presented below leads us to conclude that when the information effects of dividend changes are taken into account, the apparent price effects of the split will vanish.[5]

3. SAMPLE AND METHODOLOGY

a. *The data.* We define a "stock split" as an exchange of shares in which at least five shares are distributed for every four formerly outstanding. Thus this definition of splits includes all stock dividends of 25 per cent or greater. We also decided, arbitrarily, that in order to get reliable estimates of the parameters that will be used in the analysis, it is necessary to have at least twenty-four successive months of price-dividend data around the split date. Since the data cover only common stocks listed on the New York Stock Exchange, our rules require that to qualify for inclusion in the tests a split security must be listed on the Exchange for at least twelve months before and twelve months after the split. From January, 1927, through December, 1959, 940 splits meeting these criteria occurred on the New York Stock Exchange.[6]

b. *Adjusting security returns for general market conditions.* Of course, during this 33 year period, economic and hence general stock market conditions were far from static. Since we are interested in isolating whatever *extraordinary* effects a split and its associated dividend history may have on returns, it is necessary to abstract from general market conditions in examining the returns on securities during months surrounding split dates. We do this in the following way: Define

P_{jt} = price of the j-th stock at end of month t.

$P'_{jt} = P_{jt}$ adjusted for capital changes in month $t + 1$. For the method of adjustment see Fisher [5].

D_{jt} = cash dividends on the j-th security during month t (where the dividend is taken as of the ex-dividend data rather than the payment date).

$R_{jt} = (P_{jt} + D_{jt})/P'_{j,t-1}$ = price relative of the j-th security for month t.

L_t = the link relative of Fisher's "Combination Investment Performance Index" [6, (table A1)]. It will suffice here to note that L_t is a com-

---

[5] It is important to note that our hypothesis concerns the information content of dividend changes. There is nothing in our evidence which suggests that dividend *policy* per se affects the value of a firm. Indeed, the information hypothesis was first suggested by Miller and Modigliani in [15, (430)], where they show that, aside from information effects, in a perfect capital market dividend policy will not affect the total market value of a firm.

[6] The basic data were contained in the master file of monthly prices, dividends, and capital changes, collected and maintained by the Center for Research in Security Prices (Graduate School of Business, University of Chicago). At the time this study was conducted, the file covered the period January, 1926 to December, 1960. For a description of the data see Fisher and Lorie [7].

plicated average of the R_{jt} for all securities that were on the N.Y.S.E. at the end of months t and $t-1$. L_t is the measure of "general market conditions" used in this study.[7]

One form or another of the following simple model has often been suggested as a way of expressing the relationship between the monthly rates of return provided by an individual security and general market conditions:[8]

$$(1) \qquad \log_e R_{jt} = \alpha_j + \beta_j \log_e L_t + u_{jt} ,$$

where α_j and β_j are parameters that can vary from security to security and u_{jt} is a random disturbance term. It is assumed that u_{jt} satisfies the usual assumptions of the linear regression model. That is, (a) u_{jt} has zero expectation and variance independent of t; (b) the u_{jt} are serially independent; and (c) the distribution of u_j is independent of $\log_e L$.

The natural logarithm of the security price relative is the rate of return (with continuous compounding) for the month in question; similarly, the log of the market index relative is approximately the rate of return on a portfolio which includes equal dollar amounts of all securities in the market. Thus (1) represents the monthly rate of return on an individual security as a linear function of the corresponding return for the market.

c. *Tests of model specification.* Using the available time series on R_{jt} and L_t, least squares has been used to estimate α_j and β_j in (1) for each of the 622 securities in the sample of 940 splits. We shall see later that there is strong evidence that the expected values of the residuals from (1) are non-zero in months close to the split. For these months the assumptions of the regression model concerning the disturbance term in (1) are not valid. Thus if these months were included in the sample, estimates of α and β would be subject to specification error, which could be very serious. We have attempted to avoid this source of specification error by excluding from the estimating samples those months for which the expected values of the

---

[7] To check that our results do not arise from any special properties of the index L_t, we have also performed all tests using Standard and Poor's Composite Price Index as the measure of market conditions; in all major respects the results agree completely with those reported below.

[8] Cf. Markowitz [13, (96-101)], Sharpe [17, 18] and Fama [4]. The logarithmic form of the model is appealing for two reasons. First, over the period covered by our data the distribution of the monthly values of $\log_e L_t$ and $\log_e R_{jt}$ are fairly symmetric, whereas the distributions of the relatives themselves are skewed right. Symmetry is desirable since models involving symmetrically distributed variables present fewer estimation problems than models involving variables with skewed distributions. Second, we shall see below that when least squares is used to estimate α and β in (1), the sample residuals conform well to the assumptions of the simple linear regression model.

Thus, the logarithmic form of the model appears to be well specified from a statistical point of view and has a natural economic interpretation (i.e., in terms of monthly rates of return with continuous compounding). Nevertheless, to check that our results do not depend critically on using logs, all tests have also been carried out using the simple regression of R_{jt} on L_t. These results are in complete agreement with those presented in the text.

residuals are apparently non-zero. The exclusion procedure was as follows: First, the parameters of (1) were estimated for each security using all available data. Then for each split the sample regression residuals were computed for a number of months preceding and following the split. When the number of positive residuals in any month differed substantially from the number of negative residuals, that month was excluded from subsequent calculations. This criterion caused exclusion of fifteen months before the split for all securities and fifteen months after the split for splits followed by dividend decreases[9].

Aside from these exclusions, however, the least squares estimates $\hat{\alpha}_j$ and $\hat{\beta}_j$ for security j are based on all months during the 1926–60 period for which price relatives are available for the security. For the 940 splits the smallest effective sample size is 14 monthly observations. In only 46 cases is the sample size less than 100 months, and for about 60 per cent of the splits more than 300 months of data are available. Thus in the vast majority of cases the samples used in estimating α and β in (1) are quite large.

Table 1 provides summary descriptions of the frequency distributions of the estimated values of α_j, β_j, and r_j, where r_j is the correlation between monthly rates of return on security j (i.e., $\log_e R_{jt}$) and the approximate monthly rates of return on the market portfolio (i.e., $\log_e L_t$). The table indicates that there are indeed fairly strong relationships between the market and monthly returns on individual securities; the mean value of the $\hat{r}_j$ is 0.632 with an average absolute deviation of 0.106 about the mean.[10]

TABLE 1

SUMMARY OF FREQUENCY DISTRIBUTIONS OF ESTIMATED COEFFICIENTS
FOR THE DIFFERENT SPLIT SECURITIES

Statistic	Mean	Median	Mean absolute deviation	Standard deviation	Extreme values	Skewness
$\hat{\alpha}$	0.000	0.001	0.004	0.007	−0.06, 0.04	Slightly left
$\hat{\beta}$	0.894	0.880	0.242	0.305	−0.10*, 1.95	Slightly right
$\hat{r}$	0.632	0.655	0.106	0.132	−0.04*, 0.91	Slightly left

* Only negative value in distribution.

Moreover, the estimates of equation (1) for the different securities conform fairly well to the assumptions of the linear regression model. For example,

[9] Admittedly the exclusion criterion is arbitrary. As a check, however, the analysis of regression residuals discussed later in the paper has been carried out using the regression estimates in which no data are excluded. The results were much the same as those reported in the text and certainly support the same conclusions.

[10] The sample average or mean absolute deviation of the random variable x is defined as

$$\frac{\sum\limits_{t=1}^{N} |x_t - \bar{x}|}{N}$$

where $\bar{x}$ is the sample mean of the x's and N is the sample size.

the first order auto-correlation coefficient of the estimated residuals from (1) has been computed for every twentieth split in the sample (ordered alphabetically by security). The mean (and median) value of the forty-seven coefficients is −0.10, which suggests that serial dependence in the residuals is not a serious problem. For these same forty-seven splits scatter diagrams of (a) monthly security return versus market return, and (b) estimated residual return in month $t+1$ versus estimated residual return in month t have been prepared, along with (c) normal probability graphs of estimated residual returns. The scatter diagrams for the individual securities support very well the regression assumptions of linearity, homoscedasticity, and serial independence.

It is important to note, however, that the data do not conform well to the normal, or Gaussian linear regression model. In particular, the distributions of the estimated residuals have much longer tails than the Gaussian. The typical normal probability graph of residuals looks much like the one shown for Timken Detroit Axle in Figure 1. The departures from normality in the distributions of regression residuals are of the same sort as those noted by Fama [3] for the distributions of returns themselves. Fama (following

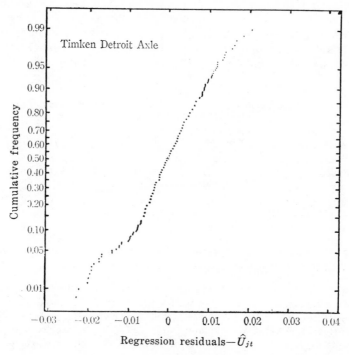

FIGURE 1

NORMAL PROBABILITY PLOT OF RESIDUALS*

* The lower left and upper right corners of the graph represent the most extreme sample points. For clarity, only every tenth point is plotted in the central portion of the figure.

Mandelbrot [12]) argues that distributions of returns are well approximated by the non-Gaussian (i.e., infinite variance) members of the stable Paretian family. If the stable non-Gaussian distributions also provide a good description of the residuals in (1), then, at first glance, the least squares regression model would seem inappropriate.

Wise [19] has shown, however, that although least square estimates are not "efficient," for most members of the stable Paretian family they provide estimates which are unbiased and consistent. Thus, given our large samples, least squares regression is not completely inappropriate. In deference to the stable Paretian model, however, in measuring variability we rely primarily on the mean absolute deviation rather than the variance or the standard deviation. The mean absolute deviation is used since, for long-tailed distributions, its sampling behavior is less erratic than that of the variance or the standard deviation[11].

In sum we find that regressions of security returns on market returns over time are a satisfactory method for abstracting from the effects of general market conditions on the monthly rates of return on individual securities. We must point out, however, that although (1) stands up fairly well to the assumptions of the linear regression model, it is certainly a grossly over-simplified model of price formation; general market conditions alone do not determine the returns on an individual security. In (1) the effects of these "omitted variables" are impounded into the disturbance term u. In particular, if a stock split is associated with abnormal behavior in returns during months surrounding the split date, this behavior should be reflected in the estimated regression residuals of the security for these months. The remainder of our analysis will concentrate on examining the behavior of the estimated residuals of split securities in the months surrounding the splits.

3. "EFFECTS" OF SPLITS ON RETURNS: EMPIRICAL RESULTS

In this study we do not attempt to determine the effects of splits for individual companies. Rather we are concerned with whether the process of splitting is in general associated with specific types of return behavior. To abstract from the eccentricities of specific cases we can rely on the simple process of averaging; we shall therefore concentrate attention on the behavior of cross-sectional averages of estimated regression residuals in the months surrounding split dates.

a. *Some additional definitions.* The procedure is as follows: For a given split, define month 0 as the month in which the effective date of a split occurs. (Thus month 0 is not the same chronological date for all securities, and indeed some securities have been split more than once and hence have more than one month 0).[12] Month 1 is then defined as the month immediately

[11] Essentially, this is due to the fact that in computing the variance of a sample, large deviations are weighted more heavily than in computing the mean absolute deviation. For empirical evidence concerning the reliability of the mean absolute deviation relative to the variance or standard deviation see Fama [3, (94–8)].

[12] About a third of the securities in the master file split. About a third of these split more than once.

following the split month, while month -1 is the month preceding, etc. Now define the average residual for month m (where m is always measured relative to the split month) as

$$u_m = \frac{\sum_{j=1}^{N_m} \hat{u}_{jm}}{N_m}$$

where $\hat{u}_{jm}$ is the sample regression residual for security j in month m and n_m is the number of splits for which data are available in month m.[13] Our principal tests will involve examining the behavior of u_m for m in the interval $-29 \leq m \leq 30$, i.e., for the sixty months surrounding the split month.

We shall also be interested in examining the cumulative effects of abnormal return behavior in months surrounding the split month. Thus we define the cumulative average residual U_m as

$$U_m = \sum_{k=-29}^{m} u_k .$$

The average residual u_m can be interpreted as the average deviation (in month m relative to the split month) of the returns of split stocks from their normal relationships with the market. Similarly, the cumulative average residual U_m can be interpreted as the cumulative deviation (from month -29 to month m); it shows the cumulative effects of the wanderings of the returns of split stocks from their normal relationships to market movements.

Since the hypothesis about the effects of splits on returns expounded in Section 2 centers on the dividend behavior of split shares, in some of the tests to follow we examine separately splits that are associated with increased dividends and splits that are associated with decreased dividends. In addition, in order to abstract from general changes in dividends across the market, "increased" and "decreased" dividends will be measured relative to the average dividends paid by all securities on the New York Stock Exchange during the relevant time periods. The dividends are classified as follows: Define the dividend change ratio as total dividends (per equivalent unsplit share) paid in the twelve months after the split, divided by total dividends paid during the twelve months before the split.[14] Dividend "increases" are then defined as cases where the dividend change ratio of the split stock is greater than the ratio for the Exchange as a whole, while dividend "decreases" include cases of relative dividend decline.[15] We then define u_m^+, u_m^- and U_m^+,

[13] Since we do not consider splits of companies that were not on the New York Stock Exchange for at least a year before and a year after a split, n_m will be 940 for $-11 \leq m \leq 12$. For other months, however, $n_m < 940$.

[14] A dividend is considered "paid" on the first day the security trades ex-dividend on the Exchange.

[15] When dividend "increase" and "decrease" are defined relative to the market, it turns out that dividends were never "unchanged." That is, the dividend change ratios of split securities are never identical to the corresponding ratios for the Exchange as a whole.

(*Continued on next page*)

U_m^- as the average and cumulative average residuals for splits followed by "increased" $(+)$ and "decreased" $(-)$ dividends.

These definitions of "increased" and "decreased" dividends provide a simple and convenient way of abstracting from general market dividend changes in classifying year-to-year dividend changes for individual securities. The definitions have the following drawback, however. For a company paying quarterly dividends an increase in its dividend rate at any time during the nine months before or twelve months after the split can place its stock in the dividend "increased" class. Thus the actual increase need not have occurred in the year after the split. The same fuzziness, of course, also arises in classifying dividend "decreases." We shall see later, however, that this fuzziness fortunately does not obscure the differences between the aggregate behavior patterns of the two groups.

b. *Empirical Results*. The most important empirical results of this study are summarized in Tables 2 and 3 and Figures 2 and 3. Table 2 presents the average residuals, cumulative average residuals, and the sample size for each of the two dividend classifications ("increased," and "decreased") and for the total of all splits for each of the sixty months surrounding the split. Figure 2 presents graphs of the average and cumulative average residuals for the total sample of splits and Figure 3 presents these graphs for each of the two dividend classifications. Table 3 shows the number of splits each year along with the end of June level of the stock price index.

Several of our earlier statements can now be substantiated. First, Figures 2a, 3a and 3b show that the average residuals (u_m) in the twenty-nine months prior to the split are uniformly positive for all splits and for both classes of dividend behavior. This can hardly be attributed entirely to the splitting process. In a random sample of fifty-two splits from our data the median time between the announcement date and the effective date of the split was 44.5 days. Similarly, in a random sample of one hundred splits that occurred between 1/1/1946 and 1/1/1957 Jaffe [9] found that the median time between announcement date and effective date was sixty-nine days. For both samples in only about 10 per cent of the cases is the time between announcement date and effective date greater than four months. Thus it seems safe to say that the split cannot account for the behavior of the regression residuals as far as two and one-half years in advance of the split date. Rather we suggest the obvious—a sharp improvement, relative to the market, in the earnings prospects of the company sometime during the years immediately preceding a split.

Thus we conclude that companies tend to split their shares during "abnormally" good times—that is during periods of time when the prices of their shares have increased much more than would be implied by the normal

---

In the remainder of the paper we shall always use "increase" and "decrease" as defined in the text. That is, signs of dividend changes for individual securities are measured relative to changes in the dividends for all N.Y.S.E. common stocks.

TABLE 2
ANALYSIS OF RESIDUALS IN MONTHS SURROUNDING THE SPLIT

	Splits followed by dividend "increases"			Splits followed by dividend "decreases"			All splits		
(1) Month m	(2) Average u_m^+	(3) Cumulative U_m^+	(4) Sample size N_m^+	(5) Average u_m^-	(6) Cumulative U_m^-	(7) Sample size N_m^-	(8) Average u_m	(9) Cumulative U_m	(10) Sample size N_m
-29	0.0062	0.0062	614	0.0033	0.0033	252	0.0054	0.0054	866
-28	0.0013	0.0075	617	0.0030	0.0063	253	0.0018	0.0072	870
-27	0.0068	0.0143	618	0.0007	0.0070	253	0.0050	0.0122	871
-26	0.0054	0.0198	619	0.0085	0.0155	253	0.0063	0.0185	872
-25	0.0042	0.0240	621	0.0089	0.0244	254	0.0056	0.0241	875
-24	0.0020	0.0259	623	0.0026	0.0270	256	0.0021	0.0263	879
-23	0.0055	0.0315	624	0.0028	0.0298	256	0.0047	0.0310	880
-22	0.0073	0.0388	628	0.0028	0.0326	256	0.0060	0.0370	884
-21	0.0049	0.0438	633	0.0131	0.0457	257	0.0073	0.0443	890
-20	0.0044	0.0482	634	0.0005	0.0463	257	0.0033	0.0476	891
-19	0.0110	0.0592	636	0.0102	0.0565	258	0.0108	0.0584	894
-18	0.0076	0.0668	644	0.0089	0.0654	260	0.0080	0.0664	904
-17	0.0072	0.0739	650	0.0111	0.0765	260	0.0083	0.0746	910
-16	0.0035	0.0775	655	0.0009	0.0774	260	0.0028	0.0774	915
-15	0.0135	0.0909	659	0.0101	0.0875	260	0.0125	0.0900	919
-14	0.0135	0.1045	662	0.0100	0.0975	263	0.0125	0.1025	925
-13	0.0148	0.1193	665	0.0099	0.1074	264	0.0134	0.1159	929
-12	0.0138	0.1330	669	0.0107	0.1181	266	0.0129	0.1288	935
-11	0.0098	0.1428	672	0.0103	0.1285	268	0.0099	0.1387	940
-10	0.0103	0.1532	672	0.0082	0.1367	268	0.0097	0.1485	940
-9	0.0167	0.1698	672	0.0152	0.1520	268	0.0163	0.1647	940
-8	0.0163	0.1862	672	0.0140	0.1660	268	0.0157	0.1804	940
-7	0.0159	0.2021	672	0.0083	0.1743	268	0.0138	0.1942	940
-6	0.0194	0.2215	672	0.0106	0.1849	268	0.0169	0.2111	940
-5	0.0194	0.2409	672	0.0100	0.1949	268	0.0167	0.2278	940
-4	0.0260	0.2669	672	0.0104	0.2054	268	0.0216	0.2494	940
-3	0.0325	0.2993	672	0.0204	0.2258	268	0.0289	0.2783	940
-2	0.0390	0.3383	672	0.0296	0.2554	268	0.0363	0.3147	940
-1	0.0199	0.3582	672	0.0176	0.2730	268	0.0192	0.3339	940
0	0.0131	0.3713	672	-0.0090	0.2640	268	0.0068	0.3407	940
1	0.0016	0.3729	672	-0.0088	0.2552	268	-0.0014	0.3393	940
2	0.0052	0.3781	672	-0.0024	0.2528	268	0.0031	0.3424	940
3	0.0024	0.3805	672	-0.0089	0.2439	268	-0.0008	0.3416	940
4	0.0045	0.3851	672	-0.0114	0.2325	268	0.0000	0.3416	940
5	0.0048	0.3898	672	-0.0003	0.2322	268	0.0033	0.3449	940
6	0.0012	0.3911	672	-0.0038	0.2285	268	-0.0002	0.3447	940

(*Continued on next page*)

TABLE 2
(continued)

(1) Month m	Splits followed by dividend "increases"			Splits followed by dividend "decreases"			All splits		
	(2) Average u_m^+	(3) Cumulative U_m^+	(4) Sample size N_m^+	(5) Average u_m^-	(6) Cumulative U_m^-	(7) Sample size N_m^-	(8) Average u_m	(9) Cumulative U_m	(10) Sample size N_m
7	0.0008	0.3919	672	−0.0106	0.2179	268	−0.0024	0.3423	940
8	−0.0007	0.3912	672	−0.0024	0.2155	268	−0.0012	0.3411	940
9	0.0039	0.3951	672	−0.0065	0.2089	268	0.0009	0.3420	940
10	−0.0001	0.3950	672	−0.0027	0.2062	268	−0.0008	0.3412	940
11	0.0027	0.3977	672	−0.0056	0.2006	268	0.0003	0.3415	940
12	0.0018	0.3996	672	−0.0043	0.1963	268	0.0001	0.3416	940
13	−0.0003	0.3993	666	0.0014	0.1977	264	0.0002	0.3418	930
14	0.0006	0.3999	653	0.0044	0.2021	258	0.0017	0.3435	911
15	−0.0037	0.3962	645	0.0026	0.2047	258	−0.0019	0.3416	903
16	0.0001	0.3963	635	−0.0040	0.2007	257	−0.0011	0.3405	892
17	0.0034	0.3997	633	−0.0011	0.1996	256	0.0021	0.3426	889
18	−0.0015	0.3982	628	0.0025	0.2021	255	−0.0003	0.3423	883
19	−0.0006	0.3976	620	−0.0057	0.1964	251	−0.0021	0.3402	871
20	−0.0002	0.3974	604	0.0027	0.1991	246	0.0006	0.3409	850
21	−0.0037	0.3937	595	−0.0073	0.1918	245	−0.0047	0.3361	840
22	0.0047	0.3984	593	−0.0018	0.1899	244	0.0028	0.3389	837
23	−0.0026	0.3958	593	0.0043	0.1943	242	−0.0006	0.3383	835
24	−0.0022	0.3936	587	0.0031	0.1974	238	−0.0007	0.3376	825
25	0.0012	0.3948	583	−0.0037	0.1936	237	−0.0002	0.3374	820
26	−0.0058	0.3890	582	0.0015	0.1952	236	−0.0037	0.3337	818
27	−0.0003	0.3887	582	0.0082	0.2033	235	0.0021	0.3359	817
28	0.0004	0.3891	580	−0.0023	0.2010	236	−0.0004	0.3355	816
29	0.0012	0.3903	580	−0.0039	0.1971	235	−0.0003	0.3352	815
30	−0.0033	0.3870	579	−0.0025	0.1946	235	−0.0031	0.3321	814

relationships between their share prices and general market price behavior. This result is doubly interesting since, from Table 3, it is clear that for the exchange as a whole the number of splits increases dramatically following a general rise in stock prices. Thus splits tend to occur during general "boom" periods, and the particular stocks that are split will tend to be those that performed "unusually" well during the period of general price increase.

It is important to note (from Figure 2a and Table 2) that when all splits are examined together, the largest positive average residuals occur in the three or four months immediately preceding the split, but that after the split the average residuals are randomly distributed about 0. Or equivalently, in Figure 2b the *cumulative* average residuals rise dramatically up to the split month, but there is almost no further systematic movement thereafter. Indeed during the first year after the split, the cumulative average residual

TABLE 3

NUMBER OF SPLITS PER YEAR AND LEVEL OF THE STOCK MARKET INDEX

Year	Number of splits	Market Index* (End of June)
1927	28	103.5
28	22	133.6
29	40	161.8
1930	15	98.9
31	2	65.5
32	0	20.4
33	1	82.9
34	7	78.5
35	4	73.3
36	11	124.7
37	19	147.4
38	6	100.3
39	3	90.3
1940	2	91.9
41	3	101.2
42	0	95.9
43	3	195.4
44	11	235.0
45	39	320.1
46	75	469.2
47	46	339.9
48	26	408.7
49	21	331.3
1950	49	441.6
51	55	576.1
52	37	672.2
53	25	691.9
54	43	818.6
55	89	1190.6
56	97	1314.1
57	44	1384.3
58	14	1407.3
59	103	1990.6

* Fisher's "Combination Investment Performance Index" shifted to a base January, 1926=100. See [6] for a description of its calculation.

changes by less than one-tenth of one percentage point, and the total change in the cumulative average residual during the two and one-half years following the split is less than one percentage point. This is especially striking since 71.5 per cent (672 out of 940) of all splits experienced greater percentage dividend increases in the year after the split than the average for all securities on the N.Y.S.E.

We suggest the following explanation for this behavior of the average residuals. When a split is announced or anticipated, the market interprets this (and correctly so) as greatly improving the probability that dividends

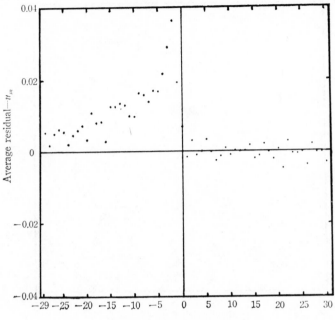

Month relative to split—m

FIGURE 2a

AVERAGE RESIDUALS—ALL SPLITS

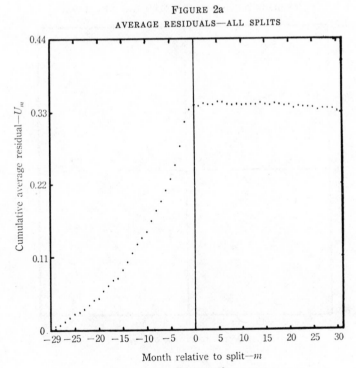

Month relative to split—m

FIGURE 2b

CUMULATIVE AVERAGE RESIDUALS—ALL SPLITS

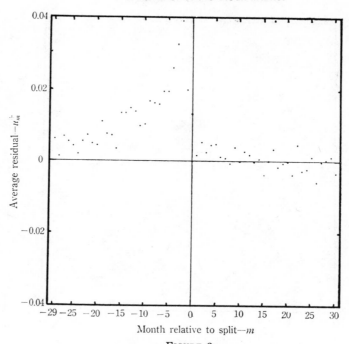

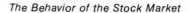

FIGURE 3a

AVERAGE RESIDUALS FOR DIVIDEND "INCREASES"

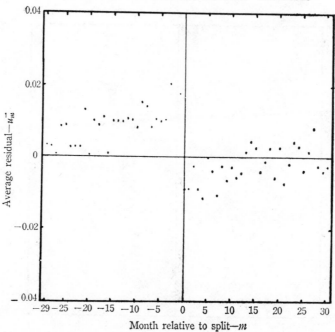

FIGURE 3b

AVERAGE RESIDUALS FOR DIVIDEND "DECREASES"

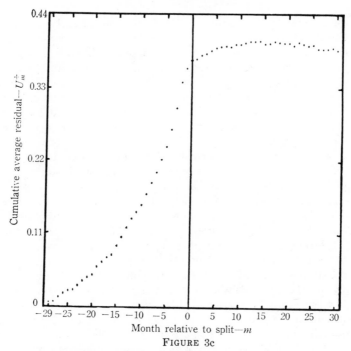

FIGURE 3c

CUMULATIVE AVERAGE RESIDUALS FOR DIVIDEND "INCREASES"

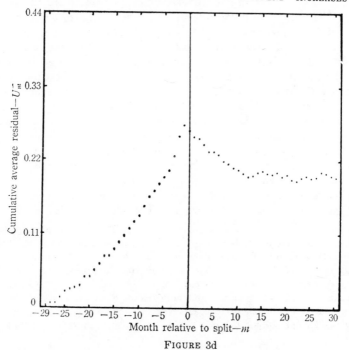

FIGURE 3d

CUMULATIVE AVERAGE RESIDUALS FOR DIVIDEND "DECREASES"

will soon be substantially increased. (In fact, as noted earlier, in many cases the split and dividend increase will be announced at the same time.) If, as Lintner [10] suggests, firms are reluctant to reduce dividends, then a split, which implies an increased expected dividend, is a signal to the market that the company's directors are confident that future earnings will be sufficient to maintain dividend payments at a higher level. If the market agrees with the judgments of the directors, then it is possible that the large price increases in the months immediately preceding a split are due to altering expectations concerning the future earning potential of the firm (and thus of its shares) rather than to any intrinsic effects of the split itself.[16]

If the information effects of actual or anticipated dividend increases do indeed explain the behavior of common stock returns in the months immediately surrounding a split, then there should be substantial differences in return behavior subsequent to the split in cases where the dividend increase materializes and cases where it does not. In fact it is apparent from Figure 3 that the differences are substantial—and we shall argue that they are in the direction predicted by the hypothesis.

The fact that the cumulative average residuals for both dividend classes rise sharply in the few months before the split is *consistent* with the hypothesis that the market recognizes that splits are usually associated with higher dividend payments. In some cases, however, the dividend increase, if it occurs, will be declared sometime during the year after the split. Thus it is not surprising that the average residuals (Figure 3a) for stocks in the dividend "increased" class are in general slightly positive, in the year after the split, so that the cumulative average residuals (Figure 3c) drift upward. The fact that this upward drift is only very slight can be explained in two (complementary) ways. First, in many cases the dividend increase associated with a split will be declared (and the corresponding price adjustments will take place) before the end of the split month. Second, according to our hypothesis when the split is declared (even if no dividend announcement is made), there is some price adjustment in anticipation of future dividend increases. Thus only a slight *additional* adjustment is necessary when the dividend increase actually takes place. By one year after the split the returns on stocks which have experienced dividend "increases" have resumed their normal relationships to market returns since from this point onward the average residuals are small and randomly scattered about zero.

The behavior of the residuals for stock splits associated with "decreased" dividends, however, provides the strongest evidence in favor of our split

---

[16] If this stock split hypothesis is correct, the fact that the average residuals (where the averages are computed using all splits (Figure 2) are randomly distributed about 0 in months subsequent to the split indicates that, on the average, the market has *correctly* evaluated the implications of a split for future dividend behavior and that these evaluations are fully incorporated in the price of the stock by the time the split occurs. That is, the market not only makes good forecasts of the dividend implications of a split, but these forecasts are fully impounded into the price of the security by the end of the split month. We shall return to this point at the end of this section.

hypothesis. For stocks in the dividend "decreased" class the average and cumulative average residuals (Figures 3b and 3d) rise in the few months before the split but then plummet in the few months following the split, when the anticipated dividend increase is not forthcoming. These split stocks with poor dividend performance on the average perform poorly in each of the twelve months following the split, but their period of poorest perform-ance is in the few months immediately after the split—when the improved dividend, if it were coming at all, would most likely be declared.[17] The hy-pothesis is further reinforced by the observation that when a year has passed after the split, the cumulative average residual has fallen to about where it was five months prior to the split which, we venture to say, is probably about the earliest time reliable information concerning a possible split is likely to reach the market.[18] Thus by the time it has become clear that the anticipated dividend increase is not forthcoming, the apparent effects of the split seem to have been completely wiped away, and the stock's returns have reverted to their normal relationship with market returns. In sum, our data suggest that once the information effects of associated dividend changes are properly considered, a split *per se* has no net effect on common stock returns.[19]

Finally, the data present important evidence on the speed of adjustment of market prices to new information. (a) Although the behavior of post-split returns will be very different depending on whether or not dividend "increases" occur, and (b) in spite of the fact that a substantial majority of split securities *do* experience dividend "increases," when all splits are examined together (Figure 2), the average residuals are randomly distributed about 0 during the year after the split. Thus there is no net movement either up or down in the cumu-lative average residuals. According to our hypothesis, this implies that on the average the market makes unbiased dividend forecasts for split securities and these forecasts are fully reflected in the price of the security by the end of the split month.

5. SPLITS AND TRADING PROFITS

Although stock prices adjust "rapidly" to the dividend information implicit in a split, an important question remains: Is the adjustment so rapid that splits can in no way be used to increase trading profits? Unfortunately our

[17] Though we do not wish to push the point too hard, it is interesting to note in Table 2 that after the split month, the largest negative average residuals for splits in the dividend "decreased" class occur in months 1, 4, and 7. This "pattern" in the residuals suggests, perhaps, that the market reacts most strongly during months when dividends are declared but not increased.

[18] In a random sample of 52 splits from our data in only 2 cases is the time be-tween the announcement date and effective date of the split greater than 162 days. Similarly, in the data of Jaffe [9] in only 4 out of 100 randomly selected splits is the time between announcement and effective date greater than 130 days.

[19] It is well to emphasize that our hypothesis centers around the information value of dividend changes. There is nothing in the empirical evidence which indicates that dividend policy *per se* affects the market value of the firm. For further dis-cussion of this point see Miller and Modigliani [15, (430)].

data do not allow full examination of this question. Nevertheless we shall proceed as best we can and leave the reader to judge the arguments for himself.

First of all, it is clear from Figure 2 that expected returns cannot be increased by purchasing split securities after the splits have become effective. After the split, on the average the returns on split securities immediately resume their normal relationships to market returns. In general, prices of split shares do not tend to rise more rapidly after a split takes place. Of course, if one is better at predicting which of the split securities are likely to experience "increased" dividends, one will have higher expected returns. But the higher returns arise from superior information or analytical talents and not from splits themselves.

Let us now consider the policy of buying splitting securities as soon as information concerning the possibility of a split becomes available. It is impossible to test this policy fully since information concerning a split often leaks into the market before the split is announced or even proposed to the shareholders. There are, however, several fragmentary but complementary pieces of evidence which suggest that the policy of buying splitting securities as soon as a split is *formally announced* does not lead to increased expected returns.

First, for a sample of 100 randomly selected splits during the period 1946–1956, Bellemore and Blucher [1] found that in general, price movements associated with a split are over by the day after the split is announced. They found that from eight weeks before to the day after the announcement, 86 out of 100 stocks registered percentage price increases greater than those of the Standard and Poor's stock price index for the relevant industry group. From the day after to eight weeks after the announcement date, however, only 43 stocks registered precentage price increases greater than the relevant industry index, and on the average during this period split shares only increased 2 per cent more in price than nonsplit shares in the same industry. This suggests that even if one purchases as soon as the announcement is made, split shares will not in general provide higher returns than nonsplit shares.[20]

Second, announcement dates have been collected for a random sample of 52 splits from our data. For these 52 splits the analysis of average and cumulative average residuals discussed in Section 4 has been carried out first using the split month as month 0 and then using the announcement month as month 0. In this sample the behavior of the residuals after the announcement date is almost identical to the behavior of the residuals after the split date. Since the evidence presented earlier indicated that one could

---

[20] We should note that though the results are Bellemore and Blucher's, the interpretation is ours.

Since in the vast majority of cases prices rise substantially in the eight weeks prior to the announcement date, Bellemore and Blucher conclude that if one has advance knowledge concerning a contemplated split, it can probably be used to increase expected returns. The same is likely to be true of all inside information, however.

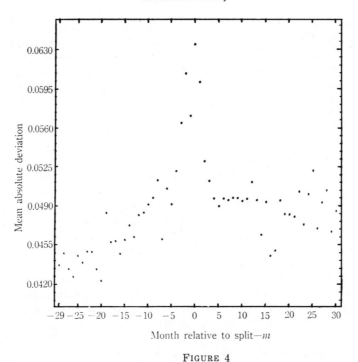

FIGURE 4

CROSS SECTIONAL MEAN ABSOLUTE DEVIATION OF RESIDUALS—ALL SPLITS

not systematically profit from buying split securities after the effective date of the split, this suggests that one also cannot profit by buying after the announcement date.

Although expected returns cannot in general be increased by buying split shares, this does not mean that a split should have no effect on an investor's decisions. Figure 4 shows the cross-sectional mean absolute deviations of the residuals for each of the sixty months surrounding the split. From the graph it is clear that the variability in returns on split shares increases substantially in the months closest to the split. The increased riskiness of the shares during this period is certainly a factor which the investor should consider in his decisions.

In light of some of the evidence presented earlier, the conclusion that splits cannot be used to increase expected trading profits may seem a bit anomalous. For example, in Table 2, column (8), the cross-sectional average residuals from the estimates of (1) are positive for at least thirty months prior to the split. It would seem that such a strong degree of "persistence" could surely be used to increase expected profits. Unfortunately, however, the behavior of the *average* residuals is not representative of the behavior of the residuals for *individual securities*; over time the residuals for individual securities are much more randomly distributed about 0. We can see this more clearly by comparing the average residuals for all splits (Figure 2a) with the month by month behavior of the cross-sectional mean absolute deviations of residuals for all splits (Figure 4). For each month before the split the mean absolute deviation of residuals is well over twice as large as the corresponding average residual, which indicates that for each month the residuals for many *individual* securities are negative. In fact, in examining residuals for individual securities the following pattern was typical: Prior to the split, successive sample residuals from (1) are almost completely independent. In most cases, however, there are a few months for which the residuals are abnormally large and positive. These months of large residuals differ from security to security, however, and these differences in timing explain why the signs of the *average* residuals are uniformly positive for many months preceding the split.

Similarly, there is evidence which suggests that the extremely large positive average residuals in the three or four months prior to the split merely reflect the fact that, from split to split, there is a variable lag between the time split information reaches the market and the time when the split becomes effective. Jaffe [9] has provided announcement and effective dates for the 100 randomly chosen splits used by herself and Bellemore [1]. The announcement dates occur as follows: 7 in the first month before the split, 67 in the second and third months, 14 in the fourth month, and 12 announcements more than four months before the split. Looking back at Table 2, column (8), and Figure 2a we see that the largest average residuals follow a similar pattern: The largest average residuals occur in the second and third months before the split; though smaller, the average residuals for one and four months before the split are larger than those of any other months.

This suggests that the pattern of the average residuals immediately prior to the split arises from the averaging process and thus cannot be assumed to hold for any particular security.

6. CONCLUSIONS

In sum, in the past stock splits have very often been associated with substantial dividend increases. The evidence indicates that the market realizes this and uses the announcement of a split to re-evaluate the stream of expected income from the shares. Moreover, the evidence indicates that on the average the market's judgments concerning the information implications of a split are fully reflected in the price of a share at least by the end of the split month but most probably almost immediately after the announcement date. Thus the results of the study lend considerable support to the conclusion that the stock market is "efficient" in the sense that stock prices adjust very rapidly to new information.

The evidence suggests that in reacting to a split the market reacts only to its dividend implications. That is, the split causes price adjustments only to the extent that it is associated with changes in the anticipated level of future dividends.

Finally, there seems to be no way to use a split to increase one's expected returns, unless, of course, inside information concerning the split or subsequent dividend behavior is available.

University of Chicago, University of Rochester, and
Carnegie-Mellon University, U.S.A.

REFERENCES

[1] BELLEMORE, DOUGLAS H. and Mrs. LILLIAN BLUCHER (JAFFE), "A Study of Stock Splits in the Postwar Years," *Financial Analysts Journal*, XV (November, 1956), 19-26.

[2] COOTNER, PAUL H., ed., *The Random Character of Stock Market Prices* (Cambridge, Mass.: M.I.T. Press, 1964).

[3] FAMA, EUGENE F., "The Behavior of Stock-Market Prices," *Journal of Business*, XXXVIII (January, 1965), 34-105.

[4] ————, "Portfolio Analysis in a Stable Paretian Market," *Management Science*, XI (January, 1965), 404-19.

[5] FISHER, LAWRENCE, "Outcomes for 'Random' Investments in Common Stocks Listed on the New York Stock Exchange," *Journal of Business*, XXXVIII (April, 1965), 149-61.

[6] ————, "Some New Stock Market Indexes," *Journal of Business*, XXXIX (Supplement, January, 1966), 191-225.

[7] ———— and JAMES H. LORIE, "Rates of Return on Investments in Common Stocks," *Journal of Business*, XXXVII (January, 1964), 1-21.

[8] GODFREY, MICHAEL D., CLIVE W. J. GRANGER and OSKAR MORGENSTERN, "The Random Walk Hypothesis of Stock Market Behavior," *Kyklos*, XVII (1964), 1-30.

[9] JAFFE (BLUCHER), LILLIAN H., "A Study of Stock Splits, 1946-1956," Unpublished Master's Thesis, Graduate School of Business Administration, New York University (1957).

[10] LINTNER, JOHN, "Distribution of Incomes of Corporations Among Dividends, Retained Earnings and Taxes," *American Economic Review*, XLVI (May, 1956), 97-113.

[11] MANDELBROT, BBNOIT, "Forecasts of Future Prices, Unbiased Markets, and 'Martingale' Models," *Journal of Business*, XXXIX (Supplement, January, 1966), 242-255.

[12] ————, "The Variation of Certain Speculative Prices," *Journal of Business*, XXXVI (October, 1963), 394-419.

[13] MARKOWITZ, HARRY, *Portfolio Selection: Efficient Diversification of Investments* (New York: Wiley, 1959).

[14] MICHAELSEN, JACOB B., "The Determinants of Dividend Policies: A Theoretical and Empirical Study," Unpublished Doctoral Dissertation, Graduate School of Business, University of Chicago (1961).

[15] MILLER, MERTON H. and FRANCO MODIGLIANI, "Dividend Policy, Growth and the Valuation of Shares," *Journal of Business*, XXXIV (October, 1961), 411-33.

[16] SAMUELSON, PAUL A., "Proof That Properly Anticipated Prices Fluctuate Randomly," *Industrial Management Review* (Spring, 1965), 41-49.

[17] SHARPE, WILLIAM F., "Capital Asset Pricing: A Theory of Market Equilibrium under Conditions of Risk," *Journal of Finance*, XIX (September, 1964), 425-42.

[18] ————, "A Simplified Model for Portfolio Analysis," *Management Science*, IX (January, 1963), 277-93.

[19] WISE, JOHN, "Linear Estimators for Linear Regression Systems Having Infinite Variances," paper presented at the Berkeley-Stanford Mathematical Economics Seminar (October, 1963).

11

THE MARKET FOR SECURITIES:
SUBSTITUTION VERSUS PRICE PRESSURE
AND THE
EFFECTS OF INFORMATION ON SHARE PRICES

Myron S. Scholes

INTRODUCTION*

Many authors in the theoretical literature in finance assume that a firm can regard the price of its shares, given its operating policies, as essentially independent of the number of shares it, or any shareholder, chooses to sell. The shares a firm sells are not unique works of art, but abstract rights to an uncertain income stream for which close counterparts exist either directly or indirectly via combinations of assets of various kinds. Hence, if the firm expands and increases the amount of its shares outstanding, the additional shares can be sold at the going market price for income streams of that particular quality.

But although perfect substitution is one view it is by no means the only one. There is a substantial body of opinion which implies that the firm's share price will be affected by new sales of securities. It is argued that this fact must be taken into account by managers in carrying out investment and financial policies on behalf of shareholders, by regulatory authorities in utility commission hearings, by judges in considering the effects of divestiture in antitrust suits, and by shareholders when selling quantities of a company's stock.

They would argue that securities in the capital market are not closely related and that the uniqueness or characteristics particular to an individual asset make each asset stand apart from other assets in the market. Hence, when the firm increases the amount of its shares outstanding, the additional shares will have to be sold at a discount from existing market prices in

* This paper is adapted from my Ph.D. thesis at the University of Chicago. I would like to acknowledge a great deal of debt to my dissertation committee; Eugene Fama, Merton Miller, Harry Roberts, and Joel Segall who took great pains to suggest how to improve the research and its presentation. I would also like to thank Larry Fisher for his many helpful comments as well as members of the Finance Workshop at the University of Chicago for many stimulating and helpful discussions, especially M. Blume, P. Brown, D. Duvel, M. Jensen, and R. Roll. I would also like to thank my many friends who prodded me into publication of these findings.

Reprinted from *The Journal of Business*, XLV, No. 2 (April, 1972), by permission of the author and the University of Chicago Press. Copyright 1972 by the University of Chicago.

order to attract new buyers to this particular issue. The magnitude of the discount is an increasing function of the size of the issue.

Although the price effects of share sales have been debated at length, the elasticity of demand for a firm's shares can be determined only by empirical tests. This paper presents empirical tests of the predictions of each hypothesis. In the following sections we will discuss the predictions of each hypothesis, the data used, the methodology of the testing procedure and the empirical findings.

The Price Pressure Hypothesis

Few people will quarrel with the idea that buyers and sellers of shares on an organized exchange such as the New York Stock Exchange can buy and sell small quantities of stock at approximately the prevailing market price. But when the size of the trade is large relative to these small trades, there is a belief that the price of the stock must fall to induce investors to purchase these additional shares. This inducement, or "sweetener" as it is called, results from an increase in the quantity of shares that must be held by market participants. If the excess demand curve for shares is downward sloping, the additional shares will only be held at lower prices. The direct consequence of buying shares at lower prices to purchasers is a subsequent extra profit or sweetener.

To illustrate that the implied price effects of sales or purchases of stock are very large, we can quote from testimony and theoretical discussions on the issue. In the rate regulation literature, a key issue is a discussion of allowances to rate of return for the necessary "underpricing" of new issues. Bonbright, [3] in a standard textbook discussion, states:

> But there must be a step up in the allowed rate of earnings to provide for underpricing and stock flotation expense. . . . A 10 percent discount for these named items is not infrequently held to be reasonable.

More to the issue itself, Gordon, [15] in a recent utility rate case, testified:

> Probably the most important reason for the high rate of return investors require on A.T.&T. is its extraordinary reliance on stock financing. Whatever rate investors require to hold the outstanding stock of a company, they will require a higher rate of return to more or less continuously absorb increasing amounts of its stock.

In antitrust cases, the courts have frequently been concerned with the effects of divestiture on the price of the divested company's stock. The duPont–General Motors divestiture suit [27] is the classic example both of the issue itself and the judicial view that selling pressure is enormous. In the court's summation to the case we found evidence from experts in the securities business that the price of General Motors' stock could fall by 50 percent. Irwin Friend presented evidence of the effects of issues, in general, on the price of a company's shares. In the summation to the case we found:

> Dr. Friend agreed that there had never been anything in the past com-

parable to the sales contemplated by the Government plan. He also testified that an increase in supply of stock of 10 percent had in the past brought about a decline in price of 5 percent, that an increase of 20 percent had been associated with price declines of between 10 percent and 15 percent.

There are numerous other examples of implied price effects of additional share issues. In the theoretical literature of finance, authors have used the price pressure arguments to determine optimum capital structures for firms. Durand [6] used the uniqueness argument and institutional restrictions to dispute the common assumption that firms can issue shares or shareholders can sell shares at existing market prices. Vickers [30] uses essentially the same argument. In both cases, imperfections in the capital markets, a less than perfectly elastic demand curve for shares or bonds, lead to a kind of monopolistic price discrimination approach to using bond or share financing for capital projects. Given the relative elasticities of demand for these two instruments, an optimal debt to equity mix for the firm can be determined. Still another case is dividend policy, where Lintner [20] has argued that the downward sloping demand curve for a firm's shares gives advantage to the retention of earnings, and therefore dividend reductions, in lieu of external stock issues to finance investment.

Lintner argues that even if shareholder expectations of terminal share values are unchanged by the new share issues, the market price of the shares must fall to induce old shareholders to purchase additional shares, and to attract new shareholders to the issue. To turn the argument around, a price discount with unchanged expectations of terminal value implies that investors who purchase these new shares expect to receive higher returns subsequent to their purchase or else there is no real inducement or "sweetener." The selling pressure hypotheses would predict that the larger the sale of securities, the larger the price effect and consequently the larger the expected rate of return subsequent to the sale.

The Substitution Hypothesis

An alternative hypothesis to the price pressure hypothesis can be called the substitution hypothesis. The purchase of risky assets provides the investor with future consumption streams. To obtain a desired consumption-investment program, investors can buy various combinations of assets. Each security is a potential candidate for inclusion into investor portfolios. When trying to measure the market for a security, it must be defined in a broader context than the security itself, or its particular industry grouping. A risky asset is a small percentage of all assets that investors may hold in their portfolios. As a result, the demand curve facing individual shareholders is essentially horizontal.

Similarly, the corporation, which issues additional claims to finance investment, adds to the stock of assets that must be held, but this addition is assumed to be a small percentage of assets that must be held. At the time of a new issue there should be no effect on the market price of the firm's existing shares. This is not to say that the price of the shares won't change to reflect changes in the quality of the uncertain income streams that the firm will produce with the additional assets, or that the price of the shares won't adjust to reflect noncompetitive opportunities that these additional assets will provide. However, these adjustments would occur even in the absence of new share issues to finance investment. They will occur to equate prices of similar income streams of market assets which are close substitutes. The adjustments (tax considerations aside) are not the result of the firm's use of one particular method of financing as opposed to any other method of financing.[1]

The market will price assets such that the expected rates of return on assets of similar risk are equal. If any particular asset should be selling to yield a higher expected return due solely to the increase in the quantity of shares outstanding, this would indicate that investors would expect to realize abnormal returns on this asset. This would imply that profit opportunities exist in the market. But investors seeing these profit opportunities would soon arbitrage them away. The substitution hypothesis implies that there cannot be profit opportunities that result from the increase in the quantity of shares that must be held. Since assets are substitutes in investor portfolios, the pure price effects of corporate new issues or investor purchases and sales must be very small. The substitution hypothesis would imply that the inducement necessary to sell large quantities of stock would be close to zero.

A Resolution of Some of the Differences: The Information Hypothesis

In recent years there has been considerable discussion and testing of the "efficient" market model. Fama [12, 6] has defined an efficient market as a market in which security prices reflect all available information. A market that is efficient prevents traders with no special information from making abnormal profits. New information that becomes available is quickly reflected in a security's price. As a consequence of the almost immediate adjustment of stock prices to new information, prices will follow a random walk. There has been considerable testing of the random walk model [4, 6, 9] and the adjustment of stock prices to new information. The Fama paper [12] presents an excellent discussion of both the theory and the empirical findings. Most evidence suggests that the "efficient" market model is an accurate description of price behavior in the securities market.

When investors sell quantities of a company's stock, they sell for various reasons. In some cases, investors liquidate positions for consumption needs or for portfolio rebalancing considerations; in other cases, they may feel that they possess adverse information about the company's prospects that, if known, would cause an immediate downward adjustment in the price of the company's stock. The same arguments apply to purchases of shares. If some investors desire shares for wealth allocation or portfolio rebalancing purposes, other investors purchase shares because they feel that they possess information that, if known, would cause an upward adjustment in the company's share price.

The efficient market model would predict that the average value of this information would be small. Since so many investors are competing for

---

[1] For a detailed discussion of these issues see Miller and Modigliani [22, 23].

information, it is unlikely that investors who possess information have information of sufficient value to cause a large rise or fall in the market price of the shares in which they trade.

If a sale of securities is an indication that the seller possesses information, the price of the shares would fall in the market to reflect the expected value of the information in each trade. In other words, a buyer of shares who purchases only to rebalance his portfolio may expect to pay not only the regular exchange commissions but also the value of the information possessed by the seller.

There are substantial costs to finding information of value and one would suspect that the sellers of a large block of stock possess more information of value than sellers of small quantities of stock. The small trades on the exchange are likely to contain many more portfolio adjustment trades than information trades. The large block trades are likely to contain more information trades than portfolio adjustment trades. Therefore, small trades may be effected at very little information discount from the previous trade, while large trades could only be sold at a lower price to reflect the expected value of information in these trades.[1]

The information hypothesis states that when a large block of stock is sold in the market, we should expect to see a downward price adjustment in the price of the stock. This fall is the expected value of information contained in large block trades. It is a permanent adjustment in the stock price and not an inducement followed by abnormal returns in the future as the price pressure hypothesis suggests. Whether or not the value of information is an increasing function of the size of the trade, or is relatively constant once a trade is deemed large, is an empirical question. But casual observation of trading in markets has led the price pressure adherents to conclude that the price adjustments are due to downward sloping demand curves for shares and not due to a change in the equilibrium value of the firm.

The efficient market model would imply that the value of information in trades would be much smaller than the implied effects suggested by the price pressure adherents. In our discussions we have devised testable implications of each hypothesis. The substitution-information hypothesis would predict that, on average, share prices would fully adjust to the expected value of information in trades and that, on average, this adjustment would be a permanent adjustment and not imply an inducement in the form of subsequent abnormal profits for share purchasers.

For the corporation issuing additional shares the separation of the value of information from the sale of additional shares is necessitated by the requisite registration statements and the announcement of an impending new issue prior to actual sale. Market participants would have ample time to assess the planned use of the funds and would reflect the value of this information in the share price prior to issue. At the time of issue, firms will

[1] There is no argument here pertaining to the most efficient size trade for investors who hold a large quantity of a company's stock. It may or may not be economical for mutual funds to trade in larger quantities than the regular 100 share lots. However, if a fund for example disposes of a large quantity of shares quickly, when it could adjust its portfolio by using many different issues, this evidence might suggest that the fund possessed adverse information.

be able to sell shares at the new equilibrium price irrespective of whether the price adjusted upward or downward to the value of the information.

DATA AND TEST METHODOLOGY

The particular set of quantity changes that will be used to test the various hypotheses with respect to the degree of market imperfection are those large block sales of stock called secondary distributions.[1] These distributions, unlike primary distributions, are initiated not by the company but by one or more shareholders to whom the future proceeds from the sale of the secondary distribution will accrue. The distributions are typically underwritten on a principal or agency basis by an investment banking group that buys the entire block of stock from the selling shareholder. The shares are then sold to subscribers after normal trading hours at a price known as the "subscription price," typically set at or near the closing price of the shares in the open market on the day of the sale. The subscriber to shares in a secondary distribution pays only the subscription price and does not pay the regular stock exchange or other brokerage commissions on the transaction. The selling shareholder does pay a specific commission to the selling group (normally twice the round lot commission) and this fee is subtracted from the proceeds of the sale before the funds are turned over to the selling shareholder.[2]

There are two types of secondary distributions—registered and unregistered. The Securities and Exchange Commission requires that a distribution be registered if the shares involved in the sale represent "a control relationship" to the issuer [28]. If a distribution is registered, registration statements, including a prospectus, must be prepared and the vendor must wait twenty days after the registration before the actual sale can take place. An unregistered distribution, however, may take place without a waiting period after approval by the Exchange is obtained. The unregistered secondary is publicly announced by the underwriters on the ticker tape or the broad tape on the day of the sale and the Securities and Exchange Commission is formally notified by the Exchange only after the sale has occurred.

No very specific rules have been issued by the Securities and Exchange Commission with respect to registration requirements for secondaries. Registration is left for the most part to the discretion of the vendors, who in some cases protect themselves by obtaining a "no action letter" from the Commission's Division of Corporation Finance. This letter, as the name implies, binds the Division not to recommend to the Commission that any action be taken under the Securities Act if the securities are sold without registration. Economically, the only importance of the distinction between

---

[1] Sales rather than purchases of shares were chosen for two reasons. First, the main focus of the relevant controversies in finance has been on the price effects of the issuance of new shares, so that sales of shares would be the counterpart in the secondary market. Second, large block purchases of securities often reflect attempts to acquire control of the firm rather than the more normal kind of investment demand which is our main concern here.

[2] For a more extensive discussion of the legal and institutional background see the report of the Special Study of Securities Markets of the Securities and Exchange Commission, Part 1 [28].

the two types of distributions is that the presumed price impact of the sale may well tend to be concentrated at different points of time—the actual day of the sale for an unregistered distribution and twenty or so days previous to the distribution for a registered issue.

Secondary distributions were chosen in lieu of primary distributions because new issues are often associated with important events such as expansion programs, changes in capital structure and the like. These events and what they mean to management's views and intentions have not always been completely anticipated and discounted by the market so that price adjustments, sometimes of fairly substantial size, accompany the announcement of a new issue by the firm. In many cases, where the news happens to be particularly good, there may well be a sizeable price increase on the announcement. In other cases, there may be a substantial fall and these differing and variable announcement effects will inevitably complicate the task of isolating the pure price-pressure effects, if any. By contrast, secondary distributions, basically events taking place outside the company, are the result of decisions that are presumably independent of the factors affecting company operations. To this extent, we are more nearly in a position of holding "all other things constant" when we look at secondaries rather than primaries.

For the secondary distributions, also, there may well be information or announcement effects that make the offering an occasion for revaluing the firm. The vendor of the distribution may, for example, possess information which, if it became generally known, would cause a downward adjustment in the market price of the security. The sale of a secondary may then provide the impetus for other market traders to commit resources to the re-evaluation of the company's prospects. Nevertheless, the prospects of controlling for this kind of information effect in secondaries are much more favorable than in primaries for several reasons.

We shall see that it is possible to identify the seller of the secondary distribution. If it is possible to determine whether or not the seller is likely to possess information, this may permit us to determine the average value of information, and the market's adjustment to the value of this information. Also, since no one is likely to sell if he has good information, we only have to worry about information effects in one direction.

In any attempt to measure the slope of a demand curve, it is, of course, essential to specify the relevant time span. In the very shortest of short runs, all demand curves will be almost perfectly inelastic. Yet, by waiting perhaps only a trivial length of time until news of a proposed sale had spread throughout the market, the sale might be effectuated without price pressure effects. How much time is to be regarded as a "reasonable" interval over which to measure price pressure can only be determined by reference to the technology of the market in question. The secondary distributions provide a unique advantage in that investment bankers inform potential buyers that a large block is for sale. In recent years, the secondary distribution has been overshadowed to some extent by the addition of third and fourth market positioning of large blocks, and the introduction of computer technology to store information on block trade interest.

In this paper, the relevant time unit for analysis will be taken as one trading day. Short as this may seem, it is actually a substantial overestimate in many cases. A tabulation undertaken for the Special Study [28] showed that of the 80 secondary distributions in 1961, 9 took less than 15 minutes to complete, 22 less than 1 hour, 12 took 1 to 4 hours, 32 were completed by the close of the following day, and only 5 remained open for a longer period. The one day time unit (which is also the most convenient in terms of data availability) would thus seem to be a reasonable starting point and one that can hardly be accused of loading the dice against the traditional selling pressure view. We will also be able to extend the interval by measuring the effect of the trade over the following trading days and also over an extended period of months to measure whether or not traders received an inducement to buy the shares of a secondary distribution.

The Actual Sample

A complete list of all secondary distributions for listed New York Stock Exchange firms was compiled for the period January 1947 to December 1965 from the Investment Dealers Digest [18]. From this source we obtained the company name, the date of the distribution, the subscription price, and whether or not the secondary was registered. The SEC Statistical Bulletin [29] was used to check the validity of the reported information in the Digest and to obtain information on the vendor of the secondary.[1]

Since daily price data was available from July 1961 to December 1965, most of the analysis will be concentrated over this time period; a period in which there were 345 secondary distributions. Monthly data on prices were

TABLE 1

DECILES OF THE DISTRIBUTIONS OF SUMMARY STATISTICS OF THE SECONDARY DISTRIBUTIONS

Fractile *	Dollar Value of Issue ($000)	Proportion of Firm Traded
.1	456.	.0018
.2	714.	.0032
.3	1045.	.0050
.4	1353.	.0071
.5	1606.	.0099
.6	2451.	.0135
.7	3200.	.0191
.8	4538.	.0286
.9	7987.	.0494
Mean	4721.	.0216

* Each frequency distribution is a marginal distribution for the variable in question: e.g., $456,000 does not correspond with .0018, etc.

[1] The vendors are classified in 5 general categories: Investment Companies, Insurance Companies and Banks, Individuals, Corporations or Corporate Officers, and Estates and Trusts. More will be said about these vendor categories and their relevance for the test design in a later section.

available for the period 1947 to 1965.[1] The longer period will be used to confirm the analysis of the daily data sample. Over the 1947 to 1965 period 1,207 secondary distributions were recorded.

Table 1 gives the deciles of the frequency distributions of the dollar value of the secondary distribution and the percentage of the firm's shares involved in the trade. These summary statistics indicate that a secondary usually represents a nontrivial percentage of the firm traded and also represents considerable market value. Over 5 percent of the firm's shares were traded in 10 percent of the cases. The largest percentage of the firm traded was 37 percent. This range contains the largest blocks of securities traded. It is also representative of the range of corporate new security issues. Some distributions had market values of over one hundred million dollars.

The Methodology

Movements in security prices are associated with market wide information that differentially affects the value of securities. To isolate the effects of the sales of a large block of securities on the price of the security it is necessary to control for the differential effects of market wide information on individual security returns. The market model proposed by Sharpe [25] and tested by Blume [1] provides a particularly simple and effective way to do so.[2] The model assumes that individual security returns, $\tilde{R}_{i,t}$, are linearly related to the returns on a market portfolio, $\tilde{R}_{m,t}$, and that the usual assumptions of the regression model are satisfied.[3] The market model asserts that,

$$\tilde{R}_{i,t} = a_i + \beta_i \tilde{R}_{m,t} + \tilde{u}_{i,t} \tag{1}$$

where $\tilde{R}_{i,t}$ = return for period t on the i'th security (dividends plus capital gains divided by initial price)

$\tilde{R}_{m,t}$ = average return on a market portfolio of all assets on the Exchange or a representative sample of all securities such as the return on the Standard & Poor 500 Composite Index

a_i, β_i = parameters that are to be estimated by least squares

$\tilde{u}_{i,t}$ = the disturbance term for period t

[1] For a discussion of the construction and composition of the monthly price file see Fisher and Lorie [17].

[2] The methodology to be used was an adaptation of the methodology used by Fama, Fisher, Jensen, and Roll [10] who used this methodology to analyze the price effects of stock splits.

[3] Extensive tests of this model by Blume [1] Fama et al. [10] indicate that the assumptions of linearity, stationarity, and serial independence of the residuals are not violated. The estimated residuals, however, appear to be more closely approximated by a member of the stable class of distributions with characteristic exponent less than 2. However, experimental sampling of Fama and Roll [11] and simulations by Fama and Babiak [14] and Blattberg and Sargent [2] indicate that for securities the mean is almost as efficient an estimator of the location parameter of the distribution as the median or nonlinear estimators such as truncated means. Thus, the use of the regression model, a generalization of estimation by means, appears to be appropriate.

The systematic part of a security's return is presumed to be captured by its normal relationship to the returns on the market portfolio. Any returns not accounted for by a security's normal relationship to the market will be impounded in the disturbance, $\tilde{u}_{i,t}$, which thus presumably captures the effects of company-specific influences. One such company-specific event, of course, is a secondary distribution.

A secondary distribution is an infrequent event for any particular company. But, the main concern of this study is not with the experience of any particular security at the time of a secondary distribution, but with the effects of secondaries in general on security prices. The econometric problem is to find an efficient method of combining the time series returns of all firms in the sample so as to estimate the average effect of a secondary distribution on the prices of the securities involved.[1]

The parameters of the market model were estimated using 100 days of return data on each security in the sample around the day of the secondary but excluding the 6 observations prior to the secondary and 7 observations including and subsequent to the day of the secondary.[2] An estimated prediction error, $\hat{E}_{i,t}$, was computed for a period of 25 days prior to the secondary and for 14 days subsequent to the distribution. The prediction error is defined as

$$\hat{E}_{i,t} = R_{i,t} - [\hat{a}_i + \hat{b}_i R_{m,t}] \tag{2}$$

where $R_{i,t}$ is the actual return for security i on day t, $R_{m,t}$ is the return on the Standard and Poor Composite Index for day t, and $\hat{a}_i$ and $\hat{b}_i$ are the estimated coefficients of the market model.[3]

Each security's prediction errors can be used to compute an average prediction error for each day relative to the day of the sale. The day of the sale is defined as day zero. The prediction errors for each day relative to the distribution day were cross-sectionally averaged over all securities. That is, the average error, $\bar{E}_d$, for day d, relative to the distribution day $d = 0$ is

$$\bar{E}_d = \frac{1}{N} \sum_{i=1}^{N} \hat{E}_{i,d} \qquad \text{where } i = 1, \ldots, N \text{ the number of securities in the sample} \tag{3}$$

The average error is the average estimated percentage deviation of the returns of the securities in the sample from their normal relationship to

[1] Fama, et al. [10] used a similar approach in their study, but used the logarithmic or continuously compounded rate of return on securities. Since we are using daily data, the arithmetic one day return is approximately equal to the continuously compounded rate of return; and when this alternative specification was tried, the results to be presented below were the same in all essential respects.

[2] The returns for these days were deleted in forming the estimates because if there are price effects of a secondary distribution, the expected value of the disturbance for the day of the distribution and possibly for days around the distribution are non-zero. The inclusion of these days in forming the regression estimates would lead to a specification error in the regression model and would bias the coefficient estimates. As we will see, the data are informative on indicating how many days to exclude and for this reason we left out these 13 days.

[3] The prediction error is not the same as the residual since observations to be predicted were not included in the estimation procedure. Thus, the mean values of the prediction errors are usually non-zero.

the market. Using the average error and its standard error we can estimate the significance of the effects of secondaries on market prices.

Another informative statistic which we called an abnormal performance index was constructed to answer the question: What abnormal return would an investor achieve over time if at the start of day d he bought a portfolio of all securities that subsequently experienced a secondary and held this portfolio from day d until sometime after the distribution? This index is defined as:

$$API_D = \frac{1}{N} \sum_{i=1}^{N} \left[\prod_{\tau=d}^{D} (1 + \hat{E}\tau) \right] \tag{4}$$

The index traces out the value of one dollar invested in equal amounts in each of the N securities in the sample at time τ and held until the end of period, D, after abstracting from general market effects on returns. An equivalent but perhaps more intuitively appealing interpretation is as follows:

Suppose two individuals A and B agree on the following proposition. B is to construct a portfolio consisting of one dollar invested in equal amounts in the N securities that had experienced a secondary distribution. The securities will be purchased at the beginning of period τ and held as a portfolio to the end of period D. B contracts with A to take only the normal gains and losses as described by the market model, and to return to A, at the end of period D, one dollar plus or minus any non-market gains or losses. The expected value of the return to B is the expectation of the API_D of (4) above, *viz.*,

$$E(API_D) = E \left\{ \frac{1}{N} \sum_{i=1}^{N} \left[\prod_{\tau=d}^{D} (1 + \hat{E}\tau) \right] \right\}$$

$$\simeq \frac{1}{N} \sum_{i=1}^{N} \prod_{\tau=d}^{D} (1 + E(\hat{E}\tau)) \tag{5}$$

which in the absence of any abnormal returns would be approximately [1] equal to 1.0.

From the Abnormal Performance Index, it is possible to find the marginal rate of return from holding this portfolio from period D to period $D + \tau$. This marginal rate of return is simply:

$$\frac{API_{D+\tau}}{API_D} - 1 \tag{6}$$

This will allow us to calculate the returns on this portfolio for various holding periods.

---

[1] This is only approximate since

$$E \left[\prod_{t=1}^{T} (1 + u_t) \right] \neq \prod_{t=1}^{T} [(1 + E(u_t))]$$

if there is any serial correlation in the u_t. All evidence (Blume, [1] Fama, et al. [10]) indicates that for individual securities the serial correlation is small enough to be ignored.

The methodology described in this section will provide a means of estimating the average effects of the sale of large block distributions on security prices. The estimated prediction errors are abnormal returns, a return not accounted for by the security's normal relationship to the market as described by the market model. By taking averages of the prediction errors for each day relative to the distribution day we will be able to estimate the average abnormal return on each day associated with the sale of the large block distributions. The abnormal performance index will be used to estimate the cumulative abnormal performance through time of a portfolio of secondaries purchased at the start of the period of interest and held through the end of the period of interest.

THE EMPIRICAL RESULTS

The implications of the competing hypotheses—the price pressure hypothesis and the substitution hypothesis—will be tested in this section. The first test will simply be to calculate the average errors and the value of the abnormal performance index for each day relative to the distribution day. The price pressure hypothesis predicts that we will observe negative average abnormal returns at the time of the distribution. If there are price declines we can then test to see (1) if the amount of the price decline relative to the market is a function of the supply of shares sold in the large block distribution, and (2) if new shareholders receive abnormal returns after they purchase the shares of the secondary. The price pressure hypothesis implies that the larger the secondary distribution the greater the necessary inducement. We can then test to see if the abnormal return subsequent to the distribution is also a function of the size of the sale.

In contrast, the substitution hypothesis implies that the pure price pressure effects should be virtually zero and not a function of the supply of additional shares sold through a secondary distribution. Also, the substitution hypothesis implies that on average there should be no observable inducements necessary to sell large blocks of shares.

We will now turn to the results of the analysis. We will use the daily sample in the first tests and then use the monthly sample to confirm the results found in the daily analysis.

A First Look at the Total Sample Results

The methodology described in the previous chapter was applied to the total daily sample of 345 secondary distributions. Table 2 gives the standard table summarizing the results of the analysis. The first column, entitled "day," references the days relative to the day of the distribution, $d = 0$. The next two columns give for each day the average error, $\bar{E}_d$, and then the value of the abnormal performance index, assuming that one dollar was invested in the portfolio of secondaries twenty-five days prior to the distribution day. The fourth column, entitled "standard deviation," contains for each day, d, the standard deviation of the prediction errors, $\hat{E}_{id}$.[1] The last column gives the fraction of negative prediction errors for each day. Figure 1 presents the abnormal performance index for the total daily sample.

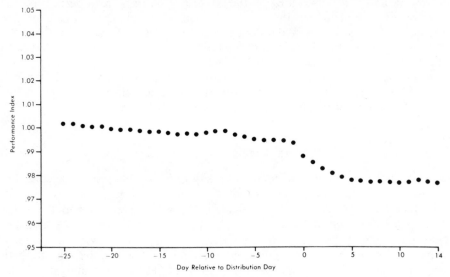

Figure 1. Secondary Distribution Daily Data, Market Adjustments

The abnormal performance index falls from an initial level of 1.0 to a final value of .977, fourteen days subsequent to the distribution, a decline of 2.2 percent. The absolute value of the average error is greater on each of the six days including and subsequent to day 0 than on any single day not in this period. On the day of the secondary the average error was —.5 percent. This initial evidence in some respects is consistent with selling pressure and in some respects inconsistent with selling pressure. Since the mean percentage of the firm traded was 2 percent and the mean price effect appears to be 2 percent, the elasticity of demand would appear to be —1. But, the price effect appears to be permanent for by the end of the fourteenth day after the distribution the abnormal performance index has not returned to its initial level of 1.0. Over this period there is no inducement for buyers of shares of a secondary. This evidence is contrary to the predictions of the price pressure adherents.

Although price pressure adherents may believe that the evidence is consistent with price pressure, we can also test to see whether or not the adverse returns are a function of the size of the distribution. We used two measures of size, the percentage of the firm traded in the distribution which appears to be the natural size variable, and also the dollar value of

[1] The standard deviation of the prediction errors, S_d, will be used as a descriptive statistic and is defined as

$$S_d = \left(\frac{1}{N-1} \sum_{i=1}^{N} (\hat{E}_{id} - \bar{E}_d)^2 \right)^{\frac{1}{2}}$$

TABLE 2

SUMMARY RESULTS OF TOTAL DAILY SAMPLE ANALYSIS
SAMPLE SIZE 345

Day	Average Error (%)	Performance Index	Standard Deviation	Fraction Negative
−25	.113	1.001	.0170	.50
−24	.054	1.002	.0163	.54
−23	−.053	1.001	.0153	.53
−22	−.053	1.001	.0155	.54
−21	.035	1.001	.0174	.54
−20	−.092	1.000	.0143	.56
−19	−.069	0.999	.0150	.53
−18	.055	1.000	.0144	.51
−17	−.076	0.999	.0150	.50
−16	.007	0.999	.0161	.54
−15	.010	0.999	.0146	.54
−14	−.092	0.998	.0153	.53
−13	−.057	0.997	.0147	.54
−12	.023	0.998	.0150	.48
−11	−.121	0.996	.0152	.51
−10	.082	0.997	.0152	.49
− 9	.121	0.998	.0167	.49
− 8	.026	0.998	.0144	.53
− 7	−.156	0.997	.0143	.54
− 6	−.095	0.996	.0139	.54
− 5	−.115	0.995	.0144	.55
− 4	.038	0.995	.0158	.53
− 3	−.020	0.995	.0151	.54
− 2	.025	0.995	.0153	.52
− 1	−.035	0.995	.0152	.54
0	−.552	0.989	.0166	.63
1	−.252	0.987	.0133	.55
2	−.229	0.984	.0150	.56
3	−.191	0.983	.0129	.55
4	−.168	0.981	.0134	.57
5	−.189	0.979	.0139	.54
6	−.068	0.978	.0185	.53
7	−.039	0.978	.0138	.52
8	.017	0.978	.0141	.51
9	−.011	0.978	.0166	.51
10	.019	0.978	.0144	.53
11	.034	0.978	.0135	.48
12	.085	0.979	.0139	.50
13	−.089	0.978	.0164	.53
14	−.044	0.977	.0149	.51

the distribution which can be considered another measure of increased supply.

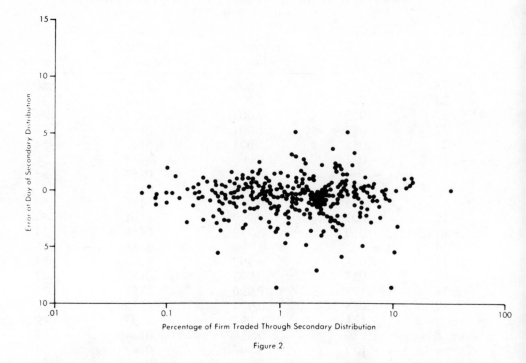

Figure 2.

In Figure 2 and Figure 3 the prediction errors for the day of the distribution, $\hat{E}_{i0}$, are plotted against the logarithm of the percentage of the firm traded and the logarithm of the dollar value of the issue, respectively.[1] As can readily be seen from these scatters, there appears to be no association between the prediction error at the day of the distribution and the size of the distribution as measured either in relative or absolute terms. For what it may be worth, least squares regressions were fitted so as to obtain numerical approximations to the implied elasticities of demand.[2] They turned out to be approximately —3000 for the relative case and —2500 for the absolute case. To help put these numbers in perspective

---

[1] The logarithm of the size variable was used as the independent variable for purposes of presentation, since the distributions of the size variables have long right tails. The regressions were also run using the percentages and dollar values. The results were exactly the same in all essential respects.

[2] The fitted equations were:

$$\hat{E}_{i0} = -.0069 - .00029 \log P \qquad R^2 = .0004$$
$$(.00078)$$

and
$$\hat{E}_{i0} = -.0022 - .00042 \log V \qquad R^2 = .0009$$
$$(.00080)$$

where P is percentage of firm traded and V is dollar value of the issue.

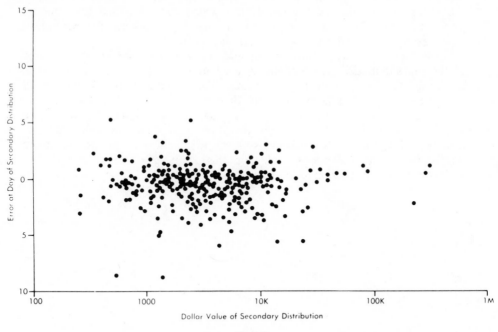

Figure 3.

we may note that an estimated elasticity cf —3000 would imply that if the percentage of the firm traded were to increase from 1.0 percent to 20.0 percent, the abnormal return would decline an additional .0063 percent or less than 1 cent on a security priced at $50 a share. This evidence, in sum, is inconsistent with the prediction of the price pressure hypothesis and implies that we cannot assume that the size of the large block sale is the cause of the observed abnormal return experience. Some evidence as to the likely source of this adjustment will be introduced in the next section.

Abnormal Return Experience of the Buyer of Secondary Distributions

The buyer of shares sold through a secondary distribution pays only the subscription price. The selling pressure hypothesis implies that an inducement, which takes the form of a price discount followed by an abnormally positive return, is necessary to find buyers for the shares of the large block sale. The substitution hypothesis predicts that the total abnormal return subsequent to the distribution should be the same as the purchase of shares of any other security. Since investors would be aware of any opportunities for abnormal returns and compete for them, the net result of this completion will be the elimination of opportunities for abnormal returns and the absence of pure price pressure.

A test of these alternative predictions involves merely substitution of the subscription price for the actual closing market price on the day of the secondary for each of the securities in the sample. Two returns change: the return on the day of the secondary, which can be called the vendor's gross last day return, and the return for the day following the secondary, which could be called the buyer's first day return.[1]

Since these two days were left out in computing the estimated coefficients of the market model, the coefficients used to estimate the prediction errors for each day, $\hat{E}_{i,d}$, will be the same. The estimated prediction errors, however, might be different for the day of the distribution and the day subsequent to the distribution. The average errors or average abnormal returns for each day relative to the distribution day and the abnormal performance index were recomputed using the new estimated prediction errors. Table 3 gives the standard table for this analysis.[2] The abnormal performance index is presented in Figure 4.

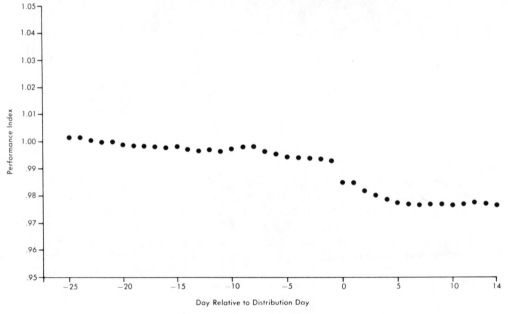

Figure 4. Seller-Buyer Adjustments

The performance index has a value of .986 on day zero. If the portfolio of all secondaries was purchased on day zero at the subscription price, this is equivalent to purchasing the abnormal performance index for 98.6 cents. If this portfolio was held until the end of day 14, the abnormal performance index has a value of .977. This indicates that the purchaser of the portfolio of all secondaries would lose approximately 1.0 percent on his purchase by the end of day 14. In fact, the value of the abnormal performance index reaches .977 by the end of day 6. The loss of 1.0 percent after the purchase

[1] Two returns change when one price changes simply because the same price is used as the terminal price on the day of the price change and the base price for the following day.

[2] Eight securities were dropped in this substitution because the subscription price of the secondary was not available.

TABLE 3

SUMMARY RESULTS OF DAILY DATA ANALYSIS—SUBSTITUTION
OF SUBSCRIPTION PRICE AT DAY OF SECONDARY
Sample Size 337

Day	Average Error (%)	Performance Index	Standard Deviation	Fraction Negative
−25	.102	1.001	.0171	.50
−24	.027	1.001	.0161	.54
−23	−.076	1.000	.0152	.54
−22	−.044	1.000	.0156	.53
−21	.030	1.000	.0175	.54
−20	−.090	0.999	.0144	.56
−19	−.086	0.998	.0151	.54
−18	.055	0.999	.0146	.51
−17	−.065	0.998	.0151	.50
−16	.019	0.998	.0163	.53
−15	.017	0.998	.0147	.54
−14	−.090	0.998	.0154	.53
−13	−.056	0.997	.0148	.54
−12	.027	0.997	.0149	.48
−11	−.141	0.996	.0148	.53
−10	.083	0.997	.0153	.50
− 9	.121	0.998	.0168	.49
− 8	.030	0.998	.0144	.53
− 7	−.172	0.996	.0143	.55
− 6	−.099	0.995	.0139	.54
− 5	−.116	0.994	.0145	.55
− 4	.032	0.994	.0158	.53
− 3	−.010	0.994	.0150	.55
− 2	.015	0.994	.0152	.51
− 1	−.033	0.994	.0152	.54
0	−.744	0.986	.0151	.72
1	−.019	0.986	.0175	.49
2	−.235	0.984	.0152	.56
3	−.203	0.982	.0130	.55
4	−.149	0.980	.0134	.57
5	−.199	0.978	.0140	.55
6	−.062	0.977	.0186	.53
7	−.052	0.977	.0139	.53
8	.025	0.977	.0141	.50
9	.030	0.977	.0146	.51
10	.018	0.977	.0145	.54
11	.039	0.978	.0135	.48
12	.085	0.978	.0139	.49
13	−.093	0.977	.0164	.53
14	−.043	0.977	.0150	.50

of shares of the distribution at the subscription price indicates that, contrary to the predictions of the price pressure hypothesis, positive abnormal returns subsequent to the purchase of the secondary distribution do not materialize over this period.

When the secondary is purchased at the subscription price, the buyer does not pay any commissions for the shares. But, in effect, the purchaser does pay a commission of 1.0 percent in the form of a subsequent negative abnormal return experience. This commission is approximately equal to the regular commissions paid to brokers on a round lot purchase of shares on the New York Stock Exchange.

This is a powerful piece of evidence in support of the substitution hypothesis. On average, the results of the analysis indicate that the buyers of all secondaries pay the regular round lot commissions on their purchase even if they buy on a supposedly commission free basis. There was no subsequent price recovery in the market over this period that served as inducement to purchase the shares of the secondary. The purchaser receives, on average, the same normal returns as if he had bought a round lot of 100 shares of any other security, after paying the regular transactions costs for the purchase. The large block sales are sold not at a reduced price but at the market price adjusted for the commissions. However, an investor who purchases the shares in the open market in the 6 day period after the distribution will pay the 1.0 percent commission but will still lose an additional amount in subsequent price adjustments in the market. There is, however, no incentive for traders to sell short after the announcement of the distribution and buy back after the 6 day period, for transaction costs would eliminate the gross profits from using such a scheme.

Abnormal Return Experience and Size of Sale

Although the prediction errors at day 0 were not associated with the size variable, and although, on average, the abnormal return experience subsequent to the distribution was negative, it is still necessary to check that the larger distributions did not have positive abnormal returns subsequent to the distribution while the smaller distributions had negative abnormal returns.

The 345 secondary distributions in the daily sample were partitioned into subsamples according to the size variables. For the percentage of the firm traded, 169 distributions that represented less than 1.2 percent of the firm traded were included in subsample P1 and 176 distributions that represented more than 1.2 percent of the firm traded were placed in subsample P2. For the dollar value subsamples, 164 distributions that represented sales of less than 2.7 million dollars were included in subsample V1 while the remaining 181 secondaries were included in subsample V2.

The average errors and the value of the performance index for each day, d, were computed for each of the subsamples. Table 4 summarizes for each of the subsamples, the average error at the day of the distribution, the performance index return for day zero, and the value of the performance index at strategic days relative to the distribution day.

Consistent with the previous results, we see that the average errors at day 0 are approximately the same for each subsample. Of more importance is the fact that the value of the abnormal performance index for each of the subsamples is lower on day 10 than on day 0. It falls approximately 1.3 percent for subsample P1 and approximately 1.0 percent for subsample P2. This evidence is again inconsistent with the implications of the price pressure hypothesis. The larger distributions do not experience a larger abnormal return than the smaller distributions subsequent to the day of the sale. Over this period, at least, there appears to have been no inducement in the form of an abnormal return as a function of the size of the distribution.

TABLE 4

THE EFFECT OF SIZE OF THE SECONDARY
ON MARKET PERFORMANCE

Subsample	Average Error at Day 0	Performance Index Return Day 0	Value of Performance Index at Day				
			−10	−2	0	+6	+10
P1	−.006	−.006	1.002	1.000	.993	.980	.980
P2	−.004	−.004	.992	.990	.986	.976	.976
V1	−.003	−.003	.999	.995	.992	.979	.978
V2	−.007	−.007	.995	.995	.987	.977	.978

A Check on the Results with Monthly Data

Although the evidence appears to be more consistent with the assumptions of the substitution hypothesis, monthly data were used to confirm the daily sample findings. The period covered included 1947–1964, a much longer time period than the daily sample period and over 1,200 secondary distributions were analyzed. With the monthly data we will be able to measure the abnormal return experience over many more months than in the daily sample period.

The analysis was repeated using the monthly data sample. The average prediction error was —2.15 percent in the month of the secondary. This confirms the evidence presented in the daily sample analysis. The value of the abnormal performance index was 1.01 at the end of the month of the secondary, 1.01 at the end of month 1, 1.01 at the end of month 5 and 1.00 at the end of month 18 after the secondary. No inducement in the form of an abnormal return was realized over the 18 month period subsequent to the distribution. This is a substantial period of time in which to realize the increased rate of return implied by the selling pressure hypothesis.

The abnormal performance index was computed for four portfolios constructed according to the size of the distribution. The first portfolio contained the 25 percent of the secondary distributions that represented the largest percentage of the firm traded. Once again there was no apparent relationship between the change in the index and the size of the distribution in the month of issue or in the months subsequent to the distribution.

In conclusion, the examination of abnormal returns both on a daily and on a monthly basis shows a permanent average 2 percent loss associated with the sale of a secondary distribution. Contrary to the selling pressure hypothesis, however, this decline does not seem to be associated with the crucial size variables. Nor are there, on the average, excess returns earned for those who buy shares of a large block distribution of securities. We will now see what additional light the data throw on the source and significance of the once and for all 2 percent price decline.

INFORMATION AND SECONDARY DISTRIBUTIONS

We have already stated that one possible explanation for the 2 percent price decline may be that the secondary distribution is associated with adverse information about the firm. That is, the seller may possess information that if generally known would cause an immediate downward adjustment in the market price of the security. An investor investigating the operations of the firm might conclude from an analysis of information not readily available to others that the shares were overvalued in the market. He therefore sells and his sale may well act in turn as a signal to others to commit resources to the re-examination of the firm's prospects. If there was indeed information of value in this sale, the price of the shares should adjust by the value of this information.

Secondary distributions, however, are sold for other than informational reasons. The classic example would be that of an investor who has held a particular stock in his portfolio for a considerable period of time and who now feels it represents a larger proportion of his wealth than he desires to hold in this form. Such an investor need have no information about the firm of any value to other traders. Although he has the option to sell his securities over time in smaller quantities on the exchange, he may feel that it is more efficient to sell them in a single offering.

The vendors of the secondary were classified into five general categories in the *SEC Statistical Bulletin* [29]. These categories were: (1) Investment Companies, (2) Banks and Insurance Companies, (3) Individuals, (4) Corporations or Corporate Officers, and (5) Estates and Trusts. The likelihood that a sale contained adverse information is very different among these categories, although, of course, no absolutely hard and fast classification can be made along these lines.

On the one hand are Estates, Trusts, Individuals, Banks and Insurance Companies, who are typically furthest from the day to day operations of the firm, and who may have motives to sell other than for informational reasons; an Estate to meet tax obligations, to make philanthropic donations or other distributions to legatees; an individual to adjust a portfolio imbalance or for consumption needs, and so on. Though some vendors in these categories undoubtedly sell for informational reasons or because they feel they possess adverse information, the vast majority probably sell for reasons having nothing to do with the prospects of the firm.

At the other extreme is the category Corporations and Officers. A Corporation which holds a large proportion of another company's stock is almost certainly in close contact with the operations of the firm it sells, and the same is obviously true for corporation officers. In their study of insider trading and stock prices, for example, Lorie and Niederhoffer [21] found strong evidence that the information available to officers did have substantial value.[1] They also found that by the time the information was publicly available that an "insider" had made a purchase or a sale, there were no further profits to be made from acting on the published data. Thus, not only do insiders close to the operations of the firm possess information, but it is plausible to imagine that a secondary distribution might be an indication to other market traders that the sellers may possess adverse information. Similarly, Investment Companies and Mutual Funds have large "research" staffs and their close contacts with brokers and underwriters make it at least plausible that some part of their sales may reflect adverse inside information.[2]

On the day of the secondary, the vendor is not generally known. If the announcement of a secondary distribution conveys information to the market, we should thus expect that on the day of the sale all the average errors should be negative and of about the same order of magnitude. Thereafter the company's prospects are actively re-evaluated and if no adverse information is discovered, the price of the shares should return to the predistribution price. If the value of the information exceeded the expected value of information contained in secondaries, then the price will fall to the new equilibrium price.

The abnormal performance index and the average prediction errors

TABLE 5

VENDOR CLASSIFICATION AND DAILY SAMPLE

Subsample	Average Error at Day 0	Number of Observations	Value of Performance Index at Day				
			−10	−2	0	+6	+10
Investment Co. and Mutal Fund	−.0042	192	1.000	.994	.989	.974	.975
Bank and Insurance	−.0053	31	.998	1.003	.995	.991	.995
Individuals	−.0045	36	.986	.983	.982	.977	.975
Corporations and Officers	−.0113	23	.992	.992	.984	.964	.963
Estates and Trusts	−.0071	50	.991	.996	.989	.986	.984

[1] They conclude: "When insiders accumulate a stock intensively, the stock can be expected to outperform the market during the next six months. Insiders tend to buy more often than usual before large price increases and to sell more than usual before price decreases. We have been unable to find companies in which the insiders are consistently more successful in predicting price movements than are insiders in general" [pp. 52–53].

[2] To quote the *Special Study* [28]: "An official of a large mutual fund selling organization stated to the study that the funds sponsored by it sometimes used secondary distributions to dispose of 'sick' situations rapidly."

TABLE 6

ABNORMAL RETURN ON PERFORMANCE INDEX
BY VENDOR CLASSIFICATION

Subsample	Percentage Abnormal Return on Performance	
	−10 to +10	*0 to +10*
Investment Companies		
and Mutual Funds	−2.5	−1.4
Banks and Insurance	− .3	−0.7
Individuals	−1.1	−0.0
Corporations and		
Officers	−2.9	−2.1
Estates	− .7	− .5

were computed for each of the five vendor categories. These results are summarized in Table 5 and 6. As can be seen in Table 5 the average errors at day 0 are indeed approximately the same order of magnitude for all groups with the exception of the corporation category. Though the sample size for that group may be too small for any firm judgment, assuming that it is a real difference, the obvious explanation would be that some information as to the vendor and cause of the sale leaks to the market prior to the sale. After the distribution, as can be seen from Table 6, the absolute magnitude of the postdistribution abnormal return is largest for Corporations followed by Mutual Funds and smallest for Banks, Estates and Individuals, which is what one would have expected on the basis of our earlier a priori classification by likelihood of adverse information.

Table 7 indicates how a buyer would have fared on purchasing each category of secondary at the subscription price. If he had bought Insurance Company, Individual or Estate secondaries, he would effectively have paid

TABLE 7

RETURN EXPERIENCE OF SELLER AND RETURN
EXPERIENCE OF BUYER OF SECONDARY

Subsample	Average Error at Day 0	Percentage Abnormal Return On Performance Index	
		Seller Day −10 to 0	*Buyer Day 0 to +10*
Investment Companies	−.0067	−1.5	−1.2
Insurance Companies	−.0077	− .5	+ .2
Individuals	−.0058	− .5	− .6
Corporations	−.0100	− .8	−2.0
Estates	−.0089	− .5	− .1

less than 1.0 percent in commissions. However, if he had bought Investment Company or Corporation distributions, he would effectively have paid more than a 1.0 percent commission.

As noted earlier, the distributions are initiated and concluded so quickly that the vendor is not generally known on the day of the distribution. Insiders do not have to report purchases and sales for a period of up to six days and, by that time, the market has adjusted to announcement effects contained in the distribution. Since the buyer of any particular secondary does not yet know the vendor he also does not yet know the effective commission he is paying. If he was unfortunate and bought the Corporation secondary he paid twice the normal commission. If he was fortunate and bought the Insurance Company secondary he in effect paid no commission. On the average he would pay the normal round-lot commission.

The monthly data sample was used to confirm the data sample evidence. The results of the analysis are summarized in Table 8.

TABLE 8

SUMMARY OF MONTHLY RUNS BY VENDOR

Vendor	E_0	Return on API for Various Periods %		Size
		Month −18 to −1	Month +1 to +18	
Investment Co.	−.031	−1.0	−1.0	361
Bank & Insurance	−.018	1.5	−1.5	220
Individuals	−.009	6.0	0.0	181
Corporations & Officers	−.031	8.0	−6.0	128
Estates and Trusts	−.013	2.0	3.0	195
Unknown *	−.022	N.A.	N.A.	112

* It was not possible to obtain the vendor for these 112 distributions. The average error at the month of the secondary was approximately the same as the total sample.

For the Individual category, the abnormal performance index has risen substantially prior to the sale and remains flat subsequent to the sale. This is consistent with the proposition that individuals tend to sell when a security has experienced positive returns to correct portfolio imbalances. Once again, the most striking evidence in favor of the information hypothesis is the experience of the Corporation and Corporate Officers category. Their sale does contain information of significant value. They sell when the security has experienced positive abnormal returns and is considered to be overvalued in the market, and the post distribution experience of the security confirms their analysis.

Other tests of the significance of the information effect versus the price pressure effect were also run. A two-way analysis of variance was conducted. The prediction errors at the month of secondary conditional on the size variables and the vendor showed that the F statistic for the vendor classification was highly significant while the F statistic for each of the size variables was insignificant. Also of interest was the finding that the possible interaction between vendor and size variable was also insignificant. Even though the cross-sectional tests overstate the significance of the relationships, the price pressure variables are not significant.

The evidence in this section is more consistent with the substitution cum information hypotheses than the selling pressure hypothesis. There does appear to be significant differences by vendor and thus information, but no evidence of price pressure or inducements for purchasers of secondary distributions.

Registration of Secondary and Price Effects

Since the evidence in the last section indicated that the selling pressure hypothesis could not account for the abnormal returns observed at the sale of a secondary distribution, it is possible to give additional evidence that the observed price effects of a secondary distribution are the result of adverse economic information about the firm. If the seller of shares in a secondary distribution has a "control relationship" to the firm, the Securities and Exchange Commission requires registration and a twenty day waiting period before the shares of the secondary can be sold.

Since registration occurs 20 days prior to the actual sale, market traders have time to re-examine the prospects of the firm prior to the sale date. If there was information of value in the sale, the price of the shares would adjust to the value of the information prior to this sale date. On the actual day of the sale there should be no price adjustment.

For those secondary distributions that were not registered, the market did not have time to re-examine the prospects for the firm prior to the sale, and therefore, if there is, on average, adverse information contained in the sale of a secondary distribution, the price effects should be observed on the day of the sale and the days following the sale as market traders confirm that there was information of value in the sale.

In the daily data there were 73 distributions that were registered out of the total sample of 345. The average errors for each day relative to the distribution day and the value of the abnormal performance index for each day relative to the distribution day were computed for each classification; registered and nonregistered distributions. Table 9 summarizes the results of the analysis.

For the nonregistered secondaries the average abnormal return on the day of the distribution was —.6 percent, slightly lower than the figure for the total sample of —.5 percent. The performance index falls from a level of .989 on the day of the secondary to .975, 10 days subsequent to day zero, a return of —1.4 percent. For the registered secondaries the average error on the day of the secondary was —.099 percent. The performance index falls from a level of .992 on day zero to .988 on day 10, a return of —.4 percent. Of interest is the average error of —.26 percent of day —20, and the error of —.41 percent on day —19. This is the announcement date of the registered secondary. From 20 days to 1 day prior to the secondary the performance index drops from a level of 1.005 to .99, a return of

TABLE 9

ABNORMAL RETURNS OVER DIFFERENT SUBPERIODS

Period	Registered Secondary	Nonregistered Secondary
Day Relative To Distribution Day	Performance Index Return	Performance Index Return
−20 to −1	−1.3	−0.4
0	−0.099	−0.6
0 to + 10	−0.4	−1.4
−20 to +14	−1.7	−2.4

—1.3 percent. For the same period for the nonregistered secondaries the performance index falls —.4 percent.

It appears that the registered secondaries have less total effect on market prices than the nonregistered secondaries. Since registration is left partially to the discretion of the vendor, the distributions that did not contain information might tend to be registered since the need for an immediate sale is not as pressing for these vendors, and they would wish to let other traders have time to confirm that there was no informational content in the distributions. However, to register a distribution is more costly than non-registration for three reasons. First, there are the necessary registration statements which are expensive to prepare. Second, the underwriting group which becomes a formal organization when registration occurs charges a higher price for its services which include distribution of a prospectus, meeting Securities and Exchange Commission requirements and the expensive advisory meetings. Third, the vendor must wait twenty days and this waiting time is also a potential cost to the vendor since the market conditions could change during the waiting period.

Therefore, distributions that occur simply to change a portfolio holding are not always registered. And on the other hand, some vendors who feel they possess adverse information may be forced to register because they are close to the operations of the firm, but since only 21 percent of the distributions were registered, this does not appear to be a great constraint.

For the registered distributions the magnitude of the price effects was quite small on the day of the sale and the days subsequent to the sale, while for the nonregistered distributions the price effects were much larger on the day of the sale and days subsequent to the sale. This evidence is consistent with the hypothesis that the secondary distribution may signal adverse economic information about a firm's prospects.

In conclusion to this section, it is of interest to state the recommendations of the Securities and Exchange Commission's Special Study of the Securities Markets [28, p. 567] in reference to unregistered secondary distributions. To quote the study:

The speed with which these distributions occur is evidence of the efficiency of the marketing facility of the financial community, but rapid distribution may not be conducive to an unhurried, informed, and careful consideration of the investment factors applicable to the securities involved.

Continuing from the study [p. 569]:

From the point of view of public customers they are often indistinguishable from registered distributions in respect to disclosure needs. Yet they occur, for the most part, without even the minimum disclosure protections that would seem practical and with a speed that does not permit careful consideration of the merits of the security being distributed.

The study then recommended that more disclosure of information and a waiting time be instituted. The evidence presented here indicates that neither are necessary. New shareholders do not suffer dire consequences when they buy the shares of an unregistered distribution. On the contrary they, in effect, pay approximately the regular exchange commissions as on any other market trade. Also, the dispersion of the distribution of prediction errors on day zero for both registered and nonregistered distributions is approximately the same as on the other days in the sample period. The requirement of registration of any secondary and its increased direct expense does not seem to be warranted.

CONCLUSION

The purpose of this paper has been to test empirically two alternative hypotheses concerning the operations of the securities markets. The substitution hypothesis defines the market for securities as all securities that the investor considers for investment. Securities or combinations of securities provide him with potential income streams of essentially similar characteristics. Since securities provide similar potential consumption streams, they are close substitutes. The substitution hypothesis implies that individuals as well as corporations can alter their holdings in securities at approximately the prevailing market price.

The alternative hypothesis, the selling pressure hypothesis, assumes that investors consider a security to be a unique commodity with a low cross-elasticity of demand with other securities. It is argued that lack of information, institutional constraints and investor speculation dominate trading in the securities markets. Keynes [19] likened the security markets to a game of Old Maid or Snap in which market traders buy and sell securities without regard to economic values but in expectation of outguessing other market traders. It is also argued that individuals have differing expectations concerning the terminal values of particular securities, and as a result will only hold increasing amounts of a security if they expect to achieve higher rates of return. Large block sales of securities would cause price declines as a function of the size of the trade as an inducement to investors to purchase the shares.

The competing hypotheses could only be resolved through testing empirically the predictions of each model. A sample of the largest block distributions of securities, secondary distributions, were considered to be the best data available to test the alternative hypotheses. The data gave consistent and strong support to the assumptions of the substitution hypothesis. The testing procedure allowed for the differential effects of changing economic conditions on security prices. Once the effects of market wide movements in security prices had been accounted for, it was possible to estimate prediction errors. The prediction errors for each security are defined as the security's abnormal returns, not associated with market wide movements. Regressions of the prediction error of each security in the sample on two supply variables; the percentage of the firm traded and the dollar value of the distribution indicated that estimated elasticities of demand were very large and negative. This evidence could only be interpreted as strong support for the substitution hypothesis. The range of the percentage of the firm traded was from less than 1.0 percent of the firm to more than 35.0 percent. If selling pressure wasn't found in this range, there most likely won't be selling pressure for trades of greater amounts. In every phase of the analysis, whether the daily sample or the monthly sample was used, the size or supply variables were not associated with the abnormal return experience of securities at the time of the large block distributions of securities.

Market Adjustments to Information

Secondary distributions were chosen in lieu of primary distributions because it was felt that many of the variables that affect the firm's prospects would be held constant. However, even for secondary distributions it was not possible to "hold all other things constant."

Certainly some sellers of a large block of stock wish to alter their portfolio holdings to affect a better balance between the expected return on their portfolios and the riskiness of their holdings. Some sales occur after the market price of a security has adjusted to some "unfavorable news" about a company's prospects. But, also, it is possible that sellers of a block of stock possess information that has economic value. The sale of a secondary distribution may be a signal to other market traders to incur the costs of re-analysis of the firm's prospects. For some firms this re-evaluation may take only one day, for other firms the task may take longer than one day. But, once the re-evaluation takes place, the market price should adjust immediately to the value of the information. It appears that the total adjustment to the sale of a secondary distribution takes approximately 6 days, from day 0 through day 5. We saw in Table 2 that the average errors from day —25 to day —1 are very close to zero. There are 12 positive average errors and 13 negative average errors with no apparent clustering of the signs of the average errors through time. Also, from day 6 through day 14, there are 4 positive and 5 negative average errors. The adjustment period doesn't imply that prices of securities adjust slowly to new equilibrium values. On the contrary, the percentage of negative prediction errors on any one day from day 1 through day 5 indicates that there is only a slight excess of negative prediction errors on any particular day. Though the average errors are negative in this period, a considerable proportion of securities experience positive prediction errors on each of the six days.

It must also be remembered that the vendor of the distribution is not generally known at the time of the distribution though there certainly are leaks in the system since brokers and investment bankers certainly know the vendor. Officially, corporate insiders must report their transactions in their own company's stock to the Securities and Exchange Commission within six days after the distribution. By the time official reporting is necessary, the market has fully adjusted for the value of the information.

Though this six day period could be an adjustment period to the value of the information it can be disputed on two counts:

(1) All distributions are not initiated and completed on a single day, but may take several days to conclude. The distribution may be "hanging" over the market and this continued selling pressure could be the cause of the observed decline subsequent to the distribution.

(2) The second objection to the adjustment period is the assertion that the investment banking group "eases" the price adjustment in the market by engaging in price stabilization.

To test these propositions, 226 secondaries were examined in the period 1961 through 1963 to find the closing date on the investment banker's books.[1] Of the 226 secondaries in these years, 51.0 percent of the distributions were initiated and completed on day zero, while 42.0 percent of the distributions were closed out the next day, and only 7.0 percent of distributions took longer than 1 day to complete. This evidence indicates that the sale period is too short to account for the entire length of the adjustment period in the market. Also, if the books are closed quickly, there is no need for further buying or selling by the selling group.

Of extreme interest is the fact that approximately 93.0 percent of the distributions are initiated and completed within one day. In a very short period of time, large holdings of securities can be sold without the price pressure to induce traders to purchase the shares.

Although it was possible to determine a vendor effect, Corporations and Officers the strongest—Individuals the weakest, of more interest was the finding that the average errors were approximately the same on the day of the sale, and as the vendor or more importantly, the value of his information became known the market price adjusted to the new equilibrium price. Also there was no apparent association between the size of the sale and the value of information contained in the secondary distribution.

Inducements: Reality or Myth?

There are various interested parties in a secondary distribution. These interested parties include (1) the buyer of shares of the secondary, (2) the vendor of the secondary, (3) the current holders of the shares, and (4) other market traders.

---

[1] A distribution ends when the Investment Banker closes his books after matching all orders with available shares. This may take longer than the actual period involved in the sale, especially for large distributions.

(1) The buyer of shares of a secondary distribution pays only the subscription price and does not pay commissions for the purchase. The imperfect market hypothesis implies that the buyer must receive an inducement to purchase the shares of a secondary distribution. This inducement could come in the form of a price discount and subsequent price recovery. On the surface it appears that the buyer of shares of a secondary distribution does receive an inducement in the form of a commission saving of approximately 1.0 percent. However, subsequent to his purchase at the subscription price, the investor, on average, lost 1.0 percent in market price adjustments. This loss was a permanent loss in that, on the average, over an 18 month period subsequent to the sale there were no observed abnormal returns. Also, the 1.0 percent adjustment in the market price was independent of the size of the sale. In effect, as the substitution hypothesis implies, the buyer of shares of a secondary distribution pays the same commissions on his purchase as he would if he purchased 100 shares of any other security on the Exchange.

But the buyer of shares does not have to buy at the subscription price. He can always wait the five days after the secondary and then purchase the shares after the adjustment period has been completed. The buyer saves the 1.0 percent price adjustment in the market subsequent to the secondary, but he must pay a commission of 1.0 percent on his purchase. The buyer is then indifferent to the purchase of a secondary at the subscription price or the shares in the open market at the end of the period. This is a powerful piece of evidence in support of the substitution hypothesis and the workings of competitive markets.

(2) The vendor of a secondary may possess information that, on the average, is worth approximately 2.0 percent. If the vendor uses a secondary distribution he incurs the following costs. First, the market price adjustment was approximately —.3 percent before the sale. Second, he sells at the subscription price and pays an additional .7 percent. Third, he pays for the services of the investment banker, an additional 2.0 percent. The vendor then pays 3.0 percent to sell his shares. If he waited until the market had adjusted to the value of his information, he would lose 2.0 percent, on the average, but have to pay an additional 1.0 percent in commissions. For this strategy his total cost would be 3.0 percent.

(3) The present holder of the shares, on average, suffers a 2.0 percent loss. If he sold after the announcement of a secondary and assume he could sell at the closing market price on the day of the secondary, he loses .9 percent on the sale and pays an additional cost of 1.0 percent in brokerage. If he holds the securities and doesn't sell, he also pays approximately 2.0 percent. Once the secondary is announced, it is no longer necessary for the present shareholder to trade. This is also a direct implication of an efficient market.

(4) Other market traders can buy and sell shares at any time. After a secondary is announced there is no incentive for them to use a mechanical trading scheme to increase profits for the price fall after the announcement is well within transactions costs on a two way trade. Even knowledge of an impending secondary distribution just prior to the announcement could not result in abnormal profits. The market price falls approximately 1.6

percent from day —1 to day +6. There is no incentive to sell short and buy back the shares in the market to mechanically increase profits.

However, shareholders who do buy shares of secondary distributions in the open market within the six day period subsequent to the sale pay effectively more than 1.0 percent in commissions. The adjustment to information in the sale seems to fall on these investors.

Sales of Other Assets—Stocks and Bonds

Though the analysis in this paper was carried out on a sample of large block distributions of already outstanding shares, the implications of this analysis carry over to new issues of common stock as well as bonds. The only reason a sample of new issues wasn't chosen was the problem of market adjustments to factors not specifically related to the issue itself such as new investment, mergers and recapitalizations. There is no reason to believe that new issues should be any different than secondary distributions in terms of price pressure. To support this contention, a sample of 696 rights issues was also collected for the period 1926 to 1966. The standard analysis was applied to this sample as well. The average error at the month of the rights issue of common stock was —.3 percent. Though the securities in the rights issue sample experienced abnormally positive returns prior to the issue, at the month of the rights issue there was no appreciable effect on market price of the increased quantity of securities. After the issue there appeared, on average, to be no further abnormal gains or losses. When the rights issue sample was classified into subsamples according to the ratio of the value of the new capital to the total market value of the outstanding shares, there also was no appreciable change in the average errors at the month of the rights issue for different stratifications by this classification. This evidence is consistent with the findings of the effects of secondary distributions on market price. Corporations like individuals can sell shares at existing market prices.

Implications of the Results

These findings have positive implications for financial managers of corporations. Since the empirical evidence suggests that price discounts are not necessary to sell new issues, managers can concentrate on the investment worth of projects, and not commit energies to the evaluation of the effects of selling quantities of stock on share prices. In reference to dividend policy versus new issues of securities, the effects of the increased quantity of stock on security prices is not a relevant variable.

Utility rate commissions can also consider the present market price as reflecting potential sale prices for new issues of utility shares without allowing higher rates of return to cover the hypothetical selling pressure associated with new issues.

To the individual shareholder, these results also give assurance that his holdings, though a relatively large percentage of the outstanding shares of the firm, can be sold at approximately the prevailing market price without suffering financial loss in the event of a necessary sale. When considering an individual shareholder, it is possible to include Mutual Funds, on other large financial institutions in this class as well. It has been argued that funds have an increasing and large percentage of the value of outstanding shares. It is asserted that they contain the financial power to make markets in certain securities by their buying and selling activities. All funds are not buying the same security; they compete against each other and hold many different assets in their portfolios. The size of their holdings should not be measured as a percentage of market value of only New York Stock Exchange securities, but all market wealth. The proportion of total market wealth of any one mutual fund is very small. Massachusetts Investors Trust, a one billion dollar fund, still holds less than .1 percent of the value of all New York Stock Exchange firms.

There has been considerable discussion connected with antitrust divestiture suits as to the long-run depressing effects on the price of the shares of the firm to be divested. It is apparent from the analysis that the distribution of a large block of a corporation's stock by a holding company will not have a long-run depressing effect on share prices. If there were monopoly returns associated with the holdings, this would have been reflected in the .price of the two companies at the time the decision was handed down. A recommendation to the courts would be to terminate testimony on this point and concentrate on more substantive issues.

Future Research

Work must be continued to understand the process of adjustment to new information in the market. Though the preliminary results of the rights issue samples were consistent with the findings of the secondary samples, the rights issue and new issues in general contain more information than secondary distributions. One can only speculate on the adjustment process to the value of information contained in a new issue. Also, new issues are sold in clusters when economic prospects are favorable. Why firms issue bonds at one time and stock at another time has to be answered as well.

REFERENCES

1. Blume, Marshall. "The Assessment of Portfolio Performance" (unpublished Ph.D. dissertation, University of Chicago, 1968).
2. Blattberg, Robert, and Thomas Sargent. "Regression With Non-Gaussian Stable Disturbances: Some Sampling Results," *Econometrica*, May, 1971, Vol. 39, No. 3, pages 501–510.
3. Bonbright, James C. *Principles of Public Utility Rates*, New York: Columbia University Press, 1961.
4. Cootner, Paul H., ed. *The Random Character of Stock Market Prices*, Cambridge: M.I.T. Press, 1964.
5. Cramer, Harold. *Mathematical Methods of Statistics*, Princeton, New Jersey: Princeton University Press, 1946.
6. Durand, David. "The Cost of Capital, Corporation Finance, and the Theory of Investment: Comment," *The American Economic Review*, XLIX, September, 1959, pages 639–655.
7. Fama, Eugene. "The Behavior of Stock Market Prices," *Journal of Business*, XXXVIII, January, 1965, pages 34–105.
8. ————. "Portfolio Analysis in a Stable Paretian Market," *Management Science*, XI, January, 1965, pages 404–419.
9. ————. and Marshall Blume, "Filter Rules and Stock Market Trading," *Journal of Business*, XXXIX, January, 1966, pages 226–241.
10. ————. Lawrence Fisher, Michael C. Jensen, and Richard Roll, "The Adjustment

of Stock Prices to New Information," *International Economic Review,* X, February, 1969, pages 1–21.

11. ———. and Richard Roll, "Some Properties of Symmetric Stable Distributions," *Journal of the American Statistical Association,* September, 1968.

12. Fama, Eugene. "Efficient Capital Markets: A Review of Theory and Empirical Work," *The Journal of Finance,* Vol. XXV, May, 1970, pages 383–417.

13. Fama, Eugene, and Merton Miller. "The Theory of Valuation" (unpublished manuscript, University of Chicago, 1971).

14. ———. and Harvey Babiak, "Dividend Policy: An Empirical Analysis," *Journal of the American Statistical Association,* Vol. 63, No. 324, December, 1968, pages 1132–1161.

15. Federal Communications Commission. "American Telephone and Telegraph Company and the Associated Bell System Companies, et al.," Docket No. 16258, et al., *CSA Reporting Corporation,* Washington, D.C., 1968.

16. Feller, William. *An Introduction to Probability Theory and Its Applications,* Vol. II, New York: John Wiley and Sons, Inc., 1966, chapter 17.

17. Fisher, Lawrence, and James H. Lorie. "Rates of Return on Investments in Common Stocks," *Journal of Business,* XXXVII, January, 1964, pages 1–21.

18. *Investment Dealers' Digest,* "Corporate Financing Section," New York: The Dealers' Digest Publishing Company, Inc., January and July editions, 1947–1966.

19. Keynes, John M. *The General Theory of Employment, Interest and Money,* London: Macmillan and Company, 1936.

20. Lintner, John. "Dividends, Earnings, Leverage, Stock Prices and the Supply of Capital to Corporations," *The Review of Economics and Statistics,* XLIV, August, 1962, pages 243–269.

21. Lorie, James H., and Victor Niederhoffer. "Predictive and Statistical Properties of Insider Trading," *The Journal of Law and Economics,* XI, April, 1968, pages 35–54.

22. Miller, Merton H., and Franco Modigliani. "Dividend Policy, Growth, and the Valuation of Shares," *The Journal of Business,* XXXIV, October, 1961, pages 411–433.

23. Modigliani, Franco, and Merton Miller. "The Cost of Capital, Corporation Finance, and the Theory of Investment," *The American Economic Review,* XLVIII, June, 1958, pages 261–297.

24. Samuelson, Paul A. "Proof That Properly Anticipated Prices Fluctuate Randomly," *Industrial Management Review,* VI, Spring, 1965, pages 41–49.

25. Sharpe, William F. "A Simplified Model for Portfolio Analysis," *Management Science,* January, 1963, pages 277–293.

26. Sharpe, William F. "Capital Asset Prices: A Theory of Market Equilibrium Under Conditions of Risk," *Journal of Finance,* XIX, September, 1964, pages 425–442.

27. United States *vs.* E. I. duPont de Nemours and Company, General Motors Corporation, et al.," *Court Decisions,* 69, 461, Commerce Clearing House, 1959, pages 75, 760–75, 806.

28. United States Government: *Report of Special Study of Securities Markets of the Securities and Exchange Commission,* Part I, 88th Congress, 1st Session, House Document No. 95, U.S. Government Printing Office, Washington, D.C., 1963.

29. United States Securities and Exchange Commission: *Statistical Bulletin,* Government Printing Office, Washington, D.C.

30. Vickers, Douglas. *The Theory of the Firm: Production, Capital, and Finance,* New York: McGraw-Hill, 1968.

12

THE PERFORMANCE OF MUTUAL FUNDS
IN THE PERIOD 1945-64

Michael C. Jensen *

I. INTRODUCTION

A CENTRAL PROBLEM IN FINANCE (and especially portfolio management) has been that of evaluating the "performance" of portfolios of risky investments. The concept of portfolio "performance" has at least two distinct dimensions:

1) The ability of the portfolio manager or security analyst to increase returns on the portfolio through successful prediction of future security prices, and
2) The ability of the portfolio manager to minimize (through "efficient" diversification) the amount of "insurable risk" born by the holders of the portfolio.

The major difficulty encountered in attempting to evaluate the performance of a portfolio in these two dimensions has been the lack of a thorough understanding of the nature and measurement of "risk." Evidence seems to indicate a predominance of risk aversion in the capital markets, and as long as investors correctly perceive the "riskiness" of various assets this implies that "risky" assets must on average yield higher returns than less "risky" assets.[1] Hence in evaluating the "performance" of portfolios the effects of differential degrees of risk on the returns of those portfolios must be taken into account.

Recent developments in the theory of the pricing of capital assets by Sharpe [20], Lintner [15] and Treynor [25] allow us to formulate explicit measures of a portfolio's performance in each of the dimensions outlined above. These measures are derived and discussed in detail in Jensen [11]. However, we shall confine our attention here *only* to the problem of evaluating a portfolio manager's *predictive ability*—that is his ability to earn returns through successful prediction of security prices which are higher than those which we could expect *given* the level of riskiness of his portfolio. The foundations of the model and the properties of the performance measure suggested here (which is somewhat different than that proposed in [11]) are discussed in Section II. The model is illustrated in Section III by an application of it to the evaluation of the performance of 115 open end mutual funds in the period 1945-1964.

A number of people in the past have attempted to evaluate the performance of portfolios[2] (primarily mutual funds), but almost all of these authors have

---

* University of Rochester College of Business. This paper has benefited from comments and criticisms by G. Benston, E. Fama, J. Keilson, H. Weingartner, and especially M. Scholes.

1. Assuming, of course, that investors' expectations are on average correct.
2. See for example [2, 3, 7, 8, 9, 10, 21, 24].

Reprinted from *The Journal of Finance*, XXIII, No. 2 (May, 1968), 389–416, by permission of the author and the publisher.

relied heavily on relative measures of performance when what we really need is an absolute measure of performance. That is, they have relied mainly on procedures for ranking portfolios. For example, if there are two portfolios A and B, we not only would like to know whether A is better (in some sense) than B, but also whether A and B are good or bad relative to some absolute standard. The measure of performance suggested below is such an absolute measure.[3] It is important to emphasize here again that the word "performance" is used here only to refer to a fund manager's forecasting ability. It does not refer to a portfolio's "efficiency" in the Markowitz-Tobin sense. A measure of "efficiency" and its relationship to certain measures of diversification and forecasting ability is derived and discussed in detail in Jensen [11]. For purposes of brevity we confine ourselves here to an examination of a fund manager's forecasting ability which is of interest in and of itself (witness the widespread interest in the theory of random walks and its implications regarding forecasting success).

In addition to the lack of an absolute measure of performance, these past studies of portfolio performance have been plagued with problems associated with the definition of "risk" and the need to adequately control for the varying degrees of riskiness among portfolios. The measure suggested below takes explicit account of the effects of "risk" on the returns of the portfolio.

Finally, once we have a measure of portfolio "performance" we also need to estimate the measure's sampling error. That is we want to be able to measure its "significance" in the usual statistical sense. Such a measure of significance also is suggested below.

II. The Model

The Foundations of the Model.—As mentioned above, the measure of portfolio performance summarized below is derived from a direct application of the theoretical results of the capital asset pricing models derived independently by Sharpe [20], Lintner [15] and Treynor [25]. All three models are based on the assumption that (1) all investors are averse to risk, and are single period expected utility of terminal wealth maximizers, (2) all investors have identical decision horizons and homogeneous expectations regarding investment opportunities, (3) all investors are able to choose among portfolios solely on the basis of expected returns and variance of returns, (4) all transactions costs and taxes are zero, and (5) all assets are infinitely divisible. Given the additional assumption that the capital market is in equilibrium, all three models yield the following expression for the expected one period return,[4] $E(\tilde{R}_J)$, on any security (or portfolio) j:

$$E(\tilde{R}_J) = R_F + \beta_J[E(\tilde{R}_M) - R_F] \tag{1}$$

where the tildes denote random variables, and

3. It is also interesting to note that the measure of performance suggested below is in many respects quite closely related to the measure suggested by Treynor [24].

4. Defined as the ratio of capital gains plus dividends to the initial price of the security. (Note, henceforth we shall use the terms asset and security interchangeably.)

R_F = the one-period risk free interest rate.

β_j = $\dfrac{\text{cov}(\tilde{R}_j, \tilde{R}_M)}{\sigma^2(\tilde{R}_M)}$ = the measure of risk (hereafter called systematic risk) which the asset pricing model implies is crucial in determining the prices of risky assets.

$E(\tilde{R}_M)$ = the expected one-period return on the "market portfolio" which consists of an investment in each asset in the market in proportion to its fraction of the total value of all assets in the market.

Thus eq. (1) implies that the expected return on any asset is equal to the risk free rate plus a risk premium given by the product of the systematic risk of the asset and the risk premium on the market portfolio.[5] The risk premium on the market portfolio is the difference between the expected returns on the market portfolio and the risk free rate.

Equation (1) then simply tells us what any security (or portfolio) can be expected to earn given its level of systematic risk, β_j. If a portfolio manager or security analyst is able to predict future security prices he will be able to earn higher returns that those implied by eq. (1) and the riskiness of his portfolio. We now wish to show how (1) can be adapted and extended to provide an estimate of the forecasting ability of any portfolio manager. Note that (1) is stated in terms of the *expected* returns on any security or portfolio j and the *expected* returns on the market portfolio. Since these expectations are strictly unobservable we wish to show how (1) can be recast in terms of the objectively measurable *realizations* of returns on any portfolio j and the market portfolio M.

In [11] it was shown that the single period models of Sharpe, Lintner, and Treynor can be extended to a multiperiod world in which investors are allowed to have heterogeneous horizon periods and in which the trading of securities takes place continuously through time. These results indicate that we can generalize eq. (1) and rewrite it as

$$E(\tilde{R}_{jt}) = R_{Ft} + \beta_j[E(\tilde{R}_{Mt}) - R_{Ft}] \tag{1a}$$

where the subscript t denotes an interval of time arbitrary with respect to length and starting (and ending) dates.

It is also shown in [5] and [11] that the measure of risk, β_j, is approximately equal to the coefficient b_j in the "market model" given by:

$$\tilde{R}_{jt} = E(\tilde{R}_{jt}) + b_j\tilde{\pi}_t + \tilde{e}_{jt} \qquad j = 1,2,\ldots,N \tag{2}$$

where b_j is a parameter which may vary from security to security and $\tilde{\pi}_t$ is an unobservable "market factor" which to some extent affects the returns on all

---

5. Note that since $\sigma^2(\tilde{R}_M)$ is constant for all securities the risk of any security is just $\text{cov}(\tilde{R}_j, \tilde{R}_M)$. But since $\text{cov}(\tilde{R}_M, \tilde{R}_M) = \sigma^2(\tilde{R}_M)$ the risk of the market portfolio is just $\sigma^2(\tilde{R}_M)$, and thus we are really measuring the riskiness of any security relative to the risk of the market portfolio. Hence the systematic risk of the market portfolio, $\text{cov}(\tilde{R}_M, \tilde{R}_M)/\sigma^2(\tilde{R}_M)$, is unity, and thus the dimension of the measure of systematic risk has a convenient intuitive interpretation.

securities, and N is the total number of securities in the market.[6] The variables $\tilde{\pi}_t$ and the $\tilde{e}_{jt}$ are assumed to be independent normally distributed random variables with

$$E(\tilde{\pi}_t) = 0 \tag{3a}$$

$$E(\tilde{e}_{jt}) = 0 \qquad j = 1,2,\ldots,N \tag{3b}$$

$$\text{cov}(\tilde{\pi}_t, \tilde{e}_{jt}) = 0 \qquad j = 1,2,\ldots,N \tag{3c}$$

$$\text{cov}(\tilde{e}_{jt}, \tilde{e}_{it}) = \begin{cases} 0 & j \neq i \\ \sigma^2(\tilde{e}_j), & j = i \end{cases} \qquad j = 1,2,\ldots,N \tag{3d}$$

It is also shown in [11] that the linear relationships of eqs. (1a) and (2) hold for any length time interval as long as the returns are measured as continuously compounded rates of return. Furthermore to a close approximation the return on the market portfolio can be expressed as[7]

$$\tilde{R}_{Mt} \cong E(\tilde{R}_{Mt}) + \tilde{\pi}_t. \tag{4}$$

Since evidence given in [1, 11] indicates that the market model, given by eqs. (2) and (3a) $\cong$ (3d), holds for portfolios as well as individual securities,

---

6. The "market model" given in eqs. (2) and (3a)-(3d) is in spirit identical to the "diagonal model" analyzed in considerable detail by Sharpe [19, 22] and empirically tested by Blume [1]. The somewhat more descriptive term "market model" was suggested by Fama [5]. The "diagonal model" is usually stated as

$$\tilde{R}_{jt} = a_j + b_j\tilde{I}_t + \tilde{u}_{jt} \tag{2a}$$

where $\tilde{I}$ is some index of market returns, $\tilde{u}_j$ is a random variable uncorrelated with $\tilde{I}$, and a_j and b_j are constants. The differences in specification between (2) and (2a) are necessary in order to avoid the overspecification (pointed out by Fama [5]) which arises if one chooses to interpret the market index I as an average of security returns or as the returns on the market portfolio, M (cf., [15, 20]). That is, if $\tilde{I}$ is some average of security returns then the assumption that $\tilde{u}_j$ is uncorrelated with $\tilde{I}$ (equivalent to (3c)) cannot hold since $\tilde{I}$ contains $\tilde{u}_j$.

7. The return on the market portfolio is given by $\tilde{R}_M = \sum_{j=1}^{N} X_j\tilde{R}_j$ where X_j is the ratio of the total value of the j'th asset to the total value of all assets. Thus by substitution from (2) we have

$$\tilde{R}_{Mt} = \sum_j X_j E(\tilde{R}_{jt}) + \sum_j X_j b_j \tilde{\pi}_t + \sum_j X_j \tilde{e}_{jt}.$$

Note that the first term on the right hand side of (3) is just $E(\tilde{R}_{Mt})$, and since the market factor π is unique only up to a transformation of scale (cf. [5]) we can scale π such that $\sum_j X_j b_j = 1$ and the second term becomes just π. Furthermore by assumption, the $\tilde{e}_{jt}$ in the third term are independently distributed random variables with $E(\tilde{e}_{jt}) = 0$, and empirical evidence indicates that the $\sigma^2(\tilde{e}_j)$ are roughly of the same order of magnitude as $\sigma^2(\tilde{\pi})$ (cf. [1, 13]). Hence the variance of the last term on the right hand side of (3), given by

$$\sigma^2\left(\sum_j X_j\tilde{e}_j\right) = \sum_j X_j^2 \sigma^2(\tilde{e}_j)$$

will be extremely small since on average X_j will be equal to 1/N, and N is very large. But since the expected value of this term $\left(\sum_j X_j e_{jt}\right)$ is zero, and since we have shown its variance is extremely small, it is unlikely that it will be very different from zero at any given time. Thus to a very close approximation the returns on the market portfolio will be given by eq. (4).

we can use (2) to recast (1a) in terms of ex post returns.[8] Substituting for $E(\tilde{R}_{Mt})$ in (1a) from (4) and adding $\beta_j\tilde{\pi}_t + \tilde{e}_{jt}$ to both sides of (1a) we have

$$E(\tilde{R}_{jt}) + \beta_j\tilde{\pi}_t + \tilde{e}_{jt} \cong R_{Ft} + \beta_j[\tilde{R}_{Mt} - \tilde{\pi}_t - R_{Ft}] + \beta_j\tilde{\pi}_t + \tilde{e}_{jt}. \tag{5}$$

But from (2) we note that the left hand side of (5) is just $\tilde{R}_{jt}$. Hence (5) reduces to:[9]

$$\tilde{R}_{jt} = R_{Ft} + \beta_j[\tilde{R}_{Mt} - R_{Ft}] + \tilde{e}_{jt}. \tag{6}$$

Thus assuming that the asset pricing model is empirically valid,[10] eq. (6) says that the *realized* returns on any security or portfolio can be expressed as a linear function of its systematic risk, the *realized* returns on the market portfolio, the risk free rate and a random error, $\tilde{e}_{jt}$, which has an expected value of zero. The term R_{Ft} can be subtracted from both sides of eq. (6), and since its coefficient is unity the result is

$$\tilde{R}_{jt} - R_{Ft} = \beta_j[\tilde{R}_{Mt} - R_{Ft}] + \tilde{e}_{jt}. \tag{7}$$

The left hand side of (7) is the risk premium earned on the j'th portfolio. As long as the asset pricing model is valid this premium is equal to $\beta_j[\tilde{R}_{Mt} - R_{Ft}]$ plus the random error term $\tilde{e}_{jt}$.

The Measure of Performance.—Furthermore eq. (7) may be used directly for empirical estimation. If we wish to estimate the systematic risk of any individual security or of an unmanaged portfolio the constrained regression estimate of β_j in eq. (7) will be an efficient estimate[11] of this systematic risk. However, we must be very careful when applying the equation to managed portfolios. If the manager is a superior forecaster (perhaps because of special knowledge not available to others) he will tend to systematically select securities which realize $\tilde{e}_{jt} > 0$. Hence his portfolio will earn more than the "normal" risk premium for its level of risk. We must allow for this possibility in estimating the systematic risk of a managed portfolio.

Allowance for such forecasting ability can be made by simply not constraining the estimating regression to pass through the origin. That is, we allow for the possible existence of a non-zero constant in eq. (7) by using (8) as the estimating equation.

$$\tilde{R}_{jt} - R_{Ft} = \alpha_j + \beta_j[\tilde{R}_{Mt} - R_{Ft}] + \tilde{u}_{jt}. \tag{8}$$

8. Note that the parameters β_j (in (1a)) and b_j (in (2)) are not subscripted by t and are thus assumed to be stationary through time. Jensen [11] has shown (2) to be an empirically valid description of the behavior of the returns on the portfolios of 115 mutual funds, and Blume [1] has found similar results for the behavior of the returns on individual securities.

In addition it will be shown below that any non-stationarity which might arise from attempts to increase returns by changing the riskiness of the portfolio according to forecasts about the market factor π lead to relatively few problems.

9. Since the error of approximation in (6) is very slight (cf. [11], and note 7), we henceforth use the equality.

10. Evidence given in [11] suggests this is true.

11. In the statistical sense of the term.

The new error term $\tilde{u}_{jt}$ will now have $E(\tilde{u}_{jt}) = 0$, and should be serially independent.[12]

Thus if the portfolio manager has an ability to forecast security prices, the intercept, α_j, in eq. (8) will be positive. Indeed, it represents the average incremental rate of return on the portfolio per unit time which is due solely to the manager's ability to forecast future security prices. It is interesting to note that a naive random selection buy and hold policy can be expected to yield a zero intercept. In addition if the manager is not doing as well as a random selection buy and hold policy, α_j will be negative. At first glance it might seem difficult to do worse than a random selection policy, but such results may very well be due to the generation of too many expenses in unsuccessful forecasting attempts.

However, given that we observe a positive intercept in any sample of returns on a portfolio we have the difficulty of judging whether or not this observation was due to mere random chance or to the superior forecasting ability of the portfolio manager. Thus in order to make inferences regarding the fund manager's forecasting ability we need a measure of the standard error of estimate of the performance measure. Least squares regression theory provides an estimate of the dispersion of the sampling distribution of the intercept α_j. Furthermore, the sampling distribution of the estimate, $\hat{\alpha}_j$, is a student t distribution with $n_j - 2$ degrees of freedom. These facts give us the information needed to make inferences regarding the statistical significance of the estimated performance measure.

It should be emphasized that in estimating α_j, the measure of performance, we are explicitly allowing for the effects of risk on return as implied by the asset pricing model. Moreover, it should also be noted that if the model is valid, the particular nature of general economic conditions or the particular market conditions (the behavior of π) over the sample or evaluation period has no effect whatsoever on the measure of performance. Thus our measure of performance can be legitimately compared across funds of different risk levels and across differing time periods irrespective of general economic and market conditions.

The Effects of Non-Stationarity of the Risk Parameter.—It was pointed out earlier[13] that by omitting the time subscript from β_j (the risk parameter in eq. (8)) we were implicitly assuming the risk level of the portfolio under consideration is stationary through time. However, we know this need not be strictly true since the portfolio manager can certainly change the risk level of his portfolio very easily. He can simply switch from more risky to less risky equities (or vice versa), or he can simply change the distribution of the assets of the portfolio between equities, bonds and cash. Indeed the portfolio manager may consciously switch his portfolio holdings between equities, bonds and cash in trying to outguess the movements of the market.

This consideration brings us to an important issue regarding the meaning

---

12. If $\tilde{u}_{jt}$ were not serially independent the manager could increase his return even more by taking account of the information contained in the serial dependence and would therefore eliminate it.

13. See note 8 above.

of "forecasting ability." A manager's forecasting ability may consist of an ability to forecast the price movements of individual securities and/or an ability to forecast the general behavior of security prices in the future (the "market factor" π in our model). Therefore we want an evaluation model which will incorporate and reflect the ability of the manager to forecast the market's behavior as well as his ability to choose individual issues.

Fortunately the model outlined above will also measure the success of these market forecasting or "timing" activities as long as we can assume that the portfolio manager attempts on average to maintain a given level of risk in his portfolio. More formally as long as we can express the risk of the j'th portfolio at any time t as

$$\tilde{\beta}_{jt} = \beta_j + \tilde{\varepsilon}_{jt} \qquad (9)$$

where β_j is the "target" risk level which the portfolio manager wishes to maintain on average through time, and $\tilde{\varepsilon}_{jt}$ is a normally distributed random variable (at least partially under the manager's control) with $E(\tilde{\varepsilon}_{jt}) = 0$. The variable $\tilde{\varepsilon}_{jt}$ is the vehicle through which the manager may attempt to capitalize on any expectations he may have regarding the behavior of the market factor $\tilde{\pi}$ in the next period. For example if the manager (correctly) perceives that there is a higher probability that π will be positive (rather than negative) next period, he will be able to increase the returns on his portfolio by increasing its risk,[14] i.e., by making ε_{jt} positive this period. On the other hand he can reduce the losses (and therefore increase the average returns) on the portfolio by reducing the risk level of the portfolio (i.e., making ε_{jt} negative) when the market factor π is expected to be negative. Thus if the manager is able to forecast market movements to some extent, we should find a positive relationship between $\tilde{\varepsilon}_{jt}$ and $\tilde{\pi}_t$. We can state this relationship formally as:

$$\tilde{\varepsilon}_{jt} = a_j \tilde{\pi}_t + \tilde{w}_{jt} \qquad (10)$$

where the error term $\tilde{w}_{jt}$ is assumed to be normally distributed with $E(\tilde{w}_{jt}) = 0$. The coefficient a_j will be positive if the manager has any forecasting ability and zero if he has no forecasting ability. We can rule out $a_j < 0$, since as a conscious policy this would be irrational. Moreover, we can rule out $a_j < 0$ caused by perverse forecasting ability since this also implies knowledge of $\tilde{\pi}_t$ and would therefore be reflected in a positive a_j as long as the manager learned from past experience. Note also that eq. (10) includes no constant term since by construction this would be included in β_j in eq. (9). In addition we note that while a_j will be positive *only* if the manager can forecast $\tilde{\pi}$, its size will depend on the manager's willingness to bet on his forecasts. His willingness to bet on his forecasts will of course depend on his attitudes towards taking these kinds of risks and the certainty with which he views his estimates.

Substituting from (9) into (8) the more general model appears as

$$\tilde{R}_{jt} - R_{Ft} = \alpha_j + (\beta_j + \tilde{\varepsilon}_{jt}) \, [\tilde{R}_{Mt} - R_{Ft}] + \tilde{u}_{jt}. \qquad (11)$$

---

14. Perhaps by shifting resources out of bonds and into equities, or if no bonds are currently held, by shifting into higher risk equities or by borrowing funds and investing them in equities.

Now as long as the estimated risk parameter $\hat{\beta}$ is an unbiased estimate of the average risk level β_j, the estimated performance measure $(\hat{\alpha}_j)$ will also be unbiased. Under the assumption that the forecast error $\tilde{w}_{jt}$ is uncorrelated with π_t (which is certainly reasonable), it can be shown[15] that the expected value of the least squares estimator $\hat{\beta}_j$ is:

$$E(\hat{\beta}_j) = \frac{\text{cov}[(\tilde{R}_{jt} - R_{Ft}), (\tilde{R}_{Mt} - R_{Ft})]}{\sigma^2(\tilde{R}_M)} = \beta_j - a_j E(R_M). \qquad (12)$$

Thus the estimate of the risk parameter is biased downward by an amount given by $a_j E(\tilde{R}_M)$, where a_j is the parameter given in eq. (10) (which describes the relationship between $\tilde{\varepsilon}_{jt}$ and $\tilde{\pi}_t$). By the arguments given earlier a_j can never be negative and will be equal to zero when the manager possesses no market forecasting ability. This is important since it means that if the manager is unable to forecast general market movements we obtain an unbiased estimate of his ability to increase returns on the portfolio by choosing individual securities which are "undervalued."

However, if the manager does have an ability to forecast market movements we have seen that a_j will be positive and therefore as shown in eq. (12) the estimated risk parameter will be biased downward. This means, of course, that the estimated performance measure $(\hat{\alpha})$ will be biased upward (since the regression line must pass through the point of sample means).

Hence it seems clear that if the manager can forecast market movements at all we most certainly should see evidence of it since our techniques will tend to overstate the magnitude of the effects of this ability. That is, the performance measure, α_j, will be positive for two reasons: (1) the extra returns actually earned on the portfolio due to the manager's ability, and (2) the positive bias in the estimate of α_j resulting from the negative bias in our estimate of β_j.

III. The Data and Empirical Results

The Data.—The sample consists of the returns on the portfolios of 115 open end mutual funds for which net asset and dividend information was available in Wiesenberger's *Investment Companies* for the ten-year period 1955-64.[16] The funds are listed in Table 1 along with an identification number and code denoting the fund objectives (growth, income, etc.). Annual data were gathered for the period 1955-64 for all 115 funds and as many additional observations as possible were collected for these funds in the period 1945-54.

---

15. By substitution from (11) into the definition of the covariance and by the use of eq. (10), the assumptions of the market model given in (3a)-(3d), and the fact that $\sigma^2(\tilde{R}_M) \cong \sigma^2(\tilde{\pi})$ (see note 7).

16. The data were obtained primarily from the 1955 and 1965 editions of Wiesenberger [26], but some data not available in these editions were taken from the 1949-54 editions. Data on the College Retirement Equities Fund (not listed in Wiesenberger) were obtained directly from annual reports.

All per share data were adjusted for stock splits and stock dividends to represent an equivalent share as of the end of December 1964.

TABLE 1
LISTING OF 115 OPEN END MUTUAL FUNDS IN THE SAMPLE

ID Number	Code[1]	Fund
140	0	Aberdeen Fund
141	0	Affiliated Fund, Inc.
142	2	American Business Shares, Inc.
144	3	American Mutual Fund, Inc.
145	4	Associated Fund Trust
146	0	Atomics, Physics + Science Fund, Inc.
147	2	Axe-Houghton Fund B, Inc.
1148	2	Axe-Houghton Fund A, Inc.
2148	0	Axe-Houghton Stock Fund, Inc.
150	3	Blue Ridge Mutual Fund, Inc.
151	2	Boston Fund, Inc.
152	4	Broad Street Investing Corp.
153	3	Bullock Fund, Ltd.
155	0	Canadian Fund, Inc.
157	0	Century Shares Trust
158	0	The Channing Growth Fund
1159	0	Channing Income Fund, Inc.
2159	3	Channing Balanced Fund
160	3	Channing Common Stock Fund
162	0	Chemical Fund, Inc.
163	4	The Colonial Fund, Inc.
164	0	Colonial Growth + Energy Shares, Inc.
165	2	Commonwealth Fund—Plan C
166	2	Commonwealth Investment Co.
167	3	Commonwealth Stock Fund
168	2	Composite Fund, Inc.
169	4	Corporate Leaders Trust Fund Certificates, Series "B"
171	3	Delaware Fund, Inc.
172	0	De Vegh Mutual Fund, Inc. (No Load)
173	0	Diversified Growth Stock Fund, Inc.
174	2	Diversified Investment Fund, Inc.
175	4	Dividend Shares, Inc.
176	0	Dreyfus Fund Inc.
177	2	Eaton + Howard Balanced Fund
178	3	Eaton + Howard Stock Fund
180	3	Equity Fund, Inc.
182	3	Fidelity Fund, Inc.
184	3	Financial Industrial Fund, Inc.
185	3	Founders Mutual Fund
1186	0	Franklin Custodian Funds, Inc.—Utilities Series
2186	0	Franklin Custodial Funds, Inc.—Common Stock Series
187	3	Fundamental Investors, Inc.
188	2	General Investors Trust
189	0	Growth Industry Shares, Inc.
190	4	Group Securities—Common Stock Fund
1191	0	Group Securities—Aerospace—Science Fund
2191	2	Group Securities—Fully Administered Fund
192	3	Guardian Mutual Fund, Inc. (No Load)
193	3	Hamilton Funds, Inc.
194	0	Imperial Capital Fund, Inc.
195	2	Income Foundation Fund, Inc.

TABLE 1 (*Continued*)

ID Number	Code[1]	Fund
197	1	Incorporated Income Fund
198	3	Incorporated Investors
200	3	The Investment Company of America
201	2	The Investors Mutual, Inc.
202	3	Investors Stock Fund, Inc.
203	1	Investors Selective Fund, Inc.
205	3	Investment Trust of Boston
206	2	Istel Fund, Inc.
207	3	The Johnston Mutual Fund Inc. (No-Load)
208	3	Keystone High-Grade Common Stock Fund (S-1)
1209	4	Keystone Income Common Stock Fund (S-2)
2209	0	Keystone Growth Common Stock Fund (S-3)
210	0	Keystone Lower-Priced Common Stock Fund (S-4)
1211	1	Keystone Income Fund—(K-1)
2211	0	Keystone Growth Fund (K-2)
1212	1	The Keystone Bond Fund (B-3)
2212	1	The Keystone Bond Fund (B-4)
215	2	Loomis-Sayles Mutual Fund, Inc. (No Load)
216	0	Massachusetts Investors Growth Stock Fund, Inc.
217	3	Massachusetts Investors Trust
218	2	Massachusetts Life Fund
219	4	Mutual Investing Foundation, MIF Fund
220	2	Mutual Investment Fund, Inc.
221	0	National Investors Corporation
222	4	National Securities Stock Series
1223	0	National Securities—Growth Stock Series
2223	1	National Securities—Income Series
224	1	National Securities—Dividend Series
225	2	Nation-Wide Securities Company, Inc.
226	2	New England Fund
227	4	Northeast Investors Trust (No Load)
231	3	Philadelphia Fund, Inc.
232	4	Pine Street Fund, Inc. (No Load)
233	3	Pioneer Fund, Inc.
234	0	T. Rowe Price Growth Stock Fund, Inc. (No Load)
235	1	Puritan Fund, Inc.
236	2	The George Putnam Fund of Boston
239	2	Research Investing Corp.
240	2	Scudder, Stevens + Clark Balanced Fund, Inc. (No Load)
241	3	Scudder, Stevens + Clark Common Stock Fund, Inc. (No Load)
243	3	Selected American Shares, Inc.
244	2	Shareholders' Trust of Boston
245	3	State Street Investment Corporation (No Load)
246	2	Stein Roe + Farnham Balanced Fund, Inc. (No Load)
247	0	Stein Roe + Farnham International Fund, Inc. (No Load)
249	0	Television-Electronics Fund, Inc.
250	0	Texas Fund, Inc.
251	3	United Accumulative Fund
252	4	United Income Fund
253	0	United Science Fund
254	1	The Value Line Income Fund, Inc.
255	0	The Value Line Fund, Inc.

TABLE 1 *(Continued)*

ID Number	Code[1]	Fund
256	4	Washington Mutual Investors Fund, Inc.
257	2	Wellington Fund, Inc.
259	3	Wisconsin Fund, Inc.
260	2	Composite Bond and Stock Fund, Inc.
1261	3	Crown Western-Diversified Fund (D-2)
2261	2	Dodge + Cox Balanced Fund (No Load)
2262	2	Fiduciary Mutual Investing Company, Inc.
263	4	The Knickerbocker Fund
267	4	Southwestern Investors, Inc.
1268	2	Wall Street Investing Corporation
2268	2	Whitehall Fund, Inc.
1000	0	College Retirement Equities Fund

[1] Wiesenberger classification as to fund investment objectives: 0 = Growth, 1 = Income, 2 = Balanced, 3 = Growth-Income, 4 = Income-Growth.

For this earlier period, 10 years of complete data were obtained for 56 of the original 115 funds.

Definitions of the Variables.—The following are the exact definitions of the variables used in the estimation procedures:

$\tilde{S}_t$ = Level of the Standard and Poor Composite 500 price index[17] at the end of year t.

$\tilde{D}_t$ = Estimate of dividends received on the market portfolio in year t as measured by annual observations on the four quarter moving average[18] of the dividends paid by the companies in the composite 500 Index (stated on the same scale as the level of the S & P 500 Index).

$\tilde{R}_{Mt} = \log_e \left(\dfrac{\tilde{S}_t + \tilde{D}_t}{S_{t-1}} \right)$ = The estimated annual continuously compounded rate of return on the market portfolio M for year t.

$\tilde{NA}_{jt}$ = Per share net asset value of the j'th fund at the end of year t.

$\tilde{ID}_{jt}$ = Per share "income" dividends paid by the j'th fund during year t.

$\tilde{CG}_{jt}$ = Per share "Capital gains" distributions paid by the j'th fund during year t.

$\tilde{R}_{jt} = \log_e \left(\dfrac{\tilde{NA}_{jt} + \tilde{ID}_{jt} + \tilde{CG}_{jt}}{NA_{j,\,t-1}} \right)$ = The annual continuously compounded rate of return on the j'th fund during year t. (Adjusted for splits and stock dividends.)[19]

17. Obtained from [23]. Prior to March 1, 1957, the S & P index was based on only 90 securities (50 industrials, 20 rails and 20 utilities) and hence for the earlier period the index is a poorer estimate of the returns on the market portfolio.

18. Obtained from [23]. Since the use of this moving average introduces measurement errors in the index returns it would be preferable to use an index of the actual dividends, but such an index is not available.

19. Note that while most funds pay dividends on a quarterly basis we treat all dividends as though they were paid as of December 31 only. This assumption of course will cause the measured returns on the fund portfolios on average to be below what they would be if dividends were

r_t = Yield to maturity of a one-year government bond at the beginning of year t (obtained from Treasury Bulletin yield curves).

R_{Ft} = $\log_e(1 + r_t)$ = Annual continuously compounded risk free rate of return for year t.

n_j = The number of yearly observations of the j'th fund. $10 \leqslant n_j \leqslant 20$.

The Empirical Results.—Table 2 presents some summary statistics of the frequency distributions of the regression estimates of the parameters of eq. (8) for all 115 mutual funds using all sample data available for each fund in the period 1945-64. The table presents the mean, median, extreme values, and mean absolute deviation of the 115 estimates of α, β, r^2, and $\rho(u_t, u_{t-1})$ (the first order autocorrelation of residuals). As can be seen in the table the average intercept was —.011 with a minimum value of —.078 and a maximum value of .058. We defer a detailed discussion of the implications of these estimated intercepts for a moment.

TABLE 2

SUMMARY OF ESTIMATED REGRESSION STATISTICS FOR EQUATION (8) FOR
115 MUTUAL FUNDS USING ALL SAMPLE DATA AVAILABLE IN THE
PERIOD 1945-64. RETURNS CALCULATED NET OF ALL EXPENSES

$$\widetilde{R}_{jt} - R_{Ft} = \alpha_j + \beta_j[\widetilde{R}_{Mt} - R_{Ft}] + \widetilde{u}_{jt} \quad j = 1,2,\ldots,115 \quad (8)$$

| Item | Mean Value | Median Value | Extreme Values | | Mean Absolute Deviation* |
			Minimum	Maximum	
$\hat{\alpha}$	—.011	—.009	—0.080	0.058	.016
$\hat{\beta}$	.840	.848	0.219	1.405	.162
$\hat{r}^2$	.865	.901	0.445	0.977	.074
$\hat{\rho}(\widetilde{u}_t,\widetilde{u}_{t-1})$**	—.077	—.064	—0.688	0.575	.211
n	17.0	19.0	10.0	20.0	3.12

* Defined as $\dfrac{\sum\limits_{i=1}^{115} |\overline{X} - X_i|}{115}$.

** First order autocorrelation of residuals. The average $\hat{\rho}^2$ is .075.

Since the average value of β was only .840, on average these funds tended to hold portfolios which were less risky than the market portfolio. Thus any attempt to compare the average returns on these funds to the returns on a market index without explicit adjustment for differential riskiness would be biased against the funds. The average squared correlation coefficient, $\hat{r}^2$, was .865 and indicates in general that eq. (8) fits the data for most of the funds quite closely. The average first order autocorrelation of residuals, —.077, is quite small as expected.

Our primary concern in this paper is the interpretation of the estimated

considered to be reinvested when received, but the data needed to accomplish this are not easily available. However, the resulting bias should be quite small. In addition, the same bias is incorporated into the measured returns on the market portfolio.

TABLE 3
ESTIMATED INTERCEPTS, $\hat{\alpha}$, AND "t" VALUES FOR INDIVIDUAL MUTUAL
FUNDS CALCULATED FROM EQUATION 8 AND ALL SAMPLE DATA
AVAILABLE IN THE PERIOD 1945-64 USING NET RETURNS

Fund ID Number	$\hat{\alpha}$	$t(\hat{\alpha}) = \dfrac{\hat{\alpha}}{\sigma(\hat{\alpha})}$	Number of Observations
1191	−.0805	−1.61	13
2211	−.0783	−1.91	14
198	−.0615	−4.82	20
222	−.0520	−4.43	20
160	−.0493	−2.41	17
146	−.0425	−1.80	11
1261	−.0424	−2.47	18
2148	−.0417	−1.89	20
184	−.0416	−4.44	20
2209	−.0412	−2.07	14
224	−.0411	−1.72	13
158	−.0410	−2.08	13
164	−.0376	−1.58	13
254	−.0372	−2.17	12
2223	−.0370	−3.27	20
194	−.0346	−1.27	13
171	−.0337	−2.57	20
220	−.0332	−2.74	20
155	−.0324	−1.61	12
263	−.0320	−1.88	20
255	−.0305	−1.10	14
210	−.0299	−1.00	13
247	−.0294	−1.35	10
1223	−.0281	−1.27	18
205	−.0278	−0.60	20
167	−.0256	−1.60	11
253	−.0249	−1.25	14
189	−.0229	−1.27	18
145	−.0224	−2.16	20
231	−.0220	−1.53	14
190	−.0213	−1.53	20
193	−.0210	−1.53	16
147	−.0207	−2.51	20
173	−.0191	−0.54	12
243	−.0190	−1.82	20
187	−.0189	−2.04	20
174	−.0188	−1.75	20
2191	−.0176	−1.49	20
197	−.0157	−0.80	10
249	−.0155	−0.74	16
140	−.0155	−1.22	20
1148	−.0143	−1.02	20
182	−.0136	−1.26	20
1211	−.0134	−0.80	14
251	−.0122	−0.95	20
1159	−.0120	−0.67	11
241	−.0117	−1.04	20
216	−.0116	−0.76	20

TABLE 3 (*Continued*)

Fund ID Number	$\hat{\alpha}$	$t(\hat{\alpha}) = \dfrac{\hat{\alpha}}{\sigma(\hat{\alpha})}$	Number of Observations
219	—.0115	—1.12	20
195	—.0111	—1.23	20
180	—.0111	—1.15	20
202	—.0111	—0.86	19
1209	—.0108	—0.79	14
153	—.0103	—0.99	20
150	—.0099	—1.14	13
2159	—.0094	—0.85	13
252	—.0093	—0.85	20
188	—.0089	—0.84	20
200	—.0088	—0.75	20
239	—.0087	—0.23	10
165	—.0082	—0.52	10
235	—.0081	—0.55	17
259	—.0080	—0.53	20
2212	—.0080	—0.44	14
244	—.0080	—0.73	16
166	—.0080	—0.97	20
163	—.0076	—0.39	20
240	—.0073	—0.82	20
2261	—.0061	—0.66	20
185	—.0061	—0.69	20
217	—.0050	—0.91	20
236	—.0050	—0.46	20
1212	—.0037	—0.24	14
168	—.0022	—0.22	15
260	—.0017	—0.14	20
218	—.0014	—0.14	16
207	.0001	0.00	17
203	.0002	0.01	19
257	.0006	0.07	20
141	.0006	0.02	20
245	.0009	0.08	20
232	.0011	0.12	15
172	.0011	0.05	14
221	.0017	0.07	20
176	.0019	0.08	17
201	.0024	0.26	20
142	.0030	0.18	20
256	.0037	0.31	12
1000	.0040	0.30	12
208	.0044	0.40	14
1268	.0048	0.58	19
175	.0048	0.57	20
192	.0054	0.46	14
178	.0055	0.46	20
144	.0056	0.65	14
177	.0060	0.69	20
157	.0060	0.20	20
152	.0065	0.59	20
215	.0074	0.50	20

TABLE 3 (*Continued*)

Fund ID Number	$\hat{\alpha}$	$t(\hat{\alpha}) = \dfrac{\hat{\alpha}}{\sigma(\hat{\alpha})}$	Number of Observations
151	.0108	0.82	20
226	.0108	0.85	20
246	.0112	1.06	15
2268	.0125	1.88	17
225	.0139	1.31	20
2262	.0140	1.43	15
250	.0145	1.02	15
2186	.0164	0.65	14
206	.0165	1.09	11
227	.0170	1.40	14
169	.0191	1.89	20
267	.0198	0.99	10
234	.0219	1.21	14
162	.0219	0.86	20
233	.0232	1.34	20
1186	.0582	2.03	14

intercepts. They are presented in Table 3 along with the fund identification number and the "t" values and sample sizes. The observations are ordered from lowest to highest on the basis of $\hat{\alpha}$. The estimates range from —.0805

TABLE 4

FREQUENCY DISTRIBUTION OF ESTIMATED INTERCEPTS FOR EQUATION (8) FOR 115 MUTUAL FUNDS FOR SEVERAL TIME INTERVALS. FUND RETURNS CALCULATED BOTH NET AND GROSS OF EXPENSES

Class Interval	All Funds Entire Sample Period*		56 Funds 20 Years 1945-64	All Funds 10 Years 1955-64
	Net Returns	Gross Returns	Gross Returns	Gross Returns
	(1)	(2)	(3)	(4)
$.06 \leqslant \hat{\alpha} < .07$	0	1	0	0
$.05 \leqslant \hat{\alpha} < .06$	1	0	0	1
$.04 \leqslant \hat{\alpha} < .05$	0	0	0	0
$.03 \leqslant \hat{\alpha} < .04$	0	1	1	1
$.02 \leqslant \hat{\alpha} < .03$	3	9	2	12
$.01 \leqslant \hat{\alpha} < .02$	12	16	8	15
$.0 \leqslant \hat{\alpha} < .01$	23	21	13	31
$-.01 < \hat{\alpha} < .0$	22	29	17	12
$-.02 < \hat{\alpha} \leqslant -.01$	21	14	6	13
$-.03 < \hat{\alpha} \leqslant -.02$	12	11	5	12
$-.04 < \hat{\alpha} \leqslant -.03$	9	9	2	3
$-.05 < \hat{\alpha} \leqslant -.04$	8	1	1	1
$-.06 < \hat{\alpha} \leqslant -.05$	1	1	1	1
$-.07 < \hat{\alpha} \leqslant -.06$	1	0	0	0
$-.08 < \hat{\alpha} \leqslant -.07$	1	2	0	0
$-.09 < \hat{\alpha} \leqslant -.08$	1	0	0	1
Average $\hat{\alpha}$	—.011	—.004	—.032	—.001

* Sample sizes range from 10 to 20 annual observations among the funds.

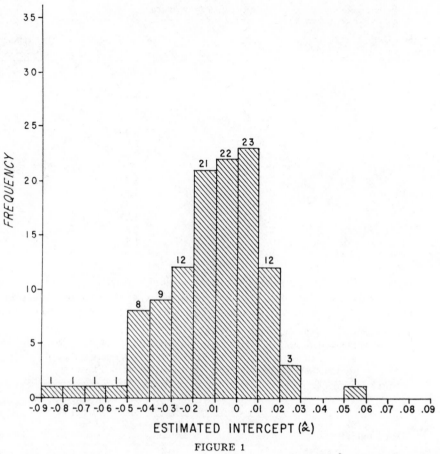

FIGURE 1

Frequency distribution (from col. (1), Table 4) of estimated intercepts ($\hat{\alpha}$) for eq. (8) for 115 mutual funds for all years available for each fund. Fund returns calculated *net* of all expenses.

to $+.0582$. Table 4 and Figures 1-4 present summary frequency distributions of these estimates (along with the distributions of the coefficients estimated for several other time intervals which will be discussed below).

In order to obtain additional information about the forecasting success of fund managers eq. (8) was also estimated using fund returns calculated before deduction of fund expenses as well as after. Fund loading charges were ignored in all cases.[20] Columns 1 and 2 of Table 4 and Figures 1 and 2 present the frequency distributions of the estimated α's obtained by using *all* sample data available for each fund. The number of observations in the estimating equation varies from 10 to 20 and the time periods are obviously not all identical. Column 1 and Figure 1 present the frequency distribution of the

20. The loading charges have been ignored since our main interest here is not to evaluate the funds from the standpoint of the individual investor but only to evaluate the fund managers' forecasting ability.

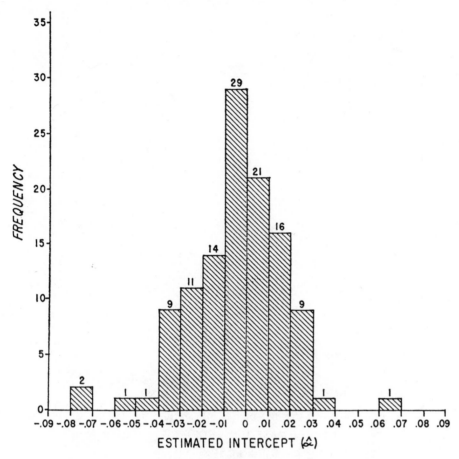

FIGURE 2

Frequency distribution (from col. (2), Table 4) of estimated intercepts ($\hat{\alpha}$) for eq. (8) for 115 mutual funds for all years available for each fund. Fund returns calculated *gross* of all management expenses.

115 intercepts estimated on the basis of fund returns calculated *net* of all expenses. Column 2 of Table 4 and Figure 2 present the frequency distributions of the estimates obtained from the fund returns calculated before deductions of management expenses (as given by Wiesenberger [26][21]).

The average value of $\hat{\alpha}$ calculated net of expenses was $-.011$ which indicates that on average the funds earned about 1.1% less per year (compounded continuously) than they should have earned given their level of systematic risk. It is also clear from Figure 1 that the distribution is skewed to the low side with 76 funds having $\hat{\alpha}_j < 0$ and only 39 with $\hat{\alpha}_j > 0$.

21. Actual expense data were available only for the 10 years 1955-64. Therefore in estimating gross returns for the years 1945-54 the expense ratio for 1955 was added (before adjustment to a continuous base) to the returns for these earlier years.

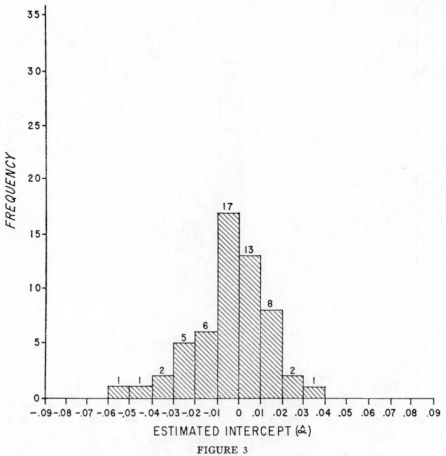

FIGURE 3

Frequency distribution (from col. (3), Table 4) of estimated intercepts ($\hat{\alpha}$) for eq. (8) for 56 mutual funds for which complete data were available in the period 1945-64. Fund returns calculated *gross* of all management expenses.

The model implies that with a random selection buy and hold policy one should expect on average to do no worse than $\alpha = 0$. Thus it appears from the preponderance of negative $\hat{\alpha}$'s that the funds are not able to forecast future security prices well enough to recover their research expenses, management fees and commission expenses.

In order to examine this point somewhat more closely the α's were also estimated on the basis of returns calculated gross of all management expenses.[22] That is $\tilde{R}_{jt}$ was taken to be

$$\tilde{R}_{jt} = \log_e \left(\frac{\tilde{NA}_{jt} + \tilde{CG}_{jt} + \tilde{ID}_{jt} + \tilde{E}_{jt}}{NA_{j,\,t-1}} \right)$$

22. It would be desirable to use the fund returns gross of all expenses including brokerage commissions as well as the management expenses. However, overall commission data are not yet available.

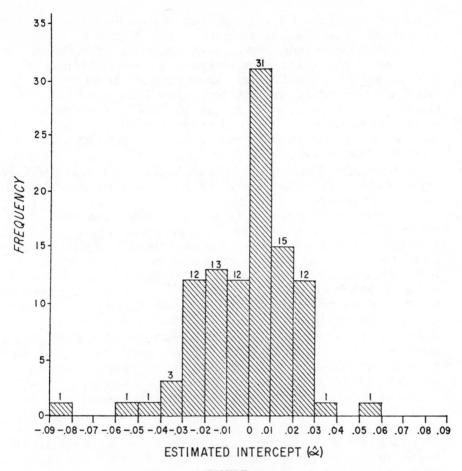

FIGURE 4

Frequency distribution (from col. (4), Table 4) of estimated intercepts ($\hat{\alpha}$) for eq. (8) for 115 mutual funds for the 10 years 1955-64. Fund returns calculated *gross* of all management expenses.

where E_{jt} is the estimated per share dollar value of all expenses except broker-age commissions, interest and taxes (the latter two of which are small) for the j'th fund in year t obtained from [26]. Now when the estimates are based on gross returns *any* forecasting success of the funds (even if not sufficient to cover their expenses) should be revealed by positive $\hat{\alpha}$'s.

The results shown in Column 2 of Table 4 indicate the average $\hat{\alpha}$ estimated from gross return data was —.004 or —.4% per year, with 67 funds for which $\hat{\alpha} < 0$ and 48 for which $\hat{\alpha} > 0$. The frequency distribution, plotted in Figure 2, is much more symmetric than the distribution obtained from the net returns. Thus it appears that on average during this 20-year period the funds were not able to increase returns enough by their trading activities to recoup even their brokerage commissions (the only expenses which were not added back to the fund returns).

In order to avoid the difficulties associated with non-identical time periods and unequal sample sizes, the measures for the 56 funds for which data were available for the entire 20-year period are summarized in Column 3 of Table 4 and Figure 3. The results indicate an average $\hat{\alpha}$ of $-.032$ with 32 funds for which $\hat{\alpha}_j < 0$ and 24 funds for which $\hat{\alpha}_j > 0$. It is very likely that part of this apparently poorer gross performance is due to the method used in approximating the expenses for the years prior to 1955. It was noted earlier that the expenses for these earlier years were assumed to be equal to the expenses for 1955. But since these expense ratios were declining in the earlier period these estimates are undoubtedly too low.

Finally in order to avoid any difficulty associated with the estimates of the expenses before 1955, the measures were estimated for each of the 115 funds using only the gross return data in the 10-year period 1955-64. The frequency distribution of the $\hat{\alpha}$'s is given in Column 4 of Table 4 and Figure 4. The average $\hat{\alpha}$ for this period was $-.001$ or $-.1\%$ per year with 55 funds for which $\hat{\alpha} < 0$ and 60 funds for which $\hat{\alpha} > 0$. The reader must be careful about placing too much significance on the seemingly larger number of funds with $\hat{\alpha} > 0$. It is well known that measurement errors (even though unbiased) in any independent variable will cause the estimated regression coefficient of that variable to be attenuated towards zero (cf. [12, chap. 6]). Since we know that there are undoubtedly some errors in the measurement of both the riskless rate and the estimated returns on the market portfolio, the coefficients $\hat{\beta}_j$ are undoubtedly slightly downward biased. This of course results in an upward bias in the estimates of the α_j since the least squares regression line must pass through the point of means.

There is one additional item which tends to bias the results slightly against the funds. That is, the model implicitly assumes the portfolio is fully invested. But since the mutual funds face stochastic inflows and outflows they must maintain a cash balance to meet them. Data presented in [8, pp. 120-127] indicate that on average the funds appear to hold about 2% of their total net assets in cash. If we assume the funds had earned the riskless rate on these assets (about 3% per year) this would increase their returns (and the average $\hat{\alpha}$) by about $(.02)(.03) = .0006$ per year. Thus the adjusted average $\hat{\alpha}$ is about $-.0004$, and it is now getting very difficult to say that this is really different from zero. Thus, let us now give explicit consideration to these questions of "significance."

The "Significance" of the Estimates.—We now address ourselves to the question regarding the statistical significance of the estimated performance measures. Table 3 presents a listing of the "t" values for the individual funds, the intercepts, and the number of observations used in obtaining each estimate. We noted earlier that it is possible for a fund manager to do worse than a random selection policy since it is easy to lower a fund's returns by unwisely spending resources in unsuccessful attempts to forecast security prices. The fact that the $\hat{\alpha}$'s shown in Table 3 and Figure 1 are skewed to the left indicate this may well be true. Likewise an examination of the "t" values given in Table 3 and plotted in Figure 5 indicates that the t values for 14 of

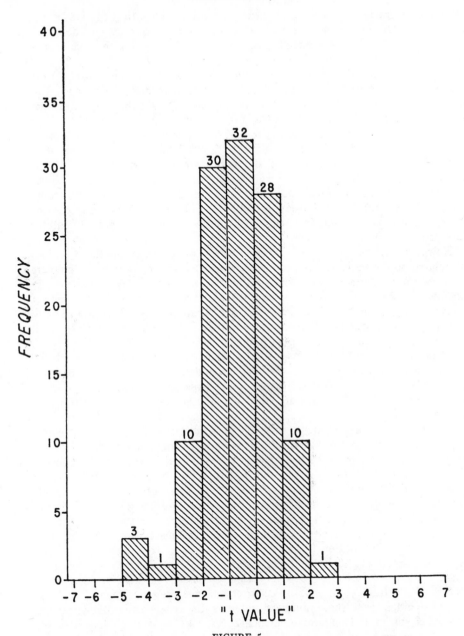

FIGURE 5

Frequency distribution (from col. (1), Table 5) of "t" values for estimated intercepts in eq. (8) for 115 mutual funds for all years available for each fund. Fund returns calculated *net* of all expenses.

the funds were less than -2 and hence are all significantly negative at the 5% level.[23] However, since we had little doubt that it was easy to do worse than a random policy we are really interested mainly in testing the significance of the large positive performance measures.

An examination of Column 3 of Table 3 reveals only 3 funds which have performance measures which are significantly positive at the 5% level. But before concluding that these funds are superior we should remember that even if all 115 of these funds had a true α equal to zero, we would expect (merely because of random chance) to find 5% of them or about 5 or 6 funds yielding t values "significant" at the 5% level. Thus, henceforth we shall concentrate on an examination of the entire frequency distribution of the estimated t values to see whether we observe more than the expected number of significant values. Unfortunately because of the differing degrees of freedom among the observations plotted in Figure 5 and Figure 6 (which contains the gross estimates), the frequency distributions are somewhat difficult to interpret.

However Figure 7 presents the frequency distribution of the t values calculated on the basis of gross returns for the 56 funds for which 20 complete years of data were available. The t value for the one-tail 2.5% level of significance is 2.1, and thus we expect $(.025)(56) = 1.4$ observations with t values greater than 2.1. We observe just one. Again we also observe a definite skewness towards the negative values and no evidence of an ability to forecast security prices. It is interesting to note that if the model is valid and if we have indeed returned all expenses to the funds, these distributions should be symmetric about zero. However, we have not added back any of the brokerage commissions and have used estimates of the expenses for the years 1945-54 which we strongly suspect are biased low. Thus the results shown in Figure 7 are not too surprising.

As mentioned above, in order to avoid some of these difficulties and to test more precisely whether or not the funds were on average able to forecast well enough to cover their brokerage expenses (even if not their other expenses) the performance measures were estimated just for the period 1955-64. The frequency distribution for the t values of the intercepts of the 115 funds estimated from gross returns is given in Figure 8 and column 4 of Table 5. All the observations have 8 degrees of freedom, and the maximum and minimum values are respectively $+2.17$ and -2.84. It seems clear from the symmetry of this distribution about zero and especially from the lack of any values greater than $+2.2$ that there is very little evidence that any of these 115 mutual funds in this 10-year period possessed substantial forecasting ability. We refrain from making a strict formal interpretation of the statistical significance of these numbers and warn the reader to do likewise since there is a substantial amount of evidence (cf. [4, 18]) which indicates the normality assumptions on the residuals, $\tilde{u}_{jt}$, of (8) may not be valid. We also point out that one could also perform chi-square goodness of fit tests on the t distributions presented, but for the same reasons mentioned above we refrain

23. The t value for 5% level of significance (one-tail) with 8 degrees of freedom (the minimum in the sample) is 1.86 and for 18 degrees of freedom (the maximum in the sample) is 1.73.

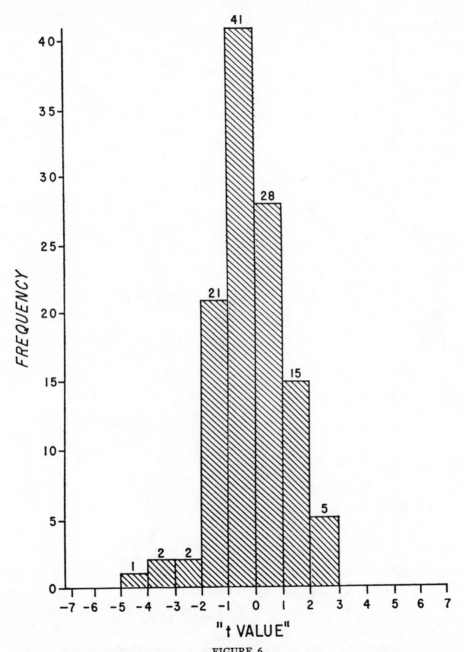

FIGURE 6

Frequency distribution (from col. (2), Table 5) of "t" values for estimated intercepts in eq. (8) for 115 mutual funds for all years available for each fund. Fund returns calculated *gross* of all expenses.

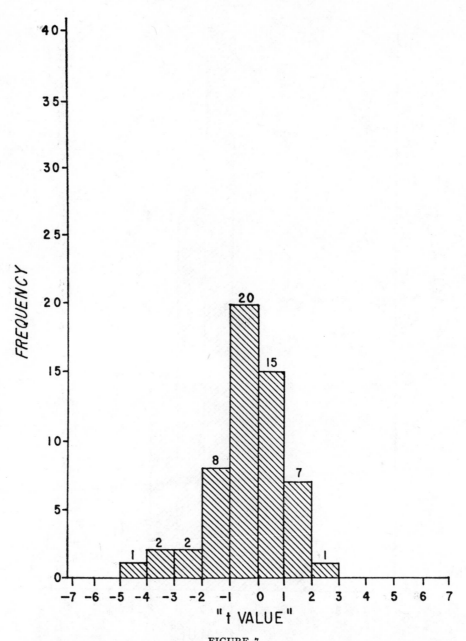

FIGURE 7
Frequency distribution (from col. (3), Table 5) of "t" values for estimated intercepts in eq. (8) for 56 mutual funds for which complete data were available in the period 1945-64. Fund returns calculated *gross* of all management expenses.

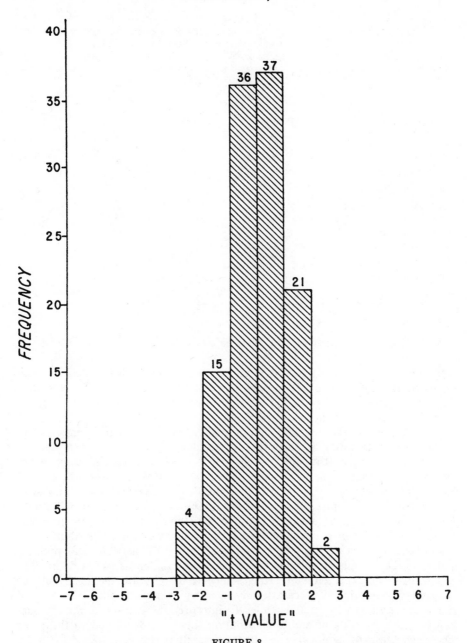

FIGURE 8

Frequency distribution (from col. (4), Table 5) of "t" values for estimated intercepts in eq. (8) for 115 mutual funds for the 10 year period 1955-64. Fund returns calculated *gross* of all management expenses.

TABLE 5
FREQUENCY DISTRIBUTION OF "t" VALUES* FOR ESTIMATED INTERCEPTS IN
EQUATION (8) FOR 115 MUTUAL FUNDS FOR SEVERAL TIME INTERVALS.
FUND RETURNS CALCULATED BOTH NET AND GROSS OF EXPENSES

Class Interval	All Funds Entire Sample Period**		56 Funds 20 Years 1945-64	All Funds 10 Years 1955-64
	Net Returns	Gross Returns	Gross Returns	Gross Returns
	(1)	(2)	(3)	(4)
$4 \leqslant t(\hat{\alpha}) < 5$	0	0	0	0
$3 \leqslant t(\hat{\alpha}) < 4$	0	0	0	0
$2 \leqslant t(\hat{\alpha}) < 3$	1	5	1	2
$1 \leqslant t(\hat{\alpha}) < 2$	10	15	7	21
$0 \leqslant t(\hat{\alpha}) < 1$	28	28	15	37
$-1 < t(\hat{\alpha}) < 0$	32	41	20	36
$-2 < t(\hat{\alpha}) \leqslant -1$	30	21	8	15
$-3 < t(\hat{\alpha}) \leqslant -2$	10	2	2	4
$-4 < t(\hat{\alpha}) \leqslant -3$	1	2	2	0
$-5 < t(\hat{\alpha}) \leqslant -4$	3	1	1	0

* Defined as $t(\hat{a}_j) = \dfrac{\hat{a}_j}{\sigma(\hat{a}_j)}$.

** Sample sizes from 10 to 20 annual observations among the funds.

from doing so. That is, if the residuals are not normally distributed the estimates of the parameters will not be distributed according to the student t distribution, and therefore it doesn't really make sense to make formal goodness of fit tests against the "t" distribution.

However, while the possible non-normality of these disturbances causes problems in attempting to perform the usual types of significance tests, it should be emphasized that the model itself is in no way crucially dependent on this assumption. Wise [27] has shown that the least squares estimates of b_j in (2) are unbiased and consistent if the disturbance terms u_j conform to the symmetric and finite mean members of the stable class of distributions. Furthermore, Fama [6] has demonstrated that the capital asset pricing model results (eq. (1)) can still be obtained in the context of these distributions. A complete discussion of the issues associated with this distributional problem and their relationship to the portfolio evaluation problem is available in [11] and will not be repeated here. It is sufficient to reiterate the fact that the normality assumption is necessary only in order to perform the strict tests of significance, and we warn the reader to interpret these tests as merely suggestive until the state of stable distribution theory is developed to the point where strict tests of significance can be legitimately performed.

It is important to note in examining the empirical results presented above that the mutual fund industry (as represented by these 115 funds) shows very little evidence of an ability to forecast security prices. Furthermore there is surprisingly little evidence that indicates any individual funds in the sample might be able to forecast prices. These results are even stronger when one realizes that the biases in the estimates[24] all tend to either exaggerate the magnitude of any forecasting ability which might exist[25] or tend to show evidence of forecasting ability where none exists.

IV. CONCLUSION

The evidence on mutual fund performance discussed above indicates not only that these 115 mutual funds were *on average* not able to predict security prices well enough to outperform a buy-the-market-and-hold policy, but also that there is very little evidence that any *individual* fund was able to do significantly better than that which we expected from mere random chance. It is also important to note that these conclusions hold *even* when we measure the fund returns gross of management expenses (that is assume their bookkeeping, research, and other expenses except brokerage commissions were obtained free). Thus on average the funds apparently were not quite successful enough in their trading activities to recoup even their brokerage expenses.

It is also important to remember that we have not considered in this paper the question of diversification. Evidence reported elsewhere (cf. Jensen [11]) indicates the funds on average have done an excellent job of minimizing the "insurable" risk born by their shareholders. Thus the results reported here should not be construed as indicating the mutual funds are not providing a socially desirable service to investors; that question has not been addressed here. The evidence does indicate, however, a pressing need on the part of the funds themselves to evaluate much more closely both the costs and the benefits of their research and trading activities in order to provide investors with maximum possible returns for the level of risk undertaken.

REFERENCES

1. Marshall Blume. "The Assessment of Portfolio Performance," (unpublished Ph.D. dissertation, University of Chicago, 1968).
2. Kalman J. Cohen and Jerry A. Pogue. "An Empirical Evaluation of Alternative Portfolio Selection Models," *Journal of Business,* XXXX (April, 1967), 166-193.
3. Peter Dietz. *Pension Funds: Measuring Investment Performance.* New York: The Free Press, 1966.
4. Eugene Fama. "The Behavior of Stock-Market Prices," *Journal of Business,* XXXVII (January, 1965), 34-105.
5. ——————. "Risk, Return and Equilibrium: Some Clarifying Comments," *Journal of Finance,* XXIII (March, 1968), 29-40.
6. ——————. "Risk, Return, and General Equilibrium in a Stable Paretian Market," (unpublished manuscript, University of Chicago, 1967).
7. Donald E. Farrar. *The Investment Decision Under Uncertainty.* Englewood Cliffs, N.J.: Prentice Hall, Inc., 1962.
8. Irwin Friend, F. E. Brown, Edward S. Herman and Douglas Vickers. *A Study of Mutual Funds.* Washington, D.C.: U.S. Government Printing Office, 1962.
9. —————— and Douglas Vickers. "Portfolio Selection and Investment Performance," *Journal of Finance,* XX (September, 1965), 391-415.
10. Ira Horowitz. "A Model for Mutual Fund Evaluation," *Industrial Management Review,* VI (Spring, 1965), 81-92.

24. Except for the assumption of a fully invested portfolio which we **have** allowed for by assuming cash earned interest at the riskless rate.

25. See Section II.

11. Michael C. Jensen. "Risk, the Pricing of Capital Assets, and the Evaluation of Investment Portfolios," (unpublished preliminary draft of Ph.D. Thesis, University of Chicago, July, 1967).

12. J. Johnston. *Econometric Methods*. New York: McGraw Hill, Inc., 1963.

13. Benjamin F. King. "Market and Industry Factors in Stock Price Behavior," *Journal of Business,* XXXIX, Part II (January, 1966), 139-190.

14. John Lintner. "The Valuation of Risk Assets and the Selection of Risky Investments in Stock Portfolios and Capital Budgets," *Review of Economics and Statistics,* XLVII (February, 1965), 13-37.

15. ————. "Security Prices, Risk, and Maximal Gains from Diversification," *Journal of Finance,* XX (December, 1965), 587-616.

16. Benoit Mandelbrot. "The Variation of Certain Speculative Prices," *Journal of Business,* XXXVI (October, 1963), 394-419.

17. H. M. Markowitz. *Portfolio Selection: Efficient Diversification of Investments.* Cowles Foundation Monograph No. 16. New York: John Wiley & Sons, Inc., 1959.

18. Richard Roll. "The Efficient Market Model Applied to U.S. Treasury Bills," (unpublished Ph.D. dissertation, University of Chicago, 1968).

19. William F. Sharpe. "A Simplified Model for Portfolio Analysis," *Management Science* (January, 1963), 277-293.

20. ————. "Capital Asset Prices: A Theory of Market Equilibrium Under Conditions of Risk," *Journal of Finance,* XIX (September, 1964), 425-442.

21. ————. "Mutual Fund Performance," *Journal of Business* XXXIX, Part 2 (January, 1966), 119-138.

22. ————. "Linear Programming Algorithm for Mutual Fund Portfolio Selection," *Management Science,* XIII (March, 1967), pp. 499-510.

23. Standard and Poor's. *Trade and Securities Statistics: Security Price Index Record.* (Orange, Conn.: Standard and Poor's Corporation, 1964).

24. Jack L. Treynor. "How to Rate Management of Investment Funds," *Harvard Business Review,* XLIII (January-February, 1965), 63-75.

25. ————. "Toward a Theory of Market Value of Risky Assets," (unpublished manuscript, undated).

26. Arthur Wiesenberger. *Investment Companies.* New York: Arthur Wiesenberger & Company, 1955 and 1965.

27. John Wise. "Linear Estimators for Linear Regression Systems Having Infinite Variances," (unpublished paper presented at the Berkeley-Stanford Mathematical Economics Seminar, October, 1963).

13

RELATIONSHIP BETWEEN INSIDER TRADING AND RATES OF RETURN FOR NYSE COMMON STOCKS, 1960–66

Shannon P. Pratt and Charles W. DeVere

This report is on the relationship between insider trading and subsequent market performance. In many respects it is academically very much a lightweight topic compared with anything we have heard at this seminar up to this point, but I think it is interesting. Victor Niederhoffer summarized the literature and research that has been done in this area at the meeting of this seminar six months ago, so I will not review the previous work but get on to what we are doing now.

I will divide my report to you into three parts, the first of which will be a description of the data file that we are creating and part of which we used in the study you will hear about this morning. The second part will be the methodology of the inquiry I'm presently reporting. The third part will be the findings.

I. DESCRIPTION OF DATA FILE

The data file in computer readable form starts with 1960 and is intended to cover every transaction by insiders in every stock on the New York Stock Exchange. We may go on and do stocks on the American Exchange and over-the-counter stocks as well. At present we have on file 52,000 transactions completely punched and verified. These 52,000 transactions constitute insider trading for about 800 companies, or approximately two-thirds of the New York Stock Exchange. That is the population on which the report of this morning is based. We had hoped to have data on the entire New York Stock Exchange punched and analyzed in time for the report at this meeting, but we simply didn't get that far with the file. When we got to the point where we didn't have too much lead time left, we had to go ahead and analyze on the two-thirds of the Exchange that was completed.

The file contains the company name and a company number which we have assigned. It includes the kinds of stock in which the transaction was made and, from 1962, the date of the transaction. Prior to 1962, we had

Unpublished paper presented to the Seminar on the Analysis of Security Prices, May, 1968, University of Chicago. Printed by permission of the authors.

Financial support for this research was provided by Black & Co., Inc. of Portland, Oregon.

available only the month of the transaction. The file includes an insider number which identifies not only the individual but also whether he is an officer, a director or a beneficial owner of ten per cent or more of the stock, or some combination of those things.

This report confines itself entirely to common stock transactions. The file also includes the character of the transaction, that is, whether it is an option purchase, or a gift, etc. This was an interesting classification, because in working through the insider report by the Securities and Exchange Commission, we found a lot of transactions which didn't have a special transaction code assigned to them in the report, but which were described in footnotes. In poring over these data we came up with several additional classifications of the character of transactions in addition to the ones that they identified. We came up with 13 categories altogether, plus the fourteenth one, "too miscellaneous to classify."

The file also includes the nature of the ownership, the number of shares that the insider purchased during the month, the number of shares the insider disposed of during the month, and the final balance held at the end of the month. For the 52,000 transactions that we now have recorded and verified, we believe that our machine readable file is considerably more accurate than the printed SEC insider report.

II. METHODOLOGY OF THE INQUIRY

Essentially we started on January 1, 1960, and we go through June 30, 1966. We are regarding for the purpose of this inquiry only open-market transactions. Option purchases and transactions of character other than open-market cash transactions are totally ignored. Furthermore, if the insider reported out of sequence, that is ignored on the basis that we would not have had the information in time for it to be useful to us. Also, we regarded only owners in categories one through three as defined by the SEC, and considered only those situations in which the aggregate purchases or sales for an insider were equal to or greater than 100 shares.

In deriving the "insider buy signals" and "insider sell signals," we looked at insider trading data for only one month at a time. We counted the number of different insiders that bought, the number of different insiders that sold, and the number of different insiders that did both. We kept a count of those companies where there was one, two, three, four, five or more than five insiders either buying or selling. For the purpose of this study, the only situations we considered were those in which three or more insiders made cash purchases and none sold. In other words, we did not net out the number of buyers against sellers to get a net consensus, so to speak. We called this the "unanimity principle." The transactions all had to be going the same way. Then we used the shadow reflection of that, three or more insiders selling during a particular month and none buying.

There were a few situations in which one insider both bought and sold. Those cases we ignored, because we believe that in most of those situations somebody who has some relationship with the company is making a trading market in the stock, and we felt that that kind of transaction should not affect our unanimity principle.

Those, then, were our selection criteria. Every time during the six-year period January, 1960 through December, 1965 that we found a company which met either the "insider buying" or "insider selling" criterion, we counted that an action signal, either a "buy signal" or a "sell signal" as we called them. However, we used what we called a "six-months skip period," that is, if we got an action signal on a stock in one month then that stock was ineligible to give us another signal (that is, to be hypothetically purchased by us) for another six months. The result is that, within any six-month time period, we do not have the same stock considered twice.

At the point when we got the signal, we computed the rate of return on that stock forward through the end of the tape, up through June of 1966, using for price and investment performance data the University of Chicago Investment Performance Relative Tape. That is why this particular study terminates in the middle of 1966, because we wanted to have the same kind of price data for the entire analysis.

III. FINDINGS

By our selection criteria, during the six-year period, we had 211 so-called buy signals and 272 so-called sell signals. We presume that the main reason for the considerably larger number of sell signals is that we totally ignored option purchases. The essence of the results is contained in Table I.

"No lag" in Table I means that we assumed that we bought the stock at the end of the month during which the insider trading took place. In other words, for insider transactions that took place in January, we assumed we made the purchase of that stock on January 31. As a practical matter, that would have been difficult, because only a small portion of the transactions actually would have been reported to the SEC and the Stock Exchange by that time.

"One-month lag" means that we assumed that the purchase of the stock at the end of the month following the month in which the transaction took place. For example, for insider transactions that took place in January, it assumes we made the purchase on February 28.

"Two-months lag" assumes that for insider transactions that took place in January we acted on March 31. By that time everybody in the United States who was interested had had the complete SEC insider report in his hands for two weeks. Anyone would have had time to look it over and act on it if he so chose.

The rates of return shown in Table I are simply average investment performance relatives minus one. The investment performance relative for any individual stock for any number of months is the product of the investment performance relatives for that stock for those months as they appear on the Chicago tapes, that is, assuming the reinvestment of all dividends and other distributions of value in the stock which issued them.

Consider, for example, the 12-month holding period in the "no lag" column. This says that, for all of those approximately 200 buy signals that we got, if we added up the investment performance relative for the 12-month period following the time that we got the buy signal in each case, and simply divided that sum by the number of stocks, our average investment per-

TABLE I

COMPARATIVE INVESTMENT PERFORMANCE OF STOCK BOUGHT
BY 3 OR MORE INSIDERS VS. STOCKS SOLD BY 3 OR MORE INSIDERS

No. Mos. Held	No Lag "Buy" Group	"Sell" Group	1-Mo. Lag "Buy" Group	"Sell" Group	2-Mo. Lag "Buy" Group	"Sell" Group
1	.034	.006	.027	.003	.013	.000
2	.063	.009	.038	.003	.031	.011
3	.074	.009	.060	.014	.031	.018
4	.098	.022	.060	.020	.044	.026
5	.099	.029	.076	.029	.067	.037
6	.116	.038	.100	.039	.093	.041
7	.141	.046	.128	.042	.115	.055
8	.171	.049	.149	.055	.141	.070
9	.192	.061	.177	.069	.161	.084
10	.220	.074	.197	.084	.191	.091
11	.240	.088	.227	.091	.209	.093
12	.271	.096	.243	.094	.240	.099
13	.284	.099	.275	.099	.254	.098
14	.315	.107	.290	.100	.262	.093
15	.329	.108	.298	.097	.265	.100
16	.338	.103	.302	.104	.284	.101
17	.343	.111	.321	.106	.296	.110
18	.362	.113	.331	.115	.325	.112
19	.366	.120	.361	.116	.345	.130
20	.398	.122	.385	.133	.338	.134
21	.423	.140	.378	.137	.337	.127
22	.416	.146	.376	.130	.355	.137
23	.413	.136	.394	.140	.367	.166
24	.431	.145	.407	.170	.382	.181
25	.447	.176	.425	.185	.420	.188
26	.463	.192	.464	.193	.444	.206
27	.500	.200	.489	.209	.486	.203
28	.524	.217	.532	.209	.533	.226
29	.567	.215	.573	.232	.548	.232
30	.608	.238	.590	.237	.592	.271
31	.629	.245	.634	.277	.613	.302
32	.670	.286	.656	.307	.631	.337
33	.695	.318	.675	.342	.617	.344
34	.711	.354	.668	.344	.597	.349
35	.707	.356	.655	.350	.622	.369
36	.685	.361	.683	.369	.586	.443

formance relative was 1.271 for those stocks which three or more insiders purchased, or an arithmetic average rate of return of 27.1 per cent. Our investment performance relative average was 1.096 for all of those stocks which three or more insiders sold, or an arithmetic average rate of return of only 9.6 per cent.

If we didn't act on this until a month later, you can see by looking in the one-month lag column on the 12-month holding period line that we lost a little of our advantage. That is to say, if we had known about it sooner, our probability would have been a bit higher. If we waited until the end of the month following the month in which the transactions occurred and bought all those for which we had a buy signal in the previous month, our average performance relative for the one-year period was 1.243. If we bought all those which had a sell signal in the previous month, the average investment performance relative would have been 1.094, or a difference of .149 (1.243 — 1.094) between the average performance of the "buy" group and the average performance of the "sell" group.

If we waited another month before buying, until the published report was actually out and in everyone's hands for two weeks, the average investment performance relative was 1.240 for those the insiders had been buying and 1.099 for those which the insiders had been selling.

In other words, the figures for each set of holding periods of the various time lengths represent the average investment performance relatives for holding periods of that length of time. Looking up and down the table at the figures for holding periods of various durations you can see that there are rather substantial differences in average investment performance in all cases between those stocks where three or more insiders have bought and none sold and those stocks which three or more insiders have sold and none bought.

Furthermore, I think it is interesting that this is not just a short-term phenomenon, but that the rather substantial difference in invesment performance between these groups of stocks is fairly persistent. The "insider buy" group continues to outperform the "insider sell" group for over a year after the insider trading takes place.

These are arithmetic averages, and we have computed geometric averages so far only for six-month holding periods. Naturally, the geometric averages would be a bit lower and, since these transactions are partly sequential and partly overlapping, the actual investment performance that one would have been able to achieve following these mechanical procedures would have been slightly less than that shown by the arithmetic averages, somewhere in between the arithmetic and geometric averages.

Table II is constructed from Table I, with the figures transformed to an annualized basis by the formula.

$$AR = (1 + R)^{\frac{12}{m}} - 1$$

where:

AR = annualized rate of return
R = average rate of return for the period (average of the investment performance relatives of the individual stocks, minus one)
m = number of months in the holding period

TABLE II

COMPARATIVE INVESTMENT PERFORMANCE OF STOCK BOUGHT
BY 3 OR MORE INSIDERS VS. STOCK SOLD BY 3 OR MORE INSIDERS
ANNUALIZED RATES OF RETURN
(Not Including Commission)

No. Mos. Held	No Lag		1-Mo. Lag		2-Mo. Lag	
	"Buy" Group	*"Sell" Group*	*"Buy" Group*	*"Sell" Group*	*"Buy" Group*	*"Sell" Group*
1	0.494	0.074	0.377	0.037	0.168	0.000
2	0.443	0.055	0.251	0.018	0.201	0.068
3	0.331	0.036	0.262	0.057	0.130	0.074
4	0.324	0.067	0.191	0.061	0.138	0.080
5	0.254	0.071	0.192	0.071	0.168	0.091
6	0.245	0.077	0.210	0.080	0.195	0.084
7	0.254	0.080	0.229	0.073	0.205	0.096
8	0.267	0.074	0.232	0.084	0.219	0.107
9	0.264	0.082	0.243	0.093	0.220	0.114
10	0.269	0.089	0.241	0.102	0.233	0.110
11	0.264	0.096	0.250	0.100	0.230	0.102
12	0.271	0.096	0.243	0.094	0.240	0.099
13	0.260	0.091	0.251	0.091	0.232	0.090
14	0.265	0.091	0.244	0.085	0.221	0.079
15	0.256	0.086	0.232	0.077	0.207	0.079
16	0.244	0.076	0.219	0.077	0.206	0.075
17	0.231	0.077	0.217	0.074	0.201	0.076
18	0.229	0.074	0.210	0.075	0.206	0.073
19	0.218	0.074	0.215	0.072	0.206	0.080
20	0.223	0.072	0.216	0.078	0.191	0.078
21	0.223	0.078	0.201	0.076	0.181	0.071
22	0.209	0.077	0.190	0.069	0.180	0.073
23	0.198	0.069	0.189	0.071	0.177	0.083
24	0.196	0.070	0.186	0.082	0.176	0.087
25	0.194	0.081	0.185	0.085	0.183	0.086
26	0.192	0.084	0.192	0.085	0.185	0.090
27	0.197	0.084	0.194	0.088	0.192	0.086
28	0.198	0.088	0.201	0.085	0.201	0.091
29	0.204	0.084	0.206	0.090	0.198	0.090
30	0.209	0.089	0.204	0.089	0.204	0.101
31	0.208	0.089	0.209	0.099	0.203	0.108
32	0.212	0.099	0.208	0.106	0.201	0.115
33	0.212	0.106	0.206	0.113	0.191	0.114
34	0.209	0.113	0.198	0.110	0.180	0.111
35	0.201	0.110	0.189	0.108	0.180	0.114
36	0.190	0.108	0.189	0.110	0.166	0.130

Table III is also constructed from Table I, except that the figures in Table I are adjusted by subtracting .02, assumed to be the average round trip commissions, before applying the formula used to construct Table I.

TABLE III

COMPARATIVE INVESTMENT PERFORMANCE OF STOCK BOUGHT
BY 3 OR MORE INSIDERS VS. STOCK SOLD BY 3 OR MORE INSIDERS
ANNUALIZED RATES OF RETURN
(Including Commission)

No. Mos. Held	No Lag "Buy" Group	No Lag "Sell" Group	1-Mo. Lag "Buy" Group	1-Mo. Lag "Sell" Group	2-Mo. Lag "Buy" Group	2-Mo. Lag "Sell" Group
1	0.182	−0.156	0.087	−0.186	−0.081	−0.215
2	0.287	−0.064	0.113	−0.098	0.068	−0.053
3	0.234	−0.043	0.170	−0.024	0.045	−0.008
4	0.253	0.006	0.125	0.000	0.074	0.018
5	0.200	0.022	0.140	0.022	0.117	0.041
6	0.201	0.036	0.166	0.038	0.151	0.042
7	0.216	0.045	0.192	0.038	0.168	0.061
8	0.235	0.044	0.200	0.053	0.187	0.076
9	0.236	0.055	0.215	0.066	0.192	0.086
10	0.245	0.065	0.216	0.077	0.209	0.086
11	0.242	0.074	0.228	0.078	0.208	0.080
12	0.251	0.076	0.223	0.074	0.220	0.079
13	0.241	0.073	0.233	0.073	0.214	0.072
14	0.248	0.074	0.227	0.068	0.204	0.062
15	0.240	0.070	0.217	0.061	0.192	0.064
16	0.230	0.062	0.205	0.062	0.192	0.060
17	0.218	0.063	0.204	0.060	0.188	0.063
18	0.217	0.061	0.198	0.062	0.194	0.060
19	0.206	0.062	0.204	0.060	0.195	0.068
20	0.212	0.060	0.205	0.066	0.180	0.067
21	0.213	0.067	0.191	0.065	0.170	0.060
22	0.200	0.067	0.181	0.059	0.171	0.062
23	0.189	0.059	0.180	0.061	0.168	0.074
24	0.188	0.061	0.178	0.072	0.167	0.077
25	0.186	0.072	0.177	0.076	0.175	0.077
26	0.184	0.076	0.185	0.076	0.177	0.082
27	0.190	0.076	0.186	0.080	0.185	0.078
28	0.191	0.080	0.194	0.077	0.194	0.084
29	0.198	0.077	0.200	0.083	0.192	0.083
30	0.203	0.082	0.198	0.082	0.198	0.094
31	0.202	0.082	0.204	0.093	0.198	0.101
32	0.207	0.092	0.203	0.099	0.196	0.109
33	0.206	0.099	0.201	0.107	0.186	0.107
34	0.204	0.107	0.193	0.104	0.174	0.106
35	0.196	0.104	0.184	0.103	0.175	0.108
36	0.185	0.103	0.185	0.105	0.161	0.125

Table III suggests that an "optimal" average holding period for purchases based on insider buying, with a two-month lag, might be about 12 months, where the average rate of return after commissions was 22%.

Table IV shows a more detailed analysis of the data for the six-month holding periods. (The decision to do the detailed analysis on the six-month holding periods was made before we had the data that suggested that holding periods of about 12 months might be closer to "optimal," and we hope to do a similar analysis for 12-month holding periods at some time in the near future.)

The X's in Table IV represent the arithmetic average of the investment performance relatives following unlagged purchases, for six-month holding periods, minus one. In other words, for the "buy" group, adding up the 211 investment performance relatives for six-month holding periods and dividing by 211, we got 1.116. The .248 in parenthesis is simply the 1.116 squared, minus one. That is an approximation of the annualized rate of return, assuming that you turned your portfolio over every six months.

For the other group, where three or more insiders were selling, the average investment performance relative in the following six months was 1.038, or on an annualized basis, about 7.8 per cent. The difference in the parentheses is simply the difference between the annualized figure for the "buy" group and the annualized figure for the "sell" group. Table V is constructed the same as Table IV, except that the assumed purchases are lagged two months from the end of the month in which the relevant insider transactions occurred.

Here, then, we seem to have identified two groups of stocks which have rather substantially different expected rates of return. The next question is, how about some measure of the risk, or the dispersion, of these results. Usually, when we identify two groups of stock which do have substantially different returns from each other on the average, the higher return group turns out to have some rather bad characteristics in terms of the dispersion of the results. We were delighted to find that the standard deviation of the investment performance relatives was almost the same for the two groups. There is really very little difference. There is even less difference when we compare the coefficients of variation.

The right-hand portions of Tables IV and V show similar analyses on the basis of the geometric means. What we have called the "standard deviation about the geometric mean" is simply the standard deviation of the natural logarithms of the investment performance relatives.

We also broke down the results on the basis of the relative frequencies of occurrences of returns of different sizes on the basis of standard deviations from the mean. In the buy group, about 58 per cent are below the mean and 42 per cent are above the mean. I think that is fairly typical. In the sell group, interestingly enough, only about 51 per cent are below the mean and 49 per cent are above the mean, but of course it is a far lower mean. In the buy group, about 74 per cent are within plus or minus one standard deviation of the mean, and, in the sell group, about 75 per cent are within plus or minus one standard deviation of the mean. Although we have not detailed them in Table V, distributions of rates of return following two-month lagged purchases follow a similar pattern.

In Table VI we have given the exact distribution of the so-called buy and sell signals throughout the six-year time period. Something that is pleasing about that is that they seem to be fairly randomly distributed

TABLE IV

Average Investment Performance, Jan. '60–June '66
for Stocks Meeting "$\geq$ 3 Buy" and "$\geq$ 3 Sell" Insider Trading Criteria
Purchases Made at End of Month in Which Signal Received
6-Month Holding Periods

	Sample Size	$\bar{X}^{1,2}$	$S.D.(\bar{X})$	$C.V.(\bar{X})$	$\bar{G}^{1,2}$	$S.D.(\bar{G})$	$C.V.(\bar{G})$
"Buy" Group	211	1.116(.248)	.221	.198	1.090(.188)	.193	.173
"Sell" Group	272	1.038(.078)	.212	.204	1.018(.036)	.200	.193
Difference		.078(.170)			.072(.152)		

Relative frequency of results on basis of standard deviations from mean:

	≤3	$3\leq2$	$2\leq1$	$1\leq0$	$0\geq1$	$1\geq2$	$2\leq3$	≥3
Deviations from $\bar{X}$:								
"Buy" Group	0	.010	.124	.442	.285	.114	.010	.019
"Sell" Group	0	.011	.132	.368	.375	.088	.015	.011
Deviations from $\bar{G}$:								
"Buy" Group	.005	.019	.119	.360	.351	.123	.014	.010
"Sell" Group	.004	.026	.118	.324	.415	.092	.015	.007

[1] Figures in parentheses represent rates of return on an annualized basis.
[2] Differences between means statistically significant at level of .001.

TABLE V

AVERAGE INVESTMENT PERFORMANCE, MAR. '60–JUNE '66

FOR STOCKS MEETING "$\geq$ 3 BUY" AND "$\geq$ 3 SELL" INSIDER TRADING CRITERIA

PURCHASES MADE AT END OF MONTH 2 MONTHS FOLLOWING MONTH IN WHICH SIGNAL RECEIVED

6-MONTH HOLDING PERIODS

	Sample Size	$\overline{X}^{1,2}$	$S.D.(\overline{X})$	$C.V.(\overline{X})$	$\overline{G}^{1,2}$	$S.D.(\overline{G})$	$C.V.(\overline{G})$
"Buy" Group	205	1.093(.195)	.229	.209	1.068(.140)	.202	.189
"Sell" Group	262	1.041(.084)	.197	.190	1.022(.044)	.192	.188
Difference		.052(.111)			.046(.096)		

Relative frequency of results on basis of standard deviations from mean closely comparable to distribution shown in Table IV.

[1] Figures in parentheses represent rates of return on an annualized basis.
[2] Differences between means statistically significant at level of .001.

through time and fairly evenly distributed. That is, it is a rare month when we don't have any signals at all on the basis of this criterion, and the most that we have at any time is nine on the buy side and ten on the sell side.

We haven't done any real analysis on the timing of insider buying and selling relative to market, but in looking it over lightly, it appears that insiders might have had a little better timing relative to the market than the folklore of Wall Street gives them credit for. However, the main things shown by Table VI is that these signals were fairly well distributed through time.

We made other breakdowns besides these, but they are not shown in the tables. For example, we broke it down by "large" as opposed to "small" companies. Our criterion for what we called large companies is an arbitrary one. Our so-called large companies are the 100 companies for which the odd-lot trading data for the individual companies is reported monthly. (We happen to have the data broken down that way for other purposes.)

It was surprising to us at first to see that the average investment performance of the large companies following an "insider buy" signal was better than the average of the smaller companies. We hadn't quite expected this, because we thought, in a small company, if there are only a few insiders

TABLE VI

Time Distribution of "Buy Group" and "Sell Group" Signals

Month	Number "Buy" Signals	Number "Sell" Signals	Month	Number "Buy" Signals	Number "Sell" Signals	Month	Number "Buy" Signals	Number "Sell" Signals
Jan. 60	7	7	Jan. 62	6	1	Jan. 64	8	6
Feb. 60	7	3	Feb. 62	1	2	Feb. 64	6	6
Mar. 60	3	1	Mar. 62	2	0	Mar. 64	2	6
Apr. 60	2	0	Apr. 62	4	0	Apr. 64	3	1
May 60	1	2	May 62	7	1	May 64	6	4
Jun. 60	1	6	Jun. 62	7	2	Jun. 64	7	4
July 60	4	4	July 62	1	1	July 64	1	5
Aug. 60	4	4	Aug. 62	1	4	Aug. 64	2	4
Sept. 60	0	1	Sept. 62	2	2	Sept. 64	4	4
Oct. 60	1	2	Oct. 62	4	0	Oct. 64	2	2
Nov. 60	2	1	Nov. 62	2	4	Nov. 64	5	3
Dec. 60	3	8	Dec. 62	2	2	Dec. 64	7	5
Jan. 61	5	5	Jan. 63	2	8	Jan. 65	9	10
Feb. 61	6	7	Feb. 63	4	2	Feb. 65	2	7
Mar. 61	1	8	Mar. 63	4	7	Mar. 65	0	4
Apr. 61	1	7	Apr. 63	2	8	Apr. 65	1	7
May 61	2	8	May 63	1	3	May 65	0	7
Jun. 61	3	2	Jun. 63	2	3	Jun. 65	8	2
July 61	2	4	July 63	3	4	July 65	2	1
Aug. 61	0	8	Aug. 63	6	7	Aug. 65	2	4
Sept. 61	1	3	Sept. 63	4	1	Sept. 65	2	8
Oct. 61	0	2	Oct. 63	4	9	Oct. 65	6	8
Nov. 61	4	3	Nov. 63	5	2	Nov. 65	3	5
Dec. 61	4	3	Dec. 63	3	6	Dec. 65	4	6

and several of them are buying, that would probably be more significant than if it were a large company with a lot of insiders and only a few of them buying. But then we got to thinking about it. We were basing this study on a "unanimity principle," and we said that there had to be no insiders selling. This meant that in a large company with, say, 40 to 50 insiders, there would be a much higher probability ex ante of one or more selling and we excluded the company from our signals if even a single one sold. In retrospect, we felt perhaps that was the explanation for large companies doing better by these criteria than the small companies.

We also broke down the study by those situations where you had exactly three insiders buying and none selling, exactly four, exactly five and six or more. Then we did breakdowns for exactly three and for four or more. We found that those situations where exactly three bought and none sold did better than those of four or more. These, I think, would tend to be the smaller companies. Those two findings are not antithetical to each other when you consider them, I think. They might seem so at first but they are really not.

Also, before we put these results together as presented here, we ran the study on the basis of two groups of 26,000 transactions each. We did that because we wanted to study the pattern for one group, run the same study on another group, and see whether the pattern was the same. Indeed it was. The magnitudes were somewhat different, but the pattern was consistent.

As a matter of fact, for all the different breakdowns that we made (by different numbers of insiders, by size of company, and between the two arbitrarily divided groups), in all situations in which we had a sample size of eight or more, the pattern of results was the same as the pattern of results for the over-all study. Of course, when we got down to smaller sample sizes for these various breakdowns, the average magnitudes varied quite a bit.

These findings tend to suggest that knowledge of insider trading is useful in getting some kind of an idea of the possible future performance of the stock in some kind of probabilistic sense. We believe we have identified two groups of situations here, those characterized by insider buying and those characterized by insider selling, one of which has a much higher probability of success in the future than the other.

Furthermore, these results tend to support previous results, particularly those reported by Victor Niederhoffer here at the last session. Our methodology was in some respects closest to that used by Rogoff, in his doctoral thesis, which Victor described as "probably the most incisive doctoral thesis in the area." We are gratified that these results tend to support what has been found before, particularly by the more rigorous of the previous research.

That completes the report on our findings up to this point. We are continuing to develop the data file, and plan to do many more types of analyses on it.

PART II

PORTFOLIO MANAGEMENT

Portfolio Theory

14

INTRODUCTION:
WHY NOT JUST PICK THE "BEST" STOCKS?

If the idea of an efficient market is the most important idea in this volume, Markowitz's concept of portfolio theory is certainly the second most important. In 1952, he published an article that radically changed thinking not only about portfolio management but also about the entire field of investments as well. Before that time, almost all texts and other writings assumed, implicitly or explicitly, that the way to pick a portfolio was to form judgments about the relative attraction of individual stocks and then select the "best" stocks. On the rare occasions that writers commented on the theory of portfolio selection, they tended to state that the maximization of expected return was an appropriate criterion for selection.

Markowitz pointed out that the common practice of diversification was not consistent with such a goal. If the goal were to be faithfully pursued, most investors would concentrate their funds in the single asset, or the two or three assets, with the greatest expected returns. The explanation of their failure to do so lies in the fact, now generally accepted as true and even obvious, that investors are concerned not only with the expected return on their investment but also with its riskiness. Diversification in itself attests to the investor's concern with risk.

If investors do not simply maximize expected returns, they must choose investments according to some other criterion. The basic assumptions of modern portfolio theory are that investors seek to maximize "expected utility," and that they act as if additional amounts of money have diminishing marginal utility. The notion is a plausible one—an extra ten dollars means less to Onassis or Getty than it does to the authors or to almost all readers. This section, therefore, starts with an extract from a book by Grayson (Chapter 15) that discusses the concept of utility and describes an experiment to measure the utility functions of oil and gas operators.

This is followed by Markowitz's 1952 article (Chapter 16), which merits study both for its historical significance and its explication of an important idea. Markowitz's work assumes that possible returns are normally distributed, and that the investor acts as if money had diminishing marginal utility. Under these conditions, expected utility will be maximized if the investor holds one of a set of portfolios, each of which maximizes expected return for a given variance (or risk) and minimizes variance for a given expected return. Markowitz shows that the variance of portfolio returns is a weighted average of the covariances between the returns on the individual holdings. Given the investor's estimates of the expected return from each security, and the degree of covariance between these prospects, the selection of an optimal portfolio becomes a problem in quadratic programming. Markowitz's article is not easy reading, but it deserves the effort.

One of the difficulties with Markowitz's solution to the portfolio problem is that it requires an unmanagable volume of data and number of computations. If one, for example, were selecting a portfolio from a list of 1,000 securities, more than 500,000 statistics would be required as input, and the amount of necessary computer time would be economically unfeasible. In the next article (Chapter 17), Sharpe takes advantage of a suggestion by Markowitz to simplify the procedure. He assumes that all the covariation between securities can be explained by movements in the general market. The advantage of this assumption is that any holding can be treated as if it were an investment in an individual security plus an investment in the market index. The riskiness of the stock depends both on the uncertainty that would exist even if the future market return were known and on the additional uncertainty that stems from ignorance of market prospects. Diversification can progressively reduce the former kind of uncertainty but not the latter. Not only does Sharpe offer a helpful way of thinking of the portfolio manager's problem, he also simplifies considerably the task of computing the optimal portfolio and reduces the necessary volume of input in our hypothetical example from over 500,000 statistics to 3,000.

Although this simplified model offers a considerable reduction in data requirements, the user still needs to quantify his assessment of the outlook for each stock. In practice most portfolio managers are prone to over-state their views. In Chapter 18 Hodges and Brealey demonstrate that such exaggeration leads to over trading and poor portfolio performance. They show how it is possible to adjust the manager's forecasts before using them in a portfolio model and they examine some of the general characteristics of an efficiently managed portfolio.

The model proposed by Sharpe and examined by Hodges and Brealey is an admitted over-simplification. In Chapter 19 we therefore return to a more complex situation. Treynor emphasizes that stock prices are influenced by a large number of economic factors: securities, he suggests, "are merely incidental vehicles for taking positions in underlying factors" It is very difficult for a manager to know how much he is exposed to these influences if he just receives unconditional recommendations or forecasts from each analyst. Treynor, therefore, would like to see the portfolio manager employ a much more specific model of the manner in which his securities are affected by these influences. Although Treynor's description of this alternative approach is condensed and difficult, his final comments on the practical consequences for investment management are easily understood and extremely perceptive.

15

DECISIONS UNDER UNCERTAINTY:
DRILLING DECISIONS BY OIL AND GAS OPERATORS

C. Jackson Grayson

As POINTED OUT in the preceding chapter, expression of the consequences of acts-events in monetary terms alone is not always a reasonable guide to action for every individual or firm.

The loss or acquisition of a dollar has different meaning for an operator of limited means, for example, as opposed to one who is extremely wealthy. And it also has different meaning to a man wanting to take great risks to make a fortune in a hurry, versus another wanting to take a slower, more careful road to increased fortune. Therefore, filling a payoff table with dollars that have different values to different people will not always result in a satisfactory guide to action for particular individuals or firms with unique financial conditions, goals, and preferences for risk taking.

This chapter, therefore, discusses a concept, "utility," whereby dollars are made to take on individual meaning. Instead of describing the consequences of act-events in terms of dollars, we can describe them in terms of their utility to the individual or firm. These utility values can then be entered in the payoff table as consequences, and an "expected" *utility* value can be used as the decision guide for the *particular* individual or firm.

THE UTILITY CONCEPT

A mathematician, Daniel Bernoulli, was one of the first to present the general idea of introducing *subjective values* of dollars into expectation calculations, rather than dollars themselves. He proposed that dollars be converted to their *utility value* by utilizing a logarithmic curve, the now familiar

C. Jackson Grayson, Chapter 10, "Utility," from *Decisions Under Uncertainty: Drilling Decisions by Oil and Gas Operators,* Division of Research, Harvard Business School, 1960, pp. 279–313. Reprinted by permission.

"diminishing marginal utility" curve. Probabilities could then be multiplied times the utility of the dollar consequences to get *expected utility value,* or, as he termed it, "moral expectation." And, if an individual has two gambles before him, he presumed that the individual would seek to maximize expected utility, that is, to choose the gamble which has the greatest excess of positive utility over negative utility.

Bernoulli's idea provided a useful way for incorporating values into expectations in an aggregate way. But, as the marginal utility curve was supposedly a representative Everyman's curve, it was deficient as a guide to action for a *particular* individual. Later, the utility concept was expanded by Von Neumann and Morgenstern [1] who proposed a system for determining an *individual's* utility function.

An individual is presented with a series of hypothetical situations in which he is asked to make a choice. When the individual answers, he is responding as an individual with a certain amount of funds, certain goals, and certain preferences for risk taking. These answers are unique to him, and they can be processed in such a way that the individual's utility function is revealed in graphic form. Then, the individual's "utility" for various monetary consequences can be multiplied by the probabilities of certain events to determine the expected utility value of a gamble (or drilling venture) to the individual.

Actually, such individual utility values are taken into consideration implicitly in every decision that an operator makes. Von Neumann and Morgenstern merely proposed a method for extracting and recording these values, so that they can be explicitly used as a guide to action—and what is particularly important, as a guide to *consistent action.* With utility values explicitly stated, ventures can be selected that follow the individual's true preferences, thereby achieving consistency in

[1] John Von Neumann and Oskar Morgenstern, *Theory of Games and Economic Behavior,* Princeton University Press, Princeton, 2d edition, 1947.

action. If utility values are mixed in a complex decision in an implicit way, there is a possibility of action that is inconsistent with an operator's true values. This is demonstrated later in the chapter.

Why such a premium on consistency?

Consistency permits a person to work in the most effective manner toward some goal. Inconsistency causes a person to meander, act in opposite ways to previous actions, possibly nullifying earlier gains. As the authors point out in *Decision Making: An Experimental Approach*,[2] if a person makes decisions inconsistent with the view of maximizing expected utility, he does not have a rational pattern of preferences and expectations. Thus, he has, in effect, a "Dutch book." It would be possible for a clever bettor to make book against him so that he would lose.

Inconsistency can also lead to frustrations, i.e., acting one way one minute and another the next creates confusion and tension within the individual. The fact that consistent action by maximizing expected utility is advanced as a recommended, or normative, guide does not intimate that all people are consistent. It is a commonplace observance that they are not. However, this does not destroy the need for pointing out such illogic or inconsistency and saying, "here is a more effective way to work toward some goal, use it if you will."

As Jacob Marschak writes, it is not asserted that norms are obeyed by all or even a sizable proportion of people, just as logicians and mathematicians do not assert that all or a majority of the people are immune to errors of logic or arithmetic. "It is merely recommended that these errors be avoided. Recommended norms and actual habits are not the same thing." [3]

[2] Donald Davidson, et al., *Decision Making: An Experimental Approach*, p. 2.

[3] Jacob Marschak, "Probability in the Social Sciences," in Paul F. Lazarsfeld, Editor, *Mathematical Thinking in the Social Sciences*, The Free Press, Glencoe, Illinois, 1954, p. 186.

The concept of using expected utility value as a decision guide also has another advantage over expected monetary value. It has been a criticism of expected monetary value that it overlooks the consequence of widely varying possible outcomes on individual action; that is, any expectation is really a weighted average. As such, it focuses attention for action on the average. Yet, there may be varying ranges of possible outcomes from a large loss to a large gain, which strongly influence an individual's decision, regardless of the expectation.

Expected utility value overcomes this objection by incorporating these variance influences directly into the computations. A large loss may be assigned a large negative utility by the individual, or he may assign a very great positive utility to a large increment in wealth, thus automatically bringing variance influences into the decision.

As decision by expected utility value seems to have certain advantages as a guide for individual action, the next question is, how can it be applied by operators in making drilling decisions?

Decision by Maximizing Expected Utility Value

First, assume for the moment that a utility function of dollars can be obtained for a particular operator and that it is an accurate representation of his preferences. It may look something like the one in Exhibit 10-1.

The origin represents the operator's asset position at a particular point in time, say today. The values on the horizontal axis represent increments (gains) and decrements (losses) in dollars. The values on the vertical axis are the operator's utility assignments for increments to, and decrements from, his asset position. These utility values are measured in units called "utiles," which is explained later.

EXHIBIT 10-1. A UTILITY FUNCTION

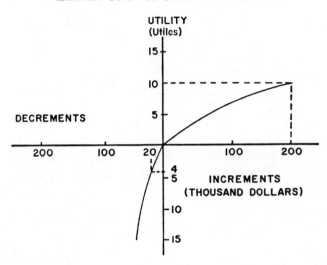

To illustrate how such a utility function could be used in making decisions, suppose that a drilling venture is presented that requires an *investment* of $20,000. This may include land, seismic, drilling costs, brokerage fees—any cost associated with the venture that may result in a decrement to the individual's asset position.

Also, suppose that the operator has, through a present value caculation described in the preceding chapter, determined the monetary consequence of each act-event. To keep this illustration simple, let us use just one successful event, the discovery of 220,000 barrels, valued at $220,000. After deduction of the investment of $20,000, the net monetary consequence of a success would be $200,000.

Finally, suppose that the personal probability (P) of hitting a producer is estimated to be 1 chance out of 4, or .25.

The payoff table would be constructed as follows to determine expected monetary value (hereafter, EMV) :

POSSIBLE EVENTS	PROBABILITY	POSSIBLE ACTS	
		Don't Drill	*Drill*
Dry Hole	.75	$0	− $20,000
220,000 bbls.	.25	0	200,000
EMV		$0	$35,000

As the act "drill" has a positive EMV of $35,000, the venture would be accepted under the decision rule of the preceding chapter (assuming that the discount rate used to calculate present value represents the required rate of return).

Under the utility concept, however, monetary consequences are not used in the payoff table. Utility values are used. And to obtain the utility values, an operator can refer to his utility function. In the example, the dotted lines on the graph show that, for this particular operator, the:

Utility of a loss, or decrement, of $20,000 is −4 utiles
Utility of a gain, or increment, of $200,000 is +10 utiles

These utiles are then put in the payoff table as consequences, and expected utility value is computed (hereafter EUV) :

POSSIBLE EVENTS	PROBABILITY	POSSIBLE ACTS	
		Don't Drill	*Drill*
Dry Hole	.75	0	−4
220,000 bbls.	.25	0	+10
EUV		0	−0.5

The act, "drill," has an EUV of −0.5. Because the act "don't drill" has a *higher* EUV, 0, this act should be accepted, and the venture would accordingly be rejected.

EMV indicates that the best decision is to drill. EUV indicates that the best decision is not to drill. Why?

The answer lies in the individual's preferences. *He as-*

signed a large negative utility to a possible monetary loss of $20,000 which was too large to take odds of 1 in 4 for a possible monetary gain of only $200,000. Had the monetary gain been estimated at $350,000, or 20 utiles, the EUV of the venture would have been a positive 2 utiles—and the act "drill" would have been preferred by this individual.

Expected Utility Value of act "drill": (.25) (20) + (.75) (−4)
Expected Utility Value = 2 utiles

More complicated problems can be handled by EUV. Suppose that the following ventures were presented to an operator for decision, and that the only acts he is considering are "don't drill" and "drill." The probabilities of the occurrence of certain events and associated monetary consequences of act "drill" are as follows:

VENTURE 1		VENTURE 2		VENTURE 3	
Investment $50,000		Investment $20,000		Investment $30,000	
Monetary Consequences	*P*	*Monetary Consequences*	*P*	*Monetary Consequences*	*P*
− $50,000	.60	− $20,000	.30	− $30,000	.70
$100,000	.20	$100,000	.40	$300,000	.20
$200,000	.10	$240,000	.30	$500,000	.05
$500,000	.07			$600,000	.05
$1,000,000	.03				

Which venture, or ventures, should the operator select, if any?

It would be a difficult decision to make merely by looking at the figures. It would be nice to make a $1 million in Venture 1, but there is only a probability of this outcome of .03; the surest is Venture 2 with only a .30 probability of being dry, etc. It would be quite a mental calculating job weaving in probabilities and desirabilities. This is where EUV can assist.

Suppose that the operator's utility function were as shown

in Exhibit 10-2. The utility associations (U) for each monetary consequence could be obtained and then multiplied by
the probabilities (P) of each event to obtain the EUV of
drilling each venture.

EXHIBIT 10-2. A UTILITY FUNCTION WITH UTILITY VALUES
OF VARIOUS INCREMENTS AND DECREMENTS
TO WEALTH INDICATED

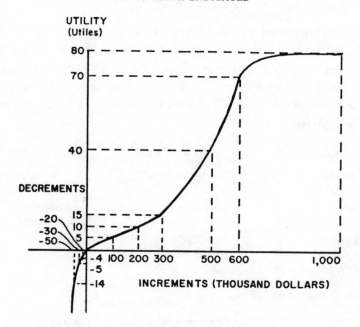

ACT: DRILL

VENTURE 1			VENTURE 2			VENTURE 3		
U	P	EUV	U	P	EUV	U	P	EUV
(−14)	(.60)	−8.4	(−4)	(.30)	−1.2	(−5)	(.70)	−3.5
(5)	(.20)	1.0	(5)	(.40)	2.0	(15)	(.20)	3.0
(10)	(.10)	1.0	(12)	(.30)	3.6	(40)	(.05)	2.0
(40)	(.07)	2.8				(70)	(.05)	3.5
(80)	(.03)	2.4						
		−1.2			4.4			5.0

Venture 3 has the highest EUV and should be selected first, Venture 2 next, and Venture 1 not at all. This does not follow if using EMV on the same ventures.

EUV		EMV	
Venture #3	5.0 Accept	Venture #2	$106,000 Accept
#2	4.4 Accept	#3	94,000 Accept
#1	−1.2 Reject	#1	75,000 Accept

Not only does decision by maximizing EUV provide a useful way for selecting between ventures so as to act consistently within a person's or a firm's preferences; there are also other uses of this concept in decision making. Consider also the possibilities for *delegating* decision-making authority.

An operator could hand his utility function to a subordinate (during his absence or just to relieve his decision-making load), and the subordinate could make decisions in accordance with the *operator's* preferences, not the preferences of the subordinate. In large firms, the top executive's utility function (which theoretically is representative of all stockholders' utility functions) could be handed to the exploration committee, or on downward to division and district levels if the firm has decentralized its decision making. The entire organization would then take action under explicitly stated criteria reflecting management's preferences. Thereby, the chances for consistent action throughout the firm would be increased.

Still another way that EUV can be of assistance is in helping an operator to decide *how much* of the investment in a venture to keep and how much to share with others.

Look at Venture 1 in the preceding illustration that was rejected because of its negative utility. (The act "don't drill" with an EUV of 0 was higher.) If an interest in the venture is sold, the operator's investment decreases, and his share of the possible payoff also decreases. But, because of the shape of the operator's utility curve, the decrease in negative utility may be more than the decrease in positive utility. And, by referring to his utility curve, the operator can determine if it is possible to spread the investment in order to change the negative utility of the act "drill" to a positive utility, greater than zero, and also to determine where the point of maximum EUV occurs. Consider the following illustration:

VENTURE 1

POSSIBLE EVENTS	PROB. OF EVENT OCCUR- RING	Don't Drill	POSSIBLE ACTS			
			Drill			
			Keep All	Sell ¼	Sell ½	Sell ¾
Dry Hole	.60	$0	− $50,000	− $37,500	− $25,000	− $12,500
100,000 bbls.	.20	0	100,000	75,000	50,000	25,000
200,000 bbls.	.10	0	200,000	150,000	100,000	50,000
500,000 bbls.	.07	0	500,000	375,000	250,000	125,000
1,000,000 bbls.	.03	0	1,000,000	750,000	500,000	250,000
Expected Monetary Value		$0	$75,000	$56,250	$37,500	$18,750

The EUV of each act would be:

VENTURE 1

POSSIBLE EVENTS	PROB. OF EVENT OCCURRING	Don't Drill	POSSIBLE ACTS			
			Drill			
			Keep All	Sell ¼	Sell ½	Sell ¾
Dry Hole	.60	0	(−14)	(−10)	(−4.2)	(−2.0)
100,000 bbls.	.20	0	(5)	(3.8)	(2.5)	(1.2)
200,000 bbls.	.10	0	(10)	(7.5)	(5.0)	(2.5)
500,000 bbls.	.07	0	(40)	(26.0)	(12.5)	(6.2)
1,000,000 bbls.	.03	0	(80)	(75.0)	(40.0)	(12.5)
Expected Utility Value		0	−1.2	−0.4	0.6	0.1

Thus, if the operator sells one-fourth interest, the expected negative utility of "drill-keep all" decreases from −1.2 to

−0.4, but the venture would still be rejected at this level: "don't drill" has a higher utility at 0. But, if the operator sells one-half interest, the utility shifts to a positive utility greater than 0 and the venture could be accepted. At one particular investment level, the EUV will be at its maximum, and this point, provided it is above zero, should be selected as the desirable level for investment, as illustrated below.

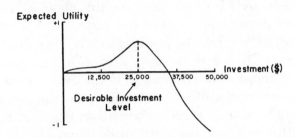

This graph of EUV for Venture 1 at various investment levels is rough, for only four investment levels are plotted. The true apex may be more or less than $25,000, and in a realistic decision, more points would have to be determined to find the desirable investment level. Of course, it may not be possible to find a positive EUV for every venture: the probabilities of success may be too low, or the negative utility assignments to decrements may be too great.

But this technique does provide the operator with a useful tool for finding the desirable investment level—for him or for his firm—in any venture. Perhaps it may not be possible to strike a bargain exactly at this level, but the operator will now have information which will be useful in *trading*. He will know how far he can go before the venture will have negative utility for him.[4]

4 Trying to find a way, mathematically, to help a man decide how much he should place in a gamble in proportion to his resources was explored by William A. Whitworth in *Choice and Chance*, G. E. Stechert & Co., New York, 1927. He arrived at a formula which purported to tell a man how much of his funds to place in a gamble "each time on a scale proportionate to his funds at that time," so that he would be left neither richer nor poorer

EUV may also be useful in another way in trading between operators. In Chapter 8, it was pointed out that trades often occur very rapidly, making it difficult for operators to visualize mentally all the possible future effects of the many combinations of deals. Another complication is that both operators probably mask their true evaluations of the deal in order to try to outmaneuver the other in trading. In these situations, it is entirely possible that bargains may be struck with which neither party is very well satisfied.

By using EUV it may be possible to formalize this bargaining process so that a *third party* can assist the operators in reaching a more optimal trade. If the two operators give their personal probabilities and utility functions to an arbiter, he may be able to suggest alternatives that they both will prefer to the one that they will probably arrive at over the bargaining table.

In summary, this section of the chapter has shown how, if a utility function can be obtained, EUV can be used as a decision guide by an individual operator, or by a decision maker within a firm, to:

1. Select an act within a single venture, and to compare different ventures for selection.

---

in the long run. This formula was picked up by a geologist, John Hayward, in 1934, who attempted to apply it to drilling decisions (John Hayward, "Probabilities and Wildcats Tested Through Mathematical Manipulation," *The Oil and Gas Journal,* November 15, 1934, pp. 129–131). Mr. Hayward gave examples of ventures with varying investments and probabilities and scaled the investment to fit the resources of the operator. His assumption was that any investment less than Whitworth's figure for the "correct" investment was a good investment for the operator. This idea was explored again in a series of articles by Sylvain J. Pirson, "Probability Theory Applied to Oil Exploitation Ventures," *The Petroleum Engineer,* February–May issues, 1941.

These are interesting attempts to arrive at an objective method for risk sharing. The utility concept is more advantageous as a decision guide, however, for it avoids any frequency interpretation and also brings in individual risk preferences.

2. Delegate decision making to subordinates or to decentralized units.
3. Decide how much of an investment in a venture to keep and how much to trade out.
4. Help a third party to suggest a trading bargain that may be preferred to one that the parties might arrive at by themselves.

The next logical question is, how can this utility function be obtained?

Obtaining a Utility Function for an Individual

The desire to measure utility has been expressed for many years. And the question of whether an individual's utility is measurable, even if he has a consistent pattern of preferences, is still debated by some. To enter this debate would require an inordinate amount of time, and a good summary of the debate, plus a bibliography for further reading, is given by Ward Edwards.[5]

In my research, I tentatively accepted the idea that utility can be measured in accordance with the ideas advanced by Von Neumann and Morgenstern. If a person can express preferences over a series of alternative gambles, then it is possible to introduce utility associates to these alternatives, provided that there is an element of consistency in his tastes. Once determined, the function can be used by the individual to guide himself by EUV and thereby act in accordance with his true tastes.

A simple example follows.

Suppose a man is offered two alternatives: (1) obtain $25 for certain, or (2) have a 50-50 chance of winning $75 or nothing. And suppose he replies that he feels that these two

[5] Ward Edwards, "The Theory of Decision Making, *Psychological Bulletin,* 51, 1954, pp. 380–417.

are about equal, i.e., he is "indifferent" between the two alternatives. To this individual, these alternatives have the same utility. Another individual may want a 50-50 chance to win $100 or $150 before he feels that the alternatives are equal. This individual has a different utility function. The reasons may be that he has less money and the $25 certain payment has more attraction, or that he just does not like gambling with dollars to that extent.

A series of such alternatives can be given to an individual, with different amounts of dollars and different probabilities. His answers can be plotted on a graph converting dollars into a utility function, measured in terms of utiles. It is difficult for some people to understand that these utiles have no meaning of their own. Utiles are merely a measuring device and could just as easily have been called petiles or qwertiles.

Returning to the first answer where $25 is the certain equivalent of a 50-50 chance of winning $75 or nothing: It can be said that the utility of $0 is 0 utiles, and the utility of $75 is 10 utiles. These point selections are purely arbitrary. The utiles of $0 and $75 could just as easily have been set at 1 and 100; it does not matter since *this is a scale unique to this individual.*[6] Just as someone arbitrarily chose to set the freezing point of water at 32 degrees, the utility origin of 0 and the units of measurement were arbitrarily chosen. After these points are selected, the utility of $100 can be determined from the individual's answers:

Utility of $25 = .50 [Utility ($75)] + .50 [Utility ($0)]
Utility of $25 = .50 [10 utiles]   + .50 [0 utiles]
Utility of $25 =   5 utiles

[6] "Another way of stating this uniqueness result is that the consistency axioms . . . determine a linear utility function which is unique up to its zero point and its unit." (R. Duncan Luce and Howard Raiffa, *Games and Decisions,* John Wiley & Sons, Inc., New York, 1957, p. 33.) Because of this uniqueness, comparison of utiles between persons is difficult. However, the over-all shape of the curve can be compared, for its shape would not be affected by the placement of the original zero point or choice of scale.

Plotted on a graph, it would look like this:

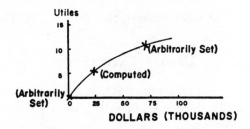

This is merely the plot of one gamble. Because only a few points can be obtained with one gamble, a series of such gambles are given to the individual, and these are also plotted. If there is an element of consistency in his tastes, the plots can be extended over a wider range of dollars to form a general utility function. What happens if the plots of the alternatives do not tend to follow some general configuration, i.e., the individual gives answers that are widely varying or inconsistent with a previous answer?

If the indiivdual is consistent in his tastes, this will not happen. But it is a fact of life that it does happen.

If people prefer A to B to C, they should not prefer C to A if they are consistent. But, often, this happens. The research points this out. There are many reasons offered for this behavior, but those interested in the normative application merely say to the individual:

> Look, this demonstrates the difficulty of your trying to behave consistently. You said you would take this venture, but a few moments later, with an identical asset position, you said you would not take this venture. This is inconsistent. Which of these two really represents your preference?

After the individual thinks this over, he may modify the first or second to bring them into consistency. These inconsistencies, or "intransitivities" in mathematics, are disturbing, but not unexpected. Modifying them is a process whereby the individual is removing inconsistencies in his answers, so that in the future, action can be taken on a consistent basis. There is a further discussion of this later in the chapter.

UTILITY EXPERIMENT

With these thoughts about the Von Neumann and Morgenstern method of obtaining an individual's utility function, I devised an experiment to try to capture an operator's utility function under field conditions.

If this concept is ever to be used in real world decisions, the function should be determined under choice-making situations that represent actual situations. Therefore, I constructed a series of hypothetical ventures in which the operator was asked to accept or reject a venture on the basis of information about the investment, payoff, and probability of success.

For example, he might have been asked to accept or reject a venture where the investment was $10,000, the total payoff was $110,000 and the probability of success was .60. If he rejected this venture, I then offered it to him at a higher probability, say .80. If he accepted this venture, I then offered it at .70. At this point, he might say that this was a hazy area: he might take it or not. This was the indifference point searched for. Therefore:

$$\text{(Gain)} \qquad\qquad \text{(Loss)}$$
$$.70 \text{ Utility } [(\$100,000)] + .30 \text{ [Utility } (-\$10,000)] = 0 \text{ utiles}$$

The zero was not put in the offer in an explicit way, but it can be presumed that if the decision maker is indifferent, then he feels that the venture has no plus or negative utility —thus zero utility. And zero utiles represent status quo, which is merely a convenient convention without loss of generality.

I presented the hypothetical gambles to small independent

operators but did not extend the utility experiment to decision makers in larger firms. The problems of obtaining an individual utility function for an individual owner-operator in a small firm were difficult enough, and there was just not sufficient time to extend the research and necessary thought about how the concept might be used in large corporations, with multilevel decision points and with divided owner-decision maker situations. I am convinced that the concept could be applicable, but all that is reported in this chapter are the results of the experiment with independent operators.

This was the procedure that I followed.

First, I explained very briefly the idea behind decision making by EUV. This had to be done to enlist operators' cooperation in participating in the experiment. Perhaps not all understood the entire idea, but they at least understood most of the concept. Then, instructions for responding to the ventures were presented informally in words like these:

I will give you a series of hypothetical drilling deals, and I want you to listen to each deal as I present it and give me an answer as to whether you would accept that deal today or reject it.

There will be three items of information that I will give you on each deal—the cost of the investment in the deal, the payoff to you if you hit, and the probability of finding oil or gas. For example, I might offer you a deal that has an investment of $30,000, a payoff of $100,000, and a 70% chance of striking. Now I want to explain each of these.

The *investment* represents the total dollar cost of going into this particular deal. You may be buying into a deal, or it may represent the cost of land, brokerage fees, drilling costs, etc. Taxes always alter the "effective" cost of a deal to you, and different deals have different tax effects. So that you will know that this variable effect is the same on all deals, just assume that this is the after-tax investment to you in hard dollars. (Note: Several operators said that they never considered taxes in decisions on individual ventures, only in the aggregate, so these operators responded to a before-tax investment figure.)

The *payoff* represents the present worth to you of any oil or gas that you may find. For example, if I say that a venture has a $100,000 payoff, that means that this is the total value today that you assign to that oil or gas that may be produced over the next five, ten, or fifteen years. You must remember that this is the total present value of the oil or gas. You will have to recover your investment out of this. Thus, the true net payoff is the difference between the investment and the total payoff, or, in this illustration, $70,000. I will remind you of this on each deal.

The *probability* means the estimate of the chance that you may find oil or gas. As you well know, there is no certainty that petroleum is down there. There is only a chance. This estimate will vary with the information you have from seismic, other wells, etc. You may call this chance a 1 in 5 shot, a 3 to 1 bet, or just a good shot. To make certain that we are talking about the same kind of chance, I am going to give you degrees of chance from 0 to 100. Any chance that is close to 100 is almost certain—a cinch. Any chance that is close to 0 has very little chance of striking. A 50-50 chance means just what it sounds like—an equal chance of getting a well or a duster. These chances, or probabilities, are the very best that you can get, and have been obtained from a source you regard as reliable, perhaps your geologist.

Putting these together, the proposition would be a venture with a $30,000 investment that has a total possible payoff of $100,000 (net $70,000), and a 70% probability of striking. Would you accept this deal today? If you would, I might ask if you would accept it with a 30% probability, or a 50% probability and so on, until I find a point where you are on the borderline. Once this point is found, we'll forget this deal, and go on to the other one. Each deal is separate.

In thinking of these deals, I want you to think of them as being presented to you this very minute. If you invest your money, it may be tied up until the well pays out, which may be several years typically. Or, if you prefer, it might be possible to sell out. Do your best to think of these as actual deals, and if you accept, you would have to sign a check.

In actual deals, you might wish other information, but for the purpose of this transaction, assume that all the other information has been explored and that there is nothing adverse. Please understand that no particular response or probabilities are being looked for. There are no "correct" solutions. All I want is your realistic response. Think of these as individual deals, and don't try to recall how you acted on a previous deal.

You may take as long as you wish to decide, and use pencil and paper if you wish.

RESULTS OF UTILITY EXPERIMENT

As was expected, I had mixed success with the utility experiment. Much was learned about the differences in risk preferences of operators and members of their organizations, the problems of utility function determination under field conditions, and the acceptance by operators of the idea of using EUV as a decision-making guide. From these standpoints, the experiment was successful.

But there were difficulties encountered in determining a "true" utility function. Part of the trouble arose from the design of the experiment and part from the operators' difficulty in responding to hypothetical situations in a real world setting. For example, one operator simply could not think in terms of probabilities, and another was so confused by the whole idea that the results were not worthwhile recording.

The successes and failures of the experiment are discussed in the remainder of the chapter. But first are presented the actual results of the experiment:

1. The form used in presenting the hypothetical ventures and recording indifference probabilities, which is self-explanatory (Exhibit 10-3),

Exhibit 10-3. Form for Recording Reactions to Hypothetical Drilling Propositions

Date_____

Individual_____ Position_____

Company_____ Location_____

Invest-ment	Total Payoff	Net Payoff	Indiff. Prob.	Invest-ment	Total Payoff	Net Payoff	Indiff. Prob.
$10	$20	$10		$100	$200	$100	
	30	20			350	250	
	40	30			450	350	
	60	50			600	500	
	100	90			1,000	900	
20	40	20		150	300	150	
	50	30			500	350	
	120	100			650	500	
	170	150			1,000	850	
50	100	50		250	400	150	
	150	100			500	250	
	400	350			750	500	
	800	750			1,000	750	
75	165	90			1,250	1,000	
	425	350		500	1,000	500	
	825	750			1,500	1,000	
	1,000	925			2,000	1,500	

2. A table of indifference probabilities (Exhibit 10-4, pages 300–301), and

3. Rough utility functions drawn for some of the operators and members of their organization.

Table of Indifference Probabilities

Without even looking at the plotted functions, the differences among operators' risk preferences can be seen from the table of indifference probabilities given in Exhibit 10-4. For example, look at the venture of $75,000 investment with a total possible payoff of $425,000. The indifference probabilities run from .10 to .70. And, by looking at the trends of indifference probabilities in columns, it can be seen which operators, in general, are willing to assume more risks than others.

Also, note that in two of the firms—Bannister Oil and Beard Oil—answers are recorded from different members of the organization. This was done in order to get more experience with utility function determination, and to examine the differences in preferences among members of a firm. This led to some interesting results which are described when the various functions themselves are presented.

The cutoff points indicate points beyond which operators would not take any venture, regardless of the probabilities offered.

A last explanation concerns the two sets of figures for Bill Beard. The first set came from a pilot study conducted in October 1957. The second set of figures was obtained when the main research was done in February 1958. The same type of hypothetical venture presentation was made both times, but from lessons learned in the pilot study, the dollar amounts of the ventures were largely changed for the main research.

How Utility Functions Were Plotted [7]

The concept behind plotting the data is exactly like that in the Von Neumann-Morgenstern example given earlier. Here are a few probabilities taken from Mr. Elliott's answers to demonstrate the method.

Investment	Total Payoff	Net Payoff	Indifference Probability
$10,000	$ 20,000	$10,000	.80
	30,000	20,000	.60
	40,000	30,000	.60
	60,000	50,000	.30
	100,000	90,000	.20
20,000	40,000	20,000	.90

[7] I am indebted to Professor Howard Raiffa for assistance in furnishing ideas for plotting the data.

Exhibit 10-4. Table of Indifference Possibilities

								Main Research			
Venture							Operators				
(Thousands)									(Bannister)		
Invest-ment	Total Payoff	Net Payoff	S. F. Bishop	R. F. Mellon	Owen Elliott	J. P. Fluitt	Bill Gordy	Robert Holladay	James Garrison	Charles Scott	Bill Beard
$10	20	10	.50	.80	.80	No	No	No	.90	.75	.90
	30	20	.25	.70	.60	.90	No	.75	.90	.65	.70
	40	30	.25	.50	.60	.80	.90	.60	.80	.65	.45
	60	50	.25	.40	.30	.50	.40	.40	.70	.75	.40
	100	90	.25	.25	.20	.30	.20	.10	.60	.25	.30
20	40	20	.40	.90	.90	No	No	No	.90	.70	.90
	50	30	.25	.90	.85	No	No	No	.85	.60	.75
	120	100	.20	.60	.40	.90	.25	.60	.70	.20	.50
	170	150	.15	.40	.30	.60	.10	.50	.60	.25	.25
50	100	50	.20	.90	.85	No	No	No	No	.75	No
	150	100	.15	.90	.75	No	.80	.75	.85	.75	.80
	400	350	.12	.40	.30	.80	.20	.40	.60	.40	.40
	800	750	.10	.20	.20	.80	.20	.10	.50	.25	.20
75	165	90	.15	.90	.90		.80	No	.90	No	No
	425	350	.10	.60	.60		.25	.60	.70	.40	.70
	825	750	.10	.30	.30		.10	.20	.60	.25	.45
	1,000	925	.10	.20	.25		.10	.10	.35	.10	.40
100	200	100	.10	No	.90			No	No	No	No
	350	250	.08	.90	.70			.75	No	No	.90
	450	350	.08	.80	.70			.50	.90	No	.80
	600	500	.08	.75	.50			.40	.80	No	.70
	1,000	900	.05	.60	.30			.20	.60	.75	.60
150	300	150	.50	No	No			No	No	No	No
	500	350	.50	.80	No			.75	No	No	.90
	650	500	.50	.80	.80			.60	.90	.90	.90
	1,000	850	.40	.70	.75			.40	.90	.75	.90
250	400	150	No	No				No	No		No
	500	250	.80	No				No	No		No
	750	500	.50	No				.90	No	.95	
	1,000	750	.50	.80				.80	.90	.95	
	1,250	1,000	.50	.70				.75	.90	.90	

First, $0 was arbitrarily set at 0 utility. Also, the loss of $10,000 was arbitrarily set at −1 utility. The equation for the first plot is:

.80 [Utility ($10,000)] + .20 [Utility (−$10,000)] = 0

As the utility of −$10,000 was set at −1 utiles, then, by the equation, the utility of $10,000 must be .25 utiles.

IN UTILITY EXPERIMENT

PILOT STUDY					
VENTURE			OPERATORS		
(In Thousands)			(BEARD OIL)		
In-vest-ment	*Total Pay-off*	*Net Payoff*	Bill Beard	John Beard	Fred Hartman
$15–30	$15	.70	.80	.90
15–50	35	.50	.40	.60
15–75	60	.40	.25	.40
15–100	85	.30	.20	.40
30–50	20	.75	.80	.90
30–75	45	.60	.50	.50
30–100	70	.40	.35	.40
30–500	470	.15	.15	.05
30–1,000	970	.10	.10	.01
50–60	10	.95	No	.90
50–75	25	.85	.90	.80
50–100	50	.70	.75	.40
50–500	450	.20	.30	.01
50–1,000	950	.15	.15	.01
100–125	25	.80	No	.80
100–150	50	.85	.95	.80
100–200	100	.80	.80	.50
100–500	400	.60	.50	.40
100–1,000	900	.50	.25	.05
150–200	50	.95	No	.95
150–300	150	.90	.80	.40
150–500	350	.80	.50	.40
150–1,000	850	.80	.30	.20
150–1,500	1,350	.70	.25	.10
250–300	50	No	No	No
250–500	250	.90	.80	.90
250–1,000	750	.80	.50	.70
250–1,500	1,250	.70	.40	.70

The three utile points $(-1, 0, .25)$ are plotted at the respective net payoff points $(-\$10,000, \$0,$ and $\$10,000)$.[8]

[8] Note that utiles are plotted at net payoff points, not total payoff points, for the net payoff represents the real increase in dollar position of the operator. The experiment could have been worded so as to give net payoffs to operators. However, from the pilot study, I learned that operators are more accustomed to talking in terms of total payoffs when ventures are discussed. Regardless, this point was explained in the instructions, and reinforced verbally as the experiment progressed.

Similar plots are made with other net payoffs at the $10,000 level. These points can now be connected with a free hand curve, and this is the utility function for the individual over the ranges of −$10,000 and $90,000.[9] But this does not cover a wide enough operational range for most operators, and thus far there is no way of checking the answers of the operator within this range to verify if his answers are consistent with his own tastes.

This is why a series of ventures were given in ascending ranges with *overlapping* net payoff points. If a person were completely consistent throughout his whole set of answers, the same utility value would be obtained for the overlapping net payoffs. This would be done unconsciously by the operator through his adjustment of the indifference probability.

In plotting the second set of data at the −$20,000 level, trial-and-error was used to set the utility of −$20,000. An arbitrary figure, say, −5 utiles, was initially selected from a visual extension of the initial rough curve. Then, I computed the utiles for the net payoffs at that level, observing whether they agreed with the utility values for overlapping net payoffs in the first plot.

If they did not agree, then an adjustment was made in the utility of −$20,000, from −5 perhaps to −6 or to −3, to determine if a point could be found that would make the overlapping payoffs consistent. If so, these were overlaid and the range extended, with the process repeated at each level. Where the points could not be made to fit exactly, and this was often the case, utility assignments were made to bring the points to as close a fit as possible, and a rough curve was drawn through them. Some points were very far away from

[9] One of the assumptions made in construction of a utility function, by means of a curve connecting determined points, is that the function is continuous between the points. It would certainly behoove an operator to check the curve at the intervening magnitudes to see if it accurately represents his preference.

the "best fit" curve, indicating an answer widely inconsistent with others.

Clearly, these curves are only approximations, for the operators answered fairly rapidly and an "error" of a few points in probabilities, particularly in the extremes, throws points far apart. As suggested earlier, to remove these errors the operator could be shown the points of inconsistency and asked which came closest to reflecting his true preferences.

There was no time in the research to plot the curves and then present them to the operators for modification, except with one operator, Bill Beard, who had been visited during the pilot study. He looked at his curve, checked the points of inconsistency, and reduced the variances to a nominal amount.

Next, the utility functions of several operators are presented, with a discussion of some of the salient features of each.

Operators' Utility Functions

(1) The first set of utility functions is that obtained in the Beard Oil Company during the *pilot* study. The three curves are those of Bill and John Beard, the owners, and Fred Hartman, the geologist (Exhibit 10-5). All were plotted with the same zero point, unit of scale, and first arbitrary point ($-\$15,000 = -3$ utiles). Thus, comparisons can be made.

Note the difference in shapes, or slopes, of the curves.

The geologist, Fred Hartman, has less preference for small increments in dollar gains (his curve is lower at smaller dollar values) than the two Beards. But when larger amounts of dollar increments are involved, he attaches much greater utility to these increments (the curve rises steeply) than do the Beards. On the negative side of the curve, note that Hartman does not consider increasing losses much more seriously than small losses (the curve is almost flat), until he passes

EXHIBIT 10-5. UTILITY FUNCTIONS OF INDIVIDUALS IN BEARD OIL

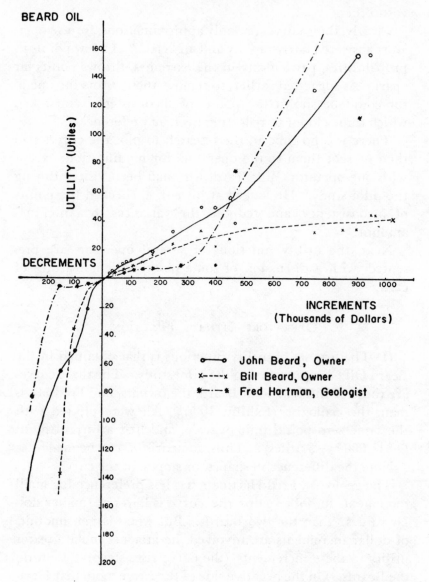

$150,000 where the curve falls off sharply. This could be a reflection of his own nature, or the fact that, as a geologist, he feels less direct involvement in losses.[10]

John Beard prefers small increments more than Hartman or Bill Beard (the curve rises at a steeper rate), but he also attaches greater negative utility to small decrements. When the stakes get higher, John Beard assigns even more utility to increments, though not as much as Hartman. Correspondingly, he assigns less negative utility to decrements (the curve is not as steep past losses of $100,000).

Bill Beard falls between the other two curves. Like his brother, he prefers small increments more than Hartman, but he attaches less negative utility than his brother to small decrements. However, when possible decrements pass $100,-000, he assigns much greater negative utility than either of the other two. Note that his curve resembles more closely the diminishing marginal utility curve.

Plotting these three curves on one graph highlights the varying risk-taking preferences in the organization. When John Beard might take a venture at certain probabilities, Bill might refuse. As the decision making is split between the two, there is a possibility that the firm, as a whole, is taking risks on an inconsistent basis in the sense that they are not maximizing any one utility function. More consistent action would result if they would look at the functions, talk over their goals, preferences, funds, and so on, and draw a new function that captures certain features of each. This composite function would be used in the future as the "firm" utility function. Or, they could decide to adopt one of the functions, as is, to guide their actions.

When the Beards saw these differences, they said that, in

---

10 No insinuation is intended that a utility function should look one way or another, or that people should behave one way or another. These are only representations of choices made by individuals, and there is no "right" way to make the choice.

EXHIBIT 10-6. UTILITY FUNCTIONS OF BILL BEARD IN
DIFFERENT TIME PERIODS

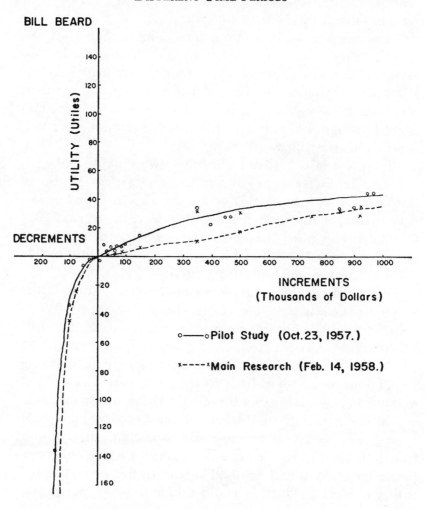

general, they were aware that they had different risk-taking preferences, but that they had never thought about it in a conscious way before.

This brings out several points that could be important in decision making by a firm:

1. The utility function demonstrates in a graphic way the varying risk taking preferences of different individuals in a firm.
2. These differences create opportunities for inconsistent action if the decision-making authority is divided, or if deals are being rejected by the screener operating under a different risk-taking function.
3. If so, two adjustments can be made. One, a composite utility function might be adopted so that the firm will take consistent action. Or, one function might be selected to guide the firm's actions.

On the second graph (Exhibit 10-6) are plotted two curves. One represents Bill Beard's responses during the research pilot study; the other his responses during the main research three months later. Although the amounts of dollar investments contained in the hypothetical ventures were largely different during the two presentations, there was one overlap point at an investment of $50,000. Thus, after the first curve representing the data gathered during the pilot study had been plotted, the second curve representing the data from the main research could be plotted by making the common point —a $50,000 decrement—have the same negative utility— minus 7 utiles.

On the increment side, note that Bill Beard assigned less utility to increments in dollars during the main research than in the earlier pilot study. And on the decrement side, he assigned a little less negative utility to decrements up to $50,000. But past $50,000, he assigned greater negative utility. On the whole this indicates a shift by the time of the main research to a more conservative behavior, which is also evident from the generally higher indifference probabilities shown in Exhibit 10-6.

When asked why he had responded with higher probabilities in the main research, Mr. Beard replied that he had decided during the intervening period that wildcatting, a risky

EXHIBIT 10-7. UTILITY FUNCTIONS OF INDIVIDUALS
IN BANNISTER OIL

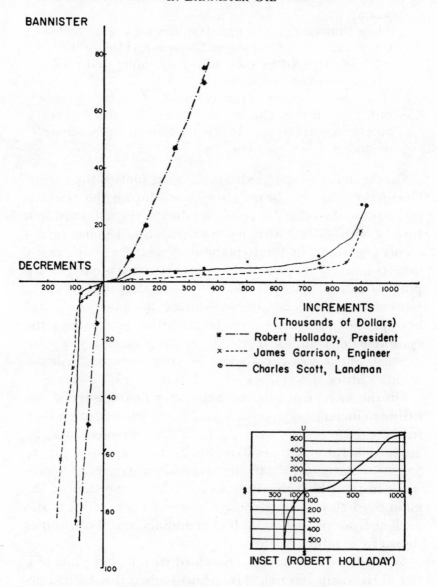

INSET (ROBERT HOLLADAY)

business, was not so favorable for investment of their funds as taking land positions in the hopes of offsets. Thus, he would require "better" deals before taking ventures. This is an illustration of the ephemeral nature of utility curves.

(2) The next set of curves (Exhibit 10-7) is that of Robert Holladay, President, Bannister Oil and Gas, and two members of his organization—James Garrison, engineer, and Charles Scott, landman.

Note that Mr. Holladay's curve is flat at low increments from $10,000 to $30,000. The curve begins to rise slowly at $30,000 and breaks upward at $50,000. Because the scale on this graph had to be small to accommodate the other members of the organization on the same graph, it does not show what happens to Mr. Holladay's curve in larger increments. The inset in the lower righthand corner of the graph shows Mr. Holladay's curve extended on a larger scale. Now it can be seen that a large inflection occurs at about a $300,000 increment, and continues upward at about the same rate to $900,000 where it tips over. Evidently in this range the increments were very attractive. The data were rough in plotting his curve because of the great variations caused by a small change in probabilities at these higher levels, but the general shape is apparent.

This curve was roughly sketched during the research and shown to Mr. Holladay. He agreed that this looked like a general representation of his preferences: he does not want to take great risks when possible gains are small, but is willing to take risks if the gains are potentially large. His utility function reflects this.

Also, note on the same graph, utility functions for two other members of the Bannister organization. The two shapes are about the same, but widely different from that of Mr. Holladay's. The same observations about different risk preferences among members of an organization as made for Beard Oil would apply here.

EXHIBIT 10-8.   UTILITY FUNCTION OF O. F. ELLIOTT

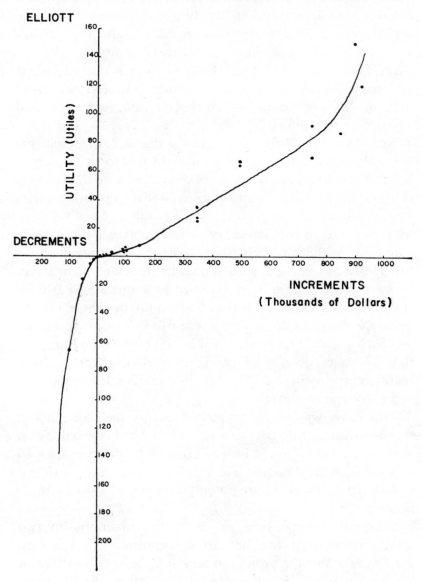

(3) The curve of Mr. Elliott, of Carson-Elliott (Exhibit 10-8) reflects almost a linear utility function in increments past $150,000; i.e., each increment in dollars is about as desirable as the preceding one. This linearity is contrary to the traditional model of diminishing marginal utility, but it should be remembered that this is a special class of men—by their nature, risk takers.

There is a sharp drop in negative utility of decrements beginning with $50,000, indicating his preference for avoiding such possible losses past that point.

(4) Mr. Mellon's curve (Exhibit 10-9) does not rise so steeply on the positive side as do some of the other curves, but observe that he has the same upward inflection at about $200,000.

(5) The final curve shown (Exhibit 10-10) is that of Mr. Bishop, a wealthy independent operator. This one is very oddly shaped. The results show that he assigns no greater negative utility to a possible loss of $100,000 any more than to a possible loss of $10,000! This is strange. One possible inference is that losses, to him, are just part of the normal operations in drilling. Losses of $10,000 are to be expected as well as losses of $100,000, so all losses are regarded as about the same within this range. Past this point, however, the negative utility of decrements increases more normally.

On the positive side, increments of dollars have increasing utility, but the rate of increase is not nearly so rapid as in some of the other curves. Perhaps the explanation is similar to that of the loss side—gains are part of the normal operations, and he attaches only slightly more utility to larger increments.

From a descriptive point of view, it would be interesting to relate these utility functions to actual decisions made by each of the operators. But this would require a record of the operators' past decisions with knowledge of the assessment of

EXHIBIT 10-9. UTILITY FUNCTION OF R. F. MELLON

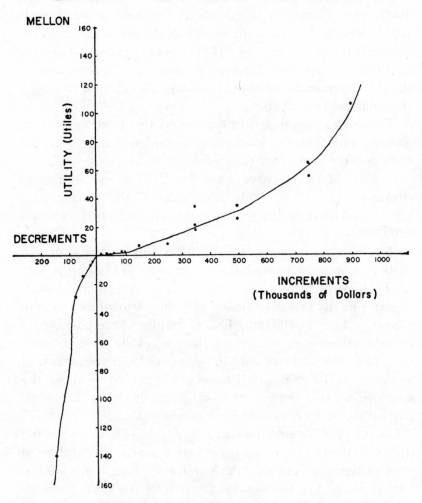

payoffs and probabilities that existed in the operator's mind when he entered into the venture. Records were not kept in this manner by any of the operators. Thus, the emphasis of this research remained with the normative prescription.

EXHIBIT 10-10. UTILITY FUNCTION OF S. F. BISHOP

BISHOP

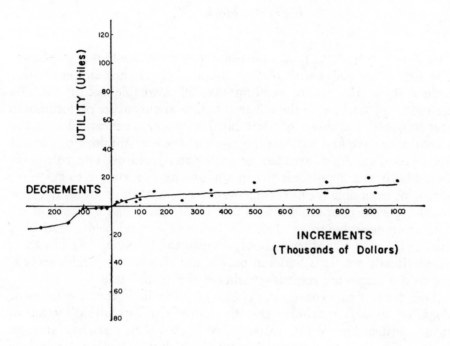

16

PORTFOLIO SELECTION *

Harry M. Markowitz

THE PROCESS OF SELECTING a portfolio may be divided into two stages. The first stage starts with observation and experience and ends with beliefs about the future performances of available securities. The second stage starts with the relevant beliefs about future performances and ends with the choice of portfolio. This paper is concerned with the second stage. We first consider the rule that the investor does (or should) maximize discounted expected, or anticipated, returns. This rule is rejected both as a hypothesis to explain, and as a maximum to guide investment behavior. We next consider the rule that the investor does (or should) consider expected return a desirable thing *and* variance of return an undesirable thing. This rule has many sound points, both as a maxim for, and hypothesis about, investment behavior. We illustrate geometrically relations between beliefs and choice of portfolio according to the "expected returns—variance of returns" rule.

One type of rule concerning choice of portfolio is that the investor does (or should) maximize the discounted (or capitalized) value of future returns.[1] Since the future is not known with certainty, it must be "expected" or "anticipated" returns which we discount. Variations of this type of rule can be suggested. Following Hicks, we could let "anticipated" returns include an allowance for risk.[2] Or, we could let the rate at which we capitalize the returns from particular securities vary with risk.

The hypothesis (or maxim) that the investor does (or should) maximize discounted return must be rejected. If we ignore market imperfections the foregoing rule never implies that there is a diversified portfolio which is preferable to all non-diversified portfolios. Diversification is both observed and sensible; a rule of behavior which does not imply the superiority of diversification must be rejected both as a hypothesis and as a maxim.

* This paper is based on work done by the author while at the Cowles Commission for Research in Economics and with the financial assistance of the Social Science Research Council. It will be reprinted as Cowles Commission Paper, New Series, No. 60.

1. See, for example, J. B. Williams, *The Theory of Investment Value* (Cambridge, Mass.: Harvard University Press, 1938), pp. 55–75.

2. J. R. Hicks, *Value and Capital* (New York: Oxford University Press, 1939), p. 126. Hicks applies the rule to a firm rather than a portfolio.

Reprinted from *The Journal of Finance*, VII, No. 1 (March, 1952), 77–91, by permission of the publisher.

The foregoing rule fails to imply diversification no matter how the anticipated returns are formed; whether the same or different discount rates are used for different securities; no matter how these discount rates are decided upon or how they vary over time.[3] The hypothesis implies that the investor places all his funds in the security with the greatest discounted value. If two or more securities have the same value, then any of these or any combination of these is as good as any other.

We can see this analytically: suppose there are N securities; let r_{it} be the anticipated return (however decided upon) at time t per dollar invested in security i; let d_{it} be the rate at which the return on the ith security at time t is discounted back to the present; let X_i be the relative amount invested in security i. We exclude short sales, thus $X_i \geqslant 0$ for all i. Then the discounted anticipated return of the portfolio is

$$R = \sum_{t=1}^{\infty} \sum_{i=1}^{N} d_{it} r_{it} X$$

$$= \sum_{i=1}^{N} X_i \left(\sum_{t=1}^{\infty} d_{it} r_{it} \right)$$

$R_i = \sum_{t=1}^{\infty} d_{it} r_{it}$ is the discounted return of the ith security, therefore

$R = \Sigma X_i R_i$ where R_i is independent of X_i. Since $X_i \geqslant 0$ for all i and $\Sigma X_i = 1$, R is a weighted average of R_i with the X_i as non-negative weights. To maximize R, we let $X_i = 1$ for i with maximum R_i. If several Ra_a, $a = 1, \ldots, K$ are maximum then any allocation with

$$\sum_{a=1}^{K} Xa_a = 1$$

maximizes R. In no case is a diversified portfolio preferred to all non-diversified portfolios.[4]

It will be convenient at this point to consider a static model. Instead of speaking of the time series of returns from the ith security $(r_{i1}, r_{i2}, \ldots, r_{it}, \ldots)$ we will speak of "the flow of returns" (r_i) from the ith security. The flow of returns from the portfolio as a whole is

3. The results depend on the assumption that the anticipated returns and discount rates are independent of the particular investor's portfolio.

4. If short sales were allowed, an infinite amount of money would be placed in the security with highest r.

$R = \Sigma X_i r_i$. As in the dynamic case if the investor wished to maximize "anticipated" return from the portfolio he would place all his funds in that security with maximum anticipated returns.

There is a rule which implies both that the investor should diversify and that he should maximize expected return. The rule states that the investor does (or should) diversify his funds among all those securities which give maximum expected return. The law of large numbers will insure that the actual yield of the portfolio will be almost the same as the expected yield.[5] This rule is a special case of the expected returns—variance of returns rule (to be presented below). It assumes that there is a portfolio which gives both maximum expected return and minimum variance, and it commends this portfolio to the investor.

This presumption, that the law of large numbers applies to a portfolio of securities, cannot be accepted. The returns from securities are too intercorrelated. Diversification cannot eliminate all variance.

The portfolio with maximum expected return is not necessarily the one with minimum variance. There is a rate at which the investor can gain expected return by taking on variance, or reduce variance by giving up expected return.

We saw that the expected returns or anticipated returns rule is inadequate. Let us now consider the expected returns—variance of returns ($E\text{-}V$) rule. It will be necessary to first present a few elementary concepts and results of mathematical statistics. We will then show some implications of the $E\text{-}V$ rule. After this we will discuss its plausibility.

In our presentation we try to avoid complicated mathematical statements and proofs. As a consequence a price is paid in terms of rigor and generality. The chief limitations from this source are (1) we do not derive our results analytically for the n-security case; instead, we present them geometrically for the 3 and 4 security cases; (2) we assume static probability beliefs. In a general presentation we must recognize that the probability distribution of yields of the various securities is a function of time. The writer intends to present, in the future, the general, mathematical treatment which removes these limitations.

We will need the following elementary concepts and results of mathematical statistics:

Let Y be a random variable, i.e., a variable whose value is decided by chance. Suppose, for simplicity of exposition, that Y can take on a finite number of values $y_1, y_2, \ldots, y_N$. Let the probability that $Y =$

5. Williams, *op. cit.*, pp. 68, 69.

y_1, be p_1; that $Y = y_2$ be p_2 etc. The expected value (or mean) of Y is defined to be

$$E = p_1 y_1 + p_2 y_2 + \ldots + p_N y_N$$

The variance of Y is defined to be

$$V = p_1 (y_1 - E)^2 + p_2 (y_2 - E)^2 + \ldots + p_N (y_N - E)^2 .$$

V is the average squared deviation of Y from its expected value. V is a commonly used measure of dispersion. Other measures of dispersion, closely related to V are the standard deviation, $\sigma = \sqrt{V}$ and the coefficient of variation, σ/E.

Suppose we have a number of random variables: $R_1, \ldots, R_n$. If R is a weighted sum (linear combination) of the R_i

$$R = a_1 R_1 + a_2 R_2 + \ldots + a_n R_n$$

then R is also a random variable. (For example R_1, may be the number which turns up on one die; R_2, that of another die, and R the sum of these numbers. In this case $n = 2$, $a_1 = a_2 = 1$).

It will be important for us to know how the expected value and variance of the weighted sum (R) are related to the probability distribution of the $R_1, \ldots, R_n$. We state these relations below; we refer the reader to any standard text for proof.[6]

The expected value of a weighted sum is the weighted sum of the expected values. I.e., $E(R) = a_1 E(R_1) + a_2 E(R_2) + \ldots + a_n E(R_n)$ The variance of a weighted sum is not as simple. To express it we must define "covariance." The covariance of R_1 and R_2 is

$$\sigma_{12} = E\{ [R_1 - E(R_1)] [R_2 - E(R_2)] \}$$

i.e., the expected value of [(the deviation of R_1 from its mean) times (the deviation of R_2 from its mean)]. In general we define the covariance between R_i and R_j as

$$\sigma_{ij} = E\{ [R_i - E(R_i)] [R_i - E(R_j)] \}$$

σ_{ij} may be expressed in terms of the familiar correlation coefficient (ρ_{ij}). The covariance between R_i and R_j is equal to [(their correlation) times (the standard deviation of R_i) times (the standard deviation of R_j)]:

$$\sigma_{ij} = \rho_{ij} \sigma_i \sigma_j$$

6. E.g., J. V. Uspensky, *Introduction to Mathematical Probability* (New York: McGraw-Hill, 1937), chapter 9, pp. 161–81.

The variance of a weighted sum is

$$V(R) = \sum_{i=1}^{N} a_i^2 V(X_i) + 2 \sum_{i=1}^{N} \sum_{i>1}^{N} a_i a_j \sigma_{ij}$$

If we use the fact that the variance of R_i is σ_{ii} then

$$V(R) = \sum_{i=1}^{N} \sum_{j=1}^{N} a_i a_j \sigma_{ij}$$

Let R_i be the return on the ith security. Let μ_i be the expected value of R_i; σ_{ij}, be the covariance between R_i and R_j (thus σ_{ii} is the variance of R_i). Let X_i be the percentage of the investor's assets which are allocated to the ith security. The yield (R) on the portfolio as a whole is

$$R = \sum R_i X_i$$

The R_i (and consequently R) are considered to be random variables.[7] The X_i are not random variables, but are fixed by the investor. Since the X_i are percentages we have $\Sigma X_i = 1$. In our analysis we will exclude negative values of the X_i (i.e., short sales); therefore $X_i \geqslant 0$ for all i.

The return (R) on the portfolio as a whole is a weighted sum of random variables (where the investor can choose the weights). From our discussion of such weighted sums we see that the expected return E from the portfolio as a whole is

$$E = \sum_{i=1}^{N} X_i \mu_i$$

and the variance is

$$V = \sum_{i=1}^{N} \sum_{j=1}^{N} \sigma_{ij} X_i X$$

7. I.e., we assume that the investor does (and should) act as if he had probability beliefs concerning these variables. In general we would expect that the investor could tell us, for any two events (A and B), whether he personally considered A more likely than B, B more likely than A, or both equally likely. If the investor were consistent in his opinions on such matters, he would possess a system of probability beliefs. We cannot expect the investor to be consistent in every detail. We can, however, expect his probability beliefs to be roughly consistent on important matters that have been carefully considered. We should also expect that he will base his actions upon these probability beliefs—even though they be in part subjective.

This paper does not consider the difficult question of how investors do (or should) form their probability beliefs.

For fixed probability beliefs (μ_i, σ_{ij}) the investor has a choice of various combinations of E and V depending on his choice of portfolio $X_1, \ldots, X_N$. Suppose that the set of all obtainable (E, V) combinations were as in Figure 1. The E-V rule states that the investor would (or should) want to select one of those portfolios which give rise to the (E, V) combinations indicated as efficient in the figure; i.e., those with minimum V for given E or more and maximum E for given V or less.

There are techniques by which we can compute the set of efficient portfolios and efficient (E, V) combinations associated with given μ_i

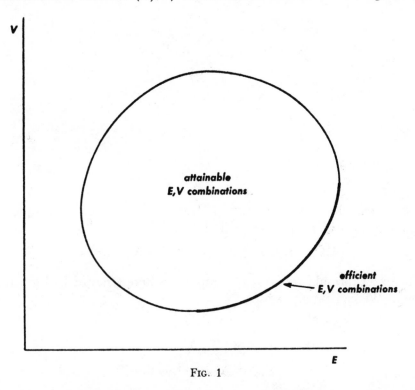

FIG. 1

and σ_{ij}. We will not present these techniques here. We will, however, illustrate geometrically the nature of the efficient surfaces for cases in which N (the number of available securities) is small.

The calculation of efficient surfaces might possibly be of practical use. Perhaps there are ways, by combining statistical techniques and the judgment of experts, to form reasonable probability beliefs (μ_i, σ_{ij}). We could use these beliefs to compute the attainable efficient combinations of (E, V). The investor, being informed of what (E, V) combinations were attainable, could state which he desired. We could then find the portfolio which gave this desired combination.

Two conditions—at least—must be satisfied before it would be prac tical to use efficient surfaces in the manner described above. First, the investor must desire to act according to the E-V maxim. Second, we must be able to arrive at reasonable μ_i and σ_{ij}. We will return to these matters later.

Let us consider the case of three securities. In the three security case our model reduces to

1) $$E = \sum_{i=1}^{3} X_i \mu_i$$

2) $$V = \sum_{i=1}^{3} \sum_{j=1}^{3} X_i X_j \sigma_{ij}$$

3) $$\sum_{i=1}^{3} X_i = 1$$

4) $$X_i \geqslant 0 \quad \text{for} \quad i = 1, 2, 3 .$$

From (3) we get

3') $$X_3 = 1 - X_1 - X_2$$

If we substitute (3') in equation (1) and (2) we get E and V as functions of X_1 and X_2. For example we find

1') $$E = \mu_3 + X_1 (\mu_1 - \mu_3) + X_2 (\mu_2 - \mu_3)$$

The exact formulas are not too important here (that of V is given below).[8] We can simply write

a) $$E = E (X_1, X_2)$$

b) $$V = V (X_1, X_2)$$

c) $$X_1 \geqslant 0, X_2 \geqslant 0, 1 - X_1 - X_2 \geqslant 0$$

By using relations (a), (b), (c), we can work with two dimensional geometry.

The attainable set of portfolios consists of all portfolios which satisfy constraints (c) and (3') (or equivalently (3) and (4)). The attainable combinations of X_1, X_2 are represented by the triangle $\overline{abc}$ in Figure 2. Any point to the left of the X_2 axis is not attainable because it violates the condition that $X_1 \geqslant 0$. Any point below the X_1 axis is not attainable because it violates the condition that $X_2 \geqslant 0$. Any

8. $V = X_1^2(\sigma_{11} - 2\sigma_{13} + \sigma_{33}) + X_2^2(\sigma_{22} - 2\sigma_{23} + \sigma_{33}) + 2X_1X_2(\sigma_{12} - \sigma_{13} - \sigma_{23} + \sigma_{33})$
$+ 2X_1 (\sigma_{13} - \sigma_{33}) + 2X_2(\sigma_{23} - \sigma_{33}) + \sigma_{33}$

point above the line $(1 - X_1 - X_2 = 0)$ is not attainable because it violates the condition that $X_3 = 1 - X_1 - X_2 \geqslant 0$.

We define an *isomean* curve to be the set of all points (portfolios) with a given expected return. Similarly an *isovariance* line is defined to be the set of all points (portfolios) with a given variance of return.

An examination of the formulae for E and V tells us the shapes of the isomean and isovariance curves. Specifically they tell us that typically[9] the isomean curves are a system of parallel straight lines; the isovariance curves are a system of concentric ellipses (see Fig. 2). For example, if $\mu_2 \neq \mu_3$ equation 1' can be written in the familiar form $X_2 = a + bX_1$; specifically (1)

$$X_2 = \frac{E - \mu_3}{\mu_2 - \mu_3} - \frac{\mu_1 - \mu_3}{\mu_2 - \mu_3} X_1.$$

Thus the slope of the isomean line associated with $E = E_0$ is $-(\mu_1 - \mu_3)/(\mu_2 - \mu_3)$ its intercept is $(E_0 - \mu_3)/(\mu_2 - \mu_3)$. If we change E we change the intercept but not the slope of the isomean line. This confirms the contention that the isomean lines form a system of parallel lines.

Similarly, by a somewhat less simple application of analytic geometry, we can confirm the contention that the isovariance lines form a family of concentric ellipses. The "center" of the system is the point which minimizes V. We will label this point X. Its expected return and variance we will label E and V. Variance increases as you move away from X. More precisely, if one isovariance curve, C_1, lies closer to X than another, C_2, then C_1 is associated with a smaller variance than C_2.

With the aid of the foregoing geometric apparatus let us seek the efficient sets.

X, the center of the system of isovariance ellipses, may fall either inside or outside the attainable set. Figure 4 illustrates a case in which X falls inside the attainable set. In this case: X is efficient. For no other portfolio has a V as low as X; therefore no portfolio can have either smaller V (with the same or greater E) or greater E with the same or smaller V. No point (portfolio) with expected return E less than E is efficient. For we have $E > E$ and $V < V$.

Consider all points with a given expected return E; i.e., all points on the isomean line associated with E. The point of the isomean line at which V takes on its least value is the point at which the isomean line

9. The isomean "curves" are as described above except when $\mu_1 = \mu_2 = \mu_3$. In the latter case all portfolios have the same expected return and the investor chooses the one with minimum variance.

As to the assumptions implicit in our description of the isovariance curves see footnote **12.**

is tangent to an isovariance curve. We call this point $\hat{X}(E)$. If we let E vary, $\hat{X}(E)$ traces out a curve.

Algebraic considerations (which we omit here) show us that this curve is a straight line. We will call it the critical line l. The critical line passes through X for this point minimizes V for all points with $E(X_1, X_2) = E$. As we go along l in either direction from X, V increases. The segment of the critical line from X to the point where the critical line crosses

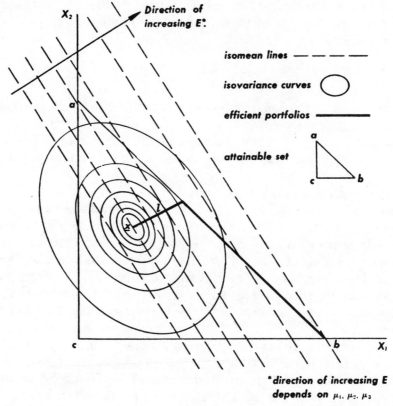

Direction of increasing E*

isomean lines — — — —

isovariance curves

efficient portfolios ——————

attainable set

*direction of increasing E depends on μ_1, μ_2, μ_3

Fig. 2

the boundary of the attainable set is part of the efficient set. The rest of the efficient set is (in the case illustrated) the segment of the $\overline{ab}$ line from d to b. b is the point of maximum attainable E. In Figure 3, X lies outside the admissible area but the critical line cuts the admissible area. The efficient line begins at the attainable point with minimum variance (in this case on the $\overline{ab}$ line). It moves toward b until it intersects the critical line, moves along the critical line until it intersects a boundary and finally moves along the boundary to b. The reader may

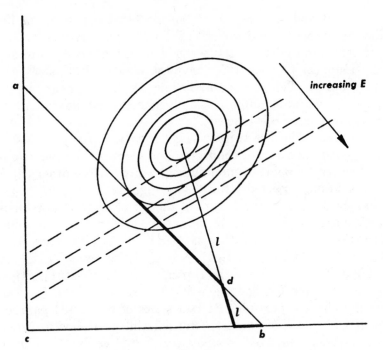

FIG. 3

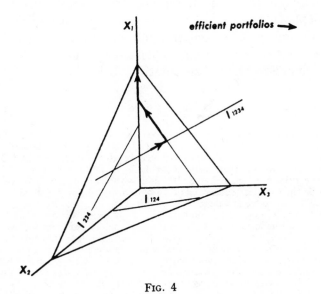

FIG. 4

wish to construct and examine the following other cases: (1) X lies outside the attainable set and the critical line does not cut the attainable set. In this case there is a security which does not enter into any efficient portfolio. (2) Two securities have the same μ_i. In this case the isomean lines are parallel to a boundary line. It may happen that the efficient portfolio with maximum E is a diversified portfolio. (3) A case wherein only one portfolio is efficient.

The efficient set in the 4 security case is, as in the 3 security and also the N security case, a series of connected line segments. At one end of the efficient set is the point of minimum variance; at the other end is a point of maximum expected return[10] (see Fig. 4).

Now that we have seen the nature of the set of efficient portfolios, it is not difficult to see the nature of the set of efficient (E, V) combinations. In the three security case $E = a_0 + a_1 X_1 + a_2 X_2$ is a plane; $V = b_0 + b_1 X_1 + b_2 X_2 + b_{12} X_1 X_2 + b_{11} X_1^2 + b_{22} X_2^2$ is a paraboloid.[11] As shown in Figure 5, the section of the E-plane over the efficient portfolio set is a series of connected line segments. The section of the V-paraboloid over the efficient portfolio set is a series of connected parabola segments. If we plotted V against E for efficient portfolios we would again get a series of connected parabola segments (see Fig. 6). This result obtains for any number of securities.

Various reasons recommend the use of the expected return-variance of return rule, both as a hypothesis to explain well-established investment behavior and as a maxim to guide one's own action. The rule serves better, we will see, as an explanation of, and guide to, "investment" as distinguished from "speculative" behavior.

10. Just as we used the equation $\sum_{i=1}^{4} X_i = 1$ to reduce the dimensionality in the three security case, we can use it to represent the four security case in 3 dimensional space. Eliminating X_4 we get $E = E(X_1, X_2, X_3)$, $V = V(X_1, X_2, X_3)$. The attainable set is represented, in three-space, by the tetrahedron with vertices $(0, 0, 0)$, $(0, 0, 1)$, $(0, 1, 0)$, $(1, 0, 0)$, representing portfolios with, respectively, $X_4 = 1$, $X_3 = 1$, $X_2 = 1$, $X_1 = 1$.

Let s_{123} be the subspace consisting of all points with $X_4 = 0$. Similarly we can define $s_{a1}, \ldots, aa$ to be the subspace consisting of all points with $X_i = 0$, $i \neq a_1, \ldots, aa$. For each subspace $s_{a1}, \ldots, aa$ we can define a *critical line* $la_1, \ldots aa$. This line is the locus of points P where P minimizes V for all points in $s_{a1}, \ldots, aa$ with the same E as P. If a point is in $s_{a1}, \ldots, aa$ and is efficient it must be on $la_1, \ldots, aa$. The efficient set may be traced out by starting at the point of minimum available variance, moving continuously along various $la_1, \ldots, aa$ according to definite rules, ending in a point which gives maximum E. As in the two dimensional case the point with minimum available variance may be in the interior of the available set or on one of its boundaries. Typically we proceed along a given critical line until either this line intersects one of a larger subspace or meets a boundary (and simultaneously the critical line of a lower dimensional subspace). In either of these cases the efficient line turns and continues along the new line. The efficient line terminates when a point with maximum E is reached.

11. See footnote 8.

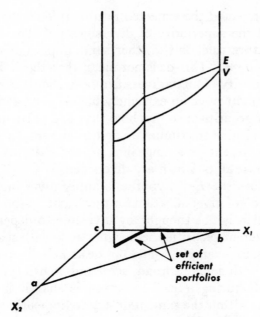

Fig. 5

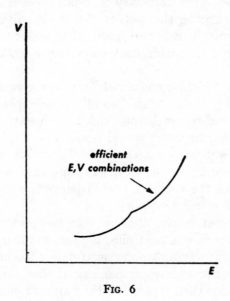

Fig. 6

Earlier we rejected the expected returns rule on the grounds that it never implied the superiority of diversification. The expected return-variance of return rule, on the other hand, implies diversification for a wide range of μ_i, σ_{ij}. This does not mean that the E-V rule never implies the superiority of an undiversified portfolio. It is conceivable that one security might have an extremely higher yield and lower variance than all other securities; so much so that one particular undiversified portfolio would give maximum E and minimum V. But for a large, presumably representative range of μ_i, σ_{ij} the E-V rule leads to efficient portfolios almost all of which are diversified.

Not only does the E-V hypothesis imply diversification, it implies the "right kind" of diversification for the "right reason." The adequacy of diversification is not thought by investors to depend solely on the number of different securities held. A portfolio with sixty different railway securities, for example, would not be as well diversified as the same size portfolio with some railroad, some public utility, mining, various sort of manufacturing, etc. The reason is that it is generally more likely for firms within the same industry to do poorly at the same time than for firms in dissimilar industries.

Similarly in trying to make variance small it is not enough to invest in many securities. It is necessary to avoid investing in securities with high covariances among themselves. We should diversify across industries because firms in different industries, especially industries with different economic characteristics, have lower covariances than firms within an industry.

The concepts "yield" and "risk" appear frequently in financial writings. Usually if the term "yield" were replaced by "expected yield" or "expected return," and "risk" by "variance of return," little change of apparent meaning would result.

Variance is a well-known measure of dispersion about the expected. If instead of variance the investor was concerned with standard error, $\sigma = \sqrt{V}$, or with the coefficient of dispersion, σ/E, his choice would still lie in the set of efficient portfolios.

Suppose an investor diversifies between two portfolios (i.e., if he puts some of his money in one portfolio, the rest of his money in the other. An example of diversifying among portfolios is the buying of the shares of two different investment companies). If the two original portfolios have *equal* variance then typically[12] the variance of the resulting (compound) portfolio will be less than the variance of either original port-

12. In no case will variance be increased. The only case in which variance will not be decreased is if the return from both portfolios are perfectly correlated. To draw the iso-variance curves as ellipses it is both necessary and sufficient to assume that no two distinct portfolios have perfectly correlated returns.

folio. This is illustrated by Figure 7. To interpret Figure 7 we note that a portfolio (P) which is built out of two portfolios $P' = (X_1', X_2')$ and $P'' = (X_1'', X_2'')$ is of the form $P = \lambda P' + (1 - \lambda)P'' = (\lambda X_1' + (1 - \lambda)X_1'', \lambda X_2' + (1 - \lambda)X_2'')$. P is on the straight line connecting P' and P''.

The E-V principle is more plausible as a rule for investment behavior as distinguished from speculative behavior. The third moment[13] M_3 of

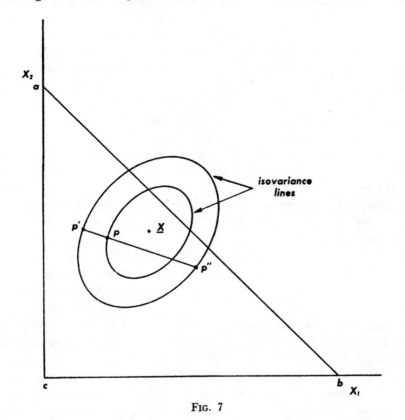

FIG. 7

the probability distribution of returns from the portfolio may be connected with a propensity to gamble. For example if the investor maximizes utility (U) which depends on E and $V(U = U(E, V), \partial U/\partial E > 0, \partial U/\partial E < 0)$ he will never accept an actuarially fair[14] bet. But if

13. If R is a random variable that takes on a finite number of values $r_1, \ldots, r_n$ with probabilities $p_1, \ldots, p_n$ respectively, and expected value E, then $M_3 = \sum\limits_{i=1}^{n} p_i(r_i - E)^3$

14. One in which the amount gained by winning the bet times the probability of winning is equal to the amount lost by losing the bet, times the probability of losing.

$U = U(E, V, M_3)$ and if $\partial U/\partial M_3 \neq 0$ then there are some fair bets which would be accepted.

Perhaps—for a great variety of investing institutions which consider yield to be a good thing; risk, a bad thing; gambling, to be avoided—E, V efficiency is reasonable as a working hypothesis and a working maxim.

Two uses of the E-V principle suggest themselves. We might use it in theoretical analyses or we might use it in the actual selection of portfolios.

In theoretical analyses we might inquire, for example, about the various effects of a change in the beliefs generally held about a firm, or a general change in preference as to expected return versus variance of return, or a change in the supply of a security. In our analyses the X_i might represent individual securities or they might represent aggregates such as, say, bonds, stocks and real estate.[15]

To use the E-V rule in the selection of securities we must have procedures for finding reasonable μ_i and σ_{ij}. These procedures, I believe, should combine statistical techniques and the judgment of practical men. My feeling is that the statistical computations should be used to arrive at a tentative set of μ_i and σ_{ij}. Judgment should then be used in increasing or decreasing some of these μ_i and σ_{ij} on the basis of factors or nuances not taken into account by the formal computations. Using this revised set of μ_i and σ_{ij}, the set of efficient E, V combinations could be computed, the investor could select the combination he preferred, and the portfolio which gave rise to this E, V combination could be found.

One suggestion as to tentative μ_i, σ_{ij} is to use the observed μ_i, σ_{ij} for some period of the past. I believe that better methods, which take into account more information, can be found. I believe that what is needed is essentially a "probabilistic" reformulation of security analysis. I will not pursue this subject here, for this is "another story." It is a story of which I have read only the first page of the first chapter.

In this paper we have considered the second stage in the process of selecting a portfolio. This stage starts with the relevant beliefs about the securities involved and ends with the selection of a portfolio. We have not considered the first stage: the formation of the relevant beliefs on the basis of observation.

15. Care must be used in using and interpreting relations among aggregates. We cannot deal here with the problems and pitfalls of aggregation.

17

A SIMPLIFIED MODEL FOR
PORTFOLIO ANALYSIS *

William F. Sharpe †

This paper describes the advantages of using a particular model of the relationships among securities for practical applications of the Markowitz portfolio
analysis technique. A computer program has been developed to take full advantage of the model: 2,000 securities can be analyzed at an extremely
low cost—as little as 2% of that associated with standard quadratic programming codes. Moreover, preliminary evidence suggests that the relatively
few parameters used by the model can lead to very nearly the same results obtained with much larger sets of relationships among securities. The possibility of low-cost analysis, coupled with a likelihood that a relatively small
amount of information need be sacrificed make the model an attractive candidate for initial practical applications of the Markowitz technique.

1. Introduction

Markowitz has suggested that the process of portfolio selection be approached
by (1) making probabilistic estimates of the future performances of securities,
(2) analyzing those estimates to determine an *efficient set* of portfolios and
(3) selecting from that set the portfolios best suited to the investor's preferences
[1, 2, 3]. This paper extends Markowitz' work on the second of these three stages
—*portfolio analysis*. The preliminary sections state the problem in its general form
and describe Markowitz' solution technique. The remainder of the paper presents
a simplified model of the relationships among securities, indicates the manner in
which it allows the portfolio analysis problem to be simplified, and provides evidence on the costs as well as the desirability of using the model for practical
applications of the Markowitz technique.

2. The Portfolio Analysis Problem

A security analyst has provided the following predictions concerning the future
returns from each of N securities:

$E_i \equiv$ the expected value of R_i (the return from security i)
C_{i1} through C_{in} ; C_{ij} represents the covariance between R_i and R_j (as
    usual, when $i = j$ the figure is the variance of R_i)

* Received December 1961.
  † The author wishes to express his appreciation for the cooperation of the staffs of both
the Western Data Processing Center at UCLA and the Pacific Northwest Research Computer Laboratory at the University of Washington where the program was tested. His
greatest debt, however, is to Dr. Harry M. Markowitz of the RAND Corporation, with
whom he was privileged to have a number of stimulating conversations during the past
year. It is no longer possible to segregate the ideas in this paper into those which were his,
those which were the author's, and those which were developed jointly. Suffice it to say that
the only accomplishments which are unquestionably the property of the author are those
of authorship—first of the computer program and then of this article.

Reprinted from *Management Science*, IX, No. 2 (January, 1963), 277–93, by permission of the author and publisher.

The portfolio analysis problem is as follows. Given such a set of predictions, determine the set of *efficient portfolios*; a portfolio is efficient if none other gives either (a) a higher expected return and the same variance of return or (b) a lower variance of return and the same expected return.

Let X_i represent the proportion of a portfolio invested in security i. Then the expected return (E) and variance of return (V) of any portfolio can be expressed in terms of (a) the basic data (E_i-values and C_{ij}-values) and (b) the amounts invested in various securities:

$$E = \sum_i X_i E_i$$

$$V = \sum_i \sum_j X_i X_j C_{ij}.$$

Consider an objective function of the form:

$$\phi = \lambda E - V$$

$$= \lambda \sum_i X_i E_i - \sum_i \sum_j X_i X_j C_{ij}.$$

Given a set of values for the parameters (λ, E_i's and C_{ij}'s), the value of ϕ can be changed by varying the X_i values as desired, a^ long as two basic restrictions are observed:

1. The entire portfolio must be invested:[1]

$$\sum_i X_i = 1$$

and 2. no security may be held in negative quantities:[2]

$$X_i \geqq 0 \quad \text{for all} \quad i.$$

A portfolio is described by the proportions invested in various securities—in our notation by the values of X_i. For each set of admissable values of the X_i variables there is a corresponding predicted combination of E and V and thus of ϕ. Figure 1 illustrates this relationship for a particular value of λ. The line ϕ_1 shows the combinations of E and V which give $\phi = \phi_1$, where $\phi = \lambda_k E - V$; the other lines refer to larger values of ϕ ($\phi_3 > \phi_2 > \phi_1$). Of all possible portfolios, one will maximize the value of ϕ;[3] in figure 1 it is portfolio C. The relationship between this solution and the portfolio analysis problem is obvious. The E, V combination obtained will be on the boundary of the set of attainable combinations; moreover, the objective function will be tangent to the set at that point. Since this function is of the form

$$\phi = \lambda E - V$$

---

[1] Since cash can be included as one of the securities (explicitly or implicitly) this assumption need cause no lack of realism.

[2] This is the standard formulation. Cases in which short sales are allowed require a different approach.

[3] This fact is crucial to the critical line computing procedure described in the next section.

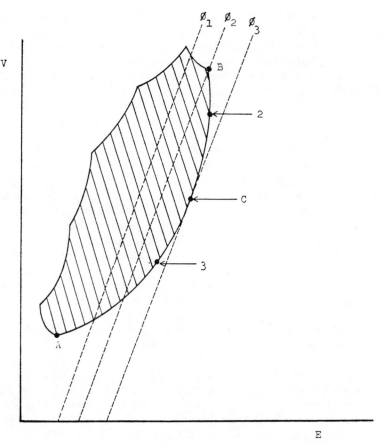

FIGURE 1

the slope of the boundary at the point must be λ; thus, by varying λ from $+\infty$ to 0, every solution of the portfolio analysis problem can be obtained.

For any given value of λ the problem described in this section requires the maximization of a quadratic function, ϕ (which is a function of X_i, X_i^2, and X_iX_j terms) subject to a linear constraint ($\sum_i X_i = 1$), with the variables restricted to non-negative values. A number of techniques have been developed to solve such *quadratic programming problems*. The critical line method, developed by Markowitz in conjunction with his work on portfolio analysis, is particularly suited to this problem and was used in the program described in this paper.

3. The Critical Line Method

Two important characteristics of the set of efficient portfolios make systematic solution of the portfolio analysis problem relatively straightforward. The first concerns the relationships among portfolios. Any set of efficient portfolios can be described in terms of a smaller set of *corner portfolios*. Any point on the E, V curve (other than the points associated with corner portfolios) can be obtained with a portfolio constructed by dividing the total investment between the two adjacent corner portfolios. For example, the portfolio which gives E, V combination C in Figure 1 might be some linear combination of the two corner portfolios with E, V combinations shown by points 2 and 3. This characteristic allows the analyst to restrict his attention to corner portfolios rather than the complete set of efficient portfolios; the latter can be readily derived from the former.

The second characteristic of the solution concerns the relationships among corner portfolios. Two corner portfolios which are adjacent on the E, V curve are related in the following manner: one portfolio will contain either (1) all the securities which appear in the other, plus one additional security or (2) all but one of the securities which appear in the other. Thus in moving down the E, V curve from one corner portfolio to the next, the quantities of the securities in efficient portfolios will vary until either one drops out of the portfolio or another enters. The point at which a change takes place marks a new corner portfolio.

The major steps in the critical line method for solving the portfolio analysis problem are:

1. The corner portfolio with $\lambda = \infty$ is determined. It is composed entirely of the one security with the highest expected return.[4]
2. Relationships between (a) the amounts of the various securities contained in efficient portfolios and (b) the value of λ are computed. It is possible to derive such relationships for any section of the E, V curve between adjacent corner portfolios. The relationships which apply to one section of the curve will not, however, apply to any other section.
3. Using the relationships computed in (2), each security is examined to determine the value of λ at which a change in the securities included in the portfolio would come about:
   a. securities presently in the portfolio are examined to determine the value of λ at which they would drop out, and
   b. securities not presently in the portfolio are examined to determine the value of λ at which they would enter the portfolio.
4. The next largest value of λ at which a security either enters or drops out of the portfolio is determined. This indicates the location of the next corner portfolio.
5. The composition of the new corner portfolio is computed, using the relationships derived in (2). However, since these relationships held only for the section of the curve between this corner portfolio and the preceding one, the solution process can only continue if new relationships are derived. The method thus returns to step (2) unless $\lambda = 0$, in which case the analysis is complete.

The amount of computation required to complete a portfolio analysis using

---

[4] In the event that two or more of the securities have the same (highest) expected return, the first efficient portfolio is the combination of such securities with the lowest variance.

this method is related to the following factors:

1. The number of securities analyzed
   This will affect the extent of the computation in step (2) and the number of computations in step (3).

2. The number of corner portfolios
   Steps (2) through (5) must be repeated once to find each corner portfolio.

3. The complexity of the variance-covariance matrix
   Step (2) requires a matrix be inverted and must be repeated once for each corner portfolio.

The amount of computer memory space required to perform a portfolio analysis will depend primarily on the size of the variance-covariance matrix. In the standard case, if N securities are analyzed this matrix will have $\frac{1}{2}(N^2 + N)$ elements.

4. The Diagonal Model

Portfolio analysis requires a large number of comparisons; obviously the practical application of the technique can be greatly facilitated by a set of assumptions which reduces the computational task involved in such comparisons. One such set of assumptions (to be called the diagonal model) is described in this article. This model has two virtues: it is one of the simplest which can be constructed without assuming away the existence of interrelationships among securities and there is considerable evidence that it can capture a large part of such interrelationships.

The major characteristic of the diagonal model is the assumption that the returns of various securities are related only through common relationships with some basic underlying factor. The return from any security is determined solely by random factors and this single outside element; more explicitly:

$$R_i = A_i + B_iI + C_i$$

where A_i and B_i are parameters, C_i is a random variable with an expected value of zero and variance Q_i, and I is the level of some index. The index, I, may be the level of the stock market as a whole, the Gross National Product, some price index or any other factor thought to be the most important single influence on the returns from securities. The future level of I is determined in part by random factors:

$$I = A_{n+1} + C_{n+1}$$

where A_{n+1} is a parameter and C_{n+1} is a random variable with an expected value of zero and a variance of Q_{n+1}. It is assumed that the covariance between C_i and C_j is zero for all values of i and $j (i \neq j)$.

Figure 2 provides a graphical representation of the model. A_i and B_i serve to locate the line which relates the expected value of R_i to the level of I. Q_i indicates the variance of R_i around the expected relationship (this variance is assumed to be the same at each point along the line). Finally, A_{n+1} indicates the expected value of I and Q_{n+1} the variance around that expected value.

The diagonal model requires the following predictions from a security analyst:

1) values of A_i, B_i and Q_i for each of N securities
2) values of A_{n+1} and Q_{n+1} for the index I.

The number of estimates required from the analyst is thus greatly reduced: from 5,150 to 302 for an analysis of 100 securities and from 2,003,000 to 6,002 for an analysis of 2,000 securities.

Once the parameters of the diagonal model have been specified all the inputs required for the standard portfolio analysis problem can be derived. The relationships are:

$$E_i = A_i + B_i(A_{n+1})$$

$$V_i = (B_i)^2(Q_{n+1}) + Q_i$$

$$C = (B_i)(B_j)(Q_{n+1})$$

A portfolio analysis could be performed by obtaining the values required by the diagonal model, calculating from them the full set of data required for the standard portfolio analysis problem and then performing the analysis with the derived values. However, additional advantages can be obtained if the portfolio analysis problem is restated directly in terms of the parameters of the diagonal model. The following section describes the manner in which such a restatement can be performed.

5. The Analogue

The return from a portfolio is the weighted average of the returns from its component securities:

$$R_p = \sum_{i=1}^{N} X_i R_i$$

The contribution of each security to the total return of a portfolio is simply $X_i R_i$ or, under the assumptions of the diagonal model:

$$X_i(A_i + B_i I + C_i).$$

The total contribution of a security to the return of the portfolio can be broken into two components: (1) an investment in the "basic characteristics" of the security in question and (2) an "investment" in the index:

(1) $$X_i(A_i + B_i I + C_i) = X_i(A_i + C_i)$$

(2) $$+ X_i B_i I$$

The return of a portfolio can be considered to be the result of (1) a series of investments in N "basic securities" and (2) an investment in the index:

$$R_p = \sum_{i=1}^{N} X_i(A_i + C_i) + \left[\sum_{i=1}^{N} X_i B_i \right] I$$

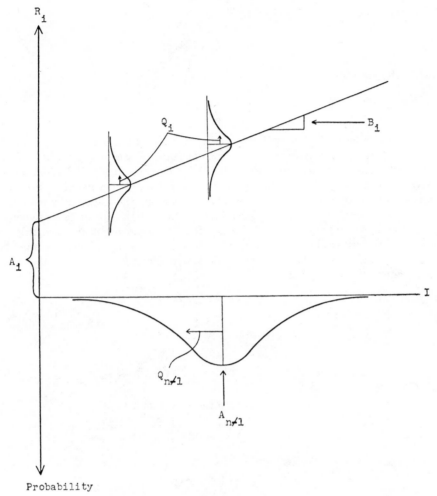

Probability

FIGURE 2

Defining X_{n+1} as the weighted average responsiveness of R_p to the level of I:

$$X_{n+1} \equiv \sum_{i=1}^{N} X_i B_i$$

and substituting this variable and the formula for the determinants of I, we obtain:

$$R_p = \sum_{i=1}^{N} X_i (A_i + C_i) + X_{n+1}(A_{n+1} + C_{n+1})$$

$$= \sum_{i=1}^{N+1} X_i (A_i + C_i).$$

The expected return of a portfolio is thus:

$$E = \sum_{i=1}^{N+1} X_i A_i$$

while the variance is:[5]

$$V = \sum_{i=1}^{N+1} X_i^2 Q_i$$

This formulation indicates the reason for the use of the parameters A_{n+1} and Q_{n+1} to describe the expected value and variance of the future value of I. It also indicates the reason for calling this the "diagonal model". The variance-covariance matrix, which is full when N securities are considered, can be expressed as a matrix with non-zero elements only along the diagonal by including an $(n + 1)$st security defined as indicated. This vastly reduces the number of computations required to solve the portfolio analysis problem (primarily in step 2 of the critical line method, when the variance-covariance matrix must be inverted) and allows the problem to be stated directly in terms of the basic parameters of the diagonal model:

$$\text{Maximize:} \quad \lambda E - V$$

$$\text{Where:} \quad E = \sum_{i=1}^{N+1} X_i A_i$$

$$V = \sum_{i=1}^{N+1} X_i^2 Q_i$$

$$\text{Subject to:} \quad X_i \geqq 0 \text{ for all } i \text{ from 1 to } N$$

$$\sum_{i=1}^{N} X_i = 1$$

$$\sum_{i=1}^{N} X_i B_i = X_{n+1}.$$

6. The Diagonal Model Portfolio Analysis Code

As indicated in the previous section, if the portfolio analysis problem is expressed in terms of the basic parameters of the diagonal model, computing time and memory space required for solution can be greatly reduced. This section describes a machine code, written in the FØRTRAN language, which takes full advantage of the characteristics of the diagonal model. It uses the critical line method to solve the problem stated in the previous section.

The computing time required by the diagonal code is considerably smaller than that required by standard quadratic programming codes. The RAND QP

---

[5] Recall that the diagonal model assumes $\text{cov}(C_i, C_j) = 0$ for all i and j $(i \neq j)$.

code[6] required 33 minutes to solve a 100-security example on an IBM 7090 computer; the same problem was solved in 30 seconds with the diagonal code. Moreover, the reduced storage requirements allow many more securities to be analyzed: with the IBM 709 or 7090 the RAND QP code can be used for no more than 249 securities, while the diagonal code can analyze up to 2,000 securities.

Although the diagonal code allows the total computing time to be greatly reduced, the cost of a large analysis is still far from insignificant. Thus there is every incentive to limit the computations to those essential for the final selection of a portfolio. By taking into account the possibilities of borrowing and lending money, the diagonal code restricts the computations to those absolutely necessary for determination of the final set of efficient portfolios. The importance of these alternatives, their effect on the portfolio analysis problem and the manner in which they are taken into account in the diagonal code are described in the remainder of this section.

A. The "lending portfolio"

There is some interest rate (r_l) at which money can be lent with virtual assurance that both principal and interest will be returned; at the least, money can be buried in the ground $(r_l = 0)$. Such an alternative could be included as one possible security $(A_i = 1 + r_l, B_i = 0, Q_i = 0)$ but this would necessitate some needless computation.[7] In order to minimize computing time, lending at some pure interest rate is taken into account explicitly in the diagonal code.

The relationship between lending and efficient portfolios can best be seen in terms of an E, σ curve showing the combinations of expected return and standard deviation of return $(= \sqrt{V})$ associated with efficient portfolios. Such a curve is shown in Figure 3 (FBCG); point A indicates the E, σ combination attained if all funds are lent. The relationship between lending money and purchasing portfolios can be illustrated with the portfolio which has the E, σ combination shown by point Z. Consider a portfolio with X_z invested in portfolio Z and the remainder $(1 - X_z)$ lent at the rate r_l. The expected return from such a portfolio would be:

$$E = X_z E_z + (1 - X_z)(1 + r_l)$$

and the variance of return would be:

$$V = X_z^2 V_z + (1 - X_z)^2 V_l + 2X_z(1 - X_z)(\text{cov}_{zl})$$

---

[6] The program is described in [4]. Several alternative quadratic programming codes are available. A recent code, developed by IBM, which uses the critical line method is likely to prove considerably more efficient for the portfolio analysis problem. The RAND code is used for comparison since it is the only standard program with which the author has had experience.

[7] Actually, the diagonal code cannot accept non-positive values of Q_i; thus if the lending alternative is to be included as simply another security, it must be assigned a very small value of Q_i. This procedure will give virtually the correct solution but is inefficient.

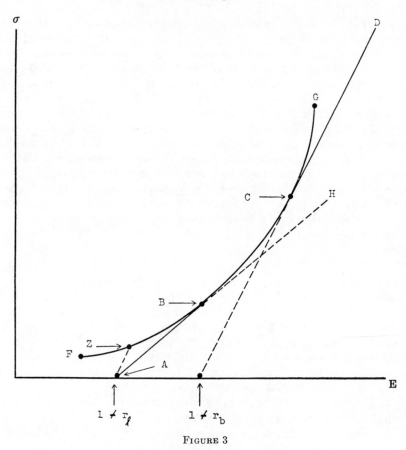

Figure 3

But, since V_l and cov_{zl} are both zero:

$$V = X_z^2 V_z$$

and the standard deviation of return is:

$$\sigma = X_z \sigma_z .$$

Since both E and σ are linear functions of X_z, the E, σ combinations of all portfolios made up of portfolio Z plus lending must lie on a straight line connecting points Z and A. In general, by splitting his investment between a portfolio and lending, an investor can attain any E, σ combination on the line connecting the E, σ combinations of the two components.

Many portfolios which are efficient in the absence of the lending alternative becomes inefficient when it is introduced. In Figure 3, for example, the possibility of attaining E, σ combinations along the line AB makes all portfolios along the original E, σ curve from point F to point B inefficient. For any desired level of

E below that associated with portfolio B, the most efficient portfolio will be some combination of portfolio B and lending. Portfolio B can be termed the "lending portfolio" since it is the appropriate portfolio whenever some of the investor's funds are to be lent at the rate r_l. This portfolio can be found readily once the E, σ curve is known. It lies at the point on the curve at which a ray from $(E = 1 + r_l, \sigma = 0)$ is tangent to the curve. If the E, σ curve is not known in its entirety it is still possible to determine whether or not a particular portfolio is the lending portfolio by computing the rate of interest which *would* make the portfolio in question the lending portfolio. For example, the rate of interest associated in this manner with portfolio C is r_b, found by extending a tangent to the curve down to the E-axis. The diagonal code computes such a rate of interest for each corner portfolio as the analysis proceeds; when it falls below the previously stated lending rate the code computes the composition of the lending portfolio and terminates the analysis.

B. The "borrowing portfolio"

In some cases an investor may be able to borrow funds in order to purchase even greater amounts of a portfolio than his own funds will allow. If the appropriate rate for such borrowing were r_b, illustrated in figure 3, the E, σ combinations attainable by purchasing portfolio C with both the investor's funds and with borrowed funds would lie along the line CD, depending on the amount borrowed. Inclusion of the borrowing alternative makes certain portfolios inefficient which are efficient in the absence of the alternative; in this case the affected portfolios are those with E, σ combinations along the segment of the original E, σ curve from C to G. Just as there is a single appropriate portfolio if any lending is contemplated, there is a single appropriate portfolio if borrowing is contemplated. This "borrowing portfolio" is related to the rate of interest at which funds can be borrowed in exactly the same manner as the "lending portfolio" is related to the rate at which funds can be lent.

The diagonal code does not take account of the borrowing alternative in the manner used for the lending alternative since it is necessary to compute all previous corner portfolios in order to derive the portion of the E, σ curve below the borrowing portfolio. For this reason all computations required to derive the full E, σ curve above the lending portfolio must be made. However, the code does allow the user to specify the rate of interest at which funds can be borrowed. If this alternative is chosen, none of the corner portfolios which will be inefficient when borrowing is considered will be printed. Since as much as 65% of the total computer time can be spent recording (on tape) the results of the analysis this is not an insignificant saving.

7. The Cost of Portfolio Analysis with the Diagonal Code

The total time (and thus cost) required to perform a portfolio analysis with the diagonal code will depend upon the number of securities analyzed, the number of corner portfolios and, to some extent, the composition of the corner portfolios. A formula which gives quite an accurate estimate of the time required to perform an analysis on an IBM 709 computer was obtained by analyzing a series of runs during which the time required to complete each major segment of the program was recorded. The approximate time required for the analysis will be:[8]

Number of seconds = .6
+ .114 × number of securities analyzed
+ .54 × number of corner portfolios
+ .0024 × number of securities analyzed × number of corner portfolios.

Unfortunately only the number of securities analyzed is known before the analysis is begun. In order to estimate the cost of portfolio analysis before it is performed, some relationship between the number of corner portfolios and the number of securities analyzed must be assumed. Since no theoretical relationship can be derived and since the total number of corner portfolios could be several times the number of securities analysed, it seemed desirable to obtain some crude notion of the typical relationship when "reasonable" inputs are used. To accomplish this, a series of portfolio analyses was performed using inputs generated by a Monte Carlo model.

Data were gathered on the annual returns during the period 1940–1951 for 96 industrial common stocks chosen randomly from the New York Stock Exchange. The returns of each security were then related to the level of a stock market index and estimates of the parameters of the diagonal model obtained. These parameters were assumed to be samples from a population of A_i, B_i and Q_i triplets related as follows:

$$A_i = \bar{A} + r_1$$
$$B_i = \bar{B} + \psi A_i + r_2$$
$$Q_i = \bar{Q} + \theta A_i + \gamma B_i + r_3$$

where r_1, r_2 and r_3 are random variables with zero means. Estimates for the parameters of these three equations were obtained by regression analysis and estimates of the variances of the random variables determined.[9] With this information the characteristics of any desired number of securities could be generated. A random number generator was used to select a value for A_i; this value, together with an additional random number determined the value of B_i; the value of Q_i was then determined with a third random number and the previously obtained values of A_i and B_i.

Figure 4 shows the relationship between the number of securities analyzed

---

[8] The computations in this section are based on the assumption that no corner portfolios prior to the lending portfolio are printed. If the analyst chooses to print all preceding portfolios, the estimates given in this section should be multiplied by 2.9; intermediate cases can be estimated by interpolation.

[9] The random variables were considered normally distributed; in one case, to better approximate the data, two variances were used for the distribution—one for the portion above the mean and another for the portion below the mean.

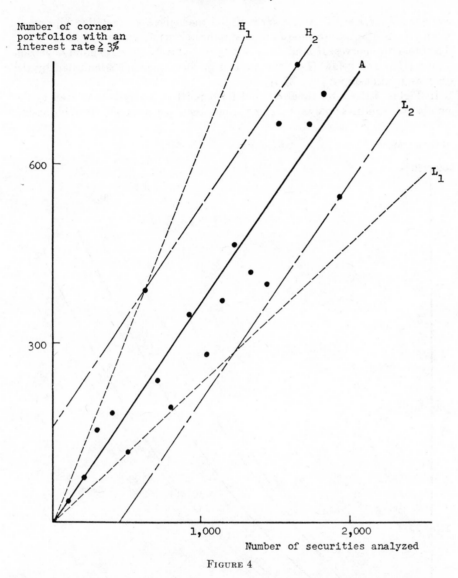

Number of corner
portfolios with an
interest rate $\geq$ 3%

Number of securities analyzed

FIGURE 4

and the number of corner portfolios with interest rates greater than 3% (an approximation to the "lending rate"). Rather than perform a sophisticated analysis of these data, several lines have been used to bracket the results in various ways. These will be used subsequently as extreme cases, on the presumption that most practical cases will lie within these extremes (but with no presumption that these limits will never be exceeded). Curve A indicates the average relationship between the number of portfolios and the number of securities:

337

average $(N_p/N_s) = .37$. Curve H_1 indicates the highest such relationship: maximum $(N_p/N_s) = .63$; the line L_1 indicates the lowest: minimum $(N_p/N_s) = .24$. The other two curves, H_2 and L_2, indicate respectively the maximum deviation above (155) and below (173) the number of corner portfolios indicated by the average relationship $N_p = .37 \ N_s$.

In Figure 5 the total time required for a portfolio analysis is related to the number of securities analyzed under various assumptions about the relationship

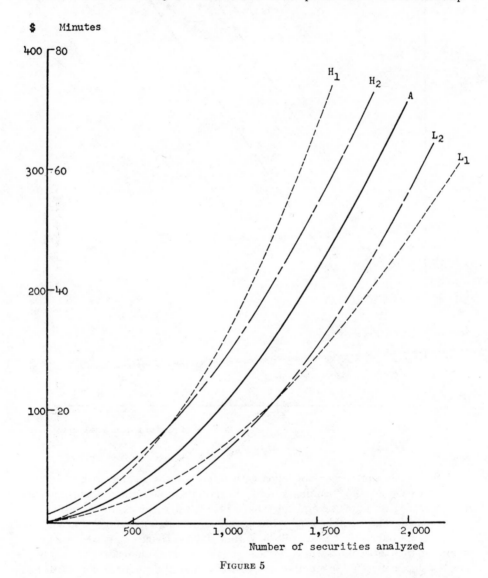

FIGURE 5

between the number of corner portfolios and the number of securities analyzed. Each of the curves shown in Figure 5 is based on the corresponding curve in Figure 4; for example, curve *A* in Figure 5 indicates the relationship between total time and number of securities analyzed on the assumption that the relationship between the number of corner portfolios and the number of securities is that shown by curve *A* in Figure 4. For convenience a second scale has been provided in Figure 5, showing the total cost of the analysis on the assumption that an IBM 709 computer can be obtained at a cost of $300 per hour.

8. The Value of Portfolio Analysis Based on the Diagonal Model

The assumptions of the diagonal model lie near one end of the spectrum of possible assumptions about the relationships among securities. The model's extreme simplicity enables the investigator to perform a portfolio analysis at a very small cost, as we have shown. However, it is entirely possible that this simplicity so restricts the security analyst in making his predictions that the value of the resulting portfolio analysis is also very small.

In order to estimate the ability of the diagonal model to summarize information concerning the performance of securities a simple test was performed. Twenty securities were chosen randomly from the New York Stock Exchange and their performance during the period 1940–1951 used to obtain two sets of

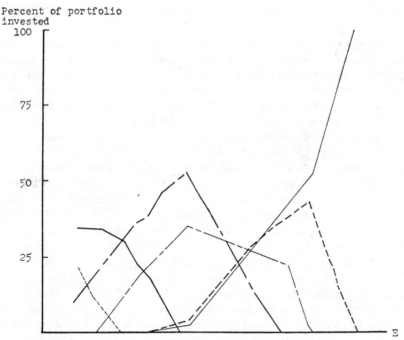

Fig. 6a. Composition of efficient portfolios derived from the analysis of the parameters of the diagonal model.

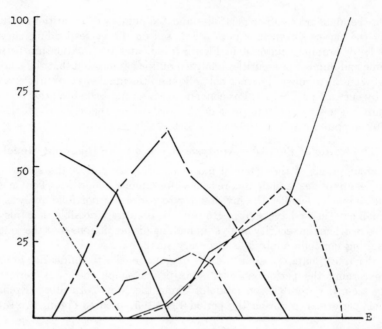

Fɪɢ. 6b. Composition of efficient portfolios derived from the analysis of historical data

data: (1) the actual mean returns, variances of returns and covariances of returns during the period and (2) the parameters of the diagonal model, estimated by regression techniques from the performance of the securities during the period. A portfolio analysis was then performed on each set of data. The results are summarized in Figures 6a and 6b. Each security which entered any of the efficient portfolios in significant amounts is represented by a particular type of line; the height of each line above any given value of E indicates the percentage of the efficient portfolio with that particular E composed of the security in question. The two figures thus indicate the compositions of all the efficient portfolios chosen from the analysis of the historical data (Figure 6b) and the compositions of all the portfolios chosen from the analysis of the parameters of the diagonal model (Figure 6a). The similarity of the two figures indicates that the 62 parameters of the diagonal model were able to capture a great deal of the information contained in the complete set of 230 historical relationships. An additional test, using a second set of 20 securities, gave similar results.

These results are, of course, far too fragmentary to be considered conclusive but they do suggest that the diagonal model may be able to represent the relationships among securities rather well and thus that the value of portfolio analyses based on the model will exceed their rather nominal cost. For these reasons it appears to be an excellent choice for the initial practical applications of the Markowitz technique.

References

1. MARKOWITZ, HARRY M., *Portfolio Selection, Efficient Diversification of Investments*, New York, John Wiley and Sons, Inc., 1959.
2. MARKOWITZ, HARRY M., "Portfolio Selection", *The Journal of Finance*, Vol. 12, (March 1952), 77–91.
3. MARKOWITZ, HARRY M., "The Optimization of a Quadratic Function Subject to Linear Constraints," *Naval Research Logistics Quarterly*, Vol. 3, (March and June, 1956), 111–133.
4. WOLFE, PHILIP, "The Simplex Method for Quadratic Programming," *Econometrica*, Vol. 27, (July, 1959), 382–398.

18

Risk, Market Sensitivity and Diversification

by William F. Sharpe

The notion of risk is central to both security analysis and portfolio selection. The primary source of risk for an individual security is uncertainty about its future price. And the primary source of risk for a portfolio is uncertainty about its future market value.

Clearly, some securities are riskier than others, and some portfolios are riskier than others. Moreover, the riskiness of a portfolio is related to the riskiness of the securities it contains. Few would quarrel with these statements. To go farther, however, one must adopt quantitative measures. This paper describes two such measures. The first, market sensitivity, (or "beta"), has been advocated by a number of authors |2, 3, 4, 5|* and is being used increasingly within the investment community |6|. The second measure, portfolio *diversification*, attempts to make more precise a notion that has been used for a great many years.

In the remaining sections we will argue: (1) that much is to be learned about the risk of a portfolio by measuring its market sensitivity and diversification, (2) that such measures can be calculated simply, using corresponding measures for the securities in the portfolio, and (3) that straightforward analysis of past data can lead to values of such measures for securities that will prove useful in this process.

Market and Non-Market Risk

To begin, it is important to divide risk into two important, but quite different, components. Why is it difficult to predict the future price of a security? Partly, because it is difficult to predict the future level of the overall market. This source of risk can be termed the security's *market risk*. But even if the future course of the market were known, some risk would remain. The price of a security depends at least partly on the fortunes of the issuer — independent of the course of the

---

*References [ ] appear at end of article.

WILLIAM F. SHARPE *is Professor of Business, Stanford University and Adviser, Computer Research Department, Merrill Lynch, Pierce, Fenner & Smith, Inc.*

market or overall economy. This source can be termed the security's *non-market risk*.

The market risk of a security or portfolio depends on the extent to which its price is sensitive to market swings. Our first measure is intended to quantify this relationship.

The non-market risk of a portfolio depends to a considerable extent on its diversification. Our second measure is intended to quantify this relationship. It is designed so that two portfolios with comparable "diversification" will be likely to have comparable amounts of non-market risk.

Market Sensitivity

When there is a major change in the market, it is a rare security indeed that does not go along, to a greater or lesser extent. A market swing generally results when investors change their opinions about the future of the economy. Some companies are affected more by such changes than are others. In terms of price action, some securities are more sensitive to market changes than are others. It is a relatively simple matter to express this relationship quantitatively. Consider the following statement:

> If the market goes up one per cent more than expected, the price of XYZ will be ___ , per cent greater than expected.

The number used to fill in the blank can be defined as XYZ's *market sensitivity*. If the value is less than 1.0, the security is defensive—it moves less than the typical stock in market swings. On the other hand, if the market sensitivity is greater than 1.0, the security is aggressive—it moves more than a typical stock in market swings.

It is possible to define a number of such measures: one for a one per cent increase in the market, one for a one per cent decrease, one for a two per cent increase, etc. But this would add little but complexity. It is common practice to use one number, with the accompanying assumption that the percentage change in the price of a security from its expected value is most likely to equal its market sensitivity times the percentage change in the market from its expected value.

The market sensitivity of a portfolio is simply the weighted average of the market sensitivities of its component securities, using the relative values as weights |3|. Table 1 provides an example.

Diversification

Why do investment managers advocate at least some diversification when constructing a portfolio? Because it can reduce risk. More precisely: because it can reduce non-market risk. When one security does worse than expected (given the market's overall behavior), another is likely to do better than expected. And, generally, the more securities in a portfolio, the greater the likelihood that sufficient good fortune will appear to balance off the bad fortune.

But it is not quite that simple. The number of securities in a portfolio provides a fairly crude measure of diversification. Imagine two portfolios, each with ten securities. Portfolio A's funds are divided equally among its ten securities, but half of portfolio B's funds are invested in a single security. Portfolio A would seem to be more diversified than portfolio B. To further complicate the matter, some securities have more non-market risk than others. A portfolio of ten securities, each of which has a large amount of this type of risk, is likely to offer less effective diversification than another with ten securities, each of which has a small amount of non-market risk.

There are other considerations. For example, a portfolio of ten chemical securities is likely to offer less effective diversification than one of ten securities, each from a different industry. This type of difference is difficult to capture in a simple formula. But differences in relative holdings and securities' non-market risks can be accommodated quite easily.

The first step requires an estimate of each security's non-market risk, relative to that of a

Table 1. Calculation of a Portfolio's Estimated Market Sensitivity

Security	Current Market Price Per Share	Number of Shares in Portfolio	Current Market Value	Relative Value	Estimated Market Sensitivity	Relative Value times Market Sensitivity
ABC	$13.00	1,000	$13,000	.325	.80	.26
DEF	50.00	300	15,000	.375	1.20	.45
GHI	30.00	400	12,000	.300	1.30	.39
			$40,000	1.000		1.10
						Portfolio Estimated Market Sensitivity

Table 2. Calculation of a Portfolio's Diversification

Security	Current Market Price Per Share	Number of Shares in Portfolio	Current Market Value	(V) Relative Value	(R) Relative Non-Market Risk	V × R	(V × R)²
ABC	$13.00	1,000	$13,000	.325	0.5	.163	.027
DEF	50.00	300	15,000	.375	1.0	.375	.141
GHI	30.00	400	12,000	.300	1.5	.450	.203
			$40,000	1.000			.371

$$\text{Diversification} = \frac{1}{.371} = 2.70$$

typical security. A value of 1.0 indicates that a security is typical in this respect. A value of .5 indicates that it has half as much non-market risk as a typical security. A value of 2.0 indicates it has twice as much, etc.

Once such estimates have been obtained, it is easy to estimate the effective *diversification* of the portfolio. Table 2 provides an example.

As the table shows, a number of values must be added together—one for each security. Each value is calculated by squaring the product of (1) the relative value invested in the security times (2) its relative non-market risk. The sum (.371 in this example) is then divided into 1.0 to determine the portfolio's diversification. In this case, it is 2.70.

Table 3 provides some insight into the meaning of this measure.

Each security listed in Table 3 provides an equal proportion of the portfolio's market value; moreover, each security is typical with respect to non-market risk. And the effective diversification of the portfolio is 5.0. Thus a portfolio of five typical stocks, each representing an equal proportion of overall market value, has a calculated diversification of 5.0.

Table 3. Diversification of an Evenly-Balanced Portfolio of Typical Securities

Security	(V) Relative Value	(R) Relative Non-Market Risk	$V \times R$	$(V \times R)^2$
A	.2	1.0	.2	.04
B	.2	1.0	.2	.04
C	.2	1.0	.2	.04
D	.2	1.0	.2	.04
E	.2	1.0	.2	.04
	1.0			.20

$$\text{Diversification} = \frac{1}{.20} = 5.0$$

This example illustrates the interpretation of the diversification measure:

A balanced portfolio with a diversification of $\underline{X}$ will have as much non-market risk as a balanced portfolio of $\underline{X}$ securities, each with

a typical amount of non-market risk, and each worth an equal dollar amount at current market prices. The term "balanced" is included to rule out portfolios with heavy concentrations of similar securities. Such portfolios will generally be less diversified than indicated by the calculation described here—i.e., they will have more non-market risk.

In cases such as that shown in Table 2, where a round number is not obtained for diversification, the result can be interpreted as lying between two alternatives. Thus a portfolio with a diversification of 2.70 is less diversified than a portfolio of three typical securities held in equal proportions; but it is more diversified than one of two typical securities, held in equal proportions.

Diversification and Non-Market Risk

The non-market risk of a portfolio will, of course, depend on more than its calculated level of diversification. However, it is possible to provide a set of benchmarks for portfolios which have been designed to avoid undue concentrations of similar securities. Figure 1 shows the general relationship. The vertical axis measures non-market risk relative to that of a typical security. Thus a portfolio with a diversification of 1.0 has a full 100 per cent of such risk.

As diversification increases, the amount of non-market risk can be expected to decrease, but not proportionately. Thus a portfolio with a diversification of 4.00 is likely to have 50 per cent as much risk as one with a diversification of 1.00.*

The basis for this relationship, and the choice of the measure of diversification itself, is described in the appendix. Here we concentrate on a more practical question: how should the needed values for individual securities be estimated?

Estimates for Securities

Two values are required for every security in a portfolio: the security's market sensitivity and its

---

*Well-diversified portfolios have another advantage. In general, the greater the diversification, the more accurate will be the estimate of the portfolio's market sensitivity. In statistical terms: the standard error of beta is smaller, the smaller the standard deviation of the residual.

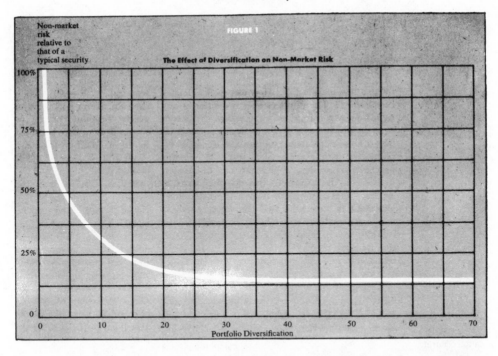

Non-market risk relative to that of a typical security

FIGURE 1

The Effect of Diversification on Non-Market Risk

Portfolio Diversification

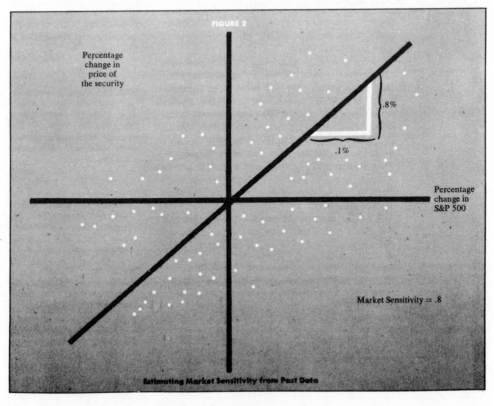

FIGURE 2

Percentage change in price of the security

Percentage change in S&P 500

.8%

.1%

Market Sensitivity = .8

Estimating Market Sensitivity from Past Data

relative non-market risk. How can such estimates be obtained? The problem does not differ in any significant way from that of estimating, say, future earnings per share. Careful analysis of past data, expert knowledge about the firm and the industry, interviews with management, study of investor psychology—all these ingredients can be brought to bear on the problem. But this may provide accuracy that costs more than it is worth. It is important to remember that the values obtained for individual securities are to be combined to calculate comparable values for a portfolio. And the accuracy of a portfolio estimate is far more important than the accuracy of the individual security estimates.

A number of rather inaccurate estimates for securities may combine to form an exceptionally accurate estimate for a portfolio, thanks to the law of large numbers. The estimate for one security may be too high, and another too low, with the result that the average is "just right." To borrow the statistician's jargon: if predictions about securities are subject to error but unbiased*, predictions about fairly well-diversified portfolios may be quite accurate.

This suggests the possibility of using past data exclusively to obtain estimates of the relevant attributes of securities. Figure 2 provides an example.

For each of 60 months, the percentage change in Standard and Poor's 500-stock index is determined. This represents the overall "market." Next, the percentage change in the price of the security in question is calculated for each of the 60 months. Then each month is plotted and a straight line fit through the points (either visually or via statistical methods). The slope of this line is the security's market sensitivity.

A useful measure of relative non-market risk can also be obtained from past data. First, the statistician's "standard error" is calculated for the

security[3]. Roughly, this is the vertical distance from the line in a diagram such as Figure 2 within which two-thirds of the points fall. After the standard error has been calculated, it is divided by the standard error for a typical security.† The result is a measure of the security's relative non-market risk.

Several firms produce estimates of market sensitivity on a continuing basis. Methods differ, as do names ("beta" and "volatility" are quite common). The most accessible source is *Value Line*, which covers 1400 securities. Some brokerage houses provide coverage of even more (e.g., Merrill Lynch provides estimates for over 3000 stocks with monthly updating). At present, values of relative non-market risk are not quite as accessible. However, Merrill Lynch provides values from which they can be readily computed, and uses them in the manner described here.

No two measures can tell all there is to know about a portfolio's risk. But the relatively simple measures presented here can greatly increase one's understanding of the characteristics of a portfolio. It behooves the thoughtful analyst to make such calculations. ◆

*And the errors are uncorrelated.

†E.g., the median or average value of the standard errors for a representative cross-section of securities.

References

1. Cohen, Kalman J. and Jerry A. Pogue, "An Empirical Evaluation of Alternative Portfolio Selection Models," *Journal of Business*, April 1967, pp. 166-193.
2. Sharpe, William F., "A Simplified Model for Portfolio Analysis," *Management Science*, January 1963, pp. 277-293.
3. ————, *Portfolio Theory and Capital Markets* (McGraw-Hill, 1970).
4. Treynor, Jack L., "How to Rate Management of Investment Funds," *Harvard Business Review*, January-February 1965, pp. 63-75.
5. Treynor, Jack L., William W. Priest, Jr., Lawrence Fisher, and Catherine A. Higgins, "Using Portfolio Composition to Estimate Risk," *Financial Analyst's Journal*, September-October 1968. pp. 93-100.
6. Welles, Chris, "The Beta Revolution: Learning to Live with Risk," *The Institutional Investor*, September 1971, pp. 21-64.

APPENDIX

This paper uses standard statistical measures of variation to represent risk. The risk of a security is measured by a standard deviation:

σ_i = the standard deviation of R_i

R_i = the rate of return on security i

= the percentage price change plus dividend yield

The rate of return on a security is assumed to equal its yield plus a linear function of the percentage change in the overall market:

$$R_i \approx y_i + a_i + b_i R_m + c_i$$

where:

y_i = the dividend yield on security i

a_i = some constant

b_i = the market sensitivity of security i

R_m = the percentage change in the overall market

c_i = the difference between the return on security i and that predicted by its relationship with the overall market

The risk of the security thus depends on two components:

$$\sigma_i^2 = b_i^2 \sigma_m^2 + \sigma_{ei}^2$$

where:

$b_i^2 \sigma_m^2$ = the market risk of security i

σ_m = the standard deviation of R_m

σ_{ei}^2 = the non-market risk of security i

σ_{ei} = the standard deviation of c_i

If the values of the c_i's for various securities are independent of one another and of the overall level of the market, * the risk of a portfolio will also depend on two components:

$$\sigma_p^2 = b_p^2 \sigma_m^2 + \sum_i X_i^2 \sigma_{ei}^2$$

where:

σ_p = the standard deviation of R_p (the rate of return on the portifolo)

b_p = the market sensitivity of the portfolio
$= \sum_i X_i b_i$

X_i = the proportion of the portfolio's value invested in security i

The term representing the non-market risk of the portfolio can be modified to form the measure of diversification advocated in the text. Let $\sigma_{e\bullet}$ represent any more or less arbitrarily chosen "typical" level of σ_{ei}. Then:

$$\sum_i X_i^2 \sigma_{ei}^2 = \sigma_{e\bullet}^2 \sum_i X_i^2 \left(\frac{\sigma_{ei}}{\sigma_{e\bullet}} \right)^2$$

The term in parentheses measures a security's relative non-market risk:

r_i = the relative non-market risk of security i

$$= \frac{\sigma_{ei}}{\sigma_{e\bullet}}$$

Diversification is defined in the text as follows:

$$D = \frac{1}{\sum_i (X_i r_i)^2}$$

so that:

$$\sum_i X_i^2 \sigma_{ei}^2 = \sigma_{e\bullet}^2 \left(\frac{1}{D} \right)$$

We take as a specific measure of the non-market risk of a portfolio the standard error of its return. But this is simply the square root of the sum:

$$\sqrt{\sum_i X_i^2 \sigma_{ei}^2} = \frac{\sigma_{e\bullet}}{\sqrt{D}}$$

The non-market risk relative to that of a typical security is this amount divided by $\sigma_{e\bullet}$, or:

$$\frac{1}{\sqrt{D}}$$

This is the relationship plotted in Figure 1.

An interpretation of the measure of diversification is provided. by considering a portfolio of n stocks, each typical with respect to non-market risk, and each worth the same dollar value. In other words:

$$r_1 = r_2 = \cdots = r_n = 1$$

$$X_1 = X_2 = \cdots = X_n = \frac{1}{n}$$

Obviously:

$$D = \frac{1}{\sum_i (X_i r_i)^2} = \frac{1}{\frac{1}{n^2} + \frac{1}{n^2} + \cdots + \frac{1}{n^2}}$$

$$= \frac{1}{n \left(\frac{1}{n^2} \right)} = n$$

If the values of the c_i's are independent, a portfolio with a diversification of D will thus have the same amount of non-market risk as one with D typical stocks, held in equal proportions (as asserted in the text).

*This assumption, which has been widely employed, should prove acceptable in most cases. For further discussion, see [1, 3].

by S. D. Hodges and R. A. Brealey

Portfolio Selection in a Dynamic and Uncertain World

The authors are respectively Senior Research Officer and Prudential Research Fellow at the London Graduate School of Business Studies. They would like to thank Mrs. Gira Gratier for her assistance with the computations.

1. Introduction

Many objections have been made to the practical implementation of portfolio selection models, but three of them predominate. Firstly, it is often suggested that the principal potential gains are from superior security analysis and that those from more efficient portfolio construction are relatively insignificant. The accumulating evidence that professional investors have only very limited access to monopolistic information has been taken to imply that, if any effort is to be devoted towards better performance, it should be concentrated on the task of obtaining better prediction of rates of return rather than on the more efficient use of mediocre predictions. Secondly, it is often argued that, regardless of the theoretical merits of the model, the solutions it indicates usually imply a rapid turnover of highly concentrated portfolios and are too far removed from practice to be acceptable. Thirdly, investors have been concerned that the solutions are very sensitive to minor changes in current stock prices or in analysts' estimates of possible future prices. The concern is accentuated by the fact that these estimates are notoriously difficult to obtain and therefore liable to considerable error.

This article contends that these objections are often exaggerated, and that if the investor's fore-casting ability is known, the diagonal model can be used to manage funds over time quite successfully, even when that ability is very limited. A simulation study is used to examine the performance that might be obtained from an all-stock portfolio, managed entirely on the basis of the diagonal model. The model is able to take into account the costs of transactions and adjustments are made for the poor quality of the forecasts.

More specifically, we explore the following topics:

1. The relationship between portfolio performance and ability.
2. The importance of refining the data inputs supplied to the portfolio selection model to compensate for the presence of errors.
3. The importance of being able to forecast the performance of the market, as against that of individual stocks.
4. The advantages likely to be gained from analyzing a large population of stocks.
5. The importance of using sophisticated selection rules such as the diagonal model in preference to simpler decision rules.
6. The implications of our work for the measurement of portfolio performance.

2. The Selection Model

The selection model used in our study was a diagonal model as described by Sharpe[1] in 1963, but with some minor, though important, modifications. Instead of merely computing the ideal port-

---

1. Footnotes and references appear at end of article.

folio to hold, our model is an adaptive one that will compute the best portfolio to change to. We take into account the transactions costs in making changes to the current portfolio. This requires the inclusion of some off-diagonal terms in the co-variance matrix, but these are easily taken care of and the computational advantages of the diagonal model are retained.

We have reported in an earlier article[2] on the use of this model and on its sensitivity to errors in the data inputs. One of our findings was that the model is extremely sensitive to the spread of the expected returns of the stocks analyzed. If there is a wide variation in the outlook for different stocks, the selected portfolios become highly concentrated and are turned over rapidly. Since analysts may be liable to exaggerate their ability to distinguish between the prospects for different stocks, we have been led to consider in this article the effect of adjusting analysts' forecasts so that they will constitute suitable inputs for the model. The procedure is described in Section 4 below.

In using the diagonal model a criterion is needed for choosing among various efficient portfolios. In our previous study we assumed that the portfolio manager was free to adjust his risk by borrowing or lending at a single pure rate of interest, and this assumption defined his preferred portfolio of stocks. In this study we are concerned with the management of a fully invested fund, so we have instead assumed that the portfolio manager maintains a constant trade-off between expected return and variance. Over a period of eight years this criterion should yield approximately the highest expected terminal wealth ratio for a given variance.

3. The Population of Stocks

We have assumed that no dividends are paid and that the annual wealth ratio P_t/P_{t-1} of each stock in the population is related to our index I by the usual equation:

$$\log\left(\frac{P_t}{P_t-1}\right) = \alpha + \beta \log\left(\frac{I_t}{I_t-1}\right) + u_t$$

where u_t is a disturbance term which has mean zero. We have chosen values for the α's, β's and the standard deviations of the u terms to correspond closely to what in practice is found in the stock market. Table 1 gives the actual values employed in the study. The β's were generated randomly from a normal distribution with mean 1.0 and standard deviation 0.3. The α's were cal-

culated from the β's according to the capital asset pricing model[3] by which

$$\alpha = (1 - \beta)\rho$$

where ρ is a pure interest rate, which we took to be 0.07 (or seven per cent).[4] To decide on values for the standard deviation of the disturbance term

Table 1. Characteristics of the Stocks

Stock	$\alpha \times 10^2$	β	Sd (u) $\times 10^2$
1	7.0	-.01	18.3
2	1.8	.74	14.1
3	-1.3	1.19	16.4
4	-3.9	1.56	17.0
5	-2.3	1.33	18.3
6	-2.0	1.29	22.1
7	1.6	.77	14.3
8	0.3	.95	23.3
9	0.7	.90	15.6
10	-1.0	1.14	12.7
11	0.8	.89	19.8
12	-2.7	1.39	32.3
13	2.2	.68	21.0
14	1.1	.84	31.1
15	0.1	.98	23.2
16	-3.3	1.47	37.6
17	-1.1	1.16	20.1
18	2.4	.65	27.9
19	1.6	.77	25.2
20	-0.1	1.01	21.7
21	-0.2	1.02	25.3
22	3.2	.55	37.0
23	0.7	.90	19.5
24	-0.2	1.02	21.2
25	-0.4	1.05	13.4
26	1.6	.78	12.6
27	-0.7	1.10	16.5
28	-2.2	1.31	29.1
29	1.2	.83	22.2
30	-2.1	1.30	12.7
31	3.4	.51	16.8
32	-0.6	1.09	23.5
33	3.1	.56	18.3
34	0.8	.89	13.2
35	-1.9	1.27	22.1
36	-0.5	1.07	37.7
37	-0.0	1.00	19.6
38	0.1	.99	28.7
39	0.0	1.00	29.2
40	1.7	.76	35.4

u of each share we examined both American and British empirical work[5] and concluded that the values should range between 0.1 and 0.4 and contribute typically about two-thirds of the variance in the returns of each stock. The values used (shown in Table 1) were generated as random numbers from a lognormal distribution with a median of 0.2 and values of 0.41 and 0.10 at the plus or minus two standard deviation marks.

We have assumed that both the logarithms of the index changes $\log(I_t/I_{t-1})$ and the u_t terms for each stock are normally distributed. This means that the wealth ratio of each stock follows a lognormal distribution. We took 10 per cent as the expected (arithmetic) return on the index and 17 per cent as its standard deviation. These numbers imply a mean of 0.084 and a standard deviation of 0.154 for $\log(I_t/I_{t-1})$. The 40 stocks shown in Table 1 were kept unchanged in all the simulations, but in some simulations additional stocks (generated from the same distributions) were added.

4. The Forecasts and Their Refinement

Our imaginary investor is trying to forecast each year the single year wealth ratios of all the stocks. We suppose that he forecasts the performance of the market index, that he knows the β coefficient for each stock, and that he forecasts the u term for each stock.

If he had no forecasting ability at all, then he should expect the actual u value to be drawn from a probability distribution (which is assumed to be normal) with mean zero. This prior distribution should be modified when a forecast is available in a way that depends on the degree of forecasting ability. We have generated the forecast F(u) by the formula:

$$F(u) = R.u + v$$

where v is an unknown, normally distributed disturbance term with zero mean. It is no real restriction to suppose that the forecasts of u are scaled to have the same variance as u itself, and so we have also assumed:

$$var(v) = (1 - R^2)var(u).$$

In this case R is the coefficient of correlation between the forecasts and the actuals. We shall therefore refer to R as the "forecasting quality."

The conditional distribution of u, given the forecast F(u), has the following mean and variance:

$$E(u|F(u)) = R.F(u)$$
$$Var(u|F(u)) = (1 - R^2)Var(u).$$

It is these refined values that should be fed into the

Table 2. Example of Forecasts and Efficient Portfolio: Run 2 Simulation 1 Year 8

Stock	Crude Forecast	Adjusted Forecast	Actual Return	Initial Holding	New Holding
1	-20.1%	4.3%	-13.1%	20.0%	7.6%
2	49.8	-15.6	6.9	-	3.3
3	33.6	15.8	-6.8	-	-
4	22.3	16.2	-4.6	-	-
5	7.0	13.0	12.8	-	-
6	-10.8	10.6	-23.2	-	-
7	35.7	14.1	3.7	0.6	0.6
8	37.9	16.9	-14.0	-	-
9	24.9	13.3	20.7	-	-
10	12.8	12.1	-0.8	-	-
11	39.5	16.0	-1.7	-	-
12	-18.8	12.5	-24.5	1.5	-
13	13.0	11.9	50.5	0.6	0.6
14	63.4	22.0	-5.0	-	9.5
15	4.3	12.2	-16.5	5.2	-
16	30.7	23.5	4.0	2.7	2.7
17	19.0	14.4	-7.1	-	-
18	30.8	16.2	13.9	-	4.2
19	68.5	20.3	16.2	-	12.4
20	33.9	16.2	-2.3	1.6	1.6
21	61.5	20.6	-10.4	-	6.6
22	60.7	23.0	-1.8	6.6	11.0
23	25.7	14.2	4.6	-	-
24	39.9	16.9	-1.3	1.9	1.9
25	8.8	11.2	-20.1	-	-
26	43.2	14.7	6.5	-	-
27	7.3	11.7	-21.7	-	-
28	34.8	19.9	-27.8	6.2	6.2
29	2.1	11.0	-0.8	7.0	-
30	79.0	20.9	-1.7	-	2.8
31	-7.5	7.3	-12.2	30.2	-
32	5.7	12.9	-10.8	-	-
33	13.3	11.1	5.1	7.0	7.0
34	10.2	10.8	-12.3	-	-
35	23.7	16.1	-22.7	4.1	3.0
36	-2.5	16.3	12.2	2.8	2.8
37	30.1	15.2	42.3	-	-
38	8.0	14.4	7.4	-	-
39	4.3	14.0	-32.9	-	-
40	132.7	30.1	-30.9	2.0	16.1
Index	31.1	13.2	-0.1		

	Expected Return	Standard Deviation	Actual Return
Old Portfolio	11.3	13.7	-9.9
New Portfolio	16.9	17.9	-8.6
40 Shares	-	-	-3.0

Table 3. Examples of Fund Performance - Run 2

Simulation 1

	Cumulative Wealth Index		Annual Return		Fund	Number of	Largest
Year	Fund	Index	Fund	Index	Turnover	Holdings	Holding
1	117.7	121.2	17.7%	21.2%.	100.0%	9	32.8%
2	152.0	185.2	29.2	52.9	27.8	11	24.1
3	155.3	201.7	2.2	8.9	34.1	15	19.4
4	157.6	170.7	1.5	-15.4	39.2	14	24.1
5	179.7	172.7	14.0	1.2	30.1	18	25.2
6	191.0	171.0	6.3	-0.9	36.8	14	30.7
7	174.8	147.0	-8.5	-14.0	49.7	16	30.8
8	159.8	142.6	-8.6	-3.0	57.3	18	16.1

Simulation 44

	Cumulative Wealth Index		Annual Return		Fund	Number of	Largest
Year	Fund	Index	Fund	Index	Turnover	Holdings	Holding
1	93.1	102.9	-6.9%	2.9%	100.0%	14	20.4%
2	125.3	135.2	34.6	31.5	27.6	12	17.4
3	126.3	135.4	0.8	0.1	36.3	13	20.7
4	116.0	97.3	-8.2	-28.1	34.7	10	30.0
5	108.6	85.7	-6.4	-11.9	29.1	11	27.5
6	129.6	93.4	19.3	8.9	31.7	12	31.6
7	146.7	96.7	13.2	3.6	16.9	13	31.0
8	177.6	108.5	21.0	12.2	23.6	12	35.3

Simulation 81

	Cumulative Wealth Index		Annual Return		Fund	Number of	Largest
Year	Fund	Index	Fund	Index	Turnover	Holdings	Holding
1	118.0	115.8	18.0%	15.8%	100.0%	11	20.8%
2	152.5	147.9	29.2	27.7	44.2	14	19.6
3	196.2	194.8	28.7	31.7	43.2	11	25.2
4	213.7	216.3	8.9	11.1	11.5	11	26.9
5	200.5	222.0	-6.2	2.6	43.3	11	16.4
6	217.2	271.1	8.3	22.1	43.9	11	34.4
7	278.4	407.9	28.2	50.4	41.9	14	31.5
8	305.7	477.1	9.8	17.0	39.5	14	19.9

Mean of 100 Simulations

	Cumulative Wealth Index		Annual Return		Fund	Number of	Largest
Year	Fund	Index	Fund	Index	Turnover	Holdings	Holding
8	298.3 a)	260.6 b)	17.5%	15.8%	37.8%	14.5	22.2%

a) standard deviation 126.1
b) standard deviation 122.0

diagonal model to provide the correct expected returns and diagonal variances, rather than the crude forecasts and estimated variances. Only if the investor has perfect forecasting ability ($R = 1$) should the variance across expected returns equal the variance of ex post returns. Forecasts of the market index and their refinements were calculated in an exactly analogous way as

$$F(I_R) = 0.084 + R.u_i + v, \text{ with}$$
$$E(I_R | F(I_R)) = 0.084 + R.(F(I_R) - 0.084), \text{ and}$$
$$\text{Var}(I_R | F(I_R)) = (1 - R^2)(0.154)^2$$

We have assumed that the investor knows *a priori* his forecasting quality R, and we have used the simulations to compare the effect of making appropriate adjustments to the forecasts with that of using the crude forecasts directly in the model. In both cases it is necessary to convert the forecasts from the logarithmic to arithmetic form in order to obtain the necessary inputs. Some degree of approximation is implied by this procedure.

Table 2 shows a typical set of crude and refined forecasts simulated as a part of the study. An overoptimistic forecast of the market return accounts for much of the disparity between the forecasts and actual returns.

The normative relationship between security analysis and portfolio selection has also been explored by Treynor and Black,[6] who develop similar formulae to our own and stress the importance of the correlation between forecast and actual returns. Much of the criticism of portfolio selection models stems from failure to allow for the possibility that this correlation may typically be quite low. In practice the quality of forecasts is likely to vary over time, and among securities and analysts. Since it can be only estimated imperfectly, adjustments will generally be less efficient than those made in this study. Although this study provides some encouragement for the use of portfolio models, the critical difficulty of estimating the quality of analysts' forecasts remains.

5. The Simulations Performed

We have performed some 58 different simulation runs. Each run simulates 100 times what might have happened to the portfolio over an eight-year period. At the beginning of the period only cash is held. Forecasts and revisions to the portfolio are made annually and transactions costs on a switch are charged at five per cent. The mean and standard deviation of the 100 different ex post

eight-year wealth ratios make it possible to measure performance objectively.

Table 2 shows the results of a single year's simulation. On the basis of the forecasts adjusted for a forecasting ability of 0.15 there was a 57 per cent turnover in the portfolio. This consisted mainly of switching out of Stocks 1, 29 and 31, and into Stocks 14, 19 and 40. Note that some of Stock 1 is retained as a hedge against uncertainty in spite of its poor prospects, and that Stock 16 is considered too risky for its holding to be increased. The revised portfolio did not perform well in this case, for its value declined by nearly nine per cent against an unexpected three per cent fall in the market. Even so the transactions conferred some benefit, for the value of the old portfolio would have declined by 10 per cent.

Table 3 lists in rather less detail the performance of the fund over the eight-year simulation period. It gives the year to year and cumulative performance of both the fund and the index, and information on fund turnover and diversification. The table also contains similar figures for two other eight-year simulations and summary statistics for the 100 simulations of this run. A complete set of summary figures for all the simulations is contained in Table 4 on pp. 60-61 this issue. It should be noted that the index used in the assessment of performance is an equally weighted average of the annual wealth ratios, and different from the index used to generate their returns.

In interpreting our results we caution the reader against placing too much reliance on the numerical values we obtain. The figures from the simulations are all subject to sampling errors. Comparisons between portfolios with different standard deviations are necessarily approximate.

6. The Effect of Differences in Forecasting Ability

One of our first tasks was to examine the effect on the efficient frontier of differences in the portfolio manager's forecasting ability. Figure 1 shows that, as the correlation between forecast and outcome is reduced to 0.05, the frontier shifts significantly to the left and becomes steeper.[7] Yet even in this case, with forecasts that are able to explain only one-quarter per cent of the variance in actual returns, and paying initial and subsequent transactions costs of five per cent, the investor is still able to outperform the market by 0.6 per cent per annum for an equivalent degree of risk. The re-

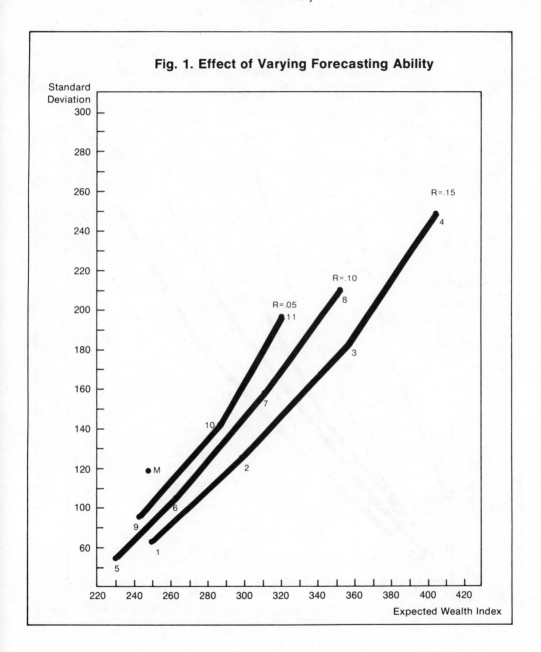

Fig. 1. Effect of Varying Forecasting Ability

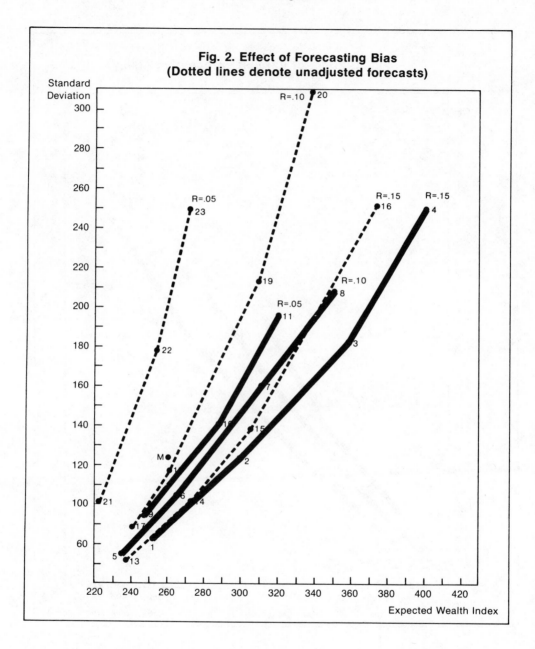

Fig. 2. Effect of Forecasting Bias
(Dotted lines denote unadjusted forecasts)

duction in forecasting ability requires important changes in the way that the portfolio is managed. In the portfolio that offers the same risk as the market, the number of holdings is increased from approximately 15 to 25, and the rate of portfolio turnover declines from about 35 to seven per cent. In practice, institutions turn over their portfolios much more rapidly than this without making such large gains.[8] One plausible explanation is that portfolio managers employ relatively inefficient selection procedures.

7. The Effect of Using Exaggerated Forecasts

The analysis so far has assumed that we could effectively eliminate any exaggeration from the expected return and variances. We have argued that in practice most investors tend to make extravagant claims as to their forecasting abilities and find it very difficult to provide the expected values. We suspect that users of portfolio selection models have seldom made any serious attempt to overcome this problem, but have simply relied on forecasts as given by the analyst. The costs of such a procedure are illustrated in Figure 2.

In each case the disadvantages of using crude forecasts are most marked at the top of the efficient set. This stems from the fact that with such limited forecasting abilities much larger adjustments need to be made to the expected returns than to the variances.

The costs of employing unadjusted forecasts are also highest when the investor's forecasting powers are weakest. In these circumstances the investor is induced to undertake a much larger number of transactions than is justified. If the investor cannot recognize that there are limitations in his forecasts, the correlation between prediction and outcome must be at least 0.1 if he is not to lose money by following apparently efficient selection procedures. No such requirement is involved when the investor acts on the basis of unadjusted forecasts, for the rate of turnover will always correctly reflect the quality of the forecasts. This distinction is illustrated in Runs 12 and 24, where we consider an investor with zero forecasting ability.

An interesting aspect of these results is the wide range of cases in which crude forecasts produce portfolios only marginally inferior to those produced from the adjusted forecasts. This is not because the two methods lead to similar courses of action, for the portfolios differ greatly in terms of turnover, diversification and identity of holdings.

Indeed, a major disadvantage to using crude forecases may lie in the appearance of the portfolio rather than its performance. For instance, the portfolio with the same risk as the market index typically has six to nine holdings, and the rate of turnover averages 70 to 80 per cent. It is this kind of result, rather than the portfolio's subsequent performance, that has led to the lack of acceptance of selection models by the investment community. If the inputs are adjusted, the resultant portfolios conform much more closely with investment practice. (See Section 6)

There is another disadvantage to the use of exaggerated forecasts, for the investor who employs them may never know the true position of the efficient set. Figures 3 and 4 illustrate this. The former shows the one year efficient frontier when using unadjusted forecasts. The horizontal scale of expected returns extends as far as 130 per cent. Faced with such apparently golden opportunities the investor might be tempted to seek the maximum amount of leverage. It is only when the forecasts have been adjusted beforehand that the efficient frontier (shown in Figure 4) can offer any real guidance as to the proportion of assets that ought to be invested in common stock.

8. The Importance of Forecasting the Market

We have hitherto assumed that the portfolio manager's forecasting ability is identical for the market component and for each individual stock. In this section we relax this assumption, permitting the investor's ability to predict market and residual return to differ. In the next section we shall consider the consequences of being able to forecast the prospects better for some stocks than for others.

Figure 5 illustrates the case in which the investor can predict only the market or the residual return. Since the market explains a relatively small proportion of a security's return, it is not surprising that the gains for a given level of forecasting ability are significantly less when that ability is confined to market prospects. However, although the market is treated in the Sharpe model as if it were simply an additional security, it is possible for the investor to deal in varying amounts of this security for a given level of transaction costs. Since he is compelled to remain fully invested, his gains come solely from moving between high and low β stocks. His success in this activity is apparent in the association between the mean β of his portfolio and the actual market returns. For example, in

Run 30, where the quality of the market forecast was 0.3, the correlation between β and market returns in years six to eight was 0.22 ($\sigma = 0.058$). In this case the investor's actions produced a gain in equivalent return of 0.4 per cent.

The investor who achieves a particular level of performance solely through his capacity to predict market returns will tend to be significantly less active than the investor who has wider forecasting powers. The amount of activity will also vary sharply from year to year, dwindling to zero when the expected market return is close to the interest rate.

Figure 5 also provides information on the opposite case, in which the investor can predict only the residual returns. Within the range of abilities that we examined, ignorance of the market is not a serious disadvantage. This is not because market knowledge goes unused, for in Run 58 there was a correlation of 0.26 between the mean β and the

market returns. However, the value of this market information is almost entirely outweighed by the value of the residual information that the investor is compelled to ignore. In these circumstances the two kinds of information may be more valuable if they are acquired sequentially, so that the investor's assessment of market prospects determines the universe of stocks for more detailed analysis.

The dotted lines in Figure 5 show the effect of employing exaggerated forecasts. Once again, ignorance of his limitations is liable to prove costly for the investor who possesses relatively little superior information.

These differences in performance and behavior are likely to be highly dependent on the constraints that we have assumed to be imposed on the fund manager. Clearly, the benefits of forecasting residual returns would be greatly enhanced if the fund manager were free to eliminate market risk by short selling. Correspondingly, he would be

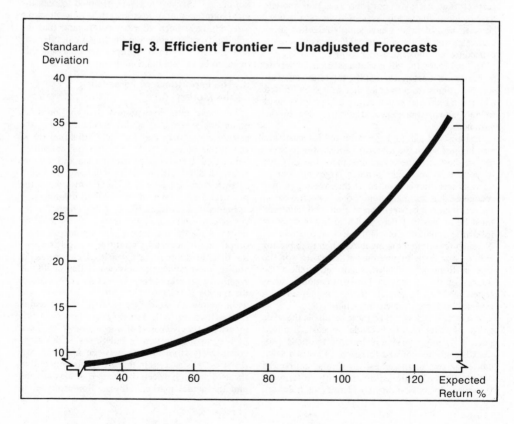

Fig. 3. Efficient Frontier — Unadjusted Forecasts

Standard Deviation

Expected Return %

better able to capitalize on any knowledge of the market if he were not obliged to remain fully invested.

9. The Number of Stocks Analyzed

A further constraint that we have imposed on the fund manager is that he should select his holdings from a universe of just 40 stocks. The benefits of analyzing an additional 40 securities are illustrated in Figure 6. Direct comparisons with earlier runs are hindered by the fact that the performance of this wider universe is slightly better than that of the original 40 securities. Nevertheless, the gains from portfolio management appear to be significantly increased by the broader coverage. There is some indication that the higher incidence of extreme price changes justifies a greater rate of fund turnover and a greater degree of diversification.

Figure 6 also illustrates the benefits of a wider universe of securities to a fund manager whose predictive powers are confined either to the market or to the residual price movements. Although the relative gains from forecasting residuals are undiminished, the costs of this wider coverage are likely to be much less for the investor who ignores the residual returns.

In practice an investor is unlikely to be equally familiar with the prospects for each of the stocks that he examines. We examined this possibility briefly in Run 55. Here we assumed that the investor forecast the residual returns of 40 stocks with a correlation of 0.15, and the residual returns of a further 40 stocks with a correlation of 0.075. He was assumed to have no ability to forecast the market. The interesting feature of this run is the very limited extent to which he is justified in holding stocks with which he is relatively unfamiliar. On the average only 26 per cent of his funds were invested in this group.

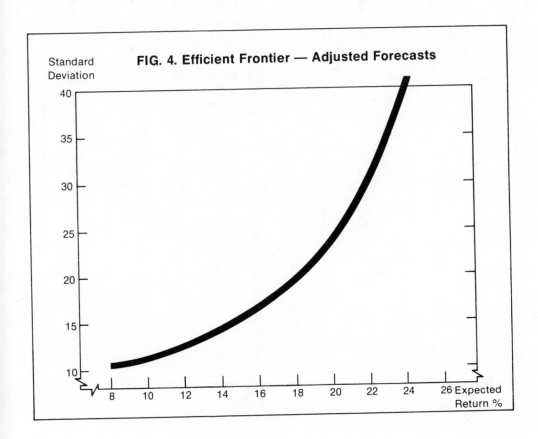

FIG. 4. Efficient Frontier — Adjusted Forecasts

Table 4. Summary of Results

Run Number	Sample Size	Adjustment	Forecast Quality		Return/Variance Trade Off	Exp. Wealth Index	S.D. Wealth Index	Exp. Annual Return ÷ Eq. S.D.	Year 8		
			Index	Residual					Turnover	No. of Holdings	Largest Holding
40 Shares*						261	122	12.7%			
80 Shares*						254	110	12.3			
The Effect of Differences in Forecasting Ability											
1	40	Adj.	.15	.15	4	252	84	14.2	24%	19	26%
2	40	"	.15	.15	2	298	126	14.4	38	15	22
3	40	"	.15	.15	1	356	135	14.4	51	10	25
4	40	"	.15	.15	.5	401	253	13.8	58	6	37
5	40	"	.10	.10	4	234	76	13.3	12	22	26
6	40	"	.10	.10	2	264	106	13.6	20	19	22
7	40	"	.10	.10	1	310	159	13.6	30	14	20
8	40	"	.10	.10	.5	349	210	13.4	36	8	31
9	40	"	.05	.05	2	248	97	13.1	7	29	22
10	40	"	.05	.05	1	287	142	13.3	7	23	17
11	40	"	.05	.05	.5	319	197	12.9	9	9	25
12	40	"	.00	.00	.8	302	165	13.1	2	13	23
The Effect of Using Exaggerated Forecasts											
13	40	Unadj.	.15	.15	40	237	73	13.8	48	13	30
14	40	"	.15	.15	20	272	103	14.2	67	10	32
15	40	"	.15	.15	12.5	304	139	14.1	79	8	37
16	40	"	.15	.15	5	372	232	13.2	91	4	55
17	40	"	.10	.10	20	241	89	13.0	67	10	32
18	40	"	.10	.10	12.5	261	118	12.9	79	8	37
19	40	"	.10	.10	5	308	213	12.1	91	4	55
20	40	"	.10	.10	2.5	337	311	11.4	95	3	72
21	40	"	.05	.05	12.5	224	102	11.2	79	8	36
22	40	"	.05	.05	5	254	178	10.9	91	4	55
23	40	"	.05	.05	2.5	272	251	10.4	95	3	72
24	40	"	.00	.00	2.5	216	190	9.1	94	3	71
The Importance of Forecasting the Market											
25	40	Adj.	.15	.00	2	251	99	13.2	3	21	23
26	40	"	.15	.00	1	290	144	13.3	4	15	20
27	40	"	.15	.00	.5	326	212	12.7	3	10	30
28	40	"	.30	.00	2	260	106	13.4	7	22	24
29	40	"	.30	.00	1	297	147	13.5	11	14	23
30	40	"	.30	.00	.5	329	200	13.1	11	9	31
31	40	"	.00	.15	2	289	120	14.3	30	15	21
32	40	"	.00	.15	1	349	182	14.3	42	11	24
33	40	"	.00	.15	.5	396	249	13.8	49	7	35
34	40	"	.00	.30	8	280	91	15.5	30	16	29
35	40	"	.00	.30	4	353	136	16.3	47	13	27
36	40	"	.00	.30	2	465	215	16.5	62	10	26
37	40	Unadj.	.15	.00	10	201	101	9.5	81	7	39
38	40	"	.15	.00	5	214	147	9.5	90	4	54
39	40	"	.15	.00	2	226	211	9.3	94	2	75
40	40	"	.30	.00	10	208	105	9.9	81	7	39
41	40	"	.30	.00	5	221	150	9.8	90	4	54
42	40	"	.30	.00	2	232	211	9.5	94	2	74
43	40	"	.00	.15	40	233	71	13.7	45	13	30
44	40	"	.00	.15	20	264	97	14.1	65	10	32
45	40	"	.00	.15	10	308	152	13.8	82	7	39
46	40	"	.00	.30	40	289	90	16.1	46	13	30
47	40	"	.00	.30	20	365	140	16.5	66	10	32
48	40	"	.00	.30	10	482	244	16.0	82	7	40

10. A Simpler Selection Rule

These simulations have suggested that, as long as the investor is made aware of the limitations in his forecasts, mean-variance efficient portfolios are likely to provide very good long-term performance even when the correlation between forecast and out-turn is as low as 0.05. These findings do not support Hakansson's forebodings about the use of a mean-variance model in a sequential context,[9] but we cannot conclude that alternative models are in any sense less desirable.

In order to judge whether the gains could be matched by more naive selection procedures, we have simulated the effect of employing a rule of thumb which causes the manager to invest most heavily in stocks offering the highest prospective premium per unit of risk. Runs 56 and 57 suggest that the benefits of the diagonal model amply compensate for its additional complexity.

11. Implications for Performance Measurement

Despite the good performance of the efficient portfolios, it is doubtful whether their merits would be fully recognized by the investment community. Consider, for example, Run 2. We have plotted in Figure 7 the return on the fund in the eighth year against that on the market. The relatively high level of residual risk could leave the fund manager exposed to criticism. To take an extreme instance, it is unlikely that the market could ever bring itself to believe that the investor of Simulation 81 (see Table 3) was a capable forecaster and an efficient portfolio manager. His deteriorating performance over the eight-year period is more likely to be attributed to some weakening in his judgment than to a run of ill luck. We suggest that the investment community tends to form opinions and distribute rewards and penalties in such a way as to discourage efficient portfolio construction.

Formal methods of performance measurement offer little better prospect of being able to distinguish the more able fund manager solely from an analysis of fund and market rates of return. For example, suppose that we draw on the capital asset pricing model and seek to measure a fund manager's ability by the statistic of excess return, $\alpha_j - \rho(1 - \beta_j)$, where ρ is the riskless rate of interest, and α_j and β_j are parameters from the regression of the annual returns of fund j on market returns.[10] Even when the fund manager confines his attention to the residual returns, it may be difficult to obtain a sufficiently accurate estimate of performance. For example, using the last three years of each simulation in Run 32, we estimate the excess return as 4.85 per cent, with a standard error 0.86. This implies that approximately 25 years of data would be needed to identify at the 95 per cent level of significance what we know to be a useful degree of forecasting ability.

These difficulties are heightened when the manager can predict market returns and varies his systematic risk accordingly. Some of the problems that arise in these circumstances have been discussed by Jensen.[11] Here we merely indicate the difficulty in detecting curvature in the characteristic line, and the lack of precision in any measure

Table 4-continued

The Number of Stocks Analyzed

49	80	Adj.	.15	.00	1	329	160	13.7	6	16	16
50	80	"	.15	.00	.5	376	242	12.9	10	11	25
51	80	"	.00	.15	1	403	201	14.6	55	11	22
52	80	"	.00	.15	.5	467	287	14.0	59	7	33
53	80	"	.15	.15	1	408	206	14.6	56	11	23
54	80	"	.15	.15	.5	475	302	13.9	61	7	34
55	80	"	.00	.15⁄.075	2	317	122	14.9	35	19	18

A Simpler Selection Rule

56	40	"	.15	.15	—	300	144	13.8	46	33	16
57	40	Unadj.	.15	.15	—	285	126	13.8	72	20	28

Implications for Performance Measurement

58	40	Adj.	.30	.15	.6	394	239	14.0	53	7	34

* Excludes Expenses.
≈ Returns adjusted so that standard deviation equals that of either the 40 share index or the 80 share index.
⁄ Forecast quality = .15 for first 40 stocks, .075 for remaining 40.

of performance that ignores this curvature. Even when the investor is able to forecast the market with some success, the curvature in the characteristic line is likely to be slight. This will be particularly true of the investor who acts on the basis of unadjusted forecasts and makes relatively few changes in his portfolio. The curvature will be least when the investor also possesses some ability to forecast residual returns, for he will tend to capitalize on this ability when the expected market return is close to the interest rate. As an illustration of this, Table 5 shows the relationship between fund and market returns for three cases when the investor could predict the market with a correlation of 0.30. Following Treynor and Mazuy,[12] we sought to measure curvature by the quadratic term in the regression $R_{jt} = \alpha_j + \beta_j R_{It} + \gamma_j R^2_{It}$, where R_{jt} denotes the percentage return on fund j in year t and R_{It} the percentage return on the market. The value of γ_j is consistently small and, despite the 300 observations, barely significant. Table 5 further demonstrates that, if we ignore the quadratic term and simply employ a linear regression, we are liable to obtain incorrect estimates of α_j and of the performance measure $\alpha_j - p(1 - \beta_j)$.

Conclusion

The consequences of using portfolio selection models in a multi-period context and with only very limited forecasting ability are not obvious nor

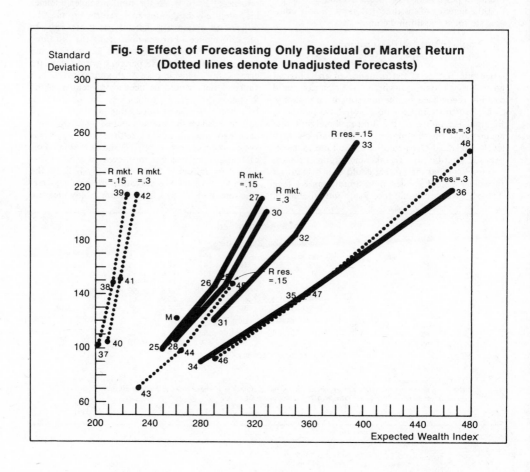

Fig. 5 Effect of Forecasting Only Residual or Market Return (Dotted lines denote Unadjusted Forecasts)

Table 5. The Measurement of Performance
When the Manager Can Forecast Market Returns

| Run No. | Adjustment | Forecast Quality | | Correlation β versus Mkt. Return | $R_{jt} = \alpha_j + \beta_j R_{It}$ | | | Performance Measure $\alpha_j \cdot \rho(1 - \beta_j)$ | $R_{jt} = \alpha_j + \beta_j R_{It} + \gamma_j R^2_{It}$ | | | |
		Market	Residual		α_j	β_j	R^2		α_j	β_j	γ_j	R^2
42	Unadj.	.30	.00	.183	-3.4769 (-1.76)	1.2069 (14.54)	.42	-2.03	-3.6943 (1.89)	.9668 (7.367)	.0063 (2.35)	.43
30	Adj.	.30	.00	.222	2.2709 (1.96)	1.1798 (24.24)	.66	3.53	2.1115 (1.85)	1.0037 (13.11)	.0046 (2.96)	.67
58	Adj.	.30	.15	.263	5.3736 (4.44)	1.1398 (22.37)	.63	6.35	5.2580 (4.36)	1.0120 (12.54)	.0033 (2.03)	.63

( ) = t value

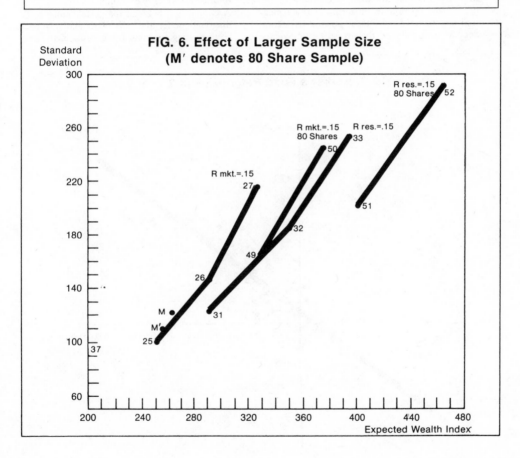

FIG. 6. Effect of Larger Sample Size (M′ denotes 80 Share Sample)

do they lend themselves to analytical solutions. The simulation model described in this article permits an assessment of the behavior of the diagonal model under controlled conditions.

The following principal conclusions emerge:

1. The single period mean-variance model performs well in a multi-period world, so that significant gains in performance relative to the market are possible even when the investor's forecasting ability is very slight.
2. Prior correction of the inputs for estimation bias produces both an improvement in portfolio efficiency and also leads to the selection of portfolios that are more acceptable to the investment community in terms of diversification and turnover. Efficient portfolio selection depends critically on the investor's knowledge

of his limitations.

3. As expected, for a given population of stocks the benefits from forecasting the factors peculiar to individual stocks are significantly greater than those that can be derived from forecasting the market factor equally well. Unless the market forecasts determine the stocks to be selected for further analysis, there is little to be gained from predicting both market and residual returns.
4. For a given degree of forecasting ability, there are significant advantages to increasing the number of stocks analyzed, at least up to the total of 80 which we examined.
5. A comparison between the performance of the diagonal model and that of a relatively naive strategy suggested that the benefits of the diag-

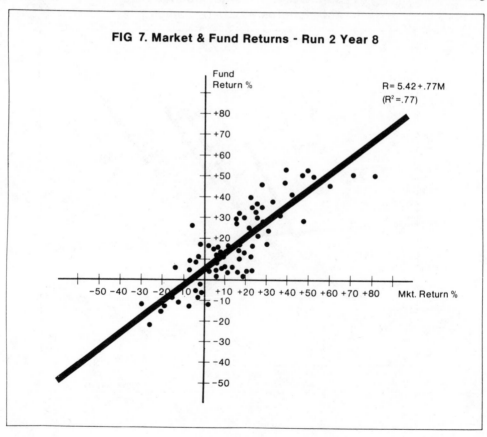

FIG 7. Market & Fund Returns - Run 2 Year 8

onal model are ample compensation for its additional complexity.

6. Despite the fact that many of the portfolios we examined have on average beaten the market by more than one per cent per annum, it would require an inordinately large amount of data to measure their success with any degree of assurance. ◆

FOOTNOTES

1. See Sharpe [11].
2. See Hodges and Brealey [3].
3. See Sharpe [10].
4. Although the pricing model we have used is widely quoted and accepted, it is not strictly the correct one in that stocks for which u has a large standard deviation have high expected values of the arithmetic return. Consequently, not only does the investor tend to prefer these stocks, but they assist his performance when held in diversified portfolios. Since completing our simulation experiments it has been pointed out to us by a referee that an additional term of $\frac{1}{2}(\beta\sigma_I^2 - \sigma^2)$ should have been included in our pricing equation, where σ_I^2 denotes Var $[\log(I_t/I_{t-1})]$ and σ^2 denotes Var $[\log(P_t/P_{t-1})]$. The derivation is given in Merton [7]. We estimate that this has the effect of biasing upwards the estimated returns from the managed portfolios by approximately 0.3 per cent per annum.
5. The principal American sources were: Cootner [1], Paine [8], King [6].
6. See Treynor and Black [12].
7. The following estimates may give the reader a clearer idea of the meaning of these differences in forecasting ability. Suppose the shares were divided into two groups of equal size, one group containing the shares with the highest forecast residual returns and the other the lowest. The difference between the expected returns from these two groups would be approximately 4.8 percentage points for a forecasting quality of 0.15 and 3.2 and 1.6 percentage points for forecasting qualities of 0.10 and 0.05.
8. See, for example, Securities and Exchange Commission [9].
9. See Hakansson [2]. The principal reason for the apparent discrepancy between our conclusion and Hakansson's arises from the difference between our assumption of log-normally distributed returns and the unusual discrete distribution in Hakansson's example.
10. Given our assumptions of a constant riskless rate, this measure differs from Jensen's only in the use of annually, rather than continuously, compounded returns. See Jensen [5]. The exam-

ples considered in the remainder of this article are unlikely to be sensitive to the choice of compounding interval. However, where α_j or β_j are sharply different from the market portfolio, the incorrect choice of compounding interval is liable to produce a spurious impression of curvature in the characteristic line.

11. See Jensen [4].
12. See Treynor and Mazuy [13].

REFERENCES

1. Cootner, P. H.: "Stock Prices: Random Walks vs. Finite Markov Chains," *Industrial Management Review* 3 (Spring 1962), pp. 24-45.
2. Hakansson, N. H.: "Capital Growth and the Mean-Variance Approach to Portfolio Selection," *Journal of Financial and Quantitative Analysis* (January 1971), pp. 517-558.
3. Hodges, S. D. and Brealey, R. A.: "Using the Sharpe Model," *Investment Analyst* 27 (September 1970), pp. 41-50.
4. Jensen, M. C.: "Optimal Utilization of Market Forecasts and the Evaluation of Investment Performance." Unpublished paper presented at the International Summer School, Universita di Venezia, September 1971.
5. Jensen, M. C.: "The Performance of Mutual Funds in the Period 1945-1964," *Journal of Finance* 23 (May 1968), pp. 389-416.
6. King, B. F.: "Market and Industry Factors in Stock Price Behavior," *Journal of Business* 39 (January 1966), pp. 139-190.
7. Merton, R. C.: "A Dynamic General Equilibrium Model of the Asset Market and Its Application to the Pricing of the Capital Structure of the Firm." Working paper 497-70, A. P. Sloan School of Management, M.I.T. December 1970.
8. Paine, N. R.: "A Case Study in Mathematical Programming of Portfolio Selections," *Applied Statistics* 15 (1966), pp. 24-36.
9. Securities and Exchange Commission. *Institutional Investor Study Report of the Securities and Exchange Commission*, Washington, D. C.: Government Printing Office, 1971.
10. Sharpe, W. F.: "Capital Asset Prices: A Theory of Market Equilibrium Under Conditions of Risk," *Journal of Finance* 19 (September 1964), pp. 425-442.
11. Sharpe, W. F.: "A Simplified Model for Portfolio Analysis," *Management Science* 9 (January 1963), pp. 277-293.
12. Treynor, J. L. and Black, F.: "How to Use Security Analysis to Improve Portfolio Selection," *Journal of Business* (forthcoming).
13. Treynor, J. L. and Mazuy, K.: "Can Mutual Funds Outguess the Market," *Harvard Business Review* 44 (July-August 1966), pp. 131-136.

Risk and Return

20

INTRODUCTION: DOES THE INVESTOR GET PAID FOR BUYING RISKY SECURITIES?

Some people like risk: One can see them either at the race tracks or in line to buy lottery tickets. Even some investors in financial assets enjoy risk, but the evidence is overwhelming that capital markets are dominated by those who do not. Part of the evidence has already been discussed in the introductory chapter to the section on portfolio theory (Chapter 15), where it was pointed out that the virtually universal practice of diversification suggests risk aversion. There is persuasive additional evidence in the returns that have, on the average, accrued to different classes of financial assets. If one arrays these assets from the least risky to the most risky, one finds a remarkably steady progression from lower average returns to higher average returns. Thus, currency normally provides a lower return than government securities, which provide lower returns than corporate bonds, which, in their turn, offer smaller returns than common stocks.

In this section, we consider just how much recompense investors require for taking additional risks. This is a question that was discussed briefly in Chapter 6, where we considered the evidence for efficient markets.

Sharpe's article of 1964 (Chapter 22) made an enormous contribution to the theory of capital asset pricing. His arguments were based upon two corollaries of portfolio-selection theory. He pointed out that the risk of a diversified portfolio of stocks corresponds to the variance or standard deviation of possible returns. However, the contribution that any individual holding makes to the over-all riskiness of the portfolio depends principally on the degree to which it is affected by adverse market movements, for this is the only source of uncertainty that cannot be reduced by diversification. As a result, an investor is likely to require additional recompense only when a security is unusually sensitive to market movements.

One way an investor can increase the sensitivity of his holdings is by increasing his stake in common stocks and reducing his investment in bonds. If he does this, the expected margin of return over the interest rate and the risk both rise in the same proportion. Sharpe argued that in an efficient market such a policy should be neither more nor less profitable than a policy of buying the more sensitive stocks. Therefore, an investor who purchases the more sensitive stocks should demand a proportionate increase in the amount by which his prospective return exceeds the interest rate. One implication of this theory is that the more risky securities are likely to outperform the market when the latter provides a higher return than the interest rate; they are likely to be relatively poor holdings when the market return falls short of the interest rate.

A number of researchers have uncovered evidence that the most variable stocks or funds have also provided, on average, the highest returns. For example. Jensen's analysis of mutual funds was reproduced in Chapter 12. The most extensive tests of capital asset pricing theory have been made by Sharpe and Cooper and by Black, Jensen, and Scholes.[1] Both studies uncover a clear relationship between return and market risk, though the rewards for risk appear to increase somewhat more slowly than the theory predicts. We have reprinted the Sharpe and Cooper article in Chapter 22.

[1]Black, F., Jensen, M.C., and Scholes, M.J. *The Capital Asset Pricing Model Some Empirical Tests,* in Jensen, M.C. (ed), *Studies in the Theory of Capital Markets.* New York: Praeger Publishers, 1972.

21

CAPITAL ASSET PRICES: A THEORY OF MARKET EQUILIBRIUM UNDER CONDITIONS OF RISK *

William F. Sharpe

I. Introduction

ONE OF THE PROBLEMS which has plagued those attempting to predict the behavior of capital markets is the absence of a body of positive microeconomic theory dealing with conditions of risk. Although many useful insights can be obtained from the traditional models of investment under conditions of certainty, the pervasive influence of risk in financial transactions has forced those working in this area to adopt models of price behavior which are little more than assertions. A typical classroom explanation of the determination of capital asset prices, for example, usually begins with a careful and relatively rigorous description of the process through which individual preferences and physical relationships interact to determine an equilibrium pure interest rate. This is generally followed by the assertion that somehow a market risk-premium is also determined, with the prices of assets adjusting accordingly to account for differences in their risk.

A useful representation of the view of the capital market implied in such discussions is illustrated in Figure 1. In equilibrium, capital asset prices have adjusted so that the investor, if he follows rational procedures (primarily diversification), is able to attain any desired point along a *capital market line.*[1] He may obtain a higher expected rate of return on his holdings only by incurring additional risk. In effect, the market presents him with two prices: the *price of time*, or the pure interest rate (shown by the intersection of the line with the horizontal axis) and the *price of risk*, the additional expected return per unit of risk borne (the reciprocal of the slope of the line).

* A great many people provided comments on early versions of this paper which led to major improvements in the exposition. In addition to the referees, who were most helpful, the author wishes to express his appreciation to Dr. Harry Markowitz of the RAND Corporation, Professor Jack Hirshleifer of the University of California at Los Angeles, and to Professors Yoram Barzel, George Brabb, Bruce Johnson, Walter Oi and R. Haney Scott of the University of Washington.

† Associate Professor of Operations Research, University of Washington.

1. Although some discussions are also consistent with a non-linear (but monotonic) curve.

Reprinted from *The Journal of Finance*, XIX, No. 3 (September, 1964), 425–42, by permission of the author and the publisher.

At present there is no theory describing the manner in which the price of risk results from the basic influences of investor preferences, the physical attributes of capital assets, etc. Moreover, lacking such a theory, it is difficult to give any real meaning to the relationship between the price of a single asset and its risk. Through diversification, some of the risk inherent in an asset can be avoided so that its total risk is obviously not the relevant influence on its price; unfortunately little has been said concerning the particular risk component which is relevant.

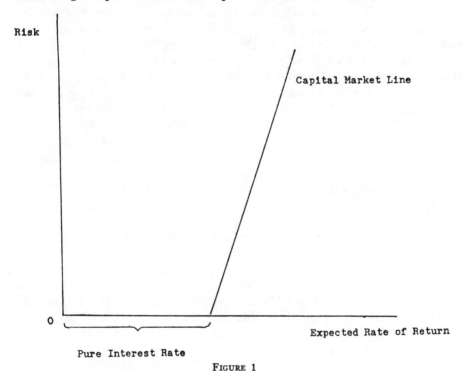

FIGURE 1

In the last ten years a number of economists have developed *normative* models dealing with asset choice under conditions of risk. Markowitz,[2] following Von Neumann and Morgenstern, developed an analysis based on the expected utility maxim and proposed a general solution for the portfolio selection problem. Tobin[3] showed that under certain conditions Markowitz's model implies that the process of investment choice can be broken down into two phases: first, the choice of a unique optimum combination of risky assets; and second, a separate choice concerning the allocation of funds between such a combination and a single riskless

2. Harry M. Markowitz, *Portfolio Selection, Efficient Diversification of Investments* (New York: John Wiley and Sons, Inc., 1959). The major elements of the theory first appeared in his article "Portfolio Selection," *The Journal of Finance*, XII (March 1952), 77-91.

3. James Tobin, "Liquidity Preference as Behavior Towards Risk," *The Review of Economic Studies*, XXV (February, 1958), 65-86.

asset. Recently, Hicks[4] has used a model similar to that proposed by Tobin to derive corresponding conclusions about individual investor behavior, dealing somewhat more explicitly with the nature of the conditions under which the process of investment choice can be dichotomized. An even more detailed discussion of this process, including a rigorous proof in the context of a choice among lotteries has been presented by Gordon and Gangolli.[5]

Although all the authors cited use virtually the same model of investor behavior,[6] none has yet attempted to extend it to construct a *market* equilibrium theory of asset prices under conditions of risk.[7] We will show that such an extension provides a theory with implications consistent with the assertions of traditional financial theory described above. Moreover, it sheds considerable light on the relationship between the price of an asset and the various components of its overall risk. For these reasons it warrants consideration as a model of the determination of capital asset prices.

Part II provides the model of individual investor behavior under conditions of risk. In Part III the equilibrium conditions for the capital market are considered and the capital market line derived. The implications for the relationship between the prices of individual capital assets and the various components of risk are described in Part IV.

II. Optimal Investment Policy for the Individual

The Investor's Preference Function

Assume that an individual views the outcome of any investment in probabilistic terms; that is, he thinks of the possible results in terms of some probability distribution. In assessing the desirability of a particular investment, however, he is willing to act on the basis of only two para-

---

4. John R. Hicks, "Liquidity," *The Economic Journal*, LXXII (December, 1962), 787-802.

5. M. J. Gordon and Ramesh Gangolli, "Choice Among and Scale of Play on Lottery Type Alternatives," College of Business Administration, University of Rochester, 1962. For another discussion of this relationship see W. F. Sharpe, "A Simplified Model for Portfolio Analysis," *Management Science*, Vol. 9, No. 2 (January 1963), 277-293. A related discussion can be found in F. Modigliani and M. H. Miller, "The Cost of Capital, Corporation Finance, and the Theory of Investment," *The American Economic Review*, XLVIII (June 1958), 261-297.

6. Recently Hirshleifer has suggested that the mean-variance approach used in the articles cited is best regarded as a special case of a more general formulation due to Arrow. See Hirshleifer's "Investment Decision Under Uncertainty," *Papers and Proceedings of the Seventy-Sixth Annual Meeting of the American Economic Association*, Dec. 1963, or Arrow's "Le Role des Valeurs Boursieres pour la Repartition la Meilleure des Risques," *International Colloquium on Econometrics*, 1952.

7. After preparing this paper the author learned that Mr. Jack L. Treynor, of Arthur D. Little, Inc., had independently developed a model similar in many respects to the one described here. Unfortunately Mr. Treynor's excellent work on this subject is, at present, unpublished.

meters of this distribution—its expected value and standard deviation.[8] This can be represented by a total utility function of the form:

$$U = f(E_w, \sigma_w)$$

where E_w indicates expected future wealth and σ_w the predicted standard deviation of the possible divergence of actual future wealth from E_w.

Investors are assumed to prefer a higher expected future wealth to a lower value, ceteris paribus ($dU/dE_w > 0$). Moreover, they exhibit risk-aversion, choosing an investment offering a lower value of σ_w to one with a greater level, given the level of E_w ($dU/d\sigma_w < 0$). These assumptions imply that indifference curves relating E_w and σ_w will be upward-sloping.[9]

To simplify the analysis, we assume that an investor has decided to commit a given amount (W_i) of his present wealth to investment. Letting W_t be his terminal wealth and R the rate of return on his investment:

$$R \equiv \frac{W_t - W_i}{W_i},$$

we have

$$W_t = R\,W_i + W_i.$$

This relationship makes it possible to express the investor's utility in terms of R, since terminal wealth is directly related to the rate of return:

$$U = g(E_R, \sigma_R).$$

Figure 2 summarizes the model of investor preferences in a family of indifference curves; successive curves indicate higher levels of utility as one moves down and/or to the right.[10]

---

8. Under certain conditions the mean-variance approach can be shown to lead to unsatisfactory predictions of behavior. Markowitz suggests that a model based on the semi-variance (the average of the squared deviations below the mean) would be preferable; in light of the formidable computational problems, however, he bases his analysis on the variance and standard deviation.

9. While only these characteristics are required for the analysis, it is generally assumed that the curves have the property of diminishing marginal rates of substitution between E_w and σ_w, as do those in our diagrams.

10. Such indifference curves can also be derived by assuming that the investor wishes to maximize expected utility and that his total utility can be represented by a quadratic function of R with decreasing marginal utility. Both Markowitz and Tobin present such a derivation. A similar approach is used by Donald E. Farrar in *The Investment Decision Under Uncertainty* (Prentice-Hall, 1962). Unfortunately Farrar makes an error in his derivation; he appeals to the Von-Neumann-Morgenstern cardinal utility axioms to transform a function of the form:

$$E(U) = a + bE_R - cE_R^2 - c\sigma_R^2$$

into one of the form:

$$E(U) = k_1 E_R - k_2 \sigma_R^2.$$

That such a transformation is not consistent with the axioms can readily be seen in this form, since the first equation implies non-linear indifference curves in the E_R, σ_R^2 plane while the second implies a linear relationship. Obviously no three (different) points can lie on both a line and a non-linear curve (with a monotonic derivative). Thus the two functions must imply different orderings among alternative choices in at least some instance.

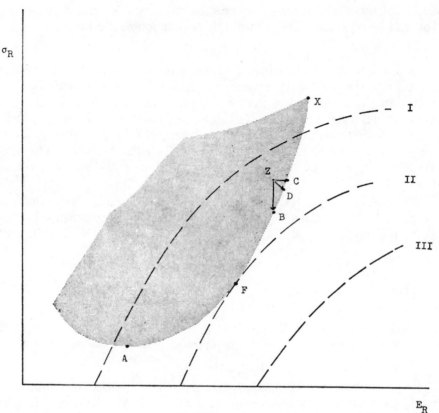

FIGURE 2

The Investment Opportunity Curve

The model of investor behavior considers the investor as choosing from a set of investment opportunities that one which maximizes his utility. Every investment plan available to him may be represented by a point in the E_R, σ_R plane. If all such plans involve some risk, the area composed of such points will have an appearance similar to that shown in Figure 2. The investor will choose from among all possible plans the one placing him on the indifference curve representing the highest level of utility (point F). The decision can be made in two stages: first, find the set of efficient investment plans and, second choose one from among this set. A plan is said to be efficient if (and only if) there is no alternative with either (1) the same E_R and a lower σ_R, (2) the same σ_R and a higher E_R or (3) a higher E_R and a lower σ_R. Thus investment Z is inefficient since investments B, C, and D (among others) dominate it. The only plans which would be chosen must lie along the lower right-hand boundary (AFBDCX)—the *investment opportunity curve*.

To understand the nature of this curve, consider two investment plans —A and B, each including one or more assets. Their predicted expected values and standard deviations of rate of return are shown in Figure 3.

If the proportion α of the individual's wealth is placed in plan A and the remainder $(1-\alpha)$ in B, the expected rate of return of the combination will lie between the expected returns of the two plans:

$$E_{Rc} = \alpha E_{Ra} + (1 - \alpha)\ E_{Rb}$$

The predicted standard deviation of return of the combination is:

$$\sigma_{Rc} = \sqrt{\alpha^2 \sigma_{Ra}{}^2 + (1 - \alpha)^2\ \sigma_{Rb}{}^2 + 2r_{ab}\ \alpha(1 - \alpha)\ \sigma_{Ra}\sigma_{Rb}}$$

Note that this relationship includes r_{ab}, the correlation coefficient between the predicted rates of return of the two investment plans. A value of $+1$ would indicate an investor's belief that there is a precise positive relationship between the outcomes of the two investments. A zero value would indicate a belief that the outcomes of the two investments are completely independent and -1 that the investor feels that there is a precise inverse relationship between them. In the usual case r_{ab} will have a value between 0 and $+1$.

Figure 3 shows the possible values of E_{Rc} and σ_{Rc} obtainable with different combinations of A and B under two different assumptions about

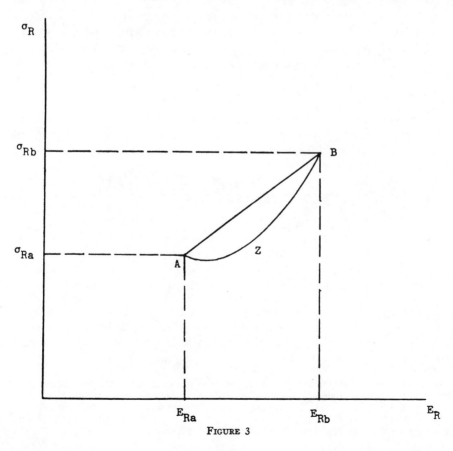

FIGURE 3

the value of r_{ab}. If the two investments are perfectly correlated, the combinations will lie along a straight line between the two points, since in this case both E_{Rc} and σ_{Rc} will be linearly related to the proportions invested in the two plans.[11] If they are less than perfectly positively correlated, the standard deviation of any combination must be less than that obtained with perfect correlation (since r_{ab} will be less); thus the combinations must lie along a curve below the line AB.[12] AZB shows such a curve for the case of complete independence ($r_{ab} = 0$); with negative correlation the locus is even more U-shaped.[13]

The manner in which the investment opportunity curve is formed is relatively simple conceptually, although exact solutions are usually quite difficult.[14] One first traces curves indicating E_R, σ_R values available with simple combinations of individual assets, then considers combinations of combinations of assets. The lower right-hand boundary must be either linear or increasing at an increasing rate ($d^2 \sigma_R/dE^2_R > 0$). As suggested earlier, the complexity of the relationship between the characteristics of individual assets and the location of the investment opportunity curve makes it difficult to provide a simple rule for assessing the desirability of individual assets, since the effect of an asset on an investor's over-all investment opportunity curve depends not only on its expected rate of return (E_{Ri}) and risk (σ_{Ri}), but also on its correlations with the other available opportunities ($r_{i1}, r_{i2}, \ldots, r_{in}$). However, such a rule is implied by the equilibrium conditions for the model, as we will show in part IV.

The Pure Rate of Interest

We have not yet dealt with riskless assets. Let P be such an asset; its risk is zero ($\sigma_{Rp} = 0$) and its expected rate of return, E_{Rp}, is equal (by definition) to the pure interest rate. If an investor places α of his wealth

11.
$$E_{Rc} = \alpha E_{Ra} + (1 - \alpha)\, E_{R_b} = E_{Rb} + (E_{R_a} - E_{R_b})\, \alpha$$
$$\sigma_{R_c} = \sqrt{\alpha^2 \sigma_{R_a}{}^2 + (1 - \alpha)^2\, \sigma_{Rb}{}^2 + 2r_{ab}\, \alpha(1 - \alpha)\, \sigma_{Ra}\, \sigma_{Rb}}$$

but $r_{ab} = 1$, therefore the expression under the square root sign can be factored:
$$\sigma_{Rc} = \sqrt{[\alpha \sigma_{Ra} + (1 - \alpha)\, \sigma_{R_b}]^2}$$
$$= \alpha\, \sigma_{Ra} + (1 - \alpha)\, \sigma_{Rb}$$
$$= \sigma_{Rb} + (\sigma_{Ra} - \sigma_{Rb})\, \alpha$$

12. This curvature is, in essence, the rationale for diversification.

13. When $r_{ab} = 0$, the slope of the curve at point A is $-\dfrac{\sigma_{Ra}}{E_{Rb} - E_{Ra}}$, at point B it is $\dfrac{\sigma_{Rb}}{E_{Rb} - E_{Ra}}$. When $r_{ab} = -1$, the curve degenerates to two straight lines to a point on the horizontal axis.

14. Markowitz has shown that this is a problem in parametric quadratic programming. An efficient solution technique is described in his article, "The Optimization of a Quadratic Function Subject to Linear Constraints," *Naval Research Logistics Quarterly*, Vol. 3 (March and June, 1956), 111-133. A solution method for a special case is given in the author's "A Simplified Model for Portfolio Analysis," *op. cit.*

in P and the remainder in some risky asset A, he would obtain an expected rate of return:

$$E_{Rc} = \alpha E_{Rp} + (1 - \alpha) E_{Ra}$$

The standard deviation of such a combination would be:

$$\sigma_{Rc} = \sqrt{\alpha^2 \sigma^2_{Rp} + (1 - \alpha)^2 \sigma_{Ra}{}^2 + 2r_{pa} \alpha(1 - \alpha) \sigma_{Rp}\sigma_{Ra}}$$

but since $\sigma_{Rp} = 0$, this reduces to:

$$\sigma_{Rc} = (1 - \alpha) \sigma_{Ra}.$$

This implies that all combinations involving any risky asset or combination of assets plus the riskless asset must have values of E_{Rc} and σ_{Rc} which lie along a straight line between the points representing the two components. Thus in Figure 4 all combinations of E_R and σ_R lying along

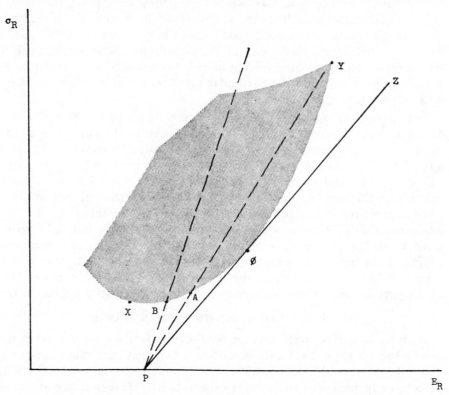

FIGURE 4

the line PA are attainable if some money is loaned at the pure rate and some placed in A. Similarly, by lending at the pure rate and investing in B, combinations along PB can be attained. Of all such possibilities, however, one will dominate: that investment plan lying at the point of the original investment opportunity curve where a ray from point P is tangent to the curve. In Figure 4 all investments lying along the original curve from X to ϕ are dominated by some combination of investment in ϕ and lending at the pure interest rate.

Consider next the possibility of borrowing. If the investor can borrow at the pure rate of interest, this is equivalent to disinvesting in P. The effect of borrowing to purchase more of any given investment than is possible with the given amount of wealth can be found simply by letting α take on negative values in the equations derived for the case of lending. This will obviously give points lying along the extension of line PA if borrowing is used to purchase more of A; points lying along the extension of PB if the funds are used to purchase B, etc.

As in the case of lending, however, one investment plan will dominate all others when borrowing is possible. When the rate at which funds can be borrowed equals the lending rate, this plan will be the same one which is dominant if lending is to take place. Under these conditions, the investment opportunity curve becomes a line (PϕZ in Figure 4). Moreover, if the original investment opportunity curve is not linear at point ϕ, the process of investment choice can be dichotomized as follows: first select the (unique) optimum combination of risky assets (point ϕ), and second borrow or lend to obtain the particular point on PZ at which an indifference curve is tangent to the line.[15]

Before proceeding with the analysis, it may be useful to consider alternative assumptions under which only a combination of assets lying at the point of tangency between the original investment opportunity curve and a ray from P can be efficient. Even if borrowing is impossible, the investor will choose ϕ (and lending) if his risk-aversion leads him to a point below ϕ on the line Pϕ. Since a large number of investors choose to place some of their funds in relatively risk-free investments, this is not an unlikely possibility. Alternatively, if borrowing is possible but only up to some limit, the choice of ϕ would be made by all but those investors willing to undertake considerable risk. These alternative paths lead to the main conclusion, thus making the assumption of borrowing or lending at the pure interest rate less onerous than it might initially appear to be.

III. Equilibrium in the Capital Market

In order to derive conditions for equilibrium in the capital market we invoke two assumptions. First, we assume a common pure rate of interest, with all investors able to borrow or lend funds on equal terms. Second, we assume homogeneity of investor expectations:[16] investors are assumed

15. This proof was first presented by Tobin for the case in which the pure rate of interest is zero (cash). Hicks considers the lending situation under comparable conditions but does not allow borrowing. Both authors present their analysis using maximization subject to constraints expressed as equalities. Hicks' analysis assumes independence and thus insures that the solution will include no negative holdings of risky assets; Tobin's covers the general case, thus his solution would generally include negative holdings of some assets. The discussion in this paper is based on Markowitz' formulation, which includes non-negativity constraints on the holdings of all assets.

16. A term suggested by one of the referees.

to agree on the prospects of various investments—the expected values, standard deviations and correlation coefficients described in Part II. Needless to say, these are highly restrictive and undoubtedly unrealistic assumptions. However, since the proper test of a theory is not the realism of its assumptions but the acceptability of its implications, and since these assumptions imply equilibrium conditions which form a major part of classical financial doctrine, it is far from clear that this formulation should be rejected—especially in view of the dearth of alternative models leading to similar results.

Under these assumptions, given some set of capital asset prices, each investor will view his alternatives in the same manner. For one set of prices the alternatives might appear as shown in Figure 5. In this situa-

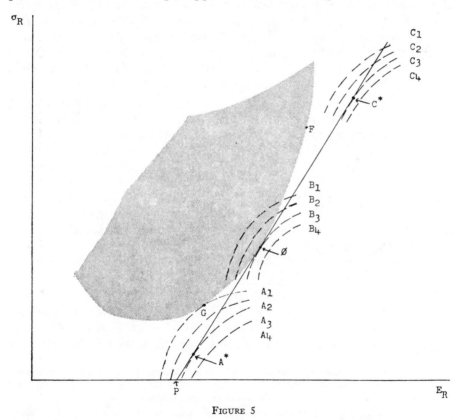

FIGURE 5

tion, an investor with the preferences indicated by indifference curves A_1 through A_4 would seek to lend some of his funds at the pure interest rate and to invest the remainder in the combination of assets shown by point ϕ, since this would give him the preferred over-all position A*. An investor with the preferences indicated by curves B_1 through B_4 would seek to invest all his funds in combination ϕ, while an investor with indifference curves C_1 through C_4 would invest all his funds plus additional (borrowed) funds in combination ϕ in order to reach his preferred position (C*). In any event, all would attempt to purchase only those risky assets which enter combination ϕ.

The attempts by investors to purchase the assets in combination ϕ and their lack of interest in holding assets not in combination ϕ would, of course, lead to a revision of prices. The prices of assets in ϕ will rise and, since an asset's expected return relates future income to present price, their expected returns will fall. This will reduce the attractiveness of combinations which include such assets; thus point ϕ (among others) will move to the left of its initial position.[17] On the other hand, the prices of assets not in ϕ will fall, causing an increase in their expected returns and a rightward movement of points representing combinations which include them. Such price changes will lead to a revision of investors' actions; some new combination or combinations will become attractive, leading to different demands and thus to further revisions in prices. As the process continues, the investment opportunity curve will tend to become more linear, with points such as ϕ moving to the left and formerly inefficient points (such as F and G) moving to the right.

Capital asset prices must, of course, continue to change until a set of prices is attained for which every asset enters at least one combination lying on the capital market line. Figure 6 illustrates such an equilibrium condition.[18] All possibilities in the shaded area can be attained with combinations of risky assets, while points lying along the line PZ can be attained by borrowing or lending at the pure rate plus an investment in some combination of risky assets. Certain possibilities (those lying along PZ from point A to point B) can be obtained in either manner. For example, the E_R, σ_R values shown by point A can be obtained solely by some combination of risky assets; alternatively, the point can be reached by a combination of lending and investing in combination C of risky assets.

It is important to recognize that in the situation shown in Figure 6 many alternative combinations of risky assets are efficient (i.e., lie along line PZ), and thus the theory does not imply that all investors will hold the same combination.[19] On the other hand, all such combinations must be perfectly (positively) correlated, since they lie along a linear border of

17. If investors consider the variability of future dollar returns unrelated to present price, both E_R and σ_R will fall; under these conditions the point representing an asset would move along a ray through the origin as its price changes.

18. The area in Figure 6 representing E_R, σ_R values attained with only risky assets has been drawn at some distance from the horizontal axis for emphasis. It is likely that a more accurate representation would place it very close to the axis.

19. This statement contradicts Tobin's conclusion that there will be a unique optimal combination of risky assets. Tobin's proof of a unique optimum can be shown to be incorrect for the case of perfect correlation of efficient risky investment plans if the line connecting their E_R, σ_R points would pass through point P. In the graph on page 83 of this article (*op. cit.*) the constant-risk locus would, in this case, degenerate from a family of ellipses into one of straight lines parallel to the constant-return loci, thus giving multiple optima.

the E_R, σ_R region.[20] This provides a key to the relationship between the prices of capital assets and different types of risk.

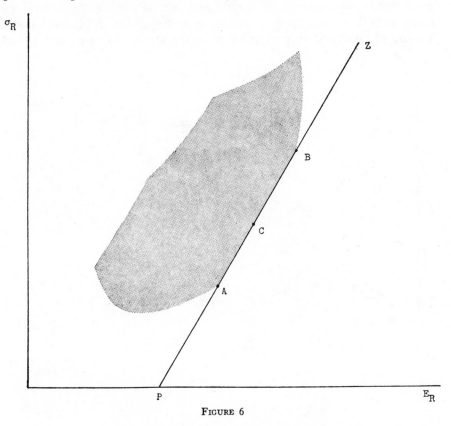

FIGURE 6

IV. THE PRICES OF CAPITAL ASSETS

We have argued that in equilibrium there will be a simple linear relationship between the expected return and standard deviation of return for efficient combinations of risky assets. Thus far nothing has been said about such a relationship for individual assets. Typically the E_R, σ_R values associated with single assets will lie above the capital market line, reflecting the inefficiency of undiversified holdings. Moreover, such points may be scattered throughout the feasible region, with no consistent relationship between their expected return and total risk (σ_R). However, there will be a consistent relationship between their expected returns and what might best be called *systematic risk*, as we will now show.

Figure 7 illustrates the typical relationship between a single capital

20. E_R, σ_R values given by combinations of any two combinations must lie within the region and cannot plot above a straight line joining the points. In this case they cannot plot below such a straight line. But since only in the case of perfect correlation will they plot along a straight line, the two combinations must be perfectly correlated. As shown in Part IV, this does not necessarily imply that the individual securities they contain are perfectly correlated.

asset (point i) and an efficient combination of assets (point g) of which it is a part. The curve igg′ indicates all E_R, σ_R values which can be obtained with feasible combinations of asset i and combination g. As before, we denote such a combination in terms of a proportion α of asset i and $(1 - \alpha)$ of combination g. A value of $\alpha = 1$ would indicate pure invest-

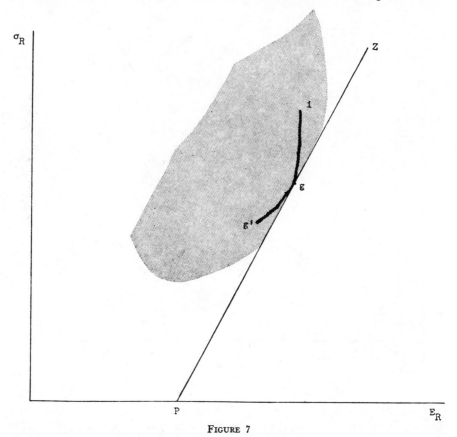

FIGURE 7

ment in asset i while $\alpha = 0$ would imply investment in combination g. Note, however, that $\alpha = .5$ implies a total investment of more than half the funds in asset i, since half would be invested in i itself and the other half used to purchase combination g, which also includes some of asset i. This means that a combination in which asset i does not appear at all must be represented by some negative value of α. Point g′ indicates such a combination.

In Figure 7 the curve igg′ has been drawn tangent to the capital market line (PZ) at point g. This is no accident. All such curves must be tangent to the capital market line in equilibrium, since (1) they must touch it at the point representing the efficient combination and (2) they are continuous at that point.[21] Under these conditions a lack of tangency would

21. Only if $r_{ig} = -1$ will the curve be discontinuous over the range in question.

imply that the curve intersects PZ. But then some feasible combination of assets would lie to the right of the capital market line, an obvious impossibility since the capital market line represents the efficient boundary of feasible values of E_R and σ_R.

The requirement that curves such as igg' be tangent to the capital market line can be shown to lead to a relatively simple formula which relates the expected rate of return to various elements of risk for all assets which are included in combination g.[22] Its economic meaning can best be seen if the relationship between the return of asset i and that of combination g is viewed in a manner similar to that used in regression analysis.[23] Imagine that we were given a number of (ex post) observations of the return of the two investments. The points might plot as shown in Fig. 8. The scatter of the R_i observations around their mean (which will approximate E_{Ri}) is, of course, evidence of the total risk of the asset — σ_{Ri}. But part of the scatter is due to an underlying relationship with the return on combination g, shown by B_{ig}, the slope of the regression line. The response of R_i to changes in R_g (and variations in R_g itself) account for

22. The standard deviation of a combination of g and i will be:

$$\sigma = \sqrt{\alpha^2 \sigma_{Ri}^2 + (1-\alpha)^2 \sigma_{Rg}^2 + 2r_{ig}\alpha(1-\alpha)\sigma_{Ri}\sigma_{Rg}}$$

at $\alpha = 0$:

$$\frac{d\sigma}{d\alpha} = -\frac{1}{\sigma}[\sigma_{Rg}^2 - r_{ig}\sigma_{Ri}\sigma_{Rg}]$$

but $\sigma = \sigma_{Rg}$ at $\alpha = 0$. Thus:

$$\frac{d\sigma}{d\alpha} = -[\sigma_{Rg} - r_{ig}\sigma_{Ri}]$$

The expected return of a combination will be:

$$E = \alpha E_{Ri} + (1-\alpha)E_{Rg}$$

Thus, at all values of α:

$$\frac{dE}{d\alpha} = -[E_{Rg} - E_{Ri}]$$

and, at $\alpha = 0$:

$$\frac{d\sigma}{dE} = \frac{\sigma_{Rg} - r_{ig}\sigma_{Ri}}{E_{Rg} - E_{Ri}}.$$

Let the equation of the capital market line be:

$$\sigma_R = s(E_R - P)$$

where P is the pure interest rate. Since igg' is tangent to the line when $\alpha = 0$, and since (E_{Rg}, σ_{Rg}) lies on the line:

$$\frac{\sigma_{Rg} - r_{ig}\sigma_{Ri}}{E_{Rg} - E_{Ri}} = \frac{\sigma_{Rg}}{E_{Rg} - P}$$

or:

$$\frac{r_{ig}\sigma_{Ri}}{\sigma_{Rg}} = -\left[\frac{P}{E_{Rg} - P}\right] + \left[\frac{1}{E_{Rg} - P}\right]E_{Ri}.$$

23. This model has been called the diagonal model since its portfolio analysis solution can be facilitated by re-arranging the data so that the variance-covariance matrix becomes diagonal. The method is described in the author's article, cited earlier.

Return on Asset 1 (R1)

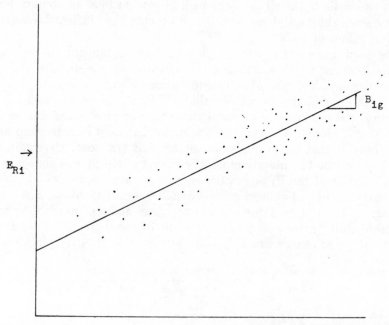

Return on Combination g (R$_g$)

FIGURE 8

much of the variation in R$_1$. It is this component of the asset's total risk which we term the *systematic* risk. The remainder,[24] being uncorrelated with R$_g$, is the unsystematic component. This formulation of the relationship between R$_1$ and R$_g$ can be employed *ex ante* as a predictive model. B$_{ig}$ becomes the *predicted* response of R$_1$ to changes in R$_g$. Then, given σ_{Rg} (the predicted risk of R$_g$), the systematic portion of the predicted risk of each asset can be determined.

This interpretation allows us to state the relationship derived from the tangency of curves such as igg' with the capital market line in the form shown in Figure 9. All assets entering efficient combination g must have (predicted) B$_{ig}$ and E$_{R1}$ values lying on the line PQ.[25] Prices will

24. *ex post*, the standard error.

25.

$$r_{ig} = \sqrt{\frac{B_{ig}{}^2\sigma_{Rg}{}^2}{\sigma_{Ri}{}^2}} = \frac{B_{ig}\sigma_{Rg}}{\sigma_{Ri}}$$

and:

$$B_{ig} = \frac{r_{ig}\sigma_{Ri}}{\sigma_{Rg}}.$$

The expression on the right is the expression on the left-hand side of the last equation in footnote 22. Thus:

$$B_{ig} = -\left[\frac{P}{E_{Rg}-P}\right] + \left[\frac{1}{E_{Rg}-P}\right] E_{Ri}.$$

adjust so that assets which are more responsive to changes in R_g will have higher expected returns than those which are less responsive. This accords with common sense. Obviously the part of an asset's risk which is due to its correlation with the return on a combination cannot be diversified away when the asset is added to the combination. Since B_{ig} indicates the magnitude of this type of risk it should be directly related to expected return.

The relationship illustrated in Figure 9 provides a partial answer to the question posed earlier concerning the relationship between an asset's risk

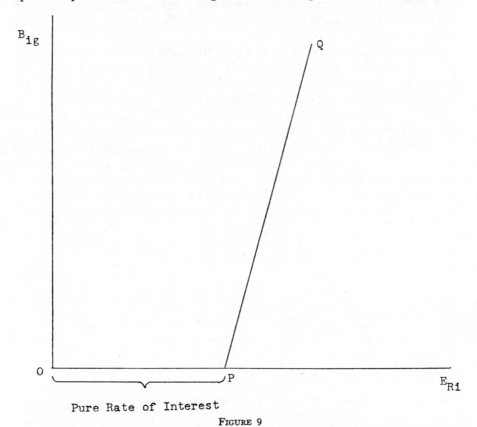

Pure Rate of Interest

FIGURE 9

and its expected return. But thus far we have argued only that the relationship holds for the assets which enter some particular efficient combination (g). Had another combination been selected, a different linear relationship would have been derived. Fortunately this limitation is easily overcome. As shown in the footnote,[26] we may arbitrarily select *any* one

26. Consider the two assets i and i*, the former included in efficient combination g and the latter in combination g*. As shown above:

$$B_{ig} = - \left[\frac{P}{E_{Rg} - P} \right] + \left[\frac{1}{E_{Rg} - P} \right] E_{Ri}$$

and:

of the efficient combinations, then measure the predicted responsiveness of *every* asset's rate of return to that of the combination selected; and these coefficients will be related to the expected rates of return of the assets in exactly the manner pictured in Figure 9.

The fact that rates of return from all efficient combinations will be perfectly correlated provides the justification for arbitrarily selecting any one of them. Alternatively we may choose instead any variable perfectly correlated with the rate of return of such combinations. The vertical axis in Figure 9 would then indicate alternative levels of a coefficient measuring the sensitivity of the rate of return of a capital asset to changes in the variable chosen.

This possibility suggests both a plausible explanation for the implication that all efficient combinations will be perfectly correlated and a useful interpretation of the relationship between an individual asset's expected return and its risk. Although the theory itself implies only that rates of return from efficient combinations will be perfectly correlated, we might expect that this would be due to their common dependence on the over-all level of economic activity. If so, diversification enables the investor to escape all but the risk resulting from swings in economic activity—this type of risk remains even in efficient combinations. And, since all other types can be avoided by diversification, only the responsiveness of an asset's rate of return to the level of economic activity is relevant in

$$B_{i \cdot g*} = - \left[\frac{P}{E_{Rg*} - P} \right] + \left[\frac{1}{E_{Rg*} - P} \right] E_{Ri*}.$$

Since R_g and R_{g*} are perfectly correlated:

$$r_{i \cdot g*} = r_{i \cdot g}$$

Thus:

$$\frac{B_{i \cdot g*} \sigma_{Rg*}}{\sigma_{Ri*}} = \frac{B_{i \cdot g} \sigma_{Rg}}{\sigma_{Ri*}}$$

and:

$$B_{i \cdot g*} = B_{i \cdot g} \left[\frac{\sigma_{Rg}}{\sigma_{Rg*}} \right].$$

Since both g and g* lie on a line which intercepts the E-axis at P:

$$\frac{\sigma_{Rg}}{\sigma_{Rg*}} = \frac{E_{Rg} - P}{E_{Rg*} - P}$$

and:

$$B_{i \cdot g*} = B_{i \cdot g} \left[\frac{E_{Rg} - P}{E_{Rg*} - P} \right]$$

Thus:

$$- \left[\frac{P}{E_{Rg*} - P} \right] + \left[\frac{1}{E_{Rg*} - P} \right] E_{Ri*} = B_{i \cdot g} \left[\frac{E_{Rg} - P}{E_{Rg*} - P} \right]$$

from which we have the desired relationship between R_{i*} and g:

$$B_{i \cdot g} = - \left[\frac{P}{E_{Rg} - P} \right] + \left[\frac{1}{E_{Rg} - P} \right] E_{Ri*}$$

$B_{i \cdot g}$ must therefore plot on the same line as does B_{ig}.

assessing its risk. Prices will adjust until there is a linear relationship between the magnitude of such responsiveness and expected return. Assets which are unaffected by changes in economic activity will return the pure interest rate; those which move with economic activity will promise appropriately higher expected rates of return.

This discussion provides an answer to the second of the two questions posed in this paper. In Part III it was shown that with respect to equilibrium conditions in the capital market as a whole, the theory leads to results consistent with classical doctrine (i.e., the capital market line). We have now shown that with regard to capital assets considered individually, it also yields implications consistent with traditional concepts: it is common practice for investment counselors to accept a lower expected return from defensive securities (those which respond little to changes in the economy) than they require from aggressive securities (which exhibit significant response). As suggested earlier, the familiarity of the implications need not be considered a drawback. The provision of a logical framework for producing some of the major elements of traditional financial theory should be a useful contribution in its own right.

22

RISK-RETURN CLASSES OF NEW YORK STOCK EXCHANGE COMMON STOCKS, 1931–67

William F. Sharpe and Guy M. Cooper

INTRODUCTION

Within the last decade economists have investigated rather thoroughly the nature of a "perfect" or "efficient" market for securities. A widely used model dealing with uncertainty is that developed by Sharpe [6], Lintner [3], Mossin [5], and Fama [2], based on the pioneering contributions of Markowitz [4] and Tobin [8]. Variously known as the "capital asset pricing model," "capital market theory," or the "market line theory," the approach deals with *ex ante* or predicted relationships. Briefly, it suggests that:

1) the appropriate measure of risk for a security or portfolio is the covariance of its rate of return with that of a portfolio composed of all risky assets, each held in proportion to its total value;
2) the expected return of any security or portfolio will equal a constant plus some other constant times its risk.

Derivation of these results can be found in Sharpe [7].

While the model provides important insights into the nature of actual capital markets, it is of limited value for the selection of an investment strategy unless additional specifications are made concerning the stability and/or predictability of key measures.

A number of investigators have performed tests of such expanded capital asset pricing models. The original specifications are augmented with assumptions about the stability of key variables through time. The expanded models suggest (1) that measurement of values during some previous period can be used to implement strategies that will in fact differ with respect to both risk and expected return; (2) that high-risk, high-return strategies will return more on the average than low-risk, low-return strategies; and (3) that high-risk, high-return strategies will bring greater losses in bear markets (i.e., have more risk) than will low-risk, low-return strategies.

An extensive study of this type was performed by Black, Jensen and Scholes [1]. They were concerned primarily with testing the validity of an expanded capital asset pricing model, and less directly with assessing the

Reprinted from the *Financial Analysts Journal*, XXVIII, No. 2, (March, April, 1972), 46 pp., by permission of the authors and the publisher.

performance of alternative investment strategies. In this paper, the general approach of Black, Jensen and Scholes is followed with modifications designed to reduce its expense as a practical investment selection technique. Moreover, we report information particularly relevant to the selection of such a technique. Our focus is primarily on assessing alternative investment strategies; by and large, we bypass issues concerned with the adequacy of various expanded capital asset pricing models.[1]

Performance Measures

For any single period, a relevant measure of performance from the investor's point of view is return:

$$\text{return} \equiv \frac{\text{ending value} + \text{dividends} - \text{beginning value}}{\text{beginning value}}$$

For securities, return can be calculated on a per-share basis, with appropriate adjustments for stock dividends and stock splits.

A related measure is appreciation:

$$\text{appreciation} \equiv \frac{\text{ending value} - \text{beginning value}}{\text{beginning value}}$$

The other component of return is yield:

$$\text{yield} = \frac{\text{dividends}}{\text{beginning value}}$$

Obviously:

$$\text{return} = \text{appreciation} + \text{yield}$$

The data used in this study were taken from the CRISP (Center for Research in Security Prices) tapes developed at the University of Chicago. Monthly returns and appreciation figures for all New York Stock Exchange stocks over the period from January 1926 through June 1968 were utilized.

Performance over a number of periods can be measured by the average return. Let R_{pt} represent the return on a portfolio of stocks in time period t. The average return from period 1 through period T is:

$$\text{average return} = \frac{1}{T} \sum_{t=1}^{T} R_{pt}$$

$$\text{(where } \sum \text{ denotes summation)}$$

[1] This paper differs from that of Black, Jensen and Scholes (BJS) in a number of respects. The differences will be summarized here, although a full understanding may require a prior reading of the remainder of this paper. First, BJS require only 24 months of data to estimate a security's risk-return class (although they use up to 60 if available); we require 60 months. Second, BJS use beta to determine risk-return classes, while we use market sensitivity. Third, BJS measure performance in terms of monthly returns; we use annual values (both because an annual holding period seems more consistent with an annual review of risk-return classes and because annual rebalancing involves smaller transactions costs than monthly rebalancing of the portfolios). Finally, we report geometric means as well as arithmetic means for those interested in long-run performance and provide data concerning stability of risk-return classes for those interested in the characteristics of individual securities.

An alternative measure of performance is the geometric instead of the arithmetic mean. The result indicates the constant return in each period that would have provided the same terminal value as the actual series of returns. The value is:

$$\text{equivalent constant return} = \left[\prod_{t=1}^{T} (1 + R_{pt}) \right]^{\frac{1}{T}} - 1$$

(where Π denotes multiplication)

Risk can be measured in a great many ways. We focus on a measure that highlights the impact of swings in the market on the return from a security or portfolio. If there were no prospects of bear markets, there would be little risk in the common meaning of the term. Stocks are considered risky because they can go down. And typically, the more sensitive a security or portfolio is to swings in the market, the more it goes down in a bear market. To measure this, we use the slope of a regression line relating return on the portfolio to the return on a broadly-based portfolio used to represent "the market." We term the slope of such a line "beta." More formally [2]:

$$\beta p = \frac{\text{Cov } (R_p, R_m)}{\text{Var } R_m}$$

Figure I provides an illustration. In the figure:

$$\text{Cov } (R_p, R_m) = \text{covariance between } R_p \text{ and } R_m$$

$$= \frac{1}{T} \left[\sum_{t=1}^{T} (R_{pt} - \bar{R}_p)(R_{mt} - \bar{R}_m) \right]$$

$$\text{Var } (R_{m}) = \text{variance of } R_m$$

$$= \frac{1}{T} \left[\sum_{t=1}^{T} (R_{mt} - \bar{R}_m)^2 \right]$$

$$\bar{R}_p = \text{average return on portfolio p}$$
$$\bar{R}_m = \text{average return on the market portfolio}$$

For purposes of this study, the Fisher market index included on the CRISP tape was used to measure R_m.

It is important to recognize that beta may not provide an adequate measure of the total risk of a portfolio. However, for well-diversified portfolios, the majority of the variation in return is attributable to changes in the return on the market, and beta will thus provide a good measure of risk.

Risk-Return Classes

In an efficient market, one rarely gets something for nothing. If investors prefer high average returns to low average returns *and* prefer low risk to high risk, prices should adjust so that the best low risk strategy provides lower returns on the average than the best high risk strategy.

The average return of a portfolio is simply the weighted average of the average returns of its component securities, with the proportions of value used as weights. Moreover, the beta of a portfolio is a weighted average of the betas of its component securities, with the proportions of value used as

---

[2] For a derivation of this relationship, see Sharpe [7].

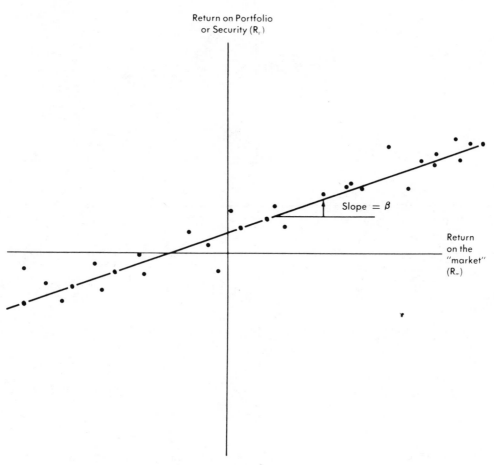

Figure 1.

weights. Finally, the beta of a well-diversified portfolio provides a good surrogate for its total risk, since almost all fluctuations in the portfolio's value will follow market swings.

A well-diversified portfolio with a high beta value will be risky. In an efficient market, it will also provide a high average return. A portfolio of this type may be constructed by choosing a large number of stocks with high beta values. Such a strategy should provide high returns on the average, but with substantial risk.

A well-diversified portfolio with a low beta value will have relatively little risk. In an efficient market, it will also provide a relatively low average return. A portfolio of this type may be constructed by choosing a large number of stocks with low beta values. Such a strategy should provide relatively low returns on the average, but with little risk.

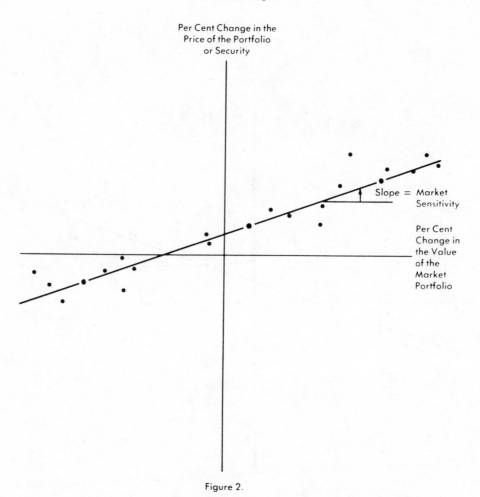

Figure 2.

In a period in which the market goes up, high-beta stocks will go up more than low-beta stocks. Unless dividend yields are strongly inversely related to beta values, average return and beta will thus be positively correlated over periods in which the market goes up. And since both history and expectations of risk-averse investors indicate that the market is more likely to go up than down, over long periods average return should be positively related to beta.

Stocks with high beta values should have high returns on the average; they may be said to be in a high *risk-return class*. On the other hand, stocks with low beta values should have low returns on the average; they may be said to be in a low *risk-return class*.

To use this relationship as a basis for an investment strategy, some means must be found to select stocks that will, in fact, have high beta values *in the future*. An obvious possibility involves the measurement of beta in the past, on the assumption that beta is reasonably stable over time. This procedure was utilized by Black, Jensen and Scholes and will be adopted here, with minor modifications.

Market Sensitivity

To measure performance it is important to use return—i.e., appreciation plus dividend yield. However, most variation in return is due to changes in appreciation, dividend yield being relatively constant over time. This suggests that the value of beta would not change significantly if dividend yield were excluded. To avoid confusion, we continue to use the term "beta" for the slope of the regression line relating the return on a portfolio or security to that of the market. The term "market sensitivity" will be used to denote the slope of a regression line relating the appreciation on a portfolio or security to that of the market. Figure II provides an illustration. To compare the two measures, the monthly returns and appreciation values for 1,572 securities during the period from January, 1960, through June, 1968, were utilized. For each security the value of beta was calculated using returns; then the value of market sensitivity was calculated, using only price changes. The results were very similar. If each of the 1,572 pairs were plotted, the points would lie almost exactly along a 45-degree line through the axis, as illustrated in Figure III. The similarity of the two measures is clear from the results obtained when the values of beta were regressed on the values of market sensitivity. The regression equation was:

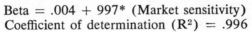

Beta = .004 + 997* (Market sensitivity)
Coefficient of determination (R^2) = .996

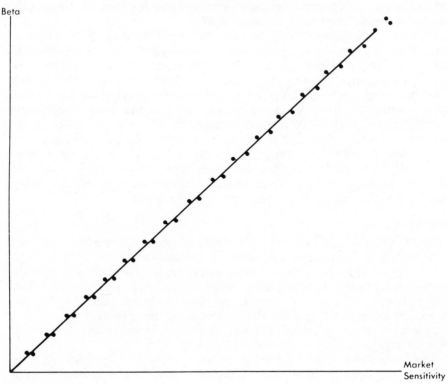

Figure 3.

This suggests that, as a practical matter, market sensitivity may be used instead of beta when classifying securities into risk-return classes. Since dividend information may be difficult to collect and verify, this makes it possible to lower the cost of implementing strategies based on risk-return classes.

Portfolio Selection Strategies

We have determined the outcomes obtained from each of ten investment strategies during the 37-year period from 1931 through 1967. For each security listed on the New York Stock Exchange, market sensitivity was calculated, based on the monthly price changes for the 60 months prior to the beginning of the investment calendar year (a security would not be included if a full 60 months of data were not available). The number of securities for which market sensitivity was calculated ranged from 478 (in 1931) to 985 (in 1967).

After the market sensitivity values were calculated, the numerical values were ranked. Based on this ranking, securities were divided into deciles. The securities in the top decile (i.e., those with the highest market sensitivities) were considered to be in risk-return class 10 at the time of classification. The securities in the next decile were considered to be in risk-return class 9, etc. The number of securities in a given risk-return class ranged from 47 (in 1931) to 99 (in 1967).

This procedure—calculation of market sensitivity, ranking of securities, and assignment to risk-return classes—was repeated for each of the possible investment years from 1931 through 1967.

Strategies are numbered from 10 to 1. Strategy 1 involves the purchase of equal dollar amounts of all stocks in risk-return class I at the beginning of each year. Every dividend received during the year is reinvested in the stock that pays it (at the beginning of the month following payment). On the first of the next year, stocks are bought and sold until the portfolio contains equal dollar amounts of all stocks in risk-return class I *at that time*. Rebalancing is thus required both to accommodate changes in the set of stocks in the specified risk-return class and to account for differential price changes.

To reduce the number of computations, the results have not been adjusted to account for transactions costs. However, these are relatively small and differ little among strategies since annual performance measures are being considered and rebalancing is done only once each year.

Performance

Figures IVa through IVd show the results obtained when each of the ten strategies was followed over the entire period studied (from 1931 through 1967). Figure IVa shows the average annual return for each strategy. On the average, strategy 10 provided a return of over 22 per cent per year, while strategy 1 provides less than 12 per cent. Although the values do not decrease uniformly, the general relationship is of the expected type—portfolios composed of securities in lower risk-return classes tend to provide lower average return.

Figure IVb shows the actual values of beta for the ten strategies. Returns obtained with strategy 10 moved 42 per cent more than the market as a whole; on the other hand, returns obtained with strategy 1 moved only 58 per cent as much as the market as a whole. Again, the values do not decrease uniformly, but the general relationship is of the expected type—portfolios composed of securities in lower risk-return classes tend to move less with swings in the market.[3]

Figure IVc shows the equivalent constant annual return for each of the ten strategies. Here the picture is far less clear. The investor concerned *only* with the very long run (in this case, 36 years) must take into account the impact of both risk and average return on his overall position. When returns vary, the geometric mean will always be smaller than the arithmetic mean, and the difference will typically be greater, the greater the variation. High risk-return classes typically offer a higher average return but also bring greater variability. The net effect over the very long term is thus relatively unpredictable. In this case, the best results would have been obtained with strategy 7. An investor who reinvested both capital and dividends every year while following strategy 7 would have accumulated as much wealth at the end of the period as if he had placed his money in a bank paying roughly 16 per cent interest per year, compounded annually. On the other hand, an investor following strategy 1 would have accumulated only as much wealth as if he had placed his funds in a bank paying roughly 10 per cent per annum, compounded annually.

Figure IVd summarizes the relationship between average return and the actual value of beta for each of the ten strategies during this period. As expected, the relationship is positive and quite significant (during this period the market rose on the average). The intercept is somewhat higher than the return on relatively safe investments during the period—a result consistent with that of Black, Jensen and Scholes—and the relationship appears to be approximately linear.[4]

[3] In general, the value of beta describes the majority of the fluctuations in returns for these portfolios. The coefficients of determination for the regressions of portfolio return on market return were:

Strategy	Coefficient of Determination
10	.94
9	.94
8	.95
7	.95
6	.98
5	.98
4	.92
3	.94
2	.88
1	.87

[4] This relationship can be derived from a model in which it is impossible to borrow without limit at the same rate of interest at which one can lend. If the portfolio used as a market surrogate is riskier than the optimal combination of risky securities for one who plans to lend part of his funds, the result follows directly as long as the market surrogate is on the efficient frontier. The true "market portfolio" (which includes all assets—e.g., corporate bonds, real estate, etc.) may well be less risky than the typical index of New York Stock Exchange common stocks such as that used in this study. It is entirely possible that, if a better surrogate for the market portfolio could be obtained, the relationship between average return and beta would intercept the average return axis very near the interest rate on safe investments.

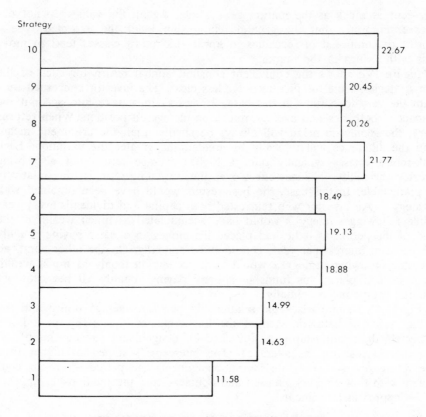

Figure 4a. Average Annual Returns 1931 Through 1967

Figures IVa, b, c, and d were produced using the Tektronix T4002 display and the Hewlett-Packard 2000C computer at the Stanford Graduate School of Business. Users of this system can obtain results for any other period between 1931 and 1967 by calling for program $GRCC and running it. The program will give instructions, request the starting and ending year, and then provide the four graphs. By and large, the results will prove consistent with expectations. When the average market return is large, high risk-return classes tend to provide higher returns on the average than lower risk-return classes. When the average market return is small or negative, high risk-return classes tend to provide smaller returns on the average than lower risk-return classes. Finally, the shorter the time-period studied, the less the results conform to expectations due to the influence of other factors.

Changes in Risk-Return Classes

The investor who holds a well-diversified portfolio need not be unduly concerned about the possibility that one or more of his stocks may move into a different risk-return class in the future. Some of the securities that were formerly in risk-return class 5 may move to class 6 (or 7, 8, 9 or 10),

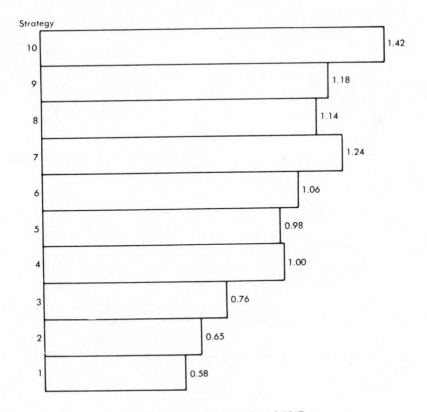

Figure 4b. Beta Values 1931 Through 1967

while some of the others may move to class 4 (or 3, 2, or 1). But the effect on the total portfolio may nonetheless be negligible, as securities moving to higher classes can be offset by those moving to lower classes. Putting it somewhat differently: it is easier to predict an average (i.e., the portfolio's beta) than the value of any single component (i.e., a given security's beta).

But changes in risk-return class membership are not unimportant. They give rise to transactions costs for the strategies described here. They are particularly relevant for those who do not (and perhaps cannot) hold well-diversified portfolios—e.g., corporate officers. And they are important when risk-return class membership is used to estimate a firm's cost of capital.

To provide some evidence on such changes, the risk-return class of every security was determined for every year between 1931 and 1967 in which price and dividend data were available for the preceding 60 months. The risk-return class in each year was compared with first the class in the succeeding year, then the class five years hence. While the first comparison uses 48 months of common data, the second involves no overlap at all. Over 27,000 combinations were used for the first set of comparisons, and over 24,000 for the second.

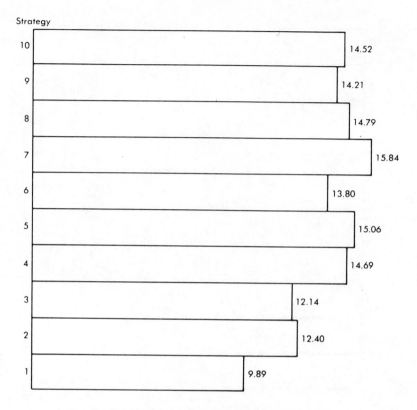

Figure 4c. Equivalent Constant Annual Returns 1931 Through 1967

Tables I and II summarize the results in transition matrices. For example, Table I shows that 74.2 per cent of the securities in risk-return class 10 in year t were still in risk-return class 10 in year t + 1. Table II shows that only 35.2 per cent remained in risk-return class 10 in year t + 5.[5] Table III provides another summary, indicating the frequencies with which securities were in the same risk-return class or within one risk-return class one and five years later. As this Table shows, there is substantial stability over time, even at the level of individual securities. For portfolios, of course, the relationship would be considerably more stable.

Some Practical Problems

23

INTRODUCTION: WHAT TO DO ABOUT PORTFOLIOS IN AN EFFICIENT MARKET

What are the joint implications of an efficient market and rationality and risk aversion of investors? The efficiency of the market suggests that ordinary security analysis is not worthwhile. Rationality and risk aversion imply that portfolio managers must form judgments about the expected returns and risks of alternative portfolios. How are these ideas reconciled, and what do they imply for the role of a portfolio manager?

In the first article in this section (Chapter 24) Black presents a fairly extreme but cogent case for a 'passive' strategy of portfolio management. He does not mean by this that the portfolio manager should become a modern Oblomov[1]. Even if the manager is not required to form judgements about individual stocks he has other important decisions to make. For example he must assess the degree of risk that his client can bear and consider whether there are any risks against which his client needs special protection. He must judge whether his risk exposure should change as his client gets older or as his wealth changes. He must ensure that the portfolio is appropriate for his client's tax position. Black provides a stimulating discussion of these problems from the viewpoint of the manager of a private client's portfolio, an endowment fund and a pension fund.

Black's article raises at least one important question, 'How do you decide what risk to take?' Our next chapter goes some way towards answering this question. O'Brien and Tito point out that it would be much easier to determine the appropriate risk level if one could have some indication of the possible consequences. Their model for stimulating the performance of a pension fund provides just this.

Since the prospective return on any investment depends on its market risk or beta, the wise portfolio manager will want to measure the beta of each stock. In Chapter 26 Blume shows that historic measures of beta provide the basis for fairly good objective estimates of future risk. This should be reassuring to the indolent.

The total risk of the portfolio depends not only on the beta of the individual holdings but also on the degree of diversification. In Chapter 27 Sharpe shows us that most of the benefits of diversification can be obtained with a fairly small number of holdings and he suggests a simple measure of the diversification of any portfolio.

---

[1] Oblomov is the central character of the nineteenth-century Russian novel *Oblomov* by Nikolai Goncharov. Rather like finance professors, Oblomov ate, drank, planned, and discussed without ever accomplishing anything.

For most purposes it is not enough to know that a portfolio earned a higher return than the market. We also need to know whether this was because the stocks were unusually volatile or because the manager was able to pick stocks that were under-valued. In chapter 28 Sharpe shows that we can take account of any differences in volatility by calculating either the reward-to-*volatility* ratio or the extent to which the reward on the portfolio differed from that on a market-based portfolio of comparable volatility. This latter measure is often called alpha and was used by Jensen to measure the ability of mutual fund managers (Chapter 13). Suppose we find that a manager has been able to pick stocks. To do this he must have accepted some residual (or non-market) risk. We might, therefore, wish to consider whether the reward was commen-surate with the *total* portfolio risk. Sharpe shows that we can measure this by calculat-ing the reward-to-*variability* ratio.

Modern performance measurement techniques do not consider just *whether* the portfolio return has been high or low but also *why* it has been high or low. In Chapter 29 Fama suggests ways in which one can extend such diagnosis.

These new measure of performance offer a vast improvement on simple compari-sons between the return of a market index and that of the fund. Nevertheless, several problems remain. For example, Friend and Blume have suggested that, if there is a tendency for differences in return to be less marked than differences in risk, such measures would underestimate the skill with which high risk funds were managed. Others have pointed to the fact that the manager may be able to alter his risk exposure to take advantage of market fluctuations. Finally, there is no indication that relatively good performance by these standards is any omen for the future, so that it is important to estimate the statistical significance of excessively high or low rates of return.

by Fischer Black

The Investment Policy Spectrum:
Individuals, Endowment Funds and Pension Funds

Investment policy, as I use the term, means such things as the choice of a risk level for an investor's portfolio, the division of the portfolio among broad classes of investments such as common stocks and bonds, the policy of taking capital losses whenever possible and letting gains go unrealized, or the reverse policy of taking capital gains and letting losses go unrealized. It means such things as the decision on how widely diversified a portfolio is to be or, conversely, how much it is to be concentrated in particular investments considered especially attractive.

I will assume, in this article, that the stock and bond markets are extremely efficient, so that the expected gains from trading stocks and bonds or from attempting to outguess movements in the market as a whole are exceeded by the total costs of doing the required analysis and executing the resulting transactions. This assumption is consistent with most of the empirical evidence on the performance of professionally managed portfolios. Only a very few portfolios give evidence of consistently superior performance.[1]

If an investor feels that buying and selling individual bonds and stocks based on his opinions of their relative attractiveness is worthwhile, then he may wish to use some of the concepts developed by Treynor and Black.[2] Those concepts are broadly

1. Footnotes appear at end of article.

Fischer Black is Professor of Finance, Sloan School of Management, Massachusetts Institute of Technology. This article was written while he was at the Graduate School of Business, University of Chicago. Dr. Black is grateful to Jacques Dreze, Richard Ennis, Merton Miller, Dennis Tito and Peter Williamson for comments on earlier versions of the article.

consistent with the ideas in this article.

I will assume also that markets are efficient in the sense that the value of a company's stock reflects everything that is known (to at least a few investors) about the company.[3] For example, I will assume that the effects of a company's pension fund policy on the company's current and future earnings are fully discounted in the price of its stock. This means that when the value of the pension fund assets declines, the value of the company's stock will tend to decline too, because the contributions that the company has to make to the pension fund will have increased. This will be particularly true in a company whose pension fund assets have a value equal to a substantial fraction of the value of the company's other assets.

The article is written from the point of view of an individual investor who has a relatively clear idea of the risks he is taking in all his investments, who thinks of the risk of his total portfolio as the standard deviation (or variance) of the portfolio return over a short future interval, and who wants to maximize his expected return at a chosen level of risk. It is written primarily from the point of view of a pension fund or endowment fund manager who is concerned with the welfare of those who ultimately receive the gains or losses in the fund, rather than from the point of view of a fund manager who is concerned with the welfare of corporate managers or endowment fund trustees. In practice, however, the welfare of the managers and trustees is often an important consideration, so some attention is given to their interests.

INDIVIDUALS

For an individual, the main investment policy decision is how much risk to take in his portfolio. Given what we know about the ability of investment managers to select stocks that will do better than other stocks, the individual will normally want to buy and hold a highly diversified portfolio of stocks, mixed with some form of borrowing or lending.[4] He will not be doing any trading on information about stocks. In principle it will be better for the individual to hold mutual fund shares. If there are no funds available that come close to meeting his investment objectives, however, then he may be forced to hold his stocks directly.

The stock portion of his portfolio may be close to the market portfolio. For example, he may be able to find a mutual fund that holds a portfolio like the Standard & Poor's 500 stock portfolio, with each stock weighted by the total dollar amount of that stock outstanding.

There is some evidence that low beta stocks tend to be underpriced relative to high beta stocks, and therefore give higher returns than one would expect given their betas.[5] If the investor believes this evidence, then he may want to put more emphasis on low beta stocks than the Standard & Poor's 500 provides.

Some major classes of assets—such as residential real estate and foreign assets—are not included in the Standard & Poor's 500. The investor may also want to put more emphasis on these assets than the Standard & Poor's 500 provides. One asset that deserves special attention is the investor's "human capital," the present value of his lifetime income from sources other than his financial assets. Since his human capital may form a major part of the investor's portfolio of risky assets, and since he can't sell any substantial portion of his human capital, he may want to eliminate financial assets the values of which correlate highly with the value of his human capital. For example, an investor may want to avoid holding his employer's common stock, unless he gets special inducements from the employer to hold it.

The investor's tax bracket will affect his portfolio in several ways. If he holds bonds and is in a very high tax bracket, he will often choose tax-exempt bonds over taxable bonds. And so long as interest rates are substantially higher than dividend rates on stocks, the high tax bracket investor is more likely to borrow than the low tax bracket investor: The higher his tax bracket, the lower the after-tax interest rate is relative to the expected after-tax return on stocks.

Investors in high tax brackets will try to realize losses and to avoid realizing gains. They may use put and call options, commodities futures, real estate, and other "tax shelters" to convert income into capital gains, or to transfer income from one year to the next, or to eliminate taxable income or

capital gains altogether.

There is even a form of investment company that makes it possible for an investor to avoid both taxes on realized capital gains and taxes on dividend income.[6] The investment company does not pay out its dividend income, so it is not eligible to be taxed as an investment company. But any corporation, including an investment company, has an exclusion for tax purposes equal to 85 per cent of its dividend income. If the expenses of the investment company amount to 15 per cent of its dividend income, and if it avoids realizing capital gains, then it won't have any taxes to pay.

To avoid realizing capital gains, the company can have a policy of not selling stock unless forced to do so by redemptions. If it is a closed end investment company, there are no redemptions, and it doesn't have even this problem. When it does have to sell for any reason, it will sell whatever stocks are below cost. If markets are efficient, this method for choosing stocks to sell will not hurt performance of the portfolio. Most funds find that, when there are no redemptions, there are usually many stocks selling below cost. Only when all the remaining stocks are selling above cost and there is no tax loss carryforward will this strategy give any taxable realized capital gains.

If the shareholders of such an investment company don't sell their shares, neither the company nor its shareholders will pay any taxes on the dividend income or capital gains from its portfolio. The shareholders will be able to reduce or eliminate their tax liabilities.

Thus an individual's stock portfolio should be close to a market portfolio, with possible extra holdings of assets not well represented in the market portfolio, and minus holdings of assets closely related in value to his human capital. It should be managed insofar as possible to avoid giving him taxable distributions. The remaining policy decision that the individual has to make is how much of this portfolio to hold—in other words, how much risk to take. Higher risk is undesirable in itself, but higher risk in a well diversified portfolio generally means higher expected return. The investor must decide how much to increase both his expected return and his risk by increasing the amount of money he keeps in risky assets. He can invest part of his wealth in bonds or savings accounts or the like, and part in stocks; or he can invest all of it in stocks; or he can borrow to invest more than his wealth in stocks.

Actually, he has many such decisions to make. He must decide at each point in his lifetime how much risk to take, and thus how much of his wealth to hold in stocks. He has to decide how to shift his holdings as the value of his portfolio fluctuates. When his portfolio goes up because the market goes up, does he sell off some of his stocks? Or buy more stocks? Or leave his holdings of stocks unchanged? How does he revise his portfolio when he learns of an unexpected inheritance?

It turns out that how he revises his portfolio over his lifetime can make a big difference. For example, suppose an individual switches back and forth between the market and a savings account every year at the start of the year. If he is in the market,

he gets out; and if he is out, he gets in. This is a variant of what he might be doing if he were trying to forecast the market. Half the time, he will have all his money in the market, and half the time, he will have all his money in a savings account.

An alternative strategy would be to keep half his money in the market every year, and the rest in a savings account. (Note that this means selling some of his stocks after every rise in the market, and buying more stocks after every fall.) If we think of the expected return on the market as being con-

"What do you recommend for the short haul?"

stant over time, then this strategy will have the same expected return as the strategy of switching back and forth between the market and a savings account. But it would have much lower risk. In fact, if we measure risk by the variance of the return on the whole portfolio over a two-year period, this strategy would have half the risk of the first strategy.

The reason why the second strategy has lower risk than the first is that it involves a form of diversification to have money in the market in two successive years. The investor may gain in the first year and lose in the second, or he may lose in the first year and gain in the second. It is the same sort of diversification that he gets when he puts money into two different stocks. His losses on one may be offset by gains on the other. This kind of diversification I call "time diversification."* Diversification across time reduces risk just like diversification across stocks.

One way for an investor to get good time diversification is to keep a constant fraction of his wealth invested in stocks. Suppose for example, that he intends to keep half his wealth invested in stocks at all times. If his stocks go up in value by $1000 over some short period of time, he will sell stocks worth $500 and put the proceeds in his savings account. Similarly, if the value of his stocks goes down by $1000, he will take $500 out of his savings account and invest it in stocks. Following the conservative strategy of keeping half in the market and half in a savings account means selling after the market goes up and buying after the market goes down.

On the other hand, an investor may choose an aggressive strategy. Consider, for example, an investor who borrows to keep one and a half times his wealth in the market at all times. Then if his stocks go up in value by $1000, he is going to borrow an additional $500 to invest in stocks. And if his stocks go down by $1000, he will sell stocks worth $500 and use the proceeds to reduce his loan. Following this aggressive strategy means buying after the market goes up and selling after the market goes down. If there is no serial correlation in market returns, then an increase in the market is no more likely to be followed by another increase than a decrease, so neither of these strategies is better than buy-and-hold so far as market timing is concerned. Both strategies give time diversification: The choice between them is simply a matter of how much risk the individual wants to take.

An individual will lose very little by limiting himself to one of the family of strategies that entails keeping a constant fraction of his wealth in stocks. If he chooses a strategy from this family, then the only major policy decision he has to make is what that fraction will be. He can ignore, at least as a first approximation, all the other elements that might influence the amount of risk he wants to take, like his age and his wealth.

ENDOWMENT FUNDS

In talking about endowment funds, I will refer most often to college and university endowment funds, but many of the points I make will be applicable in slightly modified form to other kinds of endowment funds.

For part of an endowment fund, the investment policy may be limited by the terms of the gift that created the endowment. For example, the donor may have given stock with the understanding that it will not be sold for a period of time. Or the terms of the gift may be interpreted as specifying that only the dividend and interest income may be spent, and this may have some influence on investment policy. But in most universities there is also a part of the endowment fund that is unrestricted in both its investment and the rate at which it may be spent. If this is a large enough part of the fund, we can treat the fund as a whole as if its investment policy and the rate at which it may be spent were unrestricted.

It is important to see the endowment fund as just one of the university's sources of income. In most universities, the endowment fund provides a relatively small fraction of the budget. The other sources of income include tuition, alumni contributions, government grants and foundation grants. For the university, and for anyone interested in the university, with the possible exception of those responsible for managing the endowment fund, the relevant risk is the risk of all these sources of income taken together, not just the risk of the endowment fund itself.

All the sources of income include "market risk" that cannot be diversified away. When the economy does well, contributions to universities rise, tuition payments are easier to make, and the government gets more taxes, which makes it more apt to give money to universities. So it is not only the endowment fund that is able to provide more to a university when times are good.

The non-market risk in the endowment fund, the part of the risk that can be diversified away, is in fact pretty well diversified away when it is mixed with the risk in the other sources of income for the university. The endowment fund is in effect only a small part of the university portfolio, thinking of these other sources of income as the remainder of the portfolio. This means that an endowment fund needs to be much less concerned about diversification than an individual. Normally, no great harm will be done if the endowment fund contains just four stocks, for example. However, the rules governing the behavior of endowment fund trustees and the interests of the trustees as well generally lead them to choose relatively well diversified portfolios. If a poorly diversified portfolio happens to do very badly, the trustees are likely to suffer. The conflict between the interests of the trustees and the interests of the ultimate beneficiaries of the fund suggests that the rules governing trustees may be in need of revision.

In setting the level of market risk in the endowment fund, the market risk in the university's other sources of income should be taken into account at the same time. If the endowment fund provides only ten per cent of the university's income, then a ten per cent change in the market risk of the endowment fund means only a one per cent change in the market risk of the university's income as a whole.

In other words, when setting the objectives of an endowment fund, it should really be treated as a small part of a portfolio, not as a total portfolio.

Not only is the endowment fund a small part of the university portfolio, the university portfolio may be a small part of the portfolios of the individuals who have a financial interest in the university. But who are those individuals? If the university were a privately owned corporation, we could say that the individuals with the primary financial interest in the university, who bear most of the risk in the university portfolio, are the individuals who own shares in the university.

But most universities are not privately owned. The typical university is a non-profit institution, like the typical hospital or savings and loan association or mutual insurance company. A non-profit institution has just as much risk as a privately owned institution of the same type, but the risk is borne by different people. For example, much of the risk in a mutual insurance company is borne by the policyholders, while the risk in a stock insurance company is borne primarily by the shareholders. (The managers may bear a substantial amount of risk in both mutual and stock insurance companies.)

The equity interest in a university is spread among all the people associated with the university. The people who benefit if the university gets more income are the faculty, the administration, the staff, the trustees and the students. Future students and faculty members also bear some of the university risk. So do those who would be students or faculty members if the university's income were high enough. Because none of these people can buy or sell their equity interests in the university, they have an interest only during (and to some extent, before) their association with the university.

So there is a large group of people who are actually or potentially affiliated with the university who have an equity interest in it. The income that each such person gets from the university is part of his total income. And the risk that he gets from the risk in the university's income is part of his total risk. He will have other risky assets such as common stock or real estate, and he will have other risky sources of income. The endowment fund risk is a small part of the university's income risk, and the university's income risk will be a small part of the total risk of most individuals associated with the university. The endowment fund risk will be a very small part of the typical individual's total risk.

This means that the degree of diversification in the endowment fund portfolio is particularly unimportant when viewed in the light of its effect on the diversification of the total portfolios of most of those who bear the endowment fund risk. It means that the level of market risk in the endowment fund is not very important either. It is very easy for the typical individual to make changes in his portfolio to offset any changes in risk in the endowment fund. If the endowment fund goes from a beta of 1.0 to a beta of 2.0, that will change the typical individual's risk who has an interest in it very slightly, and he could offset it by decreasing the beta of another part of his portfolio.

This does not mean that the endowment fund can simply aim at maximizing its expected return and ignore the risk it incurs in doing so. It means that so long as the expected return of the fund is related to its beta in the way that the capital asset pricing model suggests, both the risk and the expected return of the fund are unimportant to the individual.[9] So long as the fund gets an expected return commensurate with its market risk, the typical individual doesn't care how much risk it takes, because it is only a small part of his portfolio.

The people for whom the endowment fund is most important are those who are with the university for the longest period of time and who get a large part of their income from the university. For these people, the level of market risk in the fund and the extent to which the fund is diversified may not be a matter of indifference. This includes the faculty, especially the tenured faculty, the administration, and some of the staff. So it is their utility functions and preferences that should be taken into account in setting objectives for the endowment fund, if we say that it makes a difference what objectives are set for the endowment fund. But even if we say this, it's not likely to be clear what they would like to have done.

Some, who have income primarily from the university, might be conservative and prefer a conservative investment policy that minimizes fluctuations in their income or the risks of being fired. Others wanting to take a lot of risk without any convenient way to do so in their personal portfolios at reasonable cost, might prefer an aggressive investment policy in their endowment fund.

One possible way to resolve this conflict of interest would be for those affiliated with the university on a long-term basis to vote on the investment policy of the endowment fund. This would represent such a break with tradition that it is probably not possible. And if the endowment fund really makes up only a small part of each of their portfolios, then the investment policy of the endowment fund is probably not important enough to justify the expense of setting up a voting procedure and informing those who are to vote.

Moreover, in practice there is usually a relatively small group of individuals who control a university and who could not get positions of equivalent power with other organizations. These individuals are usually able to control the policies of the endowment fund, and tend to have more interest in its success than other individuals. If the university suffers a decline in income, many of the faculty and most of the students can switch jobs or schools. Those who cannot, because of their positions of power within the university, are the ones who suffer most.

It is sometimes claimed that because the endowment fund is going to be around for a long time, it can afford to take a lot of risk. I have been unable to find any sense in which this seems correct. The risk in the endowment fund must be borne ultimately by individuals. Most of the risk will be borne by individuals who are currently affiliated with the university. To some extent, the risk can be transferred from those currently associated with the university to their successors. It may even be transferred in part to individuals who have not yet been born. But it must be attributed to individuals, and the extent to which it can be passed on to future generations is limited. If a decline in the value of the endowment fund is not met by a decline in the rate of spending from the endowment fund in a short time, the expected future value of the endowment fund will be greatly reduced.

Let us look for a moment at the endowment funds of all the universities in the country as a group. At one time it was claimed that the performance of university endowment funds was inferior to the performance of other funds, and that our educational system faced a crisis unless endowment fund performance was improved. We now know that there is no evidence that the risk-adjusted performance of endowment funds has been worse than that of other funds, so the only meaning that this statement might have is that endowment funds have been taking too little risk. Indeed, in recent years, endowment funds have been increasing their risk levels, partly by switching from bonds to stocks. But it is not clear that this makes much sense, if we take a broad enough point of view.

If society wants to increase the amount it spends on education, there are much more direct ways of doing it. The most obvious is an increase in tuition levels. An increase in the risk taken by endowment funds will tend to increase the fraction of its income that society spends on education only when economic conditions are exceptionally good. When economic conditions are exceptionally bad, a high level of risk in endowment funds will tend to mean a reduction in the fraction of income spent on education.

PENSION FUNDS

For a non-insured corporate pension fund, the individuals with the most interest in the gains and losses of the fund are the corporation's shareholders.[10] The pension benefits are fixed by contract. So long as the pension plan is not changed, and so long as the corporation does not go out of business, the pension benefits are independent of the gains and losses in the fund.

The corporation promises certain pension benefits to its employees, and then makes contributions to a fund out of which the benefits are to be paid. But the corporation has a responsibility for paying the benefits regardless of the level of funding of the pension fund. In other words, the corporation could conceivably not make any contributions to the pension fund, and it would still have to pay the benefits when they come due, if it is able.[11]

In that situation, any gains or losses in the pension fund portfolio accrue primarily to the corporation, and thus to its shareholders. Gains in the pension fund benefit the pension beneficiaries to some extent, because a larger pension fund seems to make it easier for employees to extract higher pension benefits from their employer, and because a larger pension fund makes it less likely that the corporation will be unable to pay the promised benefits.

If the pension fund does well, then future contributions by the corporation to the pension fund will be reduced. If the pension fund does poorly, then future corporate contributions will be increased. Assuming that stock prices accurately reflect future earnings prospects, an increase in the value of the pension fund will mean an increase in the value of the company's stock, and a decrease in the value of the pension fund will mean a decrease in the value of the company's stock. This is how the gains and losses in a corporation's pension fund are transmitted to its shareholders.

Thus we have a situation very much like that of the endowment fund: The pension fund is a corporate asset, and is normally a relatively small part of the total value of the corporation. The corporate shares are themselves held by individuals who hold other assets in their portfolios as well. So the pension fund represents a small part of the portfolio of assets held by the typical corporate shareholder.

We can conclude again that, from the point of view of those with the major financial interest in the pension fund, diversification is not very important. An individual wants his total portfolio to be well diversified, but he does not care about the diversification of a particular small part of the portfolio. The major exceptions to this statement are the pension fund trustees, who are legally responsible for the management of the fund, and who may derive considerable economic power from managing the fund. They will generally have an interest in diversifying the portfolio, and will be in a position to make sure it is diversified. The potential liability of a trustee when a poorly diversified fund does badly will often be large compared with the value of his entire portfolio of risky assets.

Similarly, it is not very important to anyone but the trustees how much market risk the pension fund portfolio has. The corporate shareholders will simply take whatever risk they find into account in adjusting the risk of their total portfolios. If the pension fund goes from a beta of 1.0 to a beta of 2.0, the shareholders can offset this by reducing the betas of other assets they hold, or by changing the amount of his borrowing or lending they do.

When there is a significant risk that the corporation will go out of business and leave a pension fund portfolio that is not large enough to pay the promised benefits, however, the level of risk in the pension fund can make a difference. It may make a difference to the corporate shareholders, to the pension beneficiaries, and to the government, where the government is insuring payments to the beneficiaries. When there is a significant risk that the corporation will go out of business, an increase in the risk of the pension fund—either because of an increase in beta or because of a reduced level of

diversification—will cause an increase in the probability that neither the pension fund assets nor the corporate assets will be sufficient to pay the promised benefits. Such an increase in risk will reduce the value of the claim that the pension beneficiaries have on the corporation, and will increase the value of the claim they have on the insuring agency of the government.

The extreme case of a pension fund portfolio that increases the risk that the pension beneficiaries will not be paid by the corporation is where the pension fund holds only shares in the corporation of which it is a part. Then the circumstances under which the corporation would go bankrupt and lose its value in satisfying pension beneficiaries are exactly the same as the circumstances under which the pension fund would go to zero value. Under these circumstances, the beneficiaries would collect only from the government. So that particular policy can be quite risky for the government.

Tax considerations are important in determining the yield objective for the pension fund and in deciding when to realize gains and losses. If the pension fund can trade off yield for unrealized capital appreciation, or if it can trade off realized capital gains for unrealized gains, then the corporation will be able to make larger deductible contributions to the fund, and will thus be able to postpone some of its tax liabilities. A corporation that defers tax payments saves an amount equal to the interest on those tax payments.

If a corporation takes the opposite approach, and tries to maximize the yield and realized gains in its pension fund, then it will reduce its current contributions to the pension fund. This will increase current reported earnings, but at the expense of increasing taxes and reducing the rate of growth of earnings. The rate of growth of earnings will be reduced for two reasons: because the reduction in current pension fund contributions means higher contributions will have to be made later on, and because the present value of the company's tax liability is increased. If the market takes all this into account in pricing the company's stock, the policy of maximizing yield and realized gains at the expense of unrealized gains will result in a lower stock price than the opposite policy. The increase in the company's current reported earnings will be more than offset by a fall in its price-earnings ratio.

Thus the pension fund should be managed as if its income and capital gains were taxable. The effective taxes that the corporation has to pay on the pension fund income and capital gains are quite different than the taxes an individual would have to pay, however. Municipal bonds do not have tax advantages for the pension fund. Realized capital gains are effectively taxed at the full corporate income tax rate, to the extent that they are brought into pension fund income. But they are brought into income only over a period of years, which reduces the effective tax rate. Even unrealized gains must eventually be brought into income, so it is not possibile for the pension fund to delay realizing gains indefinitely, as an individual can.

If the stock market takes into account such things as the value of a company's pension fund and the magnitude of its potential tax liabilities in valuing its stock, if there is very little chance that the company will go out of business, and if a fully funded pension fund will not induce the employees to demand much higher pensions, then the company should try to *maximize* its tax deductible contributions to the pension fund. It should try to keep the fund "overfunded," rather than underfunded, so long as the IRS allows contributions to the pension fund to be deducted from income for tax purposes. It should do this in spite of the fact that higher contributions to the pension fund may mean lower current reported earnings per share. It should do this even if it has to borrow money or sell stock to make its pension fund contributions.

It is not a question of whether investments in the pension fund are more or less profitable than other investments the company makes. The investments in the pension fund are profitable in themselves, and should be made regardless of what other investments the company has to make. If the company needs additional funds to make other profitable investments, the efficient U. S. capital markets will supply them readily.

Having a low realized return on the pension fund may even help the company influence the actuarial rate of return used in calculating the required payments to the pension fund (and the payments that the IRS will allow the company to deduct). The actuaries have some latitude in choosing an assumed rate of return. The usual practice is for the company to encourage the actuaries to choose a high return, so the company can minimize its contributions and increase its current reported earnings per share. But if the company is trying to maximize its deductible contributions, it will want to encourage the actuaries to choose a low return.

If we look at the company's cash flows, rather than at its earnings, and if we combine pension fund operations with the company's other operations, it's especially easy to see the advantages of maximizing the deductible contributions to the pension fund. Assuming that the probability of bankruptcy is zero, and that the pension plan will

not be changed, the payment from the corporation to the pension fund is really just a transfer within the corporation. It doesn't count as a cash inflow or outflow. So if the corporation is able to increase its deductible contributions to the pension fund, the only effect on the company's cash flows is the reduction in its tax payments. There is no evidence that a policy that increases a company's cash flows, both present and future, while reducing its reported earnings, will have a negative effect on its stock price. More likely, this policy will increase the price of the stock. However, these effects may well be dominated by the effects of the level of funding on future changes in the terms of the plan. A more fully funded plan is more likely to be liberalized, which will help the beneficiaries at the expense of the corporation and its shareholders. A less fully funded plan is more likely to be restricted, partly because the corporation will have more to gain by restricting it. So, in the end, a corporation may do well to resist higher contributions to the pension fund, not because of the impact of the level of contributions on reported earnings, but rather because of the impact of the level of contributions on the terms of the plan. ∎

Footnotes

1. For evidence of this, see Michael C. Jensen, "The Performance of Mutual Funds in the Period 1945-1964," *Journal of Finance* (May 1968), pp. 389-419.
2. See Jack L. Treynor and Fischer Black, "How to Use Security Analysis to Improve Portfolio Selection," *Journal of Business* (January 1973), pp. 66-86.
3. See Eugene F. Fama, "Efficient Capital Markets: A Review of Theory and Empirical Evidence," *Journal of Finance* (May 1970), pp. 383-417.
4. See J. Peter Williamson, "Measuring and Forecasting of Mutual Fund Performance: Choosing an Investment Strategy," *Financial Analysts Journal* (November/December 1972), pp. 78ff.
5. See Fischer Black, Michael C. Jensen, and Myron Scholes, "The Capital Asset Pricing Model: Some Empirical Tests," *Studies in the Theory of Capital Markets*, Michael C. Jensen, ed. (New York: Praeger, 1972), pp. 79-121.
6. Since this was written, I have discovered that such an investment company exists. It is called American Birthright Trust, 210 Royal Palm Way, Palm Beach, Florida. Standard Shares, a closed-end investment company, also uses these methods.
7. This does not mean that a taxable investor should avoid high yield stocks. See Fischer Black and Myron Scholes, "The Effects of Dividend Yield and Dividend Policy on Common Stock Prices and Returns," *Journal of Financial Economics* (May 1974), pp. 1-22.
8. This concept was originated by James Tobin, in

"The Theory of Portfolio Selection," *The Theory of Interest Rates,* F. H. Hahn and F. P. R. Brechling, eds. (London: Macmillan, 1965), pp. 3-51.

9. For a description of the capital asset pricing model, see Michael C. Jensen, "Capital Markets: Theory and Evidence," *Bell Journal of Economics and Management Science* (Autumn 1972), pp. 357-398.

10. For a discussion of pension fund strategy under somewhat different assumptions, see Irwin Tepper, "Optimal Financial Strategies for Trusteed Pension Plans," *Journal of Financial and Quantitative Analysis* (June 1974), pp. 357-376.

11. Actually, corporations also have the ability to change the terms of a pension plan, and thereby reduce their obligations. For an enlightening discussion of the risks borne by pension beneficiaries and corporate shareholders, see Walter Bagehot, "Risk and Reward in Corporate Pension Funds," *Financial Analysts Journal* (January/February 1972), pp. 80-84.

25

THE IMPLICATIONS OF PENSION FUND INVESTMENT POLICY

John O'Brien and Dennis Tito

We will first talk about the general implications of pension fund investment policy. Then, to help bring these implications into quantitative terms and describe them in a particular corporate situation, we will talk specifically about the model developed at O'Brien Associates. "Implications" is not a definitive term in that people who associate with management immediately think we are talking about cost implications to the corporation, and those associated with labor think we are talking about implications of investment policy in the likelihood that benefits will be realized. We are actually talking about implications measured in such a way that insight can be gained into both the likelihood of benefits being paid and the costs to the corporation of seeing that they are.

Most of our discussion will revolve around the funding agent. Typically, it is a corporation or public entity. The first problem usually addressed is the future level of benefits and when, in time, they occur. Having ascertained these answers, future costs are discounted to the present and expressed as a present value of remaining costs or future costs--or the present value of the pension fund liability.

The discounting process is one area in which the actuary becomes involved. If one thought future benefits should be discounted at the equivalent of a riskless rate, one would then have several choices. The riskless rate could be thought of in terms of providing a nominal dollar value at some future point in time. That rate would include inflationary expectations. One could also think in terms of a rate designed to preserve the current buying power of future dollars to be paid. In this case, inflationary expectations would be removed from the rate used. Another possible approach to getting present value would be to price a riskless bond portfolio which would have coupons and maturities that roll out in such a way as to pay the benefits as they are anticipated to occur in the future.

Of interest is how obligations are going to change over time. For example, what is the expected cost for the coming year? Typically, a corporation sees an actuarily computed number as its cost. This number does not necessarily immediately fund all future obligations. Normally, it will bring in some method of smoothing the current difference between present value of future benefits and market value of present assets over some future period of time. Most generally, it will not use a discounting process or attempt to estimate a riskless rate of interest. This implies that the assumed rate of return being used has a risk premium built in. The argument in favor of a built-in risk premium, from a corporate view, is as follows: If we can earn a higher rather than lower rate of return on our assets, the present value of our future benefit payments will be reduced. This will cause less drain on corporate resources, thereby providing added earnings per share, which in turn improves share value and stockholder wealth.

The argument against this line of reasoning, and it is a powerful one, was first introduced to us by Fischer Black. It says that if earnings of the corporation are to be increased in an expected value sense, there will also be an increase in the risk of the assets producing those earnings. The increase in earnings expectations for the future will accrue an additional discount over the former earnings. The amount of that discount will be precisely that amount required to return the share value, and therefore the shareholder wealth, to its present position. Thus, in effect, it is immaterial what risk level may be maintained in the pension fund. Indeed, the argument can be generalized as being indifferent to the risk level at which the corporation operates.

An extension of the argument is that if tax considerations are included, then a corporation would like to incur all the tax savings it could as soon as possible. This would lead to a corporation which, rather than being indifferent to risk level in its pension fund, would prefer zero risk in the pension fund. That, in turn, could presumably lead to a situation justifying the most rapid funding possible and therefore accruing the tax benefits of that funding as soon as possible. In any case, these implications are based on economic theory not yet verified by the ability of the analyst to sense changes in risk level and discount rates.

It is certainly of interest to ask who is taking the risk and who is gaining the reward. If corporate management does increase risk in its pension system, and, if, over a period of time, that risk is rewarded with additional return, then that added value of the pension system accrues to the owners of the corporation. The costs of the pension system to the corporation will be reduced. There is no change in benefit to the beneficiary. However, if a risk should turn out to be actually not receiving a rate of return even equal to riskless rates at the time the investment was made, bankruptcy could ensue. The loss incurred by discontinuation of the plan would be shared by both the stockholders of the firm and the beneficiaries of the plan. Hence, the plan beneficiary shares risk but not reward.

An excellent article by Jack Treynor in the <u>Financial Analysts Journal</u>[1] pointed out three ways around this inequity. One is simply to require pension funds to invest in riskless assets. The second is to make the beneficiaries of a plan the owners and allow them to establish their own risk levels. Corporate obligation would end at the point of making contributions. The third is to think of the corporation in terms of an augmented balance sheet. Added to the normal asset side of the corporate balance sheet would be the assets of the pension system. Added to the liability side would be the liabilities of the pension system. This, in most instances, will change the apparent stockholder or corporate equity. That equity is a buffer that could be used to ensure that the slack would be taken up if the corporation took a risk in a pension plan and was not rewarded.

In order for the third solution to be effective the pension benefits must be guaranteed. However, in practically every instance corporate plans do not at this time provide guaranteed benefits to their beneficiaries. A way around this is to make the beneficiary a first creditor of the corporation. If the beneficiary were a first creditor of the corporation, examination of the financial strength and policies of the firm would include not only the standard operating aspects of the company but also the pension system.

We now want to bring investment policy into the analysis. We want investment counselors to describe the different policies that they have available to the corporation in terms of future investment outcome. The corporation, knowing its liability structure, can then presumably develop the impact of any one of those policies on the likelihood that benefits could be paid given the general financial strength of the corporation. Of particular importance to investment management and trustees are the distribution of potential annual costs, and the distribution of the unfunded liability at any point in time. The first two costs are fairly obvious. Why the third is of interest is probably best seen in view of the augmented balance sheet. If, at any point in time, the liability could grow significantly because of investment policy, then that policy could potentially bankrupt the firm.

After seeing how we would hope to describe investment policy and what kinds of implications we are looking for, the problem is to then find where to go from descriptions of probabilities. We have done probably what any systems analysis or operations research kind of firm might do--construct a systems model of the pension system. But our model is designed to account for the fact that many of the parameters are stochastic. We use Monte Carlo simulation techniques to develop the stochastic outputs from the stochastic inputs. In particular, those outputs are in terms of costs--costs as a function of policy. More clearly, the outputs are in terms of the kinds of financial data that corporate management and other types of management are familiar with, and not in terms of beta and other intermediate parameters.

In order to present the essence of the model and the manner in which results are displayed, we will begin by describing a pension system simulation approach that provides future projections of cash flows and other financial parameters. Later, we will present examples of the applications of the model to the retirement system of a major corporation.

Annual pension costs are subject to significant variations, largely as a result of period-to-period fluctuations in pension assets. For this reason we chose a Monte Carlo simulation approach, in lieu of a deterministic approach that would assume a fixed rate of return on pension investments. The Monte Carlo method provides information on cost dispersions above or below expected levels in addition to expected costs.

Exhibit 1 presents an illustration of how actuarily computed liabilities and applied asset values are combined to produce simulated pension system parameters. The Work Force Projection Model takes as input initial values of

work force parameters. It uses assumed growth rates of work force and
salary levels as well as an assumed distribution of new hires. Also
included in this model are actuarial assumptions such as mortality tables,
separation rates, retirement rates, disability rates, and salary scales
information. The output from the Work Force Projection Model serves as
input to the Actuarial Liability Computation Model. The Actuarial Liability
Computation Model replicates what the actuary would produce in any given
year given the demographic characteristics of the employee population. The
model uses the same actuarial assumptions, together with an actuarial interest
rate used to discount the benefits, in order to obtain the present value of
liabilities. The outputs of this model include normal costs and present
value of liabilities for both the active and retired work force.

EXHIBIT 1

PENSION SIMULATION MODEL

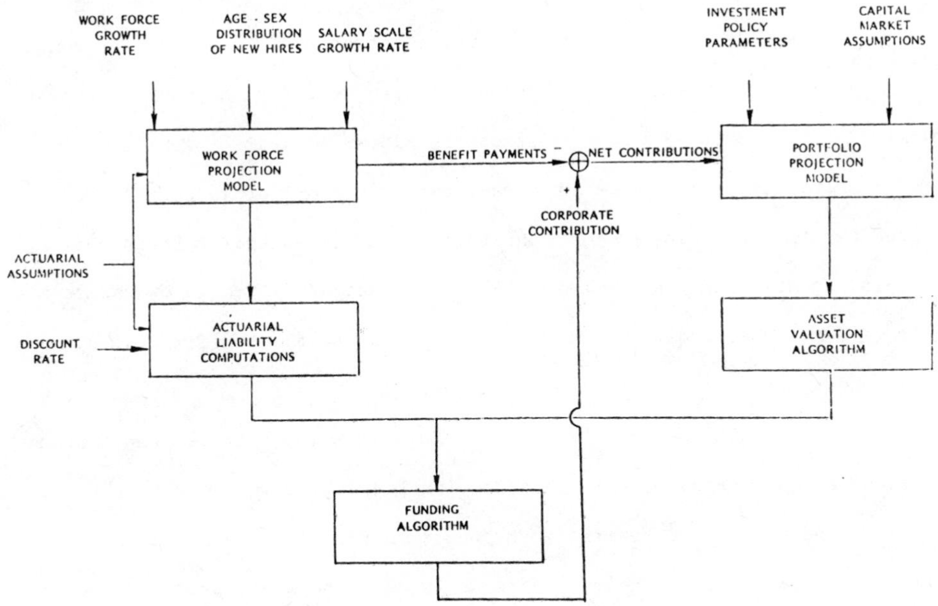

The Portfolio Projection Model takes as input, assumptions pertaining to the probability distribution of relevant market parameters. This includes both equity, fixed income, and money market characteristics. The investment policy parameters are specified by alternative probability distributions of investment returns, and in certain instances, would be conditional upon market returns.

In this simulation, the Capital Asset Pricing Model was used to describe the relationship between portfolio returns and market returns. This allowed specification of investment policy alternatives in terms of the beta coefficient and the diversification of the portfolio. The previously mentioned market assumptions together with the investment policy parameters were used to generate simulated rates of return which were then applied to initial portfolio market values and book values. These values were progressed in time and adjusted each year for the net additions and/or withdrawals to the pension fund.

The Asset Valuation Algorithm used in the simulation utilized the market and/or book value as input to compute applied assets. (The scheme for computing applied assets varies from corporation to corporation. Some corporations rely exclusively on book value while others add an adjustment for unrealized capital gains due to increases in market value over and above book.) The applied assets were combined with the total liabilities and/or the normal costs in a particular year to determine the amount of funding that was required in that year. The funding requirement was offset by the benefit payments in that year to provide a net contribution to the fund.

Exhibit 2 details the Work Force Projection Model. It is seen that new hires, separations and retirements affecting the active work force in Period 0 flow into the active and retired work forces in Period 1. Also shown is the effect of mortalities on the retired work force. The model progresses the populations from Period 0 to Period 1 by aging the active employees one year and by increasing their service by one year. The retired group is updated by aging the participants one year and adding to that the retirees from Period 0. This process is repeated until desired planning horizon is reached. The payroll and benefits in each year are computed by aggregating the various age, service, and sex categories in both the active and retired employee populations.

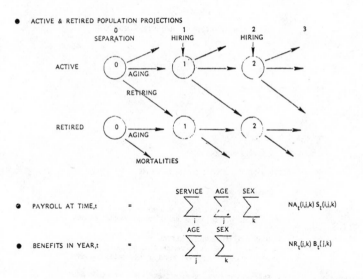

EXHIBIT 2
WORK FORCE PROJECTION MODEL

- ACTIVE & RETIRED POPULATION PROJECTIONS

PAYROLL AT TIME,t $= \displaystyle\sum_{i}^{SERVICE} \sum_{j}^{AGE} \sum_{k}^{SEX} NA_t(i,j,k)\, S_t(i,j,k)$

BENEFITS IN YEAR,t $= \displaystyle\sum_{j}^{AGE} \sum_{k}^{SEX} NR_t(j,k)\, B_t(j,k)$

WHERE: $NA_t(i,j,k)$ = Number of active employees during period t for each age, service, sex category
$NR_t(j,k)$ = Number of retired employees during period t for each age, sex category
$S_t(i,j,k)$ = Average salary during period t for each age, service, sex category
$B_t(j,k)$ = Average benefit payments during period t for each age, sex category

As mentioned earlier, the investment portfolio return could be described by the Capital Asset Pricing Model which relates returns on the portfolio to market returns. This relationship is represented by the equation shown in Exhibit 3. The tildas represent stochastic variables which are sampled randomly from an assumed probability distribution. To obtain a representative sample of investment outcomes, we have simulated hundreds of sequences of market returns to represent simulations of different experiences that the pension system could be exposed to as a result of different market environments.

EXHIBIT 3

INVESTMENT PORTFOLIO PROJECTION MODEL

$$\widetilde{RP} = RF + \beta \cdot (\widetilde{RM} - RF) + \widetilde{\epsilon}$$

WHERE:

$\widetilde{RP}$ = SIMULATED RETURN PORTFOLIO

RF = RISK-FREE RETURN

β = PORTFOLIO RELATIVE EQUITY EXPOSURE

$\widetilde{RM}$ = SIMULATED MARKET RETURN

$E(\widetilde{RM}) = r$, MEAN EQUITY MARKET RETURN
$E(\widetilde{RM} - r)^2 = \sigma_{RM}^2$, VARIANCE OF EQUITY MARKET RETURN

$\widetilde{\epsilon}$ = SIMULATED INDEPENDENT RETURN
$E(\widetilde{\epsilon}) = \propto$, MEAN INDEPENDENT RETURN
$E(\widetilde{\epsilon} - \propto)^2 = \sigma_u^2$, VARIANCE OF INDEPENDENT RETURN

DIVERSIFICATION (ρ^2) = FRACTION OF TOTAL VARIANCE EXPLAINED BY THE MARKET

$$= 1 - \frac{\sigma_u^2}{\sigma_{R.P.}^2}$$

$$= 1 - \frac{\sigma_u^2}{\beta^2 \sigma_{RM}^2 + \sigma_u^2}$$

Exhibit 4 lists the assumptions used in applying this model to the retirement system of a large corporation. In the Work Force Projection Model, we assumed a growth rate of 1 percent per annum, a salary scale growth rate of 3-1/2 percent, and a male/female hiring ratio of 1.3. The salary growth rate includes increases due to inflation as well as increased productivity. Progression that would occur as an individual experienced increases in years of service is handled in the actuarial table of salary scales. In the actuarial liability computation, we assumed a discount rate of 3-1/2 percent. The capital market assumptions were 9-1/2 percent rate of return for the Standard & Poor's "500," with a standard deviation of 16 percent. We also assumed a riskless rate of return of 4-1/2 percent. For the investment policy parameters, we assumed a portfolio that had R^2 of 95 percent, turnover of 20 percent per annum, dividend yield of 3 percent, beta range of 0-1.2, and alpha of 0 percent.

EXHIBIT 4

ASSUMPTIONS USED IN EXAMPLE SIMULATION

- WORK FORCE PROJECTION MODEL
  WORK FORCE GROWTH = 1% PER ANNUM
  SALARY SCALE GROWTH = 3½% PER ANNUM
  MALE/FEMALE HIRING RATIO = 1:3

- ACTUARIAL LIABILITY COMPUTATION
  DISCOUNT RATE = 3½% PER ANNUM

- INVESTMENT PORTFOLIO PROJECTION MODEL
  CAPITAL MARKET ASSUMPTIONS
    MEAN EQUITY MARKET RETURN = 9½% PER ANNUM
    STANDARD DEVIATION OF EQUITY MARKET RETURN = 16% PER ANNUM
    RISKLESS RATE OF RETURN 4½% PER ANNUM

  INVESTMENT POLICY PARAMETERS
    PORTFOLIO DIVERSIFICATION = 95%
    TURNOVER = 20% PER ANNUM
    DIVIDEND YIELD = 3.0% PER ANNUM
    RELATIVE EQUITY EXPOSURE (β) RANGE = 0.0 - 1.2
    MEAN INDEPENDENT RETURN (α) = 0.0% PER ANNUM

Exhibit 5 shows the history of wages and benefits developed from the Work Force Projection Model using the assumptions shown in Exhibit 4. One can see that benefits nearly doubled. Wages went up approximately 250 percent as a result of the rather large growth rate in the salary scale assumed, together with the increase of 1 percent per annum in the work force population. It should be noted that we could expect a completely different relationship between these two variables for other retirment plans.

EXHIBIT 5
COMPARISON OF ANNUAL WAGE AND BENEFIT PAYMENTS

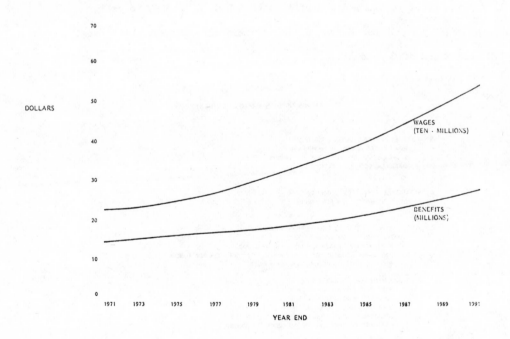

Exhibit 6 illustrates the results of the actuarial computation and shows
the present value of future liabilities for both retired and active employees.
Active employees represent a large portion of the liabilities incurred by the
plan and are largely responsible for increases in future years. This is
attributable to the lagging effect of the benefits. On the average, benefits
are obtained 35 years after a person enters the work force. The effect of
salary growth rate is realized only when the person retires, because the
benefits are computed on the basis of salary at retirement.

EXHIBIT 6
GROWTH OF LIABILITIES

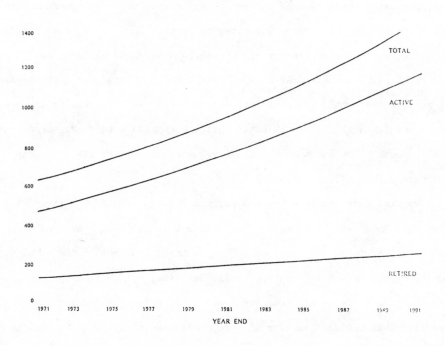

Exhibit 7 is an example of a simulation obtained by combining the pension benefit and liability data obtained from the Work Force Projection Model and Liability Computation Model with the asset valuations obtained from the Monte Carlo simulation approach. We purposely selected this simulation because it exemplifies a market time series that shows a rather high growth rate. The time series of market returns was generated using a random sampling technique. In this case, the population of market returns was assumed to be normal with a mean of 9-1/2 percent and a standard deviation of 16 percent. The simulated returns for the Standard & Poor's "500" are shown in the first row. The returns on the investment portfolio, assuming a beta of 0.7, are shown in the second row. The market and book values shown were developed using these returns and an initial market value of approximately $500 million. The book value was obtained by updating the prior book value and adding it to the dividend yield of the portfolio and any realization of capital gains occurring as a result of portfolio turnover. Inflationary assumptions were implicit in the market assumption and the results are presented in nominal dollars. It may be noted that the applied assets are approximately equal to book value and that the asset valuation algorithm has not taken advantage of unrealized capital gains.

We also show the benefits and payroll figures produced by the Work Force Projection Model. As you can see, the total liabilities of the fund and the unfunded liabilities are obtained by taking the difference of the total liabilities and the applied assets. For this particular example, the funding approach was to take the present value of remaining costs as a ratio to present value of future payroll. This produced an accrual rate percentage which was then applied to payroll in order to determine the cost. An accrual rate of 10 percent would therefore give a pension cost of 10 percent of payroll.

The total cost, represented by the bottom line, drops off as we progress into the future. As you can see, total cost varies from year to year. We have a zero cost for years 15 and 16 when the pension system is overfunded. This is largely a result of the high rate of return that began with the Standard & Poor's "500" that ultimately had a beneficial effect on the pension system.

Exhibit 8 is an example of a simulation producing low returns. It is interesting to note this particular time series projection of the Standard & Poor's "500" assumes the same market parameters as the preceding example. Over a 15 year period the level of the Standard & Poor's "500" is approximately

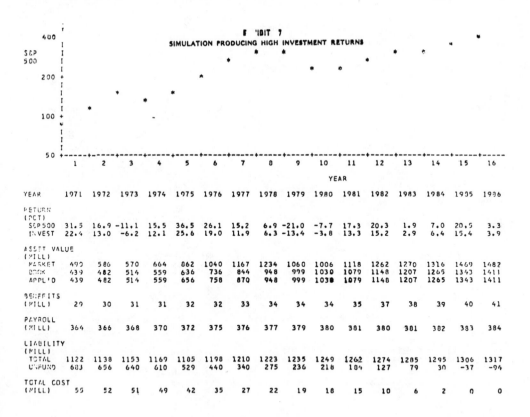

YEAR	1971	1972	1973	1974	1975	1976	1977	1978	1979	1980	1981	1982	1983	1984	1985	1986
RETURN (PCT)																
S&P500	31.5	16.9	-11.1	15.5	36.5	26.1	15.2	6.9	-21.0	-7.7	17.3	20.3	1.9	7.0	20.5	3.3
INVEST	22.4	13.0	-6.2	12.1	25.6	19.0	11.9	6.3	-13.4	-3.8	13.3	15.2	2.9	6.4	15.4	3.9
ASSET VALUE (MILL)																
MARKET	490	586	570	664	862	1040	1167	1234	1060	1006	1118	1262	1270	1316	1469	1482
BOOK	439	482	514	559	636	736	844	948	999	1030	1079	1148	1207	1265	1343	1411
APPL'D	439	482	514	559	656	758	870	948	999	1030	1079	1148	1207	1265	1343	1411
BENEFITS (MILL)	29	30	31	31	32	32	33	34	34	34	35	37	38	39	40	41
PAYROLL (MILL)	364	366	368	370	372	375	376	377	379	380	381	380	381	382	383	384
LIABILITY (MILL)																
TOTAL	1122	1138	1153	1169	1185	1198	1210	1223	1235	1249	1262	1274	1285	1295	1306	1317
UNFUND	683	656	640	610	529	440	340	275	236	218	184	127	79	30	-37	-94
TOTAL COST (MILL)	55	52	51	49	42	35	27	22	19	18	15	10	6	2	0	0

the same as it was at the beginning. The total cost shown on the bottom
line did not drop off as in the first simulation. This is due to the lower
returns on the portfolio that resulted from the adverse performance of the
Standard & Poor's "500."

After running several hundred simulations we attempted to summarize the
data in the form of a frequency distribution. From this distribution, we
obtained the expected value together with a measure of dispersion as represented
here by the 5th and 95th percentile. This allowed us to use the 95th percentile
cost as a measure of risk and the mean or expected value as a measure of reward.

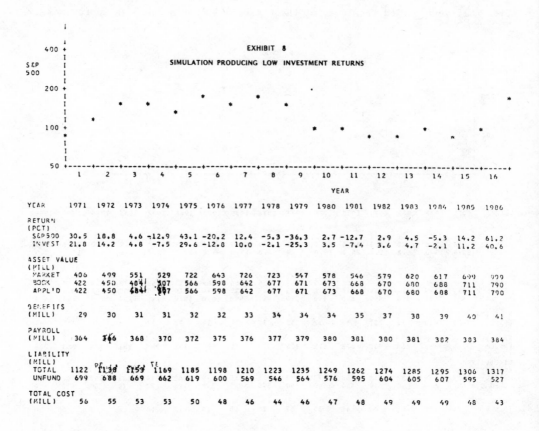

EXHIBIT 8

SIMULATION PRODUCING LOW INVESTMENT RETURNS

YEAR	1971	1972	1973	1974	1975	1976	1977	1978	1979	1980	1981	1982	1983	1984	1985	1986
RETURN (PCT)																
S&P500	30.5	18.8	4.6	-12.9	43.1	-20.2	12.4	-5.3	-36.3	2.7	-12.7	2.9	4.5	-5.3	14.2	61.2
INVEST	21.8	14.2	4.8	-7.5	29.6	-12.0	10.0	-2.1	-25.3	3.5	-7.4	3.6	4.7	-2.1	11.2	40.6
ASSET VALUE (MILL)																
MARKET	406	499	551	529	722	643	726	723	547	578	546	579	620	617	699	909
BOOK	422	450	404	507	566	598	642	677	671	673	668	670	680	688	711	790
APPL'D	422	450	484	547	566	598	642	677	671	673	668	670	680	688	711	790
BENEFITS (MILL)	29	30	31	31	32	32	33	34	34	34	35	37	38	39	40	41
PAYROLL (MILL)	364	366	368	370	372	375	376	377	379	380	381	380	381	382	303	384
LIABILITY (MILL)																
TOTAL	1122	1138	1153	1169	1185	1198	1210	1223	1235	1249	1262	1274	1285	1295	1306	1317
UNFUND	699	688	669	662	619	600	569	546	564	576	595	604	605	607	595	527
TOTAL COST (MILL)	56	55	53	53	50	48	46	44	46	47	48	49	49	49	48	43

Exhibit 9 plots market and book value as a function of relative equity exposure, or beta. In this example, we chose as our investment alternative an investment policy that was determined by market-related risk level of the portfolio. Expected levels of both market and book values increase with the higher betas. This is attributable to the assumption of a positive risk premium (excess of expected market returns over the risk free rate). A mean market return of 9-1/2 percent and a risk-free return of 4-1/2 percent produce higher expected market values in 20 years as represented by this particular example. However, the 5th percentile, or worst case, does not drop off substantially with increasing risk. It illustrates that if one focuses on a horizon 20 years into the future little additional risk is incurred by increasing the market risk of the portfolio.

EXHIBIT 9

PROJECTED VALUE OF ASSETS - TWENTIETH YEAR
(MARKET ASSUMPTION LF - H)

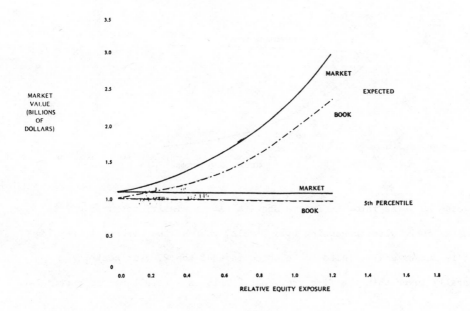

Exhibit 10 illustrates pension costs as a percentage of payroll as a function of relative equity exposure (beta). Results are shown for both the 5th and 20th years. The pension cost percentage for the fifth year ranges from 6-1/2 percent to 8 per cent of payroll. As a result of increasing the relative equity exposure it is seen that the expected cost decreases five years into the future. Notice also that there is a risk of increasing cost due to the added market risk characteristic of higher equity exposures.

EXHIBIT 10

IMPACT OF INVESTMENT POLICY ON ANNUAL PENSION PLAN COST
(MARKET ASSUMPTION LF · H)

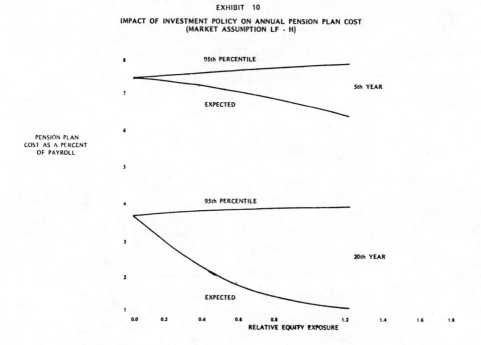

The case 20 years into the future shows a rather significant drop off in expected costs with increasing risk levels, whereas the risk of increasing cost is rather small. Also to be noted is that the 20 year cost is generally lower than the five year cost. This is a result of the particular funding method used in the plan. At present, the plan has prior service costs that still have to be amortized. These are costs that are incurred at the inception of the plan or as the result of changes in the benefits which apply to past service of employees that have to be amortized over the future periods. Once these prior-service costs are amortized, and no further plan changes take place, accrual rates of pension costs would be expected to level off.

In summary, the modeling procedures presented here integrate three basic disciplines. The first is the liability valuation approach presently being used by actuaries. The second is in the area of corporate planning and forecasting. Here we attempted to project the demographic characteristics of the employee work force and retired work force into the future. The third discipline is in the area of investment counseling. We attempted to quantify that discipline by defining investment policy parameters in terms of the Capital Asset Pricing Model.

The model combines the three disciplines in such a manner that the simulation results provide corporate management with information pertaining to key financial parameters. Although the model may seem rather complex, it produces extremely fundamental information about the pension system. Moreover, this information is presented in terms of cash flow parameters which are most useful in financial planning.

FOOTNOTES

[1] Bagehot, Walter, "Risk and Reward in Corporate Pension Funds," <u>Financial Analysts Journal</u>, Vol. 28, No. 1 (January-February, 1972).

26

The Coming Revolution in Investment Management

Jack L. Treynor

This paper has three parts. The first considers the implication of investment risk for the investment management process and concludes that because of the problems introduced by risk an approach to security analysis independent of any explicit macroeconomic forecasting is highly desirable. The second considers whether such an approach to security analysis is theoretically possible and feasible. The third explores some of the practical consequences of separating security analysis from macroeconomic forecasting, including consequences for the way the investment-management task is organized.

I. The Implications of Risk

Exhibit I depicts in a summary way investment management as it is commonly practiced today. Macroeconomic forecasts logically precede industry forecasts, and industry forecasts logically precede sales forecasts for individual companies within the industry. Price estimates are derived largely independently of cost estimates and of sales volume projections. From these considerations the analyst projects the future cash flows; these are discounted to determine an estimate of the current worth of the company's shares. Comparison with current share price generates trading recommendations, which are then forwarded to the portfolio manager for a final decision. The main justification for the current procedure is that if the macroeconomic analysis, the analysis that translates macro forecasts into industry forecasts, and analysis of the company based on the industry forecast are all correct, then a recommendation based on a comparison of the resulting appraisal with current market price can scarcely fail to be correct in turn. This mode of investment management has one great advantage. At each stage the analysis builds unconditionally on the results of the previous stage. It is rarely necessary to take a backward look at the prior stages of analysis until the recommendation reaches the final decision maker. (At that point, of course, any step in the process may be called into question.) Because the analysis proceeds unconditionally from one stage to the next, the fruit of each stage can be expressed in numbers rather than algebra. This is a consequence with undeniable appeal for most practicing security analysts and portfolio managers.

The great disadvantage of the current procedure is that it is based on a faulty premise: namely, that the forecasts generated at each stage of the process are certain. Wiesenberger's Mutual Fund Annuals used to carry (and perhaps still do carry) demonstrations of how rich one would become if he could anticipate and trade (at no cost) on daily fluctuations in the market averages. In a few years the man gifted with this kind of forecasting ability is richer than the richest men in history, and in a generation or two he owns the world. The consequences of perfect foresight contrast sharply with the actual record of professional investors. Professor Michael Jensen of the University of Rochester found, for example, that out of the several hundred mutual funds (chosen for study because their results are public knowledge) only two or three departed sufficiently far from neutral performance to defy an explanation on the grounds of mere good luck. Almost one-third of the time, price variations in over a year's time in NYSE common stocks exceed 20 percent of their initial value. If professional investors were able to anticipate even a fraction of price movements of this magnitude, their performance would improve significantly. One is forced to conclude that, of the price movement observed in the securities held in professionally managed portfolios, the great bulk is surprise—even to professional investors. These surprises are the fundamental source of investment risk. It is clear from the numbers already cited that the risks are large.

Broadly speaking, the risks are of two kinds: those specific to a single company or a few companies; and those shared by a large number of companies. The former obviously tend to be risks relating to market share and the success of new technologies. The latter tend by their nature to be the risks surrounding variables with broad economic impact.

There are two ways of eliminating the impact of a security on the riskiness of a portfolio (short of selling the security):

1. *Hedging*. Hedging works only for risks common to a large number of securities. In principle it is not difficult to take a position in a second security that will "cancel out" portfolio exposure to a given risk through a first security. In taking a position in the second security, however, the portfolio may become exposed to other sources of investment risk not shared in the same proportion by the first security. Thus hedging is practical only when it is possible to isolate a particular source of risk.
2. *Diversification*. Risks affecting large numbers of securities can be isolated through diversification. In portfolios containing large numbers of securities, common factors tend to become very important and factors unique to the individual securities relatively unimportant.

Diversification can be used to minimize the contribution to portfolio risk of unique factors, but will not work for common factors; hedging can be very effective in eliminating common factors, but will not ordinarily work for unique factors. Used together, however, the two techniques represent powerful complementary instruments for focusing portfolio exposure on those risk factors a portfolio manager is most confident he can predict while minimizing the exposure to the others. To a remarkable degree, they transform the task of portfolio balancing from one of choosing among securities to one of choosing among causal factors. Securities are merely incidental vehicles for taking positions in underlying factors.

Conventional security analysis implies that if a recommendation to take a position in a security is accepted by the portfolio manager, his decision represents a commitment to expose his portfolio to the uncertainties surrounding variables at every stage of the analysis—even though the degree of confidence may differ radically from one variable to another. Hedging can focus on the specifics to the exclusion of the market. On the other hand, diversification used alone can emphasize a portfolio's exposure to market risk while minimizing all other sources of investment risk.

In order to take proper advantage of these possibilities, however, two things must be true: (1) The uncertainties surrounding point forecasts of both kinds of factors—systematic and unique—must be known and quantified. (2) It must be possible to estimate the difference between the portfolio manager's assessment of specifics for the company and the market's assessment.

Present investment management practice, as summarized in Exhibit I, frustrates both requirements. In particular, present practice tends to leave the portfolio manager unenlightened as to whether a buy recommendation is due to a bullish macroeconomic forecast, a bullish assessment of specifics, or both. Thus he has no basis for deciding that he might prefer to emphasize exposure to the specifics of the security in question, or the underlying economic factors. In effect, what is required is a comparison of the specifics implicit in current market price with the portfolio manager's (or perhaps more appropriately the security analyst's) assessment of the specifics.

It is of course impossible to know what specifics are assumed by the market. But a meaningful comparison can be made in the price domain—provided the macroeconomic assumptions underlying the analyst's appraisal are identical to the macroeconomic assumptions implicit in the market consensus. On the other hand, the market consensus regarding macroeconomic factors is not directly measurable, any more than the market consensus regarding specific factors.

Nevertheless, the task is far from impossible. It is obvious that there will always be some macroeconomic forecast so sanguine that the current price of almost any security sensitive to economic conditions can be shown to be underpriced in terms of that forecast; or some forecast so gloomy that the price of virtually any security dependent on economic conditions will be higher than the price warranted by the latter forecast. To define "underpriced" and "overpriced" in terms of the conventional appraisal procedure outlined in Exhibit I is clearly unsatisfactory. Although the prices of individual securities may be too high or too low at a point in time, the general level of security prices implies a certain economic outlook. A more meaningful definition for "underpriced" and "overpriced" is that the security in question is respectively under priced or overpriced in relation to the current market consensus regarding the outlook implicit in the observed prices of other securities.

II. A New Approach to Security Analysis

With this thought in mind, let us consider a highly schematic model—a model far too simple to capture those features of the real world of importance to the portfolio manager, but still perhaps complex enough for our immediate purposes. In this model the only uncertainty revolves around the future level of final demand, which is assumed henceforth to be constant as a function of time. The model is therefore a static model (ignoring any transients generated by initial conditions!) and avoids accelerator problems that are actually very important to the portfolio manager.

Let:

z_j = final demand on j industry.

c_{ij} = input-output coefficients (input from i industry required per unit of j industry output).

x_i = derived demand on the i industry.

v_i = $a_i + b_i x_i$ = gross market value of the i industry as a function of derived demand, where a_i and b_i are constants specific to the industry.

It is clear from these definitions that we have achieved a complete dichotomy between macroeconomic forecasts and forecasts of industry specifics. Dichotomy in this sense is very desirable, for reasons to be discussed in the next section. (The discounting process is submerged in the constants A and B.) The constants A and B incorporate everything specific to the i industry that determines what level of gross market value for an industry will correspond to a given level of derived demand. Under our assumptions, the macroeconomic forecasting problem is of course confined to the Z. No comment on the C seems necessary at this point, except perhaps to say that they are defined consistent with whatever dimensions we assign to the z and x.

It will be convenient to adopt the convention whereby capital letters represent vectors and matrices constructed from the corresponding small letters. Thus we have a final demand vector Z, a derived demand vector X, and a vector of equilibrium market values V. We also have a matrix C of input-output coefficients. Using these definitions, we arrive immediately at the relation between equilibrium market values and final demand.

$$V = A + B \, [I - C]^{-1} \, Z$$

There is no point of course to security analysis if market prices always satisfy the equilibrium relationships implied by one's model. In the unlikely case in which those relationships can be represented faithfully by the model under discussion, a vector P of observed market prices will differ from the vector V of equilibrium market values by a vector E of error terms.

$$P = A + B \, [I - C]^{-1} \, Z + E$$

At this point the task of security analysis can be restated as finding those values for the components of Z for which the difference between estimated V and the observed P is minimized—doubtless in terms of the traditional least squares metric. In effect the components of P are the dependent variable, the components of A and $B \, [I - C]^{-1}$ are respectively independent variables, and the components of Z representing the unknown market consensus regarding final demand play the role of undetermined coefficients. In this formulation it is quite clear that security appraisal (in the sense of what Wall Street calls fundamental analysis) is in fact a regression problem. It is a linear regression problem in my example only, because my model is so unrelentingly (and unrealistically) linear.

It should also be noted that, unless some constraints are imposed on the components of Z, no meaningful regression analysis is possible, since there are as many components of Z as there are observations. In general, the more severely the components of Z are constrained, the more accurately they can be estimated. The extreme would be a one-sector model in which final demand for each industry moves up and down in strict proportion with final demand for every other industry. It is of course more realistic to recognize several sectors including, for example, consumer durables, capital goods, defense spending, and so forth. The number of observations is limited only by the degree of disaggregation in the input-output data incorporated in the model. Since as a practical matter the data will provide several hundred observations, one can afford to distinguish several independent final demand sectors without encountering a real degrees-of-freedom problem.

A faulty model will lead to serious specification problems in estimating the market consensus of the Z, and this in turn will lead to serious errors in estimating the V. To put the same statement in terms that Wall Street can understand: You can lose a lot of money acting on security appraisals based on the wrong model. The writer expects, in particular, that a portfolio manager could lose money very rapidly relying on security appraisals derived using the purely schematic model presented in this paper.

Practical Consequences for Investment Management

The approach to security analysis described above has far-reaching consequences for the way security analysts and portfolio managers define their jobs and the way they organize to make portfolio decisions. The easiest way to see how sweeping the consequences will be is to refer once again to Exhibit I. As security analysis is conventionally practiced, the analyst's first step is to form a judgment regarding the underlying macroeconomic variables. He may of course listen to a large number of expert economists before arriving at his judgment; nevertheless, determination of the values of these variables for his purposes is unavoidably a matter of judgment.

When the analyst communicates his opinion of the security in question to the portfolio manager it is couched, more often than not, in terms of a recommendation. On the face of it a recommendation to buy, sell, or hold from the security analyst is absurd, since portfolio decisions can only be made in the context of information regarding other securities, many of which will commonly be outside the analyst's ken. The reason for couching the analyst's opinions in terms of recommendations seem to be that, if instead, the analyst's opinion were couched in terms of his opinion of the value of the security in question, it would be obsoleted almost before he could convey it to the portfolio manager by changes in the underlying macroeconomic variables.

More often than not, analyst's recommendations to portfolio managers are recommendations to buy rather than sell. On the face of it this is surprising because, if securities were being valued in practice in relation to the observed prices of other securities, one would expect to find roughly as many securities overpriced as underpriced. This curious practice stems from the portfolio manager's difficulty in measuring the quality of the individual analyst's advice.

The reason the quality is difficult to measure is that, in the conventional investment management process, there is no way for the portfolio manager to know what macroeconomic assumptions are underlying the analyst's advice. Nor, since the entire process is carried through in terms of numbers rather than algebra, is there any opportunity for the portfolio manager to determine what the analyst's recommendation would have been if his macroeconomic assumptions had been those which in hindsight turned out to be correct. Without such knowledge, however, the portfolio manager is powerless to determine whether the analyst's advice was good or bad. The practical consequence has been that the analysts who get recognized and rewarded are those who (1) succeeded in persuading portfolio managers to buy their recommendations, and (2) whose recommended securities appreciate.

The current mode of investment management has a number of practical consequences:

1. As just noted, it is impossible for portfolio managers to measure meaningfully the quality of the advice they get from individual analysts.
2. There is no way for a portfolio manager to make consistent comparisons between securities recommended by different analysts if the analysts are free to base their recommendations on different sets of macroeconomic assumptions.

3. Even if it were possible to appraise all securities on the basis of the same set of macroeconomic assumptions, the present approach would bias the selection process; some securities are more sensitive to the underlying macroeconomic assumptions than others and would thus benefit, for example, from assumptions more bullish than those implicit in current market prices.

4. Because analysts tend to communicate to portfolio managers primarily in terms of recommendations to buy and because, as explained above, the analyst often has little hope of recognition unless he succeeds in getting his recommendations accepted, the conventional investment management process transforms the various analysts supplying information to a portfolio manager into rivals. The portfolio manager typically has limited funds with which to buy, and acceptance of one analyst's recommendation is likely to preclude acceptance of another's. It is obvious from the nature of the rivalry that it encourages analysts to bias their recommendations upward. Although systematic means for adjusting for analysts' bias can be devised, the high probability that the degree of bias is changing over time leads, as a practical matter, to a very substantial degradation in the quality of the information reaching the portfolio manager. (The rivalry system is nevertheless popular with many portfolio managers, chiefly because it transforms the portfolio manager into an administrator adjudicating conflicts among his subordinates. The present system maintains and enhances the status of the portfolio manager even while it degrades the quality of his product.)

5. Measurement of the quality of analyst's advice is essential—not only for any just system for rewarding analysts and their employers, but also because these quality measurements play an essential role in deciding whether portfolio should be exposed to the unique risk associated with a given security. The fraction of price variance not anticipated by the analyst may of course vary over time, and the analyst himself may have an opinion whether it is currently higher or lower than his long-run batting average (that opinion may be termed "confidence" and can obviously be quantified). Unless the portfolio manager knows the analyst's long-run batting average, however, he is unable to apply the analyst's current confidence and estimate the current residual risk.

In the face of these problems it would be quite remarkable if conventional investment management were able to make any contribution to portfolio performance whatever.

It would be tedious to review the alternative approach suggested here, pointing out that in each case the problems raised by the conventional approach are absent. But it would be wrong to end this paper without pointing out that the approach suggested here will radically redefine the jobs of the security analyst and portfolio manager.

As noted above, the analyst's job becomes estimating the value of those factors specific to the company in question and its industry that have some demonstrated bearing on future rents. Because the determination of how the capital market discounts risky future rents can be done more efficiently once and for all by the portfolio manager rather than repeated for each individual security, and because consistency here is as important as consistency elsewhere, this burden will be removed from the security analyst and centralized with the portfolio manager. This is only the first step, however, in what the writer expects to become a trend. More and more, the analysts' task will be restricted to estimating or forecasting factors in non-financial terms, while leaving the determination of the financial significance to the portfolio manager. It is not clear that, when this trend has run its course, any special knowledge of economics or finance will remain that a security analyst will need to know in order to do his job.

Instead of challenging the assumptions made by individual analysts, the portfolio manager will be free to concentrate on perfecting the model that relates one industry to others, and all industries to the macroeconomy, and to perfect his model of how the capital markets value risky future rents. He will also be concerned with the larger system, in which this model is embedded, that measures the quality of analysts' advice, reports any bias and determines whether the portfolio in question is adhering to its stated objectives (quantified in terms of risk). The portfolio manager will finally become something more than an adjudicator and a kibitzer.

Portfolio management will have ceased to be an administrative art and will have become, instead, a technology.

Exhibit I

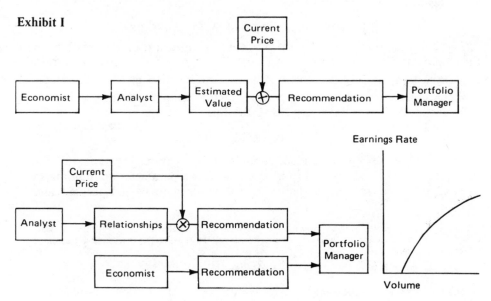

27

ON THE ASSESSMENT OF RISK

Marshall E. Blume *

INTRODUCTION

THE CONCEPT OF RISK has so permeated the financial community that no one needs to be convinced of the necessity of including risk in investment analysis. Still of controversy is what constitutes risk and how it should be measured. This paper examines the statistical properties of one measure of risk which has had wide acceptance in the academic community: namely the coefficient of non-diversifiable risk or more simply the beta coefficient in the market model.

The next section defines this beta coefficient and presents a brief non-rigorous justification of its use as a measure of risk. After discussing the sample and its basic properties in Section III, Section IV examines the stationarity of this beta coefficient over time and proposes a method of obtaining improved assessments of this measure of risk.

II. THE RATIONALE OF BETA AS A MEASURE OF RISK

The interpretation of the beta coefficient as a measure of risk rests upon the empirical validity of the market model. This model asserts that the return from time (t-1) to t on asset i, $\tilde{R}_{it}$,[1] is a linear function of a market factor common to all assets $\tilde{M}_t$, and independent factors unique to asset i, $\tilde{\varepsilon}_{it}$.

Symbolically, this relationship takes the form

$$\tilde{R}_{it} = \alpha_i + \beta_i \tilde{M}_t + \tilde{\varepsilon}_{it}, \tag{1}$$

where the tilde indicates a random variable, α_i is a parameter whose value is such that the expected value of $\tilde{\varepsilon}_{it}$ is zero, and β_i is a parameter appropriate to asset i.[2] That the random variables $\tilde{\varepsilon}_{it}$ are assumed to be independent and

---

* University of Pennsylvania.

1. In this paper, return will be measured as the ratio of the value of the investment at time t with dividends reinvested to the value of the investment at time (t-1). Dividends are assumed reinvested at time t.

2. The parameter β_i is defined as Cov $(\tilde{R}_i, \tilde{M})/$Var $(\tilde{M})$.

Reprinted from *The Journal of Finance*, XXVI, No. 1 (March, 1971), 1–10, by permission of the author and the publisher.

unique to asset i implies that Cov ($\tilde{\varepsilon}_{it}$, $\tilde{M}_t$) is zero and that Cov ($\tilde{\varepsilon}_{it}$, $\tilde{\varepsilon}_{jt}$), $i \neq j$, are zero. This last conclusion is tantamount to assuming the absence of industry effects.

The empirical validity of the market model as it applies to common stocks listed on the NYSE has been examined extensively in the literature.[3] The principal conclusions are: (1) The linearity assumption of the model is adequate.[4] (2) The variables $\tilde{\varepsilon}_{it}$ cannot be assumed independent between securities because of the existence of industry effects. However, these industry effects, as documented by King,[5] probably account for only about ten percent of the variation in returns, so that as a first approximation they can be ignored. (3) The unique factors $\tilde{\varepsilon}_{it}$ correspond more closely to non-normal stable variates than to normal ones. This conclusion means that variances and covariances of the unique factors do not exist. Nonetheless, this paper will make the more common assumption of the existence of these statistics in justifying the beta coefficient as a measure of risk since Fama[6] and Jensen[7] have shown that this coefficient can still be interpreted as a measure of risk under the assumption that the $\tilde{\varepsilon}_{it}$'s are non-normal stable variates.

That the beta coefficient, β_i, in the market model can be interpreted as a measure of risk will be justified in two different ways: the portfolio approach and the equilibrium approach.

A. *The Portfolio Approach*

The important assumption underlying the portfolio approach is that individuals evaluate the risk of a portfolio as a whole rather than the risk of each asset individually. An example will illustrate the meaning of this statement. Consider two assets, each of which by itself is extremely risky. If, however, it is always the case that when one of the assets has a high return, the other has a low return, the return on a combination of these two assets in a portfolio may be constant. Thus, the return on the portfolio may be risk free whereas each of the assets has a highly uncertain return. The discussion of such an

---

3. See Marshall E. Blume, "Portfolio Theory: A Step Towards Its Practical Application," forthcoming *Journal of Business;* Eugene F. Fama, "The Behavior of Stock Market Prices," *Journal of Business* (1965), 34-105; Eugene F. Fama, Lawrence Fisher, Michael Jensen, and Richard Roll, "The Adjustment of Stock Prices to New Information," *International Economic Review* (1969), 1-21; Michael Jensen, "Risk, the Pricing of Capital Assets, and the Evaluation of Investment Portfolios," *Journal of Business* (1969), 167-247; Benjamin F. King, "Market and Industry Factors in Stock Price Behavior," *Journal of Business* (1966), 139-90; and William F. Sharpe, "Mutual Fund Performance," *Journal of Business* (1966), 119-38.

4. The linearity assumption of the model should not be confused with the equilibrium requirement of William F. Sharpe, "Capital Asset Prices: A Theory of Market Equilibrium Under Conditions of Risk," *Journal of Finance* (1964), 425-42, which states that $\alpha_i = (1 - \beta_i) R_F$, where R_F is the risk free rate. It is quite possible that this equality does not hold and at the same time that the market model is linear.

5. King, *op. cit.*

6. Eugene F. Fama, "Risk, Return, and Equilibrium" (Report No. 6831, University of Chicago, Center for Mathematical Studies in Business and Economics, June, 1968).

7. Jensen, *op. cit.*

obvious point may seem unwarranted, but there is very little empirical work which indicates that people do in fact behave according to it.

Now if an individual is willing to judge the risk inherent in a portfolio solely in terms of the variance of the future aggregate returns, the risk of a portfolio of n securities with an equal amount invested in each, according to the market model, will be given by

$$\text{Var}\,(\tilde{W}_t) = \left(\sum_{i=1}^{n} \frac{1}{n}\beta_i\right)^2 \text{Var}\,(\tilde{M}_t) + \sum_{i=1}^{n} \left(\frac{1}{n}\right)^2 \text{Var}\,(\tilde{\varepsilon}_{it}) \qquad (2)$$

where $\tilde{W}_t$ is the return on the portfolio. Equation (2) can be rewritten as

$$\text{Var}\,(\tilde{W}_t) = \bar{\beta}^2 \text{Var}\,(\tilde{M}_t) + \frac{\overline{\text{Var}\,(\tilde{\varepsilon})}}{n} \qquad (3)$$

where the bar indicates an average. As one diversifies by increasing the number of securities n, the last term in equation (3) will decrease. Evans and Archer[8] have shown empirically that this process of diversification proceeds quite rapidly, and with ten or more securities most of the effect of diversification has taken place. For a well diversified portfolio, Var $(\tilde{W}_t)$ will approximate $\bar{\beta}^2$ Var $(\tilde{M}_t)$. Since Var $(\tilde{M}_t)$ is the same for all securities, $\bar{\beta}$ becomes a measure of risk for a portfolio and thus β_i, as it contributes to the value of $\bar{\beta}$, is a measure of risk for a security. The larger the value of β_i, the more risk the security will contribute to a portfolio.[9]

B. *The Equilibrium Approach*

Using the market model, Sharpe[10] and Lintner,[11] as clarified by Fama,[12] have developed a theory of equilibrium in the capital markets. This theory relates the risk premium for an individual security, $E(\tilde{R}_{it}) - R_F$, where R_F is the risk free rate, to the risk premium of the market, $E(\tilde{M}_t) - R_F$, by the formula

$$E(\tilde{R}_{it}) - R_F = \beta_i[E(\tilde{M}_t) - R_F]. \qquad (4)$$

The risk premium for an individual security is proportional to the risk premium for the market. The constant of proportionality β_i can therefore be interpreted as a measure of risk for individual securities.

8. John L. Evans and Stephan H. Archer, "Diversification and the Reduction of Dispersion: An Empirical Analysis," *Journal of Finance* (1968), 761-68.

9. This argument has been extended to a non-Gaussian, symmetric stable world by E. F. Fama, "Portfolio Analysis in a Stable Paretian Market," *Management Science* (1965), 404-19; and P. A. Samuelson, "Efficient Portfolio Selection for Pareto-Levy Investments," *Journal of Financial and Quantitative Analysis* (1967), 107-22.

10. Sharpe, "Capital Asset Prices," *op. cit.*

11. John Lintner, "The Valuation of Risk Assets and the Selection of Risky Investments in Stock Portfolios and Capital Budgets," *Review of Economics and Statistics* (1965), 13-37.

12. Eugene F. Fama, "Risk, Return, and Equilibrium: Some Clarifying Comments," *Journal of Finance* (1968), 29-40.

This theory of equilibrium, although theoretically sound, is based upon numerous assumptions which obviously do not hold in the real world. A theoretical model, however, should not be judged by the accuracy of its assumptions but rather by the accuracy of its predictions. The empirical work of Friend and Blume[13] suggests that the predictions of this model are seriously biased and that this bias is primarily attributable to the inaccuracy of one key assumption, namely that the borrowing and lending rates are equal and the same for all investors. Therefore, although Sharpe's and Lintner's theory of equilibrium can be used as a justification for β_i as measure of risk, it is a weaker and considerably less robust justification than that provided by the portfolio approach.

III. The Sample and Its Properties

The sample was taken from the updated Price Relative File of the Center for Research in Security Prices at the Graduate School of Business, University of Chicago. This file contains the monthly investment relatives, adjusted for dividends and capital changes of all common stocks listed on the New York Stock Exchange during any part of the period from January 1926 through June 1968, for the months in which they were listed. Six equal time periods beginning in July 1926 and ending in June 1968 were examined. Table 1 lists these six periods and the number of companies in each for which there was a complete history of monthly return data. This number ranged from 415 to 890.

The investment relatives for a particular security and a particular period were regressed[14] upon the corresponding combination market link relatives, which were originally prepared by Fisher[15] as a measure of the market factor. This process was repeated for each security and each period, yielding, for instance, in the July 1926 through June 1933 period, 415 separate regressions. The average coefficient of determination of these 415 regressions was 0.51. The corresponding average coefficients of determination for the next five periods were, respectively, 0.49, 0.36, 0.32, 0.25, and 0.28. These figures are consistent with King's findings[16] in that the proportion of the variance of returns explained by the market declined steadily until 1960 when his sample terminated. Since 1960, the importance of the market factor has increased slightly according to these figures.

Table 1, besides giving the number of companies analyzed, summarizes the distributions of the estimated beta coefficients in terms of the means, standard deviations, and various fractiles of these distributions. In addition, the number of estimated betas which were less than zero is given. In three of the periods,

13. Irwin Friend and Marshall Blume, "Measurement of Portfolio Performance Under Uncertainty," *American Economic Review* (1970), 561-75.

14. John Wise, "Linear Estimators for Linear Regression Systems Having Infinite Variances," (Berkeley-Stanford Mathematics-Economics Seminar, October, 1963) has given some justification for the use of least squares in estimating coefficients of regressions in which the disturbances are non-normal symmetric stable variates.

15. Lawrence Fisher, "Some New Stock-Market Indexes," *Journal of Business* (1966), 191-225.

16. King, *op. cit.*

TABLE 1

Descriptive Summary of Estimated BETA Coefficients

Period	Number of Companies	Mean	Standard Deviation	Number of BETAS less than Zero	Fractiles					
					.10	.25	.50	.75	.90	
7/26-6/33	415	1.051	0.462	1	0.498	0.711	1.023	1.352	1.616	
7/33-6/40	604	1.036	0.474	0	0.436	0.701	1.015	1.349	1.581	
7/40-6/47	731	0.990	0.504	0	0.500	0.643	0.872	1.186	1.606	
7/47-6/54	870	1.010	0.409	2	0.473	0.727	0.996	1.263	1.565	
7/54-6/61	890	0.998	0.423	0	0.458	0.678	0.984	1.250	1.558	
7/61-6/68	847	0.962	0.390	4	0.475	0.681	0.934	1.199	1.491	

none of the estimated betas was negative. Of the 4357 betas estimated in all six periods, only seven or 0.16 per cent were negative. This means that although the inclusion of a stock which moves counter to the market can reduce the risk of a portfolio substantially, there are virtually no opportunities to do this. Nearly every stock appears to move with the market.[17]

IV. The Stationarity of Beta over Time

No economic variable including the beta coefficient is constant over time. Yet for some purposes, an individual might be willing to act *as if* the values of beta for individual securities were constant or stationary over time. For example, a person who wishes to assess the future risk of a well diversified portfolio is really interested in the behavior of averages of the β_i's over time and not directly in the values for individual securities. For the purposes of evaluating a portfolio, it may be sufficient that the historical values of β_i be unbiased estimates of the future values for an individual to act *as if* the values of the β_i's for individual securities are stationary over time. This is because the errors in the assessment of an average will tend to be less than those of the components of the average providing that the errors in the assessments of the components are independent of each other.[18] Yet, a statistician or a person who wishes to assess the risk of an individual security may have completely different standards in determining whether he would act as if the β_i's are constant over time. The remainder of the paper examines the stationarity of the β_i's from the point of view of a person who wishes to analyze a portfolio.

A. *Correlations*

To examine the empirical behavior of the risk measures for portfolios over time, arbitrary portfolios of n securities were selected as follows: The estimates of β_i were derived using data from the first period, July 1926 through June 1933, and were then ranked in ascending order.[19] The first portfolio of n securities consisted of those securities with the n smallest estimates of β_i. The second portfolio consisted of those securities with the next n smallest estimates of β_i, and so on until the number of securities remaining was less than n. The number of securities n was allowed to vary over 1, 2, 4, 7, 10, 20, 35, 50, 75, and 100. This process was repeated for each of the next four periods.

Table 2 presents the product moment and rank order correlation coefficients between the risk measures for portfolios of n securities assuming an equal investment in each security estimated in one period and the corresponding risk

17. The use of considerably less than seven years of monthly data such as two or three years to estimate the beta coefficient results in a larger proportion of negative estimates. This larger proportion is probably due to sampling errors which, as documented in Richard Roll, "The Efficient Market Model Applied to U. S. Treasury Bill Rates," (Unpublished Ph.D. thesis, Graduate School of Business, University of Chicago, 1968) may be quite large for models with non-normal symmetric stable disturbances.

18. This property of averages does not hold for all distributions (*cf.* Eugene F. Fama, "Portfolio Analysis in a Stable Paretian Market"), but for the distributions associated with stock market returns it almost certainly holds.

19. Only securities which also had complete data in the next seven year period were included in this ranking.

measure for the same portfolio estimated in the next period.[20] The risk measure calculated using the earlier data might be regarded as an individual's assessment of the future risk, and the measure calculated using the later data can be regarded as the realized risk. Thus, these correlation coefficients can be interpreted as a measure of the accuracy of one's assessments, which in this case are simple extrapolations of historical data.

TABLE 2

PRODUCT MOMENT AND RANK ORDER CORRELATION COEFFICIENTS
OF BETAS FOR PORTFOLIOS OF N SECURITIES

Number of Securities per Portfolio	7/26-6/33 and 7/33-6/40		7/33-6/40 and 7/40-6/47		7/40-6/47 and 7/47-6/54		7/47-6/54 and 7/54-6/61		7/54-6/61 and 7/61-6/68	
	P.M.	Rank	P.M.	Rank	P.M.	Rank	P.M.	Rank	P.M.	Rank
1	0.63	0.69	0.62	0.73	0.59	0.65	0.65	0.67	0.60	0.62
2	0.71	0.75	0.76	0.83	0.72	0.79	0.76	0.76	0.73	0.74
4	0.80	0.84	0.85	0.90	0.81	0.89	0.84	0.84	0.84	0.85
7	0.86	0.90	0.91	0.93	0.88	0.93	0.87	0.88	0.88	0.89
10	0.89	0.93	0.94	0.95	0.90	0.95	0.92	0.93	0.92	0.93
20	0.93	0.99	0.97	0.98	0.95	0.98	0.95	0.96	0.97	0.98
35	0.96	1.00	0.98	0.99	0.95	0.99	0.97	0.98	0.97	0.97
50	0.98	1.00	0.99	0.98	0.98	0.99	0.98	0.98	0.98	0.97

The values of these correlation coefficients are striking. For the assessments based upon the data from July 1926 through June 1933 and evaluated using data from July 1933 through June 1940, the product moment correlations varied from 0.63 for single securities to 0.98 for portfolios of 50 securities. The high value of the latter coefficient indicates that substantially all of the variation in the risk among portfolios of 50 securities can be explained by assessments based upon previous data. The former correlation suggests that assessments for individual securities derived from historical data can explain roughly 36 per cent of the variation in the future estimated values, leaving about 64 per cent unexplained.[21]

These results, which are typical of the other periods, suggest that at least as measured by the correlation coefficients, naively extrapolated assessments of future risk for larger portfolios are remarkably accurate, whereas extrapolated assessments of future risk for individual securities and smaller portfolios are of some, but limited value in forecasting the future.

B. *A Closer Examination*

Table 3 presents the actual estimates of the risk parameters for portfolios of 100 securities for successive periods. For all five different sets of portfolios, the rank order correlations between the successive estimates are one, but there is obviously some tendency for the estimated values of the risk parameter to

20. Because of the small number of portfolios of 100 securities, correlations are not presented in Table 2 for these portfolios.

21. This large magnitude of unexplained variation may make the beta coefficient an inadequate measure of risk for analyzing the cost of equity for an individual firm although it may be adequate for cross-section analyses of cost of equity.

TABLE 3
ESTIMATED BETA COEFFICIENTS FOR PORTFOLIOS OF 100 SECURITIES
IN TWO SUCCESSIVE PERIODS

Portfolio	7/26- 6/33	7/33- 6/40	7/33- 6/40	7/40- 6/47	7/40- 6/47	7/47- 6/54	7/47- 6/54	7/54- 6/61	7/54- 6/61	7/61- 6/68
1	0.528	0.610	0.394	0.573	0.442	0.593	0.385	0.553	0.393	0.620
2	0.898	1.004	0.708	0.784	0.615	0.776	0.654	0.748	0.612	0.707
3	1.225	1.296	0.925	0.902	0.746	0.887	0.832	0.971	0.810	0.861
4			1.177	1.145	0.876	1.008	0.967	1.010	0.987	0.914
5			1.403	1.354	1.037	1.124	1.093	1.095	1.138	0.995
6					1.282	1.251	1.245	1.243	1.337	1.169

change gradually over time. This tendency is most pronounced in the lowest risk portfolios, for which the estimated risk in the second period is invariably higher than that estimated in the first period. There is some tendency for the high risk portfolios to have lower estimated risk coefficients in the second period than in those estimated in the first. Therefore, the estimated values of the risk coefficients in one period are biased assessments of the future values, and furthermore the values of the risk coefficients as measured by the estimates of β_1 tend to regress towards the means with this tendency stronger for the lower risk portfolios than the higher risk portfolios.

C. *A Method of Correction*

In so far as the rate of regression towards the mean is stationary over time, one can in principle correct for this tendency in forming one's assessments. An obvious method is to regress the estimated values of β_1 in one period on the values estimated in a previous period and to use this estimated relationship to modify one's assessments of the future.

Table 4 presents these regressions for five successive periods of time for individual securities.[22] The slope coefficients are all less than one in agreement with the regression tendency, observed above. The coefficients themselves do change over time, so that the use of the historical rate of regression to correct

TABLE 4
MEASUREMENT OF REGRESSION TENDENCY OF ESTIMATED BETA COEFFICIENTS
FOR INDIVIDUAL SECURITIES

Regression Tendency Implied Between Periods	$\beta_2 = a + b\beta_1$
7/33-6/40 and 7/26-6/33	$\beta_2 = 0.320 + 0.714\beta_1$
7/40-6/47 and 7/33-6/40	$\beta_2 = 0.265 + 0.750\beta_1$
7/47-6/54 and 7/40-6/47	$\beta_2 = 0.526 + 0.489\beta_1$
7/54-6/61 and 7/47-6/54	$\beta_2 = 0.343 + 0.677\beta_1$
7/61-6/68 and 7/54-6/61	$\beta_2 = 0.399 + 0.546\beta_1$

22. The reader should not think of these regressions as a test of the stationarity of the risk of securities over time but rather merely as a test of the accuracy of the assessments of future risk which happen to be derived as historical estimates. In this test of accuracy, the independent variable in these regressions is measured without error, so that the estimated coefficients are unbiased. In the test of the stationarity of the risk measures over time, the independent variable would be measured with error, so that the coefficients in Table 4 would be biased.

for the future rate will not perfectly adjust the assessments and may even overcorrect by introducing larger errors into the assessments than were present in the unadjusted data.

To examine the efficacy of using historical rates of regression to correct one's assessments, the estimated risk coefficients for the individual securities for the period from July 1933 through June 1940 were modified using the first equation in Table 4 to obtain adjusted risk coefficients under the assumption that the future rate of regression will be the same as the past. This process was repeated for each of the next three periods using respectively the next three equations in Table 4 to estimate the rate of regression.

Table 5 compares these adjusted assessments with the unadjusted assessments which were used in Tables 2 and 3. For the portfolios selected previously using the data from July 1933 through June 1940, both the unadjusted

TABLE 5

MEAN SQUARE ERRORS BETWEEN ASSESSMENTS AND FUTURE ESTIMATED VALUES

Number of Sec./ Port.	Assessments Based Upon							
	7/33-6/40		7/40-6/47		7/47-6/54		7/54-6/61	
	unadjusted	adjusted	unadjusted	adjusted	unadjusted	adjusted	unadjusted	adjusted
1	0.1929	0.1808	0.1747	0.1261	0.1203	0.1087	0.1305	0.1013
2	0.0915	0.0813	0.1218	0.0736	0.0729	0.0614	0.0827	0.0535
4	0.0538	0.0453	0.0958	0.0483	0.0495	0.0381	0.0587	0.0296
7	0.0323	0.0247	0.0631	0.0276	0.0387	0.0281	0.0523	0.0231
10	0.0243	0.0174	0.0535	0.0220	0.0305	0.0189	0.0430	0.0169
20	0.0160	0.0090	0.0328	0.0106	0.0258	0.0139	0.0291	0.0089
35	0.0120	0.0055	0.0266	0.0080	0.0197	0.0101	0.0302	0.0089
50	0.0096	0.0046	0.0192	0.0046	0.0122	0.0097	0.0237	0.0064
75	0.0081	0.0035	0.0269	0.0067	0.0112	0.0078	0.0193	0.0056
100	0.0084	0.0020	0.0157	0.0035	0.0114	0.0084	0.0195	0.0056

and adjusted assessments of future risk were obtained. The accuracy of these two alternative methods of assessment were compared through the mean squared errors of the assessments versus the estimated risk coefficients in the next period, July 1940 through June 1947.[23] This process was repeated for each of the next three periods.

For individual securities as well as portfolios of two or more securities, the assessments adjusted for the historical rate of regression are more accurate than the unadjusted or naive assessments. Thus, an improvement in the accuracy of one's assessments of risk can be obtained by adjusting for the historical rate of regression even though the rate of regression over time is not strictly stationary.

23. The mean square error was calculated by $\dfrac{\Sigma(\beta_1 - \beta_2)^2}{n}$ where β_1 is the assessed value of the future risk, β_2 is the estimated value of the risk, and n is the number of portfolios. In using an estimate of beta rather than the actual value, the mean square error will be biased upwards, but the effect of this bias will be the same for both the adjusted and unadjusted assessments.

V. Conclusion

This paper examined the empirical behavior of one measure of risk over time. There was some tendency for the estimated values of these risk measures to regress towards the mean over time. Correcting for this regression tendency resulted in considerably more accurate assessments of the future values of risk.

28

Adjusting for risk in portfolio performance measurement

Measurable risk is the hallmark of accurate performance evaluations.

William F. Sharpe

A common human failing is the desire for simple answers to difficult questions. Evaluation of investment performance is no exception. How well did a security or portfolio do in the past? Most people would like to have such a question answered with a single number. Which security or portfolio did best? Most would like an unambiguous reply.

Faced with this kind of question, analysts have, until recently, tended to go to one of two extremes. Some provided direct answers using either: 1) a measure of average return over some period, or 2) a measure relating terminal value to initial value. Others simply rejected the question on the grounds that performance is far too complicated to measure in any simple way; that every portfolio has its own unique characteristics; and that one simply can't compare apples with oranges.

There is, of course, much truth in the latter position. Securities and portfolios really *are* different. Any attempt to measure performance with one number *must* involve some simplification. On the other hand, simplification is the essence of science. It is impossible to compare everything with everything. Some abstraction is necessary.

Take as given the assumption that performance is to be measured with only one number. Then one must consider the obvious question: Which number? Only the investigation of the best single measure can provide an adequate basis for answering the prior question: Is one enough?

Consider the problem of measuring the performance of a mutual fund from, say, January 1, 1969 through December 31, 1973. One traditional approach would be to compute the annual returns for each of the five years, then average them. Another would assume an investment of, say, $10,000 on January 1, 1969, then compute the terminal value on December 31, 1973, assuming that all interim dividends and capital gains had been reinvested in the fund.

Numbers such as these are far from irrelevant, but they fail to take *risk* into account. We know that there is risk in the world, and that investors generally dislike it. There is substantial theoretical and empirical support for the assertion that security prices reflect this fact. As a result, there is a trade-off between risk and return. On the average, the best high-risk portfolio provides a greater return than the best low-risk portfolio. If this were not the case, the former would not be held by knowledgeable people. Because of the lack of large numbers of foolish investors, security prices must adjust so that anyone who takes the pains to be fairly well-diversified can obtain higher returns on average only by taking on more risk.

A reasonable goal is thus to find a measure of performance that takes risk into account. This article describes some of the leading candidates. Although all are based on a rather elegant theory of equilibrium capital asset prices, it is instructive to present them simply as useful measures of past performance. Thus no assumptions about market equilibrium, equality of *ex post* and *ex ante* values, etc., will be invoked. Nor will questions concerning the "significance" of differences in past performance be considered to avoid an extended discussion of statistical procedures.

EXCESS RETURNS

To begin, decisions must be made about the *period* to be covered and the *differencing interval* to be used. No simple prescription is available since the proper choice depends on the purpose for which performance is being measured. For concreteness, we will assume that a period of five years is to be covered, with a quarterly differencing interval. Of course, the procedures to be described can also be applied to other combinations of periods and intervals.

The first task is to compute the rate of return for each of the twenty quarters. If great precision seems desirable, the actual dates of the cash flows, plus information on interim values, can be used to compute the time-weighted rate of return for a quarter. Alternatively, an internal rate of return can be computed. It sometimes suffices to simply assume that all cash flows are held until the end of the quarter in which they are received.

This leads to the familiar formula whereby the return on a security or a portfolio in any given period is equal to the sum of the starting price, plus income received, less the price at the end of the period as a percent of the starting price.

While this calculation measures the performance of a security or a portfolio during a particular quarter, it fails to differentiate quarters in which interest rates were generally low. To measure the differences in return from prevailing interest rates, one must compute the *excess return*, which is of course the difference between the actual return and the return on a riskless security such as a 90-day Treasury bill over the same period of time.

All the measures described in this article will be defined in terms of excess returns. In some cases, definitions proposed in other sources have been modified slightly. When short-term interest rates did not vary significantly, there was less reason to use excess returns. Now, however, it is especially important for us to do so.

THE REWARD-TO-VARIABILITY RATIO

We consider first a measure designed to assess the performance of a portfolio representing most or all of an investor's capital. It is both simple and intuitively appealing. The "reward" provided by a portfolio is measured by its average quarterly excess return. This can be considered the reward obtained for bearing risk. The risk actually borne is measured by the "variability," or standard deviation of quarterly excess returns around the average value. This is computed by measuring the deviation of each quarter's excess return from the average, then squaring it; the resulting values are averaged and the square root taken. The final figure measures the extent to which the excess returns deviate from their average; in a typical case, approximately two thirds of the values will be within one standard deviation of the average.

Although the standard deviation of excess return may not completely accord with one's interpretation of the term "risk," it is generally highly correlated

with more familiar measures and thus provides an adequate surrogate.

The reward-to-variability ratio is simply the ratio of reward (which is good) to variability (which is bad). It indicates the reward per unit of risk borne. The larger the ratio, the better the performance.

This seems an *ad hoc* argument at best, and it is. Fortunately, a much stronger case may be made. Consider Figure 1. Points i and j plot the average excess return and standard deviation of excess return for portfolios i and j. Point π shows the results for investment solely in 90-day Treasury bills. Since such a strategy results in an excess return of zero in every quarter, the point is located at the origin (i.e., both the average excess return as well as the standard deviation are zero).

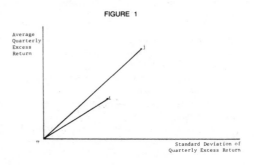

FIGURE 1

Average Quarterly Excess Return

Standard Deviation of Quarterly Excess Return

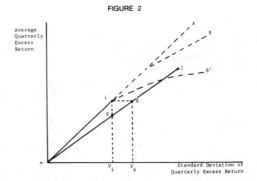

FIGURE 2

Average Quarterly Excess Return

Standard Deviation of Quarterly Excess Return

Now consider a strategy involving investment in portfolio i and Treasury bills. If half an investor's funds had been in Treasury bills each quarter and the other half in portfolio i, the average quarterly excess return on his account would have been half that of Treasury bills (zero) plus half that on portfolio i. A similar relationship holds for the standard deviation (but only because the standard deviation of the excess returns from Treasury bills is zero). Thus the performance of a 50-50 mix of Treasury bills and portfolio i would plot halfway between point π and point i. Similarly, an account with 70% in Treasury bills and 30% in portfolio i each quarter would plot 70% of the way between point i and point π. Thus portfolio i plus Treasury bills could have provided any desired point along line πi.

Similarly, portfolio j plus Treasury bills could have provided any desired point along line πj. By recognizing the opportunity to split funds between a portfolio and Treasury bills, we can replace the point associated with a portfolio by the line associated with strategies using only that portfolio plus treasury bills.

In the case shown in Figure 1, portfolio j is clearly superior to portfolio i. For any level of variability attainable with portfolio i plus Treasury bills, a higher average return could have been obtained with portfolio j plus Treasury bills. Moreover, some high-variability, high-average return alternatives are not even available with portfolio i plus Treasury bills. In this case, at least, the portfolio with the steeper line is clearly the better.

But note that the slope of such a line *is* the reward-to-variability ratio. The portfolio with the steeper line has the higher reward-to-variability ratio, and vice-versa.

The portfolio with the higher reward-to-variability ratio may not be better in all cases. Figure 2 provides a counterexample. Here, the portfolio with the smaller average excess return has the larger reward-to-variability ratio, but it is not unambiguously better.

Consider an investor who wanted an overall standard deviation below V_i. For such a person, portfolio i clearly was better. But what about a more adventuresome investor? Note that point i dominates all points from X to Z along line πj, since it gives more average return and less variability. Only in the range above V_z might portfolio j provide a more desirable investment strategy.

If the possibility of borrowing funds were taken into account, the case in favor of portfolio i in Figure 2 is likely to be even stronger. By investing his own funds, plus some borrowed money, in portfolio i, an investor could have attained a result lying to the right of point i. The actual location would depend on both the amount borrowed and the interest rate paid. If the investor could have borrowed without limit at the rate paid by the U.S. Treasury, points along line iA (the extension of π₁) could have been attained, and portfolio i would clearly have been superior to portfolio j. In fact, investors often "borrow" from themselves for such purposes, by withdrawing money from savings accounts or by paying off a mortgage at a slower rate.

Up to a point, then, the cost of "borrowed" funds may be close to the Treasury bill rate. Beyond that point, however, a loan must be obtained, and the interest rate for such a loan is likely to exceed the Treasury bill rate. Moreover, the rate may increase with the amount borrowed. All of this implies that the result may lie along a curve such as iB or iB'. Only in the latter case might portfolio j be a reasonable choice, and only then for adventuresome investors.

Despite the rather robust nature of the reward-to-variability ratio, it is wise to avoid comparisons involving portfolios with significantly different variabilities. But over a reasonable range of risk, the reward-to-variability ratio can provide an adequate risk-adjusted measure of portfolio performance.

COMPARISONS WITH THE MARKET

The reward-to-variability ratio provides an absolute measure of the performance of a portfolio. Subject to the qualifications mentioned earlier, two or more portfolios can be compared using it. Perhaps more important, the performance of a portfolio can be compared with that of one selected by a so-called "naive investor."

The usual model of a naive investor is someone who blindly "buys the averages." Thus a portfolio composed of the stocks used to compute the Standard and Poor's 500 Stock Composite Index might be selected for the comparison. In any event, some sort of *market portfolio* is used to represent the results obtained with virtually no investment management or skill.

FIGURE 3

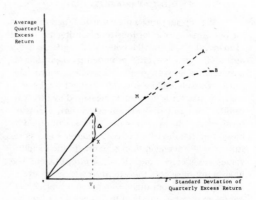

In Figure 3, point M represents the market portfolio and point i the portfolio to be evaluated. In this case, the portfolio's excess return was less variable than that of the market, so it is possible to compare portfolio i directly with a *combination* of the market portfolio and Treasury bills — a combination chosen to have the same variability as portfolio i.

Point X in Figure 3 represents such a *market based portfolio of comparable variability*. In this case, its average excess return was less than that of portfolio i. Portfolio i's *average quarterly differential return* (Δ) indicates how much better (for positive values) or worse (for negative values) portfolio i was on the average than a market-based portfolio of comparable variability.

The situation is more complex if the portfolio's excess return were more variable than that of the market. A naive investor who desired *less* variability than that provided by the market could clearly have divided his money between Treasury bills and the market portfolio. Neither more nor less than this was assumed in the previous case. But what results would have been obtained by the market? If he could have borrowed sufficient funds at the Treasury bill rate, of course, a point lying along line MA (the extension of πM) could have been attained. But what if this had not been possible? Could a portfolio plotting on MA have been found, or one along some curve such as MB?

No categorical answer is possible, since this is essentially an empirical question. One might plot the points representing a number of well-diversified portfolios of securities chosen more or less at random in an attempt to estimate the relevant curve. In practice, however, this is seldom done. Instead, the alternatives are assumed (sometimes implicitly) to lie along the straight line from the origin through the point M. For portfolios with returns that were substantially more variable than those of the market, this may be a questionable procedure. Little harm may be done however, if, in the final analysis, the resultant performance measures are compared with those of portfolios in roughly the same risk class.

VOLATILITY

Variability (standard deviation of excess returns) is an adequate measure of the risk of an entire portfolio. But it is not a satisfactory measure of the risk of a portion of that portfolio — be it a smaller portfolio or a single security — for the variability of the whole does not usually equal a weighted average of the variabilities of the parts.

The general relationship between the risk of an overall portfolio and that of its component securities is complex. Empirical evidence supports the assertion, however, that the most relevant single measure of risk is the *volatility* of a security or a portfolio.

From 30 to 40% of the variation in the typical stock's rate of return is attributable to the co-movement of its price with the overall level of the market. For well-diversified portfolios, the proportion is generally more than 90%. The responsiveness of rate of return to market swings is clearly the most important single measure of risk.

The idea is simple enough. The excess rate of return on a security or portfolio is regressed on the excess rate of return on a market portfolio to obtain a *characteristic line*.

The slope of this line is the *volatility* (more commonly termed *beta*). If the value is less than one, the security or portfolio was *defensive* — it tended to move less than the average security during market swings. If the volatility is more than one, the security or portfolio was *aggressive* — it tended to move more than the average security during market swings. Treasury bills always have a volatility of zero. And, by definition, the market portfolio always has a volatility of one.

No investor averse to risk is likely to invest all his money in a single security. Moreover, many portfolios constitute only a portion of their investor's overall wealth (for example, people combine mutual fund shares with other securities). For evaluating most securities and many portfolios, *volatility* is thus a more relevant measure of risk than *variability*.

It is an easy matter to redefine the performance measures described earlier to account for this. The reward-to-variability ratio is replaced with the *reward-to-volatility ratio*. All the arguments in its favor and questions regarding its universal applicability are similar to those presented earlier. The average differential return can also be computed, but with the comparison related to a market-based portfolio of equal *volatility*. The same line of reasoning applies as does the same line of reservations.

The real meaning of such comparisons can best be seen in conjunction with the characteristic line. Assume that portfolio i is to be evaluated. We begin with the quarter-by-quarter excess returns. The problem is to compare them with those of a relevant naive investment strategy. As before, the goal is to compare two alternatives of equal risk. In this case, the relevant naive strategy should have had the same volatility as the portfolio in question. This requires the determination of the portfolio's characteristic line, as shown in Figure 4. For concreteness, assume that the slope is 0.6. The "comparable-volatility market-based portfolio" will be based on a strategy of investing 60% of the total funds in the market portfolio and 40% in Treasury bills. Every quarter's excess return for such a portfolio will fall precisely along a straight line through the origin with a slope of 0.6 (as intended).

The two lines are parallel (by construction).

For each quarter, the excess return on portfolio i can be compared with that of the comparison portfolio and the *differential return* computed. For example, in Figure 4 the differential return is positive (d_1) in period 1 and negative (d_2) in period 2. By the nature of the least-squares regression procedure, the vertical intercept of portfolio i's characteristic line will equal its *average differential return* (Δ) over a market-based portfolio of comparable volatility. This important measure is also called *alpha*.

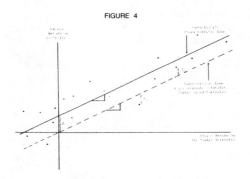

The vertical intercept of a security or portfolio's characteristic line can easily be interpreted as a measure of performance. It indicates the percent per quarter by which the excess return exceeded (for positive values) or fell below (for negative values) that obtainable to the investor from a market-based portfolio of comparable volatility.

Needless to say, this measure is subject to all the reservations mentioned earlier. It may thus be unwise to use it to compare the performance of securities and portfolios of markedly different volatilities. But over a reasonable range of variation, it should provide a good risk-adjusted measure of performance.

STOCK SELECTION AND DIVERSIFICATION

If a portfolio is highly diversified, its performance will be described almost perfectly by its characteristic line: all variation in its rate of return may be attributed to market swings and the portfolio's volatility. But if a portfolio is not highly diversified, its excess return will vary around its characteristic line, leading to additional overall variability. The average differential return over a market-based portfolio of comparable *volatility* provides a measure of the manager's superiority or inferiority vis-a-vis *stock selection*, disregarding the extent to which the portfolio is diversified. The average differential return over a market-based portfolio of comparable *variability* provides a measure that takes into account both the manager's ability to select stocks and his ability to provide diversification. For a perfectly diversified portfolio, the two measures will be the same; for an imperfectly diversified portfolio, the latter will generally be smaller. The difference can be considered the decline in performance resulting from lack of diversification.

In a real sense, *the* problem of portfolio management is to achieve an appropriate balance between stock selection and diversification. The answer is clearly not to select the one (supposedly) best stock. On the other hand, to achieve near perfect diversification, a manager would have to select hundreds of stocks — almost certainly resulting in average performance. Comparison of the two measures of average differential return can provide at least some insight into the way in which a portfolio manager has performed this delicate balancing act.

ABNORMAL PERIODS

In a "normal" period, the average excess return on a market portfolio of risky assets is positive. This is reflected in all the diagrams used thus far. And it accords with the expectations that *must* be held by the majority of (risk-averse) investors. But nature sometimes does the unexpected. It is possible for the average quarterly excess return on the market portfolio over a five-year period to be zero, or even negative. In the former case, adjustment for risk would be harmless, at best, since the average excess return of every market-based portfolio would equal zero. In the latter case, however, the average excess return of a market-based portfolio would be smaller (i.e., more negative), the larger the portfolio's variability or volatility, leading to somewhat different results.

Figure 5 provides an example. The market portfolio's average excess return was negative, so line πMA slopes downward. The "reward" for bearing the risk of portfolio M was negative; thus, both the reward-to-variability and the reward-to-volatility ratios were negative. Although one can easily explain this (abnormal times give abnormal results), the intuitive meaning of both measures is lost.

Average differential return fares somewhat better, as the figure shows. For example, portfolio i's performance is rated superior to that of a market-based portfolio of comparable variability, as is that of portfolio j. Moreover, portfolio j's performance was given a superior rating.

Why? Because it was compared with M_j — a market-based portfolio of greater variability than that of M_i, with which portfolio i was compared. Of course, during this abnormal period, one was penalized for taking on risk. But it is still important to assess performance relative to that achieved by a naive investor holding a portfolio of comparable risk. The measures of average differential return do this, even when the market is more perverse than usual.

FIGURE 5

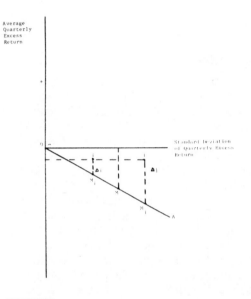

CONCLUSIONS

There is much more to be said about performance measurement. We have only provided an introduction to some of the modern approaches. The hallmark of all such procedures is the explicit consideration of risk. The evidence is, by now, almost overwhelming: Measures that account for risk (although perhaps imperfectly) are generally superior to those that do not. This is widely recognized in the academic community and, increasingly, in the investment community. Several firms now offer performance measurement services using procedures similar to those described here, and at least one has gone well beyond, to provide detailed diagnoses of the performance of components of each portfolio. Risk-adjusted performance is clearly here to stay.

REFERENCES

This paper draws from the previous work of a number of authors. The interested reader will find more details in the following references (arranged in chronological order):

Treynor, Jack L., "How to Rate Management of Investment Funds," *Harvard Business Review* (January-February, 1965) pp. 63-75.

Sharpe, William F., "Mutual Fund Performance," *Journal of Business* (January, 1966) pp. 119-138.

Jensen, Michael C., "The Performance of Mutual Funds in the Period 1945-1964," *The Journal of Finance* (May, 1968) pp. 389-416.

Fama, Eugene F., *Risk and the Evaluation of Pension Fund Portfolio Performance*, (Park Ridge, Ill.: Bank Administration Institute, 1968).

Jensen, Michael C., "Risk, the Pricing of Capital Assets and the Evaluation of Investment Portfolios," *Journal of Business* (April, 1969) pp. 167-247.

Sharpe, William F., *Portfolio Theory and Capital Markets*, (McGraw-Hill, 1970).

Williamson, J. Peter, *Investments: New Analytic Techniques* (Praeger Publishers, 1970).

Fama, Eugene F., "Components of Investment Performance," *The Journal of Finance* (June, 1972) pp. 551-567.

Merrill Lynch, Pierce, Fenner and Smith, Inc., "Merrill Lynch Presents IPA: Investment Performance Analysis," 1973.

29

COMPONENTS OF INVESTMENT PERFORMANCE *

Eugene F. Fama

I. INTRODUCTION

This paper suggests methods for evaluating investment performance. The topic is not new. Important work has been done by Sharpe [21, 22], Treynor [23], and Jensen [13, 14]. This past work has been concerned with measuring performance in two dimensions, return and risk. That is, how do the returns on the portfolios examined compare with the returns on other "naively selected" portfolios with similar levels of risk?

This paper suggests somewhat finer breakdowns of performance. For example, methods are presented for distinguishing the part of an observed return that is due to ability to pick the best securities of a given level of risk ("selectivity") from the part that is due to predictions of general market price movements ("timing"). The paper also suggests methods for measuring the effects of foregone diversification when an investment manager decides to concentrate his holdings in what he thinks are a few "winners."

Finally, most of the available work concentrates on single period evaluation schemes. Since almost all of the relevant theoretical material can be presented in this context, much of the analysis here is likewise concerned with the one-period case. Eventually, however, a multiperiod model that allows evaluations both on a period-by-period and on a cumulative basis is presented.

II. FOUNDATIONS

The basic notion underlying the methods of performance evaluation to be presented here is that the returns on managed portfolios can be judged relative to those of "naively selected" portfolios with similar levels of risk. For purposes of exposition, the definitions of a "naively selected" portfolio and of "risk" are obtained from the two-parameter market equilibrium model of Sharpe [20], Lintner [15, 16], Mossin [18] and Fama [10, 11]. But it is well to note that the two-parameter model just provides a convenient and somewhat familiar set of naively selected or "benchmark" portfolios against which the investment performance of managed portfolios can be

* Research on this paper was supported by a grant from the National Science Foundation.

evaluated. As indicated later, other risk-return models could be used to obtain benchmark portfolios consistent with the same general methods of performance evaluation.

In the simplest one-period version of the two-parameter model, the capital market is assumed to be perfect—that is, there are no transactions costs or taxes, and all available information is freely available to everybody—and investors are assumed to be risk averse expected utility maximizers who believe that return distributions for all portfolios are normal. Risk aversion and normally distributed portfolio returns imply that the expected utility maximizing portfolio for any given investor is mean-standard deviation efficient.[1] In addition, investors are assumed to have the same views about distributions of one-period returns on all portfolios (an assumption usually called "homogeneous expectations"), and there is assumed to be a riskless asset f, with both borrowing and lending available to all investors at a riskless rate of interest R_f.

It is then possible to show that in a market equilibrium all efficient portfolios are just combinations of the riskless asset f and one portfolio of risky assets m, where m, called the "market portfolio," contains every asset in the market, each weighted by the ratio of its total market value to the total market value of all assets. That is, if $\tilde{R}_m$, $E(\tilde{R}_m)$ and $\sigma(\tilde{R}_m)$ are the one-period return, expected return, and standard deviation of return for the market portfolio m, and if x is the proportion of investment funds put into the riskless asset f, then all efficient portfolios are formed according to [2]

$$\tilde{R}_x = xR_f + (1 - x)\tilde{R}_m \quad x \leq 1 , \tag{1}$$

so that

$$E(\tilde{R}_x) = xR_f + (1 - x)E(\tilde{R}_m) \tag{2}$$

$$\sigma(\tilde{R}_x) = (1 - x)\sigma(\tilde{R}_m) \tag{3}$$

Geometrically, the situation is somewhat as shown in Figure 1. The curve b m d represents the boundary of the set of portfolios that only include risky assets. But efficient portfolios are along the line from R_f through m. Points below m (that is, $x \geq 0$) involve lending some funds at the riskless rate R_f and putting the remainder in m, while points above m (that is, $x < 0$) involve borrowing at the riskless rate with both the borrowed funds and the initial investment funds put into m.

In this model the equilibrium relationship between expected return and risk for any security j is

$$E(\tilde{R}_j) = R_f + \left[\frac{E(\tilde{R}_m) - R_f}{\sigma(\tilde{R}_m)}\right] \frac{cov(\tilde{R}_j,\tilde{R}_m)}{\sigma(\tilde{R}_m)} \quad (Ex\ ante\ \text{market line}). \tag{4}$$

Here $cov(\tilde{R}_j,\tilde{R}_m)$ is the covariance between the return on asset j and the return on the market portfolio m. In the two-parameter model $\sigma(\tilde{R}_m)$ is a measure of the total risk in the return on the market portfolio m. Since

---

[1] By definition a mean-standard deviation efficient portfolio must have the following property: No portfolio with the same or higher expected one-period return has lower standard deviation of return.

[2] Tildes ($\sim$) are used throughout to denote random variables. When we refer to realized values of these variables, the tildes are dropped.

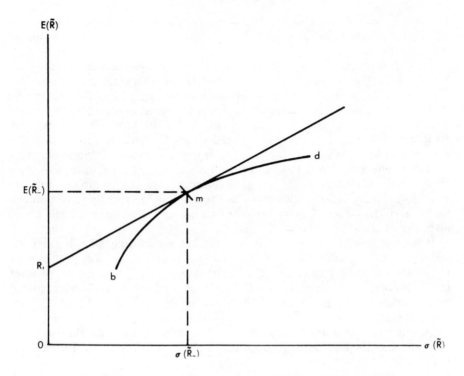

Figure 1. The Efficient Set with Riskless Borrowing and Lending

the only risky assets held by any investor are "shares" of m, it would seem that, from a portfolio viewpoint, the risk of an asset should be measured by its contribution to $\sigma(\tilde{R}_m)$. In fact this contribution is just $\text{cov}(\tilde{R}_j, \tilde{R}_m)/\sigma(\tilde{R}_m)$. Specifically, if x_{jm} is the proportion of asset j, $j = 1$, ..., N, in the market portfolio m

$$\sigma(\tilde{R}_m) = \sum_{j=1}^{N} x_{jm} \frac{\text{cov}(\tilde{R}_j, \tilde{R}_m)}{\sigma(\tilde{R}_m)} \tag{5}$$

In this light (4) is a relationship between expected return and risk which says that the expected return on asset j is the riskless rate of interest R_f plus a risk premium that is $[E(\tilde{R}_m) - R_f]/\sigma(\tilde{R}_m)$, called the market price per unit of risk, times the risk of asset j, $\text{cov}(\tilde{R}_j, \tilde{R}_m)/\sigma(\tilde{R}_m)$.

Equation (4) provides the relationship between expected return and risk for portfolios as well as for individual assets. That is, if x_{jp} is the proportion of asset j in the portfolio p (so that $\sum_{j=1}^{N} x_{jp} = 1$), then multiplying both sides of (4) by x_{jp} and summing over j, we get

$$E(\tilde{R}_p) = R_f + \left[\frac{E(\tilde{R}_m) - R_f}{\sigma(\tilde{R}_m)} \right] \frac{\text{cov}(\tilde{R}_p, \tilde{R}_m)}{\sigma(\tilde{R}_m)} \tag{6}$$

where, of course,

$$\tilde{R}_p = \sum_{j=1}^{N} x_{jp}\tilde{R}_j.$$

But (4) and (6) are expected return-risk relations derived under the assumption that investors all have free access to available information and all have the same views of distributions of returns on all portfolios. In short, the market setting envisaged is a rather extreme version of the "efficient markets" model in which prices at any time "fully reflect" available information. (See, for example [7].) But in the real world a portfolio manager may feel that he has access to special information or he may disagree with the evaluations of available information that are implicit in market prices. In this case the "homogeneous expectations" model under-lying (4) provides "benchmarks" for judging the manager's ability to make better evaluations than the market.

The benchmark or naively selected portfolios are just the combinations of the riskless asset f and the market portfolio m obtained with different values of x in (1). Given the *ex post* or realized return R_m for the market portfolio, for the naively selected portfolios, *ex post* return is just

$$R_x = xR_f + (1 - x)R_m, \tag{7}$$

that is, (1) without the tildes. Moreover,[1]

$$\beta_x = \frac{\text{cov}(\tilde{R}_x,\tilde{R}_m)}{\sigma(\tilde{R}_m)} = \frac{\text{cov}([1-x]\tilde{R}_m,\tilde{R}_m)}{\sigma(\tilde{R}_m)} = (1 - x)\sigma(\tilde{R}_m) = \sigma(\tilde{R}_x). \tag{8}$$

That is, for the benchmark portfolios risk and standard deviation of return are equal. And the result is quite intuitive: In the homogeneous expecta-tions model these portfolios comprise the efficient set, and for efficient portfolios risk and return dispersion are equivalent.

For the naively selected portfolios, (7) and (8) imply the following relationship between risk β_x and *ex post* return R_x

$$R_x = R_f + \left(\frac{R_m - R_f}{\sigma(\tilde{R}_m)}\right)\beta_x \quad \text{(ex post market line)}. \tag{9}$$

That is, for the naively selected portfolios there is a linear relationship between risk and return that is of precisely the same form as (4) except that the expected returns that appear in (4) are replaced by realized returns in (9).

In the performance evaluation models to be presented, (9) provides the benchmarks against which the returns on "managed" portfolios are judged. These "benchmarks" are used in a sequence of successively more complex suggested performance evaluation settings. First we are concerned with one-period models in which a portfolio is chosen by an investor at the beginning of the period, its performance is evaluated at the end of the period, and there are no intermediate cash flows or portfolio decisions. Then we consider multiperiod evaluation models that also allow for fund flows and portfolio decisions between evaluation dates. We find, though, that almost all of the important theoretical concepts in performance evalua-tion can be treated in a one-period context.

---

[1] Henceforth the risk $\text{cov}(\tilde{R}_j,\tilde{R}_m)/\sigma(\tilde{R}_m)$ of an asset or portfolio j will be denoted as β_j.

III. The Benchmark Portfolios: Some Empirical Issues

Before introducing the evaluation models, however, it is well to discuss some of the empirical issues concerning the so-called "market lines" (4) and (9). Since this paper is primarily theoretical, and since empirical problems are best solved in the context of actual applications, the discussion of empirical issues will be brief.

First of all, to use (9) as a benchmark for evaluating *ex post* portfolio returns requires estimates of the risk, β_p, and dispersion, $\sigma(\tilde{R}_p)$, of the managed portfolios as well as an estimate of $\sigma(\tilde{R}_m)$, the dispersion of the return on the market portfolio. If performance evaluation is to be objective, it must be possible to obtain reliable estimates of these parameters from historical data. Fortunately, Blume's evidence [3, 4, 5] suggests that at least for portfolios of ten or more securities, β_p and $\sigma(\tilde{R}_p)$ seem to be fairly stationary over long periods of time (e.g., ten years), and likewise for $\sigma(\tilde{R}_m)$.

But other empirical evidence is less supportive. Thus throughout the analysis here normal return distributions are assumed, though the data of Fama [6], Blume [3], Roll [19] and others suggest that actual return distributions conform more closely to non-normal two-parameter stable distributions. It would conceptually be a simple matter to allow for such distributions in the evaluation models (cf. Fama [11]). But since the goal here is just to suggest some new approaches to performance evaluation, for simplicity attention will be restricted to the normal model.

Finally, the available empirical evidence (e.g., Friend and Blume [12], Miller and Scholes [17], and Black, Jensen and Scholes [2]) indicates that the average returns over time on securities and portfolios deviate systematically from the predictions of (4). Though the observed average return-risk relationships seem to be linear, the tradeoff of risk for return (the price of risk) is in general less than would be predicted from (4) or (9). In short, the evidence suggests that (4) and (9) do not provide the best benchmarks for the average return-risk tradeoffs available in the market from naively selected portfolios.

Even these results do little damage to the performance evaluation models. They indicate that other benchmark portfolios than those that lead to (9) might be more appropriate, but given such alternative "naively selected" portfolios, the analysis could proceed in exactly the manner to be suggested. For example, Black, Jensen and Scholes [2] compute the risks (β's) for each security on the New York Stock Exchange, rank these, and then form ten portfolios, the first comprising the .1N securities with the highest risks and the last comprising the .1N securities with the lowest risks, where N is the total number of securities. They find that over various subperiods from 1931–65 the average monthly returns among these portfolios are highly correlated, and when plotted against risk the average returns on these portfolios lie along a straight line with slope somewhat less than would be implied by the "price of risk" in (4) or (9). As benchmarks for performance evaluation models, their empirical risk-return lines seem to be natural alternatives to (9). And with these alternative benchmarks, performance evaluation could proceed precisely as suggested here. But again, for simplicity, we continue on with the more familiar benchmarks given by (9).

It would be misleading, however, to leave the impression that all important empirical problems relevant in the application of performance evaluation models have been solved. To a large extent the practical value of such models depends on the empirical validity of the model of market equilibrium —that is, the expected return-risk relationship—from which the benchmark or "naively selected" portfolios are derived. And though much interesting work is in progress, it would be rash to claim that all empirical issues concerning models of market equilibrium have been settled.

For example, an important (and unsolved) empirical issue in models of market equilibrium is the time interval or "market horizon period" over which the hypothetical expected return-risk relationship is presumed to hold. Does the model hold continuously (instant by instant), or is the market horizon period some discrete time interval? This is an important issue from the viewpoint of performance evaluation since if the market horizon period is discrete, evaluation periods should be chosen to coincide with horizon periods.

The evidence of Friend and Blume [12] and that of Black, Jensen, and Scholes [2] suggests that meaningful relationships between average returns and risk can be obtained from monthly data, while the evidence of Miller and Scholes [17] indicates that this is not true for annual periods. Within these broad bounds, however, the sensitivity of risk-return relations to the time interval chosen remains an open issue.

But unsolved empirical questions are hardly a cause for disheartenment. It is reasonable to expect that some of the empirical issues will be solved in the process of applying the theory. And in any case, application of a theory invariably involves some empirical approximations. The available evidence on performance evaluation, especially Jensen's [13, 14], suggests that the required approximations need not prevent even more complicated evaluation models from yielding useful results.

IV. PERFORMANCE EVALUATION IN A ONE-PERIOD MODEL WHEN THERE ARE NO INTRAPERIOD FUND FLOWS

Let $V_{a,t}$ and $V_{a,t+1}$ be the total market values at t and t + 1 of the actual (a = actual) portfolio chosen by an investment manager at t. With all portfolio activity occurring at t and t +1, that is, assuming that there are no intraperiod fund flows, the one-period percentage return on the portfolio is

$$R_a = \frac{V_{a,t+1} - V_{a,t}}{V_{a,t}}.$$

One benchmark against which the return R_a on the chosen portfolio can be compared is provided by $R_x(\beta_a)$, which by definition is the return on the combination of the riskless asset f and the market portfolio m that has risk β_x equal to β_a, the risk of the chosen portfolio a. One measure of the performance of the chosen portfolio a is then

$$\text{Selectivity} = R_a - R_x(\beta_a). \tag{10}$$

That is, *Selectivity* measures how well the chosen portfolio did relative to a naively selected portfolio with the same level of risk.

Selectivity, or some slight variant thereof, is the sole measure of performance in the work of Sharpe [21, 22], Treynor [23] and Jensen [13, 14]. But more detailed breakdowns of performance are possible. Thus consider

$$\overbrace{[R_a - R_f]}^{\text{Overall Performance}} = \overbrace{[R_a - R_x(\beta_a)]}^{\text{Selectivity}} + \overbrace{[R_x(\beta_a) - R_f]}^{\text{Risk}}. \quad (11)$$

That is, the *Overall Performance* of the portfolio decision is the difference between the return on the chosen portfolio and the return on the riskless asset. The Overall Performance is in turn split into two parts, *Selectivity* (as above) and *Risk*. The latter measures the return from the decision to take on positive amounts of risk.[1] It will be determined by the level of risk chosen (the value of β_a) and, from (9), by the difference between the return on the market portfolio, R_m, and the return on the riskless asset, R_f.

These performance measures are illustrated in Figure 2. The curly bracket along the vertical axis shows Overall Performance which in this case is positive. The breakdown of performance given by (11) can be found along the vertical line from β_a. In this example, *Selectivity* is positive: A portfolio was chosen that produced a higher return than the corresponding "naively selected" portfolio along the market line with the same level of risk. *Risk* is also positive, as it is whenever a positive amount of risk is taken and the return on the market portfolio turns out to be higher than the riskless rate.

A. *Selectivity: A Closer Look*

If the portfolio chosen represents the investor's total assets, in the mean-variance model the risk of the portfolio to him is measured by $\sigma(\tilde{R}_a)$, the standard deviation of its return. And the risk of the portfolio to the investor, $\sigma(\tilde{R}_a)$, will be greater than what might now be called its "market risk," β_a, as long as the portfolio's return is less than perfectly correlated with the return on the market portfolio.

To see this note that the correlation coefficient k_{am} between R_a and R_m is

$$k_{am} = \frac{\text{cov}(\tilde{R}_a, \tilde{R}_m)}{\sigma(\tilde{R}_a)\sigma(\tilde{R}_m)}.$$

It follows that

$$\beta_a = \frac{\text{cov}(\tilde{R}_a, \tilde{R}_m)}{\sigma(\tilde{R}_m)} = k_{am}\sigma(\tilde{R}_a)$$

so that $\beta_a \lessgtr \sigma(\tilde{R}_a)$ depending on whether $k_{am} \lessgtr 1$.[2]

---

[1] For greater descriptive accuracy, we should, of course, say "return from risk" or even "return from bearing risk," rather than just Risk. Likewise, "return from selectivity," would be more descriptive than Selectivity. But (hopefully) the shorter names save space without much loss of clarity.

[2] In fact the naively selected portfolios are the only ones whose returns are literally perfectly correlated with those of the market portfolio (cf. equation (8)). But the theoretical work of Fama [9] and the empirical work of Black, Jensen and Scholes [2] suggests that the return on any well-diversified portfolio will be very highly correlated with R_m.

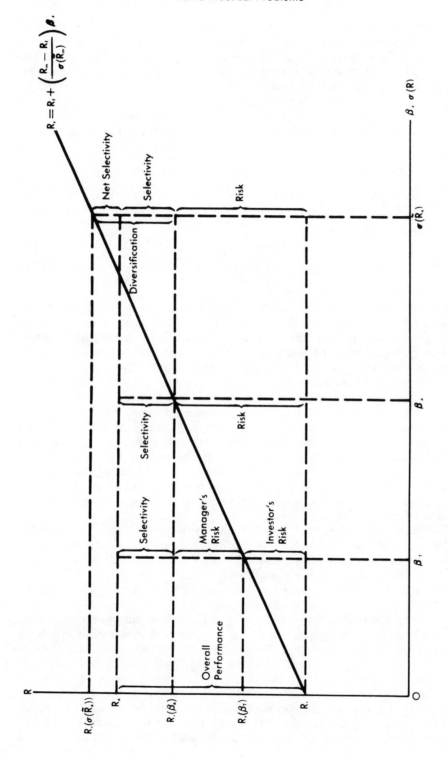

Figure 2. An Illustration of the Performance Measures of Equations (11), (12), and (13).

Intuitively, to some extent the portfolio decision may have involved putting more eggs into one or a few baskets than would be desirable to attain portfolio efficiency—that is, the manager places his bets on a few securities that he thinks are winners. In other words, to the extent that $\sigma(\check{R}_a) > \beta_a$, the portfolio manager decided to take on some portfolio dispersion that could have been diversified away because he thought he had some securities in which it would pay to concentrate resources. The results of such a decision can be evaluated in terms of the following breakdown of Selectivity:

$$\overbrace{[R_a - R_x(\beta_a)]}^{\text{Selectivity}} = \text{Net Selectivity} + \overbrace{[R_x(\sigma(\check{R}_a)) - R_x(\beta_a)]}^{\text{Diversification}}; \quad (12a)$$

or

$$\text{Net selectivity} = \overbrace{[R_a - R_x(\beta_a)]}^{\text{Selectivity}} - \overbrace{[R_x(\sigma(\check{R}_a)) - R_x(\beta_a)]}^{\text{Diversification}}. \quad (12b)$$

By definition, $R_x(\sigma(\check{R}_a))$ is the return on the combination of the riskless asset f and the market portfolio m that has return dispersion equivalent to that of the actual portfolio chosen. Thus *Diversification* measures the extra portfolio return that the manager's winners have to produce in order to make concentration of resources in them worthwhile. If *Net Selectivity* is not positive the manager has taken on diversifiable risk that his winners have not compensated for in terms of extra return.

Note that, as defined in (12), Diversification is always non-negative, so that Net Selectivity is equal to or less than Selectivity. When $R_m > R_f$, Diversification measures the additional return that would just compensate the investor for the diversifiable dispersion (that is, $\sigma(\check{R}_a) - \beta_a$) taken on by the manager. When $R_m < R_f$ (so that the market line is downward sloping), diversification measures the lost return from taking on diversifiable dispersion rather than choosing the naively selected portfolio with market risk *and* standard deviation both equal to β_a, the market risk of the portfolio actually chosen.

The performance measures of (12) are illustrated in Figure 2 along the dashed vertical line from $\sigma(\check{R}_a)$. In the example shown, Selectivity is positive but Net Selectivity is negative. Though the manager chose a portfolio that outperformed the naively selected portfolio with the same level of market risk, his Selectivity was not sufficient to make up for the avoidable risk taken, so that Net Selectivity was negative.

The breakdown of Selectivity given by (12) is the only one that is considered here. The rest of section IV is concerned with successively closer examinations of the other ingredient of Overall Performance, Risk. Before moving on, though, we should note that (12) itself is *only* relevant when diversification is a goal of the investor. And this is the case only when the portfolio being evaluated constitutes the investor's entire holdings, and the investor is risk averse. For example, an investor might allocate his funds to many managers, encouraging each only to try to pick winners, with the investor himself carrying out whatever diversification he desires on personal account. In this case Selectivity is the relevant measure of the managers' performance, and the breakdown of Selectivity of (12) is of no concern.

B. *Risk: A Closer Look*

If the investor has a target risk level β_T for his portfolio, the part of *Overall Performance* due to *Risk* can be allocated to the investor and to the portfolio manager as follows:

$$\overbrace{[R_x(\beta_a) - R_f]}^{\text{Risk}} = \overbrace{[R_x(\beta_a) - R_x(\beta_T)]}^{\text{Manager's Risk}} + \overbrace{[R_x(\beta_T) - R_f]}^{\text{Investor's Risk}} \qquad (13)$$

$R_x(\beta_T)$ is the return on the naively selected portfolio with the target level of market risk. Thus *Manager's Risk* is that part of *Overall Performance* and of *Risk* that is due to the manager's decision to take on a level of risk β_a different from the investor's target level β_T, while *Investor's Risk* is that part of Overall Performance that results from the fact that the investor's target level of risk is positive. These performance measures are illustrated in Figure 2 along the dashed vertical line from β_T.

Manager's Risk might in part result from a timing decision. That is, in part at least the manager might have chosen a portfolio with a level of risk higher or lower than the target level because he felt risky portfolios in general would do abnormally well or abnormally poorly during the period under consideration. But if an estimate of $E(\tilde{R}_m)$ is available, a more precise measure of the results of such a timing decision can be obtained.[1] Specifically, making use of the *ex ante* market line of (4)[2] we can subdivide *Risk* as follows:

$$\overbrace{[R_x(\beta_a) - R_f]}^{\text{Risk}} = \left\{ \underbrace{\overbrace{[R_x(\beta_a) - E(\tilde{R}_x(\beta_a))]}^{\text{Manager's Timing}} - \underbrace{[R_x(\beta_T) - E(\tilde{R}_x(\beta_T))]}_{\text{Market Conditions}}}_{\text{Total Timing}} \right\} (14)$$

$$+ \underbrace{[E(\tilde{R}_x(\beta_a)) - E(\tilde{R}_x(\beta_T))]}_{\text{Manager's Exp. Risk}} + \underbrace{[R_x(\beta_T) - R_f]}_{\text{Investor's Risk}}.$$

---

[1] $E(\tilde{R}_m)$ might be estimated from past average returns on the market portfolio m. Alternatively, past data might be used to estimate the average difference between R_m and R_f. In any case, it should become clear that the expected values used must be naive or mechanical estimates (or at least somehow external to those being evaluated), otherwise the value of the timing measures is destroyed.

Admittedly, given the current status of empirical work on the behavior through time of average returns on risky assets, we can at most speculate about the best way to estimate $E(\tilde{R}_m)$. Hopefully empirical work now in progress will give more meaningful guidelines. And perhaps the development of theoretical methods of performance evaluation will itself stimulate better empirical work on estimation procedures. In any case, the discussion in the text should help to emphasize that one cannot obtain precise measures of returns from timing decisions without mechanical or naive estimates of equilibrium expected returns.

[2] That is,

$$E(\tilde{R}_x(\beta_a)) = R_f + \left[\frac{E(\tilde{R}_m) - R_f}{\sigma(\tilde{R}_m)} \right] \beta_a$$

and similarly for $E(\tilde{R}_x(\beta_T))$.

The first three terms here sum to the *Manager's Risk* of (13). *Manager's Expected Risk* is the incremental expected return from the manager's decision to take on a nontarget level of risk. *Market Conditions* is the difference between the return on the naively selected portfolio with the target level of risk and the expected return of this portfolio. It answers the question: By how much did the market deviate from expectations at the target level of risk? *Total Timing* is the difference between the *ex post* return on the naively selected portfolio with risk β_a and the *ex ante* expected return. It is positive when $R_m > E(\check{R}_m)$ (and then more positive the larger the value of β_a), and it is negative when $R_m < E(\check{R}_m)$ (and then more negative the larger the value of β_a). The difference between *Total Timing* and *Market Conditions* is *Manager's Timing*: it measures the excess of *Total Timing* over timing performance that could have been generated by choosing the naively selected portfolio with the target level of risk. *Manager's Timing* is only positive when the sign of the difference between β_a and β_T is the same as the sign of the difference between R_m and $E(\check{R}_m)$, that is, when the chosen level of market risk is above (below) the target level and R_m is above (below) $E(\check{R}_m)$. It is thus somewhat more sensitive than *Total Timing* as a measure of the results of a timing decision.

A target level of risk will not always be relevant in evaluating a manager's performance. For example, an investor may allocate his funds to many managers, with the intention that each concentrates on selectivity and/or timing, with the investor using borrowing or lending on personal account to attain his desired level of market risk.

If a target level of risk is not relevant but the expected value or *ex ante* market line is still available, a breakdown of *Risk* similar to (14) can be obtained by treating the market portfolio (or the appropriate proxy) [1] as the target portfolio. That is,

$$
\underbrace{[R_x(\beta_a) - R_f]}_{\text{Risk}} = \left\{ \underbrace{\overbrace{[R_x(\beta_a) - E(\check{R}_x(\beta_a))]}^{\text{Manager's Timing}}}_{\text{Total Timing}} - \underbrace{[R_m - E(\check{R}_m)]}_{\text{Market Conditions}} \right\} \quad (15)
$$

$$
+ \underbrace{[E(\check{R}_x(\beta_a)) - E(\check{R}_m)]}_{\substack{\text{Expected Deviation} \\ \text{from Market}}} + \underbrace{[R_m - R_f]}_{\text{Market Risk}}.
$$

The idea here is that even in the absence of a target level of risk, the measure of *Manager's Timing* must be standardized for the deviation of the market return from the expected market return, that is, for the "average" spread between the *ex post* and *ex ante* market lines.

Finally, the goal of this paper is mainly to suggest some ways in which available theoretical and empirical results on portfolio and asset pricing models can provide the basis of useful procedures for performance evaluation. But the various breakdowns of performance suggested above are hardly unique. Indeed any breakdown chosen should be tailored to the

---

[1] For example, if one were faced with portfolio evaluation in a multiperiod context, one might use the average of past levels of market risk chosen by the manager as a proxy for the target risk level when the latter is not explicitly available.

situation at hand. For example, if a target level of risk is relevant but the subdivision of Risk given by (14) is regarded as too complicated, then the approximate effects of the timing decision might still be separated out as follows:

$$
\overbrace{[R_x(\beta_a) - R_f]}^{\text{Risk}} = \overbrace{[R_x(\beta_a) - E(\tilde{R}_x(\beta_a))]}^{\text{Total Timing}} + \overbrace{[E(\tilde{R}_x(\beta_a)) - E(\tilde{R}_x(\beta_T))]}^{\text{Manager's Expected Risk}}
$$
$$
\tag{16}
$$
$$
+ \overbrace{[E(\tilde{R}_x(\beta_T)) - R_f]}^{\text{Investor's Expected Risk}}.
$$

The one new term here is *Investor's Expected Risk*, which measures the expected contribution to Overall Performance of the investor's decision to have a positive target level of risk. Alternatively if a target level of risk is not relevant for the situation at hand, but an expected value line is available, *Risk* can nevertheless be subdivided as follows,

$$
\overbrace{[R_x(\beta_a) - R_f]}^{\text{Risk}} = \overbrace{[R_x(\beta_a) - E(\tilde{R}_x(\beta_a))]}^{\text{Total Timing}} + \overbrace{[E(\tilde{R}_x(\beta_a)) - R_f]}^{\text{Total Expected Risk}}. \tag{17}
$$

And these few suggestions hardly exhaust the possibilities.

V. Components of Performance: Multiperiod Models with Intraperiod Fund Flows

In the one-period evaluation model presented above, (i) the time at which performance is evaluated is assumed to correspond to the portfolio horizon date, that is, the time when portfolio funds are withdrawn for consumption; and (ii) there are assumed to be no portfolio transactions or inflows and outflows of funds between the initial investment and withdrawal dates, so that there is no reinvestment problem. If in a multiperiod context we are likewise willing to assume that (i) though there are many of them, evaluation dates nevertheless correspond to the dates when some funds are withdrawn for consumption, and (ii) all reinvestment decisions and other portfolio transactions are also made at these same points in time, then generalization of the one-period model to the multiperiod case is straightforward.[1] Indeed the basic procedure could be period-by-period application of the performance measures presented in the one-period model. The major embellishments would not be in the nature of new theory, but rather would arise from the fact that multiperiod performance histories allow statistically more reliable estimates of the various one-period performance measures.

But this pure case is unlikely to be met in any real world application. Often performance evaluation would be carried out by someone with little or no knowledge of the dates when funds are needed for consumption by the portfolio's owner, and often (e.g., in the case of a mutual fund or a pension fund) the portfolio is owned by many different investors with dif-

---

[1] For the development of the underlying models of consumer and market equilibrium for this case see [8].

ferent consumption dates. As a result evaluation dates, withdrawal dates, and reinvestment dates do not usually coincide.

The rest of this paper is concerned with how the concepts of the one-period model must be adjusted to deal with such intraevaluation period (or more simply, intraperiod) fund flows. The procedure is first to present detailed definitions of variables of interest in models involving intraperiod fund flows, and then to talk about actual measures of performance. And it is well to keep in mind that though the analysis is carried out in a multi-period context, the problems to be dealt with arise from intraperiod fund flows. With such fund flows, the same problems would arise in a one-period evaluation model.

A. *Definitions*

Suppose the investment performance of a portfolio is to be evaluated at discrete points in time, but that there can be cash flows between evaluation dates. That is, there can be intraperiod inflows in the form of either cash receipts (dividends, interest) on existing portfolio holdings or net new contributions of capital by new or existing owners. And there can be intraperiod outflows in the form of dividend payments to the portfolio's owner(s) (e.g., a mutual fund declares dividends) or withdrawals of capital (e.g., by a mutual fund's shareholders).

In simplest terms, the major problem with intraperiod cash flows is obtaining a measure of the return on the beginning of period market value of a portfolio that abstracts from the effects of intraperiod new contributions and withdrawals on the end of period value of the portfolio. One approach is what might be called the mutual fund method. Specifically, when performance evaluation is first contemplated, the market value of the portfolio is subdivided into "shares." Subsequently, whenever there are contributions of new capital or withdrawals of capital from the portfolio, the current market value of a share is computed and the number of shares outstanding is adjusted to reflect the effects of the cash flow.[1]

Thus let evaluation dates correspond to integer values of t and define

$V'_{a,t}$ = actual market value of the portfolio at time t. It thus includes the effects of investment of new capital or reinvestment of any cash income received on securities held in the portfolio, and it is net of any dividends paid out to owners or other withdrawals of funds prior to t.

$V_{a,t}$ = market value the portfolio would have had at t if no dividends were paid out to owners since the previous evaluation date. In computing $V_{a,t}$ it is simply assumed that dividends paid to the portfolio's owners were instead reinvested in the entire portfolio. At the beginning of each evaluation period, however, $V_{a,t}$ is set equal to $V'_{a,t}$.

n_t = number of shares outstanding in the portfolio at t. As indicated above, this is adjusted when new capital comes into the portfolio

---

[1] This is in fact the method of accounting used by open end mutual funds. It is also closely related to the "time-weighted rate of return" approach developed by Professor Lawrence Fisher. On this point see [1, Appendix I and p. 218].

and when capital is withdrawn, but it is unaffected by reinvestment of cash income received on securities held or by dividends paid to the portfolio's owners.

$p'_{a,t} = V'_{a,t}/n_t$ = actual market value at t of a share in the portfolio.

$p_{a,t}$ $V_{a,t}/n_t$ = value of a share at t under the assumption that dividends paid to owners of the portfolio were instead reinvested in the entire portfolio.

$R_{a,t} = (p_{a,t} - p'_{a,t-1})/p'_{a,t-1}$. Assuming t corresponds to an evaluation date, this is the one-period return on a share with reinvestment of all dividends paid on a share since the last evaluation date.

$R_{a,t}$ is an unambiguous measure of the return from $t - 1$ to t on a dollar invested in the portfolio at $t - 1$. This is not to say, however, that it is unaffected by intraperiod fund flows. Such fund flows are usually associated with redistributions of portfolio holdings across securities and these affect the return on a share. Moreover, $R_{a,t}$ as defined above is not the only unambiguous measure of the return from $t - 1$ to t on funds invested in the portfolio at $t - 1$. For example, one could define $R_{a,t} = (p'_{a,t} + d_t - p'_{a,t - 1})/p'_{a,t - 1}$, where d_t is the dividend per share paid during the evaluation period to the portfolio's owners. The more complicated definition, that is, with dividends assumed to be reinvested, is "purer" (especially for the purpose of interportfolio comparisons of performance) in the sense that funds invested at the beginning of a period remain invested for the entire period, but it is less pure in the sense that it assumes a reinvestment policy not actually followed in the portfolio.

The next step is to define prices per share for the benchmark or naively selected portfolios that also take account of intraperiod fund flows.

$p_{xt}(\beta_T)$ = price at t per share of the naively selected portfolio with the target risk level. To avoid double-counting of past performance, at the beginning of any evaluation period (for example, just after an evaluation takes place at $t - 1$) this price is set equal to the price per share of the actual portfolio. Then this amount is invested in the naively selected portfolio with the target risk level, and the behavior of the market value of this portfolio during the evaluation period determines the end-of-period price per share, $p_{xt}(\beta_T)$. Any intraperiod cash income generated by the securities of this naively selected portfolio is assumed to be reinvested in this portfolio.

These conventions for the treatment of beginning-of-period values and intraperiod cash income will be taken to apply in the definitions of all the benchmark portfolios. Thus

$p_t(R_f)$ = price at t per share of the naively selected portfolio obtained by investing all funds available at $t - 1$ in the riskless asset.

The benchmarks provided by $p_{xt}(\beta_T)$ and $p_t(R_f)$ are unaffected by intraperiod fund flows in the actual portfolio. This is not true of the following two benchmarks

$p_{xt}(\beta_a) =$ price at t per share of the naively selected portfolio with market risk equal to that of the actual portfolio. At the beginning of any evaluation period and after any transaction in the actual portfolio during an evaluation period (that is, after any cash flow or exchange of shares in the actual portfolio) the market risk of the actual portfolio is measured, and the current price per share of this benchmark is shifted into the naively selected portfolio with that level of market risk. Thus the value of β_a could be shifting more or less continuously through time as a result of inflows and outflows of funds and decisions to shift the holdings in the portfolio.[1]

$p_{xt}(\sigma(\tilde{R}_a)) =$ price at t per share of the naively selected portfolio with return dispersion equal to that of the actual portfolio. The definition of $p_{xt}(\sigma(\tilde{R}_a))$ is obtained by substituting $\sigma(\tilde{R}_a)$ for β_a in the definition of $p_{xt}(\beta_a)$ above.

Thus $p_{xt}(\beta_a)$ and $p_{xt}(\sigma(\tilde{R}_a))$ take account of changes in β_a and $\sigma(\tilde{R}_a)$ that result from intraperiod fund flows and portfolio shifts. Computationally, keeping track of β_a and $\sigma(\tilde{R}_a)$ in the way required for these benchmarks is not a difficult problem. At any point in time the market risk β_a of the chosen portfolio is just the weighted average of the market risks of the individual assets in the portfolio, where the weights are the proportions of total portfolio market value represented by each asset. Thus if one has estimates of the market risks of the assets from which portfolios are chosen, the value of β_a is updated by combining these with current measures of the weights of individual assets in the chosen portfolio. And a similar procedure can be followed with respect to updating values of $\sigma(\tilde{R}_a)$.[2]

B. *Multiperiod Measures of Performance*

Given the beginning and end-of-period prices per share for these benchmark portfolios, their one-period returns are obtained in the usual way. Then the performance history of a portfolio can be built up (for example) through period-by-period application of the breakdowns given by (11)–(13). Alternatively, one can define performance measures in terms of profit per share rather than return. Thus, in line with (13) and using end of evaluation period prices, define

$$
\overbrace{[p_{a,t} - p_t(R_f)]}^{\substack{\text{Overall}\\\text{Performance}}} = \overbrace{[p_{a,t} - p_{xt}(\beta_a)]}^{\text{Selectivity}} +
$$

$$
\overbrace{[p_{xt}(\beta_a) - p_{xt}(\beta_T)]}^{\text{Manager's Risk}} + \overbrace{[p_{xt}(\beta_T) - p_t(R_f)]}^{\text{Investor's Risk}}. \tag{18}
$$

[1] Indeed even if there are no transactions taking place, the value of β_a shifts continuously through time as a result of shifts in the relative market values of individual securities in the portfolio. Aside from adjusting the value of β_a at the beginning of each evaluation period, we have chosen to ignore the effects of such "non-discretionary" shifts here.

[2] Keeping track of $\sigma(\tilde{R}_a)$ is especially simple if one assumes that returns are generated by the so-called market model. On this, and for additional computational suggestions, see Blume [3, 4, 5].

This type of breakdown can of course be computed both period-by-period and cumulatively. And from such multiperiod histories one can get more reliable measures of a portfolio manager's true abilities than can be obtained from a one-period analysis. For example, one can determine whether his Selectivity is systematically positive or simply randomly positive in some periods.

For some purposes one may wish to compare the multiperiod performance histories of different portfolios. For example, an investment company may be interested in the relative abilities of its different security analysts and portfolio managers. Or an investor who has allocated his funds to more than one manager may be interested in comparing their performances. On a period-by-period basis such performance comparisons can be carried out in terms of percentage returns. Alternatively, if the prices of shares in different portfolios are set equal at the beginning of comparison periods, profit-based performance measures such as (18) could be computed both on a period-by-period basis and cumulatively.

One must not get the impression, however, that all the problems caused by intraperiod fund flows have been solved. Though the performance of a "share" during any given evaluation period (or across many periods) gives an unambiguous picture of the investment history of funds invested in a given portfolio at a given point in time, comparisons of the performances of shares in different portfolios are not completely unambiguous. This is due to the fact that even when things are done on a per share basis, intra-period fund flows necessitate portfolio decisions that usually have some effect on the performance of a share. And when such fund flows occur at different times (and thus during different market conditions) in different portfolios, the observed performances of shares in the portfolios may differ, even if the portfolios are managed by the same person trying to follow the same policies in all of his portfolio decisions. But though such ambiguities seem unavoidable and to some extent unsolvable, their effects on perform-ance comparisons should be minor except in cases where portfolios experi-ence large cash flows (relative to their total market values) in short periods of time and/or when evaluation periods are long.

Finally, if an *ex ante* market line is available to compute expected values through time for the three benchmarks, $p_{xt}(\beta_T)$, $p_{xt}(\beta_a)$ and $p_{xt}(\sigma(\tilde{R}_a))$, then the one-period performance breakdowns of (14)–(17) can be carried out either in terms of returns or market values, and these can be used as the basis of even more detailed multiperiod performance histories.

But we terminate the discussion at this point. We do this not because of a lack of additional interesting problems, but because in the absence of actual applications, suggested solutions become increasingly speculative and thus of less likely usefulness.

VI. Summary

Some rather detailed methods for evaluating portfolio performance have been suggested, and some of the more important problems that would arise in implementing these methods have also been discussed. In general terms. we have suggested that the return on a portfolio can be subdivided into two parts: the return from security selection (Selectivity) and the return from bearing risk (Risk). Various finer subdivisions of both Selectivity and Risk have also been presented.

To a large extent the suggested models can be viewed as attempts to combine concepts from modern theories of portfolio selection and capital market equilibrium with more traditional concepts of what constitutes good portfolio management.

For example, the return from Selectivity is defined as the difference between the return on the managed portfolio and the return on a naively selected portfolio with the same level of market risk. Both the measure of risk and the definition of a naively selected portfolio are obtained from modern capital market theory, but the goal of the performance measure itself is just to test how good the portfolio manager is at security analysis. That is, does he show any ability to uncover information about individual securities that is not already implicit in their prices?

Likewise, traditional discussions of portfolio management distinguish between security analysis and market analysis, the latter being prediction of general market price movements rather than just prediction of the special factors in the returns on individual securities. The various timing measures suggested in this paper provide estimates of the returns obtained from such attempts to predict the market. And modern capital market theory again plays a critical role in defining these estimates.

REFERENCES

1. Bank Administration Institute. *Measuring the Investment Performance of Pension Funds.* Park Ridge, Illinois: B.A.I., 1968.
2. Black, Fisher, Jensen, Michael, and Scholes, Myron. "The Capital Asset Pricing Model: Some Empirical Tests." To appear in *Studies in the Theory of Capital Markets,* edited by Michael Jensen and published by Praeger.
3. Blume, Marshall. "The Assessment of Portfolio Performance." Unpublished Ph.D. dissertation, University of Chicago, 1968.
4. ———. "Portfolio Theory: A Step Toward Its Practical Application." *Journal of Business,* XLIII (April, 1970), 152–173.
5. ———. "On the Assessment of Risk." *Journal of Finance,* XXVI (March, 1971), 1–10.
6. Fama, Eugene F. "The Behavior of Stock Market Prices." *Journal of Business,* XXXVIII (January, 1965), 34–105.
7. ———. "Efficient Capital Markets: A Review of Theory and Empirical Work." *Journal of Finance,* XXV (May, 1970), 383–417.
8. ———. "Multiperiod Consumption-Investment Decisions." *American Economic Review,* XL (March, 1970), 163–174.
9. ———. "Portfolio Analysis in a Stable Paretian Market.' *Management Science,* XII (January, 1965), 404–419.
10. ———. "Risk, Return and Equilibrium: Some Clarifying Comments." *Journal of Finance,* XXIII (March, 1968), 29–40.
11. ———. "Risk, Return, and Equilibrium." *Journal of Political Economy,* LXXIX (January–February, 1971), 30–55.
12. Friend, Irwin, and Blume, Marshall. "Measurement of Portfolio Performance under Uncertainty." *American Economic Review,* XL (September, 1970), 561–575.
13. Jensen, Michael. "The Performance of Mutual Funds in the Period 1945–64." *Journal of Finance,* XXIII (May, 1968), 389–416.
14. ———. "Risk, the Pricing of Capital Assets, and the Evaluation of Investment Portfolios." *Journal of Business,* XLII (April, 1969), 167–247.
15. Lintner, John. "Security Prices, Risk, and Maximal Gains from Diversification." *Journal of Finance,* XX (December, 1965), 587–615.

16. ———. "The Valuation of Risk Assets and the Selection of Risky Investments in Stock Portfolios and Capital Budgets." *Review of Economics and Statistics,* XLVII (February, 1965), 13–37.
17. Miller, Merton, and Scholes, Myron. "Rates of Return in Relation to Risk: A Re-examination of Some Recent Findings." To appear in *Studies in the Theory of Capital Markets,* edited by Michael Jensen and published by Praeger.
18. Mossin, Jan. "Equilibrium in a Capital Asset Market." *Econometrica,* XXXIV (October, 1966), 768–783.
19. Roll, Richard. *The Behavior of Interest Rates: Application of the Efficient Market Model to U.S. Treasury Bills.* New York: Basic Books, Inc., 1970.
20. Sharpe, William F. "Capital Assets Prices: A Theory of Market Equilibrium under Conditions of Risk." *Journal of Finance,* XIX (September, 1964), 425–442.
21. ———. "Mutual Fund Performance." *Journal of Business,* XXXIX (Special Supplement, January, 1966), 119–138.
22. ———. "Risk Aversion in the Stock Market." *Journal of Finance,* XX (September, 1965), 416–422.
23. Treynor, Jack L. "How to Rate Management of Investment Funds." *Harvard Business Review,* XLIII (January–February, 1965), 63, 75.

PART III

VALUATION OF SECURITIES

Valuation Theory

30

INTRODUCTION: WHAT DETERMINES A
SECURITY'S VALUE

Securities sell for different prices relative to current or expected earnings, and these relative prices change almost continuously. Until recently, the study of investments was almost exclusively devoted to the problem of security valuation. Modern theories about efficient markets and portfolio construction have highlighted the importance of other subjects, but security analysis remains a flourishing activity.

The theory of valuation is tantalizing. There is widespread agreement about what determines the value of securities, and what an investor must estimate or forecast in order to discriminate profitably among them. Unfortunately, neither theory nor sages have been able to tell him how to make those estimates or forecasts with superior skill.

A remarkable exposition of the principles of valuation appeared more than thirty years ago in a book by J. B. Williams.[1] Chapter 31 contains a section from that book. Williams points out that the present value of a stock or bond is the discounted stream of benefits it is expected to provide. Williams chose to define present value in terms of a perpetual stream of dividends, but we could equally well express present value as a function of the dividend receipts over a limited number of years and the expected worth of the security at the end of that period. Alternatively, we could define present value in terms of the anticipated stream of earnings and the pay-out rate. There is more room for controversy about the proper discount rate. It is, however, one of those pleasant controversies in which the participants recognize that no one so far knows the right answer, and probably no one ever will. Yet, there is at least general agreement that the rate of discount must recognize that a dollar today is worth more than a dollar tomorrow, and that a certain income stream is worth more than an uncertain one.

The second article in this section is Durand's elegant discussion of the Petersburg paradox. The paradox stems from the fact that a security should theoretically have infinite value if the expected rate of growth in benefits

[1] Williams, J. B. *The Theory of Investment Value*. Cambridge, Massachusetts: Harvard University Press, 1938.

is higher than the rate at which these benefits are discounted. Although it is sometimes assumed that securities with such growth rates exist, no securities of infinite value are currently on the market, or, if they are, they are underpriced. Durand's discussion of the possible resolution of the paradox raises some important issues about the process of valuation. Four principal explanations have been offered. One of these assumes that perpetually high rates of growth are impossible; another, that more distant benefits need to be discounted at a higher rate; the third states that the utility of a growing dividend stream is less than the discounted monetary value; and the fourth, which is not considered by Durand, argues that the required return on securities must rise until their present value matches investors' resources.

The next article (Chapter 33) is one of the classics in the development of the theory of finance. A lively controversy has existed for years about the relative values of a dollar of retained earnings and a dollar of dividends. Will the price of a stock be higher if the dollar is paid to stockholders rather than retained and reinvested by the firm? Miller and Modigliani discuss the logic of the problem and indicate that, in the absence of market imperfections, the two dollars should be valued equally. In the course of their analysis, the authors say a good deal about the effect of a firm's investment and financial decisions on the valuation of its stock.

The final chapter in this section describes the first published, respectable, formal procedure for determining the relative values of common stocks. The authors, Whitbeck and Kisor, show that relative price-earnings ratios depend on the expected growth in earnings, an estimate of risk, and the dividend-payout ratio. Subsequent and more elaborate valuation models differ in technical details, but the same three variables appear in almost all of them. All of these models do very well in explaining the current "structure of share prices" or relative price-earnings ratios. None of them, to our knowledge, does nearly as well in identifying undervalued and overvalued securities. Although the models succeed in identifying the principal things that need to be forecast, they tell us nothing about the vexing problem of how to make these forecasts.

31

EVALUATION BY THE RULE OF PRESENT WORTH

John Burr Williams

I. FUTURE DIVIDENDS, COUPONS, AND PRINCIPAL

Now that we have disposed of the troublesome misconception that stock prices are somehow determined in accordance with a quantity theory of money, we are at last ready to take up the main thesis of this book.

Let us define the investment value of a stock as the present worth of all the dividends [1] to be paid upon it. Likewise let us define the investment value of a bond as the present worth of its future coupons and principal. In both cases, dividends, or coupons and principal, must be adjusted for expected changes in the purchasing power of money. The purchase of a stock or bond, like other transactions which give rise to the phenomenon of interest, represents the exchange of present goods for future goods — dividends, or coupons and principal, in this case being the claim on future goods. To appraise the investment value, then, it is necessary to estimate the future payments. The annuity of payments, adjusted for changes in the value of money itself, may then be discounted at the pure interest rate demanded by the investor. This definition of investment value can be expressed by the following equations: [2]

[1] Cf. Robert F. Wiese, "Investing for True Values," *Barron's*, September 8, 1930, p. 5: "*The proper price of any security, whether a stock or bond, is the sum of all future income payments discounted at the current rate of interest in order to arrive at the present value.*" See also Chapter I, § 2.

[2] *Note for the non-technical reader:* It is not necessary to master all of the algebra in the following chapters to understand the rest of this book, for the text between the equations has been so written as to summarize the argument and make it possible to take the derivation of the formulas for granted. The symbols used in the formulas are defined one by one when first introduced, but for

For stocks —

(1a) $$V_o = \sum_{t=1}^{t=\infty} \pi_t v^t = \pi_1 v + \pi_2 v^2 + \pi_3 v^3 + \cdots$$

where V_o = investment value at start
           π_t = dividend in year t

(2) $v = \dfrac{1}{1+i}$, by definition

           i = interest rate sought by the investor

For bonds —

(1b) $$V_o = \sum_{t=1}^{t=n} \pi_t v^t + C v^n$$

where π_t = coupon in year t
           C = face value, or principal, of bond
           n = number of years to maturity

---

easy reference they are reprinted with explanations in a systematic "Table of Symbols" at the end of the book.

The subscripts 1, 2, 3, etc., attached to the Greek letter π in the equations below signify the first, second, third, etc., value of the variable π. Thus π_1 is the amount of the dividend in the first year, π_2 in the second year, π_3 in the third, etc., and π_t in the tth year, where t means time.

The series of terms $\pi_1 v + \pi_2 v^2 + \pi_3 v^3 + \cdots$ is called an infinite series because there is no end to the number of terms. In this particular series each term is constructed according to the rule that the exponent of the factor v shall be the same as the subscript of the factor π, thus $\pi_3 v^3$, $\pi_t v^t$, etc. In certain special cases the sum of all the terms in an infinite series is a finite number, and not infinity, even though the number of terms is infinite; under these circumstances, the series is said to be convergent. Suffice it to say that a series will often be convergent if each additional term is smaller than the preceding one; any further discussion of convergency would take us too far into higher mathematics.

Two ways of denoting an infinite series are as follows:

$$\pi_1 v + \pi_2 v^2 + \pi_3 v^3 + \cdots\cdots$$

and

$$\sum_{t=1}^{t=\infty} \pi_t v^t$$

The second notation, using the Greek letter Σ, means exactly the same as the first, but is briefer. This notation is read "Summation from t equals one, to

The way in which dividends, or coupons and principal, should be adjusted for changes in the value of money in future years will be discussed later.[3]

2. FUTURE EARNINGS OF STOCKS

Most people will object at once to the foregoing formula for stocks by saying that it should use the present worth of future *earnings*, not future *dividends*.[4] But should not earnings and dividends both give the same answer under the implicit assumptions of our critics? If earnings not paid out in dividends are all successfully reinvested at compound interest for the benefit of the stockholder, as the critics imply, then these earnings should produce dividends later; if not, then they are money lost. Furthermore, if these reinvested earnings will produce dividends, then our formula will take account of them when it takes account of all future dividends; but if they will not, then our formula will rightly refrain from including them in any discounted annuity of benefits.

Earnings are only a means to an end, and the means should not be mistaken for the end. Therefore we must say that a stock derives its value from its dividends, not its earnings. In short, a stock is worth only *what you can get out of it*. Even so spoke the old farmer to his son:

---

t equals infinity, of pi sub t, times v to the tth power." It should be noted that

$$\sum_{t=1}^{t=\infty}$$

is not a factor to be multiplied by the other factors π_t and v^t, but is an operational sign applied to these two factors taken together.

If the series runs from $t = 1$ to $t = n$, as in formula (1b) applying to bonds, the series is a finite series instead of an infinite series, because the number of terms is limited and is given in this case by the number of coupons payable during the life of the bond.

A series of the kind under discussion here, whether finite or infinite, is known as a geometric progression if π_t is constant.

[3] See Chapter VIII, § 2, and Chapter IX.

[4] See also Chapter XXII, "U. S. Steel," especially § 13.

A cow for her milk,
A hen for her eggs,
And a stock, by heck,
For her dividends.

An orchard for fruit
Bees for their honey,
And stocks, besides,
For their dividends.

The old man knew where milk and honey came from, but he made no such mistake as to tell his son to buy a cow for her cud or bees for their buzz.

In saying that dividends, not earnings, determine value, we seem to be reversing the usual rule that is drilled into every beginner's head when he starts to trade in the market; namely, that earnings, not dividends, make prices. The apparent contradiction is easily explained, however, for we are discussing permanent investment, not speculative trading, and dividends for years to come, not income for the moment only. Of course it is true that low earnings together with a high dividend for the time being should be looked at askance, but likewise it is true that these low earnings mean low dividends *in the long run*. On analysis, therefore, it will be seen that no contradiction really exists between our formula using dividends and the common precept regarding earnings.

How to estimate the future dividends for use in our formula is, of course, the difficulty. In later chapters ways of making an estimate will be given for such stocks as we now know how to deal with. In so doing, this book seeks to make its most important contribution to Investment Analysis.

3. PERSONAL VS. MARKET RATE OF INTEREST

In applying the foregoing formulas, each investor should use his own personal rate of interest. If one investor demands 10 per cent and another 2 per cent as minimum wages of abstinence, then the same stock or bond will be accorded a lower value by the one than by the other.

The only case in which the market rate of interest should be applied is when the analyst is speaking not for himself personally but for investors in general. Then he should use the pure interest rate as it is expected to be found in the open market in the years to come.[5]

4. COMPOUND INTEREST AT A CHANGING RATE

In the usual discussion of compound interest, it is always assumed that the rate of interest stays the same throughout the period in question. The assumption of a changing rate is never met with, and apparently the possibility of such a thing is not even considered.[6] Yet in theory a changing rate is easily conceivable, and so provision for it, when it occurs, should be made in our formula, thus:

(1c)
$$V_o = \sum_{t=1}^{t=\infty} \pi_t v_1 v_2 \cdots v_t$$

where

(2)
$$v_1 = \frac{1}{1 + i_1}; \; v_2 = \frac{1}{1 + i_2}; \text{ etc.}$$

and

$i_1 =$ interest rate in first year
$i_2 =$ interest rate in second year
$i_t =$ interest rate in tth year

The interest rate i_t in every case is that for one-year loans made at the beginning of the year t, and paid at the end of it.

[5] See Chapter XX, § 21.

[6] An exceptional case in which the possibility of changing interest rates is in fact considered occurs in life insurance, where actuaries of non-participating companies occasionally use a split rate in computing premiums and making other calculations.

The meaning of the equation can be shown by an example. Suppose that investors think that the interest rate for one-year loans, as determined by the equilibrium of the demand and supply for new savings, will be

$$i_1 = \tfrac{1}{2}\% \text{ in } 1937$$
$$i_2 = 1\% \text{ in } 1938$$
$$i_3 = 1\tfrac{1}{2}\% \text{ in } 1939$$
$$i_4 = 2\% \text{ in } 1940$$
$$i_5 = 2\tfrac{1}{2}\% \text{ in } 1941$$
$$i_6 = 3\% \text{ in } 1942$$

Then the present worth of π dollars payable

at the end of 1937 will be $\dfrac{\pi}{(100\tfrac{1}{2}\%)}$

at the end of 1938 will be $\dfrac{\pi}{(100\tfrac{1}{2}\%)\,(101\%)}$

at the end of 1939 will be $\dfrac{\pi}{(100\tfrac{1}{2}\%)\,(101\%)\,(101\tfrac{1}{2}\%)}$

and at the end of t years will be $\pi v_1 v_2 \cdots v_t$.

Long-term interest rates are not a genus wholly distinct from short-term interest rates, and they are not determined separately from short-term rates by independent considerations. Rather, long-term rates are only a thing derived, an average of a special kind, a mere figure of substitution that can be used in place of the series of short-term rates for the years covered. This average is not an ordinary arithmetic average, nor even a geometric average, but is a more complicated average whose formula is given implicitly by the formula for the value of the bond or stock under consideration.[7]

[7] For a further discussion of this point, see Chapter X, "Bonds with Interest Rates Changing."

5. RIGHTS AND ASSESSMENTS

In the case of growing companies,[8] rights to subscribe to additional shares may be offered from time to time, and this will affect the annuity of payments received by the stockholder. Such an issue of rights is equivalent to a stock dividend paid to the stockholder together with an assessment levied on him. Since it is well recognized that a stock dividend, like a split-up, does not change the values behind a given percentage of a company's stock, it follows that an offering of "rights," in so far as it increases the number of shares outstanding but leaves unchanged the percentage owned by each stockholder, adds nothing to the value of the stockholder's equity. And in so far as the offering brings new money into the company's treasury, it is like any other assessment in building up the stockholder's equity. But in so far as the offering draws this money out of the stockholder's pocket, it increases the total cost of his commitment. This latter.fact is clearly reflected by the change in the market worth of an issue of stock when it goes ex-rights. Then the new value of the entire issue becomes greater than that of the old by exactly the amount of new money paid in, and the stockholders' bank accounts become less by the same amount. The operation is thus exactly the opposite of the payment of a cash dividend, in that the payment of dividends re-

[8] Cf. Gabriel A. D. Preinreich, *The Nature of Dividends* (New York: Lancaster Press, Inc., 1935), p. 9: "There are various kinds of corporations. Some are unable to reinvest their earnings, others can do so only in part, still others can use every cent they earn and there are cases where the retention of the entire earnings is insufficient to provide for expansion. It is an important duty of the corporate management to formulate dividend policies which conform to these conditions. A company which can not reinvest its earnings must distribute them; slowly expanding companies will distribute the difference between the total earnings and that portion which can be reinvested, while rapidly expanding companies will not only endeavor to retain all earnings but must in addition attract new capital."

duces the value of the stockholders' investment and increases the value of their bank accounts, while the exercise of rights does the reverse.

But, it may be asked, will not the new money collected by the company be invested at a good profit, and so will not the stock rise as the profits accrue in the future? No, it may be answered, the rise will not occur in the future, because it has already occurred in the past. The price does not ordinarily wait for the profits to accrue, or even for the funds to be collected, but responds as soon as the investment opportunity appears, because usually there is no question as to the power of a company to secure such new money as may be needed to enable it to exploit any new opportunities that may arise. For established companies, the mechanism of issuing rights to take advantage of recognized opportunities for profit is known to be so sure that when the feat is successfully accomplished each time, the market sees no cause for surprised elation. The assessment is viewed as merely a routine operation in the company's growth.

That the word "assessment" used above carries an invidious connotation is true. The word "contribution" could have been used instead, but such a choice of terms would have been less challenging to old views. Just because my opponents call the contribution a "right," I shall retort by calling it an "assessment." [9] In either case, however, innuendo obscures the real facts. Assessments and dividends are opposite aspects of the same thing, differing only with respect to the direction in which the money flows. A company which pays liberal cash dividends and offers frequent rights should not be considered doubly

[9] Cf. Stephen Heard, in *Stock Growth and Discount Tables*, by S. E. Guild (Boston: Financial Publishing Company, 1931). Heard says on page 293, in an appendix written by him for that book, "If, therefore, a stockholder wishes to maintain his position, rights are in reality an assessment."

generous — the usual interpretation of such a policy — but rather as taking back with one hand what it doles out with the other. Its *gross* dividend is offset by an assessment which often makes its *net* dividend very small, or even negative. Nevertheless, such a course does not affect the intrinsic, long-run value of the stock, for, be it remembered, the investment value of a common stock is the present worth of its *net* dividends to perpetuity.

"Rights" should not be treated as income. Methods of evaluation based on such a treatment involve endless difficulties and often certain bad errors. A method which assumes, for instance, that the investor is to sell some of his rights to provide cash for subscribing with the rest makes it necessary to know the price at which these rights can be sold, and thus also the price of the stock at intervals during the period treated. If the past is drawn upon, as is sometimes done, to provide a figure for the worth of rights, then the answer becomes dependent on the general level of stock prices prevailing in the past, with the result that this method of evaluation becomes of no use in estimating the price which should prevail in the future. Not what has been but what should be the price of a given stock is our problem; and we must not use the widely fluctuating and hence mostly incorrect prices of the past as data in our calculations.[10]

The relation which exists between gross dividends, subscriptions, and net dividends may be expressed by the following equation:

(3a)
$$\pi = \kappa - \sigma$$

where

π = pure, or net, dividend in any given year ⎫ per share
κ = actual, or gross, dividend in any given year ⎬ of original
σ = subscription, or assessment in any given year ⎭ stock

[10] Heard's method of adjusting for rights (Guild, *Stock Growth and Discount Tables*, pp. 296–297) would seem to be open to this objection.

If no rights are issued in a particular year, then the assessment, or subscription, in that year will be nil, and $\sigma = 0$. It usually happens that assessments are large but infrequent, hence in the years when they do occur, σ exceeds κ and π becomes temporarily negative. Even though the assessments do not come every year, however, and even though they are spaced at irregular intervals, we may still treat them as items in an annuity (a negative one this time), and then find their present worth, and deduct this sum from the present worth of the gross dividends, to get a figure for the fair value of a stock, thus:

$$(\text{1d}) \qquad V_o = \sum_{t=1}^{t=\infty} \kappa_t v^t - \sum_{t=1}^{t=\infty} \sigma_t v^t$$

From the foregoing discussion of the place of rights in the evaluation of common stocks, it should be clear that nothing but *cash* dividends ought to be included in the formulas for appraisal,[11] and that neither rights nor stock dividends nor option warrants nor any other form of distribution should be considered except in terms of the cash payments to which it may later give rise.

6. THE FORMATION POINT FOR INCOME

If, as argued above, assessments add to the value of one's stockholdings only so much as they subtract from one's bank account, and if dividends do only the opposite, how can either operation add to one's wealth, and how can anyone get rich from his stockholdings? Surely income accrues sometime, somewhere. The behavior of stock prices indicates, and reason confirms, the conclusion that a man's income arises and his wealth increases at that point in the chain between customer and stockholder where

[11] Cf. Chapter XXIV, § 2, dealing with the rights offered on American Telephone.

a company's earnings reach its cash account. When a corporation, after making and paying for its wares and selling them at a profit, finally collects the cash due on them, then at last it realizes its profit. From that moment on, shareholders may take their money at will.[12] The date of distribution does not matter. But when the dividend is once allotted, on that day the stock goes ex-dividend by the amount of the payment, and then what a man gains in cash assets he loses in invested assets.

The reason for drawing the line at the time when profits reach the cash account instead of earlier in their development is because at the cash stage they are no longer among the earning assets of a business. Plant, inventories, receivables, all in their proper proportions, make up a going concern, and are expected to earn a higher return than cash assets. Cash assets, however, if loaned in the money market, yield the same return to all companies, just as they would to their individual stockholders; but invested assets yield varying returns to different companies. A stockholder does not give his cash to a corporation to be lent for him, but to be invested in bricks and mortar, or in current assets. He can do his own lending. When profits are still in the form of invested assets, their final cash equivalent is uncertain, but when they reach the cash account, their exact amount is known, and no variation results from the mere processes of distribution or contribution. Hence the place to draw the line is between cash and other assets.

Of course if cash piles up in a company's treasury, and is then spent again, unwisely this time, that is another story, and the stockholders' wealth decreases when the unwise expenditure is made. It still remains true, nevertheless, that the stockholders' wealth had previously increased when operations succeeded in yielding a cash profit.

[12] Cf. Schabacker, *Stock Market*, p. 348, section entitled "Dividends not a Fundamental Benefit."

7. THE VALUE OF A RIGHT

After each assessment, or offering of new stock, the old shares go ex-rights, and change their value because the number of shares and the cash assets of the company have increased. The value of a right is derived as follows:

Let

M = market price rights-on

$\hat{M}$ = market price ex-rights [13]

M_w = market price of right, or subscription warrant

S = subscription price of new stock offered

N = number of rights required for subscription to one new share

Since

N = total number of shares held before subscription to one new share

NM = total value of shares held before subscription to one new share

and

$N + 1$ = total number of shares held after subscription

$NM + S$ = total value of holdings after subscription

and

$\hat{M}(N + 1)$ = total value of shares held after subscription

therefore

(4a) $\hat{M}(N + 1) = NM + S$

and

(4b) $\hat{M} = \dfrac{NM + S}{N + 1}$, the price of the stock ex-rights [14]

and

(5) $M_w = M - \hat{M}$, the price of a right

[13] The symbol $\hat{M}$ is read "M-cap," and may be thought of as meaning "M after recapitalization in the manner specified."

[14] The application of this formula is illustrated in Chapter XXIV, § 8, dealing with American Telephone.

8. UNCERTAINTY AND THE PREMIUM FOR RISK

If the investor is uncertain about the future, he cannot tell for sure just what is the present worth of the dividends or of the interest and principal he will receive. He can only say that under one set of possible circumstances it will have one value and under another, another. Each of these possible values will have a different probability, however, and so the investor may draw a probability curve to express the likelihood that any given value, V, will prove to be the true value. Thus, if he is appraising a risky twenty-year bond bearing a 4 per cent coupon and selling at 40 to yield 12 per cent to maturity, even though the pure interest seems to be only 4 per cent, he may conclude that the probabilities are as shown in Diagram 6.

The various possible values, V, of the bond, from zero to par, are shown by the abscissae of the curve, while the likelihood, $f(V)$, that any given value will prove to be the true value, is shown by the ordinates. A uni-modal curve, of the form usual for probability curves, could not be used in this case, because it would fail to show the relatively high chances of receiving all or none of the interest and principal.

Whenever the value of a security is uncertain and has to be expressed in terms of probability, the correct value to choose is the mean value,[15]

$$
(6) \qquad \overline{V} = \int_0^\infty \frac{V \ f(V)dV}{\int_0^\infty f(V)dV}
$$

The customary way to find the value of a risky security has always been to add a "premium for risk" to the pure interest rate, and then use the sum as the interest rate for

---

[15] The value of the denominator is always unity because the sum of all the separate probabilities is necessarily one. For values of V above the maximum, $f(V) = 0$.

discounting future receipts. In the case of the bond under discussion, which at 40 would yield 12 per cent to matu-

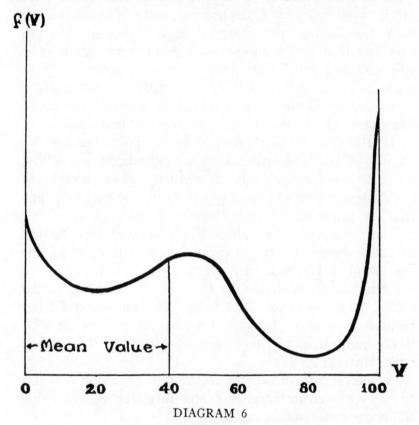

DIAGRAM 6

PROBABILITY CURVE FOR TRUE VALUE

rity,[16] the "premium for risk" is 8 per cent when the pure interest rate is 4 per cent.

Strictly speaking, however, there is no risk in buying the bond in question if its price is right. Given adequate diversification, gains on such purchases will offset losses,

[16] See, for instance, *High Yield Tables of Bond Values* (Boston: Financial Publishing Co., and London: George Rutledge and Sons, Ltd., 1919), p. 83.

and a return at the pure interest rate will be obtained. Thus the *net risk* turns out to be nil. To say that a "premium for risk" is needed is really an elliptical way of saying that payment of the full face value of interest and principal is not to be expected on the average. This leads to the mathematical definition of the "premium for risk" as the value of x that will satisfy the following two equations:

(7)
$$x = i - \hat{\imath}$$

(1e)
$$\bar{V} = \sum_{t=1}^{t=n} \frac{\pi_t}{(1 + i)^t} + \frac{C}{(1 + i)^n}$$

where

$x =$ premium for risk
$i =$ yield, at face value of interest and principal
$\hat{\imath} =$ pure interest rate [17]
$\bar{V} =$ mean of all possible values of bond, as defined in equation (6)
$\pi =$ face value of coupons
$C =$ face value of principal
$n =$ number of years to maturity of bond

If the mean value, $\bar{V}$, is known, equation (1e) can be solved for i, the proper yield. Or, if i is known, the same equation can be solved for $\bar{V}$. The problem can be approached in either way. Most people are used to going about it in the latter way, however, and find it easier to think in terms of interest and principal at face value heavily discounted than in terms of interest and principal at reduced value lightly discounted. They think they can make a better estimate of the proper rate of discount in

[17] Although it would make a more consistent notation to use $\bar{\imath}$ instead of i for the risk-inclusive rate, so as to correspond with $\bar{V}$ for the risk-inclusive value, the more common symbol was made the simpler, and i was used for the risk-inclusive, $\hat{\imath}$ for the riskless, rate of interest.

The economic "premium for risk" is not to be confused with the accounting "premium" on a bond bought above par.

any given situation than of the various possibilities of partial or complete default. If they can, their method has the advantage of being quicker and easier, because it requires the calculation of the present worth of one simple, instead of many varied, annuities. The final choice depends on whether the element of uncertainty in forecasts can be handled by the mind more easily in the one way or the other. Usually the method of using an enlarged discount rate will prove to be the simpler to think of, and so we shall generally employ it in the pages to follow.[18]

9.   SENIOR AND JUNIOR ISSUES OF THE SAME CONCERN

As everyone knows, the risk factor varies between the several securities of the same company. Usually the bonds are considered safer than the shares, with the underlying bonds having a better rating than the junior bonds, and the preferred stock than the common stock. Sometimes, however, this rule appears to be refuted by actual market prices, especially in the case of overcapitalized enterprises that nevertheless enjoy good speculative prospects. With such enterprises, the senior securities usually sell to give a high yield, the common stock a low yield. Yet the market is quite right in thus reversing the usual rule, for if the venture should fail, the bondholders would lose much; but if it should succeed, they would gain little, since all the profits in excess of stipulated interest would go to the common stockholders, who have but little to lose and much to gain. A notable instance of the foregoing was the United States Steel Corporation at the beginning of its career. As discussed in a later chapter,[19] its senior securities sold to yield 6.5 per cent on the average soon after it was

[18] See also the discussion of risk and uncertainty in connection with option warrants and convertible bonds in Chapter XIV, and in connection with government bonds during inflation in Chapter XIX, § 20.

[19] Chapter XXII, § 17, Table 25.

formed, while its stock sold at a high price-earnings ratio, because the success of the new trust was then still in doubt, although the company was thought to have great speculative possibilities.

The proper yield on the *common* stock of such an enterprise is fixed and determined, after the manner of a dependent variable, once the proper yield on the *senior* securities and on the enterprise as a whole are agreed upon, as the following algebraic analysis shows. (For simplicity a horizontal trend of earnings is assumed.)

Let

V_b = investment value of bonds, per share of common
V_c = investment value of stock, per share of common
V_a = investment value of entire enterprise, per share of common

Then

(18a) $\qquad V_a = V_b + V_c$

Likewise let

β = bond interest, per share of common
π = pure dividend, per share of common
i_b = fair interest rate for bonds
i_c = fair interest rate for common stock
i_a = fair interest rate for entire enterprise

Then

(8c) $\qquad V_b = \dfrac{\beta}{i_b}$ (see Chapter VI, § 2. For simplicity, the bonds are assumed to be perpetual bonds.)

(8a) $\qquad V_c = \dfrac{\pi}{i_c}$

(8b) $\qquad V_a = \dfrac{\beta + \pi}{i_a}$

Combining (18a) and (8b), we get

(8d) $\qquad V_b + V_c = \dfrac{\beta + \pi}{i_a}$

and combining (8c) and (8a) with (8d), we get

$$\frac{\beta}{i_b} + \frac{\pi}{i_c} = \frac{\beta + \pi}{i_a}$$

$$\frac{\pi}{i_c} = \frac{\beta + \pi}{i_a} - \frac{\beta}{i_b}$$

whence

$$(8e) \qquad i_c = \frac{\pi}{\dfrac{\beta + \pi}{i_a} - \dfrac{\beta}{i_b}}$$

Q. E. F.

The foregoing formula [20] shows the proper yield for a common stock once the fair yield for the senior securities and the enterprise as a whole have been decided upon.

10. THE LAW OF THE CONSERVATION OF INVESTMENT VALUE

If the investment value of an enterprise as a whole is by definition the present worth of all its future distributions to security holders, whether on interest or dividend account, then this value in no wise depends on what the company's capitalization is. Clearly if a single individual or a single institutional investor owned all the bonds, stocks, and warrants issued by a corporation, it would not matter to this investor what the company's capitalization was.[21] Any earnings collected as interest could not be collected as dividends. To such an individual it would be perfectly obvious that total interest- and dividend-paying power was in no wise dependent on the kind of securities issued to the company's owner. Furthermore, no *change* in the investment value of the enterprise as a whole would

[20] The application of this formula is illustrated in Chapter XXII, § 17, dealing with U. S. Steel.

[21] Except for details concerning the income tax.

result from a *change* in its capitalization. Bonds could be retired with stock issues, or two classes of junior securities (i.e., common stock and warrants) could be combined into one, without changing the investment value of the company as a whole. Such constancy of investment value is analogous to the indestructibility of matter or energy; it leads us to speak of the Law of the Conservation of Investment Value, just as physicists speak of the Law of the Conservation of Matter, or the Law of the Conservation of Energy.

Since market value does not usually conform exactly to investment value, no "conservation of market value" is to be found in general. Only to a rough extent do total market values remain the same regardless of capitalization. The exceptions in practice are important enough to afford many opportunities for profit by promoters and investment bankers.[22]

II. REFUNDING OPERATIONS

If a bond issue matures, or if general interest rates decline enough to allow the replacement of a callable issue with another bearing a lower interest rate, a refunding operation may be undertaken that will alter the corporation's interest charges and change the investment value of its common stock. Since the distributable fraction of a company's quasi-rents is independent of its capital structure and is entirely available for taxes, interest, and dividends, any saving in interest can be used for dividends, and any increase in interest must come out of dividends. Hence the resulting increment or decrement in earnings per share must be capitalized at a different rate from the original earnings per share. If by refunding its bonds at a lower rate and replacing its preferred stock with low-coupon

[22] See discussion of United Corporation in Chapter XXV.

notes, for instance, a company saves a dollar a share in senior charges, then — assuming that dividends are capitalized at 5 per cent, and earnings at 10 per cent (the usual rule of thumb) — it adds twenty dollars a share, and not ten, to the value of its common stock. If, on the other hand, a company is forced to refund a maturing issue at a higher rate, as might happen if its bonds came due during a banking crisis, then the decrease in earnings per share, resulting from the higher interest charges, would have to be capitalized at twenty times, and not at ten as would an ordinary change in earnings.

12.   MARKETABILITY

Marketability, or salability, or liquidity, is an attribute of an investment to which many buyers of necessity attach great importance. Yet it would not be helpful to amend our definition of investment value in such a way as to make it take cognizance of marketability. Risk, to be sure, should be covered by the definition, as done above, but not marketability, for the inclusion of marketability would only lead to confusion. Better to treat intrinsic value as one thing, salability as another. Then we can say, for instance, that a given investment is both cheap and liquid, not that it is cheap partly because it is liquid; the latter phraseology would only raise the question of how much of the cheapness was due to liquidity and how much to other factors. To divorce liquidity, or salability, or marketability, from the concept of investment value is in conformity, moreover, with accepted usage outside the field of investment. In speaking of goods and services, for instance, one does not say that a pound of sugar is cheap at six cents because it is so "salable." Nothing of the sort; for the sugar is bought for consumption and not for resale. By the same token, why should one say that a bond is cheap because it is so salable? For if the bond is bought for investment, as by a life insurance company, it is not intended for resale at all, but for holding to maturity. Of course, if the buyer is a speculator, that is another matter, since investment value is only one of several things considered by a speculator. But even a speculator should not confuse salability with cheapness, any more than he should confuse popularity with cheapness.[23] Just as market price determined by marginal opinion is one thing, and investment value determined by future dividends is another, so also salability is one thing and cheapness another.

Likewise *stability* is a thing distinct from investment value, and from marketability as well. While the expected stability of the price of a security in future years is a consideration of great importance to some investors, particularly banks, yet it is not a component of investment value as the latter term ought to be defined. Many individual investors who buy and hold for income do not need to concern themselves with stability any more than with liquidity; hence to include the concept of stability in the definition of investment value would only make investment value mean something different for each and every investor, according to his own personal need for stability as compared with other things.

In conclusion, therefore, it may be said that neither marketability nor stability should be permitted to enter into the meaning of the term *investment value.*

[23] Cf. Chapter III, § 7.

32

GROWTH STOCKS AND THE PETERSBURG PARADOX *

David Durand

AT A TIME like the present, when investors are avidly seeking opportunities for appreciation, it is appropriate to consider the difficulties of appraising growth stocks. There is little doubt that when other things are equal the forward-looking investor will prefer stocks with growth potential to those without. But other things rarely are equal—particularly in a sophisticated market that is extremely sensitive to growth. When the growth potential of a stock becomes widely recognized, its price is expected to react favorably and to advance far ahead of stocks lacking growth appeal, so that its price-earnings ratio and dividend yield fall out of line according to conventional standards. Then the choice between growth and lack of growth is no longer obvious, and the astute investor must ask whether the market price correctly discounts the growth potential. Is it possible that the market may, at times, pay too much for growth?

Most problems encountered in appraising growth stocks seem to fall into two categories. First there are the practical difficulties of forecasting sales, earnings, and dividends. Then come the theoretical difficulties of reducing these forecasts to present values. For a long time it seems to have been assumed, altogether too casually, that the present value of a forecasted dividend stream could be represented simply as the sum of all expected future payments discounted at a uniform rate. Doubts, however, are beginning to manifest themselves. As early as 1938, J. B. Williams suggested non-uniform discount rates, varying from payment to payment.[1] More recently, Clendenin and Van Cleave have shown that discounting forecasted dividends at a uniform rate in perpetuity may lead to absurdities or paradoxes,

* Financial assistance was received from a grant by the Sloan Research Fund of the School of Industrial Management at Massachusetts Institute of Technology. Intellectual assistance, in the form of ideas, helpful suggestions, and critical comment was received from William Beranek, Joseph N. Froomkin, Myron J. Gordon, J. Arthur Greenwood, Avram Kisselgoff, Paul A. Samuelson, Eli Shapiro, Volkert S. Whitbeck, and from various persons interviewed by the author while touring Wall Street as a guest of the Joint Committee on Education representing the American Securities Business. All this assistance is gratefully acknowledged, but the author must assume full responsibility, since some of the views expressed here are controversial.

1. John B. Williams, *The Theory of Investment Value* (Cambridge, Mass.: Harvard University Press, 1938), pp. 50–60.

Reprinted from *The Journal of Finance*, XII, No. 3 (September, 1957), 348–63, by permission of the author and the publisher.

since implied present values of infinity sometimes result. "We have not yet seen any growth stocks marketed at the price of infinity dollars per share," they remark, "but we shall hereafter be watching. Of course, many investors are skeptical and would probably wish to discount the very large and remote dividends in this perpetually growing series at a high discount rate, thus reducing our computed value per share to a figure somewhat below the intriguing value of infinity."[2] Clendenin and Van Cleave might have made a good point even better had they noticed a remarkable analogy between the appraisal of growth stocks and the famous Petersburg Paradox, which commanded the attention of most of the important writers on probability during the eighteenth and nineteenth centuries.

THE PETERSBURG PARADOX

In 1738 Daniel Bernoulli presented before the Imperial Academy of Sciences in Petersburg a classic paper on probability, in which he

TABLE 1

Sequence of Tosses	Probability	Payment
H.................	$\frac{1}{2}$	1
TH................	$\frac{1}{4}$	2
TTH...............	$\frac{1}{8}$	4
TTTH.............	$\frac{1}{16}$	8
TTTTH............	$\frac{1}{32}$	16

discussed the following problem, attributed to his cousin Nicholas: "Peter tosses a coin and continues to do so until it should land 'heads' when it comes to the ground. He agrees to give Paul one ducat if he gets 'heads' on the very first throw, two ducats if he gets it on the second, four if on the third, eight if on the fourth, and so on, so that with each additional throw the number of ducats he must pay is doubled. Suppose we seek to determine the value of Paul's expectation."[3]

One may easily obtain a solution according to the principles of mathematical expectation by noting the sequence of payments and probabilities in Table 1: Paul's expectation is the sum of the products of probability by payment or

$$\tfrac{1}{2} + \tfrac{2}{4} + \tfrac{4}{8} + \tfrac{8}{16} + \tfrac{16}{32} + \dots.$$

2. John C. Clendenin and Maurice Van Cleave, "Growth and Common Stock Values," *Journal of Finance,* IX (1954), 365–76. Quotation appears on p. 369.

3. Daniel Bernoulli, "Exposition of a New Theory on the Measurement of Risk," *Econometrica,* XXII (1954), 23–36, which is a translation by Dr. Louis Sommer of Bernoulli's paper "Specimen Theoriae Novae de Mensura Sortis," *Commentarii Academiae Scientiarum Imperialis Petropolitanae,* V (1738), 175–92.

If the players agree to terminate the game after n tosses, whether a head shows or not, the series will contain n terms and its sum will be $n/2$; but if they agree to continue without fail until a head shows, as the rules of the game stipulate, then n is infinite and the sum $n/2$ is infinite as well. Thus the principles of mathematical expectation imply that Paul should pay an infinite price to enter this game, but this is a conclusion that virtually no one will accept. A variety of explanations have been given to show that the value of the game to Paul is, in fact, only a finite amount—usually a small finite amount; and all of these explanations are relevant to growth stock appraisal. But before considering them, we shall do well to examine an important modification of the original Petersburg problem.

One modification, which is obvious enough, consists in stipulating some figure other than $\frac{1}{2}$, say $1/(1+\cdot i)$, for the probability of tossing a tail and some figure other than 2, say $1 + g$, for the rate of growth; but this has no particular interest for security appraisal. A more extensive modification, which is of interest, provides for a series of increasing payments, instead of a single lump sum. In effect, Peter agrees to pay D ducats if the first toss is a tail, $D(1 + g)$ if the second is a tail, $D(1 + g)^2$ if the third is a tail, $D(1 + g)^3$ if the fourth is a tail, and so on until a head shows—at which point the game ceases. Then, if the probability of a tail is $1/(1 + i)$, the mathematical expectation is (see Appendix)

$$\frac{D}{1+i} + \frac{D(1+g)}{(1+i)^2} + \frac{D(1+g)^2}{(1+i)^3} + \ldots \ldots \tag{1}$$

This series is arithmetically equivalent to a discounted series of dividend payments, starting at D ducats, growing at a constant rate g, and discounted at rate i.[4] The summation of the series is a simple exercise in actuarial mathematics. The sum of the first n terms is[5]

$$D \frac{1 - (1+g)^n / (1+i)^n}{i - g}, \tag{2}$$

4. Possibly the objection may be raised that series (1) is conceptually quite different from a discounted series of dividends on the grounds that the discount rate ordinarily represents the price paid for waiting in addition to the price paid for assuming risk. To meet this objection, it suffices to discount the dividend series twice, first, by an amount just sufficient to cover the price of waiting, and second, by the amount required to cover the risk of dividend termination when Peter finally tosses a head. Then, the growth rate g in (1) would represent the real growth rate less an adjustment for waiting, and i would represent only the risk of termination.

5. See, for example, Ralph Todhunter, *The Institute of Actuaries' Text-Book on Compound Interest and Annuities-Certain*, 4th ed., revised by R. C. Simmonds and T. P. Thompson (Cambridge, England: University Press, 1937), pp. 48–49.

provided i is different from g; and the sum of an infinite or very large number of terms approaches the very simply formulated quantity

$$\frac{D}{(i-g)} \tag{3}$$

provided that i exceeds g. If, however, $g \geqslant i$, the sum of an infinite number of terms would again be infinite—as in the original Petersburg problem—and a reasonable Paul might again object to paying the price.

The applicability of formulas (2) and (3) to growth stock appraisal is not new. In 1938, for example, J. B. Williams[6] derived (3), or its equivalent, in order to appraise the retained portion of common-stock earnings. He made the derivation, using quite different notation, on essentially the following assumptions: first, that in any year j, earnings per share E_j bear a constant ratio, r, to book value, B_j; second, that dividends, D_j, bear a constant ratio, p, to E_j. Then,

$$B_{j+1} = B_j + E_j(1-p) = B_j[1 + r(1-p)].$$

Hence, book value, dividends, and earnings are all growing at the same constant rate $g = r(1-p)$ and formula (3) can be rewritten

$$\frac{D_1}{i-g} = \frac{E_1 p}{i-g} = \frac{B_1 p r}{i-g}. \tag{3a}$$

Williams realized, of course, that these formulas are valid only when i exceeds g, and he mentioned certain other limitations that are best discussed with some of the proposed solutions for the Petersburg Paradox.

ATTEMPTS TO RESOLVE THE PETERSBURG PARADOX[7]

The many attempts to resolve the paradox, summarized very briefly below, fall mostly into two broad groups: those denying the basic assumptions of the game as unrealistic, and those arguing from additional assumptions that the value of the game to Paul is less than its mathematical expectation.

The basic assumptions of the game are open to all sorts of objections from the practically minded. How, in real life, can the game

6. *Op. cit.*, pp. 87–89, 128–135.

7. For a general history of the paradox, see Isaac Todhunter, *A History of the Mathematical Theory of Probability from the Time of Pascal to that of Laplace* (reprint, New York: G. E. Stechert & Co., 1931), pp. 134, 220–222, 259–262, 275, 280, 286–289, 332, 345, 393, 470. For a briefer treatment, see John Maynard Keynes, *A Treatise on Probability* (London: Macmillan and Co., 1921), pp. 316 ff.

continue indefinitely? For example, Peter and Paul are mortal; so, after a misspent youth, a dissipated middle age, and a dissolute dotage, one of them will die, and the game will cease—heads or no heads. Or again, Peter's solvency is open to question, for the stakes advance at an alarming rate. With an initial payment of one dollar, Peter's liability after only 35 tails exceeds the gold reserve in Fort Knox, and after only three more, it exceeds the volume of bank deposits in the United States and approximately equals the national debt. With this progression, the sky is, quite literally, the limit. Even if Peter and Paul agree to cease after 100 tosses, the stakes, though finite, stagger the imagination.

Despite these serious practical objections, a number of writers chose to accept the assumption of an indefinitely prolonged game at face value, and to direct their attention toward ascertaining the value of such a game to Paul. First among these was the Swiss mathematician Gabriel Cramer, who early in the eighteenth century proposed two arbitrary devices for resolving the Petersburg Paradox by assuming that the utility of money is less than proportional to the amount held.[8] First, if the utility of money is proportional to the amount up to $2^{24} = 166,777,216$ ducats and constant for amounts exceeding 2^{24}, so that the utility of the payments ceases to increase after the 24th toss, Paul's so-called moral expectation is about 13 ducats. Second, if the utility of money is assumed equal to the square root of the amount held, Paul's moral expectation is only about 2.9 ducats. Cramer believed that 2.9 was a more reasonable entrance fee than 13.

A little later and apparently independently, Daniel Bernoulli devised a solution only slightly different from Cramer's. Assuming that the marginal utility of money is inversely proportional to the amount held, he derived a formula that evaluates Paul's expectation in terms of his resources at the beginning of the game. From this formula, which does not lend itself to lightning computation, Bernoulli estimated roughly that the expectation is worth about 3 ducats to Paul when his resources are 10 ducats, about 4 ducats when his resources are 100, and about 6 when his resources are 1000.[9] At this rate, Paul must have infinite resources before he can value his expectation at infinity; but then, even his infinite valuation will constitute only an infinitesimally small fraction of his resources.

An interesting variant of Bernoulli's approach was proposed about

8. Cf. Bernoulli, *op. cit.,* pp. 33 ff.
9. *Ibid.,* pp. 32 ff.

a century later by W. A. Whitworth[10]—at least some of us would consider it a variant, though its author considered it an entirely different argument. Whitworth was, in fact, seeking a solution to the Petersburg Problem that would be free of arbitrary assumptions concerning the utility of money; and he derived a solution by considering the risk of gamblers' ruin, which is always present when players have limited resources. Thus, for example, if A with one dollar matches pennies indefinitely against B with $10, it is virtually certain that one of them will eventually be cleaned out; furthermore, A has 10 chances out of 11 of being the victim. Accordingly, a prudent A might demand some concession in the odds as the price of playing against B. But how much concession? Whitworth attacked this and other problems by assuming a prudent gambler will risk a constant proportion of his resources, rather than a constant amount, on each venture; and he devised a system for evaluating ventures that entail risk of ruin. Applied to the Petersburg Game, this system indicates that Paul's entrance fee should depend upon his resources. Thus Whitworth's solution is reminiscent of Bernoulli's—particularly when one realizes that Whitworth's basic assumption implies an equivalence between a dime bet for A with $1 and a dollar bet for B with $10. Bernoulli, of course, would have argued that the utility of a dime to A was equal to the utility of a dollar to B. Finally, the notion of a prudent gambler seeking to avoid ruin has strong utilitarian undertones, for it implies that the marginal utility of money is high when resources are running out.

But Whitworth's approach—regardless of its utilitarian subtleties—is interesting because it emphasizes the need for diversification. The evaluation of a hazardous venture—be it dice game, business promotion, or risky security—depends not only on the inherent odds, but also on the proportion of the risk-taker's resources that must be committed. And just as the prudent gambler may demand odds stacked in his favor as the price for betting more than an infinitesimal proportion of his resources, so may the prudent portfolio manager demand a greater than normal rate of return (after allowing for the inherent probability of default) as the price of investing more than an infinitesimal proportion of his assets in a risky issue.[11]

10. W. A. Whitworth, *Choice and Chance* (Cambridge, England: Deighton, Bell & Co., 4th edition, enlarged, 1886), chap. 9.

11. Section 87 of the New York Insurance Law states: "Except as more specifically provided in this chapter, no domestic insurer shall have more than ten per cent of its total admitted assets invested in, or loaned upon, the securities of any one institution; . . ." Section 81, subsection 13, places additional restrictions on common stock investment.

Although the preceding historical account of the Petersburg Paradox has been of the sketchiest, it should serve to illustrate an important point. The various proposed solutions, of which there are many, all involve changing the problem in one way or another. Thus some proposals evaluate the cash value of a finite game, even when the problem specifies an infinite game; others evaluate the utility receipts, instead of the cash receipts, of an infinite game; and still others foresake evaluation for gamesmanship and consider what Paul as a prudent man should pay to enter. But although none of these proposals satisfy the theoretical requirements of the problem, they all help to explain why a real live Paul might be loath to pay highly for his infinite mathematical expectation. As Keynes aptly summed it up, "We are unwilling to be Paul, partly because we do not believe Peter will pay us if we have good fortune in the tossing, partly because we do not know what we should do with so much money . . . if we won it, partly because we do not believe we should ever win it, and partly because we do not think it would be a rational act to risk an infinite sum or even a very large sum for an infinitely larger one, whose attainment is infinitely unlikely."[12]

Implications of Petersburg Solutions
for Growth-Stock Appraisal

If instead of tossing coins, Peter organizes a corporation in a growth industry and offers Paul stock, the latter might be deterred from paying the full discounted value by any of the considerations that would deter him from paying the full mathematical expectation to enter the Petersburg game. And again, these considerations fall into two categories: first, those denying the basic assumptions concerning the rate of indefinitely prolonged growth; and, second, those arguing that the value of the stock to Paul is less than its theoretical discounted value.

Underlying J. B. Williams' derivation of formula (3) is the assumption that Peter, Inc., will pay dividends at an increasing rate g for the rest of time. Underlying the derivation in the Appendix is a slightly different assumption: namely, that Peter will pay steadily increasing dividends until the game terminates with the toss of a head, and that the probability of a head will remain forever constant at $i/(1+i)$. Under neither assumption is there any provision for the rate of growth ever to cease or even decline. But astronomers now predict the end of the world within a finite number of years—some-

---

12. Keynes, *op. cit.*, p. 318.

where in the order of 10,000,000,000—and realistic security analysts may question Peter, Inc.'s ability to maintain a steadily increasing dividend rate for anywhere near that long. Williams, in fact, regarded indefinitely increasing dividends as strictly hypothetical, and he worked up formulas for evaluating growth stocks on the assumption that dividends will follow a growth curve (called a logistic by Williams) that increases exponentially for a time and then levels off to an asymptote.[13] This device guarantees that the present value of any dividend stream will be finite, no matter how high the current, and temporary, rate of growth. Clendenin and Van Cleave, though not insisting on a definite ceiling, argued that continued rapid growth is possible only under long-run price inflation.

The assumption of indefinitely increasing dividends is most obviously objectionable when the growth rate equals or exceeds the discount rate $(g \geqslant i)$ and the growth series (1) sums to infinity; then formula (3) does not even apply. If Peter, Inc., is to pay a dividend that increases at a constant rate $g \geqslant i$ per year, it is absolutely necessary, though not sufficient, that he earn a rate on capital, $r = E/B$, that is greater than the rate of discount—more exactly, $r \geqslant i/(1 - p)$. But this situation poses an anomaly, at least for the equilibrium theorist, who argues that the marginal rate of return on capital must equal the rate of interest in the long run. How, then, can Peter, Inc., continually pour increasing quantities of capital into his business and continue to earn on these accretions a rate higher than the standard rate of discount? This argument points toward the conclusion that growth stocks characterize business situations in which limited, meaning finite though not necessarily small, amounts of capital can be invested at rates higher than the equilibrium rate. If this is so, then the primary problem of the growth-stock appraiser is to estimate how long the departure from equilibrium will continue perhaps by some device like Williams' growth curve.

If, for the sake of argument, Paul wishes to assume that dividend growth will continue indefinitely at a constant rate, he can still find reasons for evaluating Peter's stock at somewhat less than its theoretical value just as he found reasons for evaluating his chances in the Petersburg Game at less than the mathematical expectation. The decreasing-marginal-utility approach of Cramer and Bernoulli implies that the present utility value of a growing dividend stream is less than the discounted monetary value, because the monetary value of the large dividends expected in the remote future must be sub-

13. Williams, *op. cit.*, pp. 89–94.

stantially scaled down in making a utility appraisal. Or again, Whitworth's diversification approach implies that a prudent Paul with finite resources can invest only a fraction of his fortfolio in Peter's stock; otherwise he risks ruinous loss. And either argument is sufficient to deter Paul from offering an infinite price, unless, of course, his resources should be infinite.

The Problem of Remote Dividends

There is, moreover, another important limitation on Paul's evaluation of a growth stock that has not arisen in the discussion of the Petersburg Paradox, namely, the remoteness of the large dividend payments. Conventional theory argues that a dividend n years hence is adequately evaluated by the discount factor $1/(1 + i)^n$, but this is open to question when n is very large. The question is, of course, academic for ordinary instruments like long-term bonds or preferred stock, since discounted coupons or preferred dividends many years hence are negligible when discounted in the conventional manner. Thus, for example, if $5.00 a year in perpetuity is worth exactly $100.00 (assuming 5 per cent compounded annually), then $99.24 is attributable to the first 100 payments. But for a stock growing according to series (1) and with $g \geqslant i$, the discounted value of remote dividends, say 10,000 years hence, is anything but negligible; in fact, it may be astronomic. But how should Paul evaluate such remote growth dividends?

If Paul is a real live person without heirs or other incentives for founding an estate, his problem is fairly clearcut. Dividends payable beyond his reasonable life span are useless to him as income, although claims on them may be convertible into useful income through the medium of the market place. At retirement, for example, he might easily be able to increase his income for the remainder of his life by selling long-term securities and buying an annuity. If, however, Paul has heirs, he may look forward several generations and place a very real value on dividends that will be payable to his grandchildren and great-grandchildren. But even here his investment horizon may be limited by the uncertainty of planning for offspring not yet born.

If Paul is a life insurance company, he has a special interest in evaluating remote dividends; for the shades of obligations currently contracted may extend far into the future as the following fanciful though not impossible sketch will indicate. In 1956 John Doe, aged 21, buys for his own benefit a whole life policy containing the customary guaranty of a rate of interest if the insured elects to settle the proceeds in instalments. In 2025, aged 90, John Doe decides to settle this policy on his newborn great-grandson Baby Doe and directs the insurance company to accumulate the proceeds at the guaranteed rate of interest until Baby Doe shall reach the age of 21 and thereupon pay them out to him as a life income, according to the table of guarantied rates in the policy. Encouraged by his monthly checks, Baby Doe now lives to the ripe old age of 105, so that only in 2130 does the insurance company finally succeed in discharging its obligation of 1956, based on the then current forecasts of long-term interest rates.

Even though the case of John Doe may be a bit out of the ordinary, it illustrates forcefully why life insurance companies must concern themselves with dividend income up to perhaps 200 years hence and how a future decline in the earning rate on assets may threaten the solvency of an insurance fund. Although the purchase of long-term bonds is an obvious form of protection against falling interest rates, it is not entirely effective when the liabilities extend too far into the future. To illustrate the difficulty of long-term protection, it will be convenient at this point to introduce a concept called "duration" by Macaulay,[14] which may apply to an individual security, a portfolio of securities, or even to a block of liabilities. Duration, incidentally, must not be confused with a related concept known as "equated time."

The duration of an individual security or a portfolio is the arithmetic mean of the several coupon or maturity dates, each date weighted by the present value at the valuation rate of interest of the expected income on that date. The duration of an E bond or non-interest-bearing note is simply the term to maturity; and the duration of a portfolio consisting, for example, of two $100 E bonds due two years hence and a $500 E bond due five years hence would be

$$\left[\frac{2 \times 200}{(1.03)^2} + \frac{5 \times 500}{(1.03)^5} \right] \div \left[\frac{200}{(1.03)^2} + \frac{500}{(1.03)^5} \right],$$

if evaluated at 3 per cent compounded annually. The duration of an interest-bearing bond is less than the term to maturity, because the long term of the principal payment at maturity must be averaged against the shorter terms of the various coupons. Macaulay's formula for the duration of interest-paying bonds is somewhat complex;

14. F. R. Macaulay, *Some Theoretical Problems Suggested by the Movement of Interest Rates, Bond Yields and Stock Prices in the United States since 1856* (New York: National Bureau of Economic Research, 1938), pp. 44–51.

but for perpetuities, such as Canadian Pacific debenture 4's, it simplifies to $(1 + i)/i$.[15] At $i = .03$, the duration of a perpetuity is therefore about 34 years.

In seeking suitable methods for matching the assets of a fund to its liabilities so as to minimize risk of loss from fluctuations in the interest rate, British actuaries have shown that the possible loss is very small when both present value and duration of the assets equal present value and duration of the liabilities; and, indeed, they have given examples where the "loss" is a small gain for fluctuations either up or down.[16] But although the portfolio manager can ordinarily achieve satisfactory matching by merely selecting long- and short-term bonds in such proportions that their average duration equals that of the liabilities, he runs into difficulty when the duration of the liabilities is exceptionally long. Thus, for example, the duration of the liability of a pension fund with many young workers and only a few pensioners can easily exceed 40 years: and this is too long to be matched by a portfolio consisting wholly of perpetuities, whose duration at current interest rates is only about 30 years. In such a difficulty, however, growth stocks offer a possible solution; for when dividends are growing according to series (1), the duration is longer than a perpetuity. In fact, if we define

$$1 + b = \frac{1 + i}{1 + g}.$$

then $(1 + b)b$ is the duration of the series.[17] Thus growth stocks provide a possible means of increasing the average duration of a portfolio when the composition of the liabilities requires this. W. Perks has, in fact, hinted as much.[18]

15. Macaulay, *op. cit.*, pp. 49–50. In Macaulay's formula for perpetuities (p. 50) let $R = 1 + i$.

16. See, for example, J. B. H. Pegler, "The Actuarial Principles of Investment," *Journal of the Institute of Actuaries* (England), Vol. 74 (1948), pp. 179–211; F. M. Redington, "Review of the Principles of Life-Office Valuations," *ibid.*, Vol. 78 (1952), pp. 286–340; G. V. Bayley and W. Perks, "A Consistent System of Investment and Bonus Distribution for a Life Office," *ibid.*, Vol. 79 (1953), pp. 14–73; A. T. Haynes and R. J. Kirton, "The Financial Structure of a Life Office," *Transactions of the Faculty of Actuaries* (Scotland), Vol. 21 (1953), pp. 141–218; D. J. Robertson and I. L. B. Sturrock, "Active Investment Policy Related to the Holding of Matched Assets," *ibid.*, Vol. 22 (1954), pp. 36–96. Also see Paul A. Samuelson, "The Effect of Interest Rate Increases on the Banking System," *American Economic Review*, XXXV (1945), 16–27, especially p. 19.

Interest of the British in this subject, which seems to be greater than that of the Americans, may be due in part to their relative freedom from liability for policy loans. Although the British companies are prepared to make such loans, they are not forced to do so.

17. This can be proved by using Macaulay's method of finding the duration of a perpetuity and making the substitution $b = i$.

18. See his remarks following the paper by Redington, *op. cit.*, p. 327.

There is, in fact, no theoretical limit to the duration of a stock with dividends growing as in (1). When $g = .05$ and $i = .06$, say, the duration is approximately 100 years; and as the difference between g and i decreases, durations of 1,000 years, 10,000 years, or even 1,000,000 years might result. Moreover, when $g \geqslant i$, $b \leqslant 0$ and formula $(1 + b)/b$ is no longer valid; then the duration is infinite as well as the present value. But although securities with a duration of 100 years might be useful to British life companies for increasing average duration of pension fund assets, or for providing protection against contingencies illustrated by the case of John Doe above, securities with much greater duration would begin to lose appeal. The essential characteristic of a very long duration is that the security holder or his legatees must expect to wait a long time before the security begins to pay a substantial return; and with those hypothetical securities having infinite duration, the legatees must literally expect to wait forever. Even the most forward looking of investors, who are probably those who leave bequests to such institutions as universities and religious organizations, cannot afford to look that far into the future; for, to paraphrase Keynes, it would not be a rational act to risk an infinite sum or even a very large sum for an infinitely larger one, whose attainment is infinitely remote. In effect, the very remote dividends in series (1) cannot be worth their actuarially discounted value when g is large; whether they are worth it when g is small is probably academic, for then the discounted value will be negligible.

To allow for various uncertainties in evaluating dividends in the very remote future, Clendenin and Van Cleave made a significant suggestion, namely, to increase the discount rate applicable to the more remote dividends. The difficulty, of course, is to find some reasonable, objective basis for setting up an appropriate schedule of rates. To illustrate their suggestion, Clendenin and Van Cleave worked out valuations for hypothetical securities by discounting the first twenty years of dividends at 4 per cent, the second twenty at 6 per cent, the third twenty at 8 per cent, and considering all subsequent dividends as worthless. But although such a schedule, totally disregarding all dividends after 60 years, might appeal to a man aged 40 without heirs, it would not appeal to insurance companies and pension managers, who have to look forward 150 to 200 years; and it would certainly not appeal to the loyal alumnus, who wishes to leave a bequest to alma mater. But the essential point is that by setting up a schedule of discount rates that increase fast enough to render very remote dividends negligible, one can assure himself that the present value of any increasing stream of dividends will be finite. And although many investors would object to neglecting dividends after 60 years, few would object to neglecting them after 600.

SUMMARY AND IMPLICATIONS FOR SECURITY APPRAISAL IN GENERAL

There are, to sum up, a number of potent reasons any one of which suffices to dissuade Paul from paying an infinite price for a growth stock under even the most favorable circumstances, namely when $g \geqslant i$ and the sum of series (1) is infinite. Moreover, these reasons do not lose all their force when $g < i$ and the sum of (1) is finite. In appraising any growing stream of dividends, Paul might wish to make provision for eventual decline and perhaps cessation of the growth rate, as suggested by J. B. Williams; he might adjust large dividends to allow for the decreasing marginal utility of money, somewhat in the manner of Cramer and Bernoulli; or again he might apply Whitworth's reasoning and scale down his valuation to a sum he can afford to risk, given his resources; or finally he might, following Clendenin and Van Cleave, apply a very high discount rate to remote dividends that have no significance to him. And he might, of course, apply a combination of such approaches.

But, oddly enough, the very fact that Paul has so many good reasons for scaling down the sum of series (1) when g is high, and so many ways to accomplish this end, leaves him with no clear basis for arriving at any precise valuation. Thus, the possible adjustments for the decreasing marginal utility of money are many and varied. Cramer's two proposals yielded very different solutions for the Petersburg Problem and would yield very different appraisals if applied to rapidly growing growth stocks; and Daniel Bernoulli's proposal would yield yet another result. Or again, there are many ways by which Paul can allow for an eventual decline in the current rate of growth, all of which entail major forecasting problems. Williams' formula, for example, which is stated here in the form[19]

$$V = D\left[\frac{(1+g)^n - (1+i)^n}{(g-i)(1+i)^n} + \frac{(2g+i+2gi)(1+g)^n}{i(g+i+gi)(1+i)^n}\right]$$

after the substitution $D = \Pi_0(1+g)$ and some rearrangement, rests on the somewhat restrictive assumption that dividends grow annually at a constant rate g for n years and then taper off exponen-

19. Williams, *op. cit.*, formula (27a), p. 94.

tially to a level equal to exactly twice the dividend in the nth year. Even when the assumptions are acceptable in principle, practical application of the formula may require more accurate information on g, i, and n than one could possibly expect to obtain. This is particularly true when n is large and g is only slightly larger than i; then $g - i$ in the denominator of the first fraction is small and tremendously sensitive to errors in either g or i. Nor is this difficulty peculiar to Williams' formula. Table 2, abridged from Clendenin and Van Cleave,[20] gives the present value of 60 dividend payments discounted at 5 per cent. It is assumed that the initial dividend rate of $1.00 grows at either 4 per cent or 5 per cent for a period of years and then remains constant for the remainder of the 60-year period, after which dividends either cease or are considered worthless. This

TABLE 2

| | RATE OF GROWTH | |
GROWTH PERIOD	5 Per Cent	4 Per Cent
0	$18.93	$18.93
10	$28\frac{1}{4}$	26
20	37	$32\frac{1}{4}$
30	$45\frac{1}{4}$	$37\frac{1}{2}$
40	$52\frac{1}{4}$	$41\frac{1}{2}$
50	$57\frac{3}{4}$	$44\frac{1}{4}$
60	60	$45\frac{1}{2}$

table again illustrates the difficulty of making appraisals without an accurate forecast of the growth rate and the length of the growth period.

More conventional securities such as bonds and preferred stocks, though much less troublesome than growth stocks, still present some of the same difficulties of evaluation, and a single example should make this clear. In evaluating bonds—even bonds of supposedly uniform quality—one must make some adjustment for term to maturity. Ordinarily one does this by summing a discounted series of coupons and principal

$$\frac{C}{1+i_n} + \frac{C}{(1+i_n)^2} + \ldots + \frac{C}{(1+i_n)^n} + \frac{P}{(1+i_n)^n}$$

in which the uniform discount factor depends on the number of years to maturity. Alternatively, however, one could follow the suggestion of Clendenin and Van Cleave, which would entail summing the series

$$\frac{C}{1+i_1} + \frac{C}{(1+i_2)^2} + \frac{C}{(1+i_3)^3} + \ldots + \frac{C}{(1+i_n)^n} + \frac{P}{(1+i_n)^n}$$

20. *Op. cit.*, Table 4, p. 371.

in which each discount factor i_1, i_2, etc. depends on the date of the coupon or principal payment discounted. But whether one prefers the conventional method or the alternative, the issue is clear: one cannot apply a standard discount factor i uniformly to all bonds; some adjustment for the length, or duration, of the payment stream is essential.

The moral of all this is that conventional discount formulas do not provide completely reliable evaluations. Presumably they provide very satisfactory approximations for high-grade, short-term bonds and notes. But as quality deteriorates or duration lengthens, the approximations become rougher and rougher. With growth stocks, the uncritical use of conventional discount formulas is particularly likely to be hazardous; for, as we have seen, growth stocks represent the ultimate in investments of long duration. Likewise, they seem to represent the ultimate in difficulty of evaluation. The very fact that the Petersburg Problem has not yielded a unique and generally acceptable solution to more than 200 years of attack by some of the world's great intellects suggests, indeed, that the growth-stock problem offers no great hope of a satisfactory solution.

APPENDIX

PROOF OF FORMULA (1) FOR PAUL'S EXPECTATION IN THE MODIFIED PETERSBURG GAME

The table below lists a few possible outcomes, with associated probabilities, for the modified Petersburg Game, in which Peter pays Paul a series of dividends according to the number of tails that occur before a head finally shows. There is, of course, an infinite number of such possible outcomes, because every finite

Sequence of Tosses	Prob-ability	Divi-dend	Total Pay (Cumulated Dividends)
H..............	$i/(1+i)$	0	0
TH..............	$i/(1+i)^2$	D	D
TTH.............	$i/(1+i)^3$	$D(1+g)$	$D+D(1+g)$
TTTH..........	$i/(1+i)^4$	$D(1+g)^2$	$D+D(1+g)+D(1+g)^2$

sequence of tails, no matter how long, has a finite, though possibly very small, probability of occurring. It is assumed, moreover, that throughout even the longest sequence, the probability of a tail remains constant at $1/(1+i)$, leaving $i/(1+i)$ as the probability of a head.

Paul's mathematical expectation is obtained by summing the products of probability in the second column by payout in the fourth. Thus, the sequence TTH, for example, has probability $i/(1+i)^3$ and results in the payout of two dividends, D and $D(1 + g)$. The product appears in the table below along with similar products for the sequences H, TH, and TTTH.

Sequence	Product
H.................	0
TH..............	$Di/(1+i)^2$
TTH.............	$[D+D(1+g)]i/(1+i)^3$
TTTH..........	$[D+D(1+g)+D(1+g)^2]i/(1+i)^4$

To sum these products, it is convenient to break them up and to rearrange the parts in powers of $1 + g$. Thus, for example, all elements containing $(1 + g)^2$ form an infinite series

$$\frac{Di\,(1+g)^2}{(1+i)^4}\left[1+\frac{1}{1+i}+\frac{1}{(1+i)^2}+\ldots\right],$$

where the factor in the bracket is a well-known actuarial form having the sum to infinity $(1 + i)/i$. Thus, the sum of all elements in $(1 + g)^2$ is $D(1 + g)^2/(1 + i)^3$, which is one of the terms in series (1). The other terms are obtained in an analogous manner.

33

DIVIDEND POLICY, GROWTH, AND THE VALUATION OF SHARES *

Merton H. Miller † and Franco Modigliani ‡

T HE effect of a firm's dividend policy on the current price of its shares is a matter of considerable importance, not only to the corporate officials who must set the policy, but to investors planning portfolios and to economists seeking to understand and appraise the functioning of the capital markets. Do companies with generous distribution policies consistently sell at a premium over those with niggardly payouts? Is the reverse ever true? If so, under what conditions? Is there an optimum payout ratio or range of ratios that maximizes the current worth of the shares?

Although these questions of fact have been the subject of many empirical studies in recent years no consensus has yet been achieved. One reason appears to be the absence in the literature of a complete and reasonably rigorous statement of those parts of the economic theory of valuation bearing directly on the matter

of dividend policy. Lacking such a statement, investigators have not yet been able to frame their tests with sufficient precision to distinguish adequately between the various contending hypotheses. Nor have they been able to give a convincing explanation of what their test results do imply about the underlying process of valuation.

In the hope that it may help to overcome these obstacles to effective empirical testing, this paper will attempt to fill the existing gap in the theoretical literature on valuation. We shall begin, in Section I, by examining the effects of differences in dividend policy on the current price of shares in an ideal economy characterized by perfect capital markets, rational behavior, and perfect certainty. Still within this convenient analytical framework we shall go on in Sections II and III to consider certain closely related issues that appear to have been responsible for considerable misunderstanding of the role of dividend policy. In particular, Section II will focus on the longstanding debate about what investors "really" capitalize when they buy shares; and Section III on the much mooted relations between price, the rate of growth of

* The authors wish to express their thanks to all who read and commented on earlier versions of this paper and especially to Charles C. Holt, now of the University of Wisconsin, whose suggestions led to considerable simplification of a number of the proofs.

† Professor of finance and economics, University of Chicago.

‡ Professor of economics, Northwestern University.

profits, and the rate of growth of dividends per share. Once these fundamentals have been established, we shall proceed in Section IV to drop the assumption of certainty and to see the extent to which the earlier conclusions about dividend policy must be modified. Finally, in Section V, we shall briefly examine the implications for the dividend policy problem of certain kinds of market imperfections.

I. EFFECT OF DIVIDEND POLICY WITH PERFECT MARKETS, RATIONAL BEHAVIOR, AND PERFECT CERTAINTY

The meaning of the basic assumptions. --Although the terms "perfect markets," "rational behavior," and "perfect certainty" are widely used throughout economic theory, it may be helpful to start by spelling out the precise meaning of these assumptions in the present context.

1. In "perfect capital markets," no buyer or seller (or issuer) of securities is large enough for his transactions to have an appreciable impact on the then ruling price. All traders have equal and costless access to information about the ruling price and about all other relevant characteristics of shares (to be detailed specifically later). No brokerage fees, transfer taxes, or other transaction costs are incurred when securities are bought, sold, or issued, and there are no tax differentials either between distributed and undistributed profits or between dividends and capital gains.

2. "Rational behavior" means that investors always prefer more wealth to less and are indifferent as to whether a given increment to their wealth takes the form of cash payments or an increase in the market value of their holdings of shares.

3. "Perfect certainty" implies complete assurance on the part of every investor as to the future investment program and the future profits of every corporation. Because of this assurance, there is, among other things, no need to distinguish between stocks and bonds as sources of funds at this stage of the analysis. We can, therefore, proceed as if there were only a single type of financial instrument which, for convenience, we shall refer to as shares of stock.

The fundamental principle of valuation.—Under these assumptions the valuation of all shares would be governed by the following fundamental principle: the price of each share must be such that the rate of return (dividends plus capital gains per dollar invested) on every share will be the same throughout the market over any given interval of time. That is, if we let

$d_j(t)$ = dividends per share paid by firm j during period t

$p_j(t)$ = the price (ex any dividend in $t-1$) of a share in firm j at the start of period t,

we must have

$$\frac{d_j(t) + p_j(t+1) - p_j(t)}{p_j(t)} \quad (1)$$
$$= \rho(t) \text{ independent of } j;$$

or, equivalently,

$$p_j(t) = \frac{1}{1+\rho(t)}[d_j(t)+p_j(t+1)] \quad (2)$$

for each j and for all t. Otherwise, holders of low-return (high-priced) shares could increase their terminal wealth by selling these shares and investing the proceeds in shares offering a higher rate of return. This process would tend to drive down the prices of the low-return shares and drive up the prices of high-return shares until the differential in rates of return had been eliminated.

The effect of dividend policy.—The implications of this principle for our problem of dividend policy can be seen somewhat more easily if equation (2) is restated in terms of the value of the enterprise as a whole rather than in terms of the value of an individual share. Dropping the firm subscript j since this will lead to no ambiguity in the present context and letting

$n(t) =$ the number of shares of record at the start of t

$m(t + 1) =$ the number of new shares (if any) sold during t at the ex dividend closing price $p(t + 1)$, so that

$n(t + 1) = n(t) + m(t + 1)$

$V(t) = n(t) p(t) =$ the total value of the enterprise and

$D(t) = n(t) d(t) =$ the total dividends paid during t to holders of record at the start of t,

we can rewrite (2)

$$V(t) = \frac{1}{1+\rho(t)} [D(t) + n(t) p(t+1)]$$

$$= \frac{1}{1+\rho(t)} [D(t) + V(t+1)$$

$$- m(t+1) p(t+1)]. \quad (3)$$

The advantage of restating the fundamental rule in this form is that it brings into sharper focus the three possible routes by which current dividends might affect the current market value of the firm $V(t)$, or equivalently the price of its individual shares, $p(t)$. Current dividends will clearly affect $V(t)$ via the first term in the bracket, $D(t)$. In principle, current dividends might also affect $V(t)$ indirectly via the second term, $V(t + 1)$, the new ex dividend market value. Since $V(t + 1)$ must depend only on future and not on past events, such could be the case, however, only if both (a) $V(t + 1)$ were a function of future dividend policy and (b) the current distribution $D(t)$ served to convey some otherwise unavailable information as to what that future dividend policy would be. The first possibility being the relevant one from the standpoint of assessing the effects of dividend policy, it will clarify matters to assume, provisionally, that the future dividend policy of the firm is known and given for $t + 1$ and all subsequent periods and is independent of the actual dividend decision in t. Then $V(t + 1)$ will also be independent of the current dividend decision, though it may very well be affected by $D(t + 1)$ and all subsequent distributions. Finally, current dividends can influence $V(t)$ through the third term, $-m(t + 1) p(t + 1)$, the value of new shares sold to outsiders during the period. For the higher the dividend payout in any period the more the new capital that must be raised from external sources to maintain any desired level of investment.

The fact that the dividend decision effects price not in one but in these two conflicting ways—directly via $D(t)$ and inversely via $-m(t) p(t + 1)$—is, of course, precisely why one speaks of there being a dividend policy *problem*. If the firm raises its dividend in t, given its investment decision, will the increase in the cash payments to the current holders be more or less than enough to offset their lower share of the terminal value? Which is the better strategy for the firm in financing the investment: to reduce dividends and rely on retained earnings or to raise dividends but float more new shares?

In our ideal world at least these and related questions can be simply and immediately answered: the two dividend effects must always exactly cancel out so that the payout policy to be followed in t will have *no* effect on the price at t.

We need only express $m(t+1) \cdot p(t+1)$ in terms of $D(t)$ to show that such must indeed be the case. Specifically, if $I(t)$ is the given level of the firm's investment or increase in its holding of physical assets in t and if $X(t)$ is the firm's total net profit for the period, we know that the amount of outside capital required will be

$$m(t+1)p(t+1) = I(t)$$
$$- [X(t) - D(t)]. \quad (4)$$

Substituting expression (4) into (3), the $D(t)$ cancel and we obtain for the value of the firm as of the start of t

$$V(t) \equiv n(t)p(t)$$
$$= \frac{1}{1+\rho(t)}[X(t)-I(t)+V(t+1)]. \quad (5)$$

Since $D(t)$ does not appear directly among the arguments and since $X(t)$, $I(t)$, $V(t+1)$ and $\rho(t)$ are all independent of $D(t)$ (either by their nature or by assumption) it follows that the current value of the firm must be independent of the current dividend decision.

Having established that $V(t)$ is unaffected by the current dividend decision it is easy to go on to show that $V(t)$ must also be unaffected by any future dividend decisions as well. Such future decisions can influence $V(t)$ only via their effect on $V(t+1)$. But we can repeat the reasoning above and show that $V(t+1)$—and hence $V(t)$—is unaffected by dividend policy in $t+1$; that $V(t+2)$—and hence $V(t+1)$ and $V(t)$—is unaffected by dividend policy in $t+2$; and so on for as far into the future as we care to look. Thus, we may conclude that given a firm's investment policy, the dividend payout policy it chooses to follow will affect neither the current price of its shares nor the total return to its shareholders.

Like many other propositions in economics, the irrelevance of dividend policy, given investment policy, is "obvious, once you think of it." It is, after all, merely one more instance of the general principle that there are no "financial illusions" in a rational and perfect economic environment. Values there are determined solely by "real" considerations— in this case the earning power of the firm's assets and its investment policy— and not by how the fruits of the earning power are "packaged" for distribution.

Obvious as the proposition may be, however, one finds few references to it in the extensive literature on the problem.[1] It is true that the literature abounds with statements that in some "theoretical" sense, dividend policy ought not to count; but either that sense is not clearly specified or, more frequently and especially among economists, it is (wrongly) identified with a situation in which the firm's internal rate of return is the same as the external or market rate of return.[2]

A major source of these and related misunderstandings of the role of the dividend policy has been the fruitless concern and controversy over what investors "really" capitalize when they buy shares. We say fruitless because as we shall now proceed to show, it is actually possible to derive from the basic principle of valuation (1) not merely one, but several valuation formulas each starting from one of the "classical" views of what is being capitalized by investors. Though differing somewhat in outward appearance, the various formulas can be shown to be equivalent in all essential respects including, of course, their implication that dividend policy is irrelevant. While the

[1] Apart from the references to it in our earlier papers, especially [16], the closest approximation seems to be that in Bodenborn [1, p. 492], but even his treatment of the role of dividend policy is not completely explicit. (The numbers in brackets refer to references listed below, pp. 432–33).

[2] See below p. 424.

controversy itself thus turns out to be an empty one, the different expressions do have some intrinsic interest since, by highlighting different combinations of variables they provide additional insights into the process of valuation and they open alternative lines of attack on some of the problems of empirical testing.

II. WHAT DOES THE MARKET "REALLY" CAPITALIZE?

In the literature on valuation one can find at least the following four more or less distinct approaches to the valuation of shares: (1) the discounted cash flow approach; (2) the current earnings plus future investment opportunities approach; (3) the stream of dividends approach; and (4) the stream of earnings approach. To demonstrate that these approaches are, in fact, equivalent it will be helpful to begin by first going back to equation (5) and developing from it a valuation formula to serve as a point of reference and comparison. Specifically, if we assume, for simplicity, that the market rate of yield $\rho(t) = \rho$ for all t,[3] then, setting $t = 0$, we can rewrite (5) as

$$V(0) = \frac{1}{1+\rho}[X(0) - I(0)] \\ + \frac{1}{1+\rho} V(1). \quad (6)$$

Since (5) holds for all t, setting $t = 1$ permits us to express $V(1)$ in terms of $V(2)$ which in turn can be expressed in terms of $V(3)$ and so on up to any arbitrary terminal period T. Carrying out these substitutions, we obtain

$$V(0) = \sum_{t=0}^{T-1} \frac{1}{(1+\rho)^{t+1}}[X(t) - I(t)] \\ + \frac{1}{(1+\rho)^T} V(T). \quad (7)$$

In general, the remainder term $(1+\rho)^{-T} \cdot V(T)$ can be expected to approach zero

as T approaches infinity[4] so that (7) can be expressed as

$$V(0) = \lim_{T \to \infty} \sum_{t=0}^{T-1} \frac{1}{(1+\rho)^{t+1}} \\ \times [X(t) - I(t)], \quad (8)$$

which we shall further abbreviate to

$$V(0) = \sum_{t=0}^{\infty} \frac{1}{(1+\rho)^{t+1}}[X(t) - I(t)]. \quad (9)$$

The discounted cash flow approach.— Consider now the so-called discounted cash flow approach familiar in discussions of capital budgeting. There, in valuing any specific machine we discount at the market rate of interest the stream of cash receipts generated by the machine; plus any scrap or terminal value of the machine; and minus the stream of cash outlays for direct labor, materials, repairs, and capital additions. The same approach, of course, can also be applied to the firm as a whole which may be thought of in this context as simply a large, composite machine.[5] This ap-

---

[3] More general formulas in which $\rho(t)$ is allowed to vary with time can always be derived from those presented here merely by substituting the cumbersome product

$$\prod_{\tau=0}^{t}[1+\rho(\tau)] \quad \text{for} \quad (1+\rho)^{t+1}.$$

[4] The assumption that the remainder vanishes is introduced for the sake of simplicity of exposition only and is in no way essential to the argument. What is essential, of course, is that $V(0)$, i.e., the sum of the two terms in (7), be finite, but this can always be safely assumed in economic analysis. See below, n. 14.

[5] This is, in fact, the approach to valuation normally taken in economic theory when discussing the value of the *assets* of an enterprise, but much more rarely applied, unfortunately, to the value of the liability side. One of the few to apply the approach to the shares as well as the assets is Bodenhorn in [1], who uses it to derive a formula closely similar to (9) above.

proach amounts to defining the value of the firm as

$$V(0) = \sum_{t=0}^{T-1} \frac{1}{(1+\rho)^{t+1}}$$

$$\times [\mathcal{R}(t) - \mathcal{O}(t)] + \frac{1}{(1+\rho)^T} V(T),$$

(10)

where $\mathcal{R}(t)$ represents the stream of cash receipts and $\mathcal{O}(t)$ of cash outlays, or, abbreviating, as above, to

$$V(0) = \sum_{t=0}^{\infty} \frac{1}{(1+\rho)^{t+1}} [\mathcal{R}(t) - \mathcal{O}(t)]. \quad (11)$$

But we also know, by definition, that $[X(t) - I(t)] = [\mathcal{R}(t) - \mathcal{O}(t)]$ since, $X(t)$ differs from $\mathcal{R}(t)$ and $I(t)$ differs from $\mathcal{O}(t)$ merely by the "cost of goods sold" (and also by the depreciation expense if we wish to interpret $X(t)$ and $I(t)$ as net rather than gross profits and investment). Hence (11) is formally equivalent to (9), and the discounted cash flow approach is thus seen to be an implication of the valuation principle for perfect markets given by equation (1).

The investment opportunities approach. —Consider next the approach to valuation which would seem most natural from the standpoint of an investor proposing to buy out and operate some already-going concern. In estimating how much it would be worthwhile to pay for the privilege of operating the firm, the amount of dividends to be paid is clearly not relevant, since the new owner can, within wide limits, make the future dividend stream whatever he pleases. For him the worth of the enterprise, as such, will depend only on: (a) the "normal" rate of return he can earn by investing his capital in securities (i.e., the market rate of return); (b) the earning power of the physical assets currently held by the firm; and (c) the opportunities, if any, that the firm offers for making additional investments in real assets that will yield more than the "normal" (market) rate of return. The latter opportunities, frequently termed the "good will" of the business, may arise, in practice, from any of a number of circumstances (ranging all the way from special locational advantages to patents or other monopolistic advantages).

To see how these opportunities affect the value of the business assume that in some future period t the firm invests $I(t)$ dollars. Suppose, further, for simplicity, that starting in the period immediately following the investment of the funds, the projects produce net profits at a constant rate of $\rho^*(t)$ per cent of $I(t)$ in each period thereafter.[6] Then the present worth as of t of the (perpetual) stream of profits generated will be $I(t) \rho^*(t)/\rho$, and the "good will" of the projects (i.e., the difference between worth and cost) will be

$$I(t) \frac{\rho^*(t)}{\rho} - I(t) = I(t) \left[\frac{\rho^*(t) - \rho}{\rho} \right].$$

The present worth as of now of this future "good will" is

$$I(t) \left[\frac{\rho^*(t) - \rho}{\rho} \right] (1+\rho)^{-(t+1)},$$

and the present value of all such future opportunities is simply the sum

$$\sum_{t=0}^{\infty} I(t) \frac{\rho^*(t) - \rho}{\rho} (1+\rho)^{-(t+1)}.$$

Adding in the present value of the (uniform perpetual) earnings, $X(0)$, on the as-

---

[6] The assumption that $I(t)$ yields a uniform perpetuity is not restrictive in the present certainty context since it is always possible by means of simple, present-value calculations to find an equivalent uniform perpetuity for any project, whatever the time shape of its actual returns. Note also that $\rho^*(t)$ is the *average* rate of return. If the managers of the firm are behaving rationally, they will, of course, use ρ as their cut-off criterion (cf. below p. 418). In this event we would have $\rho^*(t) \geq \rho$. The formulas remain valid, however, even where $\rho^*(t) < \rho$.

sets currently held, we get as an expression for the value of the firm

$$V(0) = \frac{X(0)}{\rho} + \sum_{t=0}^{\infty} I(t)$$

$$\times \frac{\rho^*(t) - \rho}{\rho}(1+\rho)^{-(t+1)}. \qquad (12)$$

To show that the same formula can be derived from (9) note first that our definition of $\rho^*(t)$ implies the following relation between the $X(t)$:

$$X(1) = X(0) + \rho^*(0) I(0),$$

$$\cdots \cdots \cdots \cdots \cdots \cdots \cdots \cdots$$

$$X(t) = X(t-1) + \rho^*(t-1) I(t-1)$$

and by successive substitution

$$X(t) = X(0) + \sum_{\tau=0}^{t-1} \rho^*(\tau) I(\tau),$$

$$t = 1, 2 \ldots \infty .$$

Substituting the last expression for $X(t)$ in (9) yields

$$V(0) = [X(0) - I(0)] (1+\rho)^{-1}$$

$$+ \sum_{t=1}^{\infty} \left[X(0) + \sum_{\tau=0}^{t-1} \rho^*(\tau) I(\tau) \right.$$

$$\left. - I(t) \right](1+\rho)^{-(t+1)}$$

$$= X(0) \sum_{t=1}^{\infty} (1+\rho)^{-t}$$

$$- I(0)(1+\rho)^{-1}$$

$$+ \sum_{t=1}^{\infty} \left[\sum_{\tau=0}^{t-1} \rho^*(\tau) I(\tau) - I(t) \right]$$

$$\times (1+\rho)^{-(t+1)}$$

$$= X(0) \sum_{t=1}^{\infty} (1+\rho)^{-t}$$

$$+ \sum_{t=1}^{\infty} \left[\sum_{\tau=0}^{t-1} \rho^*(\tau) I(\tau) - I(t-1) \right.$$

$$\left. \times (1+\rho) \right](1+\rho)^{-(t+1)}.$$

The first expression is, of course, simply a geometric progression summing to $X(0)/\rho$, which is the first term of (12). To simplify the second expression note that it can be rewritten as

$$\sum_{t=0}^{\infty} I(t) \left[\rho^*(t) \sum_{\tau=t+2}^{\infty} (1+\rho)^{-\tau} \right.$$

$$\left. - (1+\rho)^{-(t+1)} \right].$$

Evaluating the summation within the brackets gives

$$\sum_{t=0}^{\infty} I(t) \left[\rho^*(t) \frac{(1+\rho)^{-(t+1)}}{\rho} \right.$$

$$\left. - (1+\rho)^{-(t+1)} \right]$$

$$= \sum_{t=0}^{\infty} I(t) \left[\frac{\rho^*(t) - \rho}{\rho} \right](1+\rho)^{-(t+1)},$$

which is precisely the second term of (12).

Formula (12) has a number of revealing features and deserves to be more widely used in discussions of valuation.[7] For one thing, it throws considerable light on the meaning of those much abused terms "growth" and "growth stocks." As can readily be seen from (12), a corporation does not become a "growth stock" with a high price-earnings ratio merely because its assets and earnings are growing over time. To enter the glamor category, it is also necessary that $\rho^*(t) > \rho$. For if $\rho^*(t) = \rho$, then however large the growth in assets may be, the second term in (12) will be zero and the firm's price-earnings ratio would not rise above a humdrum $1/\rho$. The essence of "growth," in short, is not expansion, but the existence of opportunities to invest significant quantities of funds at higher than "normal" rates of return.

[7] A valuation formula analogous to (12) though derived and interpreted in a slightly different way is found in Bodenhorn [1]. Variants of (12) for certain special cases are discussed in Walter [20].

Notice also that if $\rho^*(t) < \rho$, investment in real assets by the firm will actually reduce the current price of the shares. This should help to make clear among other things, why the "cost of capital" to the firm is the same regardless of how the investments are financed or how fast the firm is growing. The function of the cost of capital in capital budgeting is to provide the "cut-off rate" in the sense of the minimum yield that investment projects must promise to be worth undertaking from the point of view of the current owners. Clearly, no proposed project would be in the interest of the current owners if its yield were expected to be less than ρ since investing in such projects would reduce the value of their shares. In the other direction, every project yielding more than ρ is just as clearly worth undertaking since it will necessarily enhance the value of the enterprise. Hence, the cost of capital or cut-off criterion for investment decisions is simply ρ.[8]

Finally, formula (12) serves to emphasize an important deficiency in many recent statistical studies of the effects of dividend policy (such as Walter [19] or Durand [4, 5]). These studies typically involve fitting regression equations in which price is expressed as some function of current earnings and dividends. A finding that the dividend coefficient is significant—as is usually the case—is then interpreted as a rejection of the hypothesis that dividend policy does not affect

[8] The same conclusion could also have been reached, of course, by "costing" each particular source of capital funds. That is, since ρ is the going market rate of return on equity any new shares floated to finance investment must be priced to yield ρ; and withholding funds from the stockholders to finance investment would deprive the holders of the chance to earn ρ on these funds by investing their dividends in other shares. The advantage of thinking in terms of the cost of capital as the cut-off criterion is that it minimizes the danger of confusing "costs" with mere "outlays."

valuation.

Even without raising questions of bias in the coefficients,[9] it should be apparent that such a conclusion is unwarranted since formula (12) and the analysis underlying it imply only that dividends will not count given current earnings *and growth potential*. No general prediction is made (or can be made) by the theory about what will happen to the dividend coefficient if the crucial growth term is omitted.[10]

The stream of dividends approach.— From the earnings and earnings opportunities approach we turn next to the dividend approach, which has, for some reason, been by far the most popular one in the literature of valuation. This approach too, properly formulated, is an entirely valid one though, of course, not the only valid approach as its more enthusiastic proponents frequently suggest.[11] It does, however, have the disadvantage in contrast with previous approaches of obscuring the role of dividend policy. In particular, uncritical use of the

[9] The serious bias problem in tests using current reported earnings as a measure of $X(0)$ was discussed briefly by us in [16].

[10] In suggesting that recent statistical studies have not controlled adequately for growth we do not mean to exempt Gordon in [8] or [9]. It is true that his tests contain an explicit "growth" variable, but it is essentially nothing more than the ratio of retained earnings to book value. This ratio would not in general provide an acceptable approximation to the "growth" variable of (12) in any sample in which firms resorted to external financing. Furthermore, even if by some chance a sample was found in which all firms relied entirely on retained earnings, his tests then could not settle the question of dividend policy. For if all firms financed investment internally (or used external financing only in strict proportion to internal financing as Gordon assumes in [8]) then there would be no way to distinguish between the effects of dividend policy and investment policy (see below p. 424).

[11] See, e.g., the classic statement of the position in J. B. Williams [21]. The equivalence of the dividend approach to many of the other standard approaches is noted to our knowledge only in our [16] and, by implication, in Bodenhorn [1].

dividend approach has often led to the unwarranted inference that, since the investor is buying dividends and since dividend policy affects the amount of dividends, then dividend policy must also affect the current price.

Properly formulated, the dividend approach defines the current worth of a share as the discounted value of the stream of dividends to be paid on the share in perpetuity. That is

$$p(t) = \sum_{\tau=0}^{\infty} \frac{d(t+\tau)}{(1+\rho)^{\tau+1}}. \quad (13)$$

To see the equivalence between this approach and previous ones, let us first restate (13) in terms of total market value as

$$V(t) = \sum_{\tau=0}^{\infty} \frac{D_t(t+\tau)}{(1+\rho)^{\tau+1}}, \quad (14)$$

where $D_t(t+\tau)$ denotes that portion of the total dividends $D(t+\tau)$ paid during period $t+\tau$, that accrues to the shares of record as of the start of period t (indicated by the subscript). That equation (14) is equivalent to (9) and hence also to (12) is immediately apparent for the special case in which no outside financing is undertaken after period t, for in that case

$$D_t(t+\tau) = D(t+\tau)$$
$$= X(t+\tau) - I(t+\tau).$$

To allow for outside financing, note that we can rewrite (14) as

$$V(t) = \frac{1}{1+\rho} \left[D_t(t) \right.$$
$$\left. + \sum_{\tau=1}^{\infty} \frac{D_t(t+\tau)}{(1+\rho)^{\tau}} \right]$$
$$\quad (15)$$
$$= \frac{1}{1+\rho} \left[D(t) \right.$$
$$\left. + \sum_{\tau=0}^{\infty} \frac{D_t(t+\tau+1)}{(1+\rho)^{\tau+1}} \right].$$

The summation term in the last expression can be written as the difference between the stream of dividends accruing to all the shares of record as of $t+1$ and that portion of the stream that will accrue to the shares newly issued in t, that is,

$$\sum_{\tau=0}^{\infty} \frac{D_t(t+\tau+1)}{(1+\rho)^{\tau+1}} = \left(1 - \frac{m(t+1)}{n(t+1)} \right)$$
$$\quad (16)$$
$$\times \sum_{\tau=0}^{\infty} \frac{D_{t+1}(t+\tau+1)}{(1+\rho)^{\tau+1}}.$$

But from (14) we know that the second summation in (16) is precisely $V(t+1)$ so that (15) can be reduced to

$$V(t) = \frac{1}{1+\rho} \left[D(t) \right.$$
$$+ \left(1 - \frac{m(t+1) p(t+1)}{n(t+1) p(t+1)} \right)$$
$$\left. \times V(t+1) \right] \quad (17)$$
$$= \frac{1}{1+\rho} \left[D(t) + V(t+1) \right.$$
$$\left. - m(t+1) p(t+1) \right],$$

which is (3) and which has already been shown to imply both (9) and (12).[12]

There are, of course, other ways in which the equivalence of the dividend approach to the other approaches might

[12] The statement that equations (9), (12), and (14) are equivalent must be qualified to allow for certain pathological extreme cases, fortunately of no real economic significance. An obvious example of such a case is the legendary company that is expected *never* to pay a dividend. If this were literally true then the value of the firm by (14) would be zero; by (9) it would be zero (or possibly negative since zero dividends rule out $X(t) > I(t)$ but not $X(t) < I(t)$); while by (12) the value might still be positive. What is involved here, of course, is nothing more than a discontinuity at zero since the value under (14) and (9) would be positive and the equivalence of both with (12) would hold if that value were also positive as long as there was some period T, however far in the future, beyond which the firm would pay out $\epsilon > 0$ per cent of its earnings, however small the value of ϵ.

have been established, but the method presented has the advantage perhaps of providing some further insight into the reason for the irrelevance of dividend policy. An increase in current dividends, given the firm's investment policy, must necessarily reduce the terminal value of existing shares because part of the future dividend stream that would otherwise have accrued to the existing shares must be diverted to attract the outside capital from which, in effect, the higher current dividends are paid. Under our basic assumptions, however, ρ must be the same for all investors, new as well as old. Consequently the market value of the dividends diverted to the outsiders, which is both the value of their contribution and the reduction in terminal value of the existing shares, must always be precisely the same as the increase in current dividends.

The stream of earnings approach.— Contrary to widely held views, it is also possible to develop a meaningful and consistent approach to valuation running in terms of the stream of earnings generated by the corporation rather than of the dividend distributions actually made to the shareholders. Unfortunately, it is also extremely easy to mistake or misinterpret the earnings approach as would be the case if the value of the firm were to be defined as simply the discounted sum of future total earnings.[13] The trouble with such a definition is not, as is

[13] In fairness, we should point out that there is no one, to our knowledge, who has seriously advanced this view. It is a view whose main function seems to be to serve as a "straw man" to be demolished by those supporting the dividend view. See, e.g., Gordon [9, esp. pp. 102–3]. Other writers take as the supposed earnings counter-view to the dividend approach not a relation running in terms of the *stream* of earnings but simply the proposition that price is proportional to current earnings, i.e., $V(0) = X(0)/\rho$. The probable origins of this widespread misconception about the earnings approach are discussed further below (p. 424).

often suggested, that it overlooks the fact that the corporation is a separate entity and that these profits cannot freely be withdrawn by the shareholders; but rather that it neglects the fact that additional capital must be acquired at some cost to maintain the future earnings stream at its specified level. The capital to be raised in any future period is, of course, $I(t)$ and its opportunity cost, no matter how financed, is ρ per cent per period thereafter. Hence, the current value of the firm under the earnings approach must be stated as

$$V(0) = \sum_{t=0}^{\infty} \frac{1}{(1+\rho)^{t+1}}$$
$$\times \left[X(t) - \sum_{\tau=0}^{t} \rho I(\tau) \right]. \quad (18)$$

That this version of the earnings approach is indeed consistent with our basic assumptions and equivalent to the previous approaches can be seen by regrouping terms and rewriting equation (18) as

$$V(0) = \sum_{t=0}^{\infty} \frac{1}{(1+\rho)^{t+1}} X(t)$$
$$- \sum_{t=0}^{\infty} \left(\sum_{\tau=t}^{\infty} \frac{\rho I(t)}{(1+\rho)^{\tau+1}} \right)$$
$$= \sum_{t=0}^{\infty} \frac{1}{(1+\rho)^{t+1}} X(t) \quad (19)$$
$$- \sum_{t=0}^{\infty} \frac{1}{(1+\rho)^{t+1}}$$
$$\times \left(\sum_{\tau=0}^{\infty} \frac{\rho I(t)}{(1+\rho)^{\tau+1}} \right).$$

Since the last inclosed summation reduces simply to $I(t)$, the expression (19) in turn reduces to simply

$$V(0) = \sum_{t=0}^{\infty} \frac{1}{(1+\rho)^{t+1}} [X(t) - I(t)], \quad (20)$$

which is precisely our earlier equation (9).

Note that the version of the earnings approach presented here does not depend for its validity upon any special assumptions about the time shape of the stream of total profits or the stream of dividends per share. Clearly, however, the time paths of the two streams are closely related to each other (via financial policy) and to the stream of returns derived by holders of the shares. Since these relations are of some interest in their own right and since misunderstandings about them have contributed to the confusion over the role of dividend policy, it may be worthwhile to examine them briefly before moving on to relax the basic assumptions.

III. EARNINGS, DIVIDENDS, AND GROWTH RATES

The convenient case of constant growth rates.—The relation between the stream of earnings of the firm and the stream of dividends and of returns to the stockholders can be brought out most clearly by specializing (12) to the case in which investment opportunities are such as to generate a constant rate of growth of profits in perpetuity. Admittedly, this case has little empirical significance, but it is convenient for illustrative purposes and has received much attention in the literature.

Specifically, suppose that in each period t the firm has the opportunity to invest in real assets a sum $I(t)$ that is k per cent as large as its total earnings for the period; and that this investment produces a perpetual yield of ρ^* beginning with the next period. Then, by definition

$$X(t) = X(t-1) + \rho^* I(t-1)$$
$$= X(t-1)[1 + k\rho^*] \quad (21)$$
$$= X(0)[1 + k\rho^*]^t$$

and $k\rho^*$ is the (constant) rate of growth of total earnings. Substituting from (21) into (12) for $I(t)$ we obtain

$$V(0) = \frac{X(0)}{\rho} + \sum_{t=0}^{\infty} \left(\frac{\rho^* - \rho}{\rho}\right)$$
$$\times kX(0)[1 + k\rho^*]^t$$
$$\times (1 + \rho)^{-(t+1)} \quad (22)$$
$$= \frac{X(0)}{\rho}\left[1 + \frac{k(\rho^* - \rho)}{1 + \rho}\right.$$
$$\left. \times \sum_{t=0}^{\infty}\left(\frac{1 + k\rho^*}{1 + \rho}\right)^t\right].$$

Evaluating the infinite sum and simplifying, we finally obtain[14]

$$V(0) = \frac{X(0)}{\rho}\left[1 + \frac{k(\rho^* - \rho)}{\rho - k\rho^*}\right]$$
$$= \frac{X(0)(1 - k)}{\rho - k\rho^*}, \quad (23)$$

which expresses the value of the firm as a function of its current earnings, the rate of growth of earnings, the internal rate of return, and the market rate of return.[15]

[14] One advantage of the specialization (23) is that it makes it easy to see what is really involved in the assumption here and throughout the paper that the $V(0)$ given by any of our summation formulas is necessarily finite (cf. above, n. 4). In terms of (23) the condition is clearly $k\rho^* < \rho$, i.e., that the rate of growth of the firm be less than market rate of discount. Although the case of (perpetual) growth rates greater than the discount factor is the much-discussed "growth stock praradox" (e.g. [6]), it has no real economic significance as we pointed out in [16, esp. n. 17, p. 664]. This will be apparent when one recalls that the discount rate ρ, though treated as a constant in partial equilibrium (relative price) analysis of the kind presented here, is actually a variable from the standpoint of the system as a whole. That is, if the assumption of finite value for all shares did not hold, because for some shares $k\rho^*$ was (perpetually) greater than ρ, then ρ would necessarily rise until an over-all equilibrium in the capital markets had been restored.

[15] An interesting and more realistic variant of (22), which also has a number of convenient features from the standpoint of developing empirical tests, can be obtained by assuming that the special invest-

Note that (23) holds not just for period 0, but for every t. Hence if $X(t)$ is growing at the rate $k\rho^*$, it follows that the value of the enterprise, $V(t)$, also grows at that rate.

The growth of dividends and the growth of total profits.—Given that total earnings (and the total value of the firm) are growing at the rate $k\rho^*$ what is the rate of growth of dividends per share and of

---

ment opportunities are available not in perpetuity but only over some finite interval of T periods. To exhibit the value of the firm for this case, we need only replace the infinite summation in (22) with a summation running from $t = 0$ to $t = T - 1$. Evaluating the resulting expression, we obtain

$$V(0) = \frac{X(0)}{\rho} \left\{ 1 + \frac{k(\rho^* - \rho)}{\rho - k\rho^*} \right.$$

$$\left. \times \left[1 - \left(\frac{1 + k\rho^*}{1 + \rho}\right)^T \right] \right\}. \quad (22a)$$

Note that (22a) holds even if $k\rho^* > \rho$, so that the so-called growth paradox disappears altogether. If, as we should generally expect, $(1 + k\rho^*)/(1 + \rho)$ is close to one, and if T is not too large, the right hand side of (22a) admits of a very convenient approximation. In this case in fact we can write

$$\left[\frac{1 + k\rho^*}{1 + \rho}\right]^T \cong 1 + T(k\rho^* - \rho)$$

the approximation holding, if, as we should expect, $(1 + k\rho^*)$ and $(1 + \rho)$ are both close to unity. Substituting this approximation into (22a) and simplifying, finally yields

$$V(0) \cong \frac{X(0)}{\rho} \left[1 + \frac{k(\rho^* - \rho)}{\rho - k\rho^*} \right.$$

$$\left. \times T(\rho - k\rho^*) \right]$$

$$= \left[\frac{X(0)}{\rho} + kX(0) \right. \quad (22b)$$

$$\left. \times \left(\frac{\rho^* - \rho}{\rho}\right) T \right].$$

The common sense of (22b) is easy to see. The current value of a firm is given by the value of the earning power of the currently held assets plus the market value of the special earning opportunity multiplied by the number of years for which it is expected to last.

the price per share? Clearly, the answer will vary depending on whether or not the firm is paying out a high percentage of its earnings and thus relying heavily on outside financing. We can show the nature of this dependence explicitly by making use of the fact that whatever the rate of growth of dividends per share the present value of the firm by the dividend approach must be the same as by the earnings approach. Thus let

$g =$ the rate of growth of dividends per share, or, what amounts to the same thing, the rate of growth of dividends accruing to the shares of the current holders (i.e., $D_0(t) = D_0(0)[1 + g]^t$);

$k_r =$ the fraction of total profits retained in each period (so that $D(t) = X(0)[1 - k_r]$);

$k_e = k - k_r =$ the amount of external capital raised per period, expressed as a fraction of profits in the period.

Then the present value of the stream of dividends to the original owners will be

$$D_0(0) \sum_{t=0}^{\infty} \frac{(1 + g)^t}{(1 + \rho)^{t+1}} = \frac{D(0)}{\rho - g}$$

$$= \frac{X(0)[1 - k_r]}{\rho - g}. \quad (24)$$

By virtue of the dividend approach we know that (24) must be equal to $V(0)$. If, therefore, we equate it to the right-hand side of (23), we obtain

$$\frac{X(0)[1 - k_r]}{\rho - g} = \frac{X(0)[1 - (k_r + k_e)]}{\rho - k\rho^*}$$

from which it follows that the rate of growth of dividends per share and the rate of growth of the price of a share must be[16]

---

[16] That g is the rate of price increase per share as well as the rate of growth of dividends per share fol-

Valuation of Securities

$$g = k\rho^* \frac{1-k_r}{1-k} - k_\bullet\rho \frac{1}{1-k}. \quad (25)$$

Notice that in the extreme case in which all financing is internal ($k_e = 0$ and $k = k_r$), the second term drops out and the first becomes simply $k\rho^*$. Hence the growth rate of dividends in that special

tive $k\rho^*$, if $\rho^* < \rho$ and if the firm pays out a large fraction of its income in dividends. In the other direction, we see from (25) that even if a firm is a "growth" corporation ($\rho^* > \rho$) then the stream of dividends and price per share must grow over time even though $k_r =$

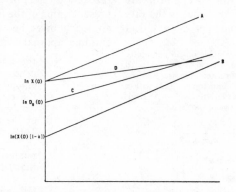

Fig. 1.—Growth of dividends per share in relation to growth in total earnings:
A. Total earnings: $\ln X(t) = \ln X(0) + k\rho^*t$;
B. Total earnings minus capital invested: $\ln [X(t) - I(t)] = \ln X(0) [1 - k] + k\rho^*t$;
  Dividends per share (all financing internal): $\ln D_0(t) = \ln D(0) + gt = \ln X(0) [1 - k] + k\rho^*t$;
C. Dividends per share (some financing external): $\ln D_0(t) = \ln D(0) + gt$;
D. Dividends per share (all financing external): $\ln D_0(t) = \ln X(0) + [(k/1 - k) (\rho^* - \rho)]t$.

case is exactly the same as that of total profits and total value and is proportional to the rate of retention k_r. In all other cases, g is necessarily less than $k\rho^*$ and may even be negative, despite a posi-

lows from the fact that by (13) and the definition of g

$$p(t) = \sum_{\tau=0}^{\infty} \frac{d(t+\tau)}{(1+\rho)^{\tau+1}}$$

$$= \sum_{\tau=0}^{\infty} \frac{d(0)[1+g]^{t+\tau}}{(1+\rho)^{\tau+1}}$$

$$= (1+g)^t \sum_{\tau=0}^{\infty} \frac{d(\tau)}{(1+\rho)^{\tau+1}}$$

$$= p(0)[1+g]^t.$$

0, that is, even though it pays out *all* its earnings in dividends.

The relation between the growth rate of the firm and the growth rate of dividends under various dividend policies is illustrated graphically in Figure 1 in which for maximum clarity the natural logarithm of profits and dividends have been plotted against time.[17]

Line *A* shows the total earnings of the firm growing through time at the constant rate $k\rho^*$, the slope of *A*. Line *B* shows the growth of (1) the stream of total earnings minus capital outlays and

[17] That is, we replace each discrete compounding expression such as $X(t) = X(0) [1 + k\rho^*]^t$ with its counterpart under continuous discounting $X(t) = X(0)e^{k\rho^*t}$ which, of course, yields the convenient linear relation $\ln X(t) = \ln X(0) + k\rho^*t$.

(2) the stream of dividends to the original owners (or dividends per share) in the special case in which all financing is internal. The slope of B is, of course, the same as that of A and the (constant) difference between the curves is simply $\ln(1 - k)$, the ratio of dividends to profits. Line C shows the growth of dividends per share when the firm uses both internal and external financing. As compared with the pure retention case, the line starts higher but grows more slowly at the rate g given by (25). The higher the payout policy, the higher the starting position and the slower the growth up to the other limiting case of complete external financing, Line D, which starts at $\ln X(0)$ and grows at a rate of $(k/1 - k) \cdot (\rho^* - \rho)$.

The special case of exclusively internal financing.—As noted above the growth rate of dividends per share is not the same as the growth rate of the firm except in the special case in which all financing is internal. This is merely one of a number of peculiarities of this special case on which, unfortunately, many writers have based their entire analysis. The reason for the preoccupation with this special case is far from clear to us. Certainly no one would suggest that it is the only empirically relevant case. Even if the case were in fact the most common, the theorist would still be under an obligation to consider alternative assumptions. We suspect that in the last analysis, the popularity of the internal financing model will be found to reflect little more than its ease of manipulation combined with the failure to push the analysis far enough to disclose how special and how treacherous a case it really is.

In particular, concentration on this special case appears to be largely responsible for the widely held view that, even under perfect capital markets, there is an optimum dividend policy for the firm that depends on the internal rate of return. Such a conclusion is almost inevitable if one works exclusively with the assumption, explicit or implicit, that funds for investment come *only* from retained earnings. For in that case *dividend policy* is indistinguishable from *investment policy;* and there *is* an optimal investment policy which does in general depend on the rate of return.

Notice also from (23) that if $\rho^* = \rho$ and $k = k_r$, the term $[1 - k_r]$ can be canceled from both the numerator and the denominator. The value of the firm becomes simply $X(0)/\rho$, the capitalized value of current earnings. Lacking a standard model for valuation more general than the retained earnings case it has been all too easy for many to conclude that this dropping out of the payout ratio $[1 - k_r]$ when $\rho^* = \rho$ must be what is meant by the irrelevance of dividend policy and that $V(0) = X(0)/\rho$ must constitute the "earnings" approach.

Still another example of the pitfalls in basing arguments on this special case is provided by the recent and extensive work on valuation by M. Gordon.[18] Gordon argues, in essense, that because of increasing uncertainty the discount rate $\hat{\rho}(t)$ applied by an investor to a future dividend payment will rise with t, where t denotes not a specific date but rather the distance from the period in which the investor performs the discounting.[19]

[18] See esp. [8]. Gordon's views represent the most explicit and sophisticated formulation of what might be called the "bird-in-the-hand" fallacy. For other, less elaborate, statements of essentially the same position see, among others, Graham and Dodd [11, p. 433] and Clendenin and Van Cleave [3].

[19] We use the notation $\hat{\rho}(t)$ to avoid any confusion between Gordon's purely subjective discount rate and the objective, market-given yields $\rho(t)$ in Sec. I above. To attempt to derive valuation formulas under uncertainty from these purely subjective discount factors involves, of course, an error essentially

Hence, when we use a single uniform discount rate ρ as in (22) or (23), this rate should be thought of as really an average of the "true" rates $\hat{\rho}(t)$ each weighted by the size of the expected dividend payment at time t. If the dividend stream is growing exponentially then such a weighted average ρ would, of course, be higher the greater the rate of growth of dividends g since the greater will then be the portion of the dividend stream arising in the distant as opposed to the near future. But if all financing is assumed to be internal, then $g = k_r \rho^*$ so that given ρ^*, the weighted average discount factor ρ will be an increasing function of the rate of retention k_r which would run counter to our conclusion that dividend policy has no effect on the current value of the firm or its cost of capital.

For all its ingenuity, however, and its seeming foundation in uncertainty, the argument clearly suffers fundamentally from the typical confounding of dividend policy with investment policy that so frequently accompanies use of the internal financing model. Had Gordon not confined his attention to this special case (or its equivalent variants), he would have seen that while a change in dividend policy will necessarily affect the size of the expected dividend payment on the share in any future period, it need not, in the general case, affect either the size of the *total* return that the investor expects during that period or the degree of uncertainty attaching to that total return. As should be abundantly clear by now, a change in dividend policy, given investment policy, implies a change only in the distribution of the total return in any period as between dividends and capital gains. If investors behave rationally, such a change cannot affect market valuations. Indeed, if they valued shares according to the Gordon approach and thus paid a premium for higher payout ratios, then holders of the low payout shares would actually realize consistently higher returns on their investment over any stated interval of time.[20]

Corporate earnings and investor returns. —Knowing the relation of g to $k\rho^*$ we can answer a question of considerable interest to economic theorists, namely: What is the precise relation between the earnings of the corporation in any period $X(t)$ and the total return to the owners of the stock during that period?[21] If we let $G_t(t)$ be the capital gains to the owners during t, we know that

$$D_t(t) + G_t(t) = X(t) \times (1 - k_r) + g V(t) \quad (26)$$

[20] This is not to deny that growth stocks (in our sense) may well be "riskier" than non-growth stocks. But to the extent that this is true, it will be due to the possibly greater uncertainty attaching to the size and duration of future growth opportunities and hence to the size of the future stream of total returns quite apart from any questions of dividend policy.

[21] Note also that the above analysis enables us to deal very easily with the familiar issue of whether a firm's cost of equity capital is measured by its earnings/price ratio or by its dividend/price ratio. Clearly, the answer is that it is measured by neither, except under very special circumstances. For from (23) we have for the earnings/price ratio

$$\frac{X(0)}{V(0)} = \frac{\rho - k\rho^*}{1 - k},$$

which is equal to the cost of capital ρ, only if the firm has no growth potential (i.e., $\rho^* = \rho$). And from (24) we have for the dividend/price ratio

$$\frac{D(0)}{V(0)} = \rho - g,$$

which is equal to ρ only when $g = 0$; i.e., from (25), either when $k = 0$; or, if $k > 0$, when $\rho^* < \rho$ and the amount of external financing is precisely

$$k_e = \frac{\rho^*}{\rho} k [1 - k_r],$$

analogous to that of attempting to develop the certainty formulas from "marginal rates of time preference" rather than objective market opportunities.

so that the gain from the retention of earnings exactly offsets the loss that would otherwise be occasioned by the unprofitable investment.

since the rate of growth of price is the same as that of dividends per share. Using (25) and (26) to substitute for g and $V(t)$ and simplifying, we find that

$$D_t(t) + G_t(t) = X(t)\left[\frac{\rho(1-k)}{\rho - k\rho^*}\right]. \quad (27)$$

The relation between the investors' return and the corporation's profits is thus seen to depend entirely on the relation between ρ^* and ρ. If $\rho^* = \rho$ (i.e., the firm has no special "growth" opportunities), then the expression in brackets becomes 1 and the investor returns are precisely the same as the corporate profits. If $\rho^* < \rho$, however, the investors' return will be less than the corporate earnings; and, in the case of growth corporations the investors' return will actually be greater than the flow of corporate profits over the interval.[22]

Some implications for constructing empirical tests.—Finally the fact that we have two different (though not independent) measures of growth in $k\rho^*$ and g and two corresponding families of valuation formulas means, among other things, that we can proceed by either of two routes in empirical studies of valuation. We can follow the standard practice of the security analyst and think in terms of price per share, dividends per share, and the rate of growth of dividends per

share; or we can think in terms of the total value of the enterprise, total earnings, and the rate of growth of total earnings. Our own preference happens to be for the second approach primarily because certain additional variables of interest—such as dividend policy, leverage, and size of firm—can be incorporated more easily and meaningfully into test equations in which the growth term is the growth of total earnings. But this can wait. For present purposes, the thing to be stressed is simply that two approaches, properly carried through, are in no sense *opposing* views of the valuation process; but rather equivalent views, with the choice between them largely a matter of taste and convenience.

IV. THE EFFECTS OF DIVIDEND POLICY UNDER UNCERTAINTY

Uncertainty and the general theory of valuation.—In turning now from the ideal world of certainty to one of uncertainty our first step, alas, must be to jettison the fundamental valuation principle as given, say, in our equation (3)

$$V(t) = \frac{1}{1 + \rho(t)}\,[D(t) + n(t)\,p(t+1)]$$

and from which the irrelevance proposition as well as all the subsequent valua-

---

[22] The above relation between earnings per share and dividends plus capital gains also means that there will be a systematic relation between retained earnings and capital gains. The "marginal" relation is easy to see and is always precisely one for one regardless of growth or financial policy. That is, taking a dollar away from dividends and adding it to retained earnings (all other things equal) means an increase in capital gains of one dollar (or a reduction in capital loss of one dollar). The "average" relation is somewhat more complex. From (26) and (27) we can see that

$$G_t(t) = k_r X(t) + kX(t)\,\frac{\rho^* - \rho}{\rho - k\rho^*}.$$

Hence, if $\rho^* = \rho$ the total capital gain received will be exactly the same as the total retained earnings per share. For growth corporations, however, the

capital gain will always be greater than the retained earnings (and there will be a capital gain of

$$kX(t)\left[\frac{\rho^* - \rho}{\rho - k\rho^*}\right]$$

even when all earnings are paid out). For non-growth corporations the relation between gain and retentions is reversed. Note also that the absolute difference between the total capital gain and the total retained earnings is a constant (given, ρ, k and ρ^*) unaffected by dividend policy. Hence the *ratio* of capital gain to retained earnings will vary directly with the payout ratio for growth corporations (and vice versa for non-growth corporations). This means, among other things, that it is dangerous to attempt to draw inferences about the relative growth potential or relative managerial efficiency of corporations solely on the basis of the ratio of capital gains to retained earnings (cf. Harkavy [12, esp. pp. 289–94]).

tion formulas in Sections II and III were derived. For the terms in the bracket can no longer be regarded as given numbers, but must be recognized as "random variables" from the point of view of the investor as of the start of period t. Nor is it at all clear what meaning can be attached to the discount factor $1/[1 + \rho(t)]$ since what is being discounted is not a given return, but at best only a probability distribution of possible returns. We can, of course, delude ourselves into thinking that we are preserving equation (3) by the simple and popular expedient of drawing a bar over each term and referring to it thereafter as the mathematical expectation of the random variable. But except for the trivial case of universal linear utility functions we know that $V(t)$ would also be affected, and materially so, by the higher order moments of the distribution of returns. Hence there is no reason to believe that the discount factor for expected values, $1/[1 + \rho(t)]$, would in fact be the same for any two firms chosen arbitrarily, not to mention that the expected values themselves may well be different for different investors.

All this is not to say, of course, that there are insuperable difficulties in the way of developing a testable theory of rational market valuation under uncertainty.[23] On the contrary, our investigations of the problem to date have convinced us that it is indeed possible to construct such a theory—though the construction, as can well be imagined, is a

fairly complex and space-consuming task. Fortunately, however, this task need not be undertaken in this paper which is concerned primarily with the effects of dividend policy on market valuation. For even without a full-fledged theory of what *does* determine market value under uncertainty we can show that dividend policy at least is *not* one of the determinants. To establish this particular generalization of the previous certainty results we need only invoke a corresponding generalization of the original postulate of rational behavior to allow for the fact that, under uncertainty, choices depend on expectations as well as tastes.

"Imputed rationality" and "symmetric market rationality."—This generalization can be formulated in two steps as follows. First, we shall say that an individual trader "imputes rationality to the market" or satisfies the postulate of "imputed rationality" if, in forming expectations, he assumes that every other trader in the market is (*a*) rational in the previous sense of preferring more wealth to less regardless of the form an increment in wealth may take, and (*b*) imputes rationality to all other traders. Second, we shall say that a market as a whole satisfies the postulate of "symmetric market rationality" if every trader both behaves rationally and imputes rationality to the market.[24]

Notice that this postulate of sym-

[23] Nor does it mean that all the previous certainty analysis has no relevance whatever in the presence of uncertainty. There are many issues, such as those discussed in Sec. I and II, that really relate only to what has been called the pure "futurity" component in valuation. Here, the valuation formulas can still be extremely useful in maintaining the internal consistency of the reasoning and in suggesting (or criticizing) empirical tests of certain classes of hypotheses about valuation, even though the formulas themselves cannot be used to grind out precise numerical values for specific real-world shares.

[24] We offer the term "symmetric market rationality" with considerable diffidence and only after having been assured by game theorists that there is no accepted term for this concept in the literature of that subject even though the postulate itself (or close parallels to it) does appear frequently. In the literature of economics a closely related, but not exact counterpart is Muth's "hypothesis of rational expectations" [18]. Among the more euphonic, though we feel somewhat less revealing, alternatives that have been suggested to us are "putative rationality" (by T. J. Koopmans), "bi-rationality" (by G. L. Thompson), "empathetic rationality" (by Andrea Modigliani), and "pan-rationality" (by A. Ando).

metric market rationality differs from the usual postulate of rational behavior in several important respects. In the first place, the new postulate covers not only the choice behavior of individuals but also their expectations of the choice behavior of others. Second, the postulate is a statement about the market as a whole and not just about individual behavior. Finally, though by no means least, symmetric market rationality cannot be deduced from individual rational behavior in the usual sense since that sense does not imply imputing rationality to others. It may, in fact, imply a choice behavior inconsistent with imputed rationality unless the individual actually believes the market to be symmetrically rational. For if an ordinarily rational investor had good reason to believe that other investors would not behave rationally, then it might well be rational for him to adopt a strategy he would otherwise have rejected as irrational. Our postulate thus rules out, among other things, the possibility of speculative "bubbles" wherein an individually rational investor buys a security he knows to be overpriced (i.e., too expensive in relation to its expected *long-run* return to be attractive as a permanent addition to his portfolio) in the expectation that he can resell it at a still more inflated price before the bubble bursts.[25]

[25] We recognize, of course, that such speculative bubbles have actually arisen in the past (and will probably continue to do so in the future), so that our postulate can certainly not be taken to be of universal applicability. We feel, however, that it is also not of universal inapplicability since from our observation, speculative bubbles, though well publicized when they occur, do not seem to us to be a dominant, or even a fundamental, feature of actual market behavior under uncertainty. That is, we would be prepared to argue that, as a rule and on the average, markets do not behave in ways which do not obviously contradict the postulate so that the postulate may still be useful, at least as a first approximation, for the analysis of long-run tendencies in organized

The irrelevance of dividend policy despite uncertainty.—In Section I we were able to show that, given a firm's investment policy, its dividend policy was irrelevant to its current market valuation. We shall now show that this fundamental conclusion need not be modified merely because of the presence of uncertainty about the future course of profits, investment, or dividends (assuming again, as we have throughout, that investment policy can be regarded as separable from dividend policy). To see that uncertainty about these elements changes nothing essential, consider a case in which current investors believe that the future streams of total earnings and total investment whatever actual values they may assume at different points in time will be identical for two firms, 1 and 2.[26] Suppose further, provisionally, that the same is believed to be true of future total dividend payments from period one on so that the only way in which the two firms differ is possibly with respect to the prospective dividend in the current period, period 0. In terms of previous notation we are thus assuming that

$$\bar{X}_1(t) = \bar{X}_2(t) \qquad t = 0 \ldots \infty$$
$$\bar{I}_1(t) = \bar{I}_2(t) \qquad t = 0 \ldots \infty$$
$$\bar{D}_1(t) = \bar{D}_2(t) \qquad t = 1 \ldots \infty$$

capital markets. Needless to say, whether our confidence in the postulate is justified is something that will have to be determined by empirical tests of its implications (such as, of course, the irrelevance of dividend policy).

[26] The assumption of two identical firms is introduced for convenience of exposition only, since it usually is easier to see the implications of rationality when there is an explicit arbitrage mechanism, in this case, switches between the shares of the two firms. The assumption, however, is not necessary and we can, if we like, think of the two firms as really corresponding to two states of the same firm for an investor performing a series of "mental experiments" on the subject of dividend policy.

the subscripts indicating the firms and the tildes being added to the variables to indicate that these are to be regarded from the standpoint of current period, not as known numbers but as numbers that will be drawn in the future from the appropriate probability distributions. We may now ask: "What will be the return, $\tilde{R}_1(0)$ to the current shareholders in firm 1 during the current period?" Clearly, it will be

$$\tilde{R}_1(0) = \tilde{D}_1(0) + \tilde{V}_1(1) - \tilde{m}_1(1)\,\tilde{p}_1(1)\,. \quad (28)$$

But the relation between $\tilde{D}_1(0)$ and $\tilde{m}_1(1)\,\tilde{p}_1(1)$ is necessarily still given by equation (4) which is merely an accounting identity so that we can write

$$\tilde{m}_1(1)\,\tilde{p}_1(1) = \tilde{I}_1(0) - [\tilde{X}_1(0) - \tilde{D}_1(0)], \quad (29)$$

and, on substituting in (28), we obtain

$$\tilde{R}_1(0) = \tilde{X}_1(0) - \tilde{I}_1(0) + \tilde{V}_1(1) \quad (30)$$

for firm 1. By an exactly parallel process we can obtain an equivalent expression for $\tilde{R}_2(0)$.

Let us now compare $\tilde{R}_1(0)$ with $\tilde{R}_2(0)$. Note first that, by assumption, $\tilde{X}_1(0) = \tilde{X}_2(0)$ and $\tilde{I}_1(0) = \tilde{I}_2(0)$. Furthermore, with symmetric market rationality, the terminal values $\tilde{V}_i(1)$ can depend only on prospective future earnings, investment and dividends from period 1 on and these too, by assumption, are identical for the two companies. Thus symmetric rationality implies that every investor must expect $\tilde{V}_1(1) = \tilde{V}_2(1)$ and hence finally $\tilde{R}_1(0) = \tilde{R}_2(0)$. But if the return to the investors is the same in the two cases, rationality requires that the two firms command the same current value so that $V_1(0)$ must equal $V_2(0)$ regardless of any difference in dividend payments during period 0. Suppose now that we allow dividends to differ not just in period 0 but in period 1 as well, but still retain the assumption of equal $\tilde{X}_i(t)$ and $\tilde{I}_i(t)$ in

all periods and of equal $\tilde{D}_i(t)$ in period 2 and beyond. Clearly, the only way differences in dividends in period 1 can effect $\tilde{R}_i(0)$ and hence $V_i(0)$ is via $\tilde{V}_i(1)$. But, by the assumption of symmetric market rationality, current investors know that as of the start of period 1 the then investors will value the two firms rationally and we have already shown that differences in the current dividend do not affect current value. Thus we must have $\tilde{V}_1(1) = \tilde{V}_2(1)$—and hence $V_1(0) = V_2(0)$—regardless of any possible difference in dividend payments during period 1. By an obvious extension of the reasoning to $\tilde{V}_i(2)$, $\tilde{V}_i(3)$, and so on, it must follow that the current valuation is unaffected by differences in dividend payments in *any* future period and thus that dividend policy is irrelevant for the determination of market prices, given investment policy.[27]

Dividend policy and leverage.—A study of the above line of proof will show it to be essentially analogous to the proof for the certainty world, in which as we know, firms can have, in effect, only two alternative sources of investment funds: retained earnings or stock issues. In an uncertain world, however, there is the additional financing possibility of debt issues. The question naturally arises, therefore, as to whether the conclusion about irrelevance remains valid even in the presence of debt financing, particularly since there may very well be inter-

[27] We might note that the assumption of symmetric market rationality is sufficient to derive this conclusion but not strictly necessary if we are willing to weaken the irrelevance proposition to one running in terms of long-run, average tendencies in the market. Individual rationality alone could conceivably bring about the latter for over the long pull rational investors could enforce this result by buying and holding "undervalued" securities because this would insure them higher long-run returns when eventually the prices became the same. They might, however, have a long, long wait.

actions between debt policy and dividend policy. The answer is that it does, and while a complete demonstration would perhaps be too tedious and repetitious at this point, we can at least readily sketch out the main outlines of how the proof proceeds. We begin, as above, by establishing the conditions from period 1 on that lead to a situation in which $\bar{V}_1(1)$ must be brought into equality with $\bar{V}_2(1)$ where the V, following the approach in our earlier paper [17], is now to be interpreted as the total market value of the firm, debt plus equity, not merely equity alone. The return to the original investors taken as a whole—and remember that any individual always has the option of buying a proportional share of both the equity and the debt—must correspondingly be broadened to allow for the interest on the debt. There will also be a corresponding broadening of the accounting identity (4) to allow, on the one hand, for the interest return and, on the other, for any debt funds used to finance the investment in whole or in part. The net result is that both the dividend component and the interest component of total earnings will cancel out making the relevant (total) return, as before, $[\bar{X}_i(0) - \bar{I}_i(0) + \bar{V}_i(1)]$ which is clearly independent of the current dividend. It follows, then, that the value of the firm must also therefore be independent of dividend policy given investment policy.[28]

The informational content of dividends. —To conclude our discussion of dividend policy under uncertainty, we might take note briefly of a common confusion about the meaning of the irrelevance proposition occasioned by the fact that in the real world a change in the dividend rate is often followed by a change in the market price (sometimes spectacularly so). Such a phenomenon would not be incompatible with irelevance to the extent that it was merely a reflection of what might be called the "informational content" of dividends, an attribute of particular dividend payments hitherto excluded by assumption from the discussion and proofs. That is, where a firm has adopted a policy of dividend stabilization with a long-established and generally appreciated "target payout ratio," investors are likely to (and have good reason to) interpret a change in the dividend rate as a change in management's views of future profit prospects for the firm.[29] The dividend change, in other words, provides the occasion for the price change though not its cause, the price still being solely a reflection of future earnings and growth opportunities. In any particular instance, of course, the investors might well be mistaken in placing this interpretation on the dividend change, since the management might really only be changing its payout target or possibly even attempting to "manipulate" the price. But this would involve no particular conflict with the irrelevance proposition, unless, of course, the price changes in such cases were not reversed when the unfolding of events had made clear the true nature of the situation.[30]

[28] This same conclusion must also hold for the current market value of all the shares (and hence for the current price per share), which is equal to the total market value minus the given initially outstanding debt. Needless to say, however, the price per share and the value of the equity at *future* points in time will not be independent of dividend and debt policies in the interim.

[29] For evidence on the prevalence of dividend stabilization and target ratios see Lintner [15].

[30] For a further discussion of the subject of the informational content of dividends, including its implications for empirical tests of the irrelevance proposition, see Modigliani and Miller [16, pp. 666–68].

V. DIVIDEND POLICY AND MARKET IMPERFECTIONS

To complete the analysis of dividend policy, the logical next step would presumably be to abandon the assumption of perfect capital markets. This is, however, a good deal easier to say than to do principally because there is no unique set of circumstances that constitutes "imperfection." We can describe not one but a multitude of possible departures from strict perfection, singly and in combinations. Clearly, to attempt to pursue the implications of each of these would only serve to add inordinately to an already overlong discussion. We shall instead, therefore, limit ourselves in this concluding section to a few brief and general observations about imperfect markets that we hope may prove helpful to those taking up the task of extending the theory of valuation in this direction.

First, it is important to keep in mind that from the standpoint of dividend policy, what counts is not imperfection per se but only imperfection that might lead an investor to have a systematic preference as between a dollar of current dividends and a dollar of current capital gains. Where no such systematic preference is produced, we can subsume the imperfection in the (random) error term always carried along when applying propositions derived from ideal models to real-world events.

Second, even where we do find imperfections that bias individual preferences —such as the existence of brokerage fees which tend to make young "accumulators" prefer low-payout shares and retired persons lean toward "income stocks"—such imperfections are at best only necessary but not sufficient conditions for certain payout policies to command a permanent premium in the mar-

ket. If, for example, the frequency distribution of corporate payout ratios happened to correspond exactly with the distribution of investor preferences for payout ratios, then the existence of these preferences would clearly lead ultimately to a situation whose implications were different in no fundamental respect from the perfect market case. Each corporation would tend to attract to itself a "clientele" consisting of those preferring its particular payout ratio, but one clientele would be entirely as good as another in terms of the valuation it would imply for the firm. Nor, of course, is it necessary for the distributions to match exactly for this result to occur. Even if there were a "shortage" of some particular payout ratio, investors would still normally have the option of achieving their particular saving objectives without paying a premium for the stocks in short supply simply by buying appropriately weighted combinations of the more plentiful payout ratios. In fact, given the great range of corporate payout ratios known to be available, this process would fail to eliminate permanent premiums and discounts only if the distribution of investor preferences were heavily concentrated at either of the extreme ends of the payout scale.[31]

Of all the many market imperfections that might be detailed, the only one that would seem to be even remotely capable of producing such a concentration is the substantial advantage accorded to capital gains as compared with dividends un-

[31] The above discussion should explain why, among other reasons, it would not be possible to draw any valid inference about the relative preponderance of "accumulators" as opposed to "income" buyers or the strength of their preferences merely from the weight attaching to dividends in a simple cross-sectional regression between value and payouts (as is attempted in Clendenin [2, p. 50] or Durand [5, p. 651]).

der the personal income tax. Strong as this tax push toward capital gains may be for high-income individuals, however, it should be remembered that a substantial (and growing) fraction of total shares outstanding is currently held by investors for whom there is either no tax differential (charitable and educational institutions, foundations, pension trusts, and low-income retired individuals) or where the tax advantage is, if anything, in favor of dividends (casualty insurance companies and taxable corporations generally). Hence, again, the "clientele effect" will be at work. Furthermore, except for taxable individuals in the very top brackets, the required difference in before-tax yields to produce equal after-tax yields is not particularly striking, at least for moderate variations in the composition of returns.[32] All this is not to say, of course, that differences in yields (market values) caused by differences in payout policies should be ignored by managements or investors merely because they may be relatively small. But it may help to keep investigators from being too surprised if it turns out to be hard to

[32] For example, if a taxpayer is subject to a marginal rate of 40 per cent on dividends and half that or 20 per cent on long-term capital gains, then a before-tax yield of 6 per cent consisting of 40 per cent dividends and 60 per cent capital gains produces an after-tax yield of 4.32 per cent. To net the same after-tax yield on a stock with 60 per cent of the return in dividends and only 40 per cent in capital gains would require a before-tax yield of 6.37 per cent. The difference would be somewhat smaller if we allowed for the present dividend credit, though it should also be kept in mind that the tax on capital gains may be avoided entirely under present arrangements if the gains are not realized during the holder's lifetime.

measure or even to detect any premium for low-payout shares on the basis of standard statistical techniques.

Finally, we may note that since the tax differential in favor of capital gains is undoubtedly the major *systematic* imperfection in the market, one clearly cannot invoke "imperfections" to account for the difference between our irrelevance proposition and the standard view as to the role of dividend policy found in the literature of finance. For the standard view is not that low-payout companies command a premium; but that, in general, they will sell at a discount![33] If such indeed were the case—and we, at least, are not prepared to concede that this has been established—then the analysis presented in this paper suggests there would be only one way to account for it; namely, as the result of systematic irrationality on the part of the investing public.[34]

To say that an observed positive premium on high payouts was due to irrationality would not, of course, make the phenomenon any less real. But it would at least suggest the need for a certain measure of caution by long-range policy-makers. For investors, however naïve they may be when they enter the market, do sometimes learn from experience; and perhaps, occasionally, even from reading articles such as this.

[33] See, among many, many others, Gordon [8, 9], Graham and Dodd [11, esp. chaps. xxxiv and xxxvi], Durand [4, 5], Hunt, Williams, and Donaldson [13, pp. 647–49], Fisher [7], Gordon and Shapiro [10], Harkavy [12], Clendenin [2], Johnson, Shapiro, and O'Meara [14], and Walter [19].

[34] Or, less plausibly, that there is a systematic tendency for external funds to be used more productively than internal funds.

REFERENCES

1. Bodenhorn, Diran. "On the Problem of Capital Budgeting," *Journal of Finance,* XIV (December, 1959), 473–92.

2. Clendenin, John. "What Do Stockholders Like?" *California Management Review,* I (Fall, 1958), 47–55.

3. CLENDENIN, JOHN, and VAN CLEAVE, M. "Growth and Common Stock Values," *Journal of Finance*, IX (September, 1954), 365–76.

4. DURAND, DAVID. *Bank Stock Prices and the Bank Capital Problem*. ("Occasional Paper," No. 54.) New York: National Bureau of Economic Research, 1957.

5. ———. "The Cost of Capital and the Theory of Investment: Comment," *American Economic Review*, XLIX (September, 1959), 639–54.

6. ———. "Growth Stocks and the Petersburg Paradox," *Journal of Finance*, XII (September, 1957), 348–63.

7. FISHER, G. R. "Some Factors Influencing Share Prices," *Economic Journal*, LXXI, No. 281 (March, 1961), 121–41.

8. GORDON, MYRON. "Corporate Saving, Investment and Share Prices," *Review of Economics and Statistics* (forthcoming).

9. ———. "Dividends, Earnings and Stock Prices," *ibid.*, XLI, No. 2, Part I (May, 1959), 99–105.

10. GORDON, MYRON, and SHAPIRO, ELI. "Capital Equipment Analysis: The Required Rate of Profit," *Management Science*, III, 1956, 102–10.

11. GRAHAM, BENJAMIN, and DODD, DAVID. *Security Analysis*. 3d ed. New York: McGraw-Hill Book Co., 1951.

12. HARKAVY, OSCAR, "The Relation between Retained Earnings and Common Stock Prices for Large Listed Corporations," *Journal of Finance*, VIII (September, 1953), 283–97.

13. HUNT, PEARSON, WILLIAMS, CHARLES, and DONALDSON, GORDON. *Basic Business Finance*. Homewood, Ill.: Richard D. Irwin, 1958.

14. JOHNSON, L. R., SHAPIRO, ELI, and O'MEARA, J. "Valuation of Closely Held Stock for Federal Tax Purposes: Approach to an Objective Method," *University of Pennsylvania Law Review*, C, 166–95.

15. LINTNER, JOHN. "Distribution of Incomes of Corporations among Dividends, Retained Earnings and Taxes," *American Economic Review*, XLVI (May, 1956), 97–113.

16. MODIGLIANI, FRANCO, and MILLER, MERTON. "'The Cost of Capital, Corporation Finance and the Theory of Investment,': Reply," *American Economic Review*, XLIX (September, 1959), 655–69.

17. ———. "The Cost of Capital, Corporation Finance and the Theory of Investment," *ibid.*, XLVIII (1958), 261–97.

18. MUTH, JOHN F. "Rational Expectations and the Theory of Price Movements," *Econometrica* (forthcoming).

19. WALTER, JAMES E. "A Discriminant Function for Earnings-Price Ratios of Large Industrial Corporations," *Review of Economics and Statistics*, XLI (February, 1959), 44–52.

20. ———. "Dividend Policies and Common Stock Prices," *Journal of Finance*, XI (March, 1956), 29–41.

21. WILLIAMS, JOHN B. *The Theory of Investment Value*. Cambridge, Mass.: Harvard University Press, 1938.

34

A NEW TOOL IN INVESTMENT
DECISION-MAKING

Volkert S. Whitbeck and Manown Kisor, Jr.

What makes stock prices? Why should the common shares of International Business Machines sell at more than 35 multiples while those of General Motors are priced at less than 18 times earnings?

If we look at *Chart I,* which depicts the historical earnings records of both, we shall find two clues to the reasons why.

Let us note first that IBM's rate of growth in net income per share, as indicated by the slope of its historical earnings path, has been considerably more rapid than that of GM. We note also that IBM's growth has been more stable, in the sense that the deviations from its trend in earnings have been much less marked than those of GM.

This double fact that IBM's growth has been both more rapid and more stable than GM's progress is readily apparent from informal, visual inspection. We may wish, however, to have more formal, statistical expressions of the past growth and stability of the two companies. Measures of this sort are easily constructed by the method of "least-squares" correlation. Without attempting to conduct a course in statistics, we may describe this procedure as a method by which the trend line of "best-fit" is drawn through the historical earnings path. More specifically, the trend line is constructed so that the sums of the *squares* of the deviations of the actual earnings from the trend line are a *minimum*—hence the term "least-squares."

Actually, if we were to take a rubber band and stretch it across the plotted data for each stock on *Chart I,* trying to get the trend line of best visual "fit," we probably would locate lines approximating the "least-squares" trends. Any two of us, however, would find slightly different lines, while the "least-squares" procedure yields one and only one path through the data. Using the logarithmic value of the actual earnings per share, as we did for the historical earnings chart, we are able to express the trend line in terms of a constant percentage rate of growth, a rate of growth which is a true "annual average" in that it does not depend directly on the selection of any two particular terminal years.

Reprinted from the *Financial Analysts Journal,* XIX, No. 3 (May–June, 1963), 55–62, by permission of the authors and the publisher.

Volkert S. Whitbeck, Vice President and Economist of The Bank of New York, received his A.B. from Princeton University in 1931 and his M.B.A. from Harvard in 1933. Manown Kisor, Jr., an Assistant Secretary of The Bank of New York, graduated in 1958 from Trinity College, Hartford, and has done graduate work at Northwestern University and New York University.

The trend lines on the historical earnings chart for IBM and GM were constructed in just such a fashion, the trend line for IBM showing an annual average rate of growth of 16.1% while that of GM indicates an average rate of only 5.3% per annum over the 15-year period.

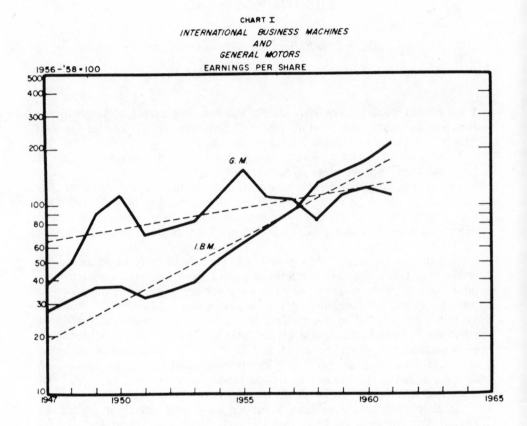

CHART I
INTERNATIONAL BUSINESS MACHINES
AND
GENERAL MOTORS
EARNINGS PER SHARE

The same least-squares procedure we attempted to describe above also provides us with a measure of the stability of the historical earnings record. Called the *standard deviation*, this measure reports the range about the trend line within which the actual earnings tended to fluctuate during the historical period. In order to provide ourselves with a measure which permits direct comparison of the stability records of different companies, we may express the standard deviation in terms of a percentage fluctuation from the trend line.

In general, this percentage figure denotes the range, on either side of the trend line, within which, in two years out of three, actual earnings were reported. In other words, if the standard deviation over the historical period were 15.0%, we might expect to find that two out of three years' actual earnings fell within 15.0% on either side of the trend line. Another way of expressing this relation is to say that the "chances" are two out of three that actual earnings in any given year were within 15.0% of the trend-line value of earnings for that year.

The lower the standard deviation in percentage terms, then, the more stable the historical record. For IBM over our 15-year period, the standard deviation of earnings about trend was 22.1%; for less stable GM, 29.9%.

It was suggested earlier that we would find, in the historical record, two clues to the reasons why IBM currently commands a price-earnings multiple more than twice that of GM. We have seen that IBM's expansion has been more stable, as well as more rapid, than GM's growth in earnings per share, and this combination of historical occurrence might itself be utilized in an attempt to explain the more generous current pricing of IBM.

The real rationale for the price differential is, however, more subtle. IBM commands a higher price-earnings ratio, not because of its past performance, but, rather, because the market, on balance, expects more *in the future* from IBM than it does from GM. As investors, we buy common stocks not simply for their records prior to our purchase, but, more fundamentally, for what we anticipate from them after our commitment.

The historical record is relevant only to the extent that past performance can provide an insight into prospective growth. To the extent that we can form an expectation (whether based on the relative growth and stability of earnings exhibited by the two companies over the past 15 years or on some other, supplemental information) that IBM will continue to outgrow GM, we are justified in paying more for a share of IBM, in terms of price earnings multiples, than for one of GM.

The question becomes: "How much more?" This is what the Valuation Study attempts to answer.

THE VALUATION STUDY

Assuming that we are in agreement in our anticipations of the future relative earnings progress of IBM and GM—that IBM's per-share earnings growth will be both more rapid and more stable than GM's—we should be willing to pay more, in terms of price-earnings multiples, for a share of IBM than for one of GM. The critical question of "How much more?" is the one to which we now direct ourselves.

In attempting to provide an answer to this vital query, we must introduce several special concepts, the most fundamental of which is that of "normalized" earnings. Most of us are well aware of the fact that, over the course of a cycle in general business, the price-multiples attached to the earnings of many firms tend to behave in a contracyclical fashion, falling as earnings rise and rising as earnings fall. *Chart II* provides an illustration of this phenomenon.

Constructed by plotting the ratio of the sample's mean earnings and earnings-multiples to those of Standard and Poor's Industrials, the chart abstracts from trends in the general market, portraying the movement of the variables *relative* to their counterparts in the market as a whole. The tendency of price-earnings ratios to move contracyclically with earnings is readily apparent, especially in the earlier years.

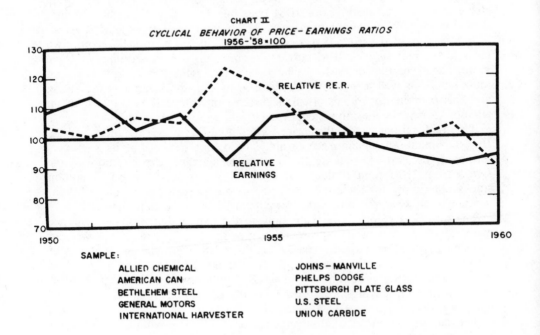

CHART II
CYCLICAL BEHAVIOR OF PRICE-EARNINGS RATIOS
1956-'58 = 100

SAMPLE:

ALLIED CHEMICAL
AMERICAN CAN
BETHLEHEM STEEL
GENERAL MOTORS
INTERNATIONAL HARVESTER

JOHNS-MANVILLE
PHELPS DODGE
PITTSBURGH PLATE GLASS
U.S. STEEL
UNION CARBIDE

    Revelation of this aspect of the market for shares carries with it an important implication for our analysis. The fact that earnings-multiples tend to fall as earnings rise and rise as earnings fall suggests that the market possesses an awareness of the inherent periodicity in the earnings of many companies.
    To be emphasized is the point that the market differentiates between the absolute cyclicality of corporate earnings as a whole and the *relative* cyclicality of the net income of individual firms. This is demonstrated in the chart, which portrays the path of the sample's earnings and price-earnings ratios relative to those of the market as a whole. And if the market recognizes the relative cyclicality of earnings of different companies, it follows that the market also has some concept of earnings normality for each firm. Reasoning from the fact that the market does not apply a constant multiplier to cyclically varying earnings, we infer that investors on balance conceive of some mid-cyclical or average level of earnings for each company.
    This notion of normalized or mid-cyclical earnings is not as nebulous as it may seem at first. For purposes of our analysis, we may conceive of the normalized earnings of a given firm as that level of net income which would

prevail currently if the economy as a whole were experiencing mid-cyclical business conditions. In terms of widely-used, general measures, we might denote the current mid-cyclical or "normal" level of the economy by a Gross National Product of $550 billion and an F.R.B. Index of Industrial Production of 117. The normalized earnings of a given company, then, would be those which would result from these general economic conditions if the company itself were experiencing "normal" operations; that is, operations not affected by such non-recurring items as strikes, natural disasters, and the like.

Since another part of this discussion is devoted entirely to the estimation of normalized earnings (and other variables which we will find fundamental to our analysis), let us, for now, simply assume that we have predetermined IBM's current normalized earning power at $10.50 per share and GM's, at $3.30 per share. We will assume also that we have projected growth in earning power from these levels at 17.0% per annum for IBM and 3.0% for GM.

The very fact that we expect IBM to grow more rapidly than GM might engender a willingness on our part to pay a higher P.E.R. for the shares of the former. Ignoring for the moment additional aspects of valuation—important considerations such as the prospective standard deviation of earnings discussed earlier—let us attempt to quantify this P.E.R. differential. *Chart III*

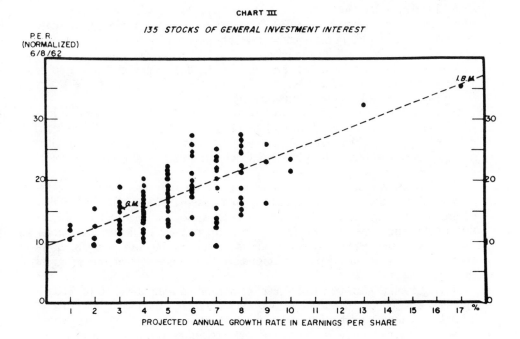

CHART III

135 STOCKS OF GENERAL INVESTMENT INTEREST

P.E.R.
(NORMALIZED)
6/8/62

PROJECTED ANNUAL GROWTH RATE IN EARNINGS PER SHARE

contains the key to our analysis. This "scatter diagram" demonstrates the relationship between the earnings-multiple and the projected rate of growth, and is constructed as follows:

Utilizing prices for all issues in the sample as of the close of business on a given date, in this case June 8, 1962, we determine the "Normalized P.E.R." for each stock by dividing price by current normalized earnings. This normalized earnings-multiple is then plotted against the projected rate of growth in earnings per share; e.g. 15.4 vs. 3.0 for GM and 35.3 vs. 17.0 for IBM.

With the entire 135 stocks in the sample so plotted, we have a visual record of the relation prevailing in the market, on June 8, between price-earnings ratios and prospective rates of growth. This visual record is readily translated into formal statistical terms by means of the least-squares procedures discussed earlier. The dashed line on the chart was computed in just such a fashion.

In the terminology of simple high-school algebra, the relevant characteristics of this line of average relationship are a slope of approximately 1.5, and a Y-intercept of 9.3, as indicated by the point where the line crosses the P.E.R. axis. Translated into terms more germane to the analysis of common stock values, a Y-intercept of 9.3 tells us that, on June 8, 1962, the market relationship was such that a stock with a zero rate of growth in earnings per share commanded, on the average, a price of slightly more than nine times earnings.

A slope of 1.5 denoted that, on our pricing date, each percentage point of positive growth added 1.5 P.E.R.'s to the 9.3 base multiple. In the case of GM, for example, our projected rate of growth of 3.0% indicated that we add 1.5 x 3.0, or 4.5, to the base multiple of 9.3 giving us a "theoretical" multiple for GM of 13.8 times earnings. For IBM, our growth projection of 17.0% combined with the base multiple to yield a theoretical P.E.R. of 9.3 plus 1.5 x 17.0, or 34.8 times earnings.

How much more should we pay for IBM than for GM? Valuing stocks solely on the basis of our expectations of their future growth, the market, on June 8, told us that IBM should sell at 34.8 times earnings and GM, at 13.8 times earnings. The differential, with the issues valued on the basis of growth alone, was, then, 21.0 multiples.

Obviously, prospective growth rates are not the only constituent in common stock valuation. We have already mentioned that the relative stability of growth is a significant factor, and it goes without saying that consideration of dividend pay-out is of fundamental importance in determining common stock values. Before we introduce these factors into our analysis, however, let us retrace our steps and emphasize the high points of our progress thus far—

Having assumed IBM's current level of normal earning power to be $10.50 and GM's to be $3.30 per share, we agreed that, if IBM were to grow at 17.0% per annum from this level while GM grew at only 3.0%, we would be willing to pay more, in terms of price-earnings ratios, for a share of IBM than for one of GM.

The vital question of "How much more?" was the one to which we directed ourselves. To answer it, we addressed *the market as a whole,* as represented by a sample of 135 stocks of general investment interest. In order to determine how much we should pay for IBM and GM, we sought the relationship between price-earnings ratios and growth rates in the general market. Through the method of least-squares, we found the *average* price-earnings ratio attached to each level of projected growth. For IBM's 17.0% rate of growth, this market-average or theoretical multiple was 34.8 for GM's 3.0% rate of growth, 13.8 times earnings. The market, in other words, told us, through our simple correlation analysis, that, if both issues were selling at their June 8 theoretical price-earnings ratios, we would be justified in paying, on the basis of prospective growth alone, 21.0 multiples more for IBM than for GM.

What, now, about the other factors in common stock valuation? Earlier, we discussed in detail the concept of the standard deviation of earnings about trend, agreeing that, in general, a relatively low anticipated standard deviation was a desirable investment characteristic. In our discussion of the cyclical behavior of price-earnings ratios, we emphasized the tendency of multiples to rise as earnings fall, and fall as earnings rise. Important to note now is that fact that, although price-earnings ratios tend to move contracyclically with earnings, in general their progress is not in direct proportion to the movement of earnings.

Multiples rise as earnings fall, but not as rapidly. The prices of stocks with high standard deviations of earnings do fall relative to the market as a whole as their earnings decline. And, conversely, as earnings of these issues increase again, their prices rise relative to the general market. On the other hand, stocks with more stable earnings, those with low standard deviations, tend to fluctuate in price less widely than the market as a whole. For investors desiring price stability, then, a relatively low prospective standard deviation of earnings becomes a distinctly desirable investment characteristic.

For these investors, an anticipated standard deviation of zero—in other words, an absolutely straight earnings path—would be an optimum trait, and anything less than this optimum would be a detractor from investment value. And if it is this category of investor which dominates the market as a whole, we would expect that, of two stocks with identical growth prospects, the one with the lower anticipated standard deviation would command the higher price-earnings ratio.

Having concluded that high prospective rates of growth and low expected standard deviations of earnings per share, are, in general, characteristics which enhance investment value, let us turn now to the consideration of a third factor in common stock valuation, *dividend pay-out.*

To the extent that investors as a whole consider current dividends a desirable investment characteristic, we would expect high dividend pay-out ratios to contribute positively to the prices of common stocks. That is to say, if we had two issues identical with respect to anticipated growth and stability, we might expect to find the one with the greater prospective pay-out selling at a higher P.E.R. than the one with the smaller dividend-earnings ratio.

On the other hand, if investors on balance did *not* desire current income, the opposite relation could be anticipated. In this case, of our two otherwise identical stocks, the one with the *lower* pay-out policy would command the higher price-earnings ratio. The effect on price of the dividend pay-out ratio, is, then, determined by the balance of market sentiment.

A Study 'in Combination'

We have examined individually the three principal constituents of common stock valuation—growth, stability, and pay-out of earnings. Our task now is to consider them in combination, to analyze their joint effect on common stock prices. To do so, we must expand the concepts introduced in our discussion of growth alone. There, we saw the nature of a two-dimensional scatter diagram and the use of a simple least-squares analysis.

The problem there was to determine the statistical relation between two variables—the normalized price-earnings ratio and the expected rate of growth in earnings per share. Here, we must examine the multiple relationship among four variables—the normalized price-earnings ratio, the projected growth rate, the anticipated standard deviation, and the prospective ratio of dividends to earnings. The tool we can utilize is directly akin to the two-dimensional least-squares analysis employed before. In the terminology of statistics, our tool before was "simple correlation;" now it will be "*multiple* correlation," a least-squares analysis in four dimensions.

The simple correlation of earnings-multiples and growth rates gave us the average price-earnings ratio prevailing in the market for each rate of growth. The multiple correlation analysis to which we now turn will give us the average price-earnings ratio for each *combination* of prospective growth, stability, and pay-out of earnings.

Utilizing the same sample of 135 stocks of general investment interest, all priced as of June 8's closing, as before, and applying our multiple correlation procedure, we are able to express the then-prevailing market relationships in terms of a simple equation:

Theoretical P.E.R. = 8.2 + 1.5 (Growth Rate)
+ 6.7 (Pay-Out)
− 0.2 (Standard Deviation)

Remembering that this equation describes the relationships existing in the market as of a given date, let us analyze its composition in some detail, utilizing our old friends for examples.

The first component of the equation, the constant term, gives us our base multiple. It is to this base multiple that we add to (or subtract from) the effects of the valuation factors—the prospective growth, stability, and pay-out of earnings. The second component of the equation describes the contribution made by each per cent of projected growth. The effect of dividend pay-out is denoted by the third segment of the equation.

As we can see from the positive sign attached to the factor by which we multiply the prospective pay-out ratio, the market on June 8 considered current dividends a desirable investment characteristic. The equation's fourth segment describes the effect on valuation of the anticipated stability of earnings. Anything less than perfect stability, as denoted by a zero standard deviation, is a detractor from investment value.

Utilizing our 17.0% projected growth rate for IBM, and assuming that its dividend pay-out will be .25 and its standard deviation, 5.0%, we compute the company's theoretical price-earnings ratio as follows:

Theoretical P.E.R.

$$= 8.2 + 1.5 \ (17.0) + 6.7 \ (.25) - 0.2 \ (5.0)$$
$$= 8.2 + 25.5 + 1.7 - 1.0$$
$$= 34.4$$

For GM, given a growth rate of 3.0%, a prospective pay-out of .75, and an expected standard deviation of 20.0%, we have:

Theoretical P.E.R.
$$= 8.2 + 1.5 \ (3.0) + 6.7 \ (.75) - 0.2 \ (20.0)$$
$$= 8.2 + 4.5 + 5.0 - 4.0$$
$$= 13.7$$

With these two theoretical price-earnings ratios so computed, we are in a position now to introduce the vital concept of the *price ratio*—the ratio of market price to theoretical price. On June 8, IBM was selling at 371, 35.3 times normalized earnings of $10.50 per share. Priced at 15.4 times normalized earnings, GM was selling at 51 on that date. Dividing market price by theoretical price (market P.E.R. by theoretical P.E.R.) for each stock, we arrive at a price ratio of 1.02 for IBM and one of 1.13 for GM. On June 8, then, IBM's market price was almost identical with its theoretical price, while GM, on the other hand, was being marketed at a level 13.0% above its theoretical price.

In order to evaluate the above information, we must remind ourselves of the exact nature of the theoretical price-earnings ratio—it is that earnings-multiple prevailing in the market, at a given moment of time, for a particular combination of prospective growth, stability, and pay-out of earnings per share. Remembering this, we shall say, for purposes of our analysis, that a stock is "under-valued" if it is selling for less than its theoretical P.E.R. and "over-valued" if it is priced in excess of its theoretical P.E.R.

The shares of IBM, by this definition, were but 2.0% over-valued on June 8, while those of GM were over-valued by 13.0%, given our expectations of their prospective growth, stability, and payout. (To the extent that another investor's expectations for IBM were less favorable, and/or those for GM more favorable, he might reach an altered, even opposite, conclusion with regard to the proper pricing of the two issues—even if he were to utilize the same valuation procedure.)

On the face of our projections and analytical concepts, it would appear that, on June 8, IBM was more attractively priced than GM and that a commitment in the former would prove more successful than one in the latter. This, indeed, is the conclusion which we wish to manifest. We would draw it, however, not simply from the primarily theoretical analysis which we have undertaken so far, but from real-world results, results which are discussed here later in detail.

The point to make here concerns one more piece of pure theory—the keystone on which the entirety of our analysis rests.

Our efforts have been directed towards measuring the relative valuation of common stocks on a particular pricing date. We have answered the question "What makes stock prices?" from the standpoint of the market at a given moment in time, while the "market" itself is a succession of such moments. Because we have determined our theoretical price-earnings ratios on the basis of a single, static moment, we should expect these average relationships to change from day to day.

Underlying the average earnings-multiple for each combination of prospective growth, stability, and pay-out is the aggregate of investor "feelings," concepts, beliefs, and we know that these forces are themselves transitory in nature. The fact remains, however, that changes in market psychology come, by and large, in a slow and orderly fashion, and it is the premise which underlies our principal hypothesis:

Given the theoretical or normal price of any stock, we assume that the market price of the stock will seek this level faster than the theoretical price itself will change—this is the key to our analysis.

Price Performance: Past and Prospective

During the year which followed the pricing date of the original Valuation Study, September 23, 1960, we accumulated a wealth of data concerning the price movements of common stocks. The purpose of this part of our treatise is to examine that data and to consider future performance in the perspective of past results. In doing so, we will be dealing with what is formally termed *statistical* or *empirical* probability.

The nature of the forces inherent in stock price movements is such that we cannot calculate exactly the *mathematical probability* that a given stock will or will not increase in price. But if we cannot reduce our projections to pure mathematical form, we *can* base them upon knowledge of what has occurred on similar occasions in the past. By examining our data on past price movements, and by making the quite reasonable assumption that analogous movements will occur in the future, we are able to offer quantified projections of future performance.

Let us begin our discussion by considering the 12-month performance of the Valuation Study in the aggregate. In doing so, we will be examining the validity of our hypothesis that, given the theoretical or normal price for any given stock, the market price of the stock will seek its normal level more rapidly than the theoretical price itself will change.

The criterion of success we choose is quite simple. We say that the Valuation Study is successful whenever the group of stocks labeled "under-valued" in relation to the general market outperforms Standard and Poor's 500-Stock Index, at the same time that the "500" outperforms those issues denoted "over-valued" in relation to the market as a whole.

In the discussion which follows, we will be examining the performance of the Valuation Study groups over the three months following each of four pricing dates. The "under-valued" group consists of those stocks with price-ratios—ratios of market price to theoretical price—of less than .85, while the "over-valued" group contains issues with price-ratios of 1.15 or greater.

As can be seen in *Table I,* our criterion of success was met in all four

Valuation Studies. In each of the three-month periods following the pricing dates, the under-valued group had a mean price performance superior to that of Standard and Poor's "500," and the "500," in turn, consistently outperformed those stocks labeled over-valued in relation to the market as a whole.

If we examine the relative-to-market action of the under-valued group, we note that the average percentage difference in three-months performance was approximately 3.0%. Noting this fact from the past, we might be led directly to conclude that if Standard and Poor's "500" were to appreciate 10% over a three-month period in the future, we could expect that the mean percentage price increase of the stocks in the under-valued group would be $1.03 \times 1.10 - 1.00$ or 13.3%.

How right would we be in voicing this expectation? Isn't it possible that the seeming success of the Valuation Study in the past was due simply to the working of chance? Let us consider this possibility. We know that, for any given Study, the price performance of the three groups could be ordered by chance in six different ways, so that the probability of success as defined is $1/6$. One of the rules of probability theory tells us that the probability of four consecutive chance successes, if the probability of one success is $1/6$, is given by $1/6 \times 1/6 \times 1/6 \times 1/6$ or $1/1296$.

The odds, then, are more than 1,000 to 1 against the random occurrence of four consecutive performance orderings of the sort experienced by the Valuation Study during the year after its inception. The performance of the Valuation Study was far too consistent to be attributable to the workings of chance. One must conclude, therefore, that this performance flowed directly from the Study itself, that it was the logical concomitant of a tool which is both relevant and reliable, and that the relative-to-market appreciation of the under-valued group will continue to approximate 3.0% per quarter or 12.5% per annum.

ROLE OF THE FINANCIAL ANALYST

Throughout our discussion of the theoretical aspects of common stock valuation, we simply assumed that the various factors influencing share prices all were pre-determined. The time has come now to part the veil of pure theory and examine the practical aspects of projecting future growth, stability, and pay-out of earnings. The task of projection falls to the Financial Analyst, for it is he who is best prepared to assay the future prospects of individual firms.

His task, however, is not an easy one, for it involves a unique combination of analytic talent, sustained effort, and, in some cases, intellectual wizardry. The starting point for his analysis is a graphic record of whatever historical information he considers relevant, a record similar to our *Chart I*. In addition to portraying the past path of earnings per share, the "growth chart," as it is commonly called, contains the complementing record of per-share sales or revenues. Placing current results in a longer-term perspective, the chart permits easy examination of several fundamental relationships:

(1) The current progress of earnings may be placed in the light of the long-term trend—Between 1958 and 1960, for example, GM's earnings ex-

panded more rapidly than those of IBM. A quick glance at the chart, how-ever, would dispel any notion that this relative progress would be likely to prevail in the future. IBM's two-year movement was from a level above the fifteen-year trend; GM's expansion sprang from a cyclical low.

(2) Casual comparison of the growth charts of several firms will reveal the relative stability of earnings over the longer-term—As we noted earlier, the fact that IBM's earnings progress has been more stable than GM's is readily apparent from the record portrayed in *Chart I*.

(3) With the path of sales per share to complement the earnings record, inspection will manifest trends in profit margins, as well as the relative stability of sales or revenue—An earnings line of greater slope than the path of sales would, of course, indicate rising margins; the opposite, declining margins. We must emphasize that a rising trend in profit margins seldom can be pro-jected indefinitely into the future, and this lack of projectability is especially operative where the company's margins exceed those typical of the industry. With regard to the relative stability of sales per share, we may point out that a sales record substantially more stable than that of earnings would emphasize a high cyclicality of profit margins and engender detailed investiga-tion of "leverage" relationships.

Other factors forming a basis for projection of future growth and stability may be revealed by inspection of growth charts, but these are the most important. They must, however, be subjected to further analysis. Merely extending a stable trend from the past is not enough. The historical paths of sales and earnings per share provide a starting point for the projection of growth—but only a starting point. If our projections are to be tenable, our analysis must be more thorough. One prerequisite of projection is an ex-amination of the physical side of growth. We must have an awareness of potential product demand, and this awareness must encompass physical amounts as well as dollar volume. We need, in other words, an estimate of the prospective growth in product units, be they widgets, data processers, or tons of cold-rolled steel.

A second prerequisite of projection concerns the *financial* aspects of growth. One of the paramount problems facing the analyst concerned with the projection of per-share earnings is the question of the firm's ability to finance future growth. If our growth projections are to be realistic, they must be consistent with the present and potential capital structures of the firm. In other words, they must be consistent with the company's capital budgeting policy, as revealed in its financial structure and pay-out practice.

The projected rate of growth in per share earnings which enters our Valua-tion Study is that rate which is expected to prevail over a future of at least five years' duration. It is also that rate which could be considered "normal" for the five-year period, in that it abstracts from cyclical elements indigenous to the firm itself or the economy as a whole.

If, for example, we had estimated the current normal or mid-cyclical earn-ing power of a given firm at $2.00 per share, as contrasted with actual earn-ings of $2.50 per share, and if we projected its earnings five years into the future at a mid-cyclical level of $3.00 per share, the firm's normalized rate of growth would be in the order of 8.5% per annum, even though its actual

rate of growth (from the current level of $2.50 per share to the $3.00 anticipated five years hence) would be less than 4.0% per year. Our choice of the
first concept for our measure of "growth" is based, obviously, on one of the
arguments presented previously, that investors on balance make allowance
for cyclical phenomena.

The Standard Deviation

Our direct allowance for cyclical phenomena rests, of course, with the
inclusion of the standard deviation as an independent valuation-factor. Since
we discussed this concept of earnings stability in considerable detail earlier,
we need comment now only on the general procedure for its estimation.
Because this variable is of a formal statistical nature, the analyst is given the
computed measure for the historical period.

It then becomes his task to review the measure as calculated and to determine whether revision is required. Because the standard deviation used in the
Valuation Study is the percentage range about trend within which earnings
are *expected* to fluctuate over the next five years, the analyst is responsible
for examining the factors influencing past stability to determine if they may
be anticipated to prevail in the future. Maturity of growth in product demand, alteration in capital structure, and changes in proportion of revenues
derived from leasing are the sort of modifications of past relationships which
would engender a revision in the calculated standard deviation.

The third principal factor of valuation, the anticipated pay-out of earnings,
is, perhaps, the factor most readily projected. The procedure generally followed is to divide the sum of the past ten years' dividends by the sum of
earnings over the same period. This measure of average or normal pay-out
may then be compared with pay-out ratios in the individual years to determine
if a trend is in evidence. Final adoption of a measure for valuation work
requires examination of the consistency of anticipated pay-out with projected
growth.

Having taken a brief look at the means of projecting valuation variables,
let us stress again the vital role played by the analyst. It is his projections
which enter the valuation procedure outlined here previously. No matter how
correct in concept our method may be, the ultimate success of the Valuation
Study rests with the analyst. Our procedure is to examine the market at a
given moment in time and to determine the average price-earnings ratio for
each combination of projected growth, stability, and pay-out of earnings.

Given this theoretical earnings-multiple for each stock, we then compare
it with the actual price-earnings ratio in order to measure the share's relative
valuation. The ratio of market price to theoretical price, the *price ratio,* becomes the final product of our analysis. It is this variable upon which we
base our projections of price performance. The past success of these price
projections has been discussed. Suffice it to say here that this success has been
both impressive and persistent. It has demonstrated that combination of valuation procedure and security analysis has provided a highly efficient tool for
comparing the relative attractiveness of investment alternatives. This combination is inseparable, however. Regardless of the efficiency of the valuation
element, the results of our Studies—both past and prospective—are de-

pendent on the accuracy of the inputs. If our staff of analysts were systematically to misconceive growth, stability, and income prospects, the outcome, of course, would be negative. The results of the past Studies demonstrate that the *combination* of analysis and valuation has proved itself successful. And as individual analysts become even more adept in applying our valuation approach and at anticipating the prospective paths of earnings and dividends, the results of future Studies should be even more rewarding.

Earnings

35

INTRODUCTION: THE MAIN POINT

Successful investing is simple. All that is needed is to forecast earnings more accurately than one's rivals. This not only ensures very high rates of return, it also eliminates any obligation to read books about efficient markets, portfolio theory, capital asset pricing models, and so on.

The point can be made in many ways. For instance, in almost all valuation formulas, the most important variable is the expected growth in earnings. A more dramatic demonstration is provided in Chapter 36, in which Niederhoffer and Regan present data on earnings for the fifty stocks on the New York Stock Exchange with the highest returns in 1970 and for the fifty with the lowest returns. From two simple tables, one derives the overwhelming impression that an ability to improve on the earnings forecasts of others would have led to considerable profits. In Chapter 37, Ball and Brown make a similar point less dramatically but more scientifically. They identified unexpected changes in earnings and investigated whether they were associated with unexpected changes in stock prices.

The problem of forecasting earnings falls naturally into two parts. The first is the definition of earnings for a previous period, and the second is the prediction of changes in that measure. One would have to be very foolish to think that reported earnings per share necessarily mean the same thing for different companies or even for the same company in different years. A remarkable example was reported in the *Wall Street Journal* of May 6, 1971. The Chrysler Corporation decided to change its method of valuing inventory from FIFO (first in, first out) to LIFO (last in, first out). One consequence was to improve earnings for 1970 by $20 million; another was to create a federal income tax liability of $53 million. Although it is barely possible to imagine that the company was better off in some fundamental sense, it is much easier to imagine that Chrysler decided to pay $53 million in additional taxes to make its latest reported earnings look more favorable. Naturally, an informed and prudent investor would not accept earnings at face value without inquiring into the methods by which they were calculated.

Many of the various forms of discretion that management has in calculating earnings are discussed in Chapter 38 by Leonard Spacek, one of America's leading accountants. In the hypothetical example that he cites, two firms doing the same real things and having the same real earnings have accounting options that permit reporting almost anything from $.79 per share to $1.80 per share. And Spacek does not exhaust the list of available options. For example, companies may vary the rate of return that they assume will be earned on the assets in the pension fund. Since these pension-fund assets amount to more than half the net worth of many firms, the assumption about their rate of return can have a large impact on the firm's contribution to the fund in any year and hence on reported earnings. When General Electric made retroactive price adjustments of more than $200 million in response to claims of treble damages from an alleged price-fixing conspiracy, it was able to offset much of the adverse impact on reported earnings by assuming that the pension-fund assets would earn a higher return than had been previously thought likely. A consequence of this cheerier assumption was a reduction of many dollars in the company's contribution to its pension fund.

The difficulties in understanding reported earnings do not mean that financial statements are useless—merely that they require careful study. However, even if one copes successfully with this problem, a serious forecasting obstacle remains. Green and Segall [1] studied the public forecasts of chief executive officers as reported in the *Wall Street Journal* during 1963 and 1964 and concluded that even such well-informed men found the future murky or impenetrable. One reason for their confusion is explained and documented by Lintner and Glauber in Chapter 39. They present persuasive evidence that earnings, like stock prices, follow approximately a random walk. Growth rates are unstable, and earnings changes cannot be predicted by the study of previous changes, a startling finding that was first suggested by I. M. D. Little [2] in a study of British firms. The lesson is clear: The investor must not rely on the simple extrapolation of historical trends but should examine the manner in which earnings have been affected by nonrecurring influences and inquire diligently into the changes taking place in the individual firm.

Chapter 40 suggests that there may be an even more fundamental reason for the difficulty in forecasting reported earnings. Treynor argues that these earnings are not simply a record of cash flows, but that they in some measure represent the accountants' assessment of the change that has taken place in the value of the firm. To the extent that this is the case, it would seem that the accountant is performing a very similar function to that of the investment analyst.

Any investment analyst could do worse than read David Ricardo's classic theory of rent: —

"If all land had the same properties, if it were unlimited in quantity and uniform in quality, no charge could be made for its use, unless where it possessed peculiar advantages of situation. It is only, then, because land is not unlimited in quantity and uniform in quality, and because in the progress of population land of an inferior quality, or less advantageously situated, is called into cultivation, rent immediately commences on that of the first quality, and the amount of that rent will depend on the difference in the quality of these two pieces of land."

Ricardo's words are a useful reminder that the value of *any* capital equipment depends on the additional costs that would be incurred if it were not available. In Chapter 41 Sobotka and Schnabel describe an interesting application of this idea to estimating the value of a fleet of aircraft.

[1] Green, D. H., and Segall, J. "The Predictive Power of First-Quarter Earnings Reports." *Journal of Business,* 40 (January, 1967), 44–55.

[2] Little, I. M. D. "Higgledy Piggledy Growth." *Bulletin of Oxford Institute of Statistics,* 24 (November, 1962), 387–412.

36

EARNINGS CHANGES, ANALYSTS' FORECASTS, AND STOCK PRICES

Victor Niederhoffer and Patrick J. Regan

In their search for the philosopher's stone, security analysts have found that stock price fluctuations are closely linked to earnings changes. In this report, we present some empirical evidence which supports that hypothesis. Our investigation concerns the earnings characteristics of those NYSE stocks that registered the largest percentage price changes in calendar 1970.

THE TOP 50/BOTTOM 50 SAMPLE

We first examined the 1970 market performance of the 1,253 common stocks listed on the New York Stock Exchange. While the closely-watched Dow Jones Industrial Average recorded a modest change of +4.8% in 1970, almost half (572, or 46%) of the NYSE stocks posted gains or losses in excess of 20%. From that group, we selected the 50 best and the 50 worst performers for closer scrutiny, on the assumption that the relation between earnings and price variation, if it existed, would be magnified in this sample.

Tables 1 and 2 list the 50 stocks with the greatest percentage gains (range: +37% to +125%) and the 50 with the largest losses (range: −49% to −78%). Also included are the reported 1969, estimated 1970, and actual 1970 earnings per share for each company. The earnings data appear exactly as they were reported, before extraordinary charges, with adjustments for stock dividends and splits. The earnings predictions were taken from the March 31, 1970 edition of the Standard and Poor's "Earnings Forecaster," a summary of up-to-date estimates by the leading financial institutions. In those cases where the "Earnings Forecaster" contained more than one prediction for a given company, we selected the estimate of the institution with the largest number of forecasts in the booklet. This procedure served to eliminate certain optimistic biases, inasmuch as some investment firms have a tendency to submit unrealistically high earnings estimates for companies in which they have a vested interest. Fortunately, though, as Malkiel and Cragg have reported,[1] the correlation of forecasts by different institutions for particular companies is quite high.

Since it was our intention to compare stock performance to current earnings, we included only those companies with fiscal years ending between September and February. Under such standards, eight stocks had to be rejected from the original top 50, and 17 from the bottom 50.

Reprinted from *The Financial Analysts Journal* XXVIII, No. 3 (May–June 1972), 65–71, by permission of the author and the publishers.

TABLE 1

Fifty Best Percentage Price Changes in 1970

	Earnings Per Share					Stock Price, Act. % Change
	Actual 1969	Est. 1970	Actual 1970	Change Per $ of Price		
				Est.	Actual	
1. Overnight Transportation	$1.47	$1.47	$2.58	+.000	+.092	+125.0%
2. Coca Cola Bottling, N.Y.	1.08	1.18	1.30	+.007	+.015	+ 84.2
3. Bates Manufacturing	.02	NA	1.28	NA	+.163	+ 72.6
4. General Cigar	2.24	2.30	3.01	+.003	+.041	+ 70.5
5. Texas East. Transmission	2.40	2.50	2.70	+.003	+.009	+ 70.5
6. Credithrift Financial	1.07	NA	1.15	NA	+.007	+ 63.6
7. Green Shoe Mfg.	1.93	2.20	2.60	+.014	+.035	+ 63.6
8. Pittston Co.	1.11	1.67	2.20	+.021	+.040	+ 63.6
9. Campbell Red Lake Mining	.73	.65	.48	−.005	−.014	+ 62.3
10. Blue Bell	3.13	3.70	3.81	+.017	+.021	+ 60.0
11. Collins & Aikman	2.47	2.50	2.61	+.001	+.006	+ 59.2
12. Gamble-Skogmo	2.66	2.60	3.08	−.003	+.019	+ 57.1
13. Amerada Hess	2.41	2.55	3.22	+.005	+.027	+ 56.0
14. Giant Portland Cement	.71	NA	1.07	NA	+.042	+ 55.1
15. AMF, Inc.	1.85	2.00	2.05	+.008	+.011	+ 54.7
16. Rubbermaid, Inc.	1.28	1.40	1.44	+.005	+.007	+ 54.2
17. Cone Mills Corp.	.97	1.20	1.51	+.017	+.039	+ 53.6
18. Graniteville Co.	1.29	1.30	2.07	+.001	+.051	+ 52.5
19. Keebler	2.01	2.10	2.95	+.002	+.024	+ 51.8
20. Interco	3.13	2.80	3.31	−.012	+.007	+ 51.6
21. M. Lowenstein & Sons	2.69	2.75	2.58	+.003	−.005	+ 51.2
22. Maytag	1.62	1.70	1.70	+.004	+.004	+ 51.1
23. Cabot Corp.	2.75	2.95	3.33	+.007	+.019	+ 49.6
24. MAPCO	1.72	1.80	1.97	+.005	· +.015	+ 48.9
25. Dr. Pepper	.50	.60	.61	+.003	+.004	+ 48.4
26. Pacific Intermt. Express	1.05	1.25	.94	+.013	−.007	+ 48.4
27. International Utilities	1.80	NA	2.40	NA	+.025	+ 47.2
28. U. S. Tobacco	1.69	1.95	2.04	+.014	+.019	+ 46.4
29. Russ Togs	1.02	1.30	1.47	+.019	+.030	+ 46.3
30. American Ship Building	1.10	1.25	1.42	+.008	+.017	+ 45.3
31. Ligget & Meyers	2.92	3.00	3.86	+.002	+.029	+ 45.2
32. Genuine Parts	1.40	1.57	1.73	+.007	+.013	+ 45.0
33. General Portland Cement	1.36	1.40	1.40	+.002	+.002	+ 44.9
34. Cudahy	1.77	NA	2.01	NA	+.019	+ 44.1
35. Cleveland Cliffs Iron	3.81	3.90	4.73	+.002	+.023	+ 43.8
36. Getty Oil	5.20	5.00	5.20	−.004	.000	+ 43.8
37. American Water Works	1.11	NA	1.29	NA	+.019	+ 42.7
38. Lone Star Gas	1.58	1.75	1.99	+.009	+.022	+ 42.5
39. Broadway Hale Stores	1.99	2.40	2.04	+.010	+.001	+ 42.3
40. Kings Dept. Store	.73	.73	.85	.000	+.013	+ 41.9
41. Northwest Industries	d .23	1.40	2.21	+.132	+.197	+ 41.4
42. Weyerhaeuser	2.11	2.35	1.87	+.006	−.006	+ 41.4
43. Quaker State Oil	1.42	1.65	1.67	+.009	+.010	+ 41.1
44. Bucyrus Erie	1.84	1.70	1.72	−.007	−.006	+ 40.1
45. Louisiana Land & Explor.	2.80	2.90	2.93	+.002	+.003	+ 40.0
46. Copeland Refrigeration	2.30	2.40	3.50	+.003	+.031	+ 38.7
47. Philip Morris	2.58	3.00	3.36	+.012	+.022	+ 38.5
48. Kaufman & Broad	.80	1.00	1.12	+.004	+.007	+ 37.7
49. Helmerich & Payne	1.55	1.70	1.72	+.009	+.011	+ 37.5
50. Safeway Stores	2.01	2.10	2.70	+.004	+.028	+ 37.4

NA = not available
d = deficit

TABLE 2

Fifty Worst Percentage Price Changes in 1970

	Earnings Per Share					Stock Price, Act. % Change
	Actual 1969	Est. 1970	Actual 1970	Change Per $ of Price		
				Est.	Actual	
1. Penn Central	$ .18	$2.00	$d 13.67	+.064	—.490	—77.9%
2. University Computing	2.58	NA	d 1.28	NA	—.040	—77.7
3. Electronic Mem. & Mag.	.93	1.05	d 2.12	+.003	—.075	—76.9
4. Fairchild Camera	.23	1.00	d 4.40	+.008	—.050	—74.7
5. Scientific Resources	d .78	NA	d 1.40	NA	—.050	—72.7
6. Transcontinental Invest.	.60	1.30	d .62E	+.029	—.051	—72.5
7. FAS International	.92	1.10	.39	+.008	—.023	—71.1
8. Republic Corp.	1.48	2.75	.23	+.046	—.045	—68.2
9. Sonesta	.27	NA	d 1.17	NA	—.112	—68.0
10. Automation Industries	.81	1.20	.22	+.032	—.049	—62.9
11. GAC Corp.	3.22	4.00	1.62	+.013	—.026	—62.9
12. Sprague Electric	.43	.75	d 1.78	+.012	—.083	—61.8
13. Memorex	1.87	2.50	.83	+.004	—.007	—61.0
14. Ward Foods	1.84	NA	.40	NA	—.053	—60.6
15. Whittaker Corp.	1.51	1.25	.28	—.014	—.067	—59.2
16. Ling-Temco-Vought	d .05	NA	d 12.73	NA	—.500	—59.1
17. Dictaphone	1.09	1.15	d .74	+.003	—.079	—58.4
18. MEI Corp.	d .19	NA	d .05	NA	+.012	—58.3
19. Smith International	1.63	1.75	.98	+.010	—.016	—58.2
20. Standard Pressed Steel	.73	.70	d 1.10	—.002	—.139	—58.1
21. High Voltage Engr.	.21	.25	d 1.00	+.002	—.057	—57.4
22. Palm Beach Co.	1.01	NA	.10	NA	—.046	—57.2
23. Bourn's Inc.	1.46	1.55	1.01	+.004	—.019	—57.1
24. Copper Range	6.80	10.00	4.07	+.050	—.042	—56.9
25. North American Philips	2.49	2.65	1.00	+.003	—.027	—56.4
26. Deltec Int'l.	.96	NA	d 1.24	NA	—.198	—56.2
27. Control Data	3.08	2.50	d .40	—.005	—.030	—56.1
28. Faberge, Inc.	1.67	1.70	.41	+.001	—.038	—56.1
29. Hamilton Watch	.68	NA	d 5.52	NA	—5.82	—55.8
30. Dillingham Corp.	1.15	1.25	d .51	+.004	—.063	—55.5
31. Berkey Photo	1.13	1.00	.41	—.007	—.041	—55.4
32. Fuqua Industries	1.90	2.02	1.48	+.004	—.015	—54.8
33. Equity Funding	1.91	NA	2.21	NA	+.005	—54.7
34. Kentucky Fried Chicken	1.24	1.70	1.24	+.011	.000	—53.8
35. Seaboard World Air.	d .43	NA	d .32	NA	+.007	—52.8
36. Electronic Associates	d .85	NA	d 1.95	NA	—.110	—52.5
37. Athlone Industries	3.31	NA	1.33	NA	—.072	—52.1
38. Crowell-Collier	1.35	1.44	.55	+.003	—.031	—51.9
39. Microdot, Inc.	1.95	2.05	1.14	+.004	—.030	—51.9
40. Arlan's Dept. Stores	1.43	1.40	d 4.40	—.002	—.315	—51.4
41. National Cash Register	2.11	2.25	1.37	+.002	—.009	—51.1
42. Varian Associates	.93	1.00	.68	+.002	—.009	—51.1
43. Diversified Industries	1.33	1.80	.01	+.026	—.072	—50.7
44. Norlin Corp.	3.31	NA	2.20	NA	—.043	—50.7
45. Budget Industries	.96	1.50	d .41	+.016	—.040	—50.0
46. HCA Industries	d .15	NA	d 1.88	NA	—.204	—50.0
47. Boeing	.47	2.00	1.02	+.054	+.020	—49.3
48. Lionel	.21	.80	.08	+.066	—.015	—49.3
49. Callahan Mining	.11	NA	d .06	NA	—.009	—49.1
50. Interstate Stores	1.70	2.00	.25	+.011	—.054	—49.1

NA = not available   d = deficit   E = preliminary earnings report

ACTUAL EARNINGS CHANGES AND THE ANALYSTS' ESTIMATES

Unmistakably, the most important factor separating the best from the worst-performing stocks was profitability. In terms of reported 1970 earnings compared to year-earlier results, 45 of the top 50 registered increases, a feat achieved by only four of the bottom 50 stocks. Thus, the chances that a company experienced an increase in earnings were 11 times as great among the superior performers. Furthermore, 20 of the top 50 recorded earnings gains of at least 25%, whereas all but six of the bottom 50 suffered declines in excess of 25%.

The superior and the inferior performers also differed greatly when actual earnings were compared to the forecasts. The analysts consistently underestimated the earnings gains of the top 50, and just as consistently overestimated the same data for the bottom 50. For example, there were estimates available for 44 of the top 50 stocks. Of those 44, 39 notched earnings in excess of the estimates. But of the 34 estimates available for the bottom 50, the actual results were worse in every single case.

Another important differentiating characteristic was the size of the predicted earnings increase. A glance at Tables 1 and 2 reveals that the forecasts for the top 50 stocks were moderate, as compared to those for the bottom 50. Indeed, of the 16 issues with predicted profit gains of 25% or more, 13 finished among the bottom 50 stocks.

Since we had no standard with which to compare the size of those earnings forecasts, we supplemented our analysis with a random sample of 100 of the remaining 1,153 NYSE stocks. The results, shown in Figure 1, were striking. The median estimated percentage changes in earnings for the top 50 and the random 100 were comparable, at 7.7% and 5.8%, respectively, but neither approached the predicted 15.3% gain for the bottom 50. Such results suggest that professional investors would be wise to cast a suspicious eye on unusually optimistic estimates, since failure on the part of the firm to realize such expectations will most certainly result in a stock price decline.

The data in Figure 1 strongly underscore the relationship between estimated earnings changes, actual earnings changes and stock performance. The median actual earnings increase of 21.4% by the top 50 was exceptional, in that the net profits of the random 100 were down 10.5%. In addition, the large earnings gain came as a pleasant surprise to the analysts, who had anticipated an increase of one-third that size. Under such conditions, the 48.4% median advance in stock prices was understandable. Similarly, there was little mystery surrounding the bottom 50's 56.7% sell-off, in view of the median earnings loss of 83.0%.

Because 23 of the bottom 50 stocks recorded deficits, there was a reluctance on the part of management to report the bad news. Hence, as Figure 2 shows, only 40% of the bottom 50 companies announced their earnings within two months of the end of the fiscal year, whereas 88% of the top 50 did so. And of the five firms which took more than three months to report, four incurred deficits. Such results confirm the observation of Alan Abelson, "Barrons" leading analyst and financial sleuth, that "companies which do well generally tend to report earlier than those that do poorly." [2]

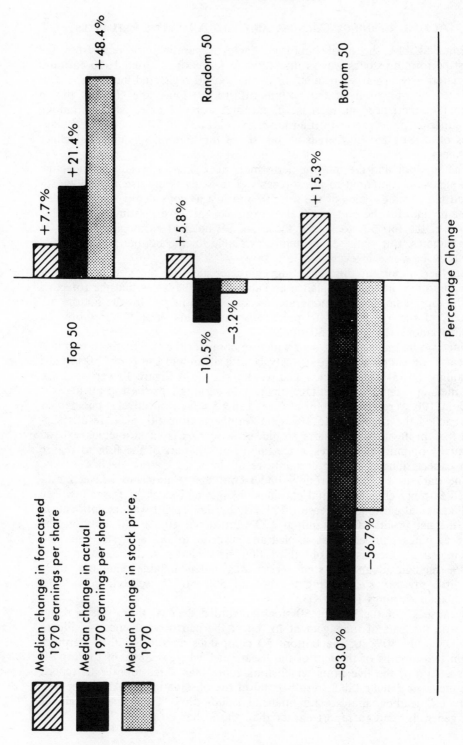

Figure 1. Median Changes in Forecasted Earnings, Actual Earnings and Stock Price, One-Year Horizon

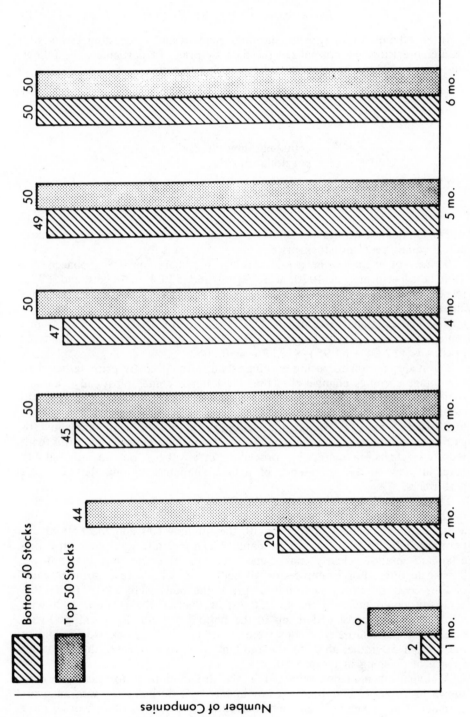

Figure 2. Companies Reporting Earnings within X Months of the End of the Fiscal Year

DATA NORMALIZED BY PRICE

In an attempt to analyze the earnings changes and forecasting errors with greater precision, we normalized the data by price. In particular, the following three variables were computed for each company:

(1) $\dfrac{F_{,1970} - E_{,1969}}{P_{,1969}}$ = estimated earnings change per dollar of price

(2) $\dfrac{E_{,1970} - E_{,1969}}{P_{,1969}}$ = actual earnings change per dollar of price

(3) $\dfrac{E_{,1970} - F_{,1970}}{P_{,1969}}$ = error in forecast per dollar of price

where E equals earnings per share, F equals forecasted earnings per share, and P equals year-end stock price.

By way of example, the actual earnings per share for U.S. Tobacco, the 28th best performer in 1970, were $1.69 and $2.04 for 1969 and 1970, respectively. Since the 1969 closing price was 18⅞, the actual earnings change per dollar of price was computed as ($2.04 - $1.69)/$18.875 = 0.019. The estimated earnings of U.S. Tobacco for 1970 were $1.95, nine cents less than the actual figure. Thus, the forecasted error per dollar of price was ($2.04 - $1.95)/$18.875 = 0.005.

The major reason for using earnings data normalized by price rather than percentage earnings changes was that the latter become statistically cumbersome whenever the base is small or negative. For example, an increase in earnings from $0.01 to $0.10 is a 900% rise, whereas a change from −$0.10 to $0.10 is a mere 200% advance. Because of this problem, many investigators have omitted from their analyses of earnings changes all firms with reported deficits,[3] a regrettable procedure in any case, but an impossibility here, in view of the abundance of deficit companies among the 50 worst performers.

The estimated and the actual earnings changes per dollar of price are listed in the fourth and fifth columns of Tables 1 and 2. The distribution of the actual earnings changes of the top 50, the random 100 and the bottom 50, normalized by price, is shown in Table 3. This simple non-parametric discriminant analysis clearly marks the areas of differentiation between the three categories. For example, for all companies with actual earnings gains of four cents or more per dollar of price, the odds were 14 to 1 that the company would finish in the top 50 rather than in the random 100, with virtually no chance of ending up in the bottom 50. But for earnings losses of eight cents or more, the odds were 20 to 1 that the stock would land in the bottom 50 rather than in the random 100. In this case, there was no chance of finishing in the top 50.

A similar phenomenon emerged in the distribution of forecasting errors, shown in Table 4. The median error in forecasts during 1970 was an overestimate of approximately one cent per dollar of price. In other words, on a

TABLE 3

DISTRIBUTION OF ACTUAL EARNINGS
CHANGES PER DOLLAR OF PRICE

Earnings Changes *	Top 50	Random 100	Bottom 50
18 and over	2		
16 to 18	2		
14 to 16			
12 to 14			
10 to 12			
8 to 10	2		
6 to 8			
4 to 6	8	1	
2 to 4	26		2
0 to 2	50	35	8
−0 to −2	10	38	16
−2 to −4		16	14
−4 to −6		4	28
−6 to −8		5	12
−8 to −10		1	2
−10 to −12			4
−12 to −14			2
−14 to −16			
−16 to −18			
−18 and over			12
	100*	100	100*

* Earnings change refers to "cents per dollar of 1969 stock price." The Top 50 and the Bottom 50 are adjusted to a total of 100 observations each, in order to facilitate comparisons with the random 100 and to offer percentage breakdowns at a glance.

$20 stock, the earnings change was overestimated by $0.20. Earlier, we noted that the worst performers were characterized by overestimates and the best stocks by underestimates. With the more precise normalized data in Table 4, we can see that when the forecast was overestimated by eight cents or more per dollar of price, the odds were nearly 17 to 1 that the stock would finish in the bottom 50 rather than in the random 100. At the other extreme, an underestimate of one cent or more per dollar of price was almost a guarantee that the stock would finish in the top 50 rather than in the random 100, since the chances were 24 out of 25. But the table does seem to vindicate the analysts' position as seers, since half of the estimates for the 100 random stocks were within one cent (normalized) of actual earnings and two-thirds were within two cents.

THE FIVE-YEAR HORIZON

As a final test, we examined the performance of 650 stocks for the five-year period ended 1970.[4] The median actual changes in stock price and

TABLE 4

DISTRIBUTION OF FORECAST ERRORS PER DOLLAR OF PRICE

Forecast Error *	Top 50	Random 100	Bottom 50	
6.0 & over	4.5			⎫
5.5 to 6.0				
5.0 to 5.5	2.3			
4.5 to 5.0				
4.0 to 4.5				
3.5 to 4.0	2.3			
3.0 to 3.5				Under-estimated
2.5 to 3.0	4.5			
2.0 to 2.5	15.9			
1.5 to 2.0	4.5	1		
1.0 to 1.5	13.6	1		
0.5 to 1.0	13.6	7		
0 to 0.5	27.2	12		⎭
−0 to −0.5		18		⎫
−0.5 to −1.0	6.8	15		
−1.0 to −1.5	2.3	6	12	
−1.5 to −2.0		9	3	
−2.0 to −2.5	2.3	7	3	
−2.5 to −3.0		5	6	
−3.0 to −3.5		2	18	
−3.5 to −4.0		3	6	
−4.0 to −4.5		3		
−4.5 to −5.0		5		
−5.0 to −5.5		1	3	Over-estimated
−5.5 to −6.0			9	
−6.0 to −6.5		1		
−6.5 to −7.0			6	
−7.0 to −7.5		1		
−7.5 to −8.0		1	3	
−8.0 to −8.5			12	
−8.5 to −9.0				
−9.0 to −9.5			6	
−9.5 to −10.0			6	
−10.0 & over		2	9	⎭
	99.8*	100	102*	

* Forecast error is equal to the actual minus the estimated earnings per share, expressed in cents per dollar of 1969 stock price. The Top 50 and the Bottom 50 are adjusted to a total of 100 observations each, in order to facilitate comparisons with the random 100 and to offer percentage breakdowns at a glance. Actually, there were 44 observations in the Top 50 and 34 in the Bottom 50.

earnings per share for the top 50, the random 100 and the bottom 50, as shown in Figure 3, confirmed the one-year results. The top 50 recorded median advances of 182% and 199% in prices and per-share profits, re-

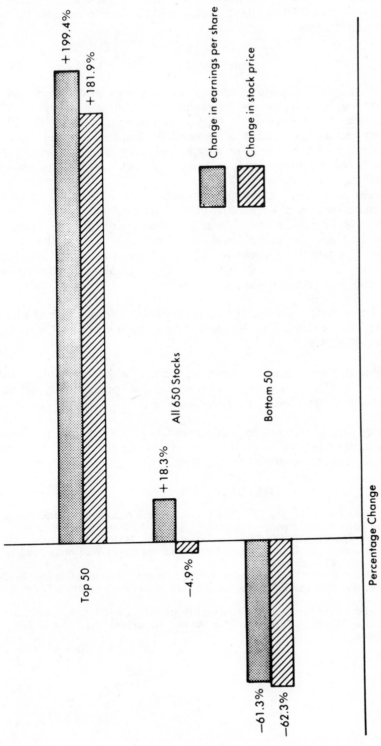

Figure 3. Median Changes in Earnings and Stock Price, Five-Year Horizon

spectively, while the bottom 50 finished with losses of 62% and 61%. Thus, by all measurements and time spans, profits held the key to superior or inferior stock performance.

CONCLUSIONS

In sum, the results of this study demonstrate that stock prices are strongly dependent on earnings changes, both absolute and relative to analysts' estimates. The common characteristics of the companies registering the best price changes included a forecast of moderately increased earnings and a realized profit gain far in excess of analysts' expectations. The worst-performing stocks were characterized by severe earnings declines, combined with unusually optimistic forecasts.

These results present both challenge and opportunity for financial analysts. If their estimates are more accurate than the conventional published forecasts of the large institutions, there is ample opportunity for differentiating between the best and the worst-performing companies. Failing that, they may be able to isolate those stocks for which the Street estimates are most reliable. At any rate, it is clear that an accurate earnings forecast is of enormous value in stock selection.

Dr. Victor Niederhoffer is President of Niederhoffer, Cross & Zeckhauser, Inc., and Assistant Professor of Business Administration at the University of California, Berkeley.

Patrick J. Regan, who recently received an M.B.A. with distinction at the University of California, is writing a book on the predictability of the market's reaction to new information.

The authors gratefully acknowledge the support they received from the Dean Witter Foundation through a grant to the Graduate School of Business Administration, University of California, Berkeley.

REFERENCES

1. J. G. Cragg and Burton G. Malkiel, "The Consensus and Accuracy of Some Predictions of the Growth of Corporate Earnings," *Journal of Finance* (March, 1968).
2. As quoted in *The 1971 Stock Trader's Almanac;* The Hirsch Organization (Old Tappan, New Jersey), p. 56. Abelson's column, "Up and Down Wall Street," adorns the cover of *Barron's* each week.
3. See, for example, Robert A. Levy and Spero L. Kripotos, "Earnings Growth, P/E's and Relative Price Strength," *Financial Analysts Journal* (November–December, 1969).
4. The five-year stock performance and earnings growth for the 650 largest corporations was taken from *Forbes* magazine's "23rd Annual Report on American Industry" (*Forbes*, January 1, 1971).

37

AN EMPIRICAL EVALUATION OF
ACCOUNTING INCOME NUMBERS

Ray Ball * *and Philip Brown* †

Accounting theorists have generally evaluated the usefulness of accounting practices by the extent of their agreement with a particular analytic model. The model may consist of only a few assertions or it may be a rigorously developed argument. In each case, the method of evaluation has been to compare existing practices with the more preferable practices implied by the model or with some standard which the model implies all practices should possess. The shortcoming of this method is that it ignores a significant source of knowledge of the world, namely, the extent to which the predictions of the model conform to observed behavior.

It is not enough to defend an analytical inquiry on the basis that its assumptions are empirically supportable, for how is one to know that a theory embraces all of the relevant supportable assumptions? And how does one explain the predictive powers of propositions which are based on unverifiable assumptions such as the maximization of utility functions? Further, how is one to resolve differences between propositions which arise from considering different aspects of the world?

The limitations of a completely analytical approach to usefulness are illustrated by the argument that income numbers cannot be defined substantively, that they lack "meaning" and are therefore of doubtful utility.[1] The argument stems in part from the patchwork development of account-

* University of Chicago.   † University of Western Australia. The authors are indebted to the participants in the Workshop in Accounting Research at the University of Chicago, Professor Myron Scholes, and Messrs. Owen Hewett and Ian Watts.

[1] Versions of this particular argument appear in Canning (1929); Gilman (1939); Paton and Littleton (1940); Vatter (1947), Ch. 2; Edwards and Bell (1961), Ch. 1; Chambers (1964), pp. 267–68; Chambers (1966), pp. 4 and 102; Lim (1966), esp. pp. 645 and 649; Chambers (1967), pp. 745–55; Ijiri (1967), Ch. 6, esp. pp. 120–31; and Sterling (1967), p. 65.

Reprinted from the *Journal of Accounting Research*, Vol. 6, No. 2 (Autumn, 1968) pp. 159–78, by permission of the publisher. Copyright Institute of Professional Accounting, 1968.

ing practices to meet new situations as they arise. Accountants have had to deal with consolidations, leases, mergers, research and development, price-level changes, and taxation charges, to name just a few problem areas. Because accounting lacks an all-embracing theoretical framework, dissimilarities in practices have evolved. As a consequence, net income is an aggregate of components which are not homogeneous. It is thus alleged to be a "meaningless" figure, not unlike the difference between twenty-seven tables and eight chairs. Under this view, net income can be defined only as the result of the application of a set of procedures $\{X_1, X_2, \cdots\}$ to a set of events $\{Y_1, Y_2, \cdots\}$ with no other definitive substantive meaning at all. Canning observes:

> What is set out as a measure of net income can never be supposed to be a fact in any sense at all except that it is the figure that results when the accountant has finished applying the procedures which he adopts.[2]

The value of analytical attempts to develop measurements capable of definitive interpretation is not at issue. What is at issue is the fact that an analytical model does not itself assess the significance of departures from its implied measurements. Hence it is dangerous to conclude, in the absence of further empirical testing, that a lack of substantive meaning implies a lack of utility.

An empirical evaluation of accounting income numbers requires agreement as to what real-world outcome constitutes an appropriate test of usefulness. Because net income is a number of particular interest to investors, the outcome we use as a predictive criterion is the investment decision as it is reflected in security prices.[3] Both the content and the timing of existing annual net income numbers will be evaluated since usefulness could be impaired by deficiencies in either.

An Empirical Test

Recent developments in capital theory provide justification for selecting the behavior of security prices as an operational test of usefulness. An impressive body of theory supports the proposition that capital markets are both efficient and unbiased in that if information is useful in forming capital asset prices, then the market will adjust asset prices to that information quickly and without leaving any opportunity for further abnormal gain.[4] If, as the evidence indicates, security prices do in fact adjust rapidly to new information as it becomes available, then changes in security prices will re-

---

[2] Canning (1929), p. 98.

[3] Another approach pursued by Beaver (1968) is to use the investment decision, as it is reflected in transactions volume, for a predictive criterion.

[4] For example, Samuelson (1965) demonstrated that a market without bias in its evaluation of information will give rise to randomly fluctuating time series of prices. See also Cootner (ed.) (1964); Fama (1965); Fama and Blume (1966); Fama, *et al.* (1967); and Jensen (1968).

flect the flow of information to the market.[5] An observed revision of stock prices associated with the release of the income report would thus provide evidence that the information reflected in income numbers is useful.

Our method of relating accounting income to stock prices builds on this theory and evidence by focusing on the information which is unique to a particular firm.[6] Specifically, we construct two alternative models of what the market expects income to be and then investigate the market's reactions when its expectations prove false.

EXPECTED AND UNEXPECTED INCOME CHANGES

Historically, the incomes of firms have tended to move together. One study found that about half of the variability in the level of an average firm's earnings per share (EPS) could be associated with economy-wide effects.[7] In light of this evidence, at least part of the change in a firm's income from one year to the next is to be expected. If, in prior years, the income of a firm has been related to the incomes of other firms in a particular way, then knowledge of that past relation, together with a knowledge of the incomes of those other firms for the present year, yields a conditional expectation for the present income of the firm. Thus, apart from confirmation effects, the amount of new information conveyed by the present income number can be approximated by the difference between the actual change in income and its conditional expectation.

But not all of this difference is necessarily new information. Some changes in income result from financing and other policy decisions made by the firm. We assume that, to a first approximation, such changes are reflected in the average change in income through time.

Since the impacts of these two components of change—economy-wide and policy effects—are felt simultaneously, the relationship must be estimated jointly. The statistical specification we adopt is first to estimate, by Ordinary Least Squares (OLS), the coefficients (a_{1jt}, a_{2jt}) from the linear regression of the change in firm j's income ($\Delta I_{j,t-\tau}$) on the change in the average income of all firms (other than firm j) in the market ($\Delta M_{j,t-\tau}$)[8] using data up to the end of the previous year ($\tau = 1, 2, \cdots, t-1$):

$$\Delta I_{j,t-\tau} = \hat{a}_{1jt} + \hat{a}_{2jt}\Delta M_{j,t-\tau} + \hat{u}_{j,t-\tau} \qquad \tau = 1, 2, \cdots, t-1, \qquad (1)$$

[5] One well documented characteristic of the security market is that useful sources of information are acted upon and useless sources are ignored. This is hardly surprising since the market consists of a large number of competing actors who can gain from acting upon better interpretations of the future than those of their rivals. See, for example, Scholes (1967); and footnote 4 above. This evaluation of the security market differs sharply from that of Chambers (1966, pp. 272–73).

[6] More precisely, we focus on information not common to all firms, since some industry effects are not considered in this paper.

[7] Alternatively, 35 to 40 per cent could be associated with effects common to all firms when income was defined as tax-adjusted Return on Capital Employed. [Source: Ball and Brown (1967), Table 4.]

[8] We call M a "market index" of income because it is constructed only from firms traded on the New York Stock Exchange.

where the hats denote estimates. The expected income change for firm j in year t is then given by the regression prediction using the change in the average income for the market in year t:

$$\Delta I_{jt} = \hat{a}_{1jt} + \hat{a}_{2jt}\Delta M_{jt}.$$

The unexpected income change, or forecast error $(\hat{u}_{jt})$, is the actual income change minus expected:

$$\hat{u}_{jt} = \Delta I_{jt} - \Delta \hat{I}_{jt}. \tag{2}$$

It is this forecast error which we assume to be the new information conveyed by the present income number.

THE MARKET'S REACTION

It has also been demonstrated that stock prices, and therefore rates of return from holding stocks, tend to move together. In one study,[9] it was estimated that about 30 to 40 per cent of the variability in a stock's monthly rate of return over the period March, 1944 through December, 1960 could be associated with market-wide effects. Market-wide variations in stock returns are triggered by the release of information which concerns all firms. Since we are evaluating the income report as it relates to the individual firm, its contents and timing should be assessed relative to changes in the rate of return on the firm's stocks net of market-wide effects.

The impact of market-wide information on the monthly rate of return from investing one dollar in the stock of firm j may be estimated by its predicted value from the linear regression of the monthly price relatives of firm j's common stock[10] on a market index of returns:[11]

---

[9] King (1966).

[10] The monthly price relative of security j for month m is defined as dividends (d_{jm}) + closing price $(p_{j,m+1})$, divided by opening price (p_{jm}):

$$PR_{jm} = (p_{j,m+1} + d_{jm})/p_{jm}.$$

A monthly price relative is thus equal to the discrete monthly rate of return plus unity; its natural logarithm is the monthly rate of return compounded continuously. In this paper, we assume discrete compounding since the results are easier to interpret in that form.

[11] Fama, *et al.* (1967) conclude that "regressions of security on market returns over time are a satisfactory method for abstracting from the effects of general market conditions on the monthly rates of return on individual securities." In arriving at their conclusion, they found that "scatter diagrams for the [returns on] individual securities [vis-à-vis the market return] support very well the regression assumptions of linearity, homoscedasticity, and serial independence." Fama, *et al.* studied the natural logarithmic transforms of the price relatives, as did King (1966). However, Blume (1968) worked with equation (3). We also performed tests on the alternative specification:

$$\ln_e (PR_{jm}) = b'_{1j} + b'_{2j}\ln_e (L_m) + v'_{jm}, \tag{3a}$$

where $\ln_e$ denotes the natural logarithmic function. The results correspond closely with those reported below.

$$[PR_{jm} - 1] = \hat{b}_{1j} + \hat{b}_{2j}[L_m - 1] + \hat{v}_{jm} , \qquad (3)$$

where PR_{jm} is the monthly price relative for firm j and month m, L is the link relative of Fisher's "Combination Investment Performance Index" [Fisher (1966)], and v_{jm} is the stock return residual for firm j in month m. The value of $[L_m - 1]$ is an estimate of the market's monthly rate of return. The m-subscript in our sample assumes values for all months since January, 1946 for which data are available.

The residual from the OLS regression represented in equation (3) measures the extent to which the realized return differs from the expected return conditional upon the estimated regression parameters (b_{1j}, b_{2j}) and the market index $[L_m - 1]$. Thus, since the market has been found to adjust quickly and efficiently to new information, the residual must represent the impact of new information, about firm j alone, on the return from holding common stock in firm j.

SOME ECONOMETRIC ISSUES

One assumption of the OLS income regression model[12] is that M_j and u_j are uncorrelated. Correlation between them can take at least two forms, namely the inclusion of firm j in the market index of income (M_j), and the presence of industry effects. The first has been eliminated by construction (denoted by the j-subscript on M), but no adjustment has been made for the presence of industry effects. It has been estimated that industry effects probably account for only about 10 per cent of the variability in the level of a firm's income.[13] For this reason equation (1) has been adopted as the appropriate specification in the belief that any bias in the estimates a_{1jt} and a_{2jt} will not be significant. However, as a check on the statistical efficiency of the model, we also present results for an alternative, naive model which predicts that income will be the same for this year as for last. Its forecast error is simply the change in income since the previous year.

As is the case with the income regression model, the stock return model, as presented, contains several obvious violations of the assumptions of the OLS regression model. First, the market index of returns is correlated with the residual because the market index contains the return on firm j, and because of industry effects. Neither violation is serious, because Fisher's index is calculated over all stocks listed on the New York Stock Exchange (hence the return on security j is only a small part of the index), and because industry effects account for at most 10 per cent of the variability in the rate

---

[12] That is, an assumption necessary for OLS to be the minimum-variance, linear, unbiased estimator.

[13] The magnitude assigned to industry effects depends upon how broadly an industry is defined, which in turn depends upon the particular empirical application being considered. The estimate of 10 per cent is based on a two-digit classification scheme. There is some evidence that industry effects might account for more than 10 per cent when the association is estimated in first differences [Brealey (1968)].

of return on the average stock.[14] A second violation results from our prediction that, for certain months around the report dates, the expected values of the v_j's are nonzero. Again, any bias should have little effect on the results, inasmuch as there is a low, observed autocorrelation in the $\hat{v}_j$'s,[15] and in no case was the stock return regression fitted over less than 100 observations.[16]

SUMMARY

We assume that in the unlikely absence of useful information about a particular firm over a period, its rate of return over that period would reflect only the presence of market-wide information which pertains to all firms. By abstracting from market effects [equation (3)] we identify the effect of information pertaining to individual firms. Then, to determine if part of this effect can be associated with information contained in the firm's accounting income number, we segregate the expected and unexpected elements of income change. If the income forecast error is negative (that is, if the actual change in income is less than its conditional expectation), we define it as bad news and predict that if there is some association between accounting income numbers and stock prices, then release of the income number would result in the return on that firm's securities being less than

---

[14] The estimate of 10 per cent is due to King (1966). Blume (1968) has recently questioned the magnitude of industry effects, suggesting that they could be somewhat less than 10 per cent. His contention is based on the observation that the significance attached to industry effects depends on the assumptions made about the parameters of the distributions underlying stock rates of return.

[15] See Table 4, below.

[16] Fama, *et al.* (1967) faced a similar situation. The expected values of the stock return residuals were nonzero for some of the months in their study. Stock return regressions were calculated separately for both exclusion and inclusion of the months for which the stock return residuals were thought to be nonzero. They report that both sets of results support the same conclusions.

An alternative to constraining the mean v_j to be zero is to employ the Sharpe Capital Asset Pricing Model [Sharpe (1964)] to estimate (3b):

$$PR_{jm} - RF_m - 1 = b'_{1j} + b'_{2j} [L_m - RF_m - 1] + v'_{jm}, \qquad (3b)$$

where RF is the risk-free ex ante rate of return for holding period m. Results from estimating (3b) (using U.S. Government Bills to measure RF and defining the abnormal return for firm j in month m now as $b'_{1j} + v'_{jm}$) are essentially the same as the results from (3).

Equation (3b) is still not entirely satisfactory, however, since the mean impact of new information is estimated over the whole history of the stock, which covers at least 100 months. If (3b) were fitted using monthly data, a vector of dummy variables could be introduced to identify the fiscal year covered by the annual report, thus permitting the mean residual to vary between fiscal years. The impact of unusual information received in month m of year t would then be estimated by the sum of the constant, the dummy for year t, and the calculated residual for month m and year t. Unfortunately, the efficiency of estimating the stock return equation in this particular form has not been investigated satisfactorily, hence our report will be confined to the results from estimating (3).

TABLE 1

Deciles of the Distributions of Squared Coefficients of Correlation, Changes in Firm and Market Income*

Variable	Decile								
	.1	.2	.3	.4	.5	.6	.7	.8	.9
(1) Net income........	.03	.07	.10	.15	.23	.30	.35	.43	.52
(2) EPS.............	.02	.05	.11	.16	.23	.28	.35	.42	.52

* Estimated over the 21 years, 1946–1966.

would otherwise have been expected.[17] Such a result ($\hat{u} < 0$) would be evidenced by negative behavior in the stock return residuals ($\hat{v} < 0$) around the annual report announcement date. The converse should hold for a positive forecast error.

Two basic income expectations models have been defined, a regression model and a naive model. We report in detail on two measures of income [net income and EPS, variables (1) and (2)] for the regression model, and one measure [EPS, variable (3)] for the naive model.

Data

Three classes of data are of interest: the contents of income reports; the dates of the report announcements; and the movements of security prices around the announcement dates.

INCOME NUMBERS

Income numbers for 1946 through 1966 were obtained from Standard and Poor's *Compustat* tapes.[18] The distributions of the squared coefficients of correlation[19] between the changes in the incomes of the individual firms and the changes in the market's income index[20] are summarized in Table 1. For the present sample, about one-fourth of the variability in the changes

---

[17] We later divide the total return into two parts: a "normal return," defined by the return which would have been expected given the normal relationship between a stock and the market index; and an "abnormal return," the difference between the actual return and the normal return. Formally, the two parts are given by: $b_{1j} + b_{2j}[L_m - 1]$; and v_{jm}.

[18] Tapes used are dated 9/28/1965 and 7/07/1967.

[19] All correlation coefficients in this paper are product-moment correlation coefficients.

[20] The market net income index was computed as the sample mean for each year. The market EPS index was computed as a weighted average over the sample members, the number of stocks outstanding (adjusted for stock splits and stock dividends) providing the weights. Note that when estimating the association between the income of a particular firm and the market, the income of that firm was excluded from the market index.

TABLE 2

Deciles of the Distributions of the Coefficients of First-Order Autocorrelation in the Income Regression Residuals*

Variable	Decile								
	.1	.2	.3	.4	.5	.6	.7	.8	.9
(1) Net income...	−.35	−.28	−.20	−.12	−.05	.02	.12	.20	.33
(2) EPS..........	−.39	−.29	−.21	−.15	−.08	−.03	.07	.17	.35

* Estimated over the 21 years, 1946–1966.

in the median firm's income can be associated with changes in the market index.

The association between the levels of the earnings of firms was examined in the forerunner article [Ball and Brown (1967)]. At that time, we referred to the existence of autocorrelation in the disturbances when the levels of net income and EPS were regressed on the appropriate indexes. In this paper, the specification has been changed from levels to first differences because our method of analyzing the stock market's reaction to income numbers presupposes the income forecast errors to be unpredictable at a minimum of 12 months prior to the announcement dates. This supposition is inappropriate when the errors are autocorrelated.

We tested the extent of autocorrelation in the residuals from the income regression model after the variables had been changed from levels to first differences. The results are presented in Table 2. They indicate that the supposition is not now unwarranted.

ANNUAL REPORT ANNOUNCEMENT DATES

The *Wall Street Journal* publishes three kinds of annual report announcements: forecasts of the year's income, as made, for example, by corporation executives shortly after the year end; preliminary reports; and the complete annual report. While forecasts are often imprecise, the preliminary report is typically a condensed preview of the annual report. Because the preliminary report usually contains the same numbers for net income and EPS as are given later with the final report, the announcement date (or, effectively, the date on which the annual income number became generally available) was assumed to be the date on which the preliminary report appeared in the *Wall Street Journal*. Table 3 reveals that the time lag between the end of the fiscal year and the release of the annual report has been declining steadily throughout the sample period.

STOCK PRICES

Stock price relatives were obtained from the tapes constructed by the Center for Research in Security Prices (CRSP) at the University of Chi-

TABLE 3

Time Distribution of Announcement Dates

Per cent of firms	Fiscal year								
	1957	1958	1959	1960	1961	1962	1963	1964	1965
25	2/07[a]	2/04	2/04	2/03	2/02	2/05	2/03	2/01	1/31
50	2/25	2/20	2/18	2/17	2/15	2/15	2/13	2/09	2/08
75	3/10	3/06	3/04	3/03	3/05	3/04	2/28	2/25	2/21

[a] Indicates that 25 per cent of the income reports for the fiscal year ended 12/31/1957 had been announced by 2/07/1958.

TABLE 4

Deciles of the Distributions of the Squared Coefficient of Correlation for the Stock Return Regression, and of the Coefficient of First-Order Autocorrelation in the Stock Return Residuals *

Coefficient name	Decile								
	.1	.2	.3	.4	.5	.6	.7	.8	.9
Return regression r^2...	.18	.22	.25	.28	.31	.34	.37	.40	.46
Residual autocorrelation..	−.17	−.14	−.11	−.10	−.08	−.05	−.03	−.01	.03

* Estimated over the 246 months, January, 1946 through June, 1966.

cago.[21] The data used are monthly closing prices on the New York Stock Exchange, adjusted for dividends and capital changes, for the period January, 1946 through June, 1966. Table 4 presents the deciles of the distributions of the squared coefficient of correlation for the stock return regression [equation (3)], and of the coefficient of first-order autocorrelation in the stock residuals.

INCLUSION CRITERIA

Firms included in the study met the following criteria:

1. earnings data available on the *Compustat* tapes for each of the years 1946–1966;

2. fiscal year ending December 31;

3. price data available on the CRSP tapes for at least 100 months; and

4. *Wall Street Journal* announcement dates available.[22]

Our analysis was limited to the nine fiscal years 1957–1965. By beginning the analysis with 1957, we were assured of at least 10 observations when

[21] The Center for Research in Security Prices at the University of Chicago is sponsored by Merrill Lynch, Pierce, Fenner and Smith Incorporated.

[22] Announcement dates were taken initially from the *Wall Street Journal Index*, then verified against the *Wall Street Journal*.

estimating the income regression equations. The upper limit (the fiscal year 1965, the results of which are announced in 1966) is imposed because the CRSP file terminated in June, 1966.

Our selection criteria may reduce the generality of the results. The sub-population does not include young firms, those which have failed, those which do not report on December 31, and those which are not represented on *Compustat*, the CRSP tapes, and the *Wall Street Journal*. As a result, it may not be representative of all firms. However, note that (1) the 261 remaining firms[23] are significant in their own right, and (2) a replication of our study on a different sample produced results which conform closely to those reported below.[24]

Results

Define month 0 as the month of the annual report announcement, and API_M , the Abnormal Performance Index at month M, as:

$$API_M = \frac{1}{N} \sum_n^N \prod_{m=-11}^M (1 + v_{nm}).$$

Then API traces out the value of one dollar invested (in equal amounts) in all securities n $(n = 1, 2, \cdots, N)$ at the end of month -12 (that is, 12 months prior to the month of the annual report) and held to the end of some arbitrary holding period $(M = -11, -10, \cdots, T)$ after abstracting from market affects. An equivalent interpretation is as follows. Suppose two individuals A and B agree on the following proposition. B is to construct a portfolio consisting of one dollar invested in equal amounts in N securities. The securities are to be purchased at the end of month -12 and held until the end of month T. For some price, B contracts with A to take (or make up), at the end of each month M, only the normal gains (or losses) and to return to A, at the end of month T, one dollar plus or minus any abnormal gains or losses. Then API_M is the value of A's equity in the mutual portfolio at the end of each month M.[25]

Numerical results are presented in two forms. Figure 1 plots API_M first for three portfolios constructed from all firms and years in which the income forecast errors, according to each of the three variables, were positive (the top half); second, for three portfolios of firms and years in which the income forecast errors were negative (the bottom half); and third, for a single portfolio consisting of all firms and years in the sample (the line which wanders just below the line dividing the two halves). Table 5 includes the numbers on which Figure 1 is based.

---

[23] Due to known errors in the data, not all firms could be included in all years. The fiscal year most affected was 1964, when three firms were excluded.

[24] The replication investigated 75 firms with fiscal years ending on dates other than December 31, using the naive income-forecasting model, over the longer period 1947–65.

[25] That is, the value expected at the end of month T in the absence of further abnormal gains and losses.

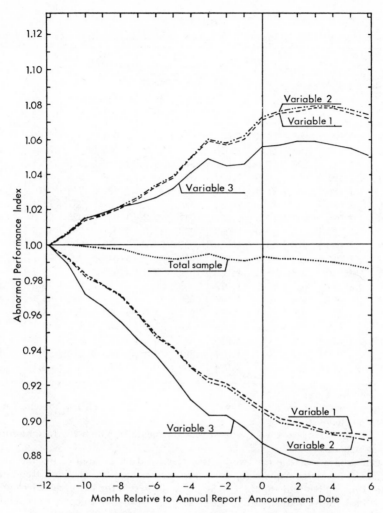

FIG. 1 Abnormal Performance Indexes for Various Portfolios

Since the first set of results may be sensitive to the distributions of the stock return disturbances,[26] a second set of results is presented. The third column under each variable heading in Table 5 gives the chi-square statistic for a two-by-two classification of firms by the sign of the income forecast error, and the sign of the stock return residual for that month.

OVERVIEW

As one would expect from a large sample, both sets of results convey essentially the same picture. They demonstrate that the information contained in the annual income number is useful in that if actual income differs

---

[26] The empirical distributions of the stock return residuals appear to be described well by symmetric, stable distributions that are characterized by tails longer than those of the normal distribution [Fama (1965); Fama, *et al.* (1967)].

TABLE 5

Summary Statistics by Month Relative to Annual Report Announcement Date

Month relative to annual report announcement date	Regression model						Naive model			Total sample
	Net income			EPS			EPS			
	(1)[a]	(2)	(3)	(1)	(2)	(3)	(1)	(2)	(3)	
−11	1.006	.992	16.5	1.007	.992	20.4	1.006	.989	24.1	1.000
−10	1.014	.983	17.3	1.015	.982	20.2	1.015	.972	73.4	.999
−9	1.017	.977	7.9	1.017	.977	3.7	1.018	.965	20.4	.998
−8	1.021	.971	9.5	1.022	.971	12.0	1.022	.956	9.1	.998
−7	1.026	.960	21.8	1.027	.960	27.1	1.024	.946	9.0	.995
−6	1.033	.949	42.9	1.034	.948	37.6	1.027	.937	19.4	.993
−5	1.038	.941	17.9	1.039	.941	21.3	1.032	.925	21.0	.992
−4	1.050	.930	40.0	1.050	.930	39.5	1.041	.912	41.5	.993
−3	1.059	.924	35.3	1.060	.922	33.9	1.049	.903	37.2	.995
−2	1.057	.921	1.4	1.058	.919	1.8	1.045	.903	0.1	.992
−1	1.060	.914	8.2	1.062	.912	8.2	1.046	.896	5.7	.991
0	1.071	.907	28.0	1.073	.905	28.9	1.056	.887	35.8	.993
1	1.075	.901	6.4	1.076	.899	5.5	1.057	.882	9.4	.992
2	1.076	.899	2.7	1.078	.897	1.9	1.059	.878	8.1	.992
3	1.078	.896	0.6	1.079	.895	1.2	1.059	.876	0.1	.991
4	1.078	.893	0.1	1.079	.892	0.1	1.057	.876	1.2	.990
5	1.075	.893	0.7	1.077	.891	0.1	1.055	.876	0.6	.989
6	1.072	.892	0.0	1.074	.889	0.2	1.051	.877	0.1	.987

[a] Column headings:
(1) Abnormal Performance Index—firms and years in which the income forecast error was positive.
(2) Abnormal Performance Index—firms and years in which the income forecast error was negative.
(3) Chi-square statistic for two-by-two classification by sign of income forecast error (for the fiscal year) and sign of stock return residual (for the indicated month).
Note: Probability (chi-square $\geq 3.84 \mid \chi^2 = 0$) $= .05$, for 1 degree of freedom.
　　　Probability (chi-square $\geq 6.64 \mid \chi^2 = 0$) $= .01$, for 1 degree of freedom.

from expected income, the market typically has reacted in the same direction. This contention is supported both by Figure 1 which reveals a marked, positive association between the sign of the error in forecasting income and the Abnormal Performance Index, and by the chi-square statistic (Table 5). The latter shows it is most unlikely that there is no relationship between the sign of the income forecast error and the sign of the rate of return residual in most of the months up to that of the annual report announcement.

However, most of the information contained in reported income is anticipated by the market before the annual report is released. In fact, anticipation is so accurate that the actual income number does not appear to cause any unusual jumps in the Abnormal Performance Index in the announcement month. To illustrate, the drifts upward and downward begin at least 12 months before the report is released (when the portfolios are first

TABLE 6

Contingency Table of the Signs of the Income Forecast Errors—by Variable

Sign of income forecast error	Sign of income forecast error					
	Variable (1)		Variable (2)		Variable (3)	
	+	−	+	−	+	−
Variable (1)						
+	1231	—	1148	83	1074	157
−	—	1109	83	1026	399	710
Variable (2)						
+	1148	83	1231	—	1074	157
−	83	1026	—	1109	399	710
Variable (3)						
+	1074	399	1074	399	1473	—
−	157	710	157	710	—	867

constructed) and continue for approximately one month after. The persistence of the drifts, as indicated by the constant signs of the indexes and by their almost monotonic increases in absolute value (Figure 1), suggests not only that the market begins to anticipate forecast errors early in the 12 months preceding the report, but also that it continues to do so with increasing success throughout the year.[27]

SPECIFIC RESULTS

1. There appears to be little difference between the results for the two regression model variables. Table 6, which classifies the sign of one variable's forecast error contingent upon the signs of the errors of the other two variables, reveals the reason. For example, on the 1231 occasions on which the income forecast error was positive for variable (1), it was also positive on 1148 occasions (out of a possible 1231) for variable (2). Similarly, on the 1109 occasions on which the income forecast error was negative for variable (1), it was also negative on 1026 occasions for variable (2). The fact that the results for variable (2) strictly dominate those for variable (1) suggests, however, that when the two variables disagreed on the sign of an income forecast error, variable (2) was more often correct.

While there is little to choose between variables (1) and (2), variable (3) (the naive model) is clearly best for the portfolio made up of firms with negative forecast errors. A contributing factor is the following. The naive model gives the same forecast error as the regression model would give if

---

[27] Note that Figure 1 contains averages over many firms and years and is not indicative of the behavior of the securities of any particular firm in any one year. While there may be, on average, a persistent and gradual anticipation of the contents of the report throughout the year, evidence on the extent of autocorrelation in the stock return residuals would suggest that the market's reaction to information about a particular firm tends to occur rapidly.

(a) the change in market income were zero, and (b) there were no drift in the income of the firm. But historically there has been an increase in the market's income, particularly during the latter part of the sample period, due to general increase in prices and the strong influence of the protracted expansion since 1961. Thus, the naive model [variable (3)] typically identifies as firms with negative forecast errors those relatively few firms which showed a decrease in EPS when most firms showed an increase. Of the three variables, one would be most confident that the incomes of those which showed negative forecast errors for variable (3) have in fact lost ground relative to the market.

This observation has interesting implications. For example, it points to a relationship between the magnitudes of the income forecast errors and the magnitudes of the abnormal stock price adjustments. This conclusion is reinforced by Figure 1 which shows that the results for positive forecast errors are weaker for variable (3) than for the other two.

2. The drift downward in the Abnormal Performance Index computed over all firms and years in the sample reflects a computational bias.[28] The bias arises because

$$E[\prod_m (1 + v_m)] \neq \prod_m [1 + E(v_m)],$$

where E denotes the expected value. It can readily be seen that the bias over K months is at least of order $(K - 1)$ times the covariance between v_m and v_{m-1}.[29] Since this covariance is typically negative,[30] the bias is also negative.

While the bias does not affect the tenor of our results in any way, it should be kept in mind when interpreting the values of the various API's. It helps explain, for example, why the absolute changes in the indexes in the bottom panel of Figure 1 tend to be greater than those in the top panel; why the indexes in the top panel tend to turn down shortly after month 0; and finally, why the drifts in the indexes in the bottom panel tend to persist beyond the month of the report announcement.

3. We also computed results for the regression model using the additional definitions of income:

> (a) cash flow, as approximated by operating income,[31] and
> (b) net income before nonrecurring items.

Neither variable was as successful in predicting the signs of the stock return

---

[28] The expected value of the bias is of order minus one-half to minus one-quarter of one per cent per annum. The difference between the observed value of the API computed over the total sample and its expectation is a property of the particular sample (see footnote 26).

[29] In particular, the approximation neglects all permutations of the product $v_s \cdot v_t$, $s = 1, 2, \cdots, K-2$, $t = s+2, \cdots, K$, as being of a second order of smallness.

[30] See Table 4.

[31] All variable definitions are specified in Standard and Poor's *Compustat Manual* [see also Ball and Brown (1967), Appendix A].

residuals as net income and EPS. For example, by month 0, the Abnormal Performance Indexes for forecast errors which were positive were 1.068 (net income, including nonrecurring items) and 1.070 (operating income). These numbers compare with 1.071 for net income [Table 5, variable (1)]. The respective numbers for firms and years with negative forecast errors were 0.911, 0.917, and 0.907.

4. Both the API's and the chi-square test in Table 5 suggest that, at least for variable (3), the relationship between the sign of the income forecast error and that of the stock return residual may have persisted for as long as two months beyond the month of the announcement of the annual report. One explanation might be that the market's index of income was not known for sure until after several firms had announced their income numbers. The elimination of uncertainty about the market's income subsequent to some firms' announcements might tend, when averaged over all firms in the sample, to be reflected in a persistence in the drifts in the API's beyond the announcement month. This explanation can probably be ruled out, however, since when those firms which made their announcements in January of any one year were excluded from the sample for that year, there were no changes in the patterns of the overall API's as presented in Figure 1, although generally there were reductions in the χ^2 statistics.[32]

A second explanation could be random errors in the announcement dates. Drifts in the API's would persist beyond the announcement month if errors resulted in our treating some firms as if they had announced their income numbers earlier than in fact was the case. But this explanation can also probably be ruled out, since all announcement dates taken from the *Wall Street Journal Index* were verified against the *Wall Street Journal*.

A third explanation could be that preliminary reports are not perceived by the market as being final. Unfortunately this issue cannot be resolved independently of an alternative hypothesis, namely that the market does take more time to adjust to information if the value of that information is less than the transactions costs that would be incurred by an investor who wished to take advantage of the opportunity for abnormal gain. That is, even if the relationship tended to persist beyond the announcement month, it is clear that unless transactions costs were within about one per cent,[33]

---

[32] The general reduction in the χ^2 statistic is due largely to the reduction in sample size.

[33] This result is obtained as follows. The ratio API_m/API_{m-1} is equal to the marginal return in month m plus unity:

$$\frac{API_m}{API_{m-1}} = (1 + r_m).$$

Similarly,

$$\frac{API_m}{API_{m-2}} = \frac{API_m}{API_{m-1}} \cdot \frac{API_{m-1}}{API_{m-2}} = (1 + r_m) \cdot (1 + r_{m-1}),$$

there was no opportunity for abnormal profit once the income information had become generally available. Our results are thus consistent with other evidence that the market tends to react to data without bias, at least to within transactions costs.

THE VALUE OF ANNUAL NET INCOME RELATIVE TO OTHER SOURCES OF INFORMATION[34]

The results demonstrate that the information contained in the annual income number is useful in that it is related to stock prices. But annual accounting reports are only one of the many sources of information available to investors. The aim of this section is to assess the relative importance of information contained in net income, and at the same time to provide some insight into the timeliness of the income report.

It was suggested earlier that the impact of new information about an individual stock could be measured by the stock's return residual. For example, a negative residual would indicate that the actual return is less than what would have been expected had there been no bad information. Equivalently, if an investor is able to take advantage of the information either by selling or by taking a short position in advance of the market adjustment, then the residual will represent, ignoring transactions costs, the extent to which his return is greater than would normally be expected.

If the difference between the realized and expected return is accepted as also indicating the value of new information, then it is clear that the value of new, monthly information, good or bad, about an individual stock is given by the absolute value of that stock's return residual for the given month. It follows that the value of all monthly information concerning the average firm, received in the 12 months preceding the report, is given by:

$$TI_0 = \frac{1}{N} \sum_{j}^{N} \left[\prod_{m=-11}^{0} (1 + |v_{jm}|) \right] - 1.00,$$

and, in general,

$$\frac{API_m}{API_s} = (1 + r_{s+1}) \cdots (1 + r_m).$$

Thus, the marginal return for the two months after the announcement date on the portfolio consisting of firms for which EPS decrease would have been $0.878/0.887 - 1 \cong -.010$; similarly, the marginal return on the portfolio of firms for which EPS increased would have been $1.059/1.056 - 1 \cong .003$. After allowing for the computational bias, it would appear that transactions costs must have been within one per cent for opportunities to have existed for abnormal profit from applying some mechanical trading rule.

[34] This analysis does not consider the *marginal* contribution of information contained in the annual income number. It would be interesting to analyze dividends in a way similar to that we have used for income announcements. We expect there would be some overlap. To the extent that there is an overlap, we attribute the information to the income number and consider the dividend announcement to be the medium by which the market learns about income. This assumption is highly artificial in that historical income numbers and dividend payments might both simply be reflections of the same, more fundamental informational determinants of stock prices.

where TI denotes total information.[35] For our sample, averaged over all firms and years, this sum was 0.731.

For any one particular stock, some of the information between months will be offsetting.[36] The value of net information (received in the 12 months preceding the report) about the average stock is given by:

$$NI_0 = \frac{1}{N} \sum_j^N \left| \prod_{m=-11}^{0} (1 + v_{jm}) - 1.00 \right|,$$

where NI denotes net information. This sum was 0.165.

The impact of the annual income number is also a net number in that net income is the result of both income-increasing and income-decreasing events. If one accepts the forecast error model,[37] then the value of information contained in the annual income number may be estimated by the average of the value increments from month -11 to month 0, where the increments are averaged over the two portfolios constructed from (buying or selling short) all firms and years as classified by the signs of the income forecast errors. That is,

$$II_0 = \frac{N1(API_0^{N1} - 1.00) - N2(API_0^{N2} - 1.00)}{(N1 + N2)},$$

where II denotes income information, and $N1$ and $N2$ the number of occasions on which the income forecast error was positive and negative respectively. This number was 0.081 for variable (1), 0.083 for variable (2), and 0.077 for variable (3).

From the above numbers we conclude:

(1) about 75 per cent [$(.731 - .165)/.731$] of the value of all information appears to be offsetting, which in turn implies that about 25 per cent persists; and

(2) of the 25 per cent which persists, about half [49 %, 50 %, and 47 %—calculated as .081/.165, .083/.165, and .077/.165—for variables (1)–(3)] can be associated with the information contained in reported income.

Two further conclusions, not directly evident, are:

(3) of the value of information contained in reported income, no more than about 10 to 15 per cent (12 %, 11 %, and 13 %) has not been anticipated by the month of the report;[38] and

---

[35] Note that the information is reflected in a value increment; thus, the original $1.00 is deducted from the terminal value.

[36] This assertion is supported by the observed low autocorrelation in the stock return residuals.

[37] Note that since we are interested in the "average firm," an investment strategy must be adopted on every sample member. Because there are only two relevant strategies involved, it is sufficient to know whether one is better off to buy or to sell short. Note also that the analysis assumes the strategy is first adopted 12 months prior to the announcement date.

[38] The average monthly yield from a policy of buying a portfolio consisting of all firms with positive forecast errors and adopting a short position on the rest would have resulted in an average monthly abnormal rate of return, from -11 to -1, of

(4) the value of information conveyed by the income number at the time of its release constitutes, on average, only 20 per cent (19%, 18%, and 19%) of the value of all information coming to the market in that month.[39]

The second conclusion indicates that accounting income numbers capture about half of the net effect of all information available throughout the 12 months preceding their release; yet the fourth conclusion suggests that net income contributes only about 20 per cent of the value of all information in the month of its release. The apparent paradox is presumably due to the fact that: (a) many other bits of information are usually released in the same month as reported income (for example, via dividend announcements, or perhaps other items in the financial reports); (b) 85 to 90 per cent of the net effect of information about annual income is already reflected in security prices by the month of its announcement; and (c) the period of the annual report is already one-and-one-half months into history.

Ours is perhaps the first attempt to assess empirically the relative importance of the annual income number, but it does have limitations. For example, our results are systematically biased against findings in favor of accounting reports due to:

1. the assumption that stock prices are from transactions which have taken place simultaneously at the end of the month;
2. the assumption that there are no errors in the data;
3. the discrete nature of stock price quotations;
4. the presumed validity of the "errors in forecast" model; and
5. the regression estimates of the income forecast errors being random variables, which implies that some misclassifications of the "true" earnings forecast errors are inevitable.

Concluding Remarks

The initial objective was to assess the usefulness of existing accounting income numbers by examining their information content and timeliness. The mode of analysis permitted some definite conclusions which we shall briefly restate. Of all the information about an individual firm which becomes available during a year, one-half or more is captured in that year's income number. Its content is therefore considerable. However, the annual income report does not rate highly as a timely medium, since most of its content (about 85 to 90 per cent) is captured by more prompt media which perhaps include interim reports. Since the efficiency of the capital market

---

0.63%, 0.66%, and 0.60% for variables (1), (2), and (3) respectively. The marginal rate of return in month 0 for that same strategy would have been 0.92%, 0.89%, and 0.94% respectively. However, relatively much more information is conveyed in the month of the report announcement than in either of the two months immediately preceding the announcement month or in the two months immediately following it. This result is consistent with those obtained by Beaver (1968).

[39] An optimum policy (that is, one which takes advantage of all information) would have yielded an abnormal rate of return of 4.9% in month 0.

is largely determined by the adequacy of its data sources, we do not find it disconcerting that the market has turned to other sources which can be acted upon more promptly than annual net income.

This study raises several issues for further investigation. For example, there remains the task of identifying the media by which the market is able to anticipate net income: of what help are interim reports and dividend announcements? For accountants, there is the problem of assessing the cost of preparing annual income reports relative to that of the more timely interim reports.

The relationship between the magnitude (and not merely the sign) of the unexpected income change and the associated stock price adjustment could also be investigated.[40] This would offer a different way of measuring the value of information about income changes, and might, in addition, furnish insight into the statistical nature of the income process, a process little understood but of considerable interest to accounting researchers.

Finally, a mechanism has been provided for an empirical approach to a restricted class of the controversial choices in external reporting.

REFERENCES

BALL, RAY AND PHILIP BROWN (1967). "Some Preliminary Findings on the Association between the Earnings of a Firm, Its Industry and the Economy," *Empirical Research in Accounting: Selected Studies, 1967*, Supplement to Volume 5 of the *Journal of Accounting Research*, pp. 55–77.

BEAVER, WILLIAM H. (1968). "The Information Content of Annual Earnings Announcements," forthcoming in *Empirical Research in Accounting: Selected Studies 1968*, Supplement to Volume 6 of the *Journal of Accounting Research*.

BLUME, MARSHALL E. (1968). "The Assessment of Portfolio Performance" (unpublished Ph.D. dissertation, University of Chicago).

BREALEY, RICHARD A. (1968). "The Influence of the Economy on the Earnings of the Firm" (unpublished paper presented at the Sloane School of Finance Seminar, Massachusetts Institute of Technology, May, 1968).

BROWN, PHILIP AND VICTOR NIEDERHOFFER (1968). "The Predictive Content of Quarterly Earnings," *Journal of Business*.

CANNING, JOHN B. (1929). *The Economics of Accountancy* (New York: The Ronald Press Co.).

CHAMBERS, RAYMOND J. (1964). "Measurement and Objectivity in Accounting," *The Accounting Review*, XXXIX (April, 1964), 264–74.

—— (1966). *Accounting, Evaluation, and Economic Behavior* (Englewood Cliffs, N.J.: Prentice-Hall).

—— (1967). "Continuously Contemporary Accounting—Additivity and Action," *The Accounting Review*, XLII (October, 1967), 751–57.

COOTNER, PAUL H., ed. (1964). *The Random Character of Stock Market Prices* (Cambridge, Mass.: The M.I.T. Press).

---

[40] There are some difficult econometric problems associated with this relationship, including specifying the appropriate functional form, the expected statistical distributions of the underlying parameters, the expected behavior of the regression residuals, and the extent and effects of measurement errors in both dependent and independent variables. (The functional form need not necessarily be linear, if only because income numbers convey information about the covariability of the income process.)

EDWARDS, EDGAR O. AND PHILIP W. BELL (1961). *The Theory and Measurement of Business Income* (Berkeley, Cal.: The University of California Press).

FAMA, EUGENE F. (1965). "The Behavior of Stock Market Prices," *Journal of Business*, XXXVIII (January, 1965), 34–105.

—— AND MARSHALL E. BLUME (1966). "Filter Rules and Stock Market Trading," *Journal of Business*, XXXIX (Supplement, January, 1966), 226–41.

——, LAWRENCE FISHER, MICHAEL C. JENSEN, AND RICHARD ROLL (1967). "The Adjustment of Stock Prices to New Information," Report No. 6715 (University of Chicago: Center for Mathematical Studies in Business and Economics; forthcoming in the *International Economic Review*).

FISHER, LAWRENCE (1966). "Some New Stock Market Indices," *Journal of Business*, XXXIX (Supplement, January, 1966), 191–225.

GILMAN, STEPHAN (1939). *Accounting Concepts of Profit* (New York: The Ronald Press Co.).

IJIRI, YUJI (1967). *The Foundations of Accounting Measurement* (Englewood Cliffs, N.J.: Prentice-Hall).

JENSEN, MICHAEL C. (1968). "Risk, the Pricing of Capital Assets, and the Evaluation of Investment Portfolios" (unpublished Ph.D. dissertation, University of Chicago).

KING, BENJAMIN F. (1966). "Market and Industry Factors in Stock Price Behavior," *Journal of Business*, XXXIX (Supplement, January, 1966), 139–90.

LIM, RONALD S. (1966). "The Mathematical Propriety of Accounting Measurements and Calculations," *The Accounting Review*, XLI (October, 1966), 642–51.

PATON, W. A. AND A. C. LITTLETON (1940). *An Introduction to Corporate Accounting Standards* (American Accounting Association Monograph No. 3).

SAMUELSON, PAUL A. (1965). "Proof That Properly Anticipated Prices Fluctuate Randomly," *Industrial Management Review*, 7 (Spring, 1965), 41–49.

SCHOLES, MYRON J. (1967). "The Effect of Secondary Distributions on Price" (unpublished paper presented at the Seminar on the Analysis of Security Prices, University of Chicago).

SHARPE, WILLIAM F. (1964). "Capital Asset Prices: A Theory of Market Equilibrium under Conditions of Risk," *Journal of Finance*, XIX (September, 1964), 425–42.

STERLING, ROBERT R. (1967). "Elements of Pure Accounting Theory," *The Accounting Review*, XLII (January, 1967), 62–73.

VATTER, WILLIAM J. (1947). *The Fund Theory of Accounting* (Chicago: The University of Chicago Press).

38

BUSINESS SUCCESS REQUIRES AN UNDERSTANDING OF UNSOLVED PROBLEMS OF ACCOUNTING AND FINANCIAL REPORTING

Leonard Spacek

I am particularly glad to talk to this class, today, because you men are at a point where you can develop an understanding of business accounting problems and practices that you will never take time to think out, once you have entered the business world. I want to be sure you understand the basis of my comments before we get into the actual accounting problems that need to be discussed.

I am not going to talk to you about whether the accounting profession should solve the accounting problems that face it, or how this should be done. It is better that we discuss the problems that exist, and consider how they should best be approached from the point of view of the public, regardless of who takes the initiative. You should understand the deficiencies in accounting from the standpoint of those segments of the public that are affected.

Your Immediate Interest Is In The Meaning and Use of Accounting Reporting In Business

Your immediate interest in accounting no doubt is in its meaning and use in today's business world. In order for you to use accounting intelligently in your future business activities, regardless of what they may be, you need first to understand the basic purposes of accounting, how it falls short of accomplishing its purposes, and what these deficiencies will mean to you as managers of or investors in business enterprises.

I want to direct my comments mainly to the uses of accounting as they will confront you. Keep in mind that you will use accounting reports to judge others, and that others will use such reports to judge you. It would be wrong to make your judgments of others, or to accept their judgments of you, without fully understanding the elasticity of the accounting that may be used in making such reports.

You Need To Know When To Rely, and When Not To Rely, On Accounting Reports

As future businessmen, you need to know when you can rely on accounting reports as a basis for business judgment, and when you cannot do so without first obtaining a definite understanding of the basis on which the reports were prepared. This is very important to you, because the choice of accounting principles and practices followed in business accounting and reporting—all within the range of acceptability—can produce vastly different financial accounting results.

An understanding of some of the principal accounting practices involved will help you to know when not to be impressed by what appear to be good reports, and what is fully as important, when to make inquiry regarding what appear to be unfavorable results in order to ascertain any favorable factors that may be causing them. Something may produce what seems to be an unfavorable present result but may, in the long run, be an exceedingly favorable development.

You probably will be unable to reconcile the various practices and the results that flow from them, from the point of view of fairness and reliability. Inquiry along these lines leads into the reasons why the various practices were originally adopted and what forces tend to keep such conflicting practices within the range of acceptability. Such questions, I believe, are mainly of interest to those whose future activities will be devoted primarily to the profession of accounting. To the extent that your interest, at least at this time, is not to be devoted to accounting practice, you will not want to spend your time on this phase. Any questions in these areas that may occur to you can be raised for discussion at the close of my comments.

Accounting, As The Principal Line Of Comunication In Our Economic System, Is Full Of Interest and Excitement

While many people believe that accounting is highly technical and uninteresting, this is because they see only those aspects of it. Actually, accounting is as exciting a field as

Reprinted by permission of the author. An Address before The Financial Accounting Class, Graduate School of Business Administration, Harvard University, September 25, 1959.

any other profession or business, if viewed from the standpoint of its value as a means of business communication. Let me illustrate.

If the electronics field were portrayed only as an assembly line for putting together a lot of small wires, fuses, switches, contacts, controls, etc., it would be unattractive, too. When you think of accounting as the routine handling of many small items and transactions, pricing material tickets, processing labor clock cards, posting invoices and bank checks, putting endless figures into ledger accounts, etc., it, too, is uninteresting. But when you visualize the purpose and use of accounting, you find it full of romance, adventure and challenge. For instance, in converting the vacuum tube and transistor as switching devices to the sorting, counting and compiling of data, there is all of the excitement and fascination that you would find in utilizing the same developments in world-wide or interplanetary communication systems.

Even the great progress in the speed and efficiency of mechanical production through automation of the repetitive assembly line operations is also present in the accounting field. The new electronic devices are rapidly eliminating the tiresome routine that you think of in handling and processing the large volume of detailed accounting work.

Accounting Reports Reflect the Results Of Actions and Decisions Of People, and They Provide The Basis For Action Thereon

Looking at accounting as a whole, we see that it is, in effect, the principal line of communication in our economic system. In accounting, we record all business activities in a common denominator called "dollars." The portrayal in dollars of the plant operations, sales activities, administration and financing has all the fascination, I think, of portraying on canvas the scenic beauty of nature. The parallel is not too remote; accounting portrays economic truth, as it results from millions of actions and decisions of people, while painting portrays the effect of millions of nature's actions, in a small area.

Since accounting does report the results of actions and decisions of people, and since the actions of people can be altered, the accounting reports reveal not only the resulting conditions, but they also provide the basis for action with respect to these conditions. Action is taken on the basis of accounting reports by business managements, directors, investors, investment advisers, the public, the government, the consumers, the labor unions, etc.

Wide Variety Of Accounting Practices Followed Greatly Affects The Results Reported

An important part in developing your business acumen is to learn when the so-called "dollars" that we use as the common denominator in accounting reports are not common denominators at all because of the wide variety of accounting practices applied in arriving at the reported results.

Now I want to mention some of the misleading but accepted beliefs in accounting. There are times when inventory costs charged off will produce future profits, and thus are not losses; when research and development costs shown as expenses (and thus as losses) are in fact future profit items; when additions to plant and equipment are made under the guise of expenses, and thus show up as losses rather than as increased plant and profit capacity. There are times when no provision is made for deferred taxes, thus, in effect, permitting them to be reported as current profits rather than as provisions for the liabilities they really are. There are times when write-downs of the goods in inventory are reported as cost of the goods that have been sold, and when obsolete items inflate profit because the loss thereon has not been recognized. Sometimes the obligations to build plants are shown on the balance sheet, yet sometimes they are not.

To be successful, you as future businessmen, must learn what is in the figures and what is not in them. Two businessmen achieving reasonably comparable results in their companies might, because of the different accounting practices followed in reporting the results, give widely different appraisals of their own success.

Because of these obvious deficiencies in accounting, our firm has devoted a great deal of time and effort in endeavoring to convince our profession that sound accounting reporting produces a dynamic and very useful tool in our economy, both from the standpoint of the management and of the national economy. The accounting field—just like law, engineering, medicine, religion, business, military or any other—has a long way to go in improving its end product to meet the surging needs of our rapidly expanding economy and to achieve fairness for all segments within it.

In the final analysis, it is the accounting reports of our economy that furnish the basis for a fair distribution among the people of their share of the economic benefits from business activities. Consequently, errors in the accounting reports produce errors in the distributions based on them.

No segment of our social or economic life and activity can stand still for long in the onrush that is occurring at an ever faster pace. If any part does stand still while there is public need for it to progress, some other force will step in to fill the vacuum created by the lack of progress. This force may be good, but usually it is evil before it becomes good. So it is with accounting.

There Are Two Broad Areas Of Accounting Reporting—Internal and Public—That Must be Understood by the Successful Businessman

The reporting of accounting facts is now so much a part of our national and world economic life that such reporting cannot be disassociated from it. But before we look at specific accounting problems, I want you to have it clearly in mind that there are two facets of accounting reporting whose objectives can be almost unrelated to each other. An understanding of the difference between these two facets may be the basis of your future success or failure—hence my desire to emphasize their great importance to you men as future operators of business enterprises.

In its most elemental as well as in its most profound sense, accounting reporting is essentially a system of business and financial communication. But I doubt that there is any other system whose communications are subject to such wide divergence of presentation and interpretation as are the reports that arise from accounting as it is practiced today. To minimize the possibility of such widely different results from the same facts, it would seem that carefully and specifically defined methods and objective standards would be required. But no such methods and standards have ever been established, and their absence multiplies many-fold the probability of misinterpretation.

These two separate areas of accounting reporting in business, which are almost wholly independent of each other, are:

(1) Internal reporting to management — the reports for the use of the management and the supervisors at the various levels, in operating the business.

(2) Public reporting on management performance—the financial reports to the shareholders, to the consumers and to labor.

INTERNAL REPORTING

Internal Reporting is a Management Tool

Accounting reporting as a tool for management use in operating a business can be quite different from the accounting reports required to present the financial results to the three groups constituting the public.

The internal reporting to management and to the supervisors within the company is probably of most immediate importance to you as future businessmen preparing to operate business enterprises. The internal reporting will be largely under your control and your responsibility.

Internal Reporting is Not Restricted by Regulatory Rules or Requirments

Never let your accounting advisers tell you that proper internal reporting for management purposes cannot be achieved because of some accounting regulation or prohibition. Any and all accounting obstacles can be overcome in a practical way for purposes of internal reporting if the end result produced is closer to the truth or is more helpful in guiding and managing the business.

Even in the case of regulated companies—such as utilities, railroads, truck lines, insurance companies, banks and savings and loan associations, which must operate under prescribed accounting rules and procedures—the regulatory authorities have co-operated in permitting the use of accounting reports which the management finds necessary in conducting or improving operations of the business, as long as the accounting system also provides the records necessary for compliance with the rules and classifications prescribed by the regulatory authorities.

The records kept for compliance purposes need not be used, and usually are not useful, except for reporting to the regulatory authority. While the regulated companies must meet certain accounting requirements, it can be fairly said that these requirements will not prevent the initiative and ingenuity in accounting that you may be able to bring to bear in improving the operations of any business you may enter or undertake.

Management Reports Must Not Only Tell What Happened, But Must Provide The Information For Corrective Action

If you are responsible for a management function, your success will require you to be sure of the usefulness of the accounting reporting system on which you depend for information and action. If there is one point I want to emphasize to you more than any other, it is that management accounting must be designed not only to tell you the truth about your business, but to give you the information that will help you run it effectively. The accounting reports to management, although they may be literally true as far as they go, can also be as antiquated and as ineffective as hand methods of production; such reports obviously are not adequate in today's rapid-fire economy.

In order to judge the adequacy of your accounting reports, make this one simple test. If, after studying the reports, you have the frustrated feeling they are like the news reports you find in the newspaper — that is, if they tell you what happened in general terms, but do not give you the information necessary to detect the operating conditions that were at fault, or to enable you to locate the individuals or machines where specific problems exist—then you do not have adequate accounting reports. But if, upon reading the accounting reports on your operations, you find yourself making extensive notes of things to do, then you are getting some measure of dynamic results from the money you are spending for your accounting communications. You must know the cause of the unfavorable developments and who is responsible before you, through management action, can take the steps necessary to improve the financial results.

In other words, for the exercise of the management function, good accounting provides continuous opportunities to improve procedures, create short cuts, apply automation and undertake innovations. These are the same opportunities that are available for the other phases of the business, such as research, design, production, distribution, etc. Too often the results of good business sense are smothered under archaic accounting practices; consequently, the areas in which management action is required are not shown to management by its accounting reports. Absence of the same careful thought and planning for improvement of accounting methods and reports that is devoted to other phases of operation, will inevitably throw any business off balance. It is like driving an automobile with brakes on one wheel—it will pull the whole car out of line.

Smooth Functioning Of Internal Accounting Is Not Enough; It Must Relate Closely To Physical Facts Of Which The Businessman Has Knowledge

The accounting methods of a business may be working well as far as the technical functioning is concerned, but at the same time may be incorrectly allocating costs or failing to assign them to the individuals responsible for incurring them. When this happens, it is like an automobile with a properly functioning speedometer or gasoline gauge, but whose indicating dials are improperly equated to the wheel or the gas tank measurements. The facts are correctly transmitted to the dials, but the dials report them incorrectly to the driver, even though there is no mechanical deficiency. The driver, in turn, relying upon these dials, makes changes in operation that are not based on the actual facts, which are not learned until the drive is completed.

Likewise, it is of little value to learn, after the goods have been sold at a loss, that because of an error in the accounting methods, the cost reports relied upon in pricing the products were wrong and the selling prices were too low. Yet this often happens. Consequently, a good business operator has to have an accounting system that has a common-sense relationship to the operations of which he has personal knowledge, so he can judge the costs reported against the physically known operating conditions.

Technical aspects of accounting systems, such as preparation of payrolls, pricing of materials used, or the computation of cost allocations, should not be allowed to obscure the businessman's view of the relationship between the physical facts of his business and the related costs.

When the company's internal accounting reports on operations are inadequate, the management is shortchanging itself as to information about its own business. This handicap is usually self-inflicted and is caused by three basic human fallacies that are present in management, as well as in all of the people against whom the management must guard.

Modern Accounting Communication and Reporting Systems Are Not Just Excess Overhead That Can Be Avoided

The first of these fallacies is the belief that accounting systems and reports are just excess overhead, and that if the operators and department heads know their jobs and everyone performs at an optimum level, everything will come out all right. Thus, it is reasoned, the additional cost of an adequate accounting system can be avoided.

This is like a seasoned traveler saying that he knows where he is and where he is going and, therefore, does not need a road map. The trouble with this concept is that nothing in life stands still, whether it be the circumstances of a company's business or a road system. So even if a person knew all of the factors affecting a corporation or the road system at one particular moment, there are so many people making decisions affecting the company or the road that an instantaneous photo at any given time is obsolete the next moment, and therefore is only history.

A communication system is needed to keep up with business history as it is being made, in order to inform all management personnel and department heads of the changes that are occurring. A road map does this for a traveler; an adequate accounting system does it for you businessmen. But neither the map nor the accounting system makes the decisions for you as you proceed. They merely give you facts so you can make the decisions and take the actions that you believe will be most helpful in reaching your objective. Advance information will help in planning the most desirable course to your objective, even though in some instances its procurement may seem to be the longer and more costly way.

So it is, that advance information on the cost of plant change-overs, material shortages, wage increases, rising costs, excess warranty claims, excessive returned goods or machine production costs, and their causes, may change your plan of operation or may affect your planning for the production of an item you thought was a high profit contributor. Or conversely, such information may indicate that an item you regarded as a low income producer is a prospectively profitable one that should be actively promoted rather than curtailed as your competitors may be doing because of their inadequate communication cost systems. Likewise, an effective production control system may dictate immediate changes in production schedules.

*There Is No Place In Modern Business
Operation For "Flying By The Seat Of
Your Pants," Where Other People's
Investments Are Involved*

Therefore, the modern businessman who
tries to operate without incurring the cost of
installing and operating a good accounting
system is himself obsolete, because he is using
a "single proprietary" concept under conditions that prevent him from succeeding.
He is "flying by the seat of his pants," as did
the airplane pilots that years ago flew from
judgment and observation, rather than from
radio communication, maps and instruments
as they now do. This may be an adventuresome method—a method which seems to reduce the number and complexity of decisions
that a good reporting system demands of you.
But it is very risky, and it is permissible only
for the flyer or businessman who, as a single
proprietor, is accountable to no one but himself and who can absorb the full consequences
of his venturesome decisions.

However, one who does operate without
adequate accounting information is guilty of
irresponsibility and recklessness if he imposes
his philosophy of operating by guess and
intuition on others without their knowledge
and consent. This is exactly what happens
if a commercial airplane pilot or the management of a publicly owned company follows
such a course. True, the responsibility for
and the consequences of "flying by the seat
of your pants," whether in a plane or with
a business, rest with those who do it. But
when trouble comes they can seldom make
good to the passengers in the plane or the
owners of the business, who have not and
would not approve of such a course. Little
satisfaction accrues to those injured, from
discharging the persons guilty of the fatal
practices. Their promises to take responsibility for the course chosen are worthless collateral for those who, in the end, pay for the
inadequate record keeping.

The argument in favor of flying a plane or
running a business in such a manner is like
that for the efficiency of a benevolent dicta-
torship in government. The gain to the people
may be great if the toss of the coin is always

rightly predicted; but one wrong decision
often means the loss of most all of the past
accomplishments. Therefore, the loss of all
gain is inevitable in such systems, as many
of us have seen in our lifetimes. So it is in
trying to run a business owned by others
without adequate accounting information.

*"Do-It-Yourself" Attempts To Design
Accounting Systems Produce Amateur
Results In Accounting As In Other
Fields*

The second fallacy that causes major deficiencies in the accounting communication
systems of business is the belief that you as
a management man can design and judge
how the accounting system should work in all
of its details.

This "design" is the most important phase
of any accounting system. It seldom can be
done by a management man just because he
has operated a business, any more than an
automobile can be designed in all of its details
by you or me just because we can drive a car.
An experienced designer has the knowledge
to bring together in a system, whether it be an
accounting system or complicated machine,
the most simple and least expensive methods
of converting the raw materials into the form
and quality the management requires.

So in accounting, the designer of a cost-
reporting system must convert the mass of
detailed data derived from payrolls, material
usage, overhead costs, etc., into the form the
management needs to run the business. It is
the management's responsibility to say what
information is required—management is the
driver, not the designer. If management were
to devote its time and energies to designing
the details of the accounting system, it would
be doing something other than its primary
function of managing. This would be like
the management designing each of the machine tools the company needs, rather than
seeing that these tools are procured and
operated to the best advantage.

The need for basic accounting knowledge
is somewhat like the need for some understanding of the automobile. Since both accounting and automobiles affect almost all

human activities, everyone today must have some knowledge of them. The housewife, the high school student or the adult must know enough about an automobile to drive it and use it. Likewise, they must know enough about accounting to understand the bills they receive, their bank accounts, their personal budgets and their tax returns.

As future businessmen, you need a basic understanding of accounting, such as you are getting here, so you can run a business with some knowledge of the fundamentals of accounting and of what it should do for you. But that does not give you the know-how to put together an accounting system so that it will function effectively. Neither does a good truck driver or a fine truck mechanic or designer, operating alone, have the ability to create a trucking business unless he also has the creative management ability. When he does have this ability and takes on the management function, he must give up his special technical work in order to become successful in management. It is the integration of these technical aspects with the many other operating functions making up a business, that calls for the ability to manage.

So it is with accounting. Businessmen cannot be expected to devote the time to design or even to be capable of designing, the accounting communication system required to properly integrate the vast assembly of minute items into the facts and reports that are needed to run the business.

Management is a dispatching function that co-ordinates and directs all phases of the business. It should strive to determine what facts are needed to run the business, and it should require the accounting system to furnish these facts as they pertain to the financial aspects. Development of such a system can only be done effectively by people skilled in design of accounting methods and procedures —who know how to accumulate the data required to furnish the needed facts on a timely basis and at a low cost. Management personnel often err by following the very human tendency of attempting to expertize outside of their management field, and thus pave the way for the failure of their own men.

Men Devoted To The Sale Of Machines Are Not Efficient Designers of Accounting Systems

The third basic fallacy that creates costly and inadequate accounting systems for management is the mistaken belief that the maker of a machine is a good designer of an assembly line.

A cost system is really nothing more than an assembly line; and if you will look at plant production methods, you will find that no two assembly lines are ever exactly alike, although they may be using similar machine tools. The reason is that the products they are making, even in competitive product lines, are never exactly alike. Competitive products emphasize different features and benefits involving quality, speed, appearance, reliability, profitability and a host of things that appeal to people.

So it is with an accounting system—it must be designed and redesigned to meet the needs and the changing requirements of the user. One accounting system may use the same machines, forms, and methods of record-keeping as another, yet it may produce completely different accounting products, depending upon the needs of the user. The designer will eliminate any controls and checks that are unnecessary for management purposes or for preservation of assets, but will achieve the controls wanted by slight changes in the sequences or steps in the assembly line without incurring significant costs.

The quality of information reports for management purposes, as well as for the cost accounting, is fundamentally determined at the worker level. Consequently, machine makers generally are not good designers of accounting systems, since their principal motive is to sell machines, not to plan accounting systems that will best meet the management needs in a particular case. Usually a machine man can install a particular machine to do a specific job. However, he may only change the method of applying the present procedures without considering possible revisions, whereas these procedures, which may have been designed around manual or less mechanized operations, include steps that are unnecessary in view of the automation now to be used.

Further and most important of all, the information furnished by the present system may be very markedly improved or extended with the new automation, and possibly the time devoted by plant workers and supervisors may be substantially reduced by the use of the new machines.

Good System Designing Requires The Will and Ability To Break With Tradition and To Pioneer In New Methods

Consequently, for the same reasons (a) that design engineers are used to convert good products into more useful ones, (b) that design engineers rather than the machine manufacturers are needed to lay out plants and determine the machines required to produce the products at the lowest cost, and (c) that architects rather than contractors are employed to design useful and functional buildings, it is necessary to have a properly qualified system designer carefully lay out the accounting system before its installation is attempted.

To be a good systems designer, one must have devoted considerable time and have had extensive experience in comparable work, so he can make use of the benefits of his experience and avoid the pitfalls in achieving optimum goals at the least cost.

The design of accounting systems is not only a field of its own, but is one that requires the imagination and initiative to break with traditional methods when they have lost their usefulness. Usefulness must be geared to the progress of life, not to traditional accounting practices. A jungle-life economy needs only a jungle-life accounting system; but a missile and atomic-age economy demands an accounting communication system that is equally advanced. Otherwise the progress of the whole economy will be retarded and thrown out of balance.

The Information The Business Manager Dreams Of Having To Guide His Operations Is Often Within Reach Of Practical Achievement

Before discussing the other broad field of accounting reporting, let me emphasize that the business manager seldom realizes the extent to which information he would like to have to properly guide and improve his business operations is not just an idle dream, but is within reach of practical achievement, often at less cost than is now being incurred. A good systems designer can build a practical and economical assembly line of accounting communication, channeling the original information, simply recorded by the plant workers and supervisors, into the dream-data wanted by the management.

Responsibility Accounting—A Method Of Reporting Costs and Expenses According To The Individuals Responsible Therefor

I have brought two films to illustrate the application of modern management reporting. Both are films of actual conditions. The first one is a simple explanation of the designing of an accounting communication system by lines of responsibility. Such systems have been specifically designed for more than 100 companies in the United States. We call these systems "Responsibility Accounting," since they are designed to report the costs and expenses according to the individuals responsible for the expenditures and to hold these individuals accountable for their own departmental operations on the same basis as if their departments were completely separate businesses. I shall be glad to answer questions concerning responsibility accounting after you have viewed this 30-minute film.

"Carfax"—A System For Railroad Car Accounting That Provides Current Information For The Operators and The Shippers

The second film shows a system for railroad car accounting. In this accounting system the management, the station agents, the yard clerks, the traffic clerks, the train crews and the accounting department are all linked into a single accounting communication system. It supplies each of them with information they never before had, but which was needed to enable the railroad to furnish its customers the information they need on freight movements and delivery schedules; to furnish the railroad operating employees with current information as to the location of the cars and what the trains are carrying on the road; to furnish the accounting department with information for billing purposes and reporting to the management; and to furnish the management with instantaneous data as to what is happening on the railroad system, thus providing the basis for action if this result is not satisfactory.

This reporting system is called "Carfax." Note its similarity to an assembly line. Note also that it is built around a particular set of conditions existing in one railroad, the Chicago and North Western Railroad. If it were to be used by another railroad, the principles might readily apply; but the application would have to be tailor-made to fit the different circumstances and requirements, and to eliminate any unnecessary steps or to add any additional features that might be needed. The layout of the assembly line would be changed altogether to conform to the different conditions that would be present.

Nothing like this "Carfax" system had ever been used by any railroad in the 100 years of railroad existence. But today's conditions demand that the fast pace of daily life be met by the railroads, too, if they are to survive and serve the country's needs under existing conditions.

Perhaps the most important point in "Carfax" is that while it is a system of accounting for railroad cars and the revenue from them, the assembly of accounting information also serves the railroad operating staff and the customers. This, in effect, makes the accounting function a by-product rather than the primary product. If this "Carfax" system were installed only to meet the accounting requirements, the railroad still would have all of the costs, but would gain only a part of the benefit. No one could deny that the

accounting system would be a good one, even if this accounting function were all that the system designer could see; but nevertheless if it served only the accounting needs, it would be only one half of a proper accounting system.

A machine manufacturer or a system designer whose only purpose was to meet the accounting requirements would have overlooked these more important service benefits. Yet the operators, or traffic clerks could not have told anyone *how* to get the information they needed. What brought about an effective system was first to find out from all of the people involved—those who initially sell the railroad's services to the shippers, those who handle and deliver the freight, those who operate and dispatch the trains, those who repair and maintain the equipment, those who do the accounting, billing, etc.—what each believed would give him optimum data that would contribute to the highest efficiency and effectiveness in his work, without asking him how to achieve it. The design problem was then to put the maximum information obtainable for each need on one assembly line of accounting data and communication.

Once installed, the system has to be carefully watched so as to detect and add any features that will contribute to profitability through lower costs, greater efficiency or increased sales, or to remove anything that has become obsolete or is not worth its incremental cost.

Such an accounting communication system is many things. It is a living, active artery that feeds the whole organization. It is a game that if well played will contribute more and more to smooth, straight-forward and understandable data that spell successful and profitable operation. It is research, invention, sales and production all woven together, connecting people with information that clearly tells them what they need to know in order to do their jobs as only they know how, with their counterparts throughout the company in other divisions.

Accounting Communication Is a Fascinating Field For Creative Work

So you see that accounting communication is not a field of boredom and routine; it is one of opportunity for creative work that will spark the imagination and emotions of those who undertake it.

With this film I complete my comments on the accounting systems which live by carrying the life blood within the corporate structure. It would be wonderful if this were the only field of accounting thought. Each accounting system would then be custom-made to hold together the many departments with their different functions, and to keep them working in perfect unison.

So far, I have dealt with internal reporting for management use, one of the two separate areas of accounting reporting that I mentioned at the start. Now I would like to take up the other area—the reporting to the other group, the public.

PUBLIC REPORTING

Public Reporting Is For Shareholders, Consumers and Labor

The public is made up of three distinct segments whose interests are independent but yet are interwoven with each other and with those of business management. The accounting principles and practices followed when it comes to reporting to the public present entanglements that clog the wheels of good reporting for management purposes. Actually these problems of public reporting need not affect the internal management reporting. But because accountants do allow the principles and practices followed in public reporting to influence the management reporting, the braking process on management reports does take place. The three segments of the public that I refer to are the shareholders of the corporation, the consumers, and the labor.

There Is Need For Authoritative, Sound Accounting Principles That Meet The Test Of Objective Standards

The so-called accounting principles followed in preparing accounting reports to the public constitute a hodge-podge of entrenched traditional practices. They have few if any objective standards, and they have grown up and gained authority largely by precedent and tradition, while the purposes for which the reports are now used have made obsolete the reasons for the original adoption of these principles.

For instance, I understand that in some towns there still are laws on the statute books requiring every motorized vehicle to be preceded by a person carrying a lantern. When such laws were passed in the horse-and-buggy days, they probably constituted reasonable requirements; but today they are so unreasonable that they are ignored, and the local governments have not even bothered to repeal them.

In accounting we, too, have principles (presumably "fundamental truths" of accounting) that were adopted in the horse-and-buggy days; but we do not ignore them, because "precedent" requires us to keep on following them.

Logic and common sense will compel you to ask why, as a profession, we do not have sufficient individual initiative and responsibility to rid ourselves of unnecessary and obsolete precedents. The answer can only be a shrug of our professional shoulders. The practices of the profession are unified through society action into practically unassailable conventions. The accounting societies, operating through committees, are in position to exercise leadership that could make the needed changes. As committees, they create the authority for practices that cannot be supported by individual practitioners. Consequently, the individual practitioner can avoid personal responsibility for his own work by conforming to established practices, irrespective of the results produced. In other words, as a group, we are all responsible, but individually none of us are responsible.

The obsolete precedents followed in accounting to the public are maintained through the use of high-sounding phrases such as "generally accepted accounting principles." "Generally accepted" is an undefined term that embraces a great many principles of accounting, the objectives of which are likewise undefined.

This lack of definition of accounting objectives confuses so-called principles with accounting conventions. It should not surprise you if a public accountant could tell you how to record a transaction but could not tell you why you should do it that way. In the accounting field, the cartoon phrase that I am sure you have all seen, *"There is no reason for it—it's just our policy,"* is no joke. It aptly describes the basis for too many of the principles and practices we follow. While many of our accounting principles are reasonably defined and have sound objectives, some of them are paralleled by other equally acceptable ones that cannot be defined or justified, and which produce wholly different financial results.

Your Management Accounting Must Give You The Truth, Regardless Of The Vagaries Of The Accounting Used In Public Reporting

Even though accounting practices followed in reporting to the public, prescribed by law and regulation in many cases, produce untrue and misleading reports, such practices should not be allowed to color or distort your internal management reports. Otherwise the internal reports you rely on to run your business will be equally misleading to you as managers, and will plant the seeds of business failure. Therefore, management reports on which you rely must always be geared to the truth of the facts, regardless of tradition or of generally accepted accounting principles used in public reporting. It is the difference in use of accounting reporting for internal management purposes and for reporting to the public that you must understand.

Choices Of Accounting Principles For Public Reporting May Produce Widely Varying Results

Now, what do these principles of accounting which are called "generally accepted," mean to you as managers? As managers of your own businesses, you can disregard the "generally accepted principles of accounting" and their misleading influence, since you are accountable only to yourselves. But as managers of publicly owned companies, your stockholders will be your employers.

Your stockholders will be interested primarily in profits and high market values for their investments. In most cases the owners (stockholders) will judge the extent of your success on the relative performance of your company's stock in the market. The prices at which the stock market values your stock will depend on the financial position and the earnings of your company.

For instance, it is common practice, in measuring market values, to multiply the earnings per share by a current rule-of-thumb multiplier that may seem reasonable under current conditions. A stock may sell, for example, at 10, 12, 15 or more times earnings, according to the industry, the market conditions, etc. Therefore, as the earnings to which such a multiplier is applied vary, the market price of the stock will also vary.

If the earnings reported are certified by a public accountant as conforming to "generally accepted accounting principles," the general public cannot be criticized if it concludes that a proper accounting must have been made, and that if made among all companies, the earnings reported must be reliable for stock-valuation purposes. The fact that stockholders' annual reports usually carry statements to the effect that they are furnished solely for information of the stockholders and not for use in connection with purchase or sale of securities, is utterly unrealistic when it is obvious that this is one of the primary uses of such reports.

Stockholders Want High Earnings and High Market Value For Stock

Now how does this affect you as managers of business enterprises, reporting to your public stockholders? Your employees want to please you by doing a good job. That is the way they get ahead. The same motives will influence you. You will want to please your stockholders by showing them that you are doing a good job for them. Let us assume that you sincerely want to report the profits in the way you feel fairly presents the true results of your company's business. You say that in doing so you will not care what any other company does, because in line with your management responsibility, you believe that the only way to keep the business healthy is to tell the truth about your operations as you see it.

This is an admirable and objective motive; but when you do this, you find that your competitor shows a relatively more favorable profit result than you do. This creates a demand for his stock, while yours lags behind. You put your analyst to work, and you find that if your competitor followed the same accounting practices you do, your results would be better than his. Or to put it the other way around, if you followed the same accounting practices that he does, your company would show up more favorably than his.

You show this analysis to your complaining stockholders. Naturally, they ask, "If this is true, and if your competitor's accounting practices are generally accepted, too, why not change your accounting practices and thus improve your profits?" At that point you try to explain why your accounting is much more factual and reliable than your competitor's. Your stockholders listen, but nothing you can say will convince them that they should give up a 20%, 50% or 100% possible increase in the market values just because you like certain accounting practices better than others.

As Bad Money Drives Out Good, Poor Accounting Practices Tend To Become Accepted, Bringing Eventual Day Of Reckoning

Eventually you, as the manager of the business, will tend to adopt the accounting that, within the range of acceptable practice, will report the most favorable financial results. Consequently, alternative accounting principles merely provide a means by which the poorer methods of accounting become the accepted ones, just as bad money drives out the good, until the cumulative effect of reaching for profits and deferring costs and losses brings disaster. When that happens a correction takes place, and the accounting principles are then raised to a higher level at one time. Such a set of conditions existed in the late 1920's and early 1930's, and played a major part in the business crash of 1932. Accounting was tremendously improved in the readjustment that followed.

Today we again have major unrecognized costs that are accumulating against business. They could reach a point where accounting recognition must be given, as in 1932. The railroads are rapidly approaching that point. Their standards of accounting are inferior to those of other businesses in several major respects; and many other businesses, too, have major deficiencies accumulating that can be carried only so far into the future.

Regulatory commissions furnish the authority for the accounting deficiencies in many respects. But regulatory authority in a nondictatorship economy cannot change the facts nor make them disappear. Therefore, neither regulatory authority nor poor accounting principles can prevent a proper accounting some day. They merely provide a respectable authority which permits today's managers of business to ignore and defer proper accounting to a later day of reckoning.

For instance, by sanction of Interstate Commerce Commission, railroads are permitted to issue financial statements with woefully inadequate depreciation provisions and reserves—something that no other business would dare do. But the Commission rules furnish the authority that enables the public accountant to ignore his professional responsibility in expressing his opinion on the railroad statements.

Also, there is a growing interest on the part of stockholders in the liberal compensation being enjoyed by corporate officers, at capital gain rates, by way of their profits on stock options. It is almost automatic, and perfectly normal, for corporate officers to prefer a substantial part of their compensation through stock options rather than in current bonus payments that are taxable at ordinary rates.

There is nothing wrong with this desire or this method of paying incentive compensation; but from an accounting standpoint, there is considerable difference in effect on the profits of the corporation. If paid as ordinary bonuses or profit sharing, the amount paid is charged to expense, thereby reducing the per-share earnings and the market value of stock; but if the incentive compensation is given in the form of stock options, no charge to expense is necessary, profits are greater, and the market price of stock is higher. The authority for this stock-option accounting is none other than the Securities and Exchange Commission. Why the Commission refused to require the corporations to record this stock-option compensation to officers as operating expense, I have never been able to understand.

Thus, as a business manager, your choice of accounting practices can have a very great effect on your stockholders. What was good for an owner of his own business may not be good for a proportionate share owner unless all publicly owned companies are required to follow the same principles of accounting. But we know they are not required to do so, thanks to the failure of the public accountant to meet his professional responsibility to the public.

Accounting Magic—Illustrating Different Results From Alternative Accounting Principles

The chart on page twenty-seven was prepared to show you how the use of alternative generally accepted accounting principles might affect the earnings reported in a given case. Column 1 shows the profit results of an assumed Company A that faces economic conditions realistically and so reports them in its earnings statement. Columns 2 to 7 show the effect of alternative accounting principles that are also generally acceptable. Column 8 shows Company B's earnings, with no change in operations except the application of alternative methods of accounting followed, yet Company B reports net profits of over twice as much as Company A.

It is wholly possible to have the stock of these two comparable companies selling at prices as much as 100% apart, merely because of the differences in accounting practices.

You can judge for yourself whether, if you were a stockholder, you would rather have the accounting of Company A or that of Company B followed by your company, if it meant the stock would bring you twice as much cash value upon sale. The answer is too obvious to dwell upon.

Now, I want to emphasize again how important it is to let your management accounting practices find the truth as it actually is, regardless of the vagaries of the accounting practices that may be followed in reporting to the public.

Thank you.

ACCOUNTING MAGIC

ALL "IN CONFORMITY WITH GENERALLY ACCEPTED ACCOUNTING PRINCIPLES"

Company B's Profits are Higher Because of

	Company A Col. 1	Use of Fifo in Pricing Inventory Col. 2	Use of Straight-Line Depreciation Col. 3	Deferring Research Costs Over 5 Years Col. 4	Funding Only the Pensions Vested Col. 5	Use of Stock Options for Incentive Col. 6	Including Capital Gain in Income Col. 7	Company B Col. 8
Sales in units	100,000 units $100 each							100,000 units $100 each
Sales in dollars	$10,000,000							$10,000,000
Costs and expenses—								
Cost of goods sold	$ 6,000,000							$ 6,000,000
Selling, general and administrative	1,500,000							1,500,000
LIFO inventory reserve	400,000	$(400,000)						–
Depreciation	400,000		$(100,000)					300,000
Research costs	100,000			$(80,000)				20,000
Pension costs	200,000				$(150,000)			50,000
Officers' compensation—								
Base salaries	200,000							200,000
Bonuses	200,000					$(200,000)		–
Total costs and expenses	$ 9,000,000	$(400,000)	$(100,000)	$(80,000)	$(150,000)	$(200,000)		$ 8,070,000
Profit before income taxes	$ 1,000,000	$ 400,000	$ 100,000	$ 80,000	$ 150,000	$ 200,000		$ 1,930,000
Income taxes	520,000	208,000	52,000	42,000	78,000	104,000		1,004,000
	$ 480,000	$ 192,000	$ 48,000	$ 38,000	$ 72,000	$ 96,000		$ 926,000
Gain on sale of property (net of income tax)	–						$150,000	150,000
Net profit reported	$ 480,000	$ 192,000	$ 48,000	$ 38,000	$ 72,000	$ 96,000	$150,000	$ 1,076,000
Per share on 600,000 shares	$ .80	$ .32	$ .08	$ .06	$ .12	$ .16	$ .25	$ 1.79
Market value at—								
10 times earnings	$ 8.00	$3.20	$ .80	$ .63	$1.20	$1.60	$2.50	$17.93
12 times earnings	$ 9.60	$3.84	$ .96	$ .76	$1.44	$1.92	$3.00	$21.52
15 times earnings	$12.00	$4.80	$1.20	$ .95	$1.80	$2.40	$3.75	$26.90

( ) Denotes deduction.

See explanation of Columns 2 to 7, inclusive, on the following page.

ACCOUNTING MAGIC

EXPLANATION OF COLUMNS 2 TO 7, INCLUSIVE

Column	Company A	Company B
2.	Uses Lifo (last in, first out) for pricing inventory	Uses Fifo (first in, first out)
3.	Uses accelerated depreciation for book and tax purposes	Uses straight-line
4.	Charges research and development costs to expense currently.	Capitalizes and amortizes over five-year period

(If R & D costs remain at same level, the difference disappears after five years. The difference of $80,000 in the chart is in the first year, where A expenses $100,000, and B capitalizes the $100,000 but amortizes 1/5.)

Column	Company A	Company B
5.	Funds the current pension costs—i.e., current service plus amortization of past service.	Funds only the present value of pensions vested

(Difference in pension charges might also arise where, as in the case of U. S. Steel in 1958, management decides that current contributions can be reduced or omitted because of excess funding in prior years and/or increased earnings of the fund or the rise in market value of the investments.)

Column	Company A	Company B
6.	Pays incentive bonuses to officers in cash	Grants stock options instead of paying cash bonuses
7.	Credits gains (net of tax thereon) directly to earned surplus (or treats them as special credits below net income)	Includes such gains (net of income tax thereon) in income

39

HIGGLEDY PIGGLEDY GROWTH IN AMERICA *

John Lintner and Robert Glauber

Someone once said that the sure road to academic success is to publish at least a few papers which anyone else working in or near the problems treated would have to footnote in subsequent work. Many other academics have said that one of the prime functions of research in universities is to test widely held tenets, presumptions, assumptions—or pieces of conventional wisdom which provide the logical starting point for decisions, policy judgments or action of most any kind—to determine whether these are or are not in fact supported by (or at least consistent with) available evidence.

On both scores Ian Little hit a home run in his famous paper on Higgledy Piggledy Growth.[1] Some of the work at Chicago, the U.S. Naval Research Laboratory and elsewhere had already conditioned us to the thought that over at least limited intervals, measured in months, weeks, days or hours, stock prices move in approximately a Brownian motion (whether or not stable Paretian). But even if so-called technical analysis of stock prices had really been dealt a mortal blow, it was still possible to believe that "fundamentals" were of basic importance over somewhat longer runs, that information itself is an economic good not uniformly distributed among mortal men, and that those who could act on earlier or better assessments of fundamentals should be expected to achieve better than average results in the market.

Apart from the risk characteristics of any company's operations and financing, surely the most fundamental of these fundamentals were prospects for growth in earnings and dividends. The British had their Marks and Spencer: we had our IBM, P&G, Kodak and many more as befits our larger and more vigorous economy. Our markets were zooming and the real rockets were the Polaroids and Xeroxes with the fastest growth records. The fast growth companies were ones with distinctive products, aggressive managements, and many of the attributes associated, in the lexicon of Industrial Organization specialists, with (product) "market power." Except perhaps for some of those viewing the economy from the shores of Lake Michigan, exceptions to

* The authors wish to express their appreciation to the Standard Statistics Company for generously making the Compustat tapes available, and to the Ford Foundation for funds for financial research granted to the Harvard Business School.

[1] Little, I. M. D. "Higgledy Piggledy Growth," Institute of Statistics, Oxford, November, 1962, Vol. 24, No. 4.

Unpublished paper presented to the Seminar on the Analysis of Security Prices, May, 1967, University of Chicago. Reprinted by permission of the authors.

purely competitive static models were not regarded as merely random nor strictly transient. It was recognized that the creation of a given set of economic rents would be rather quickly capitalized in the market, and that more intensive exploitation of *given* opportunities led to diminishing returns; but Schumpeter's dynamic bombardments were obvious to those who looked for them and it seemed reasonable to bet on the generals and the armies that had been winning the economic battles. In the long run, the equalizations of classic models would be restored; but recalling Keynes' most famous and unexceptionable dictum, living in successive shorter runs of a few years' duration, it was plausible (if not disastrously seductive) to believe that demonstrated success implied further success, that superior growth implied superior growth (and vice versa).

Little's paper for many people was like a cold shower. The evidence simply didn't square with common presumption. Though offered with no pretense of statistical sophistication, the summaries of British experience offered by Little clearly indicated that randomness was rampant in the data on successive growth rates in British companies, and the following larger study [1] with Rayner strengthened the conclusions.

But many questions remained. For instance:

1. Suppose Little's results were taken at full face value. Would the same results be found in the larger bodies of American data available to us through the Compustat tapes?
2. Most of the Little-Rayner study focused on relatively short run growth rates in earnings and to a lesser extent in dividends. But as they note in their conclusions (p. 60), "In the short run, it seems quite reasonable to suppose that fluctuations beyond the control of management should swamp any tendency to consistency that there might otherwise be." And as the authors also recognized, their extensive use of link relatives or point-to-point percentage changes as their measure of growth exaggerated the impact of noise in the primary data. While this problem is, of course, most serious when the end observation determining the earlier year's growth rate is also used as the base for the subsequent growth ratio, making negative correlations almost automatic, such measures are still generally biased toward instability even when non-overlapping periods are used and even when longer intervals are examined. Such considerations suggested that in further work on American data, attention should be focused primarily on the degree of stability (or instability if one prefers the other end of the telescope) to be found in the relative growth trends shown by companies over longer periods, and that for this purpose some measure such as the slopes of the time trends of the logarithms of the data over intervals of five or ten years should be used.
3. The British economy in the post-war period has been characterized as a stop-go operation, and we all know that except for 1961–65, growth in the American economy has also had at least some fast-slow characteristics. When real GNP alternately surges and pauses, it is probably

---

[1] Rayner, A. C., and I. M. D. Little. "Higgledy Piggledy Growth Again," Basil Blackwell, Oxford, 1966.

unreasonable to expect growth in individual companies to be very regular. Consequently it seemed worthwhile to see whether such a simple device as including the FRB index as a separate variable in the regressions would not substantially improve the stability observed in growth rates over time. If the results of this effort looked promising, more sophisticated allowance for changes in the business environment could be made in later work.

4. Since one of the basic elements in the concept of a "growth company" is that it should outperform the general economy and the general run of companies with some consistency, there also seemed to be considerable merit in examining the degree of stability between periods in the simple regression slopes of each company's performance on the FRB index itself, rather than on time as such. Our research plan consequently provided for testing the inter-period stability of growth rates based on time, with and without the FRB included as a separate variable in the intra-period regression, and also the stability between periods of the simple intra-period slope of company performance on the FRB index alone.

5. Profits are well known to be a residual and thus may be expected to reflect most if not all of the randomness of each of the components used in its determination. Also, reported earnings are subject to such exogenous events as changes in tax laws whose impact on firms, even in the same industry, is known to be quite uneven. Moreover, one might normally expect earnings per share data which is of particularly direct interest to investors to be even more random than aggregate dollar earnings because of the short run impact of the issuance of new shares, the irregular timing of conversions of outstanding hybrid securities, not to mention mergers and other such special events.

The rules for reporting corporate earnings are of course not strictly mechanical, precise and rigid. Managements (and their accountants) are clearly free to exercise their judgment—within sometimes rather broad (and in some cases, rather fuzzily bounded) ranges of discretion in reporting various forms of income and expense. Well-known examples include the timing and time pattern of the entries recognizing the realization of the income produced by equipment leased to others, and the charges for pension obligations; whether investment credits are "distributed" or "passed through"; the appropriate lives to use in depreciating equipment (especially that subject to heavy risks of obsolescence), and whether straight-line, SYD or double declining balance patterns should be used; the valuation of inventories, receivables and investments; the treatment of foreign earnings; the extent and manner of consolidating domestic operations; and so on. The existence of such multi-dimensional ranges of discretion on the one hand undoubtedly permits some managements to stabilize reported earnings over time to some extent. But the exercise of this discretion will also often have precisely the opposite effect: shifts for whatever reason from one method of reporting certain types of transactions or charge to another method (though still within the generally accepted range of discretion) may be quite *de*stabilizing to the pattern of reported earnings, as may decisions regarding so-called extraordinary or non-recurring credits and charges which may be entered above or below the line and may or may not be spread over time if entered above.

There are thus many good reasons for thinking that earnings and earnings per share may be either more or less stable than other financial series pertaining to a business, and it seemed to be worthwhile to examine the relative stability in the time patterns of other series, such as sales, operating income, EBIT and aggregate dollar earnings, as well as earnings per share and dividends.

6. The Little and Little-Rayner studies had focused on the period-to-period stability (or lack thereof) of the growth rates themselves. But it seemed reasonable to believe that the degree of stability of growth rates would vary among companies in certain regular ways. Little and Rayner had indeed tested one form of this idea by running regressions between the growth rates for non-overlapping periods among companies classified by industry groups (Table 1.9, p. 42). They found a positive relation significant at the 1% level among 30 firms in the food industry, and nine of the thirteen industry-group coefficients were positive (though the coefficient among 21 textile firms was significantly negative at the 5% level). In spite of the well-known and marked differences in the relative degree and pattern of diversification characterizing the various firms in almost every industry group, a corresponding analysis of American data grouped by industry seemed worthwhile.

But other *a priori* specifications of the degree of stability to be expected in growth rates seemed far more promising. In particular, the regression slopes measuring the mean growth rates of a given series for different companies in the initial period would have varying degrees of reliability (or within-period stability) as shown either by their τ-ratios or by the standard error of estimate. This information had not been exploited, and it seemed very relevant: one should be able to have more confidence in projecting a 6% growth rate subject to a standard error of 3% within the base interval, than in projecting either a 2% or an 8% mean growth rate which had been determined with an observed standard error of 12%.

Our efforts to examine whether Higgledy Piggledy Growth characterizes American industrial experience as much as the British thus focused on longer run 5 and 10 year growth trends measured by linear slopes in logarithmic data, and examined the relative instability of sales (S), operating income (OY), earnings before interest and taxes (EBIT), aggregate dollar earnings ($E), earnings per share (EPS) and dividends per share (DPS). Except for dividends, where we worked with the 309 companies on the Compustat industrial tapes with positive dividends in each of the years 1946 through 1965, all our regressions were run on the annual data for the 323 companies having positive earnings throughout this twenty year period. The two decades of data were broken into four five-year periods, 1946–50, 1951–55, 1956–60, and 1961–65 which are respectively denoted periods 1, 2, 3, and 4 in the accompanying tables. We also analyzed the period-to-period stability of the ten year growth rates computed as linear logarithmic slopes for the years

1946–55 and 1956–65 (which are called periods 5 and 6 or "1st 10" and "2nd 10" in the tables).

FINDINGS

1. *Observations on Basic Growth Rates.* The cross-sectional means and standard deviations of the simple regressions of our various dependent variables on time and on the FRB index are given in Table 1. The growth

TABLE 1

MEANS AND STANDARD ERRORS OF DEPENDENT VARIABLES
(in logarithms)

Slope of Following Variable on Time

Period	S		OY		EBIT		$ E		EPS	
	μ	σ	μ	σ	μ	σ	μ	σ	μ	σ
1	.1072	.0772	.1410	.1533	.1425	.1832	.1165	.1623	.1075	.1596
2	.0514	.0671	.0318	.1043	.0106	.1293	.0569	.1246	.0367	.1173
3	.0513	.0695	.0263	.1031	.0106	.1308	.0148	.1265	−.0039	.1224
4	.0885	.0625	.1059	.0893	.1180	.1243	.1401	.1169	.1295	.1126
1st 10	.0904	.0503	.0910	.0821	.0816	.0942	.0477	.0903	.0327	.0837
2nd 10	.0636	.0459	.0546	.0643	.0483	.0791	.0586	.0748	.0443	.0695

Slopes of Variables on FRB

Period	S		OY		EBIT		$ E		EPS	
1	.0303	.0192	.0447	.0386	.0476	.0461	.0397	.0400	.0375	.0393
2	.0142	.0145	.0122	.0221	.0092	.0274	.0166	.0267	.0119	.0249
3	.0133	.0120	.0129	.0185	.0135	.0249	.0143	.0253	.0112	.0245
4	.0108	.0077	.0130	.0109	.0145	.0153	.0172	.0143	.0159	.0138
1st 10	.0220	.0119	.0228	.0194	.0210	.0222	.0120	.0211	.0084	.0196
2nd 10	.0123	.0083	.0115	.0115	.0109	.0143	.0130	.0136	.0106	.0126

TABLE 2

RATIOS OF MEANS TO STANDARD ERRORS IN TABLE 1

Period	S	OY	EBIT	$ E	EPS
			On Time:		
1	1.389	0.920	0.778	0.718	0.674
2	0.766	0.305	0.082	0.457	0.313
3	0.738	0.255	0.081	0.117	neg.
4	1.416	1.185	0.949	1.198	1.150
1st 10	1.797	1.108	0.866	0.528	0.391
2nd 10	1.386	0.849	0.611	0.783	0.638
			On FRB:		
1	1.578	1.158	1.033	0.992	0.954
2	0.979	0.552	0.336	0.622	0.478
3	1.108	0.697	0.542	0.565	0.457
4	1.402	1.192	0.948	1.203	1.152
1st 10	1.849	1.175	0.946	0.568	0.429
2nd 10	1.481	1.000	0.762	0.956	0.841

rate of sales, operating income and EBIT were uniformly greatest in 1946–50, on both time and the FRB index, due to the special circumstances of the period. The time growth of earnings was largest in the final five years largely because of the change in tax laws, but earnings growth relative to the FRB was only a little higher in the current cycle expansion than within the preceding ten years.

Throughout Table 1, the cross-sectional standard deviations are large relative to the means. The average growth of each period is subject to great diversity in individual company experience. The cross-sectional standard deviation among slopes is greater for operating income than for sales, and still greater for EBIT. There is generally somewhat less cross-sectional diversity in the growth rates of aggregate dollar earnings and earnings per share than in EBIT, perhaps surprisingly, but both earnings series show more diversity in growth rates than either sales or operating income. These results are qualitatively the same whether the intra-period growth rates are based on time or the FRB index.

Table 2 shows the ratio of the mean to the standard deviation in each cell of Table 1. This ratio is considerably greater in the upper half of the table (regressions on time) than in the corresponding cell in the lower half of the table (based simply on the FRB index), with the exception that there is approximate equality in the ratios for the corresponding cells for the fourth five-year period (when the FRB has a correlation of .995 with time). Also, while every ratio based on the FRB regression is greater than that on time when ten year periods are used, the superiority of the FRB basis in this comparison is less marked than in the first three five-year periods.

2. *Inter-Period Correlations of Growth Rates, Cross-Sections of All Companies.* Table 3a summarizes the results of regressing each five and ten year periods growth rate of sales on that of the earlier periods within the two decades. Tables 3b–3e give the corresponding correlations for operating income, EBIT, aggregate dollar earnings and earnings per share. Each of the five tables in this set is divided into three sections to show in turn the results of correlating (i) the simple time-growth rates of each variable with the corresponding growth rate in other periods; (ii) the results of correlating the semi-log slopes of each variable on the FRB index with its value in other periods; and (iii) the correlations between different time periods in the *net* regression slopes of the performance variable on time, after allowing in each period for the effect of the FRB index.

Several features of these tables are worth special comment:

All the inter-period correlations are positive, but all are small and most are very small.

With the exception of the correlations of 1956–61 on 1951–55 data for sales and operating income, all the inter-period correlations between the five-year growth rates for all performance variables are greater when growth is measured relative to the FRB index rather than to calendar time within the period. (Neither basis, however, provides a correlation above .08 on any series between adjoining ten-year growth rates.)

Correspondingly, the *net* time growth rates (after allowing for the influence of the FRB) are consistently more stable than the raw time-growth rates.

TABLE 3

INTERPERIOD CROSS-SECTIONAL CORRELATIONS BETWEEN DIFFERENT
LOGARITHMIC GROWTH RATES

Part (a)(i): *Growth Rates of SALES on TIME*			
5-Year Periods Correlated	*Correlation*	*F-Ratio* *	*Standard Error of Estimate*
2 on 1	.135	5.911	.0666
3 on 2	.215	15.613	.0679
3 on 2, 1	.241	9.849	.0676
4 on 3	.095	2.919	.0623
4 on 3, 2	.112	2.016	.0623
4 on 3, 2, 1	.117	1.480	.0624
2nd on 1st 10	.080	2.074	.0459
Part (a)(ii): *Growth Rates of SALES on PRODUCTION*			
2 on 1	.190	12.013	.0143
3 on 2	.176	10.269	.0118
3 on 2, 1	.184	5.603	.0118
4 on 3	.211	14.916	.0075
4 on 3, 2	.213	7.572	.0075
4 on 3, 2, 1	.216	5.222	.0075
2nd on 1st 10	.824	2.193	.0083
Part (a)(iii): *TIME RATES of Growth in SALES, NET of FRB*			
2 on 1	.195	12.748	.0840
3 on 2	.296	30.781	.0768
3 on 2, 1	.298	15.588	.0769
4 on 3	.0227	0.165	.2237
4 on 3, 2	.042	0.280	.2239
4 on 3, 2, 1	.132	1.886	.2225
2nd on 1st 10	.249	21.188	.0742
Part (b)(i): *Growth Rates of OPERATING INCOME on TIME*			
2 on 1	.064	1.305	.1043
3 on 2	.053	0.896	.1031
3 on 2, 1	.071	0.814	.1032
4 on 3	.060	1.151	.0892
4 on 3, 2	.087	1.228	.0892
4 on 3, 2, 1	.088	0.823	.0893
2nd on 1st 10	.016	0.083	.0644
Part (b)(ii): *Growth Rates of OPERATING INCOME on PRODUCTION*			
2 on 1	.133	5.820	.0219
3 on 2	.021	0.143	.0185
3 on 2, 1	.067	0.718	.0185

* For "significance levels" see footnote 1 on page 654.

TABLE 3 (*cont.*)

INTERPERIOD CROSS-SECTIONAL CORRELATIONS BETWEEN DIFFERENT LOGARITHMIC GROWTH RATES

5-Year Periods Correlated	Correlation	F-Ratio *	Standard Error of Estimate
4 on 3	.146	7.021	.0108
4 on 3, 2	.146	3.502	.0108
4 on 3, 2, 1	.165	2.957	.0108
2nd on 1st 10	.012	0.046	.0115

Part (b)(iii): *TIME RATES of Growth In OPERATING INCOME NET of FRB*

2 on 1	.131	5.60	.1561
3 on 2	.163	8.807	.1262
3 on 2, 1	.188	5.844	.1258
4 on 3	.108	3.819	.4207
4 on 3, 2	.154	3.897	.4188
4 on 3, 2, 1	.158	2.735	.4192
2nd on 1st 10	.192	12.252	.1213

Part (c)(i): *Growth Rates of EBIT on TIME*

2 on 1	.000	0.000	.1295
3 on 2	.000	0.000	.1310
3 on 2, 1	.031	0.157	.1312
4 on 3	.106	3.667	.1238
4 on 3, 2	.125	2.531	.1237
4 on 3, 2, 1	.127	1.728	.1239
2nd on 1st 10	.055	0.960	.0791

Part (c)(ii): *Growth Rates of EBIT on PRODUCTION*

2 on 1	.084	2.279	.0274
3 on 2	.033	0.339	.0249
3 on 2, 1	.086	1.186	.0249
4 on 3	.128	5.336	.0152
4 on 3, 2	.16		
4 on 3, 2, 1	.163	2.903	.0152
2nd on 1st 10	.022	0.154	.0143

Part (c)(iii): *TIME RATES of Growth in EBIT, NET of FRB*

2 on 1	.054	0.945	.2071
3 on 2	.151	7.476	.1664
3 on 2, 1	.191	6.025	.1665
4 on 3	.099	3.168	.6516
4 on 3, 2	.152	3.800	.6482
4 on 3, 2, 1	.153	2.533	.6492
2nd on 1st 10	.184	11.297	.1593

* For "significance levels" see footnote 1 on page 654.

TABLE 3 (*cont.*)

INTERPERIOD CROSS-SECTIONAL CORRELATIONS BETWEEN DIFFERENT LOGARITHMIC GROWTH RATES

Part (d)(i): *Growth Rates of AGGREGATE EARNINGS on TIME*

5-Year Periods Correlated	Correlation	F-Ratio *	Standard Error of Estimate
2 on 1	.071	1.608	.1244
3 on 2	0	0	.1267
3 on 2, 1	.051	0.422	.1267
4 on 3	.066	1.391	.1168
4 on 3, 2	.072	0.824	.1170
4 on 3, 2, 1	.078	0.654	.1171
2nd on 1st 10	.063	1.279	.0747

Part (d)(ii):
Growth Rates of AGGREGATE INCOME on PRODUCTION

2 on 1	.109	3.873	.0266
3 on 2	.034	0.362	.0253
3 on 2, 1	.129	2.706	.0252
4 on 3	.121	4.796	.0142
4 on 3, 2	.132	2.842	.0142
4 on 3, 2, 1	.142	2.176	.0142
2nd on 1st 10	.032	0.331	.0136

Part (d)(iii):
TIME RATES of Growth in AGGREGATE INCOME, NET of FRB

2 on 1	.113	4.139	.1964
3 on 2	.135	5.910	.1599
3 on 2, 1	.152	3.778	.1597
4 on 3	.151	7.507	.5897
4 on 3, 2	.185	5.662	.5872
4 on 3, 2, 1	.186	3.826	.5879
2nd on 1st 10	.179	10.630	.1472

Part (e)(i): *Growth Rates of EPS on TIME*

2 on 1	.046	0.686	.1174
3 on 2	0	0	.1225
3 on 2, 1	.073	0.848	.1224
4 on 3	.122	4.829	.1120
4 on 3, 2	.132	2.847	.1120
4 on 3, 2, 1	.135	1.983	.1121
2nd on 1st 10	.078	1.958	.0694

Part (e)(ii): *Growth Rates of EPS on PRODUCTION*

2 on 1	.082	2.159	.0248
3 on 2	.033	0.345	.0245

* For "significance levels" see footnote 1 on page 654.

TABLE 3 (*cont.*)

INTERPERIOD CROSS-SECTIONAL CORRELATIONS BETWEEN DIFFERENT LOGARITHMIC GROWTH RATES

5-Year Periods Correlated	Correlation	F-Ratio *	Standard Error of Estimate
3 on 2, 1	.120	2.325	.0244
4 on 3	.078	1.950	.0137
4 on 3, 2	.082	1.091	.0138
4 on 3, 2, 1	.109	1.276	.0138
2nd on 1st 10	.038	0.453	.0126
Part (e)(iii): *TIME RATES of Growth in EPS, NET of FRB*			
2 on 1	.095	2.904	.1908
3 on 2	.151	7.507	.1568
3 on 2, 1	.168	4.639	.1566
4 on 3	.139	6.308	.5900
4 on 3, 2	.71	4.788	.5879
4 on 3, 2, 1	.171	3.208	.5888
2nd on 1st 10	.189	11.891	.1453

* For "significance levels" see footnote 1, below.

This is true for all the correlations between five-year growth rates for all performance variables (with the exception of those involving the 1961–65 period when time and the FRB were almost perfectly collinear). In addition, it is worth noting that—in spite of the very low correlations between simple growth rates over ten year periods based on either time or the FRB alone— the correlations between ten year *net* growth rates are among the best found anywhere in this set of tables.

It is not surprising to find that the growth rates of sales (on each of the three measurements) are less unstable than the corresponding growth rates of other performance variables. For those who like their classical statistics straight, we note that all the F ratios of correlation of 5 year sales growth rates relative to the FRB are approximately twice the levels required to pass a one per cent significance test; [1] and the same may be said of the results using both the 5 year [2] and 10 year *net* time slopes of sales. Indeed

[1] With over 300 observations, the values of the F-ratio required to satisfy classical significance tests are as follows:

number of explanatory variables	5% test value	1% test value
1	3.87	6.73
2	3.03	4.68
3	2.63	3.85

[2] Excluding 1961–65 as explained above.

TABLE 4A

CROSS-SECTIONAL MEANS, STANDARD DEVIATIONS AND TEN-YEAR CORRELATIONS
OF NET TIME GROWTH RATES * OF OPERATING INCOME WITHIN INDUSTRY GROUPS

Industry Group [1]	Number of Companies	1946–55			1956–66			Correlation	τ-Ratio	Standard Error of Estimate
		μ	σ	μ/σ	μ	σ	μ/σ			
(1)	44	.0195	.1047	.186	.0391	.0974	.401	.111	0.725	.0980
(2)	18	−.1072	.1382	−.776	.0176	.0903	.195	.199	−0.812	.0912
(3)	42	.0318	.0828	.384	.0209	.0944	.221	.167	1.074	.0943
(4)	32	.0360	.0815	.442	−.0148	.0837	−.177	.193	1.076	.0835
(5)	21	.0214	.0973	.220	.0194	.0642	.302	.088	−0.384	.0656
(6)	33	−.0462	.1629	−.284	−.0745	.1605	−.464	.130	0.730	.1617
(7)	34	−.0002	.1435	−.001	−.0975	.1566	−.623	.133	0.762	.1576
(8)	14	.0467	.1480	.275	−.0105	.0936	−.112	.189	0.667	.0957
(9)	18	−.0355	.2008	−.177	−.0434	.1266	−.343	.074	−0.298	.1301
(10)	11	.0895	.1702	.526	.0724	.1130	.641	.471	1.600	.1051
(11)	15	−.0144	.1391	−.104	−.0079	.1101	.072	.867	6.264	.0570
(12)	16	−.0350	.0732	−.478	−.1082	.1378	−.785	.139	0.524	.1412
(13)	25	.0410	.1310	.313	.0380	.0937	.406	.213	1.043	.0935
All	323	.0049	.1320	.037	−.0122	.1234	−.099	.192	3.500	.1213

* Net of FRB index.
[1] Industry identifications are given in Table 4C.

TABLE 4B

CROSS-SECTIONAL MEANS, STANDARD DEVIATIONS AND TEN-YEAR CORRELATIONS OF NET TIME GROWTH RATES * OF EPS. WITHIN INDUSTRY GROUPS

Industry Group[1]	Number of Companies	1946–55			1956–66			Correlation	τ-Ratio	Standard Error of Estimate
		μ	σ	μ/σ	μ	σ	μ/σ			
(1)	44	−.0086	.1423	−.006	.0162	.1242	.130	.174	1.145	.1238
(2)	18	−.1452	.1574	−.922	−.0434	.1255	−.346	.114	−0.458	.1285
(3)	42	.0195	.1096	.178	−.0124	.1186	−.104	.286	1.884	.1151
(4)	32	.0209	.0845	.247	−.0679	.0809	−.839	.118	0.649	.0816
(5)	21	.0078	.1251	.062	−.0491	.1104	−.445	.077	0.337	.1130
(6)	33	−.0620	.1986	−.312	−.1490	.2154	−.692	.291	1.691	.2094
(7)	34	.0131	.1393	.094	−.1484	.1501	−.989	.231	1.342	.1483
(8)	14	.0417	.1470	.284	−.0595	.1171	−.508	.107	0.373	.1211
(9)	18	−.0362	.2489	−.145	−.0992	.1423	−.697	.178	−0.725	.1444
(10)	11	.0885	.1845	.479	.0442	.1315	.336	.276	0.860	.1332
(11)	15	−.0186	.1326	−.140	−.0506	.1381	−.366	.857	6.001	.0738
(12)	16	−.0566	.1206	−.469	−.1660	.1536	−1.081	.192	0.730	.1560
(13)	25	−.0273	.2037	−.134	−.0254	.1092	−.233	.039	0.186	.1115
All	323	−.0121	.1582	−.076	−.0617	.1478	−.417	.189	3.448	.1453

* Net of FRB index.
[1] Industry identifications are given in Table 4C.

TABLE 4C

INDUSTRY GROUP DESCRIPTIONS FOR CROSS-SECTIONAL MEANS, STANDARD
DEVIATIONS AND TEN-YEAR CORRELATIONS OF NET TIME GROWTH RATES *
OF OPERATING INCOME AND EPS WITHIN INDUSTRY GROUPS

Industry Number	*Industry Description*
(1)	Food, Beverage, Tobacco, Tin Cans and Soap
(2)	Textiles, Apparel, Leather, Synthetic Fabrics
(3)	Chemicals and Drugs
(4)	Petroleum, Rubber and Plastics
(5)	Paper, Paper Products, Printing and Publishing
(6)	Primary Metals, Fabricated Metal Products
(7)	Nonelectrical Machinery
(8)	Electrical Machinery, Appliances and Home Furnishings
(9)	Transportation
(10)	Office Eqpt., Electronics, Photo Eqpt.
(11)	Distribution
(12)	Misc. Mining
(13)	Not elsewhere classified

* Net of FRB index.

using the 10 year *net* time-growth rates of sales, the F-ratio is 3½ times
the 1% significance value! But before euphoria spreads, we quickly note
that the highest inter-period correlation between growth rates of sales
"explains" less than 10% of the cross-sectional variance.

The inter-period correlations of each set of growth rates on operating
income, EBIT, aggregate earnings and EPS are so much weaker as to
require little comment other than that there is little to choose between
them. It is true that those expecting to find some predictive stability in these
important series, who also are wedded to the significance of classical
significance tests, will be pleased to see F-ratios twice the required 1% level
on the ten year *net* growth rate correlation; but those wanting to explain
more than 3.7% of the cross-sectional variance will find little encouragement in this part of the tables.

3. *Inter-Period Correlations, Cross-Sections Within Industry Groups.*
Since net time growth rates, after allowing for the FRB index, proved to
be the most stable in the overall cross-sections, we decided to examine the
gains from industry grouping in terms of these net growth rates. To keep
computations within reasonable levels, the industry analysis was run only
for operating income and EPS. The results for the cross-sectional correlations, regressing the second ten-year net growth rates on those of the
preceding ten years, are shown in Table 4A for operating income, and
Table 4B for EPS. As background, the corresponding results across all
industry groups are shown, together with the cross-sectional intra-industry
means and standard deviations of the net time growth rates in each of the
two ten-year periods.

In interpreting these mean growth rates, the reader must keep in mind
that they do reflect only the *net* rate of growth on calendar time after all

growth associated with increasing levels of industrial production has been "partialed out." Nevertheless the number of industries whose mean position was deteriorating, after allowing for growth in general output, is perhaps striking. Eleven of the thirteen groups had negative mean *net* growth rates of EPS in the second ten-year period in spite of unprecedented prosperity and massive tax cuts.

The cross-sectional dispersion of net growth rates for operating income within the first ten years covered was lower than that across all companies in only six of the thirteen groups; but in the second ten years for operating income, and in both periods for EPS, from eight to ten industries showed less intra-industry dispersion (the σ of tables 4A and B) than the entire set of 323 companies. Though the mean/σ ratio is rather ambiguous in this context, for whatever it may be worth we observe that the industry grouping has generally and often rather markedly raised the mean net growth rate relative to its dispersion.

As indicated earlier, we had substantial doubts concerning the value of industry grouping in this context before examining the data, and these "Bayesian priors" were supported with few exceptions by the "sample statistics" shown in the last three columns of Tables 4A and 4B. Interestingly, the textile group in our American data showed negative correlations in net growth rates between the decades in both operating income and EPS, but the "significance level" in our data (about 25 per cent or less on a one-tail test) is far less than the 5 per cent level Little and Rayner reported for English textiles. We also find a strong preponderance of positive signs (twenty-one of the twenty-six in the two tables) as they did in Britain. But most of the coefficients are notably low—five of the twenty-six τ-ratios fall short of a 50 per cent two-tailed level, and twelve more are below the 20 per cent level.

It is perhaps of some interest that Chemicals and Drugs fall in the 5–10 per cent range for EPS, though they fall far short of such "heights" on operating income. While five of the thirteen raw correlation coefficients in each table are larger than the overall correlation, the differences with but one exception are of no consequence after allowance is made for degrees of freedom.

The one notable success we can offer those who expected industry grouping to uncover hidden and marked stability in growth rates is provided by the distribution group. The correlation between the net growth rates of the two ten-year periods shown by the 15 firms in this industry of department stores and other retailers was a very respectable .86 for both operating income and EPS. Both correlations have τ-ratios approaching twice the values required for significance at the .001 level on two-tailed tests.

We ran a corresponding analysis of the stability of net growth rates within the same industry groups for adjacent five year periods, but there is no need to detail the results since qualitatively they merely confirmed the assessments provided by the ten-year growth rate analysis. It is, of course. quite possible that gross growth rates. on either the FRB or time, would prove to be more stable within industry groupings, even though such grouping does little to stabilize the data for net growth rates. Perhaps we will come back to test this possibility later, but especially in view of our prior judgments, the results of the tests reported on industry grouping led us to conclude that our other parts of our research plan should be pushed along for this conference.

4. *The Significance of the Standard Errors of Estimate of Growth Rates Themselves.* As indicated in the introduction, we approached this study with some presumption in our minds that whether or not a company had a reasonably well-defined growth rate in any period should have quite a lot to do with whether its mean growth in that period provided much evidence on its prospective growth in the future. We had noted that the earlier studies of Higgledy Piggledy Growth had not exploited the information provided by the standard errors of estimate (or the τ-ratios) of the growth rates in the initial period; we believed such information should be used and not thrown away.

We knew that (in the absence of other information) we would feel more comfortable about making estimates of the future growth of a company whose past growth had been defined within a "sampling error" of 2 per cent, than in projecting growth for companies whose past growth had been so "uppsy-downsy" that the standard deviation about its up-sloping trendline was 20 per cent or so. While we had a relatively open mind concerning whether the common generality of companies had stable or erratic growth patterns, we believed that those companies whose growth had been more stable within the "observation period"—on the average and in the absence of other information—could be expected to have more stable growth in the future. And if growth were to be more stable within each of two periods ("present" and "future"), the chances would seem to be good on the average that shifts between the one period and the next would be relatively smaller also. But in that case the first period's growth rate would be a better predictor of the future (or second period's) growth rate. Of course, exogenous shocks and lumpy events would often intervene, but we found such elementary observation and logic sufficiently compelling to want to give the approach a try. In short and more formally, we hypothesized that the predictive value of any observed growth rate would be inversely related to the standard error about the growth rate—or the τ-ratio of the observed growth coefficient—in the base period.

4a. *Differences in Growth Rates Relative to Their Standard Errors.* As a preliminary test of whether more refined analysis along these lines was justified, we ran a standard classical test that pairs of intra-period growth rates for each firm were equal. Table 5 tabulates the fraction of all firms for which the hypothesis of equality must be rejected at the 5 per cent level. (Even if the hypothesis of equality were true, one would expect 5 per cent of the cases to exceed the test limit.) In less technical terms, Table 5 shows the fraction of all firms whose *inter-period changes* in growth rates are greater than they would be expected on the basis of chance (*even if* they were "really equal"). Merely because of the uncertainty of each firm's own growth rates as measured by its *intra*-period standard deviations or "noise," one would expect *some* differences in growth rates between periods. The greater the noise, the greater the differences in growth rate which would be expected simply on the basis of chance, and this proposition is built into the standard test used. The results not only encouraged us to go on, but seem to have some interest in themselves.

The first three columns in the upper half of Table 5 show that one-sixth

TABLE 5

FRACTIONS OF FIRMS EXCEEDING CLASSICAL 5% ACCEPTANCE LIMITS ON
HYPOTHESIS OF EQUAL GROWTH RATES. ALL VARIABLES, ALL
TIME-COMPARISONS, SIMPLE AND NET GROWTH RATES

	Part A:	*Simple*	*Growth*	*Rates on Time*	
				Average	
	1951–55:	*1956–60:*	*1961–65:*	*5-year*	*1956–65:*
Variable	*1946–50*	*1951–55*	*1956–60*	*Comparison*	*1946–55*
Sales	24.5%	26.0%	48.0%	32.8%	62.2%
Operating Income	24.8%	18.6%	35.9%	26.4%	52.6%
EBIT	26.0%	16.4%	35.6%	26.0%	46.8%
Agg. Earnings	17.0%	24.8%	39.6%	27.1%	41.5%
EPS	18.0%	24.8%	40.3%	27.6%	38.7%
DPS	36.3%	30.7%	33.7%	33.6%	49.5%
	Part B:	*Net Time-Growth Rates, Allowing for FRB*			
Sales	5.3%	10.8%	2.2%	6.1%	15.5%
Operating Income	7.4%	11.8%	3.4%	7.5%	13.0%
EBIT	8.1%	11.8%	3.1%	7.6%	12.1%
Agg. Earnings	10.5%	17.7%	3.7%	10.6%	16.4%
EPS	9.3%	11.8%	2.5%	7.8%	15.2%
DPS	13.6%	16.8%	13.3%	14.6%	13.9%

to two-fifths of the firms had greater differences in adjacent five-year raw time-growth rates than would be expected 5 per cent of the time on the basis of the *intra*-period instability of their growth rates. Averaging the three five-year comparisons, from one-fourth to one-third (rather than the "expected" one-twentieth) fall outside. And from two-fifths to three-fifths of the paired comparisons of ten-year simple growth rates are "out of bounds."

But the second half of Table 5 shows once again the great improvement which comes from using *net* growth rates after separate allowance for the FRB index. All the fractions in the 1956–60: 1961–65 comparisons are well within the 5 per cent mark, except for dividends interestingly enough. In the first two five-year comparisons the fractions run from 5–18 per cent, and the average of the three five-year comparisons show "violative" fractions only between 6 per cent and 8 per cent except aggregate earnings (10.6 per cent) and dividends (14.6 per cent). The importance of netting out FRB is also shown in the 10-year comparisons where the "fractions exceeding expectations" fall from the previous 40–60 per cent to 12–16.4 per cent.

4b. *Correlations Between Growth Rates of Firms Classified by Intra-Period Standard Error of Estimate.* As a direct test of the hypothesis that growth rates are more stable when the observed growth rate is better

TABLE 6

CORRELATIONS OF 1961–65 AND 1956–60 GROWTH RATES OF OPERATING
INCOME ON FRB INDEX; FIRMS CLASSIFIED BY SIZE OF
STANDARD ERROR OF ESTIMATE OF 1956–60 GROWTH RATE

Part A: Cross Sectional Means and σ's of Growth Rates

	1956–60			1961–65		
*Quintiles of S.E.E.**	μ	σ	μ/σ	μ	σ	μ/σ
Smallest S.E.E.	.0087	.0099	.879	.0100	.0073	1.370
Next Smallest S.E.E.	.0145	.0164	.885	.0096	.0103	.932
3rd Smallest S.E.E.	.0136	.0136	1.000	.0126	.0089	1.415
4th Smallest S.E.E.	.0124	.0183	.678	.0143	.0119	1.202
Largest S.E.E.	.0152	.0282	.537	.0183	.0130	1.408

Part B: Intra-Quintile Correlations

	Number Firms	Correla-tion	Regression Slope	τ-ratio	Standard error of estimate
Smallest S.E.E.	64	.408	.302	3.522	.0067
Next Smallest S.E.E.	64	.391	.244	3.348	.0095
3rd Smallest S.E.E.	64	.134	−.088	1.067	.0089
4th Smallest S.E.E.	64	.109	.071	0.864	.0119
Largest S.E.E.	67	.073	.034	0.594	.0131

*Standard error of estimate in 1956–60 regression of log OY on FRB.

defined, we have run the correlations between the 1961–65 and 1956–60
Growth Rates of Operating Income relative to the FRB index cross-
sectionally for firms within each of five quintiles of our data. The quintiles
were selected by the size of the standard error of estimates of the simple
regression of the logarithm of operating income on the FRB index in the
years 1956–60. Among the 64 firms with the best defined growth rates
in 1956–60, the average standard error of estimate was only .056: the
average standard errors of estimate in the other successive quintiles are
.101, .147, .206 and .390.[1] Although the firms with the smallest S.E.E.'s
in 1956–60 also had the lowest average growth rate, there was little
difference in the average rates of growth shown by firms—the other quintiles
in this period.

The results of our correlations after this prior sorting of the firms are
given in the lower half of Table 6. The inter-period correlations and the
τ-ratios of the regression slopes "line up" over the five classes as expected.
Indeed, *relatively* speaking, they are quite respectable in the first two quintiles
with the best-determined *prior* growth rates, but their levels surely reflect
a lot of noise in the lower three-fifths of the table. Clearly the standard

[1] It may be noted that ranking by size of S.E.E. is much the same as using the τ-ratio
of the 1956–60 regression slope. The average value of these τ-ratios in our quintile are
respectively 2.101, 1.632, 1.066, 0.739, and 0.492.

errors of estimate of prior growth rates are very relevant to the issue of predictability and the stability of growth rates over time, and should be extensively used in further work in this area. It may well, for instance, be that the prior standard error of growth rates will turn out on further work to be more valuable as a screening parameter separating sheep from goats—those companies whose past statistical pattern *has* a growth rate worthy of use from those which do not in any simple sense. Alternatively, the relevance of prior standard errors of estimating growth may be involved in a more. subtle and complex and perhaps non-linear fashion.

4c. *Absolute Inter-Period Differences in Growth Rates Related to Standard Errors of Estimate of Prior Growth Rates.* It is one thing to say that inter-period correlations of growth rates are greater when prior intra-period standard errors are smaller (at least within some range) but a different thing to say that the prior intra-period standard errors can be used to predict the inter-period differences in growth rates themselves. As a preliminary test of this alternative proposition, we ran a regression in which the standard error of estimate of the growth rate within 1956–60 was used to explain the *absolute difference* (size regardless of sign) in the growth rates for 1956–60 and 1961–65. (As in 4b above growth rates of operating income relative to FRB were used.) Among the 64 firms in the lowest quintile of S.E.E.'s in 1956–60, there was very little if any relationship. The simple correlation was .098, the regression slope was an almost flat .033, and its τ-ratio was a lowly 0.78. But when this regression was run over all 323 firms, the results were quite different: the simple correlation was .40, and while the regression slope was only .041 its τ-value was a lofty 7.795. (Indeed, to throw out a still bigger number, the F-ratio of the equation was 60.769!) Apart from the effect of large numbers of degrees of freedom on classical tests, these results do indicate a strong, *broad* association between prior standard errors and subsequent period-to-period changes. But in the current jargon, the result is not "fine tuned." Nor, with a slope coefficient of .04, will it modify point estimates made on some other basis by very much.

Concluding Observations. Quite obviously, at the present stage of work on this general problem, broad sweeping conclusions would be entirely unjustified. There is indeed a great deal of randomness in the world; financial data, and specifically growth rates, clearly provide no exception. To rely on simple projections of past observed time-growth rates is indeed to give hostages to fortune. Modern econometrics is based on faith in the proposition that more sophisticated *structural* analysis of broader ranges of the *a priori* relevant data which are available can produce results superior to naive forecasting models. The elementary and preliminary analyses reported here suggest that such work in this area should continue, and we hope others will join in the effort. In the meantime, sweeping conclusions on the irrelevance of good management, superior product market position, the insights and judgments of good financial analysts—indeed any conclusion to the effect that nothing but a table of random numbers is relevant to growth in the real world—would itself be premature and unwise. If that is a general conclusion, then we have one!

40

THE TROUBLE WITH EARNINGS

Jack L. Treynor

The main objective of financial accounting has slowly but surely become providing information for security analysis. Informing the analyst was not always a primary or even a secondary objective of financial accounting, nor were accounting outputs always the primary input for security analysis; but today it is probably realistic to view the activities of the accountant and the security analyst as two parts of a larger process designed to estimate the value of corporate common stocks.

The earnings concept is the link between these ostensibly complementary activities. Yet there is no genuine communication between analysts and accountants when it comes to the meaning of earnings. The analyst treats earnings as if it were an economic concept. In view of his purpose —attaching economic value to the firm—he can scarcely do otherwise.

The accounting concept of earnings dates from a time when specialization of labor within the investment industry had scarcely begun, and when, indeed, ownership and management had not begun to separate. The accountant is, of course, the oldest of the professionals in the investment industry, and he continues to regard accounting earnings as his most important product. The accountant defines it as what he gets when he matches costs against revenues, making any necessary allocations of cost to time periods; or as the change in the equity account over the accounting period, before capital transactions. These are not *economic* definitions of earnings, but merely descriptions of the motions the accountant goes through to arrive at the earnings number. The analyst needs a definition that gives him an economic justification for using the earnings concept.

There is no way to carry on constructive discussion of an undefined concept. One approach the security analyst might take in attempting to establish meaningful communications with the accountant would be to ask him to give an economic definition of earnings. As we shall soon see, however, the accountant has very practical reasons for deferring his definition as long as possible, Accordingly, our tactic will be to narrow the accountant's room for maneuver by supplying a definition of earnings—one that has economic meaning—and then asking whether the security analyst would show much interest in the concept, given our definition. If it becomes clear that a thinking security analyst will have very little interest in our definition of earnings, then the accountant may want to repudiate it. But

Reprinted by permission of the author and the *Financial Analysts Journal*. This paper will appear in a yet to be named issue of the *Financial Analysts Journal*.

if accountants want to demonstrate that our definition imputes the wrong economic meaning to earnings, then hopefully they will be compelled to supply what they consider to be the right one.

Professor Lawrence Revsine has suggested defining earnings as an estimate of the change in present value of the firm over the accounting period—a definition that seems to accord closely with Professor Hick's celebrated definition of earnings as the measure of how much value can be withdrawn from the firm over the accounting period without leaving it worse off than before. Most practicing accountants refuse to honor the Hicks-Revsine definition. It is easy to show, however, that, given the Hicks-Revsine definition, the earnings concept is not well suited to linking the measuring and reporting function of the accountant to the judging and valuation function of the security analyst.

In simplest terms our argument runs as follows. If accounting earnings are construed as an attempt to measure changes in the present value of the firm (or, in the context of per share accounting, changes in the value of the share), then, in order to arrive at the change in value, the accountant must first arrive at the value. The accountant could save the analyst a great deal of trouble by simply reporting to him the current present value from which change in value over the period was derived.

If earnings is the difference between the worth of the firm at the beginning and the end of the accounting period, then analysis of a firm's worth logically precedes measurement of earnings, rather than the other way around.

The present joint process by which the accountant arrives at earnings by estimating or measuring the change in value over the accounting period—and the analyst in turn uses these earnings to estimate value at the end of each period—is in some danger of being logically circular. There is, of course, redundancy in having two different people estimate investment worth at two different stages of the over-all process. But the wasted effort is far less important than the fact that certain key premises (determinations of worth of major assets by the accountant) assume the conclusion (estimates of asset worth implicit in the determination of over-all worth by the investor). Aside from the fundamental difficulty in attempting to draw conclusions with real-world meaning from circular logic, there is the further problem in practice that accountants' determinations not only influence but are often influenced by analysts' determinations, closing the loop and making possible the kind of pyramiding of accounting and market values achieved by certain financial "wizards" in the late sixties.

Some may argue that circularity is avoided when changes in book values are used to produce accounting earnings figures, which are in turn used to estimate market values. Unfortunately, although there are many different kinds of markets (e.g., markets for specific productive assets on the one hand—industrial real estate, used machine tools, and so on—and markets for claims on firms owning productive assets on the other), there is only one kind of economic value. And in *every* kind of market, asset value depends on expectations of future earning power (i.e., economic rents) which are subject to continual and unpredictable change.

It is sometimes argued that, because market value fluctuates—sometimes wildly—the appropriate book figure can be a more reliable indicator of an asset's "true" or "intrinsic" value, where the latter is believed to be somehow more stable than market value. It is surprising that this notion is still taken seriously by so many, in view of the rapidly spreading recognition that, if values don't fluctuate as a random walk, they can't be true economic values.* What are these values the accountant assigns to assets at the beginning and end of the accounting period? Although, through extensive use and familiarity, they have taken on for many investors (as well as most accountants) a kind of mystical significance completely unrelated to economic reality, for purposes of security valuation, book values must be construed either as proxies for economic values or as having no meaning at all.

The process is not strictly circular when the accountant confines himself to estimating the value of such current assets as inventories and receivables in order to estimate the rate of flow of economic earnings (what economists call quasi-rents) attributable to the firm. The security analyst can choose to delegate the task of estimating a change in value (hence the value) of current assets to the accountant, accepting whatever approximating conventions the accountant may invoke in order to simplify his task, if the goal is estimating the market value of other, more important assets. Or, if the earnings of the firm are due almost entirely to the services of its employees and officers, or to special monopoly powers derived from patents or secret manufacturing processes, the use of accounting earnings by the security analyst may not be circular.

But consider, for example, the firm in which the main source of economic rents is assets—bricks and mortar and machinery—that are depreciated over time. The accountant estimates the decline in the value of these assets over the accounting period, in order to report a figure to the analyst, that the analyst extrapolates and then capitalizes to estimate the value of the firm—including the value of the assets being depreciated. Reporting the change in value over the accounting period implies an estimate of the value itself at the beginning and end of the period. The analyst cannot employ a figure based on an accountant's estimate of the change in value of assets, when these assets constitute a major source of investment value in the firm, without introducing into his reasoning a fatal circularity.

At this point, some readers will raise the standard objections to using earnings gross of depreciation for security analysis, arguing that, whereas "cash flow" fluctuates over time in ways unrelated to the firm's economic prospect, the earnings concept tends to smooth out the "spurious" fluctuations. What really matters, however, is not that the reported stream of rents be free from fluctuations, but rather that the investor's estimate of the firm's value be free from spurious fluctuations. Fluctuations in the former will translate into fluctuations in the latter only if the investor insists on capitalizing cash flow by applying a constant "P:E" ratio to the current flow, without regard for the future pattern. Needless to say, if the analyst insists on being provided with a single number so simply related to market value,

* Paul Samuelson, "Proof That Properly Anticipated Prices Fluctuate Randomly," *Industrial Management Review,* spring 1965.

then he is delegating away to whoever provides that number most of the real task of security analysis.

Why, in view of the fact that the "cash flow" concept raises fewer problems than the earnings concept, is the earnings concept almost universally preferred? Because, I suggest, it brings the user face to face with a problem he doesn't know how to solve—namely, what will happen to cash flow (i.e., economic rents) from existing assets in future time periods. Hence, the analyst prefers to delegate this painful problem to the accountant, who transforms it into a one-period problem by applying certain arbitrary rules—known as Generally Accepted Accounting Principles—to the determination of asset values at the end of the period. Suggesting that "Accounting Principles" can prevent book figures (and their impact on earnings) from misleading security analysts is roughly comparable to suggesting that bolting the steering wheel so that the front wheels of a car can only point straight ahead will reduce accidents by preventing drivers from steering off the road.

The analyst tends to treat earnings as if it were a measure of economic rent rather than a change in asset value. The only kind of asset for which these two figures are equal is a perpetuity. In effect, the analyst, in using the earnings concept, is relying on the accountant to transform the corporation, with rapidly changing markets, technology, and competition into a tidy, docile enterprise that can generate the same rents year after year. Even if the accountant could be relied on to preserve the investment value of the firm invariant through this miraculous transformation, it would still follow that the idea of "earnings growth" is, in the context of this interpretation of the earnings concept, a contradiction in terms.

Summary

The security analyst is an interloper from the accountant's point of view. The security analyst is doing something that implicitly or explicitly the accountant was doing before the security analyst came along—namely, judging the worth of a company at certain points in time. The accounting profession has had to recognize the existence of the security analyst because the analyst, by bringing to bear economic and business judgment, has been able to do a more convincing job on the determination of economic worth than the accountant. But the accountant has not accommodated the securities analyst by trimming back his own function to exclude that part of the task of determining corporate worth now performed by the analyst. Instead, he continues to encourage use by investors of accounting earnings.

Present accounting practice tends to conceal the dependence of the earnings concept on estimates of worth by substituting accounting ritual for judgment in the determination of asset values. But it is becoming more and more difficult for accountants to convince practical decision-makers that earnings figures based on such arbitrary procedures have any relevance; current trends in accounting practice (e.g., current value accounting, introduction of market values into computations of portfolio earnings) are tending to narrow the gap between book and market values. And, in removing that gap, accountants are actually moving toward Hicks's definition of earnings, whether they like to admit it or not.

It is natural and human for accountants to want to maintain the traditional scope of financial accounting; but, in their attempts to bring accounting up to date and satisfy critics' demands for greater relevance, they are bringing steadily closer the day when it will be obvious to everyone in and outside their profession that the earnings concept is not suited to the needs of investors.

In conclusion:

(1) If the roles of the accountant and the security analyst are viewed together as part of a larger process of arriving at estimates of security values, it becomes clear that no real progress can be made until we have an economic definition of earnings that is accepted by both accountant and security analyst, and until it can be established that earnings, given this definition, has any role to play in the deliberations of the analyst.

(2) On the other hand, virtually all the most heated controversies in financial accounting (e.g., the creation of artificial reserves in order to enhance reported future income, the pooling-versus-purchase controversy, full-cost accounting in the petroleum industry, bank earnings, and so on) revolve around the accounting evaluation of assets (or, equivalently, the creation of reserves against the value of fixed assets) and the impact on accounting earnings. These issues, over which the Accounting Principles Board has labored long and hard, will be seen to be empty issues once it is recognized that *no* number affected by an accountant's determinations of the value of assets contributing significantly to the investment worth of the firm can be useful to the security analyst—regardless of how the accountant's determinations are made. The hot controversies will disappear when the concept of accounting earnings loses its central role in security valuation.

(3) It is often suggested that skill in adjusting accounting data is important for the security analyst, and that skillful adjustment requires judgment. But the way to make the conventional earnings figure useful for security analysis is merely to remove the effect of any accounting determinations of worth. Hence, in any given case, there is only one correct adjustment. Very little skill—and certainly no judgment!—is required to make it.

(4) Current methods of security valuation depend on treating earnings as if they were economic rents. Far from being rents, however, accounting earnings are more like estimates of change in the value of the firm over the accounting period—if, indeed, they have any economic meaning at all. If the use of accounting earnings in security valuation is consequently circular, then the analyst will have to face the fact that he actually lacks any defensible basis for current valuation methods and start looking for better methods.

(5) If accountants want to continue to enjoy a role in the investment management process, they should prepare to focus their energies on supplying whatever data a workable theory of security valuation requires, rather than defending the present ritual.

41

LINEAR PROGRAMMING AS A DEVICE FOR PREDICTING MARKET VALUE: PRICES OF USED COMMERCIAL AIRCRAFT, 1959–65*

STEPHEN P. SOBOTKA† AND CONSTANCE SCHNABEL‡

IT WAS reported in September, 1960, that a major aircraft manufacturer had charged off "$14 million to write down to salvage value used aircraft which [the company] had acquired in connection with jet sales."[1] The aircraft involved were twenty-five DC-7's acquired by a division of the manufacturer at about $880,000 each from a leading airline in 1959.[2] Only two years before their value had sunk to the salvage level, new DC-7's were being delivered to airlines at prices in excess of $2 million each.

The rapid changes in the values of many types of aircraft owned by practically all the world's major airlines during 1959 and 1960 came as a surprise, frequently a costly one, to many in the industry; yet these price changes were predicted in substantial detail in a research paper first made available to a limited audience in February, 1959, and published in June of that year. In this paper we shall present the technique that was developed to predict the values, and hence prices, of used commercial aircraft for the period 1959–65.[3] While the method was developed for this rather limited purpose, it appears to have fairly general usefulness in predicting the values of capital goods. Since the desirability of being able to forecast values and prices of business assets is fairly obvious, the usefulness of a reasonably simple yet

---

* The results of the research project underlying this paper may be found in Stephen P. Sobotka *et al.*, "Prices of Used Commercial Aircraft, 1959–1965" (Evanston, Ill.: Transportation Center at Northwestern University, 1959 [multilithed]). The authors of this paper are indebted to Paul Keat and Margaret Wiesenfelder, who were joint authors with them in this study, and also Stanley Warner, who assisted with early phases. We are also indebted to Allen R. Ferguson for his encouragement and help as well as to the Transportation Center for its permission to reproduce portions of the original study in this paper.

† Research associate (associate professor) of business economics, Graduate School of Business, University of Chicago. Assistant director of research at the Transportation Center at Northwestern University (on leave).

‡ Research economist, Transportation Center at Northwestern University.

[1] The *Wall Street Journal*, September 23, 1960, p. 4.

[2] *Aviation Week and Space Technology*, March 21, 1960, p. 38. Other illustrations of declines in airplane value include the offering in November, 1960, of several Stratocruisers (B-377's) at prices as low as $75,000 each, which is no more than salvage value (as advertised in *Trade-A-Plane Service*, second November issue, 1960, p. 4). Also, in a recently announced merger arrangement, fifteen Viscounts are to be taken back by the manufacturer at a stated value of $450,000 each, and another airline is reported to have offered Viscounts at lower prices. Aircraft asking prices such as those quoted in *Aviation Week* (*op. cit.*) may be well above the levels

at which actual cash transactions take place. Most aircraft transactions are far more complicated than is a sale of aircraft for cash: they frequently involve leases with purchase options, sales of spares and optional equipment, long-term credit arrangements, trade-ins, and the like. This made it impossible to construct a comparison of forecast with recent actual price for each of the many aircraft types covered by the study.

[3] Used commercial aircraft were, at the time this study was started, all types of aircraft in commercial airline use during 1958. This included two- and four-engined piston-powered aircraft ranging in size, speed, and age from the DC-3 to the large four-engined DC-7's and Constellations powered by turbocompound engines, as well as the turbine-powered Viscount 700 series.

rigorous and flexible technique for accomplishing this needs no elaboration.

The theory used in this analysis is simple, and the model based on it possesses great advantages over the methods of price prediction usually employed. David Ricardo's theory for the determination of land rent, on which this analysis is based, is almost as old as economics itself and about ten or twelve times as old as the oldest aircraft for which price predictions were made.[4]

Economic theory states that the price of any capital asset, once built, is dependent entirely on its future value to its owners or potential owners. The cost of production of a unit of a commodity, once produced, in no way effects its price, although, of course, the price may be affected by the cost of production of substitute commodities. The value to its actual or potential owners, in turn, is dependent on the alternatives open to them. If the owner's only alternative is using the asset and receiving some revenue in excess of costs as opposed to not using the asset and, therefore, not earning the revenue or incurring the costs, then the value of the asset is determined by the excess of revenue over cost which can be earned by the use of the asset. The usual way of stating this proposition is to say that the value of a capital asset at any point in time is determined by the discounted value of the income stream that can be earned by its owner from its use. This statement, while theoretically correct, in most cases is insufficient as a practical guide to the determination of value.

The more common price-forecasting

[4] David Ricardo's *Principles of Political Economy and Taxation* was published in 1817; the DC-3 was introduced into airline serivce in the mid-1930's. It is still used in scheduled passenger service by both local-service and trunk airlines in the United States and by many foreign airlines.

devices that have been used by the aircraft industry have been unable to cope with the complex economic relationships that determine prices of capital goods in a period of rapid innovation. The simplest and most widely used method—a type of "naive model"—employs a depreciation rate based on some blending of historical data and guess. Such a method may work well on the average, over long period of time and many aircraft types, but it is subject to extreme errors in the area of greatest importance —the guiding of equipment design, selection, and replacement. For these decisions a measure of the average effect of age and obsolescence is nearly useless; what is needed is an estimate of how age and obsolescence will affect a particular type of aircraft.

The recent course of aircraft prices shows that different aircraft models were affected in quite different ways by the introduction of jet airplanes. In retrospect, it may be easy to see the general reasonableness of the price changes that took place: for example, the great efficiency of jets over long distances had the greatest effect on the aircraft types that were previously superior for long flights, the DC-7's being the most important example. On much shorter flights other types of aircraft had advantages in operating cost which made them superior to DC-7's even when the latter aircraft became plentiful as a result of their displacement from the longer routes. To forecast these and the resulting price changes in more than a general way requires a precise statement of the principles of price determination and the incorporation of these into a model capable of dealing with the many relevant items of information available.

The reader may be struck by the detailed data required by the model used to predict aircraft prices as well as by its apparent mathematical complexity. He may be tempted to reject the entire procedure when he finds that the "data" actually used consist of a tenuous web of trend projections based on little more than other trend projections, cost estimates based on a conglomeration of engineering and economic data mixed with hunches and guesses, as well as other "estimates" which are nothing more than statements of the expectation that present relationships will continue into the future. Moreover, the reader may be horrified by the obvious unrealism of the assumptions used to make the computations manageable.[5]

The mathematical complexity of the model used is more apparent than real. The computational problems also are minor—none require more than a desk calculator. A solution to a model requires about a day's calculations by one person.

An important feature of the model used is that it makes possible a critical evaluation of the data and assumptions used. By successive low-cost recomputations one can estimate the effect on prices of errors in the data or forecasts or of "unrealism" in the assumptions used.

The model, therefore, provides a reasonably flexible framework for the analysis of a host of interdependent relationships. This, together with its successful application in the use described in this paper, is its defense.

THE GENERAL PLAN

In this section we shall present the general plan followed in arriving at the price predictions together with the major assumptions required in order that the problem be conceptually and mathematically manageable. For the reader interested in a rigorous treatment of the problem and its solution, a mathematical statement of the method (the model) used in arriving at the price predictions is given in the Appendix.

The method employed was essentially one of comparative statics. Market-equilibrium rents were predicted for each of a series of years on the basis of forecasted supply and demand conditions for that year. These rents were then discounted to yield a predicted time series of market-equilibrium prices for the period 1959–65.[6]

In the selection of aircraft the choices open to airlines include not only the choice of using more or fewer aircraft of a single type or group of types but also a series of choices with respect to the use of different types of aircraft on the combination of routes to be served. In this study we assumed that a given quantity of service on each type of route would be provided.[7] That is, we assumed that the service to be provided is a given quantity which can be forecast and which is not a function of the prices of the aircraft providing the service. Under these conditions the alternatives open to airlines involve a series of choices among the various old and new aircraft available to them to satisfy the given quantity of service to be provided.

---

[5] Assumptions must be "unrealistic," or they would not be used. However, some of the ones used so grossly oversimplify the "real world" that they may appear ludicrous to those who have practical experience in the area of this study.

[6] No attempt was made to predict the disequilibrium time paths of prices as they adjust toward market equilibria. Since today's situation is unprecedented in aircraft markets, such predictions would have required that characteristics of the disequilibrium behavior of the buyers and sellers involved be inferred from "far-fetched" sources.

[7] Service in this context means a given quantity of seat-miles provided for the use of revenue passengers.

The various types of aircraft comprise one set of factors of production for airlines' provision of service. Since aircraft types may be substituted for each other in the production process, their demand functions are jointly dependent even when output is fixed. The nature of this dependence reflects some of the characteristics of the production process.

The quantities used of a second set of factors depend not only upon the amount and character of passenger service to be provided but also upon the particular types of aircraft employed. For the purposes of this study the second set was defined as (1) crew services, (2) goods and services required for aircraft maintenance, (3) fuel and oil, (4) public liability and property-damage insurance, and (5) rights to land at airports. The prices of these factors were assumed to be determined independently of the prices of used aircraft. Proportions employed were assumed to vary only with the type of aircraft and the length of stage (airline distance between airports) for which they are used.

Expenditures on factors in this second set were called "direct operating costs" of aircraft. Direct operating costs were estimated for each type of aircraft on each length of stage.

The number of revenue-passenger-miles to be served by the (non-Communist) world's airlines for each length of stage was assumed to be independent of prices of used aircraft. The estimated time series of these exogenous variables were based upon data the derivation of which is discussed in the next section of this paper.

The number of revenue-passenger-miles of service provided when a seat-hour of a given type of aircraft is used on a given length of stage depends upon the load factor and speed attained. Speeds were estimated from an examination of airline schedule, and engineering data and varied with both stage length and aircraft type. Load factors and speeds were assumed not to vary among airlines.

Geographical and time characteristics of airlines' route structures are such that it is sometimes highly desirable to use the same piece of equipment on stages of different lengths. It was assumed that under these conditions the airlines' choice of aircraft would be determined solely by the costs of employing aircraft on the longest of the stage lengths so related. Portions of forecast revenue-passenger-miles for shorter stage lengths, appropriately adjusted for differences in speeds and load factors, were therefore considered as part of revenue-passenger-miles to be served on longer stage lengths. These portions were estimated with the help of an analysis of airline schedules.

Load factors of aircraft were estimated from past airline experience and were assumed to vary only with length of stage. They were assumed to continue at approximately current levels for the forecast period. The possible effect of this assumption on the predictions of aircraft prices requires some explanation. Given any demand for air travel, the demand for aircraft services varies inversely with the load factor at which the aircraft fly. Under conditions of free entry but administered prices in the air transport industry,[8] one would expect load factors to drop until the expenses of operating existing aircraft were just equal

[8] The air fares charged by practically all commercial carriers are regulated either by international agreements through the International Air Transport Association or by the actions of national governments. Entry into the industry is also regulated; however, in many, though not all, cases the extent of service supplied by the firms in the industry is not. The assumption of regulated prices and free entry will therefore tend to lead to an overstatement of the amount of service rendered.

to revenues. Under these assumptions, load factors would be somewhat, but not a great deal, lower than assumed in the model which will be presented below. For a fixed number of revenue-passenger-miles the effect of a drop in load factors can be analyzed as if it were a rise in the size of the air-travel market with a given load factor. Hence, alternative solutions to the model, using different market sizes, test the sensitivity of aircraft prices to changes in both market size and load factors.

If one assumes that revenue earned per passenger-mile, the relevant unit of output, is independent of type of aircraft used,[9] then the value of aircraft relative to each other is determined by their operating cost characteristics or, more exactly, by the differences in their operating costs.

An example will illustrate this. Assume an airline system is composed of two routes, X and Y, with three types of aircraft, A, B, and C, available to fly them. Assume further that all three aircraft types are identical, except that (1) aircraft A can fly route X at one-half of B's cost on X, (2) that aircraft A can fly route Y at two-third's of B's cost on Y, and (3) that aircraft C is more expensive to fly over either route than B is.

Since A is cheapest to operate on both routes, it would be used exclusively if enough A's were available.[10] Otherwise, the A type will be used first on route X, where its cost advantage is greatest.

The B-type aircraft will be used only after all the A's are employed. If enough of A and B is available to fulfil the demand on both routes, then aircraft C will not be used. Aircraft C would have no value except for scrap, since there is no demand for its services. The value of B to the operator is determined by the additional cost which he would incur if he were forced to use a C type as a substitute for B. The value of A is determined by the additional costs incurred if B had to be substituted for A and C for B.

An airline was thought of as a multi-product firm, each of whose "products" is the provision of revenue-passenger-miles of service over some element (stage) of its route structure.

We assumed that, when an aircraft of a particular type is used to provide service on a stage of a particular length, certain costs must be incurred which vary with aircraft type and stage length. These direct operating costs were assumed not to vary with characteristics of the particular stage other than length and were assumed to be the same for all airlines providing such service. The estimation of these costs is discussed below.

We assumed further than an aircraft of a particular type allocated to a stage of a particular length has a constant marginal physical product in terms of revenue-passenger-miles of service provided per year. This number, which varies with aircraft type and length of stage, was assumed not to vary with other characteristics of the stage and was assumed to be the same for all airlines. It was computed as the product of several estimated components: annual utilization (in hours) of the type of aircraft, the number of seats in the type of aircraft, the load factor of the stage length, and

[9] This assumption was required in the case of aircraft price determination because there are some differences in the quality of service rendered by different types of aircraft. The extent to which this assumption affects the price forecast will be examined.

[10] This exposition assumes that aircraft cannot be sold out of the airline system at any value except scrap. This assumption was also used in the study.

the average speed of the aircraft on the stage length. The method of estimation of each of these components and the rationale and significance of alternative estimates are discussed below.

Finally, we assumed that the amount of service which each airline provides over each element of its route structure during a given year depends neither on the rents of aircraft nor on the particular set of aircraft which the airline chooses to employ.

Since costs and marginal physical product were assumed to vary only with length of stage and type of aircraft, it was possible, for our purposes, to consider as the same product the service provided by all airlines over all stages of the same length. This results in as many kinds of products being considered as there are different lengths of stage. To keep our problem within manageable proportions, we approximated this large set with a set of nine kinds of products, each of which represented service over a range of stage lengths of the airline system's route structure. The total of the service to be provided over stage lengths within one of these ranges was considered as service to be provided over that stage length at the midpoint of the range.

The decision to use midpoints rather than mean length of stage within each range was made after determining that in each case except the longest stage the means and medians were fairly close together. If that had not been the case, a different set of stage lengths could have been chosen. As a practical matter, aircraft operating costs, relative to each other, do not vary enough to affect greatly the results under a fairly broad set of choices of stage lengths. In computing aircraft rents, it was found that a misallocation of aircraft types to stages ad-

joining the optimal stage did not affect the resulting rents by more than a few percentage points. In fact, in all solutions of the model more than one piston aircraft was assigned to each stage in which any piston aircraft were assigned, and in all solutions for 1959–61 two or more piston aircraft were assigned to several stage lengths.

This reasoning was organized into the "basic model" used to predict aircraft rents. The solutions to the model are derived from the following assumptions and estimated parameters:

1. Service to be provided by airlines in the non-Communist world was summarized by a vector of nine elements, an element D_i representing a hypothetical number of passenger-miles of service to be provided on a single length of stage.

2. The direct operating cost, c_{if}, for a seat-hour of aircraft type f allocated to a stage length i was estimated for all types of aircraft and all lengths of stage represented in the output vector.

3. The number of passenger-miles of serivce, m_{if}, provided by the allocation to stage length i of one seat-hour of aircraft type f was also estimated for all the lengths of stage and types of aircraft.

4. The supply S_f of seat-hours of aircraft type f to exist during the year was estimated for all types of aircraft.

5. It was assumed that airlines would act as pure competitors in aircraft markets to minimize the total rental and direct operating costs of providing predetermined quantities of service on stage lengths represented by the output vector described above.

6. It was assumed that holders of aircraft would also act as pure competitors in the aircraft markets to maximize revenues to be derived from aircraft rentals. It was further assumed that there were

neither costs incurred nor alternative uses for aircraft not taken by airlines for providing the service described above.

Under these conditions, the highest rent that an airline would pay for a seat-hour of a certain type of aircraft, given the rents of other types of aircraft, would equal the decrease in the total of direct operating costs plus other aircraft rents that it would incur if it had this seat-hour to use for the year. Since aircraft of this type would be allocated by the market to those willing to pay the highest rent for them, and thus to those who stand to save the most, the aircraft would be allocated so that total direct operating costs for the airlines plus other rental costs of aircraft are minimized. The market would perform this function for each type of aircraft, however, so that aircraft would be allocated to minimize the total direct operating costs of the system, subject to the restraints imposed above.

Letting X_{if} denote the number of seat-hours of aircraft type f allocated to provide service on stage length i, the market would thus allocate aircraft to minimize

$$G \equiv \sum_i \sum_f c_{if} X_{if},$$

subject to

$$\sum_f m_{if} X_{if} = D_i \text{ for all } i,$$

$$\sum_i X_{if} \leq S_f \text{ for all } f,$$

and

$$X_{if} \geq 0 \text{ for all } i \text{ and } f.$$

This is a problem in linear programming. It is discussed further in the Appendix as are two variations of the model, one of which allows for the existence of non-airline uses of aircraft (e.g., scrap

values), the other, for the production of new aircraft.

For the years 1959–62 it was assumed that only airlines demanded aircraft and that the supply curve for any particular kind of aircraft was perfectly elastic at a zero rent for quantities less than that estimated to be in existence during the year and perfectly inelastic above a rent of zero at this quantity. The estimation of the quantity S_f of a type of aircraft f in existence during a given year is discussed below.

For the latter years of our study we assumed supply conditions such that the existing fleet could be augmented by new production if the discounted present value of any aircraft exceeded manufacturers' selling prices of that aircraft. Since the rents on piston aircraft by this time obviously did not warrant new production, these levels were estimated only for jet aircraft. The estimates of selling prices were based on 1959 contract prices.

Since the quantity of aircraft available to the system and the size of the market to be served change over time, it is necessary to recompute aircraft "rents" periodically. The prices at various times are then the discounted values of the stream of "rents" to be earned by the aircraft during its useful life. In addition, the scrap value of the aircraft at the end of its life, discounted to the initial date, has to be added to the discounted value of the income stream to yield a price. This, then, summarizes the general scheme by which aircraft prices were predicted.

THE DATA AND THEIR USE

We have outlined the basic reasoning underlying the linear-programming model. The data employed, some basic assumptions, and the resulting price predictions are described below.

The model "inputs," to be described in detail later, are the following:

1. Estimates of the passenger market (in revenue passenger miles) in the free world, divided into nine groups of stage lengths for the years 1959–65
2. Available capacity (in seat-hours) for each aircraft type, computed from estimates of the number of aircraft, seating configurations, and utilization rates.
3. The number of seat-hours used per revenue-passenger-mile of traffic carried for each aircraft type on each stage length, as determined by speeds and load factors
4. Direct operating cost per passenger mile for each aircraft by stage length

THE TRAFFIC FORECAST

The estimates made by the Port of New York Authority in 1957 were employed for the forecast of United States domestic traffic, both scheduled and non-scheduled.[11] These estimates, stated in numbers of passengers, were converted to numbers of passenger-miles through the use of a projection of the time series of average length of passenger trips for the years 1952–57. Forecast United States domestic traffic in 1965 was 50.4 billion revenue-passenger-miles.

The time series of scheduled foreign plus scheduled United States international traffic employed in this study was the forecast of these sectors made by Canadair in 1956.[12] Predicted scheduled foreign and United States international traffic for 1965 was 52.5 billion revenue-passenger-miles.

Non-scheduled foreign and non-scheduled United States international traffic,

[11] Port of New York Authority, *Air Travel Forecasting, 1965-75* (New York, 1957), p. 19.

[12] Canadair Ltd., *A Critical Review of Earlier Forecasts of Air Traffic and a New Approach* (Montreal, 1956).

estimated to be 5.4 billion revenue-passenger-miles in 1965, was predicted from meager data. In 1957, United States international non-scheduled traffic plus estimated foreign non-scheduled traffic equaled 10.25 per cent of scheduled United States international plus scheduled foreign traffic.

These estimates were combined to yield a forecast of aggregate revenue-passenger-miles for 1959–65. This in turn was broken down by stage lengths with the use of a schedule analysis[13] of all the world airlines and was adjusted for differences in load factors to yield a forecast for seat miles demanded by stage length.[14]

An adjustment was made to the seat-mile distribution because aircraft are not always used at minimal cost; that is, sometimes large, fast aircraft with relatively high operating costs on short stages are nevertheless used on these hops because of scheduling, route density, or similar reasons. The extent to which this occurs is readily ascertainable from a schedule analysis so that appropriate adjustment which, in effect, increases the long-haul and decreases the short-haul market could be made.

SUPPLY OF AIRCRAFT

The total number of aircraft available was assumed to be equal to the present fleet less attrition plus aircraft on order through 1962.[15] To determine what size

[13] A schedule analysis tells us, among other things, how the total air travel market is divided by stage lengths, types of aircraft, etc.

[14] In addition, an adjustment was made for traffic served by small numbers of "miscellaneous aircraft" ranging from JU-52 to Cessnas or Deux Ponts.

[15] Attrition rates were estimated from the *Airline Fleet Record* (London: Aviation Studies International, Ltd., October, 1958). The current rate is about 1.5 per cent per year.

of market these aircraft can serve, information on the number of seats per aircraft as well as estimates of block utilization,[16] load factors, and speeds were required.[17] This then provided an estimate of total available supply of seat-miles. It is important to note that this total available supply is not a fixed amount in any one year but is a function of the allocation of aircraft to routes.

AIRCRAFT COST AND OPERATING CHARACTERISTICS

In order to match the supply to the demand, it was then necessary to compare aircraft with respect to each other in terms of their operating costs. To do this, almost all costs not related to aircraft value which differ between aircraft were used. These were: crew costs and expenses, maintenance expenses, fuel and oil costs, employee-welfare expenditures, landing fees, and public liability and property-damage insurance.

In order to estimate costs of pilots' and copilots' salaries, eighteen contracts between trunk and local airlines and the Air Line Pilots Association were examined. Assuming a seventy-five-hour month, the total of expected hourly costs of pilots' and copilots' salaries under each of the contracts was found for each type of aircraft. From the range of these costs applicable to each particular type of aircraft, a "typical" rate was selected. The rate chosen was that of an airline with a relatively large number of aircraft of the given type, such that the selected

[16] "Block utilization" is a technical term used in the industry which refers to the number of hours per day during which an aircraft is in use.

[17] Seats per aircraft were computed from Civil Aeronautics Board "Form 41" data as of December 31, 1957. Load factor estimates were also computed from CAB data on average local service, domestic trunk and U.S. international load factors. Aircraft speeds were computed from a schedule analysis and manufacturers' specifications.

rates exhibited the same kinds of differences between types of aircraft as was found in individual contracts. The selected rates were then increased by 9 per cent to cover costs of vacation, sick leave, and training.

Four contracts between large airlines and the Flight Engineers International Association were made available for the study. The contracts did not cover all the aircraft types to which flight engineers are assigned. Examination of these contracts revealed that flight engineers received approximately fifty cents an hour less than did copilots assigned to the same type of aircraft; copilots' salaries comprised 35–37 per cent of the total of copilots' and pilots' salaries combined. Hourly salary costs for flight engineers for each type of aircraft on which flight engineers are employed were therefore estimated by taking 36 per cent of the cost of selected pilots' and copilots' salaries per hour and subtracting fifty cents. The result was then increased by 9 per cent to cover costs of vacation, sick leave, and training.

Estimates of costs of stewardesses' salaries were based upon the examination of fifteen current contracts. Rates were computed for "two-year" stewardesses assuming a seventy-five-hour month, and a "typical" figure of $4.50 per hour was selected. The number of stewardesses assigned to an aircraft is determined by its type, but the pay of a stewardess is not. It was assumed that two-engined aircraft as well as DC-4's carry one stewardess and that all other four-engined craft would carry two. The selected rate was increased by 5 per cent to cover vacation pay, etc.

In addition to salary costs, airlines must incur two minor types of expenditures for crew services. These expenses were estimated and added to salary costs.

Expenditures for the goods and services required for aircraft maintenance were estimated according to a recent version of the "ATA formula."[18] These estimates were compared to the figures on the airlines, experiences in 1957 computed from data published by the Air Transport Association. In most cases the correspondence was close, but major discrepancies existed in the cases of a few aircraft types, chiefly those which were introduced into service in 1956 or 1957. Formula estimates were employed in the model even in the latter cases, however, on the presumption that observed data reflected special maintenance problems attributable to the newness of the aircraft and random variations arising from the small number of the aircraft type for which maintenance costs had been observed.

The average fuel consumption per block hour according to airlines' reports to the Civil Aeronautics Board was computed for each type of aircraft. These figures were compared to engineering estimates by converting them to functions of distance by means of the estimated speed of aircraft as a function of distance. The curves derived from observed data were always higher than engineering estimates were; evidently this was caused by the somewhat high assumptions of speed in the latter. When discrepancies existed in the rankings of aircraft by the two methods minor adjustments were made in the figure for average hourly fuel consumption to yield the estimate used in the study.

[18] The Air Transport Association, with the help of various aircraft manufacturers and data furnished by airlines to the Civil Aeronautics Board, has devised and periodically revised a "formula" which estimates operating costs of aircraft by type. The actual formula used at the time of the study was a manufacturer's suggested revision of an earlier revision. It was proprietary.

Gasoline and oil prices per gallon, including taxes, were estimated from the records of United States airlines for the last quarter of 1957. Figures employed, including taxes of two cents per gallon on aviation gasoline and six cents per gallon on oil for piston aircraft, were used.

The cost of insurance for public liability and property damage is relatively small. The ATA-formula was accepted without investigation. The estimated cost of this factor per aircraft-hour depends on speed and thus varies with stage length.

Landing fees were estimated as nine cents per thousand pounds gross weight per departure. This figure was computed roughly by consideration of total landing fees and gross weight of total departures for each United States airline. More specific information from two airlines supported this estimate. Estimated expenditures per block hour for landing varied with stage length.

PRICE PREDICTIONS

We now have all the data necessary to solve for a minimum-cost method of serving the market. The mathematical or linear-programming model is merely a device which allocates aircraft to the market to be served so that the total costs of serving the market are minimized. The solution yields the following information: (1) which aircraft are used over what routes; and (2) how much more it would cost per aircraft-hour to substitute other aircraft. The latter figure is the value of the aircraft to the system per hour, and, when multiplied by annual utilization, is the value per year. To obtain prices, one simply discounts the annual value streams and sums them.

It may be helpful at this point to introduce some of the data employed in the computations described above before actually presenting the results. Figures 1*a* and 1*b* show the direct operating costs of aircraft for which price predictions were made.[19] Figure 2 shows the assignments of aircraft to stage lengths, which are the first result of solution of the model. The "reasonableness" of these assignments when compared with actual assignments, as revealed by an analysis of airline schedules, points to the substantial validity of the method used. Table 1 shows the values per hour of aircraft as they resulted from successive solutions of the model. These, when multiplied by expected annual utilization, yield the annual values of aircraft (Table 2). Figure 3 shows the result of discounting the annual values plus estimated scrap prices for all aircraft for the forecast period.[20]

It was stated earlier that certain simplifying assumptions were necessary in order to make the problem manageable from a conceptual and computational point of view. Once these assumptions have been made, it is important to know how large an impact changes in these assumptions would have on the results of the computation. One of the important advantages of this method of predicting price is that it makes it possible to

test the sensitivity of the conclusions to changes in assumptions or inputs in the model.

This study assumed in the first instance that the size of the market to be served can be accurately forecast. Clearly, however, the future demand for air transportation is not easily determinable; its magnitude depends on many factors entirely beyond the scope of this study. Alternative solutions 2, 3, and 4 in Table 3 show the effects of increases and decreases in the aggregate size of the market. While the changes in price predictions at first glance appear large, with the exception of those made in the case of the market 30 per cent larger than expected, they are of relatively minor importance. For example, the price of the DC-7 exceeds scrap value only in the case of the market 30 per cent greater than expected, and then only by about $150,000.

In the past, several types of aircraft have been significantly delayed in either production or testing. Others have been grounded for extended periods while the reasons for failures were investigated and corrective action taken. Alternative solution 5 is based on the possibility that the new aircraft expected to come into use will do so only with great delays or that a substantial portion of them will be grounded for an extended period of time. To give effect to this eventuality, we assumed that the aircraft expected in service in 1960 will only come into service in 1961 and that these delays are not recouped in subsequent years. The effect of this assumption on the price predictions, though marked in the case of some aircraft, does not affect others. Large four-engined aircraft continue at less than scrap prices, while smaller four-engined aircraft and some two-engined planes can be expected to

---

[19] These costs are not comparable to data on "Direct Operating Costs" as computed from figures published by the Civil Areonautics Board because we have used passenger-miles rather than aircraft-miles, thereby implying a load factor. Also the costs considered revelant for our purposes are not entirely the same as those used by the CAB.

[20] Individual transaction prices could not be expected to match the forecast values but may vary considerably. See Sobotka *et al.*, *op. cit.*, p. xiii, for a subjective judgment of the likely price ranges. A 12 per cent rate of interest was used in discounting; scrap values were estimated at 5 per cent of original cost adjusted for changes in price level. No allowance for changes in price level after 1958 was made. It is a relatively simple matter to recompute all the solutions using either a different interest rate or a different set of scrap values.

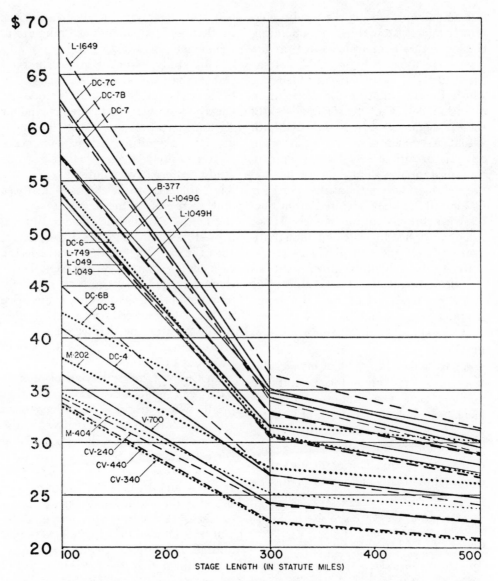

Fɪɢ. 1*a*.—Direct operating costs per thousand passenger-miles for short lengths of stage for piston aircraft and Viscount 700, calculated at midpoints of groups of stage lengths (Sobotka *et al.*, *op. cit.*, p. 45, Table 14).

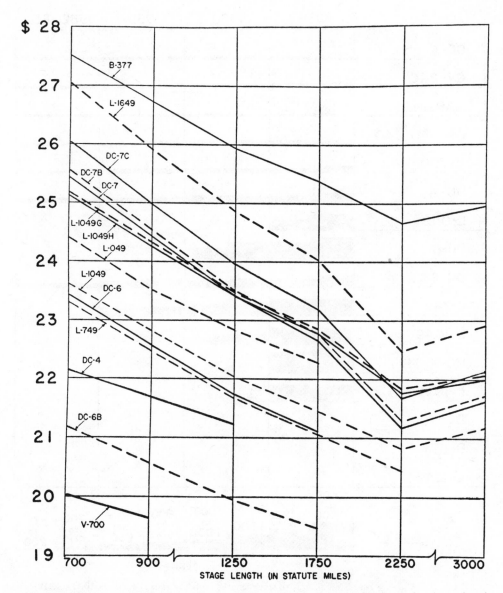

Fɪɢ. 1*b*.—Direct operating costs per thousand passenger-miles for long lengths of stage for piston aircraft and Viscount 700, calculated at midpoints of groups of stage lengths (except for 3,000) (Sobotka *et al.*, *op. cit.*, p. 45, Table 14).

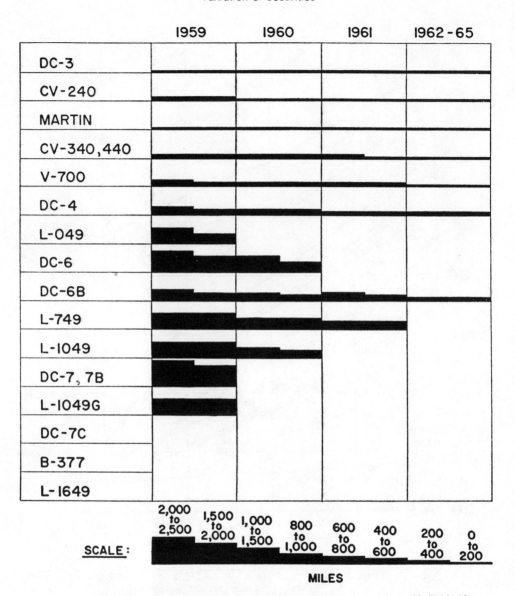

FIG. 2.—Allocation of piston aircraft to stage lengths (Sobotka *et al.*, *op. cit.*, p. 10, Table 10)

increase in value by \$100,000–\$200,000. The last two alternative solutions (6 and 7 in Table 3) are of interest because they are the results of attempts to simulate the effects of passengers' preference for certain types of aircraft. In alternative 6 it is assumed that passengers prefer aircraft with four engines over aircraft with two engines, with sufficient force to restrict twin-engined aircraft to short hauls only.[21]

[21] Twin-engined aircraft used in the model are DC-3, Martin, and Convair 240, 340, and 440.

In alternative 7 it is assumed that passengers prefer pressurized aircraft over non-pressurized ones (DC-3 and DC-4 are non-pressurized) with sufficient strength to make the latter type of aircraft uneconomical for passenger use after 1960.

The last two or three alternatives are particularly interesting because they show the ease with which the "model" can be used to show the effect of variation in changes of independent variables on the solution. By working through the

TABLE 1*

HOURLY VALUES OF PISTON AIRCRAFT, 1959-65

Model	1959	1960	1961	1962 65
DC-3.........	......	......	\$ 0.14	......
CV-240......	\$24.79	\$24.47	24.73	\$24.97
Martin......	11.95	11.95	12.18	11.95
CV-340, 440..	35.48	30.15	28.63	28.35
V-700.......	32.97	26.58	24.75	23.45
DC-4........	14.09	8.81	7.35	5.33
L-049........	4.81			
DC-6........	13.49	1.87		
DC-6B......	32.20	20.47	17.94	8.35
L-749........	14.71	2.70	......	......
L-1049.......	13.33	......	......	......
DC-7, 7B....	1.53	......	......	......
L-1049G.....	......	......	......	......
DC-7C.......	......	......	......	......
B-377.......	......	......	......	......
L-1649.......	......	......	......	......

* Stephen P. Sobotka *et al.*, "Prices of Used Commercial Aircraft, 1959-1965" (Evanston, Ill.: Transportation Center at Northwestern University, 1959 [multilithed]), p. 13, Table 3.

TABLE 2*

ANNUAL VALUES OF PISTON AIRCRAFT, 1959-65

Model	1959	1960	1961	1962–65
DC-3.........	....	....	....	....
CV-240......	\$ 63,338	\$62,521	\$58,672	\$53,589
Martin.......	30,532	30,532	28,897	26,171
CV-340, 440...	90,651	77,033	67,925	62,087
V-700........	102,289	82,464	72,270	64,194
DC-4........	36,000	22,510	17,438	11,673
L-049........	14,923	....	....	....
DC-6.........	41,853	5,802	....	....
DC-6B.......	99,901	63,508	52,385	22,858
L-749........	45,638	8,377	....	....
L-1049........	43,789	....	....	....
DC-7, 7B.....	5,026	....	....	....
L-1049G......	....	....	....	....
DC-7C.......	....	....	....	....
B-377........	....	....	....	....
L-1649........	....	....	....	....

* Sobotka *et al., op. cit.*, p. 15, Table 4.

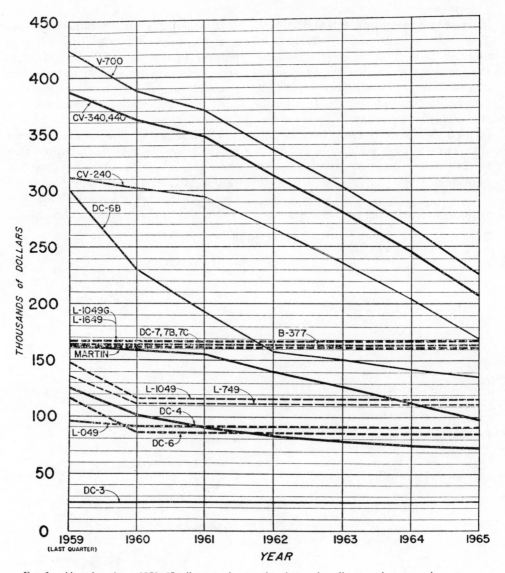

FIG. 3.—Aircraft values, 1959–65: discounted annual values, plus discounted scrap values or scrap values (higher of the two) (Sobotka *et al.*, *op. cit.*, p. 18, Table 6).

interrelationships of various types of aircraft, the model clearly shows the extent to which (large or small) changes in supply of aircraft of various types work themselves through the entire system.

SUGGESTED USES OF THE TECHNIQUE DEVELOPED FOR PREDICTING AIRCRAFT PRICES

While this study, by itself, yielded fruitful results, its extension to related fields provides a good indication of the

little new data. There is, however, a far more interesting use to which this technique can be put: one can evaluate the market potential of aircraft not yet produced. By introducing the cost characteristics of such aircraft into the model, one can determine how many aircraft the airlines of the world are likely to buy, on what types of routes they would be used, and the maximum price at which they could be sold. To do this, it is only necessary that the "new aircraft"

TABLE 3*

PRICE PROJECTIONS BASED ON ANNUAL VALUES UNDER ALTERNATIVE ASSUMPTIONS†

(Thousands of Dollars)

Aircraft	1. Basic Solution	2. Market 10 Per Cent Smaller	3. Market 10 Per Cent Greater	4. Market 30 Per Cent Greater	5. 1960 Fleet	6. Two-engined Aircraft Restricted to Short Hauls	7. DC-3 and DC-4 "Retired"
DC-3	....‡	....§	60	143	48	...	...
CV-240	273	270	398	577	391	270	466
Martin	134	132	248	412	233	132	310
CV-340, 440	316	313	452	648	458	313	526
V-700	336	319	538	826	530	442	634
DC-4	81	70	208	389	197	149	...
L-049	...	...	...	307	78	...	75
DC-6	...	...	97	399	190	...	173
DC-6B	244	136	413	777	485	292	534
L-749	...	...	116	444	212	13	196
L-1049	...	...	101	499	207	...	200
DC-7, 7B	...	...	...	282	...	...	...
L-1049G	...	...	...	323	...	...	...
DC-7C	...	...	...	205	...	...	...
B-377	...	...	...	...	...	...	...
L-1649	...	...	...	70	...	...	...

* Sobotka *et al., op. cit.,* p. 22, Table 7.
† For explanation see text.
‡ Less than $500.
§ Some aircraft of this type in use.

general value of the technique employed. There are some fairly obvious extensions of the study which require no substantial additional computations, such as forecasting the requirements for fuels, crews,[22] and those spare parts whose use is dependent on aircraft utilization. All these can be easily·computed from the models already solved with relatively

[22] For an example of this use of the model see Stephen P. Sobotka and Margaret Wiesenfelder, "Projections of Flight Crew Employment by U.S. Scheduled Airlines, 1961 and 1965," *Journal of Air Law and Commerce,* XXVII, No. 1 (Winter, 1960), 45–54.

not differ too markedly from the old, so that the passenger-preference factors of the type shown in alternatives 6 and 7 do not set limits on the predictions of value which are too wide to be useful. So much for uses of the technique within the air transport industry.

The technique as presently developed can be used to predict values of a large class of capital goods. It is obviously applicable to other transportation equipment, such as ships, locomotives, or rail cars. It appears that the technique would also be useful in estimating values of multiple-purpose machine tools—indeed, any asset which has the following characteristics: long life without physical deterioration,[23] large stocks relative to new production, multiple uses, and a reasonably stable demand for the product resulting from the use of the asset which can be predicted for a significant time period with some confidence. The technique is of no use in the prediction of value of assets of which the values are determined, among other factors, by their age or are subject to wide swings due to changes in styles.

APPENDIX

The basic form of the model is merely a generalization of Ricardo's model for the determination of land rents. The various types of aircraft are placed in the role in which Ricardo placed the various qualities of land; the various lengths of stage are placed in the role in which Ricardo placed the various kinds of products. Ricardo assumed, however, that the relative efficiencies of the various qualities of land were the same for all products, while the model used for this study allowed the relative efficiencies of aircraft types to differ with length of stage.

It was assumed that airlines produce nine kinds of outputs (service on nine lengths of stage) and that every airline acts as a pure competitor in the aircraft markets to minimize the cost of producing a predetermined quantity of each kind of output subject to the restraints of its production function. It was assumed further that the production functions of all airlines are such that, when a particular type of aircraft f is used in connection with an annual expenditure of c_{if} dollars for certain other kinds of factors required for its operation, m_{if} passenger-miles of service on stage length i are provided during the year. Operating costs c_{if}, were assumed to include expenditures on all kinds of factors other than aircraft whose proportions would vary with the type of aircraft selected to provide the predetermined quantity

of service on stage-length i. Operating costs, c_{if}, and marginal physical products, m_{if}, were assumed to be the same constants for all airlines for a given length of stage and type of aircraft. Finally, it was assumed, for the production of service on a given stage length, only another type of aircraft (used in conjunction with its own appropriate constant proportions of other kinds of factors) may be substituted for one kind of aircraft (used in conjunction with its appropriate constant proportions of other kinds of factors).

The total demand for aircraft of type f for use in providing service would be

$$\sum_i X_{if},$$

where X_{if} is the total number of aircraft of type f used to provide service on stage length i. The demand for one type of aircraft depends on the rents of other types of aircraft as well as its own, but the nature of the problem did not require that the set of demand functions be derived explicitly in terms of these variables. These functions were adequately described by listing three properties.

First, the assumptions required that

$$\sum_f m_{if} X_{if} = D_i, \qquad (1.1)$$

where D_i is the sum of the predetermined quantities of service on stage length i to be provided by airlines during the year.

Second, letting r_f represent the annual rent of aircraft type f, the assumption of cost minimization required that, if any aircraft of type f were to be used to provide service on stage length i, the corresponding ratio of "wages" to marginal physical product $(c_{if} + r_f)/m_{if}$ not exceed that of any other type of aircraft for that stage.[24] If more than one type of aircraft were to be used on the same stage length, then, their corresponding ratios of "wages" to marginal physical product had to be equal. Letting λ_i denote this ratio for stage length i, the cost-minimization assumption required that

$$\frac{c_{if} + r_{if}}{m_{if}} \geq \lambda_i \text{ for all } i \text{ and } f \quad (1.2.1)$$

[23] If deterioration does take place, it must be capable of being overcome by regular maintenance. (This requirement is imposed in order that the value of the asset is not a function of its time in use.)

[24] Otherwise the airline using aircraft f on stage length i could lower its costs by renting fewer aircraft of type f and more aircraft of the type with the lower ratio.

and that, for all i and f,

$$\frac{c_{if} + r_f}{m_{if}} = \lambda_i \text{ if } X_{if} > 0$$

$$(1.2.2)$$

Finally, numbers of aircraft allocated could not be negative, so that it was required that

$$X_{if} \geq 0 \text{ for all } i \text{ and } f . \quad (1.3)$$

The basic model was based upon the assumption that the supply of each type of aircraft in existence during the year would be fixed[25] and independent of rent and that there were neither any disposal costs for those not used nor any demand for them except that described above. Holders of this supply were assumed to act as pure competitors to maximize their annual revenues from aircraft rentals. Letting S_f denote the number of aircraft of type f in existence, the supply function of aircraft of this type would thus be perfectly elastic at a zero rent for quantities less than S_f and perfectly inelastic above a zero rent at S_f.

Equilibrium in such a market would require that

$$\sum_i X_{if} \leq S_f \text{ for all } f, \quad (2.1)$$

$$r_f \geq 0 \text{ for all } f , \quad (2.2)$$

and

$$r_f = 0 \text{ if } \sum_i X_{if} < S_f \text{ for all } f . \quad (2.3)$$

Under the conditions of supply and demand so defined, the allocation of aircraft would minimize the total of all operating costs:

$$G_a = \sum_i \sum_f c_{if} X_{if} ,$$

subject to the restrictions

$$\sum_f m_{if} X_{if} = D_i \text{ for all } i \text{ [same as (1.1)] },$$

$$\sum_i X_{if} \leq S_f \text{ for all } f \text{ [same as (2.1)] },$$

and

$$X_{if} \geq 0 \text{ for all } i \text{ and } f \text{ [same as (1.3)] } .$$

To prove this, let $\{\hat{G}_a; \hat{X}_{if}, \hat{r}_f, \lambda_i, \text{ each } i \text{ and } f\}$ be those values of the variables which satisfy all of the conditions for equilibrium, (1.1), (1.2.1), (1.2.2), (1.3), (2.1), (2.2), and (2.3). Let $\{\bar{G}_a; \bar{X}_{if}, \text{ each } i \text{ and } f\}$ be a set of values satisfying the restraints of the problem, (1.1), (2.1), and (1.3), but not necessarily the other conditions.

Then

$$\hat{G}_a = \sum_i \sum_f c_{if} \hat{X}_{if}$$

$$= \sum_i \sum_f (m_{if} \lambda_i - \hat{r}_f) \hat{X}_{if}$$

by (1.2 2),

$$= \sum_i \lambda_i \left(\sum_f m_{if} \hat{X}_{if} \right)$$

$$- \sum_f r_f \left(\sum_i \hat{X}_{if} \right)$$

$$= \sum_i \lambda_i D_i - \sum_f \hat{r}_f S_f$$

by (1.1) and by (2.1) and (2.3).

But

$$\bar{G}_a = \sum_i \sum_f c_{if} \bar{X}_{if}$$

$$\geq \sum_i \sum_f (m_{if} \lambda_i - \hat{r}_f) \bar{X}_{if}$$

by (2.2.1) applied to the first set of values and by (1.3) applied to the second set of values. (The inequality occurs because (2.2.2) does not necessarily hold here.)

We have

$$\bar{G}_a \geq \sum_i \lambda_i D_i - \sum_f \hat{r}_f S_f = \hat{G}_a$$

by (1.1) and (2.1) applied to the second set of values.

The Ricardian nature of the model is again shown by the property that, in equilibrium,

$$\sum_i \sum_f c_{if} X_{if} = \sum_i \lambda_i D_i - \sum_f r_f S_f .$$

The rent of an aircraft thus equals the increase in the total of all direct operating costs that would be required if it were necessary to substitute zero-rent aircraft for it. In this case zero-rent aircraft might be substituted indirectly, as they might not be most efficiently used on the same length of stage as would the hypothetical withdrawal, but the principle is the same as Ricardo's.

The minimization property of the competitive-equilibrium conditions is also apparent from consideration of the dual of the linear-programming problem. The dual of this problem may be written:

Maximize

$$H_a = \sum_i u_i D_i - \sum_f v_f S_f ,$$

subject to

$$m_{if} u_i - v_f \leq c_{if} \text{ for all } i \text{ and } f$$

and

$$u_i \geq 0 \text{ and } v_f \geq 0 \text{ for all } i \text{ and } f .$$

Aircraft rents and ratios of "wages" to marginal physical product of aircraft allocated comprise a feasible solution to the dual when they satisfy the equilibrium conditions:

$$m_{if} \lambda_i - \hat{r}_f \leq c_{if} \text{ by } (1.2.1) .$$

$$\hat{r}_f \geq 0 \quad \text{by } (2.3) ,$$

and

$$\lambda_i \geq 0 \quad \text{by } (1.2.2) .$$

The value of G_a that corresponds to the competitive equilibrium allocations equals the value of H_a that corresponds to this feasible solution. These must therefore be optimal because of the familiar linear-programming theorem requiring that no G_a corresponding to a feasible solution can be exceeded by an H_a corresponding to a feasible solution.

A slight modification of the basic model would have allowed considerations of scrap value to be taken into account explicitly. The difference b_f between the scrap value of an aircraft of type f at the beginning of the year and the discounted scrap value at the end of the year might have been estimated. Retaining the demand conditions of the basic model, the supply curve of each aircraft f might then have been assumed to be perfectly elastic at the rent b_f for quantities less than S_f and perfectly inelastic above b_f at S_f. Letting N_f denote the quantity of aircraft f not to be used to provide passenger service, equilibrium would require that

$$\sum_i X_{if} + N_f = S_f \text{ for all } f , \quad (3.1)$$

$$r_f \geq b_f \text{ for all } f , \quad (3.2)$$

and

$$r_f = b_f \text{ if } N_f > 0 \text{ for all } f \quad (3.3)$$

as well as conditions (1.1), 1.2.1), (1.2.2), and (1.3).

In this case the equilibrium allocation would have minimized

$$G_b = \sum_i \sum_f c_{if} X_{if} - \sum_f b_f N_f ,$$

subject to

$$\sum_f m_{if} X_{if} = D_i \text{ for all } i ,$$

$$\sum_i X_{if} + N_f = S_f \text{ for all } f ,$$

and

$$X_{if} \geq 0, \ N_f \geq 0 \text{ for all } i \text{ and } f .$$

The proof is analogous to that shown for the basic model.

A third version of the model was employed for the estimation of rents after 1962. It was assumed that, by 1963, aircraft manufacturers would be able to increase the existing stock of aircraft on hand and on order in response to demand. New aircraft prices in existence at the time of the study were transformed into annual costs, t_f, through estimated depreciation and discount rates. Retaining the demand conditions of the basic model, each supply curve was assumed at this point to be perfectly elastic at a zero rent for quantities less than S_f, perfectly inelastic at S_f for rents between zero and t_f, and then perfectly elastic again at a rent of t_f for quantities greater than S_f. Letting P_f denote the additional aircraft that are produced, the assumptions of this model require that

$$\sum_i X_{if} \leq S_f + P_f \text{ for all } f , \quad (4.1)$$

$$0 \leq r_f \leq t_f \text{ for all } f , \quad (4.2)$$

$r_f = 0$ if $\sum\limits_i X_{if} < S_f$ for all f, (4.3)

and

$r_f = l_f$ if $P_f > 0$ for all f (4.4)

in addition to conditions (1.1), (1.2.1), (1.2.2), and (1.3).

These conditions imply that the equilibrium allocation minimizes

$$G_c = \sum_i \sum_f c_{if} X_{if} + \sum_f l_f P_f,$$

subject to

$$\sum_f m_{if} X_{if} = D_i \text{ for all } i,$$

$$\sum_i X_{if} \leq S_f + P_f \text{ for all } f,$$

and

$$X_{if} \geq 0, P_f \geq 0 \text{ for all } i \text{ and } f.$$

The Level of Stock Prices

42

INTRODUCTION: A DIGRESSION ON THE MOVEMENT OF THE TIDES

The reference to "tides" in the title of this chapter is a reference to large, pervasive movements in the level of stock prices—movements exemplified by the great postwar bull markets of 1949-51, 1953-56, 1958-59, 1962-66, 1970-72 and 1975-76 and by the bear markets of 1957, 1962, 1966, 1969-70 and 1973-74. Even if the investor paid no attention to the selection of individual issues, he could earn very high rates of return by anticipating the great movements in the market as a whole. The challenge is a daunting one, for evidence from the study of mutual funds suggests that institutional portfolios have not benefited from their managers' attempts to predict market fluctuations.

Although the practical solution of the timing problem is hard to achieve, it is not so hard to understand its general nature. The total value of common stocks, like that of the individual security, is determined by the expected level of corporate earnings, the pay-out ratio, and a rate of discount that takes account of both the cost of money and the risks of equity investment. Thus, it is possible in retrospect to account for the market decline in 1973 and '74 in terms of the economic recession in the United States, the rapid rise in both inflation and interest rates and the Arab oil embargo. Similarly, the recovery in 1975-76 is plausibly explained by the decline in the inflation and interest rates, an upturn in the general economy and a reduction in political uncertainty both at home and abroad. Even the authors feel able to indulge in such retrospective explanations. However, superior performance demands that one consistently anticipate more accurately than others the future level of corporate profits, the course of interest rates, and the turmoil of domestic and international politics. This is altogether a more difficult task. Some of these questions are discussed by Julius Shiskin in Chapter 43. He demonstrates that the market is subject to an irregular, cylical movement that slightly precedes the associated business cycle. He suggests that many of the techniques employed in analyzing the business cycle may be useful in predicting the course of stock prices.

In his address to the American Economic Association in December, 1959, Arthur Burns [1] indicated the reasons that the American economy had been more stable and could be expected to become even more so in the future. He referred to changes in the tax structure and in the importance of governmental budgets, to transfer payments that soften the impact of economic fluctuations on personal income, and to increases in the relative importance of white-collar workers in the labor force. Unfortunately, as the American economy as a whole has become more stable, the sensitivity of corporate profits to changes in the economy has increased. This point is lucidly explained in Andersen's article, "Trends in Profit Sensitivity" (Chapter 44).

The increased stability to which Burns referred was in the level of output, income, and employment. He did not refer to the level of prices. Since the annual rate of inflation has averaged   seven   per cent in the last five years, this subject has become increasingly important to the investor.

Classical theory has always regarded inflation as a purely monetary phenomenon that has no effect on the *real* value of capital equipment. Therefore, if a company is unlevered, the price of its stock should vary with the general price level. Correspondingly, since payments to bondholders are fixed in money terms, the price of the stock of a levered company should actually benefit from inflation. In Chapter 45 Lintner discusses these classical theories and then sees how well they fit the facts.

---

[1] Burns, A. F. "Progress Towards Economic Stability," Presidential address delivered at the Seventy-second Annual Meeting of the American Economic Association. Washington, D.C., December 28, 1959. Published in the *American Economic Review*, 50 (March, 1960), 1–19.

[2] For a good exposition of this point, see Table 8 in Chapter 3.

[3] See Chapter 22.

43

SYSTEMATIC ASPECTS OF
STOCK PRICE FLUCTUATIONS

Julius Shiskin

I. INTRODUCTION

Economists have found it instructive to break down economic time series into systematic and irregular fluctuations. The systematic movements—the signals—usually reveal cyclical movements, long-term trends, and seasonal patterns. The irregular fluctuations—the noise—are a composite of erratic real-world occurrences and measurement errors, and resemble a series of random numbers. Like other economic time series, that on stock prices is a mixture of systematic and irregular fluctuations.[1]

The objective of this paper is to bring together the evidence that there are systematic movements in stock prices. This evidence shows that (1) while irregular fluctuations dominate the month-to-month movements in stock prices (and most other economic indicators) systematic movements dominate when longer span comparisons are made; (2) the average duration of run in stock prices is significantly higher than that of a random series, even after the strong upward trend of recent years is eliminated; (3) diffusion indexes of stock prices computed over short spans have the irregular behavior characteristic of random series, but show systematic movements with clear cyclical amplitudes and consistent leads over aggregate stock price fluctuations when the span of comparison is extended; and (4) most important of all, stock prices consistently conform to and lead broad expansions and contractions in aggregate economic activity (the composite of such measures as total employment, income, production and

---

[1] This paper utilizes methods of time series analysis familiar to students of cyclical fluctuations, and familiarity with these methods is assumed by the writer. They are described in most textbooks on business statistics, for example, Croxton, Frederick E. and Cowden, Dudley J., *Applied General Statistics,* Prentice-Hall, New York, 1955. An explanation of more recent developments utilized in this paper appear in Shiskin, J., *Electronic Computers and Business Indicators,* Occasional Paper 57, National Bureau of Economic Research, New York, 1957; Moore, Geoffrey H. and Shiskin. J., *Variable Span Diffusion Indexes,* paper given at the Sixth Annual Forecasting Conference of the American Statistical Association, New York Chapter, New York, April 17, 1964, not yet published; and Moore, Geoffrey H. and Shiskin, J., *Indicators of Business Expansions and Contractions,* National Bureau of Economic Research, New York, 1967.

The views expressed in this paper are the author's and not necessarily those of the Bureau of the Census.

Unpublished paper presented to the Seminar on the Analysis of Security Prices, May, 1968, University of Chicago. Reprinted by permission of the author.

CHART 1

Index of Stock Prices and Trend-Cycle,
Irregular and Seasonal Components

(Standard and Poor's Index of 500 Common Stocks)

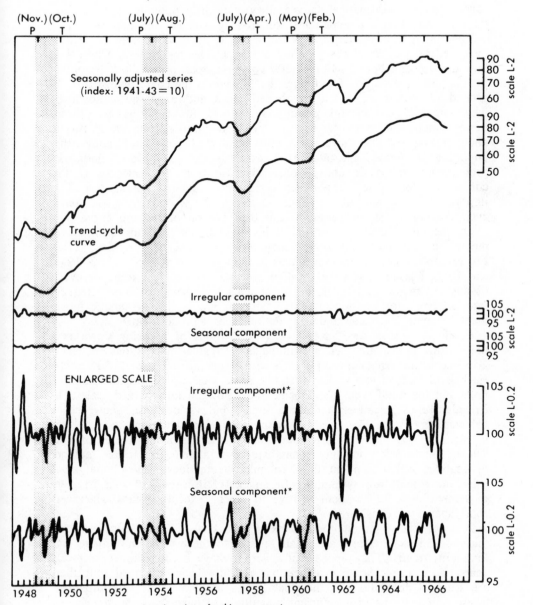

*Scale used is 10 times greater than that above for this component.

trade); this feature of stock price fluctuations distinguishes it from cumulated random series (i.e., series with random first differences) which also have systematic movements in some other ways similar to those of stock price fluctuations.

These systematic movements in stock prices are difficult to predict because, unlike mathematical curves, they vary in amplitude, pattern, and duration, and they are sometimes obscured by irregular fluctuations.

The different characteristics of stock price fluctuations can be readily discerned in a chart of the monthly averages. The top line on Chart 1 is the Standard and Poor's index of 500 common stock prices plotted monthly for the period 1948–64. The figures are plotted on the chart against a background of recessions shown by shaded areas and expansions shown by white areas. The outstanding impression from this curve is an upward trend, punctuated by shorter cycles varying in duration from about two to about five years. The short cycles are also a characteristic of many other important economic aggregates, such as gross national product, industrial production, retail sales, and so on. It is clear from an inspection of this curve that stock prices experience systematic economic fluctuations. This impression is brought out even more clearly in the second curve, the trend-cycle component of the series, a smoothed version of the top curve.

On the other hand, if one directs his attention to the short-term movements, one will see fluctuations which resemble those of a random series. For example, consider the movements in the top curve in 1951, 1952, 1955, and 1956. During these periods, stock prices show no clear trend or cycles of any systematic nature. If the movements are viewed at more frequent time intervals, for example, weekly, daily, or hourly, the systematic movements become less clear and irregular changes more evident.

Economic statisticians have developed methods of breaking down economic time series into their systematic and irregular fluctuations.[2] Chart 1 also shows the irregular and the "seasonal" components of stock prices. Each is plotted on two scales: first, the same scale as the original observations and the trend-cycle component, and below on an enlarged scale. The irregular series resembles a random series, and various tests show that it behaves very much like one. When the original observations are analyzed in such a way that the irregular fluctuations dominate, these analyses "show" that stock price movements are also random. But other methods of analysis, which iron out these irregular fluctuations, "show" that stock price movements are systematic. In any case, it is evident that irregular movements tend to be small relative to others, except perhaps when very short spans are considered.

A word about seasonal variations. Chart 1 also shows some seasonal variations. But they, too, are small relative to the cyclical movements and long-term trends. They appear, however, to have become larger in recent years, since 1954. Some evidence has recently been produced that there are seasonal fluctuations in the stock prices of some kinds of companies.[3] These appear to be of a sufficient magnitude to have made an imprint on

[2] A description of such a method appears in *Electronic Computers and Business Conditions, op. cit.*

[3] See *Fortune,* "How to Buy Stocks by the Calendar," March, 1965, p. 62.

the averages. However, the relatively small magnitude of these variations and substantial changes in their pattern over periods of six to eight years lead to doubts about the existence of true seasonal variations. In any case, seasonality would be expected virtually to disappear in a market where knowledge of its existence is generally recognized.

A chart covering earlier periods would show similar relations among the trend-cyclical and irregular components, but sometimes one would be more dominant and at other times it would be the other. Thus, during the 1930's and early 1940's the business cycle was strong relative to the long-term trend. This was also true from 1900 to 1914. But in all periods, both the cyclical and trend movements would be dominant when periods longer than a few months were considered.

The observations made above are based upon an inspection of the stock price series and are largely intuitive. However, more systematic types of studies of the relations between stock prices and other types of series, real and artificial, can and have been made. Some are provided in the pages which follow to support these impressions.

II. Short- and Long-Span Comparisons

The irregular and cyclical movements of 121 principal U.S. economic indicators [4] have been separated, and their magnitudes have been compared. These data show that the month-to-month changes in irregular component are larger than in the cyclical factor in about 65 percent of the series. If, however, the similar comparisons are made over three-month intervals, the irregular factor is larger in only about 25 percent of the series, and if comparisons are made over five-month intervals, it is larger in only a little more than 10 percent of the series. These differences arise from the fact that over varying spans the irregular factor tends to stay about the same, whereas the cyclical factor cumulates. Such calculations for stock prices

TABLE 1

PERCENTAGE OF 121 U.S. ECONOMIC SERIES FOR WHICH
NOISE-SIGNAL RATIO IS GREATER THAN ONE OVER
VARIOUS SPANS OF COMPARISON, 1953–65

Months' Span	Percent Noise-Signal Ratio Is Greater Than 1
1	66
2	46
3	27
4	18
5	12
6 or more	0

[4] The 121 series used to make up this table are those included in the study, *Indicators of Business Expansions and Contractions, op. cit.*

show that on the average the irregular factor dominates the month-to-month movements, but that over two-months and longer spans, the cyclical factor dominates.

The ratio of the average irregular movement to the average cycle-trend movement may conveniently be referred to as the noise-signal ratio. The percentage of economic series for which this ratio is greater than one for varying spans is shown in Table 1.

The effects upon the components of variations of stock prices, as the span of comparison increases, are revealed in Table 2. In the month-to-

TABLE 2

COMPONENTS OF VARIATION FOR STOCK PRICE INDEX, 500 COMMON STOCKS

	Month-to-Month *(Percent)*	3-Month Spans *(Percent)*	6-Month Spans *(Percent)*	9-Month Spans *(Percent)*	12-Month Spans *(Percent)*
Trading day	10.6	1.6	0.6	0.2	0.2
Seasonal	14.4	9.9	5.2	1.3	0.0
Irregular	37.5	7.3	2.5	1.1	1.0
Trend-cycle	37.5	81.2	91.7	97.4	98.8
Total	100.0	100.0	100.0	100.0	100.0

Period covered: January, 1953 through August, 1966.

month comparisons, the trend-cycle and the irregular factors are most important, but "seasonal" and "trading-day" factors also have a substantial role. As the span of comparison increases, the role of the trend-cycle grows, while that of the other factors declines. Thus, the trend-cycle factor accounts for only 38 percent of the month-to-month variation, but for about 92 percent of the variation in comparisons made over 6 months and almost 99 percent in comparisons over 12 months.

III. AVERAGE DURATION OF RUN

Another test of the systematic nature of an economic time series is provided by the average duration of run.[5] This measure provides another basis for determining whether the month-to-month movements of an economic series departs significantly from randomness. It equals the average number of consecutive monthly changes in the same direction. It takes into account only the signs of the changes and not their amplitudes, and it assumes the directions of change will be distributed in a random way in series without systematic movements. For a random series, short runs occur

---

[5] For an explanation of the average duration of run, its significance, and uses, see Wallis, Allen W. and Moore, Geoffrey H., *A Significance Test for Time Series*, Technical Paper 1, National Bureau of Economic Research, New York, 1941.

much more frequently than long runs, and the expected average duration of run is only 1.5 (months, quarters, or whatever the time unit in which the series is expressed). For random series with 120 observations (i.e., 10 years in monthly data) the average duration of run falls within the range 1.36 and 1.75 about 95 percent of the time.

The average duration of run for stock prices is 2.37, well above the limits for a random series. Since stock prices had a pronounced upward trend from 1948 to 1966, the average duration of run was also computed for this series after the trend was eliminated. It proved to be 2.30, also well above the limits for a random series. These figures compare with an average duration of run, for example, of 1.81 for new orders of durable goods, 2.17 for retail sales, and 3.62 for industrial production. The average duration of run for these and other series is shown in Table 4, Column 2.

IV. DIFFUSION INDEXES

Diffusion indexes offer still another way of studying the relations between random and systematic features of stock prices. A diffusion index is a simple measure which shows the percentage of component series that experience an increase in activity during a specific period computed for a succession of such periods. It takes into account only the direction of change in the series, not the magnitude of the change.

Chart 2 shows diffusion indexes for stock prices of 80 different industry groups, for example, the paper group, chemical group, and drug group. The line at the top of this chart is the Standard and Poor's index of 500 stock market prices shown in the usual way. The next line shows what percentage of the 80 industry groups experienced a rise in stock prices from month to month. The third curve from the top shows the percentage of industries for which the stock prices were higher than three months ago, the next line the percentage higher than six months ago, and so on, to the bottom line which shows the percentage higher than 12 months ago. It should be noted that all the scales for the diffusion indexes are the same.

The diffusion indexes computed over short spans are seen to have the irregular behavior characteristic of random series; however, these almost random series are converted to relatively smooth series with clear cyclical amplitudes as the span of comparison is extended. While even the longer term (9 and 12 month) diffusion indexes contain some substantial random fluctuations, the chart shows that they clearly and consistently lead the Standard and Poor's stock price index.[6]

To check the possibility that this technique of bringing out the systematic properties of stock prices by extending the span of comparisons is not an economic phenomenon, but a statistical artifact implicit in the computing techniques, similar computations were performed on 24 artificial series with random first differences, and the results are given in Chart 3.[7] The

---

[6] These series are plotted at the central rather than the last months of the comparison. This method of plotting maintains the historical timing patterns but extends the actual lead times by half the periods of comparison. The leads would still exist if the series were plotted at the end of the period.

[7] The method of constructing these artificial series is given in the Appendix.

CHART 2
Stock Prices and Diffusion Indexes of Stock Prices
over 1, 3, 6, 9, and 12 Month Spans

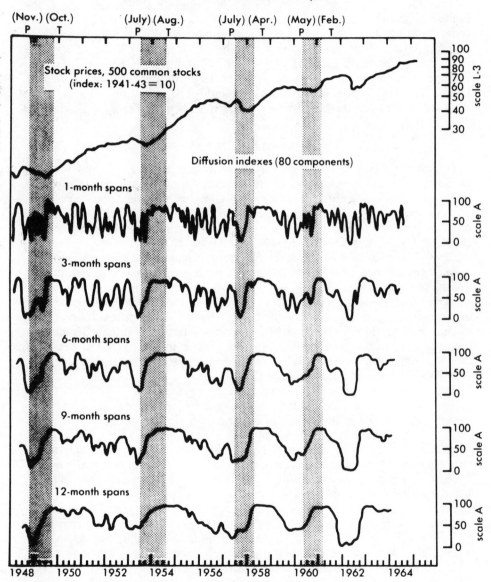

Latest data used for diffusion indexes, July, 1964; plotted at center of span.

CHART 3

Diffusion Indexes of 24 Artificial Series with Random First Differences
Computed over 1, 3, 6, 9, and 12 Month Spans

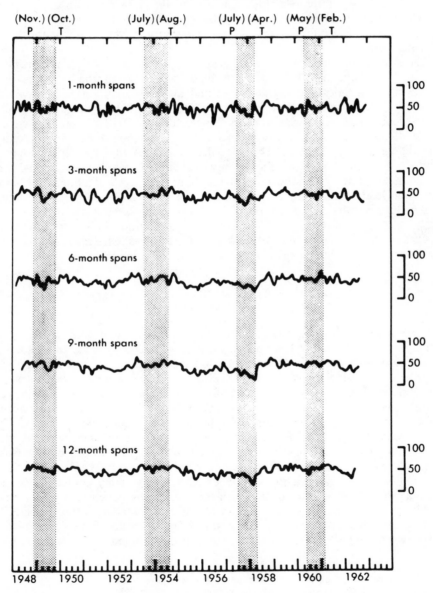

month-to-month diffusion index for the random series looks very much like that of stock prices. But the similarities between the stock prices and random series' diffusion indexes disappear, and differences come to the fore as the span of comparison increases. Thus, the diffusion indexes of the longer term random first difference series also show some persistent deviations from 50, but their amplitudes are small relative to those in stock prices, and they do not approach 100 as the size of the span increases. Other groups of economic time series show results very similar to those of stock prices.[8]

The fluctuations in rates of change are very similar to those of diffusion indexes. Consequently, the statements made above about the relations between diffusion indexes of stock prices and average stock prices apply also to rates of change and average stock prices. Rates of change for stock prices computed over variable spans for the period 1948–64 are shown in Chart 4, and similar rates are shown for an artificial series with random first differences in Chart 5. The short-term changes in both series appear random. However, whereas the changes computed over longer spans for stock prices show systematic movements with clear cyclical amplitudes and consistent leads over average stock prices, the same relations are not visible in the chart for the artificial series. If allowance for differences in scale are made, the rates of change for stock prices are quite similar to diffusion indexes of stock prices,[9] and both differ in these respects from corresponding measures for artificial series with random first differences.

V. Probability Tests of Relations to Other Types of Economic Series

Stock prices have long been identified as a leading indicator of business activity by students of cyclical analysis. This is intended to mean that usually stock prices turn down in advance of a business cycle peak and turn up in advance of a business cycle trough. Such an orderly timing sequence would exist only in series with systematic economic relations to each other. Can we demonstrate by conventional statistical methods that such a relation between stock price movements and those of other types of economic series exists?

A probability scheme for judging the significance of timing relations among economic series has been developed by Geoffrey Moore of the National Bureau of Economic Research. His scheme involves calculating the probability that as large a proportion of leads (or roughly coincidences or lags) as that observed during the business cycle turns covered by the series could have occurred by chance. In order to make this test, the "specific" turning dates in stock prices are compared with the turning dates in "general business conditions" marked off by the National Bureau. Under Moore's

---

[8] *Variable Span Diffusion Indexes, op. cit.*

[9] The movements of diffusion indexes and rates of change become even more similar when (1) the percentage change formula is modified so as to bring about a symmetrical range of fluctuations and (2) standardized so that component series, which have widely different amplitudes before adjustment, can be averaged. See Shiskin, J., *Signals of Recession and Recovery,* Occasional Paper No. 77, National Bureau of Economic Research, New York, 1961. Appendix A, especially Chart A–1, p. 126.

CHART 4

Stock Prices and Percent Changes
over 1, 3, 6, 9, and 12 Month Spans

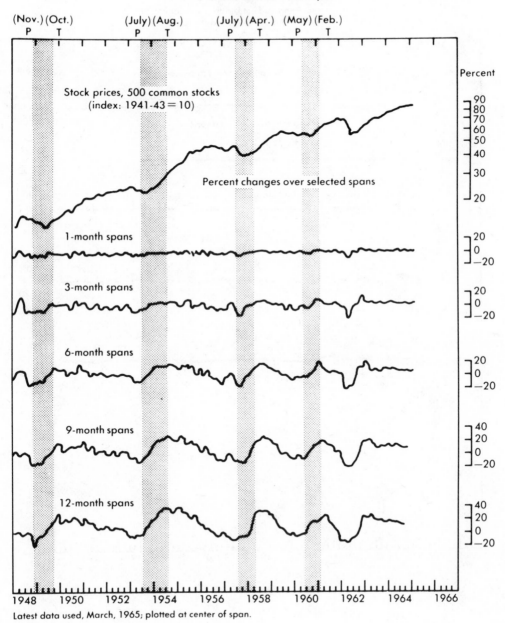

Latest data used, March, 1965; plotted at center of span.

CHART 5
Artificial Series with Random First Differences and Percent Changes
over 1, 3, 6, 9, and 12 Month Spans

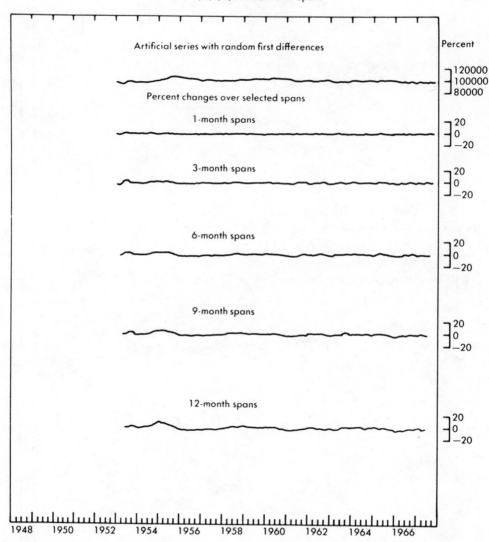

method, the probability of obtaining as many as 4 leads (or roughly coincidences or lags) out of 6 business cycle turns covered as a result of chance is .223; for 8 out of 12 the probability is .087; and for 12 out of 18, .037. The maximum acceptance level was taken to be .223; this means that it was considered unlikely that as many as 4 out of 6, 7 out of 12, or 10 out of 18 timing comparisons at business cycle turning points will be the same type (leads, coincidences, or lags) as a result of chance.[10] The results of the com-

TABLE 3

TIMING RELATIONS BETWEEN STOCK PRICES AND GENERAL BUSINESS CONDITIONS FROM 1873 TO 1961

Business Cycle Peak	Lead (−) or Lag (+) in Months	Business Cycle Trough	Lead (−) or Lag (+) in Months
Oct. 1873	−17	March 1879	−21
March 1882	− 9	May 1885	− 4
March 1887	+ 2	April 1888	+ 2
July 1890	− 2	May 1891	− 5
Jan. 1893	− 5	June 1894	+ 9
Dec. 1895	− 3	June 1897	−10
June 1899	− 2	Dec. 1900	− 3
Sept. 1902	0	Aug. 1904	−10
May 1907	− 8	June 1908	− 7
Jan. 1910	− 1	Jan. 1912	−18
Jan. 1913	− 4	Dec. 1914	0
Aug. 1918	−21	Mar. 1919	−15
Jan. 1920	− 6	July 1921	+ 1
May 1923	− 2	July 1924	− 9
Oct. 1926	N.C.	Nov. 1927	N.C.
Aug. 1929	+ 1	March 1933	− 9
May 1937	− 3	June 1938	− 2
Feb. 1945	N.C.	Oct. 1945	N.C.
Nov. 1948	− 5	Oct. 1949	− 4
July 1953	− 6	Aug. 1954	−11
July 1957	−12	April 1958	− 4
May 1960	−10	Feb. 1961	− 4
No. of timing comparisons	20	No. of timing comparisons	20
Leads	17	Leads	16
Lags	2	Lags	3
Exact coincidences	1	Exact coincidences	1
Extra turns	4	Extra turns	4

"N.C." No comparison possible

[10] Moore, Geoffrey H., *Statistical Indicators of Cyclical Revivals and Recessions*, Occasional Paper 31, National Bureau of Economic Research, New York, 1951, pp. 23–26 (reprinted in *Business Cycle Indicators*, NBER, New York, 1960, pp. 204–207). The method described here was also applied to updated series in our paper, *Indicators of Business Expansions and Contractions, op. cit.*

parison of stock prices and the NBER benchmark dates are given in Table 3 which covers the period from 1873 to date. During this period, stock prices led the National Bureau reference turning dates 33 times; it was coincident twice, and it lagged five times. The probability of having this many leads as a result of chance is very remote—.000 0. This compares, for example, with corresponding probabilities of .000 3 for new orders of durable goods and .000 5 for new housing permits. Similarly, the probability that coincidences occurred as a result of chance is .001 3 for nonagricultural employment and .066 7 for gross national product (not shown in table).

Another test of the systematic relations between stock prices and general business conditions was made, using a different National Bureau measure. Their index of conformity provides a simple measure of how faithfully each series has followed the business cycle chronology of expansions and contractions. A series which has risen during every business expansion and declined during every contraction will have an index of +100; a series which has declined during every expansion and risen during every contraction will have an index of −100. Timing differences are taken into account so that if a series typically leads, an allowance is made for the lead in computing the conformity index. The conformity index is a type of correlation coefficient between the cyclical fluctuations of each series and aggregate economic activity.

A probability scheme for judging the statistical significance of the conformity index has also been developed by Moore. Under this method, the probability that one lapse in conformity in 5 could occur as a result of chance comes to .188; 2 lapses or fewer in 10, .055; and 3 in 15, .018. The lower the probability, the more reliable the conformity index. The maximum acceptance level was taken at .188, the probability that one or fewer lapses will occur in 5 phases. This means, for example, that if a series conforms in three expansions but not in the other two, it will be rejected on the ground that there is a reasonable chance that this result could have been obtained in a series which has a random relationship to historical business cycles. But if a series conforms in eight (or more) expansions and fails to do so in two (probability .055) it will be accepted on the ground that it is unlikely that as good a result would have been obtained for a series that has a random relationship to business cycles.

The conformity index of stock prices turns out to be +77, and the probability that an index this high could have been obtained as a result of chance is also very remote—.000 0. This probability is the same for new orders (.000 0), and it is .005 9 for housing permits. The corresponding figure for industrial production is .000 0 and for gross national product .000 1.

The probabilities for 16 important economic indicators and four cumulative random series are given in Table 4. With only occasional exceptions, the economic series are shown to be systematically related to fluctuations in general business conditions, whereas the cumulated random series are not.

A recent study by Geoffrey H. Moore and myself utilized an explicit scoring plan to help in the evaluation and selection of indicators of aggregate economic activity.[11] This plan assigns scores to each series within a range

---

[11] *Indicators of Business Expansions and Contractions, op. cit.*

TABLE 4

PROBABILITY TESTS OF THE TIMING AND CONFORMITY OF STOCK PRICES AND OTHER ECONOMIC INDICATORS AND AGGREGATE ECONOMIC ACTIVITY

Series (1)	Average Duration of run [2] (2)	Timing Probability [1]			Conformity Probability [1]		
		Peaks (3)	Troughs (4)	Peaks and Troughs [3] (5)	Expansion (6)	Contraction (7)	Expansion and Contraction [4] (8)
Leading							
Stock prices	2.37	.000 5	.002 3	.000 0*	.000 0*	.002 2	.000 0*
Average workweek	2.08	.038 3	.080 6	.006 7	.019 5	.002 0	.000 1
Job opening pending	3.36	.079 5	.079 5	.006 3	.250 0	.125 0	.031 2
Nonag. placements	2.11	.112 1	.112 1	.020 2	Rej.	.062 5	.035 2
New housing permits	1.85	.046 1	.003 9	.000 5	.054 7	.054 7	.005 9
New orders, durable goods	1.81	.020 2	.220 7	.000 3	.002 0	.002 0	.000 0*
Contracts and orders, plant, eq.	1.88	.034 2	.215 5	.013 6	.125 0	.062 5	.007 8
Industrial materials price index	2.49	.020 2	.140 8	.008 0	.010 7	.010 7	.000 2
Price to labor cost ratio, mfg.	2.20	.003 1	.021 9	.000 2	.019 5	.010 7	.000 4
Coincident							
Nonag. employment, establishments	4.90	.128 2	.002 7	.001 3	.015 6	.007 8	.000 1
Index of industrial production	3.62	.133 4	.046 1	.063 8	.001 0	.001 0	.000 0*
Retail sales	2.17	Rej.	Rej.	Rej.	.001 0	.024 2	.000 1
Treasury bill rate	2.53	.080 6	.027 9	Rej.	.019 5	.006 2	.000 2
Unemployment rate	2.54	.211 8	.080 6	.211 3	.015 6	.007 8	.000 1
Personal income	4.61	.213 0	.080 6	.062 1	.002 0	.089 8	.000 7
Lagging							
Labor cost per unit of output, mfg.	2.41	.080 6	.140 8	.024 8	.054 7	.032 7	.003 6
Random first difference series (all four)	1.96	Rej.	Rej.	Rej.	Rej.	Rej.	Rej.

[1] The figures given in Cols. (3) to (5) are the probabilities that the leading indicators will lead, the coincident series will coincide, and the lagging series will lag as a result of chance; those in Cols. (6) to (8) are the probabilities that these indicators will conform to cyclical movements in aggregate economic activity with allowances for differences in timing.

[2] Period covered: January, 1953–September, 1965.

[3] Product of probabilities for peaks and troughs taken separately.

[4] Product of probabilities for expansion and contraction taken separately.

Rej.—Probability above minimum acceptance level (.223 for timing and .188 for conformity).

*—Less than .000 1 but not zero.

Average duration of run—average number of consecutive monthly changes in the same direction. For a random series the expected value is 1.5 with 95 percent of the values falling within the range 1.36 and 1.75. The figures shown above refer to the seasonally adjusted series except for those series which appear to have no systematic seasonal variations (stock prices and Treasury bill rate).

TABLE 5

SCORES FOR 25 ECONOMIC INDICATORS OF 1966 NBER SHORT LIST

Classification and Series Title (1)	Scores, Six Criteria						
	Average Score (2)	Economic Significance (3)	Statistical Adequacy (4)	Conformity (5)	Timing (6)	Smoothness (7)	(8) Currency
Leading Indicators (12 series)							
1. Avg. workweek, prod. workers, mfg.	66	50	65	81	66	60	80
30. Nonagri. placements, BES	68	75	63	63	58	80	80
38. Index of net business formation	68	75	58	81	67	80	40
6. New orders, dur. goods indus.	78	75	72	88	84	60	80
10. Contracts and orders, plant and equip.	64	75	63	92	50	40	40
29. New building permits, private housing units	67	50	60	76	80	60	80
31. Change in book value, mfg. and trade inventories	65	75	67	77	78	20	40
23. Industrial materials prices	67	50	72	79	44	80	100
19. Stock prices, 500 common stocks	81	75	74	77	87	80	100
16. Corporate profits after taxes, Q	68	75	70	79	76	60	25
17. Ratio, price to unit labor cost, mfg.	69	50	67	84	72	60	80
113. Change in consumer debt	63	50	79	77	60	60	40
Roughly Coincident Indicators (7 series)							
41. Employees in nonagri. establishments	81	75	61	90	87	100	80
43. Unemployment rate, total (inverted)	75	75	63	96	60	80	80
50. GNP in constant dollars, expenditure estimate, Q	73	75	75	91	58	80	50
47. Industrial production	72	75	63	94	38·	100	80
52. Personal income	74	75	73	89	43	100	80
816. Mfg. and trade sales	71	75	68	70	80	80	40
54. Sales of retail stores	69	75	77	89	12	80	100
Lagging Indicators (6 series)							
502. Unempl. rate, persons unempl. 15+ weeks (inverted)	69	50	63	98	52	80	80
61. Bus. expend., new plant and equip., Q	86	75	77	96	94	100	80
71. Book value, mfg. and trade inventories	71	75	67	75	66	100	40
62. Labor cost per unit of output, mfg.	68	50	70	83	56	80	80
72. Comm. and indus. loans outstanding	57	50	47	67	20	100	100
67. Bank rates on short-term bus. loans, Q	57	50	55	82	47	80	25

SOURCE: "Indicators of Business Expansions and Contractions," National Bureau of Economic Research, Inc., 261 Madison Avenue, New York, New York 10016, 1967.

of 0 to 100. The scoring of each series, admittedly arbitrary in many respects, reflects our desire not only to make as explicit as possible the criteria for selecting indicators, but also to increase the amount of information available to the user to aid in evaluating their current behavior.

Our scoring plan includes six major elements: (1) economic significance, (2) statistical adequacy, (3) historical conformity to business cycles, (4) cyclical timing record, (5) smoothness, and (6) promptness of publication. When the subheads under most of these elements are counted, some twenty different properties of series are rated in all. This list of properties provides a view of the many different considerations relevant to an appraisal of the value of a statistical series for studying current business conditions and prospects. Thus, this scoring plan not only uses the probability tests described above, but also takes into account many other factors which must be considered in appraising an economic indicator. For example, extra turns, i.e., expansions or contractions in stock prices, of the same general magnitude as cyclical movements in aggregate economic activity, which do not correspond to expansions or contractions in aggregate economic activity, are taken into account in the scoring plan, but not in the probability tests. An example of an extra contraction in stock prices is that in 1962 when there was no contraction in aggregate economic activity. The scores earned by the 25 series on the 1966 short list of indicators selected by the NBER are given in Table 5.

The score for stock prices, 81, is one of the highest. An important advantage for this series arises from the fact that it is available over a long period, since 1873, a factor which is given some extra weight in our plan. However, all series were also scored for a common period, 1948–62. Here stock prices earned a somewhat lower rating, because of the nonconforming decline in 1962, but at 72 it is still close to the top.

As a partial test of the scoring plan, a cumulated random series (i.e., a series with random first differences) was constructed from a table of random numbers to provide monthly observations over a 45-year period.[12] Scores for conformity and timing were obtained on the assumption that the series began at four alternative hypothetical dates (January, 1919, June, 1919, January, 1920, and June, 1920). In all four cases, the conformity score was 0. In three cases, the timing score was also 0, and in one it was 26. This indicates that series with cyclical properties but basically unrelated to the U.S. business cycle are unlikely to achieve scores that approach those achieved by the economic indicators included in this study.

The economic indicators included in this study are among the very best, and stock price series has one of the very best records in terms of the consistency of its relations to aggregate economic activity.

The record is, however, not perfect, and so far as the writer knows, there is no perfect economic indicator. This imperfection has led some analysts to conclude that stock prices is not a useful indicator of aggregate economic activity at all. It is reckless, however, to apply an absolute criterion in the difficult field of economic forecasting. A technique which works most, though

---

[12] This series was made up by linking together three of the random first difference series described in the Appendix.

not all, of the time may, with proper safeguards, be advantageously employed.

Statisticians have demonstrated similarities between certain types of random series and certain types of economic series, including stock market prices. The similarities are greatest between cumulated artificial series with random first differences and economic series. A random first difference series is, of course, dominated by random fluctuations, but there will also be some systematic characteristics, because cumulated series are serially correlated as a result of the inclusion of common elements in adjacent observations. It is for this reason that some analysts say that random first difference series behave like real economic series. As already pointed out, however, there is a crucial distinction between the systematic nature of a random first difference series and a real series—random first difference series have no systematic relations to each other nor, of course, to economic series, but economic series do have systematic relations to each other. Similarly, diffusion indexes of random first difference series show some systematic movements (Chart 3), but these do not have the amplitudes characteristic of diffusion indexes of stock prices and other economic series.

VI. Forecasting Stock Price Fluctuations

The evidence cited shows stock prices move systematically in relation to other economic series, more specifically that changes in stock prices usually foreshadow changes in aggregate economic activity, that is, the complex of activities covering production, employment, consumption, income, trade, and the flow of funds. However, an explanation of why the systematic relations between stock prices and aggregate economic activity exist has not been provided, nor has the question of greatest interest—how to predict future stock prices—been taken up.

A convincing economic explanation of why stock prices lead aggregate economic activity is needed to lend credence to the empirical findings. This is, of course, a very large subject in itself. All I am prepared to say here is that the relationship between stock prices and aggregate economic activity probably is indirect through causal relations with other economic activities, for example, the money supply and profits, and that it is a complex one—perhaps as complex as the intricacies of the business cycle itself.

Let me illustrate the possibilities with a familiar explanation. Say that it becomes known that a company has experienced a decline in profits for a given quarter. Stocks of this company are likely to be sold, and the price depressed. Now suppose most company reports in the quarter are similarly unfavorable. This will result in a widespread decline in stock prices. The declines will tend to be spread over the quarter as the various reports of the companies become known. There are also likely to be an interaction and a cumulative downward effect. The decline in profits may be expected to result later in a decline in investment and eventually in production and employment.

The declining trends will show up promptly in the stock price averages, which are recorded hourly, but much later in the profits statistics, which are compiled only quarterly and become available long after the quarter is over. Thus if it is true that changes in profits are primarily responsible for changing stock prices, this may not be learned from the aggregate profits statistics in time to be helpful on the market. By the time the decline in aggregate profits is revealed, the decline in stock prices will have taken place, though this may not be evident to one who studies both series in retrospect. Furthermore, it is clear from charts of these series that the timing relations between them are by no means invariant. A diffusion index of profits, which tends to lead aggregate profits, may be more helpful, but as pointed out below, such a measure has problems of its own. In addition, it seems clear that other factors also affect stock price fluctuations. For example, stock prices seem to respond promptly to changes in bond prices, as can be illustrated by the recent behavior of these series, and bond prices respond to changes in monetary policy.

With respect to the subject of greatest interest in studies of stock prices—how to forecast their future fluctuations—I believe there are some promising lines of exploration. One of the possibilities is mentioned above—through relations with profits, and especially diffusion indexes of profits. It may be helpful to mention a few others. Studies of leading indicators have recently yielded distinctions between long and short leaders, with stock prices classified as a short leader. It may be possible to forecast stock price changes by the movements of such long leaders as the rate of change in the money supply and the change in unfilled orders. Another possibility is the use of such popular stock price indicators as the high-low, odd-lot, and short interest indexes. A systematic study of the relations between such indicators and the turning dates in stock prices, using similar statistical methods to those used in establishing the relations between stock prices and aggregate economic activity, would be a way of testing this approach. In such studies, the stock price series would be "coincident," and its turning dates would be used as benchmarks in a search for "leading" indicators.

The diffusion indexes of stock prices suggest that a way may be found to forecast stock price movements from stock price data. As in the case of all other economic series, diffusion indexes of stock prices lead stock prices themselves. As can be seen in Chart 2, in every case the nine-month indexes lead not only the turning points in general business but also the turning points in the Standard and Poor's stock price index itself, though, of course, by smaller intervals. There are, however, significant obstacles in the way of taking advantage of this knowledge. The short-term diffusion indexes are so erratic that only exceptionally large changes can be interpreted as true signals. The long-term indexes use the most current information to show what has occurred over the span measured, but they do not show what has occurred within the span, and a good part of their leads may be lost for this reason. Furthermore, even the long-term diffusion indexes are sometimes fairly irregular. Finally, the leads of the diffusion indexes are variable; thus, the leads of the diffusion index over the Standard and Poor's index during the post–World War II period ranged from 3 to 22 months at peaks and 4 to 10 months at troughs.

During the past ten years, research efforts have improved our ability to use diffusion indexes to forecast future changes in GNP and industrial production, and our continuing research may yet produce still better methods.

Similar results may follow research studies of the relations between stock price changes and their own diffusion indexes. Diffusion indexes for economic processes that appear to be causally related to stock prices, such as profits, may also prove to be helpful. But to my knowledge such systematic studies of forecasting stock prices have not yet been made; so all I can say is that they offer some hope. Whether knowledge about systematic leads of stock prices, if uncovered, could be exploited in the marketplace, particularly if it were made public, is still another question.

APPENDIX

Construction of Artificial Series with Random First Differences

The series used in this experiment were constructed so that the mean is equal to 100, the expected value of the average month-to-month percent change without regard to sign $E(\bar{O})$ is equal to 5 percent, and their first differences fluctuate as random samples from a normal distribution. Following are the steps taken in the construction of these series:

(1) 24 monthly series of 15 years each were selected from the table of normal random deviates in the Rand Corporation's *A Million Random Digits*. This is equivalent to taking random samples from a normal distribution with mean 0 and variance 1.

(2) 24 new series were formed by cumulating the series derived in step (1).

(3) Each of the cumulated series was transformed, by the addition of an appropriate constant, into series with $E(\bar{O})$ equal to 5 percent.

(4) The 24 resultant series were divided by their respective constants (used in step (3) above) and multiplied by 100 to produce the final 24 artificial series with random first differences and with mean 100 and $E(\bar{O})$ equal to 5 percent. The purpose of this step was to put the series on the same base as the irregular component derived from the Census Method II seasonal adjustment program.

44

TRENDS IN PROFIT SENSITIVITY

Theodore A. Andersen *

VARIOUS JOURNALS of economics and business in recent years have
contained numerous articles which have discussed the effect of
changing profit margins on economic growth rates, inflation, and
wage rates.[1] Also, the decline in profit margins and the contributing
factors have been discussed.[2] There is, however, another important
characteristic of profits which has developed since World War II
and which has received very little attention. This is their increasing
sensitivity to business recessions.[3]

The purpose of this article is to evaluate the postwar trend in
this characteristic of profits. Part I analyzes the changing sensitivity
of total corporate profits and also compares the stability of profits in
the manufacturing industries with those in the non-manufacturing
industries. In addition to presenting the empirical evidence, an at-

---

* Associate Professor, Graduate School of Business Administration, University of California, Los Angeles.

1. N. Kaldor, "Economic Growth and the Problem of Inflation," *Economica,* August,
1959, pp. 212–26, and November, 1959, pp. 287–98. Mr. Kaldor discussed the dependence
of profit margins on the growth rate of the economy. P. W. S. Andrews and Elizabeth
Brunner, "Business Profits and the Quiet Life," *Journal of Industrial Economics,* November, 1962, pp. 72–78. Their article emphasizes the importance of the individual firm's
strenuous efforts to maximize profits. Richard G. Lipsey and M. D. Stener, "The Relation between Profits and Wage Rates," *Economica,* May, 1961, pp. 132–55. The authors
contend that the rate of increase in wage rates is more sensitive to unemployment than
profit rates in the postwar period in the United Kingdom. Rattan J. Bhatia, "Profits
and the Rate of Change in Money Earnings in the U.S., 1953–59," *Economica,* August,
1962, pp. 255–62. Mr. Bhatia argues that both the level of profits and the rate of change
in profits influence strongly changes in the United States money earnings. He sees one
of two implications in his findings. One is the so-called cost inflation which has been of
the profit-push rather than the wage-push variety. The other is that the entire postwar
period has been characterized by demand-pull inflation which first increases prices and
profits and then wages.

2. Sidney Cottle and Tate Whitman, "Twenty Years of Corporate Earnings," *Harvard
Business Review,* May–June, 1958, pp. 100–114. The authors noted that while 1955 was
in general a much more prosperous year than 1935, in most industries profit margins were
lower. J. Roger Morrison and Richard F. Neuschel, "The Second Squeeze on Profits,"
Harvard Business Review, July–August, 1962, pp. 49–66. The authors note that the
business recession in 1960–61 was mild, but profits declined more sharply than in previous recessions. They cited evidence and arguments which indicate that increasing severity
of competition rather than a wage-price squeeze was the major cause of the recent
declines in profit margins.

3. Charles L. Schultze, *Recent Inflation in the United States,* Joint Economic Committee, Congress of the United States, September, 1959, pp. 78–96. The author provides
empirical evidence of the substantial rise in overhead costs for manufacturing industries
between 1947 and 1957. From this it can be inferred that profits would become more
sensitive to decreases in sales.

Reprinted from *The Journal of Finance,* XVIII, No. 4 (December, 1963), 637–46, by
permission of the publisher.

tempt is made in Part II to evaluate the underlying causes of the trends that are shown. The changing patterns of business policies and costs, as well as the shifts in profit margins, are analyzed to determine their effect on profit sensitivity. Part III discusses the implications of these trends from the standpoint of such business policies as pricing, expansion of productive capacity, and marketing.

I. TRENDS IN PROFIT SENSITIVITY

Table 1 shows the trend in profit sensitivity during the four postwar recessions. The periods of decline were selected to show the peak level of GNP before the recession got under way and the lowest

TABLE 1

MEASURES OF PROFIT SENSITIVITY DURING
FOUR POSTWAR RECESSIONS

Period of Decline	Per Cent Change in GNP	Per Cent Change in Corporate Profits	Profit Sensitivity Ratio*
4Q48–4Q49.........	−4.3	−15.4	3.6
2Q53–2Q54.........	−2.8	−18.8	6.7
3Q57–1Q58.........	−3.8	−27.3	7.2
2Q60–1Q61.........	−0.8	−14.2	17.8

*Per cent decline in profits divided by per cent decline in GNP. For example, 15.4 ÷ 4.3 = 3.6, the profit sensitivity ratio for the 1948–49 recession.

Note: (1) All data are on a seasonally adjusted basis. Source: calculated from data on GNP and profits published by the United States Department of Commerce, *National Income*, 1951, pp. 205, 207; *Business Statistics*, 1955, pp. 2, 3; 1959, pp. 1, 2; *Economic Report of the President*, January 1963, pp. 171, 246. (2) During the 1953–54 recession, the Korean War tax on excess corporate profits was eliminated, while in the other recessions there were no changes in tax rates. Thus, to put all recessions on a comparable basis, it has been necessary to examine the profit data on a pretax basis. With the exception of the 1953–54 recession, the trends in profit sensitivity on an after-tax basis show the same pattern as on a pretax basis.

peak reached during the recession. In the first postwar recession, for example, GNP was $267.0 billion in the fourth quarter of 1948 and it declined in each succeeding quarter until it reached $255.5 billion in the fourth quarter of 1949.[4] This represented a 4.3 per cent decline.

The striking feature of this table is the strong, steady increase in the profit sensitivity ratio. Before attempting to explain the causal factors underlying this trend, it should be noted that for manufacturing industries the level of sensitivity ratios is different from that of non-manufacturing industries, although the trend for the two groups is the same. This can be seen in Table 2 and Chart 1, which were prepared on the same basis as Table 1.

4. *National Income,* 1951, United States Department of Commerce, p. 207.

TABLE 2

TRENDS IN PROFIT SENSITIVITY OF MANUFACTUR-
ING AND NON-MANUFACTURING INDUSTRIES

PERIOD OF DECLINE	PROFIT SENSITIVITY RATIO	
	Manufacturing	Non-Manufacturing
4Q48–4Q49..........	5.6	.56
2Q53–2Q54..........	7.8	5.1
3Q57–1Q58..........	8.9	4.2
2Q60–1Q61..........	24.0	11.25

Source: Federal Trade Commission–Securities Exchange Commission, *Quarterly Financial Report for Manufacturing Corporations,*
fourth quarter, 1949, p. 5; second quarter, 1954, p. 3; first quarter,
1958, p. 30; for the 1960–61 recession, the United States Department
of Commerce's figures on manufacturing profits were used rather
than FTC-SEC, because the former's were on a seasonally adjusted
basis. For the 1957–58 and prior recessions, only FTC-SEC data on
manufacturing profits were available on a quarterly basis. These
were seasonally adjusted by the author.

CHART 1

TRENDS IN PROFIT SENSITIVITY RATIOS

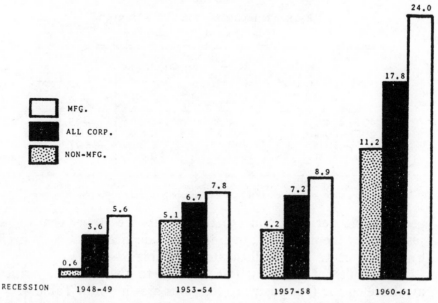

NOTE: Sensitivity ratios show ratio of per cent decline in profits to per cent decline in GNP from business cycle peak to bottom. Source: Tables 1 and 2.

The sensitivity in profits shown in Tables 1 and 2 reflects the well-known fact that costs usually drop less than sales during recessions. Because of the data available on sales, profit margins, and aggregate profits, it is possible to construct a reasonably accurate model of the proportionate decline in costs that occurred in each of the postwar recessions. For example, if the business statistics show that (*a*) sales in a given recession drop by 4 per cent and aggregate

TABLE 3

THEORETICAL MODEL SHOWING THE EFFECT ON COSTS
OF A 4 PER CENT DECLINE IN SALES

Assumptions: In Period I sales = 100, profits are 10 per cent of sales and decline by 20 per cent from Period I to Period II

	Period I	Period II	Per Cent Change
Given			
Sales......................	100	96	− 4
Profits, before taxes..........	10	8	−20
Computed (sales less profits)			
Costs......................	90	88	− 2.2

TABLE 4

ESTIMATED CHANGES IN COSTS DURING
THE POSTWAR RECESSIONS

PERIOD OF DECLINE	PER CENT CHANGE IN:		
	Sales	Costs	Profits
4Q48–4Q49.........	−4.3	−2.8	−15.4
2Q53−2Q54........	−2.8	−0.8	−18.8
3Q57−1Q58........	−3.8	−1.2	−27.3
2Q60−1Q61........	−0.8	+0.5	−14.2

Note: Allowance has been made for the fact that the ratio of profits to sales at the beginning of each recession became progressively lower after the 1948–49 slump.

profits by 20 per cent, and (*b*) that profits are 10 per cent of sales just prior to the downturn, then it can be deduced that costs decline by 2.2 per cent. This is illustrated in Table 3.

The results of applying this method to the business statistics available on the four postwar recessions are shown in Table 4.

The computed 0.5 per cent rise in total corporate costs during the 1960–61 recession is substantiated by the fact that the total wage and salary payments fell by only $1.5 billion in this period, while depreciation expense and business contributions to United States social security systems (because of an increase in tax rates) rose by $1.7 billion. Other business expenses which increased include aggregate bond interest expense and property taxes.

It may be generalized that in view of the low ratio of profits to sales—usually under 5 per cent after taxes, even during periods of relatively low unemployment—a small drop in sales not accompanied by a proportionate drop in costs can easily produce a percentage drop in profits that is many times greater than the percentage drop in sales. Table 3 showed that the combination of a 4 per cent drop in sales and a 2 per cent drop in aggregate costs produced a 20 per cent drop in profits. This is about what happened in the 1948–49 recession.

TABLE 5

AGGREGATE INDUSTRIAL RESEARCH
AND DEVELOPMENT EXPENDI-
TURES BY DECADES, 1940–70

PERIOD	AMOUNT (BILLIONS)
1941–50..................	$ 13
1951–60..................	60
1961–70..................	172

Sources: *Statistical Abstract of the United States, 1954*, p. 514; National Science Foundation, "Review of Data on R&D," September, 1961, pp. 1–3; 1941–42 and 1961–70 estimates are by the author.

II. FACTORS REDUCING COST FLEXIBILITY

The statistics on profit sensitivity indicate that business operating costs are becoming less and less susceptible to reduction during periods of sales decline.[5] There appear to be two major reasons for this trend. First, many firms are accelerating their expenditures on product development, and these costs tend to keep rising even during periods of economic recession. In 1958, for example, expenditures for research and development (R&D) were up about $1 billion or 10 per cent from 1957, while between 1948 and 1949 these expenditures remained stable. Then, too, in the 1957–58 recession, employment of engineers, scientists, and technical workers increased from 6.6 million in October, 1957, to 7.2 million in October, 1958. Again, in the 1960–61 recession, industrial R&D expenditures continued to rise and were about $1 billion higher in 1961 than in 1960.

Because R&D costs have been growing larger relative to total costs, they obviously are becoming an even more important deterrent to cost reduction. Table 5 and Chart 2 show the trends in these expenditures.

5. Schultze, *op. cit.*, pp. 78–84.

Product development, of course, involves costs other than just research. The building and testing of prototype products, tooling up to produce the new or changed product, retraining of workers, and customer education and sales promotion are extra costs which often follow industrial R&D expenditures. This complex of expenditures may well continue to expand during recessions to help contribute over the long run to a strong competitive position for the firm. With consumer discretionary income both very large and expanding rapidly, with the consumer stock of durable goods at a record high level,

CHART 2

TRENDS IN INDUSTRIAL R&D EXPENDITURES, 1940–70
(Billions of Dollars)

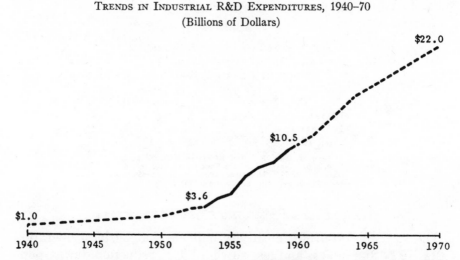

Sources: *Statistical Abstract of the United States, 1954*, p. 514; National Science Foundation, "Reviews o Data on R&D," September, 1961, pp. 1–3; 1941–42 and 1961–70 estimates are by the author.

and with technology accelerating, it seems likely that the emphasis on product development will continue to increase. This means that this upward pressure on business costs may serve over time to reduce cost flexibility continuously.

The second major factor working against major cost reductions during sales declines is the trend toward greater mechanization of production and increased efforts to plan and control business operations. For either the highly mechanized or automated business operation, costs cannot be cut as rapidly when output slumps as they could have been had that operation been handled largely or entirely by direct labor. Depreciation, obsolescence, and costs of capital have been rising as a percentage of total costs, and these types of costs, of course, do not lend themselves to reduction during periods of production decline as well as do factory direct labor costs. Between 1948 and 1958, for example, the ratio of depreciable assets to annual sales rose from 28 to 33 per cent. Thus the continuous substitution of capital for production labor means decreasing downward flexibility in total costs.

In the categories of employment which have been rising, such as industrial and systems engineers, research, accounting, finance, training, market planning, and sales promotion, little opportunity is found for reductions in employment during recessions. Thus, with the trend toward fewer workers engaged in the types of activities

TABLE 6

EFFECT OF RISING PRODUCT DEVELOPMENT AND DEPRECIATION
COSTS ON PROFIT SENSITIVITY FOR A GIVEN COMPANY

	ASSUMPTION OF PROPORTION OF SALES REPRESENTED BY PRODUCT DEVELOPMENT PLUS DEPRECIATION EXPENSES			
	Period I: 10 Per Cent		Period II: 20 Per Cent	
	Business-Cycle Peak	Business-Cycle Bottom	Business-Cycle Peak	Business-Cycle Bottom
Sales.................	100	95	100	95
Development and depreciation cost.....	10	10.5 (up 5%)	20	21.0 (up 5%)
Variable costs........	80	76.0 (down 5%)	70	66.5 (down 5%)
Total costs..........	90	86.5	90	87.5
Profits..............	10	8.5 (−15%)	10	7.5 (−25%)

where employee cuts can be made during production slumps, it is becoming increasingly difficult to reduce costs when sales decline. These shifts in the way employees are used make for higher productivity and more rapid product change, but they also make for less downward flexibility in costs.

Profit sensitivity has increased faster for manufacturing than for non-manufacturing firms because both research and depreciation expenses are much larger percentages of total sales for the former group than for the latter. Table 6 shows that if for a given company in Period I its product development plus depreciation costs equaled 10 per cent of sales and are rising, a 5 per cent sales decline would produce a relatively small drop in profits of 15 per cent. If, however, by Period II these costs equaled 20 per cent of sales and are rising, then a 5 per cent drop in sales would be accompanied by a 25 per cent drop in profits. Manufacturing firms in general have experienced an upward trend in these costs from 10 per cent of sales toward 20 per cent over the past fifteen years, and these costs have tended to rise even during recessions.

Table 7 shows that profit sensitivity is in part a function of the size of profit margins. Thus a 3 per cent decline in sales from Period I to II accompanied by no change in costs produces (*a*) a 25 per cent drop in profits if the profit-to-sales ratio is 12 per cent and (*b*) a 33.3 per cent drop in profits if the profit-to-sales ratio is 9 per cent. With the higher profit margin, the profit sensitivity ratio

TABLE 7

EFFECT OF PROFIT SQUEEZE ON PROFIT SENSITIVITY

	ASSUMING 3 PER CENT SALES DECLINE AND A 13 PER CENT PROFIT MARGIN*		ASSUMING 3 PER CENT SALES DECLINE AND A 9 PER CENT PROFIT MARGIN*	
	Period I	Period II	Period I	Period II
Sales........	100	97	100	97
Costs........	88	88	91	91
Profits......	12	9 (−25.0%)	9	6 (−33.3%)

* The ratio of profits to GNP was 12 per cent as of 4Q48, the beginning of the first postwar recession. It was 9 per cent as of 2Q60, the beginning of the fourth postwar recession.

proved to be 8.3 and with the lower profit margin, 11.1. It is believed, however, that the decline in profit margins over the postwar period was less of a contributing factor to the increase in profit sensitivity than the relatively rapid increase in the various types of overhead costs. The profit sensitivity ratios increased about fivefold over the postwar period, whereas the decline in profit margins as shown in Table 7 tended to increase the sensitivity ratio by less than 30 per cent.

III. BUSINESS POLICY IMPLICATIONS OF RISING PROFIT SENSITIVITY

The trend toward rising fixed costs might well encourage the individual business firm to become more aggressive during or in anticipation of sales slumps in attempting to maintain its unit sales in the following ways: (1) Cut prices where competition is unlikely to retaliate. (2) Cut prices if demand is quite elastic. (3) Where improvements in the product or services or both can be made in a comparatively short period of time, initiate such improvements. (4) Broaden the distribution of company products into new domestic and foreign markets. (5) Budget more for sales promotion.

Also, with rising fixed costs, manufacturing firms need to become more careful in expanding their productive capacity. The automated firm, for example, often cannot cut its costs as much when sales slump as it could if there were greater reliance on direct labor. Of course, the savings produced by automation when the utilization rate is high may more than offset the cost disadvantage incurred during periods of low production.

The growing inability to cut costs as much as previously during sales slumps may also have the effect of discouraging price increases.

TABLE 8

In Period II prices are 2 per cent higher than in Period I, unit sales are off 3 per cent, and revenue is down 1.06 per cent.*

	FIXED COSTS ARE 40 PER CENT OF TOTAL COSTS		FIXED COSTS ARE 80 PER CENT OF TOTAL COSTS	
	Period I	Period II	Period I	Period II
Fixed costs.........	4,000	4,000	8,000	8,000
Variable costs......	6,000	5,820 (−3%)	2,000	1,940 (−3%)
Total costs.....	10,000	9,820 (−1.8%)	10,000	9,940 (−0.6%)

* Assumes unit volume of 1,000 and price of $11 in Period I. Thus, total revenue in each model drops from $11,000 to $10,883, a decline of 1.06 per cent, or $117. Total costs declined by $180 when fixed costs were 40 per cent of total costs. When fixed costs were 80 per cent of total costs, however, the decline in total costs was only $60, or less than the decline in revenue.

To illustrate this point, two models have been constructed (see Table 8) which show the effect on profits of raising prices when costs are relatively (*a*) flexible and (*b*) inflexible.

When fixed costs were only 40 per cent of total costs, the 3 per cent decline in output was accompanied by a 1.8 per cent decline in costs. When fixed costs were 80 per cent, the drop in total costs was only 0.6 per cent. In general, the higher the percentage of fixed costs the less the decline in total costs when a given cut in output occurs. Since the price increases tend to exert downward pressure on unit sales, it is more and more likely that the loss of revenue which could occur if prices were raised would be greater than the decline in costs that would occur.

The assumptions used in Table 7, of course, are not always consistent with what happens in the economy. For example, rising prices and rising sales may occur simultaneously, particularly when national income is rising. For an individual firm, however, in competition with firms in its own industry and those in other industries (which produce substitute goods), an increase in price may well tend to reduce its sales volume from the level which might have been secured had prices not been raised.

In past economic recessions, a large segment of the business community has opposed federal tax reduction because it would cause the government to experience, at least in the short run, a larger budgetary deficit. Now, with fixed costs rising as a percentage of total costs, the majority of business management will be under increasing financial pressure during economic slumps to support the aggressive use of federal fiscal policies to counteract the slump. It cannot, of course, be predicted with much certainty how the businessman's attitude in the future will change toward federal fiscal policy as a countercyclical force. It seems likely, though, that the growing loss of cost flexibility will increase the amount of business support for stronger federal action to counter business downturns.

With the trend toward greater profit sensitivity, it may well be that many firms will want to depend more heavily on equity financing in the future. When costs were more flexible, debt capital could be used with less risk; but with decreasing flexibility, debt financing is becoming riskier. Creditors may also become increasingly concerned about profit instability and insist that borrowers rely more heavily on equity capital in the future.

IV. Summary

There appear to be strong and persistent reasons for rising profit sensitivity, particularly in the manufacturing industries. Product development appears to be an increasingly important part of total costs and so do mechanization and automation. Expenditures for planning and control also appear to be rising as a percentage of total costs and are relatively inflexible in the short run.

Business firms can therefore be expected to undertake progressively greater efforts to stabilize revenue, but the acceleration of technological advance is doing much to unstabilize sales for a given firm. Products have a shorter and shorter life span. This probably can explain in large part the trend toward product diversification and corporate mergers. It may also lead to more conservative financing in the future and greater business support for vigorous use of the federal government's power to moderate business cycles.

45

INFLATION AND COMMON STOCK PRICES IN A CYCLICAL CONTEXT[1]

JOHN LINTNER

Judgments of portfolio managers, investment officers of major financial institutions, and other observers regarding the impact of inflation on the returns from common stock investments have fluctuated widely over the last 25 years. Whenever there has been concern about inflation as a market factor, there has also been a currently fashionable judgment regarding the impact of inflation on prospective stock prices and thereby on the attractiveness of stocks as an investment. But a review of the record shows that these judgments have shifted repeatedly between the view that inflation would depress the returns on equity investments and the opposite view that inflation would enhance the returns on common stocks.

A review of the record suggests that this vacillation essentially generalized recent market experience. If stocks had been rising in the face of inflationary concern, inflation was regarded as good for stock prices; but if inflationary general price movements had been accompanied by falling stock prices, then inflation was an evil omen. Recall that during the inflationary surge of 1947–48, earnings considerably more than doubled, but stock prices were sluggish and price/earnings ratios fell to roughly half their prewar levels. The dominant view was that inflation had been and *would be* a major depressant on stock values because of transient inventory profits and understatements of proper charges for depreciation that impaired the quality of reported earnings. Nevertheless, during the boom in stock prices in the mid-1950s, the quickening pace of inflation was widely used as a major justification for the purchase of common stock (and mutual funds) by individuals and for increased investments of insurance company assets and pension reserves in common stocks, specifically on the grounds that equities would be a good hedge because further inflation would raise stock prices:

Similar generalizations that further inflation would enhance equity values were again widely current from 1965 to 1968. But again, in 1969–70, there was a very high inverse correlation between changes in stock prices and the most recent news or pronouncement on how the current battle against inflation was going. If the current month's annualized rate of change in the Consumer's (or the Wholesale) Price Index was higher (or lower) than the last month's, the stock market would be down (or up) after the announcement. In 1971 and 1972 there continued to be a general coincidence of periods of strongly improving stock prices with intervals of declining inflation, which undoubtedly reinforced the view that inflation is bad for the stock market. In keeping with this view, the stock market turned lower in early 1973 immediately after the announcement of a weakened price-wage control program and continued to fall as rates of inflation increased.

Although this current version of the conventional wisdom agrees with the pessimistic conclusions prevalent in the late forties, it stands in marked contrast to the optimistic conclusions of the mid-fifties and of 1965–68 when inflation was generally thought to favor equity investments as stock prices were rising along with the cost of living and product prices. This pessimistic view also runs directly counter to the traditional and widely accepted classical economic theory of the relation between inflation and stock prices.

The Classical Theory of the Relation Between Inflation and Equity Prices

Standard economic theory, from its classical origins in the last century on up into modern times, has always regarded the *real* value of unlevered equity as being invariant to inflationary or deflationary changes in the price level,

[1] This material represents one of the chapters in a larger study of the effects of inflation and inflationary expectations on common stocks, which in turn is one of five studies now underway covering different aspects of the effects of inflation on financial markets. The other related studies are reported in Part II, Section 4.

so that in principle its current *money* value will rise or fall in proportion to relative changes in the general index of prices of goods and services. In the classical formulations, this conclusion rested on essentially three basic propositions in a context of standard comparative static equilibrium analysis.

First, the *real* returns from ownership of capital goods will be invariant to the general price level, since these returns depend fundamentally on production functions or input-output relations and factor proportions that are invariant to the general level of prices. Second, the (real) market value (V^*) of these ownership claims would be equal to these real returns (X^*) on capital goods capitalized at the real rate of interest (r^*). That is,

$$V_0^* = \sum_{i=1}^{i=\infty} \frac{X^*}{(1 + r^*)^i} = X^*/r^* \qquad (1)$$

Third, the real rate of interest, r^*, is invariant to the price level per se because, as Irving Fisher demonstrated near the turn of the century,[2] market clearing equilibrium conditions require that r^* must be *simultaneously* equal (1) to the marginal real product of capital goods, and (2) to the marginal rate of substitution of real goods between adjacent time periods (which Fisher called the marginal rate of "time preference"). The second condition must be satisfied in equilibrium because self-interest ensures that consumers will have adjusted their spending and saving out of current income until they are indifferent about having x less goods and services during the current period if they can get $x (1 + r^*)$ more goods and services during the next period, and vice versa; correspondingly, profit-maximizing self-interest ensures that firm's capital stocks will have been adjusted to eliminate any discrepancy between the marginal product of their use in production and r^*. Because consumers (and producers) have no "money illusion" and act solely on the basis of exchange ratios (or "terms of trade") between

real goods and services at different points in time, the *real* rate of interest, r^*, is invariant to the price level as such in any period and consequently is invariant to the rate of inflation per se.

Since the real returns, X^*, are invariant to inflation by the first proposition, and the real rate of interest, r^*, is correspondingly invariant by proposition three, the *real* value of the equity V^* in proposition two and equation (1) must also be invariant to inflation per se (and *ceteris paribus!*). Finally, the constancy of the real value V^* of course means that the current money value $\$V_t = P_t \cdot V^*$ will vary in direct proportion to P_t, the index of the general price level. Higher or lower rates of inflation imply capital gains (in before-tax percentage terms) on unlevered equity equal to the rate of inflation.

It is instructive to notice a perhaps surprising corollary, also based on Fisher's work at the turn of the century. Fisher showed that the *nominal* or money rate of interest at any given time would be equal to the interest rate in real terms adjusted upward by the *expected* future rate of inflation.[3] It follows that the money value of unlevered common stocks at any point in time— i.e., their real value restated in terms of the prevailing price level—is *independent* of the amount of inflation *expected in the future*. In particular, as John Burr Williams argued,[4] "No common stock in a company free from debt is worth more today merely because the price level is going to go up tomorrow."

---

[2] *The Nature of Capital and Income*, Macmillan, New York, 1906; *The Rate of Interest*, Macmillan, New York, 1907; as well as the later *Theory of Interest*, Macmillan, New York, 1930, Chapters II, XV, XIX, and XX.

[3] Specifically, if in the current period money prices are expected to increase 100 p^* per cent per year, a current dollar return t years in the future would be discounted at a rate of $(1 + r^*)^t (1 + p^*)^t$. But if prices are expected to increase at 100 p^* per cent per year, the constant real returns X^* will be expected to amount to $X^*(1 + p^*)^t$ when stated in the then-current money units. Since $X^*(1 + p^*)^t/(1 + r^*)^t (1 + p^*)^t = X^*/(1 + r^*)$, *every term* in the summation on the right side of equation (1) is invariant to the value assigned to the expected inflation rate p^*.

[4] *Theory of Investment Value*, Harvard University Press, Cambridge, 1938. The quotation is from page 103. As Williams observed: "Because inflation itself makes stocks go up, most people think that the mere prospect of inflation should do so too. Yet this is not true . . . after all, why should an investor pay more in sound money today simply because a stock is going to be quoted higher in depreciated money tomorrow? Furthermore, how can stocks be a hedge against inflation, protecting their owners during inflation, if they go up before inflation? They cannot discount the same event twice. No, they should respond but once to inflation, and that during inflation, step by step, dollar for dollar, with the rise in general prices."

But notice that Williams' conclusion with respect to unlevered common stock is just a special case of the more general and fundamental conclusions that follow from the classical analysis. In particular, X^* is defined as the *total real* return to the ownership of capital goods—and the capitalization of these returns by the real rate of interest, r^*, identifies V^* in equation (1) as the *real* market value of the *total of ownership claims* against the entire real returns provided by capital goods. The invariances of real returns X^* and the real interest rate r^* from the first and third propositions thus makes (1) the total *real* market value of *all* ownership claims against the returns from capital goods invariant with respect to (a) current rates of inflation, and (b) expected future rates of inflation; (2) the total *current* market value of all these claims (a) will vary in proportion to the current realized rates of inflation, but (b) will be invariant to expected future rates of inflation. These conclusions apply directly to the value of unlevered common stock, because in the absence of debt the equity holders receive the entire return to the ownership of capital goods.

When ownership of the underlying capital goods is partially financed by debt, however, the classicists regarded the impact of inflation on the market values of equity as being even more favorable.[5] Debtors gain and creditors lose whenever there is an increase in the anticipated rate of inflation over the remaining life of the outstanding debt. But the loss in the real market value of these debts ($V_{\hat{D}}^*$) when the *ex-pected future* rates of inflation increase must be matched by an *increase* in the *real* value of levered equity ($V_{\hat{S}}^*$), since $V_{\hat{S}}^* + V_{\hat{D}}^* = V^*$, the *invariant* real capitalized value of the *total real* return to the ownership of the underlying capital goods themselves. Moreover, when this increased real value of levered equity is restated in current market prices, its market value in nominal dollars will of course *also* fully reflect any increase in the general price level. Consequently, in the classical framework, owners of levered equities benefit from a capital gain in *real* terms whenever the expected rate of inflation increases; they also receive a capital gain in nominal money equal to the full current rate of inflation in general prices.[6]

Later work in the classical tradition has of course substituted the more refined concept of "net-debtor position" (which offsets the financial assets held by a company against its debts) for leverage in the sense of long-term debt,[7] but the analysis carries through without substantive change as long as financial liabilities are larger than financial assets. Firms in a net-creditor position, however, will incur real capital losses on their net financial asset position that will at least partially offset and reduce the capital gains in current money terms otherwise associated with inflation. Kessel's classic study[8] found (in an admittedly small but random sample) that industrial firms were about evenly divided between net debtors and net creditors. More important, he found that the market equity

---

[5] For specific references, see Harry Gunnison Brown, "Rising Prices and Investments" (esp. pp. 46-49), Chapter III, in *How to Invest When Prices are Rising*, Irving Fisher, ed., 1912. Brown, then an Assistant Professor at Yale, had been a student of Fisher's. See also Irving Fisher, *The Purchasing Power of Money*, Macmillan, New York, 1920, pp. 58-59 and 170-171; J. M. Keynes, *Tract on Monetary Reform*, Macmillan, London, 1923, p. 18; and Irving Fisher, *The Money Illusion*, Adelphi, New York, 1928, esp. pp. 78-81.

It is significant that these early authors, like J. B. Williams later, specifically determined the *total* value of the firm and then subtracted the value of the debt to determine the value of the equity, precisely as required by the famous Modigliani–Miller "Proposition I," which proved that this classical relation could under certain conditions be extended to models in which risk was incorporated rigorously. (Franco Modigliani and Merton H. Miller, "The Cost of Capital, Corporation Finance and the Theory of Investment," *American Economic Review*, June 1958.)

[6] The classical arguments in this paragraph were most fully and explicitly developed in Williams, *op. cit.*, pp. 107-109, 111-114. Williams provides the following summary of the relevant conclusions on page 107: "Only for equities without leverage, however, does the rule that stocks should not rise in anticipation of inflation hold true. If senior issues are outstanding, then stocks should respond twice, or rather in two steps, to inflation; first on the promise, and second during the fulfillment, of inflation. The first response should be abrupt, and should reflect the gain by stockholders of the prospective loss by bondholders, while the second should be gradual, and should reflect the change in the purchasing power of money from month to month."

[7] Classical writers had either ignored the financial assets held by business firms, or more generally they just implicitly assumed that financial liabilities were larger than financial assets.

[8] Reuben A. Kessel, "Inflation-Caused Wealth Redistribution: A Test of a Hypothesis," *American Economic Review* (March 1956), pp. 128-141.

values of net debtors gained relative to those of net creditors during inflationary periods and fell behind relatively during deflation.[9] This confirmation of the classical expectation has generally been supported by subsequent work.[10]

The Federal Reserve's Flow of Funds data show that the consolidated balance sheet of nonfinancial corporations has consistently been in a net-debtor position since 1945. Their net financial liabilities grew from about $50 billion in the late 1950s to nearly $57 billion in 1965 and jumped to over $200 billion by 1971. Conversion of bonds and mortgages to current market values would not alter the fact of a substantial consolidated net-debtor position,[11] nor the general pattern of its strong increase in recent years. It is thus evident that economists working within the framework of the classical analysis would predict that the current market value of the equity of the large majority of corporations would at least vary directly with changes in general price levels, even though the capital gains in current money terms would not necessarily be fully proportional to current rates of inflation; and the common stock of firms in a substantial net-debtor position should show a more than proportionate capital gain in current money terms.

---

[9] Kessel also pointed out that although commercial banks were extraordinarily heavy debtors, with ratios of debts to equity several times larger than industrial corporations, their monetary assets were still larger—and as net creditors, the real value of their equity fell between 1942 and 1948, both absolutely and relative to industrial firms.

[10] G. L. Bach and Albert Ando, "The Redistributional Effects of Inflation," *Review of Economics and Statistics* (February 1957), find that "the debtor-creditor effect does occur, [although] income statement effects were generally more dominant" (p. 12)—and we return to these other factors" later. Much stronger evidence in favor of the debtor-creditor effect is found in R. A. Kessel and A. A. Alchian, "The Meaning and Validity of the Inflation-induced Lag of Wages Behind Prices," *American Economic Review* (March 1960). See also most recently G. L. Bach, *The New Inflation: Causes, Effects, Cures*, Brown University Press, Providence, 1972, esp. pp. 31-43.

[11] The New York Stock Exchange *Fact Book* (1972), p. 79, shows that the year-end ratios of the market values of all listed bonds as a percentage of par (face values were:

1966: 91.50	1968: 86.69	1970: 93.60
1967: 87.94	1969: 77.80	1971: 89.10

Applying the discounts implied by these prices to all mortgages as well as bonds in Table I-11 clearly leaves non-financial corporations in a substantial net-debtor position throughout.

TABLE I-11

Financial Assets and Liabilities
U.S. Non-Financial Corporations

Selected Years, 1945–71
(amounts in billions)

Year	Total Financial Assets	Long-term Debt[a]	Other Financial Liabilities	Net Financial Assets
1945	$ 69.3	$ 32.1	$ 43.1	$ −5.9
1948	82.0	44.0	63.6	−25.6
1951	110.9	54.1	92.9	−36.1
1955	142.2	73.6	110.2	−41.6
1958	163.4	95.4	121.9	−53.9
1962	206.5	125.0	146.0	−64.5
1965	258.7	150.6	195.0	−86.9
1968	317.1	202.9	261.2	−147.0
1969	341.0	219.7	300.0	−178.7
1970	354.5	245.2	315.6	−206.3
1971	379.8	276.3	324.1	−220.6

a. Bonds plus all mortgage debt.

Source: Flow of Funds Accounts: *Financial Assets and Liabilities Outstanding, 1945–1971*, Federal Reserve System, June 1972.

More Modern Theoretical Writings

The classical economists viewed the economy as seeking and reaching an equilibrium in real terms, and this "real" equilibrium was *independent* of the current *levels* of money prices, which depended, by way of the classical Quantity Theory of Money, on the actions of the monetary authorities. More modern theoretical (and econometric) work, building on the early insights of Keynes and Hicks in the mid-1930s, has developed increasingly complex and more realistic models of the economy in which (1) the level and equilibrium structure of activity in all the real sectors involving production, goods, and services; (2) the level and structure of money prices for all of these goods and services; and (3) the interest rates, yields, and market prices of a rich menu of financial assets are *all interrelated, interdependent, and mutually determined.* Similarly, the latter-day "monetarists" of the Friedman–Chicago–St. Louis School have also moved significantly beyond the simple dichotomies of the strict classical structure.

Most of these elaborations and developments are not directly germane to our present concerns. What needs to be recognized and emphasized here is that the basic conclusion of the classical economists that *the nominal prices of common stocks will vary directly with changes in* (the appropriate index of) *general prices*— even though not necessarily in strict proportion —is still retained and found in the more modern and sophisticated models. For instance, Lloyd Metzler in his seminal paper "Wealth, Saving and the Rate of Inflation" [12] focused on common stock as the primary security in his model and argued that "in the absence of movements in real interest rates, common stock prices rise or fall to the same extent that other prices rise or fall, so that in general inflation or deflation does not affect the real value of securities." [13] Similarly, Martin J. Bailey includes "corporate shares and other [real] assets whose [market] values tend to move with the general price level" and points out that the ownership of "real assets . . . are a significant part of the community's wealth, and other things equal, their total real value is independent of the money price level." [14]

James Tobin's various progressively more general models break the automatic tie between prices of capital stocks and consumers goods found in earlier classical models, but he too argues that "The main sources of inflation or deflation cause both capital goods and consumption goods and consumption prices to rise. Ownership of capital goods (and common stocks) is therefore a good though incomplete hedge against the risks of changes in the consumer price index." [15] Although Tobin's models

emphasize the primary importance of any divergence between the rates of return provided in the stock market to the ownership of existing capital assets and the marginal productivity of these capital assets as a primary driving force in the system, [16] the commodity price level per se "does not affect the real rate of return on capital, calculated either on reproduction cost or on current market value." [17] Franco Modigliani also explicitly retains this same classical "building-block" at the core of his model underlying the stock market equation [18] in the MIT–FRB–PENN model, which is one of the most sophisticated of the modern large-scale econometric models.

Finally, although our references to Metzler, Tobin, and Modigliani illustrate the prevalence of earlier classical judgments concerning the favorable impact of inflation on stock markets in the recent work of leading neo-Keynesians, the same premise or anterior conclusion is also retained in the work of modern neo-monetarists. For instance, Friedman and Schwartz seek to infer the expected rate of inflation by examining the difference between the current market yields of stocks and bonds; [19] such an inference is valid only if, among other things, the capital markets

---

[12] *Journal of Political Economy* (April 1951), pp. 93-116.

[13] The quotation is from page 99. In the Metzler model, if the central bank holds a constant fraction of outstanding securities at all times, the real interest rate and the real value of the common stock outstanding will be invariant to the price level as long as the nominal money supply varies in proportion (i.e., the real value of private money holdings is constant).

[14] Martin J. Bailey, *National Income and the Price Level*, McGraw-Hill, New York, 1962, pp. 106, 107.

[15] This conclusion immediately follows his observation that "Whether in the stock market or in the markets for real capital goods, the terms of trade between capital ownership and consumption goods may turn in favor of owners of capital or against them. But what happens to these terms of trade is quite independent of what happens to the terms of trade between consumption goods and money." See "An Essay on the Principles of Debt Management," in *Fiscal and Debt Management Policies*, published by the Committee on Money and Credit, 1963, and reprinted in James Tobin, *Essays in Economics*, Vol. I, Markham, Chicago, 1971. The quotation is from pages 401-402 in the second source.

[16] See his "Money, Capital and Other Stores of Value," *American Economic Review* (May 1961), reprinted in *Essays in Economics, op. cit.*, where on page 226 he writes "The strategic variable—the ultimate gauge of expansion or deflation, of monetary tightness or ease—is the rate of return that the community of wealth-owners require in order to absorb the existing capital stock (valued at current prices), no more no less, into their portfolios and balance sheets. This rate may be termed the supply price of capital. If it is lower than the marginal productivity of capital, there will be excess demand for capital, stimulating increases in prices of capital goods and additions to the stock. If the supply price of capital is higher than its marginal productivity, demand for capital will be insufficient to absorb the existing stock; its valuation will tend to fall, discouraging production of new capital goods." See also his "A General Equilibrium Approach to Monetary Theory," *Journal of Money, Credit, and Banking* (February 1969), reprinted as Chapter 18 in *Essays in Economics*. Sections 4 and 9 of this reference are especially relevant to the text above.

[17] Tobin, "General Equilibrium Approach," in *Essays in Economics*, p. 328.

[18] See Franco Modigliani, "The Valuation of Corporate Stock," mimeo., 1973, prepared for the forthcoming volume developing the econometrics of the entire model.

[19] Milton Friedman and Anna Jacobson Schwartz, *A Monetary History of the United States, 1867–1960*, National Bureau of Economic Research, New York, 1963. And see also the discussion of similar studies in Richard Roll, "Interest Rates on Monetary Assets and Commodity Price Index Changes," *The Journal of Finance* (May 1972).

are equilibrated in terms of expected real, as distinct from expected nominal, returns. The most recent study relying on this classical premise is a paper by Hendershott and Van Horne.[20]

The authors of the more recent work cited have of course abandoned the simple classical assumption that the structure of prices and returns in financial markets do not affect the equilibrium of the real sectors of the economy, and they also have moved beyond the classical preoccupation with an essentially long-run static equilibrium to deal with shorter-term equilibria and the dynamic adjustment of the economy. Especially in view of the added complexity and flexibility being introduced into their models in other respects, it is indeed striking that they still continue to rely on the classical premise that the real returns to the ownership of capital goods will be invariant to the price level—and that stock prices will consequently rise more or less in proportion to the commodity price level determined elsewhere in the system.

To be sure, there was a considerable body of other research available while these models were being developed that tended to support these conclusions. In particular, there was an impressive array of historical research covering a wide variety of countries and time periods that had uniformly concluded that wages had usually lagged behind price increases and that real wages generally had fallen during inflation.[21] In addition, during World War II and on through the early 1960s researchers focused their models on a "demand-pull" inflation and inferred such a lag[22] that increases the real rates of return to capital, and thereby should make stock market prices stated in current dollars rise *more* than proportionately to the increase in the general price level. Notice that this is very similar

in substance to the transfer of resources from creditors to debtors that made the stocks of companies in a net-debtor position rise more than the general price level in the classical analysis. But Kessel and Alchian's later careful review[23] of the evidence found that either wages had not "lagged" over any significant period as alleged, or that lagging wages could be readily explained by shifts in underlying real factor supplies and demands rather than· by inflation itself.[24] Similarly, Cargill's still more recent analysis using spectral methods on the same bodies of data found "no agreement with the wage-lag hypothesis in the frequency range identified as the short run *since wages and prices appear to be coincident* here."[25] Interestingly enough, Cargill did find weak support for a wage *lag* in the long-run frequency range.[26]

Beginning in the late 1950s, and especially in the last few years, the focus of theoretical work has shifted to the contrary "cost-push" situation in which wage increases lead price increases and in a sense may be "responsible" for them. Wages of course can "lead" and rise faster than prices without putting pressure on commodity and product prices if the increase in real wages is less than the increase in productivity—in this case, the ratio of price to unit labor cost and the gross margin before capital charges are widened. But wage increases greater than gains in productivity increase labor cost per unit of output and create a cost-push that impairs gross profit margins unless prices are raised in tandem. We will review the research dealing with cost-push and other work casting doubt on the adequacy of the classical analysis after we examine the direct evidence available on the relation between inflation and stock prices.

[20] Patric H. Hendershott and James C. Van Horne, "Expected Inflation Implied by Capital Market Rates," *The Journal of Finance* (May 1973).

[21] This earlier work is reviewed in Kessel and Alchian, *op. cit.*, and includes several studies of different countries and times by E. S. Hamilton, Wesley Mitchell, Alvin Hansen, Bresciani-Turroni, Irving Fisher, and others.

[22] J. M. Keynes, *How to Pay for the War*, Macmillan, London, 1940, pp. 61-70; A. Smithies, "The Behavior of Money National Income Under Inflationary Conditions," *Quarterly Journal of Economics*, Vol. 56 (1942), pp. 113-229; F. D. Holzman, "Income Determination in Open Inflation," *Review of Economics and Statistics*, Vol. 32 (1950), pp. 150-158.

[23] Kessel and Alchian, *op. cit.*

[24] In a separate analysis, however, they found that the relative increases in equity value of fifty-six large industrial companies between 1940 and 1952 were negatively and significantly related to the ratios of their outlays for wages to their (market) equity, contrary to the positive relation expected on the wage-lag hypothesis.

[25] T. Cargill, "An Empirical Investigation of the Wage-Lag Hypothesis," *American Economic Review* (December 1969). The quotation is from the summary, page 811 (italics added).

[26] "At the long run frequency components where *coherence* is significant only about half of the components indicate a significant time difference between prices and wages. At these components, the timing relationship is predominantly a wage-lag" (p. 811).

A Brief Review of Some Evidence

There has been surprisingly little statistical work directly relevant to the impact of inflation on stock prices. William C. Greenough's studies of United States data from 1880 to 1950 showed that common stocks had "provided a considerably better protection against inflation than debt obligations" but that it is "unwise to commit all of one's retirement savings to equity investment, since variations in prices of common stocks are much too pronounced to permit full reliance on them for the stable (real) income needed during retirement."[27] Passing over other studies (all of which, so far as is known, tend to support Greenough's conclusions), the most relevant work is Phillip Cagan's analysis of the long-term performance of the common stocks of various countries.[28] Cagan found that the common stocks represented in the comprehensive indices of stock market values in most countries tended to maintain their real values over intervals of 10 or 15 years or more in spite of inflation. I.M.F. data for almost thirty countries over the period 1939–69 show a positive relation between the percentage change in nominal equity prices and inflation, although most of the "explanatory power" depends on observations for a few severe inflations.

Michael W. Keran's study of "Expectations, Money and the Stock Market"[29] developed an econometric model of stock market prices fitted to quarterly data from the first quarter of 1953 through the second quarter of 1970. He concluded that "Expectations of increasing inflation were found to lower the level of stock prices and not to raise it as is commonly argued. Inflationary expectations increase both expected corporate earnings and the interest rate at which these earnings are discounted . . . [but] changes in inflation expectations exert a much greater influence on the rate of discount than on expected earnings. This explains the negative relationship found between the general level of stock prices and expectations of inflation." Interestingly enough, Keran's model determines the level of stock prices by the level of the current expected real corporate earnings (estimated by a 5-year distributed lag) and another (additive!) term for the long-term rate of interest. In the actual fitting, however, this interest rate is replaced by its determinants, as developed in the earlier St. Louis study[30] of interest rates—specifically distributed lags of varying length on the rates of change of the real money stock, real output, and past inflation rates—and his conclusions on the adverse effects of expected inflation on stock prices rest entirely on the negative coefficient on the inflation rate in this "reduced form" equation. Symmetry of treatment to allow for the net effects of inflationary expectations on expected earnings as well as interest rates would have suggested entering price expectations in an equation with current nominal interest rates and current nominal normalized earnings.[31]

Modigliani's more rigorous and sophisticated study previously cited leads to substantially different conclusions. Since current cash dividend payments were well estimated elsewhere in the overall MIT–FRB model, the dependent variable in the stock price equation was the current dividend yield in the market. The resulting equation was fitted to quarterly data for the seventeen years 1953 through 1969.[32] Highly significant positive coefficients were found on a risk premium term (proxied by a 15-year moving average of the absolute deviations of unemployment rates from a 4 per cent norm), and a significantly negative coefficient was found on the current "earnings cover" (E/D) of the dividend. Dividend yields, also as expected, varied strongly and very significantly with currently expected long-term interest rates, estimated as a distributed lag over the current and previous four quarter rates.

[27] William C. Greenough, *A New Approach to Retirement Income*, TIAA, New York, 1951. The quotations are from pages 13-14. Greenough's earlier studies may also be cited.

[28] See the brief description in Part II, Section 4, of this report.

[29] *St. Louis Federal Reserve Bank Review*, January 1971, pp. 16-31. The quotation is from Keran's summary, page 16.

[30] W. P. Yohe and D. S. Karnovsky, "Interest Rates and Price Level Changes, 1952–69," *St. Louis Federal Reserve Bank Review*, December 1969.

[31] This would have normalized the expected future real returns to the current price level.

[32] The equation had a standard error of estimate on dividend yields of only fifteen basic points, with low residual autocorrelation.

But of more direct relevance here, currently expected rates of inflation had a very significant *negative* effect on dividend yields—the higher the expected rate of inflation, the lower the dividend yield, and hence the higher the stock price for a given current dividend, assuming that risk premium, earnings cover, and nominal interest rates are the same. Moreover, the negative coefficient estimated on price expectations is larger in absolute terms than the positive parameter on the nominal interest rate. The fitted equations therefore suggest that even if *real* interest rates (nominal rates less price expectations) instead of nominal rates had been entered directly in the equation, the *ceteris paribus* impact of increased expectations of future price increases would still reduce dividend yields (i.e., higher expected future inflation rates raise stock prices).

For at least three reasons, however, this inference must be drawn with caution from Modigliani's work. The absolute difference in the coefficients on nominal interest rates and price expectations is less than the sum of the standard errors of the two estimates in each of his fitted equations; the respective distributed lags are five quarters for nominal rates but twelve quarters for price expectations; and as noted previously, at an early critical stage of his theoretical development, Modigliani builds on the classical proposition that the market value at current real price levels of unlevered securities is independent of the expected rate of inflation. But if this work does not justify any strong inference that greater expectations of inflation produce higher current stock prices, the good fits produced at the least cast serious doubt on Keran's contrary conclusion.

Finally, the Modigliani study justified no conclusions at all with respect to the effect of *current* realized rates of inflation on stock prices (as distinct from changes in expectations of future inflation). To some extent, of course, more serious current inflation raises expectations of future inflation, but in the fitted equations this effect is very minor, since the weights on recent inflation in Modigliani's distributed lag are small both absolutely and relative to the dominant weights found on price changes three to eight quarters back. Of most direct relevance is the strong negative relation between dividend yields and the ratio of current earnings to dividends. Even waiving the potential biases in correlating D/P with E/D, Modigliani simply used current earnings as reported and for his purposes did not need to examine the impact of current inflation rates on stock prices. If we otherwise knew that higher current rates of inflation reduce current earnings, then his fitted equations would imply higher dividend yields and lower stock prices; on the other hand, if or when more current inflation raises current earnings, his coefficients imply that more current inflations would raise stock prices. But these inferences that stock prices move with current earnings are only to be expected and are surely not novel. It remains to examine the relations to be expected between more or less inflation and the concurrent changes in corporate earnings and profits, a matter we examine in some detail later.

The evidence reviewed to this point leads to the following conclusions:

1. Cagan's work establishes that common stocks have provided a hedge in the more advanced countries against all but very extreme inflations in the long run in the sense that their real returns are positive, but he did not undertake any extensive analysis of the short-run or intermediate term effects, nor did he attempt to determine whether even the long-term positive returns were larger or smaller because of inflation than they would otherwise have been.

2. Keran's conclusion that greater expectations of future inflation depress stock prices was based entirely on their adverse effects through interest rates, and the form of the fitted equation is likely to have biased the conclusion. Modigliani's work suggests better than even odds that the *net* effect of expected future rates of inflation on current stock market prices is no worse than neutral, as the classical economists would have expected. But his study focused on the other issues, and this inference drawn from his equations would not pass standard tests of statistical significance (even though all elements of his equation did so for his own purposes).

3. These studies simply did not examine the effects of current realized inflation (as distinct from expectations of future inflation) on stock prices, although the internal evidence of these

TABLE I-12

Stock Price Trends According to Commodity Price Fluctuations

Annual Commodity Price Changes	Number of Years	Average Annual Stock Price Change		Number of Years that Stocks	
				Decline	Advance
1900 to 1966 (1971)					
–6% to –37%	7 (7)	–25.9%	(25.9)	7 (7)	0 (0)
–2 to –5	8 (8)	+7.9	(7.9)	3 (3)	5 (5)
–1 to +1	21 (23)	+15.5	(14.9)	4 (4)	17 (19)
+2 to +5	14 (17)	+8.9	(7.5)	4 (6)	10 (11)
+6 to +38	16 (16)	+7.4	(7.4)	7 (7)	9 (9)
Average +2% (2.4%)	66 (71)	Average +6.8%	(6.6%)	25 (27)	41 (44)
1946 to 1966 (1971)					
–2% to –5%	2	–4.6%	(4.6)	1 (1)	1 (1)
–1 to +1	10 (11)	+12.8	(12.4)	2 (2)	8 (9)
+2 to +23	9 (13)	+10.2	(8.0)	3 (5)	6 (8)
Average +3%	21 (26)	Average +10.0%	(8.9%)	6 (8)	15 (18)

Source: See footnote in text. We have added data through 1971 in parentheses and recomputed the entire table.

studies suggests that *this* issue turns essentially on the impact of realized inflation on contemporary corporate earnings.

The Short-Term Impact of Inflation on Stock Prices as Shown in Annual Data

In the mid-1960s, when "the Street" was most bullish on purchases of common stocks as inflation hedges, Sydney Homer, a partner in Salomon Brothers and Hutzler, argued strongly against the then common assumption that inflation is good for common stocks.[33] Using tabulations of percentage changes in annual indexes of wholesale prices and common stock prices (see Table I-12) Homer showed that in the 21 years between 1900 and 1966 when wholesale prices were essentially stable, the average gain in stock prices was 15 per cent, but that average gains were reduced to 9 per cent in the 14 years of moderate inflation (2 per cent–5 per cent) and had averaged only 7 per cent (with capital losses in *real* terms) in the 16 years of more serious inflation. When the years through 1971 are added, the average market gains in the 33 years of substantial inflation (over 2 per cent

wholesale) are only about half the 15 per cent average gain in the 23 years of essential stability in general prices; within the last quarter-century, the years of substantial inflation have shown average market gains only about two-thirds as large as those in years of price stability.

However, the stock price action in every group of years in the table was quite variable. Indeed, the within-cell standard deviation of changes in stock prices in the 11 postwar years of negligible inflation and in the 13 years of sizable inflation were, respectively, 13.1 per cent and 15.9 per cent. With so much unexplained variation in the data, the difference in the average return in these groups of years (12.4 per cent–8.0 per cent) could very easily reflect no more than chance variations in drawings from a universe in which stock price changes were really independent of changes in wholesale prices.[34] Thus the evidence that inflation is unfavorable to stock prices is weak. The evidence against the hypothesis that inflation is good for stock prices is somewhat stronger, but still far from statistically significant with such coarse groupings of the

[33] See "Inflation and the Stock Market," an address given before the Security Analysts of San Francisco, January 19, 1967.

[34] Further confirmation is provided by the non-parametric Mann–Whitney test of association. The rank sums differ from their expected value in drawing from a random ordering by less than one (.87) standard deviation. (For a description of the Mann–Whitney test see, for instance, Irwin Miller and John E. Freund, *Probability and Statistics for Engineers*, Prentice-Hall, Englewood Cliffs, N. J., 1965, pp. 214-217).

data, however suggestive they may be. Clearly, more refined regression analysis is required.[35]

1. When a simple regression between the annual percentage change in stock prices and the annual percentage change in the wholesale price index is run over the 70 years of data, there is no correlation at all. (The R^2 corrected for degrees of freedom is in fact negative.) But the results may be due to the indication shown in the table that both serious deflation and serious inflation hurt common stock returns. The deflation period would tend to produce a positive coefficient of the (negative) wholesale price change; the inflation period would tend to produce a negative coefficient on the (positive) inflation term—and the two effects may have just been offsetting each other.

In order to test the possibility that *both* deflation and serious inflation depress common stock returns, we split the wholesale price series into two separate variables. We defined $W+$ as the actual percentage change in the wholesale price index when it was algebraically greater than −2 per cent, and a constant otherwise. Correspondingly, $W-$ was the actual amount of price change when it was algebraically less (negatively greater) than −2 per cent and a constant otherwise. When these variables were entered separately in a regression to explain stock price changes, the fraction of variance in changes in stock prices explained jumped to 13 per cent and the deflation variable $W-$ was highly significant (with a *t*-ratio of 3.62), showing that a 10 per cent deflation would reduce stock market return by 15 per cent. The inflation term $W+$ was considerably weaker, with a submarginal *t*-statistic of 1.44, and the regression coefficient showed that a 10 per cent inflation would reduce stock returns by only 4.1 per cent.

2. Earnings and interest rates, of course, also affect stock prices.[36] Indeed, a simple regression of percentage stock price changes ($\dot{P}$) on contemporary percentage earnings changes ($\dot{E}$) does about as well as our more refined tests of

wholesale prices. Earnings alone explain 12 per cent of the variance in P, and have an impressive *t*-ratio of 3.35. In the simple correlation of annual data, a 10 per cent increase in earnings would increase stock prices 1.8 per cent. Moreover, an extensive series of tests adding or substituting lagged-earnings change, or moving averages, did not significantly improve these results.

3. We tested both commercial paper rates (CP) and long-term bond rates (BR) in equations to explain stock prices. Rather surprisingly, a simple regression on CP changes explained none of the stock price variance in these regressions with annual data, nor did lags or moving averages of this variable. Changes in BR, however, explained 7 per cent of the variance in stock price change, with a significant *t* of −2.67 and a simple regression coefficient, implying that a 20 per cent increase in BR (e.g., from 4 per cent to 4.8 per cent) would reduce stock prices by 15.3 per cent. Once again, lags and moving averages added nothing to the explanatory power of the long-bond rate in annual data.

4. When all of these variables are entered simultaneously in the regression, the following results were obtained when, as in all the above, all variables refer to percentage changes:

$$\dot{P} = 16.93 + 0.115\dot{E} + 3.301\dot{W}-$$
$$t: \qquad\qquad 2.19 \qquad 4.08$$
$$\text{partial:}^{37} \qquad .268 \qquad .460$$

$$-0.669\dot{W}+ -0.542\dot{B}R$$
$$-2.85 \qquad -2.09$$
$$-.341 \qquad -.257$$

All variables are significant and have the expected sign; and 33.4 per cent of the variance of stock price changes is explained. Deflation is the strongest variable when it is active; and, in particular, a 5 per cent deflation would reduce stock prices by 16.5 per cent, whereas a 5 per cent inflation reduces them by 3.35 per cent. What is perhaps most significant in this equation is that these strong deflationary impacts of inflation and deflation are *net* effects after allow-

---

[35] Peter Fortune provided able assistance in carrying through this econometric work.

[36] Since our variables are defined as percentage changes, it was necessary to drop both 1921 and 1932 (which had negative earnings), and also 1922 and 1933, from all the regressions involving the earnings variable.

[37] This line gives the partial correlation coefficient of each variable with the dependent variable.

ing for their simultaneous effects on earnings and long-term interest rates, which are also statistically significant variables in the equation.

5. As a final test, the last regression was rerun simply over the 52 years in which wholesale price changes were *positive*, with the following outcome:

$$\dot{P} = 10.10 + 0.11\dot{E} - 0.64\dot{W} + -0.60\dot{B}R$$
$$t: \qquad\qquad 1.86 \quad -2.48 \quad -2.10$$
$$partial: \qquad .27 \quad -.33 \quad -.31$$

These results are very similar to those obtained before with respect to each variable included, and the value of each separate variable continues to be significant at the 5 per cent level. Although the regression as a whole remains very significant,[38] the powerful effect of $W-$ in years of severe deflation is no longer included and the percentage of the variance of stock price changes that is explained falls to 20 per cent. We also see that the Durbin–Watson statistic[39] indicates a significant degree of autocorrelation in the residuals over the 52 years of stable or rising prices. Although no lagged variables were significant when each variable was introduced separately in our preliminary analysis, we are testing for such lags in the full model excluding years of deflation. We are also examining whether such other variables as commercial paper rates, dividends, and growth rates may also be significant factors in determining percentage changes in average stock prices in years of stable or increasing commodity prices.

It is common practice to regard percentage changes and logarithmic first-differences as interchangeable in regression analysis, but study of the data in logarithmic form permits more flexibility and we are concurrently pursuing this approach. One significant result we have confirms the appropriateness of concentrating on the simple relative first-differences in the data.[40] The resulting regression over the 52 years of

stable or rising prices, with the change in the log of the stock price index ($\Delta \ln P$) as the dependent variable, gives

$$\Delta \ln P = 4.22 + 0.27\,\Delta \ln E - 0.28\,\Delta \ln W +$$
$$.09 \qquad 3.81 \qquad -1.30$$
$$-0.18\,\Delta \ln BR$$
$$0.71$$

A comparison of this equation with the preceding one covering the same years shows marked differences. The percentage of variance of stock price changes explained is 16 per cent (instead of 20 per cent), although the F-statistic (4.69) is still very significant at the .01 level and the standard error of estimate is .109 (instead of 133). In addition, the Durbin–Watson statistic again is respectable[41] and shows no significant autocorrelation (at the 5 per cent level) of the residuals in our logarithmic equation. Even more significant, the coefficient on the earnings-change variable has more than doubled, whereas that on "inflation" has fallen to less than half its percentage-change value; and the coefficient for the long-bond rate has fallen by over two-thirds. The values of the respective t-statistics have all changed in the same proportions.

The correlation matrices in the two forms of variable measurement suggest that the stronger effect of inflation in the percentage-change analysis primarily reflects the impact of a few outlying observations,[42] which in turn suggests that some higher-order term in logarithmic inflation may be more (or additionally) significant. We are also testing for the effects of other variables suggested by theory and previous empirical work in this logarithmic equation, but these further results will have to be reported later.

Interpretations, Related Research, and Further Work

The results of our work with annual data so far indicate that the structure and conclusions of

---

[38] The F-statistic is 5.55, far above the value (4.22) required for significance at the 1 per cent level.

[39] The value has fallen from an acceptable level of 1.70 when deflation years were included to 1.30.

[40] Specifically, when we regressed the levels of all variables in logarithmic form, we found the maximum likelihood value of the Cockran–Orcutt adjustment parameter to be 1.0, which reduces the data to first-differences in the logarithms.

[41] Up to 1.64 from 1.3 in percentage-change form.

[42] These 52 years of stable or rising prices included 10 years of inflation between 10 per cent and 38 per cent and 29 years of stock price changes between 10 per cent and 45 per cent; a logarithm grows much less rapidly than the percentage change. For instance, when Δ is .10, $\Delta \ln$ is .0953; when Δ is .25, $\Delta \ln$ is .223; and when Δ is .45, $\Delta \ln$ is .372, or about one sixth smaller.

models used by both the classical and modern neo-classical economists may be substantially in error with respect to the relation between inflation and stock market prices. Assuming that our further work with annual and quarterly models continues to support this conclusion, we may appropriately consider some of the apparent reasons for such a finding.

As we saw earlier, apart from allowance for gains or losses from its net-debtor-creditor position, the classical conclusion that stock prices would rise in proportion to other prices rested essentially on the invariance to inflation of (1) the *real* returns to the ownership of capital goods, and (2) the *real* interest rate. There are substantial reasons to doubt the validity of *both* of these major premises, quite apart from the impacts of important *expectational* considerations ignored in the classical analysis, along with the implications of the theories of portfolio adjustment and multi-market equilibria that have been developed more recently.

In any given year or quarter, the *real* returns to the ownership of capital goods (a company's real after-tax earnings plus interest charges) will be invariant to inflation *only if* (1) its physical output, (2) its real gross margin per unit of output, and (3) the real after-tax value of its capital-consumption allowances are *all unaffected* by inflation.[43] Correspondingly, in a dynamic growth context, these real returns will be invariant to the current inflation rate only if the rate of growth in real output and the gross and net percentage profit margins are similarly unaffected. But we must recognize that inflation is not an exogenous force imposed on the "real" elements of an economy, but rather is a highly endogenous variable. The root cause of an inflationary "cycle" must be an increased demand for goods and services arising from a stimulating shift in the fiscal (tax and public expenditure) posture, or an easing of monetary policy, or conceivably from a spontaneous surge in private demands.

The initial acceleration and later deceleration (or decline) in the rate of change in real output

will obviously induce corresponding fluctuations in earnings (and dividends with a lag), even if gross and net (percentage) profit margins are constant. But gross (and therefore net) margins will *not* be constant. The work of Hultgren, Fabricant, Kendrick, Kuh, and Eckstein and Wilson[44] shows that the growth in productivity fluctuates about its long-term trend in resonance with the fluctuations in output growth. The resulting fluctuations in gross margins produce still larger fluctuations in profit, other things equal. But other things are not invariant because prices respond to changing demands and costs, and wages respond to changing prices, labor market tightness, induced expectations of further inflation, and other factors.

Drawing on and adapting the substantial amount of work over the last decade on the determinants of industrial prices[45] and wages,[46] one important part of our continuing research is a simulation (based on equations fitted to the last 20 years of American data) of the fluctuations in prices, wages, productivity, gross profits margins, and rates of change in gross profits that are implied by imposing different patterns of accelerating (and later stable or falling) output change on an economy otherwise in a non-

---

[43] We of course ignore the possibility of coincidentally offsetting changes in these elements. Also, for simplicity we will simply assume that the prices of variable inputs other than wages are proportional to sales (output) prices.

[44] Thor Hultgren, *Changes in Labor Cost During Cycles of Production and Business,* National Bureau of Economic Research, New York, 1960; Solomon Fabricant, *Basic Facts About Productivity Change,* National Bureau of Economic Research, New York, 1959; John W. Kendrick, *Productivity Trends: Capital and Labor,* National Bureau of Economic Research, New York, 1956, and *Productivity Trends in the United States,* National Bureau of Economic Research, New York, 1961; Edwin Kuh, *Profits, Profit Markups and Productivity,* U. S. Congress, Joint Economic Committee, 1960; Thomas A. Wilson and Otto Eckstein, "Short-Run Productivity Behavior in U.S. Manufacturing," *Review of Economics and Statistics* (February 1964).

[45] C. L. Schultze and J. L. Tryon, "Prices and Wages," *Brookings Quarterly Econometric Model of the U.S.,* 1965; Otto Eckstein and Gary Fromm, "The Price Equation," *American Economic Review* (December 1968); and the papers in *The Econometrics of Price Determination,* a conference, Board of Governors, Federal Reserve System, 1970 (published 1972).

[46] See relevant papers in preceding footnotes; Edwin Kuh, "A Productivity Theory of Wage Levels—An Alternative to the Phillips Curve," *Review of Economic Studies* (October 1967); Otto Eckstein and Roger Brinner, *The Inflation Process in the U.S.,* U.S. Congress, Joint Economic Committee, 1972; George L. Perry, "Changing Labor Markets and Inflation," *Brookings Papers on Economic Activity,* No. 3 (1970); Robert J. Gordon, "Inflation in Recession and Recovery," *Brookings Papers,* No. 1 (1971); "Wage-Price Controls and the Shifting Phillips Curve," *Brookings Papers,* No. 2 (1972); and his staff progress report appearing later in this volume.

inflationary, steady-state growth posture. The results are showing that the gross returns to capital initially are increased very substantially in an inflationary "cycle" but they later stabilize and then are sharply impaired for a considerable period. At the moment, we need only emphasize that the classical analysis of the effect of inflation on stock prices was substantially in error because all such fluctuations in gross returns were ignored.

In addition, the classical premise that the total returns to capital are invariant also requires that the real after-tax value of capital consumption allowances be unaffected by inflation. But *even if* gross margins were to be constant, as assumed in the classical framework, and if the prices of capital goods and product prices move in tandem, *net* profit margins in real terms will be impaired by increases in general price levels when taxes have to be paid on nominal profits after deducting depreciation on the basis of original costs rather than current replacement costs. *Even in a long-run steady-state*, the classical premise of constant real returns to the owners of capital goods has to be adjusted downward to allow for the reduction in the real value of the "tax shield" for depreciation under inflationary conditions. After corporate income taxes reached high levels during World War II, this matter began to receive extensive attention in the literature [47] and must surely be incorporated along with fluctuations in gross margins in an analysis of the effects of inflation on equity values.

Recall that in our work with annual data we have found a highly significant *negative* impact of inflation on the percentage changes in stock market prices, *even after* its effects on earnings and interest rates have been allowed for—and the odds are still about 9:1 that the *net* impact of inflation is negative in the logarithmic form tested. Allowance for the stream of discrepancies between historical and replacement cost depreciation under inflationary conditions for tax purposes is surely one major factor that would explain such a *net* depressing effect of a well-established inflation on stock prices. But this depressant is at least partially offset by the favorable impact of the predominantly net-debtor position of nonfinancial corporations, especially in recent years, and both of these considerations should be examined in more detail.

Recent research has shown that the classical premise of a long-term *real* rate of interest invariant to the rate of inflation is an unwarranted simplification.[48] Also, the nominal rate is not simply the real rate plus a premium equal to the expected rate of inflation during all intervals or periods when the Federal Reserve is pursuing an *active* policy of either ease or tightness. In addition, there has been growing public acceptance of the fact that restrictive fiscal and monetary policy can effectively dampen the pace of economic activity; and, based to some extent on experience of the late fifties and especially on 1966 and 1969–70, there has been a growing public *expectation* that monetary policy in particular (with at least some support from fiscal policy) *will* in fact be used to cut back the volume of activity. Although tax rates, government expenditures, and Federal Reserve actions are usually treated as exogenous variables by economists, private expectations of these exogenous responses to ongoing inflationary pressures must surely be introduced into any fully satisfactory analysis of the relation of inflation to equity values.

[47] See especially E. Cary Brown, *Effects of Taxation: Depreciation Adjustments for Price Changes*, Graduate School of Business, Division of Research, Harvard University, Cambridge, 1952; and George Terborgh, *Realistic Depreciation Policy* (1954), esp. Chapter 12; and *Essays on Inflation* (1971), esp. Chapter 2, Machinery and Allied Products Institute, Chicago. Also see Donald A. Nichols, "A Note on Inflation and Common Stock Values," *Journal of Finance* (September 1968); pp. 655-657; Brian Motley, "Inflation and Common Stock Values: Comment," *Journal of Finance* (June 1969), pp. 530-535; and most recently, James C. Van Horne and William E. Glassmire, Jr., "The Impact of Unanticipated Changes in Inflation on the Value of Common Stocks," *Journal of Finance* (December 1972), pp. 1081-1092.

[48] See Thomas Sargent, "Commodity Price Expectations and the Interest Rate," *Quarterly Journal of Economics* (February 1969); and "Interest Rates and Prices in the Long Run: A Study of the Gibson Paradox," for the Universities–National Bureau Conference on Secular Inflation, published in the *Journal of Money, Credit, and Banking*, Vol. V, No. 1, Part II (February 1973); and his papers summarized in Part II, Section 4 in this report. Also, Milton Friedman, "Factors Affecting the Level of Interest Rates," *1968 Conference Proceedings of the Conference on Savings and Residential Financing;* William E. Gibson, "Price Expectations Effects on Interest Rates," *Journal of Finance* (March 1970); and Martin Feldstein and Otto Eckstein, "The Fundamental Determinants of Interest Rates," *Review of Economics and Statistics* (November 1970).

Major developments in portfolio and capital market theory in recent years show that the adjustments of market values to changing conditions are much more subtle and complex than suspected in earlier models.[49] As part of our continuing research, we are developing a broader portfolio adjustment model simultaneously including the stock market, bond market, and short-term funds market. Among other things, this work suggests that levels, first-differences, and uncertainties regarding short-term commercial paper rates, bond rates, and equity yields, as well as expected inflation rates, be included in the market clearing equations for each interrelated sector. In particular, the insights from these efforts and related work are being incorporated in a new quarterly model of the stock market. Consistent with the known efficiency and submartingale properties of the market,[50] this model cannot provide the basis for any extraordinary risk-adjusted returns but it will hopefully add significantly to our understanding of the determinants of stock market prices and returns, including specifically the effects of inflation and of inflationary expectations.

On the basis of this work and the other work mentioned above, it would appear that our overall conclusions will finally be that *both* the unalloyed optimism of traditional economic theory and the flat pessimism of the current version of conventional wisdom are quite unjustified as *generalizations* of the relation between inflation and stock prices. In a non-inflationary setting, equity values are likely to be enhanced (in both nominal and real terms) quite significantly during the earlier stages of an inflation; in other circumstances and at other stages of a full inflation "cycle," the effects will probably be about neutral; and in still other circumstances the effects of more inflation on stock prices will surely be adverse, and very severely so for a time. But these projections of our probable conclusions will of course have to be confirmed by the detailed results of our work still underway.

---

[49] See Section V in John Lintner, *Finance and Capital Markets*, 50th Anniversary Colloquium II, National Bureau of Economic Research, New York, 1972, and references there cited.

[50] Eugene F. Fama, "Efficient Capital Markets: A Review of Theory and Empirical Work," *Journal of Finance* (May 1970).

Other Securities

46

INTRODUCTION: A FURTHER DIGRESSION

To this point, we have made almost no reference to investments in things other than common stocks.

There has been an increasing interest by both academics and investment managers in options. There are three reasons for this. The principal one is undoubtedly the remarkable success of the Chicago Board Options Exchange. A second reason is the realization how many financial contracts involve an option of some kind. In some cases this option is very obvious: for example, warrants and convertible debentures give their holder a well-defined option to acquire common stock. In other cases the option is far from obvious; for example, the price discount on a risky bond represents the value of company's option to default by handing over all its assets in settlement of the debt. A third reason for the growing interest in options is that we have learned a good deal about how they should be valued. In Chapter 47 Black explains this difficult subject of option valuation.

In Chapter 48 we introduce some basic concepts of bond analysis. Economics textbooks always speak of a one-year 'spot rate of interest', a two-year' spot rate of interest' and so on. Bond analysts always speak of a bond's 'yield to maturity' or 'redemption yield'. Schaefer's article explains these terms and tells us the relationship between them. In the process he raises some rather fundamental questions as to how bond analysis should be conducted.

A bond manager has at least three concerns. He must predict the general load of interest rates, he must predict the relative levels of long- and short-term interest rates and he must judge how much extra interest he needs on a particular bond to compensate for the risk of default. Telser's article in Chapter 49 discusses the second of these problems. He reviews two well-established theories about the 'term structure' of interest rates. The expectations theory states that long rates simply reflect investors' future expectation about the short rate. The liquidity preference theory states that, because investors are risk averse, they will be willing to pay a premium for bonds that mature when the money is most likely to be needed.

Fisher's article in Chapter 50 is concerned with the third problem, default risk. A comprehensive earlier work by Hickman [1] indicated that realized yields were lowest for bonds of the highest quality and highest for bonds of the lowest quality. The quality ratings Hickman used were those provided by Moody's. Fisher looked behind these ratings to see what it was about the operations of the firm and its capital structure that accounted for the differences in return.

[1] Hickman, W. B. *Corporate Bond Quality and Investor Experience*. National Bureau of Economic Research, Princeton, New Jersey: Princeton University Press, 1958.

by Fischer Black

Fact and Fantasy In the Use of Options

Options trading is where the action is in the securities markets these days.[1] There are some good reasons for the growing popularity of options trading, such as the fact that the brokerage charge for taking a position in options can sometimes be lower than the charge for taking an equivalent position directly in the underlying stock. But for every fact about options, there is a fantasy—a reason given for trading or not trading in options that doesn't make sense when examined carefully. It is sometimes said, for example, that covered option writers almost always gain more than they lose by writing options. This statement focuses on the premium income, and downplays the possible loss of appreciation on the stock if the option is exercised. In fact, careful study shows that an investor who writes call options against his stock will often end up with a worse position than the one he started with.

This article aims at separating fact and fantasy. It will make heavy use of the option formula developed by Black and Scholes, and of the kind of analysis that led to the formula.[2] It will make use of several refinements and extensions of the formula, some of which have been published, and some of which have not yet appeared in final form.[3]

The Option Formula

The option formula (shown in Appendix A) gives the value of a call option for any stock price and time to maturity. The simplest version of the

Fischer Black is Professor of Finance, Graduate School of Business, University of Chicago. He wishes to thank Myron Scholes and Robert Merton for extensive discussions on these issues, and Paul Blair, James Dalton and Joseph Williams for comments on an earlier draft. This work was supported in part by the Center for Research in Security Prices (sponsored by Merrill Lynch, Pierce, Fenner & Smith, Inc.) at the University of Chicago.

formula assumes that the short-term interest rate and the volatility of the stock never change, and that the stock pays no dividends. Thus there are five numbers we need to calculate an option value: (1) the stock price, (2) the time to maturity, (3) the exercise price, (4) the interest rate, and (5) the volatility of the stock.

The tables in Appendix B show the values of an option with a $40 exercise price according to the formula. The option values are arranged in three different ways, so it will be easy to see the effects of changes in any one of the four inputs other than the exercise price. The values for an option with an exercise price other than $40 can be obtained by making proportional changes in the stock price, the exercise price, and the option value.

The big unknown in the option formula is the volatility of the underlying stock. The time to maturity and the exercise price are known. The stock price and the interest rate can be observed. But the volatility of the stock must be estimated. The past volatility of the stock is very helpful in estimating its future volatility, but is not an infallible guide. The volatility of a stock can change over time, and factors other than past volatility can be helpful in predicting it.

Note that the value of an option for a given stock price does not depend on what the stock is expected to do. An option on a stock that is expected to go up has the same value, in terms of the stock, as an option on a stock that is expected to go down. An investor who thinks the stock will go up will think both the stock and the option are underpriced. An investor who thinks the stock will go down won't buy either the stock or the option.

If the price of an option on an exchange is higher than its value, and if the formula is giving the correct value, then an investor who holds the

---

1. Footnotes appear on page 72.

option should sell it, and an investor who doesn't hold the option should write it. If the price of an option on an exchange is lower than its value, and if the formula is giving the correct value, then an investor who doesn't hold the option should buy it, and an investor who has written the option should buy it back.

In other words, the rules for an option buyer are the same as the rules for an option writer. If the option is underpriced, buy it. If the option is overpriced, sell it. An option writer will generally lose if he writes underpriced options, whether he holds the underlying stock or not. His premium income on an underpriced option will be more than offset by his expected losses due to a possible increase in the price of the option over its life.

The writer's gains are the buyer's losses, and the writer's losses are the buyer's gains. If an option is overpriced when it is written, the writer is likely to gain and the buyer is likely to lose. If it is underpriced when it is written, the writer is likely to lose and the buyer is likely to gain. This is true of the writer's options position whether or not he owns the underlying stock.

The hedge ratio is the ratio of the change in the option value to the change in the stock price, for very small changes in the stock price. In Appendix B, the hedge ratios appear in parentheses, under the option values. To see the effects of larger changes in the stock price, we compare two different entries in the same table. We look down a single column at the values of the option for different stock prices.

The hedge ratio tells how to set up a "neutral hedge" between the option and the stock. A neutral hedge is one that is low in risk for small moves in the stock. The hedge ratio is the ratio of stock to option needed for a neutral hedge. For example, suppose the hedge ratio is 0.50. That means that the option value goes up or down about $0.50 when the stock goes up or down $1.00. Then a position that is short two options and long one stock or long two options and short one stock will change in value very little when the stock goes up or down $1.00.[4] The gains or losses on the long position will be offset by losses or gains on the short position. Because large moves in the stock tend to alter the hedge ratio, however, they will bring gains or losses on a fixed hedged position.

In a neutral hedge, the value of the long position need not equal the value of the short position. Suppose, in the above example, that the option price is $5 and the stock price is $40. Then the value of two options is $10, while the value of one stock is $40. The values of the two sides of the position are not even close.

Option versus Stock

The value of an option is closely related to the price of its underlying stock. For small moves in the stock over a short period of time, there is a position in the option that will give almost the same action (in dollars) as a position in the stock. The hedge ratio tells what that position is. If the hedge ratio is 0.33 at a given point in time, then three options will give the same action (in dollars) as one share of stock. This is true for both buyer and seller. Buying three option contracts gives the same action (for small price moves in the short run) as buying one round lot of stock; and selling three option contracts gives the same action as shorting one round lot of stock.

So an investor who wants the action on a stock has two ways of getting it. He can deal directly in the stock, or he can deal in the option. For equivalent dollar action, he usually has to take a larger share position in the option than he would take in the stock.

Changes in the stock price and in time to maturity cause changes in the option position that is equivalent to a stock position. As the stock price goes up, the number of option contracts needed for a position equivalent to one round lot of stock goes down. When the position is way out of the money, it may take ten contracts to give a position equivalent to one round lot. When the option is way in the money, it may take only one contract to give a position equivalent to one round lot.

Sometimes it's better for an investor who wants a position in the stock to take it directly, and sometimes it's better for him to take it via the option. If the option is underpriced—i.e., he can buy it for less than the formula says it's worth—then it may be better to buy the option than to buy the stock. If the commission on an equivalent option position is less than the commission on the stock, it may be better to deal in the option. If the investor wants a short position, it is often better to sell naked calls than to short the stock, because he may get interest on the proceeds of the sale of options. The investor may have to put up less capital to take an equivalent option position, and this can be important if he has limited capital. And finally, there may be tax reasons for dealing in the option instead of the stock.

However, these factors do not always favor options. If it takes ten $100 option contracts to get the equivalent of one round lot of stock, the commission on the ten contracts is $85, under the current commission schedule. But the commission on one round lot of a $40 stock would be about $60. So the fact that multiple option contracts are often needed to get the equivalent of a given stock position can make the option commissions higher than stock commissions.

If options are priced according to the formula, then the "net money" in a stock position is always more than the net money in an equivalent option position.[5] This means that the alternative to a long stock position is a mixture of long option positions and short-term money market instruments. For example, instead of putting up $4,000 for 100 shares of a $40 stock, the investor might pay $1,000 for two option contracts, and put the remaining $3,000 in certificates of deposit.

In the short run, the option position may go up or down just about the same amount as the stock position. In the long run, if the option position is not changed, it will do better than the stock position for large moves in the stock price, and worse than the stock position if the stock price remains about the same. If the stock ends up at the exercise price, the option will expire worthless, and the option position will be down $1,000. But if the stock goes way up, the option position will start moving up twice as fast as the stock position, and will end up with a higher value than the stock position. And if the stock goes way down, the option position will go down a maximum of $1,000, while the stock position can go down any amount up to $4,000.[6]

Thus an appropriate mixture of a long position in options with short-term money market instruments is less speculative from almost any point of view than an investment in the underlying stock. In the short run, the risk in the two positions is the same. And in the long run, the option position comes out ahead for large moves in the stock in either direction. The right mixture of options and CD's has the same expected return as the corresponding stock position, but is surely a more conservative strategy.[7]

Writing Options

Writing naked call options compared with shorting the stock is like buying call options compared with buying the stock.[8] If options are priced according to the formula, and if the hedge ratio is used to set up an equivalent position, then a short position in options will give the same gains or losses in the short run as the equivalent short position in stock. In the long run, the short option position will do better than the short stock position if the stock doesn't move much. But the short option position will do worse than the equivalent short stock position if the stock goes way up or way down and the option position is left unchanged. If buying options is less speculative than buying an equivalent amount of stock, then writing

naked options is more speculative than shorting an equivalent amount of stock.

Writing options against a stock position gives the equivalent of a long position in the stock. An investor who is long 100 shares of stock and short one option contract has a position that will go up in value if the stock goes up, and down in value if the stock goes down. This position can be compared with the two alternatives we have already discussed: a position in the underlying stock without option writing, and a long position in the option.

A position with one round lot of stock long and one option contract short is less risky in the short run than a position with just the one round lot of stock. If a long position in two option contracts is equivalent in the short run to a long position in 100 shares of stock, then a position with 100 shares of stock long and one option contract short will be equivalent to a long position in only 50 shares of stock. Thus the following positions are equivalent in the short run, if the hedge ratio is 0.50: (1) a position that is long 100 shares of stock

Drawing by B. Tobey. © 1958 The New Yorker Magazine, Inc.

*"If you want to make a fast buck,
just go in and tell them you want to make a fast buck."*

and short one option contract; (2) a position that is long 50 shares of stock; and (3) a position that is long one option contract.

These three positions involve different amounts of net money. Assuming that the stock price is $40 and the option price is $5, the net money involved in each position is: (1) $3,500; (2) $2,000; and (3) $500. To see what happens to the equivalent positions in the long run, we can assume that the investor puts up $3,500, and invests the difference between $3,500 and the net money (if any) in CD's. Thus the investment in CD's in each case is: (1) zero; (2) $1500; and (3) $3000.

The investment in CD's is the limit on the amount the investor can lose. If the stock goes to zero, the investor who buys stock and writes options will lose everything; the investor who buys stock and CD's will end up with $1,500 plus interest; and the investor who buys options and CD's will end up with $3,000 plus interest. Of these three positions, the first is the most speculative (writing covered options) and the last is the least speculative (buying options and CD's).

Writing options against a stock position is speculative because this strategy does worse for large moves in the stock than alternative strategies that have equivalent exposure to the action in the stock for small moves in the stock. If an investor writes options against his stock position and the stock doesn't move, he ends up better off than if he went to an equivalent position by selling some of his stock. But if the stock has a large move, he ends up worse off than if he went to an equivalent position by selling some of his stock.

If the formula gives the correct price for an option, and if an investor writes an option against stock at that price, he is making a fair deal. His possible gains if the stock stays at about the same price are just offset by his possible losses if the stock makes a wide move (relative to selling some of his stock instead). It is not correct to say that an investor can increase his rate of return by writing call options against his stock. In fact, he reduces his "expected return," because he creates a position that is equivalent to selling some of his stock. He creates a position in which he will come out ahead only if the stock doesn't move very much. He will come out behind if the stock moves a lot.

The only way a writer can improve expected return and retain the same exposure to small stock movements is to buy more stock and write overpriced options against his total stock position. The hedge ratio tells how much more stock to buy. If the hedge ratio is 0.50, then writing options against a stock position cuts its exposure in half; so the investor should double his stock position and write overpriced calls on all of it. If the hedge ratio is 0.33, then writing options against a stock position cuts its exposure by a third; so the investor should increase his stock position by 50 per cent, and then write overpriced calls on all of it.

Writing calls makes sense when the calls are overpriced. It does not make sense when the calls are underpriced. The fact that one position is more "speculative" than another is not important in most cases. It becomes important when a large loss has more serious consequences than loss of the money. When a large loss would lead to lawsuits and other complications, it may become important to avoid the more speculative positions. Writing overpriced calls against a stock position makes just as much sense as buying underpriced calls for most investors.

Hedging and Spreading

One way to use options is to hedge options against stock. If the hedge ratio is 0.33, then a neutral hedge will be three option contracts against one round lot of stock. A neutral hedge is achieved by going either long the stock and short the options, or short the stock and long the options. A neutral hedge is neither bullish nor bearish. If the hedge is long stock and short options, it will show gains for small moves in the stock and losses for large moves in the stock in either direction. If the hedge is long options and short stock, it will show losses for small moves in the stock and gains for large moves in the stock in either direction.[9]

When the option is underpriced, then the way to hedge is to go long options and short stock. When the option is overpriced, the way to hedge is to go long stock and short options. The farther out of line the option is, the larger the range of stock prices for which the hedge will end up profitable, and the smaller the range of stock prices for which the hedge will end up unprofitable.

Another way to use options is to spread options against one another. A "money spread" involves buying an option at one striking price and selling an option at another striking price, both on the same stock and with the same maturity. A "time spread" or "calendar spread" involves buying an option at one maturity and selling one at another; both on the same stock with the same striking price. A "butterfly spread" involves buying an option in the middle (in terms of either striking price or time) and selling one on each side, or selling an option in the middle and buying one on each side. More complicated spreads are possible too.

The hedge ratios on two options tell how to create a neutral spread between them. To find the right ratio, just divide the two hedge ratios. For example, if the hedge ratio on an October option is 0.10, and the hedge ratio on the corresponding January option is 0.30, then a neutral hedge would involve three Octobers and one January.

Once the ratio of options in a spread has been figured, the spread can be analyzed more exactly. With a 3:1 spread, we multiply the value of the first option by three, and subtract the result from the value of the second option. This is the value of the spread. Then we multiply the price of the first option by three, and subtract the result from the price of the second option. This is the price of the spread. If the value is greater than the price, it makes sense to sell the first option and buy the second. If the value is less than the price, it makes sense to buy the first option and sell the second.

A spread makes sense, of course, when the long side is underpriced and the short side is overpriced, or when the long side is more underpriced than the short side, or when the long side is less overpriced than the short side. The analysis of a spread is less sensitive to the estimated volatility of the stock than the analysis of a hedge of option against stock; an increase in the volatility estimate will increase the value of all the options on a stock. If an October option seems more overpriced than the corresponding January, and we increase the volatility estimate on the stock so that both now seem underpriced, it is likely that the October will seem less underpriced than the January. The indicated spread will be the same in either case: short the October and long the January in an appropriate ratio.

A spread that is short the near month and long a more distant month is speculative, in the sense that it makes money for small moves in the stock, and loses money for large moves in the stock. Very large moves in the stock can be disastrous if the spread is not changed. This is particularly true when the spread ratio is high. A position with one January long and ten Octobers short has great exposure to potential large losses. Similarly, a spread that is long a more in-the-money option and short a more out-of-the-money option is speculative. A position with one $60 option long and ten $80 options short has great exposure to potential large losses. The greater the difference in the exercise prices, the more speculative it is. It makes sense for an investor who is working with spreads to try to have some that are speculative and some that are conservative. Then if stocks generally move way up or way down, his gains on the conservative spreads will help offset his losses on the speculative spreads; and if stocks generally don't move very much, his gains on the speculative spreads will help offset his losses on the conservative spreads.

Estimating Volatility

The volatility of a stock can be estimated by looking at the size of the typical change in the stock price from day to day. The farther back in time we look, the more data we have to look at. If the volatility of a stock did not change, we would look as far back as possible, and would give as much weight to far distant months as to near months. But the volatility does change, so more weight should be given to recent months, and less weight should be given to distant months.

This means that when a stock seems to have a sharp increase in volatility during a month, our estimate for the future will be higher than it was, but not as high as the apparent volatility in the latest month. Sharp increases and decreases in volatility are often only temporary.

In estimating the volatility of a stock, we can also use information on the price behavior of other stocks. If the latest month shows a sharp increase in volatility for stocks generally, then it makes sense to increase our volatility estimate more for any given stock than we would if it were the only stock showing a sharp increase in volatility. If the latest month shows a sharp increase in the volatility of one of two stocks in the same industry, then the estimated volatility on the other stock should be increased too.

The direction of the price movement in a stock can also be used. A stock that drops sharply in price is likely to show a higher volatility in the future (in percentage terms) than a stock that rises sharply in price.

Sometimes other kinds of information can be useful. If we know that a company with a volatile stock is merging with a large, stable company, we may want to reduce our estimate of the future volatility of its stock. If we know that a company is starting a risky new venture, we may want to increase our estimate of the future volatility of its stock.

An increase in the estimated volatility for a stock will increase the values of all the options on the stock. Thus when the options on a stock seem generally overpriced, it is possible that the "market's estimate" of the volatility of the stock is higher than the estimate used in the formula. When the options on a stock seem generally underpriced, it is possible that the market's estimate of its volatility is lower than the estimate used in the formula. (The other possibility is that the market is simply pricing the options incorrectly.) Since the market may know some things about the future volatility in the stock that we don't know, the volatility estimate implied by the general level of option prices on a stock should be given some weight in estimating the stock's future volatility.

There are times when most traded options seem underpriced, and times when most traded options seem overpriced. Again, there are two kinds of possible explanations for this. It may be that the market is expecting volatilities to be generally lower or generally higher than the estimates used in the formula, or it may be that factors unrelated to option values are affecting the option prices.

Sometimes there should be a different volatility estimate for each option maturity. If the volatility of a stock was unusually high in the latest month, we might project a gradual decline in volatility back to more normal levels. On the other hand, if the volatility of the stock has been increasing in recent months, we might project a continued increase in volatility for a time.

Interest Rates

The interest rate in the option formula is the rate on a very low risk note that matures at the time the option expires. This means that there normally will be a different interest rate for each different option maturity. The rates on CD's and prime commercial paper are given separately for different maturities, so it makes sense to use those rates as inputs to the option formula.

Holding constant all the inputs to the option formula except the interest rate, an increase in the interest rate always increases the value of an option. To get a rough idea of why this is so, note that an increase in the interest rate reduces the present value of the exercise price. Since the exercise price is a potential liability for the holder of an option, this increases the value of the option. A one percentage point change in the interest rate does not generally have much effect on the value of an option. To see the effects of a five percentage point change in the interest rate, see Table 2 in Appendix B.

An increase in the interest rate will have a larger effect on an option with long maturity than on an option with a short maturity. Thus a change in the interest rate will change the relative values of near and far options.

An increase in the interest rate has the same effect as a reduction in the exercise price of an option, when the stock pays no dividends. A one per cent fall in the price of a CD maturing at the same time as the option has the same effect as a one per cent reduction in the exercise price.

In practice, a change in the interest rate will not occur by itself. Over the same period, there may be a change in the stock price and a change in the volatility of the stock. The change in the option price will reflect all of these changes.

Dividends

An option on a stock that pays a dividend is worth less than an option on an identical stock that pays no dividend. The higher the dividend, the less the option is worth. When a stock goes ex-dividend, the stock price usually falls, reducing the likelihood that the stock will be above its exercise price at maturity, hence the value of the option.

If the option will be exercised only at maturity, we can approximate the value of the option on a dividend paying stock by subtracting the present value of the dividends likely to be paid before maturity from the stock price. We use this adjusted stock price instead of the actual stock price in the option formula. We get the present value of the dividends by discounting them at the interest rate we are assuming. For example, if a dividend is due in three months and the interest rate is 12 per cent we discount the dividend by dividing it by about 1.03. (The number will differ slightly from 1.03 because of the effects of compounding.)

Sometimes, however, it pays to exercise an option just before it goes ex-dividend. For all dividends except the last one before the option expires, it can pay only if the annual dividend divided by the exercise price of the option is greater than the interest rate.[10] This condition is rarely satisfied. But it often pays to exercise an in-the-money option just before the last ex-dividend date. The closer the last ex-dividend date is to the expiration date of the option, the more likely it is that exercise just before the ex-dividend date will make sense.

Because there is a possibility that it will pay to exercise the option just before the last ex-dividend date, we can figure an alternative value of the option by assuming that it expires just before the last ex-dividend date. If this gives a higher value of the option than the first calculation, we will use it instead. The fact that we are using a shorter time to maturity tends to reduce the value of the option, but the fact that we are not subtracting the discounted value of the last dividend tends to increase it.

The closer the last ex-dividend date is to the maturity date, the more likely it is that the effect of leaving off the last dividend will dominate the effect of reducing the time to maturity.

Thus to figure the value of an option on a dividend-paying stock, we do two calculations of the value, and use the one that gives the higher value.[11] The first calculation subtracts the present value of all the dividends from the stock price, and uses the actual maturity date for the option. The second calculation subtracts the present value of all dividends but the last, and uses a maturity date just before the last ex-dividend date.

The holder of an option should be careful to decide whether it will pay to hold it beyond the last ex-dividend date. When the stock price is well above the exercise price just before the last ex-dividend date, it will often pay either to exercise or to sell out. This means that the writer should decide whether he wants to close his position by buying in or by having the option exercised against him. If he doesn't buy in before the stock goes ex-dividend, he may find that he has been assigned an exercise notice.

The holder of an option should keep it beyond the last ex-dividend date only if it is worth more "alive" than "dead." The value of the option alive will be its value with the stock price reduced by the dividend, with a time to maturity equal to the time between the last ex-dividend date and the date the option expires. The value of the option dead will be the stock price minus the exercise price.

The writer of an option should decide whether to buy in before the last ex-dividend date on the same basis. If he wants to avoid an exercise notice, and the option will be worth more dead than alive on the ex-dividend date, he should buy in before that date—probably several days before, because the exercise notices will start coming in faster several days before the ex-dividend date.

Transaction Costs

The transaction costs for trading in options will often be lower than the costs of making an equivalent trade in the underlying stocks. For example, assume that a six-month option with a $40 exercise price sells for $5 when the stock price is $40, and has a hedge ratio of 0.60. The round trip public commission for taking a position in the stock is now three per cent or more of the value of the stock. For a round lot of stock, this comes to $120.

To get a position that is equivalent to one round lot of stock in the short run, we need less than two option contracts. (If the hedge ratio were 0.50, we would need exactly two.) The public commission on two option contracts with a premium of $500 for each contract is $37 one way. If the option expires worthless, no further commission will be paid. If it ends up in the money, there will be a commission on the closing transaction. If it is exercised, the commission is based on the exercise price, but is no more than $65.

Taking all these possibilities into account, we get a round trip commission for the option position of around $60, which is about half the commission cost of dealing in the stock directly. This saving, however, applies only to short-term trading. If we try to take the equivalent of a long-term position in the stock by buying or selling options repeatedly, we will end up paying much more in commissions than we would in the stock.

Another element of the transaction cost on either options or stock is the market maker's or specialist's spread: the difference between the highest bid price and the lowest asked price.[12] We should use the hedge ratio to compare spreads on options with spreads on stock, just as we used it to compare commissions. When the hedge ratio is 0.50 on an option, we should compare twice the spread in the option market with the spread on the underlying stock on the stock exchange. Since it takes two option contracts to give the same action as one round lot of stock in the short run, we need to compare the spread for two option contracts with the spread for one round lot of stock.

It would not be surprising to find that the market makers' and specialists' spreads are higher on the options market than the spreads for equivalent positions in the stock market, because "information trading" may tend to shift from the market for a stock to the market for its options.

One reason why a market maker's or specialist's buying price is lower than his selling price is that he doesn't know what information those who trade with him may have. Many of them will have information about the stock that he doesn't have. He does know, however, that those who want to sell to him probably have negative information, and those who want to buy from him probably have positive information. So he protects himself to some extent by quoting a lower price to those who want to sell and a higher price to those who want to buy. He will still lose money trading with those who have important pieces of information, and this will cut into the profits he makes trading with those who do not have valuable pieces of information.

Since an investor can usually get more action for a given investment in options than he can by investing directly in the underlying stock, he may choose to deal in options when he feels he has an especially important piece of information. Also, it is easier to take a short position by writing options than by shorting the underlying stock. So many information traders will go to the options market rather than to the stock market. And many potential information traders will trade on the options market when they wouldn't bother to trade at all if the options market did not exist.

This means that in some cases a market maker or specialist will face a more dangerous trading environment on an options exchange than the specialist on the same stock faces on a stock exchange. A higher proportion of those the market maker trades with will have information that can hurt him. So he may have to set a higher bid-asked spread than the specialist in the stock does (for a corresponding position) just to break even.

The fact that the options market brings out information traders who wouldn't otherwise trade means that the market for the stock will be more efficient than it would be without the options market. Even if a piece of information shows up first on the options market, hedgers will rapidly cause the information to be incorporated in stock prices. Options trading will improve the market in the underlying stock, even if it reduces the volume of trading in the underlying stock. But because hedging brings new trading in the stock, it is unlikely that options trading will reduce the volume of trading in the underlying stock.[13]

Taxes

It appears that gains and losses for an option buyer will be taxed as capital gains and losses, while gains and losses for an option writer who buys his options back will be taxed as ordinary income or loss. A buyer who exercises his option defers realizing a gain or loss, and a writer who has an option exercised against him realizes a capital gain or loss rather than ordinary income or loss.

If everyone were in a 70 per cent tax bracket, then option values would be lower than the values given by the formula. If everyone were in the same tax bracket, then the higher the common tax bracket, the lower the option values would be. The effects of taxes are similar to the effects of dividends on the underlying stock. High taxes reduce option values, and make it profitable sometimes for an option buyer to exercise his option before it expires.

To get a rough idea of the amount by which taxes can affect option values, we can calculate a discount factor as follows. We multiply the interest rate by the common tax bracket. We multiply this by the fraction of a year that remains before the option expires, and add 1.0. We divide the stock price by this discount factor before applying the option formula. Note that the discount factor is applied to the stock price, not to the option value directly.

When the interest rate is 12 per cent, the effect on option values of assuming a common tax bracket of 50 per cent is similar to the effect of assuming that the stock pays a six per cent dividend. The effect is not huge, but it is sometimes significant.

When tax brackets differ, an option will have a different value for an investor in a high tax bracket than for an investor in a low tax bracket. The value

will be lower for the investor in a **high tax bracket**. This means that investors in high tax brackets should more often be writers of options, and investors in low tax brackets should more often be buyers of options. This is true in spite of the fact that investors in high tax brackets who buy options may get the benefit of capital gains taxation of their gains. Investors in low tax brackets also get the benefit of capital gains treatment, and they are taxed at lower rates.

In particular, it means that tax exempt institutions would generally be better off buying options than writing them, so long as they are not overpriced. Hopefully, the push to allow institutions to write options freely will be extended so that they will be allowed to buy options, too. While buying options is often considered imprudent, we have already noted that a mixture of options and CD's is actually less speculative than an equivalent combination of holding stock and writing options.

If the price of an option is $6, it may be worth $7 to a tax-exempt investor, and $5 to a taxable investor. When the taxable investor writes the option at $6, he makes $1. When the tax-exempt investor buys the option at $6, he makes $1. They both gain at the expense of the government.

Taxes affect the hedge ratios, too. An investor in a high tax bracket who wants a neutral hedge that is long stock and short options will have to write more options than an investor in a low tax bracket. Suppose, for example, that the hedge ratio is 0.50. A tax exempt investor would buy one round lot of stock and write two option contracts. But an investor in a 50 per cent tax bracket might write three or four option contracts. If he is going to continue to hold the stock, then he won't realize any gains or losses from the stock. But he will realize his gains or losses from the option. If the option goes up, he will realize an ordinary loss, so the government will pay for half of the loss. If the option goes down, he will realize ordinary income, so the government will take half the gain. In effect, the government is taking half the risk. So he needs to write twice as many options to get the same after-tax risk he would have if he were tax exempt. To get a neutral hedge, he writes four option contracts instead of two against one round lot.

If an investor in a high tax bracket writes in-the-money options, he has an additional possible advantage. If the option goes up, he will have an ordinary loss. If the option expires worthless, he will have ordinary income. But if the option goes down but ends up in the money, he can let the option be exercised against him. He can either deliver the stock he holds or buy new stock in the market, and thus realize a capital gain or loss instead of ordinary income.

To see how options can be used to save taxes, let us consider an extreme example: an option with a zero exercise price. This will allow us to illustrate the principles involved in a relatively simple manner. We will assume a $40 stock, and an option that expires in three months with an exercise price of zero. We will assume that the option can be exercised at any time, so it will have a value equal to the stock price at all times. If the stock goes ex-dividend, the option will be exercised before the ex-dividend day. We will assume no dividends.

Now suppose an investor in a 50 per cent tax bracket owns 100 shares of stock and sells options on 200 shares. He is selling options on more shares than he owns. Suppose further that he plans to keep the stock, but to buy back the options just before they expire. The gains or losses on his stock will remain unrealized, while the gains or losses on the options will become ordinary income or loss. Thus his after-tax gains or losses on the options will be only half of his before-tax gains or losses. Since he has written options on two shares of stock for each share he owns, his position is perfectly hedged. Taking taxes into account, his gains or losses on the options will exactly offset his unrealized gains or losses on the stock.

But the option premiums total $8000, while the investor has only $4000 in the stock. He has $4000 to work with until the options are exercised or until he buys them back. He can invest that $4000. His gain is the interest on $4000 for the life of the option. And he gets that without bearing any risk at all. In effect, he gets an interest-free loan of $4000 for the life of the option. The equity in his hedged position is negative. Of course, he gets this benefit only if he gets interest on the proceeds of the options he wrote naked. If he doesn't get the benefit, his brokerage firm will.

But there is more. The investor doesn't have to buy back all his options at the end. If the price of the stock is lower than it was when the options were sold, he may want to let the options on 100 shares be exercised. This will give him a capital gain or loss, depending on his cost basis for the shares. If it is a capital loss, he is clearly better off letting the options on 100 shares be exercised. If it is a capital gain, he may be better off letting them be exercised, depending on the exact amount of the gain, on whether it is long term or short term, and on how long he is likely to let the gain go unrealized if he buys the options back.

These tax benefits can be shared with the buyer of the options, especially if the buyer is an investor in a low tax bracket. One way to do this is to deal n options that have an exercise price that is not zero. For example, suppose we have an option on a $40 stock with an exercise price of $10, and suppose that both writer and buyer agree that all transactions in the option will be at the stock price minus the exercise price. A tax-exempt buyer gets the action on a $40 stock for only $30. In effect, he gets a $10 interest-free loan. His gain is the interest on $10 for each share of stock.

Suppose the writer also wants the action on 100 shares. Assuming he will buy back his options at the end, he can accomplish this by buying 200 shares of stock and writing options on 200 shares. Since his gains and losses on the options are taxable at 50 per cent, the options on 200 shares only offset the gains and losses on 100 shares of stock, so he is left with the action on 100 shares. Since the options sell initially for $3000 per 100 shares, he gets $6000 for the options, and pays $8000 for the stock. His net investment is $2000 for the action on $4000 worth of stock. In effect, he is getting a $2000 interest-free loan. His gain is the interest on $2000. Since this interest is taxable, his net gain is the interest on $1000. This is the same as the tax-exempt investor's gain.

Thus both parties to the transaction get an extra three per cent after taxes on their equity, when the interest rate is 12 per cent. They get the return on the stock plus an extra three per cent. And this doesn't count the substantial extra gain that the taxable investor may get by letting his options be exercised if the stock goes down. This should be enough to show, however, that the potential tax advantages from the use of options are truly enormous.

These factors operate on listed options, too. They probably explain why options that are well in-the-money (the stock price is well above the exercise price) often sell at tangible value (stock price minus exercise price). At that price, the option is a clear bargain for a tax-exempt investor. And a taxable investor may be able to make money writing it at the same time.

For an option sold with an exercise price equal to the stock price at the time, the right to let the option be exercised is not worth much to the writer. He will gain if the stock ends up close to the initial price (but above it). If the initial price is $40, and the option sold for $5, and the stock ends up just above $40, then the writer's ordinary income if he buys the option back is just under $5. But if he lets the option be exercised, and if he has held the stock for more than six months, he will have a long-term capital gain of $5. The profit is the same, but it is taxed as long-term capital gains, rather than as ordinary income. But he gets no benefit if the stock ends up above $45 or below

$40. If it's below $40, the option won't be exercised.

But even an option sold with an exercise price equal to the stock price at the time has a tax value to a writer in a high tax bracket. In general, high bracket investors should write options, and low bracket investors should buy them.

Individual listed options may be priced at times so high that even a tax-exempt investor should write them; or so low that even a taxable investor should buy them. The option formula may help in identifying such cases. The ideal strategy might be to use the formula to help taxable investors sell overpriced options and to help tax-exempt investors buy underpriced options.

Margin Requirements

Brokers cannot lend money for the purchase of options. But this is often not a problem, because to get the equivalent of buying a stock on margin, the investor may want to hold a mixture of options and short-term money market instruments. In that case he won't want to borrow to buy options.

The investor who wants the equivalent of a short position in the stock may be much better off writing options than shorting the stock directly. If he can keep both the amount he puts up in margin and the premiums he receives in government securities, then he will be earning interest. Even if he loses interest on one or both of these amounts, they are normally smaller than the amounts he loses interest on if he shorts the stock.

Further, a taxable investor who writes naked options realizes ordinary losses if he is wrong, while an investor who shorts the stock realizes short-term capital losses if he is wrong. Ordinary losses can be used without limit, while capital losses can only be used to offset capital gains plus a small amount of ordinary income. So writing options will be better than shorting stock for both margin reasons and tax reasons.

Actual Prices

The actual prices on listed options tend to differ in certain systematic ways from the values given by the formula. Options that are way out of the money tend to be overpriced, and options that are way into the money tend to be underpriced. Options with less than three months to maturity tend to be overpriced.

Thus the money spreads that make sense usually involve buying an option with a lower exercise price and selling a corresponding option with a higher exercise price. The time spreads that make sense usually involve buying an option with a longer maturity and selling an option with a shorter maturity. The stock option hedges that seem most profitable involve buying the stock and selling out-of-the-money options with only a little time left to go. At least this has been true so far. As time goes on, the pattern may change.

One possible explanation for this pattern is that we have left someting out of the formula. Perhaps if we assumed a more complicated pattern for changes in a stock's volatility, or for changes in interest rates, we would be able to explain the overpricing of out-of-the-money options. But this seems unlikely to give a complete explanation. The underpricing of way in-the-money options is so extreme that they often sell at "parity," where the option price is approximately equal to the stock price minus the exercise price. This means that the market is not giving the remaining time to maturity any value at all. Only tax factors, as discussed above, seem to have any chance of explaining this.

Another possible explanation for the observed pattern is that market makers and other investors have to be induced to take the indicated positions by the promise of substantial profits, because they are so speculative. A market maker who buys one option contract for $1,000 and sells ten contracts at a higher exercise price for $12.50 each is taking a great risk. A sudden large move in the stock price in either direction may give him great losses. If the stock moves down, he can lose all the money he put up. If the stock moves up, he can lose more than all the money he put up.

Those who buy short, out-of-the-money options and mix them with CD's have conservative positions. At most, they can lose all the money they put into the options. Those who write short, out-of-the-money options have speculative positions, even if they hold the underlying stock. They can lose all the money they have invested, and sometimes more. So it may be that those who want conservative positions must pay others to take the speculative positions.

Still another possible explanation is that options give a form of leverage that is otherwise unavailable because of margin restrictions, and that investors bid up their prices because of the leverage they get. This explanation seems very unlikely for two reasons. First, it can't explain why in-the-money options are usually underpriced. They can offer more leverage than the investor can get directly, yet they are underpriced. And second, it can't explain why competition among writers doesn't eliminate the overpricing of out-of-the-money options. There are great numbers of investors who have as much leverage as they want, and would be glad to earn extra money by writing overpriced options if writing options were not so speculative.

At the moment, I think we have to say that we don't know why some kinds of options are consistently overpriced according to the formula and others are consistently underpriced.

Regulation

The SEC seems to be doing a good job in regulating options trading. It has allowed the creation of exchanges that are more advanced in several respects than existing stock exchanges. Clearing facilities are more modern and lower in cost, and short positions are as easy to open as long positions.

However, the Commission has imposed restrictions on the trading of options that are way out of the money. It is hard to see how this can be in the public interest.

Apparently the Commission feels that those who buy way out-of-the-money options are throwing their money away, because there is so little chance that they will be worth anything at maturity. And in fact, the formula suggests that such options are usually overpriced. But we have already noted that careful buyers of such options are actually bearing less risk of catastrophic loss than those who write the options. If the SEC restricts trading, it will hurt those who buy options to reduce their exposure to loss as well as those who buy options to increase their potential gains. Further, no one has to buy these options. Anyone who wants to can write them instead. So this seems like a situation where any possible problems can be adequately solved through additional disclosure. ■

APPENDIX A. THE FORMULA

The simple option formula is Equation 13 on page 644 of the article by Black and Scholes (1973):

$$w(x, t) = xN(d_1) - ce^{r(t-t^*)}N(d_2)$$

$$d_1 = \frac{ln\frac{x}{c} + (r + \frac{1}{2}v^2)(t^*-t)}{v\sqrt{t^*-t}}$$

$$d_2 = \frac{ln\frac{x}{c} + (r - \frac{1}{2}v^2)(t^*-t)}{v\sqrt{t^*-t}}$$

In this formula, x is the stock price, c is the exercise price, t is the current time, t^* is the time at which the option expires, r is the interest rate, v^2 is the variance rate of the return on the stock (a measure of the stock's volatility), ln is the natural logarithm, $N(d)$ is the cumulative normal density function, and $w(x, t)$ is the value of the option at time t when the stock price is x.

The "hedge ratio" is given by Equation 14 on page 645 of the article by Black and Scholes (1973):

$$w_1(x, t) = N(d_1) .$$

In this formula, $w_1(x, t)$ is the derivative of the option formula with respect to the stock price. It is the change in the option value for a small change in the stock price, divided by the change in the stock price. Or it is the number of round lots of stock needed to balance one option contract to create a hedged position. The other symbols in this formula are defined as they are for the option formula.

APPENDIX B. TABLES OF OPTION VALUES AND HEDGE RATIOS

The tables given below show the values and hedge ratios for an option with an exercise price of $40, for different values of the other inputs to the option formula. There are six different stock prices, three maturities, three interest rates, and nine values of the volatility (annual standard deviation). The hedge ratios are in parentheses.

Table 1 makes it easy to see the influence of stock price and maturity. Reading down, we see how the value of an option changes as the stock price increases. Reading across, we see how the value changes as the maturity increases. An increase in either the stock price or the maturity will always increase the value of the option. Note that while a change of several months in maturity has a substantial effect on the value of an option, a change of a few days or a week usually has only a modest effect on the option value.

Table 2 makes it easy to see the influence of stock price and the interest rate. Reading across, we see how the value changes as the interest rate increases. An increase in the interest rate will always increase the value of the option. Note that even a five percentage point change in the interest rate usually has only a modest effect on the option value. The greatest effect of the interest rate occurs in the longest maturity options.

Table 3 makes it easy to see the influence of stock price and the volatility of the stock. Reading across, we see how the value changes as the volatility increases. An increase in the volatility will always increase the value of the option. Note that when the stock price is well below the exercise price, an increase in the volatility of the stock causes a very large percentage increase in the value of the option.

The figures in Table 2 and 3 are the same as the figures in Table 1. They are just arranged differently.

$\longrightarrow$

TABLE 1. Option Values and Hedge Ratios for Different Stock Prices and Maturities, by Standard Deviation and Interest Rate.

Annual Std Dev = 0.20   Exercise Price = 40.

	Interest Rate = 0.05			Interest Rate = 0.10			Interest Rate = 0.15		
Price	3 Months	6 Months	9 Months	3 Months	6 Months	9 Months	3 Months	6 Months	9 Months
28.	0.00	0.01	0.07	0.00	0.02	0.12	0.00	0.04	0.20
	(0.00)	(0.01)	(0.04)	(0.00)	(0.02)	(0.06)	(0.00)	(0.03)	(0.09)
32.	0.02	0.18	0.44	0.03	0.26	0.65	0.04	0.37	0.93
	(0.02)	(0.09)	(0.16)	(0.03)	(0.12)	(0.22)	(0.04)	(0.16)	(0.29)
36.	0.36	0.94	1.50	0.45	1.22	2.01	0.55	1.55	2.61
	(0.19)	(0.31)	(0.38)	(0.23)	(0.37)	(0.46)	(0.26)	(0.44)	(0.55)
40.	1.85	2.76	3.51	2.12	3.31	4.35	2.41	3.92	5.27
	(0.57)	(0.60)	(0.62)	(0.62)	(0.66)	(0.70)	(0.66)	(0.73)	(0.77)
44.	4.80	5.63	6.38	5.22	6.41	7.49	5.65	7.21	8.64
	(0.87)	(0.82)	(0.80)	(0.89)	(0.86)	(0.86)	(0.92)	(0.90)	(0.90)
48.	8.54	9.18	9.83	9.02	10.08	11.11	9.49	10.97	12.39
	(0.98)	(0.94)	(0.91)	(0.98)	(0.96)	(0.94)	(0.99)	(0.97)	(0.96)
52.	12.50	13.04	13.60	12.99	13.98	14.96	13.47	14.91	16.30
	(1.00)	(0.98)	(0.97)	(1.00)	(0.99)	(0.98)	(1.00)	(0.99)	(0.99)

Annual Std Dev = 0.30   Exercise Price = 40.

	Interest Rate = 0.05			Interest Rate = 0.10			Interest Rate = 0.15		
Price	3 Months	6 Months	9 Months	3 Months	6 Months	9 Months	3 Months	6 Months	9 Months
28.	0.02	0.18	0.45	0.02	0.23	0.59	0.03	0.29	0.76
	(0.01)	(0.07)	(0.14)	(0.02)	(0.09)	(0.17)	(0.02)	(0.11)	(0.21)
32.	0.19	0.70	1.27	0.23	0.86	1.58	0.27	1.04	1.94
	(0.09)	(0.20)	(0.28)	(0.11)	(0.24)	(0.33)	(0.12)	(0.28)	(0.38)
36.	0.92	1.89	2.72	1.05	2.21	3.25	1.19	2.56	3.84
	(0.29)	(0.39)	(0.45)	(0.32)	(0.44)	(0.51)	(0.35)	(0.49)	(0.56)
40.	2.63	3.85	4.84	2.89	4.36	5.59	3.16	4.90	6.40
	(0.56)	(0.59)	(0.61)	(0.60)	(0.63)	(0.66)	(0.63)	(0.68)	(0.71)
44.	5.36	6.55	7.54	5.73	7.22	8.50	6.11	7.91	9.49
	(0.79)	(0.75)	(0.74)	(0.81)	(0.79)	(0.78)	(0.83)	(0.82)	(0.82)
48.	8.79	9.78	10.70	9.23	10.58	11.82	9.68	11.38	12.94
	(0.92)	(0.86)	(0.84)	(0.93)	(0.89)	(0.87)	(0.94)	(0.91)	(0.90)
52.	12.59	13.37	14.18	13.06	14.24	15.41	13.53	15.11	16.63
	(0.97)	(0.93)	(0.90)	(0.98)	(0.94)	(0.92)	(0.98)	(0.96)	(0.94)

Annual Std Dev = 0.40   Exercise Price = 40.

	Interest Rate = 0.05			Interest Rate = 0.10			Interest Rate = 0.15		
Price	3 Months	6 Months	9 Months	3 Months	6 Months	9 Months	3 Months	6 Months	9 Months
28.	0.12	0.55	1.09	0.13	0.65	1.30	0.15	0.76	1.54
	(0.05)	(0.15)	(0.23)	(0.06)	(0.17)	(0.26)	(0.07)	(0.20)	(0.30)
32.	0.53	1.42	2.26	0.60	1.62	2.62	0.67	1.85	3.02
	(0.17)	(0.29)	(0.36)	(0.19)	(0.32)	(0.40)	(0.20)	(0.35)	(0.44)
36.	1.57	2.88	3.96	1.72	3.22	4.49	1.87	3.58	5.06
	(0.36)	(0.44)	(0.49)	(0.38)	(0.48)	(0.53)	(0.41)	(0.51)	(0.58)
40.	3.42	4.95	6.17	3.67	5.43	6.87	3.92	5.93	7.60
	(0.56)	(0.59)	(0.61)	(0.59)	(0.62)	(0.65)	(0.61)	(0.66)	(0.69)
44.	6.04	7.57	8.82	6.38	8.18	9.67	6.72	8.80	10.56
	(0.74)	(0.71)	(0.71)	(0.76)	(0.74)	(0.75)	(0.78)	(0.77)	(0.78)
48.	9.26	10.63	11.83	9.66	11.34	12.82	10.06	12.06	13.82
	(0.86)	(0.81)	(0.79)	(0.87)	(0.83)	(0.82)	(0.88)	(0.85)	(0.85)
52.	12.85	14.01	15.11	13.29	14.80	16.21	13.73	15.59	17.31
	(0.93)	(0.88)	(0.85)	(0.94)	(0.89)	(0.87)	(0.95)	(0.91)	(0.90)

Annual Std Dev = 0.50   Exercise Price = 40.

	Interest Rate = 0.05			Interest Rate = 0.10			Interest Rate = 0.15		
Price	3 Months	6 Months	9 Months	3 Months	6 Months	9 Months	3 Months	6 Months	9 Months
28.	0.32	1.08	1.88	0.35	1.22	2.14	0.39	1.37	2.42
	(0.11)	(0.22)	(0.30)	(0.11)	(0.24)	(0.33)	(0.12)	(0.27)	(0.36)
32.	0.99	2.23	3.32	1.07	2.46	3.71	1.16	2.71	4.12
	(0.24)	(0.35)	(0.42)	(0.25)	(0.38)	(0.45)	(0.27)	(0.40)	(0.48)
36.	2.26	3.89	5.20	2.41	4.23	5.73	2.58	4.59	6.28
	(0.40)	(0.48)	(0.52)	(0.42)	(0.51)	(0.56)	(0.44)	(0.54)	(0.59)
40.	4.21	6.05	7.49	4.44	6.51	8.15	4.69	6.97	8.83
	(0.57)	(0.60)	(0.62)	(0.59)	(0.62)	(0.65)	(0.61)	(0.65)	(0.68)
44.	6.78	8.65	10.13	7.09	9.21	10.92	7.40	9.77	11.72
	(0.71)	(0.70)	(0.70)	(0.73)	(0.72)	(0.73)	(0.74)	(0.74)	(0.76)
48.	9.85	11.60	13.07	10.22	12.25	13.96	10.59	12.91	14.87
	(0.82)	(0.78)	(0.77)	(0.83)	(0.80)	(0.79)	(0.84)	(0.82)	(0.82)
52.	13.27	14.84	16.24	13.68	15.56	17.23	14.10	16.29	18.22
	(0.89)	(0.84)	(0.82)	(0.90)	(0.86)	(0.84)	(0.91)	(0.87)	(0.86)

TABLE 1. Option Values and Hedge Ratios for Different Stock Prices and Maturities, by Standard Deviation and Interest Rate. (Continued)

Annual Std Dev = 0.60   Exercise Price = 40.

Price	Interest Rate = 0.05			Interest Rate = 0.10			Interest Rate = 0.15		
	3 Months	6 Months	9 Months	3 Months	6 Months	9 Months	3 Months	6 Months	9 Months
28.	0.62 (0.16)	1.72 (0.28)	2.76 (0.36)	0.67 (0.17)	1.88 (0.30)	3.05 (0.39)	0.72 (0.18)	2.05 (0.33)	3.35 (0.42)
32.	1.51 (0.29)	3.09 (0.40)	4.41 (0.46)	1.61 (0.30)	3.33 (0.42)	4.81 (0.49)	1.71 (0.32)	3.59 (0.45)	5.22 (0.52)
36.	2.96 (0.44)	4.91 (0.51)	6.44 (0.55)	3.12 (0.45)	5.25 (0.53)	6.95 (0.58)	3.29 (0.47)	5.60 (0.56)	7.48 (0.61)
40.	4.99 (0.58)	7.14 (0.61)	8.81 (0.63)	5.22 (0.59)	7.58 (0.63)	9.43 (0.66)	5.45 (0.61)	8.02 (0.65)	10.07 (0.68)
44.	7.54 (0.69)	9.74 (0.69)	11.46 (0.70)	7.83 (0.71)	10.26 (0.71)	12.19 (0.72)	8.13 (0.72)	10.79 (0.73)	12.93 (0.75)
48.	10.52 (0.79)	12.64 (0.76)	14.37 (0.75)	10.86 (0.80)	13.24 (0.78)	15.19 (0.77)	11.20 (0.81)	13.84 (0.79)	16.02 (0.80)
52.	13.81 (0.86)	15.79 (0.81)	17.47 (0.80)	14.20 (0.87)	16.45 (0.83)	18.38 (0.82)	14.58 (0.87)	17.12 (0.84)	19.28 (0.84)

Annual Std Dev = 0.70   Exercise Price = 40.

Price	Interest Rate = 0.05			Interest Rate = 0.10			Interest Rate = 0.15		
	3 Months	6 Months	9 Months	3 Months	6 Months	9 Months	3 Months	6 Months	9 Months
28.	0.99 (0.21)	2.42 (0.34)	3.69 (0.41)	1.05 (0.22)	2.60 (0.35)	3.99 (0.44)	1.12 (0.23)	2.78 (0.37)	4.31 (0.46)
32.	2.08 (0.33)	3.97 (0.44)	5.51 (0.50)	2.19 (0.35)	4.23 (0.46)	5.91 (0.52)	2.30 (0.36)	4.49 (0.48)	6.33 (0.55)
36.	3.67 (0.46)	5.92 (0.53)	7.67 (0.58)	3.84 (0.48)	6.26 (0.55)	8.16 (0.60)	4.01 (0.49)	6.60 (0.57)	8.67 (0.62)
40.	5.77 (0.58)	8.23 (0.62)	10.11 (0.64)	6.00 (0.60)	8.64 (0.64)	10.70 (0.67)	6.22 (0.61)	9.07 (0.66)	11.30 (0.69)
44.	8.32 (0.69)	10.84 (0.69)	12.79 (0.70)	8.59 (0.70)	11.33 (0.71)	13.47 (0.72)	8.87 (0.71)	11.83 (0.72)	14.16 (0.74)
48.	11.23 (0.77)	13.72 (0.75)	15.69 (0.75)	11.55 (0.78)	14.27 (0.76)	16.45 (0.77)	11.88 (0.79)	14.83 (0.78)	17.21 (0.79)
52.	14.44 (0.83)	16.81 (0.80)	18.76 (0.79)	14.80 (0.84)	17.42 (0.81)	19.59 (0.80)	15.16 (0.85)	18.04 (0.82)	20.43 (0.82)

Annual Std Dev = 0.80   Exercise Price = 40.

Price	Interest Rate = 0.05			Interest Rate = 0.10			Interest Rate = 0.15		
	3 Months	6 Months	9 Months	3 Months	6 Months	9 Months	3 Months	6 Months	9 Months
28.	1.42 (0.25)	3.16 (0.38)	4.64 (0.45)	1.49 (0.26,)	3.35 (0.40)	4.95 (0.48)	1.57 (0.27)	3.55 (0.41)	5.27 (0.50)
32.	2.67 (0.37)	4.87 (0.47)	6.62 (0.53)	2.79 (0.38)	5.13 (0.49)	7.01 (0.55)	2.91 (0.40)	5.40 (0.51)	7.42 (0.57)
36.	4.39 (0.49)	6.93 (0.56)	8.88 (0.60)	4.56 (0.50)	7.26 (0.57)	9.36 (0.62)	4.73 (0.51)	7.60 (0.59)	9.85 (0.64)
40.	6.55 (0.59)	9.30 (0.63)	11.39 (0.66)	6.77 (0.60)	9.70 (0.64)	11.95 (0.68)	6.99 (0.62)	10.10 (0.66)	12.52 (0.69)
44.	9.10 (0.68)	11.94 (0.69)	14.11 (0.70)	9.36 (0.69)	12.40 (0.71)	14.75 (0.72)	9.63 (0.70)	12.87 (0.72)	15.39 (0.74)
48.	11.98 (0.75)	14.81 (0.74)	17.02 (0.75)	12.28 (0.76)	15.33 (0.76)	17.73 (0.76)	12.59 (0.77)	15.85 (0.77)	18.44 (0.78)
52.	15.11 (0.81)	17.86 (0.79)	20.08 (0.78)	15.45 (0.82)	18.44 (0.80)	20.85 (0.80)	15.80 (0.83)	19.02 (0.81)	21.62 (0.81)

Annual Std Dev = 0.90   Exercise Price = 40.

Price	Interest Rate = 0.05			Interest Rate = 0.10			Interest Rate = 0.15		
	3 Months	6 Months	9 Months	3 Months	6 Months	9 Months	3 Months	6 Months	9 Months
28.	1.89 (0.29)	3.92 (0.42)	5.61 (0.49)	1.97 (0.30)	4.12 (0.43)	5.92 (0.51)	2.05 (0.31)	4.32 (0.45)	6.24 (0.53)
32.	3.28 (0.40)	5.77 (0.50)	7.72 (0.56)	3.41 (0.41)	6.03 (0.52)	8.10 (0.58)	3.53 (0.43)	6.30 (0.53)	8.50 (0.60)
36.	5.11 (0.51)	7.93 (0.58)	10.08 (0.62)	5.27 (0.52)	8.25 (0.59)	10.54 (0.64)	5.44 (0.53)	8.58 (0.61)	11.01 (0.66)
40.	7.33 (0.60)	10.36 (0.64)	12.66 (0.67)	7.54 (0.61)	10.75 (0.65)	13.19 (0.69)	7.75 (0.62)	11.14 (0.67)	13.73 (0.70)
44.	9.89 (0.68)	13.03 (0.69)	15.42 (0.71)	10.14 (0.69)	13.47 (0.71)	16.02 (0.73)	10.39 (0.70)	13.92 (0.72)	16.62 (0.74)
48.	12.74 (0.74)	15.91 (0.74)	18.35 (0.75)	13.03 (0.75)	16.40 (0.75)	19.01 (0.76)	13.32 (0.76)	16.89 (0.77)	19.67 (0.78)
52.	15.83 (0.80)	18.95 (0.78)	21.41 (0.78)	16.15 (0.81)	19.49 (0.79)	22.13 (0.79)	16.48 (0.81)	20.03 (0.80)	22.85 (0.81)

TABLE 2. Option Values and Hedge Ratios for Different Stock Prices and Interest Rates, by Standard Deviation and Maturity.

Annual Std Dev = 0.20 Exercise Price = 40.

Price	3 Months			6 Months			9 Months		
	R=0.05	R=0.10	R=0.15	R=0.05	R=0.10	R=0.15	R=0.05	R=0.10	R=0.15
28.	0.00	0.00	0.00	0.01	0.02	0.04	0.07	0.12	0.20
	(0.00)	(0.01)	(0.04)	(0.00)	(0.02)	(0.06)	(0.00)	(0.03)	(0.09)
32.	0.02	0.03	0.04	0.18	0.26	0.37	0.44	0.65	0.93
	(0.02)	(0.09)	(0.16)	(0.03)	(0.12)	(0.22)	(0.04)	(0.16)	(0.29)
36.	0.36	0.45	0.55	0.94	1.22	1.55	1.50	2.01	2.61
	(0.19)	(0.31)	(0.38)	(0.23)	(0.37)	(0.46)	(0.26)	(0.44)	(0.55)
40.	1.85	2.12	2.41	2.76	3.31	3.92	3.51	4.35	5.27
	(0.57)	(0.60)	(0.62)	(0.62)	(0.66)	(0.70)	(0.66)	(0.73)	(0.77)
44.	4.80	5.22	5.65	5.63	6.41	7.21	6.38	7.49	8.64
	(0.87)	(0.82)	(0.80)	(0.89)	(0.86)	(0.86)	(0.92)	(0.90)	(0.90)
48.	8.54	9.02	9.49	9.18	10.08	10.97	9.83	11.11	12.39
	(0.98)	(0.94)	(0.91)	(0.98)	(0.96)	(0.94)	(0.99)	(0.97)	(0.96)
52.	12.50	12.99	13.47	13.04	13.98	14.91	13.60	14.96	16.30
	(1.00)	(0.98)	(0.97)	(1.00)	(0.99)	(0.98)	(1.00)	(0.99)	(0.99)

Annual Std Dev = 0.30 Exercise Price = 40.

Price	3 Months			6 Months			9 Months		
	R=0.05	R=0.10	R=0.15	R=0.05	R=0.10	R=0.15	R=0.05	R=0.10	R=0.15
28.	0.02	0.02	0.03	0.18	0.23	0.29	0.45	0.59	0.76
	(0.01)	(0.07)	(0.14)	(0.02)	(0.09)	(0.17)	(0.02)	(0.11)	(0.21)
32.	0.19	0.23	0.27	0.70	0.86	1.04	1.27	1.58	1.94
	(0.09)	(0.20)	(0.28)	(0.11)	(0.24)	(0.33)	(0.12)	(0.28)	(0.38)
36.	0.92	1.05	1.19	1.89	2.21	2.56	2.72	3.25	3.84
	(0.29)	(0.39)	(0.45)	(0.32)	(0.44)	(0.51)	(0.35)	(0.49)	(0.56)
40.	2.63	2.89	3.16	3.85	4.36	4.90	4.84	5.59	6.40
	(0.56)	(0.59)	(0.61)	(0.60)	(0.63)	(0.66)	(0.63)	(0.68)	(0.71)
44.	5.36	5.73	6.11	6.55	7.22	7.91	7.54	8.50	9.49
	(0.79)	(0.75)	(0.74)	(0.81)	(0.79)	(0.78)	(0.83)	(0.82)	(0.82)
48.	8.79	9.23	9.68	9.78	10.58	11.38	10.70	11.82	12.94
	(0.92)	(0.86)	(0.84)	(0.93)	(0.89)	(0.87)	(0.94)	(0.91)	(0.90)
52.	12.59	13.06	13.53	13.37	14.24	15.11	14.18	15.41	16.63
	(0.97)	(0.93)	(0.90)	(0.98)	(0.94)	(0.92)	(0.98)	(0.96)	(0.94)

Annual Std Dev = 0.40 Exercise Price = 40.

Price	3 Months			6 Months			9 Months		
	R=0.05	R=0.10	R=0.15	R=0.05	R=0.10	R=0.15	R=0.05	R=0.10	R=0.15
28.	0.12	0.13	0.15	0.55	0.65	0.76	1.09	1.30	1.54
	(0.05)	(0.15)	(0.23)	(0.06)	(0.17)	(0.26)	(0.07)	(0.20)	(0.30)
32.	0.53	0.60	0.67	1.42	1.62	1.85	2.26	2.62	3.02
	(0.17)	(0.29)	(0.36)	(0.19)	(0.32)	(0.40)	(0.20)	(0.35)	(0.44)
36.	1.57	1.72	1.87	2.88	3.22	3.58	3.96	4.49	5.06
	(0.36)	(0.44)	(0.49)	(0.38)	(0.48)	(0.53)	(0.41)	(0.51)	(0.58)
40.	3.42	3.67	3.92	4.95	5.43	5.93	6.17	6.87	7.60
	(0.56)	(0.59)	(0.61)	(0.59)	(0.62)	(0.65)	(0.61)	(0.66)	(0.69)
44.	6.04	6.38	6.72	7.57	8.18	8.80	8.82	9.67	10.56
	(0.74)	(0.71)	(0.71)	(0.76)	(0.74)	(0.75)	(0.78)	(0.77)	(0.78)
48.	9.26	9.66	10.06	10.63	11.34	12.06	11.83	12.82	13.82
	(0.86)	(0.81)	(0.79)	(0.87)	(0.83)	(0.82)	(0.88)	(0.85)	(0.85)
52.	12.85	13.29	13.73	14.01	14.80	15.59	15.11	16.21	17.31
	(0.93)	(0.88)	(0.85)	(0.94)	(0.89)	(0.87)	(0.95)	(0.91)	(0.90)

Annual Std Dev = 0.50 Exercise Price = 40.

Price	3 Months			6 Months			9 Months		
	R=0.05	R=0.10	R=0.15	R=0.05	R=0.10	R=0.15	R=0.05	R=0.10	R=0.15
28.	0.32	0.35	0.39	1.08	1.22	1.37	1.88	2.14	2.42
	(0.11)	(0.22)	(0.30)	(0.11)	(0.24)	(0.33)	(0.12)	(0.27)	(0.36)
32.	0.99	1.07	1.16	2.23	2.46	2.71	3.32	3.71	4.12
	(0.24)	(0.35)	(0.42)	(0.25)	(0.38)	(0.45)	(0.27)	(0.40)	(0.48)
36.	2.26	2.41	2.58	3.89	4.23	4.59	5.20	5.73	6.28
	(0.40)	(0.48)	(0.52)	(0.42)	(0.51)	(0.56)	(0.44)	(0.54)	(0.59)
40.	4.21	4.44	4.69	6.05	6.51	6.97	7.49	8.15	8.83
	(0.57)	(0.60)	(0.62)	(0.59)	(0.62)	(0.65)	(0.61)	(0.65)	(0.68)
44.	6.78	7.09	7.40	8.65	9.21	9.77	10.13	10.92	11.72
	(0.71)	(0.70)	(0.70)	(0.73)	(0.72)	(0.73)	(0.74)	(0.74)	(0.76)
48.	9.85	10.22	10.59	11.60	12.25	12.91	13.07	13.96	14.87
	(0.82)	(0.78)	(0.77)	(0.83)	(0.80)	(0.79)	(0.84)	(0.82)	(0.82)
52.	13.27	13.68	14.10	14.84	15.56	16.29	16.24	17.23	18.22
	(0.89)	(0.84)	(0.82)	(0.90)	(0.86)	(0.84)	(0.91)	(0.87)	(0.86)

TABLE 2. Option Values and Hedge Ratios for Different Stock Prices and Interest Rates, by Standard Deviation and Maturity. (Continued)

Annual Std Dev = 0.60   Exercise Price = 40.

Price	3 Months			6 Months			9 Months		
	R=0.05	R=0.10	R=0.15	R=0.05	R=0.10	R=0.15	R=0.05	R=0.10	R=0.15
28.	0.62	0.67	0.72	1.72	1.88	2.05	2.76	3.05	3.35
	(0.16)	(0.28)	(0.36)	(0.17)	(0.30)	(0.39)	(0.18)	(0.33)	(0.42)
32.	1.51	1.61	1.71	3.09	3.33	3.59	4.41	4.81	5.22
	(0.29)	(0.40)	(0.46)	(0.30)	(0.42)	(0.49)	(0.32)	(0.45)	(0.52)
36.	2.96	3.12	3.29	4.91	5.25	5.60	6.44	6.95	7.48
	(0.44)	(0.51)	(0.55)	(0.45)	(0.53)	(0.58)	(0.47)	(0.56)	(0.61)
40.	4.99	5.22	5.45	7.14	7.58	8.02	8.81	9.43	10.07
	(0.58)	(0.61)	(0.63)	(0.59)	(0.63)	(0.66)	(0.61)	(0.65)	(0.68)
44.	7.54	7.83	8.13	9.74	10.26	10.79	11.46	12.19	12.93
	(0.69)	(0.69)	(0.70)	(0.71)	(0.71)	(0.72)	(0.72)	(0.73)	(0.75)
48.	10.52	10.86	11.20	12.64	13.24	13.84	14.37	15.19	16.02
	(0.79)	(0.76)	(0.75)	(0.80)	(0.78)	(0.77)	(0.81)	(0.79)	(0.80)
52.	13.81	14.20	14.58	15.79	16.45	17.12	17.47	18.38	19.28
	(0.86)	(0.81)	(0.80)	(0.87)	(0.83)	(0.82)	(0.87)	(0.84)	(0.84)

Annual Std Dev = 0.70   Exercise Price = 40.

Price	3 Months			6 Months			9 Months		
	R=0.05	R=0.10	R=0.15	R=0.05	R=0.10	R=0.15	R=0.05	R=0.10	R=0.15
28.	0.99	1.05	1.12	2.42	2.60	2.78	3.69	3.99	4.31
	(0.21)	(0.34)	(0.41)	(0.22)	(0.35)	(0.44)	(0.23)	(0.37)	(0.46)
32.	2.08	2.19	2.30	3.97	4.23	4.49	5.51	5.91	6.33
	(0.33)	(0.44)	(0.50)	(0.35)	(0.46)	(0.52)	(0.36)	(0.48)	(0.55)
36.	3.67	3.84	4.01	5.92	6.26	6.60	7.67	8.16	8.67
	(0.46)	(0.53)	(0.58)	(0.48)	(0.55)	(0.60)	(0.49)	(0.57)	(0.62)
40.	5.77	6.00	6.22	8.23	8.64	9.07	10.11	10.70	11.30
	(0.58)	(0.62)	(0.64)	(0.60)	(0.64)	(0.67)	(0.61)	(0.66)	(0.69)
44.	8.32	8.59	8.87	10.84	11.33	11.83	12.79	13.47	14.16
	(0.69)	(0.69)	(0.70)	(0.70)	(0.71)	(0.72)	(0.71)	(0.72)	(0.74)
48.	11.23	11.55	11.88	13.72	14.27	14.83	15.69	16.45	17.21
	(0.77)	(0.75)	(0.75)	(0.78)	(0.76)	(0.77)	(0.79)	(0.78)	(0.79)
52.	14.44	14.80	15.16	16.81	17.42	18.04	18.76	19.59	20.43
	(0.83)	(0.80)	(0.79)	(0.84)	(0.81)	(0.80)	(0.85)	(0.82)	(0.82)

Annual Std Dev = 0.80   Exercise Price = 40.

Price	3 Months			6 Months			9 Months		
	R=0.05	R=0.10	R=0.15	R=0.05	R=0.10	R=0.15	R=0.05	R=0.10	R=0.15
28.	1.42	1.49	1.57	3.16	3.35	3.55	4.64	4.95	5.27
	(0.25)	(0.38)	(0.45)	(0.26)	(0.40)	(0.48)	(0.27)	(0.41)	(0.50)
32.	2.67	2.79	2.91	4.87	5.13	5.40	6.62	7.01	7.42
	(0.37)	(0.47)	(0.53)	(0.38)	(0.49)	(0.55)	(0.40)	(0.51)	(0.57)
36.	4.39	4.56	4.73	6.93	7.26	7.60	8.88	9.36	9.85
	(0.49)	(0.56)	(0.60)	(0.50)	(0.57)	(0.62)	(0.51)	(0.59)	(0.64)
40.	6.55	6.77	6.99	9.30	9.70	10.10	11.39	11.95	12.52
	(0.59)	(0.63)	(0.66)	(0.60)	(0.64)	(0.68)	(0.62)	(0.66)	(0.69)
44.	9.10	9.36	9.63	11.94	12.40	12.87	14.11	14.75	15.39
	(0.68)	(0.69)	(0.70)	(0.69)	(0.71)	(0.72)	(0.70)	(0.72)	(0.74)
48.	11.98	12.28	12.59	14.81	15.33	15.85	17.02	17.73	18.44
	(0.75)	(0.74)	(0.74)	(0.76)	(0.76)	(0.76)	(0.77)	(0.77)	(0.78)
52.	15.11	15.45	15.80	17.86	18.44	19.02	20.08	20.85	21.62
	(0.81)	(0.79)	(0.78)	(0.82)	(0.80)	(0.80)	(0.83)	(0.81)	(0.81)

Annual Std Dev = 0.90   Exercise Price = 40.

Price	3 Months			6 Months			9 Months		
	R=0.05	R=0.10	R=0.15	R=0.05	R=0.10	R=0.15	R=0.05	R=0.10	R=0.15
28.	1.89	1.97	2.05	3.92	4.12	4.32	5.61	5.92	6.24
	(0.29)	(0.42)	(0.49)	(0.30)	(0.43)	(0.51)	(0.31)	(0.45)	(0.53)
32.	3.28	3.41	3.53	5.77	6.03	6.30	7.72	8.10	8.50
	(0.40)	(0.50)	(0.56)	(0.41)	(0.52)	(0.58)	(0.43)	(0.53)	(0.60)
36.	5.11	5.27	5.44	7.93	8.25	8.58	10.08	10.54	11.01
	(0.51)	(0.58)	(0.62)	(0.52)	(0.59)	(0.64)	(0.53)	(0.61)	(0.66)
40.	7.33	7.54	7.75	10.36	10.75	11.14	12.66	13.19	13.73
	(0.60)	(0.64)	(0.67)	(0.61)	(0.65)	(0.69)	(0.62)	(0.67)	(0.70)
44.	9.89	10.14	10.39	13.03	13.47	13.92	15.42	16.02	16.62
	(0.68)	(0.69)	(0.71)	(0.69)	(0.71)	(0.73)	(0.70)	(0.72)	(0.74)
48.	12.74	13.03	13.32	15.91	16.40	16.89	18.35	19.01	19.67
	(0.74)	(0.74)	(0.74)	(0.75)	(0.75)	(0.76)	(0.76)	(0.77)	(0.78)
52.	15.83	16.15	16.48	18.95	19.49	20.03	21.41	22.13	22.85
	(0.80)	(0.78)	(0.78)	(0.81)	(0.79)	(0.79)	(0.81)	(0.80)	(0.81)

TABLE 3. Option Values and Hedge Ratios for Different Stock Prices and Standard Deviations, by Maturity and Interest Rate.

3 Months   R = 0.05   Exercise Price = 40.

Price	S.D.=0.20	S.D.=0.30	S.D.=0.40	S.D.=0.50	S.D.=0.60	S.D.=0.70	S.D.=0.80	S.D.=0.90
28.	0.00	0.02	0.12	0.32	0.62	0.99	1.42	1.89
	(0.00)	(0.01)	(0.05)	(0.11)	(0.16)	(0.21)	(0.25)	(0.29)
32.	0.02	0.19	0.53	0.99	1.51	2.08	2.67	3.28
	(0.02)	(0.09)	(0.17)	(0.24)	(0.29)	(0.33)	(0.37)	(0.40)
36.	0.36	0.92	1.57	2.26	2.96	3.67	4.39	5.11
	(0.19)	(0.29)	(0.36)	(0.40)	(0.44)	(0.46)	(0.49)	(0.51)
40.	1.85	2.63	3.42	4.21	4.99	5.77	6.55	7.33
	(0.57)	(0.56)	(0.56)	(0.57)	(0.58)	(0.58)	(0.59)	(0.60)
44.	4.80	5.36	6.04	6.78	7.54	8.32	9.10	9.89
	(0.87)	(0.79)	(0.74)	(0.71)	(0.69)	(0.69)	(0.68)	(0.68)
48.	8.54	8.79	9.26	9.85	10.52	11.23	11.98	12.74
	(0.98)	(0.92)	(0.86)	(0.82)	(0.79)	(0.77)	(0.75)	(0.74)
52.	12.50	12.59	12.85	13.27	13.81	14.44	15.11	15.83
	(1.00)	(0.97)	(0.93)	(0.89)	(0.86)	(0.83)	(0.81)	(0.80)

3 Months   R = 0.10   Exercise Price = 40.

Price	S.D.=0.20	S.D.=0.30	S.D.=0.40	S.D.=0.50	S.D.=0.60	S.D.=0.70	S.D.=0.80	S.D.=0.90
28.	0.00	0.02	0.13	0.35	0.67	1.05	1.49	1.97
	(0.00)	(0.02)	(0.06)	(0.11)	(0.17)	(0.22)	(0.26)	(0.30)
32.	0.03	0.23	0.60	1.07	1.61	2.19	2.79	3.41
	(0.03)	(0.11)	(0.19)	(0.25)	(0.30)	(0.35)	(0.38)	(0.41)
36.	0.45	1.05	1.72	2.41	3.12	3.84	4.56	5.27
	(0.23)	(0.32)	(0.38)	(0.42)	(0.45)	(0.48)	(0.50)	(0.52)
40.	2.12	2.89	3.67	4.44	5.22	6.00	6.77	7.54
	(0.62)	(0.60)	(0.59)	(0.59)	(0.59)	(0.60)	(0.60)	(0.61)
44.	5.22	5.73	6.38	7.09	7.83	8.59	9.36	10.14
	(0.89)	(0.81)	(0.76)	(0.73)	(0.71)	(0.70)	(0.69)	(0.69)
48.	9.02	9.23	9.66	10.22	10.86	11.55	12.28	13.03
	(0.98)	(0.93)	(0.87)	(0.83)	(0.80)	(0.78)	(0.76)	(0.75)
52.	12.99	13.06	13.29	13.68	14.20	14.80	15.45	16.15
	(1.00)	(0.98)	(0.94)	(0.90)	(0.87)	(0.84)	(0.82)	(0.81)

3 Months   R = 0.15   Exercise Price = 40.

Price	S.D.=0.20	S.D.=0.30	S.D.=0.40	S.D.=0.50	S.D.=0.60	S.D.=0.70	S.D.=0.80	S.D.=0.90
28.	0.00	0.03	0.15	0.39	0.72	1.12	1.57	2.05
	(0.00)	(0.02)	(0.07)	(0.12)	(0.18)	(0.23)	(0.27)	(0.31)
32.	0.04	0.27	0.67	1.16	1.71	2.30	2.91	3.53
	(0.04)	(0.12)	(0.20)	(0.27)	(0.32)	(0.36)	(0.40)	(0.43)
36.	0.55	1.19	1.87	2.58	3.29	4.01	4.73	5.44
	(0.26)	(0.35)	(0.41)	(0.44)	(0.47)	(0.49)	(0.51)	(0.53)
40.	2.41	3.16	3.92	4.69	5.45	6.22	6.99	7.75
	(0.66)	(0.63)	(0.61)	(0.61)	(0.61)	(0.61)	(0.62)	(0.62)
44.	5.65	6.11	6.72	7.40	8.13	8.87	9.63	10.39
	(0.92)	(0.83)	(0.78)	(0.74)	(0.72)	(0.71)	(0.70)	(0.70)
48.	9.49	9.68	10.06	10.59	11.20	11.88	12.59	13.32
	(0.99)	(0.94)	(0.88)	(0.84)	(0.81)	(0.79)	(0.77)	(0.76)
52.	13.47	13.53	13.73	14.10	14.58	15.16	15.80	16.48
	(1.00)	(0.98)	(0.95)	(0.91)	(0.87)	(0.85)	(0.83)	(0.81)

6 Months   R = 0.05   Exercise Price = 40.

Price	S.D.=0.20	S.D.=0.30	S.D.=0.40	S.D.=0.50	S.D.=0.60	S.D.=0.70	S.D.=0.80	S.D.=0.90
28.	0.01	0.18	0.55	1.08	1.72	2.42	3.16	3.92
	(0.01)	(0.07)	(0.15)	(0.22)	(0.28)	(0.34)	(0.38)	(0.42)
32.	0.18	0.70	1.42	2.23	3.09	3.97	4.87	5.77
	(0.09)	(0.20)	(0.29)	(0.35)	(0.40)	(0.44)	(0.47)	(0.50)
36.	0.94	1.89	2.88	3.89	4.91	5.92	6.93	7.93
	(0.31)	(0.39)	(0.44)	(0.48)	(0.51)	(0.53)	(0.56)	(0.58)
40.	2.76	3.85	4.95	6.05	7.14	8.23	9.30	10.36
	(0.60)	(0.59)	(0.59)	(0.60)	(0.61)	(0.62)	(0.63)	(0.64)
44.	5.63	6.55	7.57	8.65	9.74	10.84	11.94	13.03
	(0.82)	(0.75)	(0.71)	(0.70)	(0.69)	(0.69)	(0.69)	(0.69)
48.	9.18	9.78	10.63	11.60	12.64	13.72	14.81	15.91
	(0.94)	(0.86)	(0.81)	(0.78)	(0.76)	(0.75)	(0.74)	(0.74)
52.	13.04	13.37	14.01	14.84	15.79	16.81	17.86	18.95
	(0.98)	(0.93)	(0.88)	(0.84)	(0.81)	(0.80)	(0.79)	(0.78)

TABLE 3. Option Values and Hedge Ratios for Different Stock Prices and Standard Deviations, by Maturity and Interest Rate. (Continued)

6 Months   R = 0.10   Exercise Price = 40.

Price	S.D.=0.20	S.D.=0.30	S.D.=0.40	S.D.=0.50	S.D.=0.60	S.D.=0.70	S.D.=0.80	S.D.=0.90
28.	0.02	0.23	0.65	1.22	1.88	2.60	3.35	4.12
	(0.02)	(0.09)	(0.17)	(0.24)	(0.30)	(0.35)	(0.40)	(0.43)
32.	0.26	0.86	1.62	2.46	3.33	4.23	5.13	6.03
	(0.12)	(0.24)	(0.32)	(0.38)	(0.42)	(0.46)	(0.49)	(0.52)
36.	1.22	2.21	3.22	4.23	5.25	6.26	7.26	8.25
	(0.37)	(0.44)	(0.48)	(0.51)	(0.53)	(0.55)	(0.57)	(0.59)
40.	3.31	4.36	5.43	6.51	7.58	8.64	9.70	10.75
	(0.66)	(0.63)	(0.62)	(0.62)	(0.63)	(0.64)	(0.64)	(0.65)
44.	6.41	7.22	8.18	9.21	10.26	11.33	12.40	13.47
	(0.86)	(0.79)	(0.74)	(0.72)	(0.71)	(0.71)	(0.71)	(0.71)
48.	10.08	10.58	11.34	12.25	13.24	14.27	15.33	16.40
	(0.96)	(0.89)	(0.83)	(0.80)	(0.78)	(0.76)	(0.76)	(0.75)
52.	13.98	14.24	14.80	15.56	16.45	17.42	18.44	19.49
	(0.99)	(0.94)	(0.89)	(0.86)	(0.83)	(0.81)	(0.80)	(0.79)

6 Months   R = 0.15   Exercise Price = 40.

Price	S.D.=0.20	S.D.=0.30	S.D.=0.40	S.D.=0.50	S.D.=0.60	S.D.=0.70	S.D.=0.80	S.D.=0.90
28.	0.04	0.29	0.76	1.37	2.05	2.78	3.55	4.32
	(0.03)	(0.11)	(0.20)	(0.27)	(0.33)	(0.37)	(0.41)	(0.45)
32.	0.37	1.04	1.85	2.71	3.59	4.49	5.40	6.30
	(0.16)	(0.28)	(0.35)	(0.40)	(0.45)	(0.48)	(0.51)	(0.53)
36.	1.55	2.56	3.58	4.59	5.60	6.60	7.60	8.58
	(0.44)	(0.49)	(0.51)	(0.54)	(0.56)	(0.57)	(0.59)	(0.61)
40.	3.92	4.90	5.93	6.97	8.02	9.07	10.10	11.14
	(0.73)	(0.68)	(0.66)	(0.65)	(0.65)	(0.66)	(0.66)	(0.67)
44.	7.21	7.91	8.80	9.77	10.79	11.83	12.87	13.92
	(0.90)	(0.82)	(0.77)	(0.74)	(0.73)	(0.72)	(0.72)	(0.72)
48.	10.97	11.38	12.06	12.91	13.84	14.83	15.85	16.89
	(0.97)	(0.91)	(0.85)	(0.82)	(0.79)	(0.78)	(0.77)	(0.77)
52.	14.91	15.11	15.59	16.29	17.12	18.04	19.02	20.03
	(0.99)	(0.96)	(0.91)	(0.87)	(0.84)	(0.82)	(0.81)	(0.80)

9 Months   R = 0.05   Exercise Price = 40.

Price	S.D.=0.20	S.D.=0.30	S.D.=0.40	S.D.=0.50	S.D.=0.60	S.D.=0.70	S.D.=0.80	S.D.=0.90
28.	0.07	0.45	1.09	1.88	2.76	3.69	4.64	5.61
	(0.04)	(0.14)	(0.23)	(0.30)	(0.36)	(0.41)	(0.45)	(0.49)
32.	0.44	1.27	2.26	3.32	4.41	5.51	6.62	7.72
	(0.16)	(0.28)	(0.36)	(0.42)	(0.46)	(0.50)	(0.53)	(0.56)
36.	1.50	2.72	3.96	5.20	6.44	7.67	8.88	10.08
	(0.38)	(0.45)	(0.49)	(0.52)	(0.55)	(0.58)	(0.60)	(0.62)
40.	3.51	4.84	6.17	7.49	8.81	10.11	11.39	12.66
	(0.62)	(0.61)	(0.61)	(0.62)	(0.63)	(0.64)	(0.66)	(0.67)
44.	6.38	7.54	8.82	10.13	11.46	12.79	14.11	15.42
	(0.80)	(0.74)	(0.71)	(0.70)	(0.70)	(0.70)	(0.70)	(0.71)
48.	9.83	10.70	11.83	13.07	14.37	15.69	17.02	18.35
	(0.91)	(0.84)	(0.79)	(0.77)	(0.75)	(0.75)	(0.75)	(0.75)
52.	13.60	14.18	15.11	16.24	17.47	18.76	20.08	21.41
	(0.97)	(0.90)	(0.85)	(0.82)	(0.80)	(0.79)	(0.78)	(0.78)

9 Months   R = 0.10   Exercise Price = 40.

Price	S.D.=0.20	S.D.=0.30	S.D.=0.40	S.D.=0.50	S.D.=0.60	S.D.=0.70	S.D.=0.80	S.D.=0.90
28.	0.12	0.59	1.30	2.14	3.05	3.99	4.95	5.92
	(0.06)	(0.17)	(0.26)	(0.33)	(0.39)	(0.44)	(0.48)	(0.51)
32.	0.65	1.58	2.62	3.71	4.81	5.91	7.01	8.10
	(0.22)	(0.33)	(0.40)	(0.45)	(0.49)	(0.52)	(0.55)	(0.58)
36.	2.01	3.25	4.49	5.73	6.95	8.16	9.36	10.54
	(0.46)	(0.51)	(0.53)	(0.56)	(0.58)	(0.60)	(0.62)	(0.64)
40.	4.35	5.59	6.87	8.15	9.43	10.70	11.95	13.19
	(0.70)	(0.66)	(0.65)	(0.65)	(0.66)	(0.67)	(0.68)	(0.69)
44.	7.49	8.50	9.67	10.92	12.19	13.47	14.75	16.02
	(0.86)	(0.78)	(0.75)	(0.73)	(0.72)	(0.72)	(0.72)	(0.73)
48.	11.11	11.82	12.82	13.96	15.19	16.45	17.73	19.01
	(0.94)	(0.87)	(0.82)	(0.79)	(0.77)	(0.77)	(0.76)	(0.76)
52.	14.96	15.41	16.21	17.23	18.38	19.59	20.85	22.13
	(0.98)	(0.92)	(0.87)	(0.84)	(0.82)	(0.80)	(0.80)	(0.79)

TABLE 3. Option Values and Hedge Ratios for Different Stock Prices and Standard Deviations, by Maturity and Interest Rate. (Continued)

9 Months   R = 0.15   Exercise Price = 40.

Price	S.D. = 0.20	S.D. = 0.30	S.D. = 0.40	S.D. = 0.50	S.D. = 0.60	S.D. = 0.70	S.D. = 0.80	S.D. = 0.90
28.	0.20	0.76	1.54	2.42	3.35	4.31	5.27	6.24
	(0.09)	(0.21)	(0.30)	(0.36)	(0.42)	(0.46)	(0.50)	(0.53)
32.	0.93	1.94	3.02	4.12	5.22	6.33	7.42	8.50
	(0.29)	(0.38)	(0.44)	(0.48)	(0.52)	(0.55)	(0.57)	(0.60)
36.	2.61	3.84	5.06	6.28	7.48	8.67	9.85	11.01
	(0.55)	(0.56)	(0.58)	(0.59)	(0.61)	(0.62)	(0.64)	(0.66)
40.	5.27	6.40	7.60	8.83	10.07	11.30	12.52	13.73
	(0.77)	(0.71)	(0.69)	(0.68)	(0.68)	(0.69)	(0.69)	(0.70)
44.	8.64	9.49	10.56	11.72	12.93	14.16	15.39	16.62
	(0.90)	(0.82)	(0.78)	(0.76)	(0.75)	(0.74)	(0.74)	(0.74)
48.	12.39	12.94	13.82	14.87	16.02	17.21	18.44	19.67
	(0.96)	(0.90)	(0.85)	(0.82)	(0.80)	(0.79)	(0.78)	(0.78)
52.	16.30	16.63	17.31	18.22	19.28	20.43	21.62	22.85
	(0.99)	(0.94)	(0.90)	(0.86)	(0.84)	(0.82)	(0.81)	(0.81)

Footnotes

1. For descriptions of options trading, see "New Game in Town" (1974), "Option Plays Are Spreading" (1973), and "The Values in Options" (1973) listed under References, and the current OCC *Prospectus*. Relevant books include Thorp and Kassouf (1967), and Malkiel and Quandt (1969).
2. See Black and Scholes (1972, 1973).
3. For some refinements and extensions, see Merton (1973).
4. More precisely, the position is short two-option contracts and long one round lot of stock, or long two-option contracts and short one round lot of stock.
5. The net money in a position is the value of any stock or options long in the investor's account minus the value of any stock or options that he is short. When he has no short positions, his net money is just the value of the stock or options in his account.
6. In fact, the $3,000 in certificates of deposit will earn interest, so the possible loss in the option position is even less than $1,000.
7. In this paragraph, I am using "speculative" and "conservative" as I take them to be used in ordinary language as related to investments.
8. Writing naked options is writing options without holding the underlying stock.
9. This assumes that the options are priced according to the formula. If they are overpriced, it may be possible to create a hedge that is long stock and short options and that shows losses only for large increases in the stock price.
10. For a proof of this, see Merton (1973, pp. 151-156).
11. This method is only an approximation. It assumes that the dividend is known for sure, and will neither be increased nor decreased. For options that expire in less than a year, this assumption gives a value

that is very close to the correct value. When there is a possibility that the option will be exercised before an early ex-dividend date, we do calculations assuming expiration just before every ex-dividend date, and use the one that gives the highest value.
12. For extensive discussions of the role of information trading in determining a market maker's spread, see Bagehot (1971) and Black (1971).
13. For a discussion of the factors affecting the quality of the market for a stock, see Black (1971).

References

Bagehot, Walter. "The Only Game in Town." *Financial Analysts Journal* (March/April 1971), pp. 12-15.

Black, Fischer. "Toward a Fully Automated Exchange." *Financial Analysts Journal*, Parts I and II (July/August and November/December 1971).

Black, Fischer, and Myron Scholes. "The Valuation of Option Contracts and a Test of Market Efficiency." *Journal of Finance* (May 1972), pp. 399-417.

_____. "The Pricing of Options and Corporate Liabilities." *Journal of Political Economy* (May/June 1973), pp. 637-654.

Malkiel, Burton G. and Richard E. Quandt. *Strategies and Rational Decisions in the Securities Options Market*. Cambridge, Massachusetts: MIT Press, 1969.

Merton, Robert G. "Theory of Rational Option Pricing." *Bell Journal of Economics and Management Science* (Spring 1973), pp. 141-183.

"New Game in Town." *Wall Street Journal* (April 22, 1974), p. 1.

"Option Plays Are Spreading." *Business Week* (December 22, 1973), p. 104.

"The Values in Options." *Fortune* (November 1973), p. 89.

Thorp, Edward O. and Sheen T. Kassouf. *Beat the Market*. New York: Random House, 1967.

by Stephen M. Schaefer

The Problem with Redemption Yields

◀ A coupon bond resembles a portfolio of pure discount bonds in that it makes payments at a number of future dates. In an efficient market, the price of a coupon bond should equal the price of the corresponding portfolio of pure discount bonds. Such a market discounts payments made by different bonds at the same point in time at the same spot rate — the rate of exchange between money today and money at a single date in the future — whereas it discounts payments made by the same bond at different points in time at different spot rates.

These properties of spot rates contrast sharply with the properties of the redemption yield — the single internal rate of return equating the discounted value of all future payments to a bond's price. Redemption yield is a derived figure; we need to know the bond's price before we compute it. The redemption yield, therefore, cannot help us estimate the bond's value.

When comparing two or more bonds, it is far more useful to estimate the relevant sequence of spot rates than to calculate the bonds' redemption yields. ▶

THE REDEMPTION YIELD is such a basic item in the bond manager's toolbox that it is sometimes useful to remember its serious limitations: Firstly, yield is an imprecise measure of investment value; secondly, since yields depend on the coupon, yields of bonds with different coupons will not generally lie along a smooth curve. Fitting a curve through points that *do* not and *should* not lie along a curve is unlikely to be a profitable exercise,

Stephen Schaefer, Prudential Research Fellow in Investment at the London Graduate School of Business Studies, is currently Visiting Assistant Professor at the University of Chicago Graduate School of Business. He is more than usually grateful to Professor Richard Brealey for his assistance in the preparation of this article, though the author is naturally responsible for any errors in the end result.

and deviations from such a curve will not imply anything about over- or underpricing. Thirdly, volatilities calculated on a yield basis are not comparable, and therefore tell us nothing about a bond's opportunity or risk.

The redemption yield on a bond is, of course, just the internal rate of return over the life of the bond. Many of the issues raised in this paper correspond to well known objections to the use of the internal rate of return as an investment criterion.

Yield as a Measure of Value

In economics, a spot interest rate usually measures the rate of exchange between money today and money at a *single* date in the future. On a coupon-bearing bond, where there are intervening payments, the spot rate is distinct from the redemption yield. If the one-year spot rate is R_1, the present value of one dollar paid in a year's time is:

$$d_1 = \frac{1}{(1 + R_1)}.$$

Similarly, if the two-year spot rate is R_2, the present value of one dollar paid in two years' time is:

$$d_2 = \frac{1}{(1 + R_2)^2}.$$

Spot rates will depend on the consensus of individuals' time preferences, expectations of future yields and degrees of risk-aversion.

We can think of d_1 as the market price of a pure discount bond promising to pay one dollar in one year's time and d_2 as the value of a similar bond promising to pay one dollar in two years' time.[1] A coupon bond resembles a *portfolio* of pure discount bonds in that it makes payments at a number of future dates. An efficient market offers little reward to packaging securities, hence the price of a coupon bond should be similar to the price of the corresponding portfolio of pure discount bonds. For example, a bond with a 10 per cent coupon and a face

---

1. Footnotes appear at end of article.

value of $100 maturing in two years would have a present value of $10d_1 + 110d_2$, which equals:

$$\frac{10}{(1 + R_1)} + \frac{110}{(1 + R_2)^2}$$

Similarly, a bond with a six per cent coupon maturing in three years would have a present value equaling:

$$\frac{6}{(1 + R_1)} + \frac{6}{(1 + R_2)^2} + \frac{106}{(1 + R_3)^3}$$

The above formulas underscore two important points: (1) Payments made by different bonds at the same point in time are discounted at the same rate and (2) payments made by the same bond at different points in time are typically discounted at different rates. Precisely the opposite is true of the redemption yield, which is the single internal rate of return equating the discounted value of all future payments to the bond's current price. Thus, if the price of the two-year 10 per cent bond is P, we calculate the redemption yield by finding the value of y that satisfies the equation:

$$P = \frac{10}{(1 + y)} + \frac{110}{(1 + y)^2}$$

This implies that payments made by the same bond at different points in time are all discounted at the same rate, y. Correspondingly, one dollar derived from a 10 per cent bond is not assumed to be worth the same as one dollar derived from a six per cent bond.

A further major disadvantage of the redemption yield lies in the fact that it is a derived figure. In our economic model, individual preferences and expectations combine to determine spot rates. Discounting the payments at the appropriate spot rates then determines the price of any coupon bond. Finally, the price and coupon payments together imply a redemption yield. In other words, we need to know the price *before* we can compute the redemption yield. Knowing the redemption yield for one bond, with its particular pattern of payments, will not tell us anything about the appropriate yield for a second bond with a different pattern of payments. Since we need to know a bond's value to compute the redemption yield, the redemption yield cannot be of any use in estimating the bond's value. We cannot reach heaven by hauling on our bootstraps.

The complexity of the yield concept brings with it a further serious shortcoming. Institutions hold portfolios, rather than individual bonds; it is the characteristics of the portfolio that are of primary interest. Although many institutions calculate the average yield on their holdings, the yield on the portfolio does *not* in fact equal the average of the yields on the individual holdings, and indeed cannot be calculated from these yields. For example, suppose we invested $100 in a three per cent five-year bond priced at 91.25 to yield five per cent and $100 in a 12 per cent five-year bond priced at 107.72 to yield 10 per cent. The average redemption yield is 7.5 per cent, but the redemption yield on the portfolio is 7.42 per cent. Its inability to tell us anything about the characteristics of the portfolio seriously limits the usefulness of the redemption yield.

In discussing the redemption yield, many investors place great emphasis on the importance of the rates at which future coupons may be reinvested. They point out that only if coupons can be reinvested at a rate equal to the redemption yield will the realized return equal the redemption yield. While correct, this fact proves quite irrelevant to the problem of assessing the relative values of riskless bonds. The important parameters are, rather, the spot rates implicit in today's prices; because they permit calculation of present values, spot rates —not future values based on some assumed reinvestment rate— represent the important quantities for the investment decision.

The Yield Curve

Since we can deduce so little from a direct comparison of redemption yields, it is perhaps not surprising that more elaborate calculations based on these measures yield little further information. As we have already indicated, the redemption yield depends not only on the spot rates and term to maturity, but also on the size of the coupon. In general, two bonds with the same maturity but different coupons will have different redemption yields. Trying to fit a smooth curve through a set of points that do not lie on the same curve is therefore pointless, and it is even more pointless to try to read omens in the deviations from the curve.

A more useful exercise is to estimate the sequence of spot rates, since we may expect these to lie on a smooth curve. There are several alternative ways to do this.[3] The most appropriate method in any particular case will depend primarily on the characteristics of the data. The calculated spot rates (or "zero-coupon yield curve") may be substantially different from the redemption yields for corresponding maturities. Figure 1 shows an estimated spot rate curve and corresponding redemption yields for the British Government Securities Market in September 1974. Notice that, while yields on 25-year bonds were approximately 15 per cent, the 25-year spot rate is estimated at over 25 per cent.

The Relationship between Redemption Yields and Spot Rates

It was suggested earlier that a coupon-bearing bond could be regarded as a portfolio of pure discount bonds. In the same way, so long as the coupon stream is uniform, we may consider an n-period bond as a portfolio containing an n-period annuity (the coupon stream) and a pure discount bond (the

principal repayment). For example, a three-year bond with a 10 per cent coupon may be regarded as a portfolio containing 10 one dollar per year three-year annuities and 100 three-year pure discount bonds, each paying one dollar at maturity.

Now, the price of an n-year annuity depends solely on the spot rates $R_1, R_2, \ldots, R_n$. Thus the redemption yield on an annuity, the *annuity yield*,

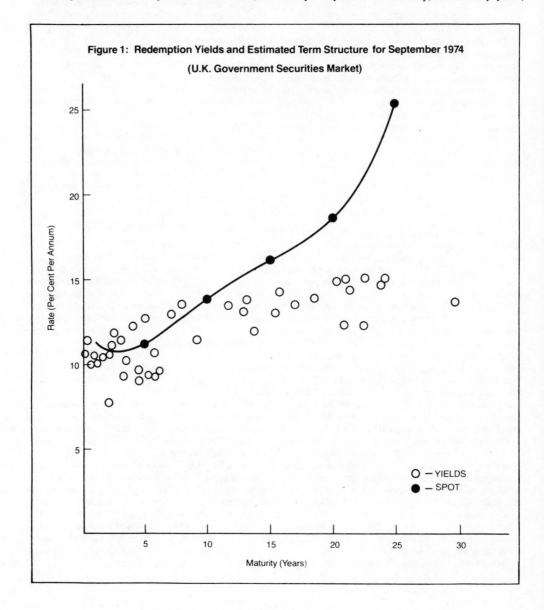

Figure 1: Redemption Yields and Estimated Term Structure for September 1974
(U.K. Government Securities Market)

also depends on $R_1, R_2, \ldots, R_n$. For any spot rate curve there exists, therefore, a corresponding annuity yield curve. The redemption yield on an n-period coupon-bearing bond is an average of the n-period annuity yield and the n-period spot rate, in the sense that the yield on the bond always lies between these two numbers.[4] Figure 2 shows a spot rate curve and the corresponding annuity yield curve; the redemption yields on all coupon-bearing bonds lie in the shaded area between the curves. Because the annuity yield is itself an average of the spot rates, the annuity yield curve will tend to lie below a rising spot rate curve and above a falling spot rate curve. It is possible for the annuity yield curve and the spot rate curve to intersect—as they do at point X in Figure 2—and in this case all coupon-bearing bonds with that maturity have the same redemption yield. We will elaborate on this point later.

Meanwhile, consider the effect of coupon size on the redemption yield when maturity is held constant. Just as a discount bond may be thought of as a zero-coupon bond, so an annuity may be considered an infinite-coupon bond. We might imagine, therefore, that as the size of the coupon increases, the redemption yield tends away from the spot rate curve towards the annuity yield curve.[5] This is indeed the case: When the spot rate is higher than the corresponding annuity yield, redemption yields decline with increasing coupon and vice versa. This result may be concisely stated as:

$$\frac{dy_n}{dc} \lessgtr 0 \text{ as } R_n \gtrless A_n'$$

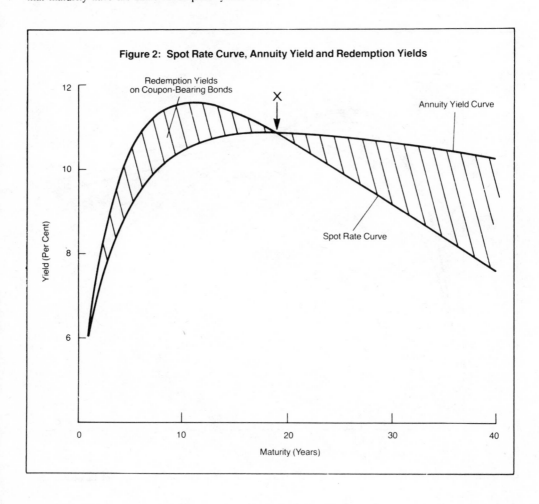

Figure 2: Spot Rate Curve, Annuity Yield and Redemption Yields

where y_n is the redemption yield on an n-period bond with coupon c, A_n is the n-period annuity yield and, as before, R_n is the n-period spot rate. Redemption yields on bonds with a given coupon will lie on a smooth curve; Figure 3 illustrates several such curves.

The result given above has to do only with the relative *location* of constant-coupon yield curves; what about their shape? In particular we might consider whether, for a given maturity, all constant-coupon yield curves have slopes with the same sign. In other words, even if we restrict our attention to constant-coupon yield curves, can we talk about yield curves rising or falling at a particular maturity without specifying the coupon size? Perhaps, surprisingly, we cannot. For example, a rising (monotonic) spot rate curve can produce hump-shaped constant-coupon yield curves for low coupon bonds. These result from the difference in characteristics between short- and long-maturity low coupon bonds. The former behave much like discount bonds, and their redemption yields are close to the spot rates. The latter, like all long-maturity bonds, are similar to annuities; when spot rates are monotonic increasing, the yield on these bonds may be substantially below the term structure and the associated yield curves may thus be humped.

If the spot rate is higher than the annuity yield and the spot rate curve has a small positive slope, a given constant-coupon yield curve can be upward sloping, at maturity n, when:

$$C/F > R_n - 1/n ,$$

where C/F is the ratio of coupon to face value and

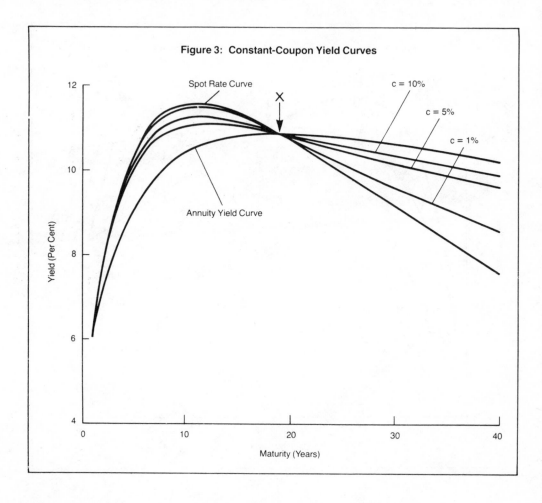

Figure 3: Constant-Coupon Yield Curves

R_n is the n-period spot rate. Yield curves for coupons lower than this value may be downward sloping at this point; all yield curves for higher coupons—including, of course, the annuity yield curve—will be upward sloping at this maturity.

Figure 4 shows a rising monotonic spot rate curve, the corresponding annuity yield curve, and constant-coupon yield curves for coupons of one per cent, five per cent and 10 per cent. The one per cent curve has a pronounced hump, the five per cent curve a slight hump and the 10 per cent curve, like the spot rate curve and the annuity yield curve, is monotonic. Notice also that all constant-coupon yield curves *except* the spot rate curve tend towards the annuity yield curve as maturity increases. They are also asymptotically horizontal no matter what shape the spot rate curve adopts. So long as spot rates are posi-

tive, this is simply a result of the arithmetic. On the other hand, there is no reason why the underlying spot rate curve should eventually become horizontal.

For practical purposes the details of these results are perhaps of only slight importance. They do illustrate, however, how difficult it is, in view of their very complex nature, to draw any sensible conclusions from the direct comparison of redemption yields. Spot rates, on the other hand, do permit logically consistent comparisons of bond prices.

Intersecting Yield Curves and the Par Yield Curve

We pointed out earlier that, when the spot rate curve and the annuity yield curve intersect, the redemption yields on all coupon-bearing bonds equal

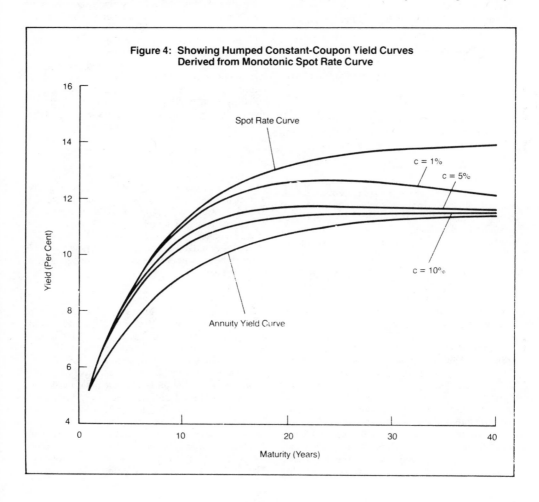

Figure 4: Showing Humped Constant-Coupon Yield Curves Derived from Monotonic Spot Rate Curve

TABLE 1: A Term Structure That Produces Intersecting Yield Curves for n = 3

Period	Spot Rate	Discount Factor	Annuity Price	Annuity Yield
j	R_j	d_j	a_j	A_j
1	0.0658	0.9383	0.9383	0.0658
2	0.1200	0.7971	1 7354	0.1000
3	0.1000	0.7513	2.4868	0.1000

the spot rate and the annuity yield at their point of intersection. This phenomenon occurs when the spot rate curve satisfies the following condition:

$$R_n = \frac{1 - d_n}{a_n} \quad,$$

where, as before, R_n is the n-period spot rate, d_n is the present value of one dollar paid at time n, or

$$d_n = \frac{1}{(1 + R_n)^n} \quad,$$

and a_n is the present value of an n-period annuity, or

$$a_n = \sum_{j=1}^{n} d_j \quad.$$

Table 1 gives an example of a term structure that satisfies this condition for n = 3. Notice that the right-hand side of the equation equals:

$$\frac{1 - d_3}{a_3} = \frac{1 - 0.7513}{2.4868} = 0.1000 \quad,$$

which is equal to R_3, the three-year spot rate. If we now calculate the price of a bond with an arbitrarily chosen coupon, we shall find that the implied redemption yield is always 10 per cent. For example, if we make the coupon 10 per cent, the price of a bond with face value $100 is given by:

$$p = 10d_1 + 10d_2 + 110d_3 = 10a_3 + 100d_3.$$

Substituting the values given in Table 1, we obtain a price of exactly $100. In other words, a three-year bond with a coupon of 10 per cent would sell at par; consequently the redemption yield must be 10 per cent.[6]

The right-hand side of the equation has another more general interpretation: It is the coupon that has to be offered to make an n-period bond sell at par. The "par yield curve," a plot of these values against maturity, will be a smooth curve and represents an alternative, logically consistent way of describing the term structure. Indeed it may appeal to practitioners more than the spot rate curve, since par yields will generally lie closer to redemption yields than spot rates do. The calculation of par yields requires estimation of spot rates as an intermediate step, how-

ever; one cannot calculate par yields directly from redemption yields. Figure 5 shows the estimated par yield curve for the data displayed in Figure 1.

Volatility

We have shown that redemption yields on bonds with different coupons are not properly comparable. The same point applies to measures based on redemption yields, of which volatility is the most common example. Volatility is usually defined as the change in price (or proportional change in price) for a given change in yield. It is used both to measure risk and to select bonds, given an assessment of future interest rates. Thus if bond A has a higher volatility than bond B, it would be argued that a given fall in yield would produce a larger proportional price increment in A than in B. We must remember, however, that redemption yields are altered by changes in spot rates, and that a given change in spot rates will generally change by different amounts the redemption yields of two bonds with different coupons. Thus, even though A has a higher volatility than B, it is quite possible that spot rates may change in such a way that B's proportional price increment will exceed A's. The relationship between price change, volatility and change in redemption yield is a tautology, and tells us nothing about how prices of different bonds will change as the underlying interest rates change.

Conclusion

The explanation for the wide use of redemption yield is obvious: Given the terms of a bond and its price, the redemption yield can be calculated unambiguously even if only one bond is available. By contrast, in the absence of pure discount bonds, we can only estimate spot rates—and then only if we have a sample of issues. Similarly, the redemption yield appears to offer the advantages of economy, for a bond has only one redemption yield, even if each payment is discounted at a different rate. But these characteristics are weaknesses, not strengths. Because a yield is unique to a security, rather than to a payment, comparison between bonds is wholly impossible. The redemption yield is calculable and un-

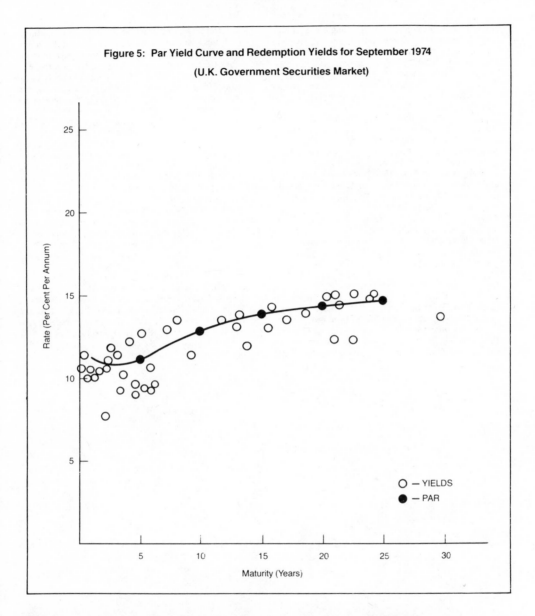

Figure 5: Par Yield Curve and Redemption Yields for September 1974

(U.K. Government Securities Market)

ambiguous only because its calculation is based on the price or value. As a summary description of the way things are, it has no place in any analysis of how things should or will be.

Bond management will make real progress only when investors start to think in terms of present values rather than future values, and they can do this only if they think in terms of the underlying spot rates, rather than the yield to maturity. ∎

Footnotes

1. $d_1, d_2 \ldots$ are sometimes called "discount factors," and $R_1, R_2 \ldots$ the term structure.

2. While this is the standard discounting formula, it is worthwhile bearing in mind the conditions under which it holds. Bonds will be priced according to a common set of spot rates provided that a bond matures in each future period and that short selling is allowed. (This guarantees a complete market.) However, it will

not hold if, for example (a) short selling is not allowed *and* (b) coupon payments and principal repayments are taxed at different rates for some investors *and* (c) there is some heterogeneity in inve ⌐r tax rates.

3. See W.T. Carleton and I.A. Cooper, "Estimation and Uses of the Term Structure of Interest Rates" (paper delivered at Annual Meeting of European Finance Association, London, September, 1975); J.H. McCulloch, "Measuring the Term Structure of Interest Rates," *Journal of Business* (January 1971), pp. 19-31; S.M. Schaefer, "On Measuring the Term Structure of Interest Rates" (London Graduate School of Business Studies, Institute of Finance and Accounting Working Paper IFA-2-74); and S.D. Hodges and S.M. Schaefer, "A Model for Bond Portfolio Improvement," forthcoming in *Journal of Financial and Quantitative Analysis.*

4. The proof of this and the other propositions in the text are not given here for the sake of brevity but are included in a supplement available from the author.

5. See A. Buse, "Expectations, Prices, Coupons and Yields," *Journal of Finance* (September 1970), pp. 809-818; J.L. Carr, P.J. Halpern and J.S. McCallum, "Correcting the Yield Curve: a Re-Interpretation of the Duration Problem" *Journal of Finance* (September 1974), pp. 1287-1294; C. Khang, "Expectation, Prices, Coupons and Yields: Comment," *Journal of Finance* (September 1975), pp. 1137-1140; B.G. Malkiel, *The Term Structure of Interest Rates* (Englewood Cliffs, N.J.: Prentice-Hall, 1966); and

Schaefer, "On Measuring the Term Structure of Interest Rates." Their results are special cases of this result. The results of these authors concern the sign of dy/dc when the term structure is rising or falling. A rising or falling term structure is sufficient but not necessary for establishing the sign of dy/dc, whereas this condition is both necessary and sufficient. In the U.K., where yields have generally increased with maturity, the relationship between redemption yields and coupon level has usually been the reverse of that predicted by the result. The explanation is connected with the tax system and, more particularly, with the fact that the conditions for the simple discounting formula to apply do not, most probably, obtain. See Footnote 2.

6. Table 1 provides a counterexample to Weingartner's proposition that "two bonds having the same term-to-maturity and the same frequency of coupons, but having different uniform coupons, cannot have the same yield-to-maturity unless the market yield curve is absolutely flat." See H.H. Weingartner, "The Generalised Rate of Return." *Journal of Financial and Quantitative Analysis* (September 1966), p. 14.

7. The Bank of England has, for some years, been publishing estimates of par yields in the *Bank of England Quarterly Bulletin.* See J.P. Burman and W.R. White, "Yield Curves for Gilt Edged Stocks," *Bank of England Quarterly Bulletin* (December 1972), pp. 467-486 and J.P. Burman, "Yield Curves for Gilt Edged Stocks," *BEQB* (September 1973), pp. 315-326 and (June 1976), pp. 212-215.

49

A CRITIQUE OF SOME RECENT EMPIRICAL RESEARCH ON THE EXPLANATION OF THE TERM STRUCTURE OF INTEREST RATES

L. G. TELSER[*]

University of Chicago

I. INTRODUCTION

MY PURPOSE is to analyze the relevance of recent empirical research on the term structure of interest rates in choosing among competing theories of the determinants of the term structure. In particular, two theories have been the subject of serious consideration. The first, known as the expectations theory, asserts that spot interest rates of loans of different maturities depend solely on market expectations of future interest rates. The current term structure forecasts the later term structure. The rival theory, known as the liquidity preference theory, denies that the current term structure provides unbiased forecasts of subsequent interest rates. Adherents of this theory claim that the risk aversion of lenders makes them value the stability of principal more than the stability of income. Principal is impaired if there is an unforeseen rise in interest rates while the stability of income is reduced from a policy of successively lending a given principal for short time periods. Supporters of the liquidity premium theory conclude that as a result long-term interest rates normally exceed short-term rates. Therefore, forecasts of future rates embodied in the

present term structure systematically overestimate the spot rates that materialize. It should be noted that this form of risk has nothing to do with the chance of borrowers' default; liquidity preference would exist even if bonds were guaranteed against default.

One would think that cash is the most liquid of all assets since, abstracting from changes in the price level, the principal is literally fixed. However, to explain why firms hold cash instead of lending on call, it is unnecessary to rely on a liquidity preference theory. In fact, if transactions costs were zero, then lending on call would be preferable to holding cash. Hence the holding of cash is explained by the fact that transactions costs are not zero. Therefore, transactions costs are one of the determinants of interest rates particularly important on loans of the shortest maturity. However, as far as I know, this is one of the most neglected determinants of the term structure in the formal treatments of the theory. The absence of formal analysis also explains the neglect of this factor in empirical work.

Interpretation of the empirical evidence relies on a careful study of the implications of these two explanations of the term structure. There are at least three sources of contention. First, universal risk aversion of both borrowers and lenders does not constrain the term structure in the way described by the

* I am grateful to Merton H. Miller for helpful discussion on this topic. I also wish to thank Dave Fand, Harry Johnson, Bert Malkiel, and the members of the Money Workshop of the University of Chicago for their comments and criticisms. Responsibility for all errors is mine.

liquidity preference theory. Risk aversion does not imply that forecasts of future interest rates are biased upward rather than downward. For example, a lender can increase his risk by purchasing short-term bonds if he has long-term payment commitments because his receipts would be subject to larger random fluctuations than his payments. Similarly, a borrower can increase his risks by long-term borrowing if he has short-term payment commitments. Risk aversion of both borrowers and lenders implies they will attempt to hedge against the risk of changes in interest rates by financial transactions intended to approximately match the timing of payments and receipts. However, it does not follow that such hedging results in a bias that can be deduced a priori.

Second, it is necessary in empirical work to specify how expectations are revised or formed. This raises the troublesome question of whether the empirical evidence refutes *the* expectations theory somehow defined or some investigator's empirical version of the formation of expectations. These difficulties are heightened by the fact that the market rates of interest reflect individual differences of expectations. Hence there are no obvious criteria that enable scholars to choose among alternative expectations models. Nor is this all.

Third, individuals change their expectations in the course of time. This makes it hard to tell whether a given term structure reflects a set of widely held beliefs about future conditions that would imply higher future interest rates (such as in the 1930's when long-term rates exceeded short-term rates) or the manifestation of liquidity preference. Perhaps expectations of lower interest rates in the future during a long period of prosperity would inspire the construction of the theories of

negative liquidity preference because the observed term structure would have higher short-term than long-term interest rates.

These three points do not question the assumption of universal risk aversion—an assumption that implies that individuals must be especially compensated for undertaking risky ventures. Yet it is well known that some individuals accept risk without special compensation, and most individuals some of the time expose themselves to risk without special compensation. Nevertheless, even if one accepts the assumption of universal risk aversion, there remains the task of deducing its empirical consequences.

II. THE ARITHMETIC OF THE TERM STRUCTURE

The link between future and present interest rates is inspired by some simple arithmetic relations implied by alternative finance programs involving the purchase and sale of bonds of different maturities. These programs show how to to fix the interest rate to be paid for a loan that will commence in the future. Interest rates on such loans are called "forward" rates. An interest rate fixed in the present for a loan that begins at once is a "spot" rate. We now derive the relations between spot and forward interest rates.

To represent the interest rates involved in the pertinent financial programs of purchases and sales of bonds of different maturities, it is necessary to adopt a somewhat cumbersome notation. I shall partly follow prevailing conventions by using R to denote spot rates and r to denote forward rates. For the former, two subscripts are necessary, the first to denote the duration of the loan and the second to give the date on which the interest rate is fixed and the loan begins.

An additional subscript is required for a forward rate since the date at which a forward loan can begin comes at any time specified following the time at which the interest rate is determined. Thus for the spot rate, let $R_{n,t}$ = the spot rate on an n period loan to begin at time t. For forward rates, let $r_{n,t,s}$ = the forward rate for a loan of n periods as determined in period t, the loan to commence at time $s \geq t$. It follows that $R_{n,t} \equiv r_{n,t,t}$.

The term structure of interest rates is the set of spot rates on loans alike in every respect save for their duration. Thus it is the sequence of spot rates as follows: $R_{1,t}, R_{2,t}, R_{3,t}, \ldots, R_{n,t}, \ldots$.

One aspect of empirical research into the term structure is the adjustment of the observed interest rates in order to make them comparable in every respect except term to maturity. These adjustments are necessary because bonds can differ in their coupons, call provisions, tax advantages, default risk, eligibility as collateral for special purposes, and so forth. In theoretical analysis it is convenient to assume that the necessary adjustments have been made so that all bonds of the same maturity are perfect substitutes. In addition, in order to avoid complicated algebra it is convenient to assume that interest is paid at the maturity date of the bonds and that transactions costs are zero.

Analysis of the forecasts of future interest rates implicit in the current term structure begins with consideration of the alternative means of finance afforded by the purchase and sale of bonds of different maturities. Since at time t it is possible to buy and sell bonds of any maturity, one can arrange for loans to begin at some future date at an interest rate presently determined. Thus if a lender at time t wishes to borrow funds for k periods to be delivered at time $t + n$ (and repaid at time $t + n + k$), he can issue a bond that matures at time $t + k + n$ and can lend the proceeds until time $t + n$ by purchasing a bond that matures in time $t + n$. This is equivalent to borrowing for k periods at the forward interest rate $r_{k,t,t+n}$. Assuming that transactions costs are zero, for the forward loan and the two transactions in the spot bonds to have the same present value it is necessary that

$$(1 + r_{k,t,t+n})^k$$
$$= (1 + R_{n+k,t})^{n+k} / (1 + R_{n,t})^n . \tag{1}$$

Formula (1) is due to Keynes (1936, chap. xiii). By means of (1) it is possible to express all spot interest rates in terms of forward interest rates for one-period loans as follows:

$$(1 + R_{n,t})^n$$
$$= (1 + r_{1,t,t})(1 + r_{1,t,t+1}) \cdots \tag{2}$$
$$(1 + r_{1,t,t+n-1}) .$$

Formula (2) is due to Hicks (1946, p. 145); it gives a canonical form for spot interest rates.[1] There is a similar expression for forward rates on n-period loans in terms of a product of forward rates on one-period loans.

Formula (2) is sometimes (incorrectly) interpreted as an arithmetic tautology without economic content. Its value depends on the possibility that any individual can buy and sell bonds of any maturity without affecting the rates. In other words, to make any sense it must be possible to engage in the kind of arbitrage used in deriving the formula. Thus if such arbitrage is possible, we

[1] See also Lutz (1940) who credits Irving Fisher. The formulas that apply in case the bond pays a periodic coupon are given by Wallace (1964) and Wonnacott (1962). Wallace also shows that in practice the effect of the coupon is slight.

would not expect any forward interest rates to be negative, although this would be consistent with the arithmetic of (2).[2]

III. THE EXPECTATIONS THEORY

By engaging in an appropriate set of purchases and sales of bonds of various maturities, an individual can borrow or lend for arbitrary periods of time at interest rates presently determined to take effect in the future. These transactions are equivalent to allowing individuals to borrow and lend at forward rates. Alternatively, an individual who wishes funds some time in the future can postpone borrowing until the time comes and then can borrow at the going spot rate. By so doing, he exposes himself to uncertainty about the interest rates that will prevail at the time he wishes the funds. Forward borrowing eliminates uncertainty about future interest rates. The availability of both alternatives suggests that the excess demand for loans depends on $r_{1,t,s}$, the forward rate at time t for delivery of a one-period loan at time $s > t$ and expectations about $R_{1,t+s}$, the spot rate for a one-period loan at time $t + s$.

The expectations theory invents the fiction of a market expectation and claims that the forward rate is the market expectation of the spot rate that will rule in the future. This claim relies on a conceptual experiment. Suppose all individuals expect interest rates to be higher in the future than they are now, although all do not necessarily expect the same rise in rates. As a result, lenders would now demand higher long-term rates because there is always the option of lending for a short time now, waiting for the appearance of the higher spot rates, and then buying bonds at the higher rates.

[2] Kessel (1965) cites an instance in September, 1960, during which for nine days the forward rate was negative.

This results in driving up long-term spot rates in the present. Conversely, if interest rates are expected to be lower in the future, borrowers would be inclined to borrow short term and wait for the lower rates to materialize in the future. As a result, the long-term interest rates now fall and reflect the expectation of lower rates to come. Thus the market responds to collective beliefs about spot rates that will prevail later on, despite individual differences of expectations.

Everyone agrees that the prevailing interest rates on loans of different maturities are equilibrium prices that clear the market in these debt instruments. To describe these rates in addition as "expectations" does not advance our understanding of the term structure. It is necessary, in addition, to demonstrate some relation between the forward rates and the subsequent spot rates. This leads to an examination of the accuracy of the forecasts provided by the forward rates. Nevertheless, although accurate forecasts would be sufficient for the validity of the expectations theory, they are not necessary since individuals can be prone to sizable errors of prophecy and still choose their actions on the basis of forward rates as expectations of subsequent spot rates.

Among the first to study the predictive accuracy of forward interest rates was Macauley. Before the establishment of the Federal Reserve, there was a pronounced seasonal in the movement of call money rates. Macauley (1938) found that time money rates did anticipate this seasonal. However, he was unable to discover evidence of successful forecasting beyond the seasonal.

Kessel (1965) repeated Macauley's test using twenty-seven- and fifty-five-day bills for the period 1959–61 and confirmed Macauley's findings that the market anticipated the seasonal in these rates.

Hickman (1943) compared the forward rates with spot rates one year hence and found a larger forecasting error than would be obtained by extrapolating the current spot rate to predict the subsequent rate. Neither Meiselman (1962) nor Kessel (1965) confirms his results; both found the current spot rate to be inferior to the forward rate as a predictor.

Kessel gives more recent evidence of forecast accuracy. For the period January, 1959–March, 1962, Kessel (1965, p. 24) compares the forward rates and the subsequent spot rates they are supposed to predict using short-term (up to six months) U.S. Treasury bills. According to his evidence, forward rates are upward-biased forecasters. His charts show that spot rates rose and fell to about their original level for the first third of the sample period and subsequently rose slightly. Moreover, when spot rates were high and rising, forward rates tended to be higher than when spot rates were nearly constant. Thus the forward rates seem to extrapolate the recent movement of spot rates. This finding is important as we shall see below.

There is another kind of somewhat qualitative evidence pertinent to the predictive accuracy of the forward rates that is implied by the cyclical behavior of interest rates. It is well known that interest rates tend to vary directly with business activity. The relation between short and long rates over the business cycle is explained by the market expectations theory in the light of the cyclical behavior of spot rates. Thus when short rates are below long rates at troughs of business activity, the market expects recovery and the rates to rise. Conversely, when short rates exceed long rates at peaks, the market anticipates decline and a fall in rates.

Hence the cyclical movement of the spread between short and long rates approximately forecasts the cyclical behavior of spot rates.

In addition, short rates have a larger amplitude over the cycle than long rates. This is consistent with the market expectations theory. Long rates depend on the path of short rates that are expected over the more distant future, while the shorter rates depend on expected spot rates for shorter stretches into the future. Since the long rates represent an average of more short rates and reflect a longer horizon, the long rates should have a smaller cyclical amplitude than the short rates.

Kessel presents data for one-, five-, and twenty-year corporate bonds for the period 1901–61. The graph of interest rates in his Chart 13 approximately confirms the implications of the market expectations theory. The Great Depression however, stands out as a unique experience. During the Great Depression the short rate remained below the long rate persistently, which implies a continuous expectation of recovery—an event that did not occur until late in the decade of the thirties. Though interest rates did rise a little from the middle of the 1930's, the rise was less than anticipated. The war intervened and with it the government price-support program on bonds. Hence it is not until the middle of the 1950's that interest rates returned to the pattern common in the first three decades of the century (Kessel, 1965, p. 79).

Lutz reports the results of a comparison between short and long rates for British data spanning 1825–1938. Omitting the cases in which the two rates were close together, he reports the long rate above the short in 764 months and the short above the long in 580 months. He also reports several periods longer than twenty months in which short rates stood above long rates, and states than the longest stretch for which this occurred is forty-two months. Aside from the Great Depression, the longest stretch for which the long rate exceeded the short rate is forty-four months (Lutz, 1940).

This type of evidence implies that presently quoted forward rates roughly predict the subsequent spot rates. However, the forecast errors are often sizable and persist in one direction. Thus the market expectations implied by the forward rates tend to adjust slowly. In addition, there is some evidence that forward rates are biased forecasts of subsequent spot rates. It is Meiselman's important contribution to propose a precise model of the formation of market expectations and obtain thereby new tests of the theory.

IV. MEISELMAN'S NEW EXPECTATIONS THEORY

Drawing upon the experience of Cagan (1956), who successfully explained the demand for money during hyperinflations with a model of how price expectations are formed, and the subsequent success with which Friedman (1957) explained consumption behavior with a model of permanent income, Meiselman proposed an original hypothesis of how expectations are revised for interest rates. Like the Cagan-Friedman models, Meiselman postulated that market expectations are revised according to the size of the error between the forecast of the spot rate given by the forward interest rate and the spot rate that subsequently appeared. Thus the forecast error in period t, E_t, is defined as follows: $E_t = R_{1,t} - r_{1,t-1,t}$. Recall that the first variable on the right side is the spot interest rate on a one-period loan in period t, and the second variable is the forward interest rate as quoted in period $t - 1$

for a loan to begin in period t. According to the market expectations theory, the latter forecasts the former. A measure of the change in expectations for one-period loans to begin in period $t + n$ is $r_{1,t,t+n} - r_{1,t-1,t+n}$. Meiselman (1962) postulates that to a linear approximation there is the following relation between the two:

$$r_{1,t,t+n} - r_{1,t-1,t+n} = a_n + b_n E_t,$$

$$n = 1, 2, 3, \ldots . \tag{3}$$

I wish to emphasize that although Meiselman's model belongs to the same family of adaptive expectations as the Cagan and Friedman models, he introduces a new feature that exploits the special fact of the market revealing its expectations in the forward rates. Meiselman correctly asserts that this model can say nothing about the *level* of expected interest rates but can only tell how expectations change. Meiselman's expected rates are the forward rates and are not weighted moving averages of past spot rates. Moreover, his model is compatible with a set of different expectations about rates to prevail at different times in the future. Thus his model implies the presence of truly extrapolative terms.

As applied to the formation of interest rate expectations, the Cagan-Friedman model gives

$$R_{t-1,t}^* = c \sum_0^\infty (1 - c)^x R_{t-1-x}, \tag{4}$$

where $R_{t-1,t}^* =$ spot rate expected to rule in period t as of period $t - 1$. Formula (4) can be generalized to show what spot rates are expected in subsequent periods as a function of past spot rates up to period $t - 1$. Moreover, the Cagan-Friedman model implies that

$$R_{t-1,t}^* = R_{t-1,t+1}^* = \ldots$$

$$= R_{t-1,t+n}^* = \ldots . \tag{5}$$

To prove this, observe that

$$R^*_{t-1,t+1} = c[R_t + (1 - c)R_{t-1}$$
$$+ (1 - c)^2 R_{t-2} + \ldots];$$
$$R^*_{t-1,t+2} = c[R_{t+1} + (1 - c)R_t$$
$$+ (1 - c)^2 R_{t-1} + \ldots],$$

and so forth. Since R_t, R_{t+1}, R_{t+2}, $\ldots$ are unknown as of period $t - 1$, we replace them by their expected values. This gives

$$R^*_{t-1,t+1} = c[R^*_{t-1,t} + (1 - c)R_{t-1}$$
$$+ (1 - c)^2 R_{t-2} + \ldots];$$
$$R^*_{t-1,t+2} = c[R^*_{t-1,t+1} + (1 - c)R^*_{t-1,t}$$
$$+ (1 - c)^2 R_{t-1} + \ldots].$$

Therefore,

$$R^*_{t-1,t+2} - (1 - c)R^*_{t-1,t+1} = cR^*_{t-1,t+1}$$
$$\ldots$$
$$R^*_{t-1,t+n} - (1 - c)R^*_{t-1,t+n-1} = cR^*_{t-1,t+n-1},$$

which yields (5).

It is well known that (4) is equivalent to

$$R^*_{t-1,t} - R^*_{t-2,t-1} = c(R_{t-1} - R^*_{t-2,t-1}),$$

or

$$R^*_{t,t+1} - R^*_{t-1,t} = c(R_t - R^*_{t-1,t}). \quad (6)$$

Hence the Cagan-Friedman model is a hypothesis about the *level* of expectations, while the Meiselman model is a hypothesis about how expectations are *revised*, which does not give implications about the level of interest rates without additional assumptions. If forward rates are substituted for expected spot rates in (6), we obtain

$$r_{t,t+1} - r_{t-1,t} = cE_t. \quad (7)$$

This equation should be compared with (3) for $n = 1$.

The Cagan-Friedman expectations model applied to interest rates implies an asymptotically flat yield curve. This follows from (5), the substitution of forward for expected rates, and from (2). Thus from (2)

$$\log(1 + R_{n,t}) = (1/n) \sum_{j=0}^{n-1} \log(1 + r_{1,t,t+j})$$

and if

$$r_{t,t+j} = R^*_{1,t,t+j},$$

then it follows from (5) that

$$\log(1 + R_{n,t}) = (1/n)\log(1 + r_{1,t,t})$$
$$+ [(n - 1)/n]\log(1 + r_{1,t,t+1}).$$

Therefore,

$$\lim_{n \to \infty} \log(1 + R_{n,t}) = \log(1 + r_{1,t,t+1}),$$

which proves that the Cagan-Friedman model implies an asymptotically flat yield curve. Moreover, the Cagan-Friedman model would be inconsistent with a humped or similarly non-linear yield curve. However, the statistical literature contains general models of which the Cagan-Friedman model is a very special case that would make the expected spot rate a more complicated moving average of past spot rates. The general models would be compatible with many shapes of the yield curve.[3] Since Meisel-

[3] The Cagan-Friedman model is a special case of a statistical model of time series. Let x_t be the observed value of a sequence such that $x_t = \xi_t + u_t$, where ξ_t is the "true value" and u_t is the measurement error which is uncorrelated with ξ_t. The true value is assumed to be generated by an nth order autoregression as follows: $A(L)\xi_t = v_t$, where v_t is a sequence of successively uncorrelated identically distributed random variables and $A(L)$ denotes an nth degree polynomial in the lag operator L (cf. n. 4). It is further assumed that the u's are also successively uncorrelated, identically distributed, and uncorrelated with the v's. Both u and v are assumed to have finite variances. This model leads to least-squares forecasts of ξ_t which are weighted moving average of past values of the observed x's. The weights are determined from the coefficients of a rational form in L. (A rational form in L is the ratio

man's model gives no information about the level of rates, it is consistent with any shaped yield curve.

Equation (3) does not fully explain the revision of expectations, and it is necessary to introduce a residual variable $u_{1,t,t+n}$ to express the fact that forward rates are responsive to other factors beside the forecast error E_t. Therefore, with the introduction of the residual, (3) becomes

$$r_{1,t,t+n} - r_{1,t-1,t+n} = a_n + b_n E_t$$
$$+ u_{1,t,t+n}, \qquad n = 1, 2, \ldots . \tag{8}$$

Meiselman fits (8) by least squares to annual data, 1901–54, for high-grade corporate bond yields for maturities of one to eight years, as estimated by Durand. The multiple correlations and b_n vary inversely with n. The intercepts, a_n, are close to zero and vary irregularly with term to maturity. Since b_n declines with n, it follows that expectations about more distant rates are more firmly held and less responsive to forecast error than expectations about rates closer to the present. Put otherwise, revisions of the more distant forward rates depend relatively more on the unexplained residual $u_{1,t,t+n}$ than on the forecast error E_t. Unfortunately, Meiselman does not examine the residuals to ascertain whether they show any systematic tendencies or whether they are successively independent.

His regressions have been replicated on annual British data for the period 1933–63 by Buse. Buse's findings (un-

published) are notable in one respect: the intercepts differ from zero. This finding is important for the liquidity preference theory as we shall see below. Buse's replication is important also because it refutes a claim by Grant who, using the same raw British data, rejected the market expectations theory because Meiselman's regressions gave very poor results. Both Buse and Fisher (1964) show that Grant's (1964a, 1964b) findings are largely an artifact of his peculiar method of calculating the term structure. When the British yields are calculated more accurately, these difficulties evaporate.

Wallace (1964) calculated (8) for U.S. Treasury bond rates using quarterly data for the period 1946–62. He also included a dummy variable in an attempt to account for the Federal Reserve–Treasury accord in 1951. Although Wallace found that the error term explains the revision of expectations, he also discovered that the intercepts a_n are positive and much larger than their standard errors. The residuals were found to be autocorrelated in his regressions.

Meiselman also tested whether the addition of lagged errors would improve the fit of his regressions. Actually, he had to use changes in the spot rates on bonds of thirty-year maturity to represent the revision of distant forward rates because it is not possible to calculate the actual forward rates for n greater than eight years using the Durand yield data. Fortunately, the error of using a thirty-year spot rate for this purpose is slight. Inclusion of both E_{t-1} and E_{t-2} reduces the standard error of estimate slightly. Since the addition of lagged errors would help assess the ability of the market to forecast turning points, it is a pity that this line of study has not been pursued.[4]

---

of two polynomials; in this case derived from $A(L)$. In the Cagan-Friedman model it is assumed that $A(L) = 1 - L$, a special case of the general model.) The general model would not necessarily imply the same forecast of successive forward rates, that is, the general case does not imply an asymptotically flat yield curve. For a complete exposition, see P. Whittle (1963, chaps. iii and viii).

[4] Bierwag and Grove (in press) estimate regressions closely resembling Meiselman's tests for the

An interesting question about Meiselman's hypothesis concerns the consistency of the revisions of the forward rates for different n. Thus for every n there is an equation (8) that purports to describe how forward rates change in response to the forecast error. The set of n equations (8) gives $2n$ parameters, n intercepts, and n slopes. These parameters are related as follows: From the first equation (8), we obtain

$$r_{t,t+2} - r_{t-1,t+2} =$$

$$a_1 + b_1(r_{t,t+1} - r_{t-1,t+1}) + u_{t,t+2}$$

$$= a_1 + b_1[a_1 + b_1(r_{t,t} - r_{t-1,t})] \quad (9)$$

$$+ \epsilon_{t,t+1}] + u_{t,t+2}$$

$$= a_1(1 + b_1) + b_1^2(r_{t,t} - r_{t-1,t})$$

$$+ u_{t,t+2} + b_1\epsilon_{t,t+1}.$$

In addition, we have from the second equation of (8) $(n = 2)$,

$$r_{t,t+2} - r_{t-1,t+2} =$$

$$a_2 + b_2(r_{t,t} - r_{t-1,t}) + \epsilon_{t,t+2}. \quad (10)$$

Equations (9) and (10) are mutually consistent provided

$$a_2 = a_1(1 + b_1),$$

$$b_2 = b_1^2,$$

$$\epsilon_{t,t+2} = u_{t,t+2} + b_1\epsilon_{t,t+1}.$$

The algebra for the general case is similar and straightforward. It gives

$$a_n = a_1(1 - b_1^n)/(1 - b_1),$$

$$b_n = b_1^n, \quad (11)$$

$$\epsilon_{t,t+n} = u_{t,t+n} + b_1u_{t,t+n-1} + \cdots$$

$$+ b_1^n\epsilon_{t,t+1}.$$

Thus the consistency of the n expectation equations implies the presence of only two basic parameters, a_1 and b_1, such that all of the others are related to these two by (11). There are, in addition, certain relations among the residuals depending on the statistical properties ascribed to the u's. For instance, if the u's are independent and identically distributed random variables, then the variances of the residuals should increase as n increases. We can determine from Meiselman's and Buse's estimates of a_n and b_n how well these parameters fit (11). Plotting b_n as a function of n shows a geometric decline as predicted by (11), but the b's do not approach zero as implied by (11). Meiselman's intercepts are approximately zero,

---

presence of lagged error terms. However, they interpret their regressions differently and conclude that there are differences among traders' expectations. To deduce this result, Bierwag and Grove depart from the Meiselman model by assuming each individual trader forms his expectations as a weighted moving average of past spot interest rates. Combined with a market equilibrium condition, this makes the market expectation depend on an infinite sequence of past rates weighted in virtually an arbitrary manner.

Since their algebra is cumbersome, a concise exposition is helpful. Let L denote the lag operator and $A(L)$ an nth degree polynomial in L defined as follows: $A(L) = 1 + a_1L + \ldots + a_nL^n$. Assume that individual j forms his expectations on the basis of the following: $R_{t(j)}^* = B_j(L)A_j(L)^{-1}R_t$, where $B_j(L)$ and $A_j(L)$ are both polynomials in L. Bierwag and Grove argue that the market expecta-

tion, R_t^*, is a weighted average of individual expectations. Assume there are N individuals. Then

$$R_t^* = \sum_{j=1}^{n} v_j R_{t(j)}^*, \quad v_j \geq 0, \quad \sum_{j=1}^{n} v_j = 1.$$

Hence the market expectations operator is

$$\sum_{j=1}^{n} v_j B_j(L) A_j(L)^{-1}.$$

This is a complicated function which, fortunately, can always be approximated by a rational form of the type $B(L) A(L)^{-1}$. Actually, Bierwag and Grove assume that $A_j(L)$ is a first-degree polynomial, omit $B_j(L)$ and assume that $N = 2$, calling this two poles of opinion.

while Buse's are positive. According to (11), the intercepts should increase and approach $a_1/(1 - b_1)$. Buse's data roughly confirms this. Although Meiselman (1962, p. 21) did attempt to relate the b_n's to n, he did not develop the implications of consistency shown in (11).

Meiselman's empirical results have been subjected to the criticism that they merely arise from a variant of the regression fallacy. Thus if the "normal" yield curve is upward sloping, meaning that short-term interest rates are less than long-term rates, and if spot interest rates are subject to independent random shocks, then the observed yield curve would bob up and down in such a way as would produce the regressions obtained by Meiselman.[5] Since it is not true that the term structure is "normal" over the past sixty years, this criticism has little force. Similar criticism can be levied against virtually any scientific hypothesis, since generally a large number of different theories are compatible with a given body of data.

Stanley Diller (1966) has taken a very interesting approach to the problem of how expectations are formed and has tested his model with the Durand and more recent data. Diller's approach is most easily described using first-order autoregressions. One may forecast spot interest rates on the basis of past spot rates by fitting autoregressions by least squares to the observed sequence of past spot rates. The autoregressions give good forecasts in the sense of minimizing the sums of squares of the deviations between actual and predicted rates. Diller postulates that the market expectations of spot rates are formed as if they were extrapolations derived from such auto-

regressions. Thus for a first-order autoregression,

$$R_t = a_0 + a_1 R_{t-1} + u_t , \qquad (12)$$

the R's are the observed one-period spot rates, and u_t is a random residual. Using (12) the forecast of subsequent spot rates is based on an extrapolation from the last observed spot rate as follows:

$$R_{t,t+n}^* = a_0(1 - a_1^n)/(1 - a_1) + a_1^n R_t . \qquad (13)$$

It is readily verified that the forecasts satisfy the same autoregression as the observed spot rates, namely,

$$R_{t,t+n}^* - a_1 R_{t,t+n-1}^* = a_0 . \qquad (14)$$

If $|a_1| < 1$, this variant of Diller's hypothesis implies that

$$\lim_{n \to \infty} R_{t, t+n} = a_0/(1 - a_1) .$$

Thus the interest rates are expected to approach a constant in the long run.

This theory also describes how expectations are revised. As of period $t - 1$, the spot rate expected to prevail in period $t + n$ is

$$R_{t-1,t+n}^* = a_0(1 - a_1^{n+1})/(1 - a_1)$$
$$+ a_1^{n+1} R_{t-1} . \qquad (15)$$

Subtracting (15) from (13) gives the revision of the expectations as follows:

$$R_{t,t+n}^* - R_{t-1,t+n}^* = [a_0/(1 - a_1)]$$
$$\times [a_1^n(a_1 - 1)] + a_1^n(R_t - a_1 R_{t-1})$$
$$= - a_1^n a_0 + a_1^n(u_t + a_0) \qquad (16)$$
$$= a_1^n u_t .$$

However,

$$R_{t-1,t}^* = a_0 + a_1 R_{t-1} ,$$
$$R_t = a_0 + a_1 R_{t-1} + u_t .$$

---

[5] This criticism is due to Buse (1967).

Therefore,

$$R_t - R^*_{t-1,t} = u_t \,,$$

which is also Meiselman's expectations error, E_t. Hence (16) implies that

$$R^*_{t,t+n} - R^*_{t-1,t+n} = a^n_1 E_t \,. \qquad (17)$$

Substituting the forward rates for the expected spot rates, Diller's hypothesis for the example of a first-order autoregression explains the change in the forward rate according to (17). It is useful to compare (17) with (11), noting that (17) has no intercept. Actually, Diller claims that a seventh-order autoregression explains the revision of the forward rates in the sense of predicting the regression coefficients of the change of forward rates on the expectation errors. In addition, he uses the same approach to predict the level of the forward rates. Thus Diller attempts to explain the forward rate in terms of past spot rates where the coefficients of the past spot rates are derived from the autoregressions of spot rates that were used to predict the revision of expectations. He also assesses the accuracy of the forward rates as predictors of subsequent spot rates and finds that the residual is correlated with an index of industrial activity and stock market prices. His work opens a promising line of research into expectations that deserves additional investigation.[6]

V. THE LIQUIDITY PREFERENCE THEORY[7]

A purchaser of long-term default-free bonds incurs the risk of a rise in interest rates and a consequent fall in bond prices. Assuming bonds bear a coupon fixed in nominal terms, such a purchaser obtains a certain nominal income in partial compensation for the principal risk. A buyer of a short-term bond incurs a smaller chance of a capital loss for a given rise in interest rates because the shorter the term to maturity, the smaller is the effect on the price of a bond of a given rise in rates. However, one who purchases short-term bonds seriatim assumes the risk of fluctuations of the nominal income stream. Therefore, an individual who expects to make a payment at some unknown time in the future and considers the alternatives of buying a long-term bond to mature on the expected payment date versus buying a sequence of short-term bonds assumes a larger principal and a smaller income risk in the first case and a larger income risk but smaller principal risk in the second. The same reasoning applies, *mutatis mutandis*, to borrowers expecting receipts.

Nevertheless, some writers, notably Hicks, have argued that there is a tendency for lenders to prefer shorter- to longer-term bonds at the same interest rate, while borrowers have the opposite preference. Hicks claims there is a "congenital weakness" on the long side of the market which results in a tendency for long rates to exceed short rates. The differential is necessary to coax lenders into the purchase of long-term bonds as compensation for the greater risk of principal loss. R. F. Kahn (1954) is among the first to criticize the Hicksian argument of a congenital weakness on one side of the market. If firms in various industries commit themselves to payments over horizons of various lengths and there is universal risk aversion, then firms, who feel incompetent or are unwilling to speculate on interest rates, would hedge

---

[6] See Diller (1966, especially chaps. ii and iii).

[7] The major earlier references are Keynes (1936), Lutz (1940), Hicks (1946), Robinson (1951), and Kahn (1954). More recent analysis is Malkiel (1962), Meiselman (1962), Culbertson (1965), and Modigliani and Sutch (1966).

payment commitments by the purchase of bonds of matching maturities. There is no a priori presumption that risk aversion weakens one side of the market instead of the other.[8]

The argument can be put in another way by considering a firm that anticipates the payment of a known amount at an unknown date in the future. The standard liquidity preference doctrine claims that if interest rates were the same for all maturities spanning the possible payment dates, then such a firm would purchase a bond to mature *before* the expected payment date, since to do otherwise would expose it to risking the loss of some of its principal. A firm, according to this theory, is induced to purchase a bond to mature on or after the expected payment date by receiving a higher interest rate on longer-term loans. Actually, the only way to secure the safety of principal *and* avoid transactions costs is to hold cash (assuming away unforeseen changes of the price level). Once a decision is made to buy a bond and given the firm's risk aversion, it does not follow on balance that the firm will choose a bond to mature before the expected date. The purchase of a bond to mature before the expected payment date exposes the firm to the risk of fluctuations of interest receipts. It does not follow from a theoretical analysis that the maturity date of the bond relative to the expected date of payment can be deduced a priori. The maturity date of the bond depends on the firm's subjective judgment about the future course of interest rates.

Despite the logical gaps in the arguments for liquidity preference, one can still maintain that as an empirical matter the market as a whole exhibits a prefer-

[8] This argument seems to have been first developed by Kahn (1954).

ence for the certainty of principal over the certainty of income. Two kinds of evidence have been offered to show that expectations alone do not explain the term structure—the bias of the forward rates as forecasts of the spot rates, and a relation between the structure of interest rates and the maturity composition of debt.

The assertion that forward rates are unbiased estimates of future interest rates implies in Meiselman's model that the intercepts, a_n, are approximately zero. Therefore, there is no tendency for forward rates to change if the error, E_t, is zero. This condition is satisfied in Meiselman's original set of regression equations. It is not satisfied in either Buse's (unpublished) estimates for British government yields or Wallace's (1964) estimates for U.S. Treasury yields. Although I have not checked this, I suspect the special character of the sample periods. In both cases, the results may be due to the fact that the yield structure was upward sloping in most of the years—the Great Depression is included in Buse's sample and both Buse's and Wallace's samples include a large number of abnormal post–World War II years. Since Meiselman's data refer to the period 1901–54, his sample contains term structures of a wider variety of shapes more representative of long-run historical experience. It would be desirable to redo Meiselman's regressions by subperiods, 1901–32, 1933–54, to check the sensitivity to choice of period. The importance of the choice of sample period and determinant of the intercept is clearly shown in Table 10 of Meiselman's study where, using the thirty-year market rate of interest in his expectations equation, he finds a zero intercept for 1901–29 and a significant positive intercept for 1930–54. Both Wood (1963) and Kessel (1965) independently point out that although a zero intercept is necessary for the forward rates to forecast spot rates unbiasedly, it is not sufficient. This is easily demonstrated. Let $R_{t,t+n}$ = the spot rate expected to rule in period $t + n$ as of period t; assume that expectations are revised according to

$$R^*_{t,t+n} - R^*_{t-1,t+n} = b_n(R_t - R^*_{t-1,t}), \quad (18)$$

and assume that the forward rate is related to the expected spot rates as follows:

$$r_{t,t+n} = R^*_{t,t+n} + L_{t,t+n}, \quad (19)$$

where $L_{t,t+n}$ denotes the liquidity premium as of time t on a forward loan to begin in time $t + n$. It follows from these assumptions and equation (6) that

$$a_n = L_{t,t+n} - L_{t-1,t+n} - b_n L_{n-1,t}. \quad (20)$$

Hence a_n can be zero under two different circumstances. Either the liquidity premiums are themselves zero, or they satisfy the additional condition

$$L_{t,t+n} - L_{t-1,t+n} = b_n L_{t-1,t}. \quad (21)$$

This simple exercise also illustrates the general proposition that empirical results implied by a theory are necessary for the truth of the theory but they are never sufficient.

Equation (21) is a theoretical curiosum. Even if we know a_n and b_n we cannot use (21) to estimate the actual liquidity premiums except in the most trivial cases, for example, if the L's are independent of both n and t. Buse, by making the heroic assumptions, $L_{t,t+n} = L_n$, $L_n - L_{n-1} > 0$, and $L_n > 0$, was still able to determine L_n only up to an arbitrary value of L_1. Finally, equation (19) makes the liquidity premium independent of the level of interest rates. This is an assumption that Kessel himself is unwilling to accept.

Kessel claims that liquidity premiums vary directly with the level of interest rates. His argument is based on the premise that nearer-term bonds are less susceptible to risk of principal than longer-term bonds and hence provide their owners with more liquidity. At high interest rates, there is a high opportunity cost of holding money. Hence if both short- and long-term bond yields were to increase by the same amount, there would be a tendency to substitute short-term for long-term bonds to secure the greater liquidity of the former. Therefore, Kessel concludes that the spread between short- and long-term rates should widen at high interest rates.

The evidence that Kessel offers in support of his argument is as follows: He regresses the forecast error, the difference between the actual and the forward rates, on the actual rate of the preceding period. He uses two sets of data. The first set is weekly closing interest rates on 91-day Treasury bills for the period January, 1959–February, 1962. The second set uses midmonthly observations of 28-day Treasury bills for the longer period October, 1949–February, 1961. In both cases, as expected on Kessel's hypothesis, the coefficient of the previous spot rate is positive. His regressions (not published in his original study and kindly made available for this paper) are as follows:

$$R_{t+n} - r_{t,t+n} = -.672 + .473 R_t;$$
$$t\text{-ratios} \quad 4.08 \quad 8.65$$

$$R_{t+n} - r_{t,t+n} = -.140 + .218 R_t.$$
$$t\text{-ratios} \quad 2.16 \quad 6.90$$

The first regression is based on 138 weekly observations of the 91-day Treasury bill rate, January, 1959–February, 1962. The second is based on 137 monthly observations of the 28-day Treasury bill rate, October, 1949–February, 1961. In both regressions, the residuals are strongly autocorrelated. For the first, which uses data at weekly intervals, the first to the fourth-order autocorrelations of the residuals are .79, .60, .46, and .42, respectively. For the second regression, the autocorrelation of the residual at one-month intervals is .41, which is nearly equal to the fourth-order autocorrelation coefficient for the regression using weekly data. The autocorrelation of these residuals leads me to suspect the omission of some important factors that are themselves autocorrelated. In addition, as Kessel himself admits, his test rely on the assumption that the forecast errors are themselves independent of liquidity premiums, and he cannot estimate the actual liquidity premiums.[9]

Meiselman's original regressions indicate that a substantial amount of the revision of forward rates cannot be explained by the forecast error E_t, especially for the more distant forward rates. This leaves ample room for the introduc-

[9] Note that Kessel's argument relating liquidity premiums to the level of interest rates raises troublesome questions about his interpretation of the intercept a_n because the latter assumes independence between liquidity premiums and the interest rates. Thus if $L_{t,t+n}$ is assumed to depend on the level of interest rates, then the presence of a_n can be due to misspecification of the equation that purports to explain the revision of expectations, for example, it may arise from the error of a linear approximation to a non-linear function. Moreover, there are functions relating the liquidity premiums to the level of interest rates that would be actually inconsistent with Kessel's interpretation of a_n. Diller (1966) makes the distinction between a liquidity trap which results from investors' reluctance to buy bonds at abnormally low interest rates for fear of a capital loss if rates should rise and liquidity preference discussed in the text. Thus the low level of short relative to long rates is evidence of a liquidity trap which, in the language of expectations theory, indicates the presence of a market expectation of a return to a normal level of rates. This phenomenon would imply an inverse relation between the forecast error and the level of rates. Van Horne (1965) attempted to demonstrate such a relation, but his work is marred by a statistical error pointed out by Roll (1966).

tion of other variables to explain changes in the forward rates (or, if you will, expectations). The troublesome question remains of identifying that part of the change in forward rates due to changes in the liquidity premiums and that part due to hitherto unexplored causes of changes in expectations.

A more direct analysis of liquidity premiums relates changes in the forward rates to changes in the maturity composition of all debt. Unfortunately, it is impossible to determine the direction of causation since the term structure of interest rates and the maturity composition of all debt are mutually dependent. This consideration led Neil Wallace to relate the forward rates on government securities to the composition of the federal debt, arguing that the latter is exogenously determined so that it affects the term structure of interest rates without in turn being affected by it. Wallace found that a shift in the maturity composition of the federal debt has a small effect on the term structure of interest rates in the direction predicted by the liquidity preference theory. Thus for a given total federal debt, an increase in its average term to maturity tends to drive up the forward interest rates. Since his regressions are not readily accessible, I reproduce them in Table 1. Despite these findings, it is consistent with the expectations theory to argue that changes in the federal debt composition can affect expectations as well as liquidity premiums (Wallace, 1964).

Modigliani and Sutch (1966) fail to find a relation between the composition of the federal debt and the term structure of rates. Using a different expectations model—one which relates the spread between long- and short-term interest rates to a weighted sum of lagged short-term rates and to the term composition of the federal debt as measured by the fraction that is short and of intermediate term—they found that the components of the debt have opposite signs and nearly equal magnitudes. This implies a trivial net effect on the term structure of rates.

VI. CONCLUSIONS AND SUGGESTIONS FOR FURTHER RESEARCH

The most challenging task for future research on the term structure of rates is the extension of the expectations model cord with business cycles? In addition, it would be desirable to try other kinds of expectation models. For instance, instead of relating the absolute change of the forward rate to the absolute forecast error, it would be interesting to relate the percentage change of the former to the forecast error expressed in percentage. This suggestion should be taken seriously if long-time series of interest rates are used and the levels of the rates widely differ.

The survey of the empirical research

TABLE 1

NEIL WALLACE'S REGRESSION RESULTS TESTING THE EFFECT OF THE MATURITY COMPOSITION OF THE FEDERAL DEBT ON THE TERM STRUCTURE OF INTEREST RATES, QUARTERLY, 1946–62,

$$r_{1,t,t+n} - r_{1,t-1,t+n} = a_n + b_n E_t + c_n[(M_{t,t+n})/M_{tt} - (M_{t-1,t+n})/(M_{t-1,t-1})] + d_n \text{ DUMMY}$$

n years	a_n	b_n	c_n	d_n	R^2	Durbin-Watson Statistic
1.............	.0020 (.0004)	.846 (.031)	.009 (.004)	−.0020 (.0005)	.94	1.37
2.............	.0021 (.0005)	.663 (.042)	.011 (.006)	−.0022 (.0007)	.84	1.48
3.............	.0023 (.0005)	.541 (.043)	.014 (.007)	−.0024 (.0007)	.75	1.54

Note: $M_{t,\,t+n}$ = outstanding marketable Treasury securities at time t that mature on or after time $t + n$. Dummy = one for all quarterly observations from March, 1946, to March, 1951, and zero thereafter. The regressions use sixty-four observations.

so as to incorporate the effects of other variables that might affect expectations in addition to the forecast error. In concrete terms, one ought to explain more of the changes in forward rates. A preliminary approach would examine the residuals of the existing regressions with a view to finding hints of left-out expectational variables. For instance, do the residuals exhibit cycles that move in accord uncovers evidence in favor of both explanations of the term structure—the expectations and the liquidity preference theory. None of these results is at all decisive, and many contain errors, shortcomings, and paradoxes. In my opinion, no verdict can yet be brought, and imaginative work remains to be done in "explaining" the formation and change of expectations.

REFERENCES

Bierwag, G. O., and Grove, M. A. "A Model of the Term Structure of Interest Rates," *Rev. Econ. and Statis.* (in press).

Buse, A. "The Term Structure of Interest Rates—Some British Experience," unpublished MS.

———. "Interest Rates, the Meiselman Model and Random Numbers," *J.P.E.*, LXXV (February, 1967), 49–62.

Cagan, Phillip. "The Monetary Dynamics of Hyperinflation," in Milton Friedman (ed.). *Studies in the Quantity Theory of Money*. Chicago: Univ. of Chicago Press, 1956.

Culbertson, J. M. "The Interest Rate Structure: Towards Completion of the Classical System," in F. H. Hahn and P. R. Brechling (eds.). *The Theory of Interest Rates*. London: Macmillian & Co., 1865.

Diller, Stanley. "Extrapolations, Anticipations and the Term Structure of Interest Rates," unpublished doctoral dissertation, Department of Economics, Columbia Univ., 1966.

Fisher, D. "The Structure of Interest Rates: A Comment," *Economica*, N.S., XXXI (November, 1964), 412–19.

Friedman, Milton. *A Theory of the Consumption Function*. Princeton, N.J.: Princeton Univ. Press, 1957.

Grant, J. A. G. "Meiselman on the Term Structure of Interest Rates," *Economica*, N.S., XXXI (February, 1964), 51–74. (*a*)

———. "A Reply," *ibid.*, pp. 419–22. (*b*)

Hickman, W. Braddock. "The Interest Structure and War Financing," National Bureau of Economic Research, unpublished, 1943.

Hicks, J. R. *Value and Capital*. 2d ed. Oxford: Oxford Univ. Press, 1946.

Kahn, R. F. "Some Notes on Liquidity Preference," *Manchester School Econ. and Soc. Studies*, XXII (September, 1954), 229–57.

Kessel, Ruben A. *The Cyclical Behavior of the Term Structure of Interest Rates*. New York: National Bureau of Economic Research, 1965.

Keynes, J. M. *The General Theory of Employment, Interest, and Money*. New York: Harcourt, Brace & Co., 1936.

Lutz, F. A. "The Structure of Interest Rates," *Q.J.E.*, LV (November, 1940, 36–63.

Macauley, F. R. *The Movements of Interest Rates, Bond Yields and Stock Prices in the United States since 1856*. New York: National Bureau of Economic Research, 1938.

Malkiel, B. G. "Expectations, Bond Prices and the Term Structure of Interest Rates," *Q.J.E.*, LXXVI (February, 1962), 197–218.

Meiselman, David. *The Term Structure of Interest Rates*. Englewood Cliffs, N.J.: Prentice-Hall, Inc., 1962.

Modigliani, Franco, and Sutch, Richard. "Innovations in Interest Rate Policy," *A.E.R.*, LVI (May, 1966), 178–97.

Robinson, Joan. "The Rate of Interest," *Econometrica*, XIX (January, 1951), 92–101.

Roll, Richard. "Interest-Rate Risk and the Term Structure of Interest Rates: Comment," *J.P.E.*, LXXIV (December, 1966), 629–32.

Van Horne, J. "Interest-Rate Risk and the Term Structure of Interest Rates," *J.P.E.*, LXXIII (August, 1965), 344–51.

Wallace, Neil. "The Term Structure of Interest Rates and Maturity Composition of the Federal Debt," unpublished doctoral dissertation, Department of Economics, Univ. of Chicago, 1964.

Whittle, P. *Prediction and Regulation*. London: English Universities Press, 1963.

Wonnacott, P. "The Height, Structure and Significance of Interest Rates," unpublished working paper prepared for the Royal Commission on Banking and Finance, Canada 1962.

Wood, J. H. "Expectations, Error and the Term Structure of Interest Rates," *J.P.E.*, LXXI (April, 1963), 160–71.

50

DETERMINANTS OF RISK PREMIUMS
ON CORPORATE BONDS [1]

Lawrence Fisher

I. INTRODUCTION

ECONOMISTS have long agreed that the rate of interest on a loan depends on the risks the lender incurs. But how lenders estimate these risks has been left largely to conjecture. This paper presents and tests a hypothesis about the determinants of risk premiums on corporate bonds. By risk premium is meant the difference between the market yield on a bond and the corresponding pure rate of interest.

My hypothesis is as follows: (1) The average risk premium on a firm's bonds depends first on the risk that the firm will default on its bonds and second on their marketability. (2) The "risk of default" can be estimated by a function of three variables: the coefficient of variation of the firm's net income over the last

nine years (after all charges and taxes), the length of time the firm has been operating without forcing its creditors to take a loss, and the ratio of the market value of the equity in the firm to the par value of the firm's debt. (3) The marketability of a firm's bonds can be estimated by a single variable, the market value of all the publicly traded bonds the firm has outstanding. (4) The logarithm of the average risk premium on a firm's bonds can be estimated by a linear function of the logarithms of the four variables just listed.

For convenience, these variables will usually be designated as follows: earnings variability, x_1; period of solvency, x_2; equity/debt ratio, x_3; and bonds outstanding, x_4. Risk premium will be called x_0. Capital letters will indicate common logarithms of the variables. Earnings variability and the equity/debt ratio are pure numbers. Risk premium will be expressed in per cent per annum, compounded semiannually; bonds outstanding, in millions of dollars; and the period of solvency, in years.[2]

[1] I am greatly indebted to Professor Arnold C. Harberger, who suggested that I undertake this research and guided me throughout the study. Professors Carl Christ and Phillip D. Cagan made valuable comments and criticisms, as did other members of the Research Group in Public Finance of the University of Chicago. An Earhart Foundation Fellowship facilitated the completion of this study.

This paper was read at the September, 1956, meeting of the Econometric Society in Detroit. An abstract was printed in *Econometrica*, XXV (1957), 366–67.

[2] Some alternative variables will be introduced below. They will be expressed in the following units: equity, x_5, and debt, x_6—millions of dollars; annual

Security analysts generally regard some form of each of these variables to be of value in appraising the "quality" of bonds. But, to the best of my knowledge, this is the first time they have been used together in an attempt to discover how much investors are influenced by various aspects of bond quality.[3]

More precise definitions of the variables will be given later, and the derivation of the hypothesis, alternative hypotheses, and statistical procedures will be explained. But first let us look at some of the main results.

II. THE MAIN RESULTS

The hypothesis was tested by least-squares regressions for cross-sections of domestic industrial corporations for five dates: December 31 of the years 1927, 1932, 1937, 1949, and 1953. The cross-sections included all firms for which I had meaningful data.[4] The cross-sections were for 71 firms in 1927, 45 firms in 1932, 89 firms in 1937, 73 firms in 1949, and 88 firms in 1953.

For each of these cross-sections the logarithms of the four variables accounted for approximately three-fourths of the variance in the logarithm of risk premium. Furthermore, I found that the elasticity[5] of risk premium with respect to each of the four variables is relatively stable over time. In view of this stability, it was possible to pool the observed variances and covariances and obtain a single set of "best" estimates of

---

volume of trading, x_7—millions of dollars a year; an alternative index of variability of earnings, x_8—the reciprocal of years.

[3] The study by Herbert Arkin, discussed in note 41, bears a superficial resemblance to this one.

[4] For the sources of data and the criteria used in selecting the firms see Section VI.

[5] Logarithmic regression coefficients are estimates of elasticities.

the elasticities. Figure 1 is the scatter of the 366 measured risk premiums against the risk premiums calculated by using this single set of elasticities. The regression equation from which these risk premiums were estimated is

$$X_0 = 0.262 X_1 - 0.223 X_2$$
$$- 0.469 X_3 - 0.290 X_4 \quad (1)$$
$$+ \text{a constant},$$

where the constant is equal to 0.966 in 1927; 1.235 in 1932; 0.918 in 1937; 0.847 in 1949; and 0.829 in 1953. This equation accounts for 81 per cent of the total variance in the logarithm of risk premium. Part of this variance, however, can be accounted for by differences in the mean of X_0 among the cross-sections. When that part of the variance is eliminated, equation (1) accounts for 74 per cent of the remaining or intra-cross-section variance. To make the data strictly comparable among the cross-sections, it would have been necessary to make adjustments for such things as changes in tax rates. But, since we do not know whether the determinants of stock prices are stable and since the market value of equity was used in computing one of the variables, these adjustments were not made. Hence there was no reason to expect the constant term of this regression equation to be the same for each date, even if investors' behavior in the bond market were perfectly stable over time.[6]

[6] The regression equation found by keeping the constant term (as well as the elasticities) the same for all cross-sections is

$$X_0 = 0.307 X_1 - 0.253 X_2$$
$$- 0.537 X_3 - 0.275 X_4 \quad (2)$$
$$+ 0.987 \ (R^2 = 0.75).$$

For a complete description of equation (2) see Table 1.

Figure 2 permits us to compare the fraction of the intra-cross-section variance in the logarithm of risk premium, X_0, that is accounted for by the pooled-variance regression, equation (1), with the squares of the multiple correlation coefficients (R^2) obtained by fitting regression equations to each cross-section separately.

Figure 3 shows the estimates of elasticities and their standard errors obtained from the pooled-variance regression, equation (1), and from the regressions for the separate cross-sections. The

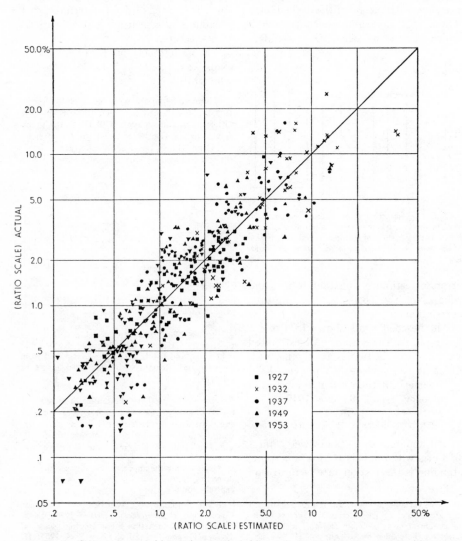

FIG. 1.—Scatter of actual risk premiums against risk premiums estimated from equation (1)

larger bars show the estimated elasticities, η. The right ends of the small bars are at points one standard error, s, greater than the estimated elasticity; the left ends are at $\eta - s$. The estimates from equation (1) may be compared with the estimates from the separate regressions with the aid of the dashed lines. These results are summarized in Table 1, which shows the elasticities, standard

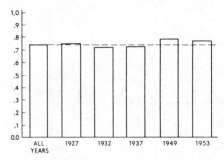

Fig. 2.—Proportion of intra-cross-section variance in the logarithms of risk premiums accounted for by the logarithms of earnings variability, period of solvency, equity/debt ratio, and bonds outstanding.

errors of estimate, constant terms, and squares of the coefficients of multiple correlation.

All the coefficients shown in Table 1 have the expected sign.[7] All estimated values of the elasticities are significantly different from zero at the 5 per cent level or lower except the estimates for period of solvency, x_2, for 1932 and 1949.[8]

III. THEORETICAL FRAMEWORK

The apparent cost of borrowed capital to a firm with publicly traded bonds outstanding is the market rate of return on

[7] See Section IV.

[8] This variable, however, was not measured with any great accuracy (see Section VI). Errors in the measurement of x_2 probably had only a negligible effect on the coefficients of equation (1) (see Section VII).

those bonds (which generally will be the pure rate of interest plus a risk premium) plus the cost of floating the issue.[9] The determinants of the pure rate of interest have long been the subject of extensive study, both theoretical and empirical. Costs of flotation have also been studied.[10] But the matter of what determines risk premiums has been left almost entirely to conjecture.

The basic theory of risk premiums on loans was stated by J. R. McCullough, who wrote:

> There are comparatively few species of security to be obtained in which there is no risk, either as to the repayment of the loans themselves, or the regular payment of the interest. . . . Other things being equal, the rate of interest must of course vary according to the sup-

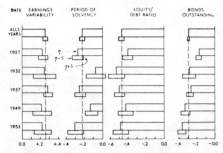

Fig. 3.—Elasticities of risk premium with respect to earnings variability, period of solvency, equity/debt ratio, and bonds outstanding estimated from cross-sections (together with standard errors of estimate).

posed risk incurred by the lender of either not recovering payment at all, or not receiving it at the stipulated term. No person of sound mind would lend on the personal security of an individual of doubtful character and solvency, and

[9] This is only the apparent cost because the cost of equity capital probably depends on the firm's capital structure.

[10] For examples see Securities and Exchange Commission, *Costs of Flotation, 1945–1949* (Washington, 1951), and Arthur Stone Dewing, *Financial Policy of Corporations* (5th ed.; New York, 1953), II, 1131–32.

on mortgage over a valuable estate, at the same rate of interest. Wherever there is risk, it must be compensated to the lender by a higher premium or interest.[11]

Mercantile bills of unquestionable credit and having two or three months to run, are generally discounted at a lower rate of interest than may be obtained for sums lent upon mortgage, *on account of the facility they afford of repossessing the principal*, and applying it in some more profitable manner.[12]

In other words, the yields on almost all securities include compensation for risk.

ments specified in the bond contract must be discounted if their present value is to equal the current market price of the bond. The corresponding pure rate of interest is defined as the market yield on a riskless bond maturing on the same day as the bond under consideration.

Risk premiums defined in this way must in general be either zero or positive if, other things being equal, bondholders prefer high incomes to low incomes. A bondholder has no expectation of re-

TABLE 1

REGRESSION EQUATIONS FOR ESTIMATING LOGARITHM OF AVERAGE RISK PREMIUM ON A FIRM'S BONDS AS A LINEAR FUNCTION OF LOGARITHMS OF EARNINGS VARIABILITY, PERIOD OF SOLVENCY, EQUITY/DEBT RATIO, AND BONDS OUTSTANDING

(Hypothesis that $X_0 = a_0 + a_1X_1 + a_2X_2 + a_3X_3 + a_4X_4$)

Equation	Date	No. of Observations	Degrees of Freedom	R^2	a_0	a_1 (s_1)	a_2 (s_2)	a_3 (s_3)	a_4 (s_4)
1.....	All	366	357	0.811*	†	+0.262 (.032)	−0.223 (.033)	−0.469 (.029)	−0.290 (.019)
2.....	All	366	361	.750	0.987	+.307 (.032)	−.253 (.036)	−.537 (.031)	−.275 (.021)
3.....	1927	71	66	.756	0.874	+.233 (.048)	−.269 (.062)	−.404 (.039)	−.169 (.031)
4.....	1932	45	40	.726	1.014	+.248 (.128)	−.067 (.114)	−.531 (.092)	−.286 (.071)
5.....	1937	89	84	.731	0.949	+.286 (.051)	−.254 (.061)	−.491 (.060)	−.271 (.038)
6.....	1949	73	68	.786	0.711	+.228 (.100)	−.124 (.076)	−.426 (.084)	−.329 (.046)
7.....	1953	88	83	0.773	1.012	+.228 (0.091)	−.300 (0.089)	−.474 (0.085)	−.363 (0.043)

* 0.741 after the effects of differences in a_0 are eliminated.

† 1927: 0.966; 1932: 1.235; 1937: 0.918; 1949: 0.847; 1953: 0.829.

These risk premiums depend on lenders' estimates of the risk of default and on the ease of turning the securities into cash. Let us consider the risk of default first.

The risk premium on a bond has been defined as the difference between its market yield to maturity and the corresponding pure rate of interest. Market yield is defined as the rate of interest at which the principal and interest pay-

[11] *The Principles of Political Economy: With a Sketch of the Rise and Progress of the Science* (2d ed.; Edinburgh, London, and Dublin, 1830), pp. 508–9.

[12] *Ibid.*, p. 508 (italics mine).

ceiving more than the payments called for by his bond and, since corporations have limited liability, he may receive less.[13] Hence, regardless of whether he

[13] There have been cases in which creditors have received equity interests in firms through reorganizations in bankruptcy, and the firms subsequently made such large profits that the bondholders ultimately received payments larger than those called for by their bonds (but it is doubtful whether, at the time of the reorganizations, the new securities received had a market value as great as the accumulated value of the bonds). But bondholders receive such payments only after expenses of the receivership have been paid and only if the earning power of the firm is underestimated at the time of reorganiza-

likes or tries to avoid being in situations of uncertain income and wealth, a bondholder will demand a risk premium as compensation for holding any bond that is not certain to be paid.[14]

A lender's estimate of the "risk of default" must depend on his estimates of the probability that a default will occur[15] and of the magnitude of his loss in the event of a default.[16] Let us assume that lenders do not behave capriciously. Then our problem is to find how a rational investor can most readily estimate the probability that a bond will be defaulted. Investors' estimates must be based on information available to them. In general, if a corporation defaults on its bonds, it is because the market value of its assets is less than its liabilities. The value of its assets—that is, the value of its total capital—depends on the earning

tion. So long as bondholders do not become stockholders, they cannot receive more than the amounts called for by their contracts. (Sinking fund and call provisions in bond indentures complicate this argument slightly, but they limit the bondholders' opportunity for capital gains; hence considering them would probably strengthen these conclusions.) We can conclude that the expectation of a bondholder's receiving more than contractual payments is negligible.

[14] That is, if a bondholder's utility is a function of his income and the first derivative of the function is positive, a dollar a year with certainty must have a greater utility than a dollar a year with probability $p < 1$ plus an amount less than one dollar a year with probability $1 - p$. This proposition is, of course, independent of the sign of the second derivative of the utility function.

[15] More precisely, the probabilities of default at each moment in time.

[16] It can easily be shown that the expected loss in the event of a default is likely to depend on two of the determinants of the probability of default—earnings variability and the equity/debt ratio. My procedure enables one to find an index of the probability of default but not to estimate the probability itself. Hence, to simplify the analysis, the magnitude of loss in the event of a default will not be discussed explicitly. Those who demand rigor may read the phrase "probability of a default" as "expected loss."

power of those assets. Hence the "risk of default" is given by the probability that the firm's earnings will not be large enough to meet the payments on its debts.

Recall that risk premium also depends on marketability. The theory of the determinants of risk premiums may then be restated: If investors are rational, the risk premium on any bond will depend on the probability that the issuing firm's earnings will be too small to permit it to pay its debts and on the ease with which the bondholder can turn the bond into cash before it matures.

Let us now turn to the problem of finding ways to measure these variables.

IV. AN OPERATIONAL HYPOTHESIS

RISK OF DEFAULT

There are three sorts of variables that it is plausible to use together in estimating risk of default: measures of the variability of the firm's earnings; measures showing how reliable the firm has been in meeting its obligations; and measures depending on the firm's capital structure.

Variability of earnings.—In 1903, J. Pease Norton suggested the probability that a firm will fail to pay interest on its bonds in any particular year could be found by computing the coefficient of variation of the firm's income in past years, over and above the amount required for fixed charges, and by looking up the probability in a table of the normal distribution.[17] This naïve procedure may be correct for non-cumulative income bonds (which are rare), but it is not correct for other types of bonds because corporations often continue to meet fixed

[17] "The Theory of Loan Credit in Relation to Corporation Economics," *Publications of the American Economic Association*, 3d ser., V (1904), 298. Cf. Irving Fisher, *The Nature of Capital and Income* (New York, 1906), p. 409.

charges during periods of losses. Nevertheless, it provides a useful point of departure.

Let us make an assumption which is implicit in Norton's procedure—that a series of observations of a firm's annual net income may be treated as a random sample from a normally distributed population of potential annual net incomes. The coefficient of variation of this series is an estimate of the coefficient of variation of the underlying population.[18] Other things being equal, a firm with a small coefficient of variation of earnings is less likely to default on its bonds than a firm with a large coefficient. Hence the variable suggested by Norton appears to be a promising one, even in analyses of bonds for which his complete procedure is invalid.

In practice, data on the earnings of a firm for its entire history are usually not available. To test the partial hypothesis that investors believe that a bond issued by a firm whose earnings have varied little is a better risk than a bond issued by a firm whose earnings have varied much, one must have comparable earnings data for the two firms. Because my tests covered a large number of firms, it was necessary to place an arbitrary limit on the number of years' earnings used in computing the coefficient of variation. Nine years was the limit selected. During the period considered, nine years was long enough for the earnings of most firms to fluctuate substantially.

In the abstract, one could take as "net earnings" either income after the payment of fixed charges or income after the payment of both charges and corporation income taxes. If taxes were proportional to income and tax rates did not

vary during the nine-year period and if one year's losses could not be deducted from another year's profits in computing taxes, the two methods would give the same computed coefficient of variation. But tax rates do vary from year to year, and there are loss carryback and carryforward provisions in our tax laws; neither measure is ideal. I did not use both measures together because, if I found that risk premium varied with the coefficient of variation in earnings, I wanted to measure the elasticity of risk premium with respect to this measure of the risk of default. And, since the two coefficients of variation were expected to be highly correlated with each other, a precise estimate of either elasticity could not be expected with both variables in the regression.

My choice was made on practical grounds. The appropriate measure of marketability, bonds outstanding, is highly correlated with size of firm. If both coefficients of variation in earnings are equally reliable, the measure that allows the use of the larger range of firms gives the more precise estimate of the elasticity of risk premium with respect to marketability. Issues of *Moody's Manual*, an important secondary source, give data on earnings after taxes for more firms than on earnings before taxes, particularly for very large and for small firms. Therefore, earnings after taxes ("net income") were taken as "earnings" and used in computing x_1, earnings variability.

In many studies it is necessary to adjust data for changes in the general price level. Since bond obligations are in "money" rather than "real" units, no such adjustment was necessary here.

Reliability in meeting obligations.—The coefficient of variation in earnings computed from a "sample" is only an

[18] The coefficient of variation is the ratio of the standard deviation of a sample (adjusted for degrees of freedom) to the arithmetic mean of the sample.

estimate of the coefficient of variation in the underlying population. This estimate may be either larger or smaller than the actual coefficient. But, other things being equal, the longer a firm has conducted its business without requiring its creditors to take a loss, the less likely it is that its estimated coefficient of variation in earnings is much less than the coefficient in the hypothetical underlying population of annual net incomes. Hence, a measure of the length of time a firm has met all its obligations—the length of time the firm has been solvent—provides a correction for the estimate of risk of default derived from earnings variability. This measure has been designated as x_2. In estimating a firm's period of solvency, I took the length of time since the latest of the following events had occurred: The firm was founded; the firm emerged from bankruptcy; a compromise was made in which creditors settled for less than 100 per cent of their claims.

Capital structure.—Thus far, variations in a firm's earnings have been treated as though they were purely random fluctuations about some mean. Now let us modify this assumption and allow not only for these "random" fluctuations but also for shifts in the underlying mean income (or permanent earning power) of the firm, because we know that industries and firms do rise and fall over the years.

Capital assets have value only because they earn income. If investors believe that the earning power of a particular collection of assets has changed, the market value of those assets will change. When earnings variability is observed, it is impossible to distinguish between "random" fluctuations about the mean and fluctuations due to shifts in the mean itself. It is reasonable to believe that investors attribute variations in earnings to both causes. Earnings variability, then, is no longer a pure measure of random fluctuations. It also gives some information about the likelihood of future shifts in the earning power of the firm—about shifts in the value of the firm's assets. The investor will then be interested in how much the firm's assets can decline in value before they become less than its liabilities and the firm becomes insolvent. A measure of this factor is the ratio of the market value of the firm's equity to the par value of its debts. When this ratio is, say, nineteen, the firm's assets may fall 95 per cent in value before it becomes insolvent. But when the equity/debt ratio is one-fourth, a default can be expected if the assets lose only 20 per cent of their value. The equity/debt ratio has been designated as x_3.

MARKETABILITY

I have developed the hypothesis that investors believe that the risk that a firm's bonds will be defaulted depends on the firm's earnings variability, its period of solvency, and its equity/debt ratio. Now let us consider the measurement of the other type of risk an investor incurs by holding a corporate bond, the risk associated with the difficulty of turning the bond into cash before it matures.

If securities markets were "perfect" (in the sense that the actions of a single individual could have only an infinitesimal effect on the price of a security), it would not be necessary to take up this topic at all; turning a bond into cash would be no problem. It is true that an investor who disposes of any interest-bearing security before maturity may have to take a loss because of changes in the pure interest rate between the time he buys his bond and the time he sells it. But such losses are allowed for by defining risk premium as the difference between the yield on the bond under consideration and the yield on a bond of the same maturity which is sure to be paid, so that compensation for possible changes in the pure rate of interest is present even in the yields on riskless bonds. Thus marketability can influence the risk premium only if it measures the degree of imperfection—the effect of a single individual's action on price—in the market for a particular security.[19]

How can an investor estimate the degree of imperfection of the market for a particular security? There are several possible ways. Imperfection of the market for bonds can be expected to result in bondholders' demanding compensation for risk because it makes the price and yield of a bond at any particular moment uncertain. Ideally, one might measure this uncertainty by finding the "random" fluctuations in the price of a bond over a short period. However, the bond market is often rather inactive.[20] Bond prices are subject both to random fluctuations and to changes caused by changes in the prospects of the firm and in the pure rate of interest. If the period of observation is made so short that the non-random changes in bond prices are negligible, it will also be too short to permit much random fluctuation.

The volume of trading and the "spread" between "bid" and "ask" prices are variables sometimes suggested as measures of marketability.[21] The vol-

ume of trading can be used only for bonds listed on some securities exchange.[22] In the abstract, "spread" could be applied to both listed and unlisted securities. But published quotations for listed bonds are "inside" (actual) prices, and quotations for over-the-counter securities are generally "outside" (nominal) prices. Hence neither of these measures can be used in this study, which includes both listed and unlisted securities.

The third variable that can be used as a measure of marketability is x_4, the total market value of the publicly traded bonds the firm has outstanding. This variable was used because it is applicable to both listed and over-the-counter securities. One of the reasons for believing that it is a good measure of marketability may be summarized as follows: Other things being equal, the smaller the amount of bonds a firm has outstanding, the less frequently we should expect its bonds to change hands. The less often its bonds change hands, the thinner the market; and the thinner the market, the more uncertain is the market price. Hence, other things being equal, the larger the market value of publicly traded bonds a firm has outstanding, the smaller is the expected risk premium on those bonds.

Thus we have the proposition that risk premium depends on estimated risk of default and on marketability. Risk of default depends on earnings variability, x_1; period of solvency, x_2; and equity/debt ratio, x_3. Marketability depends on bonds outstanding, x_4.[23]

[19] The holder of a risky bond may demand compensation simply because expectations about his bond may be subject to frequent change. But this type of "risk" is, I believe, merely an aspect of the risk of default itself.

[20] Total sales on the New York Stock Exchange of some of the listed issues included in the cross-sections were less than $50,000—50 bonds—a year. An issue may be quoted almost every day but not traded for six months or more.

[21] Cf. Graham and Dodd, *Security Analysis* (3d ed.; New York, 1951), p. 31.

[22] For a comparison of "volume of trading" with "bonds outstanding," the measure of marketability used in this study, see Section VII.

[23] This hypothesis might, perhaps, have been derived directly from Alfred Marshall's statements on

FORM OF THE FUNCTION

My hypothesis may now be stated as

$$x_0 = f(x_1, x_2, x_3, x_4).$$

To test the hypothesis, it was necessary to assume some form of the function.

If the influence of one independent variable on risk premium is independent of the magnitudes of the other independent variables, a linear function may be appropriate. If, however, the influence of one variable depends on the magnitudes of the other variables, then some other form is required.

---

the considerations involved in determining risk premiums on loans to entrepreneurs: "It is then necessary to analyse a little more carefully the extra risks which are introduced into business when much of the capital used in it has been borrowed. Let us suppose that two men are carrying on similar businesses, the one working with his own, the other chiefly with borrowed capital.

"There is one set of risks which is common to both; which may be described as the *trade risks* [A] of the particular business in which they are engaged. . . . But there is another set of risks, the burden of which has to be borne by the man working with borrowed capital, and not by the other; and we may call them *personal risks*. For he who lends capital to be used by another for trade purposes, has to charge a high interest as insurance against the chances of some flaw or deficiency in the borrower's personal character or ability.

"The borrower may be less able than he appears [B], less energetic, or less honest. He has not the same inducements [C], as a man working with his own capital has, to look failure straight in the face, and withdraw from a speculative enterprise as soon as it shows signs of going against him . . ." (*Principles of Economics* [4th ed.; London, 1898], p. 674; [8th ed.; New York, 1952], pp. 589–90 [italics his]).

My coefficient of variation of earnings can be identified with Marshall's "trade risks" [A] on the ground that the greater is the coefficient of variation, the greater are the trade risks; my period of solvency with Marshall's "the borrower may be less able than he appears" [B] on the ground that the longer a firm has operated successfully, the less likely it is that its success has been due to a run of good luck; and my equity/debt ratio directly with Marshall's "inducements" [C]. Marshall also notes the possible value of marketability (4th ed., p. 673 n.; 8th ed., p. 589 n.) and points out that investors may demand more than actuarial risk premiums (4th ed., p. 196 n.; 8th ed., p. 122 n.).

It would appear that the latter is the case here. Let us again consider the two firms, one with an equity/debt ratio of 19, the other with an equity/debt ratio of one-fourth.[24] The risk of default on bonds of the first firm will probably be very small no matter how unstable its earnings may be; for in order for bondholders to suffer much of a loss if the firm's business should become unprofitable, the resale value of its assets would have to be less than 5 per cent of their present value to the business as a going concern. But holders of the bonds of the second firm will be very much interested in how likely it is that the firm will continue to earn enough to meet its obligations; for if its current business should become unprofitable, its assets would probably not be worth enough to pay off the bonds in full. Hence, we should expect the influence of one variable on risk of default to depend on the magnitudes of the other variables. If the risk of default is small, an investor can be quite certain of what the equilibrium price of his bonds is. For when the risk of default is small, estimates of that risk are unlikely to change much over time.[25] Hence if an investor wants to liquidate his holdings, he exposes himself to little uncertainty by borrowing temporarily on the security of his bonds. But when the risk of default is large, his collateral does not enable the bondholder to obtain so large a loan at any given rate of interest. Thus the holder of a risky bond will have more incentive to sell quickly, at less than equilibrium price. Marketability, then, also becomes more important as the other variables indicate more risk of default.

[24] These numbers are well within the range of the equity/debt ratios of firms included in the cross-sections.

[25] See any recent *Moody's Manual*, p. v.

A function which behaves in the manner implied by the preceding paragraph is given in equation (8)[25a]

$$x_0 = a_0' x_1^{a_1} x_2^{a_2} x_3^{a_3} x_4^{a_4} . \qquad (8)$$

This form is particularly convenient for multiple regression analysis because the method of least squares may be applied when equation (8) is transformed to

$$X_0 = a_0 + a_1 X_1 + a_2 X_2 + a_3 X_3 + a_4 X_4 ,$$

which is the hypothesis described in the introduction.[26]

This hypothesis was tested for cross-sections of domestic industrial corporations. The results it gave will be compared with the results given by alternative hypotheses and with the results of some other studies not directly related to this one.

V. SOME ALTERNATIVE MEASURES

The independent variables used in my hypothesis are plausible, but they were selected rather arbitrarily. Some alternatives are also plausible. The use of x_1, the coefficient of variation in earnings for the last nine years, requires the implicit assumption that investors expect the firm's average annual earnings in the future to equal the average for the last nine years. We do not know that this is true. But we do know that the market value of a firm's expected future earnings is given by the market value of the firm's equity and that this market value is highly correlated with expected future earnings. Thus an alternative to x_1, earnings variability, for measuring expected variability of earnings is the ratio of the standard deviation in earnings for the last nine years to the market value of the equity in a firm. Let us call this measure x_8.

[25a] Eqs. (1)−(7) are described in Table 1.

[26] Recall that $X_i = \log_{10} x_i$.

When the equity/debt ratio is included in the function (eq. 8), the measure of marketability, x_4, becomes an inefficient measure of the size of a firm, for total debt and bonds outstanding are highly correlated. Is it not possible that investors merely prefer to invest their funds in securities issued by large firms? If the answer to this question is in the affirmative, it would be better to use a more efficient measure of firm size. When the equity/debt ratio is included, such a measure is the market value of the equity in a firm. Let us call this measure x_5.[27]

The results obtained by substituting x_8 for x_1 and x_5 for x_4 will be reported in Section VII.

VI. SUMMARY OF STATISTICAL PROCEDURES

SELECTION OF THE CROSS-SECTIONS

The hypotheses presented in Sections I and V were tested on cross-sections of domestic industrial companies. The tests were restricted to firms domiciled in the United States because a lender to a foreign corporation may incur risks of a kind not present in lending to domestic corporations. Only "industrial" corporations[28] were included because public utilities and transportation companies are subject to forms of regulation which prevent their maximizing profits.[29] In the event of a decline in earnings, the regula-

[27] Equity is the more efficient measure because, when the equity/debt ratio is held constant, total capital of a firm and equity are perfectly correlated. In this context, total debt is an equally efficient measure of firm size.

[28] For the purposes of this study, industrial firms are defined as firms which would have been included in recent issues of *Moody's Industrial Manual*. This definition includes all types of corporations except public utilities, transportation companies, financial institutions, governments, or corporations not incorporated for profit.

[29] Inclusion of financial institutions would probably require analyzing the structure of their assets.

tory bodies are presumably required to relax their restrictions enough to allow earnings to return to a "fair" level. Hence there are grounds for believing that, other things being equal, if a public utility and a manufacturing or retailing firm have the same earnings variability, the public utility is less likely to default on its bonds. If this is true, public utilities and industrial firms should not be analyzed in the same cross-section.

All domestic industrial corporations were included if meaningful data for testing the hypothesis described in Section I could be obtained for them from the sources consulted. The *Commercial and Financial Chronicle* and the *Bank and Quotation Record* were the main sources for security prices, *Moody's Industrial Manual* was the chief source of other data. In general, "meaningful data" were not available for companies with any of the following characteristics:

1. The firm's risk premium could not be estimated if
    a) Price quotations were not available for at least one bond issue at each significant level of seniority
    b) The only price quotations available for a class of bonds were for issues quoted at substantially above the call price or for issues whose quotations had obviously been affected by convertibility privileges or by the issue's having been called
    c) Substantial bond issues were those of subsidiaries or affiliates and the parent firm was not responsible for their debts
    d) The firm was in or about to go into receivership
    e) The firm had defaulted or was about to default on at least one of its bond issues
2. Earnings variability could not be estimated if
    a) Substantially complete and comparable consolidated income statements were not available for either the firm's period of solvency or for nine years
    b) The firm's period of solvency was less than two years
3. The market value of the firm's equity could

not be estimated if quotations were lacking for substantial stock issues

December 31, 1953, was chosen for the initial test because it was the most recent date for which data were available in *Moody's Industrial Manual* when this study was begun (May, 1955). The other dates were chosen in order to get the cross-sections spaced over time and from periods of widely differing business and financial conditions.

MEASUREMENT OF THE VARIABLES

Risk premium, x_0.—I have defined the risk premium on a bond as the difference between its market yield to maturity and the yield on a riskless bond having the same maturity date. When the coupon rate and maturity date of a bond are known, its yield may be found by finding its price and looking up the yield in a book of bond tables. In general, price was found by taking the last sale price on December 31 or the mean of the closing "bid" and "ask" quotations on December 31.[30] In computing yields, this price was adjusted by adding a quarter of a point (for 1927 and 1932) or half a point[31] (for 1937, 1949, and 1953) to allow for a buyer's transactions cost. Thus the yields I computed were estimates of yields facing potential buyers.

Hypothetical pure rates for 1949 and 1953 were obtained from yields on fully taxable United States treasury bonds. On the earlier dates, interest on government bonds was wholly or partially exempt from income taxes. Hence, yields on governments were not directly comparable with yields on industrials. For 1927, 1932, and 1937, estimates of pure rates were based on "basic yield" series

[30] Bond prices are in per cent of par value. Stock prices are usually in dollars a share.

[31] For bonds, a point is 1 per cent of par value; for stocks, usually one dollar a share.

compiled by the National Bureau of Economic Research for the first quarter of the year following.[32]

The average risk premium on a firm's bonds, x_0, was taken as a weighted average of the risk premiums on its individual issues.

Earnings variability, x_1.—The coefficient of variation in earnings, x_1, was generally computed from statements of consolidated net income for nine consecutive years.[33] If a firm engaged in unusual accounting practices—for example, if it had set up surplus reserves out of income or was using last-in–first-out inventory valuation—it was necessary to exclude the firm from the cross-section unless its statements could be adjusted.

Period of solvency, x_2.—The methods used to estimate this variable have been described in Section IV. It should be pointed out, however, that for many firms the information in *Moody's* permits only a very rough estimate to be made of x_2, the period of solvency.

Equity/debt ratio, x_3.—In computing the equity/debt ratio, it was first necessary to estimate equity, x_5, and debt, x_6. Equity was taken as the total market value of all shares of stock (both pre-

ferred and common) and all warrants for the purchase of stock outstanding and in the hands of the public. In general, total debt, x_6, was taken as total par value outstanding of bonds, notes, debentures, conditional sales contracts, mortgages, and judgments for which the firm was obligor or guarantor. Any current liabilities other than these were not counted because they often vary a great deal during the course of a firm's fiscal year. The equity/debt ratio, x_3, was then obtained by dividing x_5 by x_6.

Bonds outstanding, x_4.—Bonds outstanding, the market value of publicly traded debt, was found by multiplying the par value of each publicly traded issue included in a firm's total debt by its unadjusted price. I assumed that an issue was publicly traded if I had price quotations for it or if *Moody's* stated that the issue was listed or traded on an organized securities exchange or quoted in some financial center.

Volume of trading, x_7.—To find the volume of trading, total sales of each issue on each securities exchange were multiplied by the mean of the high and low sales price of the bond for the year preceding the date of the cross-section. The estimates of the volume of trading in each issue for the year were then added to get x_7, the volume of trading in a firm's publicly traded bonds. This variable was computed for firms which had all their bonds outstanding listed or traded on the New York Stock Exchange or the American Stock Exchange, provided that no issue had been offered or retired during the year and there was no issue whose price had obviously been affected by convertibility privileges.

Ratio of standard deviation in earnings to equity, x_8.—This alternative index of the variability of earnings was computed by dividing the standard deviation of

---

[32] For a description of these series see David Durand, *Basic Yields on Corporate Bonds, 1900–1942* (National Bureau of Economic Research, technical paper No. 3) (New York, 1942).

[33] If the firm's period of solvency was less than nine years, years before the beginning of the period of solvency were excluded. Except for 1949, the nine-year period ended approximately on the date for which the cross-section was taken. For 1949 the period ended near December 31, 1953. The latter date had been used for the initial cross-section; 1949 was used for the first recheck. By using the same period for the computation of x_1 for both cross-sections, much labor was saved. The partial regression coefficients of X_1 computed in this manner were identical for both cross-sections. In view of this result, it was decided not to make the effort necessary to have the data for 1949 strictly comparable with the data for the other dates.

earnings, which had been used in computing x_1, by equity, x_5.

Before any data were gathered for 1953, I had tentatively concluded that risk premium was a function of earnings variability, x_1, and equity/debt ratio, x_3. While these data were being collected, it became apparent to me that period of solvency, x_2, would probably be an empirically significant variable. The first test of this hypothesis was performed by finding the multiple regression of X_0 on X_1, X_2, X_5, and X_6 for December 31, 1953. All these variables were found to be significant, but it was also found that the simple correlation between X_0 and X_6 was negative and almost as great as the multiple correlation.[34] The necessity for finding a plausible explanation for this phenomenon led to the use of the hypothesis summarized in Section I and developed in Sections III and IV. No further change was made in this hypothesis. When data for the third cross-section (1937) were obtained, it was noted that twenty firms had to be excluded only because they had negative values of x_1, and no X_1 could be defined for them. The alternative index of variability of earnings, x_8, was thought of as a means of avoiding this restriction on the scope of the hypothesis.

VII. FURTHER RESULTS

The data from the five cross-sections are summarized in Table 2. This table and some simple calculations[35] reveal

[34] For 1953, $r_{06} = -0.76$; $R_{0.1256} = 0.89$. However, r_{06} was unstable. It was not significantly different from zero for 1932.

[35] The simple regression coefficients and simple correlation coefficients may be obtained from Table 2 b y applying the formulas

$$b_i = \sigma_{0i}^2 / \sigma_i^2 ,$$

$$r_{0i}^2 = b_i \sigma_{0i}^2 / \sigma_0^2 .$$

that, although the simple regression coefficients all have the signs which would be expected on the basis of the analysis in Section IV, these simple regression coefficients and the coefficients of simple correlation between the logarithm of risk premium, X_0, and the logarithms of the independent variables vary widely between dates.

But, as shown in Section II, both the multiple correlation coefficients and the partial regression coefficients which result from testing the hypothesis stated in the introduction are remarkably stable from cross-section to cross-section.[36]

[36] An approximate test of the significance of the differences of the partial regression coefficients among the cross-sections is provided by the following:

Suppose that the estimated partial regression coefficients, b_{it}, from the separate samples $t = 1 \ldots T$ are all estimates from the same population. Let s_{it} be the standard error of estimate of b_{it} and let

$$b_{i*} = \frac{\sum_{t=1}^{T} b_{it} / s_{it}^2}{\sum_{t=1}^{T} 1 / s_{it}^2} .$$

Then the statistic

$$y = \sum_{t=1}^{T} \frac{(b_{it} - b_{i*})^2}{s_{it}^2}$$

has approximately the χ^2 distribution with $T - 1$ degrees of freedom. Hence an improbably high value of y is cause for rejecting the hypothesis that the partial regression coefficients are estimates from the same population. (This test was suggested by David L. Wallace.)

When the test was applied to the partial regression coefficients shown in Table 1 for $t = 1927, 1932, 1937, 1949, 1953$, the results shown in the following table were obtained.

Coefficient (1)	y (2)	Probability of Obtaining as Large a χ^2 (3)	Accept Hypothesis That All Samples Have the Same Coefficient? (4)
a_1	0.72	0.95	Yes
a_2	5.13	.275	Yes
a_3	2.72	.61	Yes
a_4	16.86	0.0022	No

The partial regression coefficient is shown in column 1. The value of y actually obtained is shown in column 2. The probability of obtaining a value of χ^2

Thus we have concluded that the partial elasticities of risk premium with respect to coefficient of variation in earnings, period of solvency, equity/debt ratio, and market value of publicly traded bonds

as large as that actually found, if the regression coefficients are independent and the differences in a_i among the cross-sections are due entirely to random errors of sampling, is shown in column 3. The decision concerning the hypothesis is indicated in column 4.

Although a_4, the coefficient of bonds outstanding, appears to vary significantly, the effects of this variation are small. The root mean-square standard error of estimate of X_0 from the regressions for the separate cross-sections is 0.2076. For the pooled-moments regression (eq. [1]) it is only 0.2094—less than 1 per cent greater.

outstanding are significantly different from zero and are relatively stable over time for domestic industrial corporations.

COMPARISONS WITH ALTERNATE HYPOTHESES

Equity, x_5, was substituted for bonds outstanding, x_4, in order to use a better measure of the size of firms in the regression for each of the five cross-sections. The resulting coefficient of multiple correlation, $R_{0.1235}$, was slightly smaller than $R_{0.1234}$ for all but the 1953 cross-section, for which it was slightly larger.[37] The

[37] The difference between the R's for this sample was the third largest of five.

TABLE 2*

MEANS, VARIANCES, AND COVARIANCES OF THE COMMON LOGARITHMS OF THE VARIABLES

VARIABLE	DATE	MEAN	X_0	X_1	X_2	X_3	X_4	X_5	X_6
					VARIANCE OR COVARIANCE				
X_0	1927	0.1251	0.0740	0.0554	−0.0098	−0.0868	−0.0322	−0.1132	......
	1932	0.6997	.2008	.0871	−.0441	−.1757	−.0976	−.2130	0.1565
	1937	0.3385	.1706	.0913	−.0562	−.0936	−.1397	−.2261	.0853
	1949	0.0261	.1752	.0770	−.0970	−.0861	−.2168	−.2837	......
	1953	−0.0811	.2058	.0907	−.0717	−.0623	−.2405	−.3071	......
	Average	0.1783	.1650	.0808	−.0576	−.0933	−.1533	......	......
	Over-all	0.1783	0.2260	.1176	−.0768	−.1257	−.1684	......	......
X_1	1927	−0.0873	......	.1404	.0141	−.0578	−.0186	−.0739	......
	1932	−0.0134	......	.1238	−.0108	−.1023	−.0044	−.0774	.1426
	1937	0.1650	......	.2430	.0417	−.0289	−.0669	−.0929	.1384
	1949	−0.3240	......	.0882	−.0603	−.0378	−.1010	−.1260	......
	1953	−0.3276	......	.1045	−.0375	−.0250	−.1208	−.1415	......
	Average	−0.1219	......	.1443	−.0095	−.0443	−.0696	......	......
	Over-all	−0.1219	......	0.1843	−.0303	−.0554	−.0855	......	......
X_2	1927	1.3646	......	......	.0759	−.0232	.0118	−.0102	......
	1932	1.3692	......	......	.1163	.0487	.0271	.0642	−.0324
	1937	1.2620	......	......	.1680	.0300	.0389	.0628	.0285
	1949	1.4495	......	......	.1529	.0464	.1349	.1694	......
	1953	1.5717	......	......	.0896	.0116	.0849	.0995	......
	Average	1.4070	......	......	.1219	.0208	.0624	......	......
	Over-all	1.4070	......	......	0.1344	.0257	.0716	......	......
X_3	1927	0.4688	......	......	....	.2270	−.0735	.1419	......
	1932	−0.0522	......	......	....	.2628	.0263	.2348	−.1919
	1937	0.2942	......	......	....	.1639	−.0101	.1454	−.0594
	1949	0.3510	......	......	....	.1011	.0869	.1705	......
	1953	0.4010	......	......	....	.0896	.0360	.1126	......
	Average	0.3225	......	......	....	.1567	.0125	......	......
	Over-all	0.3225	......	......	....	0.1799	.0201	......	......
X_4	1927	1.0117	......	......	....	....	.3218	.2473	......
	1932	0.8624	......	......	....	....	.2819	.2703	−.0287
	1937	0.7000	......	......	....	....	.4217	.3876	−.0594
	1949	0.8541	......	......	....	....	.4249	.4858	......
	1953	0.9830	......	......	....	....	.4692	.4967	......
	Average	0.8792	......	......	....	....	.3972	......	......
	Over-all	0.8792	......	......	....	....	0.4112	......	......
X_5	1927	1.5265	......	......	....	....	....	.3800	......
	1932	0.9984	......	......	....	....	....	.4418	−.1732
	1937	1.1259	......	......	....	....	....	.5566	−.1399
	1949	1.3035	......	......	....	....	....	.6366	......
	1953	1.5691	......	......	....	....	....	0.6360	......
X_6	1932	0.6484	......	......	....	....	....	....	.2274
	1937	1.0368	......	......	....	....	....	....	0.1483

* For definitions of variables see text.

largest difference between corresponding values of a_1 and $b_{01.235}$, a_2 and $b_{02.135}$, and a_4 and $b_{05.123}$ was 0.035. However, the range of values for $b_{03.125}$ was -0.149 to -0.324, while the range for a_3 was only -0.404 to -0.531. Thus bonds outstanding, x_4, appears to be the better variable. It seems to lead to better prediction of risk premiums and, when it is used, the elasticity estimates are more nearly stable. This result was confirmed when it was found that when both variables are used, although the estimates of $b_{03.1245}$, $b_{04.1235}$, and $b_{05.1234}$ are all rather poor because of the multicollinearity among X_3, X_4, and X_5; the minimum ratio of $b_{04.1235}$ to its standard error is 0.86, a value exceeded by the ratio of $b_{05.1234}$ to its standard error in only two of the five cross-sections. However, we must distinguish between the two hypotheses chiefly on economic, rather than statistical, grounds. Both risk premium, x_0, and bonds outstanding, x_4, depend on market price. While the correlation between X_0 and X_4 from this source is undoubtedly very small, the multicollinearity among X_3, X_4, and X_5 is so great that the influence of the autocorrelation on $b_{04.1235}$ may not be negligible. On economic grounds, X_4 is clearly superior to X_5. Large corporations, we find, are able to borrow at lower cost than small corporations, other things being equal. Variable X_4 offers an explanation; X_5 merely repeats the statement.

My tests of the ratio of the standard deviation of earnings to equity, x_8, as an alternative to the coefficient of variation of past earnings, x_1, are also somewhat inconclusive.[38] For 1932, X_8 appears to be a slightly better variable. For 1937, X_1 appears to be a considerably better variable. Of the two, X_8 has meaning for the

larger number of firms; but X_8 is more highly correlated with X_2, X_3, and X_4 than is X_1.[39] It would appear that the market value of the equity in a firm depends not only on the expectation of the firm's earnings but also on the other factors which determine the risk premiums on the firm's bonds. Since the use of X_1 is based on the arbitrary assumption that investors expect the future average annual earnings of a firm to equal the arithmetic mean of the last nine years' earnings and since neither X_1 nor X_8 is clearly superior to the other, I am sure that an index of expected future earnings can be found that is better than that used in computing either X_1 or X_8. Such a variable could probably best be found in a study of the determinants of market value of equity organized along lines similar to those followed in this study.

The major reason for using X_8, however, was to test the applicability of the general hypothesis to firms whose net earnings have been negative. Figure 4 shows the scatter of 1937 risk premiums for the 89 firms included in regression equation (10), Table 3, and for 20 firms with negative mean earnings not included in that regression, plotted against values of x_0 estimated from that regression equation. It is obvious from Figure 4 that these 20 risk premiums are predicted with about as much precision as the 89.

Thus it appears that, where applicable, the variables of the main hypothesis, specified in Section I, are superior to the alternative variables suggested in Section V for the purpose of estimating

---

[38] Compare equations (9) and (10) (Table 3) with equations (4) and (5) (Table 1).

[39] Other things being equal, the standard errors of partial regression coefficients increase as certain elements of the inverse of the variance-covariance matrix of the independent variables increase. These elements depend in part on the collinearities among the independent variables. For 1932 and 1937, five out of six such elements were greater when X_8 was used than the corresponding elements when X_1 was used.

TABLE 3

Regression Equations under the Hypothesis That
$$X_0 = d_0 + d_8X_8 + d_2X_2 + d_3X_3 + d_4X_4$$

Equation	Date	No. of Firms	Degrees of Freedom	R^2	d_0	d_8 (s_8)	d_2 (s_2)	d_3 (s_3)	d_4 (s_4)
9....	1932	45	40	0.738	1.186	+0.295 (.123)	−0.060 (.112)	−0.415 (.117)	−0.272 (.069)
10....	1937	89	84	0.693	1.304	+ .326 (0.080)	− .254 (0.067)	− .423 (0.072)	− .261 (0.042)

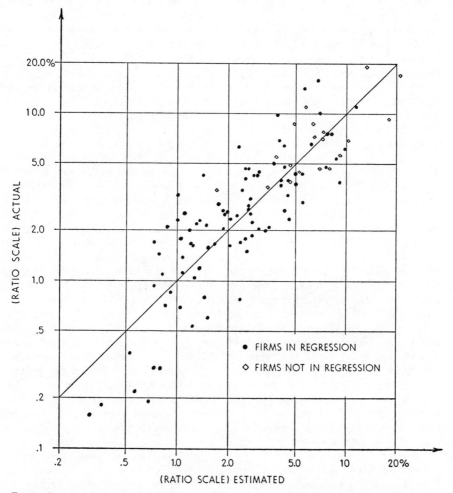

Fig. 4.—Scatter of December 31, 1937, risk premiums against risk premiums estimated from equation (10)

the elasticities of risk premium with respect to factors indicating risks incurred by lenders.

When X_0, the logarithm of risk premium, is estimated from equation (1), its standard error of estimate is 0.2094, which indicates that approximately two-thirds of the estimates of x_0, risk premium, are between 62 per cent and 162 per cent of the measured values. Let us consider the possible reasons for the errors in these estimates. If the variables I have used are proper ones and the form of the function I have used is correct, these errors must be due to four causes: errors in the measurement of risk premium; errors in the measurement of the independent variables; omission of relevant variables from the hypothesis; and randomness of bond prices or imperfect adjustment of the market prices of securities to their "equilibrium" values.

Errors in risk premiums.—Errors in the measurement of risk premium exist for two reasons. There are errors in the yields of bonds, and there are errors in the "pure rate of interest." Errors in the yields of the bonds arose because for many firms I had to rely on the mean of "bid" and "ask" prices. Since these two prices are not the same, one can observe only a range within which the true yield of a bond must lie. Given the "spread" (difference between the bid and ask prices), this uncertainty in the bond yield becomes more serious (since the logarithm of risk premium is used in the regression equations) the nearer the yield is to the pure rate and the shorter the time until the bond matures.

I believe that the errors in X_0, the logarithm of risk premium, introduced by the "random" errors in price are, in general, uniformly distributed over the range of risk premiums. For the spread in price quotations generally narrows as a bond approaches maturity and as its market yield approaches the pure rate. That part of the standard error of estimate of X_0 which is due to the uncertainty of bond prices is perhaps 0.05 (or about 11 per cent of the value of x_0). Elimination of random errors of this magnitude would raise the squares of the coefficients of multiple correlation by only about 0.02. Not much of the error in estimating risk premium can be due to this cause.

Errors in the pure rate of interest introduce both random and systematic errors in the values of X_0. Errors in the "pattern" of rates may introduce random errors in X_0. But errors in the general level of the pattern can produce non-linearities in the function, for an error of given magnitude in the pure rate will cause a larger error in the logarithm of a small risk premium than it will cause in the logarithm of a large risk premium. Overestimating the level of pure interest rates may be the cause of the slight nonlinearities of the scatter in Figure 1 for 1937 and 1953. Since I do not know the errors in the pure rates, I cannot estimate the effects of such errors on the correlation coefficients. It is interesting to note, however, that the multiple correlation coefficients for the dates before World War II are less than the multiple correlation coefficients for the postwar dates. For the former dates basic yield series of the National Bureau of Economic Research were used in estimating pure rates—these series are hypothetical; for the latter dates yields on United States government bonds were used—these series were actually observed.

Errors in independent variables.—The errors in the measurement of all independent variables except X_2 are believed to be negligible. Random errors in X_2 resulting in a standard error of estimate of X_2 of 0.0791 (20 per cent of the period of solvency, x_2) would have a negligible effect on equation (1). A standard error of 0.176 (two-thirds of observed values of x_2 between $\frac{2}{3}$ and $\frac{3}{2}$ times the actual values) would have decreased R^2 by about 0.02, a_1 by 0.005, and a_2 by 0.088 and increased a_3 by 0.012 and a_4 by 0.014 (all in absolute magnitude) from their "true" values.[40] I believe that 0.176 is larger than the actual standard error of estimate of X_2. Furthermore, it would appear that the errors in X_2 are negatively correlated with the actual values. Such errors would tend to increase the absolute magnitude of a_2. Hence it appears that the estimates of elasticities in equation (1) can be taken at their face value.

Omission of variables.—The problem of the omission of relevant variables is a difficult one. Possible omitted variables are of two kinds: those which would indicate the probability of default and expected loss in the event of a default, and those which take account of the differences in the ways in which interest income and capital gains are taxed.

The latter is a less serious problem. If a bond is bought for par or above, all income from the bond is taxed as ordinary income if the investor holds the bond until maturity. If, however, the investor buys the bond below par, only the interest payments on the bonds are taxed as ordinary income. The difference between the purchase price and the amount for which the bond is redeemed is a capital gain. This difference in tax is difficult to take into account. One would

[40] For a method of finding biases in partial regression coefficients when one independent variable is subject to (known) random error, see Gregory C. Chow, "Demand for Automobiles in the United States" (Doctoral dissertation in the University of Chicago Library), Appendix I.

expect the market yield on a bond with a high coupon rate to be higher than the yield on a bond with a low coupon rate because the former is more likely to sell above par if other things are equal. But bonds with the highest coupon rates will tend to be issued by the firms most likely to default. Hence one would expect to find the coupon rate correlated with other independent variables. Another effect also tends to obscure any effect of a high coupon rate. The investor in such a bond will get his income somewhat sooner than the investor in an equivalent bond with a low coupon rate—the high-coupon-rate bond has a shorter "duration." If the term-structure of interest rates is higher for long-term securities than for short-term securities, the high-coupon-rate bond will tend to have the lower yield—the tax and duration effects will largely offset each other. Long-term rates were substantially higher than short-term rates for all dates in this study except December 31, 1927.

Other variables that might have been taken into account are various terms contained in the bond indenture. These terms relate to the type of lien the bondholders have; the conditions, if any, under which the firm may issue additional bonds having the same or a higher lien; restrictions on dividends and sale of assets; conditions under which the indenture may be modified; sinking-fund and call provisions; the ratio of current assets to liabilities which the firm must maintain; and possibly other provisions.

One would expect that, if these provisions were included in the regressions, much of their effect on risk premiums would be obscured; for the companies least likely to default usually borrow without incurring many restrictions on their future operations. Even where this is not the case, it is difficult to appraise the effects of many indenture provisions on risk premium. Perhaps an indenture can be modified if holders of two-thirds of the issue consent, or perhaps there is no provision for modification. If the company must extend its bonds to avoid receivership, some bondholders will be better off if the indenture can be modified; others may consider themselves worse off. Hence, it is difficult to say whether a provision permitting modification will tend to raise or lower risk premium. This is an illustration of the difficulties of taking indenture provisions in-

RELATIONSHIP BETWEEN x_4 AND x_7

Some attempt was made to compare bonds outstanding, x_4, with volume of bonds traded, x_7. For each of the prewar cross-sections a correlation coefficient of about 0.8 was found between the logarithms of these variables; for the postwar cross-sections a correlation coefficient of about 0.7 was found. The annual volume of trading was about 10 per cent of bonds outstanding for the prewar years, but only about 1 per cent for the postwar years. Furthermore, the data for x_7 appear to be poor. For many issues differ-

TABLE 4

COMPARISON OF MOODY'S DAILY INDEXES OF YIELDS ON INDUSTRIAL
BONDS WITH SIMILAR INDEXES IMPLIED BY THIS STUDY

	MOODY'S DAILY INDEXES (Per Cent)			INDEXES IMPLIED BY THIS STUDY (Per Cent)		
DEC. 31	Aaa	Baa	Difference	High Grade	Medium Grade	Difference
(1)	(2)	(3)	(4)	(5)	(6)	(7)
1927.......	4.60*	5.50*	0.90*	4.59	5.71	1.12
1932.......	4.53	7.22	2.69	4.27	6.81	2.54
1937.......	2.95	4.64	1.69	2.60	4.20	1.60
1949.......	2.51	2.87	0.39	2.48	3.68	1.20
1953.......	3.07	3.64	0.57	3.03	4.42	1.39

Sources: Moody's Indexes: *Moody's Investment Survey* and *Moody's Bond Survey*. Implied indexes: Yields on bonds of firms with risk premiums implied by equation (1) (1953 constant term) of less than 0.40 per cent for high grade and between 1.00 per cent and 1.50 per cent for medium grade.
* Read from a graph, not strictly comparable with other dates.

to account. I am not a professional security analyst and was forced to neglect these provisions largely because of my lack of knowledge.[41]

[41] Herbert Arkin, in "A Statistical Analysis of the Internal Factors Affecting the Yields on Domestic Corporate Bonds" (Doctoral dissertation, Columbia University [Hewlett, N.Y., 1940]), attempted to measure the influence on bond yields of factors that are almost all specified by the bond contract. He could account for only 23 per cent and 13 per cent of the variance in yields of industrials at year-end 1927 and mid-year 1932, respectively. Since Arkin did not take the chief determinants of risk premiums into account (only coupon rate was significant in both of his industrial samples), it is difficult to say what the real importance of indenture provisions is. Arkin's is the only previous study I have found in which multiple regression analysis was used in attempting to discover how market prices of bonds are determined.

ent publications showed rather different volumes of trading. Moreover, there appears to be no relationship between residual risk premiums estimated from equation (1) and residual volume of trading estimated from bonds outstanding. These results, which show lower correlations in years of inactive markets, are consistent with the argument advanced in Section IV for bonds outstanding, x_4, as a measure of marketability.

STABILITY OF THE LEVEL OF RISK PREMIUMS

This study was not designed to measure whether the level of the regression equation is constant between cross-sections, since to do so we would have to know whether the determinants of stock prices are stable. Nevertheless, it appears that investors' behavior in the bond market is more stable than one would infer merely from inspecting the spreads between Moody's Aaa and Baa indexes of corporate bond yields. These spreads are shown in Table 4.

The coefficient of variation of the differences between Moody's Baa and Aaa indexes is 0.76. The similar coefficient for the implied indexes is only 0.365. If these spreads are assumed to be normally distributed over time, one must reject the hypothesis that the spreads between Moody's indexes are at least as stable as the spreads between the implied indexes if one uses the 10 per cent level of significance, even though each series shown in Table 4 has only four degrees of freedom. The spreads, however, are highly correlated. The coefficient of correlation between the values in columns 4 and 7 of Table 4 is 0.924, which is significantly different from zero at the 2.5 per cent level, even though this regression has only three degrees of freedom. However, if the values of x_1 and x_3 were adjusted to take changes in corporation income tax

rates into account, the spread in the implied indexes for 1932 would almost certainly be reduced.

The problem of whether or not the level of risk premiums, given the factors showing risks incurred by investors, is stable over time cannot be answered conclusively on the basis of this study. If the variables I have used should prove to give the most nearly stable level of risk premiums over time, then it is clear that investors' behavior could not be deemed stable over time. For the improvement of the estimates of risk premium which occurs when one goes from equation (2), which assumes both a stable level and stable elasticities, to equation (1), which does not assume a stable level, is clearly significant.

CONCLUSION

This study shows that economic and statistical methods are applicable to security analysis. Although by its design it could not show whether investor behavior is rational or even stable, we now know that, at least in the bond market, elasticities are reasonably stable over time.

Index

Abelson, A., 551
Accounting
  scope for discretion in practice, 545-46,
    579-97
  value of concepts, 559-578, 612-616
Aircraft valuation technique, 617-37;
  application of, to capital goods, 617,634;
  relevance of, to price prediction, 617-18,
    633;
  relevance of, to marketing new prod-
    ucts, 633
Alexander, S. S., 118, 123-25, 132 n, 149
  164
Alpha, 446. *See also* Portfolio perform-
  ance measurement
American Stock Exchange Price Index,
  88, 95-98
Anderson, T.A., 639
Ando, A., 524 n. *See also* Bach, G.L.,
  and A. Ando
Andrews, P.W.S., and E. Brunner,
  659 n.1.
Anti-trust suits, effect on price of shares
  by, 199-200, 229
Archer, S.H. *See* Evans, J.L., and S.H.
  Archer
Arkin, H., 728 n, 746 n
Arrow, K.J., 368 n
Bach, G.L., and A. Ando, 672 n10.
Bachelier, J.B.A., 117-18, 129-30
Bagehot, W., 402 n, 408 n, 690 n12.
Bailey, M.J., 673
Ball, R.J., and P. Brown, 141, 150, 545,
  561 n, 566, 572 n
Bank of New York, use of valuation model
  by, 531-44
Banks
  collective investment fund performance
    of, 1967-69, 107;
  secondary distribution by, 219-21
Bayley, G.V., and W. Perks, 502 n
Beaver, W.H., 560 n, 576
Bell, P.W. *See* Edwards, E.O., and
  P.W. Bell
Bellemore, D.H., 196
Bellemore, D.H., and L.N. Blucher,
  187 n, 194 n
Bennington, G.A. *See* Jensen, M.C.,

  and G.A. Bennington
Bernoulli, D., 275, 493 n, 496-97, 499, 504
Beta: 342, 344 n, 345-47;
  as aggressive or defensive, 342,445;
  calculation of, 343;
  relation with return, 398. *See also,* Risk,
    measurement of; Volatility
Bhatia, R.J., 659 n1.
Bierwag, G.O., and M.A. Grove, 718-19
Black, F., 395, 407, 683, 690 n12.,
  694 n13.
Black, F., M.C. Jensen, and M.J. Scholes,
  365, 384-85, 388, 391, 452-53, 454 n2.
Black, F., and M.J. Scholes, 398 n7.,
  684 n2., 694
Blattberg, R., and T. Sargent, 131,
  206 n3.
Blucher, L.N. *See* Bellemore, D.H., and
  L.N. Blucher
Blume, M.E. 123, 130, 134-36, 206 n.3.,
  208 n1., 234 n6., 235 n8., 395,
  433 n3., 452, 462 n2., 562 n11.,
  564 n14. *See also* Fama, E.F., and M.E.
  Blume; Friend, I., and M. E. Blume;
  Friend, I., M. E. Blume, and
  J. Crockett
Bodenhorn, D., 511 n, 512 n5., 514 n,
  515 n11.
Bonbright, J.C., 199
Bonds. *See* Convertible bonds; Corporate
  bonds; Coupon bonds; Interest rates
Boness, A.J., 119 n
Brealey, R.A., 52 n11., 563 n13. *See
  also* Hodges, S.D., and R.A. Brealey
Brigham, E.F., and J.L. Pappas, 44 n3.
Brinner, R. *See* Eckstein, O., and R.
  Brinner
Brokerage fees. *See* Transaction costs
Brown, E.C., 681 n47.
Brown, F.E. *See* Friend, I., F.E. Brown,
  E.S. Herman, and D. Vickers
Brown, H.G., 671 n5.
Brown, P. *See* Ball, R.J. and P. Brown
Brunner, E. *See* Andrews, P.W.S., and E.
  Brunner
Burman, J.P., and W.R. White, 708 n7.
Burns, A.F., 639
Buse, A., 705 n5., 718-22

Business cycle
  effect of earnings on, 533, 659-68;
  effect on stock prices of, 638-58
Cagan, P., 675 n28., 676, 716-18. *See
  also* Cagan-Friedman model;
  Friedman, M., and P. Cagan
Cagan-Friedman model, 716-18
Canning, J.B., 559 n, 560 n
Capital asset pricing theory. *See* Risk,
  relationship with return
Capital goods valuation. *See* Aircraft
  valuation technique
Cargill, T., 674 n25.
Carleton, W.T., and I.A. Cooper 703 n3.
Carr, J.L., P.J. Halpern, and J.S.
  McCallum, 705 n5.
Chambers, R.J., 559 n, 561 n
Chow, G.C., 745 n
Clendenin, J.C., 528 n, 529 n32.
Clendenin, J.C., and M. Van Cleave,
  492-93, 499, 503-05, 521 n18.
Clientele effect, 528-29
Cohen, K.J., and J.A. Pogue, 231 n2.,
  342 n1., 347 n
Commission costs. *See* Transaction costs
Commodities
  randomness of price changes in, 118, 115;
  realized returns from speculation in, 2
Consistency, as decision-making tool, 277
Convertible bonds, 683
Cooper, I.A. *See* Carleton, W.T., and
  I.A. Cooper
Cootner, P.H., 85 n1, 118-19, 149,
  164 n1., 177, 560 n4.
Corporate bonds
  ratings of, 729;
  realized returns from, 164-65, 175;
  risk premium of, 682, 727-747
Cost of capital, 200, 228, 515, 574 n21.
  See also Valuation theory
Cottle, S., and T. Whitman, 659 n2.
Cotton, 118
Coupon bonds
  annuity yields of, 705-08;
  redemption yields of, 702-10;
  spot rates of, 702-10
Cowden, D.J. *See* Croxton, F.E., and
  D.J. Cowden
Cowles, A., 78, 88

Cragg, J.G. *See* Malkiel, B.G., and J.G.
  Cragg
Cramer, G. and Petersburg Paradox, 496,
  499, 504
Crockett, J. *See* Friend, I., M.E. Blume,
  and J. Crockett
Croxton, F.E., and D.J. Cowden, 640 n
Culbertson, J.M., 721 n
Davidson, D., 277 n2.
Depreciation, effect of, on profit sensitiv-
  ity, 664-65
De Vere, C.W. *See* Pratt, S.P., and
  C.W. De Vere
Dewing, A.S., 730 n10.
Dietz, P.O., 232 n3.
Diffusion indexes, 645-48, 657-58
Diller, S., 720-21, 724 n
Discount rate for future dividends, 474-76,
  483-86, 492-93, 498-506, 521-22, 689-
  90, 702-04, 708. *See also* Risk,
  relationship with return
Distribution of returns across securities
  dispersion of, 42-77, 548-50;
  kurtosis of, 48;
  skewness of, 48, 98-99
Distribution of successive returns, 129-31.
  See also Pareto-Levy hypothesis
Diversification
  across time, 400;
  effect on dispersion of returns, 42 n12.,
    52-60
  justification for, 310-12, 322, 342-47;
  as key to characteristic performance,
    446,
  measurement of, 455-56;
  of mutual funds, 257;
  in Pareto-Levy market, 434
Dividend policy
  effect of, on ownership, 528-29;
  effect of, on stock price, 200, 228,
    508-30;
  informational effects of, 527. *See also*
    Valuation theory
Dodd, D.L. *See* Graham B., and D.L.
  Dodd
Donaldson, G. *See* Hunt, P., C.M.
  Williams, and G. Donaldson
Dow Jones Average, 85-87, 95, 98
Durand, D., 200, 469-70, 515, 528 n,

452-53

Friend, I., F.E. Brown, E.S. Herman, and D. Vickers, 231 n2., 250

Friend, I., M.E. Blume, and J. Crockett, 93

Fromm, G. *See* Eckstein, O., and G. Fromm

Gambler's ruin, 497

Gangolli, R. *See* Gordon, M.J., and R. Gangolli

Gibson, W.E., 680 n48.

Gilman, S., 559 n

Gini, C., 45

Gini's statistics, 45-46

Glassmire, W.E. *See* Van Horne, J.C., and W.E. Glassmire

Glauber, R. *See* Lintner, J., and R. Glauber

Godfrey, M.D., C.W.J. Granger, and O. Morgenstern, 123, 177 n2.

Gordon, M.J., 199, 515 n10., 517 n, 521-22 n, 529 n33.

Gordon, M.J., and E. Shapiro, 529 n33.

Gordon, M.J., and R. Gangolli, 368 n5.

Gordon, R.J., 680 n44.

Graham, G., and D.L. Dodd, 521 n18., 529 n33., 735 n21.

Granger, C.W.J., and O. Morgenstern, 123. *See also* Godfrey, M.D., C.W.J. Granger, and O. Morgenstern

Grant, E.L., 161 n, 162 n, 163 n

Grant, J.A.G., 718

Grayson, C.J., 273

Great Depression, 715-16, 722

Green, D.H., and J. Segall, 546

Greenough, W.C., 675 n27.

Grove, M.A. *See* Bierwag, G.O., and M.A. Grove

Growth stocks, 498-506, 514, 520

Hakansson, N.H., 359 n9.

Hald, A., 161 n, 163 n

Halpern, P.J. *See* Carr, J.L., P.J. Halpern, and J.S. McCallum

Harkavy, O., 523 n, 529 n32.

Haynes, A.T., and R.J. Kirton, 502 n16.

Hayward, J., 286 n

Heard, S., 478 n, 479 n

Hedge ratio. *See* Options trading, hedge

ratios for

Hendershott, P.H., and J.C. Van Horne, 647 n20.

Herman, E.S. *See* Friend, I., F.E. Brown, E.S. Herman and D. Vickers

Hickman, W.B., 683, 715

Hicks, J.R., 131, 310, 368, 374 n15., 613 672, 713, 721

Hirshleifer, J., 368 n6.

Hodges, S.D., and S.M. Schaefer, 703 n2.

Hodges, S.D., and R.A. Brealey, 274, 349 n2.

Homer, S., 677 n33.

Horowitz, I., 231 n2.

Hultgren, T., 680 n44.

Human capital, as component of portfolio, 398

Hunt, P., C.M. Williams, and G. Donaldson, 529 n33.

Ijiri, Y., 559 n

Indexes. *See* Market indexes

Individuals, secondary distributions by, 219-21

Industries
as factor in earnings changes, 563;
as factor in stock returns, 134, 433, 563-64

Inflation, impact of
empirical evidence, 675-77;
historiography, 669-77;
on net debtors, 671-72, 674, 680;
under classical theory, 669-72;
under modern theory, 672-74;
on pension investment plan, 407-07;
on profit margin, 659

Informational effects
of dividend payments, 527;
of secondary distributions, 141-42, 201-03, 218-22;
of stock splits, 137-40, 177-97

Insider trading
returns from 143-48, 259-70;
riskiness of stocks traded in, 266-68;
secondary distributions by, 219-21

Insurance, 475 n6., 500-03;
and restrictions on investment, 497 n11.

Insurance companies
investment performance of, 108;

secondary investments by, 219-22. *See also* Insurance

Interest rates
and business cycles, 715, 725;
effect of default on, 727-47;
forward rates, 712-25;
spot rates, 704-08, 711-17, 720-23;
term structure and efficient market hypothesis, 131-32, 711-26;
transaction costs of, 711.
See also Cagan-Friedman model; Expectations theory; Liquidity preference theory; Meiselman's new expectation theory

Inventories, valuation of, 545

Investor's preference function, 368-69

Investment management practices
criticized, 425-26, 429-30;
described, 424-31;
diversification in, as risk aversion tool, 425-26;
hedging in, as risk aversion tool, 425-26;
new approach for, proposed, 427-28;
role of portfolio manager in, 424, 428, 430-31;
role of security analyst in, 424, 428, 430-31;
systematic and unique risks in, 424-26

Investment opportunity theory, 370-72

Jaffe, L.H.(Blucher), 185, 193 n, 18., 196

James, F.E., 164

Jensen, M.C., 104, 143-48, 164-65, 172-74, 231-32, 235, 256-57, 359 n10-11., 365, 396, 397 n1., 425, 433 n3., 447 n, 448, 453-54, 560 n4. *See also* Black, F., M.C. Jensen, and M.J. Scholes; Fama, E.F., L. Fisher, M.C. Jensen, and R. Roll

Jensen, M.C., and G.A. Bennington, 103

Jet airplanes, 618

Johnson, L.R., E. Shapiro, and J. O'Meara, 529 n33.

Kahn, R.F., 721-22

Kaldor, N. 659 n1.

Karnovsky, D.S. *See* Yohe, W.P., and D.S. Karnovsky

Kassouf, S.T. *See* Thorp, E.O., and S.T. Kassouf

Kendall, M.G., 118, 123 n14., 130, 134, 155 n1.

Kendall, M.G., and A. Stuart, 45 n7.

Kendrick, J.W., 680 n44.

Keran, M.W., 675 n29., 676

Kessel, R.A., 131, 671 n8., 672, 714-15, 722-24. *See also* Kessel, R.A., and A.A. Alchian

Kessel, R.A., and A.A. Alchian, 672 n10., 674 n21.

Keynes, J.M., 224, 495 n7., 498 n, 503, 671 n5., 672, 674 n22., 713 721 n7.

Khang, C., 705 n5.

King, B.F., 79 n1., 123 n14., 134, 433 n5., 435 n16., 562 n11., 564 n14.

Kirton, R.J. *See* Haynes, A.T., and R.J. Kirton

Kisor, M.*See* Whitbeck, V., and M. Kisor

Koopmans, T.J., 524 n24.

Kripotos, S.L. *See* Levy, R.A., and S.L. Kripotos

Kruizenga, R.J., 119 n8.

Kuh, E., 680 n44.

Large price changes, 123,149;
dependence between, 126

Leading indicators. *See* Economic indicators

Leverage
effect on price of corporate bonds, 727-747;
effect on value of equity, 486-90, 526-27.
See also Corporate bonds

Levy, R.A., and portfolio upgrading rule, 164-69, 171-72, 176

Levy, R.A., and S.L. Kripotos, 554 n3.

Lim, R.S., 559 n

Limit orders, effect on price changes, 126-28

Lintner, J., 110, 113 n, 132-34, 144, 172, 178, 200, 231-34, 434 n11., 448, 527 n29., 639, 682 n49.

Lintner, J., and R. Glauber, 546

Lipsey, R.G., and M.D. Stener, 659 n1.

Liquidity preference theory, 718, 721-25

Little, I.M.D., 546, 594-95, 597

Little, I.M.D., and A.C. Rayner, 595 n1., 597, 607

Littleton, A.C. *See* Paton, W.A., and A.C. Littleton

Moving average rules, 164
Muth, J.F., 524 n24.
Mutual funds, 231-58;
  diversification in, 257;
  management expenses of, 246-50;
  performance of, 104-6, 146-48, 238-57;
  secondary distributions by, 219-21
Naive investment strategy, as foil, 445-47.
  See also Portfolio performance
  measurement
Nerlove, J. *See* Johnson, L.R., E.
  Shapiro, and J. O'Meara
Neuschel, R.F., *See* Morrison, J.R., and
  R.F. Neuschel
Neutral hedge. *See* Options trading, hedge
  ratios for
New York Stock Exchange
  composite index, 87-88, 95, 100;
  realized returns, 16-77
Nichols, D.A., 680 n47.
Niederhoffer, V. *See* Lorie, J.H., and
  V. Niederhoffer
Niederhoffer, V., and M.F.M. Osborne,
  126-29, 143, 150
Niederhoffer, V., and P.J. Regan, 545
Norton, J.P., 732-33
Oil and gas drilling decisions, 275-309
O'Meara, J. *See* Johnson, L.R., E.
  Shapiro, and J. O'Meara
Options trading, 118, 683;
  comparisons with stock trading, 685-87,
    689-92;
  estimates of volatility for, 688-89;
  ex-dividend strategies in, 689-90;
  formula for, 684, 694;
  hedge ratios for, 685-90, 694-700;
  impact of volatility on, 684, 690;
  impact of taxation on, 691-92;
  on margin, 693;
  naked writing of, 686, 696;
  neutral hedging in, 685, 687;
  price anomalies of, 693-94;
  regulation of, 694;
  rules for buying and selling in, 684-85;
  spreading strategies for, 687-88, 690,
    693;
  tax advantages of, 692-93;
  tax-exempt strategies for, 691-93
Osborne, M.F.M., 118, 126-27, 130. *See*

also Niederhoffer, V., and M.F.M.
  Osborne
Pappas, J.L. *See* Brigham, E.F., and J.L.
  Pappas
Pareto-Levy hypothesis, 3, 130, 182-83;
  implications of, 3, 123, 132, 206, 256,
    433, 437
Parker, G.G.C. *See* Van Horne, J.C., and
  G.G.C. Parker
Passive portfolio management, 395-96
Paton, W.A., and A.C. Littleton, 559 n
Pegler, J.B.H., 502 n16.
Pension funds investment policy, 402-04;
  benefits vs. costs of, 406-23;
  and capital asset pricing model, 412-14,
    419-21, 423;
  contributions to, 404, 546;
  and corporate planning/forecasting,
    410-12, 415-16, 418;
  effect of taxation on, 403-04, 408;
  equity interest in, 402-04;
  liability valuation of, 406, 409-11,
    417-19, 422-23;
  responsibility for benefits payments
    from, 402;
  role of trustees in, 403;
  a systems simulation of, 410-23;
  unimportance of risk in, 407-08;
  usefulness of Monte Carlo technique in,
    410
Performance measurement, 143-46, 172-
    75, 232-38, 396, 448-65;
  empirical analyses of, 104-8, 146-48,
    231-58;
  of diversification, 257, 456;
  of selectivity, 232-38, 453-57;
  of timing ability, 236-38, 457-59;
  treatment of horizon differences, 459
Perks, W. *See* Bayley, G.V., and W.
  Perks
Perry, G.L., 680 n44.
Petersburg paradox, 469-70, 492-507;
  implications of, 469-70, 498-500;
  solutions to, 470, 495-98, 518
Pirson, S.J., 286 n
Pogue, J.A. *See* Cohen, K.J., and J.A.
  Pogue
Poisson distributions, 130 n
Portfolio performance measurement,

H.M. Taylor

Technical analysis, 154-56, 161-77. *See also* Efficient market hypothesis, weak form

Terbough, E., 680 n47.

Thompson, G.L., 524 n24.

Thorp, E.O., and S.T. Kassouf, 684 n1.

Timing. *See* Market timing

Tobin, J., 133, 367 n3., 369 n10., 374 n15., 376 n19., 400 n8., 673

Todhunter, I., 495 n7.

Todhunter, R., 494 n5.

Transaction costs
effect of, on attitude to dividends, 528;
in efficient markets, 496;
of option trading, 690-91;
of secondary distributions, 203, 223, 227-28;
of short-term loans, 711

Treasury bill market efficiency, 131-32

Treynor, J.L., 143, 231, 232 n, 233, 342 n, 368 n7., 408, 447 n, 448, 454, 545

Treynor, J.L., and Black, F., 352 n6., 397 n2.

Tryon, J.L. *See* Schultze, C.L., and J.L. Tryon

Trusts, secondary distributions by, 219-21

Uspensky, J.V., 313 n

Utility rates, 199, 228

Utility theory, 273, 275-78;
assumption of, in portfolio theory, 368-69;
estimates of, functions, 287-309;
as guide to decisions, 278-307;
implications of, for Petersburg paradox, 496-97

Valuation theory, 469-70; 471-544;
discounted cash flow approach to, 512-13;
investment opportunities approach, 513-15;
stream of dividends approach, 471-74, 498-500, 515-17;
stream of earnings approach, 517-19;
See also Redemption yields, limitations of

Value Line Composite Average Index, 88, 95-98

Van Cleave, M. *See* Clendenin, J.C., and M. Van Cleave

Van Horne, J.C., 724 n. *See also* Henderschott, P.H., and J.C. Van Horne

Van Horne, J.C., and W.E. Glassmire, 681 n47.

Van Horne, J.C., and G.G. Parker, 164

Vatter, W.J., 559 n

Volatility, 346, 445-56;
estimates of, for options, 688-89.
See also Beta; Risk, measurement of

Vickers, D., 200. *See also* Friend, I., and D. Vickers; Friend, I., F.E. Brown, E.S. Herman, and D. Vickers

Von Neuman, J., and O. Morgenstern, 276 n, 287, 295, 367, 369 n10.

Wallace, N., 713 n, 718, 722, 724-25

Wallis, A.W., and G.H. Moore, 644 n

Wallis, A.W., and H.V. Roberts, 161 n, 162 n, 163 n

Walter, J.E., 514 n, 515, 529 n33.

Warrants, 118, 683

Waud, R.N., 141

Weingartner, H.H., 710 n6.

Welles, C., 342 n

Wheat, 118

Whitbeck, V., and M. Kisor, 470

White, W.R. *See* Burman, J.P., and W.R. White

Whitman, T. *See* Cottle, S., and T. Whitman

Whittle, P., 726

Whitworth, W.A., 285 n, 497 n10., 500

Wiese, R.F., 471 n1.

Williams, C.M. *See* Hunt, P., C.M. Williams, and G. Donaldson

Williams, J.B., 310 n1., 312 n, 469 n, 492 n, 495 n6., 498 n, 499 n, 504 n, 505 n, 515 n11., 670 n4., 671 n5.

Williamson, J.P., 398 n4., 447 n

Wilson, T.A., and O. Eckstein, 680 n44. *See also* Eckstein, O., and R. Brinner; Eckstein, O., and G. Fromm; Feldstein, M., and O. Eckstein

Wise, J., 131, 183, 256, 435 n14.

Wiesenfelder, M. *See* Sobotka, S.P., and M. Wiesenfelder

Wolfe, P., 333 n

Wonnacott, P., 713 n

Wood, J.H., 722

Working, H., 118, 155 n, 156 n, 160 n

Yohe, W.P., and D.S. Karnovsky, 675 n30.